Todd & Watt's
Cases & Materials on
Equity and Trusts

Ninth Edition

Gary Watt
Professor of Law, University of Warwick

OXFORD
UNIVERSITY PRESS

OXFORD
UNIVERSITY PRESS

Great Clarendon Street, Oxford, OX2 6DP,
United Kingdom

Oxford University Press is a department of the University of Oxford.
It furthers the University's objective of excellence in research, scholarship,
and education by publishing worldwide. Oxford is a registered trade mark of
Oxford University Press in the UK and in certain other countries

Sixth edition 2007
Seventh edition 2009
Eighth edition 2011

Impression: 1

British Library Cataloguing in Publication Data

Data available

ISBN 978–0–19–966480–1

Printed in Great Britain by
Ashford Colour Press Ltd, Gosport, Hampshire

PREFACE

You might be wondering why the cover image of this book depicts a row of shoemaker's lasts. The simple answer is that it was inspired by a line in William West's sixteenth-century treatise *Symboleography*, where he writes that 'Equity is fitly compared to a Shoomakers shop that is well furnished with all sorts and manner of lasts for men's feet, where each man may be sure to find one last or other that shall fit him, be he great or small'. The common law lays down rules of general application. It attempts, for reasons of economic efficiency, to produce rules on a one-size-fits-all basis. But we have known since the time of Aristotle that general rules cannot fit the shapes of individuals and their particular cases, so we need judges to exercise equity to make the rules fit more comfortably with the real facts of life. It may be optimistic to suppose that judges will have the time to cobble together a perfectly bespoke rule for every particular case, but the exercise of equity is at least a welcome attempt to stretch the form of rules as far as possible (without breaking them) with a view to accommodating the substance of the matter. This book contains a collection of cases and materials which you might imagine to be a shoemaker's shop in which judges, working over many years, have attempted to fashion general rules to fit particular problems. It is said that students sometimes struggle to learn the law of equity and trusts, so perhaps you will find it useful to ask yourself what you would have done if you had been a judge in the cases contained within this collection. The hard leather of the law shouldn't pinch people too hard. How would you have bent the rigid rule to get a better fit?

If all this talk of a sixteenth century shoemaker's shop seems strange, let me say that my greatest satisfaction as a lecturer and tutor in the law of trusts has been to demonstrate that a subject which some students expect will be archaic, insignificant and impenetrable is in fact highly relevant to contemporary commercial and family life, and, most importantly, is interesting and can be clearly understood. The materials chosen for inclusion in this collection have been selected to reflect the breadth of contexts in which equity and trusts operate today. One case in this book was reported as recently as 2013. (The case is *FHR European Ventures LLP v Mankarious* [2013] EWCA Civ 17.) It follows the controversial decision of the Court of Appeal in *Sinclair Investments (UK) Ltd v Versailles Trade Finance Ltd* and concerns liability to account for the proceeds of bribes and other fraudulent gains. So you can see that the law of equity and trusts continues to move on with the times!

In addition to statutes and cases I have included extracts from scholarly articles by several of the world's leading academic thinkers on the law of equity and trusts, together with extracts from Law Commission documents relating to reform of the law. There are also relevant selections from newspapers and other popular media. There are a great many new materials in this edition, including the decision of the UK Supreme Court in *Jones v Kernott* (2011), which follows the important case of *Stack v Dowden* in the field of constructive trusts of the family home. There is also the decision of the Privy Council on trustee exemption clauses in *Spread Trustee Company Ltd v Hutcheson* (2011); the decisions of the Court of Appeal in *Southgate v Sutton* (2011) on variation of trusts; *Joyce v Epsom* (2012) on remedial aspects of proprietary estoppel; *Crossco No 4 Unlimited v Jolan Ltd* (2011) on the *Pallant v Morgan* equity and *Williams v Central Bank of Nigeria* (2012) on limitation periods. The field of charitable trusts has also witnessed significant developments. For instance, the 2011 decision of The Upper Tribunal Tax and Chancery Chamber in *The Independent Schools Council v Charity Commission* (2011) is of great interest concerning the charitable status of private, fee-paying schools. There has also been a new statutory development in the field of charity law. The Charities Act 2011 makes no substantive change to charity law, but it has consolidated a number of existing charity statutes. 2013 is still young at the time of writing, but even this year there has already been a statutory development in the form of The Trusts (Capital and Income) Act 2013.

The breadth of coverage in this volume is designed to be wide enough for any undergraduate course but I have been careful to ensure that extracts from several important sources are extensive enough to facilitate deeper study and to permit readers to form new insights of their own. A deeper engagement with the materials is also encouraged throughout by means of notes, questions, and guides to further reading. Of course, it will also benefit the student to explore these cases and materials by the light of a textbook. In that regard I hope that this volume will sit as well alongside texts by other authors as it does alongside my text *Trusts and Equity* and my shorter *Equity and Trusts Law (Directions)*, both published by Oxford University Press.

The Online Resource Centre (ORC) accompanying this book will ensure that the reader is kept abreast of any significant developments that might occur after the publication of this volume. We anticipate, for instance, that the Supreme Court of the United Kingdom will shortly hear an appeal from the Court of Appeal's decision in the important case of *Pitt* v *Holt* [2011] EWCA Civ 197, which concerned the review of trustee decision-making.

Finally, a note of caution: it is not intended that this collection should be a substitute for the law library any more than watching *Match of the Day* should be a substitute for attending the game itself. The present collection will be very useful when the law library is closed, crowded or inaccessible but the law student will profit greatly from any time he or she spends alone with the original source materials, many of which can be accessed directly via the Online Resource Centre accompanying this book.

Gary Watt
University of Warwick
March 2013

ACKNOWLEDGEMENTS

Grateful acknowledgement is made to all the authors and publishers of copyright material which appears in this book, and in particular to the following for permission to reprint material from the sources indicated:

Crown copyright material reproduced with the permission of the Controller, HMSO (under the terms of the Click Use licence).

Bloomsbury International: extracts from *Trust Law International* (TLI).

Hart Publishing Ltd: extract from William Swadling (ed.): *The Quistclose Trust: Critical Essays* (2004).

Incorporated Council of Law Reporting: extracts from *Appeal Cases Law Reports* (AC), *Chancery Division Law Reports* (Ch), *King's Bench Law Reports* (KB), *Queen's Bench Law Reports* (QB), and *Weekly Law Reports* (WLR).

Jordan Publishing Ltd: extract from *Family Law Review* (FLR).

LexisNexis: extracts from *All England Law Reports* (ALL ER) and *Butterworth's Company Law Cases* (BCLC). Reproduced by permission of Reed Elsevier (UK) Limited trading as LexisNexis.

Rating Publishers Ltd: extract from *Rating & Valuation Reports*. Reproduced by kind permission of Rating Publishers Ltd.

Sweet & Maxwell: extracts from *Planning and Compensation Reports* (P & CR) and an extract from the *Civil Procedure Reports* (CP Rep); and extracts from David Goddard, 'Equity, Volunteers and Ducks' (1988) 52 *Conv* 19, and B. S. Ker 'Trustees' Powers of Maintenance' (1953) 17 *Conv* 273.

Yale Law Journal Company Inc.: extract from John H. Langbein: 'Questioning the Trust Law Duty of Loyalty: Sole Interest or Best Interest?' (2005) 114 *Yale LJ* 929.

OUTLINE CONTENTS

DETAILED CONTENTS

TABLE OF CASES

Cases and page references in bold indicate that the case is discussed fully with extracts from the judgment

TABLE OF STATUTES

Page references in bold indicate that the text is reproduced in full. Articles of the ECHR are tabled under Sch.1 to the Human Rights Act 1998.

TABLE OF STATUTORY INSTRUMENTS

PART I

Introduction to Equity and Trusts

1

Foundations of Equity and Trusts

KEY AIMS

To identify the functional distinction between equity and law and the implications of the fused administration of equity and law. To appreciate the range of different kinds of trusts. To distinguish trust from other legal ideas, and especially to distinguish trust from absolute gift and contract.

SECTION 1: INTRODUCTION

> 'Then shalt thou understand righteousness, and judgment, and equity'
>
> (Proverbs 2:9, King James Version)

The term 'equity' can be used to describe a form of social fairness or a branch of morality or even an aspect of divine justice but in the context of modern legal studies the term 'equity' connotes the law's internal capacity to depart from its general rules in the interests of better justice in particular cases. English lawyers have largely succeeded in their efforts to turn equity into something as regular as general law, but it still retains a flavour of its non-legal origins. The major means by which equity in law maintains a connection with its non-legal origins is the language of 'unconscionability'. Equity in law is still concerned to prevent 'unconscionable' assertion of general legal rights and powers. The word 'unconscionable' has lost its connection to morality and the courts try to use it as precisely as possible, in ways which vary from context to context, but it reminds us of equity's ecclesiastic origins and reminds us that equity is a broader idea than the quite narrow legal version of the concept might suggest. Language such as 'unconscionability' sits somewhat uncomfortably in modern law, but that is a good thing for keeping the law realistically and appropriately humble about its capacity to cover every possible case by means of general rules. The language of unconscionability is highly effective at keeping the general rules open to just exceptions in particular cases and particular kinds of case. For the story of equity beyond the law, and its continuing capacity to influence equity in law, you might consult my book *Equity Stirring* which is listed in the Further Reading section at the end of this chapter. In this book, we are concerned with the nature of equity and trusts in law—which is a 'story' of equity and trusts told for the most part by the legislature, judges, and legal analysts.

A brief overview of the history is essential to understanding the modern law of equity and trusts. We will see that elements of equity in English law can be traced back as far as Aristotle, but for now it will suffice to say that the legal idea of equity was developed in England in the Middle Ages by a senior clergyman called the Chancellor who originally acted as the King's private counsellor. His task was to ensure that the general 'common law', which was enforced in the King's name, was applied with justice in individual cases; equity was therefore a way of exercising a royal prerogative of mercy which was designed to ensure that the King's conscience was clear before God. The Chancellor eventually became the head of his own court, known as the Court of Chancery, and it was here that equity developed as a branch of law distinct from, and at times in competition with, the common law. The Court of Chancery came to be associated with discretionary, almost ad hoc, justice; whereas the common law courts came to be associated with certain rigid and inflexible forms of action and remedy. In his speech in *The Earl of Oxford's Case* (1615) 1 Ch Rep 1, Lord Chancellor Ellesmere observed that the 'office of the chancellor' is 'to correct men's consciences for frauds, breaches of trust, wrongs and oppressions of what nature soever they be, and to soften and mollify the extremity of the law' (pp. 6–7). In that case, the Lord Chancellor was defending the Court of Chancery from the accusation (made by Sir Edward Coke, then Chief Justice of the Court of King's Bench) that it had illegally assumed the role of court of appeal over the common law courts. The Lord Chancellor's sophisticated response was to argue that he was not criticising common law judgments, but rather the conscience of the party seeking to enforce those judgments: 'when a judgment is obtained by Oppression, Wrong and a hard Conscience, the Chancellor will frustrate and set it aside, not for any error or Defect in the Judgment, but for the hard Conscience of the Party' (p. 10). The dispute between Sir Edward Coke and Lord Chancellor Ellesmere was referred to King James I (the King who patronised the Bible translation quoted earlier). In 1616, King James decided in favour of the Chancellor and thereby established the rule that whenever equity and law conflict, equity will prevail. A few years earlier, Shakespeare had set a similar scene before King Lear in the eponymous play. To Edgar, the King says '[T]hou, robéd man of justice, take thy place' (this suggests the office of Lord Chief Justice); to the Fool he says '[a]nd thou, his yokefellow of equity, / Bench by his side' (this clearly indicates the Lord Chancellor) (William Shakespeare, *King Lear* Act III, Scene 6). This scene, which appears in the 1608 quarto edition of the play, was omitted from the 1623 first folio edition. The omission is probably attributable to the fact that the relationship between law and equity had become so politically contentious around the time of *The Earl of Oxford's Case* (1615) (see B. J. Sokol and M. Sokol, 'Shakespeare and the English Equity Jurisdiction: The Merchant of Venice and the Two Texts of King Lear' (1999) 50(200) *The Review of English Studies* 417–39).

The idea of equity that was presented by Lord Chancellor Ellesmere in *The Earl of Oxford's Case* was greatly influenced by Aristotle's idea of equity (*epieikeia*), which the Lord Chancellor received via the writings of a leading sixteenth-century jurist, Christopher St. German.

Christopher St. German, *Dialogue in English between a Doctor of Divinity and a Student in the Laws of England*
(London: Robert Wyer, c.1530), Chapter 8

What is Equity?...it is not possible to make any general Rule of the Law but that it shall fail in some case: and therefore makers of Laws take heed to such things as may often come, and not to every particular case, for they could not though they would. And therefore to follow the word of the Law were in some case both against Justice and the Common wealth. Wherefore in some cases it is necessary to leave the words of the Law, and follow that [which] Reason and Justice requireth, and to that intent Equity is ordained; that is to say, to temper and mitigate the rigor of the Law. And it is called also by some Men *Epieikeia* [see case study on Jones: 1956]; the which is no other thing but an exception of the Law of God, or of the Law of Reason, from the general Rules of the Law of Man, when they by reason of their generality would in any particular case judge against the Law of God or the Law of Reason; the which exception is secretly understood in every general Rule of general positive Law. And so it appeareth that Equity taketh not away the very right, but only that [which] seemeth to be right by the general words of the Law; nor it is not ordained against the Cruelness of the Law, for the Law in such case generally taken is good in himself; but Equity followeth the Law in all particular cases where right and Justice requireth, notwithstanding the general Rule of the Law be to the contrary.

J. Walter Jones, *The Law and Legal Theory of the Greeks*
(Oxford: Clarendon Press, 1956), pp. 64–5

EQUITY

That the existence of a system of written law is an advantage to a state is implicit in [Aristotle's] criticism of the legal arrangements in Sparta and Crete which allow the Ephors and Elders to decide cases not as directed by written law but according to their own discretion. On the other hand written law as such has its drawbacks, and he stresses various characteristics of unwritten law to set against particular defects, as they are assumed to be, of the written law. Thus it is more equitable; and in one place the equitable, *epieikeia*, the fair or fitting, is defined as that justice which runs beyond or beside the written law [*Rhetoric* i. 13.13] But it may not as such be contrary to the intention of the legislator. A well-known passage in the *Ethics* explains that, every enactment being necessarily general in scope and there being some matters which cannot be appropriately regulated in general terms, every such law must to that extent be defective, though the responsibility for the defect must not be attributed to the legislator nor regarded as peculiar to a particular law, but be ascribed to the very nature of the legislative process which cannot but deal with men and acts in the mass, without regard to the merits of any individual case.

Equity necessarily has a place in any just system of law and is not an exclusively English idea. Nevertheless, it is only in England, with its peculiar jurisdictional distinction between the courts of common law and the Court of Chancery, that equity enjoyed (or, depending upon one's point of view, endured) gradual refinement into the distinct body of law that has survived until the present day. I say 'endured', because the process of developing equity in the special Court of Chancery was a long and painful one. By the start of the eighteenth century, the Court of Chancery was hopelessly overworked and inefficient. The appointment in 1729 of the chief Chancery Master, the Master of the Rolls, to sit as a second judge hardly helped (mainly because the Chancellor remained the only judge able to hear appeals). In 1813, a Vice-Chancellor was appointed, but even that did not improve matters much. There were now three judges presiding in Chancery, where once there had been the Chancellor alone. Yet when Sir Launcelot Shadwell was asked whether the three judges could cope, he is said to have replied 'No; not three angels.' The Court of Chancery Act 1851 was an early attempt to wrestle with the procedural problems in the Court of Chancery. It was during 1851, when the newspapers were full of talk of Chancery reform, that Charles Dickens wrote his great literary complaint against chancery, *Bleak House*.

Charles Dickens, *Bleak House*
(London: Bradbury & Evans, 1852–3), Chapter 1, 'In Chancery'

The raw afternoon is rawest, and the dense fog is densest, and the muddy streets are muddiest near that leaden-headed old obstruction, appropriate ornament for the threshold of a leaden-headed old corporation, Temple Bar. And hard by Temple Bar, in Lincoln's Inn Hall, at the very heart of the fog, sits the Lord High Chancellor in his High Court of Chancery.

Never can there come fog too thick, never can there come mud and mire too deep, to assort with the groping and floundering condition which this High Court of Chancery, most pestilent of hoary sinners, holds this day in the sight of heaven and earth.

On such an afternoon, if ever, the Lord High Chancellor ought to be sitting here—as here he is-with a foggy glory round his head, softly fenced in with crimson cloth and curtains, addressed by a large advocate with great whiskers, a little voice, and an interminable brief, and outwardly directing his contemplation to the lantern in the roof, where he can see nothing but fog. On such an afternoon some score of members of the High Court of Chancery bar ought to be—as here they are—mistily engaged in one of the ten thousand stages of an endless cause, tripping one another up on slippery precedents, groping knee-deep in technicalities, running their goat-hair and horsehair warded heads against walls of words and making a pretence of equity with serious faces, as players might. On such an afternoon the various solicitors in the cause, some two or three of whom have inherited it from their fathers, who made a fortune by it, ought to be—as are they not?—ranged in a line, in a long matted well (but you might look in vain for truth at the bottom of it) between the registrar's red table and the silk gowns, with bills, cross-bills, answers, rejoinders, injunctions, affidavits, issues, references to masters, masters' reports, mountains of costly nonsense, piled before them. Well may the court be dim, with wasting candles here and there; well may the fog hang heavy in it, as if it would never get out; well may the stained-glass windows lose their colour and admit no light of day into the place; well may the uninitiated from the streets, who peep in through the glass panes in the door, be deterred from entrance by its owlish aspect and by the drawl, languidly echoing to the roof from the padded dais where the Lord High Chancellor looks into the lantern that has no light in it and where the attendant wigs are all stuck in a fog-bank! This is the Court of Chancery, which has its decaying houses and its blighted lands in every shire, which has its worn-out lunatic in every madhouse and its dead in every churchyard, which has its ruined suitor with his slipshod heels and threadbare dress borrowing and begging through the round of every man's acquaintance, which gives to monied might the means abundantly of wearing out the right, which so exhausts finances, patience, courage, hope, so over-throws the brain and breaks the heart, that there is not an honourable man among its practitioners who would not give—who does not often give—the warning, 'Suffer any wrong that can be done you rather than come here!'

The Court of Chancery and the common law courts were subsequently fused as a single Supreme Court by the Judicature Acts of 1873–5, but it would be a mistake to imagine that law (i.e. common law) and equity have become fused. All that can be said is that nowadays when a judge hears a case he or she has authority to administer the common law rules together with equitable principles and doctrines. So, for instance, if the common law remedy of damages for breach of contract is inadequate, as it would be where the contract is a contract to buy land (since all land is unique), the judge will generally order that the contract be performed as agreed. That order, known as a decree of specific performance, is an equitable remedy. Equitable remedies, together with equitable doctrines and principles (many in the form of maxims), are considered in detail in Chapter 16 of this book.

Elders Pastoral Ltd v *Bank of New Zealand*
[1989] 2 NZLR 180

SOMER J: Neither law nor equity is now stifled by its origin and the fact that both are administered by one Court has inevitably meant that each has borrowed from the other in furthering the harmonious development of the law as a whole (at 193).

NOTES

1. The rules of the common law are designed to be rules of general (or 'common') application, such as the rule that legal title to freehold land can only be transferred by a formal document called a deed and the rule that breach of contract is remedied by an award of damages. The function of equity is to modify or disapply the common law rules where to apply them strictly would cause injustice in individual cases. If, for example, B builds a house on certain land owned absolutely by A in reliance on A's oral assurance that B will thereby acquire the right to live on that land for the rest of B's life, A will no longer be able to claim absolute ownership of the land. No formal deed of transfer has been executed in favour of B so, according to the common law rule, A

remains sole legal owner of the land and is entitled to evict B from the land under a common law action in trespass, but it would bring the legal requirement of a deed into disrepute if A were able to rely on the absence of a deed to perpetrate a species of fraud on B. A cannot in good conscience claim to own the entire benefit of the land, so equity (which still describes the abuse of a legal right or power in terms of its traditional concern for conscience) intervenes to remedy or prevent A's 'unconscionable' assertion of his legal right. The usual method of equitable intervention in such a case is to recognise B to be the beneficial owner of an interest in the land. The result is a sharing of the beneficial ownership between A and B. B is the owner of an equitable life interest in the land until he dies (it is called a 'life interest'), whereas A is the equitable beneficial owner of the land from the moment B dies (A is said to have a 'remainder' interest). However, A is still the sole owner of the land in the eyes of the law, so equity requires him to hold his legal title and his legal powers (to sell the land and so forth) 'on trust' for A and B according to their beneficial shares. A is no longer the absolute owner of the land; he is a trustee. The precise process by which a trust of this informal sort may arise is discussed in Chapter 8 but the important point for now is that whenever beneficial ownership of a single asset is shared in equity, there is a trust.

2. One might conclude from the fact that equitable ownership under a trust is binding on the legal ownership of the trustee that equity always overrules the law, but that is not the case. It is true that wherever the common law rule conflicts with an equitable principle the equitable principle should prevail, but equitable principles have been developed in such a way as to ensure that they do not undermine the common law rules. Thus it is one thing for equity occasionally to recognise exceptions to the requirement for a formal legal deed, but it would be quite another thing for equity to, in effect, abolish the general requirement for a deed. Equity does not abolish the legal rules; it creates limited exceptions to the rules so as to achieve more perfect justice. Imagine the common law to be a rough and pitted stone. The common law must be as unyielding as a stone in order to apply equally in every case, for a key principle of justice is that like cases should be treated alike and certainty and predictability are economically efficient. However the common law stone has sharp edges that occasionally inflict injustice (consider the case of A and B outlined at note 1), and there are holes in the stone where it does not provide an adequate remedy (we noted earlier that damages are an inadequate remedy for breach of contract to sell land). The function of equity is to smooth away the sharp edges where the law causes injustice and fill in the holes where the legal remedies are inadequate. It would never be the function of equity to smooth away the law to the point of eroding it completely, or to overfill the cracks so as to render the stone uneven.

3. It should be clear by now that the common law applies rules of general application. One upshot of this is that everyone can claim the benefit of these rules as of right. If I pay someone to mow my lawn and they fail to turn up, it is my legal right to recover the money from them. Equity, on the other hand, does not apply in such a wide and general manner, it only applies to those cases in which it is necessary to intervene to prevent the unconscionable assertion of a legal right or power. Whether it is necessary to intervene depends upon the particular facts of the case and is said to depend, therefore, upon the discretion of the judge. Accordingly, whereas the common law applies *rules*, equity applies *principles* and *doctrines* designed, over many centuries, to guide the discretionary enforcement of relief. It is true that in some contexts equity's intervention no longer depends upon discretion but is available as of right (the most notable example being the right of a beneficial owner under an expressly created trust to claim his share), but where there is still discretion, the principles and doctrines of equity still have an important role to play in guiding the exercise of that discretion.

SECTION 2: **THE NATURE OF THE TRUST**

Before we turn to consider the juridical trust developed in the Court of Chancery, we should remind ourselves of how basic trust and entrusting are to life in all its aspects.

Matthew Harding, 'Manifesting trust'
(2009) 29(2) *Oxford Journal of Legal Studies* 245–65, p. 254

[T]rust and entrusting are not the same. Trust is an attitude, and expectations that are accompanied by the attitude of trust may also be described as trusting. Entrusting is an action that is performed in light of trust. It is important to acknowledge the distinction between trust and entrusting, because a person can trust without also entrusting to the trusted. For example, I may trust you to send my mother a birthday card on her birthday, but in no sense does that necessarily entail me exposing any interests that I care about to your discretion. Insofar as I care about my mother's interest in having her birthday acknowledged by you, an interest that I care about is exposed to your discretion. However, I have not exposed it to your discretion, and therefore I cannot be said to have entrusted it to you. [...]

In contrast, a person cannot entrust without also trusting. Just as it makes sense to describe beliefs as trusting only where they are accompanied by an attitude of trust, so it makes sense to describe an action as entrusting only if it is accompanied by that attitude and usually also those beliefs. To expose interests to the discretion of another is, broadly speaking, to rely on that other. Entrusting is one type of reliance— reliance that is accompanied by a trusting attitude—but there are other types of reliance as well, which may be accompanied by other attitudes about the choices that people will make, including distrust. For example, it makes sense to say that I rely on you to repair my train set but that I distrust you to repair it if, for example, I had no choice but to have you repair it.

Most civil law jurisdictions adopt a strict distinction between the law governing rights in property and the law governing personal obligations, but the English trust is truly a hybrid of property and obligation. As one judge put it in a recent case: 'a trust is a matter which is difficult to define, but which essentially imposes an obligation to deal with property in a particular way on behalf of another person' (*Staden* v *Jones* [2008] EWCA Civ 936, *per* Arden LJ at para. [25]). The beneficiary has a beneficial interest in the trust fund (or trust asset), which interest is in the nature of property since it is binding in equity on third parties who acquire legal title to the asset, but the trustee is also obliged to the beneficiary personally to discharge the trust reposed in him and the beneficiary can require the trustee to account personally (from the trustee's own pocket if necessary) for any trust asset which is vested in the trustee or should be under the trustee's control. The fact that the beneficiary has a property right in the trust assets is perhaps most significant in the event of the trustee's insolvency, for if the beneficiary were restricted to his personal right against his insolvent trustee, the beneficiary would be no better off than any of the trustee's general creditors. The fact that the beneficiary owns property in the trustee's hands has the effect of putting that property out of reach of the trustee's general creditors. (The right of those creditors to recover their debts from the trustee is, of course, limited to property owned by the trustee absolutely.) The fact that trust beneficiaries are property owners is also highly significant in that it allows them to bring the trust to an end and take the trust property absolutely if they all, being competent and between them absolutely entitled to the trust property, agree to such a course of action. This is the so-called 'rule in *Saunders* v *Vautier*' (discussed in depth in Chapter 9). The rule has no application where potential beneficiaries (e.g. 'grandchildren') do not yet exist. The fact that the beneficiaries' interests are remote and might be unlikely ever to vest is no basis for terminating the trust under the rule (*Thorpe* v *Revenue and Customs Commissioners* [2009] EWHC 611 (Ch)).

A trust can exist when legal and equitable title are vested in the same persons (consider joint beneficial ownership of land—see *Stack* v *Dowden* [2007] UKHL 17, [2007] 2 WLR 831, in Chapter 8) but the process of separating legal title to an asset from equitable title to the same asset will always create a trust.

In the *Westdeutsche Landesbank Girozentrale* case, Lord Browne-Wilkinson, speaking obiter, reached the surprising and unorthodox conclusion that '[e]ven in cases where the whole beneficial interest is vested in B and the bare legal interest is in A, A is not necessarily a trustee'.

Westdeutsche Landesbank Girozentrale v *Islington London Borough Council*
[1996] AC 669, House of Lords

Facts: For the facts of this case, see Chapter 5.

Held: On 'the separation of title point':

LORD BROWNE-WILKINSON: The bank's submission, at its widest, is that if the legal title is in A but the equitable interest in B, A holds as trustee for B.

Again I think this argument is fallacious. There are many cases where B enjoys rights which, in equity, are enforceable against the legal owner, A, without A being a trustee, e.g. an equitable right to redeem a mortgage, equitable easements, restrictive covenants, the right to rectification, an insurer's right by subrogation to receive damages subsequently recovered by the assured: *Lord Napier and Ettrick* v *Hunter* [1993] AC 713. Even in cases where the whole beneficial interest is vested in B and the bare legal interest is in A, A is not necessarily a trustee, e.g. where title to land is acquired by estoppel as against the legal owner; a mortgagee who has fully discharged his indebtedness enforces his right to recover the mortgaged property in a redemption action, not an action for breach of trust.

The bank contended that where, under a pre-existing trust, B is entitled to an equitable interest in trust property, if the trust property comes into the hands of a third party, X (not being a purchaser for value of the legal interest without notice), B is entitled to enforce his equitable interest against the property in the hands of X because X is a trustee for B. In my view the third party, X, is not necessarily a trustee for B: B's equitable right is enforceable against the property in just the same way as any other specifically enforceable equitable right can be enforced against a third party. Even if the third party, X, is not aware that what he has received is trust property B is entitled to assert his title in that property. If X has the necessary degree of knowledge, X may himself become a constructive trustee for B on the basis of knowing receipt. But unless he has the requisite degree of knowledge he is not personally liable to account as trustee: *Re Diplock* [1948] Ch 465, 478; *Re Montagu's Settlement Trusts* [1987] Ch 264 [see Chapter 15]. Therefore, innocent receipt of property by X subject to an existing equitable interest does not by itself make X a trustee despite the severance of the legal and equitable titles... in the present case the local authority could not have become accountable for profits until it knew that the contract was void.

NOTES
1. It is respectfully submitted that none of his Lordship's illustrations defeats this author's claim that the process of separating legal title to an asset from equitable title to the same asset will always create a trust. Let us consider his lordship's examples from land law, with which the reader may be familiar from earlier studies. Estoppel is considered in depth in Chapter 8, but suffice to say that estoppel is a cause of action that prevents the legal owner of an asset from asserting his absolute beneficial ownership of the asset, and which, having been raised, must be satisfied by a final remedial award in favour of the claimant. The final award might take the form of an equitable interest in the land, but there is no trust until then. As for the mortgage example: under the old form of mortgage, the borrower conveyed his land to the lender until repayment of the debt and retained an equity of redemption in the meantime. It is arguable that this was a situation in which legal and equitable titles were separated without producing a trust, but the argument is not strong. It is far from certain that the equity of redemption is a true estate land. Even a leading judge admitted that 'one knows in a general, if not in a critical way, what is an equity of redemption' (*Salt* v *Marquess of Northampton* [1892] AC 1, *per* Lord Bramwell at 18, HL) and one jurist wrote, in similar vein, that '[a]n equity of redemption can be more appropriately illustrated than defined or described' (J. J. Powell, *A Treatise on the Law of Mortgages*, 6th edn (Thomas Coventry ed.) (1826), Vol. I, p. 205, note A). See, generally, G. Watt, 'The Lie of the Land: Mortgage Law as Legal Fiction', in E. Cooke (ed.), *Modern Studies in Property Law*, Vol. 4 (Oxford: Hart Publishing, 2007), pp. 73–96. Equitable easements and restrictive covenants are also red herrings. They do not involve separation of equitable title from legal title to an asset. They are not forms of title at all, but rights enforceable against title.
2. The fact that the beneficiary, not the trustee, is the substantial or 'real' owner of trust assets was confirmed recently so as to allow an oil company to recover economic losses caused by the negligence of companies in control of storing and distributing its fuel. The latter companies, which were legal owners of the pipes and depot, were held to be little more than bare trustees for the oil company (*Colour Quest Ltd* v *Total Downstream UK Plc* [2010] EWCA Civ 180, [2010] 3 All ER 793

(CA (Civ)) at para. [132]). The beneficial owner could join the legal owner in the proceedings, so it did not matter that the beneficial owner was not himself in possession of the property (applying *Chappell* v *Somers & Blake* [2003] EWHC 1644 (Ch), [2004] Ch 19)—see, further, Section 3.

SECTION 3: DISTINCTIONS BETWEEN LEGAL AND EQUITABLE OWNERSHIP

A: Bringing common law claims

Where a third party owes a common law obligation to the trustee of a trust, it is the trustee as legal owner of the trust property who should enforce it. The beneficiary's entitlement is not recognised at common law and the beneficiary therefore has no right in his own capacity to bring a common law action against the third party directly. Thus, where property is leased it is the trustee who sues for rent (*Shalit* v *Joseph Nadler Ltd* [1933] 2 KB 79) and, generally speaking, it is only the legal owner of property at the time that it is damaged who can sue in negligence. Of course, the trustee is personally and directly accountable to the beneficiary, so if the trustee unreasonably refuses to sue the third party, the beneficiary can require the trustee to sue the third party and may even be permitted to sue in the trustee's stead (standing as it were in the trustee's shoes). As Lord Collins SCJ observed in *Roberts* v *Gill & Co* [2010] UKSC 22, [2010] 2 WLR 1227: 'the beneficiary has no personal right to sue, and is suing on behalf of the estate, or more accurately, the trustee' (para. [62]).

Leigh & Sullivan Ltd v *Aliakmon Shipping Co. Ltd, The Aliakmon*
[1986] AC 785, House of Lords

Facts: Buyers of a quantity of steel coils failed in a negligence action against the ship-owners who had badly stowed the cargo aboard *The Aliakmon*, as a result of which it suffered damage, because legal title in the cargo had not passed to them by the time the damage occurred. The buyers alternatively claimed that they were equitable owners of the cargo (on the grounds that equity treats as done that which ought to be done, and that property ought to pass to them).

Held: Equitable ownership does not confer the right to sue in negligence.

LORD BRANDON (on the question of equitable ownership): ... My Lords, under this head Mr Clarke [for the buyers] put forward two propositions of law. The first proposition was that a person who has the equitable ownership of goods is entitled to sue in tort for negligence anyone who by want of care causes them to be lost or damaged without joining the legal owner as a party to the action. The second proposition was that a buyer who agrees to buy goods in circumstances where, although ascertained goods have been appropriated to the contract, their legal ownership remains in the seller, acquires upon such appropriation the equitable ownership of the goods. Applying those two propositions to the facts of the present case, Mr Clarke submitted that the goods the subject-matter of the c. and f. contract had been appropriated to the contract on or before shipment at Inchon, and that from then on, while the legal ownership of the goods remained in the sellers, the buyers became the equitable owners of them, and could therefore sue the shipowners in tort for negligence for the damage done to them without joining the sellers.

In my view, the first proposition cannot be supported. There may be cases where a person who is the equitable owner of certain goods has already a possessory title to them. In such a case he is entitled, by virtue of his possessory title rather than his equitable ownership, to sue in tort for negligence anyone whose want of care has caused loss of or damage to the goods without joining the legal owner as a party to the action: see for instance *Healey* v *Healey* [1915] 1 KB 938. If, however, the person is the equitable owner of the goods and no more, then he must join the legal owner as a party to the action, either as co-plaintiff if he is willing or as co-defendant if he is not. This had always been the law in the field of equitable ownership of land and I see no reason why it should not also be so in the field of equitable ownership of goods.

With regard to the second proposition, I do not doubt that it is possible, in accordance with established equitable principles, for equitable interests in goods to be created and to exist. It seems to me, however, extremely doubtful whether equitable interests in goods can be created or exist within the confines of an ordinary contract of sale. The Sale of Goods Act 1893 [replaced in 1979], which must be taken to apply to the c. and f. contract of sale in the present case, is a complete code of law in respect of contracts for the sale of goods. The passing of the property in goods the subject-matter of such a contract is fully dealt with in ss.16 to 19 of the Act. Those sections draw no distinction between the legal and the equitable property in goods, but appear to have been framed on the basis that the expression 'property', as used in them, is intended to comprise both the legal and the equitable title. In this connection I consider that there is much force in the observations of Atkin LJ in *Re Wait* [1927] 1 Ch 606, 635–636, from which I quote only this short passage:

> It would have been futile in a code intended for commercial men to have created an elaborate structure of rules dealing with rights at law, if at the same time it was intended to leave, subsisting with the legal rights, equitable rights inconsistent with, more extensive, and coming into existence earlier than the rights so carefully set out in the various sections of the Code.

These observations of Atkin LJ were not necessary to the decision of the case before him and represented a minority view not shared by the other two members of the Court of Appeal. Moreover, Atkin LJ expressly stated that he was not deciding the point. If my view on the first proposition of law is correct, it is again unnecessary to decide the point in this appeal. I shall, therefore, say no more than that my provisional view accords with that expressed by Atkin LJ in *Re Wait*...

NOTES
1. The buyers had no equitable ownership, so that the remarks at the beginning of this passage are technically *obiter dicta*. However, they were expressly adopted by the Court of Appeal in *MCC Proceeds Inc* v *Lehman Brothers International (Europe)* [1998] 4 All ER 675, [1998] 2 BCLC 659, and applied to a conversion action. Mummery LJ observed that if the beneficiary could sue directly, the defendant would be subject to actions from both legal and equitable owners, and that there would be a problem of multiplicity of actions. Although if the claimant had had actual possession, or an immediate right to possession, of goods, a conversion claim would have lain for interference with that possessory right, beneficial title on its own will not found a claim in conversion.
2. These cases should be contrasted with *White* v *Jones* [1995] 2 WLR 187, House of Lords, upholding *Ross* v *Caunters* [1980] Ch 297. Here, an intended beneficiary under a will successfully sued the solicitors for drawing up a will in such a way as to exclude him. Of course, the intended beneficiary did not even have equitable title when the action was brought, so the case is somewhat exceptional and the decision can only be explained on the basis that the solicitor had voluntarily assumed responsibility to the intended beneficiary and the fact that nobody apart from the intended beneficiary was in any position to bring an action.

B: Equitable rights as property rights

(i) Equitable rights may be assigned

NOTE: See formalities for disposition of equitable interests in Chapter 6.

(ii) Equitable rights bind third parties

Equitable interests in property are capable of binding third parties, although unlike legal interests they do not bind the bona fide purchaser for value of the legal estate without notice. (Such a purchaser has an 'unanswerable defence'—*Pilcher* v *Rawlins* (1872) LR 7 Ch App 259 (CA)—and is sometimes referred to as equity's darling.) This is an application of the maxim 'where the equities are equal, the law prevails'. By contrast, a subsequent purchaser of an *equitable* estate is bound by the maxim 'where the equities are equal, the first in time prevails'.

NOTE: The *R. Griggs Group Ltd* v *Evans* case is included for the clear and detailed explanation it provides of the relationship between equity and law, equitable title, and legal title and rights *in personam* and rights *in rem*.

R. Griggs Group Ltd v Evans

[2004] All ER (D) 155, Chancery Division

Facts: The claimant sought to enforce copyright in a logo against a foreign defendant.

Held: It was not a breach of international comity to order the defendant to assign the foreign copyrights in the logo to Griggs, instead of leaving Griggs to bring parallel proceedings in numerous countries. Furthermore Griggs had an equity arising out of English contracts which, were the property situate in England, Griggs could enforce against the defendant. As regards the property situate abroad, it was not shown that the laws of the foreign countries would extinguish that equity; and it is not unreasonable to proceed on that basis. Hence Griggs was entitled to succeed.

PETER PRESCOTT QC (sitting as a deputy judge of the High Court):

V. The Doctrine of the Purchaser With Notice

The English Rule

In this country the general rule is well known but the reason for it sometimes forgotten. First, let us recall the rule. It is that where a vendor has entered into an obligation to transfer property to a purchaser, being an obligation which can be enforced in specie, a third party who has notice of that obligation may not validly acquire the property from the vendor, without the consent of the original purchaser. Put more accurately, the third party is defeated unless he was a purchaser for value of the legal estate in good faith without actual or constructive notice of the equity in favour of the prior purchaser, or is one claiming under such purchaser. The rule may be modified or overridden by a statutory scheme for the registration of interests in property. Absent such a scheme, the general rule applies. [para. [37]].

Every law student is taught about the rule, but nowadays if asked to explain why it is so he might be reduced to retorting: 'Well, it just is.' That will not do for the purposes of our case. For I am being asked to apply the rule to property which has no existence except under the laws of foreign states—more than 150 of them. Therefore I need to understand the inwardness of the rule. [para. [38]].

The rule was evolved by our courts of equity. Nobody has been able to come up with a satisfactory definition of 'equity', save to say that it is that body of rules and principles which, before 1875, were the peculiar province of certain special courts notably the Court of Chancery. From the beginning the courts of equity regarded themselves as courts of conscience (*per* Viscount Haldane LC in *Nocton* v *Lord Ashburton* [1914] AC 932 at 954). They ordered the defendant to behave as a righteous man would have done in that particular situation. Over time they came to accept that 'conscience' was too elastic a concept to be employed by itself (as Deane J was to put it much later in *Muschinski* v *Dodds* (1985) 160 CLR 583 at 615, it would open the door to 'idiosyncratic notions of fairness and justice'). But from that starting principle they evolved a detailed and precise body of rules. What they achieved was a kind of supplementary jurisprudence which was intended to fill up the gaps in the common law. [para. [39]].

The upshot was that the result of a case might easily differ, depending on whether it was heard by a court of common law or a court of equity. Despite this, when both sets of courts were merged in 1875 it was found that there were very few rules upon which law and equity were in conflict (Maitland, *Lectures on Equity*, 1909, 16–18). This seems an amazing paradox at first sight, but is resolved once it is appreciated that equity did not create titles rival to those of the common law, but instead acted *in personam*. A simple example will serve to bring out several of the features which were characteristic of equity, and are pertinent to our case. [para. [40]].

Suppose a man had agreed to sell his estate Blackacre yet refused to complete by the due date. The courts of common law would have said: 'You have broken your contract, and must pay damages to the buyer.' But the buyer did not want the money: he wanted Blackacre. No two estates are alike and so an award of damages was not an adequate remedy. No other remedy was available in the courts of common law. So the buyer might decide to bring a suit in a court of equity: for specific performance. I suspect that the origin of this equitable remedy is lost in the mists of time, but I believe that, originally, the court of equity would have said to the vendor something along these lines: 'If you were a man of good conscience you would not keep this estate—leaving the plaintiff to his inadequate remedy. You would keep to your bargain and convey Blackacre to him. And that is what you must do, or we shall hold you in contempt of court.' [para. [41]].

But now suppose that the vendor had already conveyed the estate to a third party—before the court of equity had made any order, of course. The courts of common law would have said: 'Well, the vendor could have chosen to pay damages and keep his estate. Then he could have sold Blackacre to anyone. Therefore he must still pay damages, but the conveyance in favour of the third party is good and effective.' In contrast, a court of equity, while not denying that the third party was the legal owner—they would have admitted that none but he could bring proceedings against a trespasser—would have added: 'It is fine if you acquired this estate as a purchaser for value without notice. But a righteous man in your position would not have acquired Blackacre if he had known that the vendor had already agreed to convey it to the original buyer. So, if you did have notice of the prior contract, we shall order you to convey the estate to the original buyer.' [para. [42]].

This illustration brings out several features characteristic of equity. Note, first, that the equity judges never sought to overrule the decisions of their common law brethren. They had not the power to do so. They were not a superior court with power to quash decisions of inferior tribunals, as in proceedings for judicial review nowadays. Instead, they achieved their aim by compelling the wrongdoing litigant himself to comply with the rule prescribed by equity. Thus equity acted *in personam*. It 'fastened upon the conscience' of the defendant and compelled him to act accordingly. The distinction may sound like mere sophism, but it was not. Show me the third party purchaser, and I will show you the difference. If equity had tried to make the third party purchaser liable, irrespective of any notice, it would not have been acting in personam. It would have been creating a title in the original purchaser good as against the whole world. Thus it would have been acting *in rem*. It would have been ousting the common law, not supplementing it. Hence, as Lord Browne-Wilkinson said in *Barclays Bank plc* v *O'Brien* [1994] AC at 195: 'The doctrine of notice lies at the heart of equity.' [para. [43]].

(iii) Taxation

Equitable rights may be subject to taxation (e.g. in *Baker* v *Archer-Shee* [1927] AC 844, an equitable owner was considered the owner of dividends for tax purposes). The trustees normally have a duty to pay tax on trust assets in their hands (see Chapter 2, Section 3, subsection A). If an owner of property wishes to settle it on trust to avoid tax, HM Revenue and Customs is very astute to spot any attempt by the settlor to reserve a beneficial interest for himself. An attempt to reserve control (by means, say, of a power to revoke, vary or regulate the trusts) might be construed as a taxable reservation of benefit. (Known as a 'gift with reservation' (Finance Act 1986, s.102(1)(a) and s.102(1)(b)). See *Inland Revenue Commissioners* v *Eversden* [2002] EWHC 1360 (Ch), [2002] STC 1109, High Court.)

■ SUMMATIVE QUESTION

1. 'Common law and equity are working in different ways towards the same ends, and it is therefore as wrong to assert the independence of one from the other as it is to assert that there is no difference between them.'

Critically discuss this statement.

FURTHER READING

Baker, J. H., 'The Court of Chancery and Equity', in *An Introduction to English Legal History*, 3rd edn (London: Butterworths, 1990); 4th edn (London: Butterworths, 2002), Chapter 6.

Cotterrell, R., 'Trusting in Law: Legal and Moral Concepts of Trust' (1993) *CLP* 75.

Goodhart, Sir William, QC, 'Trust Law for the Twenty First Century' (1996) 10(2) *TLI* 38.

Gretton, G. L., 'Trusts without Equity' (2000) 49 *ICLQ* 599.

Langbein, J. H., 'The Secret Life of the Trust as an Instrument of Commerce' (1997) 107 *Yale LJ* 165.

Lupoi, M., 'Trust and Confidence' (2009) 125 *LQR* 253–87.

Maitland, F. W. 'Uses and Trusts', in *Equity: A Course of Lectures* (rev. by J. Brunyate) (Cambridge: Cambridge University Press, 1936), p. 23.

Mason, Sir Anthony, 'The Place of Equity and Equitable Remedies in the Contemporary Common Law World' (1994) 110 *LQR* 238.

Matthews, P., 'The New Trust: Obligations without Rights?', in A. J. Oakley (ed.), *Trends in Contemporary Trust Law* (Oxford: Clarendon Press, 1996) 1.

Millett, Sir Peter, 'Equity—The Road Ahead' (1995) 9(2) *TLI* 35.

Pound, R., 'The Decadence of Equity' (1905) 5 *Columbia LR* 20.

Watt, G., *Equity Stirring: The Story of Justice Beyond Law* (Oxford: Hart Publishing, 2009).

Worthington, S., *Equity* (Oxford: Clarendon Press, 2003).

2

Trusts in Context

KEY AIMS

To locate the trust in its social and legal context. To compare and contrast the trust with other legal ideas.

SECTION 1: INTRODUCTION

It is important to place the trust in its social and legal context. The private trust is one of many institutions, such as the family, the church, and the private partnership, which lie between, or 'mediate', the individual and the State; hence in future chapters we will consider the important role played by the trust in the provision of charitable aid (Chapter 7), pensions (see Chapters 5 and 12 in particular), and home ownership (Chapter 8). Equity and trusts also play an important role in commerce, as will become clear when, for example, we examine the creation of express trusts (Chapter 3) and consider (in Part IV of the book) the implications of trusts for third parties in commercial contexts. In this chapter, we will examine the peculiar commercial device known as the '*Quistclose* trust'. However, our primary concern in this chapter is to place the trust in its legal context, by comparing and contrasting it with other legal ideas.

SECTION 2: PRIVATE TRUST CONTRASTED WITH 'GOVERNMENTAL' TRUST

Tito v *Waddell (No. 2)*

[1977] Ch 106, Court of Appeal

Facts: This action was brought by the native Banaban inhabitants of Ocean Island, a coral island located just south of the equator in the Western Pacific. Phosphate was discovered on the island in 1900 and the Pacific Islands Company moved in to extract it through mining operations. In 1920, the British Phosphate Commissioners, an unincorporated body established by the governments of the United Kingdom, Australia, and New Zealand, acquired these operations. In due course, they leased additional land from the Banabans for mining purposes. The terms of the lease and a declaration by the resident Commissioner assured the Banabans that royalties from the mining operation would be held 'on trust' by the resident Commissioner for the Banaban community generally. A subsequent ordinance omitted the word trust but still provided, *inter alia*, that the resident Commissioner would hold royalties from the phosphate for the benefit of the Banabans. The Banabans claimed that the mining profits were held on trust for them.

Held: The fiduciary claims of the Banabans failed because any obligation which the Crown owed towards the Banabans was not justiciable in the courts; it was a governmental obligation or 'trust in the higher sense'.

MEGARRY V-C: [referring to a number of principles or considerations supported by *Kinloch* v *Secretary for State for India in Council* (1882) 7 App Cas 619]. First, the use of a phrase such as 'in trust for', even in a formal document such as a Royal Warrant, does not necessarily create a trust enforceable by the courts. As Lord O'Hagan said [in *Kinloch* at 630]: 'There is no magic in the word "trust".' Second, the term 'trust' is one which may properly be used to describe not only relationships which are enforceable by the courts in their equitable jurisdiction, but also other relationships such as the discharge, under the direction of the Crown, of the duties or functions belonging to the prerogative and the authority of the Crown. Trusts of the former kind, so familiar in this Division, are described by Lord Selborne LC [in *Kinloch* at 625–6] as being 'trusts in the lower sense'; trusts of the latter kind, so unfamiliar in this Division, he called 'trusts in the higher sense'.

... There is, indeed, a certain awkwardness in describing as a trust a relationship which is not enforceable by the courts, though the so-called trusts of imperfect obligation perhaps provide some sort of parallel. Certainly in common speech in legal circles 'trust' is normally used to mean an equitable relationship enforceable in the courts and not a governmental relationship which is not thus enforceable. I propose to use the word 'trust' *simpliciter* (or for emphasis the phrase 'true trust') to describe what in the conventional sense is a trust enforceable in the courts, and to use Lord Selborne LC's compound phrase 'trust in the higher sense' to express the governmental obligation that he describes ...

The third is that it seems clear that the determination whether an instrument has created a true trust or a trust in the higher sense is a matter of construction, looking at the whole of the instrument in question, its nature and effect, and, I think, its context. Fourth, a material factor may be the form of the description given by the instrument to the person alleged to be the trustee. An impersonal description of him, in the form of a reference not to an individual but to the holder of a particular office for the time being, may give some indication that what is intended is not a true trust, but a trust in the higher sense.

SECTION 3: TRUST AND TAXATION

Ever since the days of its predecessor, the medieval 'use', the trust has been employed to separate beneficial enjoyment of an asset (originally land) from formal title to the asset in order to escape taxes charged on benefits, and duties charged on formal ownership. It is important to be aware of the general relationship between trusts and taxation. The first distinction to note is between tax avoidance and tax evasion. It is a somewhat fine distinction and one that is blurred at the margins. Broadly speaking, tax evasion is criminal financial planning carried out to avoid the payment of a tax that has already fallen due, whereas tax avoidance is legitimate financial estate planning carried out to prevent a tax from falling due in the first place. In fact, even the courts' own statutory jurisdiction to approve schemes for the variation of beneficial interests under trusts is frequently exercised for the benefit of applicants whose underlying motive is the avoidance of tax (see Chapter 9). However, whereas it is perfectly permissible to arrange one's affairs so as to reduce one's tax burden, any entirely sham or artificial steps in the arrangement of one's affairs will be ignored so as to enable HM Revenue and Customs (HMRC) to tax the transaction according to its true nature (*Ramsay* v *IRC* [1982] AC 300). Nevertheless, HMRC and the English courts can do nothing about trusts, such as 'non-resident' or 'offshore' trusts, over which they have no jurisdiction. Another preliminary point to note is that trustees and beneficiaries are subject to personal taxation, and may be taxed on trust capital and income, so the settlor and his advisers must take this into account when assessing the overall tax burden of a plan. Finally, it should be noted that one of the great benefits of charitable status is that a charitable trust is exempt from most taxes (see Chapter 7).

A: Trustees' duty to pay tax

Income and capital gains tax payable by a trust is charged to the trustees personally, although the beneficiaries are ultimately liable and the trustees can therefore recover from the trust fund any tax paid on behalf of the trust. Individual tax payers have a tax free 'personal allowance' which exempts a certain sum of income and capital gain from tax, and trusts have something similar.

Jerome v *Kelly (Her Majesty's Inspector of Taxes)*
[2004] 1 WLR 1409, House of Lords

LORD HOFFMANN (on Capital Gains Taxation of Trusts): The trustee is charged to tax, but because he is only legal owner, he is entitled to an indemnity out of the fund. The beneficiary's interest is an item of property distinct from the underlying assets but an assignment of that interest is not ordinarily treated as a disposal giving rise to a liability to tax. Otherwise a beneficiary who disposed of his interest would be taxed twice on the same gains; once through the trustee's right of indemnity and once in his own right.

SECTION 4: TRUST CONTRASTED WITH OTHER LEGAL IDEAS

In Subsections A–F, we will compare and contrast the private trust with other legal devices and ideas.

A: Trust and powers of appointment

Property held by T on trust for B *must* be held by T for the benefit of B (the beneficiary), whereas property held by P subject to a power of appointment in favour of O (the object of the power), merely gives P the *option* of conferring benefits on O. (Although if the power is given to P in P's fiduciary capacity, say because P is a trustee or solicitor, P must periodically consider whether or not to exercise the power.) Usually a power of appointment is accompanied by a gift in favour of a designated person in the event of the power not being exercised (known as a 'gift-over in default').

Re Manisty's Settlement
[1974] 1 Ch 17, Chancery Division
Facts: The settlement gave trustees a discretionary power to apply the trust fund for the benefit of a small class of the settlor's near relations, save that any member of a smaller 'excepted class' was to be excluded from the class of beneficiaries. The trustees were also given power at their absolute discretion to declare that any person, corporation, or

charity (except a member of the excepted class or a trustee) should be included in the class of beneficiaries. A power to distribute amongst the members of a class, apart from to certain excluded members, is called an intermediate power. A summons was brought to determine whether the intermediate power in this case was void for uncertainty.

Held: The power to extend the class of beneficiaries was valid.

TEMPLEMAN J: The court cannot insist upon any particular consideration being given by the trustees to the exercise of the power. If a settlor creates a power exercisable in favour of his issue, his relations and the employees of his company, the trustees may in practice for many years hold regular meetings, study the terms of the power and the other provisions of the settlement, examine the accounts and either decide not to exercise the power or to exercise it only in favour, for example, of the children of the settlor ... In my judgment it cannot be said that the trustees in those circumstances have committed a breach of trust and that they ought to have advertised the power or looked beyond the people who are most likely to be the objects of the bounty of the settlor ...

If a person within the ambit of the power is aware of its existence he can require the trustees to consider exercising the power and in particular to consider a request on his part for the power to be exercised in his favour. The trustees must consider this request, and if they decline to do so or can be proved to have omitted to do so, then the aggrieved person may apply to the court which may remove the trustees and appoint others in their place ...

The court may also be persuaded to intervene if the trustees act 'capriciously', that is to say, act for reasons which I apprehend could be said to be irrational, perverse or irrelevant to any sensible expectation of the settlor; for example, if they chose a beneficiary by height or complexion or by the irrelevant fact that he was a resident of Greater London. A special power does not show the trustees how to consider the exercise of the power in a sensible manner and does not by its terms enable the court to judge whether the power is being considered in a proper manner. The conduct and duties of trustees of an intermediate power, and the rights and remedies of any person who wishes the power to be exercised in his favour, are precisely similar to the conduct and duties of trustees of special powers and the rights and remedies of any person who wishes a special power to be exercised in his favour. In practice, the considerations which weigh with the trustees will be no different from the considerations which will weigh with the trustees of a wide special power ... In both cases the trustees have an absolute discretion and cannot be obliged to take any form of action, save to consider the exercise of the power and a request from a person who is within the ambit of the power ... The only difference between an intermediate power and a special power for present purposes is that a settlor by means of a special power cannot be certain that he has armed his trustees against all developments and contingencies ...

Logically, in my judgment, there is no reason to bless a special power which prescribes the ambit of the power by classifying beneficiaries and at the same time to outlaw an intermediate power which prescribes the ambit of the power by classifying excepted persons. It may well be that there are some classes of special power which will not be recognised by the court, but this possibility does not affect the validity of intermediate powers. The objection to the capricious exercise of a power may well extend to the creation of a capricious power. A power to benefit 'residents of Greater London' is capricious because the terms of the power negative any sensible intention on the part of the settlor. If the settlor intended and expected the trustees would have regard to persons with some claim on his bounty or some interest in an institution favoured by the settlor, or if the settlor had any other sensible intention or expectation, he would not have required the trustees to consider only an accidental conglomeration of persons who have no discernable link with the settlor or with any institution. A capricious power negatives a sensible consideration by the trustees of the exercise of the power. But a wide power, be it special or intermediate, does not negative or prohibit a sensible approach by the trustees to the consideration and exercise of their powers.

Re Hay's ST

[1982] 1 WLR 1202, [1981] 3 All ER 786, Chancery Division

Facts: Trustees of a settlement made in 1958 held the trust fund subject to a power to allocate it for the benefit of 'such persons or purposes' as they should in their discretion appoint. If they made no such appointment, the trust fund would pass to the settlor's nieces and nephews. Only the settlor, her husband, and the trustees could not be appointed to benefit from the fund. Questions arose as to how the court should supervise the exercise of such a wide discretionary power and how such a power differed from a trustee's duties under a trust.

Held: An 'intermediate' or 'hybrid' power of appointment, allowing a trustee to appoint anyone in the world except for a specified number or class of persons, did not infringe the certainty of object requirement. However, the appointment actually made was void. The trustees simply appointed the trust fund to be held by themselves for 'such person or persons and for such purposes' as the trustees should in their discretion appoint by deed within 21 years of the date of the settlement. This was not a valid appointment, since it had merely set up the mechanism for future appointments. The trustees had in effect purported to delegate their powers of appointment, rather than exercise them, and even though they had delegated them to themselves, they had infringed the rule that a trustee may not delegate his powers, including intermediate powers (*'delegatus non potest delegare'*).

SIR ROBERT MEGARRY V-C: I propose to approach the matter by stages. First, it is plain that if a power of appointment is given to a person who is not in a fiduciary position, there is nothing in the width of the power which invalidates it *per se*. The power may be a special power with a large class of persons as objects; the power may be what is called a 'hybrid' power, or an 'intermediate' power, authorising appointment to anyone save a specified number or class of persons; or the power may be a general power. Whichever it is, there is nothing in the number of persons to whom an appointment may be made which will invalidate it. The difficulty comes when the power is given to trustees as such, in that the number of objects may interact with the fiduciary duties of the trustees and their control by the court. The argument of counsel for the defendants carried him to the extent of asserting that no valid intermediate or general power could be vested in trustees.

That brings me to the second point, namely, the extent of the fiduciary obligations of trustees who have a mere power vested in them, and how far the court exercises control over them in relation to that power. In the case of a trust, of course, the trustee is bound to execute it, and if he does not, the court will see to its execution. A mere power is very different. Normally the trustee is not bound to exercise it, and the court will not compel him to do so. That, however, does not mean that he can simply fold his hands and ignore it, for normally he must from time to time consider whether or not to exercise the power, and the court may direct him to do this. When he does exercise the power, he must, of course (as in the case of all trusts and powers) confine himself to what is authorised, and not go beyond it. But that is not the only restriction. Whereas a person who is not in a fiduciary position is free to exercise the power in any way that he wishes, unhampered by any fiduciary duties, a trustee to whom, as such, a power is given is bound by the duties of his office in exercising that power to do so in a responsible manner according to its purpose. It is not enough for him to refrain from acting capriciously; he must do more. He must 'make such a survey of the range of objects or possible beneficiaries' as will enable him to carry out his fiduciary duty. He must find out 'the permissible area of selection and then consider responsibly, in individual cases, whether a contemplated beneficiary was within the power and whether, in relation to the possible claimants, a particular grant was appropriate': per Lord Wilberforce in *Re Baden (No. 1)* [1971] AC 424 at 449, 457.

I pause there. The summary of the law that I have set out above is taken from a variety of sources, principally *Re Gestetner* [1953] Ch 672, *Re Gulbenkian's Settlements* [1970] AC 508 at 518, 524–5 and *Re Baden (No. 1)* [1971] AC 424 at 456. The last proposition, relating to the survey and consideration, at first sight seems to give rise to some difficulty. It is now well settled that no mere power is invalidated by it being impossible to ascertain every object of the power; provided the language is clear enough to make it possible to say whether any given individual is an object of the power, it need not be possible to compile a complete list of every object: see *Re Gestetner* [1953] Ch 672 at 688; *Re Gulbenkian's Settlements* [1970] AC 508; *Re Baden (No. 1)* [1971] AC 424. As Harman J said in *Re Gestetner* [1953] Ch 672 at 688, the trustees need not 'worry their heads to survey the world from China to Peru, when there are perfectly good objects of the class in England'.

That brings me to the third point. How is the duty of making a responsible survey and selection to be carried out in the absence of any complete list of objects? This question was considered by the Court of Appeal in *Re Baden (No. 2)*. That case was concerned with what, after some divergences of judicial opinion, was held to be a discretionary trust and not a mere power; but plainly the require-ments for a mere power cannot be more stringent than those for a discretionary trust. The duty, I think, may be expressed along the following lines: I venture a modest degree of amplification and exegesis of what was said in *Re Baden (No. 2)* [1973] Ch 9 at 20, 27. The trustee must not simply proceed to exercise the power in favour of such of the objects as happen to be at hand or claim his attention. He must first consider what persons or classes of persons are objects of the power within the definition in the settlement or will. In doing this, there is no need to compile a complete list of the objects, or even to make an accurate assessment of the number of them: what is needed is an appre-ciation of the width of the field, and thus whether a selection is to be made merely from a dozen, or, instead, from thousands or millions ... Only when the trustee has applied his mind to 'the size of the problem' should he then consider in individual cases whether, in relation to other possible claimants, a particular grant is appropriate. In doing this, no doubt he should not prefer the undeserving to the deserving; but he is not required to make an exact calculation whether, as between deserving claim-ants, A is more deserving than B: see *Re Gestetner* [1953] Ch 672 at 688, approved in *Re Baden (No. 1)* [1971] AC 424 at 453.

If I am right in these views, the duties of a trustee which are specific to a mere power seem to be threefold. Apart from the obvious duty of obeying the trust instrument, and in particular of making no appointment that is not authorised by it, the trustee must, first, consider periodically whether or not he should exercise the power; second, consider the range of objects of the power; and third, consider the appropriateness of individual appointments. I do not assert that this list is exhaustive; but as the authorities stand it seems to me to include the essentials, so far as relevant to the case before me ...

NOTE: Because a trust must be fulfilled, the court itself will carry out a trust if no trustee can be found to do so (a trust does not fail for want of a trustee). It is said of powers, on the other hand, that since they are optional and involve a wide discretion the court will never enforce them. However, there are occasionally limited exceptions to the proposition that the courts do not enforce powers. In *Klug* v *Klug* [1918] 2 Ch 67, a mother who disapproved of her daughter's marriage without her consent capriciously refused to exercise a power in her favour. On application by the public trustee, the court ordered that the power should be exercised.

Mettoy Pension Trustees v *Evans*

[1991] 2 All ER 513, Chancery Division

Facts: Mettoy, one of whose subsidiaries manufactured the miniature toy cars known as 'Dinky Toys', had fallen victim to the recession. The company went into liquidation. The pension funds of Mettoy employees were held by a trust corporation subject to rules governing the distribution of any surplus in the event of the company being wound up. The trust corporation was appointed by the previous trustees and it was those trustees who had laid down the rules governing the distribution of surplus pension funds. In the event, the company was wound up with a surplus in the pension fund. The ques-tion arose whether the power to distribute the surplus pension funds was part of the company's assets and could be exercised by the receivers.

The rule governing the distribution of the surplus pension fund granted the trust cor-poration an 'absolute discretion' as to the mode of distribution. Accordingly, this rule granted the trust corporation a 'fiduciary power'. Such a power could not be released by the trust corporation: it could not therefore be treated as an asset of the insolvent company. As a result, the receivers had no authority to exercise the fiduciary power, and the court would have to decide the manner of its exercise. The question arose, had the trustees understood the effect of the rules governing the distribution of the surplus, would they have appointed the trust corporation subject to those rules? In other words, in appointing the trust corporation, subject to the rules, had the trustees exercised a sound discretion? If they had not, the appointment of the trust corporation would be set aside.

Held: There was no evidence to show that the trustees did not understand the effect of the rules, nor to show that they would have acted any differently had they been informed that the rules for distribution had conferred a 'fiduciary power' on the trust corporation. The appointment of the trust corporation would stand.

WARNER J: As to powers, I agree with my noble and learned friend Lord Upjohn in *Re Gulbenkian's Settlement* [1968] 3 All ER 785, [1970] AC 508 that although the trustees may, and normally will, be under a fiduciary duty to consider whether or in what way they should exercise their power, the court will not normally compel its exercise. It will intervene if the trustees exceed their powers, and possibly if they are proved to have exercised it, capriciously. But in the case of a trust power, if the trustees do not exercise it, the court will; I respectfully adopt as to this the statement in Lord Upjohn's opinion (see [1968] 3 All ER 785 at 793, [1970] AC 508 at 525). I would venture to amplify this by saying that the court, if called upon to execute the trust power, will do so in the manner best calculated to give effect to the settlor's or testator's intentions. It may do so by appointing new trustees, or by authorising or directing representative persons of the classes of beneficiaries to prepare a scheme of distribution, or even, should the proper basis for distribution appear, by itself directing the trustees so to distribute. The books give many instances where this has been done and I see no reason in principle why they should not do so in the modern field of discretionary trusts ...

B: Trust and contract

'Whilst recognising that the same transaction may involve both legal relationships, contracts and trusts are in essence two distinct legal concepts' (*Clarence House Ltd* v *Nat West Bank plc* [2009] 1 WLR 1651, *per* Judge Hodge QC at para. [18]).

If A wants B to provide certain benefits to X, A can set up a contract for the benefit of X (enforceable by X by virtue of the Contracts (Rights of Third Parties) Act 1999) or A could transfer property to B to hold on trust for X. A contract can be renegotiated between the parties and is therefore suitable when it is not intended to create permanent and irrevocable rights in favour of X, but once a trust is created it is irrevocable.

CONTRACTS (RIGHTS OF THIRD PARTIES) ACT 1999

Section 1 Right of third party to enforce contractual term

(1) Subject to the provisions of this Act, a person who is not a party to a contract (a 'third party') may in his own right enforce a term of the contract if—

(a) the contract expressly provides that he may, or

(b) subject to subsection (2), the term purports to confer a benefit on him.

(2) Subsection (1)(b) does not apply if on a proper construction of the contract it appears that the parties did not intend the term to be enforceable by the third party.

(3) The third party must be expressly identified in the contract by name, as a member of a class or as answering a particular description but need not be in existence when the contract is entered into.

(4) This section does not confer a right on a third party to enforce a term of a contract otherwise than subject to and in accordance with any other relevant terms of the contract.

(5) For the purpose of exercising his right to enforce a term of the contract, there shall be available to the third party any remedy that would have been available to him in an action for breach of contract if he had been a party to the contract (and the rules relating to damages, injunctions, specific performance and other relief shall apply accordingly).

(6) Where a term of a contract excludes or limits liability in relation to any matter references in this Act to the third party enforcing the term shall be construed as references to his availing himself of the exclusion or limitation.

(7) In this Act, in relation to a term of a contract which is enforceable by a third party—'the promisor' means the party to the contract against whom the term is enforceable by the third party, and 'the promisee' means the party to the contract by whom the term is enforceable against the promisor.

NOTES

1. The 1999 Act is concerned with X's remedies, not those of A; A's remedies are unaffected by the Act. If A can claim specific performance then there is no particular problem, but in most other cases A's damages will be nominal (since A has suffered no loss), as in *Woodar Investment Developments Ltd* v *Wimpey Construction (UK) Ltd* [1980] 1 WLR 277. There are exceptions, one of which is where A contracts as X's trustee, as in *Lloyd's* v *Harper* (1880) 16 Ch D 290. Where one party contracts as trustee for another, the contracting party's damages will be based on the beneficiary's loss; on the principles of *MCC* v *Lehman* in Chapter 1, however, the beneficiary will not be able to sue directly, but must require the trustee to sue on his behalf.

2. The insolvency of B gives rise to very significant restrictions on X's ability to enforce a contract against B, whether the contract was made between A and B or made between X and B directly. In either case X must join the queue of creditors with personal claims against B. This is the great advantage of a trust. If a trustee becomes insolvent, the beneficiaries of his trust are entitled to recover their property ahead of the trustee's personal creditors, because the beneficiaries have a proprietary entitlement to the trust property and the trust property always remains separate from the trustee's personal estate. These issues come to the fore when we consider the so-called *Quistclose* trust in Subsection C.

3. Judges are reluctant to construe contracts as trusts. So it has been said that 'Chancery mends no man's bargain' (*Maynard* v *Moseley* (1676) Swanst 651, *per* Lord Nottingham at 655) and a fiduciary duty 'cannot be prayed in aid to enlarge the scope of contractual duties' (*Clark Boyce* v *Mouat* [1994] 1 AC 428, *per* Lord Jauncey of Tullichettle at 437g–h).

C: Trust and debt

When you lend money to a friend or business partner, or deposit money in a bank account, your friend, business partner, or bank becomes a debtor, not a trustee, and you become a creditor, not a beneficiary. It should be clear from the above that a debtor will be in a very different position to a trustee. A debtor's liability to repay a loan is contractual, and therefore strict, subject to the terms of the loan. In other words, it does not require proof of negligence or bad faith. It is not avoided, for example, by the theft by a third person either of the money loaned, or of any property purchased with the money, however innocent the debtor may be. On the other hand, the property the creditor has loaned passes to the debtor, so if the debtor goes bankrupt, the creditor takes his place as one among many unsecured creditors, and is unlikely to see the return of any or all his money.

A trustee's duties are usually less strict inasmuch as a trustee is rarely liable in the absence of his own fault, and can frequently be relieved of liability if the injury to the trust was caused by another party (see, generally, Chapter 13), but in the event of a trustee's bankruptcy a beneficiary is in the position of a secured creditor, because he has retained equitable property which will be protected from the claims of the general creditors. In effect, the property never becomes part of the debtor's estate.

Both legal and equitable obligations can coexist, however, so that a loan can also constitute a trust. Thus, a creditor can also be a beneficiary, and this protects him in the event of the debtor's bankruptcy.

Barclays Bank Ltd v *Quistclose Investments Ltd*

[1970] AC 567, House of Lords

Facts: Rolls Razor Ltd were in serious financial difficulties, and had an overdraft with Barclays Bank of some £484,000 against a permitted limit of £250,000. If Rolls Razor were to stay in business, it was essential for them to obtain a loan of around £210,000 in order to pay dividends which they had declared on their ordinary shares, and which in the absence of such a loan they were unable to pay. They succeeded in obtaining the loan from Quistclose Investments Ltd (who were planning to loan Rolls Razor £1 million if they remained in business), who agreed to make the loan on the condition 'that it is used to pay the forthcoming dividend due on July 24, next'. The sum was paid into a special account with Barclays Bank, on the condition (agreed with the bank) that the account would 'only be used to meet the dividend due on 24 July 1964'.

Rolls Razor went into voluntary liquidation on 27 August, without having paid the dividend. Barclays wanted to count the money in the special account against Rolls Razor's overdraft.

Held: The House of Lords (upholding the decision of the Court of Appeal) held that Barclays held the money on trust for Quistclose, so that Quistclose was able to claim back the entire sum.

> HARMAN LJ (in the Court of Appeal [1968] 1 Ch 540): ... The money was deposited with the respondent bank, and accepted on the footing that it should only be used for payment of the dividend. That purpose was, however, frustrated by the liquidation of Rolls Razor on the following August 27 before the dividend had been paid, thus making its payment illegal.
>
> LORD WILBERFORCE (House of Lords): ... The mutual intention of the respondents [Quistclose] and of Rolls Razor Ltd, and the essence of the bargain, was that the sum advanced should not become part of the assets of Rolls Razor Ltd, but should be used exclusively for payment of a particular class of creditors, namely, those entitled to the dividend. A necessary consequence of this, simply by process of interpretation, must be that, if for any reason, the dividend could not be paid, the money was to be returned to the respondents: the word 'only' or 'exclusively' can have no other meaning or effect.
>
> That arrangements of this character for the payment of a person's creditors by a third person, give rise to a relationship of a fiduciary character or trust, in favour, as a primary trust, of the creditors, and secondarily, if the primary trust fails, of the third person, has been recognised in a series of cases over some 150 years.
>
> ...
>
> The second, and main, argument for the appellant was of a more sophisticated character. The transaction, it was said, between the respondents and Rolls Razor Ltd was one of loan, giving rise to a legal action of debt. This necessarily excluded the implication of any trust, enforceable in equity, in the respondent's favour: a transaction may attract one action or the other, it could not admit of both.
>
> My Lords, I must say that I find this argument unattractive. Let us see what it involves. It means that the law does not permit an arrangement by which one person agrees to advance money to another, on terms that the money is to be used exclusively to pay the debts of the latter, and if, and so far as not so used, rather than becoming a general asset of the latter available to his creditors at large, is to be returned to the lender. The lender is obliged, in such a case, because he is a lender, to accept, whatever the mutual wishes of lender and borrower may be, that the money he was willing to make available for one purpose only shall be freely available for others of the borrower's creditors for whom he has not the slightest desire to provide.
>
> I should be surprised if an argument of this kind—so conceptualist in character—had ever been accepted. In truth it has plainly been rejected by the eminent judges who from 1819 onwards have permitted arrangements of this type to be enforced, and have approved them as being for the benefit of creditors and all concerned. There is surely no difficulty in recognising the co-existence in one transaction of

legal and equitable rights and remedies: when the money is advanced, the lender acquires an equitable rights to see that it is applied for the primary designated purpose ... if the primary purpose cannot be carried out, the question arises if a secondary purpose (i.e., repayment to the lender) has been agreed, expressly or by implication: if it has, the remedies of equity may be invoked to give effect to it, if it has not (and the money is intended to fall within the general fund of the debtor's assets) then there is the appropriate remedy for recovery of a loan. I can appreciate no reason why the flexible interplay of law and equity cannot let in these practical arrangements, and other variations if desired: it would be to the discredit of both systems if they could not. In the present case the intention to create a secondary trust for the benefit of the lender, to arise if the primary trust, to pay the dividend, could not be carried out, is clear and I can find no reason why the law should not give effect to it.

NOTES

1. Lord Wilberforce went on to hold that the bank was bound by the trust because it had notice of it.

2. The reasoning in the above passage, that there is a primary trust in favour of the creditors and, if the primary trust fails, a secondary trust in favour of the provider of the funds, suggests that the creditors can enforce the primary trust as beneficiaries, and that the provider of the funds can enforce the secondary trust, as in *Quistclose* itself. The position may not be quite as simple as this, however. In the next passage, we are asked to consider the following question:

   A lends a sum of money to B for the specific purpose of enabling him to pay his (B's) creditors or a particular class of them, and for no other purpose. Can the creditors or any of them (C) compel B to apply the money in payment of debts owing to them? Or can A change his mind, release B from the obligation to apply the money only for the specified purpose, and either demand repayment or allow B to spend the money as he chooses for his own purposes? And where, pending its application by B, is the beneficial interest in the money?

P. J. Millett, QC, 'The Quistclose Trust: Who Can Enforce It?'

(1985) 101 *LQR* 269, pp. 275–6

It was assumed without argument in the *Quistclose* case that the primary trust for the payment of the dividend to B's shareholders failed when B went into creditors' voluntary liquidation, but ... it is far from clear why this should be so. The declaration of a dividend by resolution of the shareholders creates an immediate debt in their favour [Millett notes as authority *Re Severn and Wye and Severn Bridge Railway Co.* [1896] 1 Ch 559]. If the loan by A created a trust, and not a mere power, to discharge this debt, then it vested in the shareholders an immediate right in equity to the money in the dividend account, and there is no good reason why their right to the money should be affected by the subsequent liquidation of B. [Millett notes: 'They were not even joined as parties. If they were indeed the beneficiaries under the primary trust, it is extraordinary that they should have been given no opportunity to argue that the trust in their favour had not failed.'] In the *Northern Developments* case, Megarry V-C attempted an explanation: once the winding-up had commenced, he said, section 212(1) (g) of the Companies Act 1948, prevented the payment of the dividend in competition with other creditors, and so in the circumstances no trust for the payment of the dividend could be carried out. With respect, this is a *non sequitur*. Section 212 ... prevents the liquidator from applying the assets of the company in payment of a debt due to a member, in his character of a member, until the debts due to other creditors have been paid in full; but it does no more than this. It does not prevent a trustee from paying trust money, which *ex hypothesi* does not belong to the company, to the persons beneficially entitled thereto ...

■ QUESTION

A trust fails where its terms can no longer be carried out. So what were the terms of the *Quistclose* primary trust? What was the specific purpose? If the purpose had been 'to keep the company afloat until the dividends were paid', would there have been a trust at all? Perhaps the primary trust was 'to keep the company afloat until the dividends were paid'? If so, clearly it had failed. Must the terms of the trust be the same as the expressed purpose? Can the fact that the trust is no longer of use to the settlor be a reason for it to fail?

NOTE: It is illegal for a company which is in liquidation to pay dividends to its shareholders, at any rate using its own money, but as Millett pointed out in the passage set out above, the money did not belong beneficially to Rolls Razor Ltd. Indeed, there was no theoretical reason why Rolls Razor needed to be involved at all; the identity of the trustee was immaterial. Since the money did not belong to it, and there was no reason why anybody *apart from Rolls Razor* could not pay the amount of the dividends, it is difficult to see why the payment became illegal on the liquidation of Rolls Razor.

Carreras Rothmans v *Freeman Mathews Treasure Ltd (In liq.)*

[1985] Ch 207, Chancery Division

Facts: The claimant (cigarette manufacturer) engaged the defendant advertising agency. The defendant got into financial difficulties, but needed funds to pay its production agencies and advertising media, if it was to carry on acting for the claimant. The claimant accordingly paid a monthly sum into a special account at the defendant's bank, the money to be used for the sole purpose of paying off the agency and media creditors. The defendant later went into liquidation.

Note that the claimant (CR) was contractually obliged to pay the monthly sum to the defendants (FMT) in any event, and had it not done so could have been sued by FMT. Payment into the special account was therefore a variation of the original agreement, for which there does not appear to have been any obvious consideration, but in the ensuing litigation FMT abandoned this point, perhaps because there was an 'arrangement fee' paid of £150.

Held: The money in the special account was held for the claimant on a resulting trust, since it had been paid for a specific purpose. Accordingly, since the claimant was beneficial owner of the money in the account, the money was not part of the defendant's assets, to be distributed among the general body of creditors. The reasoning in *Barclays Bank Ltd* v *Quistclose Investments Ltd* [1970] AC 567 was adopted, and was stated to apply generally where property was transferred for a specific purpose only, and not for the recipient's own purposes. If the purpose was not carried out, equity fastened on the conscience of the recipient, and did not allow the recipient to treat the property as his own, or to use it for any other purpose.

PETER GIBSON J: There is of course ample authority that moneys paid by A to B for a specific purpose which has been made known to B are clothed with a trust. In the *Quistclose* case [1970] AC 567 at 580, Lord Wilberforce referred to the recognition, in a series of cases over some 150 years, that arrangements for the payment of a person's creditors by a third person gives rise to 'a relationship of a fiduciary character or trust, in favour, as a primary trust, of the creditors, and secondarily, if the primary trust fails, of the third person'. Lord Wilberforce in describing the facts of the *Quistclose* case said a little earlier that the mutual intention of the provider of the moneys and of the recipient of the moneys, and the essence of the bargain, was that the moneys should not become part of the assets of the recipient but should be used exclusively for payment of a particular class of its creditors. That description seems to me to be apt in relation to the facts of the present case too.

...

It is of course true that there are factual differences between the *Quistclose* case and the present case. The transaction there was one of loan with no contractual obligations on the part of the lender to make payment prior to the agreement for the loan. In the present case there is no loan but there is an antecedent debt owed by CR. I doubt if it is helpful to analyse the *Quistclose* type of case in terms of the constituent parts of a conventional settlement, though it may of course be crucial to ascertain in whose favour the secondary trust operates (as in the *Quistclose* case itself) and who has an enforceable right. In my judgment the principle in all these cases is that equity fastens on the conscience of the person who receives from another property transferred for a specific purpose only and not therefore for the recipient's own purposes, so that such person will not be permitted to treat the property as his own or to use it for other than the stated purpose. Most of the cases in this line are cases where there has been an agreement for consideration, so that in one sense each party has contributed to providing the property. But, if the common intention is that property is transferred for a specific purpose and not so as to become the property of the transferee, the transferee cannot keep the property if for any reason that purpose cannot be fulfilled. I am left in no doubt that the provider of the moneys in the present case was CR. True it is that its own witnesses said that if FMT had not agreed to the terms of the contract letter CR would not have broken its contract but would have paid its debt to FMT, but the fact remains that CR made its payment on the terms of that letter and FMT received the moneys only for the stipulated purpose. That purpose was expressed to relate only to the moneys in the account. In my judgment therefore CR can be equated with the lender in the *Quistclose* case as having an enforceable right to compel the carrying out of the primary trust.

P. J. Millett, QC, 'The Quistclose Trust: Who Can Enforce It?'

(1985) 101 *LQR* 269, pp. 275–6

... The answer to the question raised at the beginning of this article depends on A's intention, to be collected from the language used, the conduct of the parties, and the circumstances of the case.

The following, it is suggested, may be regarded as suitable guidelines by which A's intention may be ascertained:

1. If A's intention was to benefit C, or his object would be frustrated if he were to retain a power of revocation, the transaction will create an irrevocable trust in favour of C, enforceable by C, but not by A. The beneficial interest in the trust property will be in C.

2. If A's intention was to benefit B (though without vesting a beneficial interest in him), or to benefit himself by furthering some private or commercial interest of his own, and not (except incidentally) to benefit C, then the transaction will create a trust in favour of A alone, and B will hold the trust property in trust to comply with A's directions. The trust will be enforceable by A but not by C. The beneficial interest will remain in A.

3. Where A's object was to save B from bankruptcy by enabling him to pay his creditors, the prima facie inference is that set out in paragraph 2 above. Wherever that is the correct inference:

    (i)   Where A has an interest of his own, separate and distinct from any interest of B, in seeing that the money is applied for the stated purpose, B will be under a positive obligation, enforceable by A, to apply it for that purpose. Where A has no such interest, B will be regarded as having a power, but no duty, to apply it for the stated purpose, and A's remedy will be confined to preventing the misapplication of the money.

    (ii) Prima facie, A's directions will be regarded as revocable by him, but he may contract with B not to revoke them without B's consent.

    (iii) Communication to C of the arrangements prior to A's revocation will effect an assignment of A's equitable interest to C, and convert A's revocable mandate into an irrevocable trust for C.

NOTE: One of the most difficult issues when trying to understand the mysterious process by which a *Quistclose* loan becomes a *Quistclose* trust is to understand the timing of the transformation, and to identify the 'point of no return' after which the device must take effect as an ordinary loan. This was the main issue in the *Re EVTR* case.

Re EVTR

[1987] BCLC 646, Court of Appeal

Facts: The appellant, Barber, who had just won £240,000 on premium bonds, agreed to assist a company for whom he had worked in purchasing new equipment. He accordingly deposited £60,000 with the solicitors to the company, and authorised them to release it 'for the sole purpose of buying new equipment'. The money was not paid into a special fund, but was paid out by the company in pursuit of the purpose. Before the new equipment was delivered EVTR went into receivership.

Held: The Court of Appeal held that Barber was entitled to recover his money (or at any rate, the balance of £48,536, after agreed deductions) on *Quistclose* principles.

DILLON LJ: In the forefront of the appellant's case counsel for the appellant (Mr Jackson) refers to the decision of the House of Lords in *Barclays Bank Ltd* v *Quistclose Investments Ltd* [1970] AC 567. There, Quistclose had lent money to a company (Rolls Razor Ltd) on an agreed condition that the money be used only for the purpose of paying a particular dividend which the company had declared. In the event the company went into liquidation, after receiving Quistclose's money, but without having paid the dividend. It was held that Quistclose could claim the whole of the money back, as on a resulting trust, the specific purpose having failed, and Quistclose was not limited to proving as an unsecured creditor in the liquidation of the company.

In the present case the £60,000 was released by Knapp-Fishers to the company on the appellant's instructions for a specific purpose only, namely the sole purpose of buying new equipment. Accordingly, I have no doubt, in the light of *Quistclose*, that, if the company had gone into liquidation, or the receivers had been appointed, and the scheme had become abortive before the £60,000 had been disbursed by the company, the appellant would have been entitled to recover his full £60,000, as between himself and the company, on the footing that it was impliedly held by the company on a resulting trust for him as the particular purpose of the loan had failed.

At the other end of the spectrum, if after the £60,000 had been expended by the company as it was, the Encore System had been duly delivered to and accepted by, the company, there could be no doubt that the appellant's only right would have been as an unsecured creditor of the company for the £60,000. There would have been no question of the Encore System, or any interest in it, being held on any sort of trust for the appellant, and if, after it had been delivered and installed, the company had sold the system, the appellant could have had no claim whatsoever to the proceeds of sale as trust moneys held in trust for him.

The present case lies on its facts between those two extremes of the spectrum ...

On *Quistclose* principles, a resulting trust in favour of the provider of the money arises when money is provided for a particular purpose only, and that purpose fails. In the present case, the purpose for which the £60,000 was provided by the appellant to the company was, as appears from the authority to Knapp-Fishers, the purpose of (the company) buying new equipment. But in any realistic sense of the words that purpose has failed in that the company has never acquired any new equipment, whether the Encore System which was then in mind or anything else. True it is that the £60,000 was paid out by the company with a view to the acquisition of new equipment, but that was only at half-time, and I do not see why the final whistle should be blown at half-time. The proposed acquisition proved abortive and a large part of the £60,000 has therefore been repaid by the payees. The repayments were made because of, or on account of, the payments which made up the £60,000 and those were payments of trust moneys. It is a long-established principle of equity that, if a person who is a trustee receives money or property because of, or in respect of, trust property, he will hold what he receives as a constructive trustee on the trusts of the original trust property. An early application of this principle is the well-known case of *Keech* v *Sandford* (1726) Sel Cas Ch 61, but the instances in the books are legion. See also *Chelsea Estates Investment Trust Co. Ltd* v *Marche* [1955] Ch 328 where somewhat similar reasoning applied to a mortgagee. It follows, in my judgment, that the repayments made to the receivers are subject to the same trusts as the original £60,000 in the hands of the company. There is now, of course, no question of the £48,536 being applied in the purchase of new equipment for the company, and accordingly, in my judgment, it is now held on a resulting trust for the appellant.

It is irrelevant in my judgment that, if the Encore System for which the £60,000 was paid had been delivered and accepted by the company, the company's interest in that equipment would have been a general asset of the company held by the company free of any proprietary or equitable interest of the appellant by way of trust or otherwise. If that had happened, the purpose of the appellant, and any trust attaching to the money because of that purpose, would indeed have been satisfied, but it did not happen.

The company did of course have the benefit for some months of the loan of the temporary equipment. Therefore, at any rate as between the company and Quantel, there was not a total failure of consideration so far as the company was concerned. But, even assuming (contrary to submissions made by counsel for the appellant) that the appellant was at the material times aware of the loan of the temporary equipment, the loan of the temporary equipment was merely ancillary to the purchase of the Encore System to cover the gap until the Encore System was available to be delivered to the company. On the way matters developed, it was the Encore System, and not the temporary system, that the company was to purchase, and the company never got the Encore System.

In summary there are the two factors which to my mind lead to the same conclusion in this case. Firstly, the purpose of the appellant from which any trust is to be implied was, realistically, the purpose of the company acquiring new equipment, and not the purpose of the company entering into an abortive contract for the lease/purchase of new equipment. Secondly, on the repayments being made of the £48,536 by the payees of the £60,000, the same trusts must on general principle have attached to the £48,536 as attached to the original £60,000 which were trust moneys.

■ QUESTIONS

1. When did the *Quistclose* trust first take effect? Was the money in a separate account at that time? What, if anything, is the relevance of what happened subsequently?

Suggested answer: In *Quistclose*, the money was to be used for a specific purpose, that purpose was known to the recipient, and the money was paid into a special account, which could be used for no other purpose. The last requirement, for a special account, may not be absolutely rigid, but at the very least the money must be earmarked for the particular purpose *and no other*, in order to negative the inference that the payments are to be included in the general assets of the company. The setting up of a special fund negates the inference that the payments are to be included in the company's assets, but so long as that inference is negated, it may be that a special fund is not absolutely necessary. Thus in *Re EVTR*, there was no special fund. The reality is, however, that *Quistclose* trusts are used when the trustee is in liquidation. Merely to have a personal claim against the trustee is therefore useless; it is essential for the lender to be able to point to a fund of money held by the trustee and say 'that money is my property'. To be able to do this it is necessary to be able to identify the money, and this is clearly easiest where the money has been paid into a special account. It is not essential, however, so long as the money can be traced on the principles discussed in Chapter 14.

NOTES

1. In *Twinsectra Ltd* v *Yardley* [2002] AC 164, the House of Lords approved a version of Lord Millett's extra-judicial analysis of the *Quistclose* trust. (The facts of *Twinsectra* are set out in Chapter 15.) Lord Hoffmann (with whom Lords Slynn and Hutton agreed) accepted that the transferee in *Quistclose*-type cases (Rolls Razor Ltd in *Quistclose* itself) holds the transferred money on trust for the transferor subject to a power to apply it in accordance with the contract between them, and Lord Millett (with whom Lord Hutton agreed) held (at 192) that:

   The borrower is treated as holding the money on a resulting trust for the lender but with power (or in some cases a duty) to carry out the lender's revocable mandate, and [if] the lender's object in giving the mandate is frustrated, he is entitled to revoke the mandate and demand the return of money which never ceased to be his beneficially.

2. It is a somewhat unpredictable question of fact in each case whether an agreement subjecting funds to a particular purpose gives rise to a *Quistclose* trust or not. (Contrast the outcomes in *Gabriel* v *Little* [2012] EWHC 1193 (Ch) and *Global Marine Drillships Ltd* v *Landmark Solicitors LLP & Ors* [2011] EWHC 2685 (Ch).)

3. Despite the intervention of the House of Lords in *Twinsectra*, and in large part because of it, academic controversy regarding the nature of the *Quistclose* device is still ongoing. It was said of *Jarndyce* v *Jarndyce* (the fictional case at the centre of Dickens' *Bleak House*) that 'no two Chancery lawyers can talk about it for five minutes, without coming to a total disagreement as to all the premises' (from Chapter 1, 'In Chancery'). The same thing can be said of the *Quistclose* trust.

W. Swadling (ed.), *The Quistclose Trust—Critical Essays*
(Oxford: Hart Publishing, 2004)

Extract from a review by G. Watt (2004) 68 *Conv* 418–25

There is something beguiling about the *Quistclose* trust. It has the seemingly magical ability to turn a lender's personal rights under a loan for a specific purpose into proprietary rights under a trust: if the specific purpose of the loan is fulfilled the lender has its usual contractual right to repayment, but if the borrower becomes insolvent before the purpose is discharged the lender can recover the loan moneys under a trust which takes priority over the borrower's unsecured personal creditors. Yet despite all the attention that the *Quistclose* trust has received since the eponymous decision of the House of Lords, there is still no consensus upon the process by which the base personal rights under the loan are transformed into the gold of proprietary rights under a trust. The present collection of essays represents the quest for that particular philosopher's stone.

Although the *Quistclose* trust typically arises out of an emergency loan made to a borrower in a commercial context and has the effect of protecting the lender from the borrower's insolvency, the present volume was prompted, one might even say provoked, by the decision of the House of Lords in *Twinsectra Ltd* v *Yardley* [for the facts and decision, see Chapter 15] [which is] authority for the fairly remarkable conclusion that *Quistclose* trusts arise routinely whenever money is loaned for a specific purpose. This would appear to permit the casual incursion of trusts into commercial arrangements, something which has frequently been cautioned against. Accordingly, the project engaged by Mr Swadling's book is not only timely, but also of potentially great significance to our general understanding of the role of trusts and equity in commerce ...

In *Barclays Bank* v *Quistclose* the loan was advanced to a company on the brink of insolvency for the sole purpose of paying a dividend it had declared in favour of its shareholders. Swadling argues that the primary trust cannot have been a trust purely for a purpose, for the purpose not being charitable the trust would fail for infringing the orthodox beneficiary principle of trusts law. So a beneficiary is required, but Mr Swadling contends that neither the lender nor the dividend creditors could be the beneficiary of the trust. He advances a number of arguments in support of this position. All are clearly expressed, and some, such as the argument that an ordinary trade debtor cannot be a fiduciary to the lender and the general inappropriateness of the fiduciary label in commercial arms-length dealings, are compelling ...

Swadling's conclusion (that there was no trust in *Quistclose* prior to failure of the purpose of the loan) is shared by Robert Chambers. However, Chambers argues that the pre-failure arrangement in *Quistclose* was merely an equitable restriction on the borrower's freedom to use the loan moneys. Swadling ably counters this with the observation that it would be unorthodox to afford proprietary status to a mere equitable right of restraint. However, though he disagrees with Chambers' analysis of the pre-failure device, he agrees with the argument, advanced by Chambers and Birks, that the only explanation for the post-failure resulting trust is to reverse the enrichment of the transferor in circumstances which, due to lack of any intention in the transferor to confer a benefit, would make an un-reversed enrichment 'unjust'. The Birks-Chambers analysis is certainly an attractive analysis of the *Quistclose* resulting trust, but certain dangers may accompany its adoption. One danger is that we might lose sight of exceptional and unorthodox character of *Quistclose* trust and find ourselves approving Chambers' wider contention that '[a]ll resulting trusts' (even orthodox ones) 'effect restitution of what would otherwise be the unjust enrichment of the recipient'. [*Resulting Trusts* (Oxford: Clarendon Press, 1997), p. 220.] Another danger is inherent in the use of the term 'unjust' as a description of the relevant enrichment. That term remains problematic despite the impressive efforts of restitution lawyers to rationalise it. A compromise, though one that will not commend itself to the restitution theorists, would be to define 'unjust' to mean 'unjustified according to orthodox property law', for then the reversal of unjust enrichment would usefully elucidate those trusts (and only those trusts) that defy analysis in terms of orthodox property law ...

Peter Birks' chapter considers the hypothetical case of a fund collected for a campaign to oppose the building of a new road. The leader of the campaign having collected money from supporters, the proposal to build the road is withdrawn when only a small part of the fund has been spent. The leader of the campaign accepts that he owes the money to the subscribers and is anxious to repay. According to Birks this means that the leader of the campaign is unjustly enriched at the subscribers' expense until he repays. This is problematic. Until such time as he appropriates the fund to his own use and benefit the campaign leader has been enriched in a factual sense, but not in any legal sense; but that is not the problem. The problem is the suggestion that the enrichment is 'unjust' even though the subscribers voluntarily enriched the campaign leader (at least factually) and the campaign leader is anxious to repay. Here again unjust enrichment theory puts property law on a cliff-edge one perilous step away from holding that a trustee is unjustly enriched at the expense of the trust beneficiaries even where the trust is on foot and has not been breached ...

The nearest thing to consensus to be found in the present collection is an almost unanimous acknowledgement that the *Quistclose* mechanism is inconsistent with the orthodox law of property, powers and trusts. That being the case; two questions remain. The first is how to describe the unorthodox mechanism; the second is to seek to understand judicial motives for recognising the mechanism in the first place. Mr Swadling's collection represents a major advance in the doctrinal analysis of the *Quistclose* trust and so represents impressive progress in relation to the first question. The second question, though, remains largely unanswered.

With the preceding point in mind it is appropriate (though somewhat back-to front) that this review should conclude with a brief mention of Lord Millett's foreword to the present collection. In Lord Millett's words, the contributors to the collection 'demand to know whether the *Quistclose* trust is a form of express, implied, constructive or resulting trust'. To this his lordship's response is unashamedly pragmatic: 'it may be any of them ... From a commercial point of view ... the trust is simply a mechanism ... The commercial need for such a mechanism is obvious'. This appears as close as one can get to a judicial (albeit extra-judicial) admission that the *Quistclose* trust is neither led (nor constrained) by legal doctrine, but rather by the commercial need to achieve a particular outcome. It is somewhat ironic that such an admission should come from the judge who more than any other has sought to explain the *Quistclose* trust in doctrinal terms, but it serves to remind us that doctrine can take us only so far in the description and determination of legal outcomes in hard cases. The famous aphorism of Oliver Wendell Holmes also has its limitations, but the *Quistclose* trust is certainly one context in which it is helpful to recall that 'the life of the law is not logic, but experience'.

NOTES

1. In *Cooper* v *PRG Powerhouse* [2008] EWHC 498 (Ch), the departing managing director of a company paid money to the company on the understanding that it would be paid onwards to allow him to complete the private purchase of his company car. The company went insolvent before the money was paid. A *Quistclose* trust was held in the director's favour. We might be persuaded that the *Quistclose* trust is defensible where it promotes the public interest in saving a failing company, but do we doubt that the *Quistclose* trust should be employed to protect purely private contractual interests? *Mundy* v *Brown* [2011] EWHC 377 (Ch) is not quite so bad, because the accountant, who by virtue of a *Quistclose* trust recovered his fees despite the insolvency, was a truly independent party.

2. See *Re Farepak Foods and Gifts Limited (In Administration)* [2006] EWHC 3272 (Ch) (discussed in Chapter 3) for an example of an unsuccessful attempt to plead a *Quistclose* trust in favour of consumers.

3. *Quistclose* trusts are not restricted to commercial contexts. It was confirmed in *Re N (A Child)* [2009] EWHC 11 (Fam) that a court order requiring child-support monies to be paid by the child's father to the child's mother gives rise to a *Quistclose* trust in favour of the father in the event of the monies not being applied for the specified purpose (of child-support) within a reasonable time.

D: Trust and agency

Lord Millett (Sir Peter Millett, as he then was) has observed extrajudicially that there is no single test for determining whether an agent is a mere agent or a trustee. The answer depends on all the circumstances of the particular case and in particular upon the parties' express or inferred intentions.

Sir Peter Millett, 'Bribes and Secret Commissions'
[1993] *RLR* 7

[T]he usual approach is to consider whether it is appropriate to superimpose a trust relationship onto the commercial relationship which exists between the parties; or whether it was contemplated that the agent should be free to treat the money as his own, in which case no trust relationship is created.

NOTE: 'in the case of an agent employed under a contract, the scope of his fiduciary duties is determined by the terms in the underlying contract' (*Henderson* v *Merrett Syndicates Limited* [1995] 1 AC 145, House of Lords, *per* Lord Browne-Wilkinson at 206 A-D; followed in *John Youngs Insurance Services Ltd* v *Aviva Insurance Service UK Ltd* [2011] EWHC 1515 (TCC).

An interesting example of an agent who will become a constructive trustee in certain circumstances is the director of a company (see Subsection E).

E: Trust and corporation

A trust has no separate legal personality—the trustees are the owners of bare legal title to the trust assets. A corporation (or company) is, in contrast, a distinct legal person and owns corporate assets absolutely in its own right. Beneficiaries of a trust own equitable shares in the trust assets, but company shareholders do not hold equitable shares in the corporation's assets—rather, they own their shares absolutely. The company shares owned by shareholders and the corporate assets owned by the corporation are not the same thing shared, they are distinct assets owned by different legal persons. (Contrast the 'private foundation' that is popular in jurisdictions such as Panama and Liechtenstein, which performs some of the wealth-management functions of a trust, but by means of separate legal personality.)

J. J. Harrison (Properties) Ltd v Harrison

[2002] 1 BCLC 162, Court of Appeal

Facts: The director of a company bought land off the company at an undervalue in breach of his fiduciary duty to avoid a con ict between his duty to the company and his personal interests. The question was whether he was accountable merely as an agent for breach of fiduciary duty, or whether he was accountable as a trustee. If he was a trustee the company's claim would not be time-barred (see Chapter 13).

Held: The director held the land and proceeds of sale of the land on trust for the company and therefore the company's claim was not time-barred.

CHADWICK LJ: ... a director, on appointment to that office, assumes the duties of a trustee in relation to the company's property. If, thereafter, he takes possession of that property, his possession 'is coloured from the first by the trust and confidence by means of which he obtained it'. His obligations as a trustee in relation to that property do not arise out of the transaction by which he obtained it for himself. The true analysis is that his obligations as a trustee in relation to that property predate the transaction by which it was conveyed to him. The conveyance of the property to himself by the exercise of his powers in breach of trust does not release him from those obligations. He is trustee of the property because it has become vested in him; but his obligations to deal with the property as a trustee arise out of his pre-existing duties as a director; not out of the circumstances in which the property was conveyed.

NOTE: If directors take personal advantage of a business opportunity 'belonging' to their company, they will be accountable just *as if* they were trustees of property (*Foster Bryant Surveying Ltd* v *Bryant* [2007] EWCA Civ 200). See, further, Chapter 8 at pp. 268–72.

F: Trust and bailment

The division of ownership, and the nature of the enforcement, serve to distinguish the trust from other concepts with which trusts share common factors. For example, possession of personal property is often separated from ownership of the property, as in common law bailment, for example hiring or hire purchase, but both legal and equitable ownership remain in the bailor or hirer; so the relationship of the bailee to the property is quite different from that of a trustee, who is the legal owner.

If a bailee sells the goods, where this is unauthorised by the terms of the bailment, then unless the buyer can benefit from the provisions of the Factors Act 1889, ss.2, 8, and 9, or the Sale of Goods Act 1979, ss.21 and 23–26, he gets no title, even if he acts in good faith and has no notice of the existence of the bailment. This is because a bailee has no title, legal or equitable, to sell, so a purchaser from him gets neither legal nor equitable title.

If, on the other hand, a trustee sells goods in breach of trust, the buyer obtains legal title from the trustee, and is bound by any equitable title and interests only if he is unable to show that he is a bona fide purchaser for value without notice of the trust requirement (discussed in Chapter 1). If he is a bona fide purchaser, etc., he obtains legal title unencumbered by equitable interests.

FACTORS ACT 1889

2. Powers of mercantile agent with respect to disposition of goods

(1) Where a mercantile agent is, with the consent of the owner, in possession of goods or of the documents of title to goods, any sale, pledge, or other disposition of the goods, made by him when acting in the ordinary course of business of a mercantile agent, shall, subject to the provisions of this Act, be as valid as if he were expressly authorised by the owner of the goods to make the same; *provided that the person taking under the disposition acts in good faith, and has not at the time of the disposition notice that the person making the disposition has not authority to make the same.*

(2) Where a mercantile agent has, with the consent of the owner, been in possession of goods or of the documents of title to goods, any sale, pledge, or other disposition, which would have been valid if the consent had continued, shall be valid notwithstanding the determination of the consent: *provided that the person taking under the disposition has not at the time thereof notice that the consent has been determined.*

(3) Where a mercantile agent has obtained possession of any documents of title to goods by reason of his being or having been, with the consent of the owner, in possession of the goods represented thereby, or of any other documents of title to the goods, his possession of the first-mentioned documents shall, for the purposes of this Act, be deemed to be with the consent of the owner.

(4) For the purposes of this Act the consent of the owner shall be presumed in the absence of evidence to the contrary.

8. Disposition by seller remaining in possession

Where a person, having sold goods, continues, or is, in possession of the goods or of the documents of title to the goods, the delivery or transfer by that person, or by a mercantile agent acting for him, of the goods or documents of title under any sale, pledge or other disposition thereof, or under any agreement for sale, pledge or other disposition thereof, to any person receiving the same in good faith and without notice of the previous sale, shall have the same effect as if the person making the delivery or transfer were expressly authorised by the owner of the goods to make the same.

9. Disposition by buyer remaining in possession

Where a person, having bought or agreed to buy goods, obtains with the consent of the seller possession of the goods or the documents of title to the goods, the delivery or transfer, by that person or by a mercantile agent acting for him, of the goods or the documents of title under any sale, pledge or other disposition thereof, or under any agreement for sale, pledge or other disposition thereof, to any person receiving the same in good faith and without notice of any lien or other right of the original seller in

respect of the goods, shall have the same effect as if the person making the delivery or transfer were a mercantile agent in possession of the goods or documents of title with the consent of the owner. [For the purposes of this section—
   (i)   the buyer under a conditional sale agreement shall be deemed not to be a person who has bought or agreed to buy goods, and
   (ii)   'conditional sale agreement' means an agreement for the sale of goods which is a consumer credit agreement within the meaning of the Consumer Credit Act 1974 under which the purchase price or part of it is payable by instalments, and the property in the goods is to remain in the seller (notwithstanding that the buyer is to be in possession of the goods) until such conditions as to the payment of instalments or otherwise as may be specified in the agreement are fulfilled.]
[Note: words in square brackets inserted by Consumer Credit Act 1974, s.192, Sch. 4, Pt. I, para. 2.]

SALE OF GOODS ACT 1979

21. Sale by person not the owner

(1) Subject to this Act, where goods are sold by a person who is not their owner, and who does not sell them under the authority or with the consent of the owner, the buyer acquires no better title to the goods than the seller had, unless the owner of the goods is by his conduct precluded from denying the seller's authority to sell.
   (2) Nothing in this Act affects—
      (a) The provisions of the Factors Acts, or any enactment enabling the apparent owner of the goods to dispose of them as if he were their true owner.
      (b) The validity of any contract of sale under any special common law or statutory power of sale, or under the order of a court of competent jurisdiction.

22. Market overt

[Provisions concerning goods sold in England and Wales since 1967 were repealed by the Sale of Goods (Amendment) Act 1994.]

23. Sale under voidable title

Where the seller of goods has a voidable title to them, but his title has not been avoided at the time of the sale, the buyer acquires a good title to the goods, provided he buys them in good faith and without notice of the seller's defect of title.

24. Seller in possession after sale

Where a person, having sold goods, continues, or is, in possession of the goods or of the documents of title to the goods, the delivery or transfer by that person, or by a mercantile agent acting for him, of the goods or documents of title under any sale, pledge or other disposition thereof, to any person receiving the same in good faith and without notice of the previous sale, shall have the same effect as if the person making the delivery or transfer were expressly authorized by the owner of the goods to make the same.

25. Buyer in possession after sale

(1) Where a person, having bought or agreed to buy goods, obtains with the consent of the seller possession of the goods or the documents of title to the goods, the delivery or transfer, by that person or by a mercantile agent acting for him, of the goods or the documents of title under any sale, pledge or other disposition thereof, to any person receiving the same in good faith and without notice of any lien or other right of the original seller in respect of the goods, shall have the same effect as if the person making the delivery or transfer were a mercantile agent in possession of the goods or documents of title with the consent of the owner.
   (2) For the purposes of subsection (1) above—
      (a) the buyer under a conditional sale agreement shall be deemed not to be a person who has bought or agreed to buy goods, and

(b) 'conditional sale agreement' means an agreement for the sale of goods which is a consumer credit agreement within the meaning of the Consumer Credit Act 1974 under which the purchase price or part of it is payable by instalments, and the property in the goods is to remain in the seller (notwithstanding that the buyer is to be in possession of the goods) until such conditions as to the payment of instalments or otherwise as may be specified in the agreement are fulfilled.

(3) Paragraph 9 of Schedule 1 below applies in relation to a contract under which a person buys or agrees to buy goods and which is made before the appointed day.

(4) In subsection (3) above and paragraph 9 of Schedule 1 below references to the appointed day are to the day appointed for the purposes of these provisions by an order of the Secretary of State made by statutory instrument.

26. Supplementary to sections 24 and 25

In sections 24 and 25 above 'mercantile agent' means a mercantile agent having in the customary course of his business as such agent authority either—

(a) to sell goods, or
(b) to consign goods for the purpose of sale, or
(c) to buy goods, or
(d) to raise money on the security of goods.

SECTION 5: THE RECOGNITION OF TRUSTS IN OTHER JURISDICTIONS

Civil jurisdictions are generally incapable of recognising the English form of trust for the purposes of private international law unless they have ratified the 1985 Hague Convention on the Law Applicable to Trusts and on their Recognition which came into effect on 1 January 1992. It is important to be clear that it is not the purpose of the Convention to incorporate the English idea of the trust into foreign jurisdictions; the Convention does not require that the ratifying State must adopt the laws of the jurisdiction in which the trust was created, it merely empowers the recognising State to know a trust when it sees one. The usual rule of private international law, that disputes concerning the transfer and acquisition of title to property should be determined by the laws of the country in which the assets are situated (the '*lex situs*') is unaffected by the Convention. The priority of domestic laws of bankruptcy and succession (*lex successionis*) is likewise preserved, so if a settlor dies leaving assets in a civil jurisdiction his trust will not be recognised to the extent that it purports to oust the fixed entitlement of any 'heir' recognised under the civil jurisdiction's 'forced heirship' rules. The convention will not be applied in manifest conflict with the public (including fiscal) policy of any ratifying State.

The Hague Convention provides a useful description of expressly created trusts—see, generally, J. Harris, *The Hague Trusts Convention* (Oxford: Hart Publishing, 2002).

THE CONVENTION ON THE LAW APPLICABLE TO TRUSTS AND ON THEIR RECOGNITION

The Hague, 1985

For the purposes of this Convention the term 'trust' refers to the legal relationship created—*inter vivos* or on death—by a person, the settlor, when assets have been placed under the control of a trustee for the benefit of a beneficiary or for a specified purpose. A trust has the following characteristics—*a* the assets constitute a separate fund and are not part of the trustee's estate; *b* title to the trust assets stands in the name of the trustee or in the name of another person on behalf of the trustee; *c* the trustee has the power and the duty, in respect of which he is accountable, to manage, employ or dispose of the assets in accordance with the terms of the trust and the special duties imposed upon him by law. The reservation by the settlor of certain rights and powers, and the fact that the trustee may himself have rights as a beneficiary, are not necessarily inconsistent with the existence of a trust.

NOTE: Civil Jurisdiction and Judgments Order 2001 (SI 2001/3929), Sch. 1, para. 12(3) provides that '[a] trust is domiciled in a part of the United Kingdom if and only if the system of law of that part is the system of law with which the trust has its closest and most real connection' (applied in *Gomez* v *Gomez-Monche Vives*, Court of Appeal (Civil Division) [2008] EWCA Civ 1065).

■ SUMMATIVE QUESTION

online
resource
centre

'Of all the exploits of Equity the largest and the most important is the invention and development of the Trust. It is an "institute" of great elasticity and generality; as elastic, as general as contract. This perhaps forms the most distinctive achievement of English lawyers' (F. W. Maitland, 'Uses and Trusts', in *Equity: A Course of Lectures* (rev. by J. Brunyate) (Cambridge: Cambridge University Press, 1936)).

Critically discuss this statement.

FURTHER READING

Bartlett, R. T., 'When is a "Trust" not a Trust? The National Health Service Trust' (1996) 60 *Conv* 186.

Graziadei, M., Mattei, U., and Smith, L. (eds), *Commercial Trusts in European Private Law* (Cambridge: Cambridge University Press, 2005).

Hayton, D., 'Pension Trusts and Traditional Trusts: Drastically Different Species of Trusts' (2005) 18 *Conv* 229.

Langbein, J. H., 'The Contractarian Basis of the Law of Trusts' (1995) 105 *Yale LJ* 625.

Loi, K. C. F., '*Quistclose* trusts and *Romalpa* clauses: substance and *nemo dat* in corporate insolvency' (2012) 128 *LQR* 412–442.

Lupoi, M., *Trusts: A Comparative Study* (Cambridge: Cambridge University Press, 2000).

Mason, Sir Anthony, 'The Place of Equity and Equitable Remedies in the Contemporary Common Law World' (1994) 110 *LQR* 238.

Panico, P., *International Trust Laws* (Oxford: Oxford University Press, 2010).

Sealy, L. S., 'The Director as Trustee' (1967) *CLJ* 83.

Swadling, W. (ed.), *The Quistclose Trust: Critical Essays* (Oxford: Hart Publishing, 2004).

Warburton, J., 'Charitable Trusts—Unique' (1999) 63 *Conv* 20.

PART II

Creation and Recognition of Trusts

3

Trusts Created Expressly

KEY AIMS

To appreciate that a gift of an asset is presumed to be an outright gift unless it is certain that the donor intended the recipient to hold the asset on trust. To understand that, in addition to the requirement of certainty of intention, a valid express trust requires the subject matter of the trust and the object of the trust to be certain. To identify the consequences of failure to satisfy the three certainty requirements. To appreciate why, in addition to the requirement of certainty, it is necessary (subject to some anomalous exceptions) for a private trust to have an ascertainable beneficiary. To consider, in the light of this, how the law construes donations to non-charitable unincorporated associations (i.e. clubs and societies).

SECTION 1: INTRODUCTION

The great freedom of property owners to dispose of their property as they choose can be a source of great uncertainty. Sometimes it will fall to the courts to adjudicate between litigating parties with competing interpretations of the terms of a disposition. Where the question to be resolved is the very fundamental one—'was the disposition intended to take effect by way of trust or absolute gift?'—courts will hold that an absolute gift had been intended unless it is certain from the context and the expressions used that the person making the disposition had intended to create a trust. Where it is clear that a trust had been intended and the question that arises is therefore of a secondary nature, for example—'who is entitled to the benefit of this trust and in what proportions?'—courts will then endeavour, as far as they are able, to interpret the settlor's or testator's words and conduct so as to give effect to the trust. In every case, 'one reads the document within the four corners of the document itself, and taking account of such surrounding circumstances as are admissible' (*Rafferty* v *Philp* [2011] EWHC 709 at para. [41]).

Knight v *Knight*
(1840) 3 Beav 148

LORD LANGDALE MR: ... The principal question is, whether a trust in favour of the male descendants of Richard Knight is created by the will of the testator Richard Payne Knight. That the testator wished that his estates, or at least, that some estates should be preserved in the male line of his grandfather, and had a reliance, or in the popular sense, a trust that the person to whom he gave his property, and those who should succeed to it, would act upon and realise that wish, admits of no doubt. He has expressed his wish and his reliance in terms which are, to that extent, sufficiently clear. But it is not every wish or expectation which a testator may express, nor every act which he may wish his successors to do, that can or ought to be executed or enforced as a trust in this Court; and in the infinite variety of expressions which are employed, and of cases which thereupon arise, there is often the greatest difficulty in determining, whether the act desired or recommended is an act which the testator intended to be executed as a trust, or which this Court ought to deem fit to be, or capable of being enforced as such. In the construction and execution of wills, it is undoubtedly the duty of this Court to give effect to the intention of the testator whenever it can be ascertained: but in cases of this nature, and in the examination of the authorities which are to be consulted in relation to them, it is, unfortunately, necessary to make some distinction between the intention of the testator and that which the Court has deemed it to be its duty to perform; for of late years it has frequently been admitted by Judges of great eminence that, by interfering in such cases, the Court has sometimes rather made a will for the testator, than executed the testator's will according to his intention; and the observation shows the necessity of being extremely cautious in admitting any, the least, extension of the principle to be extracted from a long series of authorities, in respect of which such admissions have been made. As a general rule, it has been laid down, that when property is given absolutely to any person, and the same person is, by the giver who has power to command, recommended, or entreated, or wished, to dispose of that property in favour of another, the recommendation, entreaty, or wish shall be held to create a trust.

First, if the words are so used, that upon the whole, they ought to be construed as imperative.

Secondly, if the subject of the recommendation or wish be certain; and,

Thirdly, if the objects or persons intended to have the benefit of the recommendation or wish be also certain.

In simple cases there is no difficulty in the application of the rule thus stated ...

SECTION 2: CERTAINTY OF INTENTION

The question here is what words or conduct are sufficient to lead to the inference that a trust has been created. In a recent case, Arden LJ noted that 'a trust is a matter which is difficult to define, but which essentially imposes an obligation to deal with property in a particular way on behalf of another person', her ladyship reiterated that it does not require the express use of the word 'trust' (*Staden* v *Jones* [2008] EWCA Civ 936 at para. [25]). In *Byrnes* v *Kendle* [2011] HCA 26, High Court of Australia, the defendant tried to deny that he had intended to create a trust even though he had signed an Acknowledgment of Trust declaring that he held one undivided half interest in land as tenant in common upon trust for the claimant. The trial judge held that even if the defendant might not have fully understood what he was creating, that was irrelevant. The terms of the Acknowledgement were clear and they established a sufficient objective certainty of intention to create a trust, whatever the defendant's subjective intent might have been.

By about the middle of the nineteenth century, the courts were adopting a fairly strict view, the modern view being derived from the judgment of Cotton LJ in *Re Adams and Kensington Vestry* (1884) 27 ChD 394, 410, where it was established that there would be no trust unless this was the testator's clear intention, and a gift to the widow 'in full confidence that she would do what was right as to the disposal thereof between my children, either in her lifetime or by will after her decease' was treated as giving the widow an absolute interest unfettered by any trust in favour of the children.

It is clear, however, that trusts can be created without express words of trust, as for example in *Re Kayford* (which is considered further in this section) In *Cominsky* v *Bowring-Hanbury* [1905] AC 84, the House of Lords found a trust on the basis of words very similar to those employed in *Re Adams and Kensington Vestry*: ' ... absolutely in full confidence that she [the widow] will make such use of [the property] as I would have made myself and that at her death she will devise it to such one or more of my nieces as she may think fit'. The entire document must be construed, and it therefore cannot be said that words which create a trust in one situation will necessarily do so in another.

If, on the other hand, a testator reproduces the *exact* language of an earlier will which has previously been held to create a trust, it may be possible to infer that he intended to use the earlier will as a precedent. If so, the court in construing the later will should follow the earlier decision, at least unless that decision was clearly wrong: *Re Steele's WT* [1948] Ch 603.

For testamentary dispositions, it is naturally difficult to look beyond the terms of the will itself. For trusts created *inter vivos* there is room for greater flexibility, as we will see, for example, with cases such as *Re Kayford Ltd* [1975] 1 All ER 604 and *Paul v Constance* [1977] 1 WLR 54 (Chapter 4).

Re Kayford Ltd (In liq.)

[1975] 1 All ER 604, Chancery Division

Facts: A mail order company was in financial difficulties. In order to protect customers in the event of insolvency, the company considered setting up a separate bank account, called the 'Customers' Trust Deposit Account', to hold customers' deposits and payments until their goods were delivered, the intention of the company being that the money should be kept separate from the company's general funds. But the company took the advice of the bank, and instead of opening a new account, used a dormant account (with a small credit balance) in the company's name.

Held: On the winding up of the company, Megarry J held that the money in the account (apart from the small credit balance) was held on trust for the customers. He observed that a trust can be created without using the words 'trust' or 'confidence', so long as a sufficient intention to create a trust has been manifested, and he did not consider it fatal that the money had not been put into a separate account, but mixed with other moneys.

MEGARRY J: Now there are clearly some loose ends in the case ... Nevertheless, despite the loose ends, when I take as a whole the [evidence] I feel no doubt that the intention was that there should be a trust. There are no formal difficulties. The property concerned is pure personalty, and so writing, though desirable, is not an essential. There is no doubt about the so-called 'three certainties' of a trust. The subject-matter to be held on trust is clear, and so are the beneficial interests therein, as well as the beneficiaries. As for the requisite certainty of words, it is well settled that a trust can be created without using the words 'trust' or 'confidence' or the like: the question is whether in substance a sufficient intention to create a trust has been manifested ...

No doubt the general rule is that if you send money to a company for goods which are not delivered, you are merely a creditor of the company unless a trust has been created. The sender may create a trust by using appropriate words when he sends the money (though I wonder how many do this, even if they are equity lawyers), or the company may do it by taking suitable steps on or before receiving the money. If either is done, the obligations in respect of the money are transformed from contract to property, from debt to trust. Payment into a separate bank account is a useful (though by no means conclusive) indication of an intention to create a trust, but of course there is nothing to prevent the company from binding itself by a trust even if there are no effective banking arrangements.

. . . I should, however, add one thing. Different considerations may perhaps arise in relation to trade creditors; but here I am concerned only with members of the public, some of whom can ill afford to exchange their money for a claim to a dividend in the liquidation, and all of whom are likely to be anxious to avoid this. In cases concerning the public, it seems to me that where money in advance is being paid to a company in return for the future supply of goods or services, it is an entirely proper and honourable thing for a company to do what this company did, on skilled advice, namely, to start to pay the money into a trust account as soon as there begin to be doubts as to the company's ability to fulfil its obligations to deliver the goods or provide the services. I wish that, sitting in this court, I had heard of this occurring more frequently; and I can only hope that I shall hear more of it in the future.

NOTE: Farepak Ltd, a mail order vendor of Christmas hampers became insolvent just before Christmas 2006, creating anxiety for thousands of customers. In the three days leading up to the administration the directors sought to set up a trust of moneys received by the customers' account in that period, but the deed mistakenly failed to identify the correct customer account. The judge held that the mistake could be remedied by rectification (see Chapter 16), but that moneys received earlier in the year could not be subject to a *Quistclose* trust (see Chapter 2) in favour of customers, because there was no obligation on Farepak Ltd to keep those moneys in a separate customers' account. (*Re Farepak Foods and Gifts Limited (In Administration)* [2006] EWHC 3272 (Ch).)

Re Chelsea Cloisters Ltd (In liq.)

(1980) 41 P & CR 98, Court of Appeal

Decision: The decision in *Kayford* was applied where a 'tenants' deposit account' was set up to hold deposits against damage and breakages. The company managing the flats (Chelsea Cloisters Ltd) had gone into voluntary liquidation.

BRIDGE LJ: We are fortunate in that we do not have to speculate about Mr Iredale's intentions [who was in effective control of Chelsea Cloisters] because he has clearly disclosed them in an affidavit. It is common ground that his statements in evidence of what his intentions were at the time when the separate bank account was opened are admissible against the liquidator if they tend to support the landlords' contention that an intention to create a trust was in fact manifested. I divide up the two critical paragraphs in Mr Iredale's affidavit … into three distinct statements. It may be that each considered in isolation is insufficient to manifest the intention to create a trust; but the three considered in conjunction in my judgment, are clearly sufficient. However, it is worth examining them first in isolation to see exactly what he said. The first was: 'This'—that is to say, the opening of a separate bank account—'was a practical step, designed to ensure that the deposits would not be spent as part of the company's general cash flow.' That is entirely consistent with an intention to keep these funds from the general funds of the company in order that they should not be swallowed up by the general funds of the company. The second critical statement was this: 'I was also concerned that I and my firm could be open to criticism if deposits were spent in this way'—that is to say, if they were absorbed in the general funds of the company and spent as if they were available to be treated as part of the general funds of the company. Why was Mr Iredale apprehensive of criticism of himself and his firm? It surely can only have been that he at that time regarded the company, whose affairs he was managing, as being either under a moral or perhaps a legal duty to treat the tenants' deposits as impressed with some sort of beneficial interest in favour of the tenants and to ensure that sufficient funds were available to meet the tenants' claims to recover the deposits as and when those claims were made.

… Finally, there is the statement … : 'I regarded the tenants' deposit account as available only for repaying the deposit of any tenant who had paid a deposit on or after 18 June 1974.' That comes nearest of any of the separate statements in Mr Iredale's affidavit to amounting to a positive declaration of his intention to create a trust at the material time. When considered in conjunction with the other statements, and when considered against the background of the extremely parlous situation financially in which the company found itself, I find it possible only to construe those expressions as indicating an intention to create a trust.

NOTE: The retention of moneys in a separate account is not in itself proof of a trust. In *Re Multi Guarantee Co. Ltd* [1987] BCLC 257, Court of Appeal, MG (an insurer of domestic appliances) retained customers' premiums in a special account. MG agreed to transfer the premiums to the retailer who had collected them and the retailer agreed to indemnify MG in respect of any insurance claims. However, MG became insolvent before the terms of the indemnity had been agreed. The claim, that MG had held the premiums in the special account on trust for the retailer, failed. Nourse LJ could not conceive that the managing director of MG would have divested his company 'of all possible beneficial interest in the moneys' until he knew the terms of the indemnity.

SECTION 3: CERTAINTY OF SUBJECT MATTER

To satisfy this test it appears to be necessary that the trust property be defined in objective rather than subjective terms, or in other words so as not to be a matter on which opinions may reasonably differ. In *Palmer* v *Simmonds* (1854) 2 Drew 221, a testatrix left on trust 'the bulk' of her residuary estate, and Kindersley V-C, after consulting a dictionary, concluded that the word 'bulk' was inadequate to specify any portion of the property as trust property:

What is the meaning then of bulk? The appropriate meaning, according to its derivation, is something which bulges out ... Its popular meaning we all know. When a person is said to have given the bulk of his property, what is meant is not the whole but the greater part, and that is in fact consistent with its classical meaning. When, therefore, the testatrix uses that term, can I say that she has used a term expressing a definite, clear, certain part of her estate, or the whole of her estate? I am bound to say that she has not designated the subject as to which she expresses her confidence; and I am therefore of opinion that there is no trust created; that [the residuary legatee] took absolutely, and those claiming under him now take.

Since it was not possible to carve out from the residue that portion which was to be held on trust, the trust failed and the residuary legatee took the whole absolutely. This is an application of what later became the rule in *Hancock* v *Watson* [1902] AC 14.

Re Golay's WT

[1965] 1 WLR 969, [1965] 2 All ER 660, Chancery Division

Decision: Ungoed-Thomas J upheld a direction to executors to let 'Tossy' (Mrs Florence Bridgewater) enjoy one of the testator's flats during her lifetime 'and to receive a reasonable income from my other properties'. He took the view that the words 'reasonable income' directed an objective determinant of amount, which the court could, if necessary, apply.

NOTE: In *Re Golay's WT*, the view appears to have been taken that the yardstick was objectively defined, since it was conceded that the court would have no difficulty in quantifying 'reasonable income'. No doubt *Golay* was close to the line, because different trustees might apply the yardstick differently, so as to reach different results, but that is no different from 'residing' in *Gulbenkian* (see Section 4: Certainty of object, Subsection B: Discretionary Trusts).

■ QUESTION

Given that courts can, in principle, define anything they want to define, what is the function of certainty tests? Might it be to ensure that what the courts are doing is carrying out the settlor's wishes? Might it be to ensure that the trustees can carry out their duties without continually coming to court for directions?

Re London Wine Co. (Shippers) Ltd

[1986] PCC 121, Chancery Division

Facts: LW Ltd was a wine merchant which ran its business on the basis that wine ordered by customers was held on trust by the company from the date of each customer's order and until delivery to the customers. However, the bottles representing each order were not physically separated from the company's stocks until delivery. So, in the present case, where the customer ordered 20 bottles of Lafite 1970 out of the company's 80-bottle holding, the question arose whether the subject matter was sufficiently certain for the company to be treated as trustee of the customer's order.

Held: There was no trust of the 20 bottles. An express trust had certainly been intended by the company but the subject matter had not been removed from the company's general stock and there was therefore insufficient certainty of subject matter. To have achieved certainty of the trust of 20 bottles the company could have declared itself trustee of 'one quarter' of the general stock of 80 bottles.

OLIVER J: ... As it seems to me, to create a trust it must be possible to ascertain with certainty not only what the interest of the beneficiary is to be but to what property it is to attach. I cannot see how, for instance, a farmer who declares himself to be a trustee of two sheep (without identifying them) can be said to have created a perfect and complete trust whatever rights he may confer by such declaration as a matter of contract. And it would seem to me to be immaterial at the time he has a flock of sheep out of which he could satisfy the interest. Of course, he could by appropriate words, declare himself to be a trustee of a specified proportion of his whole flock and thus create an equitable tenancy in common between himself and the named beneficiary, so that a proprietary interest would arise in the beneficiary in an undivided share of all the flock and its produce. But the *mere* declaration that a given number of animals would be held upon trust could not, I should have thought, without very clear words pointing to such an intention, result in the creation of an interest in common in the proportion which that number bears to the number of the whole at the time of the declaration. And where the mass from which the numerical interest is to take effect is not itself ascertainable at the date of the declaration such a conclusion becomes impossible ...

Hunter v *Moss*

[1994] 1 WLR 452, [1993] 3 All ER 215, Court of Appeal

Decision: An oral declaration of trusteeship of 5 per cent of a company's issued share capital of 1,000 shares (of which the defendant was the registered holder of 950) succeeded, even though the particular shares were not ascertained or identified. However, the company was precisely identified, all the shares in that company were identical, and the quantification (50 shares) was obviously precise. Moreover, as long as the trustee retained all 950 shares there would be no point in identifying which 50 shares were subject to the trust.

DILLON LJ: ... I pass then to the second point of uncertainty. It is well established that for the creation of a trust there must be the three certainties referred to by Lord Langdale in *Knight* v *Knight* (1840) 3 Beav 148. One of those is, of course, that there must be certainty of subject matter. All these shares were identical in one class: 5 per cent was 50 shares and the defendant held personally more than 50 shares. It is well known that a trust of personalty can be created orally. We were referred to the well known passage in the judgment of Turner LJ in *Milroy* v *Lord* (1862) 4 De GF & J 264, 274–275 [see Chapter 4] ...

In the present case there was no question of an imperfect transfer. What is relied on is an oral declaration of trust. Again, it would not be good enough for a settlor to say, 'I declare that I hold 50 of my shares on trust for B,' without indicating the company he had in mind of the various companies in which he held shares. There would be no sufficient certainty as to the subject matter of the trust. But here the discussion is solely about the shares of one class in the one company.

It is plain that a bequest by the defendant to the plaintiff of 50 of his ordinary shares in MEL would be a valid bequest on the defendant's death which his executors or administrators would be bound to carry into effect. Mr Hartman sought to dispute that and to say that if, for instance, a shareholder had 200 ordinary shares in ICI and wanted to give them to A, B, C and D equally he could do it by giving 200 shares to A, B, C and D as tenants in common, but he could not validly do it by giving 50 shares to A, 50 shares to B, 50 shares to C and 50 shares to D, because he has not indicated which of the identical shares A is to have and which B is to have. I do not accept that. That such a testamentary bequest is valid, appears sufficiently from *In re Clifford* [1912] 1 Ch 29 and *In re Cheadle* [1900] 2 Ch 620. It seems to me, again, that if a person holds, say, 200 ordinary shares in ICI and he executes a transfer of 50 ordinary shares in ICI either to an individual done or to trustees, and hands over the certificate for his 200 shares and the transfer to the transferees or to brokers to give effect to the transfer, there is a valid gift to the individual or trustees/transferees of 50 of the shares without any further identification of their numbers. It would be a completed gift without waiting for registration of the transfer: see *In re Rose* [1952] Ch 499. In the ordinary way a new certificate would be issued for the 50 shares to the transferee and the transferor would receive a balance certificate in respect of the rest of his holding. I see no uncertainty at all in those circumstances.

Mr Hartman, however, relied on two authorities in particular. One is a decision of Oliver J in *In re London Wine Co. (Shippers) Ltd* [1986] PCC 121 which was decided in 1975. That was a case in which the business of the company was that of dealers in wine and over a period it had acquired stocks of wine which were deposited in various warehouses in England. Quantities were then sold to customers by the company, but in many instances the wine remained at the warehouse. There was no appropriation—on the ground, as it were—from bulk, of any wine, to answer particular contracts. But the customer received from the company a certificate of title for wine for which he had paid which described him as the sole and beneficial owner of such-and-such wine of such-and-such vintage. The customer was charged for storage and insurance, but specific cases were not segregated or identified.

Subsequently, at a stage when large stocks of wine were held in various warehouses to the order of the company and its customers, a receiver was appointed by a debenture holder. The question that arose was whether the customers who had received these certificates of title had a good title to the quantity of wine referred to in the certificate as against the receiver appointed under a floating charge. The judge held that it could not be said that the legal title to the wine had passed to individual customers and the description of the wine did not adequately link it with any given consignment or warehouse. And, furthermore, it appeared that there was a lack of comparison at the time the certificates were issued in that, in some cases, the certificates were issued before the wine which had been ordered by the company had actually been received by the company. It seems to me that that case is a long way from the present. It is concerned with the appropriation of chattels and when the property in chattels passes. We are concerned with a declaration of trust, accepting that the legal title remained in the defendant and was not intended, at the time the trust was declared, to pass immediately to the plaintiff. The defendant was to retain the shares as trustee for the plaintiff.

Mr Hartman also referred to *MacJordan Construction Ltd v Brookmount Erostin Ltd* (1991) 56 BLR 1, a decision of this court. The position there was that MacJordan were sub-contractors for Brookmount as main contractors. There was retention money kept back by Brookmount which, on the documents, was to be held on a trust for the sub-contractors, but it had not been set aside as a separate fund when a receiver was appointed by the main contractor, Brookmount's, bank. It was, consequently, held that MacJordan were not entitled to payment in full of the retention moneys in priority to the receiver and the secured creditor. It was common ground in that case that, prior to the appointment of the receivers, there were no identifiable assets of Brookmount impressed with the trust applicable to the retention fund. At best, there was merely a general bank account.

In reliance on that case Mr Hartman submitted that no fiduciary relationship can attach to an unappropriated portion of a mixed fund. The only remedy is that of a floating charge. He referred to a passage in the judgment of Lord Greene MR in *In re Diplock* [1948] Ch 465, 519–520 where he said:

> The narrowness of the limits within which the common law operated may be linked with the limited nature of the remedies available to it ... In particular, the device of a declaration of charge was unknown to the common law and it was the availability of that device which enabled equity to give effect to its wider conception of equitable rights.

So Mr Hartman submitted that the most that the plaintiff could claim is to have an equitable charge on a blended fund ... As I see it, however, we are not concerned in this case with a mere equitable charge over a mixed fund. Just as a person can give, by will, a specified number of his shares of a certain class in a certain company, so equally, in my judgment, he can declare himself trustee of 50 of his ordinary shares in MEL or whatever the company may be and that is effective to give a beneficial proprietary interest to the beneficiary under the trust. No question of a blended fund thereafter arises and we are not in the field of equitable charge.

NOTE: *Hunter v Moss* has been followed (see, for example, *Re Lewis's of Leicester Ltd* [1995] 1 BCLC 428; *Re Lehman Brothers International (Europe) (In Administration)* [2011] EWCA Civ 1544), but it has also been subjected to fairly heavy academic criticism, e.g. *Hayton* (1994) 110 LQR 335, and has been regarded as inconsistent with the Privy Council decision in *Re Goldcorp Exchange* [1995] 1 AC 74, where an argument was unsuccessfully advanced that a seller of gold bullion (who had gone into liquidation having taken money from the purchasers) had become a trustee of an undivided share in his stocks. Peter Birks ([1995] RLR 83, 87) even went so far as to argue that from the reasoning of the Privy Council in *Re Goldcorp Exchange Ltd*: 'One inference is that the Court of Appeal's decision in *Hunter* v *Moss* [1994] 1 WLR 452 must be wrong.'

■ QUESTION

Is it problematic that the distinction drawn in *Hunter* v *Moss* between trusts of tangible property (chattels) and intangible property (e.g. shares) has no counterpart in the common law of sale of goods? (The distinction was followed, with some reluctance, in *Re Harvard Securities Ltd (In liq.)* [1998] CC 567.)

SECTION 4: CERTAINTY OF OBJECT

It is incumbent upon the settlor of a trust to furnish the trustee with some means of ascertaining the intended beneficiaries. The reason is simple: an owner cannot dispose of the benefit of his property in favour of 'nobody', so either he makes a disposition to 'somebody' (this could be a human being or an 'artificial' person such as a corporation) or he makes no disposition at all. Most of the leading cases used to illustrate this point in Sections 4–6 involve express trusts in non-commercial contexts, but certainty of object is just as much a consideration where express trusts are created in commercial contexts. Thus in *OT Computers Ltd (in administration)* v *First National Tricity Finance Ltd* [2003] EWHC 1010 (Ch) a company intended to set up a trust for its 'urgent suppliers', but the trust failed because that description failed to identify the objects with sufficient certainty.

A: Fixed trusts

Under a fixed trust, such as 'to Bobby for life and Brendan in remainder' or 'for Barbara and Bill in shares of two-thirds and one-third respectively' or 'for my nephews in equal shares', the trustee has no say in the choice of beneficiaries and each beneficiary's share is fixed. It follows that, in order for trustees to effect a division of the trust fund they need to know exactly how many beneficiaries there are in total. In other words, a fixed trust will fail for uncertainty of object unless a 'fixed list' of beneficiaries can be drawn up.

IRC v Broadway Cottages Trust
[1955] Ch 20, Court of Appeal

Facts: £80,000 was settled upon trustees to apply the income within the perpetuity period in their absolute discretion, the objects being a very wide class, mostly of remote issue, contained in a schedule. There was no gift over in default of appointment, and this was an attempt to set up a trust rather than a power. Two charities (Broadway Cottages Trust and Sunnylands Trust) were among the beneficiaries, and claimed income tax exemption on income received under settlement. The IRC claimed that, the trust being void for uncertainty, the income should be taxed as belonging to the settlor.

The charities admitted that the class was not ascertainable, while the Crown conceded that the individual ascertainability test was satisfied.

Held: The trust was void for uncertainty. The whole range of objects had to be ascertainable. The income therefore belonged in equity to the settlor on resulting trust (on the principles of Chapter 5).

NOTES

1. The headnote to *McPhail* v *Doulton* (HL) (see Subsection B: Discretionary Trusts) states that *Broadway Cottages* has been overruled, but the more accurate view is that the reasoning in *Broadway Cottages* continues to apply to fixed trusts. The reasoning was that in the ultimate analysis, if distribution was not effected by the trustees, the court would be obliged to effect a distribution. Since the court could not exercise for them the discretion given to the trustees, it would have no alternative but to distribute equally (see further Note 2). This could only be done if a list of the entire class could be drawn up. If this reasoning ever had any validity, it clearly remains valid in respect of fixed trusts.

2. In the opinion of Jenkins LJ (in *Broadway*), if the trustees refused to distribute, the court could not itself exercise any discretion on their behalf. It could remove the trustees and appoint others in their place, but it might be impossible to find any other trustees prepared to execute the trust. It followed that however unlikely this eventuality may be, at the end of the day a court had to be prepared to carry out the trust itself. Since it refused to exercise any discretion, it could only divide the property equally among all the objects: 'It could not mend the invalidity of the trust by imposing an arbitrary distribution amongst some only of the whole unascertainable class.'

3. Although there is a logic to this conclusion, given the premises, equality of distribution will often not implement the intentions of the settlor, and indeed is quite likely to frustrate them. It seems that the equality principle originated in nineteenth-century family settlements (e.g. *Burrough* v *Philcox* (1840) 5 Myl & Cr 72), where it may have been the most reliable method of carrying out the settlor's intention. It is much less likely to be appropriate, however, in modern settlements, for example, dividing proceeds among employees of a company.

B: Discretionary trusts

Discretionary trusts are a very useful way of holding funds for the benefit of large numbers of people, as in the case of a large fund to make non-charitable grants to employees of a huge business. No individual potential beneficiary has an interest in the fund until the trustees' discretion is exercised in his favour. One advantage of this, which has been relied upon for tax avoidance, is that no beneficiary can be taxed on his mere *potential* to benefit under a discretionary trust; he can only be taxed on *actual* entitlements (*Gartside* v *Inland Revenue Commissioners* [1968] AC 553, HL). However, too much uncertainty leads to invalidity. So in this section we will be asking: 'Can trustees be required to distribute a trust estate "as they see fit" when it is not possible to identify all the potential beneficiaries?'

Since equality of distribution was the rule for trusts, and could only be carried out if it was possible to draw up a list of all the objects, the fixed list test originally applied to *discretionary* trusts (*Re Ogden* [1933] Ch 678, HL; *IRC* v *Broadway Cottages Trust* [1955] Ch 20, CA). One result of this was that the test for certainty was much more stringent for discretionary trusts than for powers (see *Re Gestetner Settlement*). This had two main consequences: first, many perfectly reasonable trusts failed; secondly, the courts were at pains to construe doubtful dispositions as powers, rather than discretionary trusts.

Re Gestetner's Settlement

[1953] Ch 672, Chancery Division

Facts: Trustees had power to distribute capital among a very wide class, consisting of four named persons, the descendants, spouse, widow, or widower of the settlor's father or uncle, and the directors and employees or former employees of a large number of companies. There being a gift over in default of appointment, this was a power given to a trustee. The validity of the power was challenged.

Held:

(a) Where a power does not impose a trust on the donee's conscience, it is not necessary to know all the objects in order to appoint, so that a power may be good although it is in favour of an indefinite class.

(b) But where a trustee is under a duty to select there must be certainty among those recipients.

(c) The present case concerned a power given to trustees, who had no duty to appoint, only a duty to consider whether to distribute. Although the whole class could not be ascertained, since it was a fluctuating body, the power was valid.

HARMAN J: ... If, therefore, there be no duty to distribute, but only a duty to consider, it does not seem to me that there is any authority binding on me to say that this whole trust is bad. In fact, there is no difficulty, as has been admitted, in ascertaining whether any given postulant is a member of the specified class. Of course, if that could not be ascertained the matter would be quite different, but of John Doe or Richard Doe it can be postulated easily enough whether he is or is not eligible to receive the settlor's bounty. There being no uncertainty in that sense, I am reluctant to introduce a notion of uncertainty in the other sense, by saying that the trustees must worry their heads to survey the world from China to Peru, when there are perfectly good objects of the class in England. Consequently, I am not minded to upset the scheme put forward by the settlor on the ground indicated, namely, that of uncertainty. There is no uncertainty in so far as it is quite certain whether particular individuals are objects of the power. What is not certain is how many objects there are; and it does not seem to me that such an uncertainty will invalidate a trust worded in this way. I accordingly declare the trust valid.

NOTES

1. Harman J, in the above passage, was concerned with a trust where the trustees had a power to distribute, and the problem related to the objects of the power, not to the objects of the trust.

2. The case effectively decides that the judgment required of donees of a power can be exercised without the need to ascertain the entire class. The case, which was based largely on older authorities, suggests that it is enough to satisfy the individual ascertainability test, but does examine this test with the precision of later authorities.

3. A discretionary trust may be set up for the benefit of an individual beneficiary where it is undesirable for tax and other financial planning reasons for the beneficiary to have immediate beneficial enjoyment of an entire fund (for example, where damages for serious personal injury are designed to last a lifetime, e.g. *Lindsay v Wood* [2006] EWHC 2895 (QB)).

Re Gulbenkian's Settlements, Whishaw v Stephens

[1970] AC 508, House of Lords

Facts: The case concerned the will of Calouste Gulbenkian (a well-known Armenian oil entrepreneur), made in 1929, under which the trustees had a power to apply income to maintain his son, Nubar Gulbenkian:

... and any person or persons in whose house or apartments or in whose company or under whose care or control or by or with whom the said Nubar Sarkis Gulbenkian may from time to time be employed or residing.

It was observed that the clause (which had apparently found its way into a standard book on precedents) did not make sense as it stood, but it was interpreted as meaning:

(a) any person by whom Mr Gulbenkian may from time to time be employed, and

(b) any person in whose house or in whose company or in whose care he may from time to time be residing.

No difficulties arose over limb (a), but it was argued that limb (b) was void for uncertainty.

Held: A power was not void for uncertainty if it could be said with certainty whether any given individual was or was not a member of the class, and did not fail simply because it was impossible to ascertain every member of the class. *Gestetner* was followed.

LORD UPJOHN (with whom Lords Hodson and Guest agreed): My lords, … I agree … with the Court of Appeal. Many difficult and borderline cases may occur in any one of these situations. But mere difficulty is nothing to the point. If the trustees feel difficulty or even doubt on the point the Court of Chancery is available to solve it for them. It solves many such problems every year. I cannot for myself see any insuperable difficulty arising in the solution of any given state of affairs which would make it necessary to hold that the relevant clause as I have construed it fails to comply with the test. On course I have not overlooked *Sifton* v *Sifton* [1938] AC 656, but that was the entirely different case of a divesting clause. In my opinion, this clause is not void for uncertainty, and the Court of Appeal [1968] Ch 126 were quite right to overrule the decision of Harman J in *Re Gresham's Settlements* [1956] 2 All ER 193, where he held a similar clause was void on that ground.

My lords, that is sufficient to dispose of the appeal, but, as I have mentioned earlier, the reasons of two members of the Court of Appeal went further and have been supported by counsel for the respondents with much force and so must be examined.

Lord Denning MR [1968] Ch at pp. 133, 134, propounded a test in the case of powers collateral, namely, that if you can say of one particular person meaning thereby, apparently, any one person only that he is clearly within the category the whole power is good though it may be difficult to say in other cases whether a person is or is not within the category, and he supported that view by reference to authority. Winn LJ said [1968] Ch at p. 138 that where there was not a complete failure by reason of ambiguity and uncertainty the court would give effect to the power as valid rather than hold it defeated since it will not have wholly failed, which put—though more broadly—the view expressed by Lord Denning MR. Counsel for the respondents in his second line of argument relied on these observations as a matter of principle but he candidly admitted that he could not rely on any authority. Moreover, Lord Denning MR expressed the view [1968] Ch at p. 133 that the different doctrine with regard to trust powers should be brought into line with the rule with regard to conditions precedent and powers collateral. So I propose to make some general observations on this matter.

If a donor (be he a settlor or testator) directs trustees to make some specified provision for 'John Smith', then to give legal effect to that provision it must be possible to identify 'John Smith'. If the donor knows three John Smiths then by the most elementary principles of law neither the trustees nor the court in their place can give effect to that provision; neither the trustees nor the court can guess at it. It must fail for uncertainty unless of course admissible evidence is available to point to a particular John Smith as the object of the donor's bounty.

Then, taking it one stage further, suppose the donor directs that a fund, or the income of a fund, should be equally divided between members of a class. That class must be as defined as the individual; the court cannot guess at it. Suppose the donor directs that a fund be divided equally between 'my old friends', then unless there is some admissible evidence that the donor has given some special 'dictionary' meaning to that phrase which enables the trustees to identify the class with sufficient certainty, it is plainly bad as being too uncertain. Suppose that there appeared before the trustees (or the court) two or three individuals who plainly satisfied the test of being among 'my old friends' the trustees could not consistently with the donor's intentions accept them as claiming the whole or any defined part of the fund. They cannot claim the whole fund for they can show no title to it unless they prove they are the only members of the class, which of course they cannot do, and so, too, by parity of reasoning they cannot claim any defined part of the fund and there is no authority in the trustees or the court to make any distribution among a smaller class than that pointed out by the donor. The principle is, in my opinion, that the donor must make his intention sufficiently plain as to the objects of his trust and the court cannot give effect to it by misinterpreting his intentions by dividing the fund merely among those present. Secondly, and perhaps it is the most hallowed principle, the Court of Chancery, which acts in default of trustees, must know with sufficient certainty the objects of the beneficence of the donor so as to execute the trust. Then, suppose the donor does not direct an equal division of his property among the class but gives a power of selection to his trustees among the class; exactly the same principles must apply. The trustees have a duty to select the donees of the donor's bounty from among the class designated by the donor; he has not entrusted them with any power to select the donees merely from among known claimants who are within the class, for that is constituting a narrower class and the donor has given them no power to do this.

So if the class is insufficiently defined the donor's intentions must in such cases fail for uncertainty. Perhaps I should mention here that it is clear that the question of certainty must be determined as of the date of the document declaring the donor's intention (in the case of a will, his death). Normally the question of certainty will arise because of the ambiguity of definition of the class by reason of the language employed by the donor, but occasionally owing to some of the curious settlements executed in recent years it may be quite impossible to construct even with all the available evidence anything like a class capable of definition (*Re Sayer Trust* [1957] Ch 423), though difficulty in doing so will not defeat the donor's intentions (*Re Hain's Settlement* [1961] 1 All ER 848). But I should add this: if the class is sufficiently defined by the donor the fact that it may be difficult to ascertain the whereabouts or continued existence of some of its members at the relevant time matters not. The trustees can apply to the court for directions to pay a share into court.

But when mere or bare powers are conferred on donees of the power (whether trustees or others) the matter is quite different. As I have already pointed out, the trustees have no duty to exercise it in the sense that they cannot be controlled in any way. If they fail to exercise it then those entitled in default of its exercise are entitled to the fund. Perhaps the contrast may be put forcibly in this way: in the first case it is a mere power to distribute with a gift over in default; in the second case it is a trust to distribute among the class defined by the donor with merely a power of selection within that class. The result is in the first case even if the class of appointees among whom the donees of the power may appoint is clear and ascertained and they are all of full age and *sui juris*, nevertheless they cannot compel the donees of the power to exercise it in their collective favour. If, however, it is a trust power, then those entitled are entitled (if they are of full age and *sui juris*) to compel the trustees to pay the fund over to them, unless the fund is income and the trustees have power to accumulate for the future.

Again the basic difference between a mere power and a trust power is that in the first case trustees owe no duty to exercise it and the relevant fund or income falls to be dealt with in accordance with the trusts in default of its exercise, whereas in the second case the trustees must exercise the power and in default the court will ... It is a matter of construction whether the power is a mere power or a trust power and the use of inappropriate language is not decisive (*Wilson* v *Turner* (1833) 22 ChD 521 at p. 525).

So, with all respect to the contrary view, I cannot myself see how, consistently with principle, it is possible to apply to the execution of a trust power the principles applicable to the permissible exercise by the donees, even if the trustees of mere powers; that would defeat the intention of donors completely.

But with respect to mere powers, while the court cannot compel the trustees to exercise their powers, yet those entitled to the fund in default must clearly be entitled to restrain the trustees from exercising it save among those within the power. So the trustees, or the court, must be able to say with certainty who is within and who is without the power. It is for this reason that I find myself unable to accept the broader proposition advanced by Lord Denning MR and Winn LJ mentioned earlier, and agree with the proposition as enunciated in *Re Gestetner* [1953] Ch 672 and the later cases.

My lords, I would dismiss these appeals.

NOTES

1. The exact formulation of the test is of importance: 'the trustees, or the court, must be able to say with certainty who is within and who is without the power'. Note the necessity to ascertain of any individual whether he is or is not a member of the class.

2. In the Court of Appeal, Lord Denning MR ([1968] Ch 126, 132–4) had taken the view that a power was void for uncertainty only if it was impossible to identify one single beneficiary. The argument (at 134) is that unless it is impossible to carry out the power, it will not be held bad for uncertainty. In Lord Denning MR's view, therefore, it was enough to be able to identify one individual clearly within the class.

3. The House of Lords (with Lord Donovan reserving his opinion) rejected Lord Denning MR's view, on the grounds that in order properly to exercise his discretion, *any* donee of a power must be able to ascertain whether *any* intended object was within the class of objects of the power. Even where the power gives the trustee 'absolute discretion', the discretion must be exercised in a fiduciary manner, and the donee of the power must at least consider whether to exercise it.

4. The Denning test would only really be appropriate were the trustees at liberty to distribute to the first person who came to hand, and as we have seen that is not the case. The Denning test is in any case no good for enforcement purposes, where the donees of the power propose to appoint somebody who is not an object of the power. Anybody coming to court for an injunction will have to show that he is an object, and also that the person in whose favour it is proposed to appoint is

not. That requires the ability to determine of anybody whether or not he is within the class. It is not sufficient to be able to say of one person alone.

■ QUESTION

What is the nature of the problem, in the above extract, where the donor knows three John Smiths? Is there a conceptual difficulty in defining John Smith? Or is the difficulty evidential in not knowing which John Smith is meant? Surely the difficulty must be evidential?

McPhail v *Doulton (sub nom Re Baden's Deed Trusts (No. 1))*

[1971] AC 424, House of Lords

Facts: The settlor, Bertram Baden, purported by deed to transfer shares in Matthew Hall & Co. Ltd to trustees to form the nucleus of a fund for the benefit of the staff of the company, their relatives and dependants. Clause 9, set out at p. 447, provided:

(a) The trustees shall apply the net income of the fund in making at their absolute discretion grants to or for the benefit of any of the officers and employees or ex-officers or ex-employees of the company or to any relatives or dependants of any such persons in such amounts at such times and on such conditions (if any) as they think fit and any such grant may at their discretion be made by payment to the beneficiary or to any institution or person to be applied for his or her benefit and in the latter case the trustees shall be under no obligation to see to the application of the money.

(b) The trustees shall not be bound to exhaust the income of any year or other period in making such grants as aforesaid and any income not so applied shall be dealt with as provided by clause 6(a) hereof. [Clause 6. (a) All moneys in the hands of the trustees and not required for the immediate service of the fund may be placed in a deposit or current account with any bank or banking house in the name of the trustees or may be invested as hereinafter provided.]

(c) The trustees may realise any investments representing accumulations of income and apply the proceeds as though the same were income of the fund and may also (but only with the consent of all the trustees) at any time prior to the liquidation of the fund realise any other part of the capital of the fund which in the opinion of the trustees it is desirable to realise in order to provide benefits for which the current income of the fund is insufficient.

The executors challenged the deed on behalf of the estate, on the ground that the settlement was void for uncertainty. It was argued that the disposition created a discretionary trust, not a power, and that the applicable test was therefore the class ascertainability test propounded by the Court of Appeal in *IRC* v *Broadway Cottages Trust* [1955] Ch 20, rather than the individual ascertainability test propounded by the House of Lords in *In re Gulbenkian's Settlements* [1970] AC 508. The *Gulbenkian* test, it was argued, applied only to powers.

Held: (Lords Hodson and Guest dissenting): The disposition created a discretionary trust, not a power. However, the individual ascertainability test for certainty of objects, as applied to powers, was also the correct test to be applied to discretionary trusts. *IRC* v *Broadway Cottages* was overruled, and the case was remitted to the Chancery Division for application of the correct test.

LORD WILBERFORCE: ... I therefore agree with Russell LJ and would to that extent allow the appeal, declare that the provisions of clause 9(a) constitute a trust and remit the case to the Chancery Division for determination whether on this basis clause 9 is ... valid or void for uncertainty.

This makes it necessary to consider whether, in so doing, the court should proceed on the basis that the relevant test is that laid down in *IRC* v *Broadway Cottages Trust* [1955] Ch 20 or some other test.

That decision gave the authority of the Court of Appeal to the distinction between cases where trustees are given a power of selection and those where they are bound by a trust for selection. In the former case the position as decided by this House, is that the power is valid if it can be said with certainty whether any given individual is or is not a member of the class and does not fail simply because it is impossible to ascertain every member of the class (*Re Gulbenkian's Settlements* [1970] AC 508). But in the latter case it is said to be necessary, for the trust to be valid, that the wide range of objects (I use the language of the Court of Appeal) should be ascertained or capable of ascertainment.

The respondents invited your lordships to assimilate the validity test for trusts to that which applies to powers. Alternatively they contended that in any event the test laid down in the *Broadway Cottages* case [1955] Ch 20 was too rigid, and that a trust should be upheld if there is sufficient practical certainty in its definition for it to be carried out, if necessary with the administrative assistance of the court, according to the expressed intention of the settlor. I would agree with this, but this does not dispense from examination of the wider argument. The basis for the *Broadway Cottages* principle is stated to be that a trust cannot be valid unless, if need be, it can be executed by the court, and (though it is not quite clear from the judgment where argument ends and decision begins) that the court can only execute it by ordering an equal distribution in which every beneficiary shares. So it is necessary to examine the authority and reason for this supposed rule as to the execution of trusts by the court.

Assuming, as I am prepared to do for present purposes, that the test of validity is whether the trust can be executed by the court, it does not follow that execution is impossible unless there can be equal division.

As a matter of reason, to hold that a principle of equal division applies to trusts such as the present is certainly paradoxical. Equal division is surely the last thing the settlor ever intended: equal division among all may, probably would, produce a result beneficial to none. Why suppose that the court would lend itself to a whimsical execution? And as regards authority, I do not find that the nature of the trust, and of the court's powers over trusts, calls for any such rigid rule. Equal division may be sensible and has been decreed, in cases of family trusts, for a limited class; here there is life in the maxim 'equality is equity', but the cases provide numerous examples where this has not been so, and a different type of execution has been ordered, appropriate to the circumstances ...

So I think that we are free to review the *Broadway Cottages* case [1955] Ch 20. The conclusion which I would reach, implicit in the previous discussion, is that the wide distinction between the validity test for powers and that for trust powers is unfortunate and wrong, that the rule recently fastened upon the courts by *IRC* v *Broadway Cottages Trust* ought to be discarded, and that the test for the validity of trust powers ought to be similar to that accepted by this House in *Re Gulbenkian's Settlements* [1970] AC 508 for powers, namely, that the trust is valid if it can be said with certainty that any given individual is or is not a member of the class ...

Assimilation of the validity test does not involve the complete assimilation of trust powers with powers. As to powers, I agree with my noble and learned friend Lord Upjohn in *Re Gulbenkian's Settlements* that although the trustees may, and normally will, be under a fiduciary duty to consider whether or in what way they should exercise their power, the court will not normally compel its exercise. It will intervene if the trustees exceed their powers, and possibly if they are proved to have exercised it capriciously. But in the case of a trust power, if the trustees do not exercise it, the court will: I respectfully adopt as to this the statement in Lord Upjohn's opinion (p. 525). I would venture to amplify this by saying that the court, if called upon to execute the trust power, will do so in the manner best calculated to give effect to the settlor's or testator's intentions. It may do so by appointing new trustees, or by authorising or directing representative persons of the classes of beneficiaries to prepare a scheme for distribution, or even, should the proper basis for distribution appear, by itself directing the trustees so to distribute ... Then, as to the trustees' duty of inquiry or ascertainment, in each case the trustees ought to make such a survey of the range of objects or possible beneficiaries as will enable them to carry out their fiduciary duty (cf. *Liley* v *Hey* (1842) 1 Hare 580). A wider and more comprehensive range of inquiry is called for in the case of trust powers than in the case of powers.

Two final points: first, as to the question of certainty. I desire to emphasise the distinction clearly made and explained by Lord Upjohn ([1970] AC 508, 524) between linguistic or semantic uncertainty which, if unresolved by the court, renders the gift void, and the difficulty of ascertaining the existence or whereabouts of members of the class, a matter with which the court can appropriately deal on an application for directions. There may be a third case where the meaning of the words used is clear but the definition of beneficiaries is so hopelessly wide as not to form 'anything like a class' so that the trust is administratively unworkable or in Lord Eldon's words one that cannot be executed (*Morice* v *Bishop of Durham* (1805) 10 Ves 522, 527). I hesitate to give examples for they may prejudice future cases, but perhaps 'all the residents of Greater London' will serve. I do not think that a discretionary trust for 'relatives' even of a living person falls within this category.

NOTES

1. The *ratio* of *Re Baden's Deed Trusts (No. 1)* is that the test for certainty for discretionary trusts is essentially the same as that for powers, namely the individual ascertainability test.

2. In reaching its decision, the House rejected the principle of equality of distribution, in a case where equal distribution would have made a nonsense of the settlor's intention, accepting that even in the final analysis (in other words even assuming that no trustee can be found who is prepared to execute the trust), the court could exercise the necessary discretion itself. Therefore, the reasoning in the *IRC* v *Broadway Cottages Trust* [1955] Ch 20 was inapplicable (and indeed, *Broadway Cottages Trust* was overruled).

3. Lord Wilberforce also made the point that in applying the test the courts are concerned only with conceptual uncertainty. A trust will not fail merely because there are evidential difficulties in ascertaining whether or not someone is within the class, as the court is never defeated by evidential uncertainty, and can deal with problems of proof when an application for enforcement arises:

   > I desire to emphasise the distinction clearly made ... between linguistic or semantic uncertainty which, if unresolved by the court, renders the gift void, and the difficulty of ascertaining the existence or whereabouts of members of the class, a matter with which the court can appropriately deal on an application for directions.

4. But there is not total assimilation between the tests for trusts and powers, since in considering the exercise of their discretion, the trustees must, according to Lord Wilberforce in *McPhail* v *Doulton* itself, make a survey of the entire field of objects, and consider each individual case responsibly, on its merits. A trust can fail if it is administratively unworkable, and this test may be more stringent than that for powers.

5. The trust also fails if the definition of beneficiaries is so hopelessly wide as not to form 'anything like a class'. The example given is a gift to 'all the residents of Greater London'.

6. Nothing in this case clearly affects fixed trusts. The House merely assimilated discretionary trusts and powers.

Re Baden's Trusts (No. 2)

[1973] Ch 9, Court of Appeal

Decision: The deed considered in *Re Baden's Deed Trusts (No. 1)* was remitted to the Chancery Division for application of the test propounded by the House of Lords, and was appealed for a second time to the Court of Appeal. The Court of Appeal held that the trust was valid on the individual ascertainability test.

SACHS LJ: It is first to be noted that the deed must be looked at through the eyes of a businessman seeking to advance the welfare of the employees of his firm and those so connected with the employees that a benevolent employer would wish to help them. He would not necessarily be looking at the words he uses with the same eyes as those of a man making a will. Accordingly, whether a court is considering the concept implicit in relevant words, or whether it is exercising the function of a court of construction, it should adopt that same practical and common-sense approach which was enjoined by Upjohn J in *Re Sayer* [1957] Ch 423, 436, and by Lord Wilberforce in the *Baden* case [1971] AC 424, 452, and which would be used by an employer setting up such a fund.

The next point as regards approach that requires consideration is the contention, strongly pressed by Mr Vinelott, that the court must always be able to say whether any given postulant is not within the relevant class as well as being able to say whether he is within it. In construing the words already cited from the speech of Lord Wilberforce in the *Baden* case (as well as those of Lord Reid and Lord Upjohn in [*Re Gulbenkian's Settlements* [1970] AC 508]), it is essential to bear in mind the difference between conceptual uncertainty and evidential difficulties. That distinction is explicitly referred to by Lord Wilberforce in *Re Baden's Deed Trusts* [1971] AC 424, 457 when he said:

> ... as to the question of certainty. I desire to emphasise the distinction clearly made and explained by Lord Upjohn [1970] AC 508, 524 between linguistic or semantic uncertainty which, if unresolved by the court, renders the gift void, and the difficulty of ascertaining the existence or whereabouts of members of the class, a matter with which the court can appropriately deal on an application for directions.

As Mr Vinelott himself rightly observed, 'the court is never defeated by evidential uncertainty', and it is in my judgment clear that it is conceptual uncertainty to which reference was made when the 'is or is not a member of the class' test was enunciated. (Conceptual uncertainty was in the course of argument conveniently exemplified, rightly or wrongly matters not, by the phrase 'someone under a moral obligation' and contrasted with the certainty of the words 'first cousins'.) Once the class of persons to be benefited is conceptually certain it then becomes a question of fact to be determined on evidence whether any postulant has on inquiry been proved to be within it: if he is not so proved, then he is not in it. That position remains the same whether the class to be benefited happens to be small (such as 'first cousins') or large (such as 'members of the X Trade Union' or 'those who have served in the Royal Navy'). The suggestion that such trusts could be invalid because it might be impossible to prove of a given individual that he was not in the relevant class is wholly fallacious—and only Mr Vinelott's persuasiveness has prevented me from saying that the contention is almost unarguable.

MEGAW LJ: The main argument of Mr Vinelott was founded upon a strict and literal interpretation of the words in which the decision of the House of Lords in *Re Gulbenkian's Settlements* [1970] AC 508 was expressed. That decision laid down the test for the validity of powers of selection. It is relevant for the present case, because in the previous excursion of this case to the House of Lords [1971] AC 424 it was held that there is no relevant difference in the test of validity, whether the trustees are given a power of selection or, as was held by their lordships to be the case in this trust deed, a trust for selection. The test in either case is what may be called the *Gulbenkian* test. The *Gulbenkian* test, as expressed by Lord Wilberforce at p. 450, and again in almost identical words at p. 454 is this:

> ... the power is valid if it can be said with certainty whether any given individual is or is not a member of the class and does not fail simply because it is impossible to ascertain every member of the class.

The executors' argument concentrates on the words 'or is not' in the first of the two limbs of the sentence quoted above: 'if it can be said with certainty whether any given individual is or is not a member of the class'. It is said that those words have been used deliberately, and have only one possible meaning; and that however startling or drastic or unsatisfactory the result may be—and Mr Vinelott does not shrink from saying that the consequence is drastic—this court is bound to give effect to the words used in the House of Lords' definition of the test. It would be quite impracticable for the trustees to ascertain in many cases whether a particular person was not a relative of an employee. The most that could be said is: 'There is no proof that he is a relative'. But there would still be no 'certainty' that such a person was not a relative. Hence, so it is said, the test laid down by the House of Lords is not satisfied, and the trust is void. For it cannot be said with certainty, in relation to any individual, that he is not a relative.

I do not think it was contemplated that the words 'or is not' would produce that result. It would, as I see it, involve an inconsistency with the latter part of the same sentence: 'does not fail simply because it is impossible to ascertain every member of the class'. The executors' contention, in substance and reality, is that it does fail 'simply because it is impossible to ascertain every member of the class'

.The same verbal difficulty, as I see it, emerges also when one considers the words of the suggested test which the House of Lords expressly rejected. That is set out by Lord Wilberforce in a passage immediately following the sentence which I have already quoted. The rejected test was in these terms [1971] AC 424, 450:

> ... it is said to be necessary ... that the whole range of objects ... should be ascertained or capable of ascertainment.

Since that test was rejected, the resulting affirmative proposition, which by implication must have been accepted by their lordships, is this: a trust for selection will not fail simply because the whole range of objects cannot be ascertained. In the present case, the trustees could ascertain, by investigation and evidence, many of the objects: as to many other theoretically possible claimants, they could not be certain. Is it to be said that the trust fails because it cannot be said with certainty that such persons are not members of the class? If so, is that not the application of the rejected test: the trust failing because 'the whole range' of objects cannot be ascertained'?

In my judgment, much too great emphasis is placed in the executors' argument on the words 'or is not'. To my mind, the test is satisfied if, as regards at least a substantial number of objects, it can be said with certainty that they fall within the trust; even though, as regards a substantial number of other persons, if they ever for some fanciful reason fell to be considered, the answer would have to be, not 'they are outside the trust', but 'it is not proven whether they are in or out'. What is a 'substantial number' may well be a question of common sense and of degree in relation to the particular trust: particularly where, as here, it would be fantasy, to use a mild word, to suggest that any practical difficulty would arise in the fair, proper and sensible administration of this trust in respect of relatives and dependants.

I do not think that this involves, as Mr Vinelott suggested, a return by this court to its former view which was rejected by the House of Lords in the *Gulbenkian* case. If I did so think, I should, however reluctantly, accept Mr Vinelott's argument and its consequences. But as I read it, the criticism in the House of Lords of the decision of this court in that case related to this court's acceptance of the view that it would be sufficient if it could be shown that one single person fell within the scope of the power or trust. The essence of the decision of the House of Lords in the *Gulbenkian* case, as I see it, is not that it must be possible to show with certainty that any given person is or is not within the trust; but that it is not, or may not be, sufficient to be able to show that one individual person is within it. If it does not mean that, I do not know where the line is supposed to be drawn, having regard to the clarity and emphasis with which the House of Lords has laid down that the trust does not fail because the whole range of objects cannot be ascertained. I would dismiss the appeal.

STAMP LJ: ... Counsel for the defendant executors, fastening on those words, 'if it can be said with certainty that any given individual is or is not a member of the class', submitted in this court that a trust for distribution among officers and employees or ex-officers or ex-employees or any of their relatives or dependants does not satisfy the test. You may say with certainty that any given individual is or is not an officer, employee, ex-officer or ex-employee. You may say with certainty that a very large number of given individuals are relatives of one of them; but, so the argument runs, you will never be able to say with certainty of many given individuals that they are not. I am bound to say that I had thought at one stage of counsel's able argument that this was no more than an exercise in semantics and that the phrase on which he relies indicated no more than that the trust was valid if there was such certainty in the definition of membership of the class that you could say with certainty that some individuals were members of it; that it was sufficient that you should be satisfied that a given individual presenting himself has or has not passed the test and that it matters not that having failed to establish his membership—here his relationship—you may, perhaps wrongly, reject him. There are, however, in my judgment serious difficulties in the way of a rejection of counsel's submission.

The first difficulty, as I see it, is that the rejection of counsel's submission involves holding that the trust is good if there are individuals—or even one—of whom you can say with certainty that he is a member of the class. That was the test adopted by and the decision of the Court of Appeal in the *Gulbenkian* case where what was under consideration was a power of distribution among a class conferred on trustees as distinct from a trust for distribution: but when the *Gulbenkian* case came before the House of Lords that test was decisively rejected and the more stringent test on which counsel for the defendant executors insists was adopted. Clearly Lord Wilberforce in expressing the view that the test of validity of a discretionary trust ought to be similar to that accepted by the House of Lords in the *Gulbenkian* case did not take the view that it was sufficient that you could find individuals who were clearly members of the class; for he himself remarked, towards the end of his speech as to the trustees' duty of enquiring or ascertaining, that in each case the trustees ought to make such a survey of the range of objects or possible beneficiaries as will enable them to carry out their fiduciary duty. It is not enough that trustees should do nothing but distribute the fund among those objects of the trust who happen to be at hand or present themselves. Lord Wilberforce, after citing that passage which I have already quoted from the speech of Lord Upjohn in the *Gulbenkian* case, put it more succinctly by remarking that what this did say (and he agreed) was that the trustees must select from the class, but that passage did not mean (as had been contended) that they must be able to get a complete list of all possible objects. I have already called attention to Lord Wilberforce's opinion that the trustees ought to make such a survey of the range of objects or possible beneficiaries as will enable them to carry out their fiduciary duty, and I ought perhaps to add that he indicated that a wider and more comprehensive range of enquiry is called for in the case of what I have called discretionary trusts than in the case of fiduciary powers. But, as I understand it, having made the appropriate survey, it matters not that it is not complete or fails to yield a result enabling you to lay out a list or particulars of every single beneficiary. Having done the best they can, the trustees may proceed on the basis similar to that adopted by the court where all the beneficiaries cannot be ascertained and distribute on the footing that they have been: see, for example, *Re Benjamin* [1902] 1 Ch 723. What was referred to as 'the complete ascertainment test' laid down by this court in the *Broadway Cottages* case is rejected. So also is the test laid down by this court in the *Gulbenkian* case. Validity or invalidity is to depend on whether you can say of any individual—and the accent must be on that word 'any', for it is not simply the individual whose claim you are considering who is spoken of—that he 'is or is not a member of the class', for only thus can you make a survey of the range of objects or possible beneficiaries.

If the matter rested there, it would in my judgment follow that, treating the word 'relatives' as meaning descendants from a common ancestor, a trust for distribution such as is here in question would not be valid. Any 'survey of the range of the objects or possible beneficiaries' would certainly be incomplete, and I am able to discern no principle on which such a survey could be conducted or where it should start or finish.

The most you could do, so far as regards relatives, would be to find individuals who are clearly members of the class—the test which was accepted in the Court of Appeal, but rejected in the House of Lords, in the *Gulbenkian* case.

The matter does not, however, rest there, and I must return to examine more closely Lord Wilberforce's reasons for rejecting the *Broadway Cottages* test ... He cited cases where prior to the time of Sir Richard Arden MR a discretionary trust had been executed otherwise than by equal division. *Harding* v *Glyn* (1739) 1 Atk 469, he said, was an early case where the court executed a discretionary trust for 'relations'—and it is a discretionary trust for relations that I am considering—by distributing to the next-of-kin in equal shares ...

Harding v *Glyn* accordingly cannot be regarded simply as a case where in default of appointment a gift to the next-of-kin is to be implied as a matter of construction, but as authority endorsed by the decision of the House of Lords that a discretionary trust for 'relations' was a valid trust to be executed by the court by distribution to the next-of-kin. The class of beneficiaries thus becomes a clearly defined class and there is no difficulty in determining whether a given individual is within it or without it.

Does it then make any difference that here the discretionary trust for relations was a reference not to the relations of a deceased person but of one who was living? I think not. The next-of-kin of a living person are as readily ascertainable at any given time as the next-of-kin of one who is dead. A trust for the next-of-kin of a person, without more, was not a trust for the next-of-kin according to the statutes which would regulate the distribution of the personal property of a deceased person had he died intestate, but a trust for his nearest blood relations: see *Re Gray's Settlement*. To execute a discretionary trust for the relations or relatives of a living person by distribution among his nearest blood relations appears to me a satisfactory method of so doing; and, if it were necessary to give a construction to the word 'relatives' in relating to a living person in an inter vivos settlement, to construe it as a reference to his nearest blood relations would be far more likely to give effect to the intention than a construction which embraced all who were descended from one of his ancestors. Putting aside the doctrine *ut res magis valeat quam pereat*, which would *if necessary* have persuaded me that the word 'relatives' in this settlement should be construed to mean nearest blood relations, nothing could be more improbable than that Mr Baden should have intended the trustees to be at liberty to make grants to a relative of an employee of whose very existence that employee might be ignorant. 'Nearest blood relations or dependants' makes more sense ...

In coming to these conclusions I remain haunted by a remark towards the end of Lord Wilberforce's speech when, in considering the possible unworkability of a trust, he speaks of 'relations' as if it were a very wide class; for I confess that I find a difficulty in treating a discretionary trust as one which may be executed by the trustees among a wider class than would be contemplated if the court were required to execute it ...

The only other challenge to the validity of the trust is directed against the use of the word 'dependants' which it is said introduces a linguistic or semantic uncertainty. That in the context the word connotes financial dependence I do not doubt, and although in a given case there may be a doubt whether there be a sufficient degree of dependence to satisfy the qualification of being a 'dependant', that is a question which can be determined by the court and does not introduce linguistic uncertainty.

NOTES

1. The disposition was 'to or for the benefit of any of the officers and employees or ex-officers or ex-employees of the company or to any relatives or dependants of any such persons'. It was argued by John Vinelott QC, who was challenging the disposition on behalf of the executors, that it could not be shown that any person definitely is or *is not* within the class (as required by the *Gulbenkian* test). Had this ingenious argument been accepted it would almost certainly have heralded a return to the discredited requirement that a fixed list be drawn up, so the Court of Appeal rejected the argument.

2. Sachs LJ avoided the difficulty by emphasising that the court was concerned only with conceptual certainty, so that it should not be fatal that there might be *evidential* difficulties in drawing up John Vinelott QC's list. This effectively destroys the Vinelott argument, which was addressed primarily towards *evidential* difficulties in drawing up the class. Sachs LJ also took the view that the courts would place the burden of proof, in effect, on someone claiming to be within the class. This seems acceptable if ultimate enforcement is the issue, and the test is of the *locus standi* of the claimant, but it does not help the administration of the trust.

3. Megaw LJ adopted a different solution, however, requiring that as regards a substantial number of objects, it can be shown with certainty that they fall within the class. This is rather a vague test—clearly it is not enough to be able to show that *one* person is certainly within the class, as this test was rejected in *Gulbenkian* (see the discussion of powers, above). Presumably, the test requires evidential, as well as conceptual certainty. Maybe Megaw LJ adopted it simply because he could find no other way of rejecting Mr Vinelott's argument without returning either to the rejected *Broadway* test, or to the Denning test which had been rejected in *Gulbenkian*. Indeed, none of the judges in the Court of Appeal was able to find a satisfactory solution to this difficulty. The test may have the merit, however, of ensuring that the trustees will be able to get a feel for the width of the class, which they need properly to be able to exercise their discretion.

4. Stamp LJ's test is probably the strictest of the three, and he seemed to be quite impressed by the Vinelott argument. He emphasised that it must be possible for the trustees to make a comprehensive survey of the range of objects, but he did not think it would be fatal if, at the end of the survey, it was impossible to draw up a list of every single beneficiary. He would have taken the view that the trust failed, had he not felt compelled to follow an early House of Lords authority, which had held that a discretionary trust for 'relations' was valid, 'relations' being defined narrowly for distribution purposes as 'next of kin'.

5. Sachs LJ was able to validate the trust only by adopting very wide definitions of both 'relatives' and 'dependants', enabling a clear line to be drawn between those who were within and without the class. He took the view that relatives were defined as any persons who are linked by a common ancestor. He observed that 'dependants' had already been defined by the courts, for example in relation to the Workmen's Compensation Act 1897, but he was also able to adopt a bright line definition by taking the view 'that any one wholly or partly dependent on the means of another is a "dependant" '. By contrast, Stamp LJ was able to validate the disposition only by rejecting the wide definition of 'relatives', adopted by Sachs LJ.

■ QUESTIONS

1. Is the conceptual/evidential distinction drawn by Sachs LJ, which appears to require a bright line distinction to be drawn, the same as that drawn by Lord Upjohn in *Gulbenkian*, above?

2. Would you say that Megaw and Stamp LJJ are confusing the issue by bringing ideas of administrative unworkability into the certainty test itself? If that is a mistake, is it also made by Sachs LJ?

3. Of the three tests adopted in this case, which is most likely to give effect to the wishes of the settlor? Which allows for the easiest distribution by the court, in the event that this becomes necessary? Can any other justifications be advanced for any certainty test, or for any of the particular certainty tests adopted in this case?

Re Barlow's WT

[1979] 1 WLR 278, [1979] 1 All ER 296, Chancery Division

Decision: Browne-Wilkinson J upheld a direction to an executor to sell a collection of valuable paintings, subject to provision 'to allow any member of my family and any friends of mine who may wish to do so' to purchase them at well below current market value. The issue was whether 'family' and 'friends' were conceptually uncertain, so that the gift should fail for uncertainty.

BROWNE-WILKINSON J: Counsel for the fourth defendant, who argued in favour of the validity of the gift, contended that the tests laid down in the *Gulbenkian* case [1970] AC 508 and *McPhail* v *Doulton* [1971] AC 424 were not applicable to this case. The test, he says, is that laid down by the Court of Appeal in *Re Allen* [1953] Ch 810 as appropriate in cases where the validity of a condition precedent or description is in issue, namely that the gift is valid if it is possible to say of one or more persons that he or they undoubtedly qualify even though it may be difficult to say of others whether or not they qualify.

The distinction between the *Gulbenkian* test and the *Re Allen* test is, in my judgment, well exemplified by the word 'friends'. The word has a great range of meanings; indeed, its exact meaning probably varies slightly from person to person. Some would include only those with whom they had been on intimate terms over a long period; others would include acquaintances whom they liked. Some would include people with whom their relationship was primarily one of business; others would not. Indeed, many people, if asked to draw up a complete list of their friends, would probably have some difficulty in deciding whether certain of the people they knew were really 'friends' as opposed to 'acquaintances'. Therefore, if the nature of the gift was such that it was legally necessary to draw up a complete list of 'friends' of the testatrix, or to be able to say of any person that 'he is not a friend', the whole gift would probably fail even as to those who, by any conceivable test, were friends. But in the case of a gift of a kind which does not require one to establish all the members of the class (e.g., 'a gift of £10 to each of my friends'), it may be possible to say of some people that, on any test, they qualify. Thus in *Re Allen* Evershed MR took the example of a gift to X 'if he is a tall man'; a man 6 feet 6 inches tall could be said on any reasonable basis to satisfy the test, although it might be impossible to say whether a man, say, 5 feet 10 inches high satisfied the requirement.

So in this case, in my judgment, there are acquaintances of a kind so close that, on any reasonable basis, anyone would treat them as being 'friends'. Therefore, by allowing the disposition to take effect in their favour, one would, certainly be giving effect to part of the testatrix's intention even though as to others it is impossible to say whether or not they satisfy the test.

In my judgment, it is clear that Lord Upjohn in *Re Gulbenkian* was considering only cases where it was necessary to establish all the members of the class. He made it clear that the reason for the rule is that in a gift which requires one to establish all the members of the class (e.g., 'a gift to my friends in equal shares') you cannot hold the gift good in part, since the quantum of each friend's share depends on how many friends there are. So all persons intended to benefit by the donor must be ascertained if any effect is to be given to the gift. In my judgment, the adoption of Lord Upjohn's test by the House of Lords in *McPhail* v *Doulton* is based on the same reasoning, even though in that case the House of Lords held that it was only necessary to be able to survey the class of objects of a power of appointment and not to establish who all the members were. But such reasoning has no application to a case where there is a condition or description attached to one or more individual gifts; in such cases, uncertainty as to some other persons who may have been intended to take does not in any way affect the quantum of the gift to persons who undoubtedly possess the qualification. Hence, in my judgment, the different test laid down in *Re Allen*. The recent decision of the Court of Appeal in *Re Tuck's ST* [1978] Ch 49 establishes that the test in *Re Allen* is still the appropriate test in considering such gifts, notwithstanding the *Gulbenkian* and *McPhail* v *Doulton* decisions: see per Lord Russell of Killowen.

Accordingly, in my judgment, the proper result in this case depends on whether the disposition in cl. 5(a) is properly to be regarded as a series of individual gifts to persons answering the description 'friend' (in which case it will be valid), or a gift which requires the whole class of friends to be established (in which case it will probably fail).

NOTE: To emphasise the rather subtle difference between a series of individual gifts to friends and a discretionary trust for friends, imagine that you have been left a small cellar of wine by a will. The cellar comprises ten cases of red wine and ten cases of white. You are required to give a case of red wine to any of the settlor's friends who might come forward, and to make a fair distribution of the white wine amongst the testator's friends as you think fit. The first claimant to present himself is Fred. He attended the same school as the testator and had kept in touch ever since. He always sent birthday cards and presents to the testator, a gesture that the testator had always reciprocated. You will give Fred a case of red wine because he is certainly eligible for one. However, you cannot know how many eligible friends might come forward, so you cannot know for certain how much white wine it is safe to give to Fred. Perhaps he should receive a case, perhaps only a bottle. Accordingly, the gifts of red wine will be valid, but the discretionary trust of white wine will fail due to uncertainty of object.

R v *District Auditor, ex parte West Yorkshire Metropolitan County Council*
[1986] RVR 24, Divisional Court of the Queen's Bench Division

Facts: Prior to the abolition of the Metropolitan County Councils, they were prohibited (after 1 April 1985) from incurring expenditure under the Local Government Act 1972, s.137(1): 'which in their opinion is in the interests of their area or any part of it or some or all of its inhabitants'. When West Yorkshire Metropolitan County Council realised that they were going to have a large surplus on 1 April 1985, they sought to find ways of ensuring that this money could still be spent after the 1 April deadline. In their attempt to achieve this aim, they purported to set up a discretionary trust of £400,000, having a duration of 11 months, 'for the benefit of any or all or some of the inhabitants of the County of West Yorkshire'. The trust also directed the trustees to use the fund specifically:

(a) To assist economic development in the county in order to relieve unemployment and poverty.
(b) To assist bodies concerned with youth and community problems.
(c) To assist and encourage ethnic and other minority groups.
(d) To inform all interested persons of the consequences of the proposed abolition of the Council (and the other Metropolitan County Councils) and of other programs affecting local government in the county.

Held: This was held to be administratively unworkable. The inhabitants of the County of West Yorkshire numbered about two and a half million. The range of objects was held to be so hopelessly wide as to be incapable of forming anything like a class.

There are clear statements in the case that trusts may be treated differently from powers in this regard, since a court may be called upon ultimately to execute a trust, whereas it will not of course be required to execute a power.

LLOYD LJ: ...For the creation of an express private trust three things are required. First, there must be a clear intention to create the trust. Secondly there must be certainty as to the subject matter of the trust; and thirdly there must be certainty as to the persons intended to benefit. Two of the three certainties, as they are familiarly called, were present here. Was the third? Mr Henderson argued that the beneficiaries of the trust were all or some of the inhabitants of the county of West Yorkshire. The class might be on the large side, containing as it does some $2^1/2$ million potential beneficiaries. But the definition, it was said, is straightforward and clear cut. There is no uncertainty as to the concept. If anyone were to come forward and claim to be a beneficiary, it could be said of him at once whether he was within the class or not.

I cannot accept Mr Henderson's argument. I am prepared to assume in favour of the council, without deciding, that the class is defined with sufficient clarity. I do not decide the point because it might, as it seems to me, be open to argument what is meant by 'an inhabitant' of the county of West Yorkshire. But I put that difficulty on one side. For there is to my mind a more fundamental difficulty. A trust with as many as $2^1/2$ million potential beneficiaries is, in my judgment, quite simply unworkable. The class is far too large. In *Re Gulbenkian's Settlements* [1970] AC 508, [1968] 3 All ER 785 Lord Reid said at page 518: 'It may be that there is a class of case where, although the description of a class of beneficiaries is clear enough, any attempt to apply it to the facts would lead to such administrative difficulties that it would for that reason be held to be invalid.'

In the following year in *Re Baden's Deed Trusts* [1971] AC 424, Lord Wilberforce said ... [Lloyd LJ quoted the passage on administrative unworkability, and the 'all the residents of Greater London' example]. It seems to me that the present trust comes within the ... case to which Lord Wilberforce refers. I hope I am not guilty of being prejudiced by the example which he gave. But it could hardly be more apt, or fit the facts of the present case more precisely.

I mention the subsequent decisions in *Re Baden (No. 2)* [1972] Ch 607, and on appeal [1973] Ch 9 and *Re Manisty's Settlement* [1974] Ch 17, with misgiving, since they were not cited in argument. The latter was a case of an intermediate power, that is to say, a power exercisable by trustees in favour of all the world, other than members of an excepted class. After referring to *Gulbenkian* and the two *Baden* cases, Templeman J (as he then was) said: 'I conclude ... that a power cannot be uncertain merely because it is wide in ambit'. A power to benefit, for example, the residents of Greater London might, he thought, be bad, not on the ground of its width but on the ground of capriciousness, since the settlor could have no sensible intention to benefit 'an accidental conglomeration of persons' who had 'no discernible link with the settlor'. But that objection could not apply here. The council had every reason for wishing to benefit the inhabitants of West Yorkshire. Lord Wilberforce's *dictum* has also been the subject of a good deal of academic comment and criticism, noticeably by L. McKay (1974) 38 *Conv* 269 and C. T. Emery (1982) 98 *LQR* 551. I should have welcomed further argument on these matters, but through no fault of Mr Henderson this was not possible. So I have to do the best I can.

My conclusion is that the *dictum* of Lord Wilberforce remains of high persuasive authority, despite *Re Manisty*. *Manisty's* case was concerned with a power, where the function of the court is more restricted. In the case of a trust, the court may have to execute the trust. Not so in the case of a power. That there may still be a distinction between trusts and powers in this connection was recognised by Templeman J himself in the sentence immediately following his quotation of Lord Wilberforce's *dictum*, when he said:

> In these guarded terms Lord Wilberforce appears to refer to trusts which may have to be executed and administered by the court and not to powers where the court has a very much more limited function.

There can be no doubt that the declaration of trust in the present case created a trust and not a power. Following Lord Wilberforce's dictum, I would hold that the definition of the beneficiaries of the trust is 'so hopelessly wide' as to be incapable of forming 'anything like a class'. I would therefore reject Mr Henderson's argument that the declaration of trust can take effect as an express private trust.

NOTE: A clear distinction is drawn here between trusts and powers. While it may well be that the width of the class will never cause a power to fail, it might do in the case of a discretionary trust.

■ **QUESTIONS**

1. Does Jenkins LJ's reasoning in *Broadway Cottages* still apply to fixed trusts? See Matthews (1984) 48 *Conv* 22 and Martin and Hayton (1984) 48 *Conv* 304.

2. Is the class ascertainability test an evidential or conceptual test? If it is a conceptual test, how (if at all) does it differ from the individual ascertainability test? If it is a conceptual test, were the concessions made by the charities in *Broadway Cottages* correct? Note that where there are evidential difficulties, the judge may make a *Benjamin* order ([1902] 1 Ch 723) (see, e.g. *Re Green's WT* [1985] 3 All ER 455).

3. Michael settles a fund upon trustees to be distributed equally in favour of his three sons, Paul, Quentin, and Richard. The existence and whereabouts of all three is known at the date of the settlement. Later, Richard goes on an Antarctic expedition, and much later is thought (but not known definitely) to have perished. The trustees wish to distribute. Discuss.Would your answer be different if by the time of the settlement, Richard had already embarked upon the expedition, and it was not known whether he was alive or dead?

4. Is the recognition of a certain intention to create a trust a principled response to the settlor's original intentions as expressed in the relevant document or a practical response to the facts as they have transpired by the date on which the court is asked to construe the document?

5. Is a different approach taken when there is no document and intention must be construed from conduct and other informal facts?

SECTION 5: PRIVATE PURPOSE TRUSTS

Trusts for purposes beneficial to the public are known as 'charitable' trusts; they are considered in Chapter 7. Here we are concerned with trusts established for private purposes. Such trusts are generally void for lack of a beneficiary. Purpose trusts may either be for a pure purpose (for example, a trust to advance a cause), where no individual directly benefits, or for the benefit of an ascertainable group of people (for example, a trust to build a school swimming pool). A private (non-charitable) purpose trust of the first type is usually struck down, because it is not enforceable by anyone. As learned judges have said, 'a gift on trust must have *cestui que trust*' (*Re Wood* [1949] Ch 498, *per* Harman J at 501) and '[t]here must be somebody, in whose favour the Court can decree performance' (*Morice* v *The Bishop of Durham* (1804) 9 Ves 399, *per* Sir William Grant MR at 405, Court of Appeal). This is the so-called 'beneficiary principle'.

Leahy v *Attorney-General for New South Wales*
[1959] AC 457, Privy Council

Facts: The issue arose as to the validity of a trust of property for 'such order of nuns of the Catholic Church or the Christian brothers as my executors and trustees shall select'.

Held: The trust was not charitable, and Viscount Simonds in the Privy Council thought that it would have failed as a private trust on the ground that, even though the individual members had an interest in enforcing the trust, they were not granted a full beneficial interest. The gift was saved by the Conveyancing Act 1919–54, s.37D (New South Wales), but only so far as orders other than contemplative orders of nuns were concerned (the trustees had wished to preserve their right to select such orders).

VISCOUNT SIMONDS: ... What is meant when it is said [as it had been in the High Court] that a gift is made to the individuals comprising the community and the words are added 'it is given to them for the benefit of the community'? If it is a gift to individuals, each of them is entitled to his distributive share (unless he has previously bound himself by the rules of the society that it shall be devoted to some other purpose). It is difficult to see what is added by the words 'for the benefit of the community.' If they are intended to import a trust, who are the beneficiaries? If the present members are the beneficiaries, the words add nothing and are meaningless. If some other persons or purposes are intended, the conclusion cannot be avoided that the gift is void. For it is uncertain, and beyond doubt tends to a perpetuity.

The question then appears to be whether, even if the gift to a selected Order of Nuns is prima facie a gift to the individual members of that Order, there are other considerations arising out of the terms of the will, or the nature of the society, its organisation and rules, or the subject-matter of the gift which should lead the court to conclude that, though prima facie the gift is an absolute one (absolute both in quality of estate and in freedom from restriction) to individual nuns, yet it is invalid because it is in the nature of an endowment and tends to a perpetuity or for any other reason. This raises a problem which is not easy to solve, as the divergent opinions in the High Court indicate.

The prima facie validity of such a gift (by which term their Lordships intend a bequest or demise) is a convenient starting point for the examination of the relevant law. For as Lord Tomlin (sitting at first instance in the Chancery Division) said in *In re Ogden* [1933] Ch 678, 49 TLR 341, a gift to a voluntary association of persons for the general purposes of the association is an absolute gift and prima facie a good gift. He was echoing the words of Lord Parker in *Bowman's* case [1917] AC 406, 442 that a gift to an unincorporated association for the attainment of its purposes 'may ... be upheld as an absolute gift to its members.' These words must receive careful consideration, for it is to be noted that it is because the gift can be upheld as a gift to the individual members that it is valid, even though it is given for the general purposes of the association. If the words 'for the general purposes of the association' were held to import a trust, the question would have to be asked, what is the trust and who are the beneficiaries? A gift can be made to persons (including a corporation) but it cannot be made to a purpose or to an object: so also, a trust may be created for the benefit of persons as *cestuis que trust* but not for a purpose or object unless the purpose or object be charitable. For a purpose or object cannot sue, but, if it be charitable, the Attorney-General can sue to enforce it ... It is therefore by disregarding the words 'for the general purposes of the association' (which are assumed not to be charitable purposes) and treating the gift as an absolute gift to individuals that it can be sustained ...

NOTES

1. This passage is authority for the proposition that a gift to a non-charitable unincorporated association can take effect only as a gift to the present members. If it is given for the purposes of the association it is invalid, although the members of the association have a clear interest in enforcing it.

2. It seems generally that for a trust to be valid, not only must it benefit individuals (who must be ascertainable within the certainty of object tests), but those individuals must also be the beneficiaries under the trust.

Re Denley's Trust Deed

[1969] 1 Ch 373, Chancery Division

Decision: A gift of land for use as a sports ground 'primarily for the benefit of the employees of the company and secondarily for the benefit of such other persons as the trustees may allow to use the same' was valid, despite being a private purpose trust, because the class of individuals to benefit was ascertainable.

GOFF J: I think there may be a purpose or object trust, the carrying out of which would benefit an individual or individuals, where that benefit is so indirect or intangible or which is otherwise so framed as not to give those persons any *locus standi* to apply to the court to enforce the trust, in which case the beneficiary principle would, as it seems to me, apply to invalidate the trust, quite apart from any question of uncertainty or perpetuity. Such cases can be considered if and when they arise. The present is not, in my judgment, of that character, and it will be seen that ... the trust deed expressly states that, subject to any rules and regulations made by the trustees, the employees of the company shall be entitled to the use and enjoyment of the land. Apart from this possible exception, in my judgment the beneficiary principle of *Re Astor's ST* [1952] Ch 534, which was approved in *Re Endacott (dec'd)* [1960] Ch 232, CA—see particularly by Harman LJ—is confined to purpose or object trusts which are abstract or impersonal. The objection is not that the trust is for a purpose or object *per se*, but that there is no beneficiary or *cestui que trust* ...

Where, then, the trust, though expressed as a purpose, is directly or indirectly for the benefit of an individual or individuals, it seems to me that it is in general outside the mischief of the beneficiary principle.

NOTES

1. The rationale of Goff J's judgment is not entirely clear. One view is that the test is not whether a full beneficial interest is granted, but whether individuals who are ascertainable have *locus standi* to sue. They will have so long as the benefit is not too indirect or intangible. Another view of *Denley*, however, is that Goff J construed it as a trust for individuals and not as a purpose trust at all. If this view is correct then the case breaks no new ground, and all private purpose trusts remain void, apart from the anomalous exceptions discussed in the *Astor* extracts above. This view was taken, for example, by Vinelott J in *Re Grant's WT* [1980] 1 WLR 360 (at 370):

    That case [*Denley*] on a proper analysis, in my judgment, falls outside the categories of gifts to unincorporated incorporations and purpose trusts. I can see no distinction in principle between a trust to permit a class defined by reference to employment to use and enjoy land in accordance with rules to be made at the discretion of trustees on the one hand, and, on the other hand, a trust to distribute income at the discretion of the settlor. In both cases the benefit to be taken by any member of the class is at the discretion of the trustees, but any member of the class can apply to the court to compel the trustees to administer the trust in accordance with its terms.

A similar view can be found in (1985) 101 *LQR* 269, pp. 280–2 (P. J. Millett QC).

2. Whatever the case decides, pure purpose trusts, such as *Re Astor's ST* [1952] Ch 534, are unaffected by it.

3. The duration of the trust in *Denley* was expressly limited (with a gift over to a hospital), so as to ensure that there were no perpetuity difficulties. Compare *Re Hobourn Aero Components Ltd's Air Raid Distress Fund* [1946] Ch 86, in Chapter 7.

4. In *Re St Andrew's (Cheam) Lawn Tennis Club Trust (sub nom Philippe v Cameron)* [2012] EWHC 1040 (Ch); [2012] 3 All ER 746 a trust establishing a church tennis club failed because, in the words of the judge, it represented 'an attempt to achieve the legally impossible: a perpetual trust for a non-charitable purpose' (Arnold J at para. [45]).

■ QUESTIONS

1. If the trustees decided to use the fund to install a kidney machine for the benefit of the hospital patients, rather than to maintain a sports ground for the employees, how could the trust be enforced?

2. Could the employees of the company invoke *Saunders* v *Vautier* (1841) 10 LJ Ch 354 to terminate the trust, dividing up the income amongst themselves? (See, further, Chapter 9.)

NOTE: Although the beneficiary principle has a respectable pedigree, it is only relatively recently that it has become regarded as universally applicable. The following exceptions to the principle are now considered to be anomalous and no further exceptions will be recognised: trusts to erect or maintain tombs and monuments (*Pirbright* v *Salwey* [1896] WN 86); trusts for the maintenance of specific animals (*Re Dean* (1889) 41 ChD 522); trusts for saying private masses; and, in *Re Thompson* [1934] Ch 342, a trust for the promotion and furtherance of fox hunting. (Incidentally, the ban on hunting wild mammals with dogs, which was introduced by the Hunting Act 2004, does not render the 'fox hunting' category obsolete, since hunting is exempt from the statutory prohibition in certain circumstances; one of which is stalking and flushing out vermin to be shot: the Hunting Act 2004, Sch. 1 para. 1(1).)

Re Astor's ST, Astor v *Scholfield*

[1952] Ch 534, [1952] 1 All ER 1067, Chancery Division

Facts: Trustees were instructed to hold a fund upon various trusts including 'the maintenance of good relations between nations [and] ... the preservation of the independence of newspapers'. The purposes were not charitable, but the settlement was drafted expressly (by limiting its duration) so as to be valid under the perpetuity rules.

Held: The trust was held by Roxburgh J to be void, because there were no human beneficiaries capable of enforcing it.

ROXBURGH J (after observing that it was common ground that none of the purposes offended the rule against perpetuities, and that none was charitable): The question upon which I am giving this reserved judgment is whether the non-charitable trusts of income during 'the specified period' declared by clause 5 and the third schedule of the settlement of 1945 are void. [Counsel] have submitted that they are void on two grounds: (1) that they are not trusts for the benefit of individuals; (2) that they are void for uncertainty.

Lord Parker considered the first of these two questions in his speech in *Bowman* v *Secular Society Ltd* [1917] AC 406 and I will cite two important passages. The first is [at 437]:

The question whether a trust be legal or illegal or be in accordance with or contrary to the policy of the law, only arises when it has been determined that a trust has been created, and is then only part of the larger question whether the trust is enforceable. For, as will presently appear, trusts may be unenforceable and therefore void, not only because they are illegal or contrary to the policy of the law, but for other reasons.

The second is [at 441]:

> A trust to be valid must be for the benefit of individuals, which this is certainly not, or must be in that class of gifts for the benefit of the public which the courts in this country recognize as charitable in the legal as opposed to the popular sense of that term.

Commenting on those passages [counsel for the trustees] observed that *Bowman* v *Secular Society Ltd* arose out of a will and he asked me to hold that Lord Parker intended them to be confined to cases arising under a will. But they were, I think, intended to be quite general in character. Further, [counsel] pointed out that Lord Parker made no mention of the exceptions or apparent exceptions which undoubtedly exist, and from this he asked me to infer that no such general principle can be laid down, the question is whether those cases are to be regarded as exceptional and anomalous or whether they are destructive of the supposed principle. I must later analyse them. But I will first consider whether Lord Parker's propositions can be attacked from a base of principle.

The typical case of a trust is one in which the legal owner of property is constrained by a court of equity so to deal with it as to give effect to the equitable rights of another. These equitable rights have been hammered out in the process of litigation in which a claimant on equitable grounds has successfully asserted rights against a legal owner or other person in control of property.

Prima facie, therefore, a trustee would not be expected to be subject to an equitable obligation unless there was somebody who could enforce a correlative equitable right, and the nature and extent of that obligation would be worked out in proceedings for enforcement. This is what I understand by Lord Parker's first proposition. At an early stage, however, the courts were confronted with attempts to create trusts for charitable purposes which there was no equitable owner to enforce. Lord Eldon explained in *Attorney-General* v *Brown* (1818) 1 Swans 265, 290 how this difficulty was dealt with:

> It is the duty of a court of equity, a main part, originally almost the whole, of its jurisdiction, to administer trusts; to protect not the visible owner, who alone can proceed at law, but the individual equitably, though not legally, entitled. From this principle has arisen the practice of administering the trust of a public charity: persons possessed of funds appropriated to such purposes are within the general rule; but no one being entitled by an immediate and peculiar interest to prefer a complaint, who is to compel the performance of their obligations, and to enforce their responsibility? It is the duty of the King, as *parens patriae*, to protect property devoted to charitable uses; and that duty is executed by the officer who represents the Crown for all forensic purposes. On this foundation rests the right of the Attorney-General in such cases to obtain by information the interposition of a court of equity ...

But if the purposes are not charitable, great difficulties arise both in theory and in practice. In theory, because having regard to the historical origins of equity it is difficult to visualize the growth of equitable obligations which nobody can enforce, and in practice, because it is not possible to contemplate with equanimity the creation of large funds devoted to non-charitable purposes which no court and no department of state can control, or in the case of maladministration reform. Therefore, Lord Parker's second proposition would prima facie appear to be well founded. Moreover, it gains no little support from the practical considerations that no officer has ever been constituted to take, in the case of non-charitable purposes, the position held by the Attorney-General in connection with charitable purposes, and no case has been found in the reports in which the court has ever directly enforced a non-charitable purpose against a trustee. Indeed where, as in the present case, the only beneficiaries are purposes and at present unascertainable person, it is difficult to see who could initiate such proceedings. If the purposes are valid trusts, the settlors have retained no beneficial interest and could not initiate them. It was suggested that the trustees might proceed ex parte to enforce the trusts against themselves. I doubt that, but at any rate nobody could enforce the trusts against them. This point, in my judgment, is of importance, because in most of the cases which are put forward to disprove Lord Parker's propositions the court had indirect means of enforcing the execution of the non-charitable purposes.

These cases I must now consider ...

[Roxburgh J considered a number of cases, including *Re Thompson* [1934] Ch 342, which could be justified, in his view, on the ground that there was a residuary legatee capable of enforcing the trusts. He continued:]

Let me then sum up the position so far. On the one side there are Lord Parker's two propositions with which I began. These were not new, but merely re-echoed what Sir William Grant had said as

Master of the Rolls in *Morice* v *The Bishop of Durham* as long ago as 1804 (9 Ves 399, at 405): 'There must be somebody, in whose favour the court can decree performance.' The position was recently restated by Harman J in *In re Wood* [[1949] Ch 498, 501]: 'A gift on trust must have a *cestui que trust*,' and this seems to be in accord with principle. On the other side is a group of cases relating to horses and dogs, graves and monuments—matters arising under wills and intimately connected with the deceased—in which the courts have found means of escape from these general propositions ... [These] may, I think, properly be regarded as anomalous and exceptional and in no way destructive of the proposition which traces descent from or through Sir William Grant through Lord Parker to Harman J. Perhaps the late Sir Arthur Underhill was right in suggesting that they may be concessions to human weakness or sentiment (see Underhill's *Law of Trusts and Trustees*, 8th ed., p. 79 [10th ed., p. 97]). They cannot, in my judgment, of themselves (and no other justification has been suggested to me) justify the conclusion that a Court of Equity will recognize as an equitable obligation affecting the income of large funds in the hands of trustees a direction to apply it in furtherance of enumerated non-charitable purposes in a manner which no court or department can control or enforce. I hold that the trusts here in question are void on the first of the grounds submitted by [counsel for the Attorney-General].

[Roxburgh J went on to hold that the trusts were also void for uncertainty.]

NOTES
1. This case extends and makes general the old principle that a trust will be void unless there are human beneficiaries capable of enforcing it.
2. Roxburgh J recognises that charitable trusts are an exception to this principle, since the Attorney-General can enforce them.
3. Various cases where private purpose trusts appear to have been upheld were explained by Roxburgh J as cases where there is a human beneficiary (entitled to the residue) who can enforce the trust. This is not altogether satisfactory, since the residuary beneficiary will not necessarily have any interest in enforcing it, but they were regarded as anomalous exceptions in *Re Astor's ST*, and similarly in *Re Endacott* [1960] Ch 232, where a gift 'to North Tawton Devon Parish Council for the purpose of providing some useful memorial to myself' was held void by the Court of Appeal. *Dean* and *Thompson* were again regarded as anomalous and not to be extended. It is a pity, however, that the Court of Appeal did not take the opportunity to overrule them, as it is very difficult to know exactly what they stand for, or on what principle they operate or the basis on which they are enforced.
4. All private trusts are subject to the rule against perpetuities (see Chapter 6), and if trusts such as those in *Re Dean* (1889) 41 ChD 522 and *Re Thompson* [1934] Ch 342 remain valid today, there are no beneficial interests capable of vesting. At common law, therefore, these were subject to the rule against inalienability, which rendered void any such trusts which were capable of lasting beyond 21 years.

Re Shaw, Public Trustee v Day

[1957] 1 WLR 729, [1957] 1 All ER 745, Chancery Division

Facts: The case arose from the will of George Bernard Shaw, which purported to set up a trust to research into the advantages of a new 40-letter alphabet. The issue was whether the trust was valid as a charitable or private purpose trust. Two of the residuary legatees claimed that the alphabet trusts were void, and that they were therefore entitled to come into their inheritance at once.

The purposes included the following:

(1) To institute and finance a series of inquiries to ascertain as far as possible the following statistics:
   (a) the number of extant persons who speak the English language and write it by the established and official alphabet of 26 letters (hereinafter called Dr Johnson's alphabet);
   (b) how much time could be saved per individual scribe by the substitution for the said alphabet of an alphabet containing at least 40 letters (hereinafter called the proposed British alphabet) ... ;

(c) how many of these persons are engaged in writing or printing English at any and every moment in the world;

(d) on these factors to estimate the time and labour wasted by our lack of at least 14 unequivocal single symbols;

(e) to add where possible … estimates of the loss of income in British and American currency …

(2) To employ a phonetic expert to transliterate my play entitled 'Androcles and the Lion' into the proposed British alphabet assuming the pronunciation to resemble that recorded of His Majesty our late King George V, and sometimes described as Northern English …

Held: The trust was not valid as a charity (see Chapter 7). Not being charitable, the trust failed, since there were no ascertainable beneficiaries. This conclusion was unaffected by the fact that, unlike *Astor*, the remaindermen were identifiable from the date of the will.

HARMAN J: Can, then this project be upheld apart from charity? I feel bound to say at once that, as the authorities stand, I do not think I am at liberty to hold that it can …

Lord Parker of Waddington in *Bowman* v *Secular Society Ltd* categorically states ([1917]) AC at p. 441):

A trust to be valid must be for the benefit of individuals … or must be in that class of gifts for the benefit of the public which the courts in this country recognise as charitable …

In other words, one cannot have a trust, other than a charitable trust, for the benefit, not of individuals, but of objects. The reason has been often stated, that the court cannot control the trust. The principle has been recently restated by Roxburgh J in *Re Astor's Settlement Trusts, Astor* v *Scholfield* ([1952] 1 All ER 1067), where the authorities are copiously reviewed. An object cannot complain to the court, which, therefore, cannot control the trust, and, therefore, will not allow it to continue. I must confess that I feel some reluctance to come to this conclusion. I agree at once that, if the persons to take in remainder are unascertainable, the court is deprived of any means of controlling such a trust, but if, as here, the persons taking the ultimate residue are ascertained, I do not feel the force of this objection. They are entitled to the estate except in so far it has been devoted to the indicated purposes, and in so far it is not devoted to those purposes, the money being spent is the money of the residuary legatees, or the ultimate remaindermen, and they can come to the court and sue the executor for a *devastavit*, or the trustee for a breach of trust, and thus, though not themselves interested in the purposes, enable the court indirectly to control them. This line of reasoning is not, I think, open to me …

I should have wished to regard this bequest as a gift to the ultimate residuary legatees subject to a condition by which they cannot complain of income during the first twenty-one years after the testator's death being devoted to the alphabet project. This apparently might be the way in which the matter would be viewed in the United States, for I find in Morris & Leach on the *Rule Against Perpetuities* (1956), at p. 308, the following passage quoted from the American Law Institute's *Restatement of Trusts*:

Where the owner of property transfers it upon an intended trust for a specific non-charitable purpose, and there is no definite or definitely ascertainable beneficiary designated, no trust is created; but the transferee has power to apply the property to the designated purpose, unless he is authorised so to apply the property beyond the period of the rule against perpetuities, or the purpose is capricious.

As the authors point out, this is to treat a trust of this sort as a power, for clearly there is no one who can directly enforce the trust, and if the trustees choose to pay the whole moneys to the remaindermen, no one can complain. All that can be done is to control the trustees indirectly in the exercise of their power. In my judgment, I am not at liberty to validate this trust by treating it as a power …

The result is that the alphabet trusts are, in my judgment, invalid, and must fail. It seems that their begetter suspected as much, hence his jibe about failure by judicial decision. I answer that it is not the fault of the law, but of the testator, who failed almost for the first time in his life to grasp the problem or to make up his mind what he wanted.

NOTES

1. The remaindermen argument accepted in *Astor* was rejected in *Shaw*.
2. It is possible to make provision for a pure purpose indirectly, using a device, for example where a gift is made to charity A so long as it maintains the testator's grave to the satisfaction of the testator's trustees with a gift over to charity B. Obviously, the testator wishes his grave to be

maintained for a long time, but the gift over is exempt from perpetuity rules, so long as B is a charity. If B is not a charity, the gift over will fail for perpetuity unless the gift is appropriately limited in duration: *Re Wightwick* [1950] 1 Ch 260.

Re Tyler

[1891] 3 Ch 252, Court of Appeal

Facts: A testator gave a fund to the trustees of a certain charity and as a condition of the gift he directed them to keep his family vault at Highgate Cemetery 'in good repair, and name legible, and to rebuild when it shall require'. If the trustees failed to comply with his request, the moneys were directed to pass to another charity.

Held: The condition for the maintenance and repair of the vault was valid and binding on the first charity. Further, the gift over to the second charity on failure to comply with the condition was good. The rule against perpetuities has no application to a transfer, on a certain event, of property from one charity to another.

LINDLEY LJ: ... Mr Justice Stirling has decided that the condition on which the gift over is to take effect is valid, and the appeal to us is against so much of his order as declares that the condition of repairing and rebuilding the family vault is a valid condition and binding on the defendants, the London Missionary Society; the defendants asking that that may be reversed.

There is no doubt whatever that this condition, in one sense, tends to a perpetuity. The tomb or value is to be kept in repair, and in repair for ever. There is also no doubt, and I think it is settled, that a gift of that kind cannot be supported as a charitable gift. But, then, this case is said to fall within an exception to the general rule relating to perpetuities. It is common knowledge that the rule as to perpetuities does not apply to property given to charities; and there are reasons why it should not. It is an exception to the general rule; and we are guided in the application of that doctrine by the case which has been referred to of *Christ's Hospital* v *Grainger* 1 Mac & G 460. It is sufficient for me to refer to the head-note for the facts. The bequest there was 'to the corporation of Reading, on certain trusts for the benefit of the poor of the town of Reading, with a proviso that, if the corporation of Reading should, for one whole year, neglect to observe the directions of the will, the gift should be utterly void, and the property be transferred to the corporation of London, in trust for a hospital in the town of London.' It was argued that that gift over was invalid, and Lord Cottingham disposes of the argument in this way:

> It was then argued that it was void, as contrary to the rules against perpetuities. These rules are to prevent, in the cases to which they apply; property from being inalienable beyond certain periods. Is this effect produced, and are these rules invaded by the transfer, in a certain event, of property from one charity to another? If the corporation of Reading might hold the property for certain charities in Reading, why may not the corporation of London hold it for the charity of Christ's Hospital in London? The property is neither more nor less alienable on that account.

Guided by that decision, and acting on that principle, Mr Justice Stirling held that this condition was a valid condition; and it appears to me that he was right. What is this gift when you come to look at it? It is a gift of £42,000 Russian 5 per Cent. Stock to the London Missionary Society. What for? It is for their charitable purposes. It is a gift to them for the purposes for which they exist. Then there is a gift over to another charity in a given event—that is to say, the non-repair of the testator's vault. It seems to me to fall precisely within the principle on which *Christ's Hospital* v *Grainger* was decided.

A gift to a charity for charitable purposes with a gift over on an event which may be beyond the ordinary limit of perpetuities to another charity—I cannot see that there is anything illegal in this. Mr Buckley has put it in the strongest way he can. He says that, if you give effect to this condition, you will be enabling people to evade the law relating to perpetuities. I take it this decision will not go the length—certainly I do not intend it should, so far as I am concerned—that you can get out of the law against perpetuities by making a charity a trustee. That would be absurd; but that is not this case. This property is given to the London Missionary Society for their charitable purposes. Then, there is a condition that, if the tomb is not kept in order, the fund shall go over to another charity. That appears to me, both on principle and authority, to be valid; and I do not think it is a sufficient answer to say that such a conclusion is an inducement to do that which contravenes the law against perpetuities. There is nothing illegal in keeping up a tomb; on the contrary, it is a very laudable thing to do. It is a rule of law that you shall not tie up property in such a way as to infringe what we know as the law against perpetuities; but there is nothing illegal in what the testator has done here. The appeal must be dismissed with costs.

FRY LJ: I am of the same opinion ... Keeping the tomb in repair is not an illegal object. If it were, the condition tending to bring about an illegal act would itself be illegal; but to repair the tomb is a perfectly lawful thing. All that can be said is that it is not lawful to tie up property for that purpose. But the rule of law against perpetuities applies to property, not motives; and I know of no rule which says that you may not try to enforce a condition creating a perpetual inducement to do a thing which is lawful. That is this case.

■ QUESTIONS

1. Are there any genuine exceptions to the rule that a private trust, to be valid, must have an identifiable human beneficiary?

2. Apart from capricious purposes, which are inherently invalid, is it possible to conceive of any trust for a purpose which cannot sensibly be construed as being of benefit to a person?

SECTION 6: DONATIONS TO NON-CHARITABLE UNINCORPORATED ASSOCIATIONS

In this section, we are concerned with gifts to unincorporated non-profit non-charitable associations, or, to put it in everyday language, gifts to 'clubs and societies'. Whereas a gift to an incorporated company is straightforward, a gift to an unincorporated association is problematic because the association has no separate legal personality. An unincorporated association is merely an association of individuals. A donation to an unincorporated association will normally be construed to be an absolute gift to the individual members for the time being, subject to their contractual obligation (as set out in the rules or 'constitution' of the association) to hold the donation for the purposes of the association, but sometimes the only natural and sensible course is to construe the donation as a trust; this is most obviously the case where the donation is expressly made 'on trust' or 'to trustees'. In Sections A–D, we will consider various ways of construing gifts to unincorporated associations. The list of possible constructions is now fairly comprehensive but the courts have never suggested that the list is closed.

Eastbourne Town Radio Cars Association v *Customs and Excise Commissioners*
[2001] UKHL 19, [2001] 1 WLR 794, House of Lords

'My Lords, an unincorporated association is, as I have said, not a legal entity. It is a number of legal persons having mutual rights and duties in accordance with rules which constitute the contract under which they have agreed to be associated. The property of the association is owned by or on trust for the individual members and subject to the rules. The liability of the individual members for the debts incurred for the purposes of the association is governed by the ordinary law of contract and agency. The rights of the members, as against each other, to avail themselves of the common property and facilities are governed by their contract.' ([2001] UKHL 19 at para. [32], [2001] 1 WLR 794, 803, *per* Lord Hoffmann.)

A: Trust for present and future members

At first sight, it might be thought that a *Denley*-style purpose trust (see Section 5) might be a good method of allowing property to be conveyed to a non-charitable unincorporated association; the property would be held in trust for the members of the association, for the purposes of the association, and it would be necessary only that the identity of those members was sufficiently certain. It would certainly have advantages for donors, since the property could be constrained to be used for the association's purposes, and members would not be able (for example) to dispose of it for their own benefit. If the purposes of the association were fulfilled (e.g. vivisection being abolished where the association in question was the National Anti-Vivisection Association), or became impossible (e.g. where a gun club was prohibited by legislation from carrying out its previously lawful activities), the donor would obtain any property not already used on resulting trust (see Chapter 5).

However, as we have seen in *Leahy* (see Section 5), there are difficulties in giving property for the purposes of a non-charitable unincorporated association, even though there are humans with an interest in applying the property as the donor intended. If these persons are not beneficiaries, the disposition will fail on the beneficiary principle. If the members of the association for the time being are beneficiaries then, unless membership of the association is fixed, it must be contemplated that beneficial interests will move at an unspecified future time, when old members resign or new members join, and there will be perpetuity problems unless the gift is limited to take effect within the perpetuity period, or unless (since 1964) the wait-and-see principle of the Perpetuities and Accumulations Act 1964 is applicable (see, further, Chapter 6). An express limitation (which can, since 1964, be a specified period of up to 80 years) is very rare.

B: Trust for present members only

In her article, 'Holding of Property by Unincorporated Associations' (1985) 49 *Conv* 318, Jean Warburton argues (p. 321) that:

> A trust for members for the time being would appear to be acceptable from both a conveyancing and the members' point of view as a method of holding property for an unincorporated association.
>
> First the rule, as to certainty of beneficiaries is satisfied because at any one time the beneficiaries can be ascertained by looking at the members of the association. Secondly, provided the members are free to dispose of the property, both income *and* capital, the rules against perpetuities are satisfied. There has been some debate as to the application of the rules against perpetuities to unincorporated association but an examination of the cases shows that the courts are concerned with the rule against inalienability rather than the rules against remoteness of vesting.

Warburton cites *Cocks* v *Manners* (1871) LR 12 Eq 575, *Re Clarke* [1901] 2 Ch 110, *Re Drummond* [1914] 2 Ch 90, *Re Prevost* [1930] 2 Ch 383, *Ray's WT* [1936] 1 Ch 520, *Re Taylor* [1940] 1 Ch 481, *Re Price* [1943] 1 Ch 422; *cf. Carne* v *Long* (1860) 2 De GF & J 75, *Re Topham* [1938] 1 All ER 181, and *Re Macaulay's Estate* [1943] 1 Ch 435. She continues (p. 322):

> Accordingly, a trust for members for the time being is a very useful method of holding property for an unincorporated association even though it is not generally included within the methods available. However, care should be taken to ensure that either the members have power to dispose of the whole of the capital and income of the fund or that the trust is restricted to the perpetuity period.

She then footnotes: 'But not both, *cf. Re Grant's Will Trusts* [1979] 3 All ER 359, 366–367.' (Note that *Re Grant's WT* is considered further in Subsection D: Contractual analysis.)

■ **QUESTION**

If at any time the members have power to dispose of the whole of the capital and income of the fund, is that not simply a gift to present members—albeit a gift held on bare trust for them by the officers of the club in whose names the assets of the club are for the time being held?

C: Gift to present members only

One way of avoiding perpetuity problems is to construe the donation as an absolute gift to present members only; but then you need a mechanism to prevent them from severing their share, and also to transfer rights to future members. To attempt to achieve this using a trust mechanism is likely to lead to perpetuity difficulties. However, the existing members' entitlements are normally construed as being subject to their contractual duties as members of the association, under which a member will typically be prevented from severing his share, which will accrue to the other members on his death or resignation. This now seems to be accepted as the usual basis for donations to non-charitable unincorporated associations.

The basic problem in this area is that, partly for the reasons already considered, analyses based on trusts do not work very well, whereas the contractual analysis, which can usually be made to work, seems very unfair: the donor has to give up all interests in the gift, and cannot make it conditional, neither can he prevent the club members using the property for any purpose they please, whether or not for the original purposes of the club.

Note that pension funds and mutual benefit societies do not necessarily attract the same perpetuity problems as ordinary members' clubs; for them, trusts solutions can sometimes be made to work.

D: Contractual analysis

Neville Estates v *Madden*

[1962] Ch 832, Chancery Division

Facts: The claimants, Neville Estates Ltd, sought a declaration that they were entitled to specific performance of a contract for the sale of land owned by the Catford Synagogue. The trustees of the synagogue claimed that the consent of the Charity Commissioners was required.

Held: The claimants' action failed. A gift to the Catford Synagogue, whose objects included maintaining places of worship for persons of the Jewish religion who conform to the German or Polish ritual, could not take effect as a gift to the members beneficially, subject only to their contractual rights and liabilities towards one another as members of the association, but could take effect as a charitable purpose trust. On the charitable aspect, see Chapter 7.

CROSS J: (on the holding of property by non-charitable unincorporated associations): I turn now at last to the legal issues involved. The question of the construction and effect of gifts to or in trust for unincorporated associations was recently considered by the Privy Council in *Leahy* v *Attorney-General for New South Wales* [1959] AC 457. The position, as I understand it, is as follows. Such a gift may take effect in one or other of three quite different ways. In the first place, it may, on its true construction, be a gift to the members of the association at the relevant date as joint tenants, so that any member can sever his share and claim it whether or not he continues to be a member of the association. Secondly, it may be a gift to the existing members not as joint tenants, but subject to their respective contractual rights and liabilities towards one another as members of the association. In such a case a member cannot sever his share. It will accrue to the other members on his death or resignation, even though such members include persons who became members after the gift took effect. If this is the effect of the gift, it will not be open to objection on the score of perpetuity or uncertainty unless there is something in its terms or circumstances or in the rules of the association which precludes the members at any given time from dividing the subject of the gift between them on the footing that they are solely entitled to it in equity.

Thirdly, the terms or circumstances of the gift or the rules of the association may show that the property in question is not to be at the disposal of the members for the time being, but is to be held in trust for or applied for the purposes of the association as a quasi-corporate entity. In this case the gift will fail unless the association is a charitable body. If the gift is of the second class, i.e. one which the members of the association for the time being are entitled to divide among themselves, then, even if the objects of the association are in themselves charitable, the gift would not, I think, be a charitable gift. If, for example, a number of persons formed themselves into an association with a charitable object—say the relief of poverty in some district—but if it was part of the contract between them that, if a majority of the members so desired, the association should be dissolved and its property divided between the members at the date of dissolution, a gift to the association as part of its general funds would not, I conceive, be a charitable gift.

NOTE: A gift to a non-charitable unincorporated association was held valid on the basis of the second of the above methods in *Re Lipinski's WT* [1976] Ch 235, [1976] 3 WLR 522, [1977] 1 All ER 33, where Oliver J upheld a bequest to the Hull Judeans (Maccabi) Association, to be used solely for the construction and improvements of the association's buildings, but only by striking out the condition relating to the buildings, and holding that the present members of the association were absolutely entitled, and could use the property in any way they liked. It is clear, therefore, that the members could do whatever they pleased with the property, and were not bound by the condition (see also the extract from *Re Grant's WT* (this subsection)). The requirement that 'the members at any given time [can divide] the subject of the gift between them on the footing that they are solely entitled to it in equity' can cause difficulties, however: see *Re Recher's WT* [1972] Ch 526 (this subsection).

CUCO v *Burrell*

[1982] 1 WLR 522, Court of Appeal

Decision: The Court of Appeal, applying the reasoning in *Neville Estates*, held that the Conservative and Unionist Central Office (CUCO) was not an unincorporated association (and therefore did not come within a statutory tax provision—the issue was whether corporation tax was payable on money received by Central Office and invested prior to use).

The Court held that for a body to be an unincorporated association for these purposes, its members must be subject to mutually enforceable obligations, whereas there were no enforceable mutual understandings between the members of the CUCO. In other words, the extract above, and the extract set out from *Re Recher's WT* in this section, are also used to *define* unincorporated associations for statutory purposes.

The Court of Appeal held that the local associations were, but the Parliamentary Party and Central Office were not, unincorporated associations, and there was no contractual nexus between the party members as a whole; the connection between the three parts was political not contractual; there was no control by the members over the leader of the party; there was no identifiable time when any contracts came into existence. The Conservative Party as a whole could not therefore be said to be an unincorporated association.

NOTE: The problem is, if it is not an unincorporated association, how can donations to the party through the Central Office be made? The main interest in the case is Brightman LJ's agency analysis (with which Lawton LJ agreed). This is similar to a conditional gift, with the donor being able to restrain Central Office from using the property other than for the purposes of the party, and retaining an interest in the money, *pari passu* with other donors, prior to the application of the property for party purposes. The analysis seems to be a purely personal one as between donor and recipient, however, and it seems unlikely that the agency analysis will be of general application for donations to unincorporated associations. Brightman LJ, for example, made the following observations:

> A complaining contributor might encounter problems under the law of contract after a change of the office holder to whom his mandate was originally given. Perhaps only the original recipient can be sued for the malpractices of his successors.
>
> …
>
> … The only problem which might arise in practice under the mandate theory would be the case of an attempted bequest to the Central Office funds, or to the treasurers thereof, or to the Conservative Party, since no agency could be set up at the moment of death between a testator and his chosen agent.

It seems unlikely, therefore, that an agency analysis will resolve all the problems discussed in this chapter.

Re Recher's WT

[1972] Ch 526, Chancery Division

Facts: The testatrix left some of her residuary estate to a non-charitable unincorporated association which, on the construction of her will, was identified as the London and Provincial Anti-Vivisection Society. By the date of the will, however, that society had ceased to exist, but had amalgamated with the National Anti-Vivisection Society. The question was whether the gift could take effect in favour of the National Anti-Vivisection Society.

Held:

(a) The gift could not be construed as a trust for the purposes of the London and Provincial Anti-Vivisection Society.

(b) It would have been possible to construe the gift, on the basis of Cross J's views in *Neville Estates* v *Madden* [1962] Ch 832 (above), as a gift to the members of the London and Provincial Anti-Vivisection Society, subject to the contract towards each other to which they had bound themselves as members, had the Society been in existence at the date of the testatrix's will. By then it had been dissolved, however, and the contract between the members terminated. The gift could not be construed as a gift to the members of a different association (i.e. the National Anti-Vivisection Society), and accordingly failed.

BRIGHTMAN J: A trust for non-charitable purposes, as distinct from a trust for individuals, is clearly void because there is no beneficiary. It does not, however, follow that persons cannot band themselves together as an association or society, pay subscriptions and validly devote their funds in pursuit of some lawful non-charitable purpose. An obvious example is a members' social club. But it is not essential that the members should only intend to secure direct personal advantage to themselves. The association may be one in which personal advantages to the members are combined with the pursuit of some outside purpose. Or the association may be one which offers no personal benefit at all to the members, the funds of the association being applied exclusively to the pursuit of some outside purpose. Such an association of persons is bound, I would think, to have some sort of constitution; i.e., the rights and the liabilities of the members of the association will inevitably depend on some form of contract *inter se*, usually evidenced by a set of rules. In the present case it appears to me clear that the life members, the ordinary members and the associate members of the London and Provincial Society were bound together by a contract *inter se*.

Any such member was entitled to the rights and subject to the liabilities defined by the rules. If the committee acted contrary to the rules, an individual member would be entitled to take proceedings in the courts to compel observance of the rules or to recover damages for any loss he had suffered as a result of the breach of contract. As and when a member paid his subscription to the association, he would be subjecting his money to the disposition and expenditure thereof laid down by the rules. That is to say, the member would be bound to permit, and entitled to require, the honorary trustees and other members of the society to deal with that subscription in accordance with the lawful directions of the committee. Those directions would include the expenditure of that subscription, as part of the general funds of the association, in furthering the objects of the association. The resultant situation, on analysis, is that the London and Provincial Society represented an organisation of individuals bound together by a contract under which their subscriptions became, as it were, mandated towards a certain type of expenditure as adumbrated in r. 1. Just as the two parties to a bipartite bargain can vary or terminate their contract by mutual assent, so it must follow that the life members, ordinary members and associate members of the London and Provincial Society could, at any moment of time, by unanimous agreement (or by majority vote if the rules so prescribe), vary or terminate their multipartite contract. There would be no limit to the type of variation or termination to which all might agree. There is no private trust or trust for charitable purposes or other trust to hinder the process. It follows that if all members agreed, they could decide to wind up the London and Provincial Society and divide the net assets among themselves beneficially. No one would have any *locus standi* to stop them so doing. The contract is the same as any other contract and concerns only those who are parties to it, that is to say, the members of the society. The funds of such an association may, of course, be derived not only from subscriptions of the contracting parties but also from donations from non-contracting parties and legacies from persons who have died. In the case of a donation which is not accompanied by any words which purport to impose a trust, it seems to me that the gift takes effect in favour of the existing members of the association as an accretion to the funds which are the subject-matter of the contract which such members have made *inter se*, and falls to be dealt with in precisely the same way as the funds which the members themselves have subscribed. So, in the case of a legacy. In the absence of words which purport to impose a trust, the legacy is a gift to the members beneficially, not as joint tenants or as tenants in common so as to entitle each member to an immediate distributive share, but as an accretion to the funds which are the subject-matter of the contract which the members have made *inter se*.

NOTE: This passage was adopted by Vinelott J in *Re Grant's WT* [1980] 1 WLR 360 (and also adopted by Walton J in *Re Bucks Constabulary Fund (No. 2)* [1979] 1 WLR 936 (see below)).

Re Grant's WT

[1980] 1 WLR 360, [1979] 3 All ER 359, Chancery Division

Facts: The case concerned the validity of a testamentary grant of land and personalty to the Chertsey and Walton Constituency Labour Party. The rules of the constituency party provided for, among other things, rule-making powers by the annual party conference and the National Executive Committee of the Labour Party.

Held: The gift failed. The members of the Constituency Labour Party (CLP) did not have sufficient control over its property for a gift to it to take effect under the second *Neville Estates* head.

VINELOTT J: ... The question raised by the summons is whether the gift in the will of the testator's real and personal estate is a valid gift, or is void for uncertainty or for perpetuity or otherwise; and if it is a valid gift who are the persons entitled to benefit thereunder.

Before turning to this question, it will be convenient to explain what are in my judgment the principles which govern the validity of a gift to an unincorporated association. A convenient starting point is a passage in the decision of Cross J in *Neville Estates Ltd* v *Madden* [1962] Ch 832 at 849, which is often cited [Vinelott J quoted the passage set out above and continued:] This statement, though it may require amplification in the light of subsequent authorities, is still as I see it an accurate statement of the law.

In a case in the first category, that is a gift which, on its true construction, is a gift to members of an association who take as joint tenants, any member being able to sever his share, the association is used in effect as a convenient label or definition of the class which is intended to take; but, the class being ascertained, each member takes as joint tenant free from any contractual fetter. So, for instance, a testator might give a legacy or share of residue to a dining or social club of which he had been a member with the intention of giving to each of the other members an interest as joint tenant, capable of being severed, in the subject matter of the gift. Cases within this category are relatively uncommon. A gift to an association will be more frequently found to fall within the second category. There the gift is to members of an association, but the property is given as an accretion to the funds of the association so that the property becomes subject to the contract (normally evidenced by the rules of the association) which governs the rights of the members *inter se*. Each member is thus in a position to ensure that the subject matter of the gift is applied in accordance with the rules of the association, in the same way as any other funds of the association. This category is well illustrated by the decision of Brightman J in *Re Recher's Will Trusts* [1972] Ch 526 ...

[Vinelott J quoted from the case and continued: ...] Two points should be noted. First, as Brightman J pointed out, it is immaterial in considering whether a gift falls within this category that the members of an association have not joined together for a social and recreational purpose, or to secure some personal advantage, but in pursuit of some altruistic purpose. The motive which led the testator to make the gift may have been, indeed most frequently will have been, a desire to further that purpose. It may be said that in that sense the gift is made for the furtherance of the purpose. But the testator has chosen as the means of furthering the purpose to make a gift to an association formed for the pursuit of that purpose in the expectation that the subject matter of the gift will be so used, without imposing or attempting to impose any trust or obligation on the members, or the trustees, or the committee of the association. Indeed, there are cases where the gift has been expressed as a gift for the purposes, or one of the purposes, of the association, and nonetheless has been held not to impose any purported trust ...

In the recent decision of Oliver J in *Re Lipinski* [1976] Ch 235 the gift was ' ... for the Hull Judeans (Maccabi) Association in memory of my late wife to be used solely in the work of constructing the new buildings for the association and/or improvements to the said buildings'. Oliver J said [1976] Ch 235 at 246–247:

> If a valid gift may be made to an unincorporated body as a simple accretion to the funds which are the subject-matter of the contract which the members have made *inter se*, and *Neville Estates Ltd v Madden* [1962] Ch 832 and *Re Recher's Will Trusts* [1972] Ch 526 show that it may, I do not really see why such a gift, which specifies a purpose which is within the powers of the unincorporated body and of which the members of that body are the beneficiaries, should fail. Why are not the beneficiaries able to enforce the trust or, indeed, in the exercise of their contractual rights, to terminate the trust for their own benefit? Where the donee body is itself the beneficiary of the prescribed purpose, there seems to me to be the strongest argument in common sense for saying that the gift should be construed as an absolute one within the second category, the more so where, if the purpose is carried out, the members can by appropriate action vest the resulting property in themselves, for here the trustees and the beneficiaries are the same persons.

As I read his judgment, Oliver J construed the gift as one under which the members of the association could have resolved to use the property for some other purpose, or, indeed, have divided it amongst themselves. He said [1976] Ch 235 at 249:

> There is an additional factor. This is a case in which, under the constitution of the association, the members could, by the appropriate majority, alter their constitution so as to provide, if they wished, for the division of the association's assets amongst themselves.

That leads to the second point. It must, as I see it, be a necessary characteristic of any gift within the second category that the members of the association can by an appropriate majority (if the rules so provide), or acting unanimously if they do not, alter their rules so as to provide that the funds, or part of them, shall be applied for some new purpose, or even distributed amongst the members for their own benefit. For the validity of a gift within this category rests essentially on the fact that the testator has set out to further a purpose by making a gift to the members of an association formed for the furtherance of that purpose in the expectation that, although the members at the date when the gift takes effect will be free, by a majority if the rules so provide or acting unanimously if they do not, to dispose of the fund in any way they may think fit, they and any future members of the association will not in fact do so but will employ the property in the furtherance of the purpose of the association and will honour any special condition attached to the gift.

Turning to the third category, the testator may seek to further the purpose by giving a legacy to an association as a quasi-corporate entity, that is to present and future members indefinitely, or by purporting to impose a trust. In the former case the gift will fail for perpetuity, unless confined within an appropriate period; though if it is so confined and if the members for the time being within the perpetuity period are free to alter the purposes for which the property is to be used and to distribute the income amongst themselves it will not, as I see it, fail on any other ground. In the latter case, the gift will fail on the ground that the court cannot compel the use of the property in furtherance of a stated purpose unless, of course, the purpose is a charitable one. As Lord Simonds said in *Leahy* v *Attorney-General for New South Wales* [1959] AC 457 at 478–479:

> If the words 'for the general purposes of the association' were held to import a trust, the question would have to be asked, what is the trust and who are the beneficiaries? A gift can be made to persons (including a corporation) but it cannot be made to a purpose or to an object; so, also, a trust may be created for the benefit of persons as *cestuis que trustent*, but not for a purpose or object unless the purpose or object be charitable. For a purpose or object cannot sue, but, if it be charitable, the Attorney-General can use to enforce it. (On this point something will be added later.) It is, therefore, by disregarding the words 'for the general purposes of the association' (which are assumed not to be charitable purposes) and treating the gift as an absolute gift to individuals that it can be sustained.

...

I have also been referred to the recent decision of Goff J in *Re Denley's Trust Deed* [1969] 1 Ch 373 [see Chapter 3] ... Goff J ... held that the trust deed created a valid trust for the benefit of the employees, the benefit being the right to use the land subject to and in accordance with the rules made by the trustees. That case on a proper analysis, in my judgment, falls altogether outside the categories of gifts to unincorporated associations and purpose trusts. I can see no distinction in principle between a trust to permit a class defined by reference to employment to use and enjoy land in accordance with rules to be made at the discretion of trustees on the one hand, and, on the other hand, a trust to distribute income at the discretion of trustees amongst a class, defined by reference to, for example, relationship to the settlor. In both cases the benefit to be taken by any member of the class is at the discretion of the trustees, but any member of the class can apply to the court to compel the trustees to administer the trust in accordance with its terms. As Goff J pointed out [1969] 1 Ch 373 at 388:

> The same kind of problem is equally capable of arising in the case of a trust to permit a number of persons—for example, all the unmarried children of a testator or settlor—to use or occupy a house, or to have the use of certain chattels; nor can I assume that in such cases agreement between the parties concerned would be more likely, even if that be a sufficient distinction, yet no one would suggest, I fancy, that such a trust would be void.

With those principles in mind, I return to the testator's will ...

[Vinelott J set out in detail the terms of the will and the rules of the Chertsey and Walton CLP and continued:]

Reading the gift in the will in the light of the rules governing the Chertsey and Walton CLP, it is in my judgment impossible to construe the gift as a gift made to the members of the Chertsey and Walton CLP at the date of the testator's death with the intention that it should belong to them as a collection of individuals, though in the expectation that they and any other members subsequently admitted would ensure that it was in fact used for what in broad terms has been labelled 'headquarters' purposes' of the Chertsey and Walton CLP. I base this conclusion on two grounds. First, the members of the Chertsey and Walton CLP do not control the property, given by subscription or otherwise, to the CLP. The rules which govern the CLP are capable of being altered by an outside body which could direct an alteration under which the general committee of the CLP would be bound to transfer any property for the time being held for the benefit of the CLP to the national Labour Party for national purposes. The members of the Chertsey and Walton CLP could not alter the rules so as to make the property bequeathed by the testator applicable for some purpose other than that provided by the rules; nor could they direct that property to be divided amongst themselves beneficially.

Brightman J observed in *Re Recher's Will Trusts* [1972] Ch 526 at 536 that: 'It would astonish a layman to be told there was a difficulty in his giving a legacy to an unincorporated non-charitable society which he had or could have supported without trouble during his lifetime.' The answer to this apparent paradox is, it seems to me, that subscriptions by members of the Chertsey and Walton CLP must be taken as made on terms that they will be applied by the general committee in accordance with the rules for the time being, including any modifications imposed by the annual party conference or the NEC. In the event of the dissolution of the Chertsey and Walton CLP any remaining fund representing subscriptions would (as the rules now stand) be held on a resulting trust for the original subscribers. Thus although the members of the CLP may not be able themselves to alter the purposes for which a fund representing subscriptions is to be used or to alter the rules so as to make such a fund divisible amongst themselves the ultimate proprietary right of the original subscribers remains. There is, therefore, no perpetuity and no non-charitable purpose trust. But if that analysis of the terms on which subscriptions are held is correct, it is fatal to the argument that the gift in the testator's will should be construed as a gift to the members of the Chertsey and Walton CLP at the testator's death, subject to a direction not amounting to a trust that it be used for headquarters' purposes. Equally it is in my judgment impossible, in particular having regard to the gift over to the national Labour Party, to read the gift as a gift to the members of the national Labour Party at the testator's death, with a direction not amounting to a trust, that the national party permit it to be used by the Chertsey and Walton CLP for headquarters' purposes.

That first ground is of itself conclusive, but there is another ground which reinforces this conclusion. The gift is not in terms a gift to the Chertsey and Walton CLP, but to the Labour Party Property Committee, who are to hold the property for the benefit of, that is in trust for, the Chertsey headquarters of the Chertsey and Walton CLP. The fact that a gift is a gift to trustees and not in terms to an unincorporated association militates against construing it as a gift to the members of the association at the date when the gift takes effect, and against construing the words indicating the purposes for which the property is to be used as expressing the testator's intention or motive in making the gift and not as imposing any trust. This was, indeed, one of the considerations which led the Privy Council in *Leahy's* case [1959] AC 457 to hold that the gift '… upon trust for such Order of Nuns of the Catholic Church or the Christian Brothers as my Executors and Trustees should select', would, apart from the Australian equivalent of the Charitable Trusts (Validation) Act 1954, have been invalid.

I am, therefore, compelled to the conclusion that the gift of the testator's estate fails, and that his estate accordingly devolves as on intestacy. I will make the usual order that the costs of the plaintiffs as trustees, and the defendants on a common fund basis, be taxed and paid out of the estate in due course of administration.

NOTE: *Grant, Recher,* and *Lipinski* really show up the difficulties of being unable to construe a grant to a non-charitable unincorporated association as a gift for the *purposes* of the association. In *Lipinski*, the requirement that the gift be used for the purpose stated had to be struck out for the gift to take effect. In *Re Grant*, the members of the Chertsey and Walton Constituency Labour Party were held not to have control over their own property, because they were also bound by the rules of the Labour Party nationally. Thus, a gift to the CLP could not be construed as a gift to the members of the CLP beneficially, since they could not direct that the bequest be divided among themselves as beneficial owners. The gift could take effect, if at all, only as a private purpose trust, in which case it infringed the rule against perpetuities.

The case may not be of general application, however, since the relationship between national and local labour parties was unusual, in that the local association appeared to have virtually no control over its own funds. Indeed, the national party could itself take direct control of the local party's funds, and it is not at all surprising, therefore, that Vinelott J held that the funds were owned by the national, rather than the local, party. It does not follow that gifts can never be made to local branches of federated societies, however. In *News Group Newspapers Ltd* v *SOGAT* [1986] ICR 716, the local branch of SOGAT (Society of Graphical and Allied Trades) could unilaterally secede from the national union, and was therefore held still to control its own property. Presumably therefore, it would have been possible to make a donation to the local branch. Many federated societies adopt an intermediate position, where although the local branches cannot unilaterally secede, the national society has no direct control over the local funds, the local society instead paying an annual membership subscription and agreeing to be bound, to a greater or lesser extent, by national rules. It is not clear whether the reasoning in *Re Grant's WT* applies in this situation.

■ **QUESTIONS**

1. X gives £1,000 to the Plane Truth, an unincorporated society dedicated to the proof of all unproven mathematical theorems. Assume that the Plane Truth is non-charitable. Can X prevent the members of the Plane Truth (at any time) from dissolving the society and spending the assets on beer?

2. Suppose the gift is conditional upon the Plane Truth continuing to exist as a society, with a gift over to charity if it ceases to exist. Can such a condition be placed upon

the gift? If so, does the condition have to be triggered, if at all, within a certain time, and if so, what time?

3. The law governing property owned by unincorporated associations is preoccupied with the need to identify persons within the association who can be said to own the property absolutely or under a trust—by extension of the beneficiary principle. Would it be more profitable and logical to replace the search for a personal owner with a concept of group property?

Re Horley Town Football Club

[2006] EWHC 2386 (Ch), Chancery Division

Facts: The trustees of the Club sought directions of the court as to whether they held club assets for 'temporary members' and 'Associate Members' as well as full members. *Held:* Beneficial ownership was held on bare trust for full adult and senior members of the Club only, because they could either unanimously or at an AGM call for the assets to be transferred to them.

COLLINS J: In *Re GKN Bolts & Nuts Ltd etc Works Sports and Social Club* [1982] 1 WLR 774 ... Sir Robert Megarry V-C said (at 776): 'As is common in club cases, there are many obscurities and uncertainties, and some difficulty in the law. In such cases, the court usually has to take a broad sword to the problems, and eschew an unduly meticulous examination of the rules and regulations ... ' ...

In my judgment I should adopt the same approach as Sir Robert Megarry in taking a 'broad sword' and applying fairness and common sense. In my judgment it does not make a difference that in the present case the Rules say in Rule 4 that the Club shall consist of 'members and temporary members'; or in Rule 5 provide that Associate Members will enjoy the same rights as full members except those relating to voting rights; or that Rule 15 gives a right to vote to 'independently constituted clubs enjoying Associate Membership.'

Hanchett-Stamford v Attorney-General

[2008] EWHC 330 (Ch), [2008] 4 All ER 323, Chancery Division

Held: Even a sole-surviving member of an association should take the association's assets.

LEWISON J: what I find ... difficult to accept is that a member who has a beneficial interest in an asset, albeit subject to contractual restrictions, can have that beneficial interest divested from him on the death of another member. It leads to the conclusion that if there are two members of an association which has assets of, say £2 million, they can by agreement divide those assets between them and pocket £1 million each, but if one of them dies before they have divided the assets, the whole pot goes to the Crown as *bona vacantia* ...

The thread that runs through all these cases is that the property of an unincorporated association is the property of its members, but that they are contractually precluded from severing their share except in accordance with the rules of the association; and that, on its dissolution, those who are members at the time are entitled to the assets free from any such contractual restrictions. It is true that this is not a joint tenancy according to the classical model; but since any collective ownership of property must be a species of joint tenancy or tenancy in common this kind of collective ownership must, in my judgment, be a sub-species of joint tenancy, albeit taking effect subject to any contractual restrictions applicable as between members. In some cases (such as *Cunnack* v *Edwards*) those contractual restrictions may be such as to exclude any possibility of a future claim. In others they may not. The cases are united in saying that on a dissolution the members of a dissolved association have a beneficial interest in its assets ... In addition, Article 1 of Protocol 1 of the European Convention on Human Rights and Fundamental Freedoms guarantees the peaceful enjoyment of possessions. It says that:

'No one shall be deprived of his possessions except in the public interest and subject to the conditions provided for by law ...'

On the face of it for one of two members of an unincorporated association to be deprived of his share in the assets of the association by reason of the death of the other of them, and without any compensation, appears to be a breach of this article.

■ SUMMATIVE QUESTION

Leon Easel, a renowned artist, died in 2002. His will contains the following provisions:

online resource centre

(a) To my favourite artist, Basil van Brush, I devise my country studio and gardens on the Isle of Mull absolutely in full confidence that he will make such use of them as I should have made myself and that at his death he will leave them to the Royal Academy and in default of any disposition by him thereof by his will or testament I hereby direct that all my estate and property acquired by him under this my will shall at his death be given to the Royal Academy absolutely.

(b) To my executors, my personal estate (excluding my art collection) to hold upon trust for such artists as they shall select having regard to their knowledge of my personal taste in art.

(c) To my executors, the greater part of my art collection to be held by them on trust for my favourite model, Imogen, subject to any pictures which my friends may choose.

Consider the validity of each provision, and the consequences, where relevant, of invalidity.

FURTHER READING

Gardner, S., 'A Detail in the Construction of Gifts to Unincorporated Associations' (1998) 62 *Conv* 8.

Hardcastle, I. M., 'Administrative Unworkability—A Reassessment of an Abiding Problem' (1990) 54 *Conv* 24.

Hargreaves, P., 'Charitable, Purpose and Hybrid Trusts: A Jersey Perspective' (2002) 1 *Private Client Business* 30.

Kessler, J. and Sartin, L., *Drafting Trusts and Will Trusts: A Modern Approach*, 10th revd edn (London: Sweet & Maxwell, 2010).

Matthews, P., 'Gifts to Unincorporated Associations' (1995) 59 *Conv* 302.

Pawlowski, M. and Summers, J., 'Private Purpose Trusts—A Reform Proposal' (2007) 71 *Conv* 440.

Stoljar, S. J., *Groups and Entities—An Inquiry into Corporate Theory* (Sydney: Australian University Press, 1973).

Worthington, S., 'Sorting out Ownership Interests in a Bulk: Gifts, Sales and Trusts' (1999) *Journal of Business Law* 1.

4

Constitution of Trusts: Effective Disposition of Benefit

KEY AIMS

To identify the reasons for the requirement that a trust must be completely constituted and a gift perfected. To examine the scope of the maxims 'equity will not assist a volunteer', 'equity will not perfect an imperfect gift', and 'equity will not spell out a trust from a failed gift'. To define the difference between the constitution of a trust by declaration of self as trustee and the constitution of a trust by transfer of trust assets to trustees. To consider how trusts/gifts may be constituted/perfected by accident. To examine the special case of donations made in contemplation of death.

SECTION 1: INTRODUCTION

If I give you something or promise to give you something but you neither give nor promise to give anything in return, I am said to have made my disposition or promise 'voluntarily' and you are said to be a 'volunteer'. All is well for the volunteer if an effective disposition is actually made, but what happens if an attempted disposition fails or a promise to make a disposition is not fulfilled? Suppose, for example, that I were to telephone you on your birthday to say 'I sent you a cheque in the post yesterday' or 'I will send you a present tomorrow'. If I send the cheque to you but it gets lost in the post or I forget to sign it, I am not obliged to send another one. Likewise if I decide not to fulfil my promise to send the present tomorrow, I cannot be compelled to send it. At law, a volunteer cannot enforce a voluntary gift or a voluntary promise made in their favour and, following the law, 'equity will not assist a volunteer'. (If equity were to assist volunteers, it would undermine the common law doctrine of consideration that underpins contract law.) For a gift to be 'perfect', the donor must actually complete the disposition of the subject matter in favour of the intended donee or execute a formal 'deed of gift'.

Just as a gift must be perfected before a volunteer can enforce it, so too a trust must be constituted before the beneficiary can enforce it; but *why* must a trust be completely constituted in order to be enforceable? Why is it not sufficient merely to establish that the settlor *intended* to make a trust? There are, in fact, a number of reasons for the requirement that a trust be properly constituted. First, it provides an important test of the seriousness of a donor or settlor's intent, given that a person who makes a perfect gift, or a completely constituted trust, thereby makes an irrevocable disposition of his beneficial interest in the subject matter of the gift or trust. Secondly, it prevents the casual imposition of obligations on trustees. Thirdly, it ensures that the trustees actually have the power to fulfil their trust obligations. Until the legal title is formally transferred to them, they have no legal power to deal with the trust property in any way, whether by way of sale or mortgage or lease and, crucially, they will have no power to invest the trust property or, ultimately, to distribute it to the beneficiaries. Fourthly, voluntary gifts and trusts are economically inefficient and inherently unfair because the beneficiary of the gift or trust is getting something for nothing. The economic cost and unfairness cannot be justified on the basis of the donor's intention alone, because intention can be mistakenly inferred. Intention must be joined by action.

SECTION 2: MODES OF CONSTITUTION

A: Declaration of self as trustee

A settlor can validly constitute a trust by declaring *himself* trustee of his own property, on behalf of one or more beneficiaries. The intention must be irrevocable, because trusts are of their nature irrevocable, and it must be an intention to create a trust, rather than some other transaction (e.g. an outright gift). It is more difficult to infer an intention to constitute oneself trustee than to infer an intention to make a gift, and an intention to constitute oneself trustee will not generally be inferred from a failed gift.

Richards v Delbridge

(1874) LR Eq 11, Court of Chancery

Facts: Delbridge wished to give his infant grandson, Richards, the lease he had on his place of business as a bone manure merchant. He endorsed on the lease: 'This deed and all thereto belonging I give to Edward Benetto Richards from this time forth, with all the stock-in-trade.' He gave the lease to Richards' mother to hold for Richards, but died before the lease was actually delivered to Richards himself.

Held: There had been no transfer of the lease to Richards, nor a declaration of trust in his favour.

SIR GEORGE JESSEL MR: The principle is a very simple one. A man may transfer his property, without valuable consideration, in one of two ways: he may either do such acts as amount in law to a conveyance or assignment of the property, and thus completely divest himself of the legal ownership, in which case the person who by those acts acquires the property takes it beneficially, or on trust, as the case may be; or the legal owner of the property may, by one or other of the modes recognised as amounting to a valid declaration of trust, constitute himself a trustee, and, without an actual transfer of the legal title, may so deal with the property as to deprive himself of its beneficial ownership, and declare that he will hold it from that time forward on trust for the other person. It is true that he need not use the words, 'I declare myself a trustee,' but he must do something which is equivalent to it, and use expressions which have that meaning; for, however anxious the Court may be to carry out a man's intention, it is not at liberty to construe words otherwise than according to their proper meaning.

...

The true distinction appears to me to be plain, and beyond dispute: for a man to make himself trustee there must be an expression of intention to become a trustee, whereas words of present gift shew an intention to give over property to another, and not retain it in the donor's own hands for any purpose, fiduciary or otherwise.

NOTE: In *Jones* v *Lock* (1865) LR 1 Ch App 25, the father of a baby boy handed a cheque to his nine-month-old son, uttering words which made it clear that he meant the child to have the sum represented by the cheque, although he immediately removed the cheque from the baby for safe-keeping. The father died some days later, without having endorsed the cheque, which would have been necessary to pass title in it to the child. The court refused to construe his actions as amounting to a declaration of trust, with himself as trustee, in favour of the child. Lord Cranworth LC did not think that an irrevocable intention to part with the property had been manifested. There was an intention to make an outright gift, but no gift had actually been made. It was not therefore a declaration of trust.

■ QUESTION

Jessel MR observed in *Richards* v *Delbridge* that the settlor need not use the words, 'I declare myself a trustee,' but he must do something which is equivalent to it. What do you think is meant by 'something which is equivalent to it'? Is *Paul* v *Constance* a good example of this?

Paul v Constance
[1977] 1 WLR 54, [1977] 1 All ER 195, Court of Appeal

Facts: Constance was injured at work, and obtained £950 in damages, which he put into his bank account in his name alone. It appeared, however, that the money was intended for himself and Mrs Paul, with whom he was living but not married. For this reason (according to the evidence) no joint account was opened, in order to save Mrs Paul from embarrassment.

Subsequent additions were made to the account, in particular from bingo winnings which Constance and Paul played as a joint venture. One withdrawal of £150 was also made, which was divided equally between them.

On Constance's death, Mrs Constance claimed entitlement to the £950.

Held: Constance held the money on trust for Mrs Paul, and therefore Mrs Constance was not entitled to it. The word 'trust', was not used, but regard was had to the unsophisticated character of Constance, and his relationship with Mrs Paul. Had the decision been otherwise, the money would have been regarded as Constance's, and his wife would have been entitled to succeed to it as part of her husband's estate.

SCARMAN LJ: There is no suggestion of a gift by transfer in this case. The facts of [*Jones* v *Lock* and *Richards* v *Delbridge*] do not, therefore, very much help the submission of counsel for the defendant, but he was able to extract from them this principle: that there must be a clear declaration of trust, and that means there must be clear evidence from what is said or done of an intention to create a trust or, as counsel for the defendant put it, 'an intention to dispose of a property or a fund so that somebody else to the exclusion of the disponent acquires the beneficial interest in it'. He submitted that there was no such evidence.

When one looks to the detailed evidence to see whether it goes as far as that—and I think that the evidence does have to go as far as that—one finds that from the time that Mr Constance received his damages right up to his death he was saying, on occasions, that the money was as much the plaintiff's as his. When they discussed the damages, how to invest them or what to do with them, when they discussed the bank account, he would say to her: 'The money is as much yours as mine.' The judge, rightly treating the basic problem in the case as a question of fact, reached this conclusion. He said:

> I have read through my notes, and I am quite satisfied that it was the intention of [the claimant] and Mr Constance to create a trust in which both of them were interested.

In this court the issue becomes: was there sufficient evidence to justify the judge reaching that conclusion of fact? In submitting that there was, counsel for the plaintiff draws attention first and foremost to the words used. When one bears in mind the unsophisticated character of Mr Constance and his relationship with the plaintiff during the last few years of his life, counsel for the plaintiff submits that the words that he did use on more than one occasion namely 'This money is as much yours as mine,' convey clearly a present declaration that the existing fund was as much the plaintiff's as his own. The judge accepted that conclusion. I think he was well justified in doing so and, indeed, I think he was right to do so. There are, as counsel for the plaintiff reminded us, other features in the history of the relationship between the plaintiff and Mr Constance which support the interpretation of those words as an express declaration of trust. I have already described the interview with the bank manager when the account was opened. I have mentioned also the putting of the 'bingo' winnings into the account, and the one withdrawal for the benefit of both of them.

It might, however, be thought that this was a borderline case, since it is not easy to pin-point a specific moment of declaration, and one must exclude from one's mind any case built on the existence of an implied or constructive trust; for this case was put forward at the trial and is now argued by the plaintiff as one of express declaration of trust. It was so pleaded, and it is only as such that it may be considered in this court. The question, therefore, is whether in all the circumstances the use of those words on numerous occasions as between Mr Constance and the plaintiff constituted an express declaration of trust. The judge found that they did. For myself, I think he was right so to find. I therefore would dismiss the appeal.

NOTE: This is clearly a borderline case, from which wide-ranging conclusions should not too readily be drawn.

■ QUESTIONS

1. Given that trusts are irrevocable commitments by the settlor, does it worry you that it was 'not easy to pinpoint a specific moment of declaration'?

2. In *Cooke* v *Head* [1972] 1 WLR 518, considered in Chapter 8, Mr Head's aunt gave evidence that Mr Head had said to her: 'The bungalow is as much hers [Miss Cooke's] as it is mine.' Does this suggest an alternative explanation for the decision in *Cooke* v *Head*? Would it today be regarded as a first category *Rosset* case (see, further, Chapter 8)?

3. What inference, if any, do you think should be drawn from the statement, 'This money is as much yours as mine'? Is it relevant, given that this is not land, that there was apparently no reliance on the statement?

B: Trusts by transfer to trustees

Where it is intended to create a trust by transferring the trust property to trustees (instead of making oneself trustee) it is essential to transfer the asset in the manner prescribed by law. For land this means transfer by deed (Law of Property Act 1925, s.52). For shares this now requires transfer of the shares to the transferee and registration of the transferee with the company as the new owner (Stock Transfer Act 1963, s.1; Companies Act 2006, s.771 and Part 21). Although electronic transfer of shares is now widespread, and electronic transfer of land is being introduced.

Milroy v Lord

(1862) 4 De GF & J 264, 45 ER 1185, Court of Appeal in Chancery

Facts: The settlor, Thomas Medley, executed a deed poll, purporting voluntarily to transfer shares to the defendant Samuel Lord on trust for the claimants. The deed poll was not the correct method of transferring legal title from one person to another, however, since that could only be achieved by registering the name of the transferee in the books of the bank.

Samuel Lord also held a power of attorney from Thomas Medley, which would have authorised Lord to transfer the shares to himself, but Lord did not exercise it. Legal title therefore never passed to Lord.

Held: No trust had been constituted. Samuel Lord never became trustee of the shares, nor had Thomas Medley declared himself trustee of them.

TURNER LJ:...I take the law of this court to be well settled, that, in order to render a voluntary settlement valid and effectual, the settlor must have done everything which, according to the nature of the property comprised in the settlement, was necessary to be done in order to transfer the property and render the settlement binding upon him. He may, of course, do this by actually transferring the property to the persons for whom he intends to provide, and the provision will then be effectual and it will be equally effectual if he transfers the property to a trustee for the purposes of the settlement, or declares that he himself holds it on trust for those purposes; and, if the property be personal, the trust may, as I apprehend, be declared either in writing or by parol; but, in order to render the settlement binding, one or other of these modes must...be resorted to, for there is no equity in this Court to perfect an imperfect gift. The cases I think go further to this extent, that if the settlement is intended to be effectuated by one of the modes to which I have referred, the Court will not give effect to it by applying another of those modes. If it is intended to take effect by transfer, the Court will not hold the intended transfer to operate as a declaration of trust, for then every imperfect instrument would be made effectual by being converted into a perfect trust...

The...question is, whether the defendant Samuel Lord did not become a trustee of those shares? Upon this question I have felt considerable doubt; but in the result, I have come to the conclusion that no perfect trust was ever created in him. The shares, it is clear, were never legally vested in him; and the only ground on which he can be held to have become a trustee of them is, that he held a power of attorney under which he might have transferred them into his own name; but he held that power of attorney as the agent of the settlor; and if he had been sued by the plaintiffs as trustee of the settlement for an account under the trust, and to compel him to transfer the shares into his own name as trustee, I think he might well have said—These shares are not vested in me; I have no power over them except as the agent of the settlor, and without his express directions I cannot be justified in making the proposed transfer, in converting an intended into an actual settlement. A court of equity could not, I think, decree the agent of the settlor to make the transfer, unless it could decree the settlor himself to do so, and it is plain that no such decree could have been made against the settlor. In my opinion, therefore, this decree cannot be maintained as to the 50 Louisiana Bank shares.

NOTES
1. Turner LJ recognises the two methods of creation: declaration of self as trustee, and transfer to trustees.
2. An intention to declare oneself trustee is quite different from an intention to make a gift, since one retains no obligations regarding the property in the case of a gift, whereas onerous obligations are retained in the former case. Therefore, a perfect trust will not be construed from an imperfect gift.
3. There were authorities contrary to the proposition set out in 2, but the authorities were fully reviewed, and Turner LJ's views preferred, in *Richards* v *Delbridge* (1874) LR Eq 11. They have also been adopted in most of the later cases set out here, and there can be little doubt, therefore, that they represent the law.
4. In the second case, of transfer to trustees, Turner LJ requires only that the settlor must have done everything which was necessary to be done in order to transfer the property. It is possible, therefore, for a trust to be constituted where the settlor has done all that is within his power to constitute the trust by transferring the property to a trustee, but has been thwarted by formalities which are outside his control. Equity regards the trust as constituted by the last act of the settlor.
5. However, the settlor will not have done everything in his power to transfer the property where he has used the wrong form of transfer, as in *Milroy* v *Lord*. Even if the settlor uses the correct form of transfer, as in *Re Fry, Chase National Executors and Trustees Corp.* v *Fry*, there will be no transfer of legal title where anything remains, or may remain, to be done by the settlor.

Re Fry, Chase National Executors and Trustees Corp. v *Fry*

[1946] Ch 312, Chancery Division

Facts: Fry executed transfers of shares in an English company in favour of his son. Under the Defence (Finance) Regulations 1939, the transfer could not be registered until Treasury consent was obtained. Fry had filled in the necessary forms, but died before Treasury consent was obtained.

Held: The transfer was ineffective.

ROMER J:...Now I should have thought it was difficult to say that the testator had done everything that was required to be done by him at the time of his death, for it was necessary for him to obtain permission from the Treasury for the assignment and he had not obtained it. Moreover, the Treasury might in any case have required further information of the kind referred to in the questionnaire which was submitted to him, or answers supplemental to those which he had given in reply to it; and, if so approached, he might have refused to concern himself with the matter further, in which case I do not know how anyone else could have compelled him to do so.

NOTE: This case was distinguished in *Re Rose, Midland Bank Executor and Trustee Co.* v *Rose* [1949] Ch 78, Chancery Division and the 1954 (different) case of similar name.

Re Rose, Rose v *IRC*

[1952] Ch 499, Court of Appeal

Facts: Rose executed transfers in shares in the required form in March 1943, but they could not take effect (at any rate at common law) until the directors of the company had registered them. They did this in June 1943. Rose died more than five years after executing the transfers, but less than five years after they were registered. If the effective date of the transfer was June 1943, then estate duty was payable, whereas if the transfer took effect in March, it was not.

Held: In equity, the transfer was complete when Rose had done all he could, rather than when the directors consented to and registered the transfer. Equity regarded the property as transferred by Rose's last act. Rose had done all that he could to transfer the property, but was thwarted by legal formalities which were outside his control.

EVERSHED MR: For the reasons I have stated, I do not think that *Milroy* v *Lord* covers the case.... If, as I have said, the phrase 'transfer the shares' is taken to be and to mean a transfer of all rights and interests in them, then I can see nothing contrary to the law in a man saying that so long as, pending registration, the legal estate remains in the donor, he was, by the necessary effect of his own deed, a trustee of that legal estate. Nor do I think that that is an unjustifiable addition to or gloss on the words used in the transfer. Indeed, for my part, I find it a less difficult matter in the way of interpretation than to say that this was, upon its terms, merely a conditional gift, merely a transfer as a gift to Mrs Rose of a particular right, namely the right to get herself registered and thenceforward, but not before, to enjoy the benefits which the donor previously had in these shares. That is nothing like what the deed sets out to do. I have said that I reject the proposition that the distinction between a case such as this and a case such as *Milroy* v *Lord* is, as [counsel for the Crown] urged, indefensible. I think it is sensible and real; and for these reasons I would dismiss the appeals.

JENKINS LJ:...If that was the effect of the transfers, what was the position between the delivery of the transfers and the actual registration of the transferees as the holders of the shares? [Counsel for the Crown] has referred us to the well-known case of *Milroy* v *Lord*, which has been his sheet-anchor. He says that on this authority we must be forced to the conclusion that, pending registration, the transfers had no effect at all, and he arrives at that conclusion in this way: He says that these transfers, while purporting to be transfers of the property in the shares and not declarations of trust, did not transfer the property in the shares, because registration was necessary in order to get in the legal title. He says, further, that being transfers purporting to be transfers of the property in the shares and failing of their effect as such for want of registration, they could, pending registration, have no operation at all because in the case of *Milroy* v *Lord* it was held that a defective voluntary disposition purporting to operate as a transfer or assignment of the property in question would not be given effect to in equity as a declaration of trust. I agree with my Lord that *Milroy* v *Lord* by no means covers the question with which we have to deal in the present case. If the deceased had in truth transferred the whole of his interest in these shares so far as he could transfer the same, including such right as he could pass to his transferee to be placed on the register in respect of the shares, the question arises, what beneficial interest had he then left? The answer can only be, in my view, that he had no beneficial interest left whatever: his only remaining interest consisted in the fact that his name still stood on the register as holder of the shares; but, having parted in fact with the whole of his beneficial interest, he could not, in my view, assert any beneficial title by virtue of his position as registered holder. In other words, in my view the effect of these transactions, having regard to the form and the operation of the transfers, the nature of the property transferred, and the necessity for registration in order to perfect the legal title, coupled with the discretionary power on the part of the directors to withhold registration, must be that, pending registration, the deceased was in the position of a trustee of the legal title in the shares for the transferees. Thus in the hypothetical case put by the Crown of a dividend being declared and paid (as it would have been paid in accordance with the company's articles) to the deceased as registered holder, he would have been accountable for that dividend to the transferees, on the ground that by virtue of the transfers as between himself and the transferees the owners of the shares were the transferees, to the exclusion of himself.

■ **QUESTIONS**

1. Who was trustee between March and June 1943?

2. Was the trust between March and June 1943 an express or a constructive trust? Does it matter?

3. If it is an express trust, then did Rose ever intend to declare himself trustee? If not, can *Re Rose* truly be reconciled with *Richards* v *Delbridge* (see discussion at Section 2: Modes of constitution, A: Declaration of self as trustee)?

4. In the light, for example, of the very conservative approach to the imposition of constructive trusteeship in cases such as *Westdeutsche Landesbank Girozentrale* v *Islington London Borough Council* [1996] AC 669 (see Chapter 5), is it reasonable to impose constructive trusteeship on Rose? Was his conscience affected in any way? Is it relevant that the transfer of some of the shares was in consideration of his love and affection for his wife, and in respect of the other shares, in consideration of a payment of 10 shillings? Do you think the decision would have been the same had the transfer been for no consideration?

5. It was assumed that the directors would, as a matter of course, register the shares, but they were under no obligation to do so. The headnote to the case states that under the articles of association of the company the directors were empowered, in their absolute and uncontrolled discretion and without giving any reason, to decline to register any proposed transfer of shares. That being so, can *Re Rose* truly be reconciled with *Re Fry* (above)? Does it make any difference, in your view, that the headnote continues: 'The deceased [i.e. Rose] was governing director of the company and as such had full and uncontrolled authority to determine who should be admitted from time to time to be a shareholder of the company. The other directors were the [intended recipients of the shares]?' Do you think the decision would have been the same had that not been the case?

6. Who was entitled to the dividends on the shares, had any been declared between March and June 1943? Would your view differ if the directors had eventually refused to register the shares?

7. Was *Re Rose* correctly decided? If so, on what principle was it decided?

NOTE: It is not entirely clear what mechanism is operating in *Re Rose*, and the case is not without its difficulties. One possibility is that once the settlor has done all that he needs to do to constitute a trust (or effect an out-and-out transfer), he is treated as if he has declared himself trustee of the property until legal title is actually transferred to the trustees (or transferee). The problem is that this appears to conflict with *Milroy v Lord* (1862) 4 De GF & J 264, since Rose intended to make a gift of the shares, and not to become trustee of them. Another possibility is that equity imposes a constructive trust over the intervening period.

It will not normally matter which of these approaches is correct, but arguably declarations of trust of land must be in writing unless they can be categorised as implied, resulting, or constructive trusts (see Chapter 8). In *Mascall* v *Mascall* (1984) 50 P & CR 119, the Court of Appeal applied *Re Rose* to registered land, but since the requisite writing was present, the categorisation argument was not further advanced. The transferor had executed a transfer and sent it to the Inland Revenue, and also handed to the transferee the land certificate. At this stage, before the transfer and land certificate had been sent to the Land Registry for registration of the transferee as proprietor, the transferor changed his mind, after a quarrel with the transferee. The Court of Appeal held the transfer effective, since it was for the transferee to apply to the Land Registry for registration as proprietor, and the transferor had done everything he had to do to complete the transfer.

T. Choithram International SA v Pagarani

[2001] 1 WLR 1, Privy Council

Facts: Mr Pagarani was a successful businessman who had been diagnosed as having terminal cancer. He executed a trust deed at his bedside in order to establish a foundation to be an umbrella organisation for a number of charities he had established during his life. Immediately after signing the deed, he stated that all his wealth would henceforth belong to the foundation. Mr Pagarani was a trustee of the foundation and the other trustees signed the deed the same day or soon after. Not long afterwards, the directors of four companies controlled by Mr Pagarani passed resolutions confirming that the trustees of the foundation would henceforth be the holders of the companies' shares and assets, and after Mr Pagarani's death, the companies registered the trustees of the foundation as shareholders. Members of Mr Pagarani's family brought the present action. They claimed that the donation to the foundation had been ineffective because Mr Pagarani had failed to transfer the shares before his death.

Held: Although equity will not aid a volunteer, it will not strive officiously to defeat a gift. The fact that Mr Pagarani was one of the trustees of the foundation was held to be sufficient to overcome his failure to vest the property in the remaining trustees by formal transfer.

LORD BROWNE-WILKINSON: ... Although equity will not aid a volunteer, it will not strive officiously to defeat a gift. This case falls between the two common-form situations [declaring oneself to be a trustee and transferring to another to act as trustee]. Although the words used by TCP [the donor] are those normally appropriate to an outright gift—'I give to X'—in the present context there is no breach of the principle in *Milroy* v *Lord* if the words of TCP's gift (i.e. to the foundation) are given their only possible meaning in this context. The foundation has no legal existence apart from the trust declared by the foundation trust deed. Therefore the words 'I give to the foundation' can only mean 'I give to the trustees of the foundation trust deed to be held by them on the trusts of the foundation trust deed.' Although the words are apparently words of outright gift they are essentially words of gift on trust.

But, it is said, TCP vested the properties not in *all* the trustees of the foundation but only in one, i.e. TCP. Since equity will not aid a volunteer, how can a court order be obtained vesting the gifted property in the whole body of trustees on the trusts of the foundation?...In their Lordships' view there should be no question. TCP has, in the most solemn circumstances, declared that he is giving (and later that he has given) property to a trust which he himself has established and of which he has appointed himself to be a trustee. All this occurs at one composite transaction taking place on 17 February. There can in principle be no distinction between the case where the donor declares himself to be sole trustee for a donee or a purpose and the case where he declares himself to be one of the trustees for that donee or purpose. In both cases his conscience is affected and it would be unconscionable and contrary to the principles of equity to allow such a donor to resile from his gift.

Pennington v Waine

[2002] 1 WLR 2075, Court of Appeal

Facts: Mr Pennington was a partner in a firm of auditors that acted for a private limited company in which Mrs Ada Crampton held a number of shares. She told Mr Pennington that she wished to transfer 400 of her shares in the company to her nephew, Harold, and later signed a share transfer form to that effect and gave it to Mr Pennington. He placed the form on file and took no further action prior to Ada's death, apart from to write to Harold. In the letter he informed Harold that his firm had been instructed to arrange for the transfer of the 400 shares and that Harold need take no further action. When Ada died, it emerged that her will made no specific mention of the gift of 400 shares to Harold.

Held: Ada Crampton had divested herself entirely of her interest in the 400 shares in favour of Harold before her death, and the transfer would therefore be binding on Ada's personal representatives. Arden LJ held that a stage was reached before Ada died when it would have been unconscionable for Ada to recall the gift. Schiemann LJ agreed with Arden LJ's reasoning without discussion. Clarke LJ agreed that if unconscionability was the correct test, Arden LJ had applied it correctly, but His Lordship preferred to dispose of the case on the more straightforward basis that the execution of the stock transfer form could take effect as a valid equitable assignment without the need for actual delivery of the stock transfer forms or the share certificates, provided the execution of the stock transfer forms was intended to take immediate effect.

LADY JUSTICE ARDEN: ... This appeal raises the question of what is necessary for the purposes of a valid equitable assignment of shares by way of gift. If the transaction had been for value, a contract to assign the share would have been sufficient: neither the execution nor the delivery of an instrument of transfer would have been required. However, where the transaction was purely voluntary, the principle that equity will not assist a volunteer must be applied and respected. This principle is to be found in *Milroy* v *Lord* and other cases on which Mr Weatherill relies, such as *Jones* v *Lock*, *Warriner* v *Rogers* and *Richards* v *Delbridge*: see in particular the citation from the judgment of Turner LJ set out above. Accordingly the gift must be perfected, or 'completely constituted' ...

[T]he principle that equity will not assist a volunteer at first sight looks like a hard-edged rule of law not permitting much argument or exception. Historically the emergence of the principle may have been due to the need for equity to follow the law rather than an intuitive development of equity. The principle against imperfectly constituted gifts led to harsh and seemingly paradoxical results. Before long, equity had tempered the wind to the shorn lamb (i.e. the donee). It did so on more than one occasion and in more than one way.

Firstly it was held that an incompletely constituted gift could be upheld if the gift had been completed to such an extent that the donee could enforce his right to the shares as against third parties without forcing the donor to take any further step. Accordingly, if a share transfer has been executed by the donor and duly presented to the company for registration, the donee would be entitled, if necessary, to apply to the court for an order for rectification of the share register under section 359 of the Companies Act 1985. Such an order would not, of course, be granted if for example the directors had a discretion to refuse to register the transfer and had timeously passed a valid resolution to decline to register the transfer (see *Buckley on the Companies Acts* 15 ed. (2000) paragraph [359.277]).That exception was extended in *Re Rose, Rose* v *IRC* and other cases by holding that for this exception to apply it was not necessary that the donor should have done all that it was necessary to be done to complete the gift, short of registration of the transfer. On the contrary it was sufficient if the donor had done all that it was necessary for him or her to do.

There is a logical difficulty with this particular exception because it assumes that there is a clear answer to the question, when does an equitable assignment of a share take place? In fact the question is circular. For if by handing the form of transfer to Mr Pennington in this case, Ada completed the transaction of gift and the equitable assignment of the 400 shares, Harold can bring an action against Mr Pennington to recover the shares as his property, and the principle that equity will not assist a volunteer is not infringed. If on the other hand, by handing the share transfer to Mr Pennington, Ada did not complete the transaction of gift or the equitable assignment of the shares, Harold cannot recover the shares because to do so would mean compelling the donor or the donor's agent to take some further step. The equitable assignment clearly occurs at some stage before the shares are registered. But does it occur when the share transfer is executed, or when the share transfer is delivered to the transferee, or when the transfer is lodged for registration, or when the pre-emption procedure in article 8 is satisfied or the directors resolve that the transfer should be registered? I return to this point below.

According to Counsel's researches, the situation in the present case has not arisen in any reported cases before. I note that in her recent work, *Personal Property Law Text and Materials* (Hart Publishing, 2000) Professor Worthington takes it as at axiomatic that:

> notwithstanding any demonstrable intention to make a gift, there will be no effective gift in equity if the donor simply places matters (such as completed transfer forms accompanied by the relevant share certificates) in the hand of the *donor's* agents. In those circumstances the donor remains at liberty to recall the gift simply by revoking the instructions previously given to the agent. The donor has not done all that is necessary, and the donee is not in a position to control completion of the transfer. It follows that the intended gift will not be regarded as complete either at law or in equity. (page 241)

Secondly equity has tempered the wind (of the principle that equity will not assist a volunteer) to the shorn lamb (the donee) by utilising the constructive trust. This does not constitute a declaration of trust and thus does not fall foul of the principle (see *Milroy* v *Lord* and *Jones* v *Lock*, above) that an imperfectly constituted gift is not saved by being treated as a declaration of trust. Thus, for example, in the *Choithram* case, the Privy Council held that the assets which the donor gave to the foundation of which he was one of the trustees were held upon trust to vest the same in all the trustees of the foundation on the terms of the trusts of the foundation. This particular trust obligation was not a term of the express trust constituting the foundation but a constructive trust adjunct to it. So, too, in *Re Rose, Rose* v *IRC* the Court of Appeal held that the beneficial interest in the shares passed when the share transfers were delivered to the transferee, and that consequently the transferor was a trustee of the legal estate in the shares from that date...

Thirdly equity has tempered the wind to the shorn lamb by applying a benevolent construction to words of gift. As explained above an imperfect gift is not saved by being treated as a declaration of trust. But where a court of equity is satisfied that the donor had an intention to make an immediate gift, the court will construe the words which the donor used as words effecting a gift or declaring a trust if they can fairly bear that meaning and otherwise the gift will fail. This point can also be illustrated by reference to the *Choithram* case...

Accordingly the principle that, where a gift is imperfectly constituted, the court will not hold it to operate as a declaration of trust, does not prevent the court from construing it to be a trust if that interpretation is permissible as a matter of construction, which may be a benevolent construction. The same must apply to words of gift. An equity to perfect a gift would not be invoked by giving a benevolent construction to words of gift or, it follows, words which the donor used to communicate or give effect to his gift.

The cases to which Counsel have referred us do not reveal any, or any consistent single policy consideration behind the rule that the court will not perfect an imperfect gift. The objectives of the rule obviously include ensuring that donors do not by acting voluntarily act unwisely in a way that they may subsequently regret. This objective is furthered by permitting donors to change their minds at any time before it becomes completely constituted. This is a paternalistic objective, which can outweigh the respect to be given to the donor's original intention as gifts are often held by the courts to be incompletely constituted despite the clearest intention of the donor to make the gift. Another valid objective would be to safeguard the position of the donor: suppose, for instance, that (contrary to the fact) it had been discovered after Ada's death that her estate was insolvent, the court would be concerned to ensure that the gift did not defeat the rights of creditors. But, while this may well be a relevant consideration, for my own part I do not consider that this need concern the court to the exclusion of other considerations as in the event of insolvency there are other potent remedies available to creditors where insolvents have made gifts to defeat their claims: see for example sections 339 and 423 of the Insolvency Act 1986. There must also be, in the interests of legal certainty, a clearly ascertainable point in time at which it can be said that the gift was completed, and this point in time must be arrived at on a principled basis.

There are countervailing policy considerations which would militate in favour of holding a gift to be completely constituted. These would include effectuating, rather than frustrating, the clear and continuing intention of the donor, and preventing the donor from acting in a manner which is unconscionable...

If one proceeds on the basis that a principle which animates the answer to the question whether an apparently incomplete gift is to be treated as completely constituted is that a donor will not be permitted to change his or her mind if it would be unconscionable, in the eyes of equity, vis-à-vis the donee to do so, what is the position here? There can be no comprehensive list of factors which makes it unconscionable for the donor to change his or her mind: it must depend on the court's evaluation of all the relevant considerations. What then are the relevant facts here? Ada made the gift of her own free will: there is no finding that she was not competent to do this. She not only told Harold about the gift and signed a form of transfer which she delivered to Mr Pennington for him to secure registration: her agent also told Harold that he need take no action. In addition Harold agreed to become a director of the Company without limit of time, which he could not do without shares being transferred to him. If Ada had changed her mind on (say) 10 November 1998, in my judgment the court could properly have concluded that it was too late for her to do this as by that date Harold signed the form 288A, the last of the events identified above, to occur.

There is next the pure question of law: was it necessary for Ada to deliver the form of transfer to Harold?...the *ratio* of *Re Rose, Rose* v *IRC* was as I read it that the gifts of shares in that case were completely constituted when the donor executed share transfers and delivered them to the transferees even though they were not registered in the register of members of the company until a later date.

However, that conclusion as to the *ratio* in *Re Rose, Rose* v *IRC* does not mean that this appeal must be decided in the appellants' favour. Even if I am correct in my view that the Court of Appeal took the view in *Re Rose, Rose* v *IRC* that delivery of the share transfers was there required, it does not follow that delivery cannot in some circumstances be dispensed with. Here, there was a clear finding that Ada intended to make an immediate gift. Harold was informed of it. Moreover, I have already expressed the view that a stage was reached when it would have been unconscionable for Ada to recall the gift. It follows that it would also have been unconscionable for her personal representatives to refuse to hand over the share transfer to Harold after her death. In those circumstances, in my judgment, delivery of the share transfer before her death was unnecessary so far as perfection of the gift was concerned.

It is not necessary to decide the case simply on that basis. After the share transfers were executed Mr Pennington wrote to Harold on Ada's instructions informing him of the gift and stating that there was no action that he needed to take. I would also decide this appeal in favour of the respondent on this further basis. If I am wrong in the view that delivery of the share transfers to the company or the donee is required and is not dispensed with by reason of the fact that it would be unconscionable for Ada's personal representatives to refuse to hand the transfers over to Harold, the words used by Mr Pennington should be construed as meaning that Ada and, through her, Mr Pennington became agents for Harold for the purpose of submitting the share transfer to the Company. This is an application of the principle of benevolent construction to give effect to Ada's clear wishes. Only in that way could the result 'This requires no action on your part' and an effective gift be achieved. Harold did not question this assurance and must be taken to have proceeded to act on the basis that it would be honoured.

Accordingly in my judgment the judge was right in the conclusion that he reached.

LORD JUSTICE CLARKE:...although I know that hard cases make bad law, I would have expected Harold to be entitled both to the 400 shares apparently transferred by stock transfer form and the shares bequeathed to him, with the consequence that, on Ada's death, he became entitled to 51 per cent of the issued shares in the company. I should add that, if unconscionability is the test, I agree with Arden LJ that it would have been unconscionable of Ada, as at the time of her death (if not earlier), to assert that the beneficial interest in the 400 shares had not passed to Harold. It would certainly be unconscionable of the estate to seek to resile from the transfer after Ada's death because, as at her death, she plainly intended Harold to own the shares.

The difficulty is to identify the correct approach in law and equity to the facts of this case. In addition to the facts just set out, a feature of the case which has particularly struck me stems from the role and wording of the stock transfer form. Section 1 of the Stock Transfer Act 1963 ('the 1963 Act') provides, so far as relevant, as follows:

(1) Registered securities to which this section applies may be transferred by means of an instrument under hand in the form set out in Schedule 1 to this Act (in this Act referred to as a stock transfer), executed by the transferor only and specifying (in addition to the particulars of the consideration, of the description and number or amount of the securities, and of the person by whom the transfer is made) the full name and address of the transferee.

(2) The execution of a stock transfer need not be attested;...

(3) Nothing in this section shall be construed as affecting the validity of any instrument which would be effective to transfer securities apart from this section;...

Section 1(4) sets out the securities to which the section applies. They include shares in a company...

There is nothing in the provisions of the 1963 Act which suggests that delivery is necessary to effect the transfer. On the contrary, section 1(1) provides that that registered securities 'may be transferred by means of an instrument under hand'. It does not provide that they may, let alone may only, be transferred by *delivery* of such an instrument, whether to the transferee or to the company.

Moreover, there is, so far as I am aware, no case which is authority for the proposition that an equitable assignment of shares, or perhaps strictly of the shareholder's rights to and under the shares, cannot be effective without delivery of the share certificates or the instrument of transfer. It is not, to my mind, surprising that there is no authority for such a proposition because there is no need for such a principle...

It seems to me that the signature of a donor on a stock transfer form in the statutory form used here is or should be capable, without more, of amounting to an equitable assignment. However, it does not follow that it will necessarily operate as an effective equitable assignment. Thus, the cases show that there are circumstances in which the court will not give effect to such an 'assignment'. For example, the evidence may show that, although the document was signed, the donor did not intend the assignment to take immediate (or perhaps any) effect. The classic example of such a situation is the case contemplated by Viscount Haldane in the passage from *Macedo* v *Stroud* [[1922] 2 AC 330, 337] quoted above, where the deed or instrument is delivered, or indeed executed, on the basis that it is not to have effect until some event happens or some event is performed. There is no reason why, in those circumstances, the court should not give effect to that intention.

Unless there is authority binding on this court to the contrary, I would hold that absent such an intention or some other compelling reason why equity should not give effect to the transfer, the execution of the transfer, either by itself or coupled (as here) with delivery by the transferor, as Viscount Haldane put it in the case of a deed, intending to make the transfer his own, the transfer had effect as an equitable assignment to transfer the shares in equity to the transferee...

...evidence in a particular case might lead to the conclusion that the transferor did not intend the assignment to have effect until a later date, as in the case of an escrow or other indication of an intention that the transfer should not have effect until later. However, there was no such indication either in *Re Rose, Rose* v *IRC* or the *Midland Bank Re Rose, Midland Bank* v *Rose* case or in the present case. The fact that the deed was delivered to the transferee in *Re Rose, Rose* v *IRC* and indeed in the *Re Rose, Midland Bank* v *Rose* case was an indication of the fact that the donor did indeed intend to transfer the shares to the transferee by the transfer document. So too were Ada's actions in this case, as set out by Arden LJ.

Reading the judgment of Sir Raymond Evershed, I have no doubt that he would have held that Ada's beneficial interest in the 400 shares was transferred to Harold by the stock transfer form and that her intention was amply proved by what happened thereafter. It is true that he placed some emphasis upon the fact that a deed had been used, and executed by both parties in *Re Rose, Rose* v *IRC* but I do not read his judgment as depending upon that point.

Jenkins LJ agreed with the Master of the Rolls, although it is fair to say that he placed more emphasis on the delivery of the transfer form to the donee. Nevertheless, he too emphasised the form of the transfers. Thus he said (at p. 516) that the directors, when they registered the transfers, registered them because 'by virtue of the transfers' the transferees had become owners of the shares and as such had become entitled to 'get in the legal estate' by becoming registered as owners. However he also said this by way of conclusion:

> In my view, a transfer under seal in the form appropriate under the company's regulations, coupled with delivery of the transfer and certificate to the transferee, does suffice, as between the transferor and the transferee, to constitute the transferee the beneficial owner of the share, and the circumstance that the transferee must do a further act in the form of applying for and obtaining registration in order to get in and perfect his legal title, having been equipped by the transferor with all that is necessary to enable him to do so, does not prevent the transfer from operating, in accordance with its terms as between the transferor and the transferee, and making the transferee the beneficial owner. After all, where duty is concerned, the only relevant type of ownership is beneficial ownership, and the situation of the legal estate does not affect the question.

In considering the decision in *Re Rose, Rose v IRC* it is important to note that the form had in fact been delivered to the transferee. As I see it, the *ratio* of *Re Rose, Rose v IRC* was that the gifts of the shares were completely constituted by the crucial date, which was 10th April 1943, by which time the deeds had been executed and delivered to the donee. It does not, however, follow that the decision would have been different if no such delivery had taken place. The court did not have to decide that question. I do not think that the decision would have been different because, as already stated, it seems to me that that the transferor had done everything that was necessary in order to transfer his *equitable* interest in the shares to the transferee. There was nothing further that the transferee had to do. The effect of that transfer was to create a form of trust under which the donor could have been compelled to procure the registration of the shares in the donee's name...

Moreover, I do not think that the conclusion which I have reached falls foul of the principle that the court will not convert an imperfect gift into a declaration of trust. As I see it, there was here a perfect gift of Ada's beneficial interest in the 400 shares, which, as Sir Raymond Evershed MR explained in the passage on page 510 of his judgment quoted above, took effect as a trust of the legal estate in the shares. It follows that, in my judgment, the decision in *Re Rose, Rose v IRC* does not require the appeal in the instant case to be allowed.

■ QUESTIONS

1. Arden LJ purported to apply a 'benevolent' construction so as to fulfil Ada Crompton's intentions. Is that approach consistent with Arden LJ's view that Ada Crompton was conscience-bound to complete the transfer?

2. In what ways was the decision in *Pennington* v *Waine* more generous than the decisions in *Re Rose* and *Choithram* respectively? Was the decision in *Pennington* v *Waine* generous to a fault? Consider whether a transfer of an asset to one's own agent should ever be an irrevocable binding disposition of one's beneficial interest in the asset.

3. In what sense does the doctrine of unconscionability operate at the level of policy, as suggested by Arden LJ? If it is a policy consideration should it be outweighed by the 'policy' that the court will not take active steps to remove assets from an owner when that owner has omitted to carry out the actions normally required to dispose of his property?

4. At what point is a trust constituted or a gift perfected? Is it the point at which the settlor has done everything within his power to dispose of his beneficial interest such that he is no longer in a position to resile from the transfer, or is it the point at which the donee has received everything necessary to perfect his title to the trust assets?

5. Does it seem curious that there is a rule of equity which prevents a trust from being spelled out of a failed gift, but no such rule to prevent a trust from being spelled out of a failed contract? (See the *Quistclose* trust in Chapter 2.)

6. Is the doctrine of proprietary estoppel a genuine exception to the maxim 'equity will not assist a volunteer'?

NOTE: The decision of the Court of Appeal in *Kaye* v *Zeital* [2010] EWCA Civ 159, [2010] 2 BCLC 1 was rather more orthodox. It followed the approach laid down in *Milroy* v *Lord*, holding that an intended transfer of the beneficial interest in a company share failed because the transferor had done none of the actions necessary to effect such a transfer. He had not declared himself a trustee of the beneficial interest, neither had he assigned it in writing by way of gift or trust. *Kaye* v *Zeital* was followed in *Curtis* v *Pulbrook* [2011] EWHC 167 (Ch); [2011] 1 BCLC 638, although Briggs J acknowledged that *Pennington* v *Waine* had shown three ways to perfect apparently imperfect donations:

> The first is where the donor has done everything necessary to enable the donee to enforce a beneficial claim without further assistance from the donor...The second is where some detrimental reliance by the donee upon an apparent although ineffective gift may so bind the conscience of the donor to justify the imposition of a constructive trust...The third is where by a benevolent construction an effective gift or implied declaration of trust may be teased out of the words used (para [43]).

C: Covenants to settle

It is not possible to constitute an immediate trust of future property, the best that can be done is to make a covenant (contract) to settle the property when the settlor becomes entitled to it. Most cases in this category involve marriage settlements where the parties agree to settle property to which they have not yet become entitled.

The settlement will have been made by deed of covenant, to which the trustees will be party, and consideration may move from one or more parties. Claims by trustees on the covenant are considered below. The beneficiaries are usually the issue of the marriage, and in default of issue (typically) the next of kin of the wife. It is therefore unlikely that the intended *beneficiaries* will be party to the covenant, since at the time of the covenant they will not have been born. However, if they are within the marriage consideration, specific performance can be obtained to force the settlor to constitute the trust, or damages in lieu thereof under the Chancery Amendment Act 1858.

Pullan v *Koe*

[1913] 1 Ch 9, Chancery Division

Facts: A covenant was made in consideration of marriage that the husband and wife would settle the wife's after-acquired property of the value of £100 or upwards. The wife in breach of the covenant had not settled property which she had later received (the sum of £285), part of which had been used to purchase bonds. The breach took place in 1879, when the wife failed to settle the property. On the wife's death, in 1909, the beneficiaries under the covenant (who, as issue of the marriage, were within the marriage consideration) claimed a property interest in the bonds.

Held:

(a) The beneficiaries being within the marriage consideration could obtain specific performance of the covenant, to bring the bonds within the settlement.

(b) Since where specific performance is available, equity regards as done that which ought to be done, the money was bound by the trusts of the settlement as soon as it was received by the wife. Hence the beneficial interests were created at that time, and the issue could avoid any limitation problems that would otherwise have arisen from the fact that action was not commenced until thirty years after the breach.

SWINFEN EADY J: It was contended that the bonds never in fact became trust property...In my opinion as soon as the £285 was paid to the wife it became in equity bound by and subject to the trusts of the settlement. The trustees could have claimed that particular sum...and, if it had been invested and the investment could be traced, could have followed the money, and claimed the investment.

This point was dealt with by Jessel MR in *Smith* v *Lucas* (1881) ChD 531, 543, where he said: 'What is the effect of such a covenant in equity? It has been said that the effect in equity of the covenant of the wife, as far as she is concerned, is that it does not affect her personally, but that it binds the property: that is to say, it binds the property under the doctrine of equity that that is to be considered as done which ought to be done. That is in the nature of specific performance of the contract no doubt. If, therefore, this is a covenant to settle the future-acquired property of the wife, and nothing more is done by her, the covenant will bind the property.'

...

The property being thus bound, these bonds became trust property, and can be followed by the trustees and claimed from a volunteer.

■ QUESTIONS

1. Who was the trustee from 1879 to 1909? (Note that the wife never constituted the trust as she was required to do by the settlement.)
2. What were the terms of the trust from 1879 to 1909?
3. What was the nature of the beneficiaries' interest from 1879 to 1909? (See *Oughtred* v *IRC*, considered in Chapter 6.)

NOTES

1. The beneficiaries succeeded only because equity recognises marriage consideration (which is probably best regarded as an exception to the privity of contract doctrine), and therefore the remedy of specific performance was available to sue on the covenant. Because equity regards as done that which ought to be done, the beneficiaries should be regarded as having equitable interests from the moment the wife received the property (akin to the purchaser's interest under an estate contract): see *Oughtred* v *IRC*, considered in Chapter 6.
2. The beneficiaries, as issue of the marriage, were within the marriage consideration. More remote kin, however, not being within the consideration, would be volunteers in the eyes of equity unless they had provided other consideration of value.
3. The marriage must constitute consideration. Therefore the marriage consideration doctrine only covers covenants for future marriages.
4. The effect of the doctrine is that not only parties to the contract, but also the issue *of that marriage* can sue, although otherwise volunteers.
5. The doctrine is commonly regarded as a narrow and nowadays anomalous exception to the rule that equity will not assist a volunteer. It probably developed originally to impose upon the conscience of the husband (forcing him to settle) at a time (prior to the Married Women's Property Act 1882) when the wife had no economic independence, since otherwise nobody would have been able to ensure that the issue of the marriage would benefit from the settlement. (See W. A. Lee, 'Public Policy of *Re Cook's Settlement Trusts*' (1969) 85 *LQR* 213.)

Re Cook's ST

[1965] Ch 902, Chancery Division

Facts: Sir Francis Cook covenanted, for valuable consideration, with his father, Sir Herbert Cook, and the trustees of another settlement, that if Sir Francis sold any of the valuable pictures specified in a schedule to the agreement, during his lifetime, the proceeds would be held on the terms of the settlement. The beneficiaries under this (existing) settlement were various members of Sir Francis's family (but Sir Herbert was not himself one of the beneficiaries). Sir Francis married several times, and gave (or purported to give) one of the pictures to one of his subsequent wives. The subsequent wife wanted to sell it, and the trustees of the settlement sought directions from the court.

Held: The beneficiaries could not require the trustees of the settlement to enforce the covenant against Sir Francis. Buckley J rejected the argument that the beneficiaries were within the marriage consideration.

BUCKLEY J (on the issue of marriage consideration): It is an elementary general rule of law that a contract affects only the parties to it and their successors in title and that no one but a party or the successor in title to a party can sue or be sued upon it. There are, however, exceptions to this rule, some legal, some equitable and some statutory. If there is any such exception as Mr Brightman contends, it must be equitable.

It has long since been recognised that if marriage articles or a marriage settlement contain an executory agreement to settle property, equity will assist an intended beneficiary who is issue of the marriage to enforce the agreement. Such a beneficiary is described as being within the marriage consideration... This fiction by which a child of the marriage is treated as if he were a party to and as having given consideration for his parents' marriage settlement is no doubt associated with his intimate connection with the marriage which was in fact the consideration for it, and it is, as I understand the law, because he is treated as a party who has given consideration that equity will assist him to enforce any contract to settle property which that settlement may contain... On the other hand, an intended beneficiary who is not issue of the marriage is not within the marriage consideration, is not treated as though any consideration moved from him, and will not be assisted to enforce a contract to make a settlement. Thus the next-of-kin of the covenantor who are intended to take the property which is to be brought into settlement in the event of a failure of issue cannot enforce a covenant to settle (*Re d'Angibau* [(1880) 15 ChD 228]), nor can the children by a previous marriage of one of the parties, unless maybe, their interests are interwoven with those of the children of the marriage (see *Attorney-General* v *Jacobs-Smith* [1895] 2 QB 341), nor can the children of the marriage, if the settlement is a post-nuptial one, for in such a case, though there may be consideration as between the husband and the wife, that consideration would not be their marriage but consideration of some other kind to which their children would be strangers: *Green* v *Paterson* (1886) 32 ChD 95.

These authorities show that there is an equitable exception to the general rule of law which I have mentioned where the contract is made in consideration of marriage and the intended beneficiary who seeks to have the contract enforced is within the marriage consideration. They do not support the existence of any wider exception save perhaps in the case of a beneficiary who is not within the marriage consideration but whose interests under the intended trusts are closely interwoven with interests of others who are within that consideration. They do not support the view that any such exception exists in favour of a person who was not a party to the contract and is not to be treated as though he had been and who has given no consideration and is not to be treated as if he had given consideration. Where the obligation to settle property has been assumed voluntarily it is clear that no object of the intended trusts can enforce the obligation. Thus in *Re Kay's Settlement* [1939] Ch 329, a spinster made a voluntary settlement in favour of herself and her issue which contained a covenant to settle after-acquired property. She later married and had children who, as volunteers, were held to have no right to enforce the covenant...

NOTES
1. Although it is unusual for the beneficiaries actually to be party to the deed of covenant, where they are they can sue on that and do not need to rely on the intervention of equity.
2. However, whereas contracts under seal (or covenants by deed) are recognised as valid by the common law, even where no consideration moves from the promisee, they are not recognised as valid in equity. The result is that whereas the common law remedy of damages can be obtained, the equitable remedy of specific performance, which would require the settlor actually to constitute the trust, cannot. However, a beneficiary who is party to the deed can obtain substantial damages at common law (*Cannon* v *Hartley* [1949] Ch 213, Chancery Division).

Re Plumptre's MS, Underhill v *Plumptre*
[1910] 1 Ch 609, Chancery Division

Facts: The facts were similar to those in *Pullan* v *Koe*, except that the beneficiaries were not within the marriage consideration.

The case concerned a marriage settlement made in 1878, covering presently owned and after-acquired property. The settlement was of the conventional type, so that there having been a failure of issue, the intended beneficiaries were the next of kin of the wife. In 1884, the husband made a gift of stock to his wife. On the death of the wife, intestate, in 1909, the intended beneficiaries attempted to enforce the covenant.

Held: Eve J held that the gift of stock should have been settled on the terms of the settlement, so that the husband was in breach of covenant by making an outright gift in favour of his wife. He also held, however, that the next of kin could not enforce the covenant in equity because they were volunteers.

The result was that the stock represented by the original gift (the original stock having been sold and the money reinvested) went to the husband on the intestacy of his wife, and the next of kin could not enforce the covenant.

EVE J: ... [The next of kin] are not in my opinion *cestuis que trust* under the settlement, for nothing therein amounts to a declaration of trust, or to anything more than an executory contract on the part of the husband and wife; it is, so far as the next of kin are concerned,...a voluntary contract to create a trust as distinguished from a complete voluntary trust such as existed in the case of *Fletcher* v *Fletcher* [below], on which [the next of kin] so strongly relied. The collaterals are no parties to the contract; they are not within the marriage consideration and cannot be considered otherwise than as volunteers, and in these respects it makes no difference that the covenant sought to be enforced is the husband's and that the property sought to be brought within it comes from the wife. For each of the foregoing propositions authority is to be found in the judgment of the Court of Appeal in *Re D'Angibau* (1880) 15 ChD 228; and in the same judgment is to be found this further statement—that where, as in this case, the husband has acquired a legal title as administrator of his wife to property which was subject to the contract to settle, volunteers are not entitled to enforce against that legal title the contract to create a trust contained in the settlement.

Re Pryce, Neville v *Pryce*

[1917] 1 Ch 234, Chancery Division

Facts: The case concerned a marriage settlement covering after-acquired property. Consideration moved from both the husband and the wife, but none from the trustees. The main issue concerned the wife's after-acquired property, which ought to have been caught by the covenant. There were no issue of the marriage, and the beneficiaries in default of issue were volunteers. The trustees sought directions whether they should take proceedings to enforce the covenant.

Held: The trustees ought not to take any steps to enforce the covenant.

EVE J: The position of the wife's fund is...that her next of kin would be entitled to it on her death; but they are volunteers, and although the Court would probably compel fulfilment of the contract to settle at the instance of any persons within the marriage consideration (see *per* Cotton LJ in *In re D'Angibau* (1880) 15 ChD 228, 242, 246), and in their favour will treat the outstanding property as subjected to an enforceable trust (*Pullan* v *Koe* [1913] 1 Ch 9), 'volunteers have no right whatever to obtain specific performance of a mere covenant which has remained as a covenant and has never been performed': see per James LJ in *In re D'Angibau*. Nor could damages be awarded either in this Court, or, I apprehend, at law, where, since the Judicature Act, the same defences would be available to the defendant as would be raised in an action brought in this Court for specific performance or damages.

In these circumstances, seeing that the next of kin could neither maintain an action to enforce the covenant nor for damages for breach of it, and that the settlement is not a declaration of trust constituting the relationship of trustee and *cestui que trust* between the defendant and the next of kin, in which case effect could be given to the trusts even in favour of volunteers, but is a mere voluntary contract to create a trust, ought the Court now for the sole benefit of these volunteers to direct the trustees to take proceedings to enforce the defendant's covenant? I think it ought not; to do so would be to give the next of kin by indirect means relief they cannot obtain by any direct procedure, and would in effect be enforcing the settlement as against the defendant's legal right to payment and transfer from the trustees of the parents' marriage settlement. The circumstances are not unlike those which existed in the case of *In re D'Angibau*, and I think the position here is covered by the judgments of the Lords Justices in that case.

Accordingly, I declare that the trustees ought not to take any steps to compel the transfer or payment to them of the premises assured to the wife by the deed of 12 December 1904...

■ QUESTIONS

1. Is there anything in the above passage which suggests that the trustees could not obtain damages for breach of contract, assuming that they could obtain any by suing on the deed of covenant? Or do the words 'compel the transfer or payment' suggest specific performance?

2. If the trustees had been allowed to sue, could they have obtained specific performance of the covenant?

Re Kay's Settlement, Adbent v Macnab

[1939] Ch 329, Chancery Division

Facts: The case concerns a voluntary settlement by a spinster, who only married much later. There was no marriage consideration, and hence the children of the later marriage were volunteer beneficiaries.

Held: Trustees ought not to take any steps to enforce the covenant. *Re Pryce* was followed, but the trustees were also directed not to sue for damages.

SIMONDS J (after quoting the above passage from *Re Pryce*):...It is true that in those last words the learned judge [in *Re Pryce*] does not specifically refer to an action for damages, but it is clear that he has in mind directions both with regard to an action for specific performance and an action to recover damages at law—or, now, in this Court.

In those circumstances it appears to me that I must follow the learned judge's decision and I must direct the trustees not to take any steps either to compel performance of the covenant or to recover damages through [the settlor's] failure to implement it...

■ QUESTIONS

1. Do either of these two cases decide what would have been the result had trustees actually sued, in their personal capacity?

2. If the trustees had sued for damages in *Kay*, would they have been restricted to nominal damages on the basis that they had personally suffered no loss? (See the discussion in Goddard, in this subsection.)

Re Cook's ST

[1965] Ch 902, Chancery Division

Decision: The facts have already been set out (in this Subsection). Buckley J held that the volunteer beneficiaries could not compel the trustees to enforce the covenant on their behalf.

BUCKLEY J:... As an alternative argument, Mr Brightman formulated this proposition, which he admitted not to be directly supported by any authority, but he claimed to conflict with none: that where a covenantor has for consideration moving from a third party covenanted with trustees to make a settlement of property, the court will assist an intended beneficiary who is a volunteer to enforce the covenant if he is specially an object of the intended trust or (which Mr Brightman says is the same thing) is within the consideration of the deed. In formulating this proposition Mr Brightman bases himself on language used by Cotton LJ in *Re d'Angibau* (1880) 15 ChD 228, 242, CA and by Romer J in *Cannon v Hartley* [1949] Ch 213, 223. As an example of a case to which the proposition would apply, Mr Brightman supposes a father having two sons who enters into an agreement with his elder son and with trustees whereby the father agrees to convey an estate to his elder son absolutely in consideration of the son covenanting with his father and the trustees, or with the trustees alone, to settle an expectation on trusts for the benefit of the younger son. The younger son is a stranger to the transaction, but he is also the primary (and special) beneficiary of the intended settlement. A court of equity should, and would, Mr Brightman contends, assist the younger son to enforce his brother's covenant and should not permit the elder son to frustrate the purposes of the agreement by refusing to implement his covenant although he has secured the valuable consideration given for it. This submission is not without attraction, for it is not to be denied that, generally speaking, the conduct of a man who, having pledged his word for valuable consideration, takes the benefits he has so obtained and then fails to do his part, commands no admiration. I have, therefore, given careful consideration to this part of the argument to see whether the state of the law is such as might justify me (subject to the construction point) in dealing with the case on some such grounds.

There was no consideration for Sir Francis's covenant moving from the trustees; nor, of course, was there any consideration moving from Sir Francis's children [beneficiaries]...

[Buckley J found that there was consideration moving from Sir Herbert, and continued:]... Mr Brightman distinguishes [*Kay*] from the present on the grounds that in *Re Kay's Settlement* [1939] Ch 329 the settlement and covenant were entirely voluntary, whereas Sir Francis received consideration from Sir Herbert; but Sir Francis received no consideration from his own children. Why, it may be asked, should they be accorded had Sir Herbert given no consideration? As regards them the covenant must, in my judgment, be regarded as having been given voluntarily. A plaintiff is not entitled to claim equitable relief against another merely because that latter's conduct is unmeritorious. Conduct by A which is unconscientious in relation to B so as to entitle B to equitable relief may not be unconscientious in relation to C so that C will have no standing to claim relief notwithstanding that the conduct in question may affect C. The father in Mr Brightman's fictitious illustration could after performing his part of the contract release his elder son from the latter's covenant with him to make a settlement on the younger son, and the younger son could, I think, not complain. Only the covenant with the trustees would then remain, but this covenant would be a voluntary with the trustees having given no consideration. I can see no reason why in these circumstances the court should assist the younger son to enforce the covenant with the trustees. But the right of the younger son to require the trustees to enforce their covenant could not, I think, depend on whether the father had or had not released his covenant. Therefore, as it seems to me, on principle the younger son would not in any event have an equitable right to require the trustees to enforce their covenant. In other words, the arrangement between the father and his elder son would not have conferred any equitable right or interest upon his younger son.

I reach the conclusion that Mr Brightman's proposition is not well-founded. There is no authority to support it and *Green* v *Paterson* (1886) 32 ChD 95 is, I think, authority the other way. Accordingly, the second and third defendants are not, in my judgment, entitled to require the trustees to take proceedings to enforce the covenant even if it is capable of being constructed in a manner favourable to them.

NOTES

1. Unlike *Re Pryce* [1917] 1 Ch 234 and *Re Kay's Settlement* [1939] Ch 239, *Re Cook's ST* apparently does not decide that the trustees of the settlement had no remedy, or that they should not themselves enforce the covenant, but only that they could not be compelled to do so by the beneficiaries. However, the actual order was in similar terms to that in *Re Pryce/Re Kay*.

2. Clearly, a trustee who has provided no consideration cannot sue for specific performance, but he may have a claim for damages (at any rate, if he is allowed to use it). We need now to consider further the nature of the damages claim.

David Goddard, 'Equity, Volunteers and Ducks'
(1988) 52 *Conv* 19

Donald has a wealthy uncle, Scrooge, who in an uncharacteristic moment of generosity made a promise, under seal, to pay Donald £100,000 to hold on trust for Donald's nephews, Huey, Duey and Louie. Scrooge, regretting his impulsive behaviour, now refuses to pay.
...

It is true that Donald is not, in fact, one penny worse off...

The reason that Donald did not in fact suffer any loss from Scrooge's failure to pay, is that equity would have restrained him from dealing with the money (which he would have had legal title to) otherwise than for the benefit of his nephews. But in a court of common law, prior to the Judicature Act 1873, the fact that a court of equity would have interfered with Donald's use of the money would not have been considered relevant: he would have been legal owner of the £100,000 if the promise had been honoured, but he is not—what is this but a loss *at law* of £100,000?...

In considering Donald's claim, a court of common law would have considered neither what Donald would have been required to do with the money by a court of equity, nor what Donald might be required to do with the damages by a court of equity. Worse off at law, he would have been compensated at law. Nor does the Judicature Act affect this: it did not fuse law and equity (the 'fusion fallacy'), but simply conferred jurisdiction in both on all courts. Where rules conflict, equity prevails: but it is not a *conflict* where law assesses damages on the basis of legal title, ignoring equity. Equity will not award such damages, but neither will it prevent them being sought.

Thus, Donald could in any event bring an action for damages, and recover his (legal) loss of £100,000. Such a conclusion is, in fact, hardly surprising: it displays a remarkable degree of tunnel vision to suggest that trustees who make no profit from their trust, so cannot establish loss where the trust funds are diminished by a third party's breach of contract or covenant (or tort, for that matter), cannot therefore recover substantial common law damages. Once look beyond the narrow context of cases 'on' equity and volunteers, and examples of trustees being able to recover are legion. Many trustees—especially large charity trustees—enter into a variety of contracts: they would be amazed to learn that they could not recover damages for breach. In particular, the increasing number of unit trusts would appear far less attractive as investments if it were true that the trustees had no legal remedies against defaulting purchasers and sellers of shares!...

NOTE: Goddard goes on to argue that Donald would be required to hold the damages on trust for the nephews, and that the cases set out earlier in this subsection are wrong.

■ QUESTIONS

1. Where A contracts with B that B will provide a benefit for C, if B defaults A's damages are nominal. How does this situation differ from that?

2. Do you find convincing (or relevant) the arguments that trustees can sue on behalf of the trust and claim substantial damages (presumably to be held on trust), given that here the claim is brought by someone who is not yet trustee of the disputed property?

3. Let us suppose that Goddard is correct in his assertion that Donald can recover damages of £100,000. Do you think that he should be allowed to keep them for himself?

4. If, in 3, you thought that Donald should not be allowed to keep the £100,000, you may have come to the conclusion that equity would impose on his conscience and require him to hold them on trust (perhaps adopting a principle similar to that in *Neste Oy* v *Lloyds Bank plc, The Tiiskeri* [1983] 2 Lloyd's Rep 658, where in a rather different situation the recipient of money could not in all conscience hold on to it, and was required to hold it on constructive trust). But on trust for whom? If for the beneficiaries, then is equity not assisting a volunteer?

5. What do you think is meant by the principle that equity will not assist a volunteer? Does it mean anything more than that *specific performance can be obtained* only by beneficiaries under fully constituted trusts, persons within the marriage consideration, and others who have provided consideration recognised in equity?

D: Trusts of promises

There is no reason in principle why a covenant made to trustees to settle property should not of itself form the subject matter of a trust. If there is a fully constituted trust of the promise, the beneficiaries can enforce it directly, even if volunteers, or can require the trustees to sue. *Lloyd's* v *Harper* (1880) 16 Ch D 290 (see Chapter 2) suggests that substantial damages can be obtained by the trustee, which will be held on trust for the beneficiaries.

(i) Existing property

Fletcher v *Fletcher*

(1844) 4 Hare 67, Vice Chancellor

Facts: Ellis Fletcher covenanted with trustees by deed to pay £60,000 to his trustees, on trust for his illegitimate sons, who were outside the marriage consideration and were thus volunteers.

Held: The surviving son, Jacob, was able to compel the trustees to enforce the covenant on his behalf. Though the money was never settled, Wigram V-C held that the *covenant* was held on a fully constituted trust for Jacob. Thus Jacob could enforce it in his own right, despite being a volunteer. Substantial damages were recoverable, amounting to the promised £60,000.

NOTES
1. This case has often been criticised on its facts. The trustees knew nothing of the covenant until the death of the settlor, Ellis Fletcher, and then were unwilling to enforce it. Even so, Jacob could compel the trustees to sue. However, it could be argued that the ignorance of the trustees, or their unwillingness to accept the trust, should not be a bar to a finding that Fletcher meant to give his trustees a chose in action rather than the money itself, so creating a valid trust. The relevant intention is surely that of the settlor, not of the trustees. If a trustee is unwilling to act, 'equity will not allow a trust to fail for want of a trustee', and the courts will appoint another trustee.
2. In cases since *Fletcher* v *Fletcher*, the courts have demanded much more conclusive evidence that the settlor really did intend to settle the benefit of the covenant, before construing trusts of promises: e.g. *Re Schebsman* [1944] Ch 83, and see *Smith* (1982) 46 *Conv* 352. It is probable that were the same facts to arise today, no trust would be construed, and *Fletcher* v *Fletcher* would be considered wrongly decided in this regard.

Re Cavendish Browne

[1916] WN 341, Chancery Division

Facts: Catherine Cavendish Browne made a voluntary settlement containing a covenant to 'convey and transfer to the trustees all the property, both real and personal, to which she was absolutely entitled by virtue of the joint operation of the wills of' two named persons. She died without having settled property to which she was so entitled in trust.

Held: Younger J, 'without delivering a final judgment, held...that the trustees were entitled to recover [from Catherine's administrators] substantial damages for breach of the covenant..., and that the measure of damages was the value of the property which would have come into the hands of the trustees if the covenant had been duly performed'.

NOTE: Although it is not entirely clear, it appears that Catherine was *already* entitled to the property at the time that the contract was made (i.e. this is existing property).

(ii) After-acquired property

There is some authority that only covenants to settle existing property can be held on trust.

Re Cook's ST

[1965] Ch 902, Chancery Division

Decision: The facts are set out in Section 2: Modes of constitution, C: Covenants to settle. The beneficiaries also unsuccessfully argued that there was a fully constituted trust of the promise, Buckley J taking the view that only promises to settle existing property could be held on trust.

BUCKLEY J: Counsel for the second and third defendants have contended that on the true view of the facts there was an immediate settlement of the obligation created by the covenant, and not merely a covenant to settle something in the future. It was said, as Mr Monckton put it, that by the agreement Sir Herbert bought the rights arising under the covenant for the benefit of the *cestuis que trustent* under the settlement and that, the covenant being made in favour of the trustees, these rights became assets of the trust. He relied on *Fletcher v Fletcher* (1844) 4 Hare 67; *Williamson v Codrington* (1750) 1 Ves Sen 511 and *Re Cavendish Browne's ST* [1916] WN 341. I am not able to accept this argument. The covenant with which I am concerned did not, in my opinion, create a debt enforceable at law, that is to say, a property right, which, although to bear fruit only in the future and upon a contingency, was capable of being made the subject of an immediate trust, as was held to be the case in *Fletcher v Fletcher*. Nor is this covenant associated with property which was the subject of an immediate trust as in *Williamson v Codrington*. Nor did the covenant relate to property which then belonged to the covenantor, as in *Re Cavendish Browne's ST*. In contrast to all these cases, this covenant upon its true construction is, in my opinion, an executory contract to settle a particular fund or particular funds of money which at the date of the covenant did not exist and which might never come into existence. It is analogous to a covenant to settle an expectation or to settle after-acquired property. The case, in my judgment, involves the law of contract, not the law of trusts.

E: 'Accidental' constitution

Re Ralli's WT

[1964] 1 Ch 288, Chancery Division

Facts: Helen's father left the residue of his estate on trust for his wife for her life, thence to his two daughters, Helen and Irene. Helen, by her marriage settlement, covenanted with trustees of whom the claimant (Irene's husband) was one, to settle all her existing and after-acquired property on Irene's children.

On Helen's death, in 1956, the claimant, who was the sole surviving trustee under the marriage settlement, was also appointed a trustee under Helen's father's will, and hence obtained title to Helen's residuary estate under her father's will, on the death of Helen's mother (in 1961). He brought an action to determine whether he held the property on the terms of Helen's will, or on the trusts of Helen's marriage settlement.

Held: Buckley J held that the trust had become fully constituted by the accident of the trustee obtaining legal title to the property by other means (*Ratio* One), but he also held that, by entering into the marriage settlement, Helen could be regarded as declaring herself trustee of that property (which was existing and not future property) from that moment (*Ratio* Two).

BUCKLEY J (after interpreting clause 8 of the settlement): For these reasons I think that the plaintiff's submission in this respect is right and that Helen held, and since her death the defendants have held and now hold, her equitable interest in her share of the testator's residue on the trusts of the settlement. If this is so, the rule that equity will not assist a volunteer to enforce an executory contract to make a settlement has no application to this case, for the relevant trust has been completely declared by the defendants' predecessor in title and such declaration is binding on them and is enforceable by and for the benefit of the beneficiaries under the settlement, whether they are volunteers or not…

In my judgment the circumstance that the plaintiff holds the fund because he was appointed a trustee of the will is irrelevant. He is at law the owner of the fund, and the means by which he became so have no effect upon the quality of his legal ownership. The question is: For whom, if anyone, does he hold his fund in equity? In other words, who can successfully assert an equity against him disentitling him to stand upon his legal right? It seems to me to be indisputable that Helen, if she were alive, could not do so, for she has solemnly covenanted under seal to assign the fund to the plaintiff, and the defendants can stand in no better position. It is, of course, true that the object of the covenant was not that the plaintiff should retain the property for his own benefit, but that he should hold it on the trusts of the settlement. It is also true that, if it were necessary to enforce performance of the covenant, equity would not assist the beneficiaries under the settlement, because they are mere volunteers; and that for the same reason the plaintiff, as trustee of the settlement, would not be bound to enforce the covenant and would not be constrained by the court to do so, and indeed, it seems, might be constrained by the court not to do so. As matters stand, however, there is no occasion to invoke the assistance of equity to enforce performance of the covenant. It is for the defendants to invoke the assistance of equity to make good their claim to the fund. To do so successfully they must show that the plaintiff cannot conscientiously withhold it from them. When they seek to do this, he can point to the covenant which, in my judgment, relieves him from any fiduciary obligation he would otherwise owe to the defendants as Helen's representatives. In so doing the plaintiff is not seeking to enforce an equitable remedy against the defendants on behalf of persons who could not enforce such a remedy themselves: he is relying upon the combined effect of his legal ownership of the fund and his rights under the covenant. That an action on the covenant might be statute-barred is irrelevant, for there is no occasion for such an action.

NOTES

1. In this case, the trust was constituted by Helen's entering into the contract to settle, but in general there must be a difference between entering into a contract, which is in principle revocable (should both parties to the contract so agree) and declaring oneself trustee, which is not. In *Re Ralli's*, the case turned upon the precise wording of clause 8 of the covenant, which (in Buckley J's view) indicated an irrevocable intention on Helen's part:

   … it being the intention of these presents and of the said parties hereto that by virtue and under the operation of the said covenants all the property comprised within the terms of such covenants shall become subject in equity to the settlement hereby covenanted to be made thereof.

   Therefore this part of the case should not be taken as being of general application.

2. In *Re Ralli's*, the claimant was party to the covenant in Helen's marriage settlement, but on the principles discussed in *Re Cook*, above, may not have been able to enforce that covenant. By his second line of reasoning in *Re Ralli's*, Buckley J decides that by obtaining the trust property by other means, he is relieved of the necessity of enforcing the covenant, since he already has legal title to the trust property. Helen's intention is irrelevant to this question.

3. The logic of the second line of reasoning in *Re Ralli's* extends to all cases where the trustee acquires legal title, and so long as he does so the method of acquisition is irrelevant. Thus, the principle ought still to apply if, for example, he comes by his legal title not as his executor, but as the settlor's trustee in bankruptcy, or even as a judgment creditor, or where the settlor has mortgaged his property to the trustee, and the trustee forecloses. However, it seems likely that transfer of legal title is required, and not merely physical possession.

4. Buckley J reasoned by analogy from *Strong* v *Bird* (1874) LR 18 Eq 315, where a gift was completed by the donor (testator) appointing the donee executor under his will. This is a very different situation from *Strong* v *Bird*, however, since under the rule in *Strong* v *Bird* the appointment of the executor is a voluntary act of the donor, and completion of the gift may be easily inferred from that voluntary act, whereas in *Re Ralli's* the claimant held the after-acquired capacity by a route that was independent of the wishes of the settlor under the covenant. Indeed, *Re Ralli's* would presumably allow constitution even against the wishes of the settlor, and even where the covenant was entirely voluntary. Buckley J also cited authority (*Re James* [1935] Ch 449) for the proposition that the rule in *Strong* v *Bird* operates however the donee obtained the donor's property, but this case was doubted in *Re Gonin* [1979] Ch 16. Even if *Re James* is correct, there is an additional requirement under the rule in *Strong* v *Bird* that the donor must have shown an

intention to give *inter vivos* until his death, so the *Strong* v *Bird* analogies really do not support the conclusion in *Re Ralli's*.

5. The rule in *Strong* v *Bird* could presumably be relevant if transfer of *legal* title to an executor who was also trustee under a voluntary settlement was perfected by the rule (e.g. if in a case such as *Re Stewart* [1908] 2 Ch 251, the executor was also trustee).

F: *Donatio mortis causa*

The doctrine of *donatio mortis causa* (a gift made in contemplation of death) is often cited as an exception to the maxim 'equity will not assist a volunteer' to perfect an imperfect gift. The doctrine was formulated by Lord Russell of Killowen CJ in *Cain* v *Moon* [1896] 2 QB 283 (at 286) as follows:

For an effectual *donatio mortis causa* three things must combine: first, the gift or donation must have been in contemplation, though not necessarily in expectation of death; secondly, there must have been delivery to the donee of the subject matter of the gift; and thirdly, the gift must be made under such circumstances as to show that the thing is to revert to the donor in case he should recover.

Sen v Headley
1991] 2 All ER 636, Court of Appeal

Facts: Mrs S had lived with a man for several years. On his death bed, he gave her the keys to a box containing the deeds to his house and told her that the house was hers.

Held: This was a valid *donatio mortis causa*. The court rejected the orthodox assumption that *donatio mortis causa* could not apply to gifts of land.

NOURSE LJ: ... There have been several judicial statements of what, in general terms, is necessary to constitute a *donatio mortis causa*: see *Cain* v *Moon* [1896] 2 QB 283 at 285 (Lord Russell of Killowen CJ), *Re Craven's Estate, Lloyds Bank Ltd* v *Cockburn* [1937] 3 All ER 33 (Farwell J) and *Delgoffe* v *Fader* [1939] 3 All ER 682 at 685 (Luxmoore LJ). Regard must also be had to what was said by this court in *Birch* v *Treasury Solicitor* [1950] 2 All ER 1198 the most authoritative of the modern decisions. If the question whether the subject matter is capable of passing by way of *donatio mortis causa* is put on one side, the three general requirements for such a gift may be stated very much as they are stated in *Snell's Equity* (29th edn, 1990) pp. 380–383. First, the gift must be made in contemplation, although not necessarily in expectation, of impending death. Secondly, the gift must be made upon the condition that it is to be absolute and perfected only on the donor's death, being revocable until that event occurs and ineffective if it does not. Thirdly, there must be a delivery of the subject matter of the gift, or the essential *indicia* of title thereto, which amounts to a parting with dominion and not mere physical possession over the subject matter of the gift...

We have traced the need for there to be a parting with dominion over the subject-matter of the gift, i.e. with the ability to control it, to the judgment of Lord Kenyon CJ in *Hawkings* v *Blewitt* (1798) 2 Esp 662 at 663, where he said:

In the case of a donatio mortis causa possession must be immediately given. That has been done here; a delivery has taken place; but it is also necessary that by parting with the possession, the deceased should also part with the dominion over it. That has not been done here.

A similar view was taken in *Reddel* v *Dobree* (1839) 10 Sim 244 and *Re Johnson* (1905) 92 LT 357. In each of those three cases the alleged donor delivered a locked box to the alleged donee and either retained or took back the key to it; in *Reddel* v *Dobree* he also reserved and exercised a right to take back the box. In each of them it was held that the alleged donor had retained dominion over the box and that there had been no *donatio mortis causa*.

It appears therefore that the need for there to be a parting with dominion was first identified in cases where the subject matter of the gift was a locked box and its contents. In *Birch* v *Treasury Solicitor*, as we have seen, a similar need was recognised where the subject matter of the gift was a chose in action. Without in any way questioning that need, we think it appropriate to observe that a parting with dominion over an intangible thing such as a chose in action is necessarily different from a parting with dominion over a tangible thing such as a locked box and its contents. We think that in the former case a parting with dominion over the essential *indicia* of title will *ex hypothesi* usually be enough...

We do not suggest that there might never be a state of facts where there was a parting with dominion over the essential *indicia* of title to a chose in action but nevertheless a retention of dominion over the chose itself. And it is just possible to conceive of someone, who, in contemplation of impending death, had parted with dominion over the title deeds of his house to an alleged donee, nevertheless granting a tenancy of it to a third party; for which purpose proof of the title to the freehold by production of the deeds is not usually necessary. On facts such as those there might be a case for saying that the alleged donor had not parted with dominion over the house. But nothing comparable happened here. It is true that in the eyes of the law Mr Hewett, by keeping his own set of keys to the house, retained possession of it. But the benefits which thereby accrued to him were wholly theoretical. He uttered the words of gift, without reservation, two days after his readmission to hospital, when he knew that he did not have long to live and when there could have been no practical possibility of his ever returning home. He had parted with dominion over the title deeds. Mrs Sen had her own set of keys to the house and was in effective control of it. In all the circumstances of the case, we do not believe that the law requires us to hold that Mr Hewett did not part with dominion over the house. We hold that he did.

Having now decided that the third of the general requirements for a *donatio mortis causa* was satisfied in this case, we come to the more general question whether land is capable of passing by way of such a gift...

Let it be agreed that the doctrine is anomalous, anomalies do not justify anomalous exceptions. If due account is taken of the present state of the law in regard to mortgages and choses in action, it is apparent that to make a distinction in the case of land would be to make just such an exception. A *donatio mortis causa* of land is neither more nor less anomalous than any other. Every such gift is a circumvention of the Wills Act 1837. Why should the additional statutory formalities for the creation and transmission of interests in land be regarded as some larger obstacle? The only step which has to be taken is to extend the application of the implied or constructive trust arising on the donor's death from the conditional to the absolute estate. Admittedly that is a step which the House of Lords would not have taken in *Duffield* v *Elwes* and, if the point had been a subject of decision, we would have loyally followed it in this court. But we cannot decide a case in 1991 as the House of Lords would have decided it, but did not decide it, in 1827. We must decide it according to the law as it stands today...

■ **SUMMATIVE QUESTION**

**online
resource
centre**

Explain why an appeal against the decision of the Court of Appeal in *Pennington* v *Waine* would be likely to succeed on grounds of precedent, principle, and policy.

FURTHER READING

Baker, J. H., 'Land as a *Donatio Mortis Causa*' (1993) 109 *LQR* 19.

Barton, J. L., 'Trusts and Covenants' (1975) 91 *LQR* 236.

Borkowski, A., *Deathbed Gifts: The Law of* Donatio Mortis Causa (Oxford: Blackstone Press, 1999).

Borkowski, A. and Du Plessis, P., *Textbook on Roman Law*, 4th edn (Oxford: Oxford University Press, 2010).

Garton, J., 'The Role of the Trust Mechanism in the Rule in *Re Rose*' (2003) 67 *Conv* 364.

Hopkins, J., 'Constitution of Trusts—A Novel Point' (2001) 60(3) *CLJ* 483.

Hyland, R., *Gifts: A Study in Comparative Law* (Oxford: OUP, 2009).

Jaconelli, J., 'Problems in the Rule in *Strong* v *Bird*' (2006) 70 *Conv* 432.

Rickett, C., 'Completely Constituting an *Inter Vivos* Trust: Property Rules' (2001) 65 *Conv* 515.

Tjio, H. and Yeo, T. M., '*Re Rose* Revisited: The Shorn Lamb's Equity' [2002] *LMCLQ* 296.

5

Resulting Trusts: Ineffective Disposition of Benefit

KEY AIMS

To examine the theoretical basis of the resulting trust and, in particular, the competition between the theory that resulting trusts preserve the transferor's property rights and the theory that resulting trusts reverse the transferee's unjust enrichment. To identify orthodox categories of resulting trust. To identify the circumstances in which a resulting trust arises in response to the presumed intention of the transferor, and the circumstances in which that presumption may be rebutted.

NB: The decision of the House of Lords in *Stack v Dowden* [2007] UKHL 17, [2007] 2 AC 432 has serious implications for the law of resulting trusts, but in the hope and expectation that the decision will be limited to cases involving trusts of land held in the joint names of romantic cohabitants, discussion of that case has been left to the section on Informal Trusts of Land in Chapter 8.

SECTION 1: INTRODUCTION

The word 'resulting' is derived from *saltare*, the Latin verb meaning 'to jump'. A resulting trust arises when an attempt to transfer the beneficial interest in an asset fails for some (usually unforeseen) reason, so that the benefit notionally 'jumps back' to the person who made the attempted transfer. A simple example is where someone pays money into the bank account of a company that no longer exists (see the facts of the unreported case *Omojole v HSBC Bank Plc* (1 October 2012)). The money cannot belong to the company. This leaves two possibilities. Either the money belongs to nobody, in which case it will pass to the Crown as *'bona vacantia'* ('ownerless assets') or it will return to the original owner under a resulting trust. Where the latter is possible it will be preferred (*bona vacantia* is subject to equity). One way to imagine the process is to picture the benefit of the asset as a bouncy ball that is thrown to a person who does not exist. The law is most reluctant for the benefit to be deemed ownerless and pass into Crown ownership, so it erects a barrier to keep the wealth within private hands. The bouncy ball of benefit having missed the intended donee hits the barrier raised to prevent bona vacantia and bounces straight back to the person who put the benefit in to begin with.

Vandervell v *IRC*

[1966] Ch 261

Facts: In 1958, the taxpayer, who controlled a very successful private company, decided to give £150,000 to the Royal College of Surgeons to found a chair of pharmacology. The company's issued ordinary share capital was: (i) 500,000 ordinary shares, substantially all of which were held by the taxpayer; (ii) 100,000 'A' ordinary shares held by a bank as nominee for the taxpayer; and (iii) 2,600,000 'B' ordinary shares, of which the taxpayer held 546,692 and the remaining 2,053,308 were held by VT Ltd as trustees of a family settlement. Only the first class of shares carried voting rights. In order to achieve his purpose, the taxpayer, through R his financial adviser, suggested giving to the college the 100,000 'A' ordinary shares, intending to pass to the college both the legal and beneficial interest in them. Subsequently, on the advice of R and by way of second thoughts in order to avoid any future difficulties if the company were to be converted into a public company, the taxpayer acceded to R's suggestion that the college should give an option to VT Ltd to purchase the shares for £5,000 within five years. In November 1958, R delivered to the college the transfer by the bank of the 'A' ordinary shares and an option deed. The college sealed these deeds and was registered as owner of the shares. Dividends on the 'A' shares, amounting to £145,000 less tax at the standard rate, were paid to the college. On 11 October 1961, VT Ltd exercised the option. The £5,000 was paid to the college. The taxpayer was assessed to surtax on the basis that the dividends in the years 1958–9 and 1959–60 which, with the £5,000 on the exercise of the option, made up the gift to the college, were his income or were required to be treated as his income under Income Tax Act 1952, s.415. It was not disputed that there was a settlement within the meaning of s.411(2) of that Act. The taxpayer contended that he had, by the settlement within s.411(2), divested himself absolutely of the property and thus came within the exception provided by s.415(1)(d) and (2).

Held: (i) (Lord Reid and Lord Donovan dissenting) The option to purchase the 'A' shares was vested in the trustee company in 1958, either (*per* Lord Upjohn and Lord Pearce) as a matter of inference from the primary facts on such trusts as might be declared subsequently, or (*per* Lord Wilberforce) as a matter of interpretation of the evidence on trusts which were undefined, and on either basis the consequence in law was that the option was held on a resulting trust for the taxpayer—accordingly the taxpayer had failed to divest himself absolutely of the property which was the source of the dividends paid to the college, and had not brought himself within the exempting provisions of Income Tax Act 1952, s.415(1)(d), (2), with the consequence that the assessments should stand; (ii) since a transfer of the 'A' shares had been executed by the bank, which was nominee for the taxpayer, and had been delivered on the taxpayer's behalf to the college, which became registered as owners of the shares, there had been no need for a separate transfer of the taxpayer's equitable interest in the 'A' shares and Law of Property Act 1925, s.53(1)(c) had no application.

PLOWMAN J (at first instance): a man does not cease to own property simply by saying 'I don't want it.' If he tries to give it away the question must always be, has he succeeded in doing so or not?

LORD UPJOHN: ... The question is whether, notwithstanding the plainly expressed intention of the taxpayer by himself or his agents, the absence of writing prevented any equitable or beneficial interest in the shares passing to the college so that contrary to his wishes and understanding they remained bare trustees for him. This depends entirely on the true construction of s. 53(1)(c) of the Law of Property Act 1925, which the Crown maintain makes writing necessary to pass the beneficial interest ...

... the object of the section, as was the object of the old Statute of Frauds, is to prevent hidden oral transactions in equitable interests in fraud of those truly entitled, and making it difficult, if not impossible, for the trustees to ascertain who are in truth his beneficiaries. When the beneficial owner, however, owns the whole beneficial estate and is in a position to give directions to his bare trustee with regard to the legal as well as the equitable estate there can be no possible ground for invoking the section where the beneficial owner wants to deal with the legal estate as well as the equitable estate.

I cannot agree with Diplock LJ that prima facie a transfer of the legal estate carries with it the absolute beneficial interest in the property transferred; this plainly is not so, e.g. the transfer may be on a change of trustee; it is a matter of intention in each case. If, however, the intention of the beneficial owner in directing the trustee to transfer the legal estate to X is that X should be the beneficial owner, I can see no reason for any further document or further words in the document assigning the legal estate also expressly transferring the beneficial interest; the greater includes the less. X may be wise to secure some evidence that the beneficial owner intended him to take the beneficial interest in case his beneficial title is challenged at a later date but it certainly cannot, in my opinion, be a statutory requirement that to effect its passing there must be some writing under s. 53(1)(c) ...

LORD WILBERFORCE: ... The Court of Appeal, starting from the fact that the trustee company took the option as a volunteer, thought that this was a case where the presumption of a resulting trust arose and was not displaced. For my part, I prefer a slightly different and simpler approach. The transaction has been investigated on the evidence of the settlor and his agent and the facts have been found. There is no need, or room, as I see it, to invoke a presumption. The conclusion, on the facts found, is simply that the option was vested in the trustee company as a trustee on trusts, not defined at the time, possibly to be defined later. But the equitable, or beneficial interest, cannot remain in the air: the consequence in law must be that it remains in the settlor. There is no need to consider some of the more refined intellectualities of the doctrine of resulting trust, nor to speculate whether, in possible circumstances, the shares might be applicable for Mr Vandervell's benefit: he had, as the direct result of the option and of the failure to place the beneficial interest in it securely away from him, not divested himself absolutely of the shares which it controlled.

Air Jamaica Ltd v Charlton

[1999] 1 WLR 1399, Privy Council

Facts: The pension scheme of employees of Air Jamaica was discontinued in 1994 when the company was privatised. Defined benefits were paid out under the terms of the scheme, but there remained a surplus of $400m. The claimants, who were members of the discontinued pension scheme, claimed to be entitled to the surplus under the rules of the scheme. The company purported to amend the pension scheme so as to acquire the surplus itself and had to be restrained by means of an interlocutory injunction from implementing its intended amendments.

Held: The amendments were disallowed on three grounds. First, that the power to amend the plan was void for perpetuity. Secondly, that the amendments had been made in bad faith, and, thirdly, that they infringed the trust deed. The scheme had been an ineffective attempt by the company to dispose of the entirety of its beneficial interest in the fund. The consequence was that it was entitled to recover half the surplus under a resulting trust. The members were also entitled to recover the half representing their contributions. The resulting trust operates outside ('dehors') the flawed scheme.

LORD MILLETT: Prima facie the surplus is held on a resulting trust for those who provided it. This sometimes creates a problem of some perplexity. In the present case, however, it does not. Contributions were payable by the members with matching contributions by the company. In the absence of any evidence that this is not what happened in practice, the surplus must be treated as provided as to one half by the company and as to one half by the members.

Westdeutsche v *Islington BC*

[1996] AC 669, House of Lords

Facts: In a quest to raise money to avoid the effects of rate-capping, Islington Borough Council entered into a swap agreement, the purpose of which was to advance money to the local authority in such a way as not to attract legislative controls, with Westdeutsche Landesbank Girozentrale (a bank). Under the swap agreement, Islington was the floating ratepayer and Westdeutsche the fixed ratepayer on a notional capital sum of £25 million, and Westdeutsche advanced £2.5 million to Islington in return for a reduction in the fixed-rate payment (the rate was fixed at 7.5 per cent, when market rates were approximately 9.5 per cent).

The effect of the £2.5 million advance was to allow Islington to obtain an up-front payment uninhibited (or so it was thought) by the relevant statutory controls. The reduction (compared with normal market rates) in the fixed interest rate ensured that the local authority, as floating ratepayer, at market rates, would always be paying the bank net under the swap agreement, after the initial advance. This was effectively how the loan and interest were to be repaid.

After the initial advance was made to the local authority, the local authority mixed the money with its own in a bank account which became overdrawn soon afterwards. The effect of paying the money into a mixed account was that the bank necessarily could no longer assert legal title to the money, since the common law will not trace into mixed bank accounts (see, further, Chapter 14). When the account became overdrawn, it was no longer possible to identify, even in equity, any of the money which had been paid into it.

Both parties entered into the swap agreement on the basis that it constituted an enforceable contract, but in *Hazell* v *Hammersmith and Fulham London BC* [1990] 2 QB 697 the Divisional Court (whose decision was eventually upheld in the House of Lords: [1992] 2 AC 1) held such agreements to be ultra vires. The effect of that decision was to render the agreement between Westdeutsche and Islington void *ab initio*.

Hazell was not decided until after the account into which the advance had been paid had become overdrawn. By the time of this decision, about half the capital sum had been repaid under the swap agreement by the local authority, but about half remained outstanding.

The bank claimed back the remainder of its advance, and also claimed compound interest on the outstanding sum, and succeeded both at first instance and in the Court of Appeal (both reported at [1994] 4 All ER 890). In the House of Lords, the local authority accepted that it came under an obligation to repay Westdeutsche not only the capital sum advanced, but also simple interest (simple interest being provided for in limited circumstances by statute). However, it appealed against the bank's claim for compound interest, on the grounds that there is no power to award compound interest at common law, that the equitable jurisdiction to do so is confined to fiduciary relationships, and that there was no fiduciary relationship here.

The bank claimed that it was entitled to compound interest whether or not the local authority held the money in a fiduciary capacity, but also claimed that the local authority was a resulting trustee, and hence was fiduciary for the bank.

Held: The bank was not entitled to compound interest; compound interest would be payable only if the local authority took the money in a fiduciary capacity, and this was not the case; in particular, the local authority was not a resulting trustee.

The bank's resulting trust argument: The bank's unsuccessful argument, in essence, was that the payment of the £2.5 million to the local authority was made on the assumption that the swap agreement was valid. When it was retrospectively declared void in *Hazell* v *Hammersmith and Fulham London BC* [1990] 2 QB 697, the effect was that neither legal nor equitable title passed to the local authority on receipt. However, when the local authority paid the money into a mixed account, the bank lost its legal title to the local authority. It retained its equitable title, however, with which it had never intended to part. From that moment, therefore, the local authority held the money on resulting trust for the bank.

There was thus a separation of legal and equitable title, legal title being vested in the local authority and equitable title being retained by the bank. It was necessary for the bank to argue further that from the separation of legal and equitable title between local authority and bank, it necessarily followed that the local authority was trustee for the bank; whenever there is a separation of legal and equitable titles there is a trust, and since all trusts give rise to fiduciary relationships, it therefore followed that the local authority must have been trustee for the bank. The bank was therefore entitled to compound interest in equity.

LORD BROWNE-WILKINSON (on whether there was a trust):

The argument for the bank in outline

The bank submitted that, since the contract was void, title did not pass at the date of payment either at law or in equity. The legal title of the bank was extinguished as soon as the money was paid into the mixed account, whereupon the legal title became vested in the local authority. But, it was argued, this did not affect the equitable interest, which remained vested in the bank ('the retention of title point'). It was submitted that whenever the legal interest in property is vested in one person and the equitable interest in another, the owner of the legal interest holds it on trust for the owner of the equitable title: 'the separation of the legal from the equitable interest necessarily imports a trust'. For this latter proposition ('the separation of title point') the bank, of course, relies on *Sinclair v Brougham* [1914] AC 398 and *Chase Manhattan Bank NA v Israel-British Bank (London) Ltd* [1981] Ch 105. [Both these cases are further considered in Chapter 14.]

...

It is to be noted that the bank did not found any argument on the basis that the local authority was liable to repay either as a constructive trustee or under the *in personam* liability of the wrongful recipient of the estate of a deceased person established by *In re Diplock, Diplock v Wintle* [1948] Ch 465. I therefore do not further consider those points.

The breadth of the submission

Although the actual question in issue on the appeal is a narrow one, on the arguments presented it is necessary to consider fundamental principles of trust law. Does the recipient of money under a contract subsequently found to be void for mistake or as being ultra vires hold the moneys received on trust even where he had no knowledge at any relevant time that the contract was void? If he does hold on trust, such trust must arise at the date of receipt or, at the latest, at the date the legal title of the payer is extinguished by mixing moneys in a bank account: in the present case it does not matter at which of those dates the legal title was extinguished. If there is a trust two consequences follow:

(a) the recipient will be personally liable, regardless of fault, for any subsequent payment away of the moneys to third parties even though, at the date of such payment, the 'trustee' was still ignorant of the existence of any trust: see Burrows *Swaps and the Friction between Common Law and Equity* [1995] RLR 15;

(b) as from the date of the establishment of the trust (i.e., receipt or mixing of the moneys by the 'trustee') the original payer will have an equitable proprietary interest in the moneys so long as they are traceable into whomsoever's hands they come other than a purchaser for value of the legal interest without notice.

Therefore, although in the present case the only question directly in issue is the personal liability of the local authority as a trustee, it is not possible to hold the local authority liable without imposing a trust which, in other cases, will create property rights affecting third parties because moneys received under a void contract are 'trust property'.

The practical consequences of the bank's argument

Before considering the legal merits of the submission, it is important to appreciate the practical consequences which ensue if the bank's arguments are correct. Those who suggest that a resulting trust should arise in these circumstances accept that the creation of an equitable proprietary interest under the trust can have unfortunate, and adverse, effects if the original recipient of the moneys becomes insolvent: the moneys, if traceable in the hands of the recipient, are trust moneys and not available for the creditors of the recipient. However, the creation of an equitable proprietary interest in moneys received under a void contract is capable of having adverse effects quite apart from insolvency. The proprietary interest under the unknown trust will, quite apart from insolvency, be enforceable against any recipient of the property other than the purchaser for value of a legal interest without notice.

Take the following example. T (the transferor) has entered into a commercial contract with R1 (the first recipient). Both parties believe the contract to be valid but it is in fact void. Pursuant to that contract:

  (i)   T pays £1m to R1 who pays it into a mixed bank account;
  (ii) T transfers 100 shares in X company to R1, who is registered as a shareholder. Thereafter R1 deals with the money and shares as follows:
  (iii) R1 pays £50,000 out of the mixed account to R2 otherwise than for value; R2 then becomes insolvent, having trade creditors who have paid for goods not delivered at the time of the insolvency.
  (iv) R1 charges the shares in X company to R3 by way of equitable security for a loan from R3.

If the bank's arguments are correct, R1 holds the £1m on trust for T once the money has become mixed in R1's bank account. Similarly R1 becomes the legal owner of the shares in X company as from the date of his registration as a shareholder but holds such shares on a resulting trust for T. T therefore has an equitable proprietary interest in the moneys in the mixed account and in the shares.

T's equitable interest will enjoy absolute priority as against the creditors in the insolvency of R2 (who was not a purchaser for value) provided that the £50,000 can be traced in the assets of R2 at the date of its insolvency. Moreover, if the separation of title argument is correct, since the equitable interest is in T and the legal interest is vested in R2, R2 also holds as trustee for T. In tracing the £50,000 in the bank account of R2, R2 as trustee will be treated as having drawn out his own moneys first, thereby benefiting T at the expense of the secured and unsecured creditors of R2. Therefore in practice one may well reach the position where the moneys in the bank account of R2 in reality reflect the price paid by creditors for goods not delivered by R2: yet, under the tracing rules, those moneys are to be treated as belonging in equity to T.

So far as the shares in the X company are concerned, T can trace his equitable interest into the shares and will take in priority to R3, whose equitable charge to secure his loan even though granted for value will *pro tanto* be defeated.

All this will have occurred when no one was aware, or could have been aware, of the supposed trust because no one knew that the contract was void.

I can see no moral or legal justification for giving such priority to the right of T to obtain restitution over third parties who have themselves not been enriched, in any real sense, at T's expense and indeed have had no dealings with T. T paid over his money and transferred the shares under a supposed valid contract. If the contract had been valid, he would have had purely personal rights against R1. Why should he be better off because the contract is void?

My Lords, wise judges have often warned against the wholesale importation into commercial law of equitable principles inconsistent with the certainty and speed which are essential requirements for the orderly conduct of business affairs: see *Barnes* v *Addy* (1874) LR 9 Ch App 244, 251 and 255; *Scandinavian Trading Tanker Co. AB* v *Flota Petrolera Ecuatoriana* [1983] 2 AC 694, 703–704. If the bank's arguments are correct, a businessman who has entered into transactions relating to or dependent upon property rights could find that assets which apparently belong to one person in fact belong to another; that there are 'off balance sheet' liabilities of which he cannot be aware; that these property rights and liabilities arise from circumstances unknown not only to himself but also to anyone else who has been involved in the transactions. A new area of unmanageable risk will be introduced into commercial dealings. If the due application of equitable principles forced a conclusion leading to these results, your Lordships would be presented with a formidable task in reconciling legal principle with commercial common sense. But in my judgment no such conflict occurs. The resulting trust for which the bank contends is inconsistent not only with the law as it stands but with any principled development of it.

The relevant principles of trust law

(i) Equity operates on the conscience of the owner of the legal interest. In the case of a trust, the conscience of the legal owner requires him to carry out the purposes for which the property was vested in him (express or implied trust) or which the law imposes on him by reason of his unconscionable conduct (constructive trust).

(ii) Since the equitable jurisdiction to enforce trusts depends upon the conscience of the holder of the legal interest being affected, he cannot be a trustee of the property if and so long as he is ignorant of the facts alleged to affect his conscience, i.e. until he is aware that he is intended to hold the property for the benefit of others in the case of an express or implied trust, or, in the case of a constructive trust, of the factors which are alleged to affect his conscience.

(iii) In order to establish a trust there must be identifiable trust property. The only apparent exception to this rule is a constructive trust imposed on a person who dishonestly assists in a breach of trust who may come under fiduciary duties even if he does not receive identifiable trust property.

(iv) Once a trust is established, as from the date of its establishment the beneficiary has, in equity, a proprietary interest in the trust property, which proprietary interest will be enforceable in equity against any subsequent holder of the property (whether the original property or substituted property into which it can be traced) other than a purchaser for value of the legal interest without notice.

These propositions are fundamental to the law of trusts and I would have thought uncontroversial. However, proposition (ii) may call for some expansion. There are cases where property has been put into the name of X without X's knowledge but in circumstances where no gift to X was intended. It has been held that such property is recoverable under a resulting trust ... These cases are explicable on the ground that, by the time action was brought, X or his successors in title have become aware of the facts which gave rise to a resulting trust; his conscience was affected as from the time of such discovery and thereafter he held on a resulting trust under which the property was recovered from him. There is, so far as I am aware, no authority which decides that X was a trustee, and therefore accountable for his deeds, at any time before he was aware of the circumstances which gave rise to a resulting trust.

Those basic principles are inconsistent with the case being advanced by the bank. The latest time at which there was any possibility of identifying the 'trust property' was the date on which the moneys in the mixed bank account of the local authority ceased to be traceable when the local authority's account went into overdraft in June 1987. At that date, the local authority had no knowledge of the invalidity of the contract but regarded the moneys as its own to spend as it thought fit. There was therefore never a time at which both (a) there was defined trust property and (b) the conscience of the local authority in relation to such defined trust property was affected. The basic requirements of a trust were never satisfied.

I turn then to consider the bank's arguments in detail. They were based primarily on principle rather than on authority. I will deal first with the bank's argument from principle and then turn to the main authorities relied upon by the bank, *Sinclair* v *Brougham* [1914] AC 398 and *Chase Manhattan Bank NA* v *Israel-British Bank (London) Ltd* [1981] Ch 105.

The retention of title point

It is said that, since the bank only intended to part with its beneficial ownership of the moneys in performance of a valid contract, neither the legal nor the equitable title passed to the local authority at the date of payment. The legal title vested in the local authority by operation of law when the moneys became mixed in the bank account but, it is said, the bank 'retained' its equitable title.

I think this argument is fallacious. A person solely entitled to the full beneficial ownership of money or property, both at law and in equity, does not enjoy an equitable interest in that property. The legal title carries with it all rights. Unless and until there is a separation of the legal and equitable estates, there is no separate equitable title. Therefore to talk about the bank 'retaining' its equitable interest is meaningless. The only question is whether the circumstances under which the money was paid were such as, in equity, to impose a trust on the local authority. If so, an equitable interest arose for the first time under that trust.

...

The separation of title point

[The extract of this part of His Lordship's speech can be found in Chapter 1.]

Resulting trust

This is not a case where the bank had any equitable interest which pre-dated receipt by the local authority of the upfront payment. Therefore, in order to show that the local authority became a trustee, the bank must demonstrate circumstances which raised a trust for the first time either at the date on which the local authority received the money or at the date on which payment into the mixed account was made. Counsel for the bank specifically disavowed any claim based on a constructive trust. This was plainly right because the local authority had no relevant knowledge sufficient to raise a constructive trust at any time before the moneys, upon the bank account going into overdraft, became untraceable. Once there ceased to be an identifiable trust fund, the local authority could not become a trustee: *Re Goldcorp Exchange Ltd* [1995] 1 AC 74. Therefore, as the argument for the bank recognised, the only possible trust which could be established was a resulting trust arising from the circumstances in which the local authority received the upfront payment.

Under existing law a resulting trust arises in two sets of circumstances:

(A) where A makes a voluntary payment to B or pays (wholly or in part) for the purchase of property which is vested either in B alone or in the joint names of A and B, there is a presumption that A did not intend to make a gift to B: the money or property is held on trust for A (if he is the sole provider of the money) or in the case of a joint purchase by A and B in shares proportionate to their contributions. It is important to stress that this is only a presumption, which presumption is easily rebutted either by the counter-presumption of advancement or by direct evidence of A's intention to make an outright transfer: see Underhill and Hayton, *Laws of Trusts and Trustees*, 15th ed., pp. 317 *et seq.*; *Vandervell v IRC* [1967] 2 AC 291, 312 *et seq.*; *Re Vandervell's Trusts (No. 2)* [1974] Ch 269, 288 *et seq.*

(B) Where A transfers property to B on express trusts, but the trusts declared do not exhaust the whole beneficial interest: ibid. and *Quistclose Investments Ltd v Rolls Razor Ltd (In liq.)* [1970] AC 567.

Both types of resulting trust are traditionally regarded as examples of trusts giving effect to the common intention of the parties. A resulting trust is not imposed by law against the intentions of the trustee (as is a constructive trust) but gives effect to his presumed intention. Megarry J in *Re Vandervell's Trusts (No. 2)* suggests that a resulting trust of type (B) does not depend on intention but operates automatically. I am not convinced that this is right. If the settlor has expressly, or by necessary implication, abandoned any beneficial interest in the trust property, there is in my view no resulting trust: the undisposed-of equitable interest vests in the Crown as *bona vacantia*: see *Re West Sussex Constabulary's Widows, Children and Benevolent (1930) Fund Trusts* [1971] Ch 1.

Applying these conventional principles of resulting trust to the present case, the bank's claim must fail. There was no transfer of money to the local authority on express trusts: therefore a resulting trust of type (B) above could not arise. As to type (A) above, any presumption of resulting trust is rebutted since it is demonstrated that the bank paid, and the local authority received, the upfront payment with the intention that the moneys so paid should become the absolute property of the local authority. It is true that the parties were under a misapprehension that the payment was made in pursuance of a valid contract. But that does not alter the actual intentions of the parties at the date the payment was made or the moneys were mixed in the bank account ...

NOTE: Category (A) is more narrowly defined than the *Vandervell* presumed resulting trusts category, because it only includes transfers of money. Note, however, that in *Tinsley* v *Milligan*, Lord Browne-Wilkinson had said that 'A presumption of resulting trust also arises in equity when A transfers personalty or money to B.'

■ QUESTION

If Lord Browne-Wilkinson in *Westdeutsche* really intended to exclude from category (A) transfers of personalty, do these views form part of the *ratio* of the case?

NOTES

1. On the issue of the type of property that can come within category (A), in *Tinsley* v *Milligan*, Lord Browne-Wilkinson said that:

    A presumption of resulting trust also arises in equity when A transfers personalty or money to B: ... Before 1925 there was also a presumption of resulting trust when land was voluntarily transferred by A to B; it is agrguable, however, that the position has been altered by the 1925 property legislation: see Snell (29th edn), p. 182.

In other words, transfers of money and personalty are included, but land may not be.

2. One of the problems with *Westdeutsche* is that, if the basis of both resulting and constructive trusts is the conscience of the recipient, what is the difference between them? One possibility might be to see the resulting trust as merely one variety of constructive trust. However, in *Air Jamaica Ltd* v *Charlton* [1999] 1 WLR 1399, Lord Millett said that 'Like a constructive trust, a resulting trust arises by operation of law, though unlike a constructive trust it gives effect to intention.'

   Although this statement is clearly consistent with category (A) (what used to be called presumed) resulting trusts, it seems difficult to reconcile with cases such as *Vandervell* v *Inland Revenue Commissioners* [1967] 2 AC 291 or *IRC* v *Broadway Cottages Trust* [1955] Ch 20, where a resulting trust was imposed although this would have been the last thing the settlor wanted.

3. One of the consequences of Lord Browne-Wilkinson's approach in *Westdeutsche* is to cloud the distinction between resulting and constructive trusts; indeed, it seems as though the resulting trust has become little more than a subcategory of constructive trust. In 'Restitution and Constructive Trusts' (1998) 114 *LQR* 399, Millett argues that they are quite different; unlike the constructive trust, the resulting trust (p. 401) does not depend on the unconscionable conduct of the recipient, and reverses unjust enrichment by subtraction (taking something away from the claimant) rather than unjust enrichment by wrong.

   Millett clearly accepts that all trusts are proprietary, but that not all give rise to fiduciary relationships. These are separate questions. All express trustees are fiduciaries, but resulting and constructive trustees need not be—it will depend on the circumstances in which trustee-ship is imposed. Millett states (pp. 403–4):

   > … The paradigm example of the fiduciary is the *express* trustee, not the constructive trustee: and while all fiduciaries are subject to fiduciary obligations, they are not all subject to the same fiduciary obligations.

   It is necessary to begin with two elementary observations. The first is that a trust exists whenever the legal title is in one party and the equitable title in another. The legal owner is said to hold the property in trust for the equitable owner. Lord Browne-Wilkinson denied this in the *Westdeutsche Landesbank* case, and gave examples where he said this was not the case … with respect neither is convincing … What matters is the nature of the obligation which is enforceable by equity. If it is an obligation to transfer the property to the claimant *in specie*, then the claimant has the entire equitable proprietary interest in the property itself. It has been common parlance of equity lawyers for centuries to describe the legal owner in such circumstances as a trustee and the interest of the equitable owner as arising under a trust. Lord Lindley was content to accept the usage as correct [in *Hardoon* v *Belilos* [1901] AC 118, 123]:

   > All that is necessary to establish the relation of trustee and *cestui que trust* is to prove that the legal title was in the plaintiff and the equitable title in the defendant.

   But as Lord Browne-Wilkinson himself recognised, this is essentially a question of semantics. He clearly recognises, indeed insists, that the separation of legal and equitable ownership is insufficient to give rise to fiduciary obligations. Unwilling to recognise the existence of a trust shorn of such obligations, he is forced to conclude that such separation of interests does not create a trust. It probably does not matter if we say that the relationship is not a trust relationship, so long as we call it something else. The trouble is that we have no other name for it.

   The second observation is that every fiduciary relationship is a voluntary relationship. No one can be compelled to enter into a fiduciary relationship or to accept fiduciary obligations, any more than he can be compelled to enter into a contract or to accept contractual obligations …

4. Millett argues that express trustees owe fiduciary duties to the beneficiaries because of their voluntary undertaking to the settlor. Whether resulting or constructive trustees owe fiduciary duties depends on the circumstances in which they arise. For example, the defendant in *A-G for Hong-Kong* v *Reid* ought to have owed fiduciary obligations because he knew all the relevant facts. However, the vendor of property as a constructive trustee does not owe fiduciary obligations.

   In the *Westdeutsche* context, Millett considers that the bank should have had a restitutionary personal claim, based on partial failure of consideration (which he thinks the law should recognise, although the authorities are generally against this view). Clearly, however, there was no proprietary claim for the reasons given by Lord Browne-Wilkinson; there was no constructive trust because the local authority's conscience was unaffected, and no resulting trust because the bank intended to pass legal and equitable title to the recipient. It seems probable (although the article does not make this entirely clear) that Millett would support the dissenting view taken by Lord Goff.

Millett takes the view that a resulting trust arises from the intention of the transferor, not to pass the beneficial interest to the recipient. It does not depend on the knowledge of the recipient; moreover, knowledge does not necessarily give rise to a trust—if equitable title has passed to the recipient, there will be no resulting trust, whatever knowledge the recipient later acquires. He disagrees (pp. 412–13) with Lord Browne-Wilkinson's reanalysis of *Chase Manhattan*, but thinks that the case was wrongly decided because the paying bank had parted with both legal and beneficial title to the money. There was therefore no room for a resulting trust.

■ QUESTIONS

1. Do you agree with Robert Chambers' claim (*Resulting Trusts* (Oxford: Clarendon Press, 1997)) that 'All resulting trusts effect restitution of what would otherwise be the unjust enrichment of the recipient'?

2. Contrary to Chambers' analysis, is it more accurate to say that the resulting trust positively preserves or vindicates the donor's pre-existing property rights in the transferred assets?

SECTION 2: CATEGORIES OF RESULTING TRUST

In *Re Vandervell's Trusts (No. 2)* [1974] Ch 269, Megarry J distinguished between presumed and automatic resulting trusts, as follows:

(a) The first class of case is where the transfer to B is not made on any trust … there is a rebuttable presumption that B holds on resulting trust for A. The question is not one of the automatic consequences of a dispositive failure by A, but one of presumption: the property has been carried to B, and from the absence of consideration and any presumption of advancement B is presumed not only to hold the entire interest on trust, but also to hold the beneficial interest for A absolutely. The presumption thus establishes both that B is to take on trust and also what that trust is. Such resulting trusts may be called 'presumed resulting trusts'.

(b) The second class of case is where the transfer to B is made on trusts which leave some or all of the beneficial interest undisposed of. Here B automatically holds on resulting trust for A to the extent that the beneficial interest has not been carried to him or others. The resulting trust here does not depend on any intentions or presumptions, but is the automatic consequence of A's failure to dispose of what is vested in him. Since *ex hypothesi* the transfer is on trust, the resulting trust does not establish the trust but merely carries back to A the beneficial interest that has not been disposed of. Such resulting trusts may be called 'automatic resulting trusts'.

These categories have been subjected to rigorous academic criticism and they must now be reconsidered in the light of *Westdeutsche v Islington BC* [1996] AC 669, but the *Vandervell* categorisation is still useful for structural purposes.

NOTE: The Court of Appeal has confirmed that the resulting trust arising where B acquires property in the name of A, arises at the moment of purchase and not later (*Curley v Parkes* [2004] EWCA Civ 1515, Court of Appeal).

A: Presumptions concerning intention

(i) The presumption of resulting trust

Where there is a voluntary transfer of the legal title to property (i.e. not a transfer for value) then unless there is a presumption of advancement (see (ii) The presumption of advancement), the presumption is that the equitable title does not follow the legal title but remains in the settlor, i.e. there is a resulting trust. The presumption is very old. It was orthodox by 1788 (*Dyer* v *Dyer* (1788) 2 Cox Eq Cas 92):

> ... [T]he trust of a legal estate, whether freehold, copyhold, or leasehold; whether taken in the names of the purchasers and others jointly, or in the name of others without that of the purchaser; whether in the name of one or several; whether jointly or successive, results to the man who advances the purchase money. This is a general proposition supported by all the cases, and there is nothing to contradict it; and it goes on a strict analogy to the rule of the common law, that where a feoffment is made without consideration, the use results to the feoffor. (*per* Eyre CB at 93).

The presumption is said to be fairly weak and therefore easily rebutted by evidence that some other transaction such as a gift or loan or contract was intended. In *Vajpeyi* v *Yusaf* [2003] All ER (D) 128 (Sep), (Approved judgment) the claimant, who had given the defendant money to buy a house, failed in her claim to recover the house under a resulting trust. The court held that the money had been given as a loan and the defendant's obligation to the claimant was completely discharged by repayment of the loan.

(ii) The presumption of advancement

Presumptions of advancement occur where the relationship between the parties is such as to impose a moral obligation upon one to provide for the other. Examples are the obligation of a husband to support his wife, and the obligation of a father to support his children. The effect of the presumption is that where there is a voluntary conveyance of the legal title (i.e. without consideration, in effect a gift), the equitable title passes also. In other words, the presumption is that an out-and-out gift is intended, to fulfil the moral obligation to give, whereas in other voluntary conveyances there is a presumption of resulting trust.

The presumption only applies from husband and wife and from father and child (or any other person to whom he stands *in loco parentis*, e.g. an adopted child). It does not apply from wife to husband, or at all between unmarried couples. There is authority in *Bennett* v *Bennett* (1879) 10 ChD 474, Court of Appeal for a weak presumption from mother to child.

Sekhon v *Alissa* [1989] 2 FLR 94 was decided on the basis that the presumption of resulting trust between mother and daughter had not been rebutted (there being plenty of evidence, in fact, that no gift was intended). There was no mention by Hoffmann J of a presumption of advancement. This case is discussed further in this chapter.

NOTES

1. The presumption of advancement is nowadays very weak, and when section 199 of the Equality Act 2010 becomes law the presumption will be abolished; this is because the presumption is discriminatory in so far as it applies to husbands and fathers but not to wives and mothers. (The reform will not affect existing arrangements, see note 4).
2. An interesting contemporary example of resulting trust appears from the facts of *Abrahams* v *Trustee in Bankruptcy of Abrahams* [1999] BPIR 637. A wife paid £1 each week into a National Lottery syndicate under the name of the husband, from whom she had separated. The syndicate won. The court held that the right to winnings had the character of a property right, and that

this right, though in the husband's name, was presumed to be the wife's under a resulting trust because she had contributed the winning £1. Would the result have been different if the position of husband and wife had been reversed?

3. The presumption of advancement can be rebutted if, for example, a wife is allowed to draw cheques on a joint banking account for the convenience of the husband, perhaps because the husband is ill, as in *Marshal* v *Crutwell* (1875) LR 20 Eq 328. Clearly in such a case there is no intention to make a gift to the wife, unlike, for example, *Re Figgis* [1969] 1 Ch 123, where an otherwise similar arrangement on a joint account was not merely for convenience. The presumption was rebutted in *Tribe* v *Tribe* (discussed in this section), and *McGrath* v *Wallis*, discussed in Chapter 6. It also appears that bank guarantees, for example where a husband guarantees his wife's overdraft, do not attract the operation of the presumption, but that ordinary rules of contract apply: *Anson* v *Anson* [1953] 1 QB 636. In *Lavelle* v *Lavelle* [2004] EWCA Civ 223, Court of Appeal, the presumption of advancement from father to daughter was rebutted by evidence that the transfer of land into the daughter's name had been made with the intention of avoiding inheritance tax. *Lavelle* was approved in *Kyriakides* v *Pippas* [2004] EWHC 646 (Ch).

4. We have already noted that section 199 of the Equality Act 2010 will abolish the presumption of advancement (see note 1). It has been argued that this reform is unnecessary as the presumption is already practically defunct due to the Human Rights Act 1998. Worse than being unnecessary, s.199(2) does not affect past transactions, with the result that existing discrimination is confirmed and will continue (J Glister, 'Section 199 of the Equality Act 2010: How Not to Abolish the Presumption of Advancement' (2010) 73(5) MLR 807).

(iii) Illegal transactions

Though the presumption of advancement is weak and outdated, there is one circumstance in which it can be decisive.

Tinsley v *Milligan*

[1994] 1 AC 340, House of Lords

Facts: Stella Tinsley and Kathleen Milligan were a lesbian couple who jointly purchased a home which was registered in Tinsley's name alone. On the principles governing informal trusts of land (as set out in Chapter 8), the beneficial interest would have been shared between Tinsley and Milligan in equal shares, but to both Tinsley's and Milligan's knowledge, the home was registered in Tinsley's name alone to enable Milligan to make false claims to the Department of Social Security for benefits. After a quarrel, Tinsley moved out, and claimed possession from Milligan. Milligan counterclaimed, seeking a declaration that the house was held by Tinsley on trust for both of them in equal shares. Tinsley argued that Milligan's claim was barred by the common law doctrine *ex turpi causa non oritur actio* and by the principle that 'he who comes to equity must come with clean hands'.

Held: (Lord Keith and Lord Goff dissenting): Because the presumption of resulting trust applied, Milligan could establish her equitable interest without relying on the illegal transaction, and was therefore entitled to succeed.

LORD JAUNCEY OF TULLICHETTLE: At the outset it seems to me to be important to distinguish between the enforcement of executory provisions arising under an illegal contract or other transaction and the enforcement of rights already acquired under the completed provisions of such a contract or transaction. Your Lordships were referred to a very considerable number of authorities, both ancient and modern, from which certain propositions may be derived.

First: it is trite law that the court will not give its assistance to the enforcement of executory provisions of an unlawful contract whether the illegality is apparent *ex facie* the document or whether the illegality of purpose of what would otherwise be a lawful contract emerges during the course of the trial ...

Second: it is well established that a party is not entitled to rely on his own fraud or illegality in order to assist a claim or rebut a presumption. Thus when money or property has been transferred by a man to his wife or children for the purpose of defrauding creditors and the transferee resists his claim for recovery he cannot be heard to rely on his illegal purpose in order to rebut the presumption of advancement (see ... *Tinker* v *Tinker* [1970] P 136 at 143 *per* Salmon LJ [and further in this section]).*Third*: it has, however, for some years been recognised that a completely executed transfer of property or of an interest in property made in pursuance of an unlawful agreement is valid and the court will assist the transferee in the protection of his interest provided that he does not require to found on the unlawful agreement ...

The ultimate question in this appeal is, in my view, whether the respondent in claiming the existence of a resulting trust in her favour is seeking to enforce unperformed provisions of an unlawful transaction or whether she is simply relying on an equitable proprietary interest that she has already acquired under such a transaction. The nature of a resulting trust was described by Lord Diplock in *Gissing* v *Gissing* [1971] AC 886 at 905 [see Chapter 8] ...

I find this a very narrow question but I have come to the conclusion that the transaction whereby the claimed resulting trust in favour of the respondent was created was the agreement between the parties that, although funds were to be provided by both of them, nevertheless the title to the house was to be in the sole name of the appellant for the unlawful purpose of defrauding the Department of Social Security. So long as that agreement remained unperformed neither party could have enforced it against the other. However, as soon as the agreement was implemented by the sale to the appellant alone she became trustee for the respondent who can now rely on the equitable proprietary interest which has thereby been presumed to have been created in her favour and has no need to rely on the illegal transaction which led to its creation.

My Lords, I have had the advantage of reading in draft the speech of my noble and learned friend Lord Browne-Wilkinson. I agree with it and for the reasons contained therein as well as for the reasons in this speech I would dismiss the appeal.

NOTES

1. The reasoning essentially is that whereas an unlawful agreement cannot be enforced, property can pass in pursuance of an unlawful agreement, as long as the transferee does not need to plead the unlawful agreement in order to claim that it has passed. This had long been known to be the position at common law, and Lord Jauncey is extending the same principles to equitable property. Milligan's equitable title arose from the presumption of resulting trust, so she did not need to plead the unlawful agreement in order to claim it.

2. Lord Browne-Wilkinson went further than Lord Jauncey in the above passage, taking the view (at 371) that:

    > In my judgment to draw ... distinctions between property rights enforceable at law and those which require the intervention of equity would be surprising. More than 100 years has elapsed since the fusion of the administration of law and equity. The reality of the matter is that, in 1993, English law has one single law of property made up of legal and equitable interests. Although for historical reasons legal estates and equitable estates have differing incidents, the person owning either type of estate has a right of property, a right *in rem* not merely a right *in personam*. If the law is that a party is entitled to enforce a property right acquired under an illegal transaction, in my judgment the same rule ought to apply to any property right so acquired, whether such right is legal or equitable.

    He continued (at 375):

    > ... the fusion of law and equity has led the courts to adopt a single rule (applicable both at law and in equity) as to the circumstances in which the court will enforce property interests acquired in pursuance of an illegal transaction, viz., the *Bowmakers* rule (see *Bowmakers Ltd* v *Barnet Instruments Ltd* [1945] KB 65).

    Note also that Lord Jauncey ended his speech by agreeing with Lord Browne-Wilkinson. However, as Robert Walker LJ observed in *Lowson* v *Coombes* (discussed in this section):

    > Lord Browne-Wilkinson cannot, I am sure, have intended to suggest that there are not still special principles applicable to the grant of equitable remedies of a discretionary nature, and ... [it] may be that, on the facts of *Feret* v *Hill* (1854) 15 CB 207 occurring today, it would make a difference if there had been only an agreement for a lease, since the doctrine in *Walsh* v *Lonsdale* (1882) 21 ChD 9 depends on the equitable remedy of specific performance being available. The enforcement of a resulting trust does not however in any way depend on the availability of specific performance.

    See further the remedies section in Chapter 1.

3. In *Tinsley* v *Milligan*, Milligan was able to rely on the presumption of resulting trust to claim a share in equity. Had the parties been a married couple, and legal title registered in the name of

the wife, the facts being otherwise the same, the result would undoubtedly have been different, since the husband would have had to rebut the presumption of advancement, and could not have done so without declaring the fraudulent purpose. For example, Lord Browne-Wilkinson said (at 375):

> A party to an illegality can recover by virtue of a legal or equitable property interest if, but only if, he can establish his title without relying on his own illegality. In cases where the presumption of advancement applies, the plaintiff is faced with the presumption of gift and therefore cannot claim under a resulting trust unless and until he has rebutted that presumption of gift: for those purposes the plaintiff does have to rely on the underlying illegality and therefore fails.

It does not matter how weak the presumption is for this reasoning to succeed; it matters only that there is a presumption at all. However, it now appears that the transferor can succeed, even where there is a presumption of advancement, where the fraudulent purpose has not been carried into effect; in such cases, the doctrine of the *locus poenitentiae* (interval for repentance) allows a party to withdraw from an illegal purpose, and to give evidence as to his true intention.

Tribe v Tribe

[1996] Ch 107, Court of Appeal

Facts: The claimant was concerned that he may have become liable for dilapidations on business leases, the landlords of the premises concerned having served schedules of dilapidations requiring him to carry out substantial repairs. Accordingly, he transferred his shares in a family company to the defendant, who was one of his sons and the director of the company, as a means of safeguarding his assets. The illegal purpose of the transfer was to deceive the claimant's creditors by creating an appearance that he no longer owned any shares in the company.

In the event, no repairs were carried out, because of negotiations between the claimant and the landlords of the properties. The claimant then wished to restore the position to that existing prior to the claims for repairs being made, but the defendant refused to retransfer the shares.

Held: The Court of Appeal allowed the claimant to advance evidence to rebut the presumption of advancement, where the fraud had not actually been carried out.

MILLETT LJ: Mr David Tribe transferred his shareholding in his family company to his son for a pretended consideration which was not paid and was not intended to be paid. The transfer was, therefore, made for no consideration. If the transferee had been a nephew or a trusted stranger, the transaction would have given rise to a resulting trust. In such a case equity places the burden of proving that the transfer was intended to be by way of gift upon the transferee. If he cannot discharge that burden, he holds the shares as nominee and in trust for the transferor. Mr Tribe, however, transferred the shares to his son, and accordingly the transaction gave rise to the presumption of advancement. In such a case the transfer is presumed to have been intended by way of gift. The burden of proving that it was not intended as a gift lies upon the transferor.

The judge found that Mr Tribe did not intend to make a gift of the shares to his son. The company represented his life's work, and his shareholding in the company was his largest asset. He had other children besides the son to whom in the ordinary course of things he would wish to leave his property. But he faced substantial claims for dilapidations in respect of two leasehold properties which were occupied by the company but of which he was the tenant, and he was concerned that he could lose the shares. The judge accepted his evidence that he transferred the shares to his son as a nominee in order to conceal them from his creditors, and specifically from his two landlords, by creating the appearance that he no longer owned any shares in the company. That, of course, was an illegal purpose. Ordinarily a man who makes a gratuitous transfer of property to another for an illegal purpose is not allowed to rely on his purpose in making the transfer in order to rebut the presumption of advancement: see *Tinsley v Milligan* [1994] 1 AC 340 [Millett LJ referred to the same passage quoted in note 3. on that case, and continued: ...] The question in the present case is whether there is an exception to this principle where the transferor withdraws from the transaction before any part of the illegal purpose has been carried into effect. Unless that exception applies, Mr Tribe's claim to recover his own shares from the son whom he trusted to hold them as his nominee must fail.

[Millett LJ referred again to Lord Browne-Wilkinson's reasoning in *Tinsley* v *Milligan*, and continued: ...]

The necessary consequence of this is that where he can rely on a resulting trust the transferor will normally be able to recover his property if the illegal purpose has not been carried out. In *Tinsley* v *Milligan* she recovered even though the illegal purpose had been carried out ...

The question in the present case is the converse: whether the transferor can rebut the presumption of advancement by giving evidence of his illegal purpose so long as the illegal purpose has not been carried into effect ...

[Millett LJ reviewed the authorities and concluded, on the *locus poenitentiae*:] In my opinion the following propositions represent the present state of the law

....

(3) ... the transferor can recover the property if he can do so without relying on the illegal purpose. This will normally be the case where the property was transferred without consideration in circumstances where the transferor can rely on an express declaration of trust or a resulting trust in his favour.

(4) It will almost invariably be so where the illegal purpose has not been carried out. It may be otherwise where the illegal purpose has been carried out and the transferee can rely on the transferor's conduct as inconsistent with his retention of a beneficial interest.

(5) The transferor can lead evidence of the illegal purpose whenever it is necessary for him to do so provided that he has withdrawn from the transaction before the illegal purpose has been wholly or partly carried into effect. It will be necessary for him to do so (i) if he brings an action at law or (ii) if he brings proceedings in equity and needs to rebut the presumption of advancement.

(6) The only way in which a man can protect his property from his creditors is by divesting himself of all beneficial interest in it. Evidence that he transferred the property in order to protect it from his creditors, therefore, does nothing by itself to rebut the presumption of advancement; it reinforces it. To rebut the presumption it is necessary to show that he intended to retain a beneficial interest and conceal it from his creditors.

(7) The court should not conclude that this was his intention without compelling circumstantial evidence to this effect. The identity of the transferee and the circumstances in which the transfer was made would be highly relevant. It is unlikely that the court would reach such a conclusion where the transfer was made in the absence of an imminent and perceived threat from known creditors.

■ QUESTIONS

1. Does illegality prevent the passing of legal title? Did legal title pass to Tinsley?

2. Which would be the best way forward, do you think, to abolish the 'reliance principle' or to abolish the presumption of advancement?

NOTES

1. Looking at Millett LJ's conclusions in the extract from *Tribe* v *Tribe*, proposition (3) represents the *ratio* of *Tinsley* v *Milligan*, and proposition (5), which was said to be supported by the weight of authority, justified the result in *Tribe* v *Tribe*. Propositions (6) and (7) are necessary to distinguish *Tribe* v *Tribe* from cases such as *Tinker* v *Tinker* (discussed in this section).

2. In *Tinsley* v *Milligan*, Lord Browne-Wilkinson used the existence of the *locus poenitentiae* principle to support his view that equitable title can pass, even where property is transferred for an illegal purpose:

> The principle of *locus poenitentiae* is in my judgment irreconcilable with any rule that where property is transferred for an illegal purpose no equitable proprietary right exists. The equitable right, if any, must arise at the time at which the property was voluntarily transferred to the third party or purchased in the name of the third party. The existence of the equitable interest cannot depend upon events occurring after that date. Therefore if, under the principle of *locus poenitentiae*, the courts recognise that an equitable interest did arise out of the underlying transaction, the same must be true where the illegal purpose was carried through. The carrying out of the illegal purpose cannot, by itself, destroy the pre-existing equitable interest. The doctrine of *locus poenitentiae* therefore demonstrates that the effect of illegality is not to prevent a proprietary interest in equity from arising or to produce a forfeiture of such right: the effect is to render the equitable interest unenforceable in certain circumstances. The effect of illegality is not substantive but procedural. The question therefore is: in what circumstances will equity refuse to enforce equitable

rights which undoubtedly exist? [Ed: In any event, the opportunity to revoke a donation within the *locus poenitentiae* will be lost if the donee acts to his detriment in reliance on the donation: *Q v Q* [2008] EWHC 1874 (Fam) noted Pawlowski (2009) *Conv* 145.]

3. The approach taken in *Tribe v Tribe* [1995] 3 WLR 913 should be contrasted with the approach in *Collier v Collier* [2002] BPIR 1057, where a father failed in his attempt to recover a freehold from his daughter. In order to defraud his creditors, the father had granted his daughter a lease with an option to purchase the freehold. She exercised that option and sought to take possession of the freehold from her father. The judge held that although the daughter knew that she had not received the property by way of gift, but on trust, the trust was unenforceable because it had been established for an illegal purpose.

Tinker v *Tinker*

[1970] 2 WLR 331, [1970] 1 All ER 540, Court of Appeal

Facts: The husband, who was accepted on the evidence as being an honest man, purchased a garage business, and shortly afterwards purchased the matrimonial home. Because he was worried that his business might fail through inexperience, he desired to protect the matrimonial home from any future creditors. After therefore taking the advice of his solicitor, he conveyed the matrimonial home into his wife's name, despite having paid the entirety of the purchase money himself. In the event, the business never got into financial difficulty.

Note that there was nothing unlawful in what the husband was doing, as long as it was a genuine transaction, and he really did not intend to retain any beneficial interest in the property.

The marriage having ended soon after the purchase, the husband applied for a declaration that the wife held the property in trust for him absolutely.

Held: The husband was not entitled to succeed, since the evidence was that he desired the property not to fall into the hands of creditors. This required the wife to be beneficial owner, and far from rebutting the presumption of advancement, the evidence supported the conclusion that the husband intended to make a gift of the property to his wife.

LORD DENNING MR: ... Accepting that in the present case the husband was honest—he acted, he said, on the advice of his solicitor—nevertheless I do not think that he can claim that the house belongs to him. The solicitor did not give evidence. But the only proper advice that he could give was: 'In order to avoid the house being taken by your creditors, you can put it into your wife's name; but remember that, if you do, it is your wife's and you cannot go back on it.'

But, whether the solicitor gave that advice or not, I am quite clear that the husband cannot have it both ways. So he is on the horns of a dilemma. He cannot say that the house is his own and, at one and the same time, say that it is his wife's. As against his wife, he wants to say that it belongs to him. As against his creditors, that it belongs to her. That simply will not do. Either it was conveyed to her for her own use absolutely; or it was conveyed to her as trustee for her husband. It must be one or other. The presumption is that it was conveyed to her for her own use; and he does not rebut that presumption by saying that he only did it to defeat his creditors. I think that it belongs to her.

SALMON LJ: ... A house ... was bought with money supplied by the husband. The wife did not put up a penny. The contract to purchase, however, was in her name and the house was conveyed into her name. The burden of displacing the presumption of advancement is therefore on the husband. This burden can in many cases be displaced without much effort. It seems to me, however, that in his case the husband's evidence, far from displacing the presumption, has done much to reinforce it. His explanation when he was giving evidence as to why the house was put in his wife's name was as follows:

I was advised that should the business fail the house would be taken as part of the assets of the business. Recommended therefore house should be put in wife's name.

Now, of course, if a house is made over to a wife, it is protected against the husband's creditors. No criticism can be made of a transaction such as that, providing that it is genuine; the essence of the transaction is that the husband puts the house in his wife's name, intending to convey and in reality conveying the whole interest in the house to his wife. The husband was advised by a reputable solicitor in Bodmin. For my part I have no doubt that the solicitor must have explained to him the effect of what he was doing; it would mean, therefore, that if he failed in business and his creditors came down on him and sought to take his assets, he would be able truthfully to say to them: 'You cannot touch this house; it is not mine. Look—you can see the documents; they are all in my wife's name. It has always been hers.' And this would give him and her complete protection so far as the house was concerned against the creditors. There would be nothing wrong or dishonest in doing what I have described. It seems to me to follow from the learned registrar's finding that he was an honest man and that the husband must have intended that the house should belong to the wife. That is why I say that his evidence strengthens the presumption of advancement ...

NOTE: Of *Tinker* v *Tinker*, Millett LJ observed in *Tribe* v *Tribe*:

> The dishonest man is not treated more favourably than the honest man: provided that the illegal purpose has not been carried out they are treated in the same way. The outcome is different because their intentions were different. The honest man intended a gift; the dishonest man did not.

■ QUESTIONS

1. Did Tinker really intend to make a gift to his wife? If so, is there any possible justification for allowing him later to claim an interest?

2. Should equity presume that a person's intentions are honest? Does it? Did it in *Tinker* v *Tinker*?

NOTES

1. In *Sekhon* v *Alissa* [1989] 2 FLR 94, a house to which the mother had contributed was conveyed into the daughter's sole name to enable the mother to claim exemption from capital gains tax by falsely representing that the daughter was the sole beneficial owner. The daughter argued that having allowed the solicitor (at the time of the conveyance) to act on the assumption that her contribution was a gift, the mother could not be heard to deny this. Otherwise she would be relying on her own illegal purpose, which must have been to claim exemption from capital gains tax by falsely representing that the daughter was the sole beneficial owner. However, Hoffmann J observed that: 'In this case the mother had been told in very general terms by her friend that for the purposes of capital gains tax it would not be a good idea for her name to appear as a proprietor. I do not think that she had come anywhere near to planning a fraudulent scheme of evasion, let alone carrying it into effect.'

   Unlike *Tinker* v *Tinker* or *Tribe* v *Tribe*, the reasoning was that the daughter had failed to rebut a presumption of resulting trust, there being no discussion of a presumption of advancement. Where there is evidence as to actual intention, as in both *Tinker* and *Sekhon*, the presumptions surely become irrelevant?

2. See, also, *Lavelle* v *Lavelle* [2004] EWCA Civ 223, CA where the presumption of advancement from father to daughter was rebutted by evidence that the transfer of land into the daughter's name had been made with the intention of avoiding inheritance tax.

■ QUESTION

For the mother in *Sekhon* v *Alissa* to succeed in avoiding capital gains tax, would the beneficial interest have to be vested in the daughter? If so, how is the case distinguishable from *Tinker* v *Tinker* (which incidentally was not cited)?

NOTES

1. *Tinker* v *Tinker* demonstrates that the so-called 'reliance principle'—the principle that illegality is only relevant where it is relied upon in evidence—can sometimes have an arbitrary and unfair impact upon different parties. By means of the presumption of advancement, property

law automatically grants rights to wives in circumstances in which the same rights would be denied to husbands, with the result that husbands may be forced, in an attempt to establish a right, to refer to evidence of illegality which wives in the same circumstances would have no need to raise.

2. The Law Commission recommended in its Consultation Paper No. 154, *Illegal Transactions: The Effect of Illegality on Contracts and Trusts*, published January 1999, that the 'reliance principle' should be abolished by legislation and that statute should replace it with a broad judicial discretion to decide on a case-by-case basis whether illegality should displace the application of general trust principles. The Law Commission subsequently decided to leave it to the judges to develop an appropriate response to illegality, except statutory reform was still proposed for trust cases like *Tinsley* v *Milligan*. In *The Illegality Defence: A Consultative Report* (Consultation Paper No. 189, January 2009), the Law Commission provisionally proposed that legislation should be introduced to provide judges with a discretion in cases such as *Tinsley* v *Milligan* to deprive a beneficiary of his or her interest where a trust has been created to conceal the beneficiary's interest in order to commit an offence. The Government has since decided (March 2012) that these recommendations are not a priority and has declared that it intends not to adopt the Law Commission's proposed reforms. At the time of writing the Law Commission's website now contains the rather cryptic admission that it no longer thinks its proposals are 'sufficient to remove the problems created by the illegality defence in trusts law', a state which it blames on 'further uncertainty' introduced by *Stack* v *Dowden* (2007, HL).

Lowson v *Coombes*

[1999] 2 WLR 720, [1999] 1 FLR 799, [1999] Fam Law 90, [1999] Fam Law 91, Court of Appeal

Facts: A man and woman (Douglas Lowson and Rebecca Coombes) each contributed to the purchase price of a house in which they cohabited, but the house was conveyed into Coombes' name. This was because (as she pointed out), if it were in joint names and the claimant should die, his ex-wife would have a claim on the property and the defendant could be homeless. It was clear, however, that their actual intention was to share the property beneficially.

When the relationship later broke down, Lowson claimed a declaration that the house was held by Coombes on trust for sale for them both; Coombes claimed that Lowson was precluded from giving evidence of his illegal purpose.

Held: Unlike *Tinker* v *Tinker*, Lowson's intention was dishonest. According to Nourse LJ:

a disposition, such as the conveyances in the present case, whose purpose is to prevent the other party to the marriage from being able to look to the asset disposed of in any future financial proceedings and, in the process, from seeking an order under section 37(2)(b) of the Act of 1973 [see Note 2.] is one made with an illegal purpose.

NOTES
1. Once the case was categorised as one of illegality, it was on all fours with *Tinsley* v *Milligan*; there was no presumption of advancement, and Lowson could claim his share on the basis of a resulting trust.
2. The case differed from *Tinker* v *Tinker*, in that even if the conveyance had been made to Coombes absolutely, Lowson's purpose would not have succeeded, because his ex-wife would have been able to unravel the transaction under the Matrimonial Causes Act 1973, s.37(2)(b):

   (2) Where proceedings for financial relief are sought by one person against another, the court may, on the application of the first-mentioned person ... (b) if it is satisfied that the other party has, with [the intention of defeating the claim for financial relief], made a reviewable disposition ... make an order setting aside the disposition ...

   The only point of the conveyance into Coombes' name was to hide the transaction from Lowson's ex-wife, so that her ignorance would prevent her from invoking s.37(2)(b).

B: Land and the presumption of resulting trust

LAW OF PROPERTY ACT 1925

Section 60

(3) In a voluntary conveyance a resulting trust for the grantor shall not be implied merely by reason that the property is not expressed to be conveyed for the use or benefit of the grantee.

In *Lohia* v *Lohia*, unreported, 7 July 2000, Judge Nicholas Strauss QC concluded that the Law of Property Act 1925, s.60(3) has removed the presumption of a resulting trust on the voluntary conveyance of land, but does not prevent the possibility of implying a resulting trust in the case of a voluntary conveyance, provided such implied resulting trust is not based 'merely' upon the absence of express words confirming that the grantee is to take beneficially.

C: Automatic resulting trusts

The category described by Megarry J in *Re Vandervell's Trusts (No. 2)* [1974] Ch 269, (see Section 1) arises where there has been an attempt to create a trust but the equitable interest has not been disposed of. Generally speaking, there are two possibilities: first, the trust is invalid, in which case, if legal title has been validly transferred to the trustee, the equitable title must revest in the settlor; secondly, although the trust is valid, the settlor has not made adequate provision for the disposition of the equitable interest. In the second case, a resulting trust is one, but not the only, solution.

In *Westdeutsche Landesbank Girozentrale* v *Islington London Borough Council* [1996] AC 669, Lord Browne-Wilkinson doubted whether this class of resulting trust operated automatically, but thought that, like the presumed intention trusts already considered, it too depended on intention. He did not doubt the validity of the distinction, made in *Vandervell*, between the two types, however. Lord Browne-Wilkinson's views may nevertheless affect the reasoning in *Re Gillingham Bus Disaster Fund* and *Re West Sussex Constabulary's Fund*, below.

(i) Failure to dispose of equitable interest: initial failure

If an attempt has been made to create a trust, which is invalid, there will be a resulting trust. We have already seen cases, for example, where the necessary formalities for disposing of the equitable interest are not complied with, or where the trust is void for perpetuity or uncertainty: e.g. *IRC* v *Broadway Cottages Trust* [1955] Ch 20 (see Chapter 3).

A trust can also fail for public policy reasons, for example where equity has not allowed a person to retain the fruits of criminal activities. In *Cleaver* v *Mutual Reserve Fund Life Association* [1892] 1 QB 147, the executors of a person who had effected an insurance on his life for the benefit of his wife were held by the Court of Appeal able to maintain an action on the policy where the wife had murdered the insured. The trust in favour of the wife was unenforceable, for public policy reasons. The result in *Cleaver* was that the executors held the insurance money for the estate of the insured. The result is exactly the same as in any other failed trust case: there is a resulting trust, as in the other cases in this section.

There are a number of cases where persons guilty of murder or manslaughter have been prevented from obtaining the property of the victim, either through intestacy (*Re Crippen* [1911] P 108), or through the right of survivorship (*Re K (dec'd)* [1985] 2

WLR 262, affirmed on other grounds [1986] Ch 180, although there relief was granted against forfeiture by the Forfeiture Act 1982). Where the person otherwise entitled is not allowed to take for public policy reasons, there is a trust, best categorised (I suggest) as a resulting trust, in favour of the estate.

(ii) Failure to dispose of equitable interest: subsequent surplus

Sometimes, as with the shares in *Vandervell* v *IRC* [1967] 2 AC 291 (see Section 1), the settlor may simply have failed to make any provision for the disposal of the equitable interest. In that case there was a resulting trust for Vandervell. Alternatively, the trust may presuppose the existence of an event, such as marriage, which does not happen.

Re Abbott Fund Trusts, Smith v Abbott

[1900] 2 Ch 326, Chancery Division

Decision: A fund was collected for the relief of two deaf and dumb ladies (who had been defrauded out of their rights under an earlier settlement). No provision was made for disposal of the fund on the death of the survivor. A surplus of some £367 remained when they died, and Stirling J held that this should be held on resulting trust for the subscribers.

NOTES
1. The decision is partly a matter of interpreting the intention of the donors. In *Re Abbott*, Stirling J held that the ladies themselves never became absolute owners of the fund; nor did the trustees once the purposes were accomplished. No resulting trust occurs if either beneficiary or trustee is intended to take absolutely, however.
2. The fund in *Abbott* was subscribed to by various friends of the Abbotts. On the other hand, where the whole of a specific fund is left by a single individual for the maintenance of given individuals, the courts are more likely to construe the transaction as an absolute gift to those individuals, even where the fund is expressed to be left for a particular purpose (although it depends, of course, on the intention of the donor, which is ultimately a question of fact). An example is the Court of Appeal decision in *Re Osoba* [1979] 1 WLR 247, where a testator left the whole of a fund on trust for the education of his daughter up to university level. On completion of the daughter's university education, she was held entitled to the surplus beneficially, the educational purpose being regarded merely as a statement of the testator's motive—in other words, there was no resulting trust in favour of the testator's estate.
3. In *Cunnack* v *Edwards* [1896] 2 Ch 679, an association was established using members' contributions to provide annuities for the widows of deceased members. The Court of Appeal held that the members had disposed of their contributions out-and-out, subject only to contractual rights to obtain benefits for their widows. When the fund was wound up, the Court of Appeal held that its property should go to the Crown as *bona vacantia*.
4. Anonymous donations, for example to disaster appeal funds, might also be thought to be out-and-out gifts, with the donor retaining no interest.

Re Gillingham Bus Disaster Fund

[1958] Ch 300, Chancery Division

Facts: The case concerned a fund collected to defray funeral and other expenses incurred as a result of a disaster involving the deaths of 24 Royal Marine cadets in Gillingham. The town clerk of Gillingham wrote a letter to the *Daily Telegraph* in the following terms:

Cadets' memorial. To the editor of the '*Daily Telegraph*'. Sir, The mayors of Gillingham, Rochester, and Chatham have decided to promote a Royal Marine Cadet Corps Memorial Fund to be devoted, among other things, to defraying the funeral expenses, caring for the boys who may be disabled, and then to such worthy cause or causes in memory of the boys who lost their lives, as the mayors may determine.

Harman J held that this was not a charitable purpose (see further Chapter 7), and that the last purpose, 'to such worthy cause or causes in memory of the boys who lost their lives, as the mayors may determine', was void for uncertainty. The purposes were therefore taken to be defraying the funeral expenses of the boys who lost their lives, and caring for the boys who were disabled.

Far more money (about £9,000) was collected than was necessary for these purposes, especially as there were common law actions available against the bus company. The question therefore was who owned the surplus: was it the donors, represented by the Official Solicitor, or the Crown (represented by the Treasury Solicitor), as *bona vacantia*?

Held: Harman J, following *Re Abbott*, held that the surplus should be held on resulting trust for the donors.

HARMAN J: In December, 1951, there occurred an accident with tragic consequences, in Dock Road, Gillingham, in the county of Kent, when a motor-vehicle ran into a column of cadets marching along the road, killing 24 of them and injuring a further number. There was, of course, widespread concern at so shocking an event, and the three plaintiffs, then mayors of the surrounding areas, namely, Gillingham, Rochester and Chatham, determined to open a memorial fund. According to the evidence of the town clerk of Gillingham before me at the hearing, this was done by making a statement to the press, and the press accounts of the statement were relied upon as constituting the foundations of the so-called charity. I questioned this at the time, and it now turns out that the town clerk of Gillingham wrote a letter to the editor of the *'Daily Telegraph,'* and I dare say to some other papers as well. At any rate, this letter appeared in the columns of the *'Daily Telegraph'* on 13 December 1951: 'Cadets' Memorial. To the Editor of the *'Daily Telegraph.'* Sir,—The Mayors of Gillingham, Rochester and Chatham have decided to promote a Royal Marine Cadet Corps Memorial Fund to be devoted, among other things, to defraying the funeral expenses, caring for the boys who may be disabled, and then to such worthy cause or causes in memory of the boys who lost their lives, as the Mayors may determine.' There follows another observation by the town clerk, which is not relevant, and then are given the addresses of the mayors to which donations may be sent. It was signed 'Yours faithfully, Frank Hill, Town Clerk, Gillingham.' Mr Hill had entirely forgotten the terms of the letter as written, but there it is. This appeal evoked a generous response from the public, whose subscriptions amounted to nearly £9,000, contributed partly in substantial sums by known persons, but mainly anonymously as a result of street collections, and so forth.

The result has shown that emotion is a bad foundation for such an activity. Each of the dead or injured cadets had at common law legal rights against the bus company, which were in due course asserted, with the result that compensation has been paid in full in accordance with the law. The plaintiffs administering the fund for the benefit of the victims have spent £2,368 14s. 9d., and are at a loss what to do with the balance—hence this summons. There are three claimants: first, the donors, who are represented by the Official Solicitor; second, the Crown, represented by the Treasury Solicitor, claiming the unwanted surplus of the fund as bona vacantia; and, third, the Attorney-General, claiming it for charity. It was agreed at the hearing that I should try the issue as to charity first.

Taking the town clerk's letter as the instrument constituting the trusts applicable to this money, I am constrained to say at the outset that it is most unfortunately worded. It begins by saying that the fund is to be devoted, 'among other things,' to certain objects. On the face of it, this would enable the fund to be devoted to any object in the world. I think this cannot be the true meaning, and that the words must be read so as to confine the objects to such worthy causes as shall keep green the memory of the boy victims. The money is to be spent primarily in defraying the funeral expenses of the dead and caring for the disabled, and secondarily on such other worthy causes as the mayors may determine. It was admitted at the Bar that the primary objects, namely, the funeral expenses and care of the boys, were not themselves charitable objects, there being no element of poverty involved, nor any section of the public. Further 'worthy' objects, while no doubt it would include charitable purposes, must include many others. It is perhaps a wider word even than 'benevolent.' It follows that the trust must fail for uncertainty unless the Charitable Trusts (Validation) Act, 1954, can be invoked to support it.

[Harman J concluded that the Act did not apply—see, further, Chapter 7—and continued: ...]

I have already decided that the surplus of this fund now in the hands of the plaintiffs as trustees ought not to be devoted to charitable purposes under a *cy-près* scheme. There arises now a further question, namely, whether, as the Treasury Solicitor claims, this surplus should be paid to the Crown as bona vacantia, or whether there is a resulting trust in favour of the subscribers, who are here represented by the Official Solicitor. The general principle must be that where money is held upon trust and the trusts declared do not exhaust the fund it will revert to the donor or settlor under what is called a resulting trust. The reasoning behind this is that the settlor or donor did not part with his money absolutely out and out but only sub modo to the intent that his wishes as declared by the declaration of trust should be carried into effect. When, therefore, this has been done any surplus still belongs to him. This doctrine does not, in my judgment, rest on any evidence of the state of mind of the settlor, for in the vast majority of cases no doubt he does not expect to see his money back: he has created a trust which so far as he can see will absorb the whole of it. The resulting trust arises where that expectation is for some unforeseen reason cheated of fruition, and is an inference of law based on after-knowledge of the event.

Counsel for the Crown admitted that it was for him to show that this principle did not apply to the present case. Counsel for the subscribers cited to me *In re Abbott* [1900] 2 Ch 326. In that case a fund had been subscribed for the relief of two distressed ladies who had been defrauded of their patrimony. There was no instrument of trust. When the survivor of them died the trustees had not expended the whole of the moneys subscribed and the summons asked whether this surplus resulted to the subscribers or whether it was payable to the personal representatives of the two ladies. Stirling J had no difficulty in coming to the conclusion that the ladies were not intended to become the absolute owners of the fund and therefore their personal representatives had no claim. It was never suggested in this case that any claim by the Crown to bona vacantia might arise. A similar result was reached in *In re Hobourn Aero Components Air Raid Distress Fund* [1946] Ch 86, where the judge found that the objects of the fund were charitable no general charitable intent was shown in the absence of any element of public benefit and decided that the money belonged to the subscribers upon a resulting trust. Here again no claim was made on behalf of the Crown that the surplus constituted bona vacantia.

I was referred to two cases where a claim was made to bona vacantia and succeeded. The first of these was *Cunnack* v *Edwards* [1896] 2 Ch 679. This was a case of a society formed to raise a fund by subscriptions and so forth from the members to provide for widows of deceased members. Upon the death of the last widow of a member it was found that there was a surplus. It was held by the Court of Appeal that no question of charity arose, that there was no resulting trust in favour of the subscribers, but that the surplus passed to the Crown as bona vacantia. A. L. Smith LJ said this [at 683]:

> But it was argued that the proper implication is that when the society itself came to an end, as it has done, there was then a resulting trust of what might happen to be in the coffers of the society in favour of all the personal representatives of those who had been members since the year 1810, and Chitty J has so held. Now it was never contemplated that the society would come to an end; but, on the contrary, provision was made for the introduction of new members for its perpetual existence; and the existing members had power to alter and revise the rules, so that, if it was found that the society was too affluent, provision might be made as to what was to be done with that money might not be wanted. As the member paid his money to the society, so he divested himself of all interest in this money for ever, with this one reservation, that if the member left a widow she was to be provided for during her widowhood. Except as to this he abandoned and gave up the money for ever ...
>
> In my opinion there was no resulting trust in favour of all those members who had ever subscribed to the fund.

Rigby LJ said ([1896] 2 Ch 679, 689):

> The members were not cestuis que trust of the funds or of any part thereof, but persons who, under contracts or quasi-contracts with the society, secured for valuable consideration certain contingent benefits for their widows which could be enforced by the widows in manner provided by the Acts. Any surplus would, according to the scheme of the rules, be properly used up (under appropriate amendments of the rules) either in payment of larger annuities or in reduction of contributions. It is true that no such alterations were made, and it is now too late so to distribute the funds; but I do not think that such omission can give to the contracting parties any benefit which they did not bargain for.

The *ratio decidendi* seems to have been that having regard to the constitution of the fund no interest could possibly be held to remain in the contributor who had parted with his money once and for all under a contract for the benefit of his widow. When this contract had been carried into effect the contributor had received all that he had contracted to get for his money and could not ask for any more.

...

In addition there were cited to me the three hospital cases: *In re Welsh Hospital (Netley) Fund* [1921] 1 Ch 655, *In re Hiller's Trusts* [1954] 2 All ER 59, and *In re Ulverston and District New Hospital Building Trusts* [1956] 3 All ER 164. In the first of these cases P. O. Lawrence J held that all subscribers to the hospital must be taken to have parted with their money with a general intention in favour of charity. This was the only contest in the case, between the subscribers on the one hand and charity on the other. In *Hiller's* case Upjohn J, at first instance, found that certain categories of subscribers were entitled to have their money back but that others, namely, those who had contributed to collections at entertainments and so forth, had no such right. The Court of Appeal varied this order and declared that the whole fund should go to charity but without prejudice to the right of any individual to prove that he had no general intention but only the particular intention in favour of one hospital. In the *Ulverston* case the Court of Appeal decided that the whole fund had been collected with only one object and not for general charitable purposes and that, so far as money had been received from identifiable sources, there was a resulting trust. No claim to bona vacantia was there made, and Jenkins LJ, in explaining the position in *In re Hillier's Trusts*, said this [[1956] Ch 622, 633]:

> I appreciate that anonymous contributors cannot expect their contributions back in any circumstances, at all events so long as they remain anonymous. I appreciate also the justice of the conclusion that anonymous contributors must be regarded as having parted with their money out-and-out, though I would make a reservation in the case of an anonymous contributor who was able to prove conclusively that he had in fact subscribed some specified amount to the fund. If the organisers of a fund designed exclusively and solely for some particular charitable purpose send round a collecting box on behalf of the fund, I fail to see why a person who had put £5 into the box, and could prove to the satisfaction of the court he had done so, should not be entitled to have his money back in the event of the failure of the sole and exclusive charitable purpose for which his donation was solicited and made.

Jenkins LJ, in the course of his judgment, threw out the suggestion that donations from unidentifiable donors might in such a case be treated as bona vacantia.

It was argued for the Crown that the subscribers to this fund must be taken to have parted with their money out and out, and that there was here, as in *Cunnack* v *Edwards* [1896] 2 Ch 679 ... no room for a resulting trust. But there is a difference between [that case] and this in that [that was a case] of contract and this is not. Further, it seems to me that the hospital cases are not of great help because the argument centred round general charitable intent, a point which cannot arise unless the immediate object be a charity. I have already held there is no such question here. In my judgment the nearest case is the *Hobourn* case, which, however, is no authority for the present because no claim for bona vacantia was made.

In my judgment the Crown has failed to show that this case should not follow the ordinary rule merely because there was a number of donors who, I will assume, are unascertainable. I see no reason myself to suppose that the small giver who is anonymous has any wider intention than the large giver who can be named. They all give for the one object. If they can be found by inquiry the resulting trust can be executed in their favour. If they cannot I do not see how the money could then, with all respect to Jenkins LJ, change its destination and become bona vacantia. It will be merely money held upon a trust for which no beneficiary can be found. Such cases are common and where it is known that there are beneficiaries the fact that they cannot be ascertained does not entitle the Crown to come in and claim. The trustees must pay the money into court like any other trustee who cannot find his beneficiary. I conclude, therefore, that there must be an inquiry for the subscribers to this fund.

NOTES

1. The Attorney-General appealed unsuccessfully on the issue of charitable status. See further Chapter 7.

2. One difficulty in *Gillingham* was that although some of the money had been provided by identifiable people, most had been obtained from street collections. So many of the donors were anonymous, and the trustees were therefore required to hold the fund on resulting trust for unknown people. Obviously this is most inconvenient administratively.

■ **QUESTION**

Does Harman J's conclusion depend upon his view that the doctrine does not rest on any evidence of the state of mind of the settlor, but is an inference of law based on afterknowledge of the event? If so, is it affected by Lord Browne-Wilkinson's views in *Westdeutsche Landesbank Girozentrale* v *Islington London Borough Council* [1996] AC 669?

Re West Sussex Constabulary's Widows, Children and Benevolent (1930) Fund
[1971] 1 Ch 1, Chancery Division

Facts: The purpose of the West Sussex Constabulary's Widows, Children and Benevolent (1930) Fund was to provide allowances for the widows and dependants of deceased members. Some of its revenue was derived from contributions from its own members. Some was also raised from outside sources, by:

    (a)   entertainments, raffles and sweepstakes,
    (b)   collecting boxes,
    (c)   donations, including legacies.

The fund was wound up at the end of 1967, upon the amalgamation of the constabulary with other police forces, and the question arose as to how to divide it up.

Held: (on the outside contributions): The outside contributions raised from category (c) were held on resulting trust for the contributors. Those raised by categories (a) and (b) were clearly intended to take effect as out-and-out gifts to the fund, and therefore the resulting trust doctrine did not apply to them. Having no owner, therefore, these contributions also were *bona vacantia*. The views of Harman J in *Re Gillingham Bus Disaster Fund* [1958] Ch 300, regarding street collections, were not followed.

GOFF J (on the outside contributions): ... Then counsel divided the outside moneys into three categories, first, the proceeds of entertainments, raffles and sweepstakes; secondly, the proceeds of collecting-boxes; and thirdly, donations, including legacies if any, and he took particular objections to each.

I agree that there cannot be any resulting trust with respect to the first category. I am not certain whether Harman J in *Re Gillingham Bus Disaster Fund* [1958] Ch 300 meant to decide otherwise. In starting the facts at p. 304 he referred to 'street collections and so forth'. In the further argument at p. 309 there is mention of whist drives and concerts but the judge himself did not speak of anything other than gifts. If, however, he did, I must respectfully decline to follow his judgment in that regard, for whatever may be the true position with regard to collecting-boxes, it appears to me to be impossible to apply the doctrine of resulting trust to the proceeds of entertainments and sweepstakes and such-like money-raising operations for two reasons: first, the relationship is one of contract and not of trust; the purchaser of a ticket may have the motive of aiding the cause or he may not; he may purchase a ticket merely because he wishes to attend the particular entertainment or to try for the prize, but whichever it be, he pays his money as the price of what is offered and what he receives; secondly, there is in such cases no direct contribution to the fund at all; it is only the profit, if any, which is ultimately received and there may even be none.

In any event, the first category cannot be any more susceptible to the doctrine than the second to which I now turn. Here one starts with the well-known dictum of P. O. Lawrence J in *Re Welsh Hospital (Netley) Fund* [1921] 1 Ch 655, 660 where he said:

> So far as regards the contributors to entertainments, street collections etc., I have no hesi-tation in holding that they must be taken to have parted with their money out-and-out. It is inconceivable that any person paying for a concert ticket or placing a coin in a collecting-box presented to him in the street should have intended that any part of the money so contributed should be returned to him when the immediate object for which the concert was given or the collection made had come to an end. To draw such an inference would be absurd on the face of it.

In *Re Ulverston and District New Hospital Building Trusts* [1956] Ch 622, 633, Jenkins LJ threw out a sug-gestion that there might be a distinction in the case of a person who could prove that he put a specified sum in a collecting-box, and, in the *Gillingham* case [1958] Ch 300 Harman J, after noting this, decided that there was a resulting trust with respect to the proceeds of collections. He said at p. 314:

> In my judgment the Crown has failed to show that this case should not follow the ordinary rule merely because there was a number of donors who, I will assume, are unascertainable. I see no reason myself to suppose that the small giver who is anonymous has any wider intention than the large giver who can be named. They all give for one object. If they can be found by enquiry the resulting trust can be executed in their favour. If they cannot I do not see how the money could then, with all respect to Jenkins LJ, change its destination and become *bona vacantia*. It will be merely money held upon a trust for which no beneficiary can be found. Such cases are common and where it is known that there are beneficiaries the fact that they cannot be ascertained does not entitle the Crown to come in and claim. The trustees must pay the money into court like any other trustee who cannot find his beneficiary. I conclude, therefore, that there must be an enquiry for the subscribers to this fund.

It will be observed that Harman J considered that *Re Welsh Hospital (Netley) Fund* [1921] 1 Ch 655; *Re Hillier's Trusts* [1954] 1 WLR 9 and *Re Ulverston and District New Hospital Building Trusts* [1956] Ch 622 did not help him greatly because they were charity cases. It is true that they were, and, as will presently appear, that is in my view very significant in relation to the third category, but I do not think it was a valid objection with respect to the second, and for my part I cannot reconcile the decision of Upjohn J in *Re Hillier's Trusts* with that of Harman J in the *Gillingham* case [1958] Ch 300. As I see it, therefore, I have to choose between them. On the one hand it may be said that Harman J had the advantage, which Upjohn J had not, of considering the suggestion made by Jenkins LJ. On the other hand that suggestion with all respect, seems to me somewhat fanciful and unreal. I agree that all who put their money into collecting-boxes should be taken to have the same intention, but why should they not all be regarded as intending to part with their money out and out absolutely in all circumstances? I observe that P. O. Lawrence J in *Re Welsh Hospital* [1921] 1 Ch 655, 661, used very strong words. He said that any other view was inconceivable and absurd on the face of it. That commends itself to my humble judgment, and I therefore prefer and follow the judgment of Upjohn J in *Re Hillier's Trusts*. This does not appear to me to transgress the principle which Harman J laid down in the *Gillingham* case where he said, at p. 310:

> This doctrine does not, in my judgment, rest on any evidence of the state of mind of the settlor, for in the vast majority of cases no doubt he does not expect to see his money back; he has created a trust which so far as he can see will absorb the whole of it. The resulting trust arises when that expectation is for some unforeseen reason cheated of fruition, and is an inference of law based on after-knowledge of the event.

I accept that fully but I also accept the submission of counsel for the Treasury Solicitor that equity will not impute an intention which it considers would be absurd on the face of it.

■ QUESTION

Does a resulting trust arise automatically when a donor fails to dispose of the entirety of his beneficial interest in certain assets, or does it arise only when the donor can be presumed to have intended to recover any surplus?

■ SUMMATIVE QUESTION

What is a pension fund surplus, should it be subject to a resulting trust, and, if so, in favour of whom?

online
resource
centre

FURTHER READING

Andrews, G., 'The Presumption of Advancement: Equity, Equality and Human Rights' (2007) 71 *Conv* 340.

Birks, P., 'Trusts Raised to Reverse Unjust Enrichment: The *Westdeutsche* Case' [1996] *Restitution Law Review* 3.

Chambers, R., *Resulting Trusts* (Oxford: Clarendon Press, 1997).

Davies, J. D., 'Presumptions and Illegality', in A. J. Oakley (ed.), *Trends in Contemporary Trust Law* (Oxford: Clarendon Press, 1996), p. 33.

Glister, J., 'The Presumption of Advancement' in C Mitchell (ed), *Constructive and Resulting Trusts* (Oxford: Hart Publishing, 2010) p. 289.

Martin, J., 'Fraudulent Transferors and the Public Conscience' (1992) *Conv* 153.

Millett, Sir P., 'The *Quistclose* trust: a reply' (2011) 17(1) *Trusts & Trustees* 7–16.

Rickett, C., 'Different Views on the Scope of the Quistclose Analysis' (1991) 107 *LQR* 608.

Swadling, W., 'A New Role for Resulting Trusts?' (1996) 16 *Legal Studies* 133.

Swadling, W., 'Explaining Resulting Trusts' (2008) 124 *LQR* 72.

6

Formality, Perpetuity, and Illegality: Trust Creation and Public Policy I

KEY AIMS

To observe that there is no formality for the *inter vivos* creation of an express trust (although an express trust of land is unenforceable unless evidenced in writing). To consider the formalities relating to the testamentary creation of an express trust, and to examine how secret trusts and mutual wills bypass testamentary formality requirements. To examine the formalities required for dealings with equitable interests under trusts (and, in particular) to determine whether a dealing with an equitable interest under a trust is a 'declaration' of a subtrust or an outright 'disposition' of the equitable interest. To consider when a trust will be void for reasons of public policy, including on grounds of perpetuity or illegality. We will see that the traditional justification for formality requirements is the prevention of fraud, but it is arguable that their most significant use has been as a basis for raising taxes.

SECTION 1: INTRODUCTION

There are certain safeguards in place designed to prevent the undesirable creation and operation of trusts. Amongst the most significant is the requirement that the disposition of equitable interests under trusts must be *made* in writing and the requirement that the creation of trusts of land must be *evidenced* in writing. These formality requirements seek to prevent fraud and the avoidance or evasion of tax. There is another danger inherent in the way a trust separates formal ownership from beneficial ownership, namely that the trust property might never return to the state of being owned absolutely. As long as property remains subject to a trust it will be unable to participate in the market place with complete freedom, and its ability to contribute to the national 'commonwealth' will accordingly be diminished. The rule against remoteness of vesting, which is one of the rules against perpetuity, addresses this concern by ensuring that all the interests under a trust vest in beneficiaries before the end of the 'perpetuity period'. When all the interests under a trust have vested in interest, the beneficiaries may agree, if they are all competent adults, to bring the trust to an end (see Chapter 9). Another rule against perpetuity, the rule against inalienability of capital, addresses the equally undesirable possibility that trust capital may be tied up indefinitely. This possibility is most likely when trust capital is set to one side to produce income over a long period of time for some purpose or other. Trust property dedicated to purposes beneficial to the public (charitable purposes) is exempt from this rule, but, at the other extreme, certain purposes detrimental to the public are disallowed on grounds of illegality. Courts also have jurisdiction to set aside trusts deemed to be 'shams', and courts in the Family Division of the High Court have been especially willing to strike down 'trusts' established outside England and Wales in order to treat the fund as wealth available for distribution between spouses on divorce.

A: *Inter vivos* trusts

There are no formality requirements for trusts, except those laid down by statute: these are now contained in Law of Property Act 1925, s.53. The important distinctions to bear in mind are between land and other property, and between declarations and dispositions.

Implied, resulting, and constructive trusts are expressly exempted from the statutory requirements, and so, it appears, are variations of trust carried out under the Variation of Trusts Act 1958 (on which, see Chapter 9).

LAW OF PROPERTY ACT 1925

53. Instruments required to be in writing

(1)　Subject to the provisions hereinafter contained [they are contained in s.54] with respect to the creation of interests in land by parol—

  (a)　no interest in land can be created or disposed of except by writing signed by the person creating or conveying the same, or by his agent thereunto lawfully authorised in writing, or by will, or by operation of law;

  (b)　a declaration of trust respecting any land or any interest therein must be manifested and proved by some writing signed by some person who is able to declare such trust or by his will;

  (c)　a disposition of an equitable interest or trust subsisting at the time of the disposition, must be in writing signed by the person disposing of the same, or by his agent thereunto lawfully authorised in writing or by will.

(2)　This section does not affect the creation or operation of resulting, implied or constructive trusts.

NOTE: This provision is the successor to the Statute of Frauds 1677, ss.7 and 8, but with one significant difference. The Statute of Frauds read as follows:

> AND bee it further enacted by the authoritie aforesaid that … all declarations or creations of trusts or confidences of any lands tenements or hereditaments shall be manifested and proved by some writeing signed by the partie who is by law enabled to declare such trust or by his last will in writeing or else they shall be utterly void and of none effect.
>
> PROVIDED always that where any conveyance shall be made of any lands or tenements by which a trust or confidence shall or may arise or result by the implication or construction of law or bee transferred or extinguished by an act or operation of law then and in every such case such trust or confidence shall be of like force and effect as the same would have beene if this statute had not beene made. Any thing herein before contained to the contrary notwithstanding.

The Law of Property Act 1925, s.53(1)(b) does not repeat the assertion that an informal declaration of a trust of land is *void*. It can therefore be argued that an informal declaration of a trust of land is not void but merely unenforceable until evidenced in signed writing (see *Rochefoucauld* v *Boustead* [1897] 1 Ch 196, 206).

B: Testamentary trusts

If the provisions of Wills Act 1837, s.9 are not complied with, the will is completely void, and any trusts which it purports to create will be invalid also.

WILLS ACT 1837

Section 9: Signing and attestation of wills

No will shall be valid unless—

  (a) it is in writing, and signed by the testator, or by some other person in his presence and by his direction; and

  (b) it appears that the testator intended by his signature to give effect to the will; and

  (c) the signature is made or acknowledged by the testator in the presence of two or more witnesses present at the same time; and

  (d) each witness either—

    (i) attests and signs the will; or

    (ii) acknowledges his signature, in the presence of the testator (but not necessarily in the presence of any other witness), but no form of attestation shall be necessary.

[this section substituted by Administration of Justice Act 1983 (c.53), ss.17, 73(6)]

C: Mutual wills

There is no reason in principle why A should not leave property to B on the understanding that B will leave the same property in his will to C. That was the result in *Ottaway* v *Norman* [1972] Ch 698 (see fuller discussion at Section 1: Introduction, D: Secret trusts). B simply obtains a life interest in the property. This is also a possible explanation of *Re Oldham* [1925] Ch 75, a mutual wills case. A more problematic situation is where A and B agree that each will leave all his property to the survivor on the understanding that the survivor will leave all his property to C. *Re Hagger* [1930] 2 Ch 190 suggests (contrary to *Re Oldham*) that a trust attaches to all the survivor's property, as long as the survivor accepts the legacy under the other's will.

In *Ottaway* v *Norman*, the claimants alleged that the defendant, Miss Hodges had undertaken to leave to them all furniture and other contents of the house, including Miss Hodges' own money. Brightman J accepted that the secret trust comprised such furnishings and fixtures as Miss Hodges had received under Mr Ottaway's will, but that it did not include Miss Hodges's other property and cash from whatever source.

In respect of the last, it seems that he was not convinced that so far-reaching an obligation had in fact been envisaged in the agreement, but if the intended trustee (B) has clearly accepted such an obligation, he accepted that this obligation also could be enforced against her estate. He employed the concept of a 'floating trust', derived from the Australian case of *Birmingham* v *Renfrew* (1937) 57 CLR 666, which would remain in suspense during the life of the trustee and crystallise on her death, attaching to whatever property was comprised within her estate. This, as the learned judge noted, would seem to preclude Miss Hodges from making even a small pecuniary legacy in favour of her relatives or friends. Similar reasoning was also adopted in *Re Cleaver*.

Re Cleaver

[1981] 1 WLR 939, [1981] 2 All ER 1018, Chancery Division

Decision: Mutual wills could be enforced using the 'floating trust' concept described above. The husband and wife made wills by which each left the estate to the other, subject to various legacies in favour of relatives and other gifts over. The husband died first and his widow received the whole of his net estate. She then made a new will. Nourse J held that the doctrine of mutual wills applied and that the estate of the widow was held on a constructive trust on the terms of the mutual will of the wife which she had revoked.

NOURSE J: This is a case in which it is alleged that mutual wills are enforceable. By that I mean that it is one where it is alleged that two persons (in this case husband and wife) made an enforceable agreement as to the disposal of their property and executed wills in substantially identical terms in pursuance thereof. The husband died first without having revoked his will. The wife accepted benefits under the husband's will and later made her last will in substantially different terms. She is now dead. The question is whether the persons who would have been the beneficiaries under the wife's original will can claim that her estate should be held on the trusts of that will and not of her last will.

...

   The foundations of the plaintiff's claim is the well-known case of *Dufour v Pereira* (1769) 1 Dick 419, 21 ER 332. That case is fully discussed in Hargrave's *Juridicial Arguments* (1799, vol 2, pp 304ff). That was a case where Lord Camden, relying as it appears only on the terms of a joint will executed by a husband and wife, concluded that there had been a prior agreement. There have not been so very many cases on the subject since, but in one of them, *Gray v Perpetual Trustee Co. Ltd* [1928] AC 391, [1928] All ER Rep 758, the Privy Council decided in clear terms that the mere simultaneity of the wills and the similarity of their terms are not enough taken by themselves to establish the necessary agreement. I will read what appear to me to be the material passages in the judgment of the Board, which was delivered by Viscount Haldane. The first reads as follows ([1928] AC 391 at 399–400, [1928] All ER Rep 758 at 761):

> In *Dufour* v *Pereira* the conclusion reached was that if there was in point of fact an agreement come to that the wills should not be revoked after the death of one of the parties without mutual consent, they were binding. That they were mutual wills to the same effect was at least treated as a relevant circumstance, to be taken into account in determining whether there was such an agreement. But the mere simultaneity of the wills and the similarity of their terms do not appear, taken by themselves, to have been looked on as more than some evidence of an agreement not to revoke. The agreement, which does not restrain the legal right to revoke, was the foundation of the right in equity which might emerge, although it was a fact which had in itself to be established by evidence, and in such cases the whole of the evidence must be looked at.

Their Lordships then proceeded to mention two authorities, the second of which was the decision of Astbury J in *Re Oldham* [1925] Ch 75. The judgment continues ([1928] AC 391 at 400, [1928] All ER Rep 758 at 762):

> Their Lordships agree with the view taken by Astbury J. The case before them is one in which the evidence of an agreement, apart from that of making the wills in question, is so lacking that they are unable to come to the conclusion that an agreement to constitute equitable interests has been shown to have been made. As they have already said, the mere fact of making wills mutually is not, at least by the law of England, evidence of such an agreement having been come to. And without such a definite agreement there can no more be a trust in equity than a right to damages at law.

As to the penultimate sentence of that passage it must, in the light of the earlier passage, be read as meaning that the mere fact of making mutual wills is not by itself sufficient evidence of such an agreement having been come to.

   It is therefore clear that there must be a definite agreement between the makers of the two wills, that that must be established by evidence, that the fact that there are mutual wills to the same effect is a relevant circumstance to be taken into account, although not enough of itself, and that the whole of the evidence must be looked at.

   I do not find it necessary to refer to any other English case, but I have derived great assistance from the decision of the High Court of Australia in *Birmingham v Renfrew* (1936) 57 CLR 666. That was a case where the available extrinsic evidence was held to be sufficient to establish the necessary agreement between two spouses. It is chiefly of interest because both Latham CJ and more especially Dixon J examined with some care the whole nature of the legal theory on which these and other similar cases proceed. I would like to read three passages from the judgment of Dixon J, which state, with all the clarity and learning for which the judgment of that most eminent judge are renowned, what I believe to be a correct analysis of the principles on which a case of enforceable mutual wills depends. First (at 682–683):

> I think the legal result was a contract between husband and wife. The contract bound him, I think, during her lifetime not to revoke his will without notice to her. If she died without altering her

will, then he was bound after her death not to revoke his will at all. She on her part afforded the consideration for his promise by making her will. His obligation not to revoke his will during her life without notice to her is to be implied. For I think the express promise should be understood as meaning that if she died leaving her will unrevoked then he would not revoke his. But the agreement really assumes that neither party will alter his or her will without the knowledge of the other. It has long been established that a contract between persons to make corresponding wills gives rise to equitable obligations when one acts on the faith of such an agreement and dies leaving his will unrevoked so that the other takes property under its dispositions. It operates to impose upon the survivor an obligation regarded as specifically enforceable. It is true that he cannot be compelled to make and leave unrevoked a testamentary document and if he dies leaving a last will containing provisions inconsistent with his agreement it is nevertheless valid as a testamentary act. But the doctrines of equity attach the obligation to the property. The effect is, I think, that the survivor becomes a constructive trustee and the terms of the trust are those of the will which he undertook would be his last will.

Next (at 689):

There is a third element which appears to me to be inherent in the nature of such a contract or agreement, although I do not think it has been expressly considered. The purpose of an arrangement for corresponding wills must often be, as in this case, to enable the survivor during his life to deal as absolute owner with the property passing under the will of the party first dying. That is to say, the object of the transaction is to put the survivor in a position to enjoy for his own benefit the full ownership so that, for instance, he may convert it and expend the proceeds if he choose. But when he dies he is to bequeath what is left in the manner agreed upon. It is only by the special doctrines of equity that such a floating obligation, suspended, so to speak, during the life-time of the survivor can descend upon the assets at his death and crystallize into a trust. No doubt gifts and settlements, *inter vivos*, if calculated to defeat the intention of the compact, could not be made by the survivor and his right of disposition, *inter vivos*, is, therefore, not unqualified. But, substantially, the purpose of the arrangement will often be to allow full enjoyment for the survivor's own benefit and advantage upon condition that at his death the residue shall pass as arranged.

Finally (at 690):

In *In re Oldham*, Astbury J, pointed out, in dealing with the question whether an agreement should be inferred, that in *Dufour* v *Pereira* the compact was that the survivor should take a life estate only in the combined property. It was, therefore, easy to fix the corpus with a trust as from the death of the survivor. But I do not see any difficulty in modern equity in attaching to the assets a constructive trust which allowed the survivor to enjoy the property subject to a fiduciary duty which, so to speak, crystallized on his death and disabled him only from voluntary dispositions *inter vivos*.

I interject to say that Dixon J was there clearly referring only to voluntary dispositions inter vivos which are calculated to defeat the intention of the compact. No objection could normally be taken to ordinary gifts of small value. He went on:

On the contrary, as I have said, it seems rather to provide a reason for the intervention of equity. The objection that the intended beneficiaries could not enforce a contract is met by the fact that a constructive trust arises from the contract and the fact that testamentary dispositions made upon the faith of it have taken effect. It is the constructive trust and not the contract that they are entitled to enforce.

It is also clear from *Birmingham* v *Renfrew* that these cases of mutual wills are only one example of a wider category of cases, for example secret trusts, in which a court of equity will intervene to impose a constructive trust. A helpful and interesting summary of that wider category of cases will be found in the argument of counsel for the plaintiffs in *Ottaway* v *Norman* [1972] Ch 698 at 701–702. The principle of all these cases is that a court of equity will not permit a person to whom property is transferred by way of gift, but on the faith of an agreement or clear understanding that it is to be dealt with in a particular way for the benefit of a third person, to deal with that property inconsistently with that agreement or understanding. If he attempts to do so after having received the benefit of the gift equity will intervene by imposing a constructive trust on the property which is the subject matter of the agreement or understanding. I take that statement of principle, and much else which is of assistance in this case, from the judgment of Slade J in *Re Pearson Fund Trusts* (21st October 1977, unreported; the statement of principle is at p. 52 of the official transcript). The judgment of Brightman J in *Ottaway* v *Norman* is to much the same effect.

I would emphasise that the agreement or understanding must be such as to impose on the donee a legally binding obligation to deal with the property in the particular way and that the other two certainties, namely those as to the subject matter of the trust and the persons intended to benefit under it, are as essential to this species of trust as they are to any other. In spite of an argument by counsel for Mr and Mrs Noble to the contrary, I find it hard to see how there could be any difficulty about the second or third certainties in a case of mutual wills unless it was in the terms of the wills themselves. There, as in this case, the principal difficulty is always whether there was a legally binding obligation or merely what Lord Loughborugh LC in *Lord Walpole* v *Lord Orford* (1797) 3 Ves 402 at 419, 30 ER 1976 at 1084 described as an honourable engagement.

Before turning in detail to the evidence which relates to the question whether there was a legally binding obligation on the testatrix in the present case or not I must return once more to *Birmingham* v *Renfrew*. It is clear from that case, if from nowhere else, that an enforceable agreement to dispose of property in pursuance of mutual wills can be established only by clear and satisfactory evidence. That seems to me to be no more than a particular application of the general rule that all claims relating to the property of deceased persons must be scrutinised with very great care. However, that does not mean that there has to be a departure from the ordinary standard of proof required in civil proceedings. I have to be satisfied on the balance of probabilities that the alleged agreement was made, but before I can be satisfied of that I must find clear and satisfactory evidence to that effect.

[Nourse J reviewed the evidence and continued:]

In the result, and perhaps contrary to my expectation when the case was opened, I am driven to the conclusion that the plaintiffs are entitled to succeed in this action ...

NOTE: It is not clear from the report whether the trust imposed actually bound any property not received under Arthur Cleaver's will. If it did not then the *ratio* goes no further than *Re Oldham* [1925] Ch 75, above (the widow would simply have enjoyed a life interest in the property received under Arthur Cleaver's will). However, in *Re Dale* [1994] Ch 31, Morritt J applied the mutual wills doctrine where the second testator had received no benefit at all under the first testator's will, the mutual agreement having been that their children should share equally. There the trust clearly applied to the whole of the widow's estate, since the widow had received no property to which it could apply.

The Court of Appeal in *Re Goodchild* [1997] 3 All ER 63, affirming Carnwath J [1996] 1 All ER 670, accepted the notion of the floating trust, holding also that the floating trust so created was not destroyed by the remarriage of the second testator after the death of the first. On the facts, however, Carnwath found insufficient evidence of a specific agreement that the wills were to be mutually binding. Nonetheless, this case provides further authority for the floating trust concept.

■ QUESTIONS

1. X marries his first wife Y1 and they make mutual wills at the age of 20, each agreeing to settle the whole of his/her estate on the other party at his/her death. At this time they are both childless and poor, and when Y1 dies she leaves X property worth £1,000. Later in life, X marries Y2, has a number of children by his second wife, and becomes wealthy. Suppose the reasoning in *Cleaver* is correct. To what extent, if at all, can X spend his wealth during his lifetime on himself, Y2, and his children?

2. Presumably there is no reason in principle why B should not contract that in consideration for A leaving B property in his will, B will leave all his property in his will to C. On the assumption that A dies before B, who (if anybody) could (until recently) enforce the contract against B? (NOTE: You may care to consider the privity of contract doctrine discussed in Chapter 2 and *Re Plumptre's Marriage Settlement* [1910] 1 Ch 609 (Chapter 4).) Is it likely that anybody would bring a contract claim, and what remedies would be available if he or she did? Is any of this affected by the Contracts (Rights of Third Parties) Act 1999?

3. What, if any, liabilities arise, and who, if anybody, can enforce them in each of the following circumstances? If liability is founded in trust explain whether the trust is express or constructive, and identify the trust property (if any).

(a) Alpha leaves Omega his house in his will, having previously been assured by Omega that when he dies, Omega will leave it in his will to Beta. Omega dies leaving the house to Gamma in his will.

(b) Alpha and Omega agree that each will leave all his property to the survivor on the understanding that the survivor will leave all his property to Beta. Alpha dies first and Omega takes as agreed under Alpha's will. Shortly before he dies Omega donates a large part of his property to Delta and in his will leaves another large part to Epsilon. He leaves Beta the same amount as he had himself received under Alpha's will, plus interest calculated at the equitable rate.

(c) Alpha and Omega agree that each will leave all his property to Beta. Alpha dies first leaving his property to Beta as agreed. Omega dies leaving all his property to Gamma in his will.

NOTE: In question 2 above, you may wish to consider the following passage from *Re Dale*, where Morritt J appears to take the view that specific performance of such a contract would never be possible:

> The doctrine of mutual wills is to the effect that where two individuals have agreed as to the disposal of their property and have executed mutual wills in pursuance of the agreement, on the death of the first (T1) the property of the survivor (T2), the subject matter of the agreement, is held on an implied trust for the beneficiary named in the wills. The survivor may thereafter alter his will, because a will is inherently revocable, but if he does his personal representatives will take the property subject to the trust. The basic doctrine is not in dispute. The dispute is as to the circumstances in which the doctrine applies.
>
> ... There is no doubt that for the doctrine to apply there must be a contract at law. It is apparent from all the cases, to which I shall refer later, but in particular from *Gray* v *Perpetual Trustee Co. Ltd* [1928] AC 391, [1928] All ER Rep 758, that it is necessary to establish an agreement to make and not revoke mutual wills, some understanding or arrangement being insufficient 'without such a definite agreement there can no more be a trust in equity than a right to damages at law' (see [1928] AC 391 at 400, [1928] All ER Rep 758 at 762 *per* Viscount Haldane) ... . What is necessary to obtain a decree of specific performance of a contract in favour of a third party is not, in my judgment, a relevant question when considering the doctrine of mutual wills. A will is by its very nature revocable (cf *Re Heys's Estate, Walker* v *Gaskill* [1914] P 192). It seems to me to be inconceivable that the court would order T2 to execute a will in accordance with the agreement at the suit of the personal representatives of T1 or to grant an injunction restraining T2 from revoking it. The principles on which the court acts in imposing the trust to give effect to the agreement to make and not revoke mutual wills must be found in the cases dealing with that topic, not with those dealing with the availability of the remedy of specific performance.

See, on the same point, *The Thomas and Agnes Carvel Foundation* v *Carvel* [2007] EWHC 1314 (Ch), *per* Lewison J at para. [27] and *Olins* v *Walters* [2008] EWCA Civ 782, where Mummery LJ held the person who seeks to enforce a mutual will is not a party to the contract that created the mutuality of the wills, and is not seeking anything like specific performance of a contract. His lordship approved *Snell's Principles of Equity* (31st edn), para. 22–31, which states that 'Mutual wills provide an instance of a trust arising by operation of law to give effect to the express intention of the two testators'. Writing on *Olins* v *Walters* in *The Conveyancer* and reflecting on the devastation that the litigation brought upon the family, Professor Luxton observes that '[i]t was nearly 40 years ago that Robert Burgess, writing in the pages of this journal, concluded that he would "avoid mutual wills like the plague"'. Professor Luxton asks '[i]s it not time that practitioners heeded his advice?' ((2009) 6 *Conv* 498).

D: Secret trusts

Under a fully secret trust, the testator leaves property by will to a legatee in a manner which complies with the provisions of the Act, but having come to an understanding with the legatee that he is merely trustee of it in favour of a secret beneficiary. The understanding does not comply with the formality requirements of the Act, but equity will not permit a statute to be used as an instrument of fraud and therefore enforces the secret trust against the legatee by way of a constructive trust arising to prevent unconscionable conduct (it would be unconscionable for the legatee to rely on the Wills Act to uphold his formal absolute ownership under the will). A half-secret trust is where the testator leaves property by a valid will to the legatee 'on trust', but where the beneficial interest under the trust is undeclared. The half-secret trust will be valid provided the beneficiary of the trust was communicated (orally or by sealed letter or otherwise) to the legatee before the will was executed.

McCormick v *Grogan*

(1869) LR 4 HL 82, House of Lords

Facts: In 1851, the testator had left all his property by a three-line will to his friend Mr Grogan. In 1854, he was struck down by cholera. With only a few hours to live, he sent for Mr Grogan. He told Mr Grogan, in effect, that his will and a letter would be found in his desk. The letter named various intended beneficiaries and the intended gifts to them. The letter concluded with the words:

I do not wish you to act strictly on the foregoing instructions, but leave it entirely to your own good judgment to do as you think I would, if living, and as the parties are deserving.

An intended beneficiary (an illegitimate child), whom Mr Grogan thought it right to exclude, sued.

Held: Although in principle the courts will enforce secret trusts, the terms of the letter in this particular case were not such that equity would impose on the conscience of Mr Grogan, and the secret trust alleged would not be enforced.

LORD HATHERLEY LC: ... Now this doctrine has been established, no doubt, a long time since upon a sound foundation with reference to the jurisdiction of Courts of Equity to interpose in all cases of fraud; and therefore if, for example, an heir said to a person who was competent to dispose of his property by will, 'Do not dispose of it by will, I undertake to carry into effect all such wishes as you may communicate to me.' And if the testator, acting on that representation, did not dispose of his property by will, and the heir has kept the property for himself, without carrying those instructions into effect, the Court of Equity has interposed on the ground of the fraud thus committed by the heir in inducing the testator to die intestate, upon the faith of the heir's representations that he would carry all such wishes as were confided to him into effect. And the Court has said that the heir shall not be allowed to hold the property otherwise than as trustee for those with regard to whom the testator gave him the directions in question. So again, if a legatee states to the testator that upon the testator's confiding his property, apparently disposing of it, to him, the legatee, by a regular and formal instrument, he will carry into effect all such intentions as the testator shall confide to him, then that legatee, although he apparently may be held in law to take the whole interest, shall have fastened upon his conscience the trust of carrying into full effect those instructions which he received upon such representations as I have described. And, farther than that, such an undertaking or promise on the part of the legatee has been held, in some cases, to be capable of being inferred from the conduct of the person when secret instructions have been communicated to him by the testator, which conduct has been held by the Court to be equivalent to an undertaking or promise on his part that he will abide by the instructions so communicated to him.

But this doctrine evidently requires to be carefully restricted within proper limits. It is in itself a doctrine which involves a wide departure from the policy which induced the Legislature to pass the Statute of Frauds, and it is only in clear cases of fraud that this doctrine has been applied—cases in which the Court has been persuaded that there has been a fraudulent inducement held out on the part of the apparent beneficiary in order to lead the testator to confide to him the duty which he so undertook to perform.

Now, in the case before us, Mr Grogan, the Respondent, undoubtedly stands in a very favourable position in this matter. The will was made three years before it was communicated to him. He in no way induced the testator to appoint him sole executor and sole legate of the whole property. On the contrary, it appears from the evidence that he was somewhat surprised when he was informed of the fact. There is therefore no anterior act on the part of Mr Grogan which should induce the Court to come to the conclusion upon imperfect evidence of any fraud having been meditated and perpetrated on his part. He is therefore entitled to the benefit of having his conduct regarded as that of a man who stands perfectly *rectus in curia* at the outset of the transaction.

LORD WESTBURY: My Lords, the jurisdiction which is invoked here by the Appellant is founded altogether on personal fraud. It is a jurisdiction by which a Court of Equity, proceeding on the ground of fraud, converts the party who has committed it into a trustee for the party who is injured by that fraud. Now, being a jurisdiction founded on personal fraud, it is incumbent on the Court to see that a fraud, a *malus animus*, is proved by the clearest and most indisputable evidence. It is impossible to supply presumption in the place of proof, nor are you warranted in deriving those conclusions in the absence of direct proof, for the purpose of affixing the criminal character of fraud, which you might by possibility derive in a case of simple contract. The Court of Equity has, from a very early period, decided that even an Act of Parliament shall not be used as an instrument of fraud; and if in the machinery of perpetrating a fraud an Act of Parliament intervenes, the Court of Equity, it is true, does not set aside the Act of Parliament but it fastens on the individual who gets a title under that Act, and imposes upon him a personal obligation, because he applies the Act as an instrument for accomplishing a fraud. In this way the Court of Equity has dealt with the Statute of Frauds, and in this manner, also, it deals with the Statute of Wills. And if an individual on his deathbed, or at any other time, is persuaded by his heir-at-law, or his next of kin, to abstain from making a will, or if the same individual, having made a will, communicates the disposition to the person on the face of the will benefited by that disposition, but, at the same time, says to that individual that he has a purpose to answer, which he has not expressed in the will, but which he depends on the disponee to carry into effect, and the disponee assents to it, either expressly, or by any mode of action which the disponee knows must give to the testator the impression and belief that he fully assents to the request, then, undoubtedly, the heir-at-law in the one case, and the disponee in the other, will be converted into trustees, simply on the principle that an individual should not be benefited by his own personal fraud. You are obliged, therefore, to shew most clearly and distinctly that the person you wish to convert into a trustee acted *malo animo*. You must shew distinctly that he knew that the testator or the intestate was beguiled and deceived by his conduct. If you are not in a condition to affirm that without any misgiving, or possibility of mistake, you are not warranted in affixing on the individual the *delictum* of fraud, which you must do before you convert him into a trustee.

NOTE: The jurisdiction is clearly based on fraud (not proved in this case) and requires the legatee to carry the testator's wishes into effect, not merely to hold the property on resulting trust for the estate. The precise nature of the fraud was clarified by Brightman J in *Ottaway* v *Norman* [1972] Ch 698 (discussed in this subsection).

Blackwell v *Blackwell*

[1929] AC 318, House of Lords

Facts: By a codicil to his will, a testator transferred £12,000 to five trustees, to apply the income 'for the purposes indicated by me to them', with power to pay over the capital sum of £8,000 'to such person or persons indicated by me to them'. He had given detailed oral instructions on the codicil to one of the trustees, and all five knew the general object of the codicil before its execution (and were willing to carry it out). The trustees accordingly proposed to pay the income to a lady who was not the testator's wife. The testator's legitimate family challenged the validity of the half-secret trust.

Held: The half-secret trust was valid.

VISCOUNT SUMNER: For the prevention of fraud equity fastens on the conscience of the legatee a trust, a trust, that is, which otherwise would be inoperative; in other words it makes him do what the will in itself has nothing to do with; it lets him take what the will gives him and then makes him apply it, as the Court of conscience directs, and it does so in order to give effect to wishes of the testator, which would not otherwise be effectual.

To this two circumstances must be added to bring the present case to the test of the general doctrine, first, that the will states on its face that the legacy is given on trust but does not state what the trusts are, and further contains a residuary bequest, and, second, that the legatees are acting with perfect honesty, seek no advantage to themselves, and only desire, if the Court will permit them, to do what in other circumstances the Court would have fastened it on their conscience to perform.

■ QUESTION

Is the effect of equitable intervention in a half-secret trust to prevent fraud?

Ottaway v *Norman*

[1972] 1 Ch 698, Chancery Division

Facts: Miss Hodges' employer, Mr Ottaway, left her his bungalow in his will, on terms that she would leave it by her own will to Mr Ottaway's son. Miss Hodges later changed her mind and left her property to a cousin.

According to the evidence given by the son and his wife, Miss Hodges also undertook to leave them the furniture and other contents, including her money.

Held: Brightman J accepted that there had been an arrangement between old Mr Ottaway and Miss Hodges that she should leave the bungalow to the son, and imposed a constructive trust upon the bungalow in the hands of Miss Hodges' executor. He also accepted that the secret trust comprised such furnishings and fixtures as Miss Hodges had received under Mr Ottaway's will, but not that it included all Miss Hodges' other property and cash from whatever source.

BRIGHTMAN J: ... It will be convenient to call the person upon whom such a trust is imposed the 'primary donee' and the beneficiary under that trust the 'secondary donee'. The essential elements which must be proved to exist are: (i) the intention of the testator to subject the primary donee to an obligation in favour of the secondary donee; (ii) communication of that intention to the primary donee; and (iii) the acceptance of that obligation by the primary donee either expressly or by acquiescence. It is immaterial whether these elements precede or succeed the will of the donor. I am informed that there is no recent reported case where the obligation imposed on the primary donee is an obligation to make a will in favour of the secondary donee as distinct from some form of *inter vivos* transfer. But it does not seem to me that there can really be any distinction which can validly be taken on behalf of the defendant in the present case. The basis of the doctrine of a secret trust is the obligation imposed on the conscience of the primary donee and it does not seem to me that there is any materiality in the machinery by which the donor intends that that obligation shall be carried out.

Mr Buckle, for Mr Norman, relied strongly on *McCormick* v *Grogan* (1869) LR 4 HL 82 [also discussed in this subsection] ...

Founding himself on Lord Westbury Mr Buckle sought at one stage to deploy an argument that a person could never succeed in establishing a secret trust unless he could show that the primary donee was guilty of deliberate and conscious wrongdoing of which he said there was no evidence in the case before me. That proposition, if correct, would lead to the surprising result that if the primary donee faithfully observed the obligation imposed on him there would not ever have been a trust at any time in existence. The argument was discarded, and I think rightly. Mr Buckle then fastened on the words 'clearest and most indisputable evidence' and he submitted that an exceptionally high standard of proof was needed to establish a secret trust. I do not think that Lord Westbury's words mean more than this: that if a will contains a gift which is in terms absolute, clear evidence is needed before the court will assume that the testator did not mean what he said. It is perhaps analogous to the standard of proof which this court requires before it will rectify a written instrument, for there again a party is saying that neither meant what they have written.

NOTES

1. At the time of the arrangement between Miss Hodges and the testator Ottaway, she clearly intended to carry out her promise to leave the land to Ottaway's son in her own will. There was therefore no fraud in the sense required for a deceit action at common law.
2. The fact that the trust was oral was not a bar to its enforcement, despite the Law of Property Act 1925, s.53(1)(b), because the executor was held to be a constructive trustee of the bungalow.

E: Dispositions of equitable interests

Brian Green, '*Grey, Oughtred* and *Vandervell*—A Contextual Reappraisal'
(1984) 47 *MLR* 385

In addressing itself to subsisting equitable interests, section 53(1)(c) took up the mantle of section 9 of the Statute of Frauds 1677 [Green sets out the section], and like that provision was designed (i) to prevent hidden oral transactions in equitable interests in fraud of those truly entitled and (ii) to enable trustees to know where the equitable interests behind their trusts reside at any particular time. [Green notes Lord Upjohn in *Vandervell v IRC* [1967] 2 AC 291, 311B–D] ...

Section 9 of the 1677 Act, being concerned solely with 'grants and assignments' of subsisting equitable rights, and hence exclusively with dispositions by equitable proprietors themselves, fell squarely within the twin policy objectives noted above. By replacing the words 'grants and assignments' with the single word 'disposition,' the draftsman (as a matter of language at least) potentially extended the requirement of writing to transactions effected by persons other than the equitable owner for the time being, e.g. to trustees exercising a power of revocation and new appointment: a case clearly outside the twin policy objectives in that (i) if the consent of the person entitled in equity pending the revocation and new appointment is (as is usually the case) irrelevant to the trustees exercising their power, divestment of his previously subsisting interest behind his back cannot be a cause for concern and (ii) since it is the trustees who will be exercising the power it can hardly be said that writing is necessary to enable them (at least so long as they are viewed as a single and continuing body of persons) to ascertain to whom their fiduciary duties are owed.

A principal reason for singling out subsisting equitable interests for protection is because evidence of their movement will often be the only indicator of where a particular right resides at any given time. There is no documentary paper title, nor generally is there physical possession ... : two indicia which facilitate the identification of a legal proprietor. In general there is only an invisible entitlement to certain rights perceived by courts of equity behind the veil of legal title.

NOTES
1. Green notes that there are exceptions to the position in the last paragraph, as where a life tenant has the right to occupy property.
2. The old section was probably in line with the twin policy objectives suggested by Green, but it seems from the following case that the new section is not to be interpreted as merely consolidatory, and that 'disposition' is considerably wider than 'grants and assignments'. It is not an easy term to define, but probably includes all transfers of equitable interests apart from declarations of trust, disclaimers of equitable interests (*Re Paradise Motor Co. Ltd* [1968] 1 WLR 1125), mergers of legal and equitable title (*Vandervell v IRC*) and by implication, perhaps, surrenders of equitable interests.
3. Whether or not the twin policy objectives suggested by Green were the original reasons behind the writing requirements, all the cases considered in detail here are in fact taxation cases.

Grey v IRC

[1960] AC 1, House of Lords

Facts: Mr Hunter was beneficial owner of 18,000 shares of £1 each, the legal title being held by nominees. In order to transfer his beneficial interest, Mr Hunter orally directed the nominees (one of whom was Grey) to hold the shares on trust for beneficiaries under six settlements (the nominees were also the trustees under these settlements). Later the trustees/nominees executed six deeds of declaration to this effect, which were in writing.

The issue was whether the equitable title in the shares was transferred by the oral direction, or by the deeds of declaration. If the oral direction had transferred the shares no *ad valorem* stamp duty was payable; if the transfer had been effected by the written declaration, it was.

Held: The transfer of the equitable title was effected by the written declaration. The oral direction transferred the bare legal title only. A direction by a beneficiary to the trustees to transfer his interest to someone else constitutes a disposition and must therefore be in writing, under the Law of Property Act 1925, s.53(1)(c).

Lord Radcliffe's view was that s.53(1) did not merely consolidate the earlier Statute of Frauds: this was a disposition, whether or not it was also within the mischief of s.9 of the earlier statute.

LORD RADCLIFFE: Where opinions have differed [in the courts below] is on the point whether his direction, i.e. Mr Hunter's oral direction to his trustees was a 'disposition' within the meaning of s.53(1)(c) of the Law of Property Act 1925, the argument for giving it a more restricted meaning in that context being that s.53 is to be construed as no more than a consolidation of three sections of the Statute of Frauds, ss.3, 7 and 9. So treated, 'disposition', it is said, is merely the equivalent of the former words of s.9, 'grants and assignments', except that testamentary disposition has to be covered as well, and a direction to a trustee by the equitable owner of the property prescribing new trusts upon which it is to be held is a declaration of trust but not a grant or assignment. The argument concludes, therefore, that neither before 1 January 1926 nor since did such a direction require to be in writing signed by the disponor or his agent in order to be effective.

In my opinion, it is a very nice question whether a parol declaration of trust of this kind was or was not within the mischief of s.9 of the Statute of Frauds. The point has never, I believe, been decided and perhaps it never will be. Certainly it was long established at law that while a declaration of trust respecting land or any interest therein required writing to be effective, a declaration of trust respecting personalty did not. Moreover, there is warrant for saying that a direction to his trustee by the equitable owner of trust property prescribing new trusts of that property was a declaration of trust. But it does not necessarily follow from that that such a direction, if the effect of it was to determine completely or *pro tanto* the subsisting equitable interest of the maker of the direction, was not also a grant or assignment for the purposes of section 9 and therefore required writing for its validity. Something had to happen to that equitable interest in order to displace it in favour of the new interests created by the direction: and it would be at any rate logical to treat the direction as being an assignment of the subsisting interest to the new beneficiary or beneficiaries or, in other cases, a release or surrender of it to the trustees.

I do not think, however, that that question has to be answered for the purposes of this appeal. It can only be relevant if s.53(1) of the Law of Property Act 1925, is treated as a true consolidation of the three sections of the Statute of Frauds concerned and as governed, therefore, by the general principle, with which I am entirely in agreement, that a consolidating Act is not to be read as effecting changes in the existing law unless the words it employs are too clear in their effect to admit of any other construction. If there is anything in the judgments of the majority of the Court of Appeal which is inconsistent with this principle I must express my disagreement with them. But, in my opinion, it is impossible to regard s.53 of the Law of Property Act 1925 as a consolidating enactment in this sense. It is here that the premises upon which Upjohn J and the Master of the Rolls founded their conclusions are, I believe, unsound.

[Lord Radcliffe examined the history of the 1925 legislation, and continued:]

For these reasons I think that there is no direct link between s.53(1)(c) of the Act of 1925 and section 9 of the Statute of Frauds. The link was broken by the changes introduced by the amending Act [Law of Property (Amendment) Act] of 1924, and it was those changes, not the original statute, that s.53 must be taken as consolidating. If so, it is inadmissible to allow the construction of the word 'disposition' in the new Act to be limited or controlled by any meaning attributed to the words 'grant' or 'assignment' in s.9 of the old Act.

■ QUESTION

Is this decision in line with the twin policy objectives suggested by Green (also discussed in this subsection)?

Vandervell v *IRC*

[1967] 2 AC 291, House of Lords

Facts: See Chapter 5.

LORD WILBERFORCE: The conclusion, on the facts found, is simply that the option was vested in the trustee company as a trustee on trusts, not defined at the time, possibly to be defined later. But the equitable, or beneficial interest, cannot remain in the air: the consequence in law must be that it remains in the settlor. There is no need to consider some of the more refined intellectualities of the doctrine of resulting trust, nor to speculate whether, in possible circumstances, the shares might be applicable for Mr Vandervell's benefit: he had, as the direct result of the option and of the failure to place the beneficial interest in it securely away from him, not divested himself absolutely of the shares which it controlled.

There remains the alternative point taken by the Crown that in any event, by virtue of s.53(1)(c) of the Law of Property Act 1925, the appellant never effectively disposed of the beneficial interest in the shares to the Royal College of Surgeons. This argument I cannot accept. Section 53(1)(c), a successor to the dormant s.9 of the Statute of Frauds, has recently received a new lease of life as an instrument in the hands of the Revenue. The subsection, which has twice recently brought litigants to this House (*Grey* v *IRC* [1960] AC 1; *Oughtred* v *IRC* [1960] AC 206 [both also discussed in this subsection]), is certainly not easy to apply to the varied transactions in equitable interests which now occur. However, in this case no problem arises. The shares in question, the 100,000 A shares in Vandervell Products Ltd, were, prior to 14 November 1958, registered in the name of the National Provincial Bank Ltd upon trust for the appellant absolutely. On 14 November 1958, the appellant's solicitor received from the bank a blank transfer of the shares, executed by the bank, and the share certificate. So at this stage the appellant was the absolute master of the shares and only needed to insert his name as transferee in the transfer and to register it to become the full legal owner. He was also the owner in equity. On 19 November 1958, the solicitor (or Mr Robins—the case is ambiguous) on behalf of Mr Vandervell, who intended to make a gift, handed the transfer to the college which, in due course, sealed it and obtained registration of the shares in the college's name. The case should then be regarded as one in which the appellant himself has, with the intention to make a gift, put the college in a position to become the legal owner of the shares, which the college in fact became. If the appellant had died before the college had obtained registration, it is clear that on the principle of *Re Rose* [1949] Ch 78 that the gift would have been complete, on the basis that he had done everything in his power to transfer the legal interest, with an intention to give, to the college. No separate transfer, therefore, of the equitable interest ever came to or needed to be made and there is no room for the operation of the subsection. What the position would have been had there simply been an oral direction to the legal owner (viz. the bank) to transfer the shares to the college, followed by such a transfer, but without any document in writing signed by Mr Vandervell as equitable owner, is not a matter which calls for consideration here. The Crown's argument on this point fails but, for the reasons earlier given, I would dismiss the appeal.

Re Vandervell's Trusts (No. 2)

[1974] Ch 269, Court of Appeal

Further facts: The facts follow on from the result of the previous case, and the following statement is from the judgment of Lord Denning MR.

In October 1961 the trustee company exercised the option. They did it by using the money of the children's settlement. They paid £5,000 of the children's money to the Royal College of Surgeons. In return the Royal College of Surgeons, on 27 October 1961, transferred the 100,000 A shares to the trustee company. The intention of Mr Vandervell and of the trustee company was that the trustee company should hold the shares (which had replaced the option) on trust for the children as an addition to the children's settlement. They made this clear to the Revenue authorities in an important letter written by their solicitors on 2 November 1961, which I will read:

> GA Vandervell, Esq.—Surtax
>
> Further to our letter of 7 September last, we write to inform you that in accordance with the advice tendered by counsel to Vandervell Trustees Ltd, the latter have exercised the option granted to them by the Royal College of Surgeons of 1 December 1958, and procured a transfer to

them of the shares referred to in the option, with funds held by them upon the trusts of the settlement created by Mr G. A. Vandervell and dated 30 December 1949, and consequently such shares will henceforth be held by them upon the trusts of the settlement.

Mr Vandervell believed that thenceforward the trustee company held the 100,000 A shares on trust for the children. He acted on that footing. He got his products company to declare dividends on them for the years 1962 to 1964 amounting to the large sum of £1,256,458 gross (before tax) and £769,580 10s. 9d (after tax). These dividends were received by the trustee company and added to the funds of the children's settlement. They were invested by the trustee company for the benefit of the children exclusively.

But even now Mr Vandervell had not shaken off the demands of the Revenue authorities. They claimed that, even after the exercise of the option, Mr Vandervell had not divested himself of his interest in the 100,000 A shares and that he was liable for surtax on the dividends paid to the children's settlement. Faced with this demand, Mr Vandervell, on the advice of counsel, took the final step. He executed a deed transferring everything to the trustee company on trust for the children. This ended the second period, and started the third.

On 19 January 1965, Mr Vandervell executed a deed by which he transferred to the trustee company all right, title or interest which he had on the option or the shares or in the dividends—expressly declaring that the trust company were to hold them on the trusts of the children's settlement. At last the Revenue authorities accepted the position. They recognised that from 19 January 1965, Mr Vandervell had no interest whatever in the shares or the dividends. They made no demands for surtax thenceforward.

On 27 January 1967, Mr Vandervell made his will. It was in contemplation of a new marriage. In it he made no provision for his children. He said expressly that this was because he had already provided for them by the children's settlement. Six weeks later, on 10 March 1967, he died.

Held: The Court of Appeal was concerned only with the law for the second period. Liability to surtax now depended on the whereabouts of the equitable interest in the shares during that period. It was argued that, as before, it remained with Vandervell.

The option: The option was destroyed when it was exercised by the trustee company in 1961, so Vandervell's equitable interest in it (resulting from the earlier litigation) was extinguished. This was not a disposition within s.53.

The shares: The children had the equitable interest. The shares had been placed by the trustee company on the trusts of the children's settlements, and Vandervell had now succeeded in divesting himself of the entire interest in these shares, there being no longer a resulting trust in his favour. The later trusts were precisely defined, in favour of the children's settlements, so that it was no longer necessary for the equitable interest to remain in the settlor.

Lord Denning MR analysed the position as a termination of the resulting trust of the option in favour of Vandervell, and a fresh trust of the shares declared (presumably by the trustee company) in favour of the children. As to the first part, writing is not required to terminate a resulting trust, and since the new trust was not of land no formalities were required for its creation.

LORD DENNING MR: In October and November 1961, the trustee company exercised the option. They paid £5,000 out of the children's settlement. The Royal College of Surgeons transferred the legal estate in the 100,000 A shares to the trustee company. Thereupon the trustee company became the legal owner of the shares. This was a different kind of property altogether. Whereas previously the trustee company had only a chose in action of one kind—an option—it now had a chose in action of a different kind—the actual shares. This trust property was not held by the trustee company beneficially. It was held by them on trust. On this occasion a valid trust was created at the time of the transfer. It was manifested in clear and unmistakable fashion. It was precisely defined. The shares were to be held on the trusts of the children's settlement. The evidence of intention is indisputable: (i) The trustee company used the children's money—£5,000—with which to acquire the shares. This would be a breach of trust unless they intended the shares to be an addition to the children's settlement. (ii) The trustee company wrote to the Revenue authorities the letter of 2 November 1961, declaring expressly that the shares 'will henceforth be held by them on the trusts of the children's settlement'. (iii) Thenceforward all the dividends received by the trustees were paid by them to the children's settlement and treated as part of the funds of the settlement. This was all done with the full assent of Mr Vandervell. Such being the intention, clear and manifest, at the time when the shares were conveyed to the trustee company, it is sufficient to create a trust.

Mr Balcombe for the executors admitted that the intention of Mr Vandervell and the trustee company was that the shares should be held on trust for the children's settlement. But he said that this intention was of no avail. He said that during the first period, Mr Vandervell had on equitable interest in the property, namely, a resulting trust; that he never disposed of this equitable interest (because he never knew he had it): and that in any case it was the disposition of an equitable interest which, under s.53 of the Law of Property Act 1925, had to be in writing, signed by him or his agent, lawfully authorised by him in writing (and there was no such writing produced). He cited *Grey* v *IRC* [1960] AC 1 and *Oughtred* v *IRC* [1960] AC 206 [both also discussed in this subsection].

There is a complete fallacy in that argument. A resulting trust for the settlor is born and dies without any writing at all. It comes into existence whenever there is a gap in the beneficial ownership. It ceases to exist whenever that gap is filled by someone becoming beneficially entitled. As soon as the gap is filled by the creation or declaration of a valid trust, the resulting trust comes to an end. In this case, before the option was exercised, there was a gap in the beneficial ownership. So there was a resulting trust for Mr Vandervell. But as soon as the option was exercised and the shares registered in the trustees' name, there was created a valid trust of the shares in favour of the children's settlement. Not being a trust of land, it could be created without any writing. A trust of personalty can be created without writing. Both Mr Vandervell and the trustee company had done everything which needed to be done to make the settlement of these shares binding on them. So there was a valid trust: see *Milroy* v *Lord* (1862) 4 De GF & J 264, 274, per Turner LJ.

NOTE: In 1965, Vandervell, presumably by now justifiably fed up with his scheme, expressly relinquished by deed any interest, legal or equitable, he may still have had in the shares.

■ QUESTIONS

1. So far as the formality aspects of the *Vandervell* decisions are concerned, at no stage did s.53 operate to defeat a transaction in either case. Given that none of the transactions could have been kept secret from the trustees, is this in accord with the twin policy objectives suggested by Green (in this subsection)?

2. X holds shares on trust for Y. Y wishes to transfer his equitable interest to Z, and embarks on an arrangement with X and W, where he directs X to transfer the legal and equitable interest in the shares to W, it being understood that W will declare himself trustee for Z. Is writing required at any stage?

3. Suppose W drops out of the picture, and Y surrenders his equitable interest to X, it being understood that X will declare himself trustee for Z. Can that possibly make any difference to your answer?

4. If no writing is required for 3, is this an easy way to avoid the consequences of *Grey* v *IRC*?

Oughtred v *IRC*

[1960] AC 206, House of Lords

Facts: Mrs Oughtred owned 72,700 shares in William Jackson and Son Ltd absolutely. 200,000 shares in the same company were held on trust for Mrs Oughtred for life, thence for her son, Peter absolutely. The parties orally agreed to exchange their interests, so that Mrs Oughtred would obtain Peter's reversionary interest (she would then have 200,000 shares outright), and in exchange Peter would obtain Mrs Oughtred's 72,700 shares. The contract was later performed.

The Revenue claimed stamp duty on the transfer of the reversionary interest in the 200,000 shares, the actual transfer of which involved writing. Oughtred's argument was that the equitable interest was transferred on the oral contract for sale, and that the later writing transferred only the bare legal title.

Held: (Viscount Radcliffe and Lord Cohen dissenting): The parties had intended the later written document to be part of the transaction and it should be assessed to *ad valorem* stamp duty. Their Lordships considered the agreement to exchange interests in the shares to be analogous to a simple case of a contract for sale of land. Land, like private company shares, is considered to be unique, and a constructive trust is said to arise as soon as parties to the sale of land contractually agree to the sale, but the formal deed that completes the formal transfer of legal title to the land has always been treated as stampable *ad valorem*.

LORD JENKINS: The provisions of the Stamp Act 1891 directly relevant to the claim are these:

Section 1 (which contains the charge of stamp duties) provides that stamp duties 'upon the several instruments specified in Schedule 1 to this Act shall be the several duties in the said Schedule specified'.

Section 54 provides as follows: 'For the purposes of this Act the expression' conveyance on sale 'includes every instrument ... whereby any property, or any estate or interest in any property, upon the sale thereof is transferred to or vested in a purchaser, or any person on his behalf or by his direction'.

Schedule 1 imposes under the head of charge 'conveyance or transfer on sale, of any property' (except as therein mentioned) *ad valorem* duty upon 'the amount or value of the consideration for the sale'; and under the head of charge 'conveyance or transfer of any kind not hereinbefore described' a fixed duty of 10s. [50p] ...

I am unable to accept the conclusion that the disputed transfer was prevented from being a transfer of the shares to the appellant on sale because the entire beneficial interest in the settled shares was already vested in the appellant under the constructive trust, and there was accordingly nothing left for the disputed transfer to pass to the appellant except the bare legal estate. The constructive trust in favour of a purchaser which arises on the conclusion of a contract for sale is founded upon the purchaser's right to enforce the contract in proceedings for specific performance. In other words, he is treated in equity as entitled by virtue of the contract to the property which the vendor is bound under the contract to convey to him. This interest under the contract is no doubt a proprietary interest of a sort, which arises, so to speak, in anticipation of the execution of the transfer for which the purchaser is entitled to call. But its existence has never (so far as I know) been held to prevent a subsequent transfer, in performance of the contract, of the property contracted to be sold from constituting for stamp duty purposes a transfer on sale of the property in question. Take the simple case of a contract for the sale of land. In such a case a constructive trust in favour of the purchaser arises on the conclusion of the contract for sale, but (so far as I know) it has never been held on this account that a conveyance subsequently executed in performance of the contract is not stampable *ad valorem* as a transfer on sale. Similarly, in a case like the present one, but uncomplicated by the existence of successive interests, a transfer to a purchaser of the investments comprised in a trust fund could not, in my judgment, be prevented from constituting a transfer on sale for the purposes of stamp duty by reason of the fact that the actual transfer had been preceded by an oral agreement for sale.

In truth, the title secured by a purchaser by means of an actual transfer is different in kind from, and may well be far superior to, the special form of proprietary interest which equity confers on a purchaser in anticipation of such transfer.

The difference is of particular importance in the case of property such as shares in a limited company. Under the contract the purchaser is no doubt entitled in equity as between himself and the vendor to the beneficial interest in the shares, and (subject to due payment of the purchase consideration) to call for a transfer of them from the vendor as trustee for him. But it is only on the execution of the actual transfer that he becomes entitled to be registered as a member, to attend and vote at meetings, to effect transfers on the register, or to receive dividends otherwise than through the vendor as his trustee.

VISCOUNT RADCLIFFE (dissenting): ... The reasoning of the whole matter, as I see it, is as follows. On 18 June 1956, the son owned an equitable reversionary interest in the settled shares; by his oral agreement of that date he created in his mother an equitable interest in his reversion, since the subject-matter of the agreement was property of which specific performance would normally be decreed by the court. He thus became a trustee for her of that interest sub modo; having regard to subsection (2) of s.53 of the Law of Property Act 1925, subsection (1) of that section did not operate to prevent that trusteeship arising by operation of law. On 26 June the appellant transferred to her son the shares which were the consideration for her acquisition of his equitable interest; on this transfer he became in a full sense and without more the trustee of his interest for her. She was the effective owner of all outstanding equitable interests. It was thus correct to recite in the deed of release to the trustees of the settlement, which was to wind up their trust, that the trust fund was by then held on trust for her absolutely. There was, in fact, no equity to the shares that could be asserted against her, and it was open to her, if she so wished, to let the matter rest without calling for a written assignment from her son. Given that the trustees were apprised of the making of the oral agreement and of the appellant's satisfaction of the consideration to be given by her, the trustees had no more to do than to transfer their legal title to her or as she might direct. This and no more is what they did.

It follows that, in my view, this transfer cannot be treated as a conveyance of the son's equitable reversion at all. The trustees had not got it; he never transferred or released it to them; how, then, could they convey it? With all respect to those who think otherwise, it is incorrect to say that the trustees' transfer was made either with his authority or at his direction. If the recital as to the appellant's rights was correct, as I think that it was, he had no remaining authority to give or direction to issue. A release is, after all, the normal instrument for winding-up a trust when all the equitable rights are vested and the legal estate is called for from the trustees who hold it. What the release gave the trustees from him was acquittance for the trust administration and accounts to date, and the fact that he gave it in consideration of the legal interest in the shares being vested in his mother adds nothing on this point. Nor does it, with respect, advance the matter to say, correctly, that, at the end of the day, the appellant was the absolute owner of the shares, legal and equitable. I think that she was; but that is description, not analysis. The question that is relevant for the purpose of this appeal is how she came to occupy that position; a position which, under English law, could be reached by more than one road.

NOTE: The decision in *Neville* v *Wilson* [1997] Ch 144, Court of Appeal, indicates that Mrs Oughtred and her son would have succeeded if they had simply allowed their agreement to remain informal (Watt [1997] *Nott LJ* 86).

F: Perpetuity

In addition to the many prerequisites to creating a valid trust that we have already encountered so far in this book, any private trust will be invalid if it infringes the rules against perpetuity. The three rules against perpetuity are the rule against remoteness of vesting (which is designed to ensure that all the interests under a trust vest in beneficiaries before the end of the 'perpetuity period', because at that stage the beneficiaries may agree, if they are all competent adults, to bring the trust to an end under the rule in *Saunders* v *Vautier* (1841) 10 LJ Ch 354, see Chapter 9), the rule against inalienability of capital, and the rule against accumulation of income. Calculating the perpetuity period can be complex, but as a rule of thumb it is worth bearing in mind that the perpetuity period will rarely exceed 100 years. Perpetuities rarely give rise to difficulties today, except in the context of non-charitable unincorporated associations (see Chapter 3), and are therefore not considered in detail here. The following points should be noted, however:

(a) The rule against remoteness of vesting applies to contingent dispositions, e.g. 'To X when X becomes a barrister.' It addresses the concern that the contingency might not be met until some remote future time, or to put it another way, the concern that a donee's interest in the disposition might not vest until some remote future time.

(b) At common law, the validity or otherwise of a disposition is decided at the outset. Under the common law rule against remoteness of vesting, a disposition is invalid if there is the remotest possibility, however unlikely, that the perpetuity period (a life in being plus 21 years) will be exceeded. Though the precise definition of a life in being has attracted much debate, what is certain is that a disposition will fail at common law if there is any possibility of its vesting more than 21 years after the death of the last surviving 'life in being'. A life in being is, broadly speaking, a person living when the gift is made, the duration of whose life might affect the date the gift finally vests.

(c) There was also a common law rule against inalienability, which prevented a trust for a purpose (if valid at all) from lasting more than 21 years. Since there would usually be a gift over, however (as in *Re Denley's Trust Deed* considered in Chapter 3), it would be the gift over which would be subject to perpetuity, and its validity would be determined by the rule against remoteness of vesting.

(d) The Perpetuities and Accumulations Act 1964 relaxed the common law rules, which could strike down perfectly reasonable arrangements. It introduced (among other provisions) more realistic fertility presumptions (the common law had assumed that females could bear children at any age), and a new policy of 'wait and see', which allows certain arrangements which would have been void from the outset at common law to take effect unless and until it is obvious that they must infringe the rule. However, the 1964 Act operates only prospectively, pre-1964 settlements still being governed by the common law. Moreover, the 1964 Act does not apply at all to trusts for purposes (it applies only to dispositions, which by s.15(2) require an interest in or right over property to be transferred).

(e) There are also statutory rules against excessive accumulation of income (set out in the following sections).

LAW OF PROPERTY ACT 1925

[Applicable to dispositions taking effect before 6 April 2010.]

164. General restrictions on accumulation of income

(1) No person may ... settle or dispose of any property in such manner that the income thereof shall ... be ... accumulated for any longer period than one of the following, namely:—

(a) the life of the grantor or settlor; or

(b) a term of twenty-one years from the death of the grantor, settlor or testator; or

(c) the duration of the minority or respective minorities of any person or persons living or en ventre sa mere at the death of the grantor, settlor or testator; or

(d) the duration of the minority or respective minorities only of any person or persons who under the limitations of the instrument directing the accumulations would, for the time being, if of full age, be entitled to the income directed to be accumulated.

In every case where any accumulation is directed otherwise than as aforesaid, the direction shall (save as hereinafter mentioned) be void; and the income of the property directed to be accumulated shall ... go to and be received by the person or persons who would have been entitled thereto if such accumulation had not been directed.

THE PERPETUITIES AND ACCUMULATIONS ACT 1964

[Applicable to dispositions taking effect after 15 July 1964 and before 6 April 2010.]

13 Amendment of s.164 of Law of Property Act 1925

(1) The periods for which accumulations of income under a settlement or other disposition are permitted by section 164 of the Law of Property Act 1925 shall include—

(a) a term of twenty-one years from the date of the making of the disposition, and

(b) the duration of the minority or respective minorities of any person or persons in being at that date.

(2) It is hereby declared that the restrictions imposed by the said section 164 apply in relation to a power to accumulate income whether or not there is a duty to exercise that power, and that they apply whether or not the power to accumulate extends to income produced by the investment of income previously accumulated.

LAW OF PROPERTY ACT 1925
[Applicable to dispositions taking effect before 6 April 2010.]

165. Qualification of restrictions on accumulation

Where accumulations of surplus income are made during a minority under any statutory power or under the general law, the period for which such accumulations are made is not … to be taken into account in determining the periods for which accumulations are permitted to be made by [s. 164], and accordingly an express trust for accumulation for any other permitted period shall not be deemed to have been invalidated or become invalid, by reason of accumulations also having been made as aforesaid during such minority.

PERPETUITIES AND ACCUMULATIONS ACT 2009

In 1998, the Law Commission recommended significant reform of the present law, but recognised the continuing need to prevent property being tied up in perpetuity, and stopped short of recommending abolition of the rules against perpetuities (Law Com No. 251). The essence of those recommendations have now become law in the form of the Perpetuities and Accumulations Act 2009 (which came into force on 6 April 2010). As a result of s.13 of the 2009 Act, there is no restriction on accumulations under non-charitable trusts created on or after 6 April 2010 (hence, for the purpose of such trusts, ss.162–166 of the 1925 Act have been repealed). Statutory restrictions will, however, still apply to trusts taking effect before the commencement date of the 2009 Act. According to s.14 of the 2009 Act, charitable trusts remain a special case.

14 Restriction on accumulation for charitable trusts

(1) This section applies to an instrument to the extent that it provides for property to be held on trust for charitable purposes.

(2) But it does not apply where the provision is made by a court or the Charity Commission for England and Wales.

(3) If the instrument imposes or confers on the trustees a duty or power to accumulate income, and apart from this section the duty or power would last beyond the end of the statutory period, it ceases to have effect at the end of that period unless subsection (5) applies.

(4) The statutory period is a period of 21 years starting with the first day when the income must or may be accumulated (as the case may be).

(5) This subsection applies if the instrument provides for the duty or power to cease to have effect—
    (a) on the death of the settlor, or
    (b) on the death of one of the settlors, determined by name or by the order of their deaths.

(6) If a duty or power ceases to have effect under this section the income to which the duty or power would have applied apart from this section must—
    (a) go to the person who would have been entitled to it if there had been no duty or power to accumulate, or
    (b) be applied for the purposes for which it would have had to be applied if there had been no such duty or power.

(7) This section applies whether or not the duty or power to accumulate extends to income produced by the investment of income previously accumulated.

Remoteness of vesting under the 2009 Act

According to s.12 of the Act, the trustees of *any trust created at any time* can execute an irrevocable deed to adopt a perpetuity period of 100 years if the trust specifies a perpetuity period by reference to lives in being and if the trustees express (in their deed) their belief 'that it is difficult or not reasonably practicable for them to ascertain whether the lives have ended'. Apart from trusts falling within s.12, the 2009 Act applies to all trusts taking effect on or after 6 April 2010, but not to any trusts effective before that date. The principal changes introduced by the 2009 Act can be summarised as follows:

1. The rule against perpetuities is restricted in its application to successive estates and interests in property and to powers of appointment, thereby restoring it to its original function. It ceases to

apply to rights over property such as options, rights of pre-emption, and future easements. The rule will no longer apply to occupational pension schemes, personal pension schemes, and public service pension schemes (ss.2(4), 20(4)).

2. There is a single perpetuity period of 125 years and the principle of 'wait and see' applies to this period (which will apply regardless of any express provision to the contrary).

NOTES

1. The Law Commission did not propose any reform of the rule against inalienability of capital, preferring that reform of that rule should take place as part of a more comprehensive reform of the law relating to purpose trusts.
2. For the time being we have three rules of remoteness of vesting running concurrently (common law, the 1964 Act, and the 2009 Act), an outcome that the Law Commission acknowledged to be the price of reform (Law Com No. 251, para. [1.20]). It has been argued that the price is too high and that the best thing would be to abolish the rule altogether (T. P. Gallanis 'The rule against perpetuities and the Law Commission's flawed philosophy' (2000) 59 *CLJ* 284).

■ QUESTIONS

1. What would you say are the main arguments for and against a strong rule against perpetuities? *Hint*: You may care to consider whether property today should be controlled by persons long dead. You may also consider whether people might work harder, and hence benefit the economy, if they know that they could pass on their property to their descendants.
2. If you were asked (as were economists approached by the Law Commission) how you would arrive at the ideal perpetuity period, what questions would you ask?

SECTION 2: PUBLIC POLICY LIMITATIONS ON TRUST CREATION

It is inconceivable that a court would ever recognise a trust established to advance a criminal purpose or a trust 'for the benefit of X on condition that X commits a crime', but in certain circumstances courts will even refuse to recognise a trust created for purposes or on conditions falling short of 'criminal'. Thus a trust which prejudices the settlor's creditors or which discourages a beneficiary from marrying is illegal on grounds of public policy.

NB: For the significant relationship between illegality and the presumption of resulting trust, see Chapter 5.

A: The forfeiture rule

A killer is not permitted to take the victim's property by will or intestacy (*Re Sigsworth* [1935] Ch 89), and will therefore forfeit any interest under a will trust established by the victim. However, if the killer's innocent children were next in line to inherit under the victim's intestacy, they would receive nothing if the killer is still alive, with the result that the estate may pass to some more remote relative of the victim in ways the victim would never have intended. This seems unfair, so the Law Commission have provisionally proposed that, where a potential heir is disqualified under this so-called 'forfeiture rule', the estate should be distributed on the assumption that the killer has died (*The Forfeiture Rule and the Law of Succession* Law Commission Report (Law Com No. 295),

27 July 2005). The Government has accepted this recommendation, but at the time of writing it is not yet law.

B: Trusts created to prejudice the settlor's creditors are void

Re Butterworth

(1882) 19 ChD 588, Court of Appeal

Facts: A trader, B, before embarking upon a new business, made a voluntary settlement (that is, without receiving consideration) for the benefit of his wife and children. His business eventually became insolvent, his liabilities far exceeding his assets.

Held: (*Obiter*): Irrespective of whether or not B had been solvent at the date of the settlement, the settlement was void as against the trustee in the liquidation. The settlement had clearly been executed with the intention of putting the settlor's property out of the reach of his creditors. A person is not entitled to go into a hazardous business, and immediately before doing so settle all his property voluntarily, the object being this: 'If I succeed in business, I make a fortune for myself. If I fail, I leave my creditors unpaid. They will bear the loss.' Accordingly, the settlement was void for public policy reasons as an attempt to defraud creditors.

SIR GEORGE JESSEL MR: ... The principle of *Mackay* v *Douglas* LR 14 Eq 106, and that line of cases, is this, that a man is not entitled to go into a hazardous business, and immediately before doing so settle all his property voluntarily, the object being this: 'If I succeed in business, I make a fortune for myself. If I fail, I leave my creditors unpaid. They will bear the loss.' That is the very thing which the statute of Elizabeth was meant to prevent. The object of the settlor was to put his property out of the reach of his future creditors. He contemplated engaging in this new trade and he wanted to preserve his property from his future creditors. That cannot be done by a voluntary settlement. That is, to my mind, a clear and satisfactory principle.

Now, as I understand the evidence in this case, the baker did very well as a baker, and probably he may not have recollected the old proverb *ne sutor ultra crepidam*. When he went into business as a grocer he was going into a business which it appears he did not understand, and it is obvious that the object was—(I am taking that as a fair inference)—to save his property for his wife and children in case the new business did not succeed. Well, that actually happened. The new business did not succeed; he lost money by it, and it probably brought him to bankruptcy.

His object was, as I have said, to make himself safe against that eventuality, and, if that was his object, then I think the principle of *Mackay* v *Douglas* applies, and that the deed was void also under the statute of Elizabeth. But, as I have said before, it is not really necessary to decide this point, because I am clearly of opinion that the deed is void under the 91st section of the Bankruptcy Act ...

INSOLVENCY ACT 1986

423. Transactions defrauding creditors

(1) This section relates to transactions entered into at an undervalue, and a person enters into such a transaction with another person if—

(a) he makes a gift to the other person or he otherwise enters into a transaction with the other on terms that provide for him to receive no consideration;

(b) he enters into a transaction with the other in consideration of marriage; or

(c) he enters into a transaction with the other for a consideration the value of which, in money or money's worth, is significantly less than the value, in money or money's worth, of the consideration provided by himself.

(2) Where a person has entered into such a transaction, the court may, if satisfied under the next subsection, make such order as it thinks fit for—

      (a)   restoring the position to what it would have been if the transaction had not been entered into, and

      (b)   protecting the interests of persons who are victims of the transaction.

   (3)   In the case of a person entering into such a transaction, an order shall only be made if the court is satisfied that it was entered into by him for the purpose—

      (a)   of putting assets beyond the reach of a person who is making, or may at some time make, a claim against him, or

      (b)   of otherwise prejudicing the interests of such a person in relation to the claim which he is making or may make.

   (4)   In this section 'the court' means the High Court or—

      (a)   if the person entering into the transaction is an individual, any other court which would have jurisdiction in relation to a bankruptcy petition relating to him;

      (b)   if that person is a body capable of being wound up ... any other court having jurisdiction to wind it up.

   (5)   In relation to a transaction at an undervalue, references here and below to a victim of the transaction are to a person who is, or is capable of being, prejudiced by it; and in the following two sections the person entering into the transaction is referred to as 'the debtor'.

[For an example of the application of this section see *Beckenham MC Ltd* v *Centralex Ltd* [2004] EWHC 1287 (Ch).]

NOTES:

1. The 'purpose' (intent) of the transaction is all important under section 423. For example, it was held in *Rubin* v *Dweck* [2012] BPIR 854, that the transfer of the matrimonial home by a husband to his wife did not defraud his creditors because he intended that the transaction would persuade his wife not to divorce him.

2. Two other dubious species of transaction are 'preferences' (that is, intentional attempts by the bankrupt to prefer certain creditors ahead of others, intent being presumed where the preferred creditor is a person, such as a spouse, who has a particular connection to the bankrupt: Insolvency Act 1986, s.340) and 'transfers at an undervalue' (that is, the transfer of an asset for nothing or for substantially less than its market value or in consideration of entering into a marriage or civil partnership: Insolvency Act 1986, s. 339). According to Insolvency Act 1986, s.341(2), a preference (not being a transaction at an undervalue) is voidable if entered into within six months prior to bankruptcy. Within two years prior to bankruptcy a transaction is voidable if it was a 'preference' conferred on a connected person (such as a spouse) or if it was a 'transfer at an undervalue' and beyond two years prior to bankruptcy, but still within five years prior to bankruptcy, a transfer at an undervalue is only voidable if the bankrupt person was already bankrupt at the date of the transaction, or if the transaction was a cause of their bankruptcy, or if the transaction was entered into with a non-employee associate (for example, a business partner) of the bankrupt.

TRUSTEE ACT 1925

33. Protective trusts

   (1)   Where any income, including an annuity or other periodical income payment, is directed to be held on protective trusts for the benefit of any person (in this section called 'the principal beneficiary') for the period of his life or for any less period, then, during that period (in this section called the 'trust period') the said income shall, without prejudice to any prior interest, be held on the following trusts, namely:—

      (i)   Upon trust for the principal beneficiary during the trust period or until he, whether before or after the termination of any prior interest, does or attempts to do or suffers any act or thing, or until any event happens, other than an advance under any statutory or express power, whereby, if the said income were payable during the trust period to the principal beneficiary absolutely during that period, he would be deprived of the right to receive the same or any part thereof, in any of which cases, as well as on the termination of the trust period, whichever first happens, this trust of the said income shall fail or determine;

(ii) If the trust aforesaid fails or determines during the subsistence of the trust period, then, during the residue of that period, the said income shall be held upon trust for the application thereof for the maintenance or support, or otherwise for the benefit, of all or any one or more exclusively of the other or others of the following persons (that is to say)—

    (a) the principal beneficiary and his or her wife or husband, if any, and his or her children or more remote issue, if any; or

    (b) if there is no wife or husband or issue of the principal beneficiary in existence, the principal beneficiary and the persons who would, if he were actually dead, be entitled to the trust property or the income thereof or to the annuity fund, if any, or arrears of the annuity, as the case may be;

as the trustees in their absolute discretion, without being liable to account for the exercise of such discretion, think fit …

NOTE: It has been said that protective trusts demonstrate 'the furthest extent to which English law will permit property to be denied to creditors' (Maudsley & Burn's *Trusts and Trustees*, 5th edn (1996)). Under a protective trust, the settlor grants the principal beneficiary a life interest in the trust fund that will end if a specified 'determining event' occurs. The standard determining event is the commission by the principal beneficiary of any transaction, such as 'an act of bankruptcy', that would require the trustees to pay the trust income to the principal beneficiary's trustee in bankruptcy, or any person other than the principal beneficiary. When a determining event occurs, the protective trust requires the trustees thereafter to hold the fund on a discretionary trust to distribute the income at their discretion among the members of a specified class of beneficiaries. The principal beneficiary will very often be named as a member of that specified class, but because he will now have no vested entitlement to the trust income, it will not form part of his estate and his creditors will be unable to claim it from him. Of course, when he is eventually discharged from his bankruptcy, there will be nothing to deter the trustees from choosing to pay income to him at that time. When a settlor creates a protective trust, its terms will be presumed to be those set out in the Trustee Act 1925, s.33 unless the instrument creating the trust makes express contrary provision.

C: Discrimination or choice?

Blathwayt v *Baron Cawley*
[1976] AC 397, House of Lords

Facts: A large estate (valued in 1975 at £2 million) was left in 1936 on various entailed trusts, but such that any person who became entitled was to forfeit his interest if he became a Roman Catholic (or ceased to use the name and arms of Blathwayt). It was argued that with respect to the present children, the religious condition tended to restrain the carrying out of parental duties, and was therefore void on public policy grounds.

Held: The effect of the clause may have been to force the parents to choose between material and spiritual welfare for their offspring, but this was not necessarily contrary to public policy. In the event, however, the House of Lords held by a 3:2 majority (Lords Wilberforce and Fraser of Tullybelton dissenting) that the clause did not apply on its construction.

LORD WILBERFORCE: … Finally, as to public policy. The argument under this heading was put in two alternative ways. First, it was said that the law of England was now set against discrimination on a number of grounds including religious grounds, and appeal was made to the Race Relations Act 1968 which does not refer to religion and to the European Convention of Human Rights of 1950 which refers to freedom of religion and to enjoyment of that freedom and other freedoms without discrimination on ground of religion. My Lords, I do not doubt that conceptions of public policy should move with the times and that widely accepted treaties and statutes may point the direction in which such conceptions, as applied by the courts, ought to move. It may well be that conditions such as this are, or at least are becoming, inconsistent with standards now widely accepted. But acceptance of this does not persuade me that we are justified, particularly in relation to a will which came into effect as long ago as 1936 and which has twice been the subject of judicial consideration, in introducing for the first time a rule of law which would go far beyond the mere avoidance of discrimination on religious grounds. To do so would bring about a substantial reduction of another freedom, firmly rooted in our law, namely that of testamentary disposition. Discrimination is not the same thing as choice: it operates over a larger and less personal area, and neither by express provision nor by implication has private selection yet become a matter of public policy.

...

LORD SIMON OF GLAISDALE: My Lords, on all the points dealt with in his speech, save as to the principal issue of construction, I agree with my noble and learned friend, Lord Wilberforce. In particular, I agree with what he has said about public policy as applied by the law to a religious forfeiture clause such as your Lordships are concerned with. The actual personal circumstances can differ so greatly in these matters from case to case that it is difficult to apply a general rule of public policy which is not either practically unreal in many cases or open to some logical objection. Creed or religious observance or sectarian adherence cannot be isolated from other human activities or ideologies. 'Attempt to rule the living from the grave' is a vivid phrase apt to cause revulsion from the conduct referred to: but it is difficult to see why, if public policy is invoked, a particular disposition should be more objectionable if made by will than if made inter vivos. Moreover, it would appear that the policy of English law is to allow a testator considerable freedom in the way in which he disposes of his estate: modern English law knows nothing (apart from taxation and discretionary intervention under the Inheritance (Family Provision) legislation) of a part of a deceased's estate reserved from his disposition. Balancing these various matters, I agree with my noble and learned friend, Lord Wilberforce, that in these days society's interest in a parent's conscientious choice as to what influence should be brought to bear on his own child during minority is sufficiently vindicated by the rule that a forfeiture clause shall not operate till after the lapse of a reasonable period after the child reaches the age of majority. This also accords with the contemporary view that it is for a youth himself to take the crucial decision on such a matter. He cannot hope to do so emancipated from conflicting influences and interests.

I must not be taken thereby to be implying that it is for courts of law to embark on an independent and unfettered appraisal of what they think is required by public policy on any issue. Courts are concerned with public policy only in so far as it has been manifested by parliamentary sanction or embodied in rules of law having binding judicial force. As to such rules of law your Lordships have the same power to declare, to bind and to loose as in regard to any other judicial precedent. Rules of law expressing principles of public policy therefore fall to be treated with the same respect and circumspection, the same common sense and regard to changing circumstances, as any other rules of law. So approaching the authorities expressing public policy with regard to forfeiture clauses—specifically those relating to religious and other ideologies—I agree that the law is as stated by my noble and learned friend, Lord Wilberforce.

...

LORD CROSS OF CHELSEA: ... The summons issued by the trustees of the will on 23 February 1940, asked two questions—first, whether Christopher forfeited his life interest in the property settled by the will on being received into the Roman Catholic Church on 10 November 1939, and, secondly, if the answer to the first question was 'Yes,' how the trustees were to deal with the income of the property pending the birth of a son to Christopher. I do not suppose that the legal advisers of the family at that time expected the first question to be answered otherwise than as Farwell J answered it—that is to say in the affirmative; for before the decision of this House in *Clayton* v *Ramsden* [1943] AC 320 few if any Chancery practitioners would have thought it seriously arguable that a condition subsequent forfeiting a life interest on the life tenant becoming a Roman Catholic was void. The decision in *Clayton* v *Ramsden* turned primarily on a condition for forfeiture on the beneficiary marrying a person 'not of Jewish parentage' but four of the members of the House expressed the view that a condition against marriage with a person 'not of the Jewish faith' was also void for uncertainty. If that be so then it is certainly arguable that a condition for forfeiture on the beneficiary becoming a Roman Catholic is void. That point was not however taken on behalf of Mark on the hearing of the summons taken out after his birth in 1949. That proceeded on the footing that Christopher forfeited his life interest in 1939 and that the only point to be determined was whether the interest in the income to which Justin then became entitled in possession had come to an end on Mark's birth. Your Lordships refused Mark leave to raise the issue of Christopher's forfeiture on this appeal; but the question whether the condition is or is not void emerges again in its application to Mark's estate tail. In agreement, I believe, with all your Lordships, I am clearly of opinion that the condition was not and is not void either for uncertainty or, as applied to a person of full age at the date of the will, on grounds of public policy. I accept, of course, that by the law of England a stricter test of certainty is applied to a condition subsequent than to a condition precedent but I agree with the judges both in the Irish Republic and in Northern Ireland that it would be an affront to common sense to hold that a condition for forfeiture if the beneficiary should become a Roman Catholic is open to objection on the ground of uncertainty: see *In re McKenna* [1947] IR 277 and *McCausland* v *Young* [1948] NI 72; [1949] NI 49. If I had been a member of the House which heard *Clayton* v *Ramsden*, I might well have agreed with Lord Wright that a condition for forfeiture on marriage with a person 'not of the Jewish faith' was valid. But it is a vaguer conception than being or not being a Roman Catholic and acceptance of the view of the majority does not involve the consequence that a condition of forfeiture on becoming a Roman Catholic is open to objection on the score of uncertainty. Turning to the question of public policy, it is true that it is widely thought nowadays that it is wrong for a government to treat some of its citizens less favourably than others because of differences in their religious beliefs; but it does not follow from that that it is against public policy for an adherent of one religion to distinguish in disposing of his property between adherents of his faith and those of another. So to hold would amount to saying that though it is in order for a man to have a mild preference for one religion as opposed to another it is disreputable for him to be convinced of the importance of holding true religious beliefs and of the fact that this religious beliefs are the true ones.

NOTE: As is clear from the extract from Lord Cross's speech, above, conditions subsequent can alternatively be struck down on the grounds of uncertainty, as in *Clayton* v *Ramsden* [1943] AC 320, which concerned a forfeiture on marriage to a person 'not of Jewish parentage and of the Jewish faith'. This was held to be conceptually uncertain. But it seems that so long as a clause is not uncertain the courts will be slow to strike it down on grounds of public policy, and a somewhat similar clause to the above was upheld by the Court of Appeal in *Re Tuck's ST* [1978] Ch 49, where 'an approved wife' of Jewish blood was precisely defined, cases of dispute being dealt with by the Chief Rabbi in London. Names and arms clauses (such as the other clause in *Blathwayt*) have also been upheld, for example: *Re Neeld* [1962] Ch 643 (CA).

Re Lysaght (dec'd)

[1966] 1 Ch 191, [1965] 2 All ER 888, [1965] 3 WLR 391, Chancery Division

Decision: The decision is set out in Chapter 9. For present purposes, Buckley J did not regard a racial bar (prior to the Race Relations Act 1965) as contrary to public policy.

BUCKLEY J: In *Clayton* v *Ramsden* [1943] AC 320, a condition subsequent under which a beneficiary was to forfeit a benefit in the event of her marrying a person not of Jewish parentage and of the Jewish faith was held void for uncertainty, but different considerations apply in this respect to a forfeiture provision from those applicable to a condition precedent or a qualification to take a benefit (*Re Allen, Faith* v *Allen* [1953] Ch 810). In the one case the person liable to suffer a forfeiture must be able to know with certainty what will cause a forfeiture: in the other all that any person claiming to benefit has to do is to establish that the condition or qualification is satisfied in his particular case. The fact that someone else might have difficulty in demonstrating this with certainty does not prevent someone who clearly satisfies the appropriate test from claiming to be entitled or eligible to benefit. In the present case there would be a wide field open to any trustee of the endowment fund for the selection of students who manifestly satisfy the qualification of being neither of the Jewish nor of the Roman Catholic faith. Accordingly, I do not think that this part of the trust is affected by the vice of uncertainty. Nor, in my judgment, is it contrary to public policy, as counsel for the personal representatives suggests. I accept that racial and religious discrimination is nowadays widely regarded as deplorable in many respects, and I am aware that there is a bill dealing with racial relations at present under consideration by Parliament, but I think that it is going much too far to say that the endowment of a charity, the beneficiaries of which are to be drawn from a particular faith or are to exclude adherents to a particular faith, is contrary to public policy. The testatrix's desire to exclude persons of the Jewish faith or of the Roman Catholic faith from those eligible for the studentship in the present case appears to me to be unamiable, and I would accept the suggestion of counsel for the Attorney-General that it is undesirable, but it is not, I think, contrary to public policy.

■ QUESTIONS

1. To what extent should a person be permitted to dispose of his property subject to restrictions and conditions that the general public, or significant sections of it, might consider to be odious or morally reprehensible?
2. To what extent is private property truly private?

NOTE: It might be thought that the European Convention on Human Rights (ECHR) would herald a solution to the dilemma between private dispositive choice and public discrimination, but, if anything, it compounds it. The Convention, which is incorporated into English law by the Human Rights Act 1998 (HRA), sets out a number of basic human rights and requires that public bodies (HRA, s.8) shall secure those rights 'without discrimination on any ground' (ECHR, Art. 14). However, one of the rights protected by the Convention is the citizen's right to the peaceful enjoyment of his possessions (Art. 1 of the First Protocol). So if a trust were established for certain beneficiaries on condition, say, that they abstain from joining a particular religious movement, and a court were to strike out the limitation, it would be a moot point whether the court's action should be considered consistent with Article 14 or inconsistent with the First Protocol. See, generally, Sheena Grattan, 'Testamentary Conditions in Restraint of Religion', in Elizabeth Cooke (ed.), *Modern Studies in Property Law Vol 1: Property 2000* (Oxford: Hart Publishing, 2001), p. 257 and (in the same volume) G. Watt, 'The Frontiers of Forfeiture: Property Rights and Wrongs', p. 113.

■ QUESTION

Is there any justification for the courts' refusal to enforce trusts in restraint of marriage and the courts' willingness to enforce discriminatory conditions attached to gifts?

■ SUMMATIVE QUESTION

**online
resource
centre**

Explain, with reasons, what formalities (if any) must be complied with in order to make the following actions valid and enforceable in a court of law.

(a) George, the freehold owner of Whitehouse, declares that he henceforth holds the legal title to Whitehouse on trust for his son, Junior.
(b) Tony, the sole life beneficiary under a trust set up by his father, gives notice to the trustees that he disclaims his interest in favour of his son, to whom the trustees should henceforth pay all the income from the trust.
(c) Robin, who died recently, left property to Patrick by his will, having previously informed Patrick that he should secretly hold the property as trustee for the benefit of Robin's mistress.
(d) Berty is the sole beneficial owner of a number of shares held in trust for him by a trust company wholly owned and controlled by him for the last twenty years. He now decides to instruct the company to transfer the shares to his wife.

FURTHER READING

Boughen, G., 'Mutual Wills' (1951) 15 *Conv* 28.

Enonchong, N., 'Title Claims and Illegal Transactions' (1995) 111 *LQR* 135.

Gallanis, T. P., 'The Rule Against Perpetuities and the Law Commission's Flawed Philosophy' (2000) 59 *CLJ* 284.

Grattan, S. and Conway, H., 'Testamentary Conditions in Restraint of Religion in the Twenty-First Century: An Anglo-Canadian Perspective' (2005) 50 *McGill LJ* 511.

Green, B., 'Grey, Oughtred and Vandervell—A Contextual Reappraisal' (1984) 47 *MLR* 385.

Lincaid, D., 'The Tangled Web: The Relationship Between a Secret Trust and the Will' (2000) 64 *Conv* 420.

Mee, J., 'Half Secret Trusts in England and Ireland' (1992) 56 *Conv* 202.

Norris, A. and Legge, H., 'Contract and Conscience: The Decline of the Mutual Will' (1998) 6 *Private Client Business* 332.

Parry, R., Ayliffe J. And Shivji, S., (With Anderson, H. And Trower, W.), *Transaction Avoidance in Insolvencies*, 2nd edn (Oxford: Oxford University Press, 2001).

Quint, F., 'The Perpetuities and Accumulations Bill: Clarity or Confusion?' [2009] *PCB* 126.

7

Charity: Trust Creation and Public Policy II

KEY AIMS

To identify the legal definition of charity and how it differs from everyday notions
of charity. To consider the advantages of charitable status. To examine limits on
the recognition of charitable trusts, including the requirement that purposes be
exclusively charitable, not-for-profit, and non-political. To consider whether certain categories of purpose should be presumed charitable, and which categories
they might be. To query whether the recognition of charitable status turns upon
whether the particular purpose is sufficiently beneficial to the public. To outline
the administration of charitable trusts. (The variation of charitable trusts through
the doctrine of *cy près* is considered in Chapter 9.) To appreciate the impact of the
Charities Act 2006.

NOTE: Before proceeding further in this chapter, the reader is alerted to the fact that the Charities
Act 2011 is a consolidating statute which since 14 March 2012 brings the Charities Acts 1993 and
2006 and the Recreational Charities Act 1958 under one new title without changing the substance of
the law in any significant way. Given the recent date of this change at the time of writing and in the
interests of ease of cross-referencing between this text and your study notes and existing cases and
materials, references to the 1958, 1993 and 2006 Acts are retained throughout this text with the corresponding references to the 2011 Act shown in parenthesis where appropriate. For a comprehensive
list of the section number changes brought about by the Charities Act 2011, see the official 'Table of
Destinations' on the Online Resource Centre accompanying this book.

**online
resource
centre**

SECTION 1: INTRODUCTION

The charitable status of a trust is significant for a number of reasons:

(a) *Validity.* Charitable trusts are trusts for purposes, and would be void if not charitable, on the principles in Chapter 3. It was for this reason that charitable status
was claimed in *Re Shaw (dec'd)* [1957] 1 WLR 729, set out in that chapter. See also,
e.g. *Yeap Cheah Neo* v *Ong Cheng Neo* (1875) LR 6 PC 381, *Re Pinion* [1965] Ch 85,
and *Re Koeppler's WT* [1986] Ch 423, all of which are considered in this chapter.

Charitable trusts may also exist in perpetuity (*Christ's Hospital* v *Grainger* (1849)
1 Mac & G 460), and need not satisfy certainty of objects tests (since there are
state enforcement mechanisms). Indeed, only the Attorney-General can bring
an action to establish the existence of a charitable trust, although he can be

substituted as claimant for individuals: see *Hauxwell* v *Barton-on-Humber UDC* [1974] Ch 432, where he was substituted as claimant for two individuals.

(b) *Cy près*. Where a private trust ceases to be operable, any surplus is held on resulting trust, on the principles in Chapter 5. For charitable trusts, a *cy près* scheme may be applied instead (see further Chapter 9). It was for this reason that charitable status was claimed (unsuccessfully) in *Re Gillingham Bus Disaster Fund* [1958] Ch 300, discussed in Chapter 5, and *Re Hobourn Aero Components Ltd's Air Raid Distress Fund* [1946] 1 Ch 86 (aff'd CA, [1946] 1 Ch 194). If either of those trusts had been charitable, the contributors would have got nothing back, and a *cy près* scheme would have been applied.

(c) *Tax and rates*. We have already seen that charities enjoy tax advantages; had the dispositions in favour of charities been valid in *IRC* v *Broadway Cottages Trust* [1955] Ch 20 (Chapter 3), or *Vandervell* v *IRC* [1967] 2 AC 291 (Chapters 5 and 6), the tax position would have been different (which is why the IRC was a party). In *Re South Place Ethical Society* [1980] 3 All ER 918 and *United Grand Lodge of Ancient Free & Accepted Masons of England and Wales* v *Holborn BC* [1957] 1 WLR 1080, discussed in this chapter, rates advantages were claimed, unsuccessfully, on the ground of charitable status.

If validity were the only consequence of charitable status, the courts may not have developed the strict public benefit tests in cases such as *Oppenheim* v *Tobacco Securities Trust Co. Ltd* [1951] AC 297, discussed in this chapter. Such a test is clearly appropriate where tax or rates advantages are claimed.

(d) *Public enforcement and control*. The consequence of charitable status in *Neville Estates Ltd* v *Madden* [1962] 1 Ch 832 (this chapter, and Chapter 3) was that the sale of the synagogue was subject to the approval of the Charity Commissioners.

For all the reasons set out above, the recognition of a charitable trust will have a direct or indirect impact on the public, and charitable trusts can fairly be described as 'public trusts'. It is therefore a requirement of charitable status that a charitable trust confers a public benefit.

Some questions of public benefit have proved very controversial. According to the Equality Act 2010, s.193(7) (which is not in force at the time of writing) it is not a contravention of the Act to restrict to persons of one sex participation in an activity which is carried on for the purpose of promoting or supporting a charity. However, restriction according to sexual orientation is another thing. In *Catholic Care* v *Charity Commission* [2010] EWHC 520 (Ch); [2010] 4 All ER 1041, First-Tier Tribunal (Charity) General Regulatory Chamber, Briggs J held that:

'An organisation which proposes to fulfil a purpose for the public benefit will only qualify as a charity if, taking into account any dis-benefit arising from its *modus operandi*, its activities nonetheless yield a net public benefit...Thus, a charity which proposed to apply differential treatment on grounds of sexual orientation otherwise than as a proportionate means of achieving a legitimate aim might thereby fail to achieve charitable status ...' (para [97]).

On appeal from this decision, the Upper Tribunal held the charity in this case had not demonstrated such clear net benefits that exceptional discrimination could be justified. It was acknowledged that '[t]he fact that same sex couples could seek to have access to adoption services offered elsewhere tended to reduce somewhat the immediate detrimental effect on them, but it did not remove the harm that would be caused to them through feeling that discrimination on grounds of sexual orientation was practised at some point in the adoption system' *(Catholic Care (Diocese of Leeds)* v *Charity Commission (on appeal to the Upper Tribunal)* CA/2010/0007). The decision of the Upper Tribunal shows how hard it is to balance the problem of systemic discrimination on grounds of sexual orientation against the problem of systemic discrimination on grounds of religion. Part of the Upper Tribunal's decision was to reject, as too speculative, the Catholic adoption agency's argument that potential donor's might be put off if the charity were required to place children with homosexual couples. On donations generally, see the extract from Sir Philip Christopher Ondaatje's 2007 article in the *New Statesman*.

Sir Philip Christopher Ondaatje, OC, CBE, 'Giving it all away'
New Statesman, 15 January 2007

At a recent conference organised by the Institute for Philanthropy, the institute's director, Hilary Browne-Wilkinson, argued that Britain's strong tradition of Victorian philanthropy was replaced after the Second World War by the welfare state ...She provided some helpful statistics: as a percentage of GDP, individual charitable giving in the US is more than double that in the UK. In 2002, $183.7bn was given, which represented 1.75 per cent of GDP. Using the same measure for the same year, UK individual giving was £7.3bn, or 0.76 per cent of GDP.

There are ...enormous differences between how Americans and British people give: 77 per cent of all collection methods in the UK are spontaneous, looking for loose change. In the United States, there is a culture of 'planned giving', which provides 61 per cent of the voluntary income of non-profit organisations. One critical factor is tax incentives. According to the biweekly US *Chronicle of Philanthropy*, 54 per cent of the richest US donors said that they give for the tax benefits. In Britain, the charity, rather than the individual, receives most of the refund under Gift Aid. As a result, many potential donors do not feel that the system gives them a tax break.

In addition, gifts of capital and assets in Britain do not attract an allowance similar to that on gifts of shares. A recent review published by the Treasury recommended a tax allowance to encourage getting more art into museums, but sadly nothing was done to implement this recommendation. When similar proposals were made by the Art Fund before the last Budget, they were apparently supported by Treasury officials, but then killed on the grounds that it was wrong to give tax benefits to the rich. Unfortunately, however, without obvious and understandable tax benefits, the rich in Britain are unlikely to put as much back into the community as Americans do.

'Planned giving' is vital to the US economy and it encourages individuals to feel a sense of responsibility for the welfare of others in their locality. It could be just as vital to Britain, but the government, and the Treasury in particular, must learn how to encourage a culture of philanthropic giving and must recognise that public interest lies in promoting self-interest.

NOTE: Sir Philip is a noted philanthropist. He helped fund an entire new wing of the National Portrait Gallery, which is now named after him. He remains a trustee of the gallery.

SECTION 2: DEFINITION OF CHARITY

The *Explanatory Notes* accompanying the Charities Act 2006 assert that Section 1 of the Act 'provides a general statutory definition of charity for the purposes of the law for the first time'. This definition became law from 1 April 2008. The definition is rather circular: 'charity' means 'an institution which is established for charitable purposes only' and is 'subject to the control of the High Court in the exercise of its jurisdiction with respect to charities'. The *Explanatory Notes* assert, next, that section 2 of the Act contains the first statutory definition of 'charitable purpose'. The definition provides that a purpose is charitable if it satisfies two criteria: (1) that it comes under one of the 'heads' of charity listed in the statute (we consider the list below) and (2) that it is for the public benefit; the latter requiring the conferral of real and substantial benefit on the public at large or upon a sufficient section of the community. The concept of public benefit is gloriously vague and we will see that the 'heads' of charity are open-ended. The result is that charitable purposes remain, in essence, undefined. The long list of 'heads' or categories of charitable purpose which are set down in the Act are, despite their open-endedness, at least more useful than the list which was previously relied upon. Before the Charities Act 2006, 'charitable purposes' were those which the preamble to the Charitable Uses Act 1601 (reproduced in this section), the so-called 'Statute of Elizabeth' enumerated or which 'by analogies' were deemed 'within its spirit and intendment' (Sir William Grant MR, *Morice v Bishop of Durham* (1804) 9 Ves 399, 405). The Charity Commission website contains a useful *Commentary on the Descriptions of Charitable Purposes in the Charities Act 2006* (March 2007). (References to the *Commentary* throughout the remainder of this chapter are references to that document.)

STATUTE OF CHARITABLE USES 1601

Preamble

Whereas Lands, Tenements, Rents, Annuities, Profits, Hereditaments, Goods, Chattels, Money and Stocks of Money, have been heretofore given, limited, appointed and assigned, as well as by the Queen's most excellent Majesty, and her most noble Progenitors, as by sundry other well disposed persons; some for Relief of aged, impotent and poor People, some for the Maintenance of sick and maimed Soldiers and Mariners, Schools of Learning, Free Schools, and Scholars in Universities, some for the Repair of Bridges, Ports, Havens, Causeways, Churches, Sea-Banks and Highways, some for the Education and Preferment of Orphans, some for or towards Relief, Stock or Maintenance for Houses of Correction, some for the Marriages of Poor Maids, some for Supportation, Aid and Help of young Tradesmen, Handicraftsmen and Persons decayed, and others for the Relief or Redemption of Prisoners or Captives, and for Aid or Ease of any poor Inhabitants concerning Payments of Fifteens [a tax on moveable property], setting out of Soldiers and other Taxes; which Lands, Tenements, Rents, Annuities, Profits, Hereditaments, Goods, Chattels, Money and Stocks of Money, nevertheless have not been employed according to charitable Intent of the givers and Founders thereof, by reason of Frauds, Breaches of Trust, and Negligence in those that should pay, deliver and employ the same: For Redress and Remedy whereof, Be it enacted ...

NOTE: The purposes laid down in the Preamble are many and diverse, but in *Commissioners for Special Income Tax* v *Pemsel* [1891] AC 531, the majority of the House of Lords held that 'charitable purposes' within the meaning of the Income Tax Acts were to be interpreted, not according to their popular meaning, but according to their technical legal meaning. Since it was therefore necessary to arrive at a technical legal definition of 'charity', Lord Macnaghten categorised charitable purposes under four main heads (at 544):

> 'Charity' in its legal sense comprises four principal divisions: trusts for the relief of poverty, trusts for the advancement of education, trusts for the advancement of religion, and trusts for other purposes beneficial to the community not falling under any of the preceding heads.

A: The new statutory 'definition' of charity

The Charities Act 2006 received Royal Assent on 8 November 2006 but the sections dealing with the definition of charity and the public benefit requirement became law on 1 April 2008. The Act and accompanying explanatory notes can be accessed via the online resource centre accompanying this book, or via the websites of the Charity Commission for England and Wales.

CHARITIES ACT 2006

PART I

1   Meaning of 'charity' [now Charities Act 2011, s.1]

(1) For the purposes of the law of England and Wales, 'charity' means an institution which—

   (a) is established for charitable purposes only, and

   (b) falls to be subject to the control of the High Court in the exercise of its jurisdiction with respect to charities.

(2) The definition of 'charity' in subsection (1) does not apply for the purposes of an enactment if a different definition of that term applies for those purposes by virtue of that or any other enactment.

(3) A reference in any enactment or document to a charity within the meaning of the Charitable Uses Act 1601 (c. 4) or the preamble to it is to be construed as a reference to a charity as defined by subsection (1).

2   Meaning of 'charitable purpose'

(1) [now Charities Act 2011, s.2] For the purposes of the law of England and Wales, a charitable purpose is a purpose which—

   (a) falls within subsection (2), and

   (b) is for the public benefit (see section 3).

(2) [now Charities Act 2011, s.3(1)] A purpose falls within this subsection if it falls within any of the following descriptions of purposes—

   (a) the prevention or relief of poverty;

   (b) the advancement of education;

   (c) the advancement of religion;

   (d) the advancement of health or the saving of lives;

   (e) the advancement of citizenship or community development;

   (f) the advancement of the arts, culture, heritage or science;

   (g) the advancement of amateur sport;

   (h) the advancement of human rights, conflict resolution or reconciliation or the promotion of religious or racial harmony or equality and diversity;

   (i) the advancement of environmental protection or improvement;

   (j) the relief of those in need by reason of youth, age, ill-health, disability, financial hardship or other disadvantage;

   (k) the advancement of animal welfare;

   (l) the promotion of the efficiency of the armed forces of the Crown or of the efficiency of the police, fire and rescue services or ambulance services;

   (m) any other purposes within subsection (4).

(3) [now Charities Act 2011, s.3(2)] In subsection (2)—

   (a) in paragraph (c) 'religion' includes—

      (i) a religion which involves belief in more than one god, and

      (ii) a religion which does not involve belief in a god;

   (b) in paragraph (d) 'the advancement of health' includes the prevention or relief of sickness, disease or human suffering;

   (c) paragraph (e) includes—

      (i) rural or urban regeneration, and

      (ii) the promotion of civic responsibility, volunteering, the voluntary sector or the effectiveness or efficiency of charities;

   (d) in paragraph (g) 'sport' means sports or games which promote health by involving physical or mental skill or exertion; and

   (e) paragraph (j) includes relief given by the provision of accommodation or care to the persons mentioned in that paragraph; and (f) in paragraph (l) 'fire and rescue services' means services provided by fire and rescue authorities under Part 2 of the Fire and Rescue Services Act 2004 (c. 21).

(4) The purposes within this subsection (see subsection (2)(m)) are—

    (a) any purposes not within paragraphs (a) to (l) of subsection (2) but recognised as charitable purposes under existing charity law or by virtue of section 1 of the Recreational Charities Act 1958 (c. 17) [repealed and replaced by Charities Act 2011, s.5];

    (b) any purposes that may reasonably be regarded as analogous to, or within the spirit of, any purposes falling within any of those paragraphs or paragraph (a) above; and

    (c) any purposes that may reasonably be regarded as analogous to, or within the spirit of, any purposes which have been recognised under charity law as falling within paragraph (b) above or this paragraph.

(5) Where any of the terms used in any of paragraphs (a) to (l) of subsection (2), or in subsection (3), has a particular meaning under charity law, the term is to be taken as having the same meaning where it appears in that provision.

(6) Any reference in any enactment or document (in whatever terms)—

    (a) to charitable purposes, or

    (b) to institutions having purposes that are charitable under charity law, is to be construed in accordance with subsection (1).

(7) Subsection (6)—

    (a) applies whether the enactment or document was passed or made before or after the passing of this Act, but

    (b) does not apply where the context otherwise requires.

(8) In this section—

    'charity law' means the law relating to charities in England and Wales; and 'existing charity law' means charity law as in force immediately before the day on which this section comes into force.

3   The 'public benefit' test [now Charities Act 2011, s.4]

(1) This section applies in connection with the requirement in section 2(1)(b) that a purpose falling within section 2(2) must be for the public benefit if it is to be a charitable purpose.

(2) In determining whether that requirement is satisfied in relation to any such purpose, it is not to be presumed that a purpose of a particular description is for the public benefit.

(3) In this Part any reference to the public benefit is a reference to the public benefit as that term is understood for the purposes of the law relating to charities in England and Wales.

(4) Subsection (3) applies subject to subsection (2).

4   Guidance as to operation of public benefit requirement [now Charities Act 2011, s.4]

(1) The Charity Commission for England and Wales (see section 6 of this Act) must issue guidance in pursuance of its public benefit objective.

(2) That objective is to promote awareness and understanding of the operation of the requirement mentioned in section 3(1) (see section 1B(3) and (4) of the Charities Act 1993 (c. 10), as inserted by section 7 of this Act).

(3) The Commission may from time to time revise any guidance issued under this section.

(4) The Commission must carry out such public and other consultation as it considers appropriate—

    (a) before issuing any guidance under this section, or

    (b) (unless it considers that it is unnecessary to do so) before revising any such guidance.

(5) The Commission must publish any guidance issued or revised under this section in such manner as it considers appropriate.

(6) The charity trustees of a charity must have regard to any such guidance when exercising any powers or duties to which the guidance is relevant.

5   Special provisions about recreational charities, sports clubs etc. [now Charities Act 2011, s.5]

(1) The Recreational Charities Act 1958 (c. 17) is amended in accordance with subsections (2) and (3).

(2) In section 1 (certain recreational and similar purposes deemed to be charitable) for subsection (2) substitute—

'(2) The requirement in subsection (1) that the facilities are provided in the interests of social welfare cannot be satisfied if the basic conditions are not met.

(2A) The basic conditions are—

(a) that the facilities are provided with the object of improving the conditions of life for the persons for whom the facilities are primarily intended; and

(b) that either—

(i) those persons have need of the facilities by reason of their youth, age, infirmity or disability, poverty, or social and economic circumstances, or

(ii) the facilities are to be available to members of the public at large or to male, or to female, members of the public at large.'

(3) Section 2 (miners' welfare trusts) is omitted.

(4) A registered sports club established for charitable purposes is to be treated as not being so established, and accordingly cannot be a charity.

(5) In subsection (4) a 'registered sports club' means a club for the time being registered under Schedule 18 to the Finance Act 2002 (c. 23) (relief for community amateur sports club).

CHARITIES ACT 2006

CABINET OFFICE EXPLANATORY NOTES

15. Section 1 provides a general statutory definition of charity for the purposes of the law for the first time. It follows the definition of charity in the Charities Act 1993.

16. Section 1(1) establishes the meaning of charity. By specifying that a body or trust is a charity if established for charitable purposes 'only', section 1(1)(a) preserves the current rule to the effect that a body or trust which has non-charitable as well as charitable purposes is not a charity.

...

19. Section 2 of the Act contains the first statutory definition of 'charitable purpose'. This definition still relies on a considerable body of case law.

20. The meaning of 'charitable purpose' is supplied by section 2(1), which provides that a purpose is charitable if it meets two criteria: that it falls under one or more descriptions or 'heads' of charity in section 2(2); and that it is for the public benefit.

21 Each of the paragraphs in section 2(2) is a description or 'head' of charity rather than a fully-stated purpose in itself. Within each of those descriptions lie a range of purposes all of which fit the description but each of which is a different purpose in its own right. The list of descriptions, taken as a whole with the purposes underlying the descriptions, encompasses everything which is to be a charitable purpose.

...

25. Section 3 deals with public benefit. Under the existing law there is a presumption that purposes for the relief of poverty, the advancement of education, or the advancement of religion—in other words the purposes that would fall under paragraphs (a) to (c) of section 2(2)—are for the public benefit. No other purposes benefit from that presumption. The effect of the presumption at present is that, when the status (charitable or non-charitable) of an organisation established for the relief of poverty, the advancement of education, or the advancement of religion is being considered, the organisation's purpose is presumed to be for the public benefit unless there is evidence that it is not for the public benefit. By contrast, organisations established for all other purposes, which do not benefit from that presumption, have at the time their status is being considered to provide evidence that their purpose is for the public benefit.

26. Subsection (2) of section 3 abolishes the presumption that organisations for the relief of poverty, the advancement of education, or the advancement of religion enjoy, putting all charitable purposes on the same footing. Abolishing the presumption will not by itself have the effect of depriving poverty relief, educational and religious organisations that were registered as charities while the presumption existed of their charitable status.

27. Subsection (3) makes clear that the term 'public benefit', wherever it occurs in sections 1–3, refers to the existing concept in charity law in England and Wales. The concept of public benefit will remain in the common law. Guidance that the Charity Commission issues under section 4 (see below) will explain the public benefit concept.

> **Section 4:   Guidance as to operation of public benefit requirement**
>
> 28. The Act gives the Charity Commission a set of new objectives (see section 7), one of which is to promote understanding and awareness of the operation of the public benefit requirement … .

NOTE: The Act removes the presumption of public benefit which previously applied to certain heads of charity (such as relief of poverty and the advancement of education and religion) and henceforth there will be no presumption of public benefit with regard to any category of charitable purpose.

■ QUESTION

Section 4 of the statute mandates the Charity Commission for England and Wales to issue (and from time to time revise) guidance as to the meaning of public benefit 'after such public and other consultation as it considers appropriate'. Should the interpretation of 'public benefit' have been left to the courts?

NOTE: This chapter arranges the current law on the definition of charitable purposes under the new heads of charity set out in section 3(1) of the Charities Act 2011, namely:

- the prevention or relief of poverty;
- the advancement of education;
- the advancement of religion;
- the advancement of health or the saving of lives;
- the advancement of citizenship or community development;
- the advancement of arts, culture, heritage or science;
- the advancement of amateur sport;
- the promotion of human rights, conflict resolution or reconciliation or the promotion of religious or racial harmony or equality and diversity;
- the advancement of environmental protection or improvement;
- the relief of those in need, by reason of youth, age, ill-health, disability, financial hardship or other disadvantage;
- the advancement of animal welfare;
- the promotion of the efficiency of the armed forces of the Crown or of the efficiency of the police, fire and rescue services or the ambulance services;
- [other existing charitable purposes or analogous charitable purposes. In essence, any other purpose intended to provide community benefit].

However, before we consider the particular heads of charity, it is necessary to make a number of general points about charitable status: namely that, for a trust to be recognised as charitable, its purposes must be exclusively charitable, must not be aimed at making profit, and must not be political. Furthermore, in Section 3, we will examine the crucial requirement that charity must be for the public benefit, and we will consider the reform of this requirement and how this requirement has traditionally been applied to Lord Macnaghten's original four heads of charity.

B: Purposes must be exclusively charitable

To be charitable, a trust must not merely be capable of application to charitable purposes; it must be exclusively so. If it is possible to benefit an object which is not charitable, then the trust will fail as a charity unless the courts feel able to sever the offending objects from the main corpus of the otherwise charitable purpose, as in *Re Hetherington* [1990] Ch 1, (see Section 3: Public Benefit, D:The advancement of regligion (Lord Macnaghten's third head), or to declare that the non-charitable purposes are merely subsidiary.

There are various principles of construction. For example, if a purpose is described as 'charitable *and* benevolent', it is probable that these will be construed conjunctively:

'benevolent' merely qualifies 'charitable', so only charitable purposes are included. But in *Chichester Diocesan Fund* v *Simpson* [1944] AC 341, the words 'charitable *or* benevolent' would have permitted the trustees to devote all the funds to benevolent ends which were not also charitable. The trust therefore failed, leading to further litigation because funds had already been distributed by the trustees: *Re Diplock, Minister of Health* v *Simpson* [1951] AC 251.

The notes to the *All England Reports* of the case ([1944] 2 All ER 60) state that:

The authorities are very strongly in favour of the majority decision in this case and it has long been recognised among practitioners in such matters that, while a gift for 'charitable and benevolent' purposes is valid, a gift for 'charitable or benevolent' purposes is invalid. The rule no doubt works harshly in cases, but the present decision has now put the rule, much as it is disliked, beyond question.

The rationale is that a comma, or the word 'or', is likely to lead to the listed purposes being interpreted disjunctively (i.e. as alternatives), while the word 'and' is usually read conjunctively. As Viscount Simonds observed in *Chichester*, however, the decision was made in the absence of any context tending to a contrary conclusion, and as with any matter of construction, there are no hard and fast rules.

NOTE: If a trust established for a certain class of people does not specify *any* purpose the courts may construe it to be for purely charitable purposes. This occurred in *Re Harding* [2008] Ch 235, where Lewison J held that a trust for 'for the black community of Hackney, Haringey, Islington and Tower Hamlets' was held to be charitable. The judge was content for the precise purposes to which the money should be applied to be determined by a charitable scheme settled on by the trustees. (Incidentally, the limitation in favour of the 'black community' was struck out as being in breach of Race Relations Act 1976, s.34(1); the Equality Act 2010, s.193 (which is not in force at the time of writing) requires limitations 'to persons of a class defined by reference to colour' to be ignored.)

C: Profit seeking

Generally speaking, it is incompatible with charitable status actively to seek profit as a primary objective, although fees may be charged, and incidental acquisition of profit should not disqualify. See further *Scottish Burial Reform and Cremation Society Ltd* v *Glasgow Corporation* [1968] AC 138 (at Section 2: Definition of Charity, Q: Other charitable purposes or purposes analogous to existing charitable purposes).

D: Political purposes

A trust cannot be charitable under any head if its purposes are, directly or indirectly, political. A trust to promote the aims of a particular political party is clearly not capable of being charitable, and attempts to disguise such objectives as educational trusts have generally failed.

The definition of political in this context is somewhat wider than the layman might expect, however. Where the objectives involve attempting to bring about a change in the law, they will be considered political and therefore non-charitable, unless change in the law is merely ancillary to the main purpose of the trust. This was one of the reasons for the failure of the National Anti-Vivisection Society to achieve charitable status in *National Anti-Vivisection Society* v *IRC* [1948] AC 31. Lord Simonds gave as the ostensible rationale that it is for Parliament, not the courts, to decide whether any change would be in the public benefit. He also rejected the contention that alteration in the law was merely ancillary to the purposes of the trust, since in order to abolish vivisection it would have been necessary to repeal the Cruelty of Animals Act 1876 (since replaced by the Animals (Scientific Procedures) Act 1986), and replace it with a new enactment prohibiting vivisection altogether.

(i) Change in the law of the UK

National Anti-Vivisection Society v *Inland Revenue Commissioners*
[1948] AC 31, House of Lords

Decision: The National Anti-Vivisection Society was not a charity within the fourth head, because its purposes were not beneficial for the community. The special commissioners for income tax had found that any assumed public benefit in the advancement of morals was outweighed by a detriment to medical science and research. Also, its objects (*necessarily* requiring an alteration in the law) were political. It followed that the society, not being 'a body of persons … established for charitable purposes only', was not exempt from income tax by virtue of the Income Tax Act 1918, s.37(1)(b).

LORD SIMONDS (on the question whether the object to be obtained was political): My lords, if I may deal with this second reason first, I cannot agree that in this case an alteration in the law is merely ancillary to the attainment of a good charitable object. In a sense no doubt, since legislation is not an end in itself, every law may be regarded as ancillary to the object which its provisions are intended to achieve. But that is not the sense in which it is said that a society has a political object. Here, the finding of the Commissioners is itself conclusive. 'We are satisfied', they say, 'that the main object of the society is the total abolition of vivisection … and (for that purpose) the repeal of the Cruelty to Animals Act 1876 [now replaced by the Animals (Scientific Procedures) Act 1986], and the substitution of a new enactment prohibiting vivisection altogether.' This is a finding that the main purpose of the society is the compulsory abolition of vivisection by Act of Parliament. What else can it mean? And how else can it be supposed that vivisection is to be abolished? Abolition and suppression are words that connote some form of compulsion. It can only be by Act of Parliament that that element can be supplied …

Lord Parker uses slightly different language but means the same thing when he says that the court has no means of judging whether a proposed change in the law will or will not be for the public benefit. It is not for the court to judge and the court has no means of judging. The same question may be looked at from a slightly different angle. One of the tests, and a crucial test, whether a trust is charitable, lies in the competence of the court to control and reform it. I would remind your lordships that it is the King as *parens patriae* who is the guardian of charity and that it is the right and duty of his Attorney-General to intervene and inform the court, if the trustees of a charitable trust fall short of their duty. So too it is his duty to assist the court, if need be, in the formulation of a scheme for the execution of a charitable trust. But, my lords, is it for a moment to be supposed that it is the function of the Attorney-General on behalf of the Crown to intervene and demand that a trust shall be established and administered by the court, the object of which is to alter the law in a manner highly prejudicial, as he and His Majesty's government may think, to the welfare of the State? … I conclude upon this part of the case that a main object of the society is political and for that reason the society is not established for charitable purposes only.

[His lordship continued on the question of benefit:] It is to me a strange and bewildering idea that the court must look so far and no farther, must see a charitable purpose in the intention of the society to benefit animals and thus elevate the moral character of men but must shut its eyes to the injurious results to the whole human and animal creation. I will readily concede that, if the purpose is within one of the heads of charity forming the first three classes in the classification which Lord Macnaughten borrowed from Sir Samuel Romilly's argument in *Morice* v *Bishop of Durham* (1805) 10 Ves 522, 531, the court will easily conclude that it is a charitable purpose. But even here to give the purpose the name of 'religious' or 'education' is not to conclude the matter. It may yet not be charitable, if the religious purpose is illegal or the educational purpose is contrary to public policy. Still there remains the overriding question: Is it *pro bono publico*? It would be another strange misreading of Lord Macnaughten's speech in [*Commissioners for Special Purposes of Income Tax* v *Pemsel*] [1891] AC 531 … to suggest that he intended anything to the contrary. I would rather say that, when a purpose appears broadly to fall within one of the familiar categories of charity, the court will assume it to be for the benefit of the community and, therefore, charitable, unless the contrary is shown, and further that the court will not be astute in such a case to defeat on doubtful evidence the avowed benevolent intention of a donor. But, my lords, the next step is one that I cannot take. Where on the evidence before it the court concludes that, however well-intentioned the donor, the achievement of his object will be greatly to the public disadvantage, there can be no justification for saying that it is a charitable object. If and so far as there is any judicial decision to the contrary, it must, in my opinion, be regarded as inconsistent with principle and be overruled.

NOTE: In *Hanchett-Stamford* v *H M Attorney-General* [2008] EWHC 330 (Ch), the court confirmed that the express recognition of the advancement of animal welfare in the Charities Act 2006 did not change the rule that withholds charitable status from political aims such as the aim of changing the law (in this case the organisation had been established to seek an outright ban on performing animals).

■ QUESTION

Would Lord Simonds' reasoning in the first of the above passages apply to a society whose objects were to:

(a) campaign against a change in the law which was being proposed by the government?

(b) campaign to alter the law overseas? (See (ii) below.)

NOTES

1. On the question of political objects, see further *McGovern* v *Attorney-General* [1982] Ch 321 (discussed in greater detail in this section), where similar principles were applied to a body (Amnesty International) whose objects included altering the laws of overseas jurisdictions, and *Re Koeppler's WT* [1986] Ch 423 (discussed in greater detail in this section), where alteration in the law was only an incidental object, and was not a bar to the body being an educational charity.

2. On the question of public benefit, this was treated as a question of fact, and if an object is not for the benefit of the public it cannot be charitable under any head (although Lord Simonds conceded in the last passage set out in our discussion of *National Anti-Vivisection Society* v *Inland Revenue Commissioners* that, if the object fell within one of the first three heads, public benefit would usually be assumed). Lord Simonds also recognised (at 74) that public benefit is not static, but may alter over time.

3. It follows, therefore, that any trust whose main object includes a change in the law of the United Kingdom cannot be charitable (in *Re Bushnell* [1975] 1 WLR 1596).

M. R. Chesterman, *Charities, Trusts and Social Welfare*
(London: Weidenfeld & Nicolson, 1979)

[Discussing 'progressive' charities such as international relief charities Oxfam and War on Want.] Many such charities appreciate too well that merely to distribute food and other basic amenities amongst the poor inhabitants of developing countries will at best relieve in the short term the immediate symptoms of poverty. Ultimately, more progress towards cure will be achieved if projects to stimulate local food production, distribution of locally-manufactured goods, or the building of essential amenities are undertaken; better still may be to try to persuade the foreign government to distribute the country's resources more equitably or the British government to grant more foreign aid. Yet these approaches to the problem fall foul of either or both of two rules of charity law: (a) that charities must not be 'political' in an activist sense; and (b) that activities within the fourth category of charitable purpose are not charitable if carried out abroad (except perhaps within the British Commonwealth), because such 'public' purposes fall properly within the province of the relevant foreign government. International relief charities may thus have to choose between two courses of 'political' action: continuing to hand out 'international doles', with all their politically conservative implications, or encountering opposition from the Charity Commission by pursuing courses of action which they consider much more fruitful in the long run ...

(ii) Change in the law overseas

Lord Simonds' reasoning in *National Anti-Vivisection Society* v *IRC* applies only to changes to the law in the United Kingdom, but in *McGovern* v *Attorney-General* [1982] Ch 321, Slade J frustrated Amnesty International's attempt to procure charitable status for some of its activities by creating a trust of those parts which were thought most likely to be accepted as charitable, on the ground that a main object of the trust was to secure the alteration of the laws of foreign countries.

McGovern v *Attorney-General*

[1982] Ch 321, [1981] 3 All ER 493, Chancery Division

Facts: The objects of Amnesty International included, among other things, attempting to secure the release of prisoners of conscience and procuring the abolition of torture or inhuman or degrading treatment or punishment.

The trustees applied to the Charity Commissioners for registration as a charity under the Charities Act 1960, s.4 (now Charities Act 2011, Part 4), and the Commissioners refused. Amnesty appealed.

Held: Because of the inclusion of the political objects (set out in the *Facts*), Amnesty International was not a charitable body: a direct and main object of the trust was to secure changes in the laws of foreign countries. The decision represents an extension of the principles laid down in the House of Lords in *National Anti-Vivisection Society* v *IRC* [1948] AC 31.

SLADE J: I now turn to consider the status of a trust of which a main object is to secure the alteration of the laws of a foreign country. The mere fact that the trust was intended to be carried out abroad would not be itself necessarily deprive it of charitable status. A number of trusts to be executed outside this country have been upheld as charities, though the judgment of Evershed MR in *Camille and Henry Dreyfus Foundation Inc.* v *IRC* [1954] Ch 672 at 684–5 illustrates that certain types of trust, for example trusts for the setting out of soldiers or the repair of bridges or causeways, might be acceptable as charities only if they were to be executed in the United Kingdom. The point with which I am at present concerned is whether a trust of which a direct and main object is to secure a change in the laws of a foreign country can ever be regarded as charitable under English law. Though I do not think that any authority cited to me precisely covers the point, I have come to the clear conclusion that it cannot.

I accept that the dangers of the court encroaching on the functions of the legislature or of subjecting its political impartiality to question would not be nearly so great as when similar trusts are to be executed in this country. I also accept that on occasions the court will examine and express an opinion on the quality of a foreign law. Thus, for example, it has declined to enforce or recognise rights conferred or duties imposed by a foreign law, in certain cases where it has considered that, on the particular facts, enforcement or recognition would be contrary to justice or morality. I therefore accept the particular point made by Mr Tyssen (about the law stultifying itself) has no application in this context. There is no obligation on the court to decide on the principle that any foreign law is *ex hypothesi* right as it stands; it is not obliged for all purposes to blind itself to what it may regard as the injustice of a particular foreign law.

In my judgment, however, there remain overwhelming reasons why such a trust still cannot be regarded as charitable. All the reasoning of Lord Parker in *Bowman* v *Secular Society Ltd* [1917] AC 406 seems to me to apply *a fortiori* in such a case. *A fortiori* the court will have no adequate means of judging whether a proposed change in the law of a foreign country will or will not be for the public benefit. Evershed MR in *Camille and Henry Dreyfus Foundation Inc.* v *IRC* [1954] Ch 672 at 684 expressed the prima facie view that the community which has to be considered in this context, even in the case of a trust to be executed abroad, is the community of the United Kingdom. Assuming that this is the right test, the court in applying it would still be bound to take account of the probable effects of attempts to procure the proposed legislation, or of its actual enactment, on the inhabitants of the country concerned, which would doubtless have a history and social structure quite different from that of the United Kingdom. Whatever might be its view as to the content of the relevant law from the standpoint of an English lawyer, it would, I think, have no satisfactory means of judging such probable effects on the local community.

Furthermore, before ascribing charitable status to an English trust of which a main object was to secure the alteration of a foreign law, the court would also, I conceive be bound to consider the consequences for this country as a matter of public policy. In a number of such cases there would arise a substantial prima facie risk that such a trust, if enforced, could prejudice the relations of this country with the foreign country concerned ... The court would have no satisfactory means of assessing the extent of such risk, which would not be capable of being readily dealt with by evidence and would be a matter more for political than for legal judgment. For all these reasons, I conclude that a trust of which a main purpose is to procure a change in the laws of a foreign country is a trust for the attainment of political objectives within the spirit of Lord Parker's pronouncement and, as such, is non-charitable.

Thus far, I have been considering trusts of which a main purpose is to achieve changes in the law itself or which are of a party political nature. Under any legal system, however, the government and its various authorities, administrative and judicial, will have wide discretionary powers vested in them, within the framework of the existing law. If a principal purpose of a trust is to procure a reversal of government policy or of particular administrative decisions of governmental authorities, does it constitute a trust for political purposes falling within the spirit of Lord Parker's pronouncement? In my judgment it does. If a trust of this nature is to be executed in England, the court will ordinarily have no sufficient means of determining whether the desired reversal would be beneficial to the public, and in any event could not properly encroach on the functions of the executive, acting *intra vires*, by holding that it should be acting in some other manner. If it is a trust which is to be executed abroad, the court will not have sufficient means of satisfactorily judging, as a matter of evidence, whether the proposed reversal would be beneficial to the community in the relevant sense, after all its consequences, local and international, had been taken into account.

NOTES

1. See also *Re Koeppler's WT* [1986] Ch 423 below, where *McGovern* was distinguished.
2. The decision represents an extension of the principles laid down in the House of Lords in *National Anti-Vivisection Society* v *IRC* [1948] AC 31. The reasoning adopted by Lord Simonds could not be applied directly here, but Slade J thought that to grant charitable status to such purposes might prejudice the relations of the British Government with foreign countries, and this consideration of policy could not be overlooked by the court.
3. A political taint will in any case be fatal to charitable status, whether or not a trust's direct and main object is to secure a change in the law of the United Kingdom, or of a foreign country. This can apply even to trusts seeking to promote aims which most civilised nations hold to be high aspirations. In *Re Strakosch* [1949] Ch 529, the promotion of racial harmony between English and Afrikaner communities in South Africa was held non-charitable, and registration of community councils is refused where their principal aim is the promotion of interracial accord. The same will apply where the aims are harmony and peace, if such movements overtly or covertly call upon governments to promote specific policies, such as disarmament. One reason sometimes given for denying charitable status to attempts to promote moral objectives is that they necessarily involve a propagandist element biased in favour of only one side of the argument.

(iii) Discussion of political issues, and campaigning

On the other hand, it is legitimate for an educational charity to discuss political issues, and a political object which is merely incidental will not be fatal. In *Re Koeppler's WT* [1986] Ch 423, a testamentary gift to Wilton Park, whose main function was to organise educational conferences, was upheld by the Court of Appeal as a gift for charitable purposes, although Wilton Park's objects included the promotion of informed international public opinion and the promotion of greater cooperation between East and West.

Re Koeppler's WT, Barclays Bank Trust Co. plc v Slack
[1986] Ch 423, [1985] 2 All ER 869, Court of Appeal

Facts: The issue arose over the validity of a testamentary gift to the warden of the institution known as Wilton Park. At the time of the testator's death there was no entity called Wilton Park, nor was there a warden of Wilton Park, but there was a Wilton Park project, which consisted of a series of conferences. It was accepted that the gift could only be valid if it was construed as a gift for charitable purposes.

Held: The gift was construed as a gift for the purposes of the Wilton Park project (applying the reasoning in *Re Finger's WT* [1972] 1 Ch 286, in Chapter 9). These purposes were charitable, being for the advancement of education. The political purposes of Wilton Park were of only an incidental nature, and did not invalidate the gift.

SLADE LJ (on the political issue): The organisation and conduct of the conferences which had been held since 1950 at Wiston House were clearly the central features of the Wilton Park project. The 'specific aspects' dealt with at each conference covered a wide range of topics. Examples of these specific aspects are to be found in the programmes for the four conferences immediately preceding the date of the testator's will and those for the four conferences immediately preceding his death. They were as follows:

(1) An enquiry into the 'quality of life'; ecology and the environment; participation in government and industry; tensions in free societies; (2) Europe and the emergent pattern of superpower relationships; (3) the unification of Europe; a balance sheet; (4) the requirements of Western defence and the possibilities of arms control; (5) the European Community and its external relations; (6) the media, public opinion and the decision-making process in government; (7) security issues as a factor in domestic and international politics; (8) labour and capital and the future of industrial society.

As the judge observed, those specific themes are self-evidently matters on which persons of differing political persuasions might have differing views and some of the speakers invited to speak at plenary sessions of the conferences were politicians. However, he found that 'it is clear that Wilton Park has taken pains to avoid inculcating any particular political viewpoint' (see [1984] Ch 243 at 251). There is therefore no question of the Wilton Park conferences being intended to further the interests of a particular political party ... .

There are two particular points which have caused me to hesitate before finally concluding that this gift is of a charitable nature. First, I have already mentioned the wide range of topics which are discussed at Wilton Park conferences, some of which could be said to have a political flavour. We were referred to a decision of my own in *McGovern* v *Attorney-General* [1982] Ch 321 [see discussion in this section], where I held, *inter alia*, that though certain trusts, declared in a trust deed, for research into the observance of human rights and the dissemination of the results of such research would have been charitable if they had stood alone, they failed because, read in their context, they were merely adjuncts to the political purposes declared by the earlier provisions of the deed.

However, in the present case, as I have already mentioned, the activities of Wilton Park are not of a party political nature. Nor, so far as the evidence shows, are they designed to procure changes in the laws or governmental policy of this or any other country: even when they touch on political matters, they constitute, so far as I can see, no more than genuine attempts in an objective manner to ascertain and disseminate the truth. In these circumstances I think that no objections to the trust arise on a political score, similar to those which arose in the *McGovern* case. The trust is, in my opinion, entitled to what is sometimes called a 'benignant construction', in the sense that the court is entitled to presume that the trustees will only act in a lawful and proper manner appropriate to the trustees of a charity and not, for example, by the propagation of tendentious political opinions, any more than those running the Wilton Park project so acted in the 33 years predating the testator's death: compare *McGovern* v *Attorney-General* [1982] Ch 321 at 353.

NOTE: Another authority that discussion of political issues is not necessarily fatal to charitable status is *Attorney-General* v *Ross* [1986] 1 WLR 252, where Scott J commented, at 263, that 'there is nothing the matter with an educational charity in the furtherance of its educational purposes encouraging students to develop their political awareness or to acquire knowledge of and to debate and to form views on political issues'. He also observed that there is no reason why a charitable student organisation should not affiliate to a non-charitable organisation if that enables it to further its own charitable activities for the benefit of students. That is the basis upon which student unions are entitled to affiliate to the National Union of Students, a non-charitable organisation. It is, however, essential that the purpose of the affiliation should be to benefit the student body in their capacity as students.

There are limits to the extent to which a charity can go in this direction, however. Political discussion may not be fatal to charitable status, but campaigning, in the sense of seeking to influence public opinion on political matters, undoubtedly is.

Webb v *O'Doherty and Others*

The Times, 11 February 1991, Chancery Division

Decision: Hoffmann J, distinguishing *Attorney-General* v *Ross*, granted an injunction restraining the officers of a students' union, which was an educational charity, from making any payments to the National Student Committee to Stop War in the Gulf, or to the Cambridge Committee to Stop War in the Gulf.

HOFFMANN J: There is no doubt that campaigning, in the sense of seeking to influence public opinion on political matters, is not a charitable activity. It is, of course, something which students are, like the rest of the population, perfectly at liberty to do in their private capacities, but it is not a proper object of the expenditure of charitable money ...

The law will only permit charitable money to be spent on what might be regarded as political persuasion if that is a mere incidental effect of expenditure for proper charitable educational purposes.

In this case the Student Union passed a resolution on the 22nd of January, 1991 which began by expressing various views about the Gulf War and the situation in the Middle East and then mandated the executive in the following terms: '1. To affiliate to the National Student Committee to Stop the War in the Gulf and the Cambridge Committee to stop the War in the Gulf. 2. To campaign on the above issues. 3. To support and publicise national and local demonstrations, speaker meetings and non-violent direct actions organised by CND and Committee To Stop War in the Gulf. 4. To support the teach-in on the Gulf Crisis organised by the Student Committee To Stop War this Thursday. 5. To allocate £100 from the Campaign budget to the anti-Gulf War campaign. 6. To write to the Prime Minister and Ministry of Defence outlining this policy.' All those aims are, as I have said, perfectly legitimate aims for citizens of this country to espouse, but I have absolutely no doubt that there is no way in which they can be described as 'charitable'. ...

[On the affiliation point] there is no reason why a charitable student organisation should not affiliate to a non-charitable organisation if that enables it to further its own charitable activities for the benefit of students. That is the basis upon which the union is entitled to affiliate to the National Union of Students, a non-charitable organisation, and no doubt to other non-charitable organisations as well. It is, however, essential for this purpose that the purpose of the affiliation should be to benefit the student body in their capacity as students. What is not permitted is to affiliate to a wholly non-charitable organisation simply as a way of furthering a non-charitable purpose or of channelling funds into non-charitable activities.

NOTE: An organisation (English PEN, a branch of International PEN) that promotes peace and human rights through the power of literature and free speech has been granted charitable status even though (according to its website) 25 per cent of its funds are devoted to campaigns, including the reform of English libel law on the basis that it 'has a profoundly negative impact on freedom of expression, both in the UK and around the world' (Charity Commissioners, *English PEN's Application for Registration as a Charity*, 21 July 2008, [2008] WTLR 1799).

■ QUESTION

How can the prohibition on political purposes be reconciled with the express inclusion within the 'definition' of charitable purposes of the promotion of human rights by means of such activities as 'the resolution of national or international conflicts'; 'promoting equality and diversity by the elimination of discrimination on the grounds of age, sex or sexual orientation' and 'enabling people of one faith to understand the religious beliefs of others' (Charity Commission, 'The Promotion of Human Rights' *Review of the Register* RR12). Is the Charity Commission's answer convincing?

Charity Commission, 'The Promotion of Human Rights'

Review of the Register RR12

Charities are able to engage in political campaigning in order to further their charitable purposes. Charity law draws a distinction between political purposes and political activities. An organisation which has purposes which include the promotion of human rights by seeking a change in the law, or a shift in government policy, or a reversal of a government decision has (at least in part) political purposes and cannot be a charity. However, the trustees of a charity may nonetheless use political means without jeopardising charitable status. What is important for charitable status is that political means should not be the dominant method by which the organisation will pursue its apparently charitable objects.

NOTE: In Australia (and the US), the position on the promotion of political purposes by charities is more relaxed than in the UK. See, for example, the decision of the High Court of Australia to uphold the polticial activities of a charity that acts as a 'watchdog' to scrutinise the efficacy of aid provision in foreign countries (*Aid/Watch Incorporated* v *Commissioner of Taxation* [2010] HCA 42).

E: The prevention or relief of poverty

The original basis for this head of charity was the reference to 'relief of aged, impotent and poor people' in the Preamble to the Statute of Charitable Uses 1601. It is clear that it is not necessary for the recipients of benefit to be aged, impotent, *and* poor for a bequest to be charitable: any one will do.

Joseph Rowntree Memorial Trust Housing Association Ltd v *Attorney-General*
[1983] 1 Ch 159, [1983] 2 WLR 284, [1983] 1 All ER 288, Chancery Division

Decision: Provision of housing for the aged was charitable, notwithstanding that the schemes operated by way of bargain (contract) rather than bounty (gift).

PETER GIBSON J: The views of the Charity Commissioners on schemes such as these were set out in paras. 102 to 108 of the Charity Commissioners' report for 1980 (HC Paper (1979–80) no. 608) … . I hope I summarise the objections of the Charity Commissioners fairly as being the following: (1) the schemes provide for the aged only by way of bargain on a contractual basis rather than by way of bounty; (2) the benefits provided are not capable of being withdrawn at any time if the beneficiary subsequently ceases to qualify; (3) the schemes are for the benefit of private individuals, not for a charitable class; (4) the schemes are a commercial enterprise capable of producing profit for the beneficiary.

Before I deal with these objections it is appropriate to consider the scope of the charitable purpose which the plaintiffs claim the scheme carries out, that is to say in the words of the preamble to the Statute of Elizabeth (43 Eliz I c 4, the Charitable Uses Act 1601) 'the relief of aged persons'. That purpose is indeed part of the very first set of charitable purposes contained in the preamble: 'the relief of aged, impotent and poor people'. Looking at those words without going to authority and attempting to give them their natural meaning, I would have thought that two inferences therefrom were tolerably clear. First, the words 'aged, impotent and poor' must be read disjunctively. It would be as absurd to require that the aged must be impotent or poor as it would be to require the impotent to be aged or poor, or the poor to be aged or impotent. There will no doubt be many cases where the objects of charity prove to have two or more of the three qualities at the same time. Second, essential to the charitable purpose is that it should relieve aged, impotent and poor people. The word 'relief' implies that the persons in question have a need attributable to their condition as aged, impotent or poor persons which requires alleviating, and which those persons could not alleviate, or would find difficulty in alleviating, themselves from their own resources. The word 'relief' is not synonymous with 'benefit'.

Those inferences are in substance what both counsel submit are the true principles governing the charitable purpose of the relief of aged persons. Counsel for the plaintiffs stresses that any benefit provided must be related to the needs of the aged. Thus a gift of money to the aged millionaires of Mayfair would not relieve a need of theirs as aged persons. Counsel for the Attorney General similarly emphasises that to relieve a need of the aged attributable to their age would be charitable only if the means employed are appropriate to the need. He also points out that an element of public benefit must be found if the purpose is to be charitable. I turn then to authority to see if there is anything that compels a different conclusion.

[Peter Gibson J reviewed the authorities and continued:]

These authorities convincingly confirm the correctness of the proposition that the relief of the aged does not have to be relief for the aged poor. In other words the phrase 'aged, impotent and poor people' in the preamble must be read disjunctively. The decisions in *Re Glyn's Will Trusts* [[1950] 2 All ER 1150n], *Re Bradbury* [[1950] 2 All ER 1150], *Re Robinson* [[1951] Ch 198], *Re Cottam's Will Trusts* [[1955] 1 WLR 1299] and *Re Lewis* [[1955] Ch 106] give support to the view that it is a sufficient charitable purpose to benefit the aged, or the impotent, without more. But these are all decisions at first instance and with great respect to the judges who decided them they appear to me to pay no regard to the word 'relief'. I have no hesitation in preferring the approach adopted in *Re Neal* and *Le Cras* v *Perpetual Trustee Co. Ltd* that there must be a need which is to be relieved by the charitable gift, such need being attributable to the aged or impotent condition of the person to be benefited. My attention was drawn to Picarda *The Law and Practice Relating to Charities* (1977) p. 79, where a similar approach is adopted by the learned author.

In any event in the present case, as I have indicated, the plaintiffs do not submit that the proposed schemes are charitable simply because they are for the benefit of the aged. The plaintiffs have identified a particular need for special housing to be provided for the elderly in the ways proposed and it seems to me that on any view of the matter that is a charitable purpose, unless the fundamental objections of the charity commissioners to which I have referred are correct. To these I now turn.

The first objection is, as I have stated, that the scheme makes provision for the aged on a contractual basis as a bargain rather than by way of bounty. This objection is sometimes expressed in the form that relief is charitable only where it is given by way of bounty and not by way of bargain (see 5 Halsbury's Laws (4th edn) para. 516). But as the learned editors recognise this does not mean that a gift cannot be charitable if it provides for the beneficiaries to contribute to the cost of the benefits they receive. There are numerous cases where beneficiaries only receive benefits from a charity by way of bargain. *Re Cottam* and *Le Cras* v *Perpetual Trustee Co. Ltd* provide examples. Another class of cases relates to fee-paying schools (see for example *The Abbey, Malvern Wells Ltd* v *Minister of Town and Country Planning* [1951] 2 All ER 154, [1951] Ch 728). Another example relates to a gift for the provision of homes of rest for lady teachers at a rent (*Re Estlin, Prichard* v *Thomas* (1903) 72 LJ Ch 687). It is of course crucial in all these cases that the services provided by the gift are not provided for the private profit of the individuals providing the services.

The source of the statement that charity must be provided by way of bounty and not bargain is to be found in some remarks of Rowlatt J in *IRC* v *Society for the Relief of Widows and Orphans of Medical Men* (1926) 136 LT 60 at 65. This was a case relating to the statutory provisions allowing tax relief for income applicable to charitable purposes only of trusts or bodies established for charitable purposes only. Rowlatt J said:

> It seems to me that when it is said that the relief of poverty is a charity within the meaning of the rule which we are discussing that does mean the relief of poverty by way of bounty; it does not mean the relief of poverty by way of bargain. A purely mutual society among very poor people whose dependants would quite clearly always be very poor would not, I think, be a charity: it would be a business arrangement, as has been said in one of the cases, whereby contractual benefits accrued to people whose poverty makes them very much in need of them. That would not be a charity. I think, therefore, that the crux of this case is whether this is a case of that sort.

He went on to hold that the case before him was not that of a mutual society: the beneficiaries had no right to anything.

In my judgment Rowlatt J's remarks must be understood in their limited context. They are entirely appropriate in determining whether a mutual society conferring rights on members is charitable. If a housing association were a co-operative under which the persons requiring the dwellings provided by the housing association had by that association's constitution contractual rights to the dwellings, that would no doubt not be charitable, but that is quite different from bodies set up like the trust and the association. The applicants for dwellings under the schemes which I am considering would have no right to any dwelling when they apply. The fact that the benefit given to them is in the form of a contract is immaterial to the charitable purpose in making the benefit available. I see nothing in this objection of the charity commissioners.

The second objection was that the schemes do not satisfy the requirement that the benefits they provide must be capable of being withdrawn at any time if the beneficiary ceases to qualify. No doubt charities will, so far as practical and compatible with the identified need which they seek to alleviate, try to secure that their housing stock becomes available if the circumstances of the persons occupying the premises change. But it does not seem to me to be an essential part of the charitable purpose to secure that this should always be so. The nature of some benefits may be such that it will endure for some time, if benefits in that form are required to meet the particular need that has been identified. Thus, in *Re Monk*, *Giffen v Wedd* [1927] All ER Rep 157 a testatrix set up a loan fund whereby loans for up to nine years were to be made available to the poor. This was held to be charitable. No doubt the circumstances of the borrower might change whilst the loan was outstanding. If the grant of a long-term lease-hold interest with the concomitant security of tenure that such an interest would give to the elderly is necessary to meet the identified needs of the elderly, then in my judgment that is no objection to such a grant. The plaintiffs have put in evidence that they oppose the inclusion in a lease of any provision entitling the plaintiffs to determine the lease in the event of a change in financial circumstances of the tenant. Their main reason, which to my mind is a cogent one, is the unsettling effect it could have on aged tenants. In any event the distinction between what prima facie is a short-term letting and a long lease has been rendered somewhat illusory by statute. A charity may find it no less difficult to recover possession from weekly tenants whose circumstances have changed than it would to recover possession from a tenant under a long lease.

The third objection was that the schemes were for the benefit of private individuals and not for a charitable class. I cannot accept that. The schemes are for the benefit of a charitable class, that is to say the aged having certain needs requiring relief therefrom. The fact that, once the association and the trust have selected individuals to benefit from the housing, those individuals are identified private individuals does not seem to me to make the purpose in providing the housing a non-charitable one any more than a trust for the relief of poverty ceases to be a charitable purpose when individual poor recipients of bounty are selected.

The fourth objection was that the schemes were a commercial enterprise capable of producing a profit for the beneficiary. I have already discussed the cases which show that the charging of an economic consideration for a charitable service that is provided does not make the purpose in providing the service non-charitable, provided of course that no profits accrue to the provider of the service. It is true that a tenant under the schemes may recover more than he or she has put in, but that is at most incidental to the charitable purpose. It is not a primary objective. The profit (if it be right to call the increased value of the equity a profit as distinct from a mere increase avoiding the effects of inflation, as was intended) is not a profit at the expense of the charity, and indeed it might be thought improper, if there be a profit, that it should accrue to the charity which has provided no capital and not to the tenant which has provided most if not all the capital. Again, I cannot see that this objection defeats the charitable character of the schemes.

I turn then to a consideration of the schemes themselves ...

(i) Definition of poverty

Where poverty needs to be shown we must consider its definition. In *Re Coulthurst* [1951] Ch 661, Evershed MR said of poverty (at 665–6):

It is quite clearly established that poverty does not mean destitution: it is a word of wide and somewhat indefinite import; it may not be unfairly paraphrased for present purposes as meaning persons who have to 'go short' in the ordinary acceptance of that term, due regard being had to their status in life, and so forth.

Poverty, therefore, is a relative matter, depending on one's status in life, and the courts have been willing to allow trusts to assist such categories as 'distressed gentlefolk'.

Subject to the width of the definition of poverty, it is essential that poverty should be imposed as a qualification for benefit, and that only the poor can benefit. A trust which may benefit rich persons as well as poor will fail under this head. The courts can however infer a limitation to the poor, even in the absence of an express limitation.

Re Niyazi's WT

[1978] 1 WLR 910, [1978] 3 All ER 785, Chancery Division

Decision: Megarry V-C held charitable a bequest of £15,000 'for the construction of or as a contribution towards the cost of a working men's hostel' in Famagusta, Cyprus, although there was no express limitation to the poor. He accepted that persons requiring such accommodation would necessarily be poor.

MEGARRY V-C: Certain points seem reasonably plain. First, 'poverty' is not confined to destitution, but extends to those who have small means and so have to 'go short'. Second, a gift which in terms is not confined to the relief of poverty may by inference be thus confined. In *Re Lucas* [1922] 2 Ch 52 there was a gift of 5s per week to the oldest respectable inhabitants of a village. As the law then stood, Russell J was unable to hold that a gift merely to the aged was charitable; but he held that the limitation to 5s a week indicated quite clearly that only those to whom such a sum would be of importance and a benefit were to take, and so the gift was charitable as being for the relief of poverty. I do not think that it can be said that nothing save the smallness of the benefit can restrict an otherwise unrestricted benefit so as to confine it within the bounds of charity. I think that anything in the terms of the gift which by implication prevents it from going outside those bounds will suffice. In *Re Glyn's Will Trusts* [1950] 2 All ER 1150 Danckwerts J held that a trust for building free cottages for old women of the working classes aged 60 or more provided a sufficient context to show an intention to benefit indigent persons, and so was charitable.

Thus far, I do not think that there is any serious difference between counsel for the Attorney-General and counsel for the Greek mayor on the one hand and counsel for the next-of-kin on the other. The main dispute is whether in this case there is enough in the words and their context to confine the gift to the relief of poverty. Not surprisingly, counsel for the next-of-kin strongly relied on *Re Sanders' Will Trusts* [1954] Ch 265. There the trust was to provide 'dwellings for the working classes and their families' living within five miles of Pembroke Dock. Harman J rejected the contention that this was a charitable gift, since 'working classes' was not a phrase which connoted poverty, and there was nothing about old age which might indicate those who had ceased to work. An appeal from this decision was compromised [1954] *The Times* 22nd July ...

As the arguments finally emerged, counsel for the Attorney-General's main contention was that, even if neither 'working men' nor 'hostel', by itself, could be said to confine the trust to what in law was charity, the use of these expressions in conjunction sufficed for his purpose. They were enough to distinguish *Re Sanders' Will Trusts*, especially as Harman J had not had the advantage which I have had of being able to consider what had been said in the *Guinness* case [*Guinness Trust (London Fund) founded 1890, registered 1902* v *Green* [1955] 1 WLR 872]. I think that the adjectival expression 'working mens' plainly has some flavour of 'lower income' about it, just as 'upper class' has some flavour of affluence, and 'middle class' some flavour of comfortable means. Of course there are impoverished members of the 'upper' and 'middle' classes, just as there are some 'working men' who are at least of comfortable means, if not affluence: one cannot ignore the impact of such things as football pools. But in construing a will I think that I am concerned with the ordinary or general import of words rather than exceptional cases; and, whatever may be the future meaning of 'working men' or 'working class', I think that by 1967 such phrases had not lost their general connotation of 'lower income'. I may add that nobody has suggested that any difficulty arose from the use of 'working men' as distinct from 'working persons' or 'working women'.

The connotation of 'lower income' is, I think, emphasised by the word 'hostel'. No doubt there are a number of hostels of superior quality; and one day, perhaps, I may even encounter the expression 'luxury hostel'. But without any such laudatory adjective the word 'hostel' has to my mind a strong flavour of a building which provides somewhat modest accommodation for those who have some temporary need for it and are willing to accept accommodation of that standard in order to meet the need. When 'hostel' is prefixed by the expression 'working mens', then the further restriction is introduced of the hostel being intended for those with a relatively low income who work for their living, especially as manual workers. The need, in other words, is to be the need of working men, and not of students or battered wives or anything else. Furthermore, the need will not be the need of the better paid working men who can afford something superior to mere hostel accommodation, but the need of the lower end of the financial scale of working men, who cannot compete for the better accommodation but have to content themselves with the economies and shortcomings of hostel life. It seems to me that the word 'hostel' in this case is significantly different from the word 'dwellings' in *Re Sanders' Will Trusts*, a word which is appropriate to ordinary houses in which the well-to-do may live, as well as the relatively poor.

Has the expression 'working mens hostel' a sufficient connotation of poverty in it to satisfy the require-ments of charity? On any footing the case is desperately near the borderline, and I have hesitated in reach-ing my conclusion.

On the whole, however, for the reasons that I have been discussing, I think that the trust is charitable, though by no great margin. This view is in my judgment supported by two further considerations. First, there is the amount of the trust fund, which in 1969 was a little under £15,000. I think one is entitled to assume that a testator has at least some idea of the probable value of his estate. The money is given for the purpose 'of the construction of or as a contribution towards the cost of the construction of a work-ing mens hostel'. £15,000 will not go very far in such a project, and it seems improbable that contribu-tions from other sources towards constructing a 'working mens hostel' would enable or encourage the construction of any grandiose building. If financial constraints point towards the erection of what may be called an 'economy hostel', decent but catering for only the more basic requirements, then only the relatively poor would be likely to be occupants. There is at least some analogy here to the 5s per week in *Re Lucas* [1922] 2 Ch 52. Whether the trust is to give a weekly sum that is small enough to indicate that only those in straitened circumstances are to benefit, or whether it is to give a capital sum for the construction of a building which will be of such a nature that it is likely to accommodate only those who are in straitened circumstances, there will in each case be an implied restriction to poverty.

The other consideration is that of the state of housing in Famagusta. Where the trust is to erect a build-ing in a particular area, I think that it is legitimate, in construing the trust, to erect some regard to the physical condition existing in that area. Quite apart from any question of the size of the gift, I think that a trust to erect a hostel in a slum or in an area of acute housing need may have to be construed differently from a trust to erect a hostel in an area of housing affluence or plenty. Where there is a grave housing shortage, it is plain that the poor are likely to suffer more than the prosperous, and that the provision of a 'working mens hostel' is likely to help the poor and not the rich.

In the result, then, I hold that the trust is charitable. With some hesitation I would hold this without the aid of the two further considerations that I have just mentioned, the first of which was not discussed in argument. With the aid of these considerations I remain hesitant, though less so ...

NOTES

1. Although there is here no express limitation to the poor, the context suggests the likely poverty of the recipients. The amount of money left for the purpose was relatively small, and the word 'hostel', rather than 'dwelling' suggested very inferior accommodation. 'Working men' is more limited than 'working classes', excluding, for example, battered wives and students, and Megarry V-C had regard to the deplorable housing shortage in Famagusta.
2. Note that the benefit of this charity was entirely directed overseas.

■ QUESTIONS

1. In *Re Sanders' WT* [1954] Ch 265, Harman J thought that the provision of dwellings for 'the working classes' in the Pembroke Dock area was not sufficient to limit the benefit to poor persons: the working classes and the poor were not synonymous.
2. If you think that both *Re Sanders' WT* and *Re Niyazi's WT* were correct, how do you reconcile the views of Megarry V-C and Harman J?

F: The advancement of education

The Preamble to the Act of 1601 (set out at the beginning of Section 2: Definition of Charity) speaks only of 'schools of learning, free schools, scholars in universities' and the 'education and preferment of orphans', but in modern times, this category has grown to cover a very wide range of educational and cultural activities extending far beyond the administration of formal instruction.

Schools and universities are clearly charitable, and so now are nursery schools, adult education centres, and societies dedicated to promoting training and standards within a trade or profession. Education is not limited to teaching, however, and learned societies which bring together experts in a field to share and exchange knowledge may be charitable. Museums, zoos, and public libraries may be educational to the public at large, quite apart from their research activities. Even cultural activities such as drama, music, literature, and fine arts can come within this head: see, e.g. *Re Delius* [1957] Ch 299.

Learned societies are charitable, and professional and vocational bodies which advance education, such as the Royal College of Surgeons, are also charitable, even though one of the ancillary purposes is the protection and assistance of its members. Other examples include the Royal College of Nursing, the Institute of Civil Engineers, and the Incorporated Council of Law Reporting (in *Incorporated Council of Law Reporting for England and Wales* v *Attorney-General* [1972] Ch 73, the Attorney-General tried unsuccessfully to argue that the citation of law reports in court could not be educational because judges are deemed to have complete knowledge of the law). Bodies whose chief purpose is to further the interests of the members and to promote the status of the profession will not, however, be charitable, for example, the General Nursing Council (see *General Nursing Council for England and Wales* v *St Marylebone BC* [1959] AC 540).

■ QUESTION

Is it charitable to write or publish legal textbooks?

Re Shaw (dec'd), Public Trustee v Day

[1957] 1 WLR 729, [1957] 1 All ER 745, Chancery Division

Facts: The facts are set out in Chapter 3. One of the issues was whether the alphabet trusts were valid as a charitable trust.

Held: The trust was not valid as an educational charity, because increase of knowledge is not a charitable purpose unless combined with an element of teaching or education. Nor was the trust within the category of charitable trusts for other purposes beneficial to the community, because the object of the research was to convince the public that the new alphabet would be beneficial and, analogously to the cases of trusts for political purposes advocating a change in the law (see Section D), the court was not in a position to judge whether the adoption of the new alphabet in fact would be beneficial.

Not being charitable, the trust failed, since there were no ascertainable beneficiaries. See further on this point Chapter 3.

HARMAN J: ... The Attorney-General appears as parens patriae to uphold the trusts as being charitable trusts, and counsel for the Attorney-General at my request also supported the proposition of the executor that, even if not charitable, these trusts, not being tainted with the vice of perpetuity (as it is called), are a valid exercise by a man of his power of disposing of his own money as he thinks fit [see further Chapter 3]. The claimants retort that these trusts are not charitable trusts, and it seems to me that I should address myself first to that question. It is notorious that the word 'charitable', when used by a lawyer, covers many objects which a layman would not consider to be included under that word, but excludes benevolent or philanthropic activities which the layman would consider charitable. In construing a will the lawyer's sense must prevail in the absence of some special context. The four heads of charity are set out by Lord Macnaghten in *Commissioners for Special Purposes of Income Tax* v *Pemsel* ([1891] AC 531 at p. 583). His words, as has often been pointed out, are not original, being drawn from the argument of Sir Samuel Romilly in his reply in *Morice* v *Bishop of Durham* (1805), 10 Ves 522 at p. 532). They are almost too familiar to need repetition. Shortly stated the four heads are (i) religion, (ii) poverty, (iii) education, and (iv) 'other purposes beneficial to the community'. Sir Samuel Romilly describes the last head as being 'the most difficult', and the phrase he uses is 'the advancement of objects of general public utility'. Here, again, it is trite law that not every object coming within one or other of these categories is charitable—a college for pickpockets is no charity—but that every object which is to rank as charitable must either fit into one or more of the first three categories, or, if not, may still be held charitable because of general public utility.

The first object of the alphabet trusts is to find out by inquiry how much time could be saved by persons who speak the English language and write it, by the use of the proposed British alphabet and so to show the extent of the time and labour wasted by the use of our present alphabet, and, if possible, further to state this waste of time in terms of loss of money. The second is to transliterate one of the testator's plays, 'Androcles and the Lion', into the proposed British alphabet, assuming a given pronunciation of English, and to advertise and publish the transliteration in a page by page version in the proposed alphabet on one side and the existing alphabet on the other, and, by the dissemination of copies and, in addition, by advertisement and propaganda, to persuade the government or the public or the English speaking world to adopt it. This was described by the Attorney-General as a useful piece of research beneficial to the public, because it would facilitate the education of the young and the teaching of the language and show a way to save time and, therefore, money. It was suggested that the objects could thus be brought within the third category and that a parallel could be found in the decision of Danckwerts, J, in *Crystal Palace Trustees* v *Minister of Town & Country Planning* ([1950] 2 All ER 857n.), where trusts 'for the promotion of industry, commerce and art' were held charitable. So they were, but only in the context provided by the instrument (An Act of Parliament) in which they appeared. In my opinion, if the object be merely the increase of knowledge, that is not in itself a charitable object unless it be combined with teaching or education (see the speech of Rigby, LJ, in *Re Macduff, Macduff* v *Macduff* [1896] 2 Ch 451 at p. 472) ... The research and propaganda enjoined by the testator seem to me merely to tend to the increase of public knowledge in a certain respect, namely, the saving of time and money by the use of the proposed alphabet. There is no element of teaching or education combined with this, nor does the propaganda element in the trusts tend to more than to persuade the public that the adoption of the new script would be 'a good thing', and that, in my view, is not education. Therefore I reject this element ...

NOTES

1. Harman J went on to reject an alternative argument that the trust was valid under the fourth category: see Section 3 below.
2. Harman J also held that the disposition failed as a valid non-charitable purpose trust. See further Chapter 3.
3. It would be wrong to conclude that research without a teaching element can never be charitable. The other cases in this section suggest that research with a view to publication can be charitable, as long as the results of the research (if any) are likely to be of value.

■ QUESTION

How should 'ghoti' be pronounced? *Hint*: cough, women, nation.

Re Hopkins

[1965] Ch 669, [1964] 3 WLR 840, [1964] 3 All ER 46, Chancery Division

Decision: Wilberforce J upheld as charitable a bequest to the Francis Bacon Society for the purposes of finding manuscripts which would demonstrate that Sir Francis Bacon wrote the plays popularly attributed to William Shakespeare. This was despite the fact that the manuscripts are unlikely to exist and the Bacon hypothesis is considered by virtually all leading scholars to be unsustainable.

WILBERFORCE J ... I accept that research of a private character, for the benefit only of the members of a society, would not normally be educational—or otherwise charitable— ... , but I do not think that the research in the present case can be said to be of a private character, for it is inherently inevitable, and manifestly intended, that the result of any discovery should be published to the world ...

G: The advancement of religion

As we noted earlier, the Charities Act 2006 states that 'religion' includes 'a religion which involves a belief in more than one god' and 'a religion which does not involve a belief in a god' (s.2(3)). The Charity Commission (website) lists the following characteristics of religious belief to be amongst those identified by the courts:

- 'belief in a god (or gods) or goddess (or goddesses), or supreme being, or divine or transcendental being or entity or spiritual principle ("supreme being or entity") which is the object or focus of the religion;
- a relationship between the believer and the supreme being or entity by showing worship of, reverence for or veneration of the supreme being or entity;
- a degree of cogency, cohesion, seriousness and importance;
- an identifiable positive, beneficial, moral or ethical framework.'

The law adopts a tolerant stance towards religion, and is reluctant to enter into value judgments in this area. (For example, in *Khaira* v *Shergill* [2012] EWCA Civ 983, the Court of Appeal declined to adjudicate on the claim that one of the parties was a 'holy' person according to the Sikh religion.) Cross J remarked in *Neville Estates* v *Madden* [1962] Ch 832, below, in which a trust for the members of the Catford Synagogue was held charitable: 'As between different religions the law stands neutral, but it assumes that any religion is at least likely to be better than none.' Another example is *Church of the New Faith* v *Commissioner of Payroll Tax (Victoria)* (1983) 49 ALR 65, a case concerning Australian Scientology, where Murphy J, in the High Court of Australia, stated (at 85–6) that:

Administrators and judges must resist the temptation to hold that groups or institutions are not religious because claimed religious beliefs or practices seem absurd, fraudulent, evil or novel; or because the group or institution is new, the number of adherents small, the leaders hypocrites, or because they seek to obtain the financial or other privileges which come with religious status. In the eyes of the law religions are equal ... any attempt to define religion exhaustively runs into difficulty. There is no single acceptable criterion, no essence of religion ... Some claims to be religious are not serious but merely a hoax ... but to reach this conclusion requires an extreme case ... Any body which claims to be religious, and offers a way to find meaning and purpose in life, is religious.

(It should be noted that in England and Wales, Scientology has never been recognised as a religion for the purposes of charity law. The Scientologists were turned down when they applied to the Charity Commissioners to be registered as a charity in 1999 (reported [2005] WTLR 1151).)

The Charities Act 2006 (now Charities Act 2011) takes an attitude to the meaning of 'religion' not dissimilar to that of Murphy J. For the purposes of charity law, 'religion' should now be taken to include not only monotheism and polytheism, but even some 'non-deistic', religions. Thus on 21 September 2010, the Charity Commission recognised the charitable status of the 'Druid Network', even though they worship no supreme being other than 'nature' broadly defined in its physical and spiritual aspects, and (according to the Druid Network), '[w]hilst different Druids relate to different gods, ancestors, spirits etc., all see these beings as part of Nature and, through their relationship with these beings, deepen their connection and relationship with Nature'. The previous case law referred to throughout the remainder of this Chapter has to be read in the light of this newly liberalised attitude to what counts as 'religion' for charitable purposes. The most interesting question remains—what, in the future, will *not* count as religion for charitable purposes?

The Preamble to the Statute of Charitable Uses 1601 gave little support for the tolerant approach the law has taken, the only reference to religion within it concerning the repair of churches. It may be that the explanation lies in the mortmain legislation in force from 1736 to 1891, which as we have seen rendered many gifts to charity void. Religious tolerance in this area, therefore, may have been used simply as a device to strike down testamentary gifts, the authorities from that period still having validity today.

In *Thornton* v *Howe* (1862) 31 Beav 14, for example, charitable status was extended to a devise of land to promote the writings of Joanna Southcote, the founder of a small but fervent sect in the West of England, who had proclaimed that she was with child by the Holy Ghost and would give birth to a second Messiah. The practical effect of the decision was to bring the trust within the invalidating provisions of the mortmain legislation, but the case is still seen as a landmark in establishing that any theistic belief, however obscure or remote, will fall within the meaning of religion for the purposes of charity law. The case is discussed and applied in *Re Watson* [1973] 1 WLR 1472.

Re Watson (dec'd), Hobbs v Smith

[1973] 1 WLR 1472, [1973] 3 All ER 678, Chancery Division

Decision: Plowman J held charitable a trust to publish the religious writings of a retired builder who was virtually the sole remaining adherent of a small, fundamentalist group of believers. Expert testimony regarded the theological merits of the works as very small, but confirmed the genuineness of the writer's beliefs.

PLOWMAN J (after stating the facts): So much for the evidence. There are two questions to consider. The first is, what are the purposes of the trust expressed by the will, and, secondly, whether that trust is a charitable trust. Now as to the first point, the work of God which is referred to in a number of passages in the will which I have read, to quote the will, is 'the work of God as it has been maintained by Mr H. G. Hobbs and myself since 1942 ... in propagating the truth as given in the Holy Bible'. And I accept counsel for the Attorney-General's submission that, on the true construction of the will, read in the light of the evidence of surrounding circumstances, the trust is one for the publication and distribution to the public of the religious works of Mr H. G. Hobbs. If that is right, to get one point out of the way, that trust will not, in my judgment, fail for impracticability, as counsel for the next-of-kin suggested on one view of the will that it must. On the second question, whether that trust, namely the trust for the publication and distribution to the public of the religious works of Mr Hobbs, is charitable, counsel for the next-of-kin submitted that it was not. He submitted that not every religious trust is charitable, that to be charitable there must be an element of public benefit, that whether or not there is a sufficient public benefit is a matter for the court to decide on evidence, irrespective of the opinion of the donor and that there is no sufficient element of public benefit in this case.

Counsel's submissions were based primarily on *National Anti-Vivisection Society* v *Inland Revenue Comrs* [1948] AC 31 [also discussed in this chapter] and *Gilmour* v *Coats* [1949] AC 426 [also discussed for this chapter], and he submitted that the approach of the House of Lords in those cases was inconsistent with the decision of Romilly MR in *Thornton* v *Howe* (1862) 31 Beav 14. *Thornton* v *Howe* was a well-known case about the writings of Joanna Southcote. The sidenote reads:

A trust 'for printing, publishing and propagating the sacred writings' of Joanna Southcote, is a charitable trust, which if given out of pure personality will be enforced and regulated. In respect to charitable trusts for printing and circulating works of a religious tendency, this Court makes no distinction between one sect and another, unless their tenets include doctrines adverse to the foundation of all religion or be subversive of all morality, in which case this Court will declare the bequest void.

After referring to the gift in the will Romilly MR said (1862) 31 Beav at 18:

In the first place, it is said that this, if a lawful and legitimate purpose, is a charity and therefore void, so far as the real estate is concerned, by reason of the Statute of Mortmain; and, secondly, it is also said that this is wholly void, both as to realty and personalty, by reason of the immorality and irreligious tendency of the writings of Joanna Southcote, which, by this disposition of her property, the testatrix intended to circulate and make more extensively known. On the latter point, being unacquainted with the writings of Joanna Southcote, it became my duty to look into them, for the purpose of satisfying myself on this point, and the result of my investigation is, that there is nothing to be found in them which, in my opinion, is likely to corrupt the morals of her followers, or make her readers irreligious.

And I may pause there to say that, in my judgment, is equally true of the writings of Mr H. G. Hobbs in this case. Romilly MR then went on to express his opinion of Joanna Southcote, saying that, in his opinion, she was—

> a foolish, ignorant woman, of an enthusiastic turn of mind, who had long wished to become an instrument in the hands of God to promote some great good on earth.

He said (1862) 31 Beav at 19, 20, 21:

> In the history of her life, her personal disputations and conversations with the devil, her prophecies and her inter-communings with the spiritual world, I have found much that, in my opinion, is very foolish, but nothing which is likely to make persons who read them either immoral or irreligious. I cannot, therefore, say that this devise of the testatrix is invalid by reason of the tendency of the writings of Joanna Southcote. On the other hand, the contention raised, that this is a gift to promote objects which are within the meaning of what this Court, for shortness, terms 'charitable objects', and that, consequently, it is within the provisions of the Statute of Mortmain, presents a more serious objection to this devise …

I am of opinion, that if a bequest of money be made for the purpose of printing and circulating works of a religious tendency, or for the purpose of extending the knowledge of the Christian religion, that this is a charitable bequest, and this Court will, upon a proper application being made to it, sanction and settle a scheme for this purpose, and, in truth, it is but lately that I have had in Chambers to settle and approve of a scheme of this description. In this respect, I am of opinion that the Court of Chancery makes no distinction between one sort of religion and another. They are equally bequests which are included in the general terms of charitable bequests. Neither does the Court, in this respect, make any distinction between one sect and another. It may be that the tenets of a particular sect inculcate doctrines adverse to the very foundations of all religion, and that they are subversive of all morality. In such a case, if it should arise, the Court will not assist the execution of the bequest, but will declare it to be void; but the character of the bequest, so far as regards the Statute of Mortmain, would not be altered by this circumstance. The general immoral tendency of the bequest would make it void, whether it was to be paid out of pure personality or out of real estate. But if the tendency were not immoral, and although this Court might consider the opinions sought to be propagated foolish or even devoid of foundation, it would not, on that account, declare it void, or take it out of the class of legacies which are included in the general terms charitable bequests. The words of the bequest here are, 'to propagate the sacred writings of Joanna Southcote'. The testatrix, it is clear, was a disciple or believer in Joanna Southcote, who, from her writings, it is clear, was a very sincere Christian; but she laboured under the delusion that she was to be made the medium of the miraculous birth of a child at an advanced period of her life, and that thereby the advancement of the Christian religion on earth would be occasioned. But her works, as far as I have looked at them, contain but little upon this subject, and nothing which could shake the faith of any sincere Christian. In truth, though her works are in a great measure incoherent and confused, they are written obviously with a view to extend the influence of Christianity. I cannot say that the bequest of a testator to publish and propagate works in support of the Christian religion is a charitable bequest, and, at the same time, say, that if another testator should select for this purpose some three or four authors, whose works will, in his opinion, produce that effect, such a bequest thereupon ceases to be charitable. Neither can I do so if a testator should select one single author whose works he thinks will produce that result. If a testator were to leave a fund for the purpose of propagating, at a very reduced price, the religious writings of Dr Paley or Dr Butler, I should be of opinion that the bequest was charitable in its character, and I must hold the same in respect of what the testatrix has called 'the sacred writings of the late Joanna Southcote'.

The question then arises whether *Thornton* v *Howe* is still good law. It has been treated as good law on a considerable number of occasions since it was decided and I mention certain examples which were cited to me in the course of the arguments. The first one, I think, is *Bowman* v *Secular Society Ltd* [1917] AC 406. The reference to *Thornton* v *Howe* is in the speech of Lord Parker of Waddington, where he said [1917] AC at 442:

> … a trust for the attainment of political objects has always been held invalid, not because it is illegal, for every one is at liberty to advocate or promote by any lawful means a change in the law, but because the Court has no means of judging whether a proposed change in the law will or will not be for the public benefit, and therefore cannot say that a gift to secure the change is a charitable gift. The same considerations apply when there is a trust for the publication of a book. The Court will examine the book, and if its objects be charitable in the legal sense it will give effect to the trust as a good charity: *Thornton* v *Howe*.

[Plowman J reviewed a number of other authorities, and concluded:]

Now the result of those cases, including the *Anti-Vivisection* case to which counsel for the next-of-kin referred, in my judgment, is this. First of all, as Romilly MR said in *Thornton v Howe*, the court does not prefer one religion to another and it does not prefer one sect to another. Secondly, where the purposes in question are of a religious nature—and, in my opinion, they clearly are here—then the court assumes a public benefit unless the contrary is shown. In the *Anti-Vivisection* case, Lord Wright said [1948] AC at 42:

> The test of benefit to the community goes through the whole of Lord Macnaghten's classification [in the *Pemsel* case [1891] AC 531], though, as regards the first three heads [which of course includes religion], it may be prima facie assumed unless the contrary appears.

And Lord Simonds, in his speech, said [1948] AC at 65:

> I would rather say that, when a purpose appears broadly to fall within one of the familiar categories of charity, the court will assume it to be for the benefit of the community and therefore charitable unless the contrary is shown, and further that the court will not be astute in such a case to defeat upon doubtful evidence the avowed benevolent intention of a donor.

And thirdly, that having regard to the fact that the court does not draw a distinction between one religion and another or one sect and another, the only way of disproving a public benefit is to show, in the words of Romilly MR in *Thornton v Howe*, that the doctrines inculcated are—'adverse to the very foundations of all religion, and that they are subversive of all morality'. And that in my judgment, as I have said already, is clearly not the case here, and I therefore conclude that this case is really on all fours with *Thornton v Howe* and for that reason is a valid charitable trust.

NOTE: Far from benefiting Joanna Southcote, the result of *Thornton v Howe* was to render a testamentary disposition of land void under the Mortmain legislation.

Re South Place Ethical Society, Barralet v Attorney-General
[1980] 3 All ER 918, Chancery Division

Decision: The South Place Ethical Society was not a religious charity, because although its objects included 'the study and dissemination of ethical principles', and 'the cultivation of a rational religious sentiment', its beliefs were non-theistic.

However, the society was charitable as being for the advancement of education and for purposes beneficial to the community. Advancement of education was to be construed widely: *IRC v McMullen* [1981] AC 1 applied.

DILLON J (on the issue of religion): I propose therefore to consider first the claim that the society is charitable because its objects are for the advancement of religion. In considering this, as in considering the other claims, I keep very much in mind the observation of Lord Wilberforce in the *Scottish Burial Reform and Cremation Society Ltd v Glasgow City Corpn* [1968] AC 138 at 154, that the law of charity is a moving subject which may well have evolved even since 1891. The submissions of counsel for the society seek to establish that this is indeed so, having regard to current thinking in the field of religion.

Of course it has long been established that a trust can be valid and charitable as for the advancement of religion although the religion which is sought to be advanced is not the Christian religion. In *Bowman v Secular Society Ltd* [1917] AC 406 at 448–50, Lord Parker of Waddington gave a very clear and valuable summary of the history of the approach of the law to religious charitable trusts. He said ([1917] AC 406 at 449):

> It would seem to follow that a trust for the purpose of any kind of monotheistic theism would be a good charitable trust.

Counsel for the society accepts that, so far as it goes, but he submits that Lord Parker should have gone further, even in 1917 (because the society's beliefs go back before that date) and the court should go further now. The society says that religion does not have to be theist or dependent on a god; any sincere belief in ethical qualities is religious, because such qualities as truth, love and beauty are sacred, and the advancement of any such belief is the advancement of religion ...

In a free country ... it is natural that the court should desire not to discriminate between beliefs deeply and sincerely held, whether they are beliefs in a god or in the excellence of man or in ethical principles or in Platonism or some other scheme of philosophy. But I do not see that that warrants extending the meaning of the word 'religion' so as to embrace all other beliefs and philosophies. Religion, as I see it, is concerned with man's relations with God, and ethics are concerned with man's relations with man. The two are not the same, and are not made the same by sincere inquiry into the question, What is God? If reason leads people not to accept Christianity or any known religion, but they do believe in the excellence of qualities such as truth, beauty and love, or believe in the Platonic concept of the ideal, their beliefs may be to them the equivalent of a religion, but viewed objectively they are not religion.

NOTE: In an old case in the Privy Council, *Yeap Cheah Neo v Ong Chen Neo* (1875) LR 6 PC 381, a provision for the performance of ancestor worship was held non-charitable. High ethical principles or moral philosophy, being concerned with man's relations with man, cannot amount to a religion, though they may of course be educational, and so charitable under that head. Plowman J also thought in *Re Watson* (also considered in this section), that doctrines which were averse to the foundations of all religion, and subversive of all morality, would not be charitable under this head.

Buddhism poses a problem in this context, since although it is generally accepted as being a religion, it is not clear (at any rate to the judiciary) whether or not Buddhists believe in a supernatural or supreme being. It is possible that it should be treated as an exception, since a trust to advance Buddhism is clearly charitable. Difficulties could also presumably arise where a human being sets himself up as a deity, and is worshipped as such—such religions exist, and it is unclear whether or not their advancement is charitable.

It seems that the gift must be exclusively for religious purposes, so that a gift for 'missionary work' or 'parish work' will be too wide, since such work may involve elements not wholly religious. On the other hand, in *Re Simson* [1946] Ch 299, a gift to a named clergyman 'for his work in the parish' was held to be impliedly confined to his religious duties.

G. Watt, 'Giving unto Caesar: Rationality, Reciprocity, and Legal Recognition of Religion'
in O'Dair and Lewis (eds), *Law and Religion Current Legal Issues*, Vol. 4 (Oxford: Oxford University Press, 2001), pp. 57–8

In 1976 the Goodman Committee on Charity Law reported that 'however liberal or tolerant a society may be it has the duty to determine what is and what is not beneficial to it; accordingly between good and evil it cannot be neutral. It must exclude from charitable status what it regards as evil just as it can and does outlaw what it regards as detrimental to its moral welfare' ...

... one explanation for the presence of 'evil' as a ground of exclusion [from legal recognition for charitable purposes, is] to exclude the possibility that perceived 'anti-religions' such as Satanism might otherwise be granted legal recognition. In the United Kingdom one can confidently assert that if Christianity is not a religion, then nothing is. It follows logically that any rationality which is set up in *diametric opposition* to Christianity cannot be recognised as a religion. It matters not that such a religion might satisfy all the definitions and indicia that are used to identify religions, if it is the polar opposite of the key paradigm of religion, it cannot be recognised as a religion. The problem with this approach is a practical one. Christianity, although the predominant paradigm, is not the only one. And even if Christianity were the only one, how would we identify what Christianity is and what is its opposite? Apart from the case of a group gauche enough to seek legal recognition for its avowed purpose of subverting Christianity in every way or 'subverting all currently recognised religions in every way' state agents should be wary of recourse to exclusion on the ground of evil.

■ QUESTIONS
1, There was a furore in the media when it was reported (*Sunday Telegraph*, 24 October 2004) that the Royal Navy had permitted one of its crew to practise Satanism on its ships on the ground that the Royal Navy is an 'equal opportunity employer'. Is it conceivable that Satanism should be recognised as a religion so as to attract charitable status?
2. The Charity Commission *Commentary* notes that '[b]elief in a Supreme Being' is still a 'necessary characteristic of religion in charity law' and goes on to state that a Supreme Being 'may be in the

form of one god or many gods or no god at all in the accepted understanding of the term'. Could Shakespearism qualify as a religion? Dominic Dromgoole, the Artistic Director of the Globe Theatre, professes the faith in *Will & Me: How Shakespeare Took Over My Life* (Harmondsworth: Penguin, 2006): 'Stratford was electrifying ... we went to his tomb and liked it so much we went back twice more ... I was a Catholic in Rome, a Moslem in Mecca.'

NOTE: For religious purposes to be charitable, they must actually *advance* religion in some practical way. This seems to require some positive action. As with education, the means by which religion may be advanced may be many and various. Apart from the provision and maintenance of churches, and provision of or for the benefit of clergymen, such matters as church choirs, Sunday school prizes, and even exorcism, have all been held to advance religion.

In *United Grand Lodge of Ancient Free & Accepted Masons of England and Wales v Holborn BC* [1957] 1 WLR 1080, Donovan J, in denying charitable status to freemasons (who attempted to claim rates advantages), commented (after setting out the objects of the lodge) that:

> Admirable though these objects are it seems to us impossible to say that they add up to the advancement of religion. Indeed, as already stated, the first Antient Charge, headed 'Concerning God and Religion' says, among other things, this: 'Let a man's religion or mode of worship' (the contrast is not perhaps without significance) 'be what it may, he is not excluded from the Order, provided he believe in the glorious architect of heaven and earth, and practise the sacred duties of morality'. Thus it would seem that no Mason need practise any religion, but, provided that he believes in a Supreme Being and lives a moral life, he may be and remain a Mason.
>
> Accordingly, one cannot really begin to argue that the main object of Freemasonry is to advance religion, except perhaps by saying that religion can be advanced by example as well as by precept, so that the spectacle of a man leading an upright moral life may persuade others to do likewise. The appellants did not in fact advance this argument, but even if it were accepted, it leads to no useful conclusion here. For a man may persuade his neighbour by example to lead a good life without at the same time leading him to religion. And there is nothing in the 'Constitutions', nor, apparently, in the evidence tendered to quarter sessions, to support the view that the main object of Masonry is to encourage Masons to go out in the world, and by their example lead persons to some religion or another. When one considers the work done by organisations which admittedly do set out to advance religion, the contrast with Masonry is striking. To advance religion means to promote it, to spread its message ever wider among mankind; to take some positive steps to sustain and increase religious belief; and these things are done in a variety of ways which may be comprehensively described as pastoral and missionary. There is nothing comparable to that in Masonry. This is not said by way of criticism. For Masonry really does something different. It says to a man, 'Whatever your religion or your mode of worship, believe in a Supreme Creator and lead a good moral life.' Laudable as this precept is, it does not appear to us to be the same thing as the advancement of religion. There is no religious instruction, no programme for the persuasion of unbelievers, no religious supervision to see that its members remain active and constant in the various religions they may profess, no holding of religious services, no pastoral or missionary work of any kind.

Religion may have been a necessary qualification for membership of the lodge, as it might be for a church squash club, for example, but the lodge did not advance religion, any more than a church squash club would.

Equality Act 2010

193 Charities [NB: Not in force at the time of writing]

...

(5) It is not a contravention of this Act for a charity to require members, or persons wishing to become members, to make a statement which asserts or implies membership or acceptance of a religion or belief; and for this purpose restricting the access by members to a benefit, facility or service to those who make such a statement is to be treated as imposing such a requirement.

(6) Subsection (5) applies only if—

    (a) the charity, or an organisation of which it is part, first imposed such a requirement before 18 May 2005, and

    (b) the charity or organisation has not ceased since that date to impose such a requirement.

H: The advancement of health or the saving of lives

Purposes falling under this head include charities that provide conventional and/or complementary/alternative medical treatment such as hospitals and healing centres; charities that provide services and facilities for people who are sick, convalescent, disabled, or infirm (e.g. Hospital Radio); medical research charities; charities that provide services and facilities for medical practitioners (e.g. homes for nurses); charities that ensure the proper standards of medical practice (e.g. the General Medical Council); charities set up to assist the victims of natural disasters or war; the provision of life saving or self defence classes; the provision of blood transfusion services. (Paraphrased from the Charity Commission website.)

Re Resch's WT

[1969] 1 AC 514, Privy Council

Facts: The testator left his residuary estate (then valued around $8 million) to trustees upon trust to pay two-thirds of the income 'to the Sisters of Charity for a period of 200 years so long as they shall conduct the St Vincent's Private Hospital'. The hospital did not seek to make a commercial profit, but its charges for treatment, while not necessarily excluding the poor, were not low. The question was whether this was a valid charitable trust.

Held: It was a valid charitable trust for purposes beneficial to the community. The requisite public benefit had been satisfied because evidence showed that the public needed accommodation and treatment of the type provided by the hospital. A gift for the purposes of a hospital is prima facie a good charitable gift, but the presumption could be rebutted if evidence showed that the hospital was carried on commercially for the benefit of private individuals.

LORD WILBERFORCE: ... A gift for the purposes of a hospital is prima facie a good charitable gift. This is now clearly established both in Australia and in England, not merely because of the use of the word 'impotent' in the preamble to 43 Eliz. c. 4, though the process of referring to the preamble is one often used for reassurance, but because the provision of medical care for the sick is, in modern times, accepted as a public benefit suitable to attract the privileges given to charitable institutions. This has been recognised in the High Court in Australia in *Taylor* v *Taylor* (1910) 10 CLR 218 and *Kytherian Association of Queensland* v *Sklavos* (1958) 101 CLR 56: in England in *In re Smith, decd* [1962] 1 WLR 763.

In spite of this general proposition, there may be certain hospitals, or categories of hospitals, which are not charitable institutions (see *In re Smith, decd*). Disqualifying indicia may be either that the hospital is carried on commercially, i.e. with a view to making profits for private individuals, or that the benefits it provides are not for the public, or a sufficiently large class of the public to satisfy the necessary tests of public character. Each class of objection is taken in the present case. As regards the first, it is accepted that the private hospital is not run for the profit, in any ordinary sense, of individuals. Moreover, if the purposes of the hospital are otherwise charitable, they do not lose this character merely because charges are made to the recipients of benefits—see *Inland Revenue Commissioners* v *Falkirk Temperance Café Trust* (1927) SC 261. *Salvation Army (Victoria) Property Trust* v *Fern Tree Gully Corporation* (1951) 85 CLR 159. But what is said is that surpluses are made and are used for the general purposes of the Sisters of Charity. This association, while in a broad sense philanthropic, has objects which may not be charitable in the legal sense. Furthermore its purposes, though stated in its 'constitutions' are not limited by law, other than the canon law of the Roman Catholic Church, and under this, they are empowered, and may be obliged, to alter their purposes so as to include other objects which may not be strictly charitable.

Their Lordships do not consider it necessary to enter upon these latter considerations ... The share of income given by the will must be devoted entirely to the purposes of the private hospital. The character, charitable or otherwise, of the general activities of the Sisters, is not therefore a material consideration ...

I: The advancement of citizenship or community development

Charity Commission, *Commentary on the Descriptions of Charitable Purposes in the Charities Act 2006*
(March 2007)

16. The advancement of citizenship or community development covers a broad group of charitable purposes directed towards support for social and community infrastructure which is focused on the community rather than the individual.

17. Examples of the sorts of charities and charitable purposes falling within this description include:
- The promotion of civic responsibility and good citizenship, such as good citizenship award schemes, Scout and Guide groups; etc;
- The promotion of urban and rural regeneration ... ;
- The promotion of volunteering;
- The promotion of the voluntary sector;
- Promoting the efficiency and effectiveness of charities and the effective use of charitable resources;
- The promotion of community capacity building ...
- Charities concerned with social investment.

J: The advancement of arts, culture, heritage, or science

Re Pinion (dec'd)
[1965] Ch 85, Court of Appeal

Facts: The testator left his 'studio' for the purposes of a museum to display his collection of what were claimed to be 'fine arts'. However, expert witnesses thought that the paintings were 'atrociously bad', and one 'expresse[d] his surprise that so voracious a collector should not by hazard have picked up even one meritorious object'. The question arose as to the validity of the trust, and this depended on whether it was charitable.

Held: Harman LJ described the collection as 'a mass of junk', and reversing Wilberforce J, the Court of Appeal held the trust void.

HARMAN LJ: ... there is a strong body of evidence here that as a means of education this collection is worthless. The testator's own paintings, of which there are over 50, are said by competent persons to be in an academic style and 'atrociously bad' and the other pictures without exception worthless ...

It was said that this is a matter of taste, and de gustibus non est disputandum, but here I agree with the judge that there is an accepted canon of taste on which the court must rely, for it has itself no judicial knowledge of such matters, and the unanimous verdict of the experts is as I have stated. The judge with great hesitation concluded that there was that scintilla of merit which was sufficient to save the rest. I find myself on the other side of the line. I can conceive of no useful object to be served in foisting upon the public this mass of junk. It has neither public utility nor educative value. I would hold that the testator's project ought not to be carried into effect and that his next-of-kin is entitled to the residue of his estate.

NOTE: In *Re Hummeltenberg* [1923] 1 Ch 237, the court held void a trust to train spiritualistic mediums (though perhaps disciplined research into the paranormal, undertaken on scientific principles, could be charitable). On the other hand, in *Re Delius* [1957] Ch 299, a trust for the appreciation of the works of the composer was held charitable, but Roxburgh J made it clear that the undoubted merit of Delius's music was critical.

■ QUESTIONS

1. The whole of the modern computer industry depends on quantum mechanics, and without quantum mechanics there would be no lasers, CDs, or microprocessors. Yet, in the 1920s, quantum mechanics was regarded as the purest form of science with

no possible practical application, and even when the laser was invented much later, it was seen as a solution looking for a problem. So would an association set up in the 1920s to research into quantum mechanics have been charitable?

2. Do you think it is possible to make value judgments in the area of research?

K: The advancement of amateur sport

You should refer back to the definition of sport under the Charities Act 2006 (now 2011) considered at Section 2: Definition of charity, A: The new statutory 'definition' of charity. In brief, 'sport' means 'sports or games which promote health by involving physical or mental skill or exertion'.

Re Dupree's Deed Trusts

[1945] Ch 16, Chancery Division

Decision: Vaisey J held charitable a gift of £5,000 to be applied by the trustees in promoting an annual chess tournament open to boys and young men under the age of 21 resident in the City of Portsmouth.

VAISEY J: In this case I have to decide whether the encouragement and promotion of chess-playing among the boys and young men of the city of Portsmouth is a good charitable object.

The game of chess (which, by those who follow it, as well, perhaps, as by those who do not follow it, is regarded as something rather more than a mere game) is an institution with a very long history behind it, and it possesses the somewhat notable feature that it is essentially a game of skill into which elements of chance enter, if at all, only to a negligible extent. It is a game which, I suppose, is played all over the civilized world. I have some evidence which enables me to say—and, indeed, I think I might have said it even without that evidence—that the nature of the game is such as to encourage the qualities of foresight, concentration, memory and ingenuity. Even unguided by actual evidence, I should not have been surprised if the conclusion could have been reached that the game is essentially one which does possess an educational value.

There are many pursuits possessing an educational value which may be followed to excess, and the matter is in no way concluded by any such consideration. Chess players may become so obsessed by the interest of their pursuit that they may neglect other duties, but the same thing may be said of those who range the mysterious country of the higher mathematics or indulge in the study of classical authors. I am not surprised to learn from the evidence that there are schoolmasters and persons actually concerned with the business of education who regard the playing of chess as something of so much value educationally that in some places it is actually a part of a school curriculum ...

I think that the case before me may be a little near the line, and I decide it without attempting to lay down any general propositions. One feels, perhaps, that one is on rather a slippery slope. If chess, why not draughts? If draughts, why not bezique, and so on, through to bridge and whist, and, by another route, to stamp collecting and the acquisition of birds' eggs? Those pursuits will have to be dealt with if and when they come up for consideration in connexion with the problem whether or no there is in existence an educational charitable trust. Nor do I say whether, if this trust had been without a geographical limitation, if it had been for the promotion of chess playing *in vacuo* or at large, the area of what is regarded as charitable would or would not have been over-stepped. Having regard to the evidence before me and to what is known about the game of chess by everybody, and, in particular, to the fact that the encouragement of chess playing here is for the benefit of young persons living within a well-defined area, and also that it is of the essence of the constitution of the trusteeship that two of the trustees should be persons closely connected with educational activities in the borough, I think I am bound, in the present case, to hold that there is a good charitable trust, and answer the question by declaring that the trusts constituted by the deed of June 30, 1932, are valid charitable trusts.

IRC v *McMullen and others*

[1981] AC 1, [1980] 1 All ER 884, House of Lords

Facts: The issue was whether the Football Association Youth Trust, whose objects were (in essence) to encourage football in schools and universities in the UK, was charitable. It was argued that it was charitable either as an educational charity, or under the provisions of the Recreational Charities Act 1958.

Held: The trust was charitable for the advancement of education, even though the sports and games were not required to be enjoyed as part of a school or university curriculum. The House left open the question whether it was also charitable under the Recreational Charities Act 1958.

LORD HAILSHAM LC: [Lord Hailsham quoted from Eve J in *Re Mariette* [1915] 2 Ch 284, where he said (at 288):

> No one of sense could be found to suggest that between those ages [10 to 19] any boy can be properly educated unless at least as much attention is given to the development of his body as is given to the development of his mind.

and continued:]

> Apart from the limitation to the particular institution I would think that these words apply as well to the settlor's intention in the instant appeal as to the testator's in *Re Mariette*, and I regard the limitation to the pupils of schools and universities in the instant case as a sufficient association with the provision of formal education to prevent any danger of vagueness in the object of the trust or irresponsibility or capriciousness in application by the trustees. I am far from suggesting either that the concept of education or of physical education even for the young is capable of indefinite extension. On the contrary, I do not think that the courts have as yet explored the extent to which elements of organisation, instruction or the disciplined inculcation of information, instruction or skill may limit the whole concept of education. I believe that in some ways it will prove more extensive, in others more restrictive that has been thought hitherto. But it is clear at least to me that the decision in *Re Mariette* is not to be read in a sense which confines its application for ever to gifts to a particular institution. It has been extended already in *Re Mellody* [1918] 1 Ch 228, to gifts for annual treats for schoolchildren in a particular locality (another decision of Eve J), to playgrounds for children (*Re Chesters*, 25 July 1934 unreported, possibly not educational, but referred to in *IRC* v *Baddeley* [1955] AC 572 at 596); to a children's outing (*Re Ward's Estate* (1937) 81 SJ 397), to a prize for chess to boys and young men resident in the City of Portsmouth (*Re Dupree's Deed Trusts* [1945] Ch 16, a decision of Vaisey J), and for the furthering of the Boy Scouts' movement by helping to purchase sites for camping, outfits etc. (*Re Webber* [1954] 1 WLR 1500, another decision of Vaisey J).

NOTES

1. The Court of Appeal ([1979] 1 WLR 130), whose decision was reversed, had held by a majority that this trust was not charitable under the Recreational Charities Act 1958, because the recipients of benefit were not 'deprived'. Because the House of Lords held that it was a valid educational charity, they did not need to decide this issue, and left it open.
2. A club for the time being registered under the Finance Act 2002, Sch. 18 (a Community Amateur Sports Club) enjoys some special tax relief whether or not it is a charity. In *Simpson and others (Trustees of the East Berkshire Sports Foundation)* v *Revenue and Customs Commissioners* (2008 WL 5538975) [2009] STC (SCD) 226, the Special Commissioner praised the appellants for their 'selfless generosity' in making payments to support their local amateur football club, but held that those payments had not been payments to charity and were not tax exempt, because the club was not a registered community amateur sports club.
3. The Charity Commission has recognised the charitable status of an amateur bridge club on the basis of the mental health benefits that are engendered by the card game (*Hitchen Bridge Club*, Charity Commission Decision, February 2011). Is this a bridge too far?

L: The promotion of human rights, conflict resolution, and reconciliation or the promotion of religious or racial harmony or equality and diversity

See *McGovern* v *Attorney-General* [1982] Ch 321 and the Charity Commission publication RR12, which are considered in depth at Section 2: Definition of Charity, D: Political purposes.

According to the Charity Commission (website) examples of charitable purposes falling under this head include:

- charities concerned with the promotion of human rights, at home or abroad, such as relieving victims of human rights abuse, raising awareness of human rights issues, securing the enforcement of human rights law;
- charities concerned with the promotion of restorative justice and other forms of conflict resolution or reconciliation;
- charities concerned with the resolution of national or international conflicts;
- mediation charities;
- charities promoting good relations between persons of different racial groups;
- charities promoting equality and diversity by the elimination of discrimination on the grounds of age, sex, or sexual orientation;
- charities enabling people of one faith to understand the religious beliefs of others.

M: The advancement of environmental protection or improvement

As the following decision makes clear, one of the main obstacles to the recognition of trusts for conservation and such like is that such issues are regulated by dedicated authorities under the delegated authority of Parliament. It will therefore frequently be the case that environmental purposes are political purposes.

Decision of the Charity Commissioners for England and Wales on the Application for Registration of the Wolf Trust, 30 January 2003

1. The issue before the Commissioners

The Commissioners considered an application for registration by a trust called The Wolf Trust (formerly known as 'Wild Bite') for registration as a charity. If the trust was established as a charity it should be entered on the Central Register of Charities under section 3(2) of the Charities Act 1993. This decision has been made by the Commissioners in a final review under the Commission's review procedures.

...

5.3. The Commissioners noted ... that the website makes very clear that the main thrust of the Wolf Trust's aims and activities is directed towards the reintroduction of wolves into the Highlands of Scotland. For example:—

- beneath the Wolf Trust's logo at the top of every page is a strapline referring to the reintroduction of wolves in Britain;
- the Home Page starts by saying 'The Wolf Trust is a non-profit charity educating the public about wolves ... and promoting a wolf reintroduction and recovery in Britain to the Scottish Highlands';
- the same page says that the Wolf Trust 'calls for partnership ... to further wolf reintroduction in Britain'; and
- a page about the Wolf Trust lists its first aim as being to 'promote the reintroduction and recovery of wolves back to Britain in the Scottish Highlands'.

This message is reinforced by the way in which Mr Panaman described the purpose of the Wolf Trust in his letter of 1 July 2002: 'The purpose of the Wolf Trust is to facilitate the reintroduction and recovery of wolves ... in Britain.'

6. The re-introduction of the wolf into Scotland

6.1. The Commissioners noted that the process for analysing the potential public harm against the benefits of reintroducing a predatory species into Britain and safeguarding public safety was undertaken by other authorities [in particular, it is an offence under s14(1) Wildlife and Countryside Act 1981 to release into the wild an animal, which is of a kind which is not ordinarily resident in and not a regular visitor to Great Britain in a wild state, without a licence (which in this case would need to be obtained under s16(4) (c) from the Secretary of State for Scotland)]. There would appear to be strict requirements as to any reintroduction of the species. Indeed it is recognised by the Wolf Trust that any release would need to be authorised by and involve other authorities (including Scottish Natural Heritage and the Secretary of State for Scotland) and the Wolf Trust would not be ultimately deciding whether the reintroduction of the wolf into Scotland was conducive to the public good.

7. The Commissioners' determination of the Wolf Trust's purpose

7.1. The Commissioners considered the Wolf Trust's aims and activities as set out in paragraph 5 above, together with the stated objects, in order to ascertain the true purpose for which the Wolf Trust could be said to be established. They then considered the extent to which such a purpose could be said to be charitable.

7.2. The Commissioners noted that there was a difference between a body which was established for educational and conservation purposes and which carried out an ancillary activity of promoting the reintroduction of the wolf and a body concerned with promoting the reintroduction of the wolf as an end in itself.

7.3. The Courts have held that a purpose to promote a change in the law or bring about a change in government policy is a political purpose and as such cannot be charitable. This is primarily because the Court is unable to judge whether such a change is for the benefit of the public. Similarly, a purpose designed to promote a propagandist or particular point of view, for the same reason, cannot be charitable.

7.4. The Commissioners concluded that the purpose of the Wolf Trust was primarily to secure the reintroduction of wolves into Scotland, and that the Wolf Trust's educational activities were directed at securing broad public acceptance and support for reintroduction and at influencing the authorities which would eventually have to decide whether reintroduction should be allowed. The following factors support this conclusion:—

7.4.1. The Wolf Trust's stated aims are explicitly directed at reintroduction;

7.4.2. The Wolf Trust acknowledges on its website the important connection between its educational activities, in particular the centre, and securing its aim of reintroduction. It recognises that a good case for the reintroduction of wolves must include broad public support for the proposals, and it wants to educate the public towards such support. Its website states that the centre 'will support the Highland wolf recovery with information, education, fundraising and more'. Although the subject of the educational activities is potentially wide, those activities have an underlying purpose, namely securing public support for wolves and their reintroduction into Britain;

7.4.3. The Wolf Trust also claims that one of the reasons why the government and large conservation organisations would not support wolf introduction is fear of upsetting landowners and farmers;

7.4.4. On the Wolf Trust's website it asks partners to 'contribute substantially to the wolf reintroduction in Britain'; and

7.4.5. It has published on its website a Wolf Trust resolution to Her Majesty's Government to call for it to promote public awareness about wolves and consider the possibility of reintroducing wolves into Scotland and declares that certain measures should be taken by the Government concerning the reintroduction of wolves.

8. Conclusion

The Commissioners therefore concluded that the Wolf Trust was not established for exclusively charitable purposes in that its primary purpose was to promote the reintroduction of the wolf into Scotland as an end in itself. That purpose could not be charitable as it was designed to influence the opinion of the public and the decisions of the relevant Government authorities and neither the Court nor the Commission could determine whether such a purpose was for the benefit of the public.

In consequence the Commission could not register the Wolf Trust as a charity pursuant to Section 3 of the Charities Act 1993.

N: The relief of those in need, by reason of youth, age, ill health, disability, financial hardship, or other disadvantage

According to the Charity Commission (website), examples of charitable purposes falling under this head include:
- charities concerned with the care, upbringing or establishment in life of children or young people, e.g. children's care homes, apprenticing, etc.;
- charities concerned with the relief of the effects of old age, such as those providing specialist advice, equipment or accommodation, drop-in centres, etc.;
- charities concerned with the relief of disability, such as those providing specialist advice, equipment or accommodation or providing access for disabled people, etc.;
- charities concerned with the provision of housing, such as almshouses, housing associations, and Registered Social Landlords.

Equality Act 2010

193 Charities [NB: Not in force at the time of writing]

(1) A person does not contravene this Act only by restricting the provision of benefits to persons who share a protected characteristic if—
    (a) the person acts in pursuance of a charitable instrument, and
    (b) the provision of the benefits is within subsection (2).
(2) The provision of benefits is within this subsection if it is—
    (a) a proportionate means of achieving a legitimate aim, or(b)   for the purpose of preventing or compensating for a disadvantage linked to the protected characteristic.
(3) It is not a contravention of this Act for—
    (a) a person who provides supported employment to treat persons who have the same disability or a disability of a prescribed description more favourably than those who do not have that disability or a disability of such a description in providing such employment;
    (b) a Minister of the Crown to agree to arrangements for the provision of supported employment which will, or may, have that effect.

O: The advancement of animal welfare

See *National Anti-Vivisection Society* v *Inland Revenue Commissioners* [1948] AC 31, House of Lords, and *Re Recher's WT* [1972] Ch 526 (Chapter 3) and the Charity Commissioners' decision in relation to the 'Wolf Trust'.

Re Moss (dec'd), Hobrough v *Harvey*
[1949] 1 All ER 495, 65 TLR 299, [1949] WN 93, Chancery Division

Decision: A gift for the welfare of cats and kittens needing care was a charitable gift because of the beneficial effects it had on mankind. The testatrix's will had been challenged by the next-of-kin.

ROMER J: Inasmuch as I am satisfied that this is a valid charitable object, the bequest does not fail, and I propose to base my decision on that ground. Russell LJ, in *Re Grove-Grady* [1929] 1 Ch 557 laid it down clearly that a gift in favour of animals depends for its validity on the question whether such a gift produces a benefit to mankind. He said ([1929] 1 Ch 582):

So far as I know there is no decision which upholds a trust in perpetuity in favour of animals upon any other ground than this, that the execution of the trust in the manner defined by the creator of the trust must produce some benefit to mankind. I cannot help feeling that in some instances matters have been stretched in favour of charities almost to bursting point: and that a decision benevolent to one doubtful charity has too often been the basis of a subsequent decision still more benevolent in favour of another.

Later he said (*ibid.*, 588):

In my opinion, the court must determine in each case whether the trusts are such that benefit to the community must necessarily result from their execution.

The observations of the Lord Justice on those matters received recognition in the House of Lords in *Inland Revenue Comrs* v *National Anti-Vivisection Society* [1948] AC 31 [below].

Therefore, one has to see whether the present case passes that test, namely, the test whether the gift produces some benefit to mankind. In my judgment, it passes that test with honours. It seems to me that the care of and consideration for animals which through old age or sickness or otherwise are unable to care for themselves are manifestations of the finer side of human nature, and gifts in furtherance of these objects are calculated to develop that side and are, therefore, calculated to benefit mankind. That is more especially so, perhaps, where the animals are domestic animals. That appears to have been the view of the matter taken by Lord Hanworth MR, in *Re Grove-Grady* [1929] 1 Ch 557 where, after referring to certain authorities, he said ([1929] 1 Ch 570):

From these authorities it seems clear that if the object be to enhance the condition of animals that are useful to mankind, or to secure good treatment for animals, whether those animals are useful to mankind or not (see *per* Chatterton V-C, in *Armstrong* v *Reeves* (1890) 25 LR Ir 325 and *per* Wood V-C, in *Marsh* v *Means* (1857) 30 LTOS 89, or to insure humane conduct towards, and treatment of, them whether in respect of a particular subjection of them to the use of mankind, as for food (*Re Cranston* [1898] 1 IR 431), or in what is called vivisection, such objects are to be deemed charitable.

It appears to me that, taking a fair view of this lady's activities as they emerge from her affidavit, it may truthfully be said of them that they conform to all those tests and criteria to which Lord Hanworth draws attention. I need, I think, only add that a gift to the Institution of the Home for Lost Dogs was regarded as a charitable gift in *Re Douglas* (1887) 35 ChD 472.

Counsel for the next-of-kin has urged that this is not a trust for the protection of cats and kittens or protection from cruelty, but is merely a gift for their welfare. I do not take that view of the matter. The gift in the will is not merely a gift to be used at the lady's discretion for the welfare of cats and kittens. It is for the welfare of cats and kittens needing care and attention. It is plain that a gift to prevent cruelty in relation to cats and kittens would be good as having an elevating effect on mankind. For my part, I can see no difference between that and a gift the object of which is to alleviate distress among cats and kittens. It seems to me that, that being the object which the testatrix had in mind, the object which she intended to benefit, and it being, in substance, the object of the work which this lady has carried out and is now carrying out, the gift is perfectly good as being a valid charitable bequest, and I so hold.

P: The promotion of the efficiency of the armed forces of the Crown or of the efficiency of the police, fire and rescue services, or the ambulance services

This charitable purpose did not appear in the Charities Act 2011 until a very late stage of redrafting. It originates in one of the oldest charitable purposes. The Preamble to the Statute of Elizabeth, 1601, refers to 'Maintenance of sick and maimed Soldiers and Mariners' and to the 'setting out of Soldiers and other Taxes'.

Charity Commission, *Commentary on the Descriptions of Charitable Purposes in the Charities Act 2006*
(March 2007)

35. The armed forces exist for public defence and security. It is charitable to promote the efficiency of the armed forces of the Crown as a means of defending the country. That includes ensuring that those forces are properly trained and equipped during times of conflict. It also includes providing facilities and benefits for the armed forces.

36. Examples of the sorts of charities and charitable purposes falling within this description include:
- Increasing technical knowledge of members of the armed forces through the provision of educational resources, competitions and prizes;
- Increasing physical fitness of members of the armed forces through the provision of sporting facilities, equipment and sporting competitions;
- Providing opportunities for service personnel to gain additional experience relevant to their jobs (e.g. aeroplane clubs for RAF personnel);
- Supporting messes (NCOs and Officers) and institutes (other ranks), including the provision of chattels (items of plate etc);
- Providing and maintaining band instruments and equipment;
- Promoting and strengthening bonds between allied units;
- Providing memorials to commemorate the fallen or victories;
- Maintaining chapels (e.g. regimental chapels in cathedrals) or churches;
- Researching the military history of a regiment or other unit, and publishing books about it;
- Maintaining a museum or other collection for the preservation of artefacts connected with a military unit and supporting military museums generally;
- Encouraging esprit de corps (loyalty of a member to the unit to which he or she belongs and recognition of the honour of the unit);
- Providing associations which support a unit and enable serving and former members to mix together;
- Providing facilities for military training (e.g. drill halls);
- Encouraging recruitment to the services (e.g. through exhibitions, air displays etc).

IRC v *City of Glasgow Police Athletic Association*
[1953] AC 380, House of Lords

Facts: The question arose as to the charitable status of the City of Glasgow Police Athletic Association, membership of which was restricted to officers and ex-officers of the force. The objects of the association were to encourage and promote all forms of athletic sports and general pastimes. The Special Commissioners found that the association was regarded as an essential part of the police organisation, that played an important part in the maintenance of health, morale, and *esprit de corps* within the police force, that it attracted recruits to the force, and that it helped to induce members of the force to continue in the force rather than leave it.

Held: The purposes were not exclusively charitable because of the inclusion of a social element.

Q: Other charitable purposes or purposes analogous to existing charitable purposes

The Charity Commission *Commentary* identifies a number of purposes within this 'residual' head, including the provision of facilities under the Recreational Charities Act 1958; 'The provision of public works and services and the provision of public amenities (such as the repair of bridges, ports, havens, causeways and highways, the provision of water and lighting, etc.)'; 'The promotion of certain patriotic purposes, such as war memorials'; 'The social relief, resettlement and rehabilitation of persons under a disability or deprivation (including disaster funds)'. Certain examples lend especially strong support to the thesis that charitable purposes have little to do with altruistic love and more to do with governmental concern for national wealth-generation: they are '[t]he promotion of industry and commerce', '[t]he promotion of agriculture and horticulture', '[t]he preservation of public order'; '[p]romoting the sound administration and development of the law'; '[t]he promotion of ethical standards of conduct and compliance with the law in the public and private sectors' and '[t]he rehabilitation of ex-offenders and the prevention of crime'.

RECREATIONAL CHARITIES ACT 1958
[replaced by Charities Act 2011, s.5]

1 General provision as to recreational and similar trusts, etc. (as amended by the Charities Act 2006, s.5(2))

(1) Subject to the provisions of this Act, it shall be and be deemed always to have been charitable to provide, or assist in the provision of, facilities for recreation or other leisure-time occupation, if the facilities are provided in the interests of social welfare:

Provided that nothing in this section shall be taken to derogate from the principle that a trust or institution to be charitable must be for the public benefit.

(2) The requirements of the foregoing subsection that the facilities are provided in the interests of social welfare shall not be treated as satisfied unless—

  (a) the facilities are provided with the object of improving the conditions of life for the persons for whom the facilities are primarily intended; and

  (b) either—

    (i) those persons have need of such facilities as aforesaid by reason of their youth, age, infirmity or disablement, poverty or social and economic circumstances; or

    (ii) the facilities are to be available to the members of the public at large or to male, or to female, members of the public at large.

(3) Subject to the said requirement, subsection (1) of this section applies in particular to the provision of facilities at village halls, community centres, and women's institutes, and to the provision and maintenance of grounds and buildings to be used for purposes of recreation or leisure-time occupation, and extends to the provision of facilities for those purposes by the organising of any activity.

Guild v *IRC*
[1992] 2 AC 310, House of Lords

Decision: A gift of a sports centre was a valid charitable gift for tax purposes, although the benefit was not limited to deprived persons.

LORD KEITH OF KINKEL: A Scottish court, when faced with the task of construing and applying the words 'charity' and 'charitable' in a United Kingdom tax statute, must do so in accordance with the technical meaning of these words in English law (see *Special Comrs of Income Tax* v *Pemsel* [1891] AC 531 and *IRC* v *Glasgow Police Athletic Association* [1953] AC 380). For tax purposes, and for them alone, the English law of charity is to be regarded as part of the law of Scotland. Lord Jauncey's decision in the action of multiple pointing proceeded on the general law of Scotland as regards charities, and, as the *Glasgow Police Athletic* case shows, the decision under the corresponding English common law rules would have been different. However, the *Glasgow Police Athletic* case and that of *IRC* v *Baddeley* [1955] AC 572 led to the Recreational Charities Act 1958 (the 1958 Act), and it is that Act which the executor invokes in his claim to the charitable exemption from capital transfer tax.

[Lord Keith set out s.1 of the 1958 Act and continued:]

In the course of his argument in relation to the first branch of the bequest counsel for the Crown accepted that it assisted in the provision of facilities for recreation or other leisure time occupation within the meaning of sub-s. (1) of s.1 of the 1958 Act, and also that the requirement of public benefit in the proviso to the subsection was satisfied. It was further accepted that the facilities of the sports centre were available to the public at large so that the condition of sub-s. (2)(b)(ii) was satisfied. It was maintained, however, that these facilities were not provided 'in the interests of social welfare' as required by sub-s. (1), because they did not meet the condition laid down in sub-s. (2)(a), namely that they should be 'provided with the object of improving the conditions of life for the persons for whom the facilities are primarily intended'. The reason why it was said that this condition was not met was that on a proper construction it involved that the facilities should be provided with the object of meeting a need for such facilities in people who suffered from a position of relative social disadvantage. Reliance was placed on a passage from the judgment of Walton J in *IRC* v *McMullen* [1978] 1 WLR 664. That was a case where the Football Association had set up a trust to provide facilities to encourage pupils of schools and universities in the United Kingdom to play association football and other games and sports. Walton J held that the trust was not valid as one for the advancement of education nor did it satisfy s.1 of the 1958 Act. He said (see [1978] 1 WLR 664 at 675) in relation to the words 'social welfare' in sub-s. (1):

> In my view, however, these words in themselves indicate that there is some sort of deprivation— not, of course, by any means necessarily of money—which falls to be alleviated; and I think that this is made even clearer by the terms of subsection (2)(a). The facilities must be provided with the object of improving the conditions of life for persons for whom the facilities are primarily intended. In other words, they must be to some extent and in some way deprived persons.

When the case went to the Court of Appeal (see [1979] 1 WLR 130) the majority (Stamp and Orr LJJ) affirmed the judgment of Walton J on both points, but Bridge LJ dissented. As regards the 1958 Act point he said ([1979] 1 WLR 130 at 142):

> I turn therefore to consider whether the object defined by clause 3(1) is charitable under the express terms of section 1 of the Recreational Charities Act 1958. Are the facilities for recreation contemplated in this clause to be 'provided in the interests of social welfare' under s.1(1)? If this phrase stood without further statutory elaboration, I should not hesitate to decide that sporting facilities for persons undergoing any formal process of education are provided in the interests of social welfare. Save in the sense that the interests of social welfare can only be served by the meeting of some social need, I cannot accept the judge's view that the interests of social welfare can only be served in relation to some 'deprived' class. The judge found this view reinforced by the requirement of subsection (2)(a) of s.1 that the facilities must be provided 'with the object of improving the conditions of life for the persons for whom the facilities are primarily intended; ... ' Here again I can see no reason to conclude that only the deprived can have their conditions of life improved. Hyde Park improves the conditions of life for residents in Mayfair and Belgravia as much as for those in Pimlico or the Portobello Road, and the village hall may improve the conditions of life for the squire and his family as well as for the cottagers. The persons for whom the facilities here are primarily intended are pupils of schools and universities, as defined in the trust deed, and these facilities are in my judgment unquestionably to be provided with the object of improving their conditions of life. Accordingly the ultimate question on which the application of the statute to this trust depends, is whether the requirements of s.1(2)(b)(i) are satisfied on the ground that such pupils as a class have need of facilities for games or sports which will promote their physical education and development by reason either of their youth or of their social and economic circumstances, or both. The overwhelming majority of pupils within the definition are young persons and the tiny minority of mature students can be ignored as *de minimis*. There cannot surely be any doubt that young persons as part of their education do need facilities for organised games and sports both by reason of their youth and by reason of their social and economic circumstances. They cannot provide such facilities for themselves but are dependent on what is provided for them.

In the House of Lords the case was decided against the Crown on the ground that the trust was one for the advancement of education, opinion being reserved on the point under the 1958 Act. Lord Hailsham LC said ([1981] AC 1 at 11)—

> ... I do not wish my absence of decision on the third or fourth points to be interpreted as an indorsement of the majority judgments in the Court of Appeal nor as necessarily dissenting from the contrary views contained in the minority judgment of Bridge LJ.

> ...

> The fact is that persons in all walks of life and all kinds of social circumstances may have their conditions of life improved by the provision of recreational facilities of suitable character. The proviso requiring public benefit excludes facilities of an undesirable nature. In my opinion the view expressed by Bridge LJ (see [1979] 1 WLR 130 at 142) in *IRC* v *McMullen* is clearly correct and that of Walton J (see [1978] 1 WLR 664 at 675) in the same case is incorrect ... I would therefore reject the argument that the facilities are not provided in the interests of social welfare unless they are provided with the object of improving the conditions of life for persons who suffer from some form of social disadvantage. It suffices if they are provided with the object of improving the conditions of life for members of the community generally.

■ QUESTIONS

1. Are private flying clubs charitable? Assume that anybody can join, and that the club's charges are set primarily with a view to covering the high costs of private flying (around £100 per hour), rather than with a view to making a profit. Would your answer be different if the society ran only jet aircraft costing £10,000 per hour?

2. The Charity Commission list the 'promotion of mental or moral improvement' and 'promotion of the moral or spiritual welfare or improvement of the community' amongst the sort of purpose that will fall within this head. Do you suppose that the Charity Commission or any branch of government is competent to determine when an organisation will or will not fall within these descriptions?

Scottish Burial Reform and Cremation Society, Ltd v *Glasgow City Corporation*
[1968] AC 138, [1967] 3 All ER 215, [1967] 3 WLR 1132, House of Lords

Decision: The House of Lords held a society charitable for rating purposes (under the fourth *Pemsel* head), whose main object was the promotion of sanitary methods of disposal of the dead. The society charged fees but was not profit-making.

LORD WILBERFORCE: My Lords, the Scottish Burial Reform and Cremation Society Ltd was formed in 1890 with the following main objects, as stated in clause 3 of its memorandum of association:—

(a) To promote reform in the present methods of burial in Scotland, both as regards the expense involved and the dangerous effects on the public health. (b) To promote inexpensive and at the same time sanitary methods of disposal of the dead, which shall best tend to render the remains innocuous; and, in particular to promote the method known as cremation.

The company is non-profit-making in the sense that its income and property must be applied solely towards the promotion of its objects and that its members receive no dividends nor any distribution on a winding up.

In 1890 the company was, no doubt, a pioneering venture; it must have been one of the earliest undertakings offering to provide a service of cremation for the inhabitants of Glasgow and of Scotland. Though its first object is stated as the promotion of reform in burial methods, its activity in this direction has not been by way of propaganda, but rather by way of providing services of a kind and in a manner which would progressively persuade the public of their advantages …

Was, then, the company established for charitable purposes only? I interpret its objects clause as meaning that the company was formed for a general and a particular purpose: the general purpose was to promote methods of disposal of the dead which should be inexpensive and sanitary; the particular purpose (to which the company has in fact confined itself) to promote the method known as cremation. It is this combination of purposes which has to be examined in order to see whether it satisfies the legal test of charitable purposes.

On this subject, the law of England, though no doubt not very satisfactory and in need of rationalisation, is tolerably clear. The purposes in question, to be charitable, must be shown to be for the benefit of the public, or the community, in a sense or manner within the intendment of the preamble to the statute 43 Eliz. I, c. 4. The latter requirement does not mean quite what it says; for it is now accepted that what must be regarded is not the wording of the preamble itself, but the effect of decisions given by the courts as to its scope, decisions which have endeavoured to keep the law as to charities moving according as new social needs arise or old ones become obsolete or satisfied. Lord Macnaghten's grouping of the heads of recognised charity in *Pemsel's* case [1891] AC 531, 583 is one that has proved to be of value and there are many problems which it solves. But three things may be said about it, which its author would surely not have denied: first that, since it is a classification of convenience, there may well be purposes which do not fit neatly into one or other of the headings; secondly, that the words used must not be given the force of a statute to be construed; and thirdly, that the law of charity is a moving subject which may well have evolved even since 1891.

With this in mind, approach may be made to the question whether the provision of facilities for the disposal of human remains, whether, generally, in an inexpensive and sanitary manner, or, particularly, by cremation, can be considered as within the spirit of the statute. Decided cases help us, at any rate, to the point of showing that trusts for the repair or maintenance of burial grounds connected with a church are charitable.

...

Then in *In re Eighmie* [1935] Ch 524, a trust for the maintenance of a cemetery owned and managed by a local authority was held charitable. The cemetery was an extension of a closed churchyard so that the decision can be regarded as a logical step rather than a new departure. Now what we have to consider is whether to take the further step of holding charitable the purpose of providing burial, or facilities for the disposal of mortal remains, without any connection with a church, by an independent body. I have no doubt that we should. I would regard the earlier decisions as falling on the borderline between trusts for the advancement of religion and trusts otherwise beneficial to the community. One may say either that burial purposes fall within both, or that the categories themselves shade one into the other. So I find no departure in principle in saying that purposes such as the present—which, though the company in fact provides the means for religious observance, should be regarded as independent of any religious basis—are to be treated as equally within the charitable class.

It was argued for the respondents that the company's purposes were neither for the benefit of the community nor, in any event, within the intendment of the preamble to the Statute of Elizabeth I. One or other of these arguments was accepted by the Lord Ordinary and by three members of the Inner House. As to the first of these, there was some suggestion that the necessary basis of fact had not been shown, and that the appellants should have averred, and if necessary proved, that their services were more inexpensive and more sanitary than normal methods of burial. In my opinion, the appellants rightly made no such averment, for no such comparison was called for. All they had to do was to show that the provision of inexpensive and sanitary methods, and of cremation in particular, was for the benefit of the community. As to this, the facts speak for themselves; for, it being admitted by joint minute that the company had used its premises in carrying out its objects, the scale on which the company's services were resorted to clearly showed that they met a need of the public. And it can hardly be said that to meet a need of this character is not beneficial. The second argument can be met in two ways. First, it may be said that the same evolutionary process which has carried charity from the 'repair of churches' to the maintenance of burial grounds (i) in a churchyard and (ii) in a cemetery extended from a churchyard should naturally carry it further so as to embrace the company's objects. Secondly, and more generally, the company's objects themselves may directly be seen to be within the preamble's spirit. The group 'repair of bridges, ports, havens, causeways, churches, sea banks and highways' has within it the common element of public utility and it is of interest to note that the original label of Lord Macnaghten's fourth category 'other purposes beneficial to the community' affixed by Sir Samuel Romilly in *Morice* v *Bishop of Durham* (1805) 10 Ves 522, 532 was '... the advancement of objects of general public utility.' In this context I find it of significance that Parliament in 1902 by the Cremation Act of that year placed cremation, as a public service, on the same footing as burial.

I regard, then, the provision of cremation services as falling naturally, and in their own right, within the spirit of the preamble.

One other point requires mention. The company makes charges for its services to enable it, in the words of the joint agreed minute, to fulfil effectively the objects for which it was formed. These charges, though apparently modest, are not shown to be higher or lower than those levied for other burial services. In my opinion, the fact that cremation is provided for a fee rather than gratuitously does not affect the charitable character of the company's activity, for that does not consist in the fact of providing financial relief but in the provision of services. That the charging for services for the achievement of a purpose which is in itself shown to be charitable does not destroy the charitable element was clearly, and, in my opinion, rightly, decided in *Inland Revenue Commissioners* v *Falkirk Temperance Café Trust* [1927] SC 261 as well as in English authorities.

I am therefore of opinion that the appellant makes good its claim to rating relief and I would allow the appeal.

SECTION 3: **PUBLIC BENEFIT**

Broadly speaking, it is the fact that charitable purposes are beneficial to the public, and therefore directly or indirectly save public money, that justifies the trust law and fiscal 'privileges' that charities enjoy. In *Dingle* v *Turner* [1972] AC 601, Lord Cross even went so far as to suggest that the grant or recognition of charitable status is tantamount to the endowment of 'a substantial annual subsidy at the expense of the taxpayer', and suggested, therefore, that a cost–benefit calculation should be carried out before the grant or recognition of charitable status.

■ QUESTIONS

1. Do you agree with Lord Cross that the grant or recognition of charitable status comes at the taxpayers' expense?
2. Would it be constitutionally appropriate for courts to carry out the cost–benefit test suggested by Lord Cross? (Simon Gardner has argued that it would not be: *An Introduction to the Law of Trusts* (Oxford: Clarendon Press, 1990), p. 105.)
3. Can you propose a test that could be applied to quantify the relative benefit to the public of such charitable purposes as research into a cure for cancer, education in the arts, and the advancement of religion?

A: Public benefit under the Charities Act 2006 (now 2011)

In response to the research carried out by the National Council for Voluntary Organisations (NCVO) and other bodies, the Strategy Unit of the Cabinet Office published *Private Action, Public Benefit* ('A Review of Charities and the Wider Not-For-Profit Sector', September 2002), in which it proposed that the Charity Commission should undertake ongoing checks on the public character of charities (para. 4.30) and, most significantly, that even when a charity falls under one of the heads of charitable purpose, there should be no presumption of public benefit. In other words, public benefit will have to be established in each case. The requirement of proof of public benefit now appears in the Charities Act 2011, s.4.

The Charity Commission published general guidance on public benefit for all charities in January 2008 (see discussion in this section, and consult the Online Resource Centre accompanying this book for the full text). The Charity Commission has also consulted the public on drafts of supplementary guidance on public benefit as it relates to: (1) the Advancement of Religion; (2) the Prevention or Relief of Poverty; (3) the Advancement of Education; and (4) Fee-charging. A consultation on 'Public Benefit and the Advancement of Moral or Ethical Belief Systems' was launched on 4 September 2008, and closed on 5 January 2009.

Charity Commission, 'Charities and Public Benefit: Summary Guidance for Charity Trustees'
(January 2008)

... There are two key principles of public benefit and, within each principle there are some important factors that must be considered in all cases. These are:

Principle 1: There must be an identifiable benefit or benefits
Principle 1a It must be clear what the benefits are
Principle 1b The benefits must be related to the aims
Principle 1c Benefits must be balanced against any detriment or harm
Principle 2: Benefit must be to the public, or section of the public
Principle 2a The beneficiaries must be appropriate to the aims
Principle 2b Where benefit is to a section of the public, the opportunity to benefit must not be unreasonably restricted:
   • by geographical or other restrictions; or
   • by ability to pay any fees charged
Principle 2c People in poverty must not be excluded from the opportunity to benefit
Principle 2d Any private benefits must be incidental

The principles of public benefit apply to all charities, whatever their aims. Each charity must be able to demonstrate that its aims are for the public benefit. Public benefit decisions are about whether an individual organisation is a charity and not about whether particular types of charity or groups of charities, as a whole, are for the public benefit.

B: The relief of poverty (Lord Macnaghten's first head)

In the case of relief of poverty, even benefiting a small number of people may be regarded as conferring a public benefit. It is unquestioned law that to relieve poverty is to confer a benefit upon the public at large, if only by mitigating the burden of support for the poor which would otherwise fall upon the community. The House of Lords in *Oppenheim* exempted 'poor relations' cases as anomalous, and left open the question whether the personal nexus test applies to them.

The 'poor relations' anomaly stems from the practice of Chancery in the nineteenth century when faced with trusts expressed to be for poor relations; rather than allow these to fail for uncertainty (at a time when the class ascertainability test applied) or perpetuity, the courts rescued such trusts by holding them charitable. Since then, the 'poor relations' cases have been consistently followed, which is probably why the House of Lords left them alone in *Oppenheim*. The House of Lords has since considered them directly in *Dingle* v *Turner* [1972] AC 601, and expressly upheld them. In that case, a trust for 'poor employees of E. Dingle and Co.' was held charitable, although it would have failed under the personal nexus test. The same reasoning must apply to 'poor relation'. It is clear, therefore, that the personal nexus test does not apply to this head of charity.

In order for a trust to be charitable under this head, it is however necessary that the trust should be intended to benefit a class of persons, and not simply to make a gift to an individual, or group of individuals, who happen to be poor. In *Re Scarisbrick* [1951] 1 Ch 662, Jenkins LJ stated the rule thus:

I think the true question in each case has really been whether the gift was for the relief of poverty amongst a class of persons, or ... a particular description of the poor, or was merely a gift to individuals, albeit with the relief of poverty amongst those individuals as the motive of the gift, or with a selective preference for the poor or the poorest amongst those individuals.

This statement received the approval of Lord Cross in the leading case of *Dingle* v *Turner*, considered in this subsection In *Scarisbrick* itself, the class of potential recipients was sufficiently wide as to be incapable of exhaustive ascertainment ('such relations of my said son and daughters as shall be in needy circumstances ... '), so the trust was charitable.

Assuming that Jenkins LJ's test is satisfied, however, the public benefit requirements are less stringent under this head than under the others, and the class to be benefited can be quite small.

Dingle v *Turner*
[1972] AC 601, [1972] 1 All ER 878, House of Lords

Decision: A trust to invest a large sum of money and apply the income in paying pensions to poor employees and ex-employees of E. Dingle & Co. Ltd was a valid charitable bequest for the relief of poverty. The *Oppenheim* personal nexus test does not apply to poverty charities.

LORD CROSS: The status of some of the 'poor relations' trusts as valid charitable trusts was recognised more than 200 years ago and a few of those then recognised are still being administered as charities today. In *Re Compton* [1945] Ch 123 Lord Greene MR said that it was 'quite impossible' for the Court of Appeal to overrule such old decisions and in the *Oppenheim* case [1951] AC at 309 [see Section 3: Public benefit, C: The advancement of education (Lord Macnaghten's second head)], Lord Simonds in speaking of them remarked on the unwisdom of—

> [casting] doubts on decisions of respectable antiquity in order to introduce a greater harmony into the law of charity as a whole.

Indeed counsel for the appellant hardly ventured to suggest that we should overrule the 'poor relations' cases. His submission was that which was accepted by the Court of Appeal in Ontario in *Re Cox* [1951] OR 205—namely that while the 'poor relations' cases might have to be left as long standing anomalies there was no good reason for sparing the 'poor employees' cases which only date from *Re Gosling* (1900) 48 WR 300 decided in 1900 and which have been under suspicion ever since the decision in *Re Compton* in 1945. But the 'poor members' and the 'poor employees' decisions were a natural development of the 'poor relations' decisions and to draw a distinction between different sorts of 'poverty' trusts would be quite illogical and could certainly not be said to be introducing 'greater harmony' into the law of charity. Moreover, although not as old as the 'poor relations' trusts, 'poor employees' trusts have been recognised as charities for many years; there are now a large number of such trusts in existence; and assuming, as one must, that they are properly administered in the sense that benefits under them are only given to people who can fairly be said to be, according to current standards, 'poor persons' to treat such trusts as charities is not open to any practical objection. So it seems to me it must be accepted that wherever else it may hold sway the *Compton* rule has no application in the field of trusts for the relief of poverty and that there the dividing line between a charitable trust and a private trust lies where the Court of Appeal drew it in *Re Scarisbrick* [1951] Ch 622.

The *Oppenheim* case was a case of an educational trust and although the majority evidently agreed with the view expressed by the Court of Appeal in the *Hobourn Aero* case [1946] Ch 194 [see Section 3: Public benefit, F: Self-help organisations], that the *Compton* rule was of universal application outside the field of poverty, it would no doubt be open to this House without overruling *Oppenheim* to hold that the scope of the rule was more limited. If ever I should be called on to pronounce on this question—which does not arise in this appeal—I would as at present advised be inclined to draw a distinction between the practical merits of the *Compton* rule and the reasoning by which Lord Greene MR sought to justify it. That reasoning—based on the distinction between personal and impersonal relationships—has never seemed to me very satisfactory and I have always—if I may say so—felt the force of the criticism to which my noble and learned friend Lord MacDermott subjected it in his dissenting speech in the *Oppenheim* case. For my part I would prefer to approach the problem on far broader lines. The phrase 'a section of the public' is in truth a vague phrase which may mean different things to different people. In the law of charity judges have sought to elucidate its meaning by contrasting it with another phrase 'a fluctuating body of private individuals'. But I get little help from the supposed contrast for as I see it one and the same aggregate of persons may well be describable both as a section of the public and as a fluctuating body of private individuals. The ratepayers in the Royal Borough of Kensington and Chelsea, for example, certainly constitute a section of the public; but would it be a misuse of language to describe them as a 'fluctuating body of private individuals'? After all, every part of the public is composed of individuals and being susceptible of increase or decrease is fluctuating. So at the end of the day one is left where one started with the bare contrast between 'public' and 'private'. No doubt some classes are more naturally describable as sections of the public than as private classes while other classes are more naturally describable as private classes than as sections of the public. The blind, for example, can naturally be described as a section of the public; but what they have in common—their blindness—does not join them together in such a way that they could be called a private class. On the other hand, the descendants of Mr Gladstone might more reasonably be described as a 'private class' than as a section of the public, and in the field of common employment the same might well be said of the employees in some fairly small firm. But if one turns to large companies employing many thousands of men and women most of whom are quite unknown to one another and to the directors the answer is by no means so clear. One might say that in such a case the distinction between a section of the public and a private class is not applicable at all or even that the employees in such concerns as ICI or GEC are just as much 'sections of the public' as the residents in some geographical area. In truth the question whether or not the potential beneficiaries of a trust can fairly be said to constitute a section of the public is a question of degree and cannot be by itself decisive of the question whether the trust is a charity. Much must depend on the purpose of the trust. It may well be that, on the one hand, a trust to promote some purpose, prima facie charitable, will constitute a charity even though the class of potential beneficiaries might fairly be called a private class and that, on the other hand, a trust to promote another purpose, also prima facie charitable, will not constitute a charity even though the class of potential beneficiaries might seem to some people fairly describable as a section of the public.

In answering the question whether any given trust is a charitable trust the courts—as I see it—cannot avoid having regard to the fiscal privileges accorded to charities. As counsel for the Attorney-General remarked in the course of the argument the law of charity is be devilled by the fact that charitable trusts enjoy two quite different sorts of privilege. On the one hand, they enjoy immunity from the rules against perpetuity and uncertainty and although individual potential beneficiaries cannot sue to enforce them the public interest arising under them is protected by the Attorney-General. If this was all there would be no reason for the courts not to look favourably on the claim of any 'purpose' trust to be considered as a charity if it seemed calculated to confer some real benefit on those intended to benefit by it whoever they might be and if it would fail if not held to be a charity. But that is not all. Charities automatically enjoy fiscal privileges which with the increased burden of taxation have become more and more important and in deciding that such and such a trust is a charitable trust the court is endowing it with a substantial annual subsidy at the expense of the taxpayer. Indeed, claims of trusts to rank as charities are just as often challenged by the Revenue as by those who would take the fund if the trust was invalid. It is, of course, unfortunate that the recognition of any trust as a valid charitable trust should automatically attract fiscal privileges, for the question whether a trust to further some purpose is so little likely to benefit the public that it ought to be declared invalid and the question whether it is likely to confer such great benefits on the public that it should enjoy fiscal immunity are really two quite different questions. The logical solution would be to separate them and to say—as the Radcliffe Commission proposed— that only some charities should enjoy fiscal privileges. But as things are, validity and fiscal immunity march hand in hand and the decisions in the *Compton* and *Oppenheim* cases were pretty obviously influenced by the consideration that if such trusts as were there in question were held valid they would enjoy an undeserved fiscal immunity. To establish a trust for the education of the children of employees in a company in which you are interested is no doubt a meritorious act; but however numerous the employees may be the purpose which you are seeking to achieve is not a public purpose. It is a company purpose and there is no reason why your fellow taxpayer should contribute to a scheme which by providing 'fringe benefits' for your employees will benefit the company by making their conditions of employment more attractive. The temptation to enlist the assistance of the law of charity in private endeavours of this sort is considerable—witness the recent case of the Metal Box scholarships—*IRC* v *Educational Grants Association Ltd* [1967] Ch 993—and the courts must do what they can to discourage such attempts. In the field of poverty the danger is not so great as in the field of education—for while people are keenly alive to the need to give their children a good education and to the expense of doing so, they are generally optimistic enough not to entertain serious fears of falling on evil days much before they fall on them. Consequently the existence of company 'benevolent funds', the income of which is free of tax does not constitute a very attractive 'fringe benefit'. This is a practical justification—although not, of course, the historical explanation—for the special treatment accorded to poverty trusts in charity law. For the same sort of reason a trust to promote some religion among the employees of a company might perhaps safely be held to be charitable provided that it was clear that the benefits were to be purely spiritual. On the other hand, many 'purpose' trusts falling under Lord Macnaughten's fourth head if confined to a class of employees would clearly be open to the same sort of objection as educational trusts. As I see it, it is on these broad lines rather than for the reasons actually given by Lord Greene MR that the *Compton* rule can best be justified.

NOTES

1. In the light of the comments made in the last paragraph set out above, note that only the validity of the bequest was at issue, and tax advantages were not claimed.

2. In *Re Segelman* [1996] 2 WLR 173, a trust for the 'poor and needy' of a class comprising at the time of the hearing a mere 26 people related to the testator, a multimillionaire, was held to be a valid charitable trust. Chadwick J held that, although this case very nearly infringed the rule that relief should not be restricted to named individuals, it was saved by the inclusion of after-born issue of the 26 identified beneficiaries within the class of potential beneficiaries, thereby raising the possibility of quite substantial numbers of additional beneficiaries who might themselves be, or become, poor. The removal by the 2006 Act of the presumption of public benefit should in the future prevent trusts such as that in *Re Segelman* from gaining charitable status.

Charity Commission, 'The Prevention or Relief of Poverty for the Public Benefit' (December 2008)

'Even where all the beneficiaries have to be poor, there may be circumstances in which the restrictions on who can benefit are either so limited or irrational as to outweigh the normal public character of the relief of poverty.

For example, the relief of poverty of people who have attended a specific school during a specific time and were members of the school's rugby team. This is unlikely to be considered a sufficient section of the public, even for the relief of poverty. Since, even if it can be shown there are a lot of them, unless there was clear evidence that such people had a predisposition to being poor by virtue of their having those characteristics, there is no, clear, rational link between the restrictions and the charitable aim.

However, the relief of poverty of families living in an area of social deprivation who care for vulnerable or dependent elderly relatives, or children with learning difficulties, would be considered a sufficient section of the public. This is because there is likely to be a connection between the restrictions based on the social and economic circumstances of the beneficiaries, and poverty'.

NOTE: The Charity Commission confirms that 'the issue is whether people lack the basic things in life, rather than why they lack them', so there is no possibility of returning to the invidious distinction, favoured by many Victorians, between 'deserving' and 'undeserving' poor. (See, generally, A. Rahmatian, 'The continued relevance of the "poor relations" and the "poor employees" cases under the Charities Act 2006' (2009) 73(1) *Conv* 12.)

C: The advancement of education (Lord Macnaghten's second head)

Whereas education is clearly a benefit to those in immediate receipt of it, it is not self-evident that educating a few people constitutes a benefit to the general public. Indeed, given that many of the cases under this head are in reality disputes over tax relief, it would be quite wrong if the education of a privileged few were to be regarded as charitable. Under this head it is therefore necessary that there is some additional benefit to the general public, or some appreciable sector thereof.

That is not to say that a particular form of education has to be capable of being enjoyed by everyone, so long as access to it is reasonably open. Thus public schools may be charitable as long as they are not operated as profit-making ventures, although their fees may place them beyond the means of the majority. Even scholarships or endowed chairs, which can be enjoyed only by one person at a time, present no difficulty. The problems arise where it is sought to limit the range of the potential beneficiaries within a class which is insufficiently wide to constitute a section of the public.

It is clear that it may be charitable to provide (e.g.) scholarships, open to:

(a) persons following a common profession or calling, or their children and dependants; or

(b) people of common nationality, religion, or sex; or

(c) the inhabitants of a given area, provided this is reasonably large, such as a town or county.

Special provisions for people suffering disability are also permissible, since they are a section of the public in a meaningful sense.

However, under the second head, and probably under all the *Pemsel* heads except relief of poverty, it will be fatal that the class of potential beneficiaries (however large) be defined in terms of relation to particular individuals, or a company. This approach originated in *Re Compton* [1945] Ch 123, where charitable status was denied to a trust to educate the children of three named families. It is understandable that the courts are reluctant to allow an essentially private arrangement to enjoy charitable privileges, especially tax advantages, but it seems that the principle extends to cases where the class of potential beneficiaries is defined in terms of a relationship with an employer, even where the employer is a substantial concern.

Oppenheim v *Tobacco Securities Trust Co.*
[1951] AC 297, House of Lords

Facts: The income of a trust fund was directed to be applied 'in providing for … the education of children of employees or former employees of the British-American Tobacco Co. Ltd … or any of its subsidiary or allied companies in such manner … as the acting trustees shall in their absolute discretion … think fit'. The number of present employees alone exceeded 110,000.

Held: (Lord MacDermott dissenting): The trust was not charitable, under the second head in *Pemsel's* case as being for the advancement of education, there being an insufficient element of public benefit. Although the number of potential beneficiaries was considerable, it was not charitable because of the personal nexus rule (because all the potential beneficiaries were connected with the same company).

LORD SIMONDS: It is a clearly established principle of the law of charity that a trust is not charitable unless it is directed to the public benefit. This is sometimes stated in the proposition that it must benefit the community or a section of the community. Negatively it is said that a trust is not charitable if it confers only private benefits. In the recent case of *Gilmour* v *Coates* [1949] AC 426 this principle was reasserted. It is easy to state and has been stated in a variety of ways, the earliest statement that I find being in *Jones* v *Williams* (1767) 2 Amb 651, in which Lord Hardwicke LC, is briefly reported as follows: 'Definition of charity: a gift to a general public use, which extends to the poor as well as to the rich'. With a single exception, to which I shall refer, this applies to all charities. We are apt now to classify them by reference to Lord Macnaughten's division in *Commissioners for Special Purposes of Income Tax* v *Pemsel* [1891] AC 531, 583 and, as I have elsewhere pointed out, it was at one time suggested that the element of public benefit was not essential except for charities falling within the fourth class, 'other purposes beneficial to the community'. This is certainly wrong except in the anomalous case of trusts for the relief of poverty with which I must specifically deal. In the case of trusts for educational purposes the condition of public benefit must be satisfied. The difficulty lies in determining what is sufficient to satisfy the test …

The difficulty arises where the trust is not for the benefit of any institution either then existing or by the terms of the trust to be brought into existence, but for the benefit of a class of persons at large. Then the question is whether that class of persons can be regarded as such as a 'section of the community' as to satisfy the test of public benefit. The words 'section of the community' have no special sanctity, but they conveniently indicate first, that the possible (I emphasise the word 'possible') beneficiaries must not be numerically negligible, and secondly, that the quality which distinguishes them from other members of the community, so that they form a section of it, must be a quality which does not depend on their relationship to a particular individual… . A group of persons may be numerous, but, if the nexus between them is their personal relationship to a single *propositus* or to several *propositi*, they are neither the community nor a section of the community for charitable purposes …

It must not, I think, be forgotten that charitable institutions enjoy rare and increasing privileges, and that the claim to come within that privileged class should be clearly established. With the single exception of *Re Rayner* (1920) 89 LJ Ch 369, which I must regard as of doubtful authority, no case has been brought to the notice of the House in which such a claim as this has been made, where there is no element of poverty in the beneficiaries, but just this and no more, that they are the children of those in common employment.

Learned counsel for the appellant sought to fortify his case by pointing to the anomalies that would ensue from the rejection of his argument. For, he said, admittedly those who follow a profession or calling, clergymen, lawyers, colliers, tobacco workers and so on, are a section of the public; how strange then it would be if, as in the case of railwaymen, those who follow a particular calling are all employed by one employer. Would a trust for the education of railwaymen be charitable, but a trust for the education of men employed on the railways by the Transport Board not be charitable? And what of service of the Crown whether in the civil service or the armed forces? Is there a difference between soldiers and soldiers of the King? My lords, I am not impressed by this sort of argument and will consider on its merits, if the occasion should arise, the case where the description of the occupation and the employment is in effect the same, where in a word, if you know what a man does, you know who employs him to do it. It is to me a far more cogent argument, as it was to my noble and learned friend in the *Hobourn* case [1946] Ch 194, that if a section of the public is constituted by the personal relations of employment, it is impossible to say that it is not constituted by 1,000 as by 100,000 employees, and, if by 1,000, then by 100, and if by 100, then by 10. I do not mean merely that there is a difficulty in drawing the line, though that too is significant: I have it also in mind that, though the actual numbers of employees at any one moment might be small, it might increase to any extent, just as, being large, it might decrease to any extent. If the number of employees is the test of validity, must the court take into account potential increase or decrease, and if so, as at what date?

... I would also, as I have previously indicated, say a word about the so-called 'poor relations' cases. I do so only because they have once more been brought forward as an argument in favour of a more generous view of what may be charitable. It would not be right for me to affirm or to denounce or to justify these decisions: I am concerned only to say that the law of charity, so far as it relates to 'the relief of aged, impotent and poor people' (I quote from the statute) and to poverty in general, has followed its own line, and that it is not useful to try to harmonise decisions on that branch of the law with the broad proposition on which the determination of this case must rest. It is not for me to say what fate might await those cases if in a poverty case this House had to consider them.

LORD MACDERMOTT (dissenting): But can any really fundamental distinction, as respects the personal or impersonal nature of the common link, be drawn between those employed, for example, by a particular university and those whom the same university has put in a certain category as the result of individual examination and assessment? Again, if the bond between those employed on a particular railway is purely personal, why should the bond between those who are employed as railwaymen be so essentially different? Is a distinction to be drawn in this respect between those who are employed in a particular industry before it is nationalised and those who are employed therein after that process has been completed and one employer has taken the place of many? Are miners in the service of the National Coal Board now in one category and miners at a particular pit or of a particular district in another? Is the relationship between those in the service of the Crown to be distinguished from that obtaining between those in the service of some other employer? Or, if not, are the children of, say, soldiers or civil servants to be regarded as not constituting a sufficient section of the public to make a trust for their education charitable?

It was conceded in the course of the argument that, had the present trust been framed so as to provide for the education of the children of those engaged in the tobacco industry in a named county or town, it would have been a good charitable disposition, and that even though the class to be benefited would have been appreciably smaller and no more important than is the class here.

NOTES

1. As well as standing for the personal nexus test, the case requires that the recipients of benefit must be a section of the community. This aspect of the case was applied in *Davies* v *Perpetual Trustee Co.* [1959] AC 459, where the Privy Council held non-charitable a trust which was confined to Presbyterian youths who were descended from settlers in New South Wales who had originated from the North of Ireland. Although quite large in number, this category of potential beneficiaries was held not to be a section of the public.

2. Lord Simonds apparently took the view that the test of public benefit may vary between the four heads of charity in *Pemsel's* case, and in particular excluded the 'poor relations' cases from consideration. For the question of whether the same test applies to other heads of charity, see *Inland Revenue Commissioners* v *Baddeley* [1955] AC 572 (below). For the test to be applied in the 'poor relations' cases, see *Dingle* v *Turner* [1972] AC 602.

3. Lord Simonds expressly refers to the tax concessions given to charities, and this clearly influenced his decision. This passage was also referred to with approval in *Davies* v *Perpetual Trustee* [1959] AC 459.

■ QUESTIONS

1. Suppose that the trustees had decided to use the fund to pay 15 per cent of the fees of those employees who decided to send their children to fee-paying schools.

How many employees do you suppose could have benefited in practice from such a scheme? Do you feel that the real problem in this case is the extent of the discretion given to the trustees?

2. How would you feel about paying more tax so that a trust to send the sons and daughters of a private company to public school could pay less?

3. Do you think that Lord MacDermott's railwaymen example has any force now that the railways have been privatised? Given that a trust for railwaymen set up in 1951 could have continued indefinitely whatever corporate structure was later adopted by the railway industry, do you think they have ever had any force?

In *Re Koettgen's WT* [1954] Ch 252, an educational trust succeeded despite a direction that the trustees should give preference to the families of employees, up to a maximum of 75 per cent of income. On the other hand, doubts have been expressed, and for example a preference for the grantor's family rendered a gift non-charitable in *Caffoor* v *Income Tax Commissioner, Colombo* [1961] AC 584. In *IRC* v *Educational Grants Association Ltd* [1967] Ch 123, affirmed [1967] Ch 993, between 76 per cent and 85 per cent of the income of a fund (varying from year to year) was paid out for the education of persons connected with the Metal Box Co. Ltd. In a dispute with the Inland Revenue, it was held that the money had not been paid exclusively for charitable purposes. Pennycuick J found 'considerable difficulty in the *Koettgen* decision', and thought that a preference for a private class might always be fatal (although he did not need actually to decide that).

■ **QUESTION**

Is a possible solution to this problem that the trust is valid, albeit that (following *Oppenheim*) it allows the trustees to use the property for both charitable and non-charitable purposes, but that they will be constrained to use it for charitable purposes only (as in *Hetherington* (D: The advancement of religion (Lord Macnaghten's third head))?

Fee-charging schools

Charity Commission, 'Public Benefit and Fee-Charging'
(December 2008)

'Fee-charging is likely to be a public benefit issue where:
- the service or facility that a charity charges for forms a significant part of its aims, or the way it carries out those aims; and/or
- the fees that are charged for that service or facility are high.

Charities that charge high fees must demonstrate that there is sufficient opportunity for people who cannot afford the fees to benefit in a material way that is related to the charity's aims. In general, the higher the fees that are charged, the more people there are likely to be who cannot afford the fees, and the more the charity is likely to have to do to provide those people with sufficient opportunity to benefit.

There are many different ways in which charities can ensure that there are sufficient opportunities to benefit for people who cannot afford the fees. When assessing public benefit we will take into consideration the totality of the opportunities to benefit that the charity provides for people who cannot afford the fees. Offering free or subsidised access is an obvious and, in many cases, the simplest way in which charities can provide opportunities to benefit for people who cannot afford the fees. It is also easier to show that the opportunity to benefit is material and related, not only to the charity's aims, but also to the service or facility that is charged for. It is primarily for the trustees of the charity to decide for themselves the extent to which they offer free or subsidised access, provided they can show that people who cannot afford the fees have sufficient opportunity to benefit in a material way that is related to the charity's aims. There is no 'one-size-fits-all' amount or percentage of free or subsidised access that charities must offer...'

■ **QUESTION**

The Charity Commission acknowledges that 'Some fee-charging charity trustees might wish to argue that there are wider or remote benefits to the public at large that arise from carrying out their charity's aims and that these benefits should be regarded as opportunities to benefit for people who cannot afford the fees. For example … the general relief of public expenditure from a charity doing something that the state would otherwise have to provide, such as relieving the exchequer of the cost of educating children at state schools or treating patients at NHS hospitals; or benefits to the nation from educating students who go on to become, for example, successful entrepreneurs or scientists'. Do you agree with the Charity Commission that such indirect benefits do not represent opportunities to benefit in a 'material way' for people who cannot afford the fees and are therefore irrelevant when considering the extent to which a charity meets public benefit principles?

The Independent Schools Council v *The Charity Commission for England and Wales*

[2011] UKUT 421 (TCC), The Upper Tribunal Tax and Chancery Chamber

Determination on the issue of the law governing fee-paying schools.

Held: The Charities Act 2006 'makes little, if any, difference to the legal position of the independent schools sector', but it does 'bring into focus what it is that the pre-existing law already required'. The Upper Tribunal confirmed that 'a trust which excludes the poor from benefit cannot be a charity' and therefore concluded that a school which operates *solely* for the benefit of fee-paying students is not sufficiently for the public benefit even though it undoubtedly operates for the public benefit in the general sense of advancing the overall level of education in the population at large. Taking a distinctly laissez-faire approach to an issue which the tribunal suggested ought to be resolved by politicians rather than judges, the tribunal held that it should lie within the trustees' discretion to determine what level of provision (above the minimum necessary to secure charitable status) should be made for the poor to access the educational benefits arising from a fee-paying school.

D: The advancement of religion (Lord Macnaghten's third head)

There is also a public benefit requirement for religious charities. The leading case is *Gilmour* v *Coats* [1949] AC 426, where the House of Lords had to consider a gift of £500 towards a Carmelite priory. The priory housed about 20 cloistered nuns who devoted themselves to intercessory prayer, and had no contact at all with the outside world. This was held non-charitable on the grounds that there was no contact with the outside world. Arguments based on Catholic doctrine, to the effect that everyone benefited from the intercessory prayers, were rejected as being not susceptible to legal proof. Nor could any benefit be found merely in the example of the piousness of the women, as it was too vague and intangible. The House of Lords also rejected the argument that, entry being open to all women, the priory should be treated on analogy with an educational institution offering scholarship entry, holding that an educational establishment which required its members to withdraw from the world and leave no record of their studies would not be charitable either.

On the other hand, in *Re Caus* [1934] Ch 162, Catholic masses for the dead were held charitable. This case was doubted in *Gilmour* v *Coats*, but in principle the case seems correct, since Catholic masses are normally said in public, and *Caus* was applied by Browne-Wilkinson V-C in *Re Hetherington* [1990] Ch 1.

Re Hetherington

[1990] Ch 1, Chancery Division

Decision: A gift for the saying of masses is charitable as long as the masses are said in public. The gift (which on a literal interpretation could be used for the saying of either private or public masses) must therefore be construed as a gift for public masses only, private masses not being permissible since it would not be a charitable application of the fund for a religious purpose.

SIR NICOLAS BROWNE-WILKINSON V-C: In my judgment the cases establish the following propositions.

(1) A trust for the advancement of education, the relief of poverty or the advancement of religion is prima facie charitable and assumed to be for the public benefit. *National Anti-Vivisection Society* v *Inland Revenue Commissioners* [1948] AC 31, 42 and 65. This assumption of public benefit can be rebutted by showing that in fact the particular trust in question cannot operate so as to confer a legally recognised benefit on the public, as in *Gilmour* v *Coats* [1949] AC 426.

(2) The celebration of a religious rite in public does confer a sufficient public benefit because of the edifying and improving effect of such celebration on the members of the public who attend. As Lord Reid said in *Gilmour* v *Coats* [1949] AC 426, 459:

A religion can be regarded as beneficial without it being necessary to assume that all its beliefs are true, and a religious service can be regarded as beneficial to all those who attend it without it being necessary to determine the spiritual efficacy of that service or to accept any particular belief about it.

(3) The celebration of a religious rite in private does not contain the necessary element of public benefit since any benefit by prayer or example is incapable of proof in the legal sense, and any element of edification is limited to a private, not public, class of those present at the celebration: see *Gilmour* v *Coats; Yeap Cheah Neo* v *Ong Cheng Neo* (1875) LR 6 PC 381 and *Hoare* v *Hoare* (1886) 56 LT 147.

Where there is a gift for a religious purpose which could be carried out in a way which is beneficial to the public (i.e. by public Masses) but could also be carried out in a way which would not have sufficient element of public benefit (i.e. by private Masses) the gift is to be construed as a gift to be carried out only by the methods that are charitable, all non-charitable methods being excluded: see *In re White* [1893] 2 Ch 41, 52–53; and *In re Banfield* [1968] 1 WLR 846.

Applying those principles to the present case, a gift for the saying of Masses is prima facie charitable, being for a religious purpose. In practice, those Masses will be celebrated in public which provides a sufficient element of public benefit. The provision of stipends for priests saying the Masses, by relieving the Roman Catholic Church pro tanto of the liability to provide such stipends, is a further benefit. The gift is to be construed as a gift for public Masses only on the principle of *In re White*, private Masses not being permissible since it would not be a charitable application of the fund for a religious purpose.

■ QUESTION

How do you distinguish this case from *Chichester Diocesan Board of Finance* v *Simpson* [1944] AC 341 (see Section 2: Definition of charity, B: Purposes must be exclusively charitable)

NOTE: In *Re Le Cren Clarke* [1996] 1 WLR 288, Hazel Williamson QC held faith healing to be charitable where carried out in public and in a Christian context. Any private element was ancillary only. Had it not been, however, it would not have been possible to fall back on *Re Hetherington* and simply ignore the non-charitable purpose. The distinction was drawn between a single purpose gift capable of being implemented in two different ways, where the court, as in *Hetherington*, could direct that it be carried on in one of those ways only, and a dual-purpose gift (one purpose not being charitable), which would fail.

Neville Estates v Madden

[1962] Ch 832, Chancery Division

Facts and decision: The facts of this case have already been set out in Chapter 3. The decision was that a gift to the Catford Synagogue, whose objects included maintaining of places of worship for persons of the Jewish religion who conform to the German or Polish ritual, could take effect as a charitable purpose trust. The consent of the Charity Commissioners was therefore required before an order for the sale of land could be made.

In order to hold the Catford Synagogue charitable, Cross J had to distinguish *Gilmour* v *Coats*.

CROSS J (on the question whether the purposes of the Catford Synagogue were charitable): If, as I have held, this £3,250 and the land bought with it was held by the trustees for the purposes of this synagogue, then the plaintiffs contend that the trust is not a charitable trust on two grounds. First, because the objects of the synagogue are not wholly religious. Secondly, because if the objects are wholly religious, a trust for the benefit of an unincorporated association of this sort is not a charitable trust but a private trust for the benefit of the members from time to time.

The chief purposes which a synagogue exists to achieve are the holding of religious services and the giving of religious instruction to the younger members of the congregation. But just as today church activity overflows from the church itself to the parochial hall, with its whist drives, dances and bazaars, so many synagogues today organise social activities among the members. A new clause added to the scheme of the United Synagogue in October, 1926, authorised, or purported to authorise, that body to establish, *inter alia*, halls for religious and social purposes, and the Catford Synagogue, as I have said, has erected a communal hall near the synagogue building in which social functions are held. The plaintiffs, fastening on these facts and on the wording of cl. 2 of the trust deed, argue that the trust in this case is open to the objections which proved fatal to the trust for the foundation of a community centre which came before the court in *IRC* v *Baddeley* [1955] AC 572. But in my judgment there is a great difference between that case and this. Here, the social activities are merely ancillary to the strictly religious activities. In the *Baddeley* case, on the other hand, no one sought to argue—indeed it was manifestly impossible to argue—that the trust was for the advancement of religion. No doubt it had a religious flavour in that the beneficiaries were confined to Methodists or persons likely to become Methodists, and the premises and the activities in which the beneficiaries were to engage were to be under the control of the leaders of a Methodist mission. Nevertheless the activities in themselves were directed predominantly to the social and not to the religious well-being of the beneficiaries.

In my judgment the purposes of the trust with which I am concerned are religious purposes—the social aspect is merely ancillary.

I turn now to the argument that this is a private, not a public trust. In an article which he contributed in 1946 to volume 62 of the *Law Quarterly Review*, Professor Newark argued that the courts ought not to concern themselves with the question whether or not a trust for a religious purpose confers a public benefit. Even assuming that such questions can be answered at all, judges, he said, are generally ill-equipped to answer them and their endeavours to do so are apt to cause distress to the faithful and amusement to the cynical. I confess that I have considerable sympathy with Professor Newark's views; but the decision of the House of Lords in *Gilmour* v *Coats* [1949] AC 426 has made it clear that a trust for a religious purpose must be shown to have some element of public benefit in order to qualify as a charitable trust. In that case it was held that a trust to apply the income of a fund for all or any of the purposes of a community of Roman Catholic nuns living in seclusion and spending their lives in prayer, contemplation and penance, was not charitable because it could not be shown that it conferred any benefit on the public or on any section of the public. The trust with which I am concerned resembles that in *Gilmour* v *Coats* in this, that the persons immediately benefited by it are not a section of the public but members of a private body. All persons of the Jewish faith living in or about Catford might well constitute a section of the public, but the members for the time being of the Catford Synagogue are no more a section of the public than the members for the time being of a Carmelite Priory. The two cases, however, differ from one another in that the members of the Catford Synagogue spend their lives in the world, whereas the members of a Carmelite Priory live secluded from the world. If once one refuses to pay any regard—as the courts refused to pay any regard—to the influence which these nuns living in seclusion might have on the outside world, then it must follow that no public benefit is involved in a trust to support a Carmelite Priory. As Lord Greene said in the Court of Appeal ([1948] Ch 340, 354): 'Having regard to the way in which the lives of the members are spent, the benefit is a purely private one.' But the court is, I think, entitled to assume that some benefit accrues to the public from the attendance at places of worship of persons who live in this world and mix with their fellow citizens. As between different religions the law stands neutral, but it assumes that any religion is at least likely to be better than none.

NOTE: On this view, religion can be advanced by example—so long as one mixes in the world in a *physical* sense. *Neville Estates* is authority that no more is required. It is not easy, however, to reconcile this position with *Re Warre's Wt, Wort* v *Salisbury Diocesan Board of Finance* [1953] 1 WLR 725, [1953] 2 All ER 99, Chancery Division, where Harman J refused to accord charitable status to an Anglican house of retreat open to all members of the public wishing to retire from the world for a short period of meditation and spiritual renewal. Although, technically, this is probably *obiter dicta*, since the gift in question was also void for uncertainty, the trustees being given a wide discretion, including using the property for purposes which were undoubtedly non-charitable.

E: Public benefit for other purposes beneficial to the community (Lord Macnaghten's fourth head)

Lord Simonds thought in *Oppenheim* that the test of public benefit may vary between the four heads of charity (in particular, he excluded the 'poor relations' cases entirely from consideration). It is clear that the personal nexus test applies to the fourth head, but arguably the requirement that the trust benefits a section of the public is more stringent under the fourth head than under the second.

For example, in *Williams' Trustees* v *IRC* [1947] AC 447, doubt was expressed by Lord Simonds as to whether Welsh people living in London could be a section of the public under the fourth head. In *IRC* v *Baddeley* [1955] AC 572, the House of Lords held that the persons to be benefited must either be the whole community or the inhabitants of a particular area. If some further restriction is imposed, thus creating in effect a class within a class, the test of public benefit will not be satisfied.

IRC v *Baddeley*
[1955] AC 572, House of Lords

Facts: Land was conveyed for the benefit of the Stratford Newtown Methodist Mission to be used by its leaders ' ... for the promotion of the religious social and physical well-being of persons resident in the County Boroughs of West Ham and Leyton in the County of Essex by the provision of facilities for religious services and instruction and for the social and physical training and recreation of such ... persons who for the time being are in the opinion of such leaders members or likely to become members of the Methodist Church and of insufficient means otherwise to enjoy the advantages provided by these presents and by promoting and encouraging all forms of such activities as are calculated to contribute to the health and well-being of such persons ... '.

Further land was conveyed on similar terms, but for the promotion of moral, rather than religious, welfare, but with the same additional social element, and for the benefit of the same class of people as above ('persons resident in the County Boroughs of West Ham and Leyton in the County of Essex ... who for the time being are in the opinion of such leaders members or likely to become members of the Methodist Church ... '). Provision of intoxicating liquor was firmly prohibited.

The question arose whether the gift was charitable.

Held: This was not a charitable donation. The purposes were not exclusively charitable because of the inclusion of a social element. Also, the purposes did not satisfy the public benefit requirement for the fourth head of charity.

VISCOUNT SIMONDS (on the public benefit issue): This brings me to another aspect of the case, which was argued at great length and to me at least presents the most difficult of the many difficult problems in this branch of the law. Suppose that, contrary to the view that I have expressed [in a part of his lordship's opinion not reproduced here], the trust would be a valid charitable trust, if the beneficiaries were the community at large or a section of the community defined by some geographical limits, is it the less a valid trust if it is confined to members or potential members of a particular church within a limited geographical area?

The starting point of the argument must be, that this charity (if it be a charity) falls within the fourth class in Lord Macnaughten's classification. It must therefore be a trust which is, to use the words of Sir Samuel Romilly in *Morice* v *Bishop of Durham* (1805) 10 Ves 522, 532, of 'general public utility', and the question is what these words mean. It is, indeed, an essential feature of all 'charity' in the legal sense that there must be in it some element of public benefit, whether the purpose is educational, religious or eleemosynary: see the recent case of *Oppenheim* v *Tobacco Securities Trust Co.* [1951] AC 297 [Section 3: Public benefit, C: The advancement of education (Lord Macnaghten's second head)], and, as I have said elsewhere, it is possible, particularly in view of the so-called 'poor relations' cases, the scope of which may one day have to be considered, that a different degree of public benefit is requisite according to the class in which the charity is said to fall. But it is said that if a charity falls within the fourth class, it must be for the benefit of the whole community or at least of all the inhabitants of a sufficient area.

LORD REID (dissenting): In *Oppenheim's case* [1951] AC 297 the trust was for the advancement of education, but the decision of this House was that it is not enough that the class of beneficiaries is numerous, it must also be a section of the community, and the *ratio decidendi* applies equally to a trust for the advancement of religion. So if ... the members of a religious denomination do not constitute a section of the public (or the community) then a trust solely for the advancement of religion or of education would not be a charitable trust if limited to members of a particular church. Of course, the appellants do not contend that is right: they could not but admit that the members of a church are a section of the community for the purpose of such trusts. But they maintain that they cease to be a section of the community when it comes to trusts within the fourth class ... the appellants cannot succeed on this argument unless that contention is sound. Poverty may be in a special position but otherwise I can see no justification in principle for holding that when dealing with one deed for one charitable purpose the members of the Methodist or any other church are a section of the community, but when dealing with another deed for a different charitable purpose they are only a fluctuating body of private individuals.

NOTES

1. The inclusion of a social element had the same effect as in *IRC* v *Glasgow*. It would not necessarily be fatal today, due to the subsequent enactment of the Recreational Charities Act 1958.

2. The essential difference between the approaches of Viscount Simonds and Lord Reid is that whereas the former would allow different tests of public benefit for the different heads of charity, Lord Reid would apply the same test for each head (except possibly the 'poor relations' cases). From Viscount Simonds's approach, it seems that the public benefit requirement under the fourth head is at least as stringent as the *Oppenheim* test (see Section 3: Public benefit, C: The advancement of education (Lord Macnaghten's second head)), which applies to the second head (advancement of education).

3. The 'poor relations' cases have now been reconsidered—see *Dingle* v *Turner*.

4. The *Baddeley* test seems therefore to be a different, and additional, test to that adopted in *Davies* v *Perpetual Trustee Co.* [1959] AC 459, for the second head. Indeed, the very definition of charity under the fourth head (purposes beneficial to the community) would seem to demand a more stringent test of public benefit than under any other head. However, Lord Reid thought otherwise in his dissenting speech in *IRC* v *Baddeley*.

5. It is also likely that what constitutes a section of the public depends on the purposes of the particular trust, and the courts are more likely to strike down arbitrary restrictions which are irrelevant to those purposes, but which simply serve to exclude other sections of the public. For example, in *IRC* v *Baddeley*, the limitation was to Methodists living in West Ham and Leyton, and the trust included the provision of playing fields. Lord Simonds clearly thought that the restriction to Methodists living in West Ham and Leyton was completely irrelevant to the provision of playing fields. Referring (at 592) to a rhetorical question put in argument, 'Who has ever heard of a bridge to be crossed only by impecunious Methodists?', he went on to say that what is true of a bridge for Methodists is equally true of any other public purpose falling within the fourth head, and of the adherents of any other creed. The limitation merely operated to prevent the purpose from being a public purpose; it could have had no other effect. A purpose which is not a public purpose cannot be charitable within the fourth head.

6. There is some authority that the test of public benefit can vary even within the fourth head itself. In *Re Dunlop (dec'd)* (1984) Northern Irish Judgments Bulletin (noted by Norma Dawson (1987) 51 *Conv* 114), Carswell J upheld as charitable a bequest 'to hold the remainder of my residuary estate for the Presbyterian Trust ... to found or help to found a home for Old Presbyterian persons', and a *cy près* scheme (see Chapter 9) was ordered. There was earlier Northern Irish authority that the Presbyterians of Londonderry were not a sufficient section of the public under the fourth head, and it was accepted that there was no difference between Irish and English definitions of charity. Carswell J took the view, however, that public benefit depended upon the nature of 'the advantage which the donor intends to provide for the benefit of all of the public'. A 'bridge to be used only by Methodists should clearly fail to qualify, whereas a gift for the education of the children of members of that church might be a valid charity'. But he was also prepared to distinguish between purposes within the fourth head itself.

7. It should perhaps finally be observed that neither *IRC* v *Baddeley* nor *Williams' Trustees* v *IRC* actually turned on the issue of public benefit. In the former case, the purposes were not exclusively religious, but included social purposes and the provision of playing fields; in the latter case, the purposes were exclusively social and recreational. They would therefore have failed because of the inclusion of a social content, whatever view had been taken on the public benefit issue.

F: Self-help organisations

Although self-help organisations may possibly have been regarded as charitable in the nineteenth century, when, for example, friendly societies contributed considerably to the then limited provisions for welfare, Hall V-C held in *Re Clark* (1875) 1 ChD 497 that a friendly society was not charitable because of the absence of any stipulation that benefits should be restricted to those members who were poor as well as old, disabled, or sick.

If they are not poverty charities, self-help organisations clearly fail on the *Oppenheim* personal nexus test (see Section 3: Public benefit, C: The advancement of education (Lord Macnaghten's second head)). Hall V-C envisaged that they may succeed as poverty charities, where, as we have seen, public benefit tests are less stringent, but there may be a second principle that the benefits of charity must be provided by bounty and not bargain (but note the views of Peter Gibson J in *Joseph Rowntree Memorial Trust Housing Association Ltd* v *A-G* (see Section 2: Definition of charity, E: The prevention or relief of poverty). Where, as is the case with many friendly societies, the beneficiaries have, in effect, bought their entitlement in a contractual arrangement, the element of altruism essential to charity is lacking.

Re Hobourn Aero Components Ltd's Air Raid Distress Fund, Ryan v *Forrest*
[1946] Ch 86 affirmed [1946] Ch 194, Court of Appeal

Facts: From 1940 to 1944, employees of a company situated in Coventry made weekly contributions to a fund to assist employees who had suffered damage as a result of air raids. Only contributors to the fund could benefit. The fund was closed in 1944 and the question arose what to do with surplus moneys.

Held at first instance:
(a) These funds were not held on any charitable trust, since there was an insufficient element of public benefit. It followed that a *cy près* scheme could not be directed.
(b) The contributors were entitled to distribute the fund among themselves, in proportion to the total amount each had contributed, on resulting trust principles (see Chapter 5).

Held in the Court of Appeal: The Crown appealed (arguing for a *cy près* scheme to be directed) on the issue of the charitable status of the fund alone. The Court of Appeal upheld Cohen J's decision.

LORD GREENE MR: We are not dealing with a fund put up by outside persons, although, even if we were, I should on the authority of *Re Compton* [1945] Ch 123 feel constrained to hold that such a fund would not be a good charity. The point to my mind which really puts this case beyond reasonable doubt is the fact that a number of employees of this company, actuated by motives of self-help, agreed to a deduction from their wages to constitute a fund to be applied for their own benefit without any question of poverty coming into it. Such an arrangement seems to me to stamp the whole transaction as one having a personal character, money put up by a number of people, not for the general benefit, but for their own individual benefit. I am not concerned to dispute the proposition that a fund put up for air raid distress in Coventry generally would be a good charitable gift. I have very little doubt that it would be. But there is all the difference in the world between such a fund and a fund put up by a dozen inhabitants of a street, or, it may be, a thousand employees of a firm, to provide for themselves out of the moneys subscribed by themselves some kind of immediate relief in case they suffered from an air raid.

MORTON LJ: ... there is no element of poverty in the present case. That, of course, does not prevent a trust from coming within the fourth head of Lord MacNaughten's classification in *Pemsel's case* [1891] AC 531, but the relevance of it in the present case is this: where poverty is essential in the qualification for benefits under a particular fund, there have been cases where trusts which would appear to be of a private nature have been held to be charitable. An example of this is the case of *Spiller v Maude* (1881) 32 ChD 158 n, which has been already mentioned. The reason, as was suggested by the Master of the Rolls in *Re Compton* [1945] Ch 123, may be that the relief of poverty is regarded as being in itself beneficial to the community. That element being absent in the present case, the appellant cannot rely on these cases. Mr Upjohn has argued that the provision of relief for air raid distress should be elevated to the same position as trusts for the relief of poverty. No doubt the provision of relief for air raid distress is a most excellent object, and I should not myself doubt that a fund for the relief of air raid distress in Coventry was a fund held upon charitable trusts. But I do not feel inclined to extend the somewhat anomalous line of cases where poverty has been held to take a trust out of the category of a private trust and into the category of a trust which is charitable in the legal sense.

NOTE: Morton LJ suggests that the self-help reasoning in *Hobourn Aero* may not apply to poverty trusts, where the public benefit requirement is less stringent (see, e.g. *Dingle* v *Turner*), but Lord Greene MR seemed rather less sure. Whatever may be the position regarding poverty charities, however, it is clear that a self-help scheme can never be charitable, unless it is for the relief of poverty.

G: Disaster appeals

These will be valid if for the relief of poverty, otherwise (like self-help organisations) they will fail on the grounds of public benefit (unless they are drawn up so as to benefit a large section of the community: see *Re North Devon and West Somerset Relief Fund Trusts*). This leaves the organisers of such funds with two alternatives. One possibility is that they can apply a means test criterion to the receipt of benefit, which they may regard as invidious. For example, in the Aberfan coal-tip disaster of 1966, the majority of victims were children, and far from it being easy to show that their deaths produced material deprivation among the relatives, one could actually argue that the cost of rearing the children had been saved. In fact, the Commissioners eventually held that the fund was charitable, when money was paid to enable people to move away from the area altogether. Professor Chesterman provides comprehensive coverage of this appeal in *Charities, Trusts and Social Welfare* (London: Weidenfeld & Nicolson, 1979) (see the extract in this section).

The other possibility, often favoured by fund organisers (e.g. Penlee lifeboat disaster fund in 1982), is to avoid the means test and draft the appeal in such a way as to avoid charitable status altogether. In that event, of course, the tax concessions will also be foregone. Perhaps more importantly, the *cy près* doctrine described in Chapter 9 will not apply, and there may be difficulties over distribution of any surplus left over after the purposes have been achieved. It may even be, as we have seen, that the Crown will take some or all of the surplus as *bona vacantia*—hardly the most fitting consequence of the altruism of the donors.

One of the problems with disaster appeals is that they are usually set up very quickly after the disaster has occurred, often before the full legal consequences have been considered. They may well be described as charitable, and donors may believe that their contributions are going to a charitable fund, only for the organisers later to change their minds and draft the purposes so as to avoid charitable status. An interesting question might then arise as to what happens to the money already contributed, in the (probably unlikely) event of a dispute (for example, if somebody who had contributed on the assumption that the fund was charitable was to object when he discovered that it was not).

Michael Chesterman, *Charities, Trusts and Social Welfare*
(Weidenfeld & Nicolson Law in Context Series, 1979), pp. 339–43

On 21 October 1966, a huge coal-tip belonging to the National Coal Board collapsed, crushing a schoolhouse and about forty other buildings in the small Welsh village of Aberfan. One hundred and sixteen children (belonging to 99 families) and 28 adults were killed, and another 29 children injured. A public appeal launched almost immediately by the local mayor attracted nearly 90,000 separate donations. Within about two months, the fund totalled £1.5 million and it ultimately closed at nearly £1.75 million, of which about £83,000 was earmarked for specific purposes such as the benefit of bereaved families, memorials to the dead victims and building a play-ground for the surviving children, and the balance was for the general purposes of the appeal.

... If the legal concept of charity was based solely on the notion of disinterested giving with a view to relieving the unhappiness of others, the Aberfan trust would have been indisputably charitable ... In fact, as the charity commissioners had warned in their report for 1965, disaster funds are not automatically charitable ... . 'those responsible for drawing up appeals and trust deeds should use words to show that no person will receive assistance unless he is in need' ... .

The commissioners' comments in their 1965 report clearly originated from the *Gillingham* and *Hobourn* decisions. Their view was a cautious one, because (a) the lack of 'public benefit' was conceded, without being argued, in *Gillingham* and (b) where the victims of a disaster are numerous, as in the *West Somerset* case but not in *Gillingham*, the *Gillingham* dictum may not be appropriate. Nevertheless, when the Aberfan trust deed was drawn up, both the lawyers involved and the commissioners took the view that a restriction of benefit to victims 'in need' should be included. This placed the committee in something of a quandary. Neither the local community nor the donors (to whose wishes the committee, in their capacity as agents, were bound by law to pay some respect ...) were in favour of anything in the nature of a means test. On the other hand, liability to taxation on the fund's substantial investment income and the possibility that, as in the *Gillingham* case itself, any surplus undisposed of might have to be returned to the donors on resulting trust constituted disincentives against drafting a trust which was not charitable.

... [E]ventually the charity commissioners' sanction had to be obtained to the distribution of a flat sum of £5,000 to each bereaved family, irrespective of its financial circumstances. This figure was thought sufficient to enable any family to move out of Aberfan if it so wished, or at least to start a new mode of life as an aid towards overcoming its grief ... .

SECTION 4: ADMINISTRATION OF CHARITIES

(i) Charity Commission

Charities Act 2006, s.7 (Charities Act 2011, Part 2) defines the objectives, functions, and duties of the Charity Commission. Its 'public confidence objective is to increase public trust and confidence in charities'; its 'public benefit objective is to promote awareness and understanding of the operation of the public benefit requirement'; its 'compliance objective is to promote compliance by charity trustees with their legal obligations in exercising control and management of the administration of their charities'; its 'charitable resources objective is to promote the effective use of charitable resources'; its 'accountability objective is to enhance the accountability of charities to donors, beneficiaries and the general public'. The Commission's general functions include determining whether institutions are or are not charities; encouraging and facilitating the better administration of charities; deciding whether to approve litigation with regard to a charity (Charities Act 2011, s.115; *Rai v Charity Commission* [2012] EWHC 1111 (Ch)); identifying and investigating apparent misconduct or mismanagement in the administration of charities and taking remedial or protective action in connection with misconduct or mismanagement therein; determining whether public collections certificates should be issued, and remain in force, in respect of public charitable collections; obtaining, evaluating, and disseminating information in connection with the performance of any of the Commission's functions or meeting any of its objectives (including the maintenance of an accurate and up-to-date register of charities); giving information or advice, or making proposals, to any Minister of the Crown on matters relating to any of the Commission's functions or meeting any of its objectives. The Commission's general duties require it to act, so far as is reasonably practicable, in a way which is compatible with its objectives, and which it considers most appropriate for the purpose of meeting those objectives and so as to encourage all forms of charitable giving and voluntary participation in charity work.

CHARITIES ACT 1993

3. The register of charities [now Charities Act 2011, Part 4]

(1) The Commissioners shall continue to keep a register of charities, which shall be kept by them in such manner as they think fit.

(2) There shall be entered in the register every charity not excepted by subsection (5) below; and a charity so excepted (other than one excepted by paragraph (a) of that subsection) may be entered in the register at the request of the charity, but (whether or not it was excepted at the time of registration) may at any time, and shall at the request of the charity, be removed from the register.

(3) The register shall contain—

    (a) the name of every registered charity; and

    (b) such other particulars of, and such other information relating to, every such charity as the Commissioners think fit.

(4) Any institution which no longer appears to the Commissioners to be a charity shall be removed from the register, with effect, where the removal is due to any change in its purposes or trusts, from the date of that change; and there shall also be removed from the register any charity which ceases to exist or does not operate.

(5) The following charities are not required to be registered—

    (a) any charity comprised in Schedule 2 to this Act (in this Act referred to as an 'exempt charity');

    (b) any charity which is excepted by order or regulations;

    (c) any charity which has neither—

        (i) any permanent endowment, nor

        (ii) the use or occupation of any land,

        and whose income from all sources does not in aggregate amount to more than £1,000 a year; and no charity is required to be registered in respect of any registered place of worship.

(6) With any application for a charity to be registered there shall be supplied to the Commissioners copies of its trusts (or, if they are not set out in any extant document, particulars of them), and such other documents or information as may be prescribed by regulations made by the Secretary of State or as the Commissioners may require for the purpose of the application.

(7) It shall be the duty—

(a) of the charity trustees of any charity which is not registered nor excepted from registration to apply for it to be registered, and to supply the documents and information required by subsection (6) above; and

(b) of the charity trustees (or last charity trustees) of any institution which is for the time being registered to notify the Commissioners if it ceases to exist, or if there is any change in its trusts or in the particulars of it entered in the register, and to supply to the Commissioners particulars of any such change and copies of any new trusts or alterations of the trusts.

(8) The register (including the entries cancelled when institutions are removed from the register) shall be open to public inspection at all reasonable times ...

4. Effect of, and claims and objections to, registration

(1) An institution shall for all purposes other than rectification of the register be conclusively presumed to be or to have been a charity at any time when it is or was on the register of charities.

(2) Any person who is or may be affected by the registration of an institution as a charity may, on the ground that it is not a charity, object to its being entered by the Commissioners in the register, or apply to them for it to be removed from the register; and provision may be made by regulations made by the Secretary of State as to the manner in which any such objection or application is to be made, prosecuted or dealt with.

(3) An appeal against any decision of the Commissioners to enter or not to enter an institution in the register of charities, or to remove or not to remove an institution from the register, may be brought in the High Court by the Attorney General, or by the persons who are or claim to be the charity trustees of the institution, or by any person whose objection or application under subsection (2) above is disallowed by the decision.

(4) If there is an appeal to the High Court against any decision of the Commissioners to enter an institution in the register, or not to remove an institution from the register, then until the Commissioners are satisfied whether the decision of the Commissioners is or is not to stand, the entry in the register shall be maintained, but shall be in suspense and marked to indicate that it is in suspense; and for the purposes of subsection (1) above an institution shall be deemed not to be on the register during any period when the entry relating to it is in suspense under this subsection.

(5) Any question affecting the registration or removal from the register of an institution may, notwithstanding that it has been determined by a decision on appeal under subsection (3) above, be considered afresh by the Commissioners and shall not be concluded by that decision, if it appears to the Commissioners that there has been a change of circumstances or that the decision is inconsistent with a later judicial decision, whether given on such an appeal or not.

NOTE: The role of the courts in deciding whether a body is charitable has been diminished by these sections, replacing with amendments the equivalent sections from the Charities Act 1960. An organisation seeking charitable status must normally apply for registration to the Charity Commissioners, who have power under the Act to grant or withhold registration according to their decision as to whether the proposed purposes are, in law, charitable. Registration is conclusive evidence of charitable status.

However, refusal by the Commissioners to register an organisation gives rise to a right of appeal under s.4, which is, in the first instance, an informal appeal to the board of Charity Commissioners. Such appeals are rare, usually single figures each year. Further appeal lies through the courts (as in, e.g. *Incorporated Council of Law Reporting for England and Wales* v *Attorney-General* [1972] Ch 73, and *McGovern* v *Attorney-General* [1982] Ch 321), initially the High Court, and thence to the Court of Appeal and House of Lords. The legal definition of charity is still a matter for the courts, therefore, but only as the end product of a complex administrative process.

(ii) Charity Tribunal

On 18 March 2008, the Charities Act 2006, Schs 3 and 4 came into effect, introducing the Charity Tribunal. According to the Charity Commission website:

[a] charity wishing to appeal a legal decision of the Commission can challenge this through the Commission's decision review process. Previously, if a charity was not satisfied with the final decision the only further route of appeal was by taking the case to the High Court, which tends to be an expensive and complicated process. The Tribunal provides an independent route of appeal for charities which have exhausted the Commission's decision review process.

SECTION 5: *CY PRÈS*

Where property given on trust for charitable purposes cannot be used in the precise manner intended by the donor, the court (and, since about 130 years ago, the Charity Commissioners) may make a scheme for the application of the property to purposes resembling as closely as possible the donor's original intention (see Chapter 9, Section 4 for detail).

■ SUMMATIVE QUESTION

Consider the validity of the following clauses in the will of Mr X:

online resource centre

Clause One: 'To my son, Leonard, a life interest in the income earned from my country properties, to determine if ever the income of the fund becomes payable to another person. In the event of determination of the interest the income from the properties shall be held by my trustees on trust for such of my children and in such shares as my trustees shall in their absolute discretion think fit.'

Clause Two: 'In the event of any of the beneficiaries under this will converting or marrying into Islam, the estate hereby limited to him or her shall cease and determine and be utterly void.'

Clause Three: '£100,000 to my trustees on trust to provide temporary shelter for Old Etonians who have fallen on hard times. Preference to be given to my old class mates.'

Clause Four: '£10,000 to my trustees to support research into the likely consequences for political and public life of a legal ban on the Society of Free and Accepted Masons.'

FURTHER READING

Chesterman, M., 'Foundations of Charity Law in the New Welfare State' [1999] 62(3) *MLR* 333.

Dunn, A., 'Demanding Service or Servicing Demand? Charities, Regulation and the Policy Process' [2008] *MLR* 247.

Garton, J., *Public Benefit in Charity Law: Principles and Practice* (Oxford: Oxford University Press, 2012).

Harding, M., 'Trusts for Religious Purposes and the Question of Public Benefit' [2008] *MLR* 159.

Institute for Fiscal Studies, 'Poverty and Inequality in the UK: 2011' (IFS Commentary C118).

Jones, G., *History of the Law of Charity*, 1532–1827 (Cambridge Studies in English Legal History) (Cambridge: CUP, 2008).

Luxton, P., Evans N., and Smith J., *The Law of Charities*, 2nd edn (Oxford: Oxford University Press, 2012).

McGregor-Lowndes, M. and O'Halloran, K., *Modernising Charity Law: Recent Developments and Future Directions* (Cheltenham: Edward Elgar, 2010).

Picarda, H., *Law and Practice Relating to Charities*, 4th edn (West Sussex: Bloomsbury Professional, 2010).

Warburton, J. and Morris, D. (eds), *Tudor on Charities*, 8th edn (London: Sweet & Maxwell, 1997).

8

Constructive Trusts and Informal Trusts of Land

KEY AIMS

To consider the relationship between constructive trusts and unconscionability and to demonstrate that the English constructive trust is an 'institutional' rather than a 'remedial' constructive trust. To identify common categories of constructive trust. To identify significant theoretical and practical distinctions between the principal 'methods' (resulting trust, constructive trust, and proprietary estoppel) by which equity recognises informal shared ownership of land.

SECTION 1: INTRODUCTION

A constructive trust is, in some respects, the polar opposite of an express trust. An express trust gives effect to an owner's intention to transfer a beneficial interest in his property, whereas a constructive trust may be imposed directly contrary to the owner's intentions. A constructive trust arises by operation of law where the facts are such that it would be unconscionable for an owner to deny that another person has acquired a beneficial interest in his property. Another respect in which a constructive trust is the polar opposite of an express trust concerns the relationship between the creation of the trust and the burden on the trustee's conscience. In the case of an express trust, it is the fact that property has been vested in the trustee 'on trust' that gives rise to the burden on the trustee's conscience, whereas in the case of a constructive trust, the process operates in reverse: the fact that the trustee's conscience is affected gives rise to the trust. As Sir Robert Megarry V-C stated in *Re Montagu's Settlement Trusts* [1987] Ch 264:

In determining whether a constructive trust has been created, the fundamental question is whether the conscience of the recipient is bound in such a way as to justify equity in imposing a trust on him.

And as Mr Justice Cardozo put it in *Beatty* v *Guggenheim Exploration Co.* 225 NY 380 (1919), 386:

A constructive trust is the formula through which the conscience of equity finds expression. When property has been acquired in such circumstances that the holder of the legal title may not in good conscience retain the beneficial interest, equity converts him into a trustee.

One of the most significant distinctions between express trusts and constructive trusts is that an express trust of land is unenforceable unless it is evidenced in writing, whereas a constructive trust of land is created and operates without formality (see Law of Property Act 1925, s.53, in Chapter 6). In the context of cohabitation of land, this has produced a situation in which courts routinely recognise constructive trusts on the basis of express statements and agreements which, in relation to property other than land, would have given rise to express trusts or contracts.

A: Constructive trust: property-based or free-standing remedy?

American jurists tend to see the positive benefits of a remedial constructive trust. See, for example, the observation (quoted in Section 1: Introduction) made by Judge Cardozo in *Beatty* v *Guggenheim Exploration Co.* 225 NY 380 (1919). English jurists, on the other hand, have tended on the whole to take a more negative view. Sir Peter Millett once called it 'a counsel of despair which too readily concedes the impossibility of propounding a general rationale for the availability of a proprietary remedy' ('Remedies: The Error in *Lister v. Stubbs*', in P. Birks (ed.), *The Frontiers of Liability* (Oxford: Oxford University Press, 1994), Vol. I, p. 51 at p. 52). A recent judgment accurately summarises the current position by observing that there is no English authority binding against the remedial constructive trust, but 'an English Court will be very slow indeed to adopt the US and Canadian model' (*London Allied Holdings Ltd* v *Lee* [2007] EWHC 2061 (Ch), *per* Etherton J at para. [274]).

Re Sharpe

[1980] 1 WLR 219, Chancery Division

Facts: An 82-year-old lady, who was not in good health, loaned a large sum of money (£12,000) to her nephew to enable him to purchase a house in which they could both live. The nephew later went bankrupt, and the question arose whether the old lady's money was secured, or whether it formed part of the nephew's assets, to be divided among his general creditors.

Held: Browne-Wilkinson J found for the old lady, on the basis that she was a beneficiary under a constructive trust, which bound the trustee in bankruptcy.

BROWNE-WILKINSON J: ... Even if it be right to say that the courts can impose a constructive trust as a remedy in certain cases—which to my mind is a novel concept in English law—in order to provide a remedy the court must first find a right which has been infringed. So far as land is concerned an oral agreement to create any interest in it must be evidenced in writing: see s.40 of the Law of Property Act 1925. Therefore if these irrevocable licences create an interest in land, the rights cannot rest simply on an oral contract. The introduction of an interest under a constructive trust is an essential ingredient if the plaintiff has any right at all. Therefore in cases such as this, it cannot be that the interest in property arises for the first time when the court declares it to exist. The right must have arisen at the time of the transaction in order for the plaintiff to have any right the breach of which can be remedied. Again, I think the *D. H. N. Food Distributors Ltd* case [1976] 1 WLR 852 shows that the equity pre-dates any order of the court. The right to compensation in that case depended on substantive rights at the date of compulsory acquisition, not on what remedy the court subsequently chose to grant in the subsequent litigation.

Accordingly, if I am right in holding that as between the debtor and Mrs Johnson she had an irrevocable licence to remain in the property, authority compels me to hold that that gave her an interest in the property before the bankruptcy and the trustee takes the property subject to that interest. In my judgment the mere intervention of the bankruptcy by itself cannot alter Mrs Johnson's property interest. If she is to be deprived of her interest as against the trustee in bankruptcy, it must be because of some conduct of hers which precludes her from enforcing her rights, that is to say, the ordinary principles of acquiescence and laches which apply to all beneficiaries seeking to enforce their rights apply to this case.

I am in no way criticising the trustee in bankruptcy's conduct; he tried to find out if she made any claim relating to the £12,000 before he contracted to sell the property. But I do not think that on ordinary equitable principles Mrs Johnson should be prevented from asserting her rights at this late stage. She is very old and in bad health. No one had ever advised her that she might have rights to live in the property. As soon as she appreciated that she was to be evicted she at once took legal advice and asserted her claim. This, in my judgment, is far removed from conduct which precludes enforcement by a beneficiary of his rights due to his acquiescence, the first requirement of acquiescence being that the beneficiary knows his or her rights and does not assert them.

Accordingly, I hold that Mrs Johnson is entitled as against the trustee in bankruptcy to remain in the property until she is repaid the sums she advanced. I reach this conclusion with some hesitation since I find the present state of the law very confused and difficult to fit in with established equitable principles. I express the hope that in the near future the whole question can receive full consideration in the Court of Appeal, so that, in order to do justice to the many thousands of people who never come into court at all but who wish to know with certainty what their proprietary rights are, the extent to which these irrevocable licences bind third parties may be defined with certainty. Doing justice to the litigant who actually appears in the court by the invention of new principles of law ought not to involve injustice to the other persons who are not litigants before the court but whose rights are fundamentally affected by the new principles ...

NOTE: Browne-Wilkinson J's views on when a constructive trust might arise were very wide. He thought that a constructive trust can be imposed simply because a licensee expends money or otherwise acts to his detriment. If the reasoning in this case is correct, almost any reliance on a promise relating to the occupation of property could give rise to a constructive trust. *Re Sharpe* may well be better explained on other grounds. For example, if it was the intention of the aunt and nephew that the old lady should have an interest in the property, then she may well have an interest on conventional resulting trust principles. However, the express intention to create a loan almost certainly rebuts the presumption in favour of a resulting trust.

B: Classification of constructive trusts

It is a virtually impossible task to fit every established category of constructive trust within a coherent conceptual framework. At some point in every study of constructive trusts it therefore becomes necessary simply to catalogue the somewhat disorganised collection of trusts that, rightly or wrongly, bear the name 'constructive'.

(i) Express trusts or gifts lacking formality

This includes the case of the person who receives legal title to land as a trustee in the absence of any formal declaration of trust and relies upon the lack of formality to claim absolute ownership of the land. See *Rochefoucauld* v *Boustead* [1897] 1 Ch 196, Court of Appeal (considered in *Hodgson* v *Marks* [1970] 3 WLR 956 Chancery Division, see Chapter 16). Secret trusts are also included in this category (see Chapter 6). We might also include in this category *donationes mortis causa* and the constructive trust that is said to arise when an express gift is made in favour of a trust foundation by a trustee of the foundation but without the formal transfer necessary fully to constitute the gift (*T. Choithram International SA* v *Pagarani* [2001] 1 WLR 1, see Chapter 4).

(ii) Trustees de son tort

See Chapter 15.

(iii) Trusts of property acquired with notice of express trust

A person who receives property with notice that it is subject to an express trust will hold it on trust for the beneficiary of the express trust, unless he overreaches those beneficial interests. In essence, 'notice' is knowledge of facts that have been discovered, or would have been discovered, by making reasonable inquiries appropriate to the type of property transferred. Notice is a highly technical concept in land law, the detail of which lies outside the scope of this book. The rules for overreaching also vary according to whether the trust property comprises land or other assets, but a recipient of property subject to an express trust will certainly overreach beneficial interests under the trust if he purchases the property from trustees who are acting within the scope of a legitimate power to sell it and all the trustees sign the receipt for the purchase moneys.

(iv) Trusts arising from a contract to transfer property

The most obvious candidate for inclusion in this category is the constructive trust that arises under a specifically enforceable contract for the sale of unique property such as shares in a private company or land (see *Walsh* v *Lonsdale* in Chapter 1). We can also include mutual wills within this category, because it has been held that only a fully contractual agreement to create mutual wills is sufficient to burden the conscience of the parties (see Chapter 6).

(v) Trusts that fulfil an assurance that has been relied on

When the owner of certain property (A) assures another person (B) that B has acquired, or will acquire, an interest in or over A's property and B relies on that assurance to her detriment, A will be stopped ('estopped') from denying that B has acquired whatever interest was the subject of the assurance and the detrimental reliance thereon. This proprietary estoppel arises in equity to prevent A from unconscionably asserting his strict legal rights. However, it has a positive aspect too, in that it must be fulfilled by some award of an interest in favour of B. The nature of the award lies in the discretion of the court, and frequently, especially where the interest claimed is an interest in land, the remedy awarded is a constructive trust.

(vi) Trusts under a joint venture to acquire property

Banner Homes Group plc v Luff Developments Ltd (No. 1)
[2000] Ch 372, Court of Appeal

Facts: Luff agreed *in principle* with Banner that they would create a new joint venture company in order to purchase a commercial site. They agreed to take equal shares in the new company. On that understanding, Luff purchased S Ltd (a new company) for use in the joint venture. Later, Luff began to have doubts about the proposed joint venture and started looking for a new partner. It did not tell Banner, fearing that Banner might put in an independent bid for the commercial site. Banner continued to act on the footing that the joint venture would proceed, always anticipating that Banner and Luff would enter into a formal agreement setting out the terms of the joint venture. S Ltd eventually acquired the site with funds provided by Luff, and only then did Luff inform Banner that the proposed joint venture would not be going ahead. Banner contended, *inter alia*, that it was entitled to half the shares in S Ltd under a constructive trust. At first instance, the judge rejected this contention. He held that equity could not transform the agreement, which was implicitly qualified by the right of either side to withdraw, into a binding arrangement. He also held that Banner had suffered no detriment, inasmuch as he refused to accept that Banner might have made an independent bid for the land if it had been aware of Luff's intention to abandon the proposed joint venture.

Held (allowing the appeal): An equity arose because it would have been inequitable to allow Luff to claim, outright, a site which it had acquired in furtherance of the non-contractual, pre-acquisition understanding that it would be held for the joint benefit of Luff and Banner. The Court would have held otherwise if Luff had informed

Banner soon enough to avoid advantage to Luff and detriment to Banner. (*Pallant* v *Morgan* [1952] 2 All ER 951 applied.)

CHADWICK LJ: [His Lordship began with a reference to the overview provided by Millett LJ in *Paragon Finance plc* v *D. B. Thakerar & Co.* [1999] 1 All ER 400, 408–9 of the underlying principles applicable in this area, and having referred to Robert Walker LJ in *Yaxley* v *Gotts* [2000] Ch 162, 176 he continued] … the present appeal provides the first opportunity, so far as I am aware, for this court to consider the basis and scope of what may be called the *Pallant* v *Morgan* equity in a case in which reliance has to be placed upon it by the appellant. In my view there is no doubt that such an equity does exist and is firmly based. It is an example of the wider equity to which Millett J referred in *Lonrho plc* v *Fayed (No. 2)* [1992] 1 WLR 1, 9–10:

> Equity will intervene by way of constructive trust, not only to compel a defendant to restore the plaintiff's property to him, but also to require a defendant to disgorge property which should have acquired, if at all, for the plaintiff. In the latter category of case, the defendant's wrong lies not in the acquisition of the property, which may or not have been lawful, but in his subsequent denial of the plaintiff's beneficial interest. For such to be the case, however, the defendant must either have acquired property which but for his wrongdoing would have belonged to the plaintiff, or he must have acquired property in circumstances in which he cannot conscientiously retain it against the plaintiff … .

It is important, however, to identify the features which will give rise to a *Pallant* v *Morgan* equity and to define its scope; while keeping in mind that it is undesirable to attempt anything in the nature of an exhaustive classification. As Millett J pointed out in *Lonrho plc* v *Fayed (No. 2)* [1992] 1 WLR 1, 9b, in a reference to the work of distinguished Australian commentators, equity must retain its 'inherent flexibility and capacity to adjust to new situations by reference to mainsprings of the equitable jurisdiction'. Equity must never be deterred by the absence of a precise analogy, provided that the principle invoked is sound. Mindful of this caution, it is, nevertheless, possible to advance the following propositions.

(1) A *Pallant* v *Morgan* equity may arise where the arrangement or understanding on which it is based precedes the acquisition of the relevant property by one party to that arrangement. It is the pre-acquisition arrangement which colours the subsequent acquisition by the defendant and leads to his being treated as a trustee if he seeks to act inconsistently with it. Where the arrangement or understanding is reached in relation to property already owned by one of the parties, he may (if the arrangement is of sufficient certainty to be enforced specifically) thereby constitute himself trustee on the basis that 'equity looks on that as done which ought to be done;' or an equity may arise under the principles developed in the proprietary estoppel cases. As I have sought to point out, the concepts of constructive trust and proprietary estoppel have much in common in this area. *Holiday Inns Inc* v *Broadhead*, 232 EG 951 may, perhaps, best be regarded as a proprietary estoppel case; although it might be said that the arrangement or understanding, made at the time when only the five acre site was owned by the defendant, did, in fact, precede the defendant's acquisition of the option over the 15-acre site.

(2) It is unnecessary that the arrangement or understanding should be contractually enforceable. Indeed, if there is an agreement which is enforceable as a contract, there is unlikely to be any need to invoke the *Pallant* v *Morgan* equity; equity can act through the remedy of specific performance and will recognise the existence of a corresponding trust. On its facts *Chattock* v *Muller*, 8 ChD 177 is, perhaps, best regarded as a specific performance case. In particular, it is no bar to a *Pallant* v *Morgan* equity that the pre-acquisition arrangement is too uncertain to be enforced as a contract—see *Pallant* v *Morgan* [1953] Ch 43 itself, and *Time Products Ltd* v *Combined English Stores Group Ltd*, 2 December 1974—nor that it is plainly not intended to have contractual effect—see *Island Holdings Ltd* v *Birchington Engineering Co. Ltd*, 7 July 1981.

(3) It is necessary that the pre-acquisition arrangement or understanding should contemplate that one party ('the acquiring party') will take steps to acquire the relevant property; and that, if he does so, the other party ('the non-acquiring party') will obtain some interest in that property. Further, it is necessary that (whatever private reservations the acquiring party may have) he has not informed the non-acquiring party before the acquisition (or, perhaps more accurately, before it is too late for the parties to be restored to a position of no advantage/no deteriment) that he no longer intends to honour the arrangement or understanding.

(4) It is necessary that, in reliance on the arrangement or understanding, the non-acquiring party should do (or omit to do) something which confers an advantage on the acquiring party in relation to the acquisition of the property; or is detrimental to the ability of the non-acquiring party to acquire the

property on equal terms. It is the existence of the advantage to the one, or detriment to the other, gained or suffered as a consequence of the arrangement or understanding, which leads to the conclusion that it would be inequitable or unconscionable to allow the acquiring party to retain the property for himself, in a manner inconsistent with the arrangement or understanding which enabled him to acquire it. *Pallant v Morgan* [1953] Ch 43 itself provides an illustration of this principle. There was nothing inequitable in allowing the defendant to retain for himself the lot (lot 15) in respect to which the plaintiff's agent had no instructions to bid. In many cases the advantage/detriment will be found in the agreement of the non-acquiring party to keep out of the market. That will usually be both to the advantage of the acquiring party—in that he can bid without competition from the non-acquiring party—and to the detriment of the non-acquiring party—in that he loses the opportunity to acquire the property for himself. But there may be advantage to the one without corresponding detriment to the other. Again, *Pallant v Morgan* provides an illustration. The plaintiff's agreement (through his agent) to keep out of the bidding gave an advantage to the defendant—in that he was able to obtain the property for a lower price than would otherwise have been possible; but the failure of the plaintiff's agent to bid did not, in fact, cause detriment to the plaintiff—because, on the facts, the agent's instructions would not have permitted him to outbid the defendant. Nevertheless, the equity was invoked.

(5) That leads, I think, to the further conclusions: (i) that although, in many cases, the advantage/detriment will be found in the agreement of the non-acquiring party to keep out of the market, that is not a necessary feature; and (ii) that although there will usually be advantage to the one and correlative disadvantage to the other, the existence of both advantage and detriment is not essential—either will do. What is essential is that the circumstances make it inequitable for the acquiring party to retain the property for himself in a manner inconsistent with the arrangement or understanding on which the non-acquiring party has acted. Those circumstances may arise where the non-acquiring party was never 'in the market' for the whole of the property to be acquired; but (on the faith of an arrangement or understanding that he shall have a part of that property) provides support in relation to the acquisition of the whole which is of advantage to the acquiring party. They may arise where the assistance provided to the acquiring party (in pursuance of the arrangement or understanding) involves no detriment to the non-acquiring party; or where the non-acquiring party acts to his detriment (in pursuance of the arrangement or understanding) without the acquiring party obtaining any advantage therefrom ...

The *Pallant v Morgan* equity does not seek to give effect to the parties' bargain, still less to make for them some bargain which they have not themselves made, as the cases to which I have referred make clear. The equity is invoked where the defendant has acquired property in circumstances where it would be inequitable to allow him to treat it as his own; and where, because it would be inequitable to allow him to treat the property as his own, it is necessary to impose on him the obligations of a trustee in relation to it. It is invoked because there is no bargain which is capable of being enforced; if there were an enforceable bargain there would have been no need for equity to intervene in the way that it has done in the cases to which I have referred ...

As I have sought to show, the *Pallant v Morgan* equity is invoked where it would be inequitable to allow the defendant to treat the property acquired in furtherance of the arrangement or understanding as his own. It may be just as inequitable to allow the defendant to treat the property as his own when it has been acquired by the use of some advantage which he has obtained under the arrangement or understanding as it is to allow him to treat the property as his own when the plaintiff has suffered some detriment under the arrangement or understanding. That, as it seems to me, is this case.

For those reasons I would allow this appeal. In the circumstances that it was always in contemplation that a single enterprise company—which, in the event, was Stowhelm—should acquire the site as its own asset, so that the parties should participate as the holders of shares in that company rather than as the joint owners of the site itself, my present view is that the appropriate order is that sought in the notice of appeal, namely, that the shares in Stowhelm are held, as to one-half, upon trust for Banner. If necessary, I would order a sale of all the shares in Stowhelm held by Luff and a division of the proceeds. But I am conscious that there may have been dealings in the shares in Stowhelm since the acquisition of the site; and, if the parties cannot agree on the appropriate form of order in the light of the decision of this court, I would think it right to hear further submissions on that question before reaching a concluded view.

NOTE: The prevailing judicial opinion is that the *Pallant v Morgan* equity arises on the same basis as a common intention constructive trust (*Crossco No 4 Unlimited v Jolan Ltd* [2011] EWCA Civ 1619) and therefore will not arise unless the defendant's conscience is affected by knowledge that a binding agreement was intended (*Herbert v Doyle* [2010] EWCA Civ 1095). The equity depends upon an intention that the claimant would acquire a proprietary interest in the disputed assets, but it is not necessary that the nature of the intended proprietary interest should be specified precisely in advance (*Kearns Brothers Ltd* v *Hova Developments Ltd* [2012] EWHC 2968 (Ch)).

■ **QUESTIONS**

1. Is it somewhat strange that Luff's 'conscience' was bound by Banner's *detrimental* reliance without evidence that Banner *would probably* have made an independent bid in the absence of the agreement with Luff?

2. Is the *'Pallant* v *Morgan* equity' dubious because it operates in a commercial context to confer proprietary rights under a constructive trust on a claimant who has suffered no loss of a pre-existing proprietary right? (As argued by Nicholas Hopkins, 'The *Pallant* v *Morgan* "Equity"?' (2002) 66 *Conv* 35.)

Cox v *Jones*

[2004] EWHC 1486 (Ch) (Transcript)

Facts: This case involved the acrimonious (and litigious) break-up of two barristers (Mr Jones and Miss Cox) who were formerly engaged to be married. The main dispute related to ownership of certain assets, including a flat in the name of Mr Jones.

Held: Miss Cox's claim to the flat succeeded.

MANN J: ... looking at all the evidence, I find that the basis of the acquisition of the Flat, under which both Mr Jones and Miss Cox operated, was that he was purchasing for her, as her nominee (though that word may not have been used) and not in his own right. Both parties acted on that footing—Miss Cox when she 'diverted' the purchase into what she thought was joint names and then acquiesced in a purchase in Mr Jones's sole name, when she did not pursue her idea of getting assistance from her parents; when she paid money towards the purchase price; when she accepted a loan from Mr Jones; when she managed the Flat thereafter; and when she took the utility accounts into her sole name.

... Miss Cox's belief that she would have an interest in the property was entirely reasonable—indeed, on my findings, it was the whole purpose of the acquisition. In addition she suffered some detriment in assuming a liability for the utility bills (which, in the circumstances of this case was slight), and in managing the lettings (which was more significant), and in providing part of the purchase price from her own resources (which is also significant). However, I do not think that the answer to this case lies in the line of cases principally relied on by Mr Roberts, which are the familiar cases which rely principally on some form of contribution by a cohabitee towards the acquisition or improvement of property. The answer lies in the slightly different, though probably conceptually related, line of cases involving one person standing aside from purchasing a property on the understanding that another purchaser would take the property and provide an interest to the former. The cases are identified and discussed in *Banner Homes Group plc* v *Luff Developments Ltd* [2000] Ch 372, [2000] 2 All ER 117. One of the cases cited was *Holiday Inns* v *Broadhead* 232 EG 951. During an unreported interlocutory hearing Megarry J is recorded as saying the following (as appears from the judgment in *Banner Homes* at p 391, where it is cited with apparent approval):

'It seems to me that if A and B agree that A shall acquire some specific property for the joint benefit of A and B on terms yet to be agreed, and B, in reliance on A's agreement, is thereby induced to refrain from attempting to acquire the property, equity ought not to permit A, when he acquires the property, to insist on retaining the whole benefit for himself to the exclusion of B.'

These remarks were made in the context of considering *Pallant* v *Morgan*, a case in which two parties agreed that one would not bid at auction for one of two lots on the footing that the other would bid for both and would sell one plot to the non-bidding party. The effect was that the bidding party (who was successful) held the combined property on trust for both of them. That dictum would certainly cover the facts of the present case as I have found them to be, save for the reference to "terms to be agreed", because in the present case the terms were agreed (so far as they concerned the quantum of beneficial interest), thus making equity's job slightly easier (in terms of quantification of interest).

In *Banner Homes* Chadwick LJ went on to consider the *'Pallant* v *Morgan* equity'. The case itself, and Chadwick LJ's analysis of it at p 397, makes it clear that it operates via the mechanism of the imposition of a constructive trust. He cites from *Lonrho plc* v *Fayed (No. 2)* [1991] 4 All ER 961, [1992] 1 WLR 1 at 9–10:

'Equity will intervene by way of constructive trust, not only to compel a defendant to restore the plaintiffs property to him, but also to require a defendant to disgorge property which should have been acquired, if at all, for the defendant.'

Having then referred to the inherent flexibility necessary in the implementation of equitable remedies, he then advanced (inter alia) the following propositions which can be applied to the present case:

'(1) A *Pallant* v *Morgan* equity may arise where the arrangement of understanding on which it is based precedes the acquisition of the relevant property by one party to the arrangement. It is the pre-acquisition arrangement which colours the subsequent acquisition by the defendant and leads to his being treated as a trustee if he seeks to act inconsistently with it.'

In the present case, on my findings, there was a clear arrangement that Mr Jones would hold as trustee and not beneficially at all. That was the underpinning of the whole arrangement, and it was made before the acquisition. It certainly colours the subsequent acquisition, because without it there would, I find, have been no purchase at all.

'(3) It is necessary that the pre-acquisition arrangement or understanding should contemplate that one party ('the acquiring party') will take steps to acquire the relevant property; and that, if he does so, the other party ('the non-acquiring party') will obtain some interest in that property. Further, it is necessary that (whatever private reservations the acquiring party may have) he has not informed the non-acquiring party before the acquisition (or, perhaps more accurately, before it is too late for the parties to be restored to a position of no advantage/no detriment) that he no longer intends to honour the arrangement or understanding.'

This requirement is fulfilled in the present case. Mr Jones was to acquire it, and he did not tell Miss Cox that he intended to own it beneficially until much later. Indeed, I find that on the facts it did not occur to him to do so until some time after the rift between them.

'(4) it is necessary that, in reliance on the arrangement or understanding, the non-acquiring party should do (or omit to do) something which confers an advantage on the acquiring party in relation to the acquisition of the property; or is detrimental to the ability of the non-acquiring party to acquire the property on equal terms. It is the existence of the advantage to the one, or the detriment to the other, gained or suffered as a consequence of the arrangement of understanding, which leads to the conclusion that it would be inequitable or conscionable to allow the acquiring party to retain the property for himself, in a manner inconsistent with the arrangement or understanding which enabled him to acquire it.'

These criteria are fulfilled. Mr Jones had the benefit of being able to acquire the property swiftly and in circumstances in which the market had not been tested in relation to it. He benefited from Miss Cox's good relationship with the personal representative of the deceased owner. He also had the 'benefit' of the moneys provided by Miss Cox, and of her property management activities thereafter. For her part Miss Cox suffered a detriment in that she did not pursue her own attempts to acquire the property herself in her sole name. It was not conclusively proved that those attempts would have been successful. The assistance to be provided by her parents was not finalised—indeed, it was not discussed much. However, it was far from being a merely fanciful possibility, and I find that her parents would have assisted if they could. Her stopping these activities was a clear detriment. It should be noted that in *Banner Homes* the claimant was unable to say clearly when it was that it would have sought to acquire the site itself were it not for the arrangement which left it to the defendants to acquire it (see page 382). This was still a detriment—see page 400.

'(5) ... (ii) that, although there will usually be advantage to the one and correlative disadvantage to the other, the existence of both advantage and disadvantage is not essential—either will do. What is essential is that the circumstances make it inequitable for the acquiring party to retain the property for himself in a manner inconsistent with the arrangement or understanding on which the non-acquiring party has acted.'

In the present case there is both advantage and disadvantage, and the clearest possible case for saying that it would be inequitable for Mr Jones to hold the Flat for himself absolutely. There was an understanding that it would be bought for her; on that footing she stopped her attempt to find methods of funding the purchase; she switched the purchase to joint names, then acquiesced in a purchase in his sole name; she then managed the Flat thereafter. All that makes it inequitable for Mr Jones to seek to claim it for himself, and he therefore holds it on constructive trust for her absolutely.

(vii) Trusts of property acquired 'subject to' personal rights

Bannister v *Bannister*

[1948] 2 All ER 133, Court of Appeal

Facts: The defendant was negotiating to sell two cottages to the claimant (plaintiff in the case extract), her brother-in-law, and it was understood that after the sale she would be able to continue to live in one of the cottages rent free for as long as she wished. Because of this oral arrangement the claimant obtained the cottages for only £250, as compared with their true market value of around £400.

No written agreement giving rights to the defendant was included in the conveyance, however. She relied on his oral statement 'I do not want to take any rent, but will let you stay' in one of the cottages 'as long as you like, rent free'.

After the sale, the claimant claimed possession of the cottage.

Held: The claimant held the cottage as constructive trustee of the defendant for her life.

SCOTT LJ: The conclusion ... reached by the learned county court judge was attacked in this court on substantially the following three grounds:—First, it was said that the oral undertaking found by the learned county court judge to have formed part of the agreement—namely, that the plaintiff would let the defendant stay in No. 30 as long as she liked rent free—did not, as a matter of construction of the language used, amount to a promise that the defendant should retain a life interest in No. 30, but amounted merely to a promise that the plaintiff would allow the defendant to remain in No. 30 rent free as his tenant at will. Secondly, it was said that, even if the terms of the oral undertaking were such as to amount to a promise that the defendant should retain a life interest in No. 30, a tenancy at will free of rent was, nevertheless, the greatest interest she could claim in view of the absence of writing and the provisions of ss.53 and 54 of the Law of Property Act, 1925. Thirdly, it was said that a constructive trust in favour of the defendant (which the absence of writing admittedly would not defeat) could only be raised by findings to the effect that there was actual fraud on the part of the plaintiff and that the property was sold and conveyed to him on the faith of an express oral declaration of trust which it would be fraudulent in him to deny. It was, accordingly, submitted that the learned county court judge's conclusion that there was a constructive trust could not stand since it was negatived by his finding that there was no fraud in the case and by the absence of any evidence of anything amounting to an express oral declaration of trust.

[Scott LJ rejected the first objection and continued:]

As will be seen from what is said below, the second objection (based on want of writing) in effect stands or falls with the third, and it will, therefore, be convenient to deal with that next. It is, we think, clearly a mistake to suppose that the equitable principle on which a constructive trust is raised against a person who insists on the absolute character of a conveyance to himself for the purpose of defeating a beneficial interest, which, according to the true bargain, was to belong to another, is confined to cases in which the conveyance itself was fraudulently obtained. The fraud which brings the principle into play arises as soon as the absolute character of the conveyance is set up for the purpose of defeating the beneficial interest, and that is the fraud to cover which the Statute of Frauds or the corresponding provisions of the Law of Property Act, 1925, cannot be called in aid in cases in which no written evidence of the real bargain is available. Nor is it, in our opinion, necessary that the bargain on which the absolute conveyance is made should include any express stipulation that the grantee is in so many words to hold as trustee. It is enough that the bargain should have included a stipulation under which some sufficiently defined beneficial interest in the property was to be taken by another. The above propositions are, we think, clearly borne out by ... *Rochefoucauld* v *Boustead*. We see no distinction in principle between a case in which property is conveyed to a purchaser on terms that the entire beneficial interest in some part of it is to be retained by the vendor ... and a case, like the present, in which property is conveyed to a purchaser on terms that a limited beneficial interest in some part of it is to be retained by the vendor. We are, accordingly, of opinion that the third ground of objection to the learned county court judge's conclusion also fails. His finding that there was no fraud in the case cannot be taken as meaning that it was not fraudulent in the plaintiff to insist on the absolute character of the conveyance for the purpose of defeating the beneficial interest which he had agreed the defendant should retain. The conclusion that the plaintiff was fraudulent, in this sense, necessarily follows from the facts found, and, as indicated above, the fact that he may have been innocent of any fraudulent intent in taking the conveyance in absolute form is for this purpose immaterial. The failure of the third ground of objection necessarily also destroys the second objection based on want of writing and the provisions of ss.53 and 54 of the Law of Property Act 1925.

...

In the result, we hold that the appeal fails and the order of the learned county court judge should be affirmed, but in the interests of accuracy we think his order should be varied by substituting a declaration to the effect that the plaintiff holds No. 30 in trust during the life of the defendant to permit the defendant to occupy the same for so long as she may desire to do so and subject thereto in trust for the plaintiff. A trust in this form has the effect of making the beneficiary a tenant for life within the meaning of the Settled Land Act, 1925, and, consequently, there is a very little practical difference between such a trust and a trust for life *simpliciter*. The appeal will be dismissed with that variation in the form of the order. The plaintiff must pay the costs of the appeal.

■ QUESTIONS

The following questions are directed towards the possibility of finding alternative routes to protecting the defendant, without the need to develop a general fraud doctrine leading to the imposition of a constructive trust:

1. Does it appear that the claimant fraudulently misrepresented his intentions when he told the defendant that she would be able to remain in the cottage for her life?
2. If you take property expressly subject to an undertaking that you hold it for the benefit of somebody else, why are you not an express trustee?
3. If this case is merely an example of an express declaration of trusteeship by the claimant, could he have relied on s.53(1)(b) given the decision in *Rochefoucauld* v *Boustead* (also discussed in this section)?

Sir Nicolas Browne-Wilkinson, 'Constructive Trusts and Unjust Enrichment'
(Holdsworth Club Address, 1991)

According to the conventional equitable principles, the consequences of holding that there is a constructive trust go far beyond making the constructive trustee himself personally liable to the beneficiary. The essence of the constructive trust is that the property held by the constructive trustee is itself trust property. The beneficiary ... has an equitable interest ... from the date when the constructive trust arises: that equitable interest ... is enforceable against the [property] even in the hands of third parties unless the third party is a purchaser for value without notice. Therefore, according to the conventional law of trusts, the imposition of a constructive trust may have an effect far beyond requiring someone who has been unjustly enriched to disgorge his unjust enrichment. Third parties who have not been unjustly enriched may suffer as a result of holding that there is a constructive trust.

NOTE: *Binions* v *Evans* is an example of the imposition of a constructive trust on a purchaser. In considering whether it gives rise to any potential conveyancing difficulties, on reading the details you may care to give thought to the position of a subsequent purchaser, in the event that Mr and Mrs Binions sell the property on in Mrs Evans's lifetime.

Binions v *Evans*

[1972] Ch 359, Court of Appeal

Facts: Mrs Evans's husband was employed by the Tredegar Estate (near Newport in South Wales) and lived rent-free in a cottage owned by the estate. The husband died when the defendant (Mrs Evans) was 73.

The trustees of the estate then entered into an agreement with the defendant that she could continue to live in the cottage during her lifetime as tenant at will rent-free; she undertook to keep the cottage in good condition and repair.

Subsequently, the estate sold the cottage to the claimants. The contract provided that the property was sold subject to the 'tenancy agreement'. In consequence of that provision, the claimants paid a reduced price for the cottage.

The claimants sought to eject the defendant, claiming that she was a tenant at will.

Held: The claimants' claim failed. Megaw and Stephenson LJJ decided the case on the grounds that the defendant was a tenant for life under the Settled Land Act 1925. Lord Denning MR held that the claimants took the property subject to a constructive trust for the defendant's benefit.

> LORD DENNING MR: Suppose, however, that the defendant did not have an equitable interest at the outset, nevertheless it is quite plain that she obtained one afterwards when the Tredegar Estate sold the cottage. They stipulated with the plaintiffs that they were to take the house 'subject to' the defendant's rights under the agreement. They supplied the plaintiffs with a copy of the contract: and the plaintiffs paid less because of her right to stay there. In these circumstances, this court will impose on the plaintiffs a constructive trust for her benefit: for the simple reason that it would be utterly inequitable for the plaintiffs to turn the defendant out contrary to the stipulation subject to which they took the premises. That seems to me clear from the important decision of *Bannister* v *Bannister* [1948] 2 All ER 133, which was applied by the judge, and which I gladly follow.
>
> This imposing of a constructive trust is entirely in accord with the precepts of equity. As Cardozo J once put it: 'A constructive trust is the formula through which the conscience of equity finds expression', see *Beatty* v *Guggenheim Exploration Co.* (1919) 225 NY 380, 386: or, as Lord Diplock put it quite recently in *Gissing* v *Gissing* [1971] AC 886, 905, a constructive trust is created 'whenever the trustee has so conducted himself that it would be inequitable to allow him to deny the cestui que trust a beneficial interest in the land acquired'.
>
> I know that there are some who have doubted whether a contractual licensee has any protection against a purchaser, even one who takes with full notice. We were referred in this connection to Professor Wade's article 'Licences and third parties' in (1952) 68 LQR 337, and to the judgment of Goff J in *Re Solomon, a Bankrupt, ex parte Trustee of the Bankrupt* v *Solomon* [1967] Ch 573. None of these doubts can prevail, however, when the situation gives rise to a constructive trust. Whenever the owner sells the land to a purchaser, and at the same time stipulates that he shall take it 'subject to' a contractual licence, I think it plain that a court of equity will impose on the purchaser a constructive trust in favour of the beneficiary ...
>
> In many of these cases the purchaser takes expressly 'subject to' the rights of the licensee. Obviously the purchaser then holds the land on an imputed trust for the licensee. But, even if he does not take expressly 'subject to' the rights of the licensee, he may do so impliedly. At any rate when the licensee is in actual occupation of the land, so that the purchaser must know that he is there, and of the rights which he has: see *Hodgson* v *Marks* [1971] Ch 892. Whenever the purchaser takes the land impliedly subject to the rights of the contractual licensee, a court of equity will impose a constructive trust for the beneficiary. So I still adhere to the proposition I stated in *Errington* v *Errington and Woods* [1952] 1 KB 290, 299; and elaborated in *National Provincial Bank* v *Hastings Car Mart* [1964] Ch 665, 686–9, namely, that, when the licensee is in actual occupation, neither the licensor nor anyone who claims through him can disregard the contract except a purchaser for value without notice.
>
> MEGAW LJ: In my view, Judge Bulger was right in holding that the effect was the same as the effect of the agreement considered by this court in *Bannister* v *Bannister* [1948] 2 All ER 133.

[Megaw LJ set out the facts of *Bannister* v *Bannister* (also discussed in this subsection), and continued:] The court (Scott LJ, Asquith LJ and Jenkins J) held, at p. 137:

> ... the plaintiff holds No. 30 in trust during the life of the defendant to permit the defendant to occupy the same for so long as she may desire to do so and subject thereto in trust for the plaintiff. A trust in this form has the effect of making the beneficiary a tenant for life within the meaning of the Settled Land Act 1925, and, consequently, there is very little practical difference between such a trust and a trust for life *simpliciter.*

As was said by the court, at p. 136:

> Similar words in deeds and wills have frequently been held to create a life interest determinable (apart from special considerations introduced by the Settled Land Act 1925) on the beneficiary ceasing to occupy the premises.

I confess that I have had difficulty in seeing precisely how the Settled Land Act of 1925 was applicable. But the court in *Bannister* v *Bannister* [1948] 2 All ER 133 so held, and I am certainly content, and we are probably bound, to follow that authority. I see no relevant distinction. The fact that the transaction—the creation of the trust—was there effected orally, whereas here there is an agreement in writing, surely cannot be a ground for saying that the principle is not here applicable. The fact that there is here express provision for determination by the beneficiary cannot provide a relevant distinction. The defendant in *Bannister* v *Bannister* [1948] 2 All ER 133 was free to give up occupation whenever she wished. The fact and nature of the obligations imposed upon the defendant by the agreement in the present case must tend in favour of, rather than adversely to, the creation of an interest in land, as compared with *Bannister's* case.

I realise that the application of the Settled Land Act 1925 may produce some odd consequences; but no odder than those which were inherent in the decision in *Bannister* v *Bannister* [1948] 2 All ER 133. I do not find anything in the possible, theoretical, consequences to lead me to the conclusion that *Bannister's* case should not be followed.

The plaintiffs took with express notice of the agreement which constitutes, or gives rise to, the trust. They cannot turn the defendant out of the house against her will; for that would be a breach of the trust which binds them.

If for some reason *Bannister* v *Bannister* [1948] 2 All ER 133 did not apply, so that there would then be no trust and the defendant would possibly have no 'interest in land' within the technical meaning of those words, there would none the less be a continuing contractual obligation as between the trustees and the defendant. It would then be what is sometimes called an irrevocable licence. It would be irrevocable—that is not determinable by the licensors, the trustees, without the consent of the licensee, the defendant—because it is founded on a contract. The agreement was based on consideration—the provisions made by the defendant as her side of the agreement. That irrevocable licence, that contractual right to continue in occupation, remained binding upon the trustees. They could not, and did not, free themselves from it unilaterally by selling the land to the plaintiffs. As the plaintiffs took with express notice of, and indeed expressly subject to, the agreement between the trustees and the defendant, the plaintiffs would, on ordinary principles, be guilty of the tort of interference with existing contractual rights if they were to evict the defendant. For that would be knowingly to interfere with her continuing contractual rights with a third party, the trustees. In the ordinary way, the court would intervene to prevent the plaintiffs from interfering with those rights. I should have thought that ordinary principles of equity would have operated in the same way. However, it may be that there are special technical considerations in the law relating to land which would require to be reviewed before one could confidently assert that the ordinary principles as to the protection of known contractual rights would apply. There are, for example, passages in the speech of Lord Upjohn in *National Provincial Bank* v *Hastings Car Mart* [1965] AC 1175, 1239, which indicate doubts and difficulties in this sphere. Since, in my opinion, this case is governed by *Bannister* v *Bannister* [1948] 2 All ER 133 I do not think it is necessary to pursue that topic further.

NOTES

1. Lord Denning MR started with the assertion that Mrs Evans had a contractual licence, which bound the purchasers with notice. If his reasoning were correct, then it would have been unnecessary for the Court of Appeal to consider whether Mrs Evans also had a beneficial interest, and there would have been no need for any discussion of constructive trusts at all. This line of reasoning was not very promising at the time, but looks especially unpromising in the light of the *Ashburn Anstalt* decision. Whereas in *Bannister* v *Bannister* a contractual licence may have sufficed, it seems likely that a property interest is required to protect Mrs Evans.

2. Lord Denning MR alternatively reasoned that because Mr and Mrs Binions had purchased expressly subject to the agreement, equity would impose upon their conscience, and require them to hold the property on constructive trust for Mrs Evans. The Master of the Rolls himself thought that to take *impliedly* subject to an enforceable agreement would also be enough. He also thought that a constructive trust could be imposed whenever the trustee had conducted himself in an inequitable manner.

3. The reasoning of Megaw and Stephenson LJJ was entirely different. In their view, the original agreement between the trustees and the defendant created a life tenancy. Thus, even at this stage the trustees held the property on trust for Mrs Evans for her life, thereafter for the Tredegar Estate in fee simple. The purchasers were therefore bound by an existing trust, on the ordinary principles of the equitable notice doctrine.

4. Note the alternative economic torts reasoning of Megaw LJ.

5. The constructive trust reasoning of Lord Denning MR (at any rate where the purchaser takes expressly subject to the agreement) and the economic torts reasoning of Megaw LJ were both applied, in a different context, by Browne-Wilkinson J in *Swiss Bank Corporation v Lloyds Bank* [1979] Ch 548. *Swiss Bank Corporation v Lloyds Bank* was reversed on its facts ([1982] AC 584), but no doubt was cast on Browne-Wilkinson J's views on these questions.

Ben McFarlane identifies a common 'event' underlying the imposition of constructive trusts arising on a receipt *sub conditione* of property by C from A: 'That event is the receipt by C of property subject to an undertaking that he recognise a right of B in respect of that property.' ('Constructive Trusts Arising on a Receipt of Property *Sub Conditione*' (2004) 120 *LQR* 667, p. 683.)

(viii) Trusts of mistaken payments

Chase Manhattan Bank NA v Israel-British Bank (London) Ltd [1981] Ch 105 (see Chapter 14) is a classic case of mistaken payment in which the claimant needed to establish a proprietary right in order to recover its money from the estate of an insolvent defendant. The claimant had intended to make a payment of $2 million to the defendant bank, but made the payment twice by mistake. Goulding J held that the claimant could trace the overpaid $2 million into the hands of the defendant bank, and that the defendant was a constructive trustee of the mistaken payment for B because B retained 'an equitable property in it'.

■ QUESTION

If a mistaken payment gives rise to a trust, should it be a resulting trust or a constructive trust?

(ix) Trusts of unauthorised fiduciary gains

There are authorities which state that a fiduciary holds unauthorised gains as a constructive trustee. They include: *Keech v Sandford* (1726) Sel Cas Ch 61, a case decided by Lord Chancellor King nearly 300 years ago; *Boardman v Phipps* [1967] 2 AC 46, a decision by a bare majority of the House of Lords handed down the last time England won the football World Cup; and *Attorney-General for Hong Kong v Reid* [1994] 1 AC 324, a decision of a distinguished Privy Council expressly driven by a special political concern to deter bribery.

These authorities must now be reconsidered in the light of the 2011 decision of the Court of Appeal in *Sinclair Investments (UK) Ltd v Versailles Trade Finance Ltd (In Administration)* (see, further, the discussion in the next subsection).

(x) Trusts of bribes

Bribery is a criminal offence (Bribery Act 2010), but here we are concerned with civil claims relating to bribery. In this context, a payment by X will be considered to be a bribe where it is paid secretly to the agent of a person with whom X is dealing (*Bank of Ireland* v *Jaffery* [2012] EWHC 1377 (Ch)), although it has been said that a gift can sometimes be too small to count as a bribe or incentive to conflict (*Fiona Trust & Holding Corp* v *Privalov* [2010] EWHC 3199).

Sinclair Investments (UK) Ltd v Versailles Trade Finance Ltd (In Administration)

[2011] EWCA Civ 347, Court of Appeal

Facts: The principal (the claimant company) sought a constructive trust of wrongful gains made by one of its directors when in breach of his fiduciary duty to the claimant he sold his own shares in another company at a value which had been artificially inflated as a result of misapplying the claimant's money.

Held: *AG Hong Kong* v *Reid* (also discussed in this subsection) does not alter the long line of English decisions which establishes that the beneficiary of a fiduciary's duties cannot claim a proprietary interest, but is only entitled to an equitable account, unless the asset or money was or had been beneficially the property of the beneficiary or the trustee.

NEUBERGER MR: '… there is a real case for saying that the decision in *Reid* [1994] 1 AC 324 is unsound. In cases where a fiduciary takes for himself an asset which, if he chose to take, he was under a duty to take for the beneficiary, it is easy to see why the asset should be treated as the property of the beneficiary. However, a bribe paid to a fiduciary could not possibly be said to be an asset which the fiduciary was under a duty to take for the beneficiary. There can thus be said to be a fundamental distinction between (i) a fiduciary enriching himself by depriving a Claimant of an asset and (ii) a fiduciary enriching himself by doing a wrong to the Claimant. Having said that, I can see a real policy reason in its favour (if equitable accounting is not available), but the fact that it may not accord with principle is obviously a good reason for not following it in preference to decisions of this court'. [para. 80]

Attorney-General for Hong Kong v Reid (NB: not followed by the English Court of Appeal in *Sinclair Investments (UK) Ltd* v *Versailles Trade Finance Ltd (In Administration)*)

[1994] 1 AC 324, Privy Council

Facts: Mr Reid was a senior public prosecutor in Hong Kong who accepted large sums of money in return for which he obstructed the prosecution of certain criminals. He invested the bribes in land and other investments, including a number of properties in New Zealand, and the Crown sought to claim beneficial ownership of the various tainted investments on the basis that Mr Reid had held the bribes on constructive trust.

Decision: The recipient of a bribe held it on trust for the person whose interests had been betrayed.

LORD TEMPLEMAN: Bribery is an evil practice which threatens the foundations of any civilised society. In particular, bribery of policemen and prosecutors brings the administration of justice into disrepute. Where bribes are accepted by a trustee, servant, agent or other fiduciary, loss and damage are caused to the beneficiaries, master or principal whose interests have been betrayed. The amount of loss or damage resulting from the acceptance of a bribe may or may not be quantifiable. In the present case the amount of harm caused to the administration of justice in Hong Kong by Mr Reid in return for bribes cannot be quantified.

When a bribe is offered and accepted in money or in kind, the money or property constituting the bribe belongs in law to the recipient. Money paid to the false fiduciary belongs to him. The legal estate in freehold property conveyed to the false fiduciary by way of bribe vests in him. Equity however which acts *in personam* insists that it is unconscionable for a fiduciary to obtain and retain a benefit in breach of duty. The provider of a bribe cannot recover it because he committed a criminal offence when he paid the bribe. The false fiduciary who received the bribe in breach of duty must pay and account for the bribe to the person to whom that duty was owed. In the present case, as soon as Mr Reid received a bribe in breach of the duties he owed to the Government of Hong Kong, he became a debtor in equity to the Crown for the amount of that bribe. So much is admitted. But if the bribe consists of property which increases in value or if a cash bribe is invested advantageously, the false fiduciary will receive a benefit from his breach of duty unless he is accountable not only for the original amount or value of the bribe but also for the increased value of the property representing the bribe. As soon as the bribe was received it should have been paid or transferred instanter to the person who suffered from the breach of duty. Equity considers as done that which ought to have been done. As soon as the bribe was received, whether in cash or in kind, the false fiduciary held the bribe on a constructive trust for the person injured. Two objections have been raised to this analysis. First it is said that if the fiduciary is in equity a debtor to the person injured, he cannot also be a trustee of the bribe. But there is no reason why equity should not provide two remedies, so long as they do not result in double recovery. If the property representing the bribe exceeds the original bribe in value, the fiduciary cannot retain the benefit of the increase in value which he obtained solely as a result of his breach of duty. Secondly, it is said that if the false fiduciary holds property representing the bribe in trust for the person injured, and if the false fiduciary is or becomes insolvent, the unsecured creditors of the false fiduciary will be deprived of their right to share in the proceeds of that property. But the unsecured creditors cannot be in a better position than their debtor. The authorities show that property acquired by a trustee innocently but in breach of trust and the property from time to time representing the same belong in equity to the cestui que trust and not to the trustee personally whether he is solvent or insolvent. Property acquired by a trustee as a result of a criminal breach of trust and the property from time to time representing the same must also belong in equity to his cestui que trust and not to the trustee whether he is solvent or insolvent.

When a bribe is accepted by a fiduciary in breach of his duty then he holds that bribe in trust for the person to whom the duty was owed. If the property representing the bribe decreases in value the fiduciary must pay the difference between that value and the initial amount of the bribe because he should not have accepted the bribe or incurred the risk of loss. If the property increases in value, the fiduciary is not entitled to any surplus in excess of the initial value of the bribe because he is not allowed by any means to make a profit out of a breach of duty …

It has always been assumed and asserted that the law on the subject of bribes was definitively settled by the decision of the Court of Appeal in *Lister & Co.* v *Stubbs* (1890) 45 ChD 1.

In that case the plaintiffs, Lister & Co., employed the defendant, Stubbs, as their servant to purchase goods for the firm. Stubbs, on behalf of the firm, bought goods from Varley & Co. and received from Varley & Co. bribes amounting to £5,541. The bribes were invested by Stubbs in freehold properties and investments. His masters, the firm Lister & Co., sought and failed to obtain an interlocutory injunction restraining Stubbs from disposing of these assets pending the trial of the action in which they sought inter alia £5,541 and damages. In the Court of Appeal the first judgment was given by Cotton LJ who had been party to the decision in *Metropolitan Bank* v *Heiron* (1880) 15 ChD 139. He was powerfully supported by the judgment of Lindley LJ and by the equally powerful concurrence of Bowen LJ. Cotton LJ said that the bribe could not be said to be the money of the plaintiffs (see 45 ChD 1 at 12). He seemed to be reluctant to grant an interlocutory judgment which would provide security for a debt before that debt had been established. Lindley LJ said that the relationship between the plaintiffs, Lister & Co., as masters and the defendant, Stubbs, as servant who had betrayed his trust and received a bribe:

> … is that of debtor and creditor; it is not that of trustee and cestui que trust. We are asked to hold that it is which would involve consequences which, I confess, startle me. One consequence, of course, would be that, if Stubbs were to become bankrupt, this property acquired by him with the money paid to him by Messrs Varley would be withdrawn from the mass of his creditors and be handed over bodily to Lister & Co. Can that be right? Another consequence would be that, if the appellants are right, Lister & Co. could compel Stubbs to account to them, not only for the money with interest, but for all the profit which he might have made by embarking in trade with it. Can that be right? (See 45 ChD 1 at 15.)

For the reasons which have already been advanced their Lordships would respectfully answer both these questions in the affirmative. If a trustee mistakenly invests moneys which he ought to pay over to his cestui que trust and then becomes bankrupt, the moneys together with any profit which has accrued from the investment are withdrawn from the unsecured creditors as soon as the mistake is discovered. *A fortiori*, if a trustee commits a crime by accepting a bribe which he ought to pay over to his *cestui que trust*, the bribe and any profit made therefrom should be withdrawn from the unsecured creditors as soon as the crime is discovered.

The decision in *Lister & Co.* v *Stubbs* is not consistent with the principles that a fiduciary must not be allowed to benefit from his own breach of duty, that the fiduciary should account for the bribe as soon as he receives it and that equity regards as done that which ought to be done. From these principles it would appear to follow that the bribe and the property from time to time representing the bribe are held on a constructive trust for the person injured. A fiduciary remains personally liable for the amount of the bribe if, in the event, the value of the property then recovered by the injured person proved to be less than that amount.

NOTE: *Sinclair* has rejected the reasoning of the Privy Council in *Reid* and returned English law to the approach favoured in *Lister*. *Sinclair* has since been followed by the Court of Appeal (e.g. *FHR European Ventures LLP* v *Mankarious* [2013] EWCA Civ 17), but contrast the position in Australia, which still favours proprietary awards of the sort approved in *Reid* (e.g. *Grimaldi* v *Chameleon Mining NL (No. 2)* [2012] FCAFC 6).

QUESTION

'Why should the principal take a windfall in priority to those to whom the fiduciary owes purchased obligations?' (J. W. Harris, *Property and Justice* (Oxford: Clarendon Press, 1996.)

(xi) Trusts of property inherited by a killer from his victim

See the 'forfeiture rule' in Chapter 6.

(xii) Strangers liable 'as if' they were constructive trustees

See Chapter 15.

■ QUESTIONS

1. Does a constructive trust arise flexibly by way of remedy or institutionally according to established preconditions?
2. Is the constructive trust a coherent concept or a historical miscellany of unrelated legal events?

SECTION 2: INFORMAL TRUSTS OF LAND

English law does not presume 'community of ownership' of land even when two adults have lived together in a stable relationship for a long period of time. Even as between husband and wife there is no presumption of communal ownership of the matrimonial home. If one 'newly wed' moves into a home held solely in the name of the other 'newly wed', the married couple may regard the house as jointly theirs but the law does not consider the newcomer to have acquired any interest in the house by the mere fact of marriage. If the couple divorce or are judicially separated, the court has very wide powers under the Matrimonial Causes Act 1973 to allocate the property of the parties to the marriage as it thinks fit, provided certain specified matters (child welfare being paramount) are taken into account, but even this might not lead to a straightforward declaration that the matrimonial home is owned equally by husband and wife. In the case of unmarried cohabitees, who represent an increasingly large proportion of all cohabiting couples, the court has no discretion equivalent to that conferred by the Matrimonial Causes Act 1973 (some suggest it should) so, on the breakdown of a stable non-marital relationship, ownership of the shared home is determined in strict accordance with property law, with the exception of a limited power to allocate capital for the benefit of children of the relationship. If married or unmarried cohabitees want the legal under-standing of their ownership to reflect their own understanding it is incumbent upon them to take steps to formalise their ownership position. The best way to do this is for the party or parties with legal title to the land to declare an express trust of the land, making clear who is to have a beneficial interest in the land and in what proportions beneficial ownership is to be divided. The law's ideal is, however, unrealistic. It is hard to imagine cohabitees, and perhaps least of all newly weds, choosing to regularise their property ownership by means of an express trust. The point at which a relationship is strong enough to contemplate sharing property communally is the very point at which the parties to the relationship are least likely to feel the need to regularise their property ownership by means of a formal piece of paper. Judicial recognition of informal trusts of land therefore becomes of paramount importance.

NOTE: Before the Married Women's Property Act 1882, the common law allowed a married woman very little freedom to own her own property, although to a limited extent property could be held for her on trust (see Gardner, *An Introduction to the Law of Trusts* (Clarendon Law Series, 1990), p. 30). Extending the trend started by the Married Women's Property Act 1870, the Married Women's Property Act 1882 largely abolished restrictions on the right of a married woman to own property. The effect of s.1 of the 1882 Act, coupled with the Law Reform (Married Women and Tortfeasors) Act 1935, s.2 and the Married Women (Restraint upon Anticipation) Act 1949, s.1 was entirely to remove any remaining fetters on her separate ownership of property.

Pettitt v *Pettitt*

[1970] AC 777, House of Lords

Facts: A cottage was purchased in the name of the wife, the wife providing the entirety of the purchase money. The husband significantly improved the property, using his own labour and money. He claimed an equitable interest, one of his arguments being that the Married Women's Property Act 1882, s.1 gave the courts a discretion to award him an interest in these circumstances.

Held: The husband had no interest in the cottage.

LORD REID: Many of the cases have been brought by virtue of the provisions of section 17 of the Married Women's Property Act, 1882. That is a long and complicated section: the relevant part is as follows:

> In any question between husband and wife as to the title to or possession of property, either party ... may apply by summons or otherwise in a summary way to any judge of the High Court of Justice ... and the judge ... may make such order with respect to the property in dispute ... as he thinks fit.

The main dispute has been as to the meaning of the latter words authorising the judge (including a county court judge and now a registrar) to make such order with respect to the property in dispute as he thinks fit. These are words normally used to confer a discretion on the court: where the discretion is limited, the limitations are generally expressed: but here no limitation is expressed. So it has been said that here these words confer on the court an unfettered discretion to override existing rights in the property and to dispose of it in whatever manner the judge may think to be just and equitable in the whole circumstances of the case. On the other hand it has been said that these words do not entitle the court to disregard any existing property right, but merely confer a power to regulate possession or the exercise of property rights, or, more narrowly, merely confer a power to exercise in proceedings under section 17 any discretion with regard to the property in dispute which has already been conferred by some other enactment. And other intermediate views have also been expressed.

I would approach the question in this way. The meaning of the section cannot have altered since it was passed in 1882. At that time the certainty and security of rights of property were still generally regarded as of paramount importance and I find it incredible that any Parliament of that era could have intended to put a husband's property at the hazard of the unfettered discretion of a judge (including a county court judge) if the wife raised a dispute about it. Moreover, this discretion, if it exists, can only be exercised in proceedings under section 17: the same dispute could arise in other forms of action; and I find it even more incredible that it could have been intended that such a discretion should be given to a judge in summary proceedings but denied to the judge if the proceedings were of the ordinary character. So are the words so unequivocal that we are forced to give them a meaning which cannot have been intended? I do not think so. It is perfectly possible to construe the words as having a much more restricted meaning and in my judgment they should be so construed. I do not think that a judge has any more right to disregard property rights in section 17 proceedings than he has in any other form of proceedings.

It was argued that the present case could be decided by applying the presumption regarding advancement. It was said that if a husband spends money on improving his wife's property, then, in the absence of evidence to the contrary, this must be regarded as a gift to the wife. I do not know how this presumption first arose, but it would seem that the judges who first gave effect to it must have thought either that husbands so commonly intended to make gifts in the circumstances in which the presumption arises that it was proper to assume this where there was no evidence, or that wives' economic dependence on their husbands made it necessary as a matter of public policy to give them this advantage. I can see no other reasonable basis for the presumption. These considerations have largely lost their force under present conditions, and, unless the law has lost all flexibility so that the courts can no longer adapt it to changing conditions, the strength of the presumption must have been much diminished. I do not think that it would be proper to apply it to the circumstances of the present case.

And there is another matter I must deal with before coming to the crucial questions. There are at least suggestions in some cases that property rights may be different before and after the break-up of a marriage. I can see no ground for this. There are other occasions for disputes as to rights of property besides break-up of the marriage, and it appears to me that the property rights of the spouses must be capable of determination immediately after the property has been paid for or the improvements carried out and must in the absence of subsequent agreements or transactions remain the same. There are also suggestions that agreements or arrangements made by the spouses may be rendered inoperative by, or may have a different effect after, the breakdown of the marriage. I suppose that an agreement could take an unusual form, but as a general rule I would think that most improbable. The question does not arise in the present case.

It can now come to the main question of how the law does or should deal with cases where the title to property is in one of the spouses and contributions towards its purchase-price have been made or subsequent improvements have been provided by the other. As regards contributions, the traditional view is that, in the absence of evidence to the contrary effect, a contributor to the purchase-price will acquire a beneficial interest in the property: but as regards improvements made by a person who is not the legal owner, after the property has been acquired, that person will not, in the absence of agreement, acquire any interest in the property or have any claim against the owner.

Let me suppose that a house which requires extensive renovation or improvement is acquired by one spouse putting down the deposit and taking the title. Instalments of the purchase-price and the cost of the improvements will then have to be paid. The other spouse may be willing and able to help, and as a pure matter of convenience, without any thought of legal consequences and without making any agreement, one spouse may pay the instalments of the purchase price and the other may pay for the improvements. On this view the legal position will be different according as the contributing spouse pays the instalments or the cost of the improvements. Payment of the instalments will obtain for him or her a proprietary interest in the house, but payment of the cost of the improvements will not give him or her either an interest in the house or a claim against the other spouse. That seems to me to be entirely unsatisfactory. It is true that the court will do its best to spell out an agreement to prevent this, but I shall return to that matter.

Then go a step farther. There is no question of making any improvements, but the wife who wants to contribute pays all the household bills thus enabling the husband who holds the title to the house to pay the instalments. That wife will have no claim of any kind. And go a step farther still. The wife may not be able to make any financial contribution but by good management and co-operation she may make it possible for the husband to pay the instalments regularly. Again on this view she will have no claim. Opinions may differ as to whether in one or both of these cases she should have any claim.

Views have been expressed that the law does give a claim to the contributing spouse in the first, or the first and second, or in all the three cases which I have outlined. But there has been no unanimity as to the legal basis or the legal nature of such claims. I think that broadly there are two views. One is that you ask what reasonable people in the shoes of the spouses would have agreed if they had directed their minds to the question of what claim the contributing spouse ought to have. The other is that all property used for family purposes must, in the absence of agreement, be regarded as the joint property of the spouses or as belonging to them in equal shares, no matter which spouse bought or inherited it or contributed to its acquisition.

We must first have in mind or decide how far it is proper for the courts to go in adapting or adding to existing law. Whatever views may have prevailed in the last century, I think that it is now widely recognised that it is proper for the courts in appropriate cases to develop or adapt existing rules of the common law to meet new conditions. I say in appropriate cases because I think we ought to recognise a difference between cases where we are dealing with 'lawyer's law' and cases where we are dealing with matters which directly affect the lives and interests of large sections of the community and which raise issues which are the subject of public controversy and on which laymen are as well able to decide as are lawyers. On such matters it is not for the courts to proceed on their view of public policy for that would be to encroach on the province of Parliament.

I would therefore refuse to consider whether property belonging to either spouse ought to be regarded as family property for that would be introducing a new conception into English law and not merely developing existing principles. There are systems of law which recognise joint family property or communio bonorum. I am not sure that those principles are very highly regarded in countries where they are in force, but in any case it would be going far beyond the functions of the court to attempt to give effect to them here.

But it is, I think, proper to consider whether, without departing from the principles of the common law, we can give effect to the view that, even where there was in fact no agreement, we can ask what the spouses, or reasonable people in their shoes, would have agreed if they had directed their minds to the question of what rights should accrue to the spouse who has contributed to the acquisition or improvement of property owned by the other spouse. There is already a presumption which operates in the absence of evidence as regards money contributed by one spouse towards the acquisition of property by the other spouse. So why should there not be a similar presumption where one spouse has contributed to the improvement of the property of the other? I do not think that it is a very convincing argument to say that, if a stranger makes improvements on the property of another without any agreement or any request by that other that he should do so, he acquires no right. The improvement is made for the common enjoyment of both spouses during the marriage. It would no doubt be different if the one spouse makes the improvement while the other spouse who owns the property is absent and without his or her knowledge or consent. But if the spouse who owns the property acquiesces in the other making the improvement in circumstances where it is reasonable to suppose that they would have agreed to some right being acquired if they had thought about the legal position, I can see nothing contrary to ordinary legal principles in holding that the spouse who makes the improvement has acquired such a right.

Some reference was made to the doctrine of unjust enrichment. I do not think that that helps. The term has been applied to cases where a person who has paid money sues for its return. But there does not appear to be any English case of the doctrine being applied where one person has improved the property of another. And in any case it would only result in a money claim whereas what a spouse who makes an improvement is seeking is generally a beneficial interest in the property which has been improved.

...

In whatever way the general question as to improvements is decided I think that the claim in the present case must fail for two reasons. These improvements are nearly all of an ephemeral character. Redecoration will only last for a few years and it would be unreasonable that a spouse should obtain a permanent interest in the house in return for making improvements of this character ...

LORD UPJOHN: My Lords, the facts of this case depend not upon the acquisition of property but upon the expenditure of money and labour by the husband in the way of improvement upon the property of the wife which admittedly is her own beneficial property. Upon this it is quite clearly established that by the law of England the expenditure of money by A upon the property of B stands in quite a different category from the acquisition of property by A and B.

It has been well settled in your Lordships' House (*Ramsden* v *Dyson* (1865) LR 1 HL 129) that if A expends money on the property of B, prima facie he has no claim on such property. And this, as Sir William Grant MR, held as long ago as 1810 in *Campion* v *Cotton* (1810) 17 Ves 263 is equally applicable as between husband and wife. If by reason of estoppel or because the expenditure would be rewarded, the person expending the money may have some claim for monetary reimbursement in a purely monetary sense from the owner or even, if explicitly promised to him by the owner, an interest in the land (see *Plimmer* v *Wellington Corpn.* (1884) 9 App Cas 699). But the respondent's claim here is to a share of the property and his money claim in his plaint is only a qualification of that. Plainly, in the absence of agreement with his wife (and none is suggested) he could have no monetary claim against her and no estoppel or mistake is suggested so, in my opinion, he can have no charge upon or interest in the wife's property.

It may be that as counsel for the Queen's Proctor quite rightly pointed out this case could be decided somewhat on the *Balfour* v *Balfour* [1919] 2 KB 571 principle, that the nature of the work done was of the type done by husband and wife upon the matrimonial home without giving the worker a legal interest in it. See *Button* v *Button* [1968] 1 WLR 457. But I prefer to decide this appeal upon the wider ground that in the absence of agreement, and there being no question of any estoppel, one spouse who does work or expends money upon the property of the other has no claim whatever upon the property of the other. *Jansen* v *Jansen* [1965] P 478 was a very good example of that type of case. The husband, putting it briefly, spent his short married life making very substantial improvements upon the properties of the wife which greatly increased their value as reflected in their sale price. The wife recognised that as between husband and wife he should receive some benefit and instructed her solicitor to draw up an agreement whereby he was to receive monetary recompense from the proceeds of sale of one of the properties he had improved when such sale was effected. The husband refused to accept this so the parties in fact and in law never did agree. In those circumstances it seems to me clear that the husband had no claim against the wife even personally and certainly no claim against the property itself either by way of charge or by way of a share in the property.

MATRIMONIAL PROCEEDINGS AND PROPERTY ACT 1970

37. Contributions by spouse in money or money's worth to the improvement of property

It is hereby declared that where a husband or wife contributes in money or money's worth to the improvement of real or personal property in which or in the proceeds of sale of which either or both of them has or have a beneficial interest, the husband or wife so contributing shall, if the contribution is of a substantial nature and subject to any agreement between them to the contrary express or implied, be treated as having then acquired by virtue of his or her contribution a share or an enlarged share, as the case may be, in that beneficial interest of such an extent as may have been agreed or, in default of such agreement, as may seem in all the circumstances just to any court before which the question of the existence or extent of the beneficial interest of the husband or wife arises (whether in proceedings before them or in any other proceedings).

NOTE: This section applies only to husbands, wives, and—by virtue of Law Reform (Miscellaneous Provisions) Act 1970, s.2(1)—fiancé(e)s.

Gissing v *Gissing*

[1971] AC 886, House of Lords

Facts: Mrs Gissing had been married to Mr Gissing for 16 years, and had paid a substantial sum towards furniture and the laying of a lawn, but the house had been conveyed into the name of Mr Gissing alone, and Mrs Gissing had made no direct contributions towards its purchase. On their divorce, she claimed a beneficial interest.

Held: The House of Lords held that she had no interest.

LORD DIPLOCK: Any claim to a beneficial interest in land by a person, whether spouse or stranger, in whom the legal estate in the land is not vested must be based upon the proposition that the person in whom the legal estate is vested holds it as trustee upon trust to give effect to the beneficial interest of the claimant as cestui que trust. The legal principles applicable to the claim are those of the English law of trusts and in particular, in the kind of dispute between spouses that comes before the courts, the law relating to the creation and operation of 'resulting, implied or constructive trusts.' Where the trust is expressly declared in the instrument by which the legal estate is transferred to the trustee or by a written declaration of trust by the trustee, the court must give effect to it. But to constitute a valid declaration of trust by way of gift of a beneficial interest in land to a cestui que trust the declaration is required by section 53(1) of the Law of Property Act, 1925, to be in writing. If it is not in writing it can only take effect as a resulting, implied or constructive trust to which that section has no application.

A resulting, implied or constructive trust—and it is unnecessary for present purposes to distinguish between these three classes of trust—is created by a transaction between the trustee and the cestui que trust in connection with the acquisition by the trustee of a legal estate in land, whenever the trustee has so conducted himself that it would be inequitable to allow him to deny to the cestui que trust a beneficial interest in the land acquired. And he will be held so to have conducted himself if by his words or conduct he has induced the cestui que trust to act to his own detriment in the reasonable belief that by so acting he was acquiring a beneficial interest in the land.

This is why it has been repeatedly said in the context of disputes between spouses as to their respective beneficial interests in the matrimonial home, that if at the time of its acquisition and transfer of the legal estate into the name of one or other of them an express agreement has been made between them as to the way in which the beneficial interest shall be held, the court will give effect to it—notwithstanding the absence of any written declaration of trust. Strictly speaking this states the principle too widely, for if the agreement did not provide for anything to be done by the spouse in whom the legal estate was not to be vested, it would be a merely voluntary declaration of trust and unenforceable for want of writing. But in the express oral agreements contemplated by these dicta it has been assumed *sub silentio* that they provide for the spouse in whom the legal estate in the matrimonial home is not vested to do something to facilitate its acquisition, by contributing to the purchase price or to the deposit or the mortgage instalments when it is purchased upon mortgage or to make some other material sacrifice by way of contribution to or economy in the general family expenditure. What the court gives effect to is the trust resulting or implied from the common intention expressed in the oral agreement between the spouses that if each acts in the manner provided for in the agreement the beneficial interests in the matrimonial home shall be held as they have agreed.

An express agreement between spouses as to their respective beneficial interests in land conveyed into the name of one of them obviates the need for showing that the conduct of the spouse into whose name the land was conveyed was intended to induce the other spouse to act to his or her detriment upon the faith of the promise of a specified beneficial interest in the land and that the other spouse so acted with the intention of acquiring that beneficial interest. The agreement itself discloses the common intention required to create a resulting, implied or constructive trust.

But parties to a transaction in connection with the acquisition of land may well have formed a common intention that the beneficial interest in the land shall be vested in them jointly without having used express words to communicate this intention to one another; or their recollections of the words used may be imperfect or conflicting by the time any dispute arises. In such a case—a common one where the parties are spouses whose marriage has broken down—it may be possible to infer their common intention from their conduct.

As in so many branches of English law in which legal rights and obligations depend upon the intentions of the parties to a transaction, the relevant intention of each party is the intention which was reasonably understood by the other party to be manifested by that party's words or conduct notwithstanding that he did not consciously formulate that intention in his own mind or even acted with some different intention which he did not communicate to the other party. On the other hand, he is not bound by any inference which the other party draws as to his intention unless that inference is one which can reasonably be drawn from his words or conduct. It is in this sense that in the branch of English law relating to constructive, implied or resulting trusts effect is given to the inferences as to the intention of parties to a transaction which a reasonable man would draw from their words or conduct and not to any subjective intention or absence of intention which was not made manifest at the time of the transaction itself. It is for the court to determine what those inferences are.

In drawing such an inference, what spouses said and did which led up to the acquisition of a matrimonial home and what they said and did while the acquisition was being carried through is on a different footing from what they said and did after the acquisition was completed. Unless it is alleged that there was some subsequent fresh agreement, acted upon by the parties, to vary the original beneficial interests created when the matrimonial home was acquired, what they said and did after the acquisition was completed is relevant if it is explicable only upon the basis of their having manifested to one another at the time of the acquisition some particular common intention as to how the beneficial interests should be held. But it would in my view be unreasonably legalistic to treat the relevant transaction involved in the acquisition of a matrimonial home as restricted to the actual conveyance of the fee simple into the name of one or other spouse. Their common intention is more likely to have been concerned with the economic realities of the transaction than with the unfamiliar technicalities of the English law of legal and equitable interests in land. The economic reality which lies behind the conveyance of the fee simple to a purchaser in return for a purchase price the greater part of which is advanced to the purchaser upon a mortgage repayable by instalments over a number of years, is that the new freeholder is purchasing the matrimonial home upon credit and that the purchase price is represented by the instalments by which the mortgage is repaid in addition to the initial payment in cash. The conduct of the spouses in relation to the payment of the mortgage instalments may be no less relevant to their common intention as to the beneficial interests in a matrimonial home acquired in this way than their conduct in relation to the payment of the cash deposit.

It is this feature of the transaction by means of which most matrimonial homes have been acquired in recent years that makes difficult the task of the court in inferring from the conduct of the spouses a common intention as to how the beneficial interest in it should be held. Each case must depend upon its own facts but there are a number of factual situations which often recur in the cases.

Where a matrimonial home has been purchased outright without the aid of an advance on mortgage it is not difficult to ascertain what part, if any, of the purchase price has been provided by each spouse. If the land is conveyed into the name of a spouse who has not provided the whole of the purchase price, the sum contributed by the other spouse may be explicable as having been intended by both of them either as a gift or as a loan of money to the spouse to whom the land is conveyed or as consideration for a share in the beneficial interest in the land. In a dispute between living spouses the evidence will probably point to one of these explanations as being more probable than the others, but if the rest of the evidence is neutral the prima facie inference is that their common intention was that the contributing spouse should acquire a share in the beneficial interest in the land in the same proportion as the sum contributed bore to the total purchase price. This prima facie inference is more easily rebutted in favour of a gift where the land is conveyed into the name of the wife: but as I understand the speeches in *Pettitt* v *Pettitt* four of the members of your Lordships' House who were parties to that decision took the view that even if the 'presumption of advancement' as between husband and wife still survived today, it could seldom have any decisive part to play in disputes between living spouses in which some evidence would be available in addition to the mere fact that the husband had provided part of the purchase price of property conveyed into the name of the wife.

Similarly when a matrimonial home is not purchased outright but partly out of moneys advanced on mortgage repayable by instalments, and the land is conveyed into the name of the husband alone, the fact that the wife made a cash contribution to the deposit and legal charges not borrowed on mortgage gives rise, in the absence of evidence which makes some other explanation more probable, to the inference that their common intention was that she should share in the beneficial interest in the land conveyed. But it would not be reasonable to infer a common intention as to what her share should be without taking account also of the sources from which the mortgage instalments were provided. If the wife also makes a substantial direct contribution to the mortgage instalments out of her own earnings or unearned income this would be prima facie inconsistent with a common intention that her share in the beneficial interest should be determined by the proportion which her original cash contribution bore either to the total amount of the deposit and legal charges or to the full purchase price. The more likely inference is that her contributions to the mortgage instalments were intended by the spouses to have some effect upon her share.

Where there has been an initial contribution by the wife to the cash deposit and legal charges which points to a common intention at the time of the conveyance that she should have a beneficial interest in the land conveyed to her husband, it would be unrealistic to regard the wife's subsequent contributions to the mortgage instalments as without significance unless she pays them directly herself. It may be no more than a matter of convenience which spouse pays particular household accounts, particularly when both are earning, and if the wife goes out to work and devotes part of her earnings or uses her private income to meet joint expenses of the household which would otherwise be met by the husband, so as to enable him to pay the mortgage instalments out of his moneys this would be consistent with and might be corroborative of an original common intention that she should share in the beneficial interest in the matrimonial home and that her payments of other household expenses were intended by both spouses to be treated as including a contribution by the wife to the purchase price of the matrimonial home.

Even where there has been no initial contribution by the wife to the cash deposit and legal charges but she makes a regular and substantial direct contribution to the mortgage instalments it may be reasonable to infer a common intention of the spouses from the outset that she should share in the beneficial interest or to infer a fresh agreement reached after the original conveyance that she should acquire a share. But it is unlikely that the mere fact that the wife made direct contributions to the mortgage instalments would be the only evidence available to assist the court in ascertaining the common intention of the spouses.

Where in any of the circumstances described above contributions, direct or indirect, have been made to the mortgage instalments by the spouse into whose name the matrimonial home has not been conveyed, and the court can infer from their conduct a common intention that the contributing spouse should be entitled to *some* beneficial interest in the matrimonial home, what effect is to be given to that intention if there is no evidence that they in fact reached any express agreement as to what the respective share of each spouse should be?

I take it to be clear that if the court is satisfied that it was the common intention of both spouses that the contributing wife should have a share in the beneficial interest and that her contributions were made upon this understanding, the court in the exercise of its equitable jurisdiction would not permit the husband in whom the legal estate was vested and who had accepted the benefit of the contributions to take the whole beneficial interest merely because at the time the wife made her contributions there had been no express agreement as to how her share in it was to be quantified.

In such a case the court must first do its best to discover from the conduct of the spouses whether any inference can reasonably be drawn as to the probable common understanding about the amount of the share of the contributing spouse upon which each must have acted in doing what each did, even though that understanding was never expressly stated by one spouse to the other or even consciously formulated in words by either of them independently. It is only if no such inference can be drawn that the court is driven to apply as a rule of law, and not as an inference of fact, the maxim 'equality is equity,' and to hold that the beneficial interest belongs to the spouses in equal shares.

The same result however may often be reached as an inference of fact. The instalments of a mortgage to a building society are generally repayable over a period of many years. During that period, as both must be aware, the ability of each spouse to contribute to the instalments out of their separate earnings is likely to alter, particularly in the case of the wife if any children are born of the marriage. If the contribution of the wife in the early part of the period of repayment is substantial but is not an identifiable and uniform proportion of each instalment, because her contributions are indirect or, if direct, are made irregularly, it may well be a reasonable inference that their common intention at the time of acquisition of the matrimonial home was that the beneficial interest should be held by them in equal shares and that each should contribute to the cost of its acquisition whatever amounts each could afford in the varying exigencies of family life to be expected during the period of repayment. In the social conditions of today this would be a natural enough common intention of a young couple who were both earning when the house was acquired but who contemplated having children whose birth and rearing in their infancy would necessarily affect the future earning capacity of the wife.

The relative size of their respective contributions to the instalments in the early part of the period of repayment, or later if a subsequent reduction in the wife's contribution is not to be accounted for by a reduction in her earnings due to motherhood or some other cause from which the husband benefits as well, may make it a more probable inference that the wife's share in the beneficial interest was intended to be in some proportion other than one-half. And there is nothing inherently improbable in their acting on the understanding that the wife should be entitled to a share which was not to be quantified immediately upon the acquisition of the home but should be left to be determined when the mortgage was repaid or the property disposed of, on the basis of what would be fair having regard to the total contributions, direct or indirect, which each spouse had made by that date. Where this was the most likely inference from their conduct it would be for the court to give effect to that common intention of the parties by determining what in all the circumstances was a fair share.

Difficult as they are to solve, however, these problems as to the amount of the share of a spouse in the beneficial interest in a matrimonial home where the legal estate is vested solely in the other spouse, only arise in cases where the court is satisfied by the words or conduct of the parties that it was their common intention that the beneficial interest was not to belong solely to the spouse in whom the legal estate was vested but was to be shared between them in some proportion or other.

Where the wife has made no initial contribution to the cash deposit and legal charges and no direct contribution to the mortgage instalments nor any adjustment to her contribution to other expenses of the household which it can be inferred was referable to the acquisition of the house, there is in the absence of evidence of an express agreement between the parties no material to justify the court in inferring that it was the common intention of the parties that she should have any beneficial interest in a matrimonial home conveyed into the sole name of the husband, merely because she continued to contribute out of her own earnings or private income to other expenses of the household. For such conduct is no less consistent with a common intention to share the day-to-day expenses of the household, while each spouse retains a separate interest in capital assets acquired with their own moneys or obtained by inheritance or gift. There is nothing here to rebut the prima facie inference that a purchaser of land who pays the purchase price and takes a conveyance and grants a mortgage in his own name intends to acquire the sole beneficial interest as well as the legal estate: and the difficult question of the quantum of the wife's share does not arise.

In the instant appeal the matrimonial home was purchased in 1951 for £2,695 and conveyed into the sole name of the husband. The parties had by then been married for some 16 years and both were in employment with the same firm, the husband earning £1,000 and the wife £500 per annum. The purchase price was raised as to £2,150 on mortgage repayable by instalments, as to £500 by a loan to the husband from his employers, and as to the balance of £45 and the legal charges was paid by the husband out of his own moneys. The wife made no direct contribution to the initial deposit or legal charges, nor to the repayment of the loan of £500 nor to the mortgage instalments. She continued earning at the rate of £500 per annum until the marriage broke down in 1961. During this period the husband's salary increased to £3,000 per annum. The husband repaid the loan of £500, and paid the mortgage instalments. He also paid the outgoings on the house, gave to his wife a housekeeping allowance of £8 to £10 a week out of which she paid the running expenses of the household and he paid for holidays. The only contribution which the wife made out of her earnings to the household expenses was that she paid for her own clothes and those of the son of the marriage and for some extras. No change in this arrangement was made when the house was acquired. Each spouse had a separate banking account, the wife's in the Post Office Savings Bank, and each made savings out of their respective earnings. There was no joint bank account and there were no joint savings. There was no express agreement at the time of the purchase or thereafter as to how the beneficial interest in the house should be held. The learned judge was prepared to accept that after the marriage had broken down the husband said to the wife: 'Don't worry about the house—it's yours,' but this has not been relied upon, at any rate in your Lordships' House, as an acknowledgment of a pre-existing agreement on which the wife had acted to her detriment so as to give rise to a resulting, implied or constructive trust, nor can it be relied upon as an express declaration of trust as it was oral only.

On what then is the wife's claim based? In 1951 when the house was purchased she spent about £190 on buying furniture and a cooker and refrigerator for it. She also paid about £30 for improving the lawn. As furniture and household durables are depreciating assets whereas houses have turned out to be appreciating assets it may be that she would have been wise to have devoted her savings to acquiring an interest in the freehold; but this may not have been so apparent in 1951 as it has now become. The court is not entitled to infer a common intention to this effect from the mere fact that she provided chattels for joint use in the new matrimonial home; and there is nothing else in the conduct of the parties at the time of the purchase or thereafter which supports such an inference. There is no suggestion that the wife's efforts or her earnings made it possible for the husband to raise the initial loan or the mortgage or that her relieving her husband from the expense of buying clothing for herself and for their son was undertaken in order to enable him the better to meet the mortgage instalments or to repay the loan. The picture presented by the evidence is one of husband and wife retaining their separate proprietary interests in property whether real or personal purchased with their separate savings and is inconsistent with any common intention at the time of the purchase of the matrimonial home that the wife, who neither then nor thereafter contributed anything to its purchase price or assumed any liability for it, should nevertheless be entitled to a beneficial interest in it.

Both Buckley J and Edmund Davies LJ in his dissenting judgment in the Court of Appeal felt unable on this evidence to draw an inference that there was any common intention that the wife should have any beneficial interest in the house. I think that they were right. Like them I, too, come to this conclusion with regret, because it may well be that had husband and wife discussed the matter in 1951 when the house was bought he would have been willing for her to have a share in it if she wanted to. But this is speculation, and if such an arrangement had been made between them there might well have also been a different allocation of the house-hold expenses between them in the ensuing years ...

NOTES
1. The distinction drawn in the above passage between express agreement and inferred intention is essentially the same as that drawn by Lord Bridge in *Lloyds Bank* v *Rosset* (also discussed in this section).
2. The interests of the parties were determined on the basis of their inferred intentions at the time of acquisition of the property, and not by their subsequent conduct. In the absence of express agreement, only conduct relevant to the acquisition of the property will generally be relevant.

3. Lord Diplock seems to equate initial direct contributions to purchase price (by way of deposit, say) to contributions by way of mortgage instalments, but the former is preferable in practice because the payment of mortgage instalments can be ambiguous in the absence of an agreement expressly relating to that type of payment. Payment of mortgage instalments could, for instance, be construed to be merely a payment made instead of rent. (See *Barrett* v *Barrett* [2008] EWHC 1061 (Ch) and *Carlton* v *Goodman* [2002] EWCA Civ 545, [2002] 2 FLR 259.)

4. The fact that the parties were married made no difference. The following legislation was a reaction to the decision in *Gissing* v *Gissing*.

MATRIMONIAL CAUSES ACT 1973 (AS AMENDED)

PART II FINANCIAL RELIEF FOR PARTIES TO MARRIAGE AND CHILDREN OF FAMILY

24. Property adjustment orders in connection with divorce proceedings, etc.

(1)   On granting a decree of divorce, a decree of nullity of marriage or a decree of judicial separation or at any time thereafter (whether, in the case of a decree of divorce or of nullity of marriage, before or after the decree is made absolute), the court may make any one or more of the following orders, that is to say—

(a) an order that a party to the marriage shall transfer to the other party, to any child of the family or to such person as may be specified in the order for the benefit of such a child such property as may be so specified, being property to which the first-mentioned party is entitled, either in possession or reversion;

(b) an order that a settlement of such property as may be so specified, being property to which a party to the marriage is so entitled, be made to the satisfaction of the court for the benefit of the other party to the marriage and of the children of the family or either or any of them;

(c) an order varying for the benefit of the parties to the marriage and of the children of the family or either or any of them any ante-nuptial or post-nuptial settlement (including such a settlement made by will or codicil) made on the parties to the marriage, other than one in the form of a pension arrangement ...;

(d) an order extinguishing or reducing the interest of either of the parties to the marriage under any such settlement, other than one in the form of a pension arrangement ...;

subject, however, in the case of an order under paragraph (a) above, to the restrictions imposed by section 29(1) and (3) below on the making of orders for a transfer of property in favour of children who have attained the age of eighteen.

(2)   The court may make an order under subsection (1)(c) above notwithstanding that there are no children of the family.

(3)   Without prejudice to the power to give a direction under section 30 below for the settlement of an instrument by conveyancing counsel, where an order is made under this section on or after granting a decree of divorce or nullity of marriage, neither the order nor any settlement made in pursuance of the order shall take effect unless the decree has been made absolute.

24A. Orders for sale of property

(1)   Where the court makes under section 23 or 24 of this Act a secured periodical payments order, an order for the payment of a lump sum or a property adjustment order, then, on making that order or at any time thereafter, the court may make a further order for the sale of such property as may be specified in the order, being property in which or in the proceeds of sale of which either or both of the parties to the marriage has or have a beneficial interest, either in possession or reversion.

(2)   Any order made under subsection (1) above may contain such consequential or supplementary provisions as the court thinks fit and, without prejudice to the generality of the foregoing provision, may include—

(a) provision requiring the making of a payment out of the proceeds of sale of the property to which the order relates, and

(b) provision requiring any such property to be offered for sale to a person, or class of persons, specified in the order.

(3) Where an order is made under subsection (1) above on or after the grant of a decree of divorce or nullity of marriage, the order shall not take effect unless the decree has been made absolute.

(4) Where an order is made under subsection (1) above, the court may direct that the order, or such provision thereof as the court may specify, shall not take effect until the occurrence of an event specified by the court or the expiration of a period so specified.

(5) Where an order under subsection (1) above contains a provision requiring the proceeds of sale of the property to which the order relates to be used to secure periodical payments to a party to the marriage, the order shall cease to have effect on the death or re-marriage of, or formation of a civil partnership by, that person.

(6) Where a party to a marriage has a beneficial interest in any property, or in the proceeds of sale thereof, and some other person who is not a party to the marriage also has a beneficial interest in that property or in the proceeds of sale thereof, then, before deciding whether to make an order under this section in relation to that property, it shall be the duty of the court to give that other person an opportunity to make representations with respect to the order; and any representations made by that other person shall be included among the circumstances to which the court is required to have regard under section 25(1) below...;

25. Matters to which court is to have regard in deciding how to exercise its powers under ss 23, 24 and 24A

(1) It shall be the duty of the court in deciding whether to exercise its powers under any of sections 22A to 24BB above and, if so, in what manner, to have regard to all the circumstances of the case, first consideration being given to the welfare while a minor of any child of the family who has not attained the age of eighteen.

(2) As regards the exercise of the powers of the court under section 23(1)(a), (b) or (c), [section 22A or 23 above] to make a financial provision order in favour of a party to a marriage or the exercise of its powers under section 23A, 24, 24A or 24B, 24B or 24BB above in relation to a party to the marriage, the court shall in particular have regard to the following matters—

(a) the income, earning capacity, property and other financial resources which each of the parties to the marriage has or is likely to have in the foreseeable future, including in the case of earning capacity any increase in that capacity which it would in the opinion of the court be reasonable to expect a party to the marriage to take steps to acquire;

(b) the financial needs, obligations and responsibilities which each of the parties to the marriage has or is likely to have in the foreseeable future;

(c) the standard of living enjoyed by the family before the breakdown of the marriage;

(d) the age of each party to the marriage and the duration of the marriage;

(e) any physical or mental disability of either of the parties to the marriage;

(f) the contributions which each of the parties has made or is likely in the foreseeable future to make to the welfare of the family, including any contribution by looking after the home or caring for the family;

(g) the conduct of each of the parties, whatever the nature of the conduct and whether it occurred during the marriage or after the separation of the parties or (as the case may be) dissolution or annulment of the marriage, if that conduct is such that it would in the opinion of the court be inequitable to disregard it;

(h) in the case of proceedings for divorce or nullity of marriage, the value to each of the parties to the marriage of any benefit (for example, a pension) which, by reason of the dissolution or annulment of the marriage, that party will lose the chance of acquiring.

(3) As regards the exercise of the powers of the court under section 23(1)(d), (e) or (f), (2) or (4) section 22A or 23 above to make a financial provision order in favour of a child of the family or the exercise of its powers under section 23A, 24 or 24A above in relation to a child of the family, the court shall in particular have regard to the following matters—

(a) the financial needs of the child;

(b) the income, earning capacity (if any), property and other financial resources of the child;

(c) any physical or mental disability of the child;

(d) the manner in which he was being and in which the parties to the marriage expected him to be educated or trained;

(e) the considerations mentioned in relation to the parties to the marriage in paragraphs (a), (b), (c) and (e) of subsection (2) above.

(4)   As regards the exercise of the powers of the court under any of sections 22A to 24A above against a party to a marriage in favour of a child of the family who is not the child of that party, the court shall also have regard—

(a) to whether that party assumed any responsibility for the child's maintenance, and, if so, to the extent to which, and the basis upon which, that party assumed such responsibility and to the length of time for which that party discharged such responsibility;

(b) to whether in assuming and discharging such responsibility that party did so knowing that the child was not his or her own;

(c) to the liability of any other person to maintain the child.

(5)   In relation to any power of the court to make an interim periodical payments order or an interim order for the payment of a lump sum, the preceding provisions of this section, in imposing any obligation on the court with respect to the matters to which it is to have regard, shall not require the court to do anything which would cause such a delay as would, in the opinion of the court, be inappropriate having regard—

(a) to any immediate need for an interim order;

(b) to the matters in relation to which it is practicable for the court to inquire before making an interim order; and

(c) to the ability of the court to have regard to any matter and to make appropriate adjustments when subsequently making a financial provision order which is not interim.

NOTES

1. Precisely how these sections operate is beyond the scope of this book, but it is obvious that they allow the courts to take account of factors other than pure property interests.

2. These sections apply only in the event of marital breakdown, and do not alter the law as stated in *Pettitt* v *Pettitt* [1970] AC 777 and *Gissing* v *Gissing* [1971] AC 866 where the parties are unmarried (as in *Burns* v *Burns* (this section) and *Grant* v *Edwards*, (see A: Cases where there is an express understanding), or where the parties continue to be happily married. This last situation is only likely to become an issue where the dispute involves a third party, as in *Lloyds Bank* v *Rosset* (also in this section).

3. It is obvious from the above discussion that, if the statutory provisions do not apply, great significance is attached by the courts to financial contributions, which are referable to the acquisition of the property. These contributions may take the form of provision of the initial deposit, or payment of mortgage instalments.

   By comparison, other contributions are arguably undervalued. Generally speaking, this operates to the disadvantage of the woman living in the home, since it is more likely that the man will earn more money than the woman, and it is accordingly likely that his financial contributions will be the greater. On the other hand, the woman may contribute in other ways. She may, for example, give up her job to bring up the children, pay the household expenses, or provide furniture or domestic services. Because it undervalues these other contributions, the law appears to work unjustly against the woman (which is presumably why legislation was thought necessary for married couples).

   A number of Court of Appeal decisions appeared subsequently to water down the effect of *Gissing* v *Gissing*. The basis of these decisions was the following passage from Lord Diplock's speech in *Gissing* v *Gissing* [1971] AC 886:

   > A resulting, implied or constructive trust—and it is unnecessary for present purposes to distinguish between these three classes of trust—is created ... whenever the trustee has so conducted himself that it would be inequitable to deny to the *cestui que trust* a beneficial interest in the land acquired.

   The Court of Appeal took the view that this passage allowed them a great degree of flexibility. The nature of the interest depended on all the equities of the case, and the law might consider not merely financial contributions at the time of acquisition of the property, but all types of contribution, whether at that time or subsequently. It was also argued that equity is a flexible instrument. 'Equity,' said Lord Denning MR in *Eves* v *Eves* [1975] 1 WLR 1338 at 1340, 'is not past the age of child bearing'.

However, shortly after Lord Denning's retirement, the Court of Appeal restated the conventional view in *Burns* v *Burns* [1984] Ch 317.

Burns v *Burns*

[1984] Ch 317, [1984] 1 All ER 244, Court of Appeal

Facts: The claimant, Valerie Burns, had been living with the defendant for 19 years, 17 in the house which was the subject of the dispute. She and the defendant, Patrick Burns, had never married, however. The house had been purchased in the name of the defendant and he paid the purchase price. The claimant made no contribution to the purchase price or the mortgage repayments, but had brought up their two children, performed domestic duties and recently contributed from her own earnings towards household expenses. She also bought various fittings and a washing machine, and redecorated the interior of the house. The claimant left the defendant and claimed a beneficial interest in the house.

Held: Since the couple had never married the provisions of the Matrimonial Causes Act 1973, ss.24 and 25 did not apply, and the claimant's case rested on orthodox property principles. In the absence of a financial contribution which could be related to the acquisition of the property, for example to the mortgage repayments, or a contribution enabling Patrick Burns to pay the mortgage instalments, she was not entitled to a beneficial interest in the house.

FOX LJ: For present purposes I think that such a trust could only arise (a) by express declaration or agreement or (b) by way of a resulting trust where the claimant has directly provided part of the purchase price or (c) from the common intention of the parties.

In the present case (a) and (b) can be ruled out. There was no express trust of an interest in the property for the benefit of the plaintiff; and there was no express agreement to create such an interest. And the plaintiff made no direct contribution to the purchase price. Her case, therefore, must depend on showing a common intention that she should have a beneficial interest in the property. Whether the trust which would arise in such circumstances is described as implied, constructive or resulting does not greatly matter. If the intention is inferred from the fact that some indirect contribution is made to the purchase price, the term 'resulting trust' is probably not inappropriate. Be that as it may, the basis of such a claim, in any case, is that it would be inequitable for the holder of the legal estate to deny the claimant's right to a beneficial interest.

In determining whether such a common intention exists it is, normally, the intention of the parties when the property was purchased that is important. As to that I agree with the observations of Griffiths LJ in *Bernard* v *Josephs* [1982] Ch 391 at 404. As I understand it, that does not mean that for the purpose of determining the ultimate shares in the property one looks simply at the factual position as it was at the date of acquisition. It is necessary for the court to consider all the evidence, including the contributions of the parties, down to the date of separation (which in the case of man and mistress will generally, though not always, be the relevant date). Thus the law proceeds on the basis that there is nothing inherently improbable in the parties acting on the understanding that the woman—

> should be entitled to a share which was not to be quantified immediately on the acquisition of the home but should be left to be determined when the mortagage was repaid or the property disposed of, on the basis of what would be fair having regard to the total contributions, direct or indirect, which each spouse had made by that date. (See *Gissing* v *Gissing* [1971] AC 886 at 900 per Lord Diplock.)

That approach does not, however, in my view preclude the possibility that while initially, there was no intention that the claimant should have any interest in the property, circumstances may subsequently arise from which the intention to confer an equitable interest on the claimant may arise (e.g., the discharge of a mortgage or the effecting of capital, improvements to the house at his or her own expense). Further, subsequent events may throw light on the initial intention.

MAY LJ: At the hearing of this appeal our attention was drawn to a number of authorities, to some of which I shall briefly refer, and thereafter state what I think is the general approach adopted by the courts to these disputes which can be deduced from the two leading cases in 1970 and 1971 and those which have followed them.

In *Falconer* v *Falconer* [1970] 3 All ER 449, [1970] 1 WLR 1333 the couple were married in 1960. About a year later a building plot was bought in the wife's name as a site for a house. Part of the purchase price was provided by the wife's mother and the balance was borrowed on mortgage in which the husband joined as surety. A house was then built on the plot with money raised by another mortgage of the plot with the partially erected house on it. As the plot was in the wife's name she was the mortgagor. However her husband again stood surety. The husband's father also guaranteed the repayments under the mortgage. After they moved into the house, the husband paid his wife a regular sum by way of housekeeping money. The wife herself went out to work and paid the mortgage instalments out of the total of her own earnings and her housekeeping money. About 18 months later the marriage began to go wrong and the husband moved out of the house. From that time and for two years thereafter he paid one half of the mortgage instalments and the rates on the property. Subsequently the wife formed an association with another man and the husband stopped his payments. The marriage was ultimately dissolved. On the husband's summons under s.17 of the Married Women's Property Act 1882, the county court judge held that the land itself belonged to the wife but that the husband had a half interest in the house. The wife's appeal to the Court of Appeal was dismissed and in the course of his judgment Lord Denning MR referred to the decision in *Gissing* v *Gissing* and said ([1970] 3 All ER 449 at 452, [1970] 1 WLR 1333 at 1336):

> It stated the principles on which a matrimonial home, which stands in the name of husband or wife alone, is nevertheless held to belong to them both jointly (in equal or unequal shares). It is done, not so much by virtue of an agreement, express or implied, but rather by virtue of a trust which is *imposed* by law. The law imputes to husband and wife an intention to create a trust, the one for the other. It does so by way of an *inference* from their conduct and the surrounding circumstances, even though the parties themselves made no agreement on it. This inference of a trust, the one for the other, is readily drawn when each has made a financial contribution to the purchase price or to the mortgage instalments. The financial contribution may be *direct*, as where it is actually stated to be a contribution towards the price or the instalments. It may be *indirect*, as where both go out to work, the one pays the housekeeping and the other the mortgage instalments. It does not matter which way round it is. It does not matter who pays what. So long as there is a substantial financial contribution towards the family expenses, it raises the inference of a trust. But where it is insubstantial, no such inference can be drawn, see the cases collected in the dissenting judgment of Edmund Davies LJ ([1969] 1 All ER 1043 at 1049, [1969] 2 Ch 85 at 97), which was upheld by the House. The House did, however, sound a note of warning about proportions. It is not in every case that the parties hold in equal shares. Regard must be had to their respective contributions. This confirms the practice of this court. In quite a few cases we have not given half-and-half but something different. (Lord Denning MR's emphasis).

Megaw LJ ([1970] 3 All ER 449 at 454, [1970] 1 WLR 1333 at 1338) in his judgment quoted a passage from Lord Pearson's speech in *Gissing* v *Gissing* [1970] 2 All ER 780 at 788, [1971] AC 886 at 903 which was to this effect:

> I think also that the decision of cases of this kind has been made more difficult by excessive application of the maxim. 'Equality is equity.' No doubt it is reasonable to apply the maxim in a case where there have been very substantial contributions (otherwise than by way of advancement) by one spouse to the purchase of property in the name of the other spouse but the proportion borne by the contributions to the total price or cost is difficult to fix. But if it is plain that the contributing spouse has contributed about one-quarter, I do not think it is helpful or right for the Court to feel obliged to award either one-half or nothing.

In the next case, *Hazell* v *Hazell* [1972] 1 All ER 923, [1972] 1 WLR 301, the couple were again husband and wife. They bought a house for the matrimonial home which was conveyed into the husband's name. The purchase price was obtained in part by a loan from the husband's parents and the remainder by a mortgage from a building society. In order to meet the increased expenditure involved it was agreed between the parties that the wife should go out to work and she used her earnings to supplement the limited housekeeping moneys which her husband gave her, including clothing for herself and the children. The top floor of the house was let and the rent was received by the husband. After 15 years the wife left the husband who stayed on in the house and continued to pay the outgoings. Four years later the parties were divorced. The wife applied under the 1882 Act claiming that she was entitled to a share in the matrimonial home. The deputy county court judge found that she had indeed made substantial contributions to the family expenses but decided that she was not entitled to any share of the house because there was no express or implied agreement to give her one. He went on, however, to hold that if he was wrong in so deciding on that basis, then the wife should have a share amounting to one-fifth. On the wife's appeal, this court held that she was entitled to a share in the ultimate value of the matrimonial home by virtue of the contributions which she made to supplement the housekeeping expenses. On the facts, her earnings had helped her husband to pay the mortgage instalments. In his judgment Lord Denning MR referred to what he had said in *Falconer* v *Falconer* and his reference there to *indirect* contributions by one member of a couple to the purchase price of the matrimonial home, and a little later said ([1972] 1 All ER 923 at 927, [1972] 1 WLR 301 at 305):

> Stephenson LJ suggested that it might be inferred that [the wife's] contributions were referable to the acquisition of the house. That seems to be sufficient ground from which the court could and should impute a trust. It would be inequitable for the husband to take the whole when she has helped him so much to acquire it. So I would reverse the decision of the judge and hold that the wife is entitled to a share in the house.

Lord Denning MR then upheld the deputy county court judge's assessment of one-fifth. Megaw LJ agreed and in the course of his judgment, dealing with the question of contributions, said ([1972] 1 All ER 923 at 928, [1972] 1 WLR 301 at 306):

> In my judgment it is sufficient if as a matter of common sense the wife's contribution ought to be treated as being a contribution towards the expenses of the acquisition of the matrimonial home.

In *Cooke* v *Head* [1972] 2 All ER 38, [1972] 1 WLR 518 the couple were not married. They planned to build a bungalow in which they could live after the man's wife had divorced him and they were able to get married. A plot of land was purchased in the man's name and he paid the deposit and arranged the mortgage. Both the man and the woman helped to build the bungalow, the woman's part of the work including demolishing a building, removing hard core and rubble, working a cement-mixer and painting. They both saved each week as much as they could from their earnings. They pooled their savings and used these for mortgage repayments and buying furniture. However, theirs was a relatively short-lived association, for when the bungalow was near completion but not entirely finished they separated and the man alone continued to live in it repaying the mortgage. It seems that the parties lived together for between two and three years. On an application by the woman for a declaration that the bungalow was owned jointly by herself and the man, Plowman J held that she had a one-twelfth interest in the property. She was dissatisfied and appealed. I quote brief passages from the judgment of Lord Denning MR, again with which Karminski and Orr LJJ agreed:

> The particular case of man and mistress came before the Court of Appeal in *Diwell* v *Farnes* [1959] 2 All ER 379, [1959] 1 WLR 624. The court was divided in opinion. The majority thought that a mistress was not in the same position as a wife. She could recover her actual contributions to the purchase price, but could not claim any part of the windfall on resale. Willmer LJ approached the case much as we approach cases between husband and wife. He would have given the mistress one-half. His approach is more in accord with recent development ... In the light of recent developments, I do not think it is right to approach this case by looking at the money contributions of each and dividing up the beneficial interest according to those contributions. The matter should be looked at more broadly, just as we do in husband and wife cases.
>
> We look to see what the equity is worth at the time when the parties separate. We assess the shares as at that times. If the property has been sold, we look at the amount which it has realised, and say how it is to be divided between them. Lord Diplock in *Gissing* v *Gissing* [1970] 2 All ER 780

at 793, [1971] AC 886 at 909 intimated that it is quite legitimate to infer that 'the wife should be entitled to a share which was not to be quantified immediately on the acquisition of the home but should be left to be determined when the mortgage was repaid or the property disposed of'. Likewise with a mistress.

Lord Denning MR then considered the various matters which should be taken into account in assessing the parties' share in the family home in these circumstances and ultimately held that the woman plaintiff was entitled to one-third of the net proceeds of sale, instead of the one-twelfth found by the judge at first instance.

Richards v *Dove* [1974] 1 All ER 888 also concerned an unmarried couple. They first lived as man and mistress in rented accommodation and then in a house which was bought and taken in the man's name. He paid £350 by way of deposit, of which £150 had been lent to him by his mistress. The balance of £3,150 was obtained by a mortgage to the man from the local authority. After the couple moved in, as had been the situation in their earlier rented accommodation, the mistress continued to pay for the household food and gas; the man paid all other bills including the mortgage repayments. Walton J dismissed the woman's application for a declaration that the house was vested in the man on trust for both of them. In his view it did not follow that the application of the relevant principles produced the same result whether the parties were married or not, because it was impossible to leave out of the picture the fact that as between husband and wife the former has certain legal duties relating to the maintenance of his wife, whereas between man and mistress the whole relationship is consensual, with no legal obligations imposed. In his view all that the mistress had done in the case before him was to provide the loan of £150 towards the deposit and then to carry on as they had for a number of years in rented accommodation, with the man paying off the mortgage. In truth, as the judge held, his mistress made no 'real' or 'substantial' contribution to the acquisition of the matrimonial home and accordingly was not entitled to any share of it.

Eves v *Eves* [1975] 3 All ER 768, [1975] 1 WLR 1338 also concerned an unmarried couple living together. They bought a house in the man's name partly by the sale of his previous house and partly by a mortgage which he obtained. At the time of the purchase the man told his mistress that if she had been 21 years of age he would have had the house put into their joint names as it was to be their joint home. At the subsequent trial he said that he had used the plaintiff's age as an excuse for not having had the house put into joint names. At the outset the house was in a very dirty and dilapidated condition and the couple each worked hard to improve it. Ultimately, some three years later, the man left the house and married another woman. Pennycuick V-C held that the plaintiff woman had not established a claim to be entitled to any share of the property and dismissed her application. She successfully appealed. On my reading of the judgments in this court the basis for Lord Denning MR's view that the woman was entitled to a declaration was that the untrue statement by the man that but for her age he would have put the house into their joint names amounted to a recognition by him that, in all fairness, she was entitled to a share in the house, equivalent in some way to a declaration of trust. He went on to say that the declaration was not for a particular share but for such share as was fair in view of all that she had done and was doing for the man and their children and would thereafter do. In this judgment, however, Brightman J, with whom Browne LJ agreed, referred to *Gissing* v *Gissing* and expressed his view that the actual decision in that case was that the wife had made no contribution to the acquisition of the title to the matrimonial home from which it could be inferred that the parties intended her to have any beneficial interest in it. He went on to hold that the case then before his court was different: the man clearly led the plaintiff to believe that she was to have some undefined interest in the property. That, of course, he said, was not enough by itself to create a beneficial interest in his favour but if it was part of the bargain between the parties, expressed or to be implied, that the plaintiff should contribute her labour towards the reparation of a house in which she was to have some beneficial interest, then in his view the arrangement became one to which the law could give effect. Although Pennycuick V-C had been unable to find any link in the evidence, Brightman J disagreed and found it in these circumstances ([1975] 3 All ER 768 at 774, [1975] 1 WLR 1338 at 1345):

> The house was found by them jointly. It was in poor condition. What needed to be done was plain for all to see, and must have been discussed. The plaintiff was to have some interest in the house, or so she was led to believe, although her name would not be on the deeds. They moved in. They both set to and put the house to rights. I find it difficult to suppose that she would have been wielding the 14-pound sledgehammer, breaking up the large area of concrete, filling the skip and doing other things which were carried out when they moved in, except in pursuance of some expressed or implied arrangement and on the understanding that she was helping to improve a house in which she was to all practical intents and purposes promised that she had an interest.

In the result the court held that the woman was entitled to a one-quarter share in the family home.

Of all the authorities to which our attention was drawn, I think that the facts of *Hall* v *Hall* (1981) 3 FLR 379 are the closest to those of the instant case. In *Hall's* case the couple were unmarried. The woman left her husband and went to live with the man, who was divorced. They bought a flat in the man's name, the woman contributing to the furnishings and the general household expenses. Subsequently a house was bought in the man's name, the purchase money coming partly from the proceeds of the sale of the flat, partly from the man's savings and partly by way of mortgage. Within a year the couple separated. On the woman's application to the county court for a share in the family home, she was awarded one-fifth and her appeal to the Court of Appeal against this award was dismissed. At first sight the decision in *Hall* v *Hall* might not seem to be in accord with the principles applied in the earlier authorities. However, having read the judgments in the case it is clear that the decision proceeded on a concession by counsel for the man, both before the county court and in the Court of Appeal, that in the events which had occurred there had been a resulting trust of the family house in favour of the woman. In these circumstances, save to the extent that the members of the Court of Appeal in *Hall's* case did not expressly say that they thought that this concession had been wrongly made, I think that one should be careful about reaching the conclusion that *Hall's* case extended the basis of the woman's entitlement in man/mistress cases of the type with which we are concerned. With the greatest respect and particularly having regard to the reference to *Falconer* v *Falconer* in the judgments, I think that the concession in *Hall* v *Hall* was wrongly made.

Lloyds Bank v Rosset

[1991] 1 AC 107, [1991] 1 All ER 1111, House of Lords

Facts: Mr and Mrs Rosset decided to purchase a semi-derelict farmhouse for £57,000. Mrs Rosset understood that the entire purchase money was to come out of a family trust fund, the trustees of which insisted that the house be purchased in the husband's sole name (this appears to have been the only reason for the legal title being vested in Mr Rosset alone). The house required renovation, and it was intended that this should be a joint venture. The vendors allowed Mr and Mrs Rosset to enter the property a number of weeks before completion in order to begin repairs, and render the house habitable.

During this period, Mrs Rosset spent a lot of time at the house, urging on the builders and attempting to coordinate their work (until her husband insisted that he alone should give instructions), going to builders' merchants to obtain material required by the builders, delivering the materials to the site, assisting her husband in planning the renovation and decoration of the house (she was a skilled painter and decorator), wallpapering two bedrooms, arranging the insurance of the house, arranging a crime prevention survey, and assisting in arranging the installation of burglar alarms.

Unbeknown to Mrs Rosset, Mr Rosset was unable to fund the purchase and repairs entirely from the trust fund, and obtained an overdraft of £18,000 from Lloyds Bank, executing a legal charge on the property in their favour on the same day as completion. He later defaulted on the repayments, and the bank sought possession. Mrs Rosset claimed a beneficial interest in the property, binding the bank by virtue of her actual occupation, as an overriding interest under the Land Registration Act 1925, s.70(1)(g).

Held: Mrs Rosset had no beneficial interest. There was no evidence of any agreement between the parties to share the beneficial interest, and the wife's contributions were regarded as *de minimis*.

LORD BRIDGE OF HARWICH: ... [The judge] said: The decision to transfer the property into the name of [Mr Rosset] alone was a disappointment to [Mrs Rosset], but I am satisfied that she genuinely believed that [Mr Rosset] would hold the property in his name as something which was a joint venture, to be shared between them as the family home and that the reason for it being held by [him] alone was to ensure that [his] uncle would sanction the export of trust funds from Switzerland to England for the purchase. As so often happens [Mr and Mrs Rosset] did not pursue their discussion to the extent of defining precisely what their respective interests in the property should be. It was settled that the property should be transferred into the name of [Mr Rosset] alone to achieve the provision of funds from Switzerland, but in the period from August 1982 to the 23 November 1982 when the contracts were exchanged, [the parties] did not decide whether [Mrs Rosset] should have any interest in the property. On one occasion [Mr Rosset] heard [her husband] say to her parents that he had put the house in their joint names, but she knew that he could not do that and treated what he said as an expression of what he would like to do. In these circumstances I am satisfied that the outcome of the discussions between the parties as to the name into which the property should be transferred did not exclude the possibility that [Mrs Rosset] should have a beneficial interest in the property.

...

Even if there had been the clearest oral agreement between Mr and Mrs Rosset that Mr Rosset was to hold the property in trust for them both as tenants in common, this would, of course, have been ineffective since a valid declaration of trust by way of gift of a beneficial interest in land is required by s.53(1) of the Law of Property Act 1925 to be in writing. But if Mrs Rosset had, as pleaded, altered her position in reliance on the agreement this could have given rise to an enforceable interest in her favour by way either of a constructive trust or of a proprietary estoppel ...

...

[The judge continued:]

Up to 17 December 1982 [Mrs Rosset's] contribution to the venture was: (1) to urge on the builders and to attempt to co-ordinate their work, until her husband insisted that he alone should give instructions; (2) to go to builders' merchants and obtain material required by the builders ... and to deliver the materials to the site. This was of some importance because Mr Griffin and his employees did not know the Thanet area; (3) to assist her husband in planning the renovation and decoration of the house. In this, she had some skill over and above that acquired by most housewives. She was a skilled painter and decorator who enjoyed wallpapering and decorating, and, as her husband acknowledged, she had good ideas about this work. In connection with this, she advised on the position of electric plugs and radiators and planned the design of the large breakfast room and the small kitchen of the house; (4) to carry out the wallpapering of Natasha's bedroom and her own bedroom, after preparing the surfaces of the walls and clearing up the rooms concerned before the papering began; (5) to begin the preparation of the surfaces of the walls of her son's bedroom, the den, the upstairs lavatory and the downstairs washroom for papering. All this wallpapering was completed after 17 December 1982 but by 31 December 1982; (6) to assist in arranging the insurance of the house by the Minister Insurance Co. Ltd home cover policy, in force from 3 November 1982; (7) to assist in arranging a crime prevention survey on 23 November 1982; (8) to assist in arranging the installation of burglar alarms described in a specification dated 3 December 1982.

...

The first and fundamental question which must always be resolved is whether, independently of any inference to be drawn from the conduct of the parties in the course of sharing the house as their home and managing their joint affairs, there has at any time prior to acquisition, or exceptionally at some later date, been any agreement, arrangement or understanding reached between them that the property is to be shared beneficially. The finding of an agreement or arrangement to share in this sense can only, I think, be based on evidence of express discussions between the partners, however imperfectly remembered and however imprecise their terms may have been. Once a finding to this effect is made it will only be necessary for the partner asserting a claim to a beneficial interest against the partner entitled to the legal estate to show that he or she has acted to his or her detriment or significantly altered his or her position in reliance on the agreement in order to give rise to a constructive trust or proprietary estoppel.

In sharp contrast with this situation is the very different one where there is no evidence to support a finding of an agreement or arrangement to share, however reasonable it might have been for the parties to each such an arrangement if they had applied their minds to the question, and where the court must rely entirely on the conduct of the parties both as the basis from which to infer a common intention to share the property beneficially and as the conduct relied on to give rise to a constructive trust. In this situation direct contributions to the purchase price by the partner who is not the legal owner, whether initially or by payment of mortgage instalments, will readily justify the inference necessary to the creation of a constructive trust. But, as I read the authorities, it is at least extremely doubtful whether anything less will do.

The leading cases in your Lordships' House are *Pettitt* v *Pettitt* [1969] 2 All ER 385, [1970] AC 777 and *Gissing* v *Gissing* [1970] 2 All ER 780, [1971] AC 886. Both demonstrate situations in the second category to which I have referred and their Lordships discuss at great length the difficulties to which these situations give rise. The effect of these two decisions is very helpfully analysed in the judgment of Lord MacDermott LCJ in *McFarlane* v *McFarlane* [1972] NI 59.

Outstanding examples on the other hand of cases giving rise to situations in the first category are *Eves* v *Eves* [1975] 3 All ER 768, [1975] 1 WLR 1338 and *Grant* v *Edwards* [1986] 2 All ER 426, [1986] Ch 638. In both these cases, where the parties who had cohabited were unmarried, the female partner had been clearly led by the male partner to believe, when they set up home together, that the property would belong to them jointly. In *Eves* v *Eves* the male partner had told the female partner that the only reason why the property was to be acquired in his name alone was because she was under 21 and that, but for her age, he would have had the house put into their joint names. He admitted in evidence that this was simply an 'excuse'. Similarly, in *Grant* v *Edwards* the female partner was told by the male partner that the only reason for not acquiring the property in joint names was because she was involved in divorce proceedings and that, if the property were acquired jointly, this might operate to her prejudice in those proceedings. As Nourse LJ put it ([1986] 2 All ER 426 at 433, [1986] Ch 638 at 649):

> Just as in *Eves* v *Eves*, these facts appear to me to raise a clear inference that there was an understanding between the plaintiff and the defendant, or a common intention, that the plaintiff was to have some sort of proprietary interest in the house; otherwise no excuse for not putting her name onto the title would have been needed.

The subsequent conduct of the female partner in each of these cases, which the court rightly held sufficient to give rise to a constructive trust or proprietary estopped supporting her claim to an interest in the property, fell far short of such conduct as would by itself have supported the claim in the absence of an express representation by the male partner that she was to have such an interest. It is significant to note that the share to which the female partners in *Eves* v *Eves* and *Grant* v *Edwards* were held entitled were one-quarter and one-half respectively. In no sense could these shares have been regarded as proportionate to what the judge in the instant case described as a 'qualifying contribution' in terms of the indirect contributions to the acquisition or enhancement of the value of the houses made by the female partners.

NOTE: The two types of case outlined at the start of the chapter are clearly distinguished here. In the first category discussed by Lord Bridge, A's representations would amount to a declaration of trust, except for the formality requirements for trusts of land. B's reliance prevents A from relying on lack of formality (see the maxim 'equity will not allow a statute to be used as an instrument of fraud', as considered in Chapters 6 and 16). In the second category, there are no representations, and B's interest, if any, will depend on his or her contributions. In *Rosset* itself, there were no representations, and she had not done enough to earn herself an interest in their absence.

A: Cases where there is an express understanding

If A says anything which can be construed as a declaration of trust, and B relies on this to his detriment, B obtains an interest under a constructive trust. Note that the sole function of the reliance is to get around the formality provisions (Law of Property Act 1925, s.53(1)(b), see Chapter 6). In principle, the extent of B's interest ought to depend on A's representation, with a presumption of a half share if that is unclear.

If, for some reason, A's statement cannot amount to a declaration of trust, perhaps because it does not amount to an irrevocable commitment, or because of problems of certainty of subject matter, it might still give rise to a proprietary estoppel (see C: Proprietary estoppel).

Grant v *Edwards*

[1986] Ch 638, [1986] 2 All ER 426, Court of Appeal

Facts: In 1969, a house was purchased for the claimant, Mrs Linda Grant, and the defendant, George Edwards, to live in as if married (although Linda Grant was actually married to someone else). The house was purchased in the name of Edwards and his brother. Edwards told Grant that her name would not go on the title for the time being because it would cause prejudice in the matrimonial proceedings pending between Mrs Grant and her husband. In reality, he had no intention of conveying any legal title to the claimant.

The defendant paid the deposit on the house, and most, but not all, of the repayments on the two mortgages. The claimant also contributed towards general household expenses, provided housekeeping, and brought up the children. In 1980, the couple separated, and the claimant claimed a beneficial interest in the property.

Held: Edwards's statement that Mrs Grant's name would have appeared on the title except that it could cause prejudice in the matrimonial proceedings was evidence of a common intention that Mrs Grant should have beneficial interest (a half share) in the property. Mrs Grant had relied to her detriment on the common intention, so that she was entitled to a half share on a resulting or constructive trust.

NOURSE LJ: In most of these cases the fundamental, and invariably the most difficult, question is to decide whether there was the necessary common intention, being something which can only be inferred from the conduct of the parties, almost always from the expenditure incurred by them respectively. In this regard the court has to look for expenditure which is referable to the acquisition of the house: see *Burns* v *Burns* [1984] 1 All ER 244 at 252–253, [1984] Ch 317 at 328–329 per Fox LJ. If it is found to have been incurred, such expenditure will perform the twofold function of establishing the common intention and showing that the claimant has acted on it.

There is another and rarer class of case, of which the present may be one, where, although there has been no writing, the parties have orally declared themselves in such a way as to make their common intention plain. Here the court does not have to look for conduct from which the intention can be inferred, but only for conduct which amounts to an acting on it by the claimant. And, although that conduct can undoubtedly be the incurring of expenditure which is referable to the acquisition of the house, it need not necessarily be so.

...

It seems therefore, on the authorities as they stand, that a distinction is to be made between conduct from which the common intention can be inferred on the one hand and conduct which amounts to an acting on it on the other. There remains this difficult question: what is the quality of conduct required for the latter purpose? The difficulty is caused, I think, because, although the common intention has been made plain, everything else remains a matter of inference. Let me illustrate it in this way. It would be possible to take the view that the mere moving into the house by the woman amounted to an acting on the common intention. But that was evidently not the view of the majority in *Eves* v *Eves*. And the reason for that may be that, in the absence of evidence, the law is not so cynical as to infer that a woman will only go to live with a man to whom she is not married if she understands that she is to have an interest in their home. So what sort of conduct is required? In my judgment it must be conduct on which the woman could not reasonably have been expected to embark unless she was to have an interest in the house. If she was not to have such an interest, she could reasonably be expected to go and live with her lover, but not, for example, to wield a 14–lb sledge hammer in the front garden. In adopting the latter kind of conduct she is seen to act to her detriment on the faith of the common intention.

MUSTILL LJ: I believe that the following propositions, material to this appeal, can be extracted from the authorities. (For convenience it is assumed that the 'proprietor', viz. the person who has the legal title is male and the 'claimant' who asserts a beneficial interest is female.)

(1) The law does not recognise a concept of family property, whereby people who live together in a settled relationship *ipso facto* share the rights of ownership in the assets acquired and used for the purposes

of their life together. Nor does the law acknowledge that by the mere fact of doing work on the asset of one party to the relationship the other party will acquire a beneficial interest in that asset.

(2) The question whether one party to the relationship acquires rights to property the legal title to which is vested in the other party must be answered in terms of the existing law of trusts. There are no special doctrines of equity applicable in this field alone.

(3) In a case such as the present the inquiry must proceed in two stages. First, by considering whether something happened between the parties, in the nature of bargain, promise or tacit common intention, at the time of the acquisition. Second, if the answer is yes, by asking whether the claimant subsequently conducted herself in a manner which was (a) detrimental to herself and (b) referable to whatever happened on acquisition. (I use the expression 'on acquisition' for simplicity. In fact, the event happening between the parties which, if followed by the relevant type of conduct on the part of the claimant, can lead to the creation of an interest in the claimant may itself occur after acquisition. The beneficial interests may change in the course of the relationship.)

(4) For present purposes, the event happening on acquisition may take one of the following shapes: (a) an express bargain whereby the proprietor promises the claimant an interest in the property, in return for an explicit undertaking by the claimant to act in a certain way; (b) an express but incomplete bargain whereby the proprietor promises the claimant an interest in the property, on the basis that the claimant will do something in return. The parties do not themselves make explicit what the claimant is to do. The court therefore has to complete the bargain for them by means of implication; when it comes to decide whether the proprietor's promise has been matched by conduct falling within whatever undertaking the claimant must be taken to have given *sub silencio*; (c) an explicit promise by the proprietor that the claimant will have an interest in the property, unaccompanied by any express or tacit agreement as to a quid pro quo; (d) a common intention, not made explicit, to the effect that the claimant will have an interest in the property if she subsequently acts in a particular way.

(5) In order to decide whether the subsequent conduct of the claimant serves to complete the beneficial interest which has been explicitly or tacitly promised to her the court must decide whether the conduct is referable to the bargain, promise or intention. Whether the conduct satisfied this test will depend on the nature of the conduct and the bargain, promise or intention.

(6) Thus, if the situation falls into category (a) above, the only question is whether the claimant's conduct is of the type explicitly promised. It is immaterial whether it takes the shape of a contribution to the cost of acquiring the property or is of a quite different character.

(7) The position is the same in relation to situations (b) and (d). No doubt it will often be easier in practice to infer that the quid pro quo was intended to take the shape of a financial or other contribution to the cost of acquisition or of improvement, but this need not always be so. Whatever the court decides the quid pro quo to have been, it will suffice if the claimant has furnished it.

(8) In considering whether there was a bargain or common intention, so as to bring the case within categories (b) and (d), and, if there was one, what were its terms, the court must look at the true state of affairs on acquisition. It must not impute to the parties a bargain which they never made or a common intention which they never possessed.

(9) The conduct of the parties, and in particular of the claimant, after the acquisition may provide material from which the court can infer the existence of an explicit bargain or a common intention, and also the terms of such a bargain or intention. Examining the subsequent conduct of the parties to see whether an inference can be made as to a bargain or intention is quite different from examining the conduct of the claimant to see whether it amounts to compliance with a bargain or intention which has been proved in some other way. (If this distinction is not observed, there is a risk of circularity. If the claimant's conduct is too readily assumed to be explicable only by the existence of a bargain, she will always be able to say that her side of the bargain has been performed.)

The propositions do not touch two questions of general importance. The first, is whether in the absence of a proved or inferred bargain or intention the making of subsequent indirect contributions, for instance in the shape of a contribution to general household expenses, is sufficient to found an interest. I believe the answer to be that it does not. The routes by which the members of the House reached their common conclusion in *Gissing* v *Gissing* [1971] AC 886 were not, however, the same and the point is still open. Since it does not arise here, I prefer to express no conclusion on it.

The second question is closer to the present case: namely whether a promise by the proprietor to confer an interest, but with no element of mutuality (i.e., situation (c) above), can effectively confer an interest if the claimant relies on it by acting to her detriment. This question was not directly addressed in

Gissing v *Gissing*, although the speech of Lord Diplock supports an affirmative answer (see [1971] AC 886 at 905). The plaintiff's case was not argued on this footing in the present appeal, and, since the appeal can be decided on other grounds, I prefer not to express an opinion on this important point.

NOTES

1. At first sight, it seems difficult to reconcile this case with *Burns* v *Burns* [1984] Ch 317, but it is clear that, like *Burns* v *Burns*, the case was decided on conventional property reasoning, and not on any special doctrines applicable in this area alone. The crucial element here was the statement by the defendant as to why the claimant's name would not go on to the title. This could only be explained on the basis of a common intention that she was to have a half share.

2. Because there was evidence of a common intention (independent of the contributions themselves), Linda Grant's contributions (unlike those of Valerie Burns) were relevant only in order to get round the formality provisions of the Law of Property Act 1925, s.53. Resulting and constructive trusts are excluded by virtue of s.53(2), and in *Grant* v *Edwards*, it was necessary only for Linda Grant to show that she had relied on the agreement to her detriment for a constructive trust to arise in her favour.

3. In cases like *Burns* v *Burns* by contrast, where there is no independent evidence of any agreement, evidence of intention can only be inferred from the contributions themselves. This requires a substantial contribution referable to the acquisition of the property, whereas in *Grant* v *Edwards*, all Mrs Grant had to show was that she had acted in a manner which was explicable only on the basis that she was to have an interest in the house. This is a far less stringent requirement. Further, the value of the beneficial interest was determined by the common intention (as evidenced by the defendant's statement), and not by the value of Linda Grant's contributions. In cases like *Burns*, by contrast, where there is no express evidence of a common intention, the value of the contributions will also determine the *size* of the beneficial interest (if any).

4. The case of *Rowe* v *Prance* [1999] 2 FLR 787 illustrates how the law's response to trusts of personal property differs to its treatment of trusts of land. On facts otherwise reminiscent of *Grant* v *Edwards*, the cohabitees bought a *boat* to live on. The man paid for it but frequently stated that the boat belonged to them both. His explanation ('excuse') for not registering the woman as joint owner was that she did not possess 'a relevant certificate'. The court held that he had constituted himself an express trustee of the boat for himself and the woman in equal shares. Surely *Grant* v *Edwards* would likewise have been disposed of as a case of express trust had it not been for the formality requirements in relation to express trusts of *land*.

Simon Gardner, 'Rethinking Family Property'
(1993) 109 *LQR* 263, pp. 264–5

[Footnotes have been incorporated as far as possible into the text.]

In *Eves* v *Eves* [1975] 1 WLR 1338 and *Grant* v *Edwards* [1986] Ch 638, the court found an *express* agreement that a woman should have a share in a house owned by her partner. In both, the woman's only hope of success lay with the finding of an express agreement, because she had not made the direct financial contribution needed to allow discovery of an implied agreement. But in both, the partner had explicitly told the woman that she was not to have a share. So on the face of it, there was most decidedly no agreement that she should. The courts based their contrary finding on the fact that in each case the man had added a reason for this refusal to let the woman share the house, which was in truth a bad reason. In one case, it was that at 20 years of age the woman was legally too young to have an interest in land; in the other, it was that any share she had would cause prejudice in the matrimonial proceedings she was currently undergoing with her estranged husband. In each case the court characterised this as an 'excuse,' and went on to say that the man's giving an excuse showed that he actually acknowledged the existence of an agreement that the woman should have a share [*per* Browne-Wilkinson V-C and Nourse LJ; Gardner notes that Mustill LJ took a slightly different position].

But the fact that the men's statements were excuses (i.e., neither objectively valid nor even sincerely uttered) does not mean that the men were thereby acknowledging an agreement whereby the woman should have a share. If I give an excuse for rejecting an invitation to what I expect to be a dull party, it does not mean that I thereby agree to come: on the contrary, it means that I do not agree to come, but for one reason or another find it hard to say so outright. The fallacious quality of the reasoning in *Eves* v *Eves* and *Grant* v *Edwards* is thus clear. It is hard to think that the judges concerned really believed in it … .

Ungurian v *Lesnoff*

[1990] Ch 206, [1989] 3 WLR 840, [1990] Fam Law 93, Chancery Division

Facts: Mrs Lesnoff, who was a Polish academic, gave up a flat in Poland of which she could have remained in occupation for life, her Polish nationality, and her career, in order to live with Mr Ungurian. Ungurian bought a house in London, registered in his sole name, in which he and Mrs Lesnoff lived as man and wife for four years. During that time Mrs Lesnoff installed or supervised the installation of central heating, and the rewiring and replumbing of the house, in addition to other works of improvement and redecoration. Mrs Lesnoff remained in occupation, and Ungurian brought an action for possession and the case finally came to court many years later.

Held: Vinelott J held that Mrs Lesnoff had a right to reside in the house for life, even though the case depended upon obscure recollections of conversations which were over 20 years old.

VINELOTT J: … The words spoken are … set out [in Mrs Lesnoff's defence] in the following terms:

> In Beirut, over Christmas 1968 and subsequently in London by the plaintiff to the first defendant on a number of different occasions, *inter alia*, the plaintiff used the following words of which the following are a translation from Polish to that effect, 'We will have to look for and buy a house for us in London so that you will feel secure and happy, having lost your house in Poland,' and 'You'll have to decide and find the house which you like. I want you to feel that you have something to rely on if anything happens to me.'

The words said to have been spoken and which are reported in those particulars do not support a claim that there was a clear statement by Mr Ungurian that it was to be her absolute property sufficient to found the claim that he constituted himself a bare trustee. They are consistent with the property being bought simply as a home for them both and for Mrs Lesnoff if anything should happen to Mr Ungurian.

■ QUESTIONS

1. What was the subject matter of this trust? Apparently the conversation had taken place before the parties had even begun to look for a house. Do you think there was certainty of subject matter?

2. The requirement of substantial direct financial contributions may in practice prevent women from establishing constructive trusts interests, but is this offset by the fact that a constructive trusts interest may be based on the woman's detrimental reliance upon an imperfectly remembered express statement made many years ago?

B: Cases where there is no express understanding

One way for B to obtain an interest is by way of the presumption of resulting trust discussed in Chapter 5. Under a resulting trust, a contribution towards the acquisition of land gives the contributor a beneficial share in the land proportionate to their contribution. However, the presumption of resulting trust no longer applies to land acquired by cohabitants in their joint names. In *Stack* v *Dowden* [2007] UKHL 17, [2007] 2 AC 432, the House of Lords held that where land is acquired by cohabitants and legal title is placed in their joint names, it should now be strongly presumed that equity follows the law—so as to make the parties joint tenants in equity (giving them joint beneficial ownership so long as the land is held in joint names and giving them equal shares in the proceeds of any sale of the land). Such a trust is not a resulting trust (the beneficial share does not 'jump back', i.e. 'result' in proportion to contribution); it is a constructive trust arising from the maxim 'equity follows the law'. In cases of cohabitants holding land in their joint names, the presumption that equity follows the law can be rebutted in an exceptional case by evidence that joint beneficial ownership was not intended. In *Stack* v *Dowden* itself, their Lordships held that the presumption should be rebutted in favour of unequal shares because the parties kept their general finances—income, outgoings, bank accounts—separate one from the other.

■ **QUESTION**

Were the factors which their Lordships considered to be 'exceptional' really sufficient, do you think, to rebut a so-called 'strong' presumption in favour of joint or equal beneficial ownership?

NOTES

1. Paying mortgage instalments is presumed to give rise to an interest, but only if the mortgage was an acquisition mortgage (in *McKenzie* v *McKenzie* [2003] EWHC 601 (Ch), Mr McKenzie remortgaged his land but his son, who helped pay off the instalments, failed to acquire a beneficial share in it). In *James* v *Thomas* [2007] EWCA Civ 1212, it was held that courts should be especially slow to impose a trust on land which had been acquired before the relationship between the cohabitants began.

2. Where land is acquired by non-cohabitants whose relationship is not what one might call 'analogous' to a heterosexual marriage relationship or a homosexual civil partnership, and in any case in which land is acquired in the name of one party only, then the presumption of resulting trust still applies, and so does the second route to a constructive trust set out in Lord Bridge's *obiter dictum* in *Lloyds Bank* v *Rosset*:

   > direct contributions to the purchase price by the partner who is not the legal owner, whether initially or by payment of mortgage instalments, will readily justify the inference necessary to the creation of a constructive trust. But, as I read the authorities, it is at least extremely doubtful whether anything less will do.

■ **QUESTION**

Does *Stack* v *Dowden* affect the situation anticipated by the statement in *Rosset* just set out in which land is in the name of one legal owner?

There are *obiter dicta* in *Stack* (see full details set out in this section) which suggest that the two *Rosset* routes to a constructive trust interest (express agreement plus detrimental reliance OR substantial direct financial contribution to purchase) may be too restrictively framed (Lord Walker opined that 'the law has moved on [since Rosset], and your Lordships should move it a little more in the same direction' para. [27]. It was, for instance, suggested that making improvements that added significant value to the property should be sufficient to generate an interest) but *Rosset* was a case in which land was in one name and *Stack* was a case in which land was in joint names. It follows that as regards sole legal owner cases, no court will be bound to prefer their Lordships' analysis in *Stack* to their Lordships' analysis in *Rosset*. I would go further and suggest that *Stack* does not have the authority to justify a departure from the *Rosset* orthodoxy in sole legal owner cases. The key innovation in *Stack* was to revitalise the maxim 'equity follows law'. It follows that if anything should be implied from *Stack* for sole owner cases, it should be that 'equity follows the law' to raise a very strong presumption that a sole legal owner is the sole beneficial owner. If anything, that would make it *harder* to claim a beneficial interest against a sole legal owner under *Stack* than under *Rosset*. That being so, it seems safest not to read *Stack* expansively, but to restrict its operation to cases of cohabitants who are joint legal owners.

The following section sets out the scope and significance of the decision in *Stack* v *Dowden*. Thereafter, the rest of the chapter is concerned (except where expressly indicated) with trusts that are NOT of the *Stack* v *Dowden* type.

(i) The family home where legal title is in joint names

Stack v *Dowden*
[2007] UKHL 17, [2007] 2 AC 432, House of Lords

Facts: Mr Stack and Ms Dowden began cohabiting in the early 1980s in a house which was in Ms Dowden's sole name. Mr Stack may have contributed to the deposit on that house, but the deposit was paid out of Ms Dowden's account and she provided the balance by means of a mortgage loan which she repaid. They had four children and in 1993 moved into a new home. Title to that house was registered in their joint names. There was a new mortgage on that house under which both Stack and Dowden were liable and under which they both made repayments. Ms Dowden paid all the domestic bills. They separated in 2002 and Mr Stack brought proceedings to establish a beneficial share in the house. He was awarded a half-share at first instance, but the Court of Appeal reduced that to a third (35 per cent, in fact).

Held: The award of a 35 per cent share to Stack was upheld. The task of the court is to determine 'what the parties must, in view of their conduct, be taken to have intended' (para. [61]). Where property is purchased or held in joint names there is a strong presumption that the parties intended to own the equitable interest jointly in accordance with the maxim 'equity follows the law'. According to Baroness Hale, who delivered the leading speech, 'cases in which the joint legal owners are to be taken to have intended that their beneficial interests should be different from their legal interests will be very unusual'. Lord Walker opined that 'there will be a heavy burden in establishing ... that an intention to keep a sort of balance-sheet of contributions actually existed, or should be inferred, or imputed to the parties. The presumption will be that equity follows the law' (para. [3]3). Despite the supposedly strong presumption in favour of joint beneficial ownership, in this case their Lordships held that the strong presumption in favour of equality had been rebutted and the Court of Appeal's 65per cent/35per cent division was upheld. Why? The answer seems to be that that Dowden had contributed more cash to the acquisition of the house (Baroness Hale [para. [87]] and Lord Hope [para. [11]]). Their Lordships (Hale, Hoffmann, Walker, Hope, and Neuberger) all agreed on the result, although Lord Neuberger dissented from the reasoning adopted by Baroness Hale. Lord Neuberger preferred the traditional presumption of resulting trust under which shares are presumed to correspond to the parties' financial contributions.

BARONESS HALE:

58. The issue as it has been framed before us is whether a conveyance into joint names indicates only that each party is intended to have some beneficial interest but says nothing about the nature and extent of that beneficial interest, or whether a conveyance into joint names establishes a prime facie case of joint and equal beneficial interests until the contrary is shown. For the reasons already stated, at least in the domestic consumer context, a conveyance into joint names indicates both legal and beneficial joint tenancy, unless and until the contrary is proved.

59. The question is, how, if at all, is the contrary to be proved? Is the starting point the presumption of resulting trust, under which shares are held in proportion to the parties' financial contributions to the acquisition of the property, unless the contributor or contributors can be shown to have had a contrary intention? Or is it that the contrary can be proved by looking at all the relevant circumstances in order to discern the parties' common intention?

60. The presumption of resulting trust is not a rule of law. According to Lord Diplock in *Pettitt v Pettitt* [1970] AC 777, at 823H, the equitable presumptions of intention are 'no more than a consensus of judicial

opinion disclosed by reported cases as to the most likely inference of fact to be drawn in the absence of any evidence to the contrary'. Equity, being concerned with commercial realities, presumed against gifts and other windfalls (such as survivorship). But even equity was prepared to presume a gift where the recipient was the provider's wife or child. These days, the importance to be attached to who paid for what in a domestic context may be very different from its importance in other contexts or long ago. ... The law has indeed moved on in response to changing social and economic conditions. The search is to ascertain the parties' shared intentions, actual, inferred or imputed, with respect to the property in the light of their whole course of conduct in relation to it. ...

65. Curiously, it is in the context of homes conveyed into joint names but without an express declaration of trust that the courts have sometimes reverted to the strict application of the principles of the resulting trust: see *Walker v Hall* [1984] FLR 126 and two cases decided by the same court on the same day, *Springette v Defoe* [1992] 2 FLR 388 and *Huntingford v Hobbs* [1993] 1 FLR 736; but cf *Crossley v Crossley* [2005] EWCA Civ 1581, [2006] 2 FLR 813. However, Chadwick LJ commented in *Oxley v Hiscock* [2005] Fam 211, at 235:

'47. It is, I think, important to an understanding of the reasoning in the judgments in *Springette v Defoe* that each member of this court seems to have thought that when Lord Bridge referred, in *Lloyds Bank plc v Rosset* [1991] 1 AC 107, 132F, to the need to base a 'finding of an agreement or arrangement to share in this sense' on 'evidence of express discussions between the partners' he was addressing the secondary, or consequential, question –

'what was the common intention of the parties as to the extent of their respective beneficial interests'—rather than the primary, or threshold, question—'was there a common intention that each should have a beneficial interest in the property?' ...

48. For the reasons which I have sought to explain, I think that the better view is that, in the passage in *Rosset's* case [1991] 1 AC 107, 132F, to which both Dillon LJ and Steyn LJ referred in *Springette v Defoe* [see [1992] 2 FLR 388, at 393E–F and 395B, agreed with by Sir Christopher Slade at 397G] Lord Bridge was addressing only the primary question—'was there a common intention that each should have a beneficial interest in the property?' He was not addressing the secondary question—'what was the common intention of the parties as to the extent of their respective beneficial interests?' As this court had pointed out in *Grant v Edwards* and *Stokes v Anderson*, the court may well have to supply the answer to that secondary question by inference from their subsequent conduct. ... ' In the case before us, he observed at para. 24:

' ... I have not altered my view that, properly understood, the authorities before (and after) *Springette v Defoe* do not support the proposition that, absent discussion between the parties as to the *extent* of their respective beneficial interests at the time of purchase, it must follow that the presumption of resulting trust is not displaced and the property is necessarily held in beneficial shares proportionate to the respective contributions to the purchase price.'

With these passages I entirely agree. The approach to quantification in cases where the home is conveyed into joint names should certainly be no stricter than the approach to quantification in cases where it has been conveyed into the name of one only. To the extent that *Walker v Hall*, *Springette v Defoe* and *Huntingford v Hobbs* hold otherwise, they should not be followed.

66. However, Chadwick LJ went on to say at para. 26, that: '... there is no reason in principle why the approach to the second question—'what is the extent of the parties' respective beneficial interests in the property?—should be different, in a case where the property is registered in the joint names of cohabitees, from what it would be if the property were registered in the sole name of one of them; although the fact that it has been registered in joint names is, plainly, to be taken into account when having regard "to the whole course of dealing between them in relation to the property".'

But the questions in a joint names case are not simply 'what is the extent of the parties' beneficial interests?' but 'did the parties intend their beneficial interests to be different from their legal interests?' and 'if they did, in what way and to what extent?' There are differences between sole and joint names cases when trying to divine the common intentions or understanding between the parties. I know of no case in which a sole legal owner (there being no declaration of trust) has been held to hold the property on a beneficial joint tenancy. But a court may well hold that joint legal owners (there being no declaration of trust) are also beneficial joint tenants. Another difference is that it will almost always have been a conscious decision to put the house into joint names. Even if the parties have not executed the transfer, they will usually, if not invariably, have executed the contract which precedes it. Committing oneself to spend large sums of money on a place to live is not normally done by accident or without giving it a moment's thought.

67. This is not to say that the parties invariably have a full understanding of the legal effects of their choice: there is recent empirical evidence from a small scale qualitative study to confirm that they do not (see G. Douglas, J. Pearce and H. Woodward, 'Dealing with Property Issues on Cohabitation Breakdown' [2007] *Fam Law* 36). But that is so whether or not there is an express declaration of trust and no one thinks that such a declaration can be overturned, except in cases of fraud or mistake: see para. 49 above. Nor do they always have a completely free choice in the matter. Mortgagees used to insist upon the home being put in the name of the person whom they assumed would be the main breadwinner. Nowadays, they tend to think that it is in their best interests that the home be jointly owned and both parties assume joint and several liability for the mortgage. (It is, of course, a matter of indifference to the mortgagees where the beneficial interests lie.) Here again, this factor does not invalidate the parties' choice if there is an express declaration of trust, nor should it automatically count against it where there is none.

68. The burden will therefore be on the person seeking to show that the parties did intend their beneficial interests to be different from their legal interests, and in what way. This is not a task to be lightly embarked upon. In family disputes, strong feelings are aroused when couples split up. These often lead the parties, honestly but mistakenly, to reinterpret the past in self-exculpatory or vengeful terms. They also lead people to spend far more on the legal battle than is warranted by the sums actually at stake. A full examination of the facts is likely to involve disproportionate costs. In joint names cases it is also unlikely to lead to a different result unless the facts are very unusual. Nor may disputes be confined to the parties themselves. People with an interest in the deceased's estate may well wish to assert that he had a beneficial tenancy in common. It cannot be the case that all the hundreds of thousands, if not millions, of transfers into joint names using the old forms are vulnerable to challenge in the courts simply because it is likely that the owners contributed unequally to their purchase.

69. In law, 'context is everything' and the domestic context is very different from the commercial world. Each case will turn on its own facts. Many more factors than financial contributions may be relevant to divining the parties' true intentions. These include: any advice or discussions at the time of the transfer which cast light upon their intentions then; the reasons why the home was acquired in their joint names; the reasons why (if it be the case) the survivor was authorised to give a receipt for the capital moneys; the purpose for which the home was acquired; the nature of the parties' relationship; whether they had children for whom they both had responsibility to provide a home; how the purchase was financed, both initially and subsequently; how the parties arranged their finances, whether separately or together or a bit of both; how they discharged the outgoings on the property and their other household expenses. When a couple are joint owners of the home and jointly liable for the mortgage, the inferences to be drawn from who pays for what may be very different from the inferences to be drawn when only one is owner of the home. The arithmetical calculation of how much was paid by each is also likely to be less important. It will be easier to draw the inference that they intended that each should contribute as much to the household as they reasonably could and that they would share the eventual benefit or burden equally. The parties' individual characters and personalities may also be a factor in deciding where their true intentions lay. In the cohabitation context, mercenary considerations may be more to the fore than they would be in marriage, but it should not be assumed that they always take pride of place over natural love and affection. At the end of the day, having taken all this into account, cases in which the joint legal owners are to be taken to have intended that their beneficial interests should be different from their legal interests will be very unusual.

70. This is not, of course, an exhaustive list. There may also be reason to conclude that, whatever the parties' intentions at the outset, these have now changed. An example might be where one party has financed (or constructed himself) an extension or substantial improvement to the property, so that what they have now is significantly different from what they had then.

...

Applying the law to the facts

86. The starting point is that it is for Ms Dowden to show that the common intention, when taking a conveyance of the house into their joint names or thereafter, was that they should hold the property otherwise than as beneficial joint tenants. Unfortunately, we lack precise findings on many of the factors relevant to answering that question, because the judge addressed himself to 'looking at the parties' entire course of conduct together'. He looked at their relationship rather than the matters which were

particularly relevant to their intentions about this property. He founded his conclusion on the length and nature of their relationship, which he repeatedly referred to as a partnership, despite the fact that they had maintained separate finances throughout their time together. With the best will in the world, and acknowledging the problems of making more precise findings on many issues after this length of time, this is not an adequate answer to the question. It amounts to little more than saying that these people were in a relationship for twenty-seven years and had four children together. During this time Mr Stack made unquantifiable indirect contributions to the acquisition and improvement of one house and quantifiable direct contributions to the acquisition of another. Both co-operated in looking after the home and bringing up their children.

87. In some, perhaps many, cases of real domestic partnership, there would be nothing to indicate that a contrary inference should be drawn. However, there are many factors to which Ms Dowden can point to indicate that these parties did have a different common intention. The first, of course, is that on any view she contributed far more to the acquisition of Chatsworth Road than did Mr Stack. There are many different ways of calculating this. The Court of Appeal rejected the judge's view that the Halifax account represented 'joint savings', either at the time of the Purves Road purchase or at the time of the Chatsworth Road purchase. Hence they held that the whole of the purchase price, other than the mortgage loan, had been contributed by Ms Dowden. She had also contributed more to the capital repayment of that loan, although Mr Stack had made all the payments necessary to keep it going. It is not surprising that the Court of Appeal reached the conclusion that Ms Dowden was entitled to at least the 65% she claimed.

88. On the other hand, there was some evidence that Mr Stack had made payments into the Halifax account before the Purves Road purchase and that he had made payments thereafter which would have enabled Ms Dowden to save more of her income than would otherwise have been possible. This, together with his contributions towards the substantial improvements made to Purves Road, might suffice to give him some interest in the proceeds of sale, although quantifying that share would be very difficult. It might also suffice to give him some lesser interest in the accumulated Halifax account at the time when Chatsworth Road was bought. Again, quantifying that interest would be very difficult. There was certainly little if anything to support the conclusion that these were truly 'joint' savings. But suppose that one apportions the Purves Road proceeds between them in shares of 2 to Ms Dowden and 1 to Mr Stack; the Halifax savings in shares of 3 to her and 1 to him; and shares the mortgage loan equally between them: this would yield total contributions to Chatsworth Road of roughly 64% to 36%. That calculation is, in my view, as generous to Mr Stack as it is possible to be.

89. The fact that it is possible to make two such different calculations on this sort of evidence indicates the pitfalls in an arithmetical approach to ascertaining the parties' intentions. The one thing that can clearly be said is that, when Chatsworth Road was bought, both parties knew that Ms Dowden had contributed far more to the cash paid towards it than had Mr Stack. Furthermore, although they planned that Mr Stack would pay the interest on the loan and premiums on the joint policy, they also planned to reduce the loan as quickly as they could. These are certainly factors which could, in context, support the inference of an intention to share otherwise than equally.

90. The context is supplied by the nature of the parties' conduct and attitudes towards their property and finances. This is not a case in which it can be said that the parties pooled their separate resources, even notionally, for the common good. The only things they ever had in their joint names were Chatsworth Road and the associated endowment policy. Everything else was kept strictly separate. Each made separate savings and investments most of which it was accepted were their own property. It might have been asked, 'why then did they make an exception for Chatsworth Road?' This is the obvious question. The obvious answer, which Ms Dowden has never denied, was that this time it was indeed intended that Mr Stack should have some interest in the property. In the light of all the other evidence, it cannot be conclusive as to what that interest was.

91. There are other aspects to their financial relationship which tell against joint ownership. Chatsworth Road was, of course, to be a home for the parties and their four children. But they undertook separate responsibility for that part of the expenditure which each had agreed to pay. The only regular expenditure to which it is clear that Mr Stack committed himself was the interest and premiums on Chatsworth Road. All other regular commitments in both houses were undertaken by Ms Dowden. Had it been clear that he had undertaken to pay for consumables and child minding, it might have been possible to deduce some sort of commitment that each would do what they could. But Mr Stack's evidence did not even go as far as that.

92. This is, therefore, a very unusual case. There cannot be many unmarried couples who have lived together for as long as this, who have had four children together, and whose affairs have been kept as

rigidly separate as this couple's affairs were kept. This is all strongly indicative that they did not intend their shares, even in the property which was put into both their names, to be equal (still less that they intended a beneficial joint tenancy with the right of survivorship should one of them die before it was severed). Before the Court of Appeal, Ms Dowden contended for a 65% share and in my view she has made good her case for that.

93. There remains the question of the payment for Mr Stack's alternative accommodation. This matter is governed by the Trusts of Land and Appointment of Trustees Act 1996. Section 12(1) gives a beneficiary who is beneficially entitled to an interest in land the right to occupy the land if the purpose of the trust is to make the land available for his occupation. Thus both these parties have a right of occupation. Section 13(1) gives the trustees the power to exclude or restrict that entitlement, but under section 13(2) this power must be exercised reasonably. The trustees also have power under section 13(3) to impose conditions upon the occupier. These include, under section 13(5), paying any outgoings or expenses in respect of the land and under section 13(6) paying compensation to a person whose right to occupy has been excluded or restricted. Under section 14(2)(a), both trustees and beneficiaries can apply to the court for an order relating to the exercise of these functions. Under section 15(1), the matters to which the court must have regard in making its order include (a) the intentions of the person or person who created the trust, (b) the purposes for which the property subject to the trust is held, (c) the welfare of any minor who occupies or might reasonably be expected to occupy the property as his home, and (d) the interests of any secured creditor of any beneficiary. Under section 15(2), in a case such as this, the court must also have regard to the circumstances and wishes of each of the beneficiaries who would otherwise be entitled to occupy the property.

94. These statutory powers replaced the old doctrines of equitable accounting under which a beneficiary who remained in occupation might be required to pay an occupation rent to a beneficiary who was excluded from the property. The criteria laid down in the statute should be applied, rather than in the cases decided under the old law, although the results may often be the same. In this case, the judge applied neither. The property had been bought as a home for the parties and their children. By October 2004, three of the children were still minors. Both parties had the responsibility of providing them with a home. Ms Dowden remained responsible for the upkeep and outgoings on the home until it was sold. Mr Stack had to provide himself with alternative accommodation but had nothing to pay in respect of the upkeep of the family's home until he was able to realise his share in it upon sale. While, therefore, a case could be made for compensating him for his exclusion, it has to be borne in mind that he had agreed to go in the course of proceedings under the Family Law Act 1996. The reason given by the judge took no account, as he was required to do, of the statutory criteria. The fact that the house was to be sold as soon as possible, so that Mr Stack would not be kept out his money for long, was if anything a factor telling against the exercise of this discretion. I would therefore agree with the Court of Appeal on this point.

95. In the result, therefore, I would dismiss this appeal. But the route by which I, and as I understand it the majority of your Lordships, have arrived at that result is different, both in principle and on the facts, from that taken by the Court of Appeal.

LORD NEUBERGER OF ABBOTSBURY (dissenting from the majority analysis):

...

102. ... A change in the law, however sensible and just it seems, always carries a real risk of new and unforeseen uncertainties and unfairnesses. That is a particular danger when the change is effected by the court rather than the legislature, as the change is influenced by, indeed normally based on, the facts of a particular case, there is little room for public consultation, and there is no input from the democratically elected legislature.

103. In the present type of case, while the number of unmarried cohabitants has increased very substantially over the past fifty (and even more over the past twenty) years, the change has been one of degree, and does not, in my view, justify a departure from established legal principles. I agree with Griffiths LJ (see *Bernard* v *Josephs* [1982] Ch 391 at 402) that the applicable principles are the same whether the parties are married or not, although the nature of the relationship will bear on the inferences to be drawn from their discussions and actions.

104. The Law Commission has considered this topic in the excellent Discussion and Consultation Papers described by Baroness Hale in paragraphs 44 to 47 of her opinion. The fact that the Law Commission has characterised the present state of the law as 'unduly complex, arbitrary and uncertain', does not, in my opinion, justify our changing it. The Discussion Paper refers to the impossibility of devising a scheme 'which can operate fairly and evenly across the diversity of domestic circumstances which are now to

be encountered'. This is a warning shot against the courts (as opposed to the legislature) refashioning the law. All the more so bearing in mind that, as Lord Walker says, the Law Commission may soon make specific proposals for change in this area.

105. In other words, the Law Commission's analysis may well justify the legislature changing the law in this field, but it does not support similar intervention by the courts, other than for the purpose of clarification and simplification. Similarly, the fact that the law of Scotland on this topic may differ from that of England and Wales, as explained by Lord Hope, does not justify the courts changing the law here (or indeed in Scotland), although it may well be another reason for changing and unifying the law on this topic throughout the United Kingdom[.]

106. In my judgment, it is therefore inappropriate for the law when applied to cases of this sort to depart from the well-established principles laid down over the years. It also seems to me that the law of resulting and constructive trusts is flexible enough to deal with problems such as those thrown up by cases such as this, and it would be a disservice to the important causes of certainty and consistency if we were to hold otherwise. I note that the Court of Appeal's recent decisions in this case and in *Oxley* v *Hiscock* [2004] EWCA Civ 546, [2005] Fam 211 (both of which were rightly decided) produced an outcome which would be dictated by a resulting trust solution.

107. Accordingly, while the domestic context can give rise to very different factual considerations from the commercial context, I am unconvinced that this justifies a different approach in principle to the issue of the ownership of the beneficial interest in property held in joint names. In the absence of statutory provisions to the contrary, the same principles should apply to assess the apportionment of the beneficial interest as between legal co-owners, whether in a sexual, platonic, familial, amicable or commercial relationship. In each type of case, one is concerned with the issue of the ownership of the beneficial interest in property held in the names of two people, who have contributed to its acquisition, retention or value.

108. It appears to me helpful for present purposes to consider the issue in a structured way. First, to consider how the beneficial interest is owned at the date of acquisition, which involves identifying the nature and effect of the relevant features of what transpired between the parties up to, and at, the date of acquisition of the property. Then to consider the position at the date of the hearing, which involves identifying the relevant features of what subsequently transpired between the parties, and deciding whether they justify a change in the way in which the beneficial ownership is held. As already explained, I believe that the proper approach to these highly fact-sensitive enquiries should be in accordance with established legal principles and, as far as is consistent with those principles, as simple as possible.

Beneficial ownership on acquisition: where there is no evidence

109. In the absence of any relevant evidence other than the fact that the property, whether a house or a flat, acquired as a home for the legal co-owners is in joint names, the beneficial ownership will also be joint, so that it is held in equal shares. This can be said to result from the maxims that equity follows the law and equality is equity. On a less technical, and some might say more practical, approach, it can also be justified on the basis that any other solution would be arbitrary or capricious.

Beneficial ownership on acquisition: differential contributions

110. Where the only additional relevant evidence to the fact that the property has been acquired in joint names is the extent of each party's contribution to the purchase price, the beneficial ownership at the time of acquisition will be held, in my view, in the same proportions as the contributions to the purchase price. That is the resulting trust solution. The only realistic alternative in such a case would be to adhere to the joint ownership solution. There is an argument to support the view that equal shares should still be the rule in cohabitation cases, on the basis that it may be what many parties may expect if they purchase a home in joint names, even with different contributions. However, I consider that the resulting trust solution is correct in such circumstances.

Beneficial ownership: events after the acquisition of the house

138. The fact that the ownership of the beneficial interest in a home is determined at the date of acquisition does not mean that it cannot alter thereafter. My noble and learned friend Lord Hoffmann suggested during argument that the trust which arises at the date of acquisition, whether resulting or constructive, is of an ambulatory nature. That elegant characterisation does not justify a departure from the application of established legal principles any more than such a departure is justified at the time of acquisition. It seems to me that 'compelling evidence', to use Lord Hope's expression in paragraph 11,

is required before one can infer that, subsequent to the acquisition of the home, the parties intended a change in the shares in which the beneficial ownership is held. Such evidence would normally involve discussions, statements or actions, subsequent to the acquisition, from which an agreement or common understanding as to such a change can properly be inferred. I have already discussed some of the issues arising in this connection, partly because Ms Dowden and Mr Stack had lived together in Purves Road before they acquired the house at Chatsworth Road. 139. There are, however, one or two aspects I should like to mention. I agree with Lord Walker that, subject of course to other relevant facts justifying a different conclusion, the fact that one party carries out significant improvements to the home will justify an adjustment of the apportionment of the beneficial interest in his favour. In such a case, the cost could be seen as capital expenditure which differs from regular outgoings relating to the use of the home, and is not dissimilar in financial effect, from the cost of acquiring the home in the first place. To qualify, any work must be substantial: decoration or repairs (at least unless they were very significant) would not do.

140. There is also the question of repayments of the mortgage, and payments of other outgoings. I have already discussed the effect of the parties taking a mortgage in joint names, and suggested that, in some cases, repayments of capital could have the effect of adjusting the shares in the beneficial interest. (It is conceivable that that could apply to payments of interest as well). In many cases, the repayments of capital, even if effected wholly by one party, should not be interpreted as indicating an intention to alter the way in which the beneficial interest is apportioned. Thus, the fact that one party is the home-maker (and, often, child-carer) and the other is the wage-earner would probably not justify the former having his share decreased simply because the other party repays the mortgage by instalments, but it may be different where both parties earn and share the home-making, but one of them repays the mortgage by a single capital sum.

141. Consistently with what has already been discussed, I am unconvinced that the original ownership of the beneficial interest could normally be altered merely by the way in which the parties conduct their personal and day-to-day financial affairs. I do not see how the facts that they have lived together for a long time, have been in a loving relationship, have children, operated a joint bank account, and shared the outgoings of the household, including in respect of use and occupation of the home, can, of themselves, indicate an intention to equalise their originally unequal shares any more than they would indicate an intention to equalise their shares on acquisition, as discussed earlier. So, too, the facts that they both earn and share the home-making, or that one party has a well-paid job and the other is the home-maker, seem to me to be irrelevant at least on their own. Even the fact that one party pays all the outgoings and the other does nothing would not seem to me to justify any adjustment to the original ownership of the beneficial interest (subject to the possible exception of mortgage repayments).

142. In many cases, these points may result in an outcome which would seem unfair at least to some people. However (unless and until the legislature decides otherwise) fairness is not the guiding principle as Baroness Hale says, and, at least without legislative directions, it would be a very subjective and uncertain guide. Further, it is always important to bear in mind the need for clarity and certainty.

143. It is worth repeating that one is concerned with the ownership of what will normally be the most important and valuable asset of the parties, and the way they conduct their day-to-day living and finances is, in my view, at least of itself, not a reliable guide to their intentions in relation to that ownership. Even payments on decoration, repairs, utilities and Council tax, although related to the home, are concerned with its use and enjoyment, as opposed to its ownership as a capital asset. It is also worth repeating that these factors are not irrelevant to the issue of whether there has been a change in the shares in which the beneficial interest in the home is held. They provide part of the vital background against which any alleged discussion, statement or action said to give rise to a change in the beneficial ownership is to be assessed, in relation to both whether it occurred and what its effect was.

144. I am unhappy with the formulation of Chadwick LJ in *Oxley* at paragraph 69, quoted by Baroness Hale at paragraph 61 of her opinion, namely that the beneficial ownership should be apportioned by reference to what is 'fair having regard to the whole course of dealing between [the parties] in relation to the property'. First, fairness is not the appropriate yardstick. Secondly, the formulation appears to contemplate an imputed intention. Thirdly, 'the whole course of dealing ... in relation to the property' is too imprecise, as it gives insufficient guidance as to what is primarily relevant, namely dealings which cast light on the beneficial ownership of the property, and too limited, as all aspects of the relationship could be relevant in providing the context by reference to which any alleged discussion, statement and actions must be assessed. As already explained, I also disagree with Chadwick LJ's implicit suggestion in the same paragraph that 'the arrangements which [the parties] make with regard to the outgoings' (other than

mortgage repayments) are likely to be of primary relevance to the issue of the ownership of the beneficial interest in the home.

145. I am rather more comfortable with the formulation of Gray and Gray, also quoted in paragraph 61 of Baroness Hale's opinion, that the court should 'undertak[e] a survey of the whole course of dealing between the parties ... taking account of all conduct which throws light on the question what shares were intended'. It is perhaps inevitable that this formulation begs the difficult questions of what conduct throws light, and what light it throws, as those questions are so fact-sensitive. 'Undertaking a survey of the whole course of dealings between the parties' should not, I think, at least normally, require much detailed or controversial evidence. That is not merely for reasons of practicality and certainty. As already indicated, I would expect almost all of 'the whole course of dealing' to be relevant only as background: it is with actions discussions and statements which relate to the parties' agreement and understanding as to the ownership of the beneficial interest in the home with which the court should, at least normally, primarily be concerned. Otherwise, the enquiry is likely to be trespassing into what I regard as the forbidden territories of imputed intention and fairness.

NOTES

1. Approving *Goodman* v *Gallant* [1986] Fam 106, their lordships confirmed that the parties should have declared all the nature and extent of their rights by means of an express trust (answering all the questions on the Land Registry's standard land transfer form (form TR1) will produce the same benefit of certainty). Baroness Hale confirmed that '[n]o-one now doubts that such an express declaration of trust is conclusive unless varied by subsequent agreement or affected by proprietary estoppel' (para. [49]). An express trust will deal with such matters as whether the equitable interest in the land is owned jointly or in shares (remember that the legal title to co-owned land is always, as with all forms of property held on trust, held by the trustees jointly). If the express trust declares that the co-owners own distinct equitable shares in the land, the trust should also express the size of the parties' distinct shares. The problem is that not everyone takes the sensible precaution of drawing up an express trust. In this respect, the parties in *Stack* v *Dowden* are typical. The most they did was to sign a conveyance containing the words the survivor 'can give a valid receipt for capital money arising on a disposition of the land'. It was held that this mere form of conveyance did not constitutive an express declaration of trust.

2. It is in the absence of an express trust that the decision in *Stack* v *Dowden* really becomes significant. Before *Stack* v *Dowden* a party claiming an interest under an informal trust of a family home held in joint names was allowed two bites at the cherry. She could argue that she had an interest under a resulting trust, or, in the alternative, an interest under a constructive trust. Following the decision of the House of Lords in *Stack* v *Dowden* it would appear that the resulting trust alternative is now no longer available to the claimant. That alternative died when the House of Lords held that unequal contributions to purchase price will no longer rebut the presumption of joint beneficial ownership. (You should recall that the essence of a resulting trust is to give an interest in proportion to financial contribution.)

3. A general difficulty with the decision in *Stack* v *Dowden*, is that in one fell swoop it has made the application of the settled property doctrine of resulting trust turn upon such relatively ill-defined concepts as 'family' and 'shared home'. And yet, having decided to unsettle the resulting trust doctrine, their Lordships decided that on the particular facts of *Stack* v *Dowden* the strong presumption in favour of equality had been overcome and that the parties should have interests in the property proportionate to their financial contributions to acquisition—precisely the same outcome that would have been reached on a resulting trust approach!

4. It is interesting to observe that the value of the family home was divided in almost exactly the same proportions in which, at the end of their relationship, Mr Stack and Ms Dowden had been bringing income into the 'family finances' (Ms Dowden's £42,000 salary representing 63 per cent of the whole, Mr Stack's £24,000 salary representing 37 per cent).

5. After the land has been acquired, the parties' dealings *inter se* are only relevant to the extent that such dealings elucidate their intentions regarding sharing beneficial ownership of the land (*Holman* v *Howes* [2007] EWCA Civ 877, Court of Appeal). The cohabitants in *Jones* v *Kernott* ([2011] UKSC 53; [2011] 3 WLR 1121) expressly agreed, when their relationship broke down and Mr Kernott left the family home in 1993, that they were at that time beneficial joint owners in

equity. Thereafter Ms Jones remained in occupation and met all future expenses and outgoings of maintaining the premises and paying off the mortgage. Some years later, Mr Kernott purported to sever and recover his half-share of the land, but the County Court judge awarded Ms Jones 90 per cent of the value of the land on the basis that this was 'fair and just'. That decision was upheld in the High Court. The Court of Appeal allowed Mr Kernott's appeal by a majority of two to one, where their Lordships emphasised that (following *Stack* v *Dowden*) the judges in the lower courts ought to have respected the parties' agreement to share equally in the event of sale and, in the absence of compelling evidence that the parties' intentions had changed, that initial agreement should stand ([2010] EWCA Civ 578; [2010] 3 All ER 423). However, when the matter came before the UK Supreme Court, their Lordships held that the parties' intentions *had* changed during the period of Mr Kernott's absence from the shared home and, allowing the appeal, upheld the decision of the County Court judge. Their Lordships favoured fair maintenance of the current occupants (Ms Jones and the children of her cohabitation with Kernott) over a strict allocation on the basis of initial financial contribution to purchase. The outcome of any given 'cohabitation case' is as unpredictable as ever as a result of *Jones* v *Kernott*, and it is fair to say that judicial discretion in this area is now so wide that courts are not far off the broad approach to allocation that is required by statute when married cohabitants divorce. Lord Walker and Baroness Hale summarised their judgment by saying that 'where a family home is bought in the joint names of a cohabiting couple who are both responsible for any mortgage, but without any express declaration of their beneficial interests', the starting point is that 'equity follows the law and they are joint tenants both in law and in equity'. This 'presumption can be displaced by showing (a) that the parties had a different common intention at the time when they acquired the home, or (b) that they later formed the common intention that their respective shares would change'.

6 According to Baroness Hale in *Stack* v *Dowden*, 'In law, "context is everything" and the domestic context is very different from the commercial world' [para.[69]]. This is hard to square with recent decisions in which courts have proceeded on the assumption that there is *prima facie* no substantial difference between domestic and business contexts when deciding fair shares under a constructive trust (e.g. *Gallarotti* v *Sebastianelli* [2012] EWCA Civ 865; [2012] Fam Law 1206—a case of two 'friends' living together). Note that a case is to be characterised as commercial or domestic according to the nature of the parties' dealings, not the nature of the type of property involved (*Whittaker* v *Kinnear* [2011] EWHC 1479 (QB)—a proprietary estoppel case).

■ QUESTIONS

1. In *Burns* v *Burns* [1984] Ch 317, Fox LJ said at 327:

   What is needed, I think, is evidence of a payment or payments by the plaintiff which it can be inferred was referable to the acquisition of the house ... If there is a substantial contribution by the woman to the family expenses, and the house was purchased on a mortgage, her contribution is, indirectly, referable to the acquisition of the house since, in one way or another, it enables the family to pay the mortgage instalments. Thus, a payment could be said to be referable to the acquisition of the house if, for example, the payer either (a) pays part of the purchase price or (b) contributes regularly to the mortgage instalments or (c) pays off part of the mortgage or (d) makes a substantial financial contribution to the family expenses so as to enable the mortgage instalments to be paid.

   In the light of Lord Bridge's speech in *Lloyds Bank* v *Rosset*, was Fox LJ correct to include item (d)?

   Note that Patricia Ferguson observed in (1993) 109 *LQR* 114, at p. 116: [Lord Bridge's] requirement of 'direct contributions' where there is no express agreement runs contrary to previous authorities which held that indirect financial contributions which were 'referable to the acquisition of the house'—such as F's payment of all household expenses to free M's income for mortgage instalments—were sufficient. It is difficult to know ... whether he intends to depart from this view of the law or not.

2. Even Lord Bridge would accept that mortgage contributions (payments of capital and interest) can count—and indeed this has been clear since *Gissing v Gissing*—but on what basis? Note that they do not fit happily into a resulting trust analysis. Is there anything in Lord Diplock's speech in *Gissing* which gives any indication? Is the conceptual basis of discounts similar? Can this also help determine the answer to question 1 above?

3. Do you agree with the observation by Professor J. W. Harris (set out in this section)? Does he attach too much weight to money compared to labour, do you think? Which is the more 'real' of the two?

J. W. Harris, 'Doctrine, justice, and home-sharing'

(1999) 19(3) *Oxford Journal of Legal Studies* 421

'We are here in the realm of metaphor. It seems that a person with money in her pocket is to be taken as carrying around with her both so much cash and a fixed quantity of labour-power. She "owns" both. She may transfer some portion of the one or of the other, so that there will be 'subtraction" or "deprivation" from the total sum (of money or labour-power). Restitution theory, in this respect, comes in august company. Karl Marx founded his critique of capitalist production and its appropriation of surplus values on the assumption that every service contract represents a conveyance, for the contract's duration, of the worker's entire labour-power to the employer. ...

The metaphor may be readily unravelled. When I work I may be said to "expend" physical or mental energy and I may, perhaps, feel in some way depleted. But it is not the case, as with spending money, that I cease to own some resource which formerly I did own. I have maintained that arguments for property-distribution based on labour-ownership, or the connected notion of self-ownership, are spurious. *Quantum meruit* claims were, in law, once founded on the fiction of promise. Are we better off if we erect claims arising from labour on the metaphor of depletion and transfer?'

C: Proprietary estoppel

Brian Turner v *Kim Jacob*

[2006] EWHC 1317 (Ch), Chancery Division

MR JUSTICE PATTEN: Recent authorities have emphasised that the boundaries between the creation of a constructive trust by agreement and the operation of the doctrine of proprietary estoppel which may lead to the creation of interest in the property are closely linked and have many characteristics in common. Lord Bridge, I think, recognised this [in *Lloyd's Bank* v *Rosset*] ... but it was spelt out clearly by the Court of Appeal in *Yaxley* v *Gotts* [2000] Ch 162 at p. 176 where Robert Walker LJ said this:

'At a high level of generality, there is much common ground between the doctrines of proprietary estoppel and the constructive trust, just as there is between proprietary estoppel and part performance. All are concerned with equity's intervention to provide relief against unconscionable conduct, whether as between neighbouring landowners, or vendor and purchaser, or relatives who make informal arrangements for sharing a home, or a fiduciary and the beneficiary or client to whom he owes a fiduciary obligation ... '

NOTE: Even in those cases (typically land acquisition cases) where a constructive trust appears to be the same as a proprietary estoppel, there is a crucial difference between them. Proprietary estoppel is a cause of action that arises in equity to prevent ('stop') the legal owner of certain property (A) from denying that another person (B) has or might have a proprietary interest in that property. The estoppel having thus been raised, it still needs to be satisfied or 'fed' by a remedial award made at the court's discretion. In some cases, the award of a share of the land under a constructive trust is the appropriate remedial award, and in such cases, constructive trust and proprietary estoppel are practically indistinguishable in their final effect. In other cases, an award of cash will suffice (see, for example, *Lloyd* v *Sutcliffe* [2008] EWHC 1329 (Ch)). Nevertheless, the proprietary estoppel comes first (in the nature of a cause of action) and the constructive trust comes second (to satisfy the cause of action). Note, however, that although the constructive trust is in this respect a remedy, it is not a 'remedial constructive trust' in the sense that the trust is created by the court as a remedy. Rather, the court recognises the trust which already existed according to the facts—the significant facts being that of representation and reliance such that it would be unconscionable for the legal owner to deny that the claimant has a beneficial share in the property.

Gillett v *Holt*

[2001] Ch 210, Court of Appeal

Facts: *Gillett* v *Holt* reads like a Dickensian novel. Mr Gillett was 12 years old when Mr Holt (then a 38-year-old gentleman farmer) took him under his wing. At Mr Holt's suggestion Mr Gillett left school at the age of 16 and began a long career working on Mr Holt's farm. Mr Gillett's wife and children became in due course a surrogate family to Mr Holt (who had no immediate family of his own), a fact confirmed by Mr Holt's frequent assurances (often in public) that Mr Gillett would one day inherit the farm. However, the relationship between the men eventually cooled and ultimately broke down entirely. Mr Holt wrote Mr Gillett out of his will and Mr Gillett commenced action seeking to establish an interest in the farm under proprietary estoppel, on the basis of Mr Holt's assurances and Mr Gillett's detrimental reliance upon them. The judge at first instance held that Mr Holt's representation could not be considered irrevocable and that in any event Mr Gillett had suffered no detriment in reliance upon them.

Held: The Court of Appeal rejected any need to show that the assurance was irrevocable and held that, despite the obvious material benefits of Mr Holt's patronage, it would be detrimental to deny him an interest in the farm because he had forgone the opportunity to educate himself and make alternative provision for his retirement and old age. Detriment is 'not a narrow or technical concept':

ROBERT WALKER LJ: The detriment need not consist of the expenditure of money or other quantifiable financial detriment, so long as it is something substantial. The requirement must be approached as part of a broad enquiry as to whether repudiation of an assurance is or is not unconscionable in all the circumstances.

NOTES
1. A most interesting feature is the detriment Mr Gillett was held to have suffered when Mr Holt paid the private school fees of Mr Gillett's eldest son. How is that detrimental one might ask? The answer is that Mr Gillett had another son whom he then felt obliged to educate privately at his own expense.
2. A similar case to *Gillett* v *Holt* is *Murphy* v *Burrows* [2004] EWHC 1900 (Ch), involving facts which the judge actually described as 'Dickensian' (*per* Mr Richard Sheldon QC (sitting as a Deputy Judge of the High Court) at para. [3] of the transcript).
3. If a representation is made on certain conditions, it is not enough to prove reliance on the representation. One must also show that reliance was reasonable and detrimental, and that the detriment flowed from reasonable reliance on the representation (*Hunt* v *Soady* [2007] EWCA Civ 366, Court of Appeal (Civil Division)). *Powell* v *Benney* [2007] EWCA Civ 1283 illustrates the point. The owner of a number of properties promised Mr and Mrs Powell that he would leave the properties to them in his will. They proceeded to improve the properties *on their own initiative*. When the representor died, he left no will and his property passed to Benney on intestacy. The Court of Appeal called this a 'non-bargain' estoppel and upheld the first instance award of £20,000 as reasonable to meet the Powell's expectations. For a case of outright refusal to make an award, due to the claimant's failure to make a 'sacrifice', see *Century (UK) Limited SA* v *Clibbery* [2004] EWHC 1870 (Ch).

Jennings v *Rice*

[2002] EWCA Civ 159, [2003] 1 FCR 501, Court of Appeal

ROBERT WALKER LJ: [para. [45] onwards] Sometimes the assurances, and the claimant's reliance on them, have a consensual character falling not far short of an enforceable contract ... In a case of that sort both the claimant's expectations and the element of detriment to the claimant will have been defined with reasonable clarity ... In a case like that the consensual element of what has happened suggests that the claimant and the benefactor probably regarded the expected benefit and the accepted detriment as being (in a general, imprecise way) equivalent, or at any rate not obviously disproportionate ... [para. [50]] In such a case the court's natural response is to fulfil the claimant's expectations. But if the claimant's expectations are uncertain, or extravagant, or out of all proportion to the detriment which the claimant has suffered, the court can and should recognize that the claimant's equity should be satisfied in another (and generally more limited) way. [para. 51] But that does not mean that the court should in such a case abandon expectations completely, and look to the detriment suffered by the claimant as defining the appropriate measure of relief. Indeed in many cases the detriment may be even more difficult to quantify, in financial terms, than the claimant's expectations ... In such cases the court has to exercise a wide judgmental discretion. [para. 52] It would be unwise to attempt any comprehensive enumeration of the factors relevant to the exercise of the court's discretion, or to suggest any hierarchy of factors. In my view they include ... misconduct of the claimant as in *Willis* v *Willis* [1979] Ch. 261 or particularly oppressive conduct on the part of the defendant, as in *Crabb* v *Arun District Council* [[1976] Ch. 179] or *Pascoe* v *Turner* [[1979] 1 WLR 431]. To these can safely be added the court's recognition that it cannot compel people who have fallen out to live peaceably together, so that there may be a need for a clean break; alterations in the benefactor's assets and circumstances, especially where the benefactor's assurances have been given, and the claimant's detriment has been suffered, over a long period of years; the likely effect of taxation; and (to a limited degree) the other claims (legal and moral) on the benefactor or his or her estate. No doubt there are many other factors which it may be right for the court to take into account in particular factual situations. [para. 56] ... I respectfully agree with the view expressed by Hobhouse L.J. in *Sledmore* v *Dalby*, [(1996) 72 P. & C.R. 196.] that the principle of proportionality (between remedy and detriment) ... is relevant ...

Simon Gardner, 'The Remedial Discretion In Proprietary Estoppel—Again'

(2006) 122 (Jul) *LQR* 492, pp. 493–4, 511–12

(Commenting on the preceding passage from *Jennings* v *Rice*)

Robert Walker L.J. thus divides the range of possible situations into two classes, with differing approaches to relief, as follows:

A. Where the parties have made a bargain in reasonably clear terms, defining both the claimant's expectation and the detrimental reliance required of him in order to earn that expectation. Here, the relief should vindicate the claimant's expectation.

B. Where the claimant's expectation is uncertain, or extravagant, or out of all proportion to the detriment which she has suffered. Here, the relief is arrived at by the exercise of a wide judgmental discretion, influenced—as relevant—by:

    (i) the claimant's expectation, but also proportionality with her detriment;

    (ii) the parties' conduct;

    (iii) the need for a clean break;

    (iv) alterations in the defendant's assets and circumstances;

    (v) the effect of taxation;

    (vi) other claims on the defendant or his or her estate;

    (vii) possible other factors.

... It is a striking feature of this analysis that it divides cases into 'bargain' and 'non-bargain' categories, the former entailing relief in an expectation measure, the latter requiring the exercise of a 'wide judgmental discretion'. Such a division is absent from other discussions of the subject ...

It is legitimate for the law to make use of a discretion, rather than a rigid rule, in this context. On the other hand, the courts have not done enough to make that legitimacy secure ... overall, this discretion cannot be sufficiently reconciled with the Rule of Law: it involves an unacceptable degree of rule by men (the individual judges), not laws. The reasons for this are, however, fully capable of repair. A clearer perception of the jurisdiction's aim is readily attainable, as is a practice of greater transparency in the justification of chosen outcomes, and a sharper focus in appraising the aptness of these justifications. Although it does not go far enough, Robert Walker L.J.'s analysis represents a promising start on this project: efforts should now be made take it further.

NOTES:

1. Robert Walker LJ approved the judgment of Hobhouse LJ in *Sledmore* v *Dalby* (1996) 72 P & CR 196, who had identified 'the need for proportionality' and observed: 'The essence of the doctrine of proprietary estoppel is to do what is necessary to avoid an unconscionable result, and a disproportionate remedy cannot be the right way of going about that' (p. 209). In *Sledmore* v *Dalby*, the Court of Appeal held that although there may have been grounds for an estoppel in the past, it was no longer inequitable to allow the expectation created by the benefactor (Robert Walker LJ's term—see *Jennings* v *Rice*) to be defeated. See also, *Clark* v *Clark* [2006] EWHC 275 (Ch).

2. The Court of Appeal, following *Jennings* v *Rice*, has confirmed that the remedy satisfying a proprietary estoppel should attempt to achieve an outcome that is fair and proportionate between the parties, rather than seeking merely 'the minimum equity to do justice', which was the traditional formula (*Joyce* v *Epsom* [2012] EWCA Civ 1398. See, also, *Suggitt* v *Suggitt* [2012] EWCA Civ 1140). In *Aspden* v *Elvy* [2012] EWHC 1387 (Ch); [2012] 2 FLR 807, a claimant was awarded a 25 per cent share in a barn conversion on the basis that the legal owner (his partner) had encouraged him to make substantial financial contributions to the conversion knowing that he did not intend the contributions to be a gift. The 25 per cent valuation was considered to be a proportionate response to expectation and detriment.

Yeoman's Row Management Ltd v *Cobbe*

[2008] UKHL 55, [2008] 1 WLR 1752, House of Lords

Facts: A property developer entered into an oral agreement with the owner of a block of flats (Yeoman's—controlled by Mrs Lisle-Mainwaring) under which the developer undertook to obtain planning permission to demolish the block and replace it with new town houses. A formula was agreed on price and the division of profits from the development. The developer spent 18 months acquiring planning permission to demolish a block of flats to build new town houses. It was after planning permission had been obtained, that the owner of the block purported to withdraw from the agreement. In the Court of Appeal, the developer was awarded a share in the increased value of the property attributable to the planning permission and not merely an award based on their expenditure and work, but this was overturned by the House of Lords.

Held: The developer was awarded a mere *quantum meruit* (sum deserved) sufficient to ensure that the land owner had not been unjustly enriched by the time and labour expended by the developer in pursuing the planning permission in accordance with the informal agreement. It was held that the developer had assumed the risk that the owner of the block would withdraw. The fact that withdrawal was unconscionable in the abstract did not suffice, it had to be shown that the owner had behaved in a manner traditionally considered to be unconscionable in this context. The evidence was the other way—namely, that the traditional practice was to allow parties to withdraw from an informal contract in such a case. The claimant's argument that both parties considered themselves to be bound 'in honour' to perform the contract was rejected.

LORD SCOTT OF FOSCOTE:

16. My Lords, unconscionability of conduct may well lead to a remedy but, in my opinion, proprietary estoppel cannot be the route to it unless the ingredients for a proprietary estoppel are present. These ingredients should include, in principle, a proprietary claim made by a Claimant and an answer to that claim based on some fact, or some point of mixed fact and law, that the person against whom the claim is made can be estopped from asserting. To treat a 'proprietary estoppel equity' as requiring neither

a proprietary claim by the Claimant nor an estoppel against the Defendant but simply unconscionable behaviour is, in my respectful opinion, a recipe for confusion.

...

28. The reality of this case, in my opinion, is that Etherton J and the Court of Appeal regarded their finding that Mrs Lisle-Mainwaring's behaviour in repudiating, and seeking an improvement on, the core financial terms of the second agreement was unconscionable, an evaluation from which I do not in the least dissent, as sufficient to justify the creation of a 'proprietary estoppel equity'. As Mummery LJ said (para. 123), she took unconscionable advantage of Mr Cobbe. The advantage taken was the benefit of his services, his time and his money, in obtaining planning permission for the property. The advantage was unconscionable because immediately following the grant of planning permission, she repudiated the financial terms on which Mr Cobbe had been expecting to be able to purchase the property. But to leap from there to a conclusion that a proprietary estoppel case was made out was not, in my opinion, justified. Let it be supposed that Mrs Lisle-Mainwaring were to be held estopped from denying that the core financial terms of the second agreement were the financial terms on which Mr Cobbe was entitled to purchase the property. How would that help Mr Cobbe? He still would not have a complete agreement. Suppose Mrs Lisle-Mainwaring had simply said she had changed her mind and did not want the property to be sold after all. What would she be estopped from denying? Proprietary estoppel requires, in my opinion, clarity as to what it is that the object of the estoppel is to be estopped from denying, or asserting, and clarity as to the interest in the property in question that that denial, or assertion, would otherwise defeat. If these requirements are not recognised, proprietary estoppel will lose contact with its roots and risk becoming unprincipled and therefore unpredictable, if it has not already become so. This is not, in my opinion, a case in which a remedy can be granted to Mr Cobbe on the basis of proprietary estoppel.

29. There is one further point regarding proprietary estoppel to which I should refer. Section 2 of the 1989 Act declares to be void any agreement for the acquisition of an interest in land that does not comply with the requisite formalities prescribed by the section. Subsection (5) expressly makes an exception for resulting, implied or constructive trusts. These may validly come into existence without compliance with the prescribed formalities. Proprietary estoppel does not have the benefit of this exception. The question arises, therefore, whether a complete agreement for the acquisition of an interest in land that does not comply with the section 2 prescribed formalities, but would be specifically enforceable if it did, can become enforceable via the route of proprietary estoppel. It is not necessary in the present case to answer this question, for the second agreement was not a complete agreement and, for that reason, would not have been specifically enforceable so long as it remained incomplete. My present view, however, is that proprietary estoppel cannot be prayed in aid in order to render enforceable an agreement that statute has declared to be void. The proposition that an owner of land can be estopped from asserting that an agreement is void for want of compliance with the requirements of section 2 is, in my opinion, unacceptable. The assertion is no more than the statute provides. Equity can surely not contradict the statute. As I have said, however, statute provides an express exception for constructive trusts. [At this point his lordship considered, and rejected, the possibility of a constructive trust.]

...

The Proprietary Claims: Conclusion

38. N I would for the reasons I have given reject both of the proprietary claims made on Mr Cobbe's behalf. Mr Cobbe's alternative *in personam* claims are relatively uncontroversial but before turning to them I want to reflect for a moment on the implications of the claim he has not made, namely, a claim in deceit. The findings of fact made by Etherton J suggest that well before 18 March 2004 Mrs Lisle-Mainwaring had decided to repudiate the core financial terms of the second agreement but nonetheless had continued to represent to Mr Cobbe, by conduct if not expressly, that she intended to abide by the core financial terms and regarded herself as honour bound to do so. It may be that the detriment incurred by Mr Cobbe had already been incurred and that no further detriment in reliance on any such knowingly false representations was incurred, but that may not have been so. If Mr Cobbe's proprietary claims, of proprietary estoppel and to an interest under a constructive trust, were well founded, similar claims could presumably be brought in many cases where a contract had been induced by a fraudulent misrepresentation. The dishonest representation would often have led to unrealised expectations of benefit. But, unless the representation had become a term of the contract, no one, I think, would suggest that the victim could claim to be compensated for the loss of the expected benefit. The tortious damages recoverable for the deceit would be limited to consequential loss. How could the victim be entitled to a better result than

that if there were no contract at all but simply a dishonest representation on which he had acted to his disadvantage, or, *a fortiori*, to a better result if not only had there been no contract at all but, in addition, the representation had not been dishonest? In my opinion, the representations of intention on which Mr Cobbe acted in the present case cannot, in principle, entitle him to a remedy intended to give him the value of his expectations engendered by the representations. A genuine proprietary claim enabled to succeed by the operation of a genuine proprietary estoppel would be in accordance with principle. But a claim for the imposition of a constructive trust in order to provide a remedy for a disappointed expectation engendered by a representation made in the context of incomplete contractual negotiations is, in my opinion, misconceived and cannot be sustained by reliance on unconscionable behaviour on the part of the representor.

...

LORD WALKER:

92. Here [the word 'unconscionable'] is being used (as in my opinion it should always be used) as an objective value judgment on behaviour (regardless of the state of mind of the individual in question). As such it does in my opinion play a very important part in the doctrine of equitable estoppel, in unifying and confirming, as it were, the other elements. If the other elements appear to be present but the result does not shock the conscience of the court, the analysis needs to be looked at again. In this case Mrs Lisle-Mainwaring's conduct was unattractive. She chose to stand on her rights rather than respecting her non-binding assurances, while Mr Cobbe continued to spend time and effort, between Christmas 2003 and March 2004, in obtaining planning permission. But Mr Cobbe knew that she was bound in honour only, and so in the eyes of equity her conduct, although unattractive, was not unconscionable.

NOTES

1. The decision of the House of Lords in this case makes it difficult to employ proprietary estoppel to render informal land transactions binding between the parties to a commercial negotiation conducted at arms-length, but the decision should be construed narrowly to leave other situations amenable to the assistance offered by proprietary estoppel. A welcome aspect of the decision is that it prevents the customary and reasonable expectations of commercial parties from being disturbed by the inappropriate suggestion that a party has acted 'unconsciously' (on the need for a customary conduct ceiling on unconscionability-based intervention, see G. Watt, 'Unconscionability in Property Law: A Fairy-tale Ending?', in M. Dixon and G. Griffiths (eds), *Contemporary Perspectives in Property, Equity and Trusts Law* (Oxford: Oxford University Press, 2007), pp. 117–37).

2. For a comparison between the House of Lords' approach to unjust enrichment in *Cobbe* and the Australian approach, see J. Getzler, 'Quantum meruit, estoppel, and the primacy of contract' (2009) 125 *LQR* 196.

3. In the same way that the radical decision in *Stack* v *Dowden* ought to be read so as to restrict it to its facts (i.e. domestic or 'romantic' joint legal ownership cases), so the *Yeoman* case ought to be construed restrictively to apply only to commercial cases (and perhaps only to joint venture cases). It is clear that proprietary estoppel will continue to thrive in non-commercial cases, as the decision in *Thorner* v *Major* makes clear.

Thorner v *Major (sub nom Thorner v Curtis)*

[2009] UKHL 18, [2009] 1 WLR 776, House of Lords

Facts: The owner of a farm [Peter] left it to the claimant [David] by will, but subsequently destroyed the will and died intestate. David had worked for Peter for nearly 30 years in the reasonable expectation (based on various hints, but no express representation) that he would inherit the farm.

Held: Proprietary estoppel was found in favour of David and he was awarded the farm.

LORD WALKER OF GESTINGTHORPE (at paras [61]–[62]): In my opinion it is a necessary element of proprietary estoppel that the assurances given to the claimant (expressly or impliedly, or, in standing-by cases, tacitly) should relate to identified property owned (or, perhaps, about to be owned) by the defendant. That is one of the main distinguishing features between the two varieties of equitable estoppel, that is promissory estoppel and proprietary estoppel. The former must be based on an existing legal *relationship* (usually a contract, but not necessarily a contract relating to land). The latter need not be based on an existing legal relationship, but it must relate to *identified property* (usually land) owned (or, perhaps, about to be owned) by the defendant. It is the relation to identified land of the defendant that has enabled proprietary estoppel to develop as a sword, and not merely a shield: see Lord Denning MR in *Crabb v Arun DC* [1976] Ch 179, 187.

In this case the deputy judge made a clear finding of an assurance by Peter that David would become entitled to Steart Farm. The first, 'watershed' assurance was made in 1990 at about the time that Peter made an advantageous sale of one field for development purposes, and used part (but not the whole) of the proceeds to buy more agricultural land, so increasing the farm to the maximum at about 582 acres (some merely tenanted by Peter) which Peter farmed in 1992. Both Peter and David knew that the extent of the farm was liable to fluctuate (as development opportunities arose, and tenancies came and went). There is no reason to doubt that their common understanding was that Peter's assurance related to whatever the farm consisted of at Peter's death (as it would have done, barring any restrictive language, under section 24 of the Wills Act 1837, had Peter made a specific devise of Steart Farm).

NOTES

1. In a note of *Cobbe* and *Thorner*, Martin Dixon laments the fact that in *Thorner* their Lordships missed an opportunity to explore the potential of 'unconscionability' to provide a framework for law in this area ((2009) 3 *Conv* 260–8). Also on *Cobbe* and *Thorner*, see Sloan (2009) 68(3) *CLJ* 518. If any reader has any lingering doubt about the significance of our subject, they might note that the authors McFarlane and Robertson write on *Cobbe* under the title 'The Death of Proprietary Estoppel' ([2008] *LMCLQ* 449) and *Thorner* under the title 'Apocalypse averted'! ((2009) 125 *LQR* 535).

2. The way we analyse proprietary estoppel has inheritance tax implications. It has been argued that 'until the death of the deceased who has not fulfilled his promise to the claimant, there is no trust imposed which in any way diminishes the value of his property' subject to inheritance tax (P. Reed QC (2010) 1 *PCB* 49–57), but against this it has been suggested that the value of the promisor's estate is reduced from the moment *inter vivos* that the promisor's conscience is bound (C. Whitehouse (2010) 2 *PCB* 91–4).

3. It should be noted that where an agreement gives rise to a proprietary estoppel, the terms of the agreement must be sufficiently certain, but need be no more certain than normal contractual terms (*Herbert v Doyle* [2010] EWCA Civ 1095) Court of Appeal (Civ Div). This casts doubt on the decision in *Yaxley v Gotts*.

D: Quantification of the beneficial share

If it is accepted that this area is governed by ordinary principles of property law, then quantification should pretty well be a mechanical task of adding up qualifying contributions. However, the following cases suggest a very flexible approach.

Midland Bank v *Cooke*

[1995] 4 All ER 562, [1995] 2 FLR 915, Court of Appeal

Facts: In 1971, shortly before Mr and Mrs Cooke's marriage, their matrimonial home was purchased by Mr Cooke, and registered in his name alone. The only financial contribution which she could argue was half a wedding present, of £1,100, from Mr Cooke's parents. She did not make any contributions to the mortgage instalments, but discharged other household outgoings, and devoted much time and energy to the improvement of the house and garden. In 1978, the original mortgage was replaced by a new mortgage in favour of Midland Bank, granted to Mr Cooke in his sole name, which also secured repayment of the business overdraft of Mr Cooke's company. In 1981, Mrs Cooke signed a consent form postponing her rights in the property, if any, to the bank. Later that year, a second charge was executed on the property to secure their liability under a joint guarantee, as security for a business loan. In 1984, the property was conveyed into the joint names of Mr and Mrs Cooke. In 1987, the bank brought possession proceedings, claiming outstanding amounts due under the mortgage. Mrs Cooke claimed a one half beneficial interest in the property, overriding any interests of the bank. It was common ground that at the time of purchase there had been no discussion between the parties as to how the property should be owned beneficially.

(These facts are taken as they appear in a scholarly commentary on this case by Nicola Glover and Paul Todd which is freely available online ('Inferring Share of Interest in Home: *Midland Bank* v *Cooke*' [1995] 4 *Web JCLI*).)

Held: Mrs Cooke was entitled to a half share in the matrimonial home, although this was not justified by her direct contribution to the purchase price (only some 6.47 per cent), and there had been no express discussions between the parties. The case appears to be authority for the proposition that, even though the courts have no discretion in deciding whether B acquires an interest, they have a discretion as to its quantification once an interest has been acquired.

Oxley v *Hiscock*

[2004] EWCA Civ 546, Court of Appeal

Facts: An unmarried couple disputed the extent of their respective entitlements in their shared home. The man (H) contributed £60,700 to the acquisition of the home and the woman (O) contributed £36,300. At first instance, Her Honour Judge Hallon awarded the cohabitees equal shares on the sale of their home, in accordance with the maxim 'equality is equity' should apply.

Held: (on appeal) It was held that a fair division of the proceeds of sale 'having regard to the whole course of dealing between them in relation to the property' was 60 per cent to H and 40 per cent to O.

Chadwick LJ observed that two distinct questions arise in cases where property had been purchased in the sole name of one of two cohabitees:

'The first question is whether there was evidence from which to infer a common intention, communicated by each to the other, that each should have a beneficial share in the property ... An affirmative answer to the first question leads to the second question: 'what is the extent of the parties' respective beneficial interests in the property?' ... It must now be accepted that (at least in this Court and below) the answer is that each is entitled to that share which the court considers fair having regard to the whole course of dealing between them in relation to the property. And, in that context, 'the whole course of dealing between them in relation to the property' includes the arrangements which they make from time to time in order to meet the outgoings (mortgage contributions, council tax and utilities, repairs, insurance and housekeeping) which have to be met if they are to live in the property as their home.'

NOTES

1. In *Stack* v *Dowden* [2005] EWCA Civ 857, Court of Appeal, Chadwick LJ reiterated the approach he had taken in *Oxley* v *Hiscock* [2005] Fam 211 to the quantification of beneficial shares under a cohabitation constructive trust.

2. In *Stack* v *Dowden*, Lord Neuberger cautioned against inferring a constructive trust of the shared home based only on the way the cohabitants manage their finances and share their other property (paras [113], [132]), but the majority of Lordships in *Stack* v *Dowden* agreed upon a list of factors (mostly to be found in paras [69]–[70] of the speech of Baroness Hale (see the extract in this chapter under the heading (i) The family home where legal title is in joint names)) to be amongst those a court might consider when seeking to determine the parties' intentions regarding ownership of the shared home. Baroness Hale emphasised that this list is not exhaustive, and she made the general observation that '[i]n the cohabitation context, mercenary considerations may be more to the fore than they would be in marriage, but it should not be assumed that they always take pride of place over natural love and affection'.

3. Baroness Hale was a member of the judicial committee of the Privy Council that decided the case of *Abbott* v *Abbott* [2007] UKPC 53. In that case, her ladyship emphasised this statement that she had made in *Stack* (at para. [60]): 'The law has ... moved on in response to changing social and economic conditions. The search is to ascertain the parties' shared intentions, actual, inferred or imputed, with respect to the property in the light of their whole course of conduct in relation to it'. In *Rosset* Lord Bridge had doubted that, in the absence of an express agreement and detrimental reliance, any thing less than substantial direct contributions to acquisition would suffice to establish a share, Baroness Hale takes the view that the law has moved on since then. What is not clear is whether it has merely moved in terms of factors relevant to quantification of an interest once an interest has been established, or whether the law has moved on with regard to the threshold contribution or conduct that is required to establish an interest in the first place. If the latter, it is by no means clear to what point the law has moved. It would be more certain (even if somewhat strained) to limit the *Stack* innovation as regards *establishing* a share to the presumption of joint beneficial ownership where land is in joint names, and to restrict the most radical aspect of the decision (the aspect which encourages courts to take a very wide range of factors) to the quantification stage. There is some support for such a restrictive reading in the fact that Baroness Hale in *Abbot* v *Abbot* specifically notes that in *Stack* their Lordships had approved the following passage from the Law Commission's discussion paper on *Sharing Homes* (2002, Law Com No. 278, para. 4.27):

> 'If the question really is one of the parties' "common intention", we believe that there is much to be said for adopting what has been called a "holistic approach" *to quantification*, undertaking a survey of the whole course of dealing between the parties and taking account of all conduct which throws light on the question what shares were intended.' (emphasis added)

(For an argument that *Stack* has produced a more radical change (one that supersedes *Rosset*) see Simon Gardner, 'Family Property Today' (2008) 124 *LQR* 422.)

■ QUESTIONS

1. In your view, is the following conclusion, drawn by Patricia Ferguson (1993) 109 *LQR* 114, p. 131, correct?

   > ... constructive trusts and proprietary estoppel should be distinguished: a constructive trust automatically gives rise to a proprietary right independently of any court intervention, and this result justifies higher evidentiary requirements since it thus forms a means of creating interests in land without any prior regulation by the court; a proprietary estoppel gives rise only to a remedial jurisdiction in the court, and any proprietary right granted has effect only as a result of and subsequent to the court's order; this discretion justifies lower evidentiary requirements since the court is enabled to filter out only the deserving cases to receive proprietary interests.

2. Consider whether either or both of the following two statements represents an accurate statement of the law:

   > In the absence of any declaration of trust, the parties' respective beneficial interests in the property fall to be determined not by reference to any broad concepts of justice, but by reference to the principles governing the creation or operation of resulting, implied or constructive trusts which by section 53(2) of the Law of Property Act 1925 are exempted from the general requirements of writing imposed by section 53(1). (Sir Christopher Slade in *Huntingford* v *Hobbs* [1993] 1 FCR 45)

   > ... in constructive trust cases, the court can adopt a broad brush approach to determining the parties' respective shares. (Peter Gibson LJ in *Drake* v *Whipp* [1996] 1 FLR 826)

3. Are constructive trusts of land simply express trusts that lack formality?

4. A constructive trust will arise where the legal owner of land reaches an arrangement or understanding with another person (based on express discussions) that the other will acquire some beneficial interest in the legal owner's land—provided that the other person relied on the arrangement in such a way that it

would be detrimental (and unconscionable) of the legal owner to resile from it. To what extent does this correspond to the doctrine of proprietary estoppel?

5. A constructive trust will arise where a person makes a direct financial contribution to land legally owned by another if it can be inferred that the parties had a common intention that the contributor should acquire a beneficial interest in the land. To what extent does this correspond to the concept of resulting trust?

6. Is it arguable that the only theoretical and practical distinction between interests under resulting and constructive trusts of land is that the size of the former is quantified according to a rigid calculus whereas the size of the latter is determined flexibly according to the demands of conscience?

SECTION 3: THE CIVIL PARTNERSHIP ACT

The Act applies to civil partnerships defined as a registered relationships between two people 'of the same sex' (s.3(1)(a)).

CIVIL PARTNERSHIP ACT 2004

65 Contribution by civil partner to property improvement

(1)   This section applies if—

(a)   a civil partner contributes in money or money's worth to the improvement of real or personal property in which or in the proceeds of sale of which either or both of the civil partners has or have a beneficial interest, and

(b)   the contribution is of a substantial nature.

(2)   The contributing partner is to be treated as having acquired by virtue of the contribution a share or an enlarged share (as the case may be) in the beneficial interest of such an extent—

(a)   as may have been then agreed, or

(b)   in default of such agreement, as may seem in all the circumstances just to any court before which the question of the existence or extent of the beneficial interest of either of the civil partners arises (whether in proceedings between them or in any other proceedings).

(3)   Subsection (2) is subject to any agreement (express or implied) between the civil partners to the contrary.

66 Disputes between civil partners about property

(1)   In any question between the civil partners in a civil partnership as to title to or possession of property, either civil partner may apply to—

(a)   the High Court, or

(b)   such county court as may be prescribed by rules of court.

(2)   On such an application, the court may make such order with respect to the property as it thinks fit (including an order for the sale of the property).

(3)   Rules of court made for the purposes of this section may confer jurisdiction on county courts whatever the situation or value of the property in dispute.

NOTE: The Civil Partnership Act 2004 came into force on 5 December 2005.

■ QUESTION

Is homosexual partnership the only form of civil partnership outside marriage in which registration and property distribution powers (such as those set out in ss.65 and 66) would be useful?

Cohabitation: The Financial Consequences of Relationship Breakdown

The Law Commission Report No. 307, 31 July 2007 (from the executive summary of the Report)

KEY FEATURES OF THE SCHEME

1.13 We do not think that all cohabitants should be able to obtain financial relief in the event of separation. We recommend that a remedy should only be available where:
- the couple satisfied certain eligibility requirements;
- the couple had not agreed to disapply the scheme; and
- the applicant had made qualifying contributions to the relationship giving rise to certain enduring consequences at the point of separation.

Eligibility requirements

1.14 The recommended scheme would apply only to cohabitants who had had a child together or who had lived together for a specified number of years (a 'minimum duration requirement'). The Report does not make a specific recommendation as to what the minimum duration requirement should be, but suggests that a period of between two and five years would be appropriate.

Disapplying the scheme

1.15 We reject an 'opt-in' scheme, which couples would be required to sign up to in order to be able to claim financial remedies on separation. Consultation confirmed our view that an opt-in scheme would not deal effectively with the problems of hardship created by the current law. Vulnerable individuals would be no more likely to protect themselves by registering than they are currently to marry. We are also aware that to introduce an opt-in scheme would effectively create a new status of 'registered cohabitant'. This would jeopardise the support of many who have expressed support for reform, but who are concerned to protect the institution of marriage, such as the Mission and Public Affairs Council of the Church of England.

1.16 Instead, we recommend that, as a default position, the scheme should be available between all eligible cohabitants. However, we understand the strongly held view that it is wrong to force cohabitants who have not chosen to marry or form a civil partnership into a particular legal regime against their will. We agree that it is very important to respect the autonomy of couples who wish to determine for themselves the legal consequences of their personal relationships. We therefore recommend that a new scheme should allow couples, subject to necessary protections, to disapply the statute by means of an opt-out agreement, leaving them free to make their own financial arrangements.

Qualifying contributions and their consequences: the basis for remedies

1.17 It would not be sufficient for applicants simply to demonstrate that they were eligible for financial relief and that the couple had not made a valid opt-out agreement disapplying the scheme. In order to obtain a remedy, applicants would have to prove that they had made qualifying contributions to the parties' relationship which had given rise to certain enduring consequences at the point of separation.

1.18 The scheme would therefore be very different from that which applies between spouses on divorce. Simply cohabiting, for however long, would not give rise to any presumed entitlement to share in any pool of property. Nor would the scheme grant remedies simply on the basis of a party's needs following separation, whether by making orders for maintenance or otherwise.

1.19 In broad terms, the scheme would seek to ensure that the pluses and minuses of the relationship were fairly shared between the couple. The applicant would have to show that the respondent retained a benefit, or that the applicant had a continuing economic disadvantage, as a result of contributions made to the relationship. The value of any award would depend on the extent of the retained benefit or continuing economic disadvantage. The court would have discretion to grant such financial relief as might be appropriate to deal with these matters, and in doing so would be required to give first consideration to the welfare of any dependent children.

1.20 We consider that a scheme based on these principles would provide a sound basis on which to address the hardship and other economic unfairness that can arise when a cohabiting relationship ends. It would respond, more comprehensively than the current law can, to the economic impact of the contributions made by parties to their relationship, and so to needs which arise in consequence. Where there are dependent children, the scheme would enable a remedy to be provided for the benefit of the primary carer, and so better protect those children who share their primary carer's standard of living.

By making adequate provision for the adult parties, the scheme would give more leeway to the court than it currently has to apply Schedule 1 to the Children Act 1989 for the benefit of the parties' children.

[For further analysis, see an article written by the Law Commissioner responsible for this report: Stuart Bridge, 'Cohabitation: why legislative reform is necessary' [2007] *Fam Law* 911.]

SECTION 4: SPECIAL RULES GOVERNING TRUSTS OF LAND

A: Overreaching

A purchaser is able to 'overreach' beneficial interests under trusts of land. This means that he is relieved from having to inquire of them as long as he pays the purchase money to all the trustees (provided there are at least two trustees or a trust corporation) and obtains a receipt from them. The beneficiaries are protected by being able to take a share of the purchase money, and the purchaser is not concerned with their interests (Law of Property Act 1925, s.2; s.27).

B: Trusts of Land and Appointment of Trustees Act 1996

The Trusts of Land and Appointment of Trustees Act 1996 (TOLATA) came into force on 1 January 1997. It governs all trusts of land created on or after that date and, with the exception of strict settlements, all trusts of land already in existence at that date. Strict settlements remain subject to the Settled Land Act 1925, the detail of which lies outside the scope of this book. In fact, detailed consideration of TOLATA also belongs to a specialist book on land law, but the Act is set out in this section for reference and is followed by notes and questions on those features of the Act that are relevant to our wider study of trusts.

See generally on the 1996 Act: Phillip Kenny and Ann Kenny, *The Trusts of Land and Appointment of Trustees Act 1996* (Sweet & Maxwell, 1997); Barraclough & Matthews, *A Practitioner's Guide to The Trusts of Land and Appointment of Trustees Act 1996* (CLT, 1996); Jackie Jones and Warren Palmer [1997] 1 *Web JCLI* (http://webjcli.ncl.ac.uk/1997/issue1/jones1.html).

TRUSTS OF LAND AND APPOINTMENT OF TRUSTEES ACT 1996

1. Meaning of 'trust of land'
    (1) In this Act—
        (a) 'trust of land' means (subject to subsection (3)) any trust of property which consists of or includes land, and
        (b) 'trustees of land' means trustees of a trust of land.
    (2) The reference in subsection (1)(a) to a trust—
        (a) is to any description of trust (whether express, implied, resulting or constructive), including a trust for sale and a bare trust, and
        (b) includes a trust created, or arising, before the commencement of this Act.
    (3) The reference to land in subsection (1)(a) does not include land which (despite section 2) is settled land or which is land to which the Universities and College Estates Act 1925 applies.

2. Trusts in place of settlements

(1) No settlement created after the commencement of this Act is a settlement for the purposes of the Settled Land Act 1925; and no settlement shall be deemed to be made under that Act after that commencement.

(2) Subsection (1) does not apply to a settlement created on the occasion of an alteration in any interest in, or of a person becoming entitled under, a settlement which—

    (a) is in existence at the commencement of this Act, or

    (b) derives from a settlement within paragraph (a) of this paragraph.

(3) But a settlement created as mentioned in subsection (2) is not a settlement for the purposes of the Settled Land Act 1925 if provision to the effect that it is not is made in the instrument, or any of the instruments, by which it is created.

(4) Where at any time after the commencement of this Act there is in the case of any settlement which is a settlement for the purposes of the Settled Land Act 1925 no relevant property which is, or is deemed to be, subject to the settlement, the settlement permanently ceases at that time to be a settlement for the purposes of that Act.

In this subsection 'relevant property' means land and personal chattels to which section 67(1) of the Settled Land Act 1925 (heirlooms) applies.

(5) No land held on charitable, ecclesiastical or public trusts shall be or be deemed to be settled land after the commencement of this Act, even if it was or was deemed to be settled land before that commencement.

(6) Schedule 1 has effect to make provision consequential on this section (including provision to impose a trust in circumstances in which, apart from this section, there would be a settlement for the purposes of the Settled Land Act 1925 (and there would not otherwise be a trust)).

3. Abolition of doctrine of conversion

(1) Where land is held by trustees subject to a trust for sale, the land is not to be regarded as personal property; and where personal property is subject to a trust for sale in order that the trustees may acquire land, the personal property is not to be regarded as land.

(2) Subsection (1) does not apply to a trust created by a will if the testator died before the commencement of this Act.

(3) Subject to that, subsection (1) applies to a trust whether it is created, or arises, before or after that commencement.

4. Express trusts for sale as trusts of land

(1) In the case of every trust for sale of land created by a disposition there is to be implied, despite any provision to the contrary made by the disposition, a power for the trustees to postpone sale of the land; and the trustees are not liable in any way for postponing sale of the land, in the exercise of their discretion, for an indefinite period.

(2) Subsection (1) applies to a trust whether it is created, or arises, before or after the commencement of this Act.

(3) Subsection (1) does not affect any liability incurred by trustees before that commencement.

5. Implied trusts for sale as trusts of land

(1) Schedule 2 has effect in relation to statutory provisions which impose a trust for sale of land in certain circumstances so that in those circumstances there is instead a trust of the land (without a duty to sell).

(2) Section 1 of the Settled Land Act 1925 does not apply to land held on any trust arising by virtue of that Schedule (so that any such land is subject to a trust of land).

6. General powers of trustees

(1) For the purpose of exercising their functions as trustees, the trustees of land have in relation to the land subject to the trust all the powers of an absolute owner.

(2) Where in the case of any land subject to a trust of land each of the beneficiaries interested in the land is a person of full age and capacity who is absolutely entitled to the land, the powers conferred

on the trustees by subsection (1) include the power to convey the land to the beneficiaries even though they have not required the trustees to do so; and where land conveyed by virtue of this subsection—

    (a) the beneficiaries shall do whatever is necessary to secure that it vests in them, and

    (b) if they fail to do so, the court may make an order requiring them to do so.

(3) The trustees of land have power to purchase a legal estate in any land in England or Wales.

(4) The power conferred by subsection (3) may be exercised by trustees to purchase land—

    (a) by way of investment,

    (b) for occupation by any beneficiary, or

    (c) for any other reason.

(5) In exercising the powers conferred by this section trustees shall have regard to the rights of the beneficiaries.

(6) The powers conferred by this section shall not be exercised in contravention of, or of any order made in pursuance of, any other enactment or any rule of law or equity.

(7) The reference in subsection (6) to an order includes an order of any court or of the Charity Commissioners.

(8) Where any enactment other than this section confers on trustees authority to act subject to any restriction, limitation or condition, trustees of land may not exercise the powers conferred by this section to do any act which they are prevented from doing under the other enactment by reason of the restriction, limitation or condition.

7. Partition by trustees

(1) The trustees of land may, where beneficiaries of full age are absolutely entitled in undivided shares to land subject to the trust, partition the land, or any part of it, and provide (by way of mortgage or otherwise) for the payment of any equality money.

(2) The trustees shall give effect to any such partition by conveying the partitioned land in severalty (whether or not subject to any legal mortgage created for raising equality money), either absolutely or in trust, in accordance with the rights of those beneficiaries.

(3) Before exercising their powers under subsection (2) the trustees shall obtain the consent of each of those beneficiaries.

(4) Where a share in the land is affected by an incumbrance, the trustees may either give effect to it or provide for its discharge from the property allotted to that share as they think fit.

(5) If a share in the land is absolutely vested in a minor, subsections (1) to (4) apply as if he were of full age, except that the trustees may act on his behalf and retain land or other property representing his share in trust for him.

8. Exclusion and restriction of powers

(1) Sections 6 and 7 do not apply in the case of a trust of land created by a disposition in so far as provision to the effect that they do not apply is made by the disposition.

(2) If the disposition creating such a trust makes provision requiring any consent to be obtained to the exercise of any power conferred by section 6 or 7, the power may not be exercised without that consent.

(3) Subsection (1) does not apply in the case of charitable, ecclesiastical or public trusts.

(4) Subsections (1) and (2) have effect subject to any enactment which prohibits or restricts the effect of provision of the description mentioned in them.[Section 9 is on delegation—see Chapter 10.]

10. Consents

(1) If a disposition creating a trust of land requires the consent of more than two persons to the exercise by the trustees of any function relating to the land, the consent of any two of them to the exercise of the function is sufficient in favour of a purchaser.

(2) Subsection (1) does not apply to the exercise of a function by trustees of land held on charitable, ecclesiastical or public trusts.

(3) Where at any time a person whose consent is expressed by a disposition creating a trust of land to be required to the exercise by the trustees of any function relating to the land is not of full age—

    (a) his consent is not, in favour of a purchaser, required to the exercise of the function, but

    (b) the trustees shall obtain the consent of a parent who has parental responsibility for him (within the meaning of the Children Act 1989) or of a guardian of his.

11. Consultation with beneficiaries

(1) The trustees of land shall in the exercise of any function relating to land subject to the trust—

    (a) so far as practicable, consult the beneficiaries of full age and beneficially entitled to an interest in possession in the land, and

    (b) so far as consistent with the general interest of the trust, give effect to the wishes of those beneficiaries, or (in case of dispute) of the majority (according to the value of their combined interests).

(2) Subsection (1) does not apply—

    (a) in relation to a trust created by a disposition in so far as provision that it does not apply is made by the disposition,

    (b) in relation to a trust created or arising under a will made before the commencement of this Act, or

    (c) in relation to the exercise of the power mentioned in section 6(2).

(3) Subsection (1) does not apply to a trust created before the commencement of this Act by a disposition, or a trust created after that commencement by reference to such a trust, unless provision to the effect that it is to apply is made by a deed executed—

    (a) in a case in which the trust was created by one person and he is of full capacity, by that person, or

    (b) in a case in which the trust was created by more than one person, by such of the persons who created the trust as are alive and of full capacity.

(4) A deed executed for the purposes of subsection (3) is irrevocable.

12. The right to occupy

(1) A beneficiary who is beneficially entitled to an interest in possession in land subject to a trust of land is entitled by reason of his interest to occupy the land at any time if at that time—

    (a) the purposes of the trust include making the land available for his occupation (or for the occupation of beneficiaries of a class of which he is a member or of beneficiaries in general), or

    (b) the land is held by the trustees so as to be so available.

(2) Subsection (1) does not confer on a beneficiary a right to occupy land if it is either unavailable or unsuitable for occupation by him.

(3) This section is subject to section 13.

13. Exclusion and restriction of right to occupy

(1) Where two or more beneficiaries are (or apart from this subsection would be) entitled under section 12 to occupy land, the trustees of land may exclude or restrict the entitlement of any one or more (but not all) of them.

(2) Trustees may not under subsection (1)—

    (a) unreasonably exclude any beneficiary's entitlement to occupy land, or

    (b) restrict any such entitlement to an unreasonable extent.

(3) The trustees of land may from time to time impose reasonable conditions on any beneficiary in relation to his occupation of land by reason of his entitlement under section 12.

(4) The matters to which trustees are to have regard in exercising the powers conferred by this section include—

    (a) the intentions of the person or persons (if any) who created the trust,

    (b) the purposes for which the land is held, and

    (c) the circumstances and wishes of each of the beneficiaries who is (or apart from any previous exercise by the trustees of those powers would be) entitled to occupy the land under section 12.

(5) The conditions which may be imposed on a beneficiary under subsection (3) include, in particular, conditions requiring him—

    (a) to pay any outgoings or expenses in respect of the land, or

    (b) to assume any other obligation in relation to the land or to any activity which is or is proposed to be conducted there.

(6) Where the entitlement of any beneficiary to occupy land under section 12 has been excluded or restricted, the conditions which may be imposed on any other beneficiary under subsection (3) include, in particular, conditions requiring him to—

    (a) make payments by way of compensation to the beneficiary whose entitlement has been excluded or restricted, or

(b) forgo any payment or other benefit to which he would otherwise be entitled under the trust so as to benefit that beneficiary.

(7) The powers conferred on trustees by this section may not be exercised—

(a) so as prevent any person who is in occupation of land (whether or not by reason of an entitlement under section 12) from continuing to occupy the land, or

(b) in a manner likely to result in any such person ceasing to occupy the land, unless he consents or the court has given approval.

(8) The matters to which the court is to have regard in determining whether to give approval under subsection (7) include the matters mentioned in subsection (4)(a) to (c).

14. Application for order

(1) Any person who is a trustee of land or has an interest in a property subject to a trust of land may make an application to the court for an order under this section.

(2) On an application for an order under this section the court may make any such order—

(a) relating to the exercise by the trustees of any of their functions (including an order relieving them of any obligation to obtain the consent of, or to consult, any person in connection with the exercise of any of their functions), or

(b) declaring the nature or extent of a person's interest in property subject to the trust, as the court thinks fit.

(3) The court may not under this section make any order as to the appointment or removal of trustees.

(4) The powers conferred on the court by this section are exercisable on an application whether it is made before or after the commencement of this Act.

15. Matters relevant in determining applications

(1) The matters to which the court is to have regard in determining an application for an order under section 14 include—

(a) the intentions of the person or persons (if any) who created the trust,

(b) the purposes for which the property subject to the trust is held,

(c) the welfare of any minor who occupies or might reasonably be expected to occupy any land subject to the trust as his home, and

(d) the interests of any secured creditor of any beneficiary.

(2) In the case of an application relating to the exercise in relation to any land of the powers conferred on the trustees by section 13, the matters to which the court is to have regard also include the circumstances and wishes of each of the beneficiaries who is (or apart from any previous exercise by the trustees of those powers would be) entitled to occupy the land under section 12.

(3) In the case of any other application, other than one relating to the exercise of the power mentioned in section 6(2), the matters to which the court is to have regard also include the circumstances and wishes of any beneficiaries of full age and entitled to an interest in possession in property subject to the trust or (in case of dispute) of the majority (according to the value of their combined interests).

(4) This section does not apply to an application if section 335A of the Insolvency Act 1986 (which is inserted by Schedule 3 and relates to applications by a trustee of a bankrupt) applies to it.

16. Protection of purchasers

(1) A purchaser of land which is or has been subject to a trust need not be concerned to see that any requirement imposed on the trustees by section 6(5), 7(3) or 11(1) has been complied with.

(2) Where—

(a) trustees of land who convey land which (immediately before it is conveyed) is subject to the trust contravene section 6(6) or (8), but

(b) the purchaser of the land from the trustees has no actual notice of the contravention, the contravention does not invalidate the conveyance.

(3) Where the powers of trustees of land are limited by virtue of section 8—

(a) the trustees shall take all reasonable steps to bring the limitation to the notice of any purchaser of the land from them, but

(b) the limitation does not invalidate any conveyance by the trustees to a purchaser who has no actual notice of the limitation.

(4) Where trustees of land convey land which (immediately before it is conveyed) is subject to the trust to persons believed by them to be beneficiaries absolutely entitled to the land under the trust and of full age and capacity—

    (a) the trustees shall execute a deed declaring that they are discharged from the trust in relation to that land, and

    (b) if they fail to do so, the court may make an order requiring them to do so.

(5) A purchaser of land to which a deed under subsection (4) relates is entitled to assume that, as from the date of the deed, the land is not subject to the trust unless he has actual notice that the trustees were mistaken in their belief that the land was conveyed to beneficiaries absolutely entitled to the land under the trust and of full age and capacity.

(6) Subsections (2) and (3) do not apply to land held on charitable, ecclesiastical or public trusts.

(7) This section does not apply to registered land.

17. Application of provisions to trusts of proceeds of sale

(1) Section 6(3) applies in relation to trustees of a trust of proceeds of sale of land as in relation to trustees of land.

(2) Section 14 applies in relation to a trust of proceeds of sale of land and trustees of such a trust as in relation to a trust of land and trustees of land.

(3) In this section 'trust of proceeds of sale of land' means (subject to subsection (5)) any trust of property (other than a trust of land) which consists of or includes—

    (a) any proceeds of a disposition of land held in trust (including settled land), or

    (b) any property representing any such proceeds.

(4) The references in subsection (3) to a trust—

    (a) are to any description of trust (whether express, implied, resulting or constructive), including a trust for sale and a bare trust, and

    (b) include a trust created, or arising, before the commencement of this Act.

(5)   A trust which (despite section 2) is a settlement for the purposes of the Settled Land Act 1925 cannot be a trust of proceeds of sale of land.

(6) In subsection (3)—

    (a) 'disposition' includes any disposition made, or coming into operation, before the commencement of this Act, and

    (b) the reference to settled land includes personal chattels to which section 67(1) of the Settled Land Act 1925 (heirlooms) applies.

NOTES

1. The Trusts of Land and Appointment of Trustees Act 1996 also contains provisions on the appointment and removal of trustees, their powers and their rights to delegate. These are dealt with in Chapter 11.

2. Section 3 of the Act purports to abolish the doctrine of conversion. This is the doctrine which, in accordance with the maxim 'equity sees as done that which ought to be done', holds that a trustee holding property on trust to sell it (that is, subject to a 'trust for sale') has already sold it the moment he acquires it. It should be noted, however, that the true effect of the section is merely to repeal the doctrine of conversion in relation to trusts for sale, a result which necessarily follows from the fact that trusts for sale are now 'trusts of land' according to the Act and the trustees of such trusts are under no immediate binding obligation to sell the land.

3. One of the most significant subsections of the Act is subs. 6(1), which provides that 'for the purpose of exercising their functions' the trustees of land subject to the trust of land have all the powers of an absolute owner. It should not surprise us that trustees of land have all the *powers* of an absolute owner for the crucial feature that distinguishes trustees from absolute owners is not their powers, but their *obligations*.

4. Section 8(1) allows for the powers conferred by subs. 6(1) to be expressly removed by the terms of the trust instrument. There is therefore nothing to prevent a settlor removing such basic powers as the power to sell the land or lease it out. An interesting question which then arises is whether the court has the power under s.14 to authorise the trustees to sell or lease in the face of a clause purporting to remove their powers. The answer to the question turns upon whether the powers

to sell or lease remain 'functions' of the trustee even if they have been expressly removed by the trust instrument. Charles Harpum, who was the Law Commissioner responsible for the Act, argues that the court does have the necessary power (Megarry & Wade, *The Law of Real Property*, 6th edn (London: Sweet & Maxwell, 2000), pp. 449–55) but for a contrary view, see G. Watt (1997) 61 *Conv* 263.

■ SUMMATIVE QUESTION

online resource centre

Explain by reference to appropriate authorities whether, and to what extent, Bertie may be entitled to an interest in land in each of the following situations:

(a) Bertie has moved into a house owned by his girlfriend Tania. The house is in Tania's sole name and she paid the deposit. The mortgage is also in her sole name and she pays the monthly instalments. Bertie meets the majority of the couple's other financial outgoings, including electricity, water and gas bills and grocery shopping. Tania has recently paid for a conservatory to be added to the house. She would not have had the means to do so were it not for Bertie's contribution to their general outgoings.

(b) Bertie, who is a businessman, purchased a house in the name of his daughter, Tracy. He did so for two reasons: on the one hand, to provide his daughter with accommodation during the period of her university studies, and on the other hand, to put some of his wealth out of the reach of his business creditors during a particularly difficult period of business. In the event, Bertie became insolvent and ten years later, his bankruptcy having been discharged, he sought to recover the house from Tracy. Tracy resisted, insisting that she believed the house to be a gift, on account of the fact that her university studies had finished six years earlier and her father had made no attempt to recover the house until now. Tracy is now in well-paid employment.

(c) Bertie is keen to acquire gainful employment and applies for a post advertised in the following terms:

Wanted: live-in custodian of Carlsham Castle. Successful applicant must give up all other employment and in return is guaranteed a modest salary and a home in Pink Cottage within the castle grounds for the duration of the employment.

Bertie is appointed custodian of the castle, but is concerned when the castle is sold on to a stranger.

FURTHER READING

Browne-Wilkinson, Sir Nicolas, 'Constructive Trusts and Unjust Enrichment' (1996) 10(4) *TLI* 98.

Cooke, E., *The Modern Law of Estoppel* (Oxford: Oxford University Press, 2000).

Dixon, M. J., 'Proprietary estoppel: a return to principle?' (2009) 3 *Conv* 260.

Elias, G., *Explaining Constructive Trusts* (Oxford: Clarendon Press, 1990).

Etherton, T., 'Constructive trusts and proprietary estoppel: the search for clarity and principle' (2009) 2 *Conv* 104.

Gardner, S., 'Family Property Today' (2008) 124 *LQR* 422.

Goode, R., 'Proprietary liability for secret profits – a reply' (2011) 127 *LQR* 493.

Hopkins, N., 'Regulating trusts of the home: private law and social policy' (2009) 125 *LQR* 310.

McFarlane, B., 'Constructive Trusts Arising on a Receipt of Property *Sub Conditione*' (2004) 120 *LQR* 667.

Mitchell, C. (ed), *Constructive and Resulting Trusts* (Oxford: Hart, 2010).

Neuberger (Lord) of Abbotsbury, 'The stuffing of Minerva's owl? Taxonomy and taxidermy in equity' (2009) 68(3) *CLJ* 537.

Oakley, A. J., *Constructive Trusts* (London: Sweet & Maxwell, 1997).

Piska, N., 'Intention, Fairness and the Presumption of Resulting trust after *Stack v Dowden*' (2008) 71(1) *Modern Law Review* 120.

Probert, R., 'Cohabitants and Joint Ownership: The Implications of *Stack v Dowden*' [2007] *Family Law* 924.

Rickett, C. and Grantham, R., 'Toward a More Constructive Classification of Trusts' [1999] *LMCLQ* 111.

Slade, Sir Christopher, 'The Informal Creation of Interests in Land', The Child & Co. Oxford Lecture, 2 March 1984.

Virgo, G., 'Profits obtained in breach of fiduciary duty: personal or proprietary claim?' (2011) 70(3) *CLJ* 502.

Waters, D. W. M., *Constructive Trusts* (London: Athlone Press, 1964).

PART III

The Regulation of Trusts

9

Variation of Trusts and the
Flexibility of Benefit

KEY AIMS

To recognise when a gift on trust for an infant beneficiary will carry the intermediate income so as to empower the trustees to maintain the infant out of income.
To be able to advise trustees when, and to what extent, they are permitted to apply
trust capital for the benefit of a trust beneficiary before the beneficiary becomes
entitled to it. To identify the circumstances which brought about the creation of
the Variation of Trusts Act 1958, and to examine why the Act is still widely resorted
to.

SECTION 1: INTRODUCTION

The beneficiaries of an expressly created private trust may bring the trust to an end if
they are in unanimous agreement and are all competent adults and are between them
absolutely entitled to the trust property. This is the so-called 'rule in *Saunders* v *Vautier*'
(1841) 4 Beav 115 (see Section 3: Variation of beneficial ownership, A: Inherent equitable jurisdiction, (i)). Having terminated the trust, each beneficiary will be entitled to
take his share of the fund as an absolute owner. When beneficial ownership returns
to absolute ownership, it is then at its most flexible, because an absolute owner has
a virtually unrestricted right to use and dispose of his property as he wishes. In the
meantime, before the trust is brought to an end, the nature and extent of a beneficiary's
beneficial ownership is limited by the terms of the trust. The trust may provide that the
beneficiary's interest will vest in possession the moment the trust is created, or that his
interest may be deferred until some future date (for example 'the year 2010' or 'the date
of his father's death'), or it may be expressly contingent upon the happening of some
future event that may or may not occur (for example 'when he qualifies as a barrister'
or 'when he reaches the age of 25'). The central question to be addressed in this chapter
is to what extent beneficiaries may be able to take benefits under a trust despite limitations on their beneficial ownership, and to what extent limitations on their beneficial
ownership may be varied or entirely removed. In short, we are concerned with the issue
of 'flexibility of benefit'.

SECTION 2: MAINTENANCE AND ADVANCEMENT

The powers of maintenance and advancement have the object of providing for beneficiaries who are not as yet entitled to any, or sufficient, income or capital, and who require financial support. Payments by way of maintenance are payments out of income, to provide for routine necessities such as education or board and lodging, while payments by way of advancement are sums advanced from capital, to cover major costs such as setting up the beneficiary in his profession. The statutory power of maintenance is only exercisable in favour of infants (persons under 18).

In recent decades, significant use has also been made of these powers in reducing the tax liability of trusts. For example, early advancements of capital could, until 1975, be effective to avoid liability to estate duty entirely (see, e.g. *Pilkington* v *IRC* [1964] AC 612), and even now can be used to reduce inheritance tax liability, while the purpose of maintenance payments is often to reduce liability for income tax (for an explanation of so-called 'Accumulation and Maintenance' trusts, see Chapter 2).

A: Maintenance

TRUSTEE ACT 1925

31. Power to apply income for maintenance and to accumulate surplus income during a minority

(1) Where any property is held by trustees in trust for any person for any interest whatsoever, whether vested or contingent, then, subject to any prior interests or charges affecting that property—

    (i)   during the infancy of any such person, if his interest so long continues, the trustees may, at their sole discretion, pay to his parent or guardian, if any, or otherwise apply for or towards his maintenance, education, or benefit, the whole or such part, if any, of the income of the property as may, in all the circumstances, be reasonable, whether or not there is—

        (a)   any other fund applicable to the same purpose; or

        (b)   any person bound by law to provide for his maintenance or education; and

    (ii)   if such person on attaining the age of [eighteen years] has not a vested interest in such income, the trustees shall thenceforth pay the income of that property and of any accretion thereto under subsection (2) of this section to him, until he either attains a vested interest therein or dies, or until failure of his interest.

Provided that, in deciding whether the whole or any part of the income of the property is during a minority to be paid or applied for the purposes aforesaid, the trustees shall have regard to the age of the infant and his requirements and generally to the circumstances of the case, and in particular to what other income, if any, is applicable for those purposes; and where trustees have notice that the income of more than one fund is applicable for those purposes, then, so far as practicable, unless the entire income of the funds is paid or applied as aforesaid or the court otherwise directs, a proportionate part only of the income of each fund shall be so paid or applied.

(2) During the infancy of any such person, if his interest so long continues, the trustees shall accumulate all the residue of that income in the way of compound interest by investing the same and the resulting income thereof from time to time in authorised investments, and shall hold those accumulations as follows:—

    (i)   If any such person—

        (a)   attains the age of eighteen years, or marries under that age, and his interest in such income during his infancy or until his marriage is a vested interest; or

(b) on attaining the age of eighteen years or on marriage under that age becomes entitled to the property from which such income arose in fee simple, absolute or determinable, or absolutely, or for an entailed interest;

the trustees shall hold the accumulations in trust for such person absolutely, but without prejudice to any provision with respect thereto contained in any settlement by him made under any statutory powers during his infancy, and so that the receipt of such person after marriage, and though still an infant, shall be a good discharge; and

(ii) in any other case the trustees shall, notwithstanding that such person had a vested interest in such income, hold the accumulations as an accretion to the capital of the property from which such accumulations arose, and as one fund with such capital for all purposes, and so that, if such property is settled land, such accumulations shall be held upon the same trusts as if the same were capital money arising therefrom;

but the trustees may, at any time during the infancy of such person if his interest so long continues, apply those accumulations, or any part thereof, as if they were income arising in the then current year.

(3) This section applies in the case of a contingent interest only if the limitation or trust carries the intermediate income of the property, but it applies to a future or contingent legacy by the parent of, or a person standing in loco parentis to, the legatee, if and for such period as, under the general law, the legacy caries interest for the maintenance of the legatee, and in any such case as last aforesaid the rate of interest shall (if the income available is sufficient, and subject to any rules of court to the contrary) be five pounds per centum per annum.

(4) This section applies to a vested annuity in like manner as if the annuity were the income of property held by the trustees in trust to pay the income thereof to the annuitant for the same period for which the annuity is payable, save that in any case accumulations made during the infancy of the annuitant shall be held in trust for the annuitant or his personal representatives absolutely.

(5) This section does not apply where the instrument, if any, under which the interest arises came into operation before the commencement of this Act.

NOTES
1. The section is set out as subsequently amended.
2. Power to maintain is not implied into the trust instrument. Therefore it must be expressly given, or advantage may be taken of the statutory power. The statutory power operates provided no contrary intention is expressed. But where the statutory power is expressly excluded, it cannot be used, even if an express power turns out to be useless. In *Re Erskine's ST* [1971] 1 WLR 162, a settlement contained a provision for accumulation which was void for perpetuity. But since the statutory power to maintain was excluded by the provisions of the trust instrument, the income which the trustees had accumulated could not be applied for the beneficiary, and resulted to the settlor's estate.
3. The court also has an inherent jurisdiction to approve the use of income or even capital for the maintenance of infant beneficiaries, but in practice, this is rarely necessary.

LAW OF PROPERTY ACT 1925

175. Contingent and future testamentary gifts to carry the intermediate income

(1) A contingent or future specific devise or bequest of property, whether real or personal, and a contingent residuary devise of freehold land, and a specific or residuary devise of freehold land to trustees upon trust for persons whose interests are contingent or executory shall, subject to the statutory provisions relating to accumulations, carry the intermediate income of that property from the death of the testator, except so far as such income, or any part thereof, may be otherwise expressly disposed of.

(2) This section applies only to wills coming into operation after the commencement of this Act.

B. S. Ker, 'Trustees' Powers of Maintenance'

(1953) 17 *Conv* 273

When a Gift Carries the Intermediate Income

The question now arises as to when a 'limitation or trust' carries the intermediate income of the property. The rules are as follows:—

1. A contingent gift by will of *residuary* personalty carries with it all the income it earns from the testator's death, for the simple reason that there is no one besides the residuary legatee to whom it could go. North J said in *Re Adams* [1893] 1 Ch 829, at p. 884 'Here no child has [a vested interest in the residue]. How does the matter stand as to the income? It is said that they take an interest in the income, *qua* income of the capital they take an interest in. *But it is undisposed-of income, and as such becomes part of the residue*; but, being part of the residue, the income belongs contingently to the children, in the same way as the capital belongs contingently to them.' If this income is accumulated until the contingency vesting the money in the beneficiaries happens the rules in sections 164–166 of the Law of Property Act 1925, must be observed. (See *Bective* v *Hodgson* (1864) 10 HL Cas 656.)

2. The rule as to the contingent *specific* gifts of personalty and contingent specific or residuary gifts of realty is contained in section 175 of the Law of Property Act 1925: 'A contingent or future specific devise or bequest of property, whether real or personal, and a contingent residuary devise of freehold land, and a specific or residuary devise of freehold land to trustees upon trust for persons whose interests are contingent or executory shall, subject to the statutory provisions relating to accumulations, carry the intermediate income of that property from the death of the testator, except so far as such income, or any part thereof, may be otherwise expressly disposed of.' This section applies only to *wills* coming into operation after 1925, but it has been held in *Re Raine* [1929] 1 Ch 716, not to apply to a pecuniary legacy. Further, it draws a distinction between 'land' and 'freehold land.' This is because leaseholds rank as personal property and therefore the ordinary rules (*supra* and *infra*) as to the income of contingent gifts of personalty apply: see *Guthrie* v *Walrond* (1883) 22 ChD 573, and *Re Woodin* [1895] 2 Ch 309, *per* Lindley LJ and Kay LJ.

Pecuniary Legacies

3. In view of the decision in *Re Raine (supra)* the rules of the general law as to when contingent pecuniary legacies bear interest require examination. The broad rule is that no interest is payable on a contingent pecuniary legacy from the testator's death while the gift is in suspense (see *per* Kay LJ in *Re George* (1877) 5 ChD 837). There are, however, the following exceptions in which the legacy, subject to any contrary intention in the will, carries interest from the testator's death:

(a) *Where the testator was the father of, or in loco parentis to, the infant legatee.* The idea is simple; a father is under an obligation to maintain his child and is therefore presumed to intend the income of the gift to be paid for his child's maintenance until the contingency happens. Although it is strictly an exception, we will refer to this rule hereafter for brevity's sake as 'the golden rule.' There are two exceptions to it.

First, it does not apply if the contingency is the attaining of some greater age than 21. In *Re Abrahams* [1911] 1 Ch 108, the testator gave a legacy to X contingently on his attaining 25. The judge reasoned that the legacy had clearly not been deferred simply on account of infancy, or the age specified would have been 21. All idea of X's infancy was thus ousted and hence no intention to maintain could be presumed; hence no interest was payable towards X's maintenance. The second exception is where the testator has provided another fund out of which the infant is to be maintained: *Re West* [1913] 2 Ch 345. This is a clear intention which ousts the presumed intention underlying the rule.

Section 31(1)(i)(a), however might be thought to have altered the rule. We are considering the question 'Has the golden rule been ousted?' The old law said, 'Yes, if another fund has been provided for maintenance'. But this part of section 31 says that maintenance can be paid 'whether or not there is another fund applicable to the same purpose.' However, no part of the section applies to a contingent gift at all unless the requirements of subsection (3) are satisfied. Section 31(1)(i)(a) therefore cannot come into play to oust the rule illustrated by *Re West (supra)*. Thus, where a father gives a contingent legacy to his infant child and also provides another fund for his maintenance the legacy does not carry interest and therefore section 31 does not apply to it.

(b) A contingent legacy to an infant carries interest from the date of death where the testator without being a parent of, or in loco parentis to the infant legatee, nevertheless shows an intention that the infant is to be maintained. In *Re Churchill* [1909] 2 Ch 431 a testatrix gave a legacy to a grandnephew and directed the trustees at their discretion to pay any part, etc., of it, 'towards the advancement in life or otherwise for the benefit' of the legatee. It was held that the legacy carried interest from the date of death at 4 per cent ...

(c) Where the testator segregates a fund for a legatee but makes the gift contingent. The idea here is that if the testator says 'X is to have an ear-marked sum of £10,000 when he is 21' and nothing more, he must obviously have intended him to have the accretions earned meanwhile. But there must be a segregation of the legacy required inherently in the nature of the legacy itself ...

> ... in *Re Medlock* (1886) 55 LJ Ch 738 ... the testator bequeathed £750 to trustees upon trust to pay and divide the same among three people contingently on their surviving him and attaining 21. If none got a vested interest the fund was to fall into residue. It was held that here a definite fund had been segregated by the will itself from the rest of the estate ...

B: Advancement

The power of advancement permits trustees to pay capital sums to or on behalf of a beneficiary some time before he is entitled to claim the fund. The power may be given by the trust instrument or, subject to contrary intention, the power contained in the Trustee Act 1925, s.32 may be used.

NOTE: Whatever the theoretical purpose of the power of advancement, it can obviously be used to avoid taxes on capital transfers, particularly on death, by the simple expedient of bringing the capital transfer forward.

TRUSTEE ACT 1925

32. Power of advancement

(1) Trustees may at any time or times pay or apply any capital money subject to a trust, for the advancement or benefit, in such manner as they may, in their absolute discretion, think fit, of any person entitled to the capital of the trust property or of any share thereof, whether absolutely or contingently on his attaining any specified age or on the occurrence of any other event, or subject to a gift over on his death under any specified age or on the occurrence of any other event, and whether in possession or in remainder or reversion, and such payment or application may be made notwithstanding that the interest of such person is liable to be defeated by the exercise of a power of appointment or revocation, or to be diminished by the increase of the class to which he belongs:

Provided that—

(a) the money so paid or applied for the advancement or benefit of any person shall not exceed altogether in amount one-half of the presumptive or vested share or interest of that person in the trust property; and

(b) if that person is or becomes absolutely and indefeasibly entitled to a share in the trust property the money so paid or applied shall be brought into account as part of such share; and

(c) no such payment or application shall be made so as to prejudice any person entitled to any prior life or other interest, whether vested or contingent, in the money paid or applied unless such person is in existence, and of full age and consents in writing to such payment or application.

(2) This section does not apply to capital money arising under the Settled Land Act 1925. [as amended by the Trusts of Land and Appointment of Trustees Act 1996]

(3) This section does not apply to trusts constituted or created before the commencement of this Act.

CD (a minor) v O

[2004] EWHC 1036 (Ch), Chancery Division

Facts: The powers of maintenance and advancement having been exhausted, an application was made to extend the power of advancement by varying the beneficial interests under the trust under the Variation of Trusts Act 1958.

Held: The application succeeded.

LLOYD J: ... by virtue of proviso (a) to section 32(1), no more than half of the presumptive or vested share or interest of the beneficiary may be paid or applied by way of advancement. That limit is commonly relaxed in modern trust deeds, but there is nothing to that effect in the documents in the present case. [para. [10]]

On the evidence I am satisfied that it would be for C's benefit for the limit imposed by section 32 on the application of the capital of the fund for her education to be lifted. The question is whether and on what basis the court has power to achieve this result. There are two possible sources of jurisdiction. [para. [11]]

The Court of Chancery had an ancient jurisdiction to authorise the application of income and, in more limited circumstances, capital, for the maintenance of a minor even if this was not authorised by the terms of the trust. This jurisdiction is recognised in the speeches in *Chapman* v *Chapman* [1954] AC 429: see in particular Lord Morton of Henryton at pages 455–6 and Lord Asquith of Bishopstone at 469. As to the application of capital, *Lewin on Trusts*, 17th ed., refers to a number of cases at paragraph 32–06. One of them, in which specific reference was made to the court's ability to authorise the expenditure of capital to which a minor was absolutely entitled for his or her maintenance, is *Worthington* v *M'Craer* (1856) 23 Beav 81. It seems to me that this would be a possible basis on which the court could proceed in the present circumstances. [para. [12]]

However, since the decision in *Chapman* v *Chapman*, the relevant area of law has been transformed by the Variation of Trusts Act 1958. While this Act does not take away any jurisdiction that the court already had, it seems to me that it would be more appropriate to proceed under the Act if that is possible. [para. [13]]

The 1958 Act applies 'where property ... is held on trusts arising ... under any will settlement or other disposition'. On the face of it, the proceeds of the insurance policies are held on trusts arising under a settlement, albeit that they are held for the three children in equal shares absolutely. The idea of varying a bare trust might perhaps seem a little odd, and but for the beneficiary not being of full legal capacity it is difficult to imagine how the question could arise. Given that lack of capacity, and the constraints on the extent of the statutory provisions which do authorise the trustees to act in certain ways, it does not seem to me so surprising that the Act should apply to property held on a bare trust, at least for a minor. [para. [14]]

A similar point, though in relation to a fund of a very different kind, was argued before Eveleigh J in the Queen's Bench Division, in *Allen* v *Distillers Company (Biochemicals) Ltd* [1974] QB 384. That concerned the funds to be received pursuant to the compromise of the thalidomide litigation, and the desire of many of the parents of children affected to ensure that the sums held for their children should not become their absolute property at the age of 18. The judge held that he did have power to achieve that, but he rejected the argument that he could do so under the 1958 Act. He was shown authority under the 1958 Act for the proposition that the Act could be used to defer the vesting of property in a beneficiary, if it would be for that person's benefit to do so. He did not dispute that, but he held that the Act did not apply to the money to be paid pursuant to the compromise. At page 394 he said this:

'I do not think that the payment out to the trustees in the first instance gives rise to the kind of trust contemplated by the Act. As a common lawyer struggling with this problem I am reminded of the first sentence in the chapter on trusts contained in Snell's Principles of Equity 25th edition: "No one has yet succeeded in giving an entirely satisfactory definition of a trust". An agent may hold and deal with property of his principal in such circumstances as to constitute him a trustee for his principal but leaving aside the manner in which the trust is created, no one would contemplate the possibility of there being a trust of the kind referred to in the Act. The Act contemplates the situation where a beneficial interest is created which did not previously exist and probably one which is related to at least one other beneficial interest. Moreover the Act is designed to deal with the situation where the original disposition was intended to endure according to its terms but which

> in the light of changed attitudes and circumstances it is fair and reasonable to vary. In any event I do not think that the so-called variation would be a variation at all. It would be a new trust made on behalf of an absolute owner.' [para. [15]]

Eveleigh J was not considering the sort of case of absolute entitlement with which I am concerned. In the case before him there was no prior trust of any kind. Despite the potential width of the word 'disposition', it would be difficult to conclude that money paid by an alleged tortfeasor by way of compensation for injury to a minor was 'property ... held on trusts arising ... under any will settlement or other disposition'. Accordingly I would not venture to disagree with his conclusion that the 1958 Act did not apply to the fund that he was concerned with. [para. [16]]

His observation that the Act is concerned with a trust where there is more than one beneficial interest was not necessary to his decision. If it were right the Act could not apply to C's Fund, at any rate once it is split off from the rest of the fund. In my judgment it is not correct. Whether it could be appropriate in any circumstances to exercise the power conferred by the 1958 Act in relation to a fund held for a minor absolutely so as to reduce his or her entitlement in any respect, for example as was sought in the *Allen* case by deferring the date when the person in question can call for the fund, I do not need to decide. What is proposed in the present case would have the effect, in a sense, of accelerating the benefit for C, by allowing the whole of the fund to be used for her benefit while she is still under age. In other circumstances it may be possible to use the power under section 32 in such a way that the trust property does not become vested in the beneficiary: see *Re Pilkington's Will Trusts* [1964] AC 612. On the present and foreseeable facts of this case this is no more than theoretical. It could not be for C's benefit to divert any part of the fund from her. [para. [17]]

In my judgment both the whole trust fund, and C's Fund separately, are 'property ... held on trusts arising ... under any will settlement or other disposition'. It is therefore open to the court to exercise the powers conferred by the 1958 Act in relation to the funds, so long as it is satisfied that the proposed variation of the trusts is for the benefit of the relevant beneficiary. I am satisfied that it is for C's benefit to vary the trusts applying to her fund so that the whole fund, not merely one half, may be applied pursuant to section 32 of the Trustee Act 1925. I have therefore approved on her behalf a variation of the trusts applying to C's Fund so as to permit the powers under section 32 to be exercised in relation to the whole, not only half, of the fund. [para. [18]]

NOTES

1. This decision seems a somewhat radical departure from the statutory rule restricting advancement to one-half of a beneficiary's presumptive share, but the judge was rightly fortified by the fact that the beneficiary in this case was solely entitled to the fund and would (but for her age) have been entitled to bring the trust to an end.

2. In *Wright* v *Gater* [2011] EWHC 2881, an application to postpone from age 18 to age 30 was rejected on the ground that no benefit had been shown, and because the variation would come close to being a resettlement.

Re Pilkington's WT

[1964] AC 612, House of Lords

Facts: Under a will which contained no provision either replacing or excluding the statutory power of advancement under the Trustee Act 1925, s.32, Penelope (a two-year-old girl) was entitled to a share in the capital (valued at around £90,000) at 21. The trustees proposed, under the powers contained in s.32, to advance one-half of Penelope's share to her, and resettle it.

The resettlement was theoretically disadvantageous to her. Although she was still entitled to receive the income on the resettled sum between the ages of 21 to 30, her entitlement to the capital on the advanced funds was postponed until she reached 30. Further, if Penelope died before reaching 30, the fund would be held on trust for other children, in addition to which the other income beneficiaries necessarily benefited from the postponement of her entitlement to the capital. The child was in no need of the moneys advanced, and too young for the traditional purposes of advancement to be relevant.

The reason for the advance, and the only benefit to Penelope, was the saving of estate duty which would otherwise have been payable on the death of her father, the life tenant under the trust. The usual way to avoid estate duty was to advance as much money as possible as long as possible before the death of the father (this principle also applies to inheritance tax, introduced in 1986).

The IRC challenged the lawfulness of the advancement, and one of the issues was whether there was a sufficient benefit to Penelope.

Held:

(a) There was no need to show that the advancement was to meet some personal need of the beneficiary, and the saving of estate duty was itself a sufficient benefit. Nor was it relevant that other persons might benefit, if the provision as a whole would benefit Penelope.

(b) But the resettlement infringed the rule against perpetuities as it then stood. Thus, although the advancement was valid, the resettlement was not.

VISCOUNT RADCLIFFE (on the question of benefit): I think, with all respect to the Commissioners, a good deal of their argument is infected with some of this confusion. To say, for instance, that there cannot be a valid exercise of a power of advancement that results in a deferment of the vesting of the beneficiary's absolute title (Miss Penelope, it will be remembered, is to take at 30 under the proposed settlement instead of at 21 under the will) is in my opinion to play upon words. The element of anticipation consists in the raising of money for her now before she has any right to receive anything under the existing trusts: the advancement consists in the application of that money to form a trust fund, the provisions of which are thought to be for her benefit. I have not forgotten, of course, the references to powers of advancement which are found in such cases as *Re Joicey* [1915] 2 Ch 115, CA, *Re May's Settlement* [1926] Ch 136 and *Re Mewburn's Settlement* [1934] Ch 112, to which our attention was called, or the answer supplied by Cotton LJ in *Re Aldridge* (1886) 55 LT 554, 556 to his own question 'What is advancement?'

> It is a payment to persons who are presumably entitled to, or have a vested or contingent interest in, an estate or a legacy, before the time fixed by the will for their obtaining the absolute interest in a portion or the whole of that to which they would be entitled;

but I think that it will be apparent from what I have already said that the description that he gave (it cannot be a definition) is confined entirely to the aspect of anticipation or acceleration which renders the money available and not to any description or limitation of the purposes for which it can then be applied.

I have not been able to find in the words of s.32, to which I have now referred, anything which in terms or by implication restricts the width of the manner or purpose of advancement. It is true that, if this settlement is made, Miss Penelope's children, who are not objects of the power, are given a possible interest in the event of her dying under 30 leaving surviving issue. But if the disposition itself, by which I mean the whole provision made, is for her benefit, it is no objection to the exercise of the power that other persons benefit incidentally as a result of the exercise. Thus a man's creditors may in certain cases get the most immediate advantage from an advancement made for the purpose of paying them off, as in *Lowther* v *Bentinck* (1874) LR 19 Eq 166; and a power to raise money for the advancement of a wife may cover a payment made direct to her husband in order to set him up in business (*Re Kershaw's Trusts* (1868) LR 6 EQ 322). The exercise will not be bad therefore on this ground.

NOTES

1. The House of Lords struck down the advancement, however, on the ground that it infringed against the common law perpetuity rule.

2. However widely expressed is the power of advancement, the Court of Appeal held in *Re Pauling's ST* [1964] Ch 303 that the trustees must be satisfied that the advance will be for the benefit of the advancee. Further, if the trustees decide to make him an advance for a particular purpose, they must ask themselves whether he will carry it out: they should not make a payment for a purpose and then leave him free to do with it as he pleases. The question was left open as to whether trustees can recover money which the beneficiary requests but then applies for some quite different

purpose. In that case, the life tenant and her husband habitually spent well in excess of their income, and consequently their account at the defendant bank was considerably overdrawn. The defendant bank was also trustee under the settlement, under which the claimants were remaindermen. As the claimants reached their majority, the life tenant and her husband persuaded them to consent to various advances, which were ostensibly made for a specific purpose, for example the purchase of a house or furniture, or house improvements, but which were in fact given to the life tenant and her husband, and used to reduce their overdraft. The bank was held to have acted in breach of trust in making the advances.

Re Clore's Settlement Trusts

[1966] 1 WLR 955, ChD

Facts: The beneficiary's father had established a charitable foundation to which the beneficiary felt morally obliged to contribute. It was more tax efficient for the donation to be made out of the beneficiary's trust monies rather than their private funds. The trustees sought the court's approval of such a course.

Held: The advancement was proper. The beneficiary was morally bound to make the donation. He would benefit financially from making the donation out of the trust fund as opposed to his private monies.

PENNYCUICK J: ... the crux of the present application ... is that the court has always recognised that a wealthy person has a moral obligation to make appropriate charitable donations. The court has certainly recognised this in several cases, although, generally, it has been concerned with relatively small sums of income: see, in particular, *In re Walker* [1901] 1 Ch 879. It seems to me that a beneficiary under a settlement may indeed in many cases be reasonably entitled to regard himself as under a moral obligation to make donations towards charity. The nature and amount of those donations must depend upon all the circumstances, including the position in life of the beneficiary, the amount of the fund and the amount of his other resources. Once that proposition is accepted, it seems to me that it must lie within the scope of a power such as that contained in clause 8 of this settlement for the trustees to raise capital for the purpose of relieving the beneficiary of his moral obligation towards whatever charity he may have in mind. If the obligation is not to be met out of the capital of the trust fund, he would have to meet it out of his own pocket, if at all. Accordingly, the discharge of the obligation out of the capital of the trust fund does improve his material situation... .

To avoid misunderstanding, it seems to me that in the case of a transaction of this kind, i.e., an advance of capital in discharge of a moral obligation towards charity, it is essential to a valid exercise of the power that the beneficiary himself should recognise the moral obligation. It is not open to the trustees to pay away the beneficiary's prospective capital over his head or against his will in discharge of what they consider to be his moral obligations.

NOTE: *Re Clore's Settlement Trusts* was applied in *X v A* [2006] 1 WLR 741. In that case, trustees of a marriage settlement had exercised their power of advancement to give the life tenant (the wife of the settlor) £350,000 in 1996 and £500,000 in 2000, which sums she had given to charity in accordance with her Christian beliefs. The trustees now applied for directions as to whether it was open to them to give her a very substantial part of the remaining trust capital for the purpose of enabling her to devote it to charitable causes. The judge did not criticise the earlier payments, but refused to authorise further advancement on the ground that the sums proposed to be released were too large a proportion of the whole.

■ QUESTION

Does the decision in *X v A* betray the law's inherent bias towards maintaining material wealth at the expense of moral considerations (compare the law's attitude towards ethical investment in Chapter 12)?

SECTION 3: VARIATION OF BENEFICIAL OWNERSHIP

The main reason for wishing to vary trusts is to reduce liability to taxation. Until the Variation of Trusts Act 1958, however, powers to vary were extremely limited, especially where tax planning was the motive.

Most of the jurisdiction considered in this chapter is statutory, but there are circumstances apart from those provided for by statute where variation is possible. The trust instrument itself may have been drafted so as to confer upon the trustees the power to vary the beneficial interests. There is also an inherent equitable jurisdiction considered in the following section.

Most of the modes of varying trusts considered in this chapter relate to the variation of beneficial interests under trusts and incidental administrative variations. The exception is the Trustee Act 1925, s.57, which applies solely to variations in the administration of trusts.

A: Inherent equitable jurisdiction

(i) *Saunders* v *Vautier*

In the absence of express powers, it may be possible to effect a variation in the trust by taking advantage of the rule in *Saunders* v *Vautier* (1841) 10 LJ Ch 354. Collectively, the beneficiaries, so long as they are all adult, *sui iuris*, and between them entitled to the entirety of the trust property, can bring the trust to an end and resettle the property on any terms they wish. Thus, for example, in a simple settlement of property upon a life interest for X with remainder for Y, X and Y may agree to end the trust and divide the capital between them immediately. They can also collectively consent to any act by the trustees which has the effect of varying the terms of the trust. However there are limits to the application of the *Saunders* v *Vautier* doctrine.

First, it depends on the beneficiaries all being collectively entitled. Thus, donees under a power cannot use it, and though beneficiaries under a discretionary trust usually can, they will not be able to unless the entire class of objects is ascertainable.

Secondly, the trustees must be entitled to convey the property to the beneficiaries. So where, for example, 'the subject matter of the trust is a non-assignable contract and there are outstanding obligations to be performed by the trustee, the beneficiary under the trust cannot interfere' (*Barbados Trust Company Ltd* v *Bank of Zambia* [2006] EWHC 222 (Comm); *Don King Productions Inc* v *Warren* [2000] Ch 291; *Re Brockbank* [1948] Ch 206).

Thirdly, it turns upon all the beneficiaries being able to consent to dissolve the trust, or to what would otherwise be a breach of trust by the trustees. If some of the beneficiaries are infants, or if the settlement creates any interests in favour of persons who are not yet born or ascertained, variation of the trust upon this basis will not be possible. This is a serious limitation when dealing with family settlements of the usual type, which almost invariably give interests to *non sui iuris* persons. As will be discussed, this is the difficulty tackled by the Variation of Trusts Act 1958.

Fourthly, unless the trustees also agree, the beneficiaries cannot vary an existing trust, and keep it on foot, instead of dissolving it and resettling the property. In *Re Brockbank* [1948] Ch 206, a trustee wished to retire and the beneficiaries sought to have a trust corporation appointed in place of the remaining trustees, who opposed the change on the ground of the cost to the trust of the trust corporation's fees. The beneficiaries argued that since they were all *sui iuris* and collectively entitled, the trustees were obliged to appoint in accordance with their wishes. Vaisey J rejected this argument. The beneficiaries might terminate the trust if they so wished, but they were not entitled to control the trustees' exercise of their statutory power to appoint while the trust subsisted. Although the *ratio* of the case is confined to the appointment of new trustees (in which context it has been overruled by the Trusts of Land and Appointment of Trustees Act 1996, see Chapter 11), there are remarks by Vaisey J of a much wider scope:

It seems to me that the beneficiaries must choose between two alternatives: either they must keep the trust of the will on foot. In which case those trusts must continue to be executed by trustees ... not ... arbitrarily selected by themselves; or they must, by mutual agreement, extinguish and put an end to the trusts ...

Walton J expressed similar views in *Stephenson* v *Barclays Bank* [1975] 1 WLR 88. One of the reasons he gave was that otherwise the beneficiaries could force upon the trustees duties quite different to those they had originally accepted.

Stephenson (Inspector of Taxes) v Barclays Bank Trust Co. Ltd

[1975] 1 WLR 882, [1975] 1 All ER 625, Chancery Division

Facts: Under a deed of family arrangement made in 1969, Richard and Charles were the only beneficiaries under a trust of a fund. The trustees (Barclays Bank Trust Co. Ltd) had already (before the arrangement was made) acquired the investments which were to make up the fund, but did not transfer them to Richard and Charles. On the question of the liability of the trustees to capital gains tax, the Crown contended that Richard and Charles were 'absolutely entitled as against the trustee' from 1969, as required by the Finance Act 1965, s.22(5). The trustees contended that Richard and Charles did not become absolutely entitled until the fund was actually distributed.

Held: (for the Crown): Richard and Charles were 'absolutely entitled as against the trustee' from 1969, and it could not be contended that they did not become absolutely entitled until the fund was actually distributed.

WALTON J: I now turn to a consideration of the phrase 'absolutely entitled as against the trustee', which is now of course fairly closely defined in the Finance Act 1969, sch. 19, para. 9. It is there defined as meaning that the person concerned—

has the exclusive right, subject only to satisfying any outstanding charge, lien or other right of the trustees to resort to the asset for payment of duty, taxes, costs or other outgoings, to direct how that asset should be dealt with.

Now it is trite law that the persons who between them hold the entirety of the beneficial interests in any particular trust fund are as a body entitled to direct the trustees how that trust fund is to be dealt with, and this is obviously the legal territory from which that definition derives. However, in view of the arguments advanced to me by counsel for the respondents, and more particularly that advanced by him on the basis of the decision of Vaisey J in *Re Brockbank* [1948] Ch 206 [above], I think it may be desirable to state what I conceive to be certain elementary principles. (1) In a case where the persons who between them hold the entirety of the beneficial interest in any particular trust fund are all *sui juris* and acting together ('the beneficial interest holders'), they are entitled to direct the trustees how the trust fund may be dealt with. (2) This does not mean, however, that they can at one and the same time override the pre-existing trusts and keep them in existence. Thus, in *Re Brockbank* itself the beneficial interest holders were entitled to override the pre-existing trusts by, for example, directing the trustees to transfer the trust fund to X and Y, whether X and Y were the trustees of some other trust or not, but they were not entitled to direct the existing trustees to appoint their own nominee as a new trustee of the existing trust. By so doing they would be pursuing inconsistent rights. (3) Nor, I think, are the beneficial interest holders entitled to direct the trustees as to the particular investment they should make of the trust fund. I think this follows for the same reason as the above. Moreover, it appears to me that once the beneficial inter-est holders have determined to end the trust they are not entitled, unless by agreement, to the further services of the trustees. Those trustees can of course be compelled to hand over the entire trust assets to any person or persons selected by the beneficiaries against a proper discharge, but they cannot be compelled, unless they are in fact willing to comply with the directions, to do anything else with the trust fund which they are not in fact willing to do. (4) Of course, the rights of the beneficial interest holders are always subject to the right of the trustees to be fully protected against such matters as duty, taxes, costs or other outgoings; for example, the rent under a lease which the trustees have properly accepted as part of the trust property.

NOTES

1. Walton J went on to hold that Richard and Charles were absolutely entitled from 1969, although the fund was still actually held by the bank.
2. Professor Paul Matthews has argued that on a short timescale, although useful, the rule in *Saunders* v *Vautier* is not essential to defining the right of trust beneficiaries as property rights. It is on the longer timescale (when the trust property might be rendered inalienable in perpetuity) that the rule may be essential to the beneficiaries' rights being in nature property rights, that is, rights to determine what happen to the trust assets ('The Comparative Importance of the Rule in *Saunders* v. *Vautier*' (2006) 122 LQR 266–94).

(ii) *Non sui iuris* beneficiaries

There are often in any case persons unable to give consent, especially children and unborn persons. The courts have limited power to permit a variation of trust under their inherent jurisdiction, where not all beneficiaries are adult and *sui iuris*.

It has long been recognised that the court may, in the case of necessity, permit the trustees to take measures not authorised by the trust instrument, including varying the beneficial interests. The inherent jurisdiction is narrow, encompassing for the most part only emergency and salvage. Originally, this seems to have been confined to cases where some act of salvage was urgently required, such as the mortgage of an infant's property in order to raise money for vital repairs. Gradually, it was widened to cover other contingencies not foreseen and provided for by the settlor, but the House of Lords reaffirmed in *Chapman* v *Chapman* [1954] AC 429 that some element of emergency still needs to be shown.

The courts may also approve compromises of disputes regarding the beneficial enti-tlements on behalf of infant or future beneficiaries. In *Chapman* v *Chapman*, it was argued that this jurisdiction could be extended to cover situations where no real dis-pute had arisen, but this broad conception of the inherent jurisdiction was firmly dis-approved by the House of Lords, and held to be confined to instances where a genuine element of dispute exists.

B: Variation of Trusts Act 1958

In *Re Holmden's ST* [1968] AC 685, Lord Reid took the view that a variation under the 1958 Act must be regarded as one made by the beneficiaries themselves, rather than by the court, with the court acting merely on behalf of those beneficiaries who are unable to give their own consent and approval. His view did not form part of the *ratio* of the case, nor was it explicitly shared by his brethren, but it was accepted as being good law by the Court of Appeal in *Goulding* v *James* [1997] 2 All ER 239, probably as part of the *ratio*, since it followed that the adult *sui iuris* beneficiaries could consent to the variation for themselves, and that any reservations the settlor might have had were irrelevant.

Since, however, even where all beneficiaries are *sui iuris* and consenting they may not be able to vary the trusts in all circumstances, it must follow that the jurisdiction under the Act takes the form of a *Saunders* v *Vautier* revocation, followed by a resettlement (this presumably requires the consent of the trustees, since the resettlement cannot be forced on them against their will).

On this view of the matter, however, it arguably follows that the adult beneficiaries at least ought to give their consents in writing so as to comply with the Law of Property Act 1925, s.53(1)(c). In fact, however, variations are seldom in writing. In *Re Viscount Hambleden's WT* [1960] 1 WLR 82, it had been stated that the court's approval was effective for all purposes to vary the trusts, and this has been relied upon in countless subsequent instances. The problem was posed directly in *Re Holt's Settlement* (see subsection (v) Risks), where Megarry J, aware that possibly thousands of variations had been acted upon without writing conforming with s.53(1)(c), accepted, though without enthusiasm, two grounds put forward by counsel in favour of the view that no writing was necessary. First, it might be said that in conferring express power upon the court to make an order, Parliament had impliedly created an exception to s.53. Secondly and alternatively, the arrangement might be regarded as one in which the beneficial interests passed to their respective purchasers upon the making of the agreement, that agreement itself being specifically enforceable. The original interests under the (unvaried) trusts would thus be held, from the moment of the agreement, upon constructive trusts identical to the new (varied) trusts, and as constructive trusts would be exempt from writing under s.53(2). Whether or not these reasons are regarded as adequate, the assumption that no writing is required has continued to prevail.

The point was also important in *Re Holt*, because the order of the court took effect after 15 July 1964, whereas the original trust had been set up in 1959, and Megarry J thought that the provisions of the Perpetuities and Accumulations Act 1964 (see Chapter 6) could apply. If all the court had done had been to provide consent, then the perpetuity period would have been that applicable to a 1959 instrument (i.e. the common law period).

NOTE: Following the decision of the House of Lords in *Chapman* v *Chapman*, the Law Reform Committee was asked to consider the question of the court's powers to sanction variations (see Law Reform Committee Sixth Report (*Court's Power to Sanction Variations of Trusts*), Cmnd 310). The Variation of Trusts Act 1958 was based on these recommendations.

VARIATION OF TRUSTS ACT 1958

1. Jurisdiction of courts to vary trusts

(1) Where property, whether real or personal, is held on trusts arising, whether before or after the passing of this Act, under any will, settlement or other disposition, the court may as it thinks fit by order approve on behalf of—

    (a) any person having, directly or indirectly, an interest, whether vested or contingent, under the trusts who by reason of infancy or other incapacity is incapable of assenting, or

    (b) any person (whether ascertained or not) who may become entitled, directly or indirectly, to an interest under the trusts as being at a future date or on the happening of a future event a person of any specified description or a member of any specified class of persons, so however that this paragraph shall not include any person who would be of that description, or a member of that class, as the case may be, if the said date had fallen or the said event had happened at the date of the application to the court, or

(c) any person unborn, or

(d) any person in respect of any discretionary interest of his under protective trusts where the interest of the principle beneficiary has not failed or determined, any arrangement (by whomsoever proposed, and whether or not there is any other person beneficially interested who is capable of assenting thereto) varying or revoking all or any of the trusts, or enlarging the trustees' powers of managing and administering any of the property subject to the trusts:

Provided that except by virtue of paragraph (d) of this subsection the court shall not approve an arrangement on behalf of any person unless the carrying out thereof would be for the benefit of that person.

[The remaining subsections are detailed provisions which are not reproduced.]

(i) Persons on whose behalf the court may vary trusts

The 1958 Act allows the court to give consent on behalf of *non sui iuris* beneficiaries, but the principles underlying the rule in *Saunders* v *Vautier* were preserved by the Act, in as much as the court will not provide a consent which ought properly to be sought from an ascertainable adult, *sui iuris* beneficiary. Hence the limits placed on s.1(1)(b).

The categories of person on whose behalf consent may be given are set out in s.1. They include infants and other people who are not capable by reason of capacity of assenting (e.g. those who used to be called lunatics), and unborn persons, so long as the proposed arrangement would be for their benefit. Beneficiaries under protective discretionary trusts are also included: in the last case, the statute does not expressly require that a benefit be shown.

The difficulty with s.1(1)(b) arises with interests which are very remote, such as interests in default of appointment, or in the event of a failure of the trust. It is the words after 'so however' which cause the problem, since those persons have to consent on their own behalf: the court cannot consent for them. There is no problem over, for example, potential future spouses, since they clearly have more expectation of succeeding. They clearly come within the first part of para. (b), and the court can consent on their behalf. But if somebody is named in the instrument as having a contingent interest, however unlikely that contingency is to arise, the court cannot consent on their behalf. They must consent themselves to any variation.

This can seriously limit the scope of the 1958 Act, as can be seen from *Knocker* v *Youle* [1986] 1 WLR 934.

Knocker v *Youle*

[1986] 1 WLR 934, [1986] 2 All ER 914, Chancery Division

Decision: The court could not consent on behalf of persons who would benefit only in the event of failure or determination of the trust.

WARNER J: What is said by counsel on behalf of the plaintiffs, and is supported by counsel for Mrs Youle's children, is that I have power under s.1(1)(*b*) of the Variation of Trusts Act 1958 to approve the arrangement on behalf of the cousins.

[Warner J set out the relevant part of s.1(1) and continued: ...]

There are two difficulties. First, it is not strictly accurate to describe the cousins as persons 'who may become entitled ... to an interest under the trusts'. There is no doubt of course that they are members of a 'specified class'. Each of them is, however, entitled now to an interest under the trusts, albeit a contingent one (in the case of those who are under 21, a doubly contingent one) and albeit also that it is an interest that is defeasible on the exercise of the general testamentary powers of appointment vested in Mrs Youle and Mr Knocker. None the less, it is properly described in legal language as an interest, and it seems to me plain that in this Act the word 'interest' is used in its technical, legal sense. Otherwise, the words 'whether vested or contingent' in para. (*a*) of s.1(1) would be out of place.

What counsel invited me to do was in effect to interpret the word 'interest' in s.1(1) loosely, as a layman might, so as not to include an interest that was remote. I was referred to two authorities: *Re Moncrieff's Settlement Trusts* [1962] 3 All ER 838, [1962] 1 WLR 1344 and the earlier case of *Re Suffert's Settlement, Suffert* v *Martyn-Linnington* [1960] 3 All ER 561, [1961] Ch 1. In both those cases, however, the class in question was a class of prospective next of kin, and, of course it is trite law that the prospective or presumptive next of kin of a living person do not have an interest. They have only a spes successionis, a hope of succeeding, and quite certainly they are the typical category of persons who fall within s.1(1)(*b*). Another familiar example of a person falling within that provision is a potential future spouse. It seems to me, however, that a person who has an actual interest directly conferred on him or her by a settlement, albeit a remote interest, cannot properly be described as one who 'may become' entitled to an interest.

The second difficulty (if one could think of a way of overcoming the first) is that there are, as I indicated earlier, 17 cousins who, if the failure or determination of the earlier trusts declared by the settlement had occurred at the date of the application to the court, would have been members of the specified class, in that they were then living and over 21. Therefore, they are prima facie excluded from s.1(1)(*b*) by what has been conveniently called the proviso to it, that is to say the part beginning 'so however that this paragraph shall not include … ' They are in the same boat, if I may express it in that way, as the first cousins in *Re Suffert's Settlement* and the adopted son in *Re Moncrieff's Settlement Trusts*. The court cannot approve the arrangement on their behalf; only they themselves can do so.

Counsel for the plaintiffs suggested that I could distinguish *Re Suffert's Settlement* and *Re Moncreieff's Settlement Trusts* in that respect for two reasons.

First, he suggested that the proviso applied only if there was a single event on the happening of which one could ascertain the class. Here, he said, both Mr Knocker and Mrs Youle must die without exercising their general testamentary powers of appointment to the full before any of the cousins could take anything. But it seems to me that what the proviso is referring to is the event on which the class becomes ascertainable, and that that is a single event. It is, in this case, the death of the survivor of Mrs Youle and Mr Knocker, neither of them having exercised the power to the full; in the words of cl 7 of the settlement, it is 'the failure or determination of the trusts hereinbefore declared concerning the trust fund.'

The second reason suggested by counsel for the plaintiffs why I should distinguish the earlier authorities was that the event hypothesised in the proviso was the death of the survivor of Mr Knocker and Mrs Youle on the date when the originating summonses were issued, that is to say on 6 January 1984. There is evidence that on that day there were in existence wills of both of them exercising their testamentary powers to the full. The difficulty about that is that the proviso does not say ' … so however that this paragraph shall not include any person who would have become entitled if the said event had happened at the date of the application to the court'. It says:

> … so however that this paragraph shall not include any person who would be of that description, or a member of that class, as the case may be, if the said date had fallen or the said event had happened at the date of the application to the court.

So the proviso is designed to identify the presumptive members of the class at the date of the application to the court and does not advert to the question whether at that date they would or would not have become entitled.

I was reminded by counsel of the principle that one must construe Acts of Parliament having regard to their purpose, and it was suggested that the purpose here was to exclude the need to join as parties to applications under the Variation of Trusts Act 1958 people whose interests were remote. In my view, however, that principle does not enable me to take the sort of liberty with the language of this statute that I was invited to take. It is noteworthy that remoteness does not seem to be the test if one thinks in terms of presumptive statutory next of kin. The healthy issue of an elderly widow who is on her deathbed, and who has not made a will, have an expectation of succeeding to her estate; that could hardly be described as remote. Yet they are a category of persons on whose behalf the court could, subject of course to the proviso, approve an arrangement under this Act. On the other hand, people in the position of the cousins in this case have an interest that is extremely remote. None the less, it is an interest, and the distinction between an expectation and an interest is one which I do not think that I am entitled to blur. So, with regret, having regard to the particular circumstances of this case, I have to say that I do not think that I have jurisdiction to approve these arrangements on behalf of the cousins.

(ii) What is benefit?

Benefit will usually be synonymous with financial advantage but need not be. In *Re Towler's ST* [1964] Ch 158, Wilberforce J was prepared to postpone the vesting of capital to which a beneficiary was soon to become entitled, upon evidence that she was likely to deal with it imprudently. In *Re Steed's WT* [1960] Ch 407, the proposed scheme was for the elimination of the protective element in a trust relating to land. The principal beneficiary, who was a life tenant (but not *sui iuris* because of the protective element), wanted a variation such that the trustees held the property on trust for herself absolutely. Clearly this was, in theory, to her financial advantage, but evidence suggested that advantage would in fact be taken of the life tenant's good nature by the very persons against whose importuning the settlor had meant to protect her, and the Court of Appeal refused its consent. In *Re Weston's Settlements* [1969] 1 Ch 223, the Court of Appeal refused to approve a scheme which would have removed the trusts to a tax haven (Jersey), where the family had moved three months previously, on the ground that the moral and social benefits of an English upbringing were not outweighed by the tax savings to be enjoyed by the infant beneficiaries. Harman LJ said that 'this is an essay in tax avoidance naked and unashamed', and Lord Denning MR noted (at 223) that:

There are many things in life more worthwhile than money. One of these things is to be brought up in this our England, which is still 'the envy of less happier lands'. I do not believe it is for the benefit of children to be uprooted from England and transported to another country simply to avoid tax ... Many a child has been ruined by being given too much. The avoidance of tax may be lawful, but it is not yet a virtue.

Finally, in *Re CL* [1969] 1 Ch 587, the Court of Protection held that there was a benefit to an elderly mental patient in giving up, in return for no consideration, her life interests for the benefit of adopted daughters. This was, in effect, giving approval to a straightforward gift by the beneficiary, from which in strictly material terms she could not possibly benefit. The lady's needs were otherwise amply provided for, however, and the court, in approving the arrangement, took the view that it was acting as she herself would have done, had she been able to appreciate her family responsibilities.

(iii) Extent of the court's discretion

The only constraint on the court's discretion under the Act is the requirement that it must be satisfied of a benefit, except in the case of para. (d) persons. However, even if it is clear that the court has *jurisdiction* to consent to a variation, it has an unfettered discretion to exercise its powers under the Act *'if it thinks fit'*. Thus, whereas the court cannot approve a variation except where the Act so provides it has an unlimited discretion to refuse its approval where it is given jurisdiction under the Act.

It follows that, even where a benefit is clearly shown for the persons on whose behalf approval is sought, the court is not required to approve. For para. (d) persons, it is not even required that a benefit be shown, yet the court, in its discretion, refused to approve a variation in *Re Steed's WT* [1960] Ch 407.

(iv) Relevance of the settlor's views

In *Re Steed's WT* [1960] Ch 407, the Court of Appeal was undoubtedly influenced by the views of the settlor, who had clearly in his will expressed his concern about the welfare of the beneficiary under the protective trust, for whom approval was sought. Yet though the settlor's views can be relevant, they are rarely paramount; they were overridden in *Re Remnant's ST* [1970] Ch 560, and it was the settlor who applied for the variation in *Re Weston's Settlements* [1969] 1 Ch 223. Moreover, the Court of Appeal held in *Goulding v James* [1997] 2 All ER 239 that they have no relevance at all unless they relate to someone on whose behalf the court's approval is required. In *Goulding v James*, the proposed variation (which was clearly for the benefit of the testatrix's unborn great-grandchildren for whom approval was sought) would have frustrated her desire to restrict the ability of two adult, *sui iuris* beneficiaries to touch the capital of the estate.

Since the court's approval was not required for the adult beneficiaries, however, who were able to consent for themselves, the settlor's views were entirely irrelevant.

(v) Risks

More interesting issues arise where the proposed arrangement involves some element of risk to the beneficiary for whom the court is asked to consent. An element of risk will not prevent the court from approving the arrangement, if the risk is one which an adult beneficiary would be prepared to take. Such a test was applied by Danckwerts J in *Re Cohen's WT* [1959] 1 WLR 865.

Re Robinson's ST

[1976] 1 WLR 806, [1976] 3 All ER 61, Chancery Division

Facts: The fund was held on trust for the claimant for her life, with remainders over to her children, one of whom was an infant. The claimant was 55 and expected to live for many years. The variation proposed was to divide up the fund, giving the claimant an immediate capital share of 52 per cent (the actuarial capitalised value of her share), the children dividing the balance in equal shares. The children who got their share immediately, and those who were over 18 consented to the variation. The court was asked to approve variation on behalf of Nicola (who was 17).

Before the introduction of Capital Transfer Tax in 1975, division of the fund in this way, by giving the children their interests immediately rather than on the death of the life tenant, was almost certain to reduce liability to estate duty, because at that time there was no liability to estate duty on any advance made more than seven years before the death of the life tenant. The same is true today under Inheritance Tax. However, for a short period following the Finance Act 1975, which introduced Capital Transfer Tax, all *inter vivos* gifts were also taxable, albeit that liability was lower so long as the transfer was made more than three years before the death of the life tenant.

At the time of *Re Robinson's ST*, therefore, the division would not necessarily have favoured Nicola. The transfer would have been taxed immediately, so that the value of the fund would be reduced. On the other hand, Nicola would get her share immediately, and not have to wait for the death of her mother. Whether this would be to her benefit or not would depend entirely on how long her mother was likely to live. If she died immediately, Nicola's share would be less than she would have received under the unvaried trust, since tax would have been paid on it. It was calculated, however, that, given the mother's life expectancy, the deficiency would be made up in income on her share between the date of the variation and her mother's death.

Held: The variation would be approved, subject to a policy of insurance to protect the infant's interests.

TEMPLEMAN J: I am quite satisfied that it would not be sensible to leave matters entirely as they are. There are other people interested besides the infant, and to preserve the present trusts with present, and future, rates of income and capital taxation does not seem sensible. I am satisfied that the life tenant will only receive under the arrangement a reasonable and fair proportion having regard to the value of her life interest in her present situation.

In these circumstances I think I can accept the arrangement, provided that the infant's income is to a certain extent made available for insurance in order to protect the infant's own share against loss caused by the premature death of the life tenant. A quotation has been obtained, and it would appear that to insure a shortfall of £14,000 would cost about £800 a year. Having regard to the amount of the income that seems to me to be weighing too much on the future and not enough on the present. A policy for £8,000, which with profits will yield something over £11,000 in ten years and more thereafter, will only cost about £400 a year. That will still leave a substantial income for the infant to receive straight away.

It seems to me if insurance of £8,000 with profits is effected, I can, relying on the observations of Stamp [1965] 3 All ER 139 at 144, [1965] 1 WLR 1229 at 1236 and Danckwerts JJ [1959] 3 All ER 523, [1959] 1 WLR 865, approve this arrangement, although I still think it is a borderline case. Great powers of advocacy were used to persuade me that capital transfer tax has made such a change that the possible result of a death must be disregarded, the actuarial division accepted and a risk taken. I do not take that view. I start with the principle that all these schemes should, if possible, prove that an infant is not going to be materially worse off. There are difficulties with capital transfer tax, and borderline cases, and one may then have to take a broad view, but not a galloping, gambling view.

In my judgment, taking a reasonably prudent view, insurance of £8,000 in the present instance will be sufficient, and I am prepared to sanction the arrangement thus amended.

NOTE: Templeman J took the view that the court should require evidence that the infant would at least not be materially worse off as a result of the variation. He adopted as the test whether an adult beneficiary would have been prepared to take the risk: a 'broad' view might be taken, but not a 'galloping, gambling view'. The arrangement was approved subject to a policy of insurance to protect the infant's interests, but Templeman J did not require the entirety of the possible loss to be covered, the view being taken that the saving in premium on a lesser cover was worth the small risk.

Re Cohen's ST, Eliot-Cohen v Cohen

[1965] 1 WLR 1229, [1965] 3 All ER 139, Chancery Division

Facts: A settlement made in 1909 provided that, until the death of the settlor's last surviving son, the *income* would be divided equally between his five sons. On the death of each of the first four sons to die, his share of the *income* went to his issue through all degrees. When the last surviving son died, the *capital* was to be held for the grandchildren of the settlor then living, and the issue of any grandchild then dead, but so that the issue of any dead grandchild would take between them only the share that the grandchild himself would have taken had he or she still been living.

Up until the death of the last surviving son, therefore, the beneficiaries were entitled only to a share of the income. After that, the same people who had been entitled to income up to the death of the last surviving son became entitled to a share of the capital (otherwise there would have been perpetuity problems). Only those living at the death of the last surviving son would become entitled at all (again, for perpetuity reasons).

The claimant was the last surviving son. The income of the other four sons, who were dead, was being enjoyed by their issue. Clearly, on the claimant's death, estate duty would become payable on the capital corresponding to his share of the income, and there was no attempt to avoid that. The worry was, however, that estate duty would become payable on the entire fund at the death of the claimant, since the grandchildren (or issue) who would until then be entitled only to income would become entitled to a share of the capital in the fund. The court was therefore asked to approve a scheme under the Variation of Trusts Act 1958, s.1, substituting for the claimant's death a fixed date on which interests in the capital would vest. A date of 30 June 1973 was proposed, beyond which it was unlikely that the claimant would live.

Note that those who would become entitled to a share under the proposed variation, being those grandchildren (or issue) living on 30 June 1973, could be different people from those entitled under the unvaried scheme, being those grandchildren (or issue) living on the claimant's death.

Held: The court would approve the variation on behalf of the infants, since the scheme was for their benefit, but it was possible to envisage unborn persons who could get no benefit from the scheme, and could only suffer substantial disadvantage. The court had to be satisfied that every individual for whom it was asked to consent would benefit from the scheme, not merely that the class as a whole would benefit. It could not therefore consent for those unborn persons who could clearly not benefit, so approval for the scheme would be refused.

NOTES

1. Perhaps the most important aspect of this case is that benefit must be shown on the part of *every single individual* for whom approval is sought. It is not sufficient to show merely that the class as a whole can be benefited. It follows that if one infant or unborn person can be found who will clearly not benefit, approval for the variation cannot be given. It was possible to envisage unborn persons who could not possibly benefit, and the fact that unborn persons as a class might benefit was irrelevant.

2. No problem arose for approval for the existing infants, although any who died between the death of the claimant and 30 June 1973 (assuming that the claimant did indeed die before that date) would lose out. On balance, however, the risk was worth taking given the likely saving in estate duty, and the increased chance that his parent would have died by 30 June 1973.

Re Holt's ST

[1969] 1 Ch 100, Chancery Division

Facts: The trust provided for a life interest of personal property for Mrs Wilson, and then to her children at 21 in equal shares. The variation proposed was that Mrs Wilson should surrender the income of one-half of her life interest to the fund, but another effect of the proposed variation was to postpone the vesting of the children's interests until 30. The court was asked to approve the variation on behalf of Mrs Wilson's three children who were aged 10, 7, and 6.

The surrender of the income (the real purpose of which was to reduce Mrs Wilson's liability to surtax) was also clearly to the advantage of the children, since the value of the trust property would be increased. However, the postponement to 30 (on the grounds that it would be undesirable for Mrs Wilson's children to receive a large income from 21) was clearly to their disadvantage.

Held: The variation would be approved.

MEGARRY J: I can deal with the merits of this application quite shortly. It seems to me that, subject to one reservation the arrangement proposed is for the benefit of each of the beneficiaries contemplated by the Variation of Trusts Act 1958, s.1(1). The financial detriment to the children is that the absolute vesting of their interests will be postponed from age twenty-one to age thirty. As against that, they will obtain very substantial financial benefits, both in the acceleration of their interests in a moiety of the trust fund and in the savings of estate duty to be expected in a case such as this. Where the advantages of the scheme are overwhelming, any detailed evaluation, or 'balance sheet' of advantages and disadvantages, seems to me to be unnecessary; but I can imagine cases under the Act where it may be important that an attempt should be made to put in evidence a detailed evaluation of the financial and other consequences of the changes proposed to be made, so that it may be seen whether on balance there is a sufficient advantage to satisfy the proviso to s.1(1) of the Act of 1958. But this is not such a case, and I say no more about it. I should, however, state that I fully concur in the view taken by Mrs Wilson that, speaking in general terms, it is most important that young children 'should be reasonably advanced in a career and settled in life before they are in receipt of an income sufficient to make them independent of the need to work'. The word 'benefit' in the proviso to s.1(1) of the Act of 1958 is, I think, plainly not confined to financial benefit, but may extend to moral or social benefit, as is shown by *Re Towler's Settlement Trusts* [1964] Ch 158.

The point that at one stage troubled me concerns the unborn issue. Counsel for the trustees, as in duty bound, put before me a contention that it was possible to conceive of an unborn infant who would be so circumstanced that the proposed rearrangement would be entirely to his disadvantage. He postulated the case of a child born to Mrs Wilson next year, and of Mrs Wilson dying in childbirth, or shortly after the child's birth. In such a case, he said the benefit of the acceleration of interest resulting from Mrs Wilson surrendering the moiety of her life interest would be minimal, and there would be no saving of estate duty. All that would happen in regard to such an infant would be that the vesting of his interest would be postponed from age twenty-one to age thirty, and the only possible advantage in that would be the non-financial moral or social advantage to which I have just referred. In support of this contention he referred me to the decision of Stamp J in *Re Cohen's Settlement Trusts*. There, the scheme originally proposed was not approved by the court because there was a possibility of there being a beneficiary who would get no advantage whatsoever from the proposed arrangement; it would merely be to his detriment.

Counsel for the plaintiff, however, points out that there is an essential distinction between that case and this; for there, whatever the surrounding circumstances, the unborn person contemplated could not benefit from the arrangement. In the present case, he says, all that counsel for the trustees has done is to put forward the case of an infant who might be born next year; and it would be a result of the surrounding circumstances, and not of the time of birth or the characteristics of the infant, that that infant might derive no benefit from the arrangement proposed. Counsel for the plaintiff referred me to *Re Cohen's Will Trusts* [1959] 3 All ER 523, where Danckwerts J held that in exercising the jurisdiction under the Act of 1958 the court must, on behalf of those persons for whom it was approving the arrangement, take the sort of risk which an adult would be prepared to take. Accordingly, says counsel for the plaintiff, counsel for the trustee's special infant to be born next year was in the position that although there was the chance that its mother would die immediately afterwards, there was also the alternative chance that its mother would survive his birth for a substantial period of time. In the latter event, which was the more probable, the advantages of the arrangement would accrue to the infant. In short, he distinguished the decision of Stamp J in *Re Cohen's Settlement Trusts* on the footing that that was the case of an unborn person whose prospects were hopeless, whatever the events, whereas in the present case the hypothetical unborn person has the normal prospects of events occurring which will either improve or not improve his position. Such an unborn person falls, he says, into the category of unborn persons on whose behalf the court should be prepared to take a risk if the arrangement appears on the whole to be for their benefit.

It seems to me that this is a proper distinction to make, and I accept it. Accordingly, I hold that the arrangement is for the benefit of the classes of persons specified in s.1(1) of the Act of 1958, and I approve it.

NOTES

1. If a child was born the year after the variation, and his mother died very soon afterwards, that child could not possibly benefit. The benefit from Mrs Wilson surrendering part of her income under the trust would be minimal if Mrs Wilson died soon after the birth, whereas the postponement would operate entirely to the child's disadvantage.

2. Megarry J approved the variation on the same test adopted in *Re Robinson*. *Cohen* was distinguished because here two chances had to occur: that of the unborn person being born next year, and secondly, that child having been born (and thus become a legal entity) and his or her mother dying shortly afterwards. The first chance could be disregarded on *Cohen* principles, but not the second. Both were independently unlikely possibilities, so approval for the scheme was given. Even once the theoretical unborn child had been born, he or she would still have been well advised to agree to the variation, and accept the slight risk of his or her mother dying shortly afterwards.

3. It follows that the reasoning in *Cohen* applies only when the date of *vesting in interest* (or in other words the date on closing the class) is altered, and does not apply merely to alterations in *vesting in possession*.

4. The main part of the case concerned the question whether writing was required for a variation under the Law of Property Act 1925, s.53(1)(c). Megarry J, aware that possibly thousands of variations had been acted upon without writing conforming with s.53(1)(c), accepted, though without enthusiasm, two grounds put forward by counsel in favour of the view that no writing was necessary. First, it might be said that in conferring express power upon the court to make an order, Parliament had impliedly created an exception to s.53. Secondly and alternatively, the arrangement might be regarded as one in which the beneficial interests passed to their respective purchasers upon the making of the agreement, that agreement itself being specifically enforceable. The original interests under the (unvaried) trusts would thus be held, from the moment of the agreement, upon constructive trusts identical to the new (varied) trusts, and as constructive trusts would be exempt from writing under s.53(2).

(vi) Variation not resettlement

Re Ball's ST

[1968] 1 WLR 899, Chancery Division

Decision: Following *Re Towler's ST* [1964] Ch 158, the courts will not approve a proposal for a total resettlement. This is however a question of substance not form.

Merely because an arrangement can correctly be described as effecting a revocation and resettlement, it does not follow that it cannot also be correctly described as effecting a variation of the trusts. The test is whether the arrangement alters completely the substratum of the trust. If so, the court cannot approve it.

MEGARRY J: The second point in this case concerns the jurisdiction of the court. The originating summons asks for the approval of the court of an arrangement 'revoking the trusts of the above-mentioned settlement and resettling the subject matter of the above-mentioned settlement'. What s.1(1) of the Act of 1958 authorises the court to approve is any arrangement ... varying or revoking all or any of the trusts, or enlarging the powers of the trustees of managing or administering any of the property subject to the trusts.

The word 'resettling' or its equivalent nowhere appears. Accordingly, while there is plainly jurisdiction to approve the arrangement insofar as it revokes the trusts, in my view there is equally plainly no jurisdiction to approve the arrangement as regards 'resettling' the property, at any rate *eo nomine*. In this connexion, I bear in mind the words of Wilberforce J in *Re Towler's Settlement Trusts*. He there said [[1964] Ch 158, 162]:

> ... I have no desire to cut down the very useful jurisdiction which this Act has conferred on the court, but I am satisfied that the proposal as originally made to me falls outside it. Though presented as 'a variation' it is in truth a complete new re-settlement. The former trust funds were to be got in from the former trustee and held on totally new trusts such as might be made by an absolute owner of the funds. I do not think that the court can approve this.

It seems to me that the originating summons correctly describes what is sought to be done in this case, and as so described there is clearly no jurisdiction for the court to approve the arrangement. But it does not follow that merely because an arrangement can correctly be described as effecting a revocation and resettlement, it cannot also be correctly described as effecting a variation of the trusts. The question then is whether the arrangement in this case can be so described. In the course of argument I indicated that it seemed desirable for the summons to be amended by substituting the word 'varying' for the word 'revoking' and deleting the reference to 'resettling', and that I would give leave for this amendment to be made. On the summons as so amended the question is thus whether the arrangement can fairly be said to be covered by the word 'varying' so that the court has power to approve it.

There was some discussion of the ambit of this word in *Re Holt's Settlement* [1968] 1 All ER 470. It was there held that if in substance the new trusts were recognisable as the former trusts, though with variations, the change was comprehended within the word 'varying', even if it had been achieved by a process of revocation and new declaration. In that case, the new trusts were plainly recognisable as the old trusts with variations. In the present case, the new trusts are very different from the old ... . All that remains of the old trusts are what I may call the general drift or purport, namely that a moiety of the trust fund is to be held on certain trusts for each son and certain of his issue. Is the word 'varying' wide enough to embrace so categorical a change?

... If an arrangement changes the whole substratum of the trust, then it may well be that it cannot be regarded merely as varying that trust. But if an arrangement, while leaving the substratum, effectuates the purpose of the original trust by other means, it may still be possible to regard that arrangement as merely varying the original trusts, even though the means employed are wholly different and even though the form is completely changed.

I am, of course, well aware that this view carries me a good deal farther than I went in *Re Holt*. I have felt some hesitation in the matter, but on the whole I consider that this is a proper step to take. The jurisdiction of the Act of 1958 is beneficial and, in my judgment, the court should construe it widely and not be astute to confine its beneficent operation. I must remember that in essence the court is merely contributing on behalf of infants and unborn and unascertained persons the binding assents to the arrangement which they, unlike an adult beneficiary, cannot give. So far as is proper, the power of the court to give that assent should be assimilated to the wide powers which the ascertained adults have.

In this case, it seems to me that the substratum of the original trusts remains ... . In the events which are likely to occur, the differences between the old provisions and the new may, I think, fairly be said to lie in detail rather than in substance. Accordingly, in my judgment, the arrangement here proposed, with the various revisions to it made in the course of argument, can properly be described as varying the trusts of the settlement. Subject to the summons being duly amended, I therefore approve the revised arrangement. I may add that since the hearing of this case I have considered the speeches of their lordships in *Re Holmden's Settlement Trusts, IRC v Holmden* [1968] 1 All ER 148, but although these suggest certain questions of interest and difficulty, I find in them nothing to make me resile from the views that I have expressed.

■ QUESTIONS

1. If the substratum of a trust equates to the settlor's underlying intentions, do you think the 'substratum test' has effectively been destroyed by the decision of the Court of Appeal in *Goulding* v *James*?

2. Benefit to the beneficiaries is the courts' sole concern when considering whether to approve a proposal to vary a trust. Given that many variations are sought for the purpose of avoiding tax, should the court also be concerned with the public benefit before approving a variation?

3. Do you think it could benefit the children of a settlor for the trust to be varied to grant the settlor's spouse a life interest on the settlor's death?

NOTE:

In *Ridgwell* v *Ridgwell* [2007] EWHC 2666 (Ch), the court held that such a variation would benefit the children of the settlor and his spouse. (Economically, it is hard to see how the surviving spouse could gain a benefit without the children suffering a corresponding financial loss. The court held that the arrangement was to the financial benefit of the children, but it might have been more convincing to acknowledge that this is an area in which financial benefit is not the only benefit taken into consideration.)

Where there is a resettlement there are potential (capital gains) tax consequences, so to recognise when a variation involves a resettlement is a practical necessity. In *Roome* v *Edwards* [1982] AC 279, Lord Wilberforce suggested that a new settlement (one that does not leave the old substratum intact) might be indicated by such factors as 'separate and defined property; separate trusts; and separate trustees' and, perhaps, 'a separate disposition bringing the separate settlement into existence'. This was followed in *Wyndham* v *Egremont* [2009] EWHC 2076 (Ch), where the court noted that the Inland Revenue has discontinued its practice of giving advance opinions on the tax implications of proposed arrangements to vary trusts under the 1958 Act.

(vii) Matrimonial Causes Act 1973

Sections 24 and 25 give a wide power to make orders affecting the property of parties to matrimonial proceedings, so as to avoid the unfairness which sometimes arose where the property of a married couple, in particular the matrimonial home, came under the rules governing resulting trusts (see Chapter 5). The court may order provision for either spouse to be made by payments in cash, by transfers of property, or by the creation of a settlement for the benefit of a spouse and children.

More important in the context of variation, s.24(1)(c) and (d) allow for variation of an ante- or post-nuptial settlement, including settlements made by will or codicil, and also permit the making of an order extinguishing or reducing the interest of either of the spouses under such a settlement. The term 'settlement' has been widely interpreted to include any provision (other than outright gifts) made for the benefit of the parties to a marriage, whether by themselves or by a third party, and the acquisition of a matrimonial home has been held to be a settlement (*Ulrich* v *Ulrich* [1968] 1 WLR 180). Further, the court has the power to vary or discharge any order for a settlement or variation under s.24(1) made on or after a decree of judicial separation, if the separation order is rescinded or the marriage subsequently dissolved.

(viii) Mental Capacity Act jurisdiction

The Mental Capacity Act 2005 came into force on 1 October 2007. (For consideration of the practical implications of the 2005 Act as regards trusts for the disabled see, for example, the commentary by A. Palin (2010) 2 PCB 137.) Section 16 of the 2005 Act confers powers to govern the property and affairs of persons who lack mental capacity. According to s.18, those powers extend to a range of matters, including: the control and management of P's property; the sale, exchange, charging, gift or other disposition of P's property; the acquisition of property in P's name or on P's behalf; the settlement of any P's property, whether for P's benefit or for the benefit of others; the execution for P of a will; and, the exercise of any power (including a power to consent) vested in P whether beneficially or as trustee or otherwise. Any settlement made under these powers can be varied (see the extract of the Act reproduced here).

MENTAL CAPACITY ACT 2005

SCHEDULE 2: Property and affairs: supplementary provisions

...

6. Variation of settlements

    (1) If a settlement has been made by virtue of section 18, the court may by order vary or revoke the settlement if—

        (a) the settlement makes provision for its variation or revocation,

        (b) the court is satisfied that a material fact was not disclosed when the settlement was made, or

        (c) the court is satisfied that there has been a substantial change of circumstances.

    (2) Any such order may give such consequential directions as the court thinks fit.

C: Variation of trust administration

TRUSTEE ACT 1925

57. Power of court to authorise dealings with trust property

    (1) Where in the management or administration of any property vested in trustees, any sale, lease, mortgage, surrender, release or other disposition, or any purchase, investment, acquisition, expenditure, or other transaction, is in the opinion of the court expedient, but the same cannot be effected by reason of the absence of any power for that purpose vested in the trustees by the trust instrument, if any, or by law, the court may be order confer upon the trustees, either generally or in any particular instance, the necessary power for the purpose, on such terms, and subject to such provisions and conditions, if any, as the court may think fit and may direct in what manner any money authorised to be expended, and the costs of any transaction, are to be paid or borne as between capital and income.

    (2) The court may, from time to time, rescind or vary any order made under this section, or may make any new or further order.

(3) An application to the court under this section may be made by the trustees, or by any of them, or by a person beneficially interested under the trust.

(4) This section does not apply to trustees of a settlement for the purposes of the Settled Land Act 1925.

Anker-Petersen v *Anker-Petersen*

(1991) 16 LS Gaz 32

Facts: The claimant, tenant for life of a fund held on the trusts of his father's will, applied to the court under the Trustee Act 1925, s.57, alternatively Variation of Trusts Act 1958, s.1, for approval of an extension of the trustees' powers of investment. Under the will, moneys were to be invested as from time to time sanctioned by law for the investment of trust moneys; they were thus governed by the Trustee Investments Act 1961. The proposed extensions would give the trustees power: (1) to invest in assets of any kind as if they were beneficial owners; (2) to delegate to investment managers; (3) to hold investments through nominees; (4) to borrow money for any purpose. Beneficial interests under the will were not affected and the proposals were supported by all the defendants.

Held: Judge Paul Baker QC, approving the proposals, said that where the beneficial interests under a will or settlement were unaffected, an application for extension of investment powers brought under the Trustee Act 1925, s. 57 was preferable to one under the Variation of Trusts Act 1958, s.1. The specific nature of the transactions which s.57 permitted had led to some doubt whether it could be used to enlarge a power of investment generally. There seemed no reason to adopt a restrictive construction of s.57, its manifest object being to enlarge the inherent administrative jurisdiction of the court—hitherto confined to cases of emergency—and there was a power 'either generally or in any particular instance' to effect a wide range of transactions, including investment. Despite the general terms of s.1 of the Act of 1958, they did not seem to enlarge the scope of the powers which the court could authorise. If no alterations of beneficial interests were contemplated, it was more convenient to use s.57 of the 1925 Act, because the trustees were the natural persons to make the applications, the consent of every adult beneficiary was not essential, and the court was not required to give consent on behalf of every category of beneficiary separately but—more realistically—would consider their interests collectively in income and in capital. Those factors led to a less costly application without imperilling the legitimate interests of the beneficiaries.

NOTE: This section cannot be used to vary beneficial interests under trusts, but does permit administrative changes that cause merely 'incidental' variation of beneficial interests (*Southgate* v *Sutton* [2011] EWCA Civ 637, Court of Appeal).

(i) Settled land

SETTLED LAND ACT 1925

64. General power of the tenant for life to effect any transaction under an order of the court

(1) Any transaction affecting or concerning the settled land, or any part thereof, or any other land (not being a transaction otherwise authorised by this Act, or by the settlement) which in the opinion of the court would be for the benefit of the settled land, or any part thereof, or the persons interested under the settlement, may, under an order of the court, be effected by a tenant for life, if it is one which could have been validly effected by an absolute owner.

NOTE: This section was invoked by Morritt J in *Hambro v Duke of Marlborough* [1994] Ch 158, to allow the 11th Duke of Marlborough (as tenant for life) to execute a conveyance the effect of which was to disinherit the Marquis of Blandford, who (the trustees had concluded) displayed unbusinesslike habits and lack of responsibility.

(ii) Vesting orders in relation to infants

TRUSTEE ACT 1925

53. Vesting orders in relation to infants' beneficial interests

Where an infant is beneficially entitled to any property the court may, with a view to the application of the capital or income thereof for the maintenance, education, or benefit of the infant, make an order—

    (a) appointing a person to convey such property; or

    (b) in the case of stock, or a thing in action, vesting in any person the right to transfer or call for a transfer of such stock, or to receive the dividends or income thereof, or to sue for and recover such thing in action, upon such terms as the court may think fit.

NOTE: This section allows the court to authorise dealings with an infant's property with a view to application of the capital or income for the infant's maintenance, education, or benefit. 'Benefit' has been interpreted to cover dealings having the effect of reducing estate duty for the benefit of the infant: *Re Meux* [1958] Ch 154.

In that case, the proceeds of sale of property were to be resettled upon the infant, and so could be regarded as an 'application' for the infant's benefit. However, in *Re Hayworth's Contingent Reversionary Interest* [1956] Ch 364, a proposal to sell an infant's contingent reversionary interest to the life tenant for cash, thus ending the trusts, was thought not to be for the 'benefit' of the infant. Other types of dealing approved under the section have included the barring of entails to exclude remote beneficiaries (*Re Gower's Settlement* [1934] Ch 365) or to simplify a proposed application to the court for approval of a further variation under the Variation of Trusts Act 1958 (*Re Bristol's Settled Estates* [1964] 3 All ER 939).

SECTION 4: *CY PRÈS*

This Anglo-Norman phrase (which is sometimes hyphenated) meant something like 'as near as possible', and the doctrine of *cy près* in charity law lays down that where property given on trust for charitable purposes cannot be used in the precise manner intended by the donor, the court (and, since about 130 years ago, the Charity Commissioners) may make a scheme for the application of the property to purposes resembling as closely as possible the donor's original intention. The idea, in other words, is not to frustrate the intention of the donor (who cannot be consulted if the gift is testamentary) any more than necessary. The doctrine dates back at least as far as the seventeenth century.

The question whether *cy près* can be applied can arise either because it is clear from the outset that the donor's intention cannot be fulfilled, as where the organisation which he has singled out for benefit has already ceased to exist, or because at some later time, during the continuance of the trust, it turns out that the purposes cannot be achieved. *Cy près* is more easily invoked in the latter case, for once property has been dedicated to charity, there is no possibility of a resulting trust to the donor.

Where, however, a gift fails from the start, the courts have, since the early nineteenth century, insisted that before the property can be applied *cy près*, a general or 'paramount' charitable intention must be shown.

Before proceding further in this chapter, the reader is alerted to the fact that the Charities Act 2011 is a consolidating statute which since 14 March 2012 brings the Charities Acts 1993 and 2006 under one new title without changing the substance of the law in any significant way. Given the recent date of this change and in the interests of ease of cross-referencing between this text and your study notes and existing cases and materials, references to the 1993 and 2006 Acts are retained throughout this text with the corresponding references to the 2011 Act shown in parenthesis where appropriate. For a comprehensive list of the section number changes brought about by the Charities Act 2011, see the official 'Table of Destinations' on the Online Resource Centre accompanying this book.

online resource centre

A: Initial failure

The question turns on whether the intention of the donor was specific or general. If it was to further some specific purpose which cannot be carried out, or benefit some specific institution no longer in existence, then the gift fails and the property will return to the settlor, or his estate, on a resulting trust, as discussed in Chapter 5. An example of failure *ab initio* without general charitable intent occurred in *Kings v Bultitude* [2010] EWHC 1795 (Ch). When the last surviving priest of a church denomination died, the church was deemed to have 'died' with her. She left her residuary estate to the church, but because *cy près* did not apply the residue was distributed on the basis of intestacy and other effects passed to the Attorney General.

If, however, the intention is a more general one, which might be satisfied by applying the property to a purpose or institution similar to that specified, a *cy près* scheme may be ordered. The test, then, is whether a general or 'paramount' charitable intention can be found.

(i) Charity never existed at all

Finding general charitable intention

In *Re Rymer* [1895] 1 Ch 19, a gift for a specific seminary which had ceased to exist failed. This is the general position where no paramount (or general) charitable intention can be found. Whether a general charitable intention can be shown is a question of fact, and the cases in this section are illustrations of the factors that can be taken into account, and are not cited as authorities.

If the charity specified by the donor has never existed at all, it is usually easier to discover a general charitable intention than where the charity once existed but has since ceased (as in *Re Rymer*), since only a general intention can be attributed to the donor who fails correctly to specify the beneficiary. For example, in *Re Harwood* [1936] Ch 285, a gift was made to the Peace Society in Belfast, which could not be shown ever to have existed. Farwell J found that there was an intention to benefit societies aimed at promoting peace, and the gift was therefore applied *cy près*. A second gift in the will, in favour of the Wisbech Peace Society, which had once existed but had ceased to do so prior to the testatrix's death, was held, however, to have lapsed.

Another possibility, suggested by the following case, is what is sometimes termed 'charity by association'. The authority for the existence of this doctrine cannot be said to be conclusive, however.

Re Satterthwaite's WT, Midland Bank Executor & Trustee Co. v Royal Veterinary College

[1966] 1 WLR 277, [1966] 1 All ER 919, Court of Appeal

Facts: Under the testatrix's will, her residuary estate was to be divided in approximately equal proportions among nine organisations, all of whose names appeared to show that they were concerned with animal welfare. One was unidentifiable; six were charities; another was the Animal Defence and Anti-Vivisection Society, which for a long time was considered to be a charity (but not, of course, since the *National Anti-Vivisection Society* case considered in Chapter 8), and another was the 'London Animal Hospital'. The list had been thoughtlessly compiled from the London telephone directory, the testatrix's chief concern being to divert her estate to animal charities, because she hated the whole human race. The London Animal Hospital had never existed as a charity.

Held: The Court of Appeal held that the gift to the London Animal Hospital should be applied *cy près*.

HARMAN LJ: There remains the claim of the Attorney-General that a general charitable intent is shown. On this I have felt the gravest doubts. If a particular donee were intended which cannot be identified, no general intent would follow. When one looks at the whole of the residuary bequest, however, it seems plain that each share is intended to go to some object connected with the care or the cure of animals. That anti-vivisection has been declared not to be in law a charitable object (see *National Anti-Vivisection Society* v *Inland Revenue Comrs* [1948] AC 31) is irrelevant. The society exists to save animals from suffering. The other names make the same sort of suggestion, though it is true that the evidence suggested that the word 'clinic' often indicated a place where the business of animal surgery was carried on rather than a charitable organisation.

The judge has held that there is a general charitable intent sufficient to cause share No. (8) to be applied *cy près*, and it would be inconsistent to come to a different conclusion in the case of share No. (4) if, as I have held, the object there too is not identifiable. It follows that a scheme must in this instance also be settled.

RUSSELL LJ (after stating the facts): What is the result in law of this? I have already indicated that she is to be taken as intending to benefit a charitable activity; but the organisation picked by name was not such. *Prima facie*, therefore, the bequest would fail and there would be a lapse, with the result in this case in fact—owing to the incidence of liabilities and death duties—of mere relief of other residuary objects. My assumption, however, is that the testatrix was pointing to a particular charitable application of this one-ninth of residue. If a particular mode of charitable application is incapable of being performed as such, but it can be discerned from his will that the testator has a charitable intention (commonly referred to as a general charitable intention) which transcends the particular mode of application indicated, the court has jurisdiction to direct application of the bequest to charitable purposes *cy près*. Here I have no doubt from the nature of the other dispositions by this testatrix of her residuary estate that a general intention can be discerned in favour of charity through the medium of kindness to animals. I am not in any way deterred from this conclusion by the fact that one-ninth of residue was given to an anti-vivisection society which in law—unknown to the average testator—is not charitable (see *National Anti-Vivisection Society* v *Inland Revenue Comrs* [1948] AC 31).

Accordingly in my judgment the correct answer in this case is that the one-ninth share in question is not payable to the third defendant but should be applied *cy près* and to that end the matter should be referred to chambers for settlement of a scheme.

DIPLOCK LJ: With that humility which is becoming in a common law lawyer when confronted with such an arcane branch of the Chancery law, I agree with the judgments which have been delivered.

NOTES

1. The authority for the doctrine of charity by association comes from Russell LJ's opinion, which was that a general intention to benefit animal charities could be inferred from the testatrix's known attitude towards the human race, and from the fact that all but one of the other dispositions were made in favour of genuine animal charities. But Harman LJ expressed 'the gravest

doubts', and seems to have been swayed more by Plowman J's finding (at first instance) of a general charitable intent regarding one of the other gifts. Diplock LJ agreed with both viewpoints!

2. A better explanation of *Re Satterthwaite* may be that, as with the Peace Society in Belfast in *Re Harwood* [1936] Ch 285, the London Animal Hospital had never existed as a charity. In *Re Jenkins' WT* [1966] Ch 249, Buckley J declined to hold that a gift to the British Union for the Abolition of Vivisection (which did exist but was not charitable) could be taken as charitable simply by being included in a list of gifts to unquestionably charitable organisations.

3. Sir Robert Megarry V-C refused to apply what he described as the doctrine of 'charity by association' in *Re Spence* [1979] Ch 483, on the grounds that *Re Satterthwaite* only applied where the body had never existed.

(ii) Non-existent body, but no initial failure

Even where the charity specified does not exist, it may be possible to save the gift if the institution can be said to continue to exist in some other form. In recent years, many small charities have amalgamated, and it is sometimes possible to regard the new body thus formed as being the same as the old. In *Re Faraker* [1912] 2 Ch 488, for example, a gift to 'Mrs Bailey's charity, Rotherhithe' (which was taken to mean 'Hannah Bayly's Charity') passed to the new charity formed by an amalgamation of Hannah Bayly's Charity with several others.

Another approach is to find that the gift was made for the *purpose* of the named charity, rather than for the body itself. If the body is unincorporated, then, by definition, the gift cannot be to it but must be to its purposes, and if those purposes can still be fulfilled, the gift will not fail. Since there is no failure, there is no need to show a general charitable intention. Indeed, this is not an application of *cy près* as such, but rather an instance of finding a substitute trustee to carry out the purposes of the trust. Where the body is a corporation, however, a gift to it will prima facie lapse if the corporation has ceased to exist, just as a gift to a human individual would lapse if the person concerned had died before the gift was made. The gift may be rescued only on the *cy près* principles already outlined, i.e. if the court is able to find a general charitable intention going beyond the specific aim of benefiting the named corporate charity.

Re Finger's WT, Turner v Ministry of Health

[1972] 1 Ch 286, Chancery Division

Facts: Testamentary gifts were made to the National Radium Commission, an unincorporated association, and to the National Council for Maternity and Child Welfare, which was a corporate charity. Both had ceased to exist by the time the testatrix died.

Held: The gift to the National Radium Commission was interpreted as a gift to its purposes, and since these still continued, the gift did not fail. The gift to the National Council for Maternity and Child Welfare would have failed, except that, in the case, it was possible to discern a general charitable intention which allowed for the application of the gift *cy près*.

GOFF J: If the matter were *res integra* I would have thought that there would be much to be said for the view that the status of the donee, whether corporate or incorporate, can make no difference to the question whether as a matter of construction a gift is absolute or on trust for purposes. Certainly drawing such a distinction produces anomalous results.

In my judgment, however, on the authorities a distinction between the two is well established, at all events in this court. I refer first to *Re Vernon's WT* [1972] Ch 300 where Buckley J said at p. 303C–G:

Every bequest to an unincorporated charity by name without more must take effect as a gift for a charitable purpose. No individual or aggregate of individuals could claim to take such a bequest beneficially. If the gift is to be permitted to take effect at all, it must be as a bequest for a purpose, viz., that charitable purpose which the named charity exists to serve. A bequest which is in terms made for a charitable purpose will not fail for lack of a trustee but will be carried into effect either under the Sign Manual or by means of a scheme. A bequest to a named unincorporated charity, however, may on its true interpretation show that the testator's intention to make the gift at all was dependent upon the named charitable organisation being available at the time when the gift takes effect to serve as the instrument for applying the subject-matter of the gift to the charitable purpose for which it is by inference given. If so and the named charity ceases to exist in the lifetime of the testator, the gift fails: *Re Ovey* (1885) 29 ChD 560. A bequest to a corporate body, on the other hand, takes effect simply as a gift to that body beneficially, unless there are circumstances which show that the recipient is to take the gift as a trustee. There is no need in such a case to infer a trust for any particular purpose. The objects to which the corporate body can properly apply its funds may be restricted by its constitution, but this does not necessitate inferring as a matter of construction of the testator's will a direction that the bequest is to be held in trust to be applied for those purposes: the natural construction is that the bequest is made to the corporate body as part of its general funds, that is to say, beneficially and without the imposition of any trust. That the testator's motive in making the bequest may have undoubtedly been to assist the work of the incorporated body would be insufficient to create a trust.

...

As I read the dictum in *Re Vernon's WT* [1972] Ch 300, the view of Buckley J was that in the case of an unincorporated body the gift is *per se* a purpose trust, and provided that the work is still being carried on will have effect given to it by way of a scheme notwithstanding the disappearance of the donee in the lifetime of the testator, unless there is something positive to show that the continued existence of the donee was essential to the gift. Then Buckley J put his dictum into practice and decided *Re Morrison* (1967) 111 SJ 758 on that very basis, for there was nothing in that case beyond the bare fact of a gift to a dissolved unincorporated committee. In the case of a corporation, however, *Re Vernon* shows that the position is different as there has to be something positive in the will to create a purpose trust at all ...

Accordingly I hold that the bequest to the National Radium Commission being a gift to an unincorporated charity is a purpose trust for the work of the commission which does not fail but is applicable under a scheme, provided (1) there is nothing in the context of the will to show—and I quote from *Re Vernon's WT*—that the testatrix's intention to make a gift at all was dependent upon the named charitable organisation being available at the time when the gift took effect to serve as the instrument for applying the subject matter of the gift to the charitable purpose for which it was by inference given; (2) that charitable purpose still survives; but that the gift to the National Council for Maternity and Child Welfare, 117 Piccadilly, London being a gift to a corporate body fails, notwithstanding the work continues, unless there is a context in the will to show that the gift was intended to be on trust for that purpose and not an absolute gift to the corporation.

[His Lordship went on to hold that the gift to the National Council for Maternity and Child Welfare failed (at 299A), but that a *cy près* scheme could be applied since a general charitable intention was shown. See further on this aspect of the case *Re Spence*.]

NOTES

1. If the body is unincorporated then, by definition, the gift cannot be to it but can be to its purposes if charitable. Where the body is a corporation, however, a gift to it will prima facie lapse if the corporation has ceased to exist, just as a gift to a human individual would lapse if the person concerned had died before the gift was made. The gift may be rescued only on the *cy près* principles applicable to initial failure, i.e. if the court is able to find a general charitable intention going beyond the specific aim of benefiting the named corporate charity. This was the outcome of the case itself, so far as the National Council for Maternity and Child Welfare was concerned.

2. Since the gift to the National Radium Commission was construed as a gift to its purposes, all the court needed to do was to settle a scheme to apply the property elsewhere. This is not a *cy près* scheme as such, but rather an instance of finding a substitute trustee to carry out the purposes of the trust. It would not have been necessary to look for any general charitable intention above and beyond those purposes.

3. Similar principles were applied in *Re Koeppler's WT* [1986] Ch 423 (see Chapter 7), where Slade LJ construed a gift to a non-existent body as a valid trust for educational purposes. The non-existent body there was treated as analogous to the National Radium Commission in this case.

(iii) Gifts with conditions attached

It is possible for there to be an initial failure even where the institution to whom the donation is made exists, but where there is a condition in the gift which the donee body finds unacceptable.

Re Lysaght (dec'd)

[1966] 1 Ch 191, Chancery Division

Facts: The testatrix left £5,000 to the Royal College of Surgeons in order to establish and maintain one or more studentships. There was a condition, contained in clause 11(d) of the will, which would have disqualified Jews and Roman Catholics, and the College declined to accept the gift on these terms. They were happy to accept the gift without the conditions.

Held:

(a) The conditions could not be struck out on grounds of uncertainty or public policy.

(b) The gift was saved nonetheless, because the court found a general charitable intention on the part of the testatrix, to establish medical studentships. The *cy près* doctrine therefore operated; the condition could be deleted as not being essential to the fulfilment of the general intention. A scheme was ordered on the terms of the will as it stood without the condition.

BUCKLEY J: The question in this case is whether a bequest for charitable purposes which was contained in the will, dated June 22, 1960, of a testatrix who died on January 2, 1962 is effective or whether it fails on the grounds that it is impracticable to carry it into effect. [Buckley J, stated the facts and continued]: The first question for decision is whether the trust declared by clause 11 of the will in respect of the endowment fund are effective, or whether on the true construction of the will and in the events which have happened they fail. The Royal College of Surgeons, which I shall refer to as 'the college,' when informed by the executors of the bequest, stated, through their solicitors, that the college could not accept it in the terms stated in the will because the provision that a student must not be of the Jewish or Roman Catholic faith was, as they put it, 'so invidious and so alien to the spirit of the college's work as to make the gift inoperable in that form,' but they went on to say that the college would be most happy to accept the bequest with that one provision deleted.

Mr Morris Smith for the college has submitted that the condition that a student must be not of the Jewish or Roman Catholic faith is void for uncertainty, citing *Clayton v Ramsden* [1943] AC 320 and *In re Wolffe* [1953] 2 All ER 697. He further submits that, since a charitable trust cannot fail for uncertainty (*In re Gott* [1944] Ch 193) the trusts of the endownment fund are valid.

Mr Balcombe for the personal representatives of Henry Lysaght says that, although the court can by means of a scheme cure any uncertainty in a charitable gift, it should depart no further from the terms of the will than is necessary to achieve that end, and that any scheme which the court could devise in the present case to eliminate any uncertainty in the offending provision would still leave a provision involving religious discrimination in the trusts which would consequently still be unacceptable to the college. He goes on to say that, since it was an essential feature of the testatrix's intention that the college and no one else should be the trustee of the endowment fund, it would remain impossible to carry her intention into effect, notwithstanding any such scheme, if the college were still to refuse to act as the trustee, as it is common ground that they would so long as the trusts involve religious discrimination. Mr Balcombe further says that by reason of the element of religious discrimination the trusts are void as contrary to public policy.

The Attorney-General, while he concedes on the one hand that the will discloses no general charitable intent, submits on the other that the primary object of the gift is the establishment of a medical studentship; that the detailed provisions of clause 11 are machinery and are not essential parts of that primary object; that the provision requiring religious discrimination is at least undesirable and militates against the beneficial effect of the charity, and that the court can accordingly by way of scheme eliminate it. In making such a concession and at the same time presenting such submissions, I think that the Attorney-General is giving with one hand and taking away with the other.

Let me consider for a moment the meaning of the term 'general charitable intent.' Whether a donor has or has not evinced such an intent is relevant in any case in which the donor has made a charitable gift in terms which cannot be carried out exactly. In such a case the court has to discover whether the donor's true intention can be carried out notwithstanding that it is impracticable to give effect to some part of his particular directions. I take by way of example four imaginary testators. The first bequeaths a fund for charitable purposes generally, the second for the relief of poverty, the third for the relief of poverty in the parish of 'X,' the fourth for the relief of a particular class of poor (for example, of a particular faith or of a particular age group) in the parish of 'X.' Each of them couples with his bequest an indication of a particular manner in which the gift should be carried into effect, say, by paying the fares of poor persons travelling by rail from the village of 'X' to the town of 'Y' to obtain medical advice and attention. Between the dates of the wills and of the deaths of the four testators the railway between 'X' and 'Y' is closed, so that it becomes impossible for anyone to travel by rail from the one to the other. In each case the court must consider whether it was an essential part of the testator's intention that his benefaction should be carried into effect in all respects in the particular manner indicated and no other, or whether his true intention was, in the first case to make a gift for charitable purposes without qualification; in the second, to relieve poverty; in the third, to relieve poverty in the parish of 'X' and in the fourth, to relieve the poverty of the particular class of persons in the parish of 'X'; the specification of a particular mode of giving effect to such intention being merely an indication of a desire on his part in this respect: see the well-known passage in the judgment of Parker J in *In re Wilson* [1913] 1 Ch 314 at 320, 321. If on the true construction of any of the wills the latter is the true view, the court will, if it can, carry the testator's true intention into effect in some other way *cy-près* to the impracticable method indicated by the testator. In so doing the court is not departing from the testator's intention but giving effect to his true paramount intention. Such an intention is called a general, charitable intention. It is not general in the sense of being unqualified in any way or as being confined only to some general head of charity. It is general in contrast with the particular charitable intention which would have been shown by any of the four supposed testators who upon the true construction of his will intended to benefit poor people by paying their railway fares when travelling by rail between 'X' and 'Y' to obtain medical advice and attention and in no other way. Such a general intention would not avail if the court could find no practical or legal method of giving effect to it—if, for instance, it could be shown in respect of the bequest of the fourth testator that at the relevant time there were no poor people of the particular class specified in his will to be found in the parish of 'X' and there was no reasonable likelihood of there being any such at any foreseeable time in the future. The question would then arise whether the testator's true intention was restricted to benefiting this particular class of poor people or whether he had some yet more general charitable intent to which the court could give effect.

A general charitable intention, then, may be said to be a paramount intention on the part of a donor to effect some charitable purpose which the court can find a method of putting into operation, notwithstanding that it is impracticable to give effect to some direction by the donor which is not an essential part of his true intention—not, that is to say, part of his paramount intention.

In contrast, a particular charitable intention exists where the donor means his charitable disposition to take effect if, but only if, it can be carried into effect in a particular specified way, for example, in connection with a particular school to be established at a particular place, *In re Wilson*, or by establishing a home in a particular house: *In re Packe* [1918] 1 Ch 437. The alternatives are neatly stated by Younger LJ in *In re Willis* [1921] 1 Ch 44, 54:

> The problem which in this case we have to solve is to say by which of two different principles the construction of this gift has to be controlled. The first of these principles is that if a testator has manifested a general intention to give to charity, whether in general terms or to charities of a defined character or quality, the failure of the particular mode in which the charitable intention is to be effectuated shall not imperil the charitable gift. If the substantial intention is charitable the court will substitute some other mode of carrying it into effect. The other principle which I paraphrase from the judgment of Kay J in *Biscoe* v *Jackson* (1887) 35 ChD 460 at 463 is this. If on the proper construction of the will the mode of application is such an essential part of the gift that you cannot distinguish any general purpose of charity but are obliged to say that the prescribed mode of doing the charitable act is the only one the testator intended or at all contemplated, then the court cannot, if that mode fails, apply the money *cy près*.

When, therefore, the Attorney-General submits that the primary intention of the testatrix in the present case was to found a medical studentship and that the detailed directions contained in clause 11 are not essential to that intention, he is, I think, contending, notwithstanding his concession to the contrary, that the testatrix had a general charitable intention, that is to say, a paramount intention to which the court can give effect, notwithstanding that it may be impracticable or, as Mr Clauson suggests, impolitic to give effect to that part of those detailed directions which requires religious discrimination. I proceed, therefore, to consider how far (a) the selection of the college as the trustee of the endowment fund and (b) the provision for religious discrimination, are essential parts of the testatrix's intention.

The recital with which clause 11 opens is an expression of the testatrix's motive for making a charitable gift and no more, but as such it is, I think, very relevant to the ascertainment of her true intention. It shows that her aim was to establish medical studentships in the gift of the president and council of the college ... In my judgment, upon the proper construction of clause 11 of the testatrix's will the essentials of her intention expressed in that clause were (a) to found medical studentships which (b) should be administered by the governing body of the college (c) for the purposes set out in paragraph (E) of clause 11 [para. (E) set out the purposes of the studentships]. These parts of the clause state her objective, and in them, in my judgment, the heart of her intention is to be found. The remaining provisions of clause 11 may not unfairly be said to deal with the machinery of the trust. This is ... less clearly so in the cases of paragraphs (D) and (F) dealing with eligibility [para. (F) required a student to be married and between 19 and 30], but I can find nothing ... which suggests that these regulations as to eligibility were essential parts of her objective ... I recognise that ... the whole clause should be taken in its entirety, but in doing so I am left with the clear impression that the testatrix's true and overriding intention is to be found in the recital ... and that paragraphs (D) and (F) contain directions to which the testatrix had doubtless given anxious and careful thought but which do not form essential parts of that intention ... This does not mean that, so far as they can be given effect consistently with giving effect to the paramount intention of the testatrix, they need not be complied with. It does, however, mean that, in so far as it is impossible to give effect to them, or impossible to do so consistently with carrying out the paramount intention, this will not jeopardise the validity of the bequest.

On these grounds I think that the Attorney-General is justified in his submission that clause 11 (D) is not an essential part of the primary and paramount object of the testatrix in respect of the endowment fund.

As regards the trusteeship it is noteworthy that the testatrix confers important discretionary powers upon the college ... to regulate the object which each student shall be required to pursue and the quality and conduct of students. Although another trustee could, no doubt, be found capable of exercising these discretions, the college is obviously a body particularly suited to exercise them. This circumstance alone would, I think, be insufficient to establish that the personality of the trustee was of the essence of the testatrix's intention, but, coupled with the recital of the testatrix's wish to found studentships 'within the gift of the President and Council of this College,' it satisfies me that it was the particular wish of the testatrix that the college should be the trustee of this fund because of its peculiar aptitude for the office, and that it was to the college and to no one else that she meant to confide these discretionary powers.

In my judgment, the present case is to be distinguished from cases like *Moggridge* v *Thackwell* (1803) 7 Ves 36 and *In re Willis* [1921] 1 Ch 44 where bequests were made to charities to be selected by a named person who predeceased the testator. In each of those cases the testator was held to have shown an intention to benefit charitable purposes generally, leaving only the mode of application to the selection of the named person. Selection by that person having become impossible, the court carried the testator's intention into effect by way of a scheme. In the present case, on the other hand, I reach the conclusion that the intention of the testatrix was confined to establishing a charitable trust of which the college should be the trustee and so was conditional upon the college being able and willing to accept that office.

Are, then, the circumstances such as to justify the court in permitting the trusts of the endowment fund to be administered without regard to so much of clause 11 (D) as requires religious discrimination?

[Buckley J concluded that the discrimination clauses were neither uncertain nor affected by public policy (see Chapter 6) and continued, on the issue of practicability:]

I do not understand the college to assert that it would be legally incapable of accepting the trusts of the endowment and giving them effect with due regard to the provision for religious discrimination. It is not suggested that this would be ultra vires the college. What I understand from their solicitor's letter which is in evidence and from what counsel has stated in court is that on account of the character of the college and of the purposes which it exists to serve, the college would be unalterably opposed to accepting and administering a trust containing any provision for religious discrimination.

Obviously a trustee will not normally be permitted to modify the terms of his trust on the ground that his own opinions or convictions conflict with them. If his conscience will not allow him to carry out the trust faithfully in accordance with its terms, he must make way for a trustee who can and will do so. But how, if the identity of the trustee selected by the settlor is essential to his intention? If it is of the essence of a trust that the trustees selected by the settlor and no one else shall act as the trustees of it and those trustees cannot or will not undertake the office, the trust must fail: *In re Lawton* [1936] 3 All ER 378 and see *Reeve v Attorney-General* (1843) 3 Hare 191 at 197 and *Tudor on Charities*, 5th ed., (1929), p. 128. I have already reached the conclusion that it is an essential part of the testatrix's intention that the college should be the trustee of the endowment fund. The college is, as I have said, unalterably opposed to accepting the trust if any provision for religious discrimination is an effective part of it. That part or paragraph (D) which requires religious discrimination, if it is to be insisted upon, will consequently defeat the testatrix's intention entirely, for in that case the college must disclaim the trust with the result that it will fail.

The impracticability of giving effect to some inessential part of the testatrix's intention cannot, in my judgment, be allowed to defeat her paramount charitable intention.

In *In re Robinson* [1921] 2 Ch 332 P. O. Lawrence J had to deal with a fund bequeathed many years earlier for the endowment of a church of an evangelical character to which conditions were attached, including what was called an 'abiding' condition that a black gown should be worn in the pulpit unless this should become illegal. The evidence showed that in 1923 the wearing of a black gown in the pulpit, though not illegal, would be detrimental to the teaching and practice of evangelical doctrines and services in the church in question. Lawrence J had to determine whether a scheme could properly be sanctioned dispensing with the observance of this condition.

[Buckley J set out part of the judgment and continued: ...] The judge held on the evidence that the effect of insisting upon the condition would be to defeat the main intention of the testatrix. He held that, although compliance with the condition was not impossible in an absolute sense, it was impracticable and ought to be dispensed with.

In that case compliance with the condition relating to the black gown was not impracticable at the inception of the trust in 1889, but had become so by 1923. In the present case, if the trust is impracticable, this is due to an initial difficulty, not to any change of circumstances. Since *In re Robinson* [1923] 2 Ch 332 was decided it has been recognised that different considerations govern the application of the *cy près* doctrine when impracticability supervenes after a charitable trust has once taken effect from those which apply in cases of initial impracticability. In cases of supervening impracticability it matters not whether the original donor had or had not a general charitable intention (see *In re Wright* [1954] Ch 347 at 362). It was not, however, on any such ground as this that the decision in *In re Robinson* was based. The passage which I have read from the judgment of P.O. Lawrence J makes it clear that he decided as he did because, in his opinion, the testatrix's dominant intention was to endow a church and that the condition as to wearing a black gown was not an essential part of that intention but merely subsidiary.

If I am right in the view that I have formed, that it was an essential part of the testatrix's intention in the present case that the college should be the trustee of the endowment fund, then I think that the reasoning in *In re Robinson* is precisely applicable to the present case. Just as insistence on the black gown condition would in *In re Robinson* have defeated the paramount intention of the testatrix, so insistence on the provision for religious discrimination would defeat the paramount intention of the testatrix in the present case: indeed it would destroy the trust, for it would result in the college disclaiming the trusteeship, which would occasion the failure of the trust.

Accordingly, in my judgment, the court can and should enable the college to carry the trust into effect without any element of religious discrimination.

NOTES

1. In *Re Robinson*, the gift towards an endowment for a proposed evangelical church had taken effect, and the condition was held subsequently to have become impracticable. Since there was therefore no initial failure in *Robinson*, there was no need to find a general or paramount charitable intention. In *Lysaght*, by contrast, there would be an initial failure unless a general charitable intention could be found. But once a general charitable intention could be found a *cy près* scheme could be adopted, and then the conditions could be struck out on the same basis as in *Robinson*.

2. *Re Lysaght* was followed in *Re Woodhams* [1981] 1 WLR 493, where a general charitable intention to foster musical education was found, allowing the court to remove the restriction which would have limited scholarships to boys from two named children's homes, and which also prevented the donees from accepting the gift. Unlike *Re Lysaght*, however, in *Re Woodhams*, the charitable bequest took effect subject to a prior life interest, and the donees refused to accept the gift on the termination of the prior interest.

3. It may be wondered why the gift fails unless the conditions are deleted. 'Equity will not allow a trust to fail for want of a trustee', and in principle it might be thought that the court should find a trustee who is prepared to carry out the terms of the trust on the settlor's terms. In other words, it should not be necessary to delete the repugnant condition.

In a case like *Re Lysaght*, however, the identity of the donee is essential to the purposes of the trust, and were the Royal College to decline the gift, another trustee simply could not be found to carry out the testatrix's intention. (Likewise in the case of *Kings* v *Bultitude* [2010] EWHC 1795 (Ch).)

■ QUESTION

In the light of the detailed provisions in the will in *Re Lysaght*, and the fact that the gift was clearly intended for a particular institution, can it really be said that the testatrix had displayed a general charitable intention?

B: Subsequent failure

Once property has been dedicated to charitable purposes, it remains so, and if those purposes cease to be capable of achievement, there can be no resulting trust to the settlor or his estate unless the terms on which the gift was originally made provide for this to happen. It is not necessary to search for a general charitable intention on the part of the settlor. The only relevant consideration is whether there was an outright disposition in favour of charity. Where this is so, funds which cannot be applied to the original purpose, whether because that purpose is impossible, or because there is a surplus left over after the purposes have been achieved, may be applied *cy près*.

Re Slevin

[1891] 2 Ch 236, Court of Appeal

Facts: A legacy had been left to the Orphanage of St Dominics, Newcastle-upon-Tyne. The orphanage ceased to exist after the date of the donor's death, but before the legacy could be paid over.

Held: Since the orphanage had survived its benefactor, by however short a time, the gift was effective in favour of charity and could be applied *cy près*.

KAY LJ: In the present case we think that the Attorney-General must succeed, not on the ground that there is such a general charitable intention that the fund should be administered *cy près* even if the charity had failed in the testator's lifetime, but because, as the charity existed at the testator's death, this legacy became the property of that charity, and on its ceasing to the Crown, who will apply it, according to custom, for some analogous purpose of charity.

NOTES

1. In *Re King* [1923] 1 Ch 243, a surplus was left after the purpose (the setting of a stained-glass window in a church) was carried out. Finding that the whole fund, and not just the sum sufficient for the window, had been dedicated to charity, Romer J applied the surplus *cy près* (to the setting of a second window).

2. Nor will it matter that the gift to charity was intended to be postponed until some future date under the terms of the will or gift. In other words, the relevant date is that of the original donation, even though the charity may only at that time obtain a future interest in the property. If A dies leaving property to B for his life, thereafter to C (a charity), and C ceases to exist after A's death but before B's, this is regarded as a subsequent, not an initial, failure.

C: Altering charitable objects

(i) At common law

Whereas no difficulties have ever arisen in the case of a clear failure, such as a charitable body ceasing to exist, when the *cy près* doctrine could operate on the subsequent failure, there could be problems before 1960 where charitable purposes simply became outdated and obsolete, although the original charitable body continued in existence. There was no effective system whereby moribund charities could be modernised, and of course the *cy près* doctrine could not apply if there was no failure.

Until the reforms introduced by the Charities Act 1960, the courts' only jurisdiction was their inherent jurisdiction to apply funds *cy près*, but that jurisdiction is confined to rather narrow limits, being available only where it is 'impossible' or 'impracticable' to carry out the terms of the trust. The courts' main concern was not to depart too far from the original wishes of settlors, rather than to promote the efficient administration of charities.

For example, in *Re Weir Hospital* [1910] 2 Ch 124, a testator left two houses to be used as a hospital. The premises were not suitable, and the Charity Commissioners approved a scheme to use them as a nurses' home instead, perpetuating the testator's name by renaming a hospital in his honour. The Court of Appeal held that the scheme was *ultra vires*, since the original purpose was not impossible to fulfil, merely difficult. Sir Herbert Cozens-Hardy MR's view (at 131) was that the court's primary duty was to give effect to the charitable intentions of the donor, rather than to seek the most beneficial application of the property:

The first duty of the Court is to construe the will, and to give effect to the charitable directions of the founder, assuming them not to be open to objection on the ground of public policy. The Court does not consider whether those directions are wise or whether a more generally beneficial application of the testator's property might not be founded.

Similar sentiments were echoed by Kennedy LJ, at 140–1:

But neither the Court of Chancery, nor the Board of Charity Commissioners, which has been entrusted by statute, in regard to the application of charitable fund, with similar jurisdiction, is entitled to substitute a different scheme for the scheme which the donor has prescribed in the instrument which creates the charity, merely because a coldly wise intelligence, impervious to the special predilections which inspired his liberality, and untrammelled by his directions, would have dictated a different use of his money ... If the charity can be administered according to the directions of founder or testator, the law requires that it should be so administered.

It is permissible under the courts' inherent jurisdiction, however, to eradicate a condition of the trust which, with the passage of time, has become inimical to its main purpose.

Re Dominion Students' Hall Trust, Dominion Students' Hall Trust v Attorney-General

[1947] Ch 183, Chancery Division

Decision: A colour bar was removed from a trust for the maintenance of a hostel for male students of the overseas dominions of the British Empire, since the main purpose of the trust was to promote community of citizenship among members of the Commonwealth.

EVERSHED J: The purpose of both the petition and the summons is that a restriction which has hitherto been characteristic of the charity, limiting its objects so as to exclude coloured students of the British Empire, should be removed and that the benefits of the charity should be open to all citizens from the Empire without what is commonly known as the 'colour bar'. Having regard to the interest of the Inns of Court in Imperial students, I have thought it right to be particularly careful to see that I have jurisdiction to authorize the scheme and to sanction the petition. The proposed removal of the 'colour bar' restriction has been put to a substantial number of the subscribers. Owing to the necessities of the case, it has not been possible to put it to all, but those to whom it has been put represent over 75 per cent in value of the subscription and none dissents from what is now proposed.

It is plain that I have to bear in mind the general proposition contained in the headnote to *Re Weir Hospital* [1910] 2 Ch 124, which is to the effect that funds given by a testator for a particular charitable purpose cannot be applied *cy près* by the court unless it has been shown to be impossible to carry out the testator's intention. True, the present is not a case of a testator and the court is, perhaps, not quite so strictly limited as in the case of a will. It is true, also, that the word 'impossible' should be given a wide significance: see *Re Campden Charities* (1881) 18 ChD 310; *Re Robinson* [1921] 2 Ch 332. It is not necessary to go to the length of saying that the original scheme is absolutely impracticable. Were that so, it would not be possible to establish in the present case that the charity could not be carried on at all if it continued to be so limited as to exclude coloured members of the Empire.

I have, however, to consider the primary intention of the charity. At the time when it came into being, the objects of promoting community of citizenship, culture and tradition among all members of the British Commonwealth of Nations might best have been attained by confining the Hall to members of the Empire of European origin. But times have changed, particularly as a result of the war; and it is said that to retain the condition, so far from furthering the charity's main object, might defeat it and would be liable to antagonize those students, both white and coloured, whose support and goodwill it is the purpose of the charity to sustain. The case, therefore, can be said to fall within the broad description of impossibility illustrated by *Re Campden Charities* and *Re Robinson*.

There is also this further point. On the facts of the case, as proved in evidence, including particularly the substantial promises received of further financial support if the 'colour bar' is removed, it seems clear that the original class of beneficiaries, so far from being adversely affected by the proposed change, should gain as a consequence. Notionally, there might be two complementary charities, one for white and one for coloured students, both of which the trust could administer and, in practice, should administer, together. In the circumstances, I am happy to think that I can make the order which I have been asked to make. I am also assisted by the circumstance that Mr Danckwerts, for the Attorney-General, who has considered the matter from all points of view both of charity generally and of the original subscribers, did not feel that the case was one in which he could offer opposition, either on merits or on jurisdiction.

Re J. W. Laing Trust

[1984] Ch 143, Chancery Division

Decision: Peter Gibson J was prepared to strike out a term requiring trustees to distribute, within 10 years of the settlor's death, a fund which by then had risen significantly in value (from some £15,000 in 1922 when the trust was set up, to over £24 million in 1982). The increase in value had been quite unforeseen when the trust was set up, partly because the settlor had lived much longer than expected (to the age of 98). The recipients of the income from the charity (Christian evangelical bodies) had come to depend upon it, whereas it would have been impossible to distribute such a large amount of capital in such a way as to ensure continuance of the causes which the settlor wished to support.

PETER GIBSON J (on the inherent jurisdiction of the court): On this question Mr Picarda and Mr McCall submit, and I accept, that the court is not fettered by the particular conditions imposed by section 13(1)(e)(iii), but can, and should, take into account all the circumstances of the charity, including how the charity has been distributing its money, in considering whether it is expedient to regulate the administration of the charity by removing the requirement as to distribution within ten years of the settlor's death.

The evidence before me shows that the settlor throughout his life was a man of strong religious convictions and particularly interested, and personally involved, in the activities of the religious group known as the Christian (or Open) Brethren. That group has never had any central organisation of the group's churches or their missionaries. There are approximately 450 such missionaries. The plaintiff company is now a charity. Although in 1922 it did not hold its property for exclusively charitable purposes, nevertheless it was founded to hold property for missionary purposes and for the transmission of funds for the missionary and other work of the Christian Brethren, and there can be no doubt that it was chosen by the settlor to act as trustee because of its connections with the Christian Brethren.

When the charity was founded in 1922 the 15,000 shares in John Laing & Sons Ltd were worth little more than their par value, £15,000. No doubt because of a prudent failure to diversify the charity's investments, the assets of the charity, which largely consist of shares and loan stock in Laing companies (which are now public companies), had increased by June 30, 1982, to no less than £24 million. In August 1922 no one would have foreseen either that the settlor would live for more than half a century longer and attain the age of 98 before he died on January 11, 1978, or that the assets of the charity would increase so astonishingly. The income of the charity in the year to June 30, 1982, exceeded £1.2 million.

The settlor acted as agent of the plaintiff in effecting distribution until the end of 1964. He followed an income distribution policy which fostered Christian evangelical activities, and since then the plaintiff has, in the exercise of its discretion, continued an active distribution policy, financing home and overseas evangelism and the relief of poverty. Various Christian causes have come to depend on the charity for their continued support and, in the view of the plaintiff, they are in need of continued support from the charity in the manner adopted hitherto. By far the greater part of the distributions have been to individuals or bodies not well suited to receive large sums of capital to finance their future activities. There is a particular difficulty in relation to providing for the future work of the Christian Brethren because they do not accept any organisation as a governing or controlling body but operate on an individual basis. There would be severe practical inconveniences and difficulties in distributing the very large sums of capital now held by the plaintiff in a way that would ensure continuance of the causes which the settlor wished to support by the charity. The court should always be slow to thwart a donor's wishes, but in this case the settlor himself, as early as October 5, 1932, indicated to the plaintiff by letter that he wished the plaintiff to be at liberty to disregard the requirement as to distribution. On January 26, 1939, the settlor wrote again to the plaintiff, referring to the capital value of his gift as then worth £30,000, and saying:

> considering that the capital value is more, and in view of many Christian activities, I wish to withdraw the stipulation that the capital should be distributed within 10 years of my death.

It is clear that even then, after that comparatively modest increase in capital value in that comparatively short period of the charity's existence, the settlor appreciated that the requirement as to distribution was inexpedient.

The chairman of the directors of the plaintiff, Mr Andrew Gray, in his affidavit, says of the plaintiff:

> The plaintiff, itself a registered charity in its own right, has broad experience in the field of Christian ministry and (so far as not already covered by that concept) the relief of the poor. It considers that this experience makes it sensitive to the ever-changing needs of the modern world, and enables it to adapt to such changes by shifts in the emphasis of its giving. The plaintiff would not presume to claim that no other body has this capability, but having regard to its long association with the settlor, who remained a director of the plaintiff until his death, it considers that it may reasonably suggest that it may be better able than most to fulfil his wishes for the distribution of the funds he so generously provided.

The plaintiff has considered causing another charitable body to be set up to carry on permanently the work now conducted by the charity, but it took the view that it would be unacceptable for it to adopt such a device to circumvent the restriction as to distribution. For my part, I would have thought that the plaintiff could distribute the capital to any other charitable body or bodies if it thought fit, but that merely serves to emphasise the unimportance of the requirement as to distribution.

In my judgment, the plaintiff has made out a very powerful case for the removal of the requirement as to distribution, which seems to me to be inexpedient in the very altered circumstances of the charity since that requirement was laid down 60 years ago. I take particular account of the fact that this application is one that has the support of the Attorney-General. Although the plaintiff is not fettered by the express terms of the gift as to the charitable purposes for which the charity's funds are to be applied, it is, in my view, proper for the plaintiff to wish to continue to support the causes which the settlor himself wished the charity to support from its inception, and which would suffer if that support was withdrawn as a consequence of the distribution of the charity's assets. I have no hesitation in reaching the conclusion that the court should, in the exercise of its inherent jurisdiction, approve a scheme under which the trustees for the time being of the charity will be discharged from the obligation to distribute the capital within 10 years of the death of the settlor. I shall discuss with counsel the precise form of order that is appropriate.

D: Charities Act 1993 (now Charities Act 2011)

It is no longer necessary to show that it is 'impossible' or 'impracticable' to carry out the terms of the trust. It is enough that the original purpose has been fulfilled as far as possible, or cannot be carried out according to the directions given and the spirit of the gift, or if there is a surplus left over, or if the purposes have been adequately provided for by other means, or become useless or harmful to the community. *Cy près* may also apply where the original purposes relate to an area, or class of persons, which has ceased to have any relevance, having regard to the spirit of the gift. There are also provisions for the amalgamation of small charities if that is more efficient.

CHARITIES ACT 1993

13. Occasions for applying property *cy près* [now Charities Act 2011, s.62, except see (5) below]

(1) Subject to subsection (2) below, the circumstances in which the original purposes of a charitable gift can be altered to allow the property given or part of it to be applied *cy près* shall be as follows—

(a) where the original purposes, in whole or in part—
   (i)   have been as far as may be fulfilled; or
   (ii) cannot be carried out, or not according to the directions given and to the spirit of the gift; or

(b) where the original purposes provide a use for part only of the property available by virtue of the gift; or

(c) where the property available by virtue of the gift and other property applicable for similar purposes can be more effectively used in conjunction, and to that end can suitably, regard being had to the spirit of the gift, be made applicable to common purposes; or

(d) where the original purposes were laid down by reference to an area which then was but has since ceased to be a unit for some other purpose, or by reference to a class of persons or to an area which has for any reason since ceased to be suitable, regard being had to the spirit of the gift, or to be practical in administering the gift; or

(e) where the original purposes, in whole or in part, have, since they were laid down—
   (i)   been adequately provided for by other means; or
   (ii) ceased, as being useless or harmful to the community or for other reasons, to be in law charitable; or
   (iii) ceased in any other way to provide a suitable and effective method of using the property available by virtue of the gift, regard being had to the spirit of the gift.

(2) Subsection (1) above shall not affect the conditions which must be satisfied in order that property given for charitable purposes may be applied cy près except in so far as those conditions require a failure of the original purposes.

(3) References in the foregoing subsections to the original purposes of a gift shall be construed, where the application of the property given has been altered or regulated by a scheme or otherwise, as referring to the purposes for which the property is for the time being applicable.

(4)   Without prejudice to the power to make schemes in circumstances falling within subsection (1) above, the court may by scheme made under the court's jurisdiction with respect to charities, in any case where the purposes for which the property is held are laid down by reference to any such area as is mentioned in the first column in Schedule 3 to this Act, provide for enlarging the area to any such area as is mentioned in the second column in the same entry in that Schedule.

(5)   It is hereby declared that a trust for charitable purposes places a trustee under a duty, where the case permits and requires the property or some part of it to be applied cy près, to secure its effective use for charity by taking steps to enable it to be so applied. [This subsection is now Charities Act 2011, s.61.]

■ QUESTION

Does s.13 apply only to subsequent failure, or are its terms, in your view, also appropriate to deal with issues such as those which arose in *Re Lysaght*? Do you think that 'the original purposes of a charitable gift' can have any meaning prior to the gift taking effect?

NOTE: Another case falling within s.13(1)(e)(iii), but where the original purposes were neither impractical nor impossible to achieve, is *Varsani* v *Jesani* [1999] 2 WLR 255, CA. The case concerned a charity, established in 1967 by a declaration of trust, whose purpose was to promote the faith of a Hindu sect. In 1984, the sect split into two factions, with each side accusing the other of having departed from the true faith. As long as either faction in fact adhered to the true faith, it remained possible to achieve the original purposes, but the effect of the schism was that only one of the factions was making use of the main asset of the charity, a temple in London, to the exclusion of the other faction. The Court of Appeal, upholding the decision of Carnwath J, felt that the framework within which the faith was practised in 1967 (i.e. the original purposes) had ceased to provide a suitable and effective method of enabling the property to be used in accordance with 'the spirit of the gift'; therefore the court had jurisdiction to order a *cy près* scheme. Only the jurisdictional issue was before the court, and it is not reported what was actually done (or will be done) with the property.

Oldham Borough Council v *Attorney-General*

[1993] 2 All ER 432, Court of Appeal

Facts: The Clayton Playing Fields in Oldham had been conveyed to the Council (or more accurately, the bodies which preceded it prior to the local government reorganisation in 1974) in 1962, for recreational purposes. The Borough Council proposed to sell the land for development, but also to provide a new site which (it was assumed) would be used for exactly the same charitable purposes. The Attorney-General opposed the sale.

Held: The sale would be approved. Although the Council expressly disclaimed reliance on the Charities Act 1960, since clearly none of the heads (enumerated in the extract) could apply in this case, the Court of Appeal took the view that the sale of the land would have been approved prior to the Charities Act. Dillon LJ also considered that the requirement that the actual land given should be used as playing fields was not part of the 'original purposes' within s.13.

DILLON LJ: The problem arises because of ... section 13 of the Charities Act 1960, subsections (1) and (2) of which provide as follows [Dillon LJ set out the section and continued:]

Broadly the effect of that section is that an alteration of the 'original purposes' of a charitable gift can only be authorised by a scheme for the *cy près* application of the trust property and such a scheme can only be made in the circumstances set out in subheads (a) to (e) of subsection (1) of section 13.

It follows that if the retention of a particular property is part of the 'original purposes' of a charitable trust, sale of that property would involve an alteration of the original purposes even if the proceeds of the sale were applied in acquiring an alternative property for carrying out the same charitable activities. If so, a sale of the original property could only be ordered as part of a *cy près* scheme, and then only if circumstances within one or other of sub heads (a) to (e) are made out. The particular bearing of that in the present case is that the council accepts, and the Attorney-General agrees, that the circumstances of this charity do not fall within any of these subheads.

If therefore, on a true appreciation of the deed of gift and of section 13, the retention of the existing site is part of the original purposes of the charity, the court cannot authorise any sale.

It is necessary therefore to look first at the terms of the deed of gift.

[Dillon LJ concluded that retention of the existing site was part of the original purpose of the donor, and continued:]

I come then to what I regard as the crux of this case, *viz.* the true construction of the words 'original purposes of a charitable gift' in section 13 of the 1960 Act. Do the 'original purposes' include the intention and purpose of the Donor that the land given should be used for ever for the purposes of the charity, or are they limited to the purposes of the charity, in the sense in which Lord Cranworth was using these words in the passage just cited?

Certain of the authorities cited to us can be put on one side. Thus in *Re J. W. Laing Trust* [1984] Ch 143 at 153 Peter Gibson J said, plainly correctly, that 'it cannot be right that any provision, even if only administrative, made applicable by a donor to his gifts should be treated as a condition and hence as a purpose'. In that case, however, the provision, which was held to be administrative and was plainly not a 'purpose', was a provision that the capital was to be wholly distributed within the settlor's lifetime or within 10 years of his death.

Conversely there are cases where the Donor has imposed a condition as part of the terms of his gift, which limits the main purpose of the charity in a way which, with the passage of time, has come to militate against the achievement of that main purpose. The condition was there part of the purpose, but the court found itself able on the facts to cut out the condition by way of a *cy près* scheme under the *cy près* jurisdiction, on the ground that the subsistence of the condition made the main purpose impossible or impracticable of achievement. See *Re Dominion Students' Hall Trust* [1947] Ch 183 where a condition of a trust for the maintenance of a hostel for male students of the overseas dominions of the British Empire restricted the benefits to dominion students of European origin. See also *Re Robinson* [1921] 2 Ch 332 where it was a condition of the gift of an endowment for an evangelical church that the preacher should wear a black gown in the pulpit. But unlike those conditions, the intention or purpose in the present case that the actual land given should be used as playing fields is not a condition qualifying the use of that land as playing fields.

It is necessary, in my judgment, in order to answer the crucial question of the true construction of section 13 to appreciate the legislative purpose of section 13. Pennycuick V-C has said in *Re Lepton's Charity* [1972] 1 Ch 276, 284F that the section in part restates the principles applied under the existing law but also extends those principles. But the principles with which it is concerned are the principles for applying property *cy près* and nothing else. The stringency of those principles as stated in *Re Weir Hospital* [1910] 2 Ch 124 had been somewhat mitigated, but to nothing like the extent contended for by the unsuccessful parties in *Re Weir Hospital*.

■ **QUESTION**

Is Dillon LJ implying (at the start of the above passage) that s.13(1) substitutes for, rather than reinforces, the common law definition of failure? Is this a reasonable interpretation of the section? Does it matter in practice?

CHARITIES ACT 1993

14. Application *cy près* of gifts of donors unknown or disclaiming [now Charities Act 2011, ss.63–64, 66]

(1) Property given for specific charitable purposes which fail shall be applicable *cy près* as if given for charitable purposes generally, where it belongs—

(a) to a donor who after—

(i) the prescribed advertisements and inquiries have been published and made, and

(ii) the prescribed period beginning with the publication of those advertisements has expired, cannot be identified or cannot be found; or

(b) to a donor who has executed a disclaimer in the prescribed form of his right to have the property returned.

(2) Where the prescribed advertisements and inquiries have been published and made by or on behalf of trustees with respect to any such property, the trustees shall not be liable to any person in respect of the property if no claim by him to be interested in it is received by them before the expiry of the period mentioned in subsection (1)(a)(ii) above.

(3) For the purposes of this section property shall be conclusively presumed (without any advertisement or inquiry) to belong to donors who cannot be identified, in so far as it consists—

(a) of the proceeds of cash collections made by means of collecting boxes or by other means not adapted for distinguishing one gift from another; or

(b) of the proceeds of any lottery, competition, entertainment, sale or similar money-raising activity, after allowing for property given to provide prizes or articles for sale or otherwise to enable the activity to be undertaken.

(4) The court may by order direct that property not falling within subsection (3) above shall for the purposes of this section be treated (without any advertisement or inquiry) as belonging to donors who cannot be identified where it appears to the court either—

(a) that it would be unreasonable, having regard to the amounts likely to be returned to the donors, to incur expense with a view to returning the property; or

(b) that it would be unreasonable, having regard to the nature, circumstances and amounts of the gifts, and to the lapse of time since the gifts were made, for the donors to expect the property to be returned.

(5) Where property is applied *cy près* by virtue of this section, the donor shall be deemed to have parted with all his interest at the time when the gift was made; but where property is so applied as belonging to donors who cannot be identified or cannot be found, and is not so applied by virtue of subsection (3) or (4) above—

(a) the scheme shall specify the total amount of that property; and

(b) the donor of any part of that amount shall be entitled, if he makes a claim not later than six months after the date on which the scheme is made, to recover from the charity for which the property is applied a sum equal to that part, less any expenses properly incurred by the charity trustees after that date in connection with claims relating to his gift; and

(c) the scheme may include directions as to the provision to be made for meeting any such claim.

(6) Where—

(a) any sum is, in accordance with any such directions, set aside for meeting any such claims, but

(b) the aggregate amount of any such claims actually made exceeds the relevant amount,

then, if the Commissioners so direct, each of the donors in question shall be entitled only to such proportion of the relevant amount as the amount of his claim bears to the aggregate amount referred to in paragraph (b) above; and for this purpose 'the relevant amount' means the amount of the sum so set aside after deduction of any expenses properly incurred by the charity trustees in connection with claims relating to the donors' gifts.

(7) For the purposes of this section, charitable purposes shall be deemed to 'fail' where any difficulty in applying property to those purposes makes that property or the part not applicable *cy près* available to be returned to the donors.

(8) In this section 'prescribed' means prescribed by regulations made by the Commissioners; and such regulations may, as respects the advertisements which are to be published for the purposes of subsection (1)(a) above, make provision as to the form and content of such advertisements as well as the manner in which they are to be published.

(9) Any regulations made by the Commissioners under this section shall be published by the Commissioners in such manner as they think fit.

(10) In this section, except in so far as the context otherwise requires, references to a donor include persons claiming through or under the original donor, and references to property given

include the property for the time being representing the property originally given or property derived from it.

(11) This section shall apply to property given for charitable purposes, notwithstanding that it was so given before the commencement of this Act.

■ QUESTION

Does s.14 apply where funds are raised for a charitable purpose which later fails leaving a surplus? See *Re Ulverston and District New Hospital Building Trusts* [1956] 3 All ER 164.

Re Henry Wood National Memorial Trusts, Armstrong v Moiseiwitsch

[1967] 1 All ER 238n, Chancery Division

STAMP J (on an adjourned summons to determine what were reasonable inquiries under s.14(2) of the 1960 Act, replaced by s.14(3) of the 1993 Act): The following notices, together with inquiries already made, would constitute reasonable advertisements and inquiries for identifying and finding donors who have not disclaimed, *viz.*—notices inviting a donor who does not wish to give a written disclaimer to notify his name and address in writing to the designated agents of the trustees, so as to be received by them before a specified date not less than two months after publication or posting of the notice, such a notice to be inserted in two issues of each of the following newspapers, namely, *The Times, The Daily Telegraph* and *The Scotsman*, and to be sent by ordinary post to the address, as recorded in the books and papers of the trustees, of every donor who made any such gift and has such a recorded address (not being an address of a formation or unit of Her Majesty's Forces) but who has not already given such a written disclaimer.

E: Further reform of *cy près*

CHARITIES ACT 2006

EXPLANATORY NOTES

Section 15—Application by reference to current circumstances [now Charities Act 2011, s.62(2)]

This section [of the Charities Act 2006] amends section 13 of the 1993 Act by substituting 'the appropriate considerations' for 'the spirit of the gift' in that section. The effect is to require the Charity Commission, when making a scheme to alter the purposes for which charity property is to be applied, to take into account not only the spirit of the gift of the property but also the social and economic circumstances prevailing at the time of the proposed alteration in the purpose.

Section 16—Application *cy-près* of gifts by donors unknown or disclaiming [now Charities Act 2011, s.64(2)]

This section, by amending section 14(4) of the 1993 Act, gives the Charity Commission the power to decide whether property is to be treated as belonging to donors who cannot be identified. Under the existing law only the court has that power.

Section 17—Application *cy-près* of gifts made in response to certain solicitations [subsections (1) to (8) of this section are now consolidated as Charities Act 2011, s.65]

This section inserts a new section, section 14A, into the 1993 Act. Section 14A applies to property (which includes money) given for specific charitable purposes in response to a solicitation—i.e. an appeal—containing a certain type of statement. The statement is described in subsection (2) and is to the effect that unless, at the time of making his donation, the donor asks (by making a 'relevant declaration' as described in subsection (3)) to be given the chance to reclaim his donation if the specific purposes for which he is giving it fail in future, the donation will be applied *cy-près*.

Subsections (4)–(6) set out the process to be followed where the purposes have failed and where the donor has made a relevant declaration. The trustees holding the property must notify the donor that the purposes have failed and ask him whether he wants the property (or a sum equal to its value) returned. If he does, the trustees must return it to him. If either the trustees cannot find the donor, or the donor indicates that he does not wish the property returned, then the property can be applied *cy-près* as if the donor had disclaimed his right to have it returned to him.

Subsection (7) applies where the purposes have failed and where the donor has not made a 'relevant declaration'. It allows the property to be applied *cy-près* as if the donor had disclaimed his right to have it returned to him. Paragraph (b) of subsection (8) makes clear that this section applies both where the donor has received something of value in return for his donation and where he has not. Paragraph (c) makes clear that where an appeal consists of some solicitations which contain the statement described in subsection (2) and some which do not contain that statement, the donor (unless he proves otherwise) will be regarded as having responded to a solicitation containing the statement.

Section 18—*Cy-près* schemes

This section alters the *cy-près* rule. The *cy-près* rule is a well-established legal rule that applies when the purposes for which charitable property is held are being changed by the court or by the Charity Commission. The occasions on which charitable purposes can be changed to new purposes by the court or the Commission are set out in section 13 of the 1993 Act, as amended by section 12 of this Act. At present the *cy-près* rule requires the new purposes to be as close as practicable (bearing in mind the reason why the need to change the purposes arose in the first place) to the original purposes.

Section 18 alters the *cy-près* rule by inserting into the 1993 Act a new section 14B [now Charities Act 2011, s.67], subsection (1) of which requires the court or the Commission to act, when making a scheme to change charitable purposes, in accordance with the remaining provisions (i.e. subsections (2) to (6)) of new section 14B. Subsection (2) of new section 14B requires the court or the Commission, when making a scheme changing the charitable purposes for which particular property given to a charity is held, to have regard to certain matters (see next paragraph). This applies either when the scheme is transferring the property from one charity to another or when there is no transfer and the scheme simply changes the purposes of the charity that holds the property. 'Property given' to a charity includes (by virtue of subsection (5)) both the property in the form in which it was originally given and any property derived from it. The effect is that if, for example, a piece of land was given to a charity, then sold by the charity, the money representing the proceeds of the sale would also count as the 'property given'. The three matters to which the court or the Commission must have regard in those circumstances are set out in subsection (3) of new section 14B. One of those matters is the desirability of choosing new purposes which are close to the original purposes; but that is not paramount. The court or the Commission must give equal weight to the other two matters. One of these is the spirit of the gift by which the property came to the charity. The other is the need to ensure that, once the scheme has been made, the property can be used to make a significant social and economic impact. Subsection (4) of new section 14B allows the court or the Commission, when making a scheme which transfers a charity's property to another charity, to require the trustees of the receiving charity to use the property for purposes as similar as practicable to the original purposes for which the property was held. This is to cover cases where the original purposes are still useful but the court or the Commission believe that the property can be more effectively used in conjunction with other property.

NOTE: The Charities Act 1993, s.14 [now Charities Act 2011 ss.63–64, 66] provides that surplus monies donated to collecting boxes, raffles, entertainments, and other gifts made by donors 'unknown or disclaiming' and so on may be applied *cy près* without having to obtain the donors' consent. As regards other donations, the trustees must advertise and take steps to find the donors and, if they are found, return the donation to them or obtain in writing a waiver of the donors' claims to the donation. However, this advertising and inquiry process can be dispensed with by order of the court where it appears to the court either that it would be 'unreasonable, having regard to the amounts likely to be returned to the donors, to incur expense with a view to returning the property' (s.64(2)(a)) or that it would be 'unreasonable, having regard to the nature, circumstances and amounts of the gifts, and to the lapse of time since the gifts were made, for the donors to expect the property to be returned' (s.64(2)(a)).

F: Small poverty charities

Many old charities for the relief of poverty required trustees to distribute money or goods, but the growth of state welfare reduced the attractiveness of these, and even rendered them counterproductive in some cases, because handouts can lead to a reduction in state benefit. As long ago as 1967, the Annual Report of the Charity Commissioners (paras 17–20 and App. B) recognised the problem involved in cash handouts by commenting on the undesirability of using charity funds to relieve the burdens of the DHSS and local authorities, and instead suggested other schemes, for example outings or home decoration. Yet many old trusts to relieve poverty bound trustees to distribute money or goods.

A possible solution to this problem existed under the provisions of the Charities Act 1960, but the mechanisms for the full scheme-making powers contained therein were arguably too complicated for very small charities. Following a report of a House of Lords Select Committee in 1984, the Charities Act 1985 addressed this problem. Section 2 allowed trustees of charities more than 50 years old, by a simplified procedure, to change the objects to more suitable ones, so long as they were within the spirit of the original donor's intentions. Under s.3, where the annual income of a charity was less than £200, the trustees could transfer its property to another charity having similar aims, or if its income was less than £5 a year, the trustees under s.4 could wind it up, by spending the capital as if it were income. Now trustees of a charity with a previous year's income of £5,000 or less and no land devoted to charitable purposes may transfer its property to another charity under the Charities Act 1993, s.74, the only requirement is that the trustees of the transferring trust must vote on the transfer and at least two-thirds of them must approve it on the basis that the present application of income by the transferring charity is not 'suitable and effective'. Instead of transferring the funds to another charity, the trustees may instead amend the purposes for which their trust is established, so that they become 'suitable and effective'. Crucially, there is no requirement, whether transferring or amending, for regard to be had to the original 'spirit of the gift'.

CHARITIES ACT 1993

74. Power to transfer all property, modify objects etc. [now Charities Act 2011, see subsection references to the 2011 Act in bold text in square brackets below]

(1) [**267(1)**] This section applies to a charity if—
    (a) its gross income in its last financial year did not exceed £5,000, and
    (b) it does not hold any land on trusts which stipulate that the land is to be used for the purposes, or any particular purposes, of the charity, and it is neither an exempt charity nor a charitable company.

(2) [**268(1)**] Subject to the following provisions of this section, the charity trustees of a charity to which this section applies may resolve for the purposes of this section—
    (a) that all the property of the charity should be transferred to such other charity as is specified in the resolution, being either a registered charity or a charity which is not required to be registered;

(b) that all the property of the charity should be divided, in such manner as is specified in the resolution, between such two or more other charities as are so specified, being in each case either a registered charity or a charity which is not required to be registered;

(c) that the trusts of the charity should be modified by replacing all or any of the purposes of the charity with such other purposes, being in law charitable, as are specified in the resolution;

(d) that any provision of the trusts of the charity—
    (i) relating to any of the powers exercisable by the charity trustees in the administration of the charity, or
    (ii) regulating the procedure to be followed in any respect in connection with its administration,
    should be modified in such manner as is specified in the resolution.

(3) **[268(2)]** Any resolution passed under subsection (2) above must be passed by a majority of not less than two-thirds of such charity trustees as vote on the resolution.

(4) **[268(3)]** The charity trustees of a charity to which this section applies ('the transferor charity') shall not have power to pass a resolution under subsection (2)(a) or (b) above unless they are satisfied—

(a) that the existing purposes of the transferor charity have ceased to be conducive to a suitable and effective application of the charity's resources; and

(b) that the purposes of the charity or charities specified in the resolution are as similar in character to the purposes of the transferor charity as is reasonably practicable; and before passing the resolution they must have received from the charity trustees of the charity, or (as the case may be) of each of the charities, specified in the resolution written confirmation that those trustees are willing to accept a transfer of property under this section.

(5) **[268(4)]** The charity trustees of any such charity shall not have power to pass a resolution under subsection (2)(c) above unless they are satisfied—

(a) that the existing purposes of the charity (or, as the case may be, such of them as it is proposed to replace) have ceased to be conducive to a suitable and effective application of the charity's resources; and

(b) that the purposes specified in the resolution are as similar in character to those existing purposes as is practical in the circumstances.

(6) **[268(5)]** Where charity trustees have passed a resolution under subsection (2) above, they shall—

(a) give public notice of the resolution in such manner as they think reasonable in the circumstances; and

(b) send a copy of the resolution to the Commissioners, together with a statement of their reasons for passing it.

(7) **[269(1)]** The Commissioners may, when considering the resolution, require the charity trustees to provide additional information or explanation—

(a) as to the circumstances in and by reference to which they have determined to act under this section, or

(b) relating to their compliance with this section in connection with the resolution;

and the Commissioners shall take into account any representations made to them by persons appearing to them to be interested in the charity where those representations are made within the period of six weeks beginning with the date when the Commissioners receive a copy of the resolution by virtue of subsection (6)(b) above.

(a) that the Commissioners concur with the resolution; or

(b) that they do not concur with it.

(8) **[269(2)]** Where the Commissioners have so received a copy of a resolution from any charity trustees and it appears to them that the trustees have complied with this section in connection with the resolution, the Commissioners shall, within the period of three months beginning with the date when they receive the copy of the resolution, notify the trustees in writing either—

(9) **[270]** Where the Commissioners so notify their concurrence with the resolution, then—

  (a) if the resolution was passed under subsection (2)(a) or (b) above, the charity trustees shall arrange for all the property of the transferor charity to be transferred in accordance with the resolution and on terms that any property so transferred—

    (i) shall be held and applied by the charity to which it is transferred ('the transferee charity') for the purposes of that charity, but

    (ii) shall, as property of the transferee charity, nevertheless be subject to any restrictions on expenditure to which it is subject as property of the transferor charity, and those trustees shall arrange for it to be so transferred by such date as may be specified in the notification; and

  (b) if the resolution was passed under subsection (2)(c) or (d) above, the trusts of the charity shall be deemed, as from such date as may be specified in the notification, to have been modified in accordance with the terms of the resolution.

  (10) **[272(1),(2)]** For the purpose of enabling any property to be transferred to a charity under this section, the Commissioners shall have power, at the request of the charity trustees of that charity, to make orders vesting any property of the transferor charity—

  (a) in the charity trustees of the first-mentioned charity or in any trustee for that charity, or

  (b) in any other person nominated by those charity trustees to hold the property in trust for that charity.

  (11) **[272(3)]** The Secretary of State may by order amend subsection (1) above by substituting a different sum for the sum for the time being specified there.

  (12) **[272(4)]** In this section—

  (a) 'charitable company' means a charity which is a company or other body corporate; and

  (b) references to the transfer of property to a charity are references to its transfer—

    (i) to the charity trustees, or

    (ii) to any trustee for the charity, or

    (iii) to a person nominated by the charity trustees to hold it in trust for the charity,

  as the charity trustees may determine.

■ SUMMATIVE QUESTION

Wilhelm, who died in 2011, left the residue of his estate in trust for his grandchildren, Betty and Andrew, at the age of 25, in equal shares absolutely. The trustees have invested the fund and accumulated all the income on it. The capital value of the fund is now £20,000. Betty is 19 years old; Andrew is 12. The trustees have received the following requests:

First, they have been asked to transfer £4,000 into a trust fund set up by the children's uncle in 1995 under which the fund trustees may, in their sole discretion, pay income or capital to any of his nephews or nieces who are students at university, and any capital remaining after a period of 21 years will be divided equally between all his nephews and nieces. At present, the fund is valued at £6,000 and Betty is the only eligible beneficiary.

Secondly, Andrew's parents have asked the trustees to pay all the income of the fund to them for ten years to enable them to meet the initial running costs of a riding school which they propose to establish at their home. Andrew is interested in riding and supports the proposal.

Advise whether the trustees may comply with these requests.

online
resource
centre

FURTHER READING

Garton, J., 'Justifying the *Cy-Près* Doctrine' (2007) 21(3) *Tru LI* 134.

Harris, J. W., *Variation of Trusts* (London: Sweet & Maxwell, 1975).

Ker, B. S., 'Trustees' Powers of Maintenance' (1953) 17 *Conv* 273.

Luxton, P., '*Cy-près* and Schemes', in Luxton, P., Evans N., and Smith J., *The Law of Charities,* 2nd edn (Oxford: Oxford University Press, 2012), Chapter 15.

Mulheron, R., *The Modern Cy-Pres Doctrine: Applications and Implications* (Routledge Cavendish, London, 2006).

Riddall, J. G., '*Re Ransome* Revisited or "First Good News"' (1979) 43 *Conv* 423.

Riddall, J. G., 'Does it or Doesn't it? Contingent Interests and the Variation of Trusts Act 1958' (1987) 51 *Conv* 144.

Sheridan, L.A., *The Cy-Près Doctrine* (London: Sweet & Maxwell, 1959).

Stibbard, P., 'Jersey Court Upholds Variation of Trust to Avoid Capital Gains Tax Liability of the Settlor' (2001) 1 *Private Client Business* 35.

10

The Fiduciary Duty

KEY AIMS

To appreciate that certain relationships (such as trustee–beneficiary) are presumed 'fiduciary' but that, generally, fiduciary relationships cannot be presumed and are based on evidence of a fiduciary duty. To examine the nature of the fiduciary duty and the reasons why it is strictly enforced. To consider the application of the fiduciary duty to relationships and transactions in which there is a potential conflict of interest, including cases of information received in confidence or trust. To compare and contrast fair-dealing and self-dealing, and to appreciate why the latter is void at the instance of the beneficiary or principal affected. To identify what a fiduciary should do to avoid, and if necessary extract himself from, conflicts of interest. To elucidate the duty to account for unauthorised profits acquired in a fiduciary capacity.

SECTION 1: INTRODUCTION

The fiduciary duty comprises a number of overlapping obligations concerned to promote loyalty or faithfulness. The principal obligations that make up the fiduciary duty are the trustee's duty not to put himself in a position of potential conflict with the interests of the trust, and his duty not to make an unauthorised profit from the trust property or from his position of trust. In certain circumstances, the fiduciary duty will also apply to a person who is not a trustee properly so-called. In such a case, the person subject to the duty is said to be a fiduciary. The fiduciary duty was developed in Chancery and it is equitable in the sense that it is, broadly speaking, concerned to restrain unconscionable abuse of legal power and position, but is not equitable in the usual sense of being concerned to achieve justice between the parties in a particular case. It is not concerned to achieve fairness between the trustee and the beneficiaries of his trust or between a fiduciary and his principal. On the contrary, it is a rule of public policy that is strictly applied against trustees in order to set an example and to encourage good behaviour in all who hold positions of trust. In *Parker* v *McKenna* (1874) 10 Ch App 96, James LJ went as far as to say that the strict enforcement of exemplary fiduciary propriety is required for 'the safety of mankind'. Fiduciary duties have been described as 'simple, strict and salutary' (*Towers* v *Premier Waste Ltd* [2011] EWCA Civ 923, [2012] 1 BCLC 67, CA per Mummery LJ at para. [2]).

Bristol and West Building Society v Mothew

[1998] Ch 1, Court of Appeal

Facts: In 1988, the defendant solicitor acted for a husband and wife in the purchase of a house for £73,000 and also for the claimant to whom the purchasers had applied for a loan of £59,000 to finance the purchase. The claimant offered to advance the money on the express condition that the balance of the purchase price was provided by the purchasers without resort to further borrowing, and it instructed the solicitor to report, prior to completion, any proposal that the purchasers might create a second mortgage or otherwise borrow in order to finance part of the purchase price. The solicitor knew that the purchasers were arranging for an existing bank debt of £3,350 to be secured by a second charge on the new property but, due to an oversight, he stated in his report to the claimant that the balance of the purchase price was being provided by the purchasers without resort to further borrowing. The claimant advanced the loan and the purchase was completed. When the purchasers defaulted on their mortgage repayments, the claimant enforced its security and the house was sold at a loss. The claimant sought to recover the whole of its loss on the transaction from the solicitor, alleging breach of contract, negligence, and breach of trust.

Held: (inter alia): That the solicitor's conduct in providing the claimant with the wrong information, although a breach of duty, was neither dishonest nor intentional, but due to an oversight and was unconnected to the fact that he was also acting for the purchasers; that, accordingly, his conduct and subsequent application of the money advanced by the claimant to complete the purchase was not a breach of trust or fiduciary duty; and that the order for damages for breach of trust would therefore be set aside. Appeal allowed on other grounds.

MILLETT LJ: ...A fiduciary is someone who has undertaken to act for or on behalf of another in a particular matter in circumstances which give rise to a relationship of trust and confidence. The distinguishing obligation of a fiduciary is the obligation of loyalty. The principal is entitled to the single-minded loyalty of his fiduciary. This core liability has several facets. A fiduciary must act in good faith; he must not make a profit out of his trust; he must not place himself in a position where his duty and his interest may conflict; he may not act for his own benefit or the benefit of a third person without the informed consent of his principal. This is not intended to be an exhaustive list, but it is sufficient to indicate the nature of fiduciary obligations. They are the defining characteristics of the fiduciary. As Dr Finn pointed out in his classic work *Fiduciary Obligations* (1977), p. 2, he is not subject to fiduciary obligations because he is a fiduciary; it is because he is subject to them that he is a fiduciary. (In this survey I have left out of account the situation where the fiduciary deals with his principal. In such a case he must prove affirmatively that the transaction is fair and that in the course of the negotiations he made full disclosure of all facts material to the transaction. Even inadvertent failure to disclose will entitle the principal to rescind the transaction. The rule is the same whether the fiduciary is acting on his own behalf or on behalf of another. The principle need not be further considered because it does arise in the present case. The mortgage advance was negotiated directly between the society and the purchasers. The defendant had nothing to do with the negotiations. He was instructed by the society to carry out on its behalf a transaction which had already been agreed.)

The nature of the obligation determines the nature of the breach. The various obligations of a fiduciary merely reflect different aspects of his core duties of loyalty and fidelity. Breach of fiduciary obligation, therefore, connotes disloyalty or infidelity. Mere incompetence is not enough. A servant who loyally does his incompetent best for his master is not unfaithful and is not guilty of a breach of fiduciary duty.

In the present case it is clear that, if the defendant had been acting for the society alone, his admitted negligence would not have exposed him to a charge of breach of fiduciary obligations. Before us counsel for the society accepted as much, but insisted that the fact that he also acted for the purchasers made all the difference. So it is necessary to ask: why did the fact that the defendant was acting for the purchasers as well as for the society convert the defendant's admitted breach of his duty of skill and care into a breach of fiduciary duty? To answer this question it is necessary to identify the fiduciary obligation of which he is alleged to have been in breach. It is at this point, in my judgment, that the society's argument runs into difficulty. A fiduciary who acts for two principals with potentially conflicting interests without the informed consent of both is in breach of the obligation of undivided loyalty; he puts himself in a position where his duty to one principal may conflict with his duty to the other: see *Clark Boyce* v *Mouat* [1993] 4 All ER 268 and the cases there cited. This is sometimes described as 'the double employment rule'. Breach of the rule automatically constitutes a breach of fiduciary duty. But this is not something of which the society can complain. It knew that the defendant was acting for the purchasers when it instructed him. Indeed, that was the very reason why it chose the defendant to act for it. The potential was of the society's own making (see Finn p. 254 and *Kelly* v *Cooper* [1993] AC 205) ...

That, of course, is not the end of the matter. Even if a fiduciary is properly acting for two principals with potentially conflicting interests he must act in good faith in the interests of each and must not act with the intention of furthering the interests of one principal to the prejudice of those of the other (see Finn p. 48). I shall call this 'the duty of good faith'. But it goes further than this. He must not allow the performance of his obligations to one principal to be influenced by his relationship with the other. He must serve each as faithfully and loyally as if he were his only principal. Conduct which is in breach of this duty need not be dishonest but it must be intentional. An unconscious omission which happens to benefit one principal at the expense of the other does not constitute a breach of fiduciary duty, though it may constitute a breach of the duty of skill and care. This is because the principle which is in play is that the fiduciary must not be inhibited by the existence of his other employment from serving the interests of his principal as faithfully and effectively as if he were the only employer. I shall call this 'the no inhibition principle'. Unless the fiduciary is inhibited or believes (whether rightly or wrongly) that he is inhibited in the performance of his duties to one principal by reason of his employment by the other, his failure to act is not attributable to the double employment.

Finally, the fiduciary must take care not to find himself in a position where there is an *actual* conflict of duty so that he cannot fulfil his obligations to one principal without failing in his obligations to the other: see *Moody* v *Cox* [1917] 2 Ch 71 and *Commonwealth Bank of Australia* v *Smith* (1991) 102 ALR 453. If he does, he may have no alternative but to cease to act for at least one and preferably both. The fact that he cannot fulfil his obligations to one principal without being in breach of his obligations to the other will not absolve him from liability. I shall call this 'the actual conflict rule' ...

In my judgment, the defendant was never in breach of the actual conflict rule. It is not alleged that he acted in bad faith or deliberately withheld information because he wrongly believed that his duty to the purchasers required him to do so. He was not guilty of a breach of fiduciary duty ...

Breach of trust

It is not disputed that from the time of its receipt by the defendant the mortgage money was trust money. It was client's money which belonged to the society and was properly paid into a client account. The defendant never claimed any beneficial interest in the money which remained throughout the property of the society in equity. The defendant held it in trust for the society but with the society's authority (and instructions) to apply it in the completion of the transaction of purchase and mortgage of the property. Those instructions were revocable but, unless previously revoked, the defendant was entitled and bound to act in accordance with them.

The society's instructions were not revoked before the defendant acted on them, and in my judgment there was no ground upon which the judge could properly conclude that his authority to apply the money in completing the transaction had determined.

If his judgment in the present case is considered without the benefit of his later explanation in *Bristol and West Building Society* v *May, May & Merrimans* [1996] 2 All ER 801, it would appear that the judge was of opinion that the defendant's authority to deal with the money was automatically vitiated by the fact that it (and the cheque itself) was obtained by misrepresentation. But that is contrary to principle. Misrepresentation makes a transaction voidable not void. It gives the representee the right to elect whether to rescind or affirm the transaction. The representor cannot anticipate his decision. Unless and until the representee elects to rescind the representor remains fully bound. The defendant's misrepresentations merely gave the society the right to elect to withdraw from the transaction on discovering the truth. Since its instructions to the defendant were revocable in any case, this did not materially alter the position so far as he was concerned, though it may have strengthened the society's position in relation to the purchasers.

The right to rescind for misrepresentation is an equity. Until it is exercised the beneficial interest in any property transferred in reliance on the representation remains vested in the transferee. In *El Ajou* v *Dollar Land Holdings Plc* [1993] 3 All ER 717, 734 I suggested that on rescission the equitable title might revest in the representee retrospectively at least to the extent necessary to support an equitable tracing claim. I was concerned to circumvent the supposed rule that there must be a fiduciary relationship or retained beneficial interest before resort may be had to the equitable tracing rules. The rule would have been productive of the most extraordinary anomalies in that case, and its existence continually threatens to frustrate attempts to develop a coherent law of restitution. Until the equitable tracing rules are made available in support of the ordinary common law claim for money had and received some problems will remain incapable of sensible resolution.

But all that is by the way. Whether or not there is a retrospective vesting for tracing purposes it is clear that on rescission the equitable title does not revest retrospectively so as to cause an application of trust money which was properly authorised when made to be afterwards treated as a breach of trust. In *Lipkin Gorman* v *Karpnale Ltd* [1991] 2 AC 548 Lord Goff of Chieveley said, at p. 573:

> Of course, 'tracing' or 'following' property into its product involves a decision by the owner of the original property to assert his title to the product in place of his original property. This is sometimes referred to as ratification. I myself would not so describe it, but it has, in my opinion, at least one feature in common with ratification, that it cannot be relied upon so as to render an innocent recipient a wrongdoer (cf. *Bolton Partners* v *Lambert* (1889) 41 ChD 295, 307, *per* Cotton LJ.; 'an act lawful at the time of its performance [cannot] be rendered unlawful, by the application of the doctrine of ratification.')

In *Westdeutsche Landesbank Girozentrale* v *Islington London Borough Council* [1996] AC 669 Lord Browne-Wilkinson expressly rejected the possibility that a recipient of trust money could be personally liable, regardless of fault, for any subsequent payment away of the moneys to third parties even though, at the date of such payment, he was ignorant of the existence of any trust. He said, at p. 705:

> Since the equitable jurisdiction to enforce trusts depends upon the conscience of the holder of the legal interest being affected, he cannot be a trustee of the property if and so long as he is ignorant of the facts alleged to affect his conscience, i.e. until he is aware that he is intended to hold the property for the benefit of others in the case of an express or implied trust, or, in the case of a constructive trust, of the factors which are alleged to affect his conscience.

Mutatis mutandis that passage is directly applicable in the present case. The defendant knew that he was a trustee of the money for the society; but he did not realise that he had misled the society and could not know that his authority to complete had determined (if indeed it had). He could not be bound to repay the money to the society so long as he was ignorant of the facts which had brought his authority to an end, for those are the facts which are alleged to affect his conscience and subject him to an obligation to return the money to the society.

Before us the society put forward a more sophisticated argument. The defendant's instructions, it pointed out, expressly required him to report the arrangements in question 'to the society prior to completion'. This, it was submitted, made it a condition of the defendant's authority to complete that he had complied with his obligation. Whether he knew it or not, he had no authority to complete. It was not necessary for the society to revoke his authority or withdraw from the transaction. I do not accept this. The society's standing instructions did not clearly make the defendant's authority to complete conditional on having complied with his instructions. Whether they did so or not is, course, a question of construction, and it is possible that the society could adopt instructions which would have this effect. But it would in my judgment require very clear wording to produce so inconvenient and impractical a result. No solicitor could safely accept such instructions, he could never be certain that he was entitled to complete.

In my judgment the defendant's authority to apply the mortgage money in the completion of the purchase was not conditional on his having first complied with his contractual obligations to the society, was not vitiated by the misrepresentations for which he was responsible but of which he was unaware, had not been revoked, and was effective to prevent his payment being a breach of trust. Given his state of knowledge (and, more importantly, that his authority had not been revoked), he had no choice but to complete.

Conclusion

In my judgment the defendant was not guilty of breach of trust or fiduciary duty. This makes it unnecessary to consider what the consequences of such a breach would have been. I would allow the appeal and set aside the money judgment. I would leave undisturbed the judgments for damages to be assessed for breach of contract and negligence, but make it clear that it does not follow that the society will establish any recoverable loss.

Ordinary commercial relationships, where the parties act independently in their own interests, are not fiduciary relationships. In *Re Goldcorp Exchange Ltd* [1995] 1 AC 74, the Privy Council refused to recognise the existence of any fiduciary relationship between a company which had sold gold bullion for future delivery, and its customers. Lord Mustill observed that 'the essence of a fiduciary relationship is that it creates obligations of a different character from those deriving from the contract itself', and that that was not the case here. One effect of the lack of a fiduciary relationship between the parties was that the customers were unable to trace in equity [see further Chapter 14].

NOTES

1. It should always be borne in mind that courts are reluctant to find fiduciary relationships in commercial contexts. The presumption is always in favour of simple contract or agency without a fiduciary dimension (see, for example, *Button* v *Phelps* [2006] EWHC 53 (Ch), 2006 WL 584571).

2. Canadian courts have been far more willing to recognise fiduciary relationships than courts in other commonwealth jurisdictions, even going so far as to hold that a parent is in a fiduciary relationship to their child (*M (K)* v *M (H)* [1992] 3 SCR 6). It is said that Chief Justice Mason of the High Court of Australia once quipped that in Canada there are only three categories of people: 'those who are fiduciaries, those who are about to become fiduciaries, and judges' (quoted in M. McInnes, 'A new direction for the Canadian law of fiduciary relations?' (2010) 126 *LQR* 185–8).

SECTION 2: CONFLICTS

A trustee must not grant or sell any trust property to himself (this is the rule against self-dealing) and if he purchases an equitable interest from a beneficiary the onus is on the trustee to prove that the purchase was fair (this is the fair-dealing rule). Neither must a trustee nor fiduciary place himself in a position where there may be a potential conflict of interest.

A: The self-dealing rule and the fair-dealing rule

Tito v *Waddell (No. 2)*
[1977] Ch 106, Chancery Division

MEGARRY V-C (at 225): During the argument, two agreed labels emerged for the two rules, or two elements of the one rule; and for convenience of reference I shall use those labels. Without attempting in any way to set out all the details of the rules or elements, and merely for the purposes of identification, I propose to refer to them as follows:

   (1) The self-dealing rule: if a trustee purchases trust property from himself, any beneficiary may have the sale set aside ex debito justitiae, however fair the transaction.

   (2) The fair-dealing rule: if a trustee purchases his beneficiary's beneficial interest, the beneficiary may have the sale set aside unless the trustee can establish the propriety of the transaction, showing that he had taken no advantage of his position and that the beneficiary was fully informed and received full value.

B: The duty not to put oneself in a position of potential conflict

Sargeant and another v *National Westminster Bank plc*

(1990) 61 P & CR 518, Court of Appeal

Facts: A testator let a number of farms to his children which they worked as a partnership. He then appointed his children to be executors and trustees under his will. When one of the children (Charles) died, the surviving children exercised an option to purchase the deceased child's share of the partnership. Later, they revealed plans to purchase the freehold of one of the farms of which they were tenants, and to sell the other freeholds. The administrators of the estate of the deceased child objected to these plans and argued that the surviving children would be in breach of their trust were they to sell, to themselves, the trust-owned freeholds of which they were trustees and under which they were tenants. The trustees sought a declaration that they would be entitled to sell the freeholds. This declaration was granted. The administrators appealed.

Held: The trustees were in a position where their interest as tenants might conflict with their duties as trustees, but they had not put themselves in that position. The trustees' rights as tenants pre-dated their duties as trustees and they would therefore be permitted to assert those rights. They must nevertheless endeavour to obtain the best price for the freeholds in order to fulfil their obligations to the trust.

NOURSE LJ: The rule that a trustee must not profit from his trust holds that prevention is better than cure. While it invariably requires that a profit shall be yielded up, it prefers to intervene beforehand by dissolving the connection out of which the profit may be made. At that stage the rule is expressed by saying that a trustee must not put himself in a position where his interest and duty conflict. But to express it in that way is to acknowledge that if he is put there, not by himself, but by the testator or settlor under whose dispositions his trust arises, the rule does not apply ...

In this case two of the testator's children, as the trustees of his will, are the legal owners and trustees for sale of his three freehold farms. Under the terms of the will, each of them is absolutely entitled to one third of the net proceeds of sale and the net rents and profits until sale. They are also the tenants of the farms under tenancies which the testator originally granted to them and a deceased child during his life-time. The owners of the remaining third of the beneficial interest, subject to the tenancies, are the personal representatives of the deceased child ...

I now come to the first and second arguments which were advanced by Mr Romer on behalf of the administrators. Although he sought to keep them separate, they were both founded on the rule that a trustee must not put himself in a position where his interest and duty conflict. Mr Romer relied on the following passage in the judgment of Lord Herschell in *Bray* v *Ford* [1896] AC 44 which was described by Lord Upjohn in *Boardman* v *Phipps* [1967] 2 AC 46 as the best statement of the rule:

> It is an inflexible rule of a Court of Equity that a person in a fiduciary position ... is not, unless otherwise expressly provided, entitled to make a profit, he is not allowed to put himself in a position where his interest and duty conflict. It does not appear to me that this rule is, as has been said, founded upon principles of morality. I regard it rather as based on the consideration that, human nature being what it is, there is a danger, in such circumstances, of the person holding a fiduciary position being swayed by interest rather than by duty, and thus prejudicing those whom he was bound to protect. It has, therefore, been deemed expedient to lay down this positive rule.

Mr Romer submitted that the trustees' duty is to obtain the best price for the freeholds of the farms, which admittedly can only be obtained by a sale with vacant possession, whereas their interest is to preserve their tenancies and to sell subject to them, in which event the best price will not be obtained. Mr Romer therefore submitted that if the trustees go ahead and sell subject to the tenancies, either to themselves or to a third party, they will be putting themselves in a position where their interest and duty conflict ...

What then happened on the death of Charles? He necessarily ceased to be a trustee of the will. His estate retained his beneficial interest in the farms, subject to the tenancies. The arrangements between the children might have been such that his estate retained his interest in the tenancies as well. No doubt for a short period it did. But under the provisions of the partnership deed, to which Charles himself had been a party, the trustees acquired his share in the partnership, including his share in the tenancies. Thenceforth each of the trustees continued to have the rights of a tenant and a beneficiary. But Charles' estate only had the rights of a beneficiary.

It cannot be doubted that the trustees have ever since been in a position where their interests as tenants *may* conflict with their duties as trustees to the estate of Charles. But the conclusive objection to the application of the absolute rule on which Mr Romer relies is that it is not they who have put themselves in that position. They have been put there mainly by the testator's grant of the tenancies and by the provisions of his will and partly by contractual arrangements to which Charles himself was a party and of which his representatives cannot complain. The administrators cannot therefore complain of the trustees' continued assertion of their rights as tenants.

Since the absolute rule on which Mr Romer relies does not apply, there is no absolute requirement that the trustees should appoint a new trustee before making any sale subject to the tenancies. Nor is there any absolute bar to their selling to themselves so long as the tenancies subsist. On the other hand, they must continue to discharge their fiduciary duties to Charles' estate in regard to the freeholds, in particular by obtaining the best price for them subject to the tenancies. In the end, the basis for Mr Romer's arguments was seen to be a fear or a suspicion that the trustees will not properly discharge that duty. But there is no evidence either that they have failed to discharge their duties in the past or that they will fail to do so in the future. Without such evidence, it is wholly inappropriate for the court to interfere ...

Re Mulholland's WT

[1949] 1 All ER 460, Chancery Division

WYNN-PARRY J: the principle ... that the existence of the fiduciary relationship creates an inability in the trustee to contract in regard to the trust property ... does not touch the position arising where the contract in question has been brought into existence before the fiduciary relationship.

C: The effect of retirement from a trust

Re Boles and British Land Company's Contract

[1902] 1 Ch 244, Chancery Division

Facts: One of the trustees (and executor) of a will trust retired from office by deed and with the consent of the continuing trustees. Twelve years later, the continuing trustees sold land owned by the trust to the trustee who had retired. The question arose whether the sale was valid or should be set aside.

Held: The sale was valid.

BUCKLEY J: ... Apart from any circumstances of doubt or suspicion, is there any rule of this Court that a person, who has ceased for twelve years to be a trustee of an instrument which contains a trust for sale, is precluded from becoming a purchaser of property subject to the trust? I think there is not. The principle that lies at the root of this matter is that a trustee for sale owes a duty to his *cestuis que trust* to do everything in his power for their benefit, and is therefore absolutely precluded from buying the trust property, irrespective of questions of undervalue or otherwise, because he may be thus induced to neglect his duty. Beyond that, if he retires with a view to becoming a purchaser so as to put himself in a position to do what would otherwise be a breach of trust, that will not do. But if he has retired and there is nothing to shew that at the time of the retirement there was any idea of a sale, and in fact there is no sale for twelve years after his retirement, is there anything to prevent him from becoming a purchaser? I think not ...

(i) Duty to a former client

Jefri Bolkiah v *KPMG (a firm)*
[1999] 2 AC 222, House of Lords

Facts: Over a period of 18 months between 1996 and 1998, KPMG, a global firm of chartered accountants, was retained by one of Prince Jefri's companies on his behalf and at his request to undertake a substantial investigation in connection with major litigation in which he was personally involved. In the course of the investigation, the firm was entrusted with or acquired extensive confidential information concerning the Prince's assets and financial affairs. On 14 May 1998, the Prince terminated his instructions to the firm and two months later, the Brunei Investment Agency (BIA) approached the same department of the firm with a view to instructing it to carry out certain financial investigations, including investigations into transactions carried out by the Prince. KPMG had carried out an annual audit for BIA since 1983. The firm took the view that there was no conflict of interest but they nevertheless took the precaution of putting special arrangements in place designed to prevent the disclosure of confidential information relating to the Prince. A separate office, with a separate computer server, was established to carry out work on behalf of BIA and information relating to the Prince was deleted from the firm's computers.

Held: The firm should have declined to accept the new instructions and was required to cease to act for BIA in connection with its investigation into the Prince's affairs.

LORD MILLETT: Chinese walls are widely used by financial institutions in the City of London and elsewhere. They are the favoured technique for managing the conflicts of interest which arise when financial business is carried on by a conglomerate. The Core Conduct of Business Rules published by the Financial Services Authority recognise the effectiveness of Chinese walls as a means of restricting the movement of information between different departments of the same organisation. They contemplate the existence of established organisational arrangements which preclude the passing of information in the possession of one part of the business to other parts of the business. In their consultation paper on Fiduciary Duties and Regulatory Rules (Law Com No. 124) (1992), the Law Commission describe Chinese walls as normally involving some combination of the following organisational arrangements: (i) the physical separation of the various departments in order to insulate them from each other—this often extends to such matters of detail as dining arrangements; (ii) an educational programme, normally recurring, to emphasise the importance of not improperly or inadvertently divulging confidential information; (iii) strict and carefully defined procedures for dealing with a situation where it is felt that the wall should be crossed and the maintaining of proper records where this occurs; (iv) monitoring by compliance officers of the effectiveness of the wall; (v) disciplinary sanctions where there has been a breach of the wall.

KPMG insist that, like other large firms of accountants, they are accustomed to maintaining client confidentiality not just within the firm but also within a particular team. They stress that it is common for a large firm of accountants to provide a comprehensive range of professional services including audit, corporate finance advice, corporate tax advice and management consultancy to clients with competing commercial interests. Such firms are very experienced in the erection and operation of information barriers to protect the confidential information of each client, and staff are constantly instructed in the importance of respecting client confidentiality. This is, KPMG assert, part of the professional culture in which staff work and becomes second nature to them. Forensic projects are treated as exceptionally confidential and are usually given code names. In the present case KPMG engaged different people, different servers, and ensured that the work was done in a secure office in a different building. KPMG maintain that these arrangements satisfy the most stringent test, and that there is no risk that information obtained by KPMG in the course of Project Lucy has or will become available to anyone engaged on Project Gemma.

I am not persuaded that this is so. Even in the financial services industry, good practice requires there to be established institutional arrangements designed to prevent the flow of information between separate departments ... The Chinese walls which feature in the present case, however, were established ad hoc and were erected within a single department. When the number of personnel involved is taken into account, together with the fact that the teams engaged on Project Lucy and Project Gemma each had a rotating membership, involving far more personnel than were working on the project at any one time, so that individuals may have joined from and returned to other projects, the difficulty of enforcing confidentiality or preventing the unwitting disclosure of information is very great. It is one thing, for example, to separate the insolvency, audit, taxation and forensic departments from one another and erect Chinese walls between them. Such departments often work from different offices and there may be relatively little movement of personnel between them. But it is quite another to attempt to place an information barrier between members all of whom are drawn from the same department and have been accustomed to work with each other. I would expect this to be particularly difficult where the department concerned is engaged in the provision of litigation support services, and there is evidence to confirm this. Forensic accountancy is said to be an area in which new and unusual problems frequently arise and partners and managers are accustomed to share information and expertise. Furthermore, there is evidence that physical segregation is not necessarily adequate, especially where it is erected within a single department.

In my opinion an effective Chinese wall needs to be an established part of the organisational structure of the firm, not created ad hoc and dependent on the acceptance of evidence sworn for the purpose by members of staff engaged on the relevant work.

NOTES

1. In *Rakusen* v *Ellis Munday & Clarke* [1912] 1 Ch 831, both partners of a small firm of solicitors carried on separate practices, each with his own clients and without any knowledge of the other's clients. The claimant instructed one of the partners in relation to a contentious matter and after he had terminated his instructions, the other partner, who had never met the claimant and was not aware that he had consulted his partner, was instructed by the party on the other side in the same contentious matter. An injunction restraining the firm from acting for that other party was granted at first instance but discharged by the Court of Appeal on the ground that there was no risk of disclosure of confidential information.

2. The law firm in the case of *Marks & Spencer plc* v *Freshfields Bruckhaus Deringer* [2004] EWCA Civ 741 was prohibited from accepting instructions from a company that was in the course of acquiring one of the firm's former clients.

Holder v *Holder*

[1968] Ch 353, Court of Appeal

Facts: The defendant, Victor Holder, was appointed one of the executors of his father's will. He was also tenant of two farms which were part of the estate. After the death of his father, Victor purported to renounce his office as executor, but the renunciation was technically ineffective. Nevertheless, probate was granted to two of the other executors named in the will. They put the two farms of which he was tenant up for sale by auction, where Victor, through an agent, bid successfully for them. The claimant, another member of the family, started an action to set aside the conveyance to Victor.

Held: The sale would not be set aside.

HARMAN LJ: The judge [Cross J] decided in favour of the plaintiff on this point because ... (Victor) at the time of the sale was himself still in a fiduciary position and, like any other trustee, could not purchase the trust property. I feel the force of this argument, but doubt its validity in the very special circumstances of this case. The reason for the rule is that a man may not both be vendor and purchaser; but [Victor] was never in that position here. He took no part in instructing the valuer who fixed the reserves or in the preparations for the auction. Everyone in the family knew that he was not a seller but a buyer. In this case [Victor] never assumed the duties of an executor. It is true that he concurred in signing a few cheques for trivial sums and endorsing a few insurance policies, but he never so far as appears interfered in any way with the administration of the estate. It is true he managed the farms, but he did that as tenant and not as executor. He acquired no special knowledge as executor. What he knew he knew as tenant of the farms. Another reason lying behind the rule is that there must never be a conflict of duty and interest, but in fact there was none here in the case of the third defendant, who made no secret throughout that he intended to buy ...

Of course, I feel the force of the judge's reasoning that if … [Victor] remained an executor he is within the rule, but in a case where the reasons behind the rule do not exist I do not feel bound to apply it. My reasons are that the beneficiaries never looked to the third defendant to protect their interests. They all knew he was in the market as purchaser; that the price paid was a good one and probably higher than anyone not a sitting tenant would give. Further, the first two defendants alone acted as executors and sellers: they alone could convey: they were not influenced by the third defendant in connexion with the sales.

NOTES
1. Danckwerts LJ expressed doubt whether today the self-dealing rule should apply where trust property is sold at public auctions, at least in a case where the sale is arranged by trustees other than the purchasing trustee. He also held that the claimant had acquiesced in or confirmed the sale and could not claim to have it set aside. Sachs LJ expressed the same doubt whether the self-dealing rule should apply now to a sale by auction.
2. However, *Holder* v *Holder* was limited almost to its own unusual facts by Vinelott J in *Re Thompson's Settlement* [1986] Ch 99. Vinelott J explained the decision on the narrow ground that the defendant had never acted as executor in a way which could be taken to amount to acceptance of a duty to act in the interests of the beneficiaries under his father's will. He said that the self-dealing rule (see *Wright* v *Morgan* [1926] AC 788) is an application of the wider principle that a man must not put himself in a position where duty and interest conflict or where his duty to one conflicts with his duty to another.

D: The rule against unauthorised profit

Arguably, all that is necessary is to establish the causal connection between position and profit. In *Re Macadam* [1946] Ch 73, trustees who used their position to appoint themselves to directorships of a company were held liable to account to the trust for all the fees they received as directors. This type of situation can commonly arise in private companies, because eligibility for appointment to directorships can depend on the legal ownership of a minimum number of shares, and indeed trustees may be under a duty to procure their representation on the board if it is necessary in order to safeguard the value of the trust shares.

No causal connection was established in *Re Dover Coalfield Extension* [1908] 1 Ch 65, a case similar to *Re Macadam*, but where a trustee had already become a director before becoming trustee. *Re Gee* [1948] Ch 284 is similar, where a trustee became a director after refraining from using his vote, which he had by virtue of holding trust shares. He would have been elected anyway, however, due to the votes of the other shareholders, no matter how he had voted himself; he would even have been elected if he had voted against himself. Harman J held that the remuneration received as director was not accountable to the trust. In neither of these cases could it be said that the trustees had made any profit by virtue of their position.

A closer examination of these cases suggests that they are, in reality, conflict of interest cases, since clearly a trustee who stands to gain from the choice of himself as director cannot advise the trust impartially as to the choice of who to appoint. Thus, in *Crown Dilmun* v *Sutton* [2004] 1 BCLC 468, which was an action by the claimant company against one of its former employees, the claimant was successful in preventing the defendant from taking the benefit on his own account of a business opportunity which he had acquired in the course of his employment and had declined to pursue on the company's account. It was no defence for the defendant to show that he could have acquired the information independently of his fiduciary position. Peter Smith J held that, 'Whether or not the information is confidential, if the opportunity that arises by reason of the acquisition of the information puts the fiduciary in a position of conflict, he cannot take that opportunity' (para. [187]). The disputed business opportunity in this case concerned the commercial development of Craven Cottage, the home ground of Fulham F.C.

An important case is *Keech* v *Sandford* (1726) Sel Cas Ch 61, where the trustee took over the benefit of a lease which had been devised to the trust, when that lease expired. Since the lease had expired, this is not a case of dealing in trust property. The causal connection between position and profit was presumably established, in that he would not have been in a position to take the lease had he not been trustee. The lessor had refused to renew the lease for the trust, on the grounds that the beneficiary was an infant, against whom it would be difficult to recover rent. The trustee thereupon took the lease for his personal benefit, and profited from it.

There cannot have been any actual conflict of interest, because the trust itself could not have benefited, given the views of the lessor. Nor would Lord King LC say that there was any fraud in the case. Yet he held that the trustee had to assign the benefit of the lease to the infant, and account for profits received. The trustee was the one person in the world who could not take the lease for his own benefit, because by so doing he would be profiting from his position. The same principle may apply where a trustee of a lease purchases for himself the freehold reversion: *Protheroe* v *Protheroe* [1968] 1 WLR 519 (CA) (but there are contrary authorities).

There was no mala fides in *Regal (Hastings) Ltd* v *Gulliver* [1967] 2 AC 134n (originally reported in [1942] 2 All ER 378). Regal had considered applying for shares in a subsidiary company, but had been unable to afford them, whereupon the directors subscribed for shares on their own account and made a profit. The directors would not have been in a position to profit had they not been directors, but arguably there was no conflict of interest, given that Regal was not in a position to subscribe on its own account. The directors were nevertheless held liable to account. Lord Russell of Killowen said:

The rule of equity which insists on those, who by use of a fiduciary position make a profit, being liable to account for that profit, in no way depends on fraud, or absence of *bona fides*; or upon such questions or considerations as whether the profit would or should otherwise have gone to the plaintiff, or whether the profiteer was under a duty to obtain the source of the profit for the plaintiff, or whether he took a risk or acted as he did for the benefit of the plaintiff, or whether the plaintiff has in fact been damaged or benefited by his action. The liability arises from the mere fact of a profit having, in the stated circumstances, been made.

This is a fairly clear statement that all that needs to be established is the causal connection between position and profit. Arguably, however, there was in fact a conflict of interest, as the directors themselves must have determined that the company could not afford to subscribe for the shares. It would have been difficult for them to advise impartially where they intended to subscribe for themselves, and hence obtain a profit.

Boardman v *Phipps*

[1967] 2 AC 46, House of Lords

Facts: Boardman was solicitor to a trust, which owned 8,000 of 30,000 shares in a private textile company, with whose performance Boardman was dissatisfied. The trust had no wish to buy the remaining shares, and in any case was unable to buy them, although it could have applied to court for power to do so. Boardman decided to purchase them himself, undoubtedly benefiting from information he had received in his fiduciary capacity (in knowing what price to offer), and did not obtain the consent of all beneficiaries. The shares later increased in value (partly perhaps because of Boardman's management in selling off some of the assets of the newly acquired company), so Boardman made a large profit for himself. Additionally, however, because the trust still had a large share in the same company, his activities also resulted in a large profit for the trust. There was no claim of bad faith, nor any obvious conflict of interest, since the trust did not have the power to purchase the shares itself, and in any case, the trust had positively benefited from Boardman's intervention.

In negotiating for the majority shareholding Boardman had, in good faith, obtained information in his capacity as solicitor to the trust, which he would not otherwise have obtained. Phipps, a beneficiary under the trust, sued for an account of profits.

Held: (Viscount Dilhorne and Lord Upjohn dissenting): Boardman held the shares acquired as constructive trustee for the trust, and he must account for any profits made. He was, however, entitled to remuneration on a *quantum meruit* basis.

LORD COHEN: Wilberforce J and, in the Court of Appeal, both Lord Denning MR and Pearson LJ based their decision in favour of the respondent on the decision of your lordships' House in *Regal (Hastings) Ltd* v *Gulliver*, reported at [1967] 2 AC 134. I turn, therefore, to consider that case. Mr Walton [for the trust] relied upon a number of passages in the judgments of the learned Lords who heard the appeal: in particular on (1) a passage in the speech of Lord Russell of Killowen where he says:

> The rule of equity which insists on those, who by use of a fiduciary position make a profit, being liable to account for that profit, in no way depends on fraud, or absence of bona fides; or upon such questions or considerations as whether the profit would or should otherwise have gone to the plaintiff, or whether the profiteer was under a duty to obtain the source of the profit for the plaintiff, or whether he took a risk or acted as he did for the benefit of the plaintiff, or whether the plaintiff has in fact been damaged or benefited by his action. The liability arises from the mere fact of a profit having, in the stated circumstances, been made.

(2) a passage in the speech of Lord Wright, where he says:

> That question can be briefly stated to be whether an agent, a director, a trustee or other person in an analogous fiduciary position, when a demand is made upon him by the person to whom he stands in the fiduciary relationship to account for profits acquired by him by reason of his fiduciary position, and by reason of the opportunity and the knowledge, or either, resulting from it, is entitled to defeat the claim upon any ground save that he made profits with the knowledge and assent of the other person. The most natural and typical case of this nature is that of principal and agent. The rule in such cases is compendiously expressed to be that an agent must account for net profits secretly (that is, without the knowledge of his principal) acquired by him in the course of his agency. The authorities show how manifold and various are the applications of the rule. It does not depend on fraud or corruption.

These paragraphs undoubtedly help the respondent but they must be considered in relation to the facts of that case. In that case the profit arose through the application by four of the directors of Regal for shares in a subsidiary company which it had been the original intention of the board should be subscribed for by Regal. Regal had not the requisite money available but there was no question of it being *ultra vires* Regal to subscribe for the shares. In the circumstances Lord Russell of Killowen said:

> I have no hesitation in coming to the conclusion, upon the facts of this case, that these shares, when acquired by the directors, were acquired by reason, and only by reason of the fact that they were directors of Regal, and in the course of their execution of that office.

He goes on to consider whether the four directors were in a fiduciary relationship to Regal and concludes that they were. Accordingly, they were held accountable. Mr Bagnall [for Boardman] argued that the present case is distinguishable. He puts his argument thus. The question you ask is whether the information could have been used by the principal for the purpose for which it was used by his agents? If the answer to that question is no, the information was not used in the course of their duty as agents. In the present case the information could never have been used by the trustees for the purpose of purchasing shares in the company; therefore purchase of shares was outside the scope of the appellant's agency and they are not accountable.

This is an attractive argument, but it does not seem to me to give due weight to the fact that the appellants obtained both the information which satisfied them that the purchase of the shares would be a good investment and the opportunity of acquiring them as a result of acting for certain purposes on behalf of the trustees. Information is, of course, not property in the strict sense of that word and, as I have already stated, it does not necessarily follow that because an agent acquired information and opportunity while acting in a fiduciary capacity he is accountable to his principals for any profit that comes his way as the result of the use he makes of that information and opportunity. His liability to account must depend on the facts of the case. In the present case much of the information came the appellants' way when Mr Boardman was acting on behalf of the trustees on the instructions of Mr Fox and the opportunity of bidding for the shares came because he purported for all purposes except for making the bid to be acting on behalf of the owners of the 8,000 shares in the company. In these circumstances it seems to me that the principle of the *Regal* case applies and that the courts below came to the right conclusion.

LORD HODSON: It cannot, in my opinion, be said that the purchase of shares in Lester & Harris was outside the scope of the fiduciary relationship in which Mr Boardman stood to the trust.

The confidential information which the appellants obtained at a time when Mr Boardman was admittedly holding himself out as solicitor for the trustees was obtained by him as representing the trustees, the holders of 8,000 shares of Lester & Harris. As Russell LJ put it [1965] Ch 1992, 1031:

> The substantial trust shareholding was an asset of which one aspect was its potential use as a means of acquiring knowledge of the company's affairs, or of negotiating allocations of the company's assets, or of inducing other shareholders to part with their shares.

Whether this aspect is properly to be regarded as part of the trust assets is, in my judgment, immaterial. The appellants obtained knowledge by reason of their fiduciary position and they cannot escape liability by saying that they were acting for themselves and not as agents of the trustees. Whether or not the trust or the beneficiaries in their stead could have taken advantage of the information is immaterial, as the authorities clearly show. No doubt it was but a remote possibility that Mr Boardman would ever be asked by the trustees to advise on the desirability of an application to the court in order that the trustees might avail themselves of the information obtained. Nevertheless, even if the possibility of conflict is present between personal interests and the fiduciary position the rule of equity must be applied. This appears from the observations of Lord Cranworth LC in *Aberdeen Railway Co.* v *Blaikie Brothers* (1854) 1 Macq 461, 471.

NOTES

1. It is not easy to discern the *ratio* of this 3:2 decision, although it seems that whereas the majority thought it enough simply to profit from the trust, Viscount Dilhorne and Lord Upjohn (dissenting) thought that this was insufficient, in the absence of a clear conflict of interest. They took the view that there was no conflict or possibility of a conflict between the personal interests of the appellants and those of the trust.

2. Unfortunately, the position is muddied because the majority also took the view that there was a (somewhat theoretical) conflict of interest also: the trust might have changed its mind and sought to buy the shares itself, in which case Boardman, as solicitor to the trust, would have had to advise on the application to court. It may be, therefore, that the case does not extend existing principles, except in showing how willing the courts are to find even the most theoretical possibility of a conflict of interest.

3. A further difficulty about *Boardman* v *Phipps* is that in the Court of Appeal [1965] Ch 992, Russell LJ had decided the case on an entirely different ground, that all the information acquired by Boardman, in his fiduciary capacity, became trust property. Lords Hodson and Guest also seemed to be of this view. In *A-G for Hong Kong* v *Reid*, Lord Templeman (discussing *Keech* v *Sandford*) also appears to accept that:

   > ... property which a trustee obtains by use of knowledge acquired as trustee becomes trust property.

   In *Boardman* v *Phipps*, Lord Cohen appeared less sure about the trust property point, but was happy to decide the case on causation alone.

   The property reasoning raises serious difficulties (see, e.g. Gareth Jones (1968) 84 *LQR* 472), especially where information is obtained by somebody who is trustee to several trusts, or where the information is passed on to other, innocent recipients, who also profit from it. Partly for these reasons, Viscount Dilhorne, adopting the views of Lindley LJ in *Aas* v *Benham* [1891] 2 Ch 244, said that information was not the property of the trust, and Lord Upjohn's views were similar. Certainly, the information as trust property reasoning is not part of the *ratio* in the House of Lords.

■ QUESTION

1. Do you think that this decision might stifle entrepreneurial spirit?
2. Was there any possibility that, by acting in his own interests, Boardman might have compromised the interests of the trust? Or were their interests really the same?

NOTES: Although the *ratio* of *Boardman* v *Phipps* is not very clear, the weight of authority probably supports the proposition that all that is required is to find a causal connection between the fiduciary's position and the profit obtained. If Boardman would have purchased the shares anyway, even without the information acquired by virtue of his fiduciary position, there would have been no causal connection between the position and the profit, and the case would have been like *Re Gee*. If not, the case is similar to *Re Macadam*, and Boardman was properly held to account.

Matthew Conaglen, 'The Nature and Function of Fiduciary Loyalty'
(2005) 121 *LQR* 452, pp. 461–2

The proposition that the function of fiduciary duties is to protect the proper performance of non-fiduciary duties is best illustrated by reference to the fundamental fiduciary principle that prohibits a fiduciary from acting where there is a 'real sensible possibility of conflict' between his duty and his personal interest. In *Aberdeen Railway Co* v *Blaikie Bros*, Lord Cranworth L.C. stated the principle in clear terms:

> 'it is a rule of universal application, that no one having [fiduciary] duties to discharge, shall be allowed to enter into engagements in which he has, or can have, a personal interest conflicting, or which may possibly conflict, with the interests of those whom he is bound to protect.'

... It is important to be clear here about the two kinds of duty involved: the fiduciary duty prohibits conflict between duty and interest, but there is also a non-fiduciary duty, the protection of which is the purpose of the fiduciary duty. In *Blaikie Bros*, for example, Blaikie owed a non-fiduciary duty to the company to negotiate contracts on behalf of the company on terms most beneficial to the company. That duty arose because of his position as a director of the company, but it is not a fiduciary duty. If a director acts incompetently in negotiating a contract, he acts in breach of a duty owed to the company, but he does not thereby commit a breach of fiduciary duty. The fiduciary duty is separate, designed to protect proper performance of the non-fiduciary duty from inconsistent influences; it prohibits the fiduciary from acting in a situation where he has a personal interest which is inconsistent with his non-fiduciary duty.

NOTES

1. Conaglen argues that the fiduciary duty is purely accessory or 'subsidiary' to non-fiduciary duties, the function of fiduciary duties being merely 'to protect the proper performance of non-fiduciary duties' (p. 480) by prohibiting 'the fiduciary from acting in a situation where he has a personal interest which is inconsistent with his non-fiduciary duty' (p. 462). It is a sophisticated analysis, but it may be unlikely to influence or predict the outcome of cases. We will see throughout this chapter that the enforcement of fiduciary duties is, as Conaglen himself admits, 'ultimately one of public policy' (p. 478). The same author has more recently extended his argument (that fiduciary duties are merely subsidiary to non-fiduciary duties) to the fiduciary duty to avoid conflicts between duties to different principals ('Fiduciary regulation of conflicts between duties' (2009) 125 *LQR* 111–41).
2. A trustee will not be removed simply because he has interests in conflict with the trust, provided the trust can function properly without him ever having to choose between the trust and his private interests (*Public Trustee* v *Cooper* [2001] WTLR 901), and an occasional error by a trustee is not of itself a ground for removal (*Isaac* v *Isaac* [2005] EWHC 435 (Ch) at para. [73]).
3. In *United Pan-Europe Communications NV* v *Deutsche Bank AG* [2000] 2 BCLC 461, CA, Morritt LJ stated that, if there is a fiduciary duty of loyalty and if the conduct complained of falls within the scope of that fiduciary duty, he could see no justification for any further requirement that the profit shall have been obtained by the fiduciary 'by virtue of his position'. Does His Lordship's approach necessarily require us to abandon a 'causation' basis for the fiduciary duty to account for unauthorised profits?

E: Relaxation of the strict rule of fiduciary loyalty?

John H. Langbein, 'Questioning the Trust Law Duty of Loyalty: Sole Interest or Best Interest?'

(2005) 114 *Yale LJ* 929, pp. 987–90

Because the trust relationship places the beneficiary's property under the control of the trustee, the danger inheres that the trustee will misappropriate the property for personal advantage. The duty of loyalty, which forbids that behavior, is an essential principle of trust fiduciary law. The question raised in this Article is not whether to retain the duty of loyalty but how best to formulate it. What is wrong with the duty as presently formulated in the sole interest rule is that it emphasizes a particular enforcement technique (avoiding all conflict or overlap of interest between trustee and trust property), as opposed to the underlying purpose that the technique is meant to serve, which is to maximize the beneficiary's best interest.

So long as there is no divergence between sole interest and best interest, and often there is none, nothing turns on the distinction. However, by refusing to allow the trustee to defend a particular conflict on the ground that it was prudently undertaken in the best interest of the beneficiaries, the sole interest rule conclusively presumes that all overlap or conflict of interest between trustee and trust entails misappropriation. I have explained in this Article why the law should allow inquiry into the merits of a trustee's defense that the conduct in question served the best interest of the beneficiary. In recommending that change, I have emphasized four profound historical changes over the past two centuries in the circumstances of trusteeship that have undermined the original premises of the sole interest rule:

(1) The revolution in civil procedure associated with fusion has provided trust-enforcing courts with an adequate system of fact-finding, casting doubt upon the early-nineteenth-century preference for prophylaxis over cure that is embodied in the sole interest rule. What previously had to be done by crude overdeterrence can now be done by rational inquiry into the circumstances of a transaction.

(2) As the trust has changed function, from a device for holding and transferring family real estate into its characteristic modern role as a management regime for a portfolio of financial assets, trusteeship has changed character. The gentleman amateur, serving as a matter of honor, with few duties, few powers, and no particular skills, has largely given way to the fee-paid professional, who brings managerial resources commensurate with the investment and administrative challenges of the modern trust.

(3) The professionalization of trust administration, together with the data processing revolution, has led to large improvements in trust recordkeeping and record retention. Those changes are now reflected in the standards of trust fiduciary law and are reinforced by an expanded duty of disclosure to the trust beneficiary. Thus, routine trust administration now greatly reduces the danger that so motivated the sole interest rule, the fear that without a prohibitory rule a conflicted trustee could easily conceal evidence of misappropriation.

(4) Professionalization has transformed trusteeship into a commercial relationship, now centered in the financial services industry, typically in bank trust departments. Like any other professional services industry, the trust industry is based on patterns of mutual benefit that the sole interest paradigm does not accurately capture. Professional trustees do not serve for honor, they serve for hire; accordingly, they serve not in the sole interest of the beneficiary but also to make money for themselves and their shareholders. The first great breach in the sole interest rule was the American rule allowing reasonable compensation to trustees. Thereafter, pressure to allow the economies of integration associated with in-house financial services has resulted in case law and legislation further diminishing the scope of the sole interest rule, as evidenced in the exceptions for self-deposit on the trustee's banking side, for common trust funds, and now for affiliated mutual funds. What has driven these waves of reduction in the ambit of the sole interest rule is the realization that each advances the best interest of the beneficiary. In such circumstances, a rule recognizing mutual benefit is better than insisting upon the sole interest rule. Quite similar thinking underlies the movement to permit extra compensation for trustee-provided professional services.

The central thesis of this Article is that these great changes in the character and practice of modern trusteeship make the sole interest rule outmoded. The reform urged here is to allow a conflicted trustee to defend on the ground that the particular transaction was prudently undertaken in the best interest of the beneficiaries. Permitting this defense would effectively turn the sole interest rule into a best interest rule. I have explained that, procedurally, the way to implement the change is to reduce the presumption of wrongdoing that now attaches to a conflict-tinged transaction from conclusive to rebuttable, allowing the trustee to show that the conflict was harmless or beneficial.

This Article points to the successful experience that trust law has acquired in applying the best interest standard under the long-established advance-approval doctrine. When the trustee petitions the court to authorize a conflicted transaction, the court applies the best interest test. I have also emphasized the experience in the law of corporations, where the trust law sole interest rule has been abandoned in favor of the modern corporate regime for conflicted directors' transactions, under which mutually beneficial conflicts are permitted when evaluated under appropriate safeguards for the corporation. I have pointed to a variety of reasons for thinking that the reform would be unlikely to increase, and might in fact decrease, litigation levels about loyalty matters.

The sole interest rule works needless harm on trust beneficiaries and trustees. Cases like *Boardman v Phipps* and doctrines such as the rule that the trustee cannot bid on trust property at a public auction deter trustee conduct that would be manifestly beneficial to the trust beneficiary, on the ground that the law must inflict such harm in order to prevent trustees from misappropriating trust property in quite different cases. Allowing a best interest defense would cut back on the mischief worked under the sole interest rule while still maintaining the deterrent to trustee disloyalty. In a case such as *Boardman v Phipps* or in the most embarrassing of the auction cases, the sole interest rule takes away a benefit from the trustee who earned it and awards it to the trust beneficiary. In these cases trust law works unjust enrichment, in ugly tension with the equity tradition of preventing unjust enrichment. Adjusting the duty of loyalty as suggested would eliminate that stain on our fundamentally sound tradition of encouraging faithful trusteeship.

Wrexham Association Football Club Ltd v *Crucialmove Ltd*

[2006] EWCA Civ 237, Court of Appeal (Civ Div)

SIR PETER GIBSON (para. [51]): It was said … that recent cases show that the law in this area is open to development, and reference was made to the *obiter* remarks of Arden LJ in *Murad* v *Al-Saraj* [2005] EWCA Civ 939 at paragraphs 82–83 to the effect that the harshness of the equitable principle might be tempered by a modern court in some circumstances. For my part I cannot see how any such tempering could be done by a court below the House of Lords and I very much doubt if the present case would be seen to be an appropriate case for the relaxation of the principle.

NOTES: In fact, in *Murad* v *Al-Saraj*, Arden LJ expressly acknowledged that the question of relaxing the strict rule of fiduciary loyalty and accountability 'must be left to another court' (para. [82]).

■ **QUESTION**

How does the Voltaire passage parallel the strict enforcement of the fiduciary duty?

Voltaire, *Candide*

(Paris: Sirène, 1759), Chapter 23

As they were chatting together they arrived at Portsmouth. The shore on each side of the harbour was lined with a multitude of people, whose eyes were steadfastly fixed on a robust man who was kneeling down on the deck of one of the men-of-war, with his eyes bandaged. Opposite to this person stood four soldiers, each of whom shot three bullets into his skull, with all the composure imaginable; and when it was done, the whole company went away perfectly well satisfied.

'What the devil is all this for?' said Candide, 'and what demon, or foe of mankind, lords it thus tyrannically over the world?' He then asked who was that robust man who had been sent out of the world so ceremonially. When he received for answer, that it was an admiral. 'And pray why do you put your admiral to death?'

'Because he did not put a sufficient number of his fellow creatures to death. You must know, he had an engagement with a French admiral, and it has been proved against him that he was not near enough to his antagonist.'

'But,' replied Candide, 'the French admiral must have been as far from him.'

'There is no doubt of that; but in this country it is found desirable, now and then, to put an admiral to death, in order to encourage the others' (*dans ce pays-ci il est bon de tuer de temps en temps un amiral pour encourager les autres*).

The answer, of course, is that fiduciary duties are enforced strictly to set a public example to be followed.

F: Trustee remuneration

TRUSTEE ACT 2000

PART V REMUNERATION

28. Trustee's entitlement to payment under trust instrument

(1) Except to the extent (if any) to which the trust instrument makes inconsistent provision, subsections (2) to (4) apply to a trustee if—

(a) there is a provision in the trust instrument entitling him to receive payment out of trust funds in respect of services provided by him to or on behalf of the trust, and

(b) the trustee is a trust corporation or is acting in a professional capacity.

(2) The trustee is to be treated as entitled under the trust instrument to receive payment in respect of services even if they are services which are capable of being provided by a lay trustee.

(3) Subsection (2) applies to a trustee of a charitable trust who is not a trust corporation only—

(a) if he is not a sole trustee, and

(b) to the extent that a majority of the other trustees have agreed that it should apply to him.

(4) Any payments to which the trustee is entitled in respect of services are to be treated as remuneration for services (and not as a gift) for the purposes of—

(a) section 15 of the M1Wills Act 1837 (gifts to an attesting witness to be void), and

(b) section 34(3) of the M2Administration of Estates Act 1925 (order in which estate to be paid out).

(5) For the purposes of this Part, a trustee acts in a professional capacity if he acts in the course of a profession or business which consists of or includes the provision of services in connection with—

(a) the management or administration of trusts generally or a particular kind of trust, or

(b) any particular aspect of the management or administration of trusts generally or a particular kind of trust,

and the services he provides to or on behalf of the trust fall within that description.

(6) For the purposes of this Part, a person acts as a lay trustee if he—

(a) is not a trust corporation, and

(b) does not act in a professional capacity.

29. Remuneration of certain trustees

(1) Subject to subsection (5), a trustee who—

(a) is a trust corporation, but

(b) is not a trustee of a charitable trust, is entitled to receive reasonable remuneration out of the trust funds for any services that the trust corporation provides on behalf of the trust.

(2) Subject to subsection (5), a trustee who—

(a) acts in a professional capacity, but

(b) is not a trust corporation, a trustee of a charitable trust or a sole trustee,

is entitled to receive reasonable remuneration out of the trust funds for any services that he provides on behalf of the trust if each other trustee has agreed in writing that he may be remunerated for the services.

(3) 'Reasonable remuneration' means, in relation to the provision of services by a trustee, such remuneration as is reasonable in the circumstances for the provision of those services on behalf of that trust by that trustee ...

(4) A trustee is entitled to remuneration under this section even if the services in question are capable of being provided by a lay trustee.

(5) A trustee is not entitled to remuneration under this section if any provision about his entitlement to remuneration has been made—

(a) by the trust instrument, or

(b) by any enactment or any provision of subordinate legislation.

(6) This section applies to a trustee who has been authorised under a power conferred by Part IV or the trust instrument—

(a) to exercise functions as an agent of the trustees, or

(b) to act as a nominee or custodian,

as it applies to any other trustee.

30. Remuneration of trustees of charitable trusts

(1) The Secretary of State may by regulations make provision for the remuneration of trustees of charitable trusts.

(2) The power under subsection (1) includes power to make provision for the remuneration of a trustee who has been authorised under a power conferred by Part IV or the trust instrument—

(a) to exercise functions as an agent of the trustees, or

(b) to act as a nominee or custodian.

(3) Regulations under this section may—

(a) make different provision for different cases;

(b) contain such supplemental, incidental, consequential and transitional provision as the Secretary of State considers appropriate.

(4) The power to make regulations under this section is exercisable by statutory instrument which shall be subject to annulment in pursuance of a resolution of either House of Parliament.

31. Trustees' expenses

(1) A trustee is entitled to be reimbursed out of the trust funds for expenses properly incurred when acting on behalf of the trust.

(2) This section applies to a trustee who has been authorised under a power conferred by Part IV or the trust instrument—

(a) to exercise functions as an agent of the trustees, or

(b) to act as a nominee or custodian,

as it applies to any other trustee.

Re Duke of Norfolk's ST

[1982] Ch 61, [1981] 3 All ER 220, Court of Appeal

Decision: The court has an inherent jurisdiction to authorise the payment of trustees, or increase the remuneration authorised under the trust instrument, if to do so would be beneficial to the administration of the trust.

FOX LJ: *Chapman v Chapman* [1954] AC 429 [see Chapter 9], it seems to me, was concerned with the power of the court to authorise variations in the beneficial interests as such. The present problem is different. It is concerned not with beneficial interests as such, but with the administration of the trust fund.

When the court authorises payment of remuneration to a trustee under its inherent jurisdiction it is, I think, exercising its ancient jurisdiction to secure the competent administration of the trust property just as it has done when it appoints or removes a trustee under its inherent jurisdiction. The result, in my view, is that there is nothing in the principle stated in *Chapman* v *Chapman* [1954] AC 429 which is inconsistent with the existence of an inherent jurisdiction in the court to increase the remuneration payable to trustees under the trust instrument. In my view, therefore, neither of the two objections which have been raised as to existence of such a jurisdiction is well founded.

There remains the question whether, on principle and authority, we can properly infer that the jurisdiction does exist. As to principle, it seems to me that, if the court has jurisdiction, as it has, on the appointment of a trustee to authorise remuneration though no such power exists in the trust instrument, there is no logical reason why the court should not have power to increase the remuneration given by the instrument. In many cases the latter may involve a smaller interference with the provisions of the trust instrument than the former. Further, the law has not stopped short at authorising remuneration to a trustee only if he seeks the authority at the time when he accepts the trusts ...

I conclude that the court has an inherent jurisdiction to authorise the payment of remuneration of trustees and that that jurisdiction extends to increasing the remuneration authorised by the trust instrument. In exercising that jurisdiction the court has to balance two influences which are to some extent in conflict. The first is that the office of trustee is, as such, gratuitous; the court will accordingly be careful to protect the interests of the beneficiaries against claims by the trustees. The second is that it is of great importance to the beneficiaries that the trust should be well administered. If therefore the court concludes, having regard to the nature of the trust, to the experience and skill of a particular trustee and to the amounts which he seeks to charge when compared with what other trustees might require to be paid for their services and to all the other circumstances of the case, that it would be in the interests of the beneficiaries to increase the remuneration, then the court may properly do so.

G: The duty of personal service

(i) Powers of individual delegation

TRUSTEE DELEGATION ACT 1999

4. Enduring powers

(1) Section 3(3) of the Enduring Powers of Attorney Act 1985 (which entitles the donee of an enduring power to exercise any of the donor's functions as trustee and to give receipt for capital money etc.) does not apply to enduring powers created after the commencement of this Act.

(2) Section 3(3) of the Enduring Powers of Attorney Act 1985 ceases to apply to enduring powers created before the commencement of this Act—

    (a) where subsection (3) below applies, in accordance with that subsection, and

    (b) otherwise, at the end of the period of one year from that commencement.

    ...

TRUSTEE ACT 1925

25. Delegation of trustee's functions by power of attorney [as substituted by Trustee Delegation Act 1999, s.5]

(1) Notwithstanding any rule of law or equity to the contrary, a trustee may, by power of attorney, delegate the execution or exercise of all or any of the trusts, powers and discretions vested in him as trustee either alone or jointly with any other person or persons.

(2) A delegation under this section—

    (a) commences as provided by the instrument creating the power or, if the instrument makes no provision as to the commencement of the delegation, with the date of the execution of the instrument by the donor; and

(b) continues for a period of twelve months or any shorter period provided by the instrument creating the power.

(3) The persons who may be donees of a power of attorney under this section include a trust corporation.

(4) Before or within seven days after giving a power of attorney under this section the donor shall give written notice of it (specifying the date on which the power comes into operation and its duration, the donee of the power, the reason why the power is given and, where some only are delegated, the trusts, powers and discretions delegated) to—

(a) each person (other than himself), if any, who under any instrument creating the trust has power (whether alone or jointly) to appoint a new trustee; and

(b) each of the other trustees, if any; but failure to comply with this subsection shall not, in favour of a person dealing with the donee of the power, invalidate any act done or instrument executed by the donee.

(5) A power of attorney given under this section by a single donor—

(a) in the form set out in subsection (6) of this section; or

(b) in a form to the like effect but expressed to be made under this subsection,

shall operate to delegate to the person identified in the form as the single donee of the power the execution and exercise of all the trusts, powers and discretions vested in the donor as trustee (either alone or jointly with any other person or persons) under the single trust so identified.

(6) The form referred to in subsection (5) of this section is as follows—

> 'THIS GENERAL TRUSTEE POWER OF ATTORNEY is made on [date] by [name of one donor] of [address of donor] as trustee of [name or details of one trust]
>
> I appoint [name of one donee] of [address of donee] to be my attorney [if desired, the date on which the delegation commences or the period for which it continues (or both)] in accordance with section 25(5) of the Trustee Act 1925.
>
> [To be executed as a deed]'.

(7) The donor of a power of attorney given under this section shall be liable for the acts or defaults of the donee in the same manner as if they were the acts or defaults of the donor.

(8) For the purpose of executing or exercising the trusts or powers delegated to him, the donee may exercise any of the powers conferred on the donor as trustee by statute or by the instrument creating the trust, including power, for the purpose of the transfer of any inscribed stock, himself to delegate to an attorney power to transfer, but not including the power of delegation conferred by this section.

(9) The fact that it appears from any power of attorney given under this section, or from any evidence required for the purposes of any such power of attorney or otherwise, that in dealing with any stock the donee of the power is acting in the execution of a trust shall not be deemed for any purpose to affect any person in whose books the stock is inscribed or registered with any notice of the trust.

(10) This section applies to a personal representative, tenant for life and statutory owner as it applies to a trustee except that subsection (4) shall apply as if it required the notice there mentioned to be given—

(a) in the case of a personal representative, to each of the other personal representatives, if any, except any executor who has renounced probate;

(b) in the case of a tenant for life, to the trustees of the settlement and to each person, if any, who together with the person giving the notice constitutes the tenant for life; and

(c) in the case of a statutory owner, to each of the persons, if any, who together with the person giving the notice constitute the statutory owner and, in the case of a statutory owner by virtue of section 23(1)(a) of the Settled Land Act 1925, to the trustees of the settlement.

NOTES

1. Originally, this section (which allows trustees individually to delegate all their functions, including fiduciary powers) applied only when the trustee was absent from the United Kingdom, the

idea being that it was necessary for trustees to have this power while they were temporarily abroad, but the present provision allows trustees, by power of attorney, generally to delegate all or any of their powers and discretions for a period not exceeding 12 months. The effect of s.25(7), however, is that there is no equivalent to s.30 protection where a trustee delegates under s.25, as opposed to appointing an agent under s.23: trustees are vicariously liable for the defaults of those to whom the power has been delegated under s.25.

2. Note that there is no equivalent of the original s.25(2), preventing delegation to the only other co-trustee.

(ii) Powers of collective delegation

TRUSTEE ACT 2000

PART IV AGENTS, NOMINEES AND CUSTODIANS

11. Power to employ agents

(1) Subject to the provisions of this Part, the trustees of a trust may authorise any person to exercise any or all of their delegable functions as their agent.

(2) In the case of a trust other than a charitable trust, the trustees' delegable functions consist of any function other than—

(a) any function relating to whether or in what way any assets of the trust should be distributed,

(b) any power to decide whether any fees or other payment due to be made out of the trust funds should be made out of income or capital,

(c) any power to appoint a person to be a trustee of the trust, or

(d) any power conferred by any other enactment or the trust instrument which permits the trustees to delegate any of their functions or to appoint a person to act as a nominee or custodian.

(3) In the case of a charitable trust, the trustees' delegable functions are—

(a) any function consisting of carrying out a decision that the trustees have taken;

(b) any function relating to the investment of assets subject to the trust (including, in the case of land acquired as an investment, managing the land and creating or disposing of an interest in the land);

(c) any function relating to the raising of funds for the trust otherwise than by means of profits of a trade which is an integral part of carrying out the trust's charitable purpose;

(d) any other function prescribed by an order made by the Secretary of State.

(4) For the purposes of subsection (3)(c) a trade is an integral part of carrying out a trust's charitable purpose if, whether carried on in the United Kingdom or elsewhere, the profits are applied solely to the purposes of the trust and either—

(a) the trade is exercised in the course of the actual carrying out of a primary purpose of the trust, or

(b) the work in connection with the trade is mainly carried out by beneficiaries of the trust.

(5) The power to make an order under subsection (3)(d) is exercisable by statutory instrument which shall be subject to annulment in pursuance of a resolution of either House of Parliament.

12. Persons who may act as agents

(1) Subject to subsection (2), the persons whom the trustees may under section 11 authorise to exercise functions as their agent include one or more of their number.

(2) The trustees may not authorise two (or more) persons to exercise the same function unless they are to exercise the function jointly.

(3) The trustees may not under section 11 authorise a beneficiary to exercise any function as their agent.

(4) The trustees may under section 11 authorise a person to exercise functions as their agent even though he is also appointed to act as their nominee or custodian (whether under section 16, 17 or 18 or any other power).

13. Linked functions etc.

(1) Subject to subsections (2) and (5), a person who is authorised under section 11 to exercise a function is (whatever the terms of the agency) subject to any specific duties or restrictions attached to the function.

> For example, a person who is authorised under section 11 to exercise the general power of investment is subject to the duties under section 4 in relation to that power.

(2) A person who is authorised under section 11 to exercise a power which is subject to a requirement to obtain advice is not subject to the requirement if he is the kind of person from whom it would have been proper for the trustees, in compliance with the requirement, to obtain advice.

(3) Subsections (4) and (5) apply to a trust to which section 11(1) of the Trusts of Land and Appointment of Trustees Act 1996 (duties to consult beneficiaries and give effect to their wishes) applies.

(4) The trustees may not under section 11 authorise a person to exercise any of their functions on terms that prevent them from complying with section 11(1) of the 1996 Act.

(5) A person who is authorised under section 11 to exercise any function relating to land subject to the trust is not subject to section 11(1) of the 1996 Act.

14. Terms of agency

(1) Subject to subsection (2) and sections 15(2) and 29 to 32, the trustees may authorise a person to exercise functions as their agent on such terms as to remuneration and other matters as they may determine.

(2) The trustees may not authorise a person to exercise functions as their agent on any of the terms mentioned in subsection (3) unless it is reasonably necessary for them to do so.

(3) The terms are—

   (a) a term permitting the agent to appoint a substitute;
   (b) a term restricting the liability of the agent or his substitute to the trustees or any beneficiary;
   (c) a term permitting the agent to act in circumstances capable of giving rise to a conflict of interest.

15. Asset management: special restrictions

(1) The trustees may not authorise a person to exercise any of their asset management functions as their agent except by an agreement which is in or evidenced in writing.

(2) The trustees may not authorise a person to exercise any of their asset management functions as their agent unless—

   (a) they have prepared a statement that gives guidance as to how the functions should be exercised ('a policy statement'), and
   (b) the agreement under which the agent is to act includes a term to the effect that he will secure compliance with—
       (i)   the policy statement, or
       (ii) if the policy statement is revised or replaced under section 22, the revised or replacement policy statement.

(3) The trustees must formulate any guidance given in the policy statement with a view to ensuring that the functions will be exercised in the best interests of the trust.

(4) The policy statement must be in or evidenced in writing.

(5) The asset management functions of trustees are their functions relating to—

   (a) the investment of assets subject to the trust,
   (b) the acquisition of property which is to be subject to the trust, and
   (c) managing property which is subject to the trust and disposing of, or creating or disposing of an interest in, such property.

16. Power to appoint nominees

(1) Subject to the provisions of this Part, the trustees of a trust may—

(a) appoint a person to act as their nominee in relation to such of the assets of the trust as they determine, and

(b) take such steps as are necessary to secure that those assets are vested in a person so appointed.

(2) An appointment under this section must be in or evidenced in writing.

(3) This section does not apply to any trust having a custodian trustee.

17. Power to appoint custodians

(1) Subject to the provisions of this Part, the trustees of a trust may appoint a person to act as a custodian in relation to such of the assets of the trust as they may determine.

(2) For the purposes of this Act a person is a custodian in relation to assets if he undertakes the safe custody of the assets or of any documents or records concerning the assets.

(3) An appointment under this section must be in or evidenced in writing.

(4) This section does not apply to any trust having a custodian trustee.

18. Investment in bearer securities

(1) If trustees retain or invest in securities payable to bearer, they must appoint a person to act as a custodian of the securities.

(2) Subsection (1) does not apply if the trust instrument contains provision which (however expressed) permits the trustees to retain or invest in securities payable to bearer without appointing a person to act as a custodian.

(3) An appointment under this section must be in or evidenced in writing.

(4) This section does not apply to any trust having a custodian trustee.

19. Persons who may be appointed as nominees or custodians

(1) A person may not be appointed under section 16, 17 or 18 as a nominee or custodian unless one of the relevant conditions is satisfied.

(2) The relevant conditions are that—

(a) the person carries on a business which consists of or includes acting as a nominee or custodian;

(b) the person is a body corporate which is controlled by the trustees.

(3) The question whether a body corporate is controlled by trustees is to be determined in accordance with section 840 of the Income and Corporation Taxes Act 1988.

(4) The trustees of a charitable trust which is not an exempt charity must act in accordance with any guidance given by the Charity Commissioners concerning the selection of a person for appointment as a nominee or custodian under section 16, 17 or 18.

(5) Subject to subsections (1) and (4), the persons whom the trustees may under section 16, 17 or 18 appoint as a nominee or custodian include—

(a) one of their number, if that one is a trust corporation, or

(b) two (or more) of their number, if they are to act as joint nominees or joint custodians.

(6) The trustees may under section 16 appoint a person to act as their nominee even though he is also—

(a) appointed to act as their custodian (whether under section 17 or 18 or any other power), or

(b) authorised to exercise functions as their agent (whether under section 11 or any other power).

(7) Likewise, the trustees may under section 17 or 18 appoint a person to act as their custodian even though he is also—

(a) appointed to act as their nominee (whether under section 16 or any other power), or

(b) authorised to exercise functions as their agent (whether under section 11 or any other power).

20. Terms of appointment of nominees and custodians

(1) Subject to subsection (2) and sections 29 to 32, the trustees may under section 16, 17 or 18 appoint a person to act as a nominee or custodian on such terms as to remuneration and other matters as they may determine.

(2) The trustees may not under section 16, 17 or 18 appoint a person to act as a nominee or custodian on any of the terms mentioned in subsection (3) unless it is reasonably necessary for them to do so.

(3) The terms are—

(a) a term permitting the nominee or custodian to appoint a substitute;

(b) a term restricting the liability of the nominee or custodian or his substitute to the trustees or to any beneficiary;

(c) a term permitting the nominee or custodian to act in circumstances capable of giving rise to a conflict of interest.

21. Application of sections 22 and 23

(1) Sections 22 and 23 apply in a case where trustees have, under section 11, 16, 17 or 18—

(a) authorised a person to exercise functions as their agent, or

(b) appointed a person to act as a nominee or custodian.

(2) Subject to subsection (3), sections 22 and 23 also apply in a case where trustees have, under any power conferred on them by the trust instrument—

(a) authorised a person to exercise functions as their agent, or

(b) appointed a person to act as a nominee or custodian.

(3) If the application of section 22 or 23 is inconsistent with the terms of the trust instrument, the section in question does not apply.

22. Review of agents, nominees and custodians

(1) While the agent, nominee or custodian continues to act for the trust, the trustees—

(a) must keep under review the arrangements under which the agent, nominee or custodian acts and how those arrangements are being put into effect,

(b) if circumstances make it appropriate to do so, must consider whether there is a need to exercise any power of intervention that they have, and

(c) if they consider that there is a need to exercise such a power, must do so.

(2) If the agent has been authorised to exercise asset management functions, the duty under subsection (1) includes, in particular—

(a) a duty to consider whether there is any need to revise or replace the policy statement made for the purposes of section 15,

(b) if they consider that there is a need to revise or replace the policy statement, a duty to do so, and

(c) a duty to assess whether the policy statement (as it has effect for the time being) is being complied with.

(3) Subsections (3) and (4) of section 15 apply to the revision or replacement of a policy statement under this section as they apply to the making of a policy statement under that section.

(4) 'Power of intervention' includes—

(a) a power to give directions to the agent, nominee or custodian;

(b) a power to revoke the authorisation or appointment.

23. Liability for agents, nominees and custodians

(1) A trustee is not liable for any act or default of the agent, nominee or custodian unless he has failed to comply with the duty of care applicable to him, under paragraph 3 of Schedule 1—

(a) when entering into the arrangements under which the person acts as agent, nominee or custodian, or

(b) when carrying out his duties under section 22.

(2) If a trustee has agreed a term under which the agent, nominee or custodian is permitted to appoint a substitute, the trustee is not liable for any act or default of the substitute unless he has failed to comply with the duty of care applicable to him, under paragraph 3 of Schedule 1—

    (a)   when agreeing that term, or

    (b)   when carrying out his duties under section 22 in so far as they relate to the use of the substitute.

24. Effect of trustees exceeding their powers

A failure by the trustees to act within the limits of the powers conferred by this Part—

    (a)   in authorising a person to exercise a function of theirs as an agent, or

    (b)   in appointing a person to act as a nominee or custodian,

        does not invalidate the authorisation or appointment.

25. Sole trustees

(1)   Subject to subsection (2), this Part applies in relation to a trust having a sole trustee as it applies in relation to other trusts (and references in this Part to trustees—except in sections 12(1) and (3) and 19(5)—are to be read accordingly).

(2)   Section 18 does not impose a duty on a sole trustee if that trustee is a trust corporation.

26. Restriction or exclusion of this Part etc.

The powers conferred by this Part are—

    (a)   in addition to powers conferred on trustees otherwise than by this Act, but

    (b)   subject to any restriction or exclusion imposed by the trust instrument or by any enactment or any provision of subordinate legislation.

27. Existing Trusts

This Part applies in relation to trusts whether created before or after its commencement.

(iii) Duties with regard to delegation

Fry v *Tapson*

(1884) 28 ChD 268, Chancery Division

Facts: The trustees in this case had decided to invest in a mortgage of freehold land, such an investment being authorised under the terms of their trust. However, the trustees appointed a London-based valuer to value land in Liverpool and, what is more, the valuer was an agent of the proposed mortgagor and thus had a financial interest in inflating the value of the security. The valuer had been recommended by the trustees' solicitors. In the event, the valuation turned out to have been inflated and proved to be inadequate security when the mortgagor became bankrupt in due course.

Held: The trustees did not exercise sufficient care in their choice of agent. An agent should always be chosen to act within the agent's proper sphere of expertise: a London-based solicitor should not have been chosen to value a property in Liverpool. Further, the trustees had failed to consider the accuracy of the agent's valuation, but accepted it at face value. Although it was not doubted that the trustees had acted honestly, they had failed to act as ordinary prudent persons of business would have acted in business of their own and they would accordingly be liable to account to the beneficiaries for the losses caused through their lack of prudence.

KAY J: ... *Speight* v *Gaunt* did not lay down any new rule, but only illustrated a very old one, viz., that trustees acting according to the ordinary course of business, and employing agents as a prudent man of business would do on his own behalf, are not liable for the default of an agent so employed. But an obvious limitation of that rule is that the agent must not be employed out of the ordinary scope of his business. If a trustee employs an agent to do that which is not the ordinary business of such an agent, and he performs that unusual duty improperly, and loss is thereby occasioned, the trustee would not be exonerated.

Suppose, for example, that in selling trust property, or changing an investment, trustees were to allow the trust fund to pass into the hands of their solicitors, and that it was lost in consequence, they would be liable. I take that illustration because I am afraid it not unfrequently happens that trustees do allow trust funds to be in their solicitors' hands without sufficient reason. It would be no excuse to say, as one of the witnesses said in this case, 'Solicitors often do so.' The question is not what they often do, but what is properly within the scope of their employment as solicitors.

SUMMATIVE QUESTION

online resource centre

In his book, *Property and Justice* (Oxford: Clarendon Press, 1996), Professor J. W. Harris observed that the strict rule that a fiduciary must account for unauthorised profit 'confers the windfall constituted by the fiduciary's profit, not on the community, but on his principal', with the result that the principal is entitled to claim it in preference to the fiduciary's creditors. Professor Harris asks: 'Why should the principal take a windfall in priority to those to whom the fiduciary owes purchased obligations?'

Outline the reasons why English law takes this approach, and state why, in your opinion, this is (or is not) the correct approach for the law to take.

FURTHER READING

Conaglen, M., 'The Extent of Fiduciary Accounting and the Importance of Authorisation Mechanisms' [2011] 70(3) *CLJ* 548–578.

Edelman, J., 'The Fiduciary Self-Dealing Rule' in J. Glister and P. Ridge (eds.) *Fault Lines in Equity* (Oxford: Hart Publishing, 2012) pp. 107–118.

Finn, P., *Fiduciary Obligations* (Sydney: Law Book Co., 1977).

Hicks, A. D., 'The remedial principle of *Keech v Sandford* reconsidered' (2010) *CLJ* 287.

Hilliard, J., 'The flexibility of fiduciary doctrine in trust law: how far does it stretch in practice?' (2009) 23(3) *Tru LI* 119.

Langbein, J. H., 'Questioning the trust law duty of loyalty: sole interest or best interest?' (2005) 114 *Yale LJ* 929.

McInnes, M., 'A new direction for the Canadian law of fiduciary relations?' (2010) 126 *LQR* 185.

Nolan, R. C., 'Controlling Fiduciary Power' (2009) 68(2) *CLJ* 293.

Reynolds, F. M. B., 'Solicitors and Conflicts of Duties' [1991] 107 *LQR* 536.

Salzedo, S. and Hollander, C., *Conflicts of Interest and Chinese Walls*, 3rd edn (London: Sweet & Maxwell, 2008).

Samet, I., 'Guarding the Fiduciary's Conscience—A Justification of a Stringent Profit-Stripping Rule' (2008) 28(4) *OJLS* 763.

Sealy, L. S., 'Fiduciary Obligations, Forty Years On' (1995) 9 *JCL* 37.

Simpson, E., 'Conflicts', in P. Birks and A. Pretto (eds), *Breach of Trust* (Oxford: Hart Publishing, 2002), p. 75.

11

Fulfilling and Filling the Office of Trustee

KEY AIMS

To examine the rules for appointment, retirement, and removal of trustees and to consider whether it is true that a trust will not fail for want of a trustee. To identify the range of trust duties and consider the extent to which duties laid down by the general law may be excluded or modified by the express terms of a trust instrument. To appreciate how and when trust duties and functions may be delegated.

SECTION 1: INTRODUCTION

Trustees are the legal owners of trust property and as such they have all the legal powers of an absolute owner, but trustees do not have the freedom of an absolute owner. They must exercise their trust powers for the exclusive benefit of the trust beneficiaries or otherwise for the purposes of the trust, and they must exercise their powers unanimously with the other trustees. Trustees may even be liable in certain circumstances for omitting to exercise their powers.

Unless the provisions of his particular trust instrument provide to the contrary, a trustee is subject to a number of duties laid down by the general law. One of these, the fiduciary duty, was considered at length in Chapter 10; the others, including the duty of care and the duty to exercise a sound discretion, are introduced in this chapter and demonstrated Chapter 12 in the context of trustee investment. The office of trustee must be filled if it is to be fulfilled. This point should be borne in mind throughout this chapter as we consider the various ways in which the law maintains a fine balance between the strict enforcement of trust duties and the need to attract persons to accept trust office. It should also be noted that the trust instrument plays a significant role in defining the nature and extent of a trustee's duties. The general law of trusts is really little more than the background against which settlors set out the rules that are to govern their particular trust and trustees.

Target Holdings Ltd v Redferns (a firm)

[1996] 1 AC 421, House of Lords

(For the facts and decision, see Chapter 13.)

LORD BROWNE-WILKINSON: the basic right of a beneficiary is to have the trust duly administered in accordance with the provisions of the trust instrument, if any, and the general law. [at 434A]

■ QUESTION

Is there a point beyond which the trust instrument is not permitted to go in modifying or excluding the general law of trustee obligations? Keep this important question in mind as we progress through this chapter.

Hayim v *Citibank*

[1987] AC 730, Privy Council

Facts: Two wills had been executed by the same testator, one in respect of his property in America and one in respect of his property in Hong Kong. The executors of the two wills were different persons. The dispute concerned a particular residential property in Hong Kong. Although the Hong Kong executors held legal title to the residence, they had no power to sell it without the consent of the American executors. An express clause in the trust instrument relieved the American executors of any responsibility in respect of the Hong Kong property so long as the testator's elderly brother and sister remained alive, unless the American executors received the proceeds of sale of the Hong Kong residence in the meantime. The beneficiaries of the American will were entitled to the proceeds of sale of the Hong Kong residence, and so they requested that the residence be sold. When the American executors refused consent to a sale (so as to allow the existing occupiers, the testator's elderly brother and sister, to remain in occupation), the beneficiaries of the American will brought the present action against the American executors and against the Hong Kong executors. In other words, the claimants issued proceedings against all the trustees of both trusts.

Held: The claimants failed. The Hong Kong executors owed no trust duties to the beneficiaries of the American will and the American executors had no trust duties because the Hong Kong residence had not yet been sold, so for a short period of time, no trustee was liable to account to the American beneficiaries with respect to the Hong Kong residence.

LORD TEMPLEMAN: It is of course unusual for a testator to relieve the trustee of his will of any responsibility or duty in respect of the trust property, but a testator may do as he pleases.

■ QUESTION

'[There] can be no trust where the trustee is not accountable to someone' (Paul Matthews, 'The New Trust: Obligations without Rights?', in A. J. Oakley (ed.), *Trends in Contemporary Trusts Law* (Oxford: Clarendon Press, 1996), pp. 1, 26).

   Is Professor Matthews right?

SECTION 2: FULFILLING THE OFFICE OF TRUSTEE

A: General statutory powers

TRUSTEE ACT 1925

69. Application of Act

   (1)   This Act, except where otherwise expressly provided, applies to trusts including, so far as this Act applies thereto, executorships and administratorships constituted or created either before or after the commencement of this Act.

(2)   The powers conferred by this Act on trustees are in addition to the powers conferred by the instrument, if any, creating the trust, but those powers, unless otherwise stated, apply if and so far only as a contrary intention is not expressed in the instrument, if any, creating the trust, and have effect subject to the terms of that instrument.

[(3)   repealed]

(i) Powers of sale

TRUSTEE ACT 1925

16. Power to raise money by sale, mortgage, etc.

(1)   Where trustees are authorised by the instrument, if any, creating the trust or by law to pay or apply capital money subject to the trust for any purpose or in any manner, they shall have and shall be deemed always to have had power to raise the money required by sale, conversion, calling in, or mortgage of all or any part of the trust property for the time being in possession.

(2)   This section applies notwithstanding anything to the contrary contained in the instrument, if any, creating the trust, but does not apply to trustees of property held for charitable purposes, or to trustees of a settlement for the purposes of the Settled Land Act, not being also the statutory owners.

NOTE: In exercising their powers of sale, trustees have an overriding duty to obtain the best price they can on behalf of the beneficiaries; while there may be circumstances in which it will be proper to reject the highest offer, if this is suspect, the trustees will be in breach of their duty if they permit ethical considerations to entice them into accepting a lower price. This may require trustees to resile from an agreement on later receiving a better offer. See, in general, *Fry* v *Fry* (1859) 28 LJ Ch 591.

(ii) Power to give receipts

TRUSTEE ACT 1925

14. Power of trustees to give receipts

(1)   The receipt in writing of a trustee for any money, securities, or other personal property or effects payable, transferable, or deliverable to him under any trust or power shall be a sufficient discharge to the person paying, transferring, or delivering the same and shall effectually exonerate him from seeing to the application or being answerable for any loss or misapplication thereof.

(2)   This section does not, except where the trustee is a trust corporation, enable a sole trustee to give a valid receipt for—

(a)   the proceeds of sale or other capital money arising under a trust for sale of land;

(b)   capital money arising under the Settled Land Act 1925.

(3)   This section applies notwithstanding anything to the contrary in the instrument, if any, creating the trust.

NOTE: This is s.14 as subsequently amended.

(iii) Power to insure

TRUSTEE ACT 1925 (as amended by the Trustee Act 2000)

19. Power to insure

(1)   A trustee may—

(a)   insure any property which is subject to the trust against risks of loss or damage due to any event, and

(b)   pay the premiums out of the trust funds.

(2) In the case of property held on a bare trust, the power to insure is subject to any direction given by the beneficiary or each of the beneficiaries—

    (a) that any property specified in the direction is not to be insured;

    (b) that any property specified in the direction is not to be insured except on such conditions as may be so specified.

(3) Property is held on a bare trust if it is held on trust for—

    (a) a beneficiary who is of full age and capacity and absolutely entitled to the property subject to the trust, or

    (b) beneficiaries each of whom is of full age and capacity and who (taken together) are absolutely entitled to the property subject to the trust.

(4) If a direction under subsection (2) of this section is given, the power to insure, so far as it is subject to the direction, ceases to be a delegable function for the purposes of section 11 of the Trustee Act 2000 (power to employ agents).

(5) In this section 'trust funds' means any income or capital funds of the trust...

NOTES

1. The trustees' statutory duty of care extends to the exercise of their power of insurance, so they may be personally liable if the chosen insurance is inadequate or inappropriate (Trustee Act 2000, s.2 and Sch. 1, para. 5).

2. All the above applies only to first-party insurance of the trust property. There is nothing to stop the trustees insuring *themselves* for third-party liability towards the trust in the event of their own breach, although they cannot reimburse themselves from the trust property for the premiums they pay on insuring themselves.

B: The duty of care

Trustees owe no common law duty of care to their beneficiaries but they owe a duty of care in equity. A trustee must act (trusteeship is not passive), so the question is how careful must he be? The answer is that a trustee is not liable for reasonable errors of judgment. He is 'merely' required 'to conduct the business of the trust in the same manner that an ordinary prudent man of business would conduct his own' (*Speight* v *Gaunt* (1883) 9 App Cas 1, HL). This principle is preserved and elaborated by the Trustee Act 2000.

TRUSTEE ACT 2000

1. The duty of care

(1) Whenever the duty under this subsection applies to a trustee, he must exercise such care and skill as is reasonable in the circumstances, having regard in particular—

    (a) to any special knowledge or experience that he has or holds himself out as having, and

    (b) if he acts as trustee in the course of a business or profession, to any special knowledge or experience that it is reasonable to expect of a person acting in the course of that kind of business or profession.

(2) In this Act the duty under subsection (1) is called 'the duty of care'.

2. Application of duty of care

Schedule 1 makes provision about when the duty of care applies to a trustee.

SCHEDULE 1 APPLICATION OF DUTY OF CARE

Investment

1. The duty of care applies to a trustee—

    (a) when exercising the general power of investment or a power of investment conferred on him by the trust instrument;

    (b) when carrying out a duty to which he is subject under section 4 or 5 (duties relating to the exercise of a power of investment or to the review of investments).

Acquisition of land

2. The duty of care applies to a trustee—

    (a) when exercising the power under section 8 to acquire land;

    (b) when exercising any power to acquire land conferred on him by the trust instrument;

    (c) when exercising any power in relation to land acquired under a power mentioned in sub-paragraph (a) or (b).

Agents, nominees and custodians

3. (1) The duty of care applies to a trustee—

    (a) when entering into arrangements under which a person is authorised under section 11 to exercise functions as an agent;

    (b) when entering into arrangements under which a person is appointed under section 16 to act as a nominee;

    (c) when entering into arrangements under which a person is appointed under section 17 or 18 to act as a custodian;

    (d) when entering into arrangements under which, under any power conferred by the trust instrument, a person is authorised to exercise functions as an agent or is appointed to act as a nominee or custodian;

    (e) when carrying out his duties under section 22 (review of agent, nominee or custodian, etc.).

    (2) For the purposes of sub-paragraph (1), entering into arrangements under which a person is authorised to exercise functions or is appointed to act as a nominee or custodian includes, in particular—

    (a) selecting the person who is to act,

    (b) determining any terms on which he is to act, and

    (c) if the person is being authorised to exercise asset management functions, the preparation of a policy statement under section 15.

    ...

Insurance

5. The duty of care applies to a trustee—

    (a) when exercising the power under the Trustee Act 1925 to insure property;

    (b) when exercising any corresponding power conferred on him by the trust instrument...

Bartlett v *Barclays Bank Trust Co. Ltd (No. 1)*

[1980] Ch 515, [1980] 1 All ER 139, Chancery Division

Facts: The bank, as trustee under a settlement of shares in a private company, Bartletts Trust Ltd (BTL), had a controlling interest in that company. From 1960, the board of BTL had no director representing the settlor's family or acting for the bank. The bank made no objection at the annual general meeting of BTL in 1961, when BTL altered its investment policy to go into property development. The board of BTL accordingly embarked on two hazardous development projects, without consulting the bank, and the bank did not insist on receiving a regular flow of information on the progress of these projects. Although one of these projects, at Guildford, was successful, the project at Old Bailey, London, which involved buying at a high price on the chance that planning permission for development would be granted, was unsuccessful, and BTL sustained a large loss. The beneficiaries under the settlement sued the bank.

Held:

(a) The bank was in breach of its duty as trustee.

(b) However, since the Guildford and Old Bailey projects, although separate transactions, were part of the same overall policy of BTL, the bank was entitled to set off the profit from the Guildford transaction against the loss from the Old Bailey project.

(c) The bank could not use the Trustee Act 1925, s.61 (see Chapter 13) as a defence, since that section protected only trustees who had acted honestly and reasonably. The bank had acted honestly, but not reasonably.

(d) However, in relation to income lost outside the limitation period, the bank could rely on the Limitation Act 1939, s.19 (see now the Limitation Act 1980, s.21: see Chapter 13). Under s.21(1), the limitation period does not apply in respect of a fraudulent breach of trust. The bank had not acted fraudulently, however. Although fraud for limitation purposes was wider than common law fraud or deceit, it required unconscionable conduct on the part of the trustee, something in the nature of a deliberate cover-up. Here, the bank was unaware that it was acting in breach of trust, so was not guilty of fraud for limitation purposes.

BRIGHTMAN J (on the duty of the bank): What, then was the duty of the bank and did the bank fail in its duty? It does not follow that because a trustee could have prevented a loss it is therefore liable for that loss. The questions which I must ask myself are: (1) what was the duty of the bank as the holder of 99.8 per cent of the shares in BTL and BTH [Bartlett Trust Holdings Ltd, a holding company of which BTL was a wholly owned subsidiary since 1967]? (2) was the bank in breach of duty in any and if so in what respect? (3) if so, did that breach of duty cause the loss which was suffered by the trust estate? (4) if so, to what extent is the bank liable to make good that loss? In approaching these questions, I bear in mind that the attack on the bank is based, not on wrongful acts, but on wrongful omissions, that is to say, non-feasance not misfeasance.

The cases establish that it is the duty of a trustee to conduct the business of the trust with the same care as an ordinary prudent man of business would extend towards his own affairs: see *Re Speight, Speight* v *Gaunt* (1883) 22 ChD 727 at 739, 762 per Jessel MR and Bowen LJ (affirmed on appeal (1883) 9 App Cas 1 and see Lord Blackburn at 19). In applying this principle, Lindley LJ (who was the third member of the court in *Re Speight*) added in *Re Whitely* (1886) 33 ChD 347 at 355:

> ...care must be taken not to lose sight of the fact that the business of the trustee, and the business which the ordinary prudent man is supposed to be conducting for himself, is the business of investing money for the benefit of persons who are to enjoy it at some future time, and not for the sole benefit of the person entitled to the present income. The duty of a trustee is not to take such care only as a prudent man would take if he had only himself to consider; the duty rather is to take such care as an ordinary prudent man would take if he were minded to make an investment for the benefit of people for whom he felt morally bound to provide. That is the kind of business the ordinary prudent man is supposed to be engaged in; and unless this is borne in mind the standard of a trustee's duty will be fixed too low; lower than it has ever yet been fixed, and lower, certainly than the House of Lords or this court endeavoured to fix it in *Speight* v *Gaunt*.

On appeal Lord Watson added (1887) 12 App Cas 727 at 733:

> Businessmen of ordinary prudence may, and frequently do, select investments which are more or less of a speculative character; but it is the duty of a trustee to confine himself to the class of investments which are permitted by the trust, and likewise to avoid all investments of that class which are attended with hazard.

That does not mean that the trustee is bound to avoid all risk and in effect act as an insurer of the trust fund: in *Re Godfrey* (1883) 23 ChD 483 at 493 Bacon V-C said:

> No doubt it is the duty of a trustee, in administering the trusts of a will, to deal with property intrusted into his care exactly as any prudent man would deal with his own property. But the words in which the rule is expressed must not be strained beyond their meaning. Prudent businessmen in their dealings incur risk. That may and must happen in almost all human affairs.

The distinction is between a prudent degree of risk on the one hand, and hazard on the other. Nor must the court be astute to fix liability on a trustee who has committed no more than an error of judgment, from which no businessman, however prudent, can expect to be immune: in *Re Chapman* [1896] 2 Ch 763 at 778, Lopes LJ said:

> A trustee who is honest and reasonably competent is not to be held responsible for a mere error in judgment when the question which he has to consider is whether a security of a class authorised but depreciated in value, should be retained or realised, provided he acts with reasonable care, prudence and circumspection.

[Brightman J described the hazardous nature of the Old Bailey project and continued:]

The prudent man of business will act in such manner as is necessary to safeguard his investment. He will do this in two ways. If facts come to his knowledge which tell him that the company's affairs are not being conducted as they should be, or which put him on enquiry, he will take appropriate action. Appropriate action will no doubt consist in the first instance of enquiry of and consultation with the directors, and in the last but most unlikely resort, the convening of a general meeting to replace one or more directors. What the prudent man of business will not do is to content himself with the receipt of such information on the affairs of the company as a shareholder ordinarily receives at annual general meetings. Since he has the power to do so, he will go further and see that he has sufficient information to enable him to make a responsible decision from time to time either to let matters proceed as they are proceeding, or to intervene if he is dissatisfied. This topic was considered by Cross J in *Re Lucking's WT* [1968] 1 WLR 866 [below].

[Brightman J set out the facts of *Lucking*, and quoted the judgment of Cross J on the standard of care applicable to trustees—the last paragraph in the extract in this section—and continued:]

I do not understand Cross J to have been saying that in every case where trustees have a controlling interest in a company it is their duty to ensure that one of their number is a director or that they have a nominee on the board who will report from time to time on the affairs of the company. He was merely outlining convenient methods by which a prudent man of business (as also a trustee) with a controlling interest in a private company, can place himself in a position to make an informed decision whether any action is appropriate to be taken for the protection of his asset. Other methods may be equally satisfactory and convenient, depending on the circumstances of the individual case. Alternatives which spring to mind are the receipt of the copies of the agenda and minutes of board meetings if regularly held, the receipt of monthly management accounts in the case of a trading concern, or quarterly reports. Every case will depend on its own facts. The possibilities are endless. It would be useless, indeed misleading, to seek to lay down a general rule. The purpose to be achieved is not that of monitoring every move of the directors, but of making it reasonably probable, so far as circumstances permit, that the trustee or (as in *Re Lucking's WT*) one of them will receive an adequate flow of information in time to enable the trustees to make use of their controlling interest should this be necessary for the protection of their trust asset, namely the shareholding. The obtaining of information is not an end in itself, but merely a means of enabling the trustees to safeguard the interests of their beneficiaries.

The principle enunciated in *Re Lucking's WT* appears to have been applied in *Re Miller's Deed Trusts*, decided by Oliver J. No transcript of the judgment is available but the case is briefly noted in a journal of the Law Society (1978) 75 LS Gaz 454). There are also a number of American decisions proceeding on the same lines, to which counsel has helpfully referred me.

So far, I have applied the test of the ordinary prudent man of business. Although I am not aware that the point has previously been considered, except briefly in *Re Waterman's WT* [1952] 2 All ER 1054, I am of the opinion that a higher duty of care is plainly due from someone like a trust corporation which carries on a specialised business of trust management. A trust corporation holds itself out in its advertising literature as being above ordinary mortals. With a specialist staff of trained trust officers and managers, with ready access to financial information and professional advice, dealing with and solving trust problems day after day, the trust corporation holds itself out, and rightly, as capable of providing an expertise which it would be unrealistic to expect and unjust to demand from the ordinary prudent man or woman who accepts, probably unpaid and sometimes reluctantly from a sense of family duty, the burdens of a trusteeship. Just as, under the law of contract, a professional person possessed of a particular skill is liable for breach of contract if he neglects to use the skill and experience which he professes, so I think that a professional corporate trustee is liable for breach of trust if loss is caused to the trust fund because it neglects to exercise the special care and skill which it professes to have. The advertising literature of the bank was not in evidence (other than the scale of fees) but counsel for the bank did not dispute that trust corporations, including the bank, hold themselves out as possessing a superior ability for the conduct of trust business, and in any event I would take judicial notice of that fact. Having expressed my view of the higher duty required from a trust corporation, I should add that the bank's counsel did not dispute the proposition.

In my judgment the bank wrongfully and in breach of trust neglected to ensure that it received an adequate flow of information concerning the intentions and activities of the boards of BTL and BTH. It was not proper for the bank to confine itself to the receipt of the annual balance sheet and profit and loss account, detailed annual financial statements and the chairman's report and statement, and to attendance at the annual general meetings and the luncheons that followed, which were the limits of the bank's regular sources of information…

I hold that the bank failed in its duty whether it is judged by the standard of the prudent man of business or of the skilled trust corporation.

NOTES

1. Brightman J thought that a higher standard of care is required of paid trustees than of unpaid, non-professional trustees, in that the former will be held to the standards of skill and expertise which they claim to possess.
2. In *Bartlett*, however, the bank would have been liable on the standard applied in *Speight* v *Gaunt*, and it was unnecessary to rely on the higher standard owed by professional trustees.
3. See also *Cowan* v *Scargill* [1984] 3 WLR 501 (see Chapter 12).

Re Lucking's WT, Renwick v *Lucking*
[1968] 1 WLR 866, [1967] 3 All ER 726, Chancery Division

Facts: Nearly 70 per cent of the shares of a private company (Stephen Lucking Ltd) were held by two trustees, Mr Lucking and Mr Block, as part of the estate of the deceased, Mary Lucking; about 20 per cent belonged to Mr Lucking in his own right, and 1 per cent belonged to Lucking's wife. The directors in 1954 were Mr and Mrs Lucking and Mr Dewar, who was also the manager of the business. In 1956, Block was appointed trustee to act jointly with Lucking.

The company, which was engaged in the manufacture and sale of shoe accessories, had a small factory employing about twenty people. Dewar wrongfully drew some £15,000 from the company's bank account in excess of his remuneration, and later became bankrupt. The money was lost, and a beneficiary sued the trustees for breach of trust.

Held: Lucking was in breach in failing adequately to supervise the manager, Dewar.

CROSS J: The conduct of the defendant trustees is, I think, to be judged by the standard applied in *Re Speight, Speight* v *Gaunt* (1883) 22 ChD 727, namely, that a trustee is only bound to conduct the business of the trust in such a way as an ordinary prudent man would conduct a business of his own.

Now, what steps, if any, does a reasonably prudent man who finds himself a majority shareholder in a private company take with regard to the management of the company's affairs? He does not, I think, content himself with such information as to the management of the company's affairs as he is entitled to as shareholder, but ensures that he is represented on the board. He may be prepared to run the business himself as managing director or, at least, to become a non-executive director while having the business managed by someone else. Alternatively, he may find someone who will act as his nominee on the board and report to him from time to time as to the company's affairs. In the same way, as it seems to me, trustees holding a controlling interest ought to ensure so far as they can that they have such information as to the progress of the company's affairs as directors would have. If they sit back and allow the company to be run by the minority shareholders and receive no more information than shareholders are entitled to, they do so at their risk if things go wrong.

Henderson v *Merrett Syndicates Ltd*
[1995] 2 AC 145, House of Lords

LORD BROWNE-WILKINSON: The liability of a fiduciary for the negligent transaction of his duties is not a separate head of liability but the paradigm of the general duty to act with care imposed by law on those who take it upon themselves to act for or advise others. Although the historical development of the rules of law and equity have, in the past, caused different labels to be stuck on different manifestations of the duty, in truth the duty of care imposed on bailees, carriers, trustees, directors, agents and others is the same duty: it arises from the circumstances in which the defendants were acting not from their status or description. It is the fact that they have all assumed responsibility for the property or affairs of others which renders them liable for the careless performance in what they have undertaken to do, not the description of the trade or position which they hold (at 205).

C: The duty of fairness

In a trust of the traditional form 'to A for life and B in remainder', A and B have competing interests in the fund; broadly speaking, the life beneficiary is interested in income and the remainder beneficiary is interested in capital. The trustee must act fairly in the interests of both. However, fairness does not always mean equality.

Nestle v *National Westminster Bank plc*
(1996) 10(4) TLI 11, Chancery Division

HOFFMANN J:...This brings me to the second principle on which there was general agreement, namely that the trustee must act fairly in making investment decisions which may have different consequences for different classes of beneficiaries. There are two reasons why I prefer this formulation to the traditional image of holding the scales equally between tenant for life and remainderman. The first is that the image of the scales suggests a weighing of known quantities whereas investment decisions are concerned with predictions of the future. Investments will carry current expectations of their future income yield and capital appreciation and these expectations will be reflected in their current market price, but there is always a greater or lesser risk that the outcome will deviate from those expectations.

A judgment on the fairness of the choices made by the trustees must have regard to these imponderables. The second reason is that the image of the scales suggests a more mechanistic process than I believe the law requires. The trustees have in my judgment a wide discretion. They are for example entitled to take into account the income needs of the tenant for life or the fact that the tenant for life was a person known to the settlor and a primary object of the trust whereas the remainderman is a remoter relative or a stranger. Of course these cannot be allowed to become the overriding considerations but the concept of fairness between classes of beneficiaries does not require them to be excluded. It would be an inhuman law which required trustees to adhere to some mechanical rule for preserving the real value of the capital when the tenant for life was the testator's widow who had fallen upon hard times and the remainderman was young and well off.

Capital and Income in Trusts: Classification and Apportionment
Law Commission Report No. 315 (May 2009)

4.4 [Our] proposed statutory power of allocation would enable trustees to allocate receipts and expenses to income or to capital in proportions that maintained an appropriate balance between the capital value of the fund and its income yield. Although the allocation power would in theory enable the allocation of each individual receipt (and we envisaged that such allocation could be in whole or in part), the trustees' objective would be to ensure that, over a period, a proportionate level of return was attributed to the classes of beneficiaries entitled to capital and to income. To achieve this result, trustees might need only to allocate one or two receipts, irrespective of how any imbalance had been caused. Alternatively, they might take a more global approach, not unlike a percentage trust, allocating an appropriate proportion of the entire investment return to income and capital respectively. The exercise of the power of allocation would be underpinned by the trustees' overarching duty to balance the interests of the different beneficiaries; the proposed power would only be capable of exercise in so far as necessary to discharge the duty to balance and for no other purpose.

NOTE: Following the Law Commission report, the Trusts (Capital and Income) Act 2013 received Royal Assent on 31 January 2013.

D: Exercising discretion and giving reasons

(i) Expressly unqualified discretion

Gisborne v *Gisborne*
(1877) 2 App Cas 300, House of Lords

Facts: Trustees held a fund upon trust for the maintenance of the testator's mentally infirm wife. The terms of the trust granted the trustees 'uncontrollable authority' as to how the fund should be applied. The care of 'lunatics' (the unfortunate label then applied to the mentally ill) normally lay within the powers of the court, and so a decree of the Court of Chancery had recorded the court's approval of the trustees' chosen course of action.

Held: That part of the decree should be struck out. The court had no jurisdiction to 'approve' that which was in the 'uncontrollable' discretion of trustees.

LORD CAIRNS LC:…My Lords, larger words than those, it appears to me, it would be impossible to introduce into a will. The trustees are not merely to have discretion, but they are to have 'uncontrollable,' that is, uncontrolled, 'authority.' Their discretion and authority, always supposing that there is no *mala fides* with regard to its exercise, is to be without any check or control from any superior tribunal. What is the subject-matter with regard to which they are to exercise this discretion and this authority? The subject-matter is the payment, or the application, not merely of the whole of the income of his real and personal estate, but of such portion only as they deem it proper to expend. It is for them to say whether they will apply the whole, or only a part, and if so what part. And how are they to decide, if they do not apply the whole; what is the part which they are to apply? They are to decide upon this principle, that it is to be such part as they shall think expedient, not such part as shall be sufficient, not such part as shall be demanded by or for the person to be benefited, but such part as they shall think expedient; and upon the question of what is expedient it is their discretion which is to decide, and that discretion according to which they are to decide is to be uncontrolled…

My Lords, in a case like this, where the Court of Chancery recognises that the trustees and not the Court, are to be the judges of the *quantum* to be allowed, where the trustees are willing to exercise the discretion which they claim to exercise, and where the Court allows and declares their right to exercise that discretion, I do not understand it to be the habit of the Court to go on and express any opinion as to whether the exercise of the discretion by the trustees is a wise or an unwise exercise of that discretion…

(ii) The rule in *Hastings-Bass*

Mettoy Pension Trustees Ltd v *Evans and others*
[1990] 1 WLR 1587, Chancery Division

WARNER J:…I have come to the conclusion that there is a principle which may be labelled 'the rule in *Hastings-Bass*.' I do not think that the application of that principle is confined, as Mr Nugee suggested, to cases where an exercise by trustees of a discretion vested in them is partially ineffective because of some rule of law or because of some limit on their discretion which they overlooked. If, as I believe, the reason for the application of the principle is the failure by the trustees to take into account considerations that they ought to have taken into account, it cannot matter whether that failure is due to their having overlooked (or to their legal advisers having overlooked) some relevant rule of law or limit on their discretion, or is due to some other cause.

For the principle to apply however, it is not enough that it should be shown that the trustees did not have a proper understanding of the effect of their act. It must also be clear that, had they had a proper understanding of it, they would not have acted as they did. That is apparent from *In re Hastings-Bass* [1975] Ch 25 itself,...There may well be cases where the court, giving effect to the rule in *Hastings-Bass*, comes to the conclusion that, had the trustees not failed to take into account considerations which they ought to have taken into account, they would not have acted as they did at all, but would either have done nothing or done something quite different. In such a case the court must declare void the whole of the purported exercise of the trustees' discretion. There may however be cases where the court is satisfied that the trustees would have acted in the same way but with, for instance, the omission of a particular provision in a deed. I do not see why, in such a case, the court should not declare only that provision void. It seems to me, that the remedy to be adopted by the court must depend on the circumstances of each case.

In a case such as this, where it is claimed that the rule in *Hastings-Bass* applies, three questions arise: (1) What were the trustees under a duty to consider? (2) Did they fail to consider it? (3) If so, what would they have done if they had considered it?...

I now come to the all important *third* question: what would the trustees have done if they had considered the matters that they failed to consider? In dealing with that question, two important points must be borne in mind. First, as I have said, for the rule in *Hastings-Bass* to apply it must be clear that the trustees would not have done what in fact they did. The decision in *In re Hastings-Bass* itself [1975] Ch 25 shows how stringent a requirement that is. It is not enough to show that the trustees would have realised that what they were doing was to some extent unsatisfactory. Secondly, it is implicit I think in *In re Baron Vestey's Settlement* [1951] Ch 209 and in *In re Hastings-Bass* [1975] Ch 25 that the trustees would have been correctly advised as to the effect in law of what they were doing. It cannot be right to consider what they would have done if they had been wrongly or inadequately advised...

Pitt v Holt; Futter v Futter
[2011] EWCA Civ 197, Court of Appeal

Held: the orthodox statement of the so-called 'rule in *Re Hastings-Bass*' was disapproved. Where trustees act within their powers but fail to take a relevant factor (e.g. tax consequences) into account, their action is not void, but may be voidable.

LLOYD LJ: The trustees' duty to take relevant matters into account is a fiduciary duty, so an act done as a result of a breach of that duty is voidable. Fiscal considerations will often be among the relevant matters which ought to be taken into account. However, if the trustees seek advice (in general or in specific terms) from apparently competent advisers as to the implications of the course they are considering taking, and follow the advice so obtained, then, in the absence of any other basis for a challenge, I would hold that the trustees are not in breach of their fiduciary duty for failure to have regard to relevant matters if the failure occurs because it turns out that the advice given to them was materially wrong.

(iii) No duty to give reasons

NOTE: Trustees are under no duty to disclose reasons for their decisions on trust matters (*In re Londonderry's Settlement* [1965] Ch 918, CA) but in *Schmidt v Rosewood Trust Ltd* [2003] 2 WLR 1442, the Privy Council held that disclosure may be ordered on a case by case basis as part of the courts' inherent jurisdiction to ensure the proper administration of trusts. *Schmidt* is not a binding authority in the UK jurisdiction, but it is highly persuasive. *Schmidt* is considered in *Breakspear* v *Ackland* where the leading binding authority on the issue of disclosure (*In re Londonderry's Settlement* [1965] Ch 918, CA) was considered in depth and followed.

Breakspear v *Ackland*
[2008] EWHC 220 (Ch), [2008] 3 WLR 698, Chancery Division

Facts: A settlor set up a discretionary trust for the benefit of himself and his children. By a non-binding 'wish letter' which was contemporaneous with the settlement, the settlor requested that the trustees take stated matters into account when exercising their dispositive powers. The claimants, three of the beneficiaries, asked for disclosure of the wish letter in order to evaluate their future expectations under the trust. The trustees refused that request on the ground that the wish letter was confidential and that its disclosure would cause division and family discord. By a 'Part 8' claim the claimants sought, *inter alia,* an order for disclosure of the letter.

Held: allowing the claim for disclosure, that the basis on which trustees and the court should approach a request for disclosure of a wish letter was one calling for the exercise of discretion rather than the adjudication upon a proprietary right of beneficiaries to see trust documents. Having made a decision as to disclosure the trustees were not obliged to give reasons for it although if they did so the court would not be prohibited from examining the rationality of the reasons put forward by reference, if necessary, to the contents of the wish letter. In the circumstances, the wish letter was a key document to be taken into account by the trustees and relevant to the court's approval of the scheme and the risk of family division occasioned by disclosure was outweighed by the requirement to give the claimants a proper opportunity to address the court on the question of sanction; and that, accordingly, disclosure of the wish letter to the claimants would be ordered.

BRIGGS J: The first question is whether it is either permissible or appropriate in the light of *O'Rourke* v *Darbishire* [1920] AC 581 and the *Londonderry* case [1965] Ch 918 for me to decide at first instance that the basis upon which trustees and the court should approach a request for disclosure of a wish letter (or of any other document in the possession of trustees in their capacity as such) is one calling for the exercise of discretion rather than the adjudication upon a proprietary right. In my judgment it is both permissible and appropriate to answer that question in the affirmative. My review of the authorities demonstrates that there is now virtual unanimity in the relevant common law jurisdictions to that effect. Furthermore, as I have sought to demonstrate, even the Court of Appeal in the *Londonderry* case itself found the proprietary analysis to be both inconclusive and unsatisfactory, by comparison with the recognition of a clear, principled basis for refusing disclosure even in cases where there appeared to be a prima facie proprietary right to disclosure.

On that basis, the second question is whether the *Londonderry* principle remains good law, at least in England. In my opinion, it is still good law and, in any event, law by which a first instance judge remains bound, unless and until released by some higher judicial or parliamentary authority.

At the heart of the *Londonderry* principle is the unanimous conclusion (most clearly expressed by Danckwerts LJ) that it is in the interests of beneficiaries of family discretionary trusts, and advantageous to the due administration of such trusts, that the exercise by trustees of their dispositive discretionary powers be regarded, from start to finish, as an essentially confidential process. It is in the interests of the beneficiaries because it enables the trustees to make discreet but thorough inquiries as to their competing claims for consideration for benefit without fear or risk that those inquiries will come to the beneficiaries' knowledge. They may include, for example, inquiries as to the existence of some life-threatening illness of which it is appropriate that the beneficiary in question be kept ignorant. Such confidentiality serves the due administration of family trusts both because it tends to reduce the scope for litigation about the rationality of the exercise by trustees of their discretions, and because it is likely to encourage suitable trustees to accept office, undeterred by a perception that their discretionary deliberations will be subjected to scrutiny by disappointed or hostile beneficiaries, and to potentially expensive litigation in the courts.

I recognise the force of the contrary proposition, best enunciated by the editors of Underhill & Hayton, that the conferral of a general confidentiality upon the exercise by trustees of their discretionary powers may in particular cases reduce the practical extent to which they can be held to account. Trustees undoubtedly are accountable for the exercise of those powers, but it seems to me quite wrong to suppose that the courts have been mindless of the existence of that core principle of accountability, during the period of more than 150 years when the law has been that it is better for confidentiality to be afforded. While...the principle of fiduciary accountability has gained ground in recent years, it seems to me that this is better described as a process whereby the strict principles whereby a trustee has always been accountable have spread to other areas of society, where the concept of fiduciary obligations by those w ho hold property or exercise power or authority on behalf of others, or over their affairs, has come to be more generally recognised.

Nor can I see any persuasive basis for thinking that the reasoning which led the English courts to think it appropriate in the interests of beneficiaries, and in the administration of trusts, to confer confidentiality on the exercise by family trustees of their discretionary dispositive powers has ceased to hold good. It is not obvious that the potentially disastrous consequences of a resort to civil litigation about the administration of family trust property, in terms of the expenditure of time and cost, are much less of a potential evil than they were in the 19th century. Nor is there any less need today than there always has been to avoid deterring suitable family trustees from accepting an arduous unpaid office. Of course there is a risk that the conferral of such confidentiality may enable unworthy trustees to use it as a shield for the concealment of their culpable inadequacies, but this risk cannot have been ignored in the 19th century, and now that it is recognised that the general principle of confidentiality is subject to being overridden as a matter of discretion by the court, it may fairly be supposed that the risk has if anything become more rather than less manageable.

My reason for concluding that, regardless of my own opinion, I am bound to continue to treat the *Londonderry* principle as still being good law is simply because it formed part of the ratio of that decision, it has never been overruled, and because, if anything, it received a general endorsement rather than criticism in *Schmidt* v *Rosewood Trust Ltd* [2003] 2 AC 709.

I turn therefore to the question whether, and if so in what way, the *Londonderry* principle applies to wish letters. In that context I am content to limit myself to wish letters arising in the context of family discretionary trusts, rather than employee trusts, pension trusts or other business trusts, leaving for another occasion the manner in which the *Londonderry* principle is applicable to them. The defining characteristic of a wish letter is that it contains material which the settlor desires that the trustees should take into account when exercising their (usually dispositive) discretionary powers. It is therefore brought into existence for the sole purpose of serving and facilitating an inherently confidential process. It seems to me axiomatic that a document brought into existence for the sole or predominant purpose of being used in furtherance of an inherently confidential process is itself properly to be regarded as confidential, to substantially the same extent and effect as the process which it is intended to serve.

There is nothing unusual in such an approach. It is routinely applied in the working out of the principles of legal professional privilege, litigation privilege, and public interest immunity, as well as in the application of the without prejudice principle. The critical difference is that confidence may be overridden by the exercise of the court's discretion, whereas privilege may not.

While in a sense a wish letter is the companion of the trust deed, it by no means follows that it therefore needs or ought to be afforded similar treatment in the hands of the trustees. The trust deed is a document which confers and identifies the trustees' powers. There is in principle nothing confidential about the existence and precise boundaries of those powers. By contrast, the wish letter, operating exclusively within those boundaries and purely in furtherance of the trustees' confidential exercise of discretionary powers, may properly be afforded a status of confidentiality which the trust deed itself entirely lacks.

Of course, particular wish letters may contain valuable background information relevant (under modern ICS-based principles) (see *Investors Compensation Scheme Ltd* v *West Bromwich Building Society* [1998] 1 WLR 896) to the construction of the trust deed itself, but I can see no reason why that possibility should detract from the inherent confidentiality of a wish letter. If a genuine issue as to the construction of a trust deed becomes the subject of litigation, and that issue appears likely to be illuminated by relevant background material evidenced by a wish letter, then the wish letter may become disclosable, regardless of its confidentiality, in accordance with ordinary principles of disclosure in civil litigation.

In my judgment, the effect of that analysis is broadly as described by the editors of *Lewin*, at para. 23–56, in the passage which I have quoted at para. 48 above, although I do not share their view that the judicial trend is towards disclosure. Generally, the confidence which ordinarily attaches to a wish letter is such that, for the better discharge of their confidential functions, the trustees need not disclose it to beneficiaries merely because they request it unless, in their view, disclosure is in the interests of the sound administration of the trust, and the discharge of their powers and discretions. My only reservation with the analysis in *Lewin* is that I doubt whether it is appropriate for the trustees to be greatly influenced by the subsequent giving or withholding of consent to disclosure by the settlor. ...In the absence of special terms, the confidentiality in which a wish letter is enfolded is something given to the trustees for them to use, on a fiduciary basis, in accordance with their best judgment and as to the interests of the beneficiaries and the sound administration of the trust. Once the settlor has completely constituted the trust, and sent his wish letter, it seems to me that the preservation, judicious relaxation or abandonment of that confidence is a matter for the trustees or, in an appropriate case, for the court.

SECTION 3: FILLING THE OFFICE OF TRUSTEE

If the reader wonders why a whole section of this chapter is devoted to the topic of trustee appointments, the answer is simple. If a mistake is made in this practical aspect of trusts law, the consequences can be disastrous.

Jasmine Trustees v *Wells & Hinds*
[2007] EWHC 38 (Ch), Chancery Division

Facts: The case, which was a professional negligence action brought against various solicitors' firms, arose from a 1982 deed of appointment and retirement of trustees which appointed a Mr Thornton and a trust company to act as new trustees. The new trustees were based in the Isle of Man and that was the problem. In 1982, trustees could retire provided the trustees they left behind were at least two humans or one trust corporation (Trustee Act 1925, s.37(1)(c)). Unfortunately, in this case the retiring trustees left behind one human and one trust company which (because it was incorporated outside the EU) could not be regarded as a trust corporation.

Held: The retirement of the trustees had been invalid and the retired trustees continued to be liable for trust matters. The knock-on effect of the new trustees being unaware of the fact that the trust was now invalid in the UK was to render subsequent trustees appointments void. The trustees might have hoped that this would get them off the hook, but even though they were not true trustees they continued to be liable to the trust as 'Trustees de son tort' (see Chapter 15) and liable to pay tax on the trust (which is why the *Jasmine* case was brought).

NOTES
1. The lesson of this case is never to accept appointment to the office of trustee without first checking that all trustees have been correctly appointed in the past. If an error is found at any stage all relevant parties, if living, might be persuaded to correct the error by mutual deed. Failing that, the court should be called upon to rectify the situation to whatever extent it can.
2. Section 37(1)(c) has since been amended, so this particular case would not have arisen had the deed of appointment and retirement been made today.

A: Appointment of new trustees

TRUSTEE ACT 1925

36. Power of appointing new or additional trustees

(1)   Where a trustee, either original or substituted, and whether appointed by a court or otherwise, is dead, or remains out of the United Kingdom for more than twelve months, or desires to be discharged from all or any of the trusts or powers reposed in or conferred on him, or refuses or is unfit to act therein, or is incapable of acting therein, or is an infant, then, subject to the restrictions imposed by this Act on the number of trustees—

   (a)   any person or persons nominated for the purpose of appointing new trustees by the instrument, if any, creating the trust; or

    (b) if there is no such person, or no such person able and willing to act, then the surviving or continuing trustee or trustees for the time being, or the personal representative of the last surviving or continuing trustee;

        may, by writing, appoint one or more other person (whether or not being the persons exercising the power) to be a trustee or trustees in the place of the trustee so deceased remaining out of the United Kingdom, desiring to be discharged, or being unfit or incapable, or being an infant, as aforesaid.

    (2)   Where a trustee has been removed under a power contained in the instrument creating the trust, a new trustee or new trustees may be appointed in the place of the trustee who is removed, as if he were dead, or, in the case of a corporation, as if the corporation desired to be discharged from the trust, and the provisions of this section shall apply accordingly, but subject to the restrictions imposed by this Act on the number of trustees.

    (3)   Where a corporation being a trustee is or has been dissolved, either before or after the commencement of this Act, then, for the purposes of this section and of any enactment replaced thereby, the corporation shall be deemed to be and to have been from the date of the dissolution incapable of acting in the trusts or powers reposed in or conferred on the corporation.

    (4)   The power of appointment given by subsection (1) of this section or any similar previous enactment to the personal representatives of a last surviving or continuing trustee shall be and shall be deemed always to have been exercisable by the executors for the time being (whether original or by representation) of such surviving or continuing trustee who have proved the will of their testator or by the administrators for the time being of such trustee without the concurrence of any executor who has renounced or has not proved.

    (5)   But a sole or last surviving executor intending to renounce, or all the executors where they all intend to renounce, shall have and shall be deemed always to have had power, at any time before renouncing probate, to exercise the power of appointment given by this section, or by any similar previous enactment, if willing to act for that purpose and without thereby accepting the office of executor.

    (6)   Where, in the case of any trust, there are not more than three trustees—

    (a) the person or persons nominated for the purpose of appointing new trustees by the instrument, if any, creating the trust; or

    (b) if there is no such person, or no such person able and willing to act, then the trustee or trustees for the time being; may, by writing, appoint another person to other persons to be an additional trustee or additional trustees, but it shall not be obligatory to appoint any additional trustee, unless the instrument, if any, creating the trust, or any statutory enactment provides to the contrary, nor shall the number of trustees be increased beyond four by virtue of any such appointment.

    …

    (7)   Every new trustee appointed under this section as well before as after all the trust property becomes by law, or by assurance, or otherwise, vested in him, shall have the same powers, authorities, and discretions, and may in all respects act as if he had been originally appointed a trustee by the instrument, if any, creating the trust.

    (8)   The provisions of this section relating to a trustee who is dead include the case of a person nominated trustee in a will but dying before the testator, and those relative to a continuing trustee include a refusing or retiring trustee, if willing to act in the execution of the provisions of this section.

    (9)   Where a trustee is incapable, by reason of mental disorder within the meaning of the Mental Health Act 1983, of exercising his functions as trustee and is also entitled in possession to some beneficial interest in the trust property, no appointment of a new trustee in his place shall be made by virtue of paragraph (b) of subsection (1) of this section unless leave to make the appointment has been given by the authority having jurisdiction under Part VII of the Mental Health Act 1983.

NOTE: This is s.36 as amended.

TRUSTEE ACT 1925

41. Power of court to appoint new trustees

(1)   The court may, whenever it is expedient to appoint a new trustee or new trustees, and it is found inexpedient, difficult or impracticable to do so without the assistance of the court, make an order appointing a new trustee or new trustees either in substitution for or in addition to any existing trustee or trustees, or although there is no existing trustee.

In particular and without prejudice to the generality of the foregoing provision, the court may make an order appointing a new trustee in substitution for a trustee who is incapable, by reason of mental disorder within the meaning of the Mental Health Act 1983, of exercising his functions as a trustee or is a bankrupt, or is a corporation which is in liquidation or has been dissolved.

(2)   The power conferred by this section may, in the case of a deed of arrangement within the meaning of the Deeds of Arrangement Act 1914, be exercised either by the High Court or by the court having jurisdiction in bankruptcy in the district in which the debtor resided or carried on business at the date of the execution of the deed.

(3)   An order under this section, and any consequential vesting order or conveyance, shall not operate further or otherwise as a discharge to any former or continuing trustee than an appointment of new trustees under any power for that purpose contained in any instrument would have operated.

(4)   Nothing in this section gives power to appoint an executor or administrator.

Re Tempest

[1860] 1 Ch App 485, Court of Appeal

Facts: The will of Sir C. R. Tempest, Bart. appointed Stonor and Fleming as trustees of certain real estates. A codicil to the will appointed Stonor, Fleming and Lord Camoys as trustees of certain charitable trusts. Stonor predeceased the testator. Fleming and one Arthur Tempest, the testator's uncle, were empowered by the will to appoint new trustees of the real estates, but they could not agree upon a replacement trustee. Most of the beneficiaries concurred with Arthur Tempest's choice, but Fleming opposed it on the ground that the proposed trustee was connected with a branch of the family with whom the testator had not been on friendly terms. The surviving trustees of the charitable trusts were, on the other hand, able to agree to a replacement trustee of those trusts.

Held: The trustee proposed by Arthur Tempest should not be appointed to the trusts. Certain principles were laid down to guide appointments by the court.

SIR G. J. TURNER LJ:...the discretion which the Court has and exercises in making such appointments, is not, as I conceive, a mere arbitrary discretion, but a discretion in the exercise of which the Court is, and ought to be, guided by some general rules and principles, and, in my opinion, the difficulty which the Court has to encounter in these cases lies not so much in ascertaining the rules and principles by which it ought to be guided, as in applying those rules and principles to the varying circumstances of each particular case. The following rules and principles may, I think, safely be laid down as applying to all cases of appointments by the Court of new trustees.

First, the Court will have regard to the wishes of the persons by whom the trust has been created, if expressed in the instrument creating the trust, or clearly to be collected from it. I think this rule may be safely laid down, because if the author of the trust has in terms declared that a particular person, or a person filling a particular character, should not be a trustee of the instrument, there cannot, as I apprehend, be the least doubt that the Court would not appoint to the office a person whose appointment was so prohibited, and I do not think that upon a question of this description any distinction can be drawn between express declarations and demonstrated intention. The analogy of the course which the Court pursues in the appointment of guardians affords, I think, some support to this rule. The Court in those cases attends to the wishes of the parents, however informally they may be expressed.

Another rule which may, I think, safely be laid down is this—that the Court will not appoint a person to be trustee with a view to the interest of some of the persons interested under the trust, in opposition either to the wishes of the testator or to the interests of others of the *cestuis que trusts*. I think so for this reason, that it is of the essence of the duty of every trustee to hold an even hand between the parties interested under the trust. Every trustee is in duty bound to look to the interests of all, and not of any particular member or class of members of his *cestuis que trusts*. A third rule which, I think, may safely be laid down, is,—that the Court in appointing a trustee will have regard to the question, whether his appointment will promote or impede the execution of the trust, for the very purpose of the appointment is that the trust may be better carried into execution...

...but, on the other hand, if the continuing or surviving trustee refuses to act with a trustee who may be proposed to be appointed—and I make this observation with reference to what appears to have been said by Mr Fleming, as to Mr Petre having come forward in opposition to his wishes—I think it would be going too far to say that the Court ought, on that ground alone, to refuse to appoint the proposed trustee; for this would, as suggested in the argument, be to give the continuing or surviving trustee a veto upon the appointment of the new trustee. In such a case, I think it must be the duty of the Court to inquire and ascertain whether the objection of the surviving or continuing trustee is well founded or not, and to act or refuse to act upon it accordingly. If the surviving or continuing trustee has improperly refused to act with the proposed trustee, it might be a ground for removing him from the trust. Upon the facts of this case, however, it seems to me that the objections taken by Mr Fleming to the appointment of Mr Petre were and are well founded, and upon the whole case, therefore, my opinion is, that the order under appeal, so far as it appoints Mr Petre, ought to be discharged.

TRUSTEE ACT 1925

40. Vesting of trust property in new or continuing trustees

(1) Where by a deed a new trustee is appointed to perform any trust, then—

(a) if the deed contains a declaration by the appointor to the effect that any estate or interest in any land subject to the trust, or in any chattel so subject, or the right to recover or receive any debt or other thing in action so subject, shall vest in the persons who by virtue of the deed become or are the trustees for performing the trust, the deed shall operate, without any conveyance or assignment, to vest in those persons as joint tenants and for the purposes of the trust the estate interest or rights to which the declaration relates; and

(b) [Applied by the Incumbents and Churchwardens (Trust) Measure 1964 (No. 2), s.3(3).] if the deed is made after the commencement of this Act and does not contain such a declaration, the deed shall, subject to any express provision to the contrary therein contained, operate as if it had contained such a declaration by the appointor extending to all the estates interests and rights with respect to which a declaration could have been made.

(2) Where by deed a retiring trustee is discharged under the statutory power without a new trustee being appointed, then—

(a) if the deed contains such a declaration as aforesaid by the retiring and continuing trustees, the deed shall, without any conveyance or assignment, operate to vest in the continuing trustees alone, as joint tenants, and for the purposes of the trust, the estate, interest, or right to which the declaration relates; and

(b) if the deed is made after the commencement of this Act and does not contain such a declaration, the deed shall, subject to any express provision to the contrary therein contained, operate as if it had contained such a declaration by such persons as aforesaid extending to all the estates, interests and rights with respect to which a declaration could have been made.

(3) An express vesting declaration, whether made before or after the commencement of this Act, shall, notwithstanding that the estate, interest or right to be vested is not expressly referred to, and provided that the other statutory requirements were or are complied with, operate and be deemed always to have operated (but without prejudice to any express provision to the contrary contained in the deed of appointment or discharge) to vest in the persons respectively referred to in subsections (1) and (2) of this section, as the case may require, such estates, interests and rights as are capable of being and ought to be vested in those persons.

(4) This section does not extend—

    (a) to land conveyed by way of mortgage for securing money subject to the trust, except land conveyed on trust for securing debentures or debenture stock;

    (b) to land held under a lease which contains any covenant, condition or agreement against assignment or disposing of the land without licence or consent, unless, prior to the execution of the deed containing expressly or impliedly the vesting declaration, the requisite licence or consent has been obtained, or unless, by virtue of any statute or rule of law, the vesting declaration, express or implied, would not operate as a breach of covenant or give rise to a forfeiture;

    (c) to any share, stock, annuity or property which is only transferable in books kept by a company or other body, or in manner directed by or under an Act of Parliament.

    In this subsection 'lease' includes an underlease and an agreement for a lease or underlease.

(5) For purposes of registration of the deed in any registry, the person or persons making the declaration expressly or impliedly, shall be deemed the conveying party or parties, and the conveyance shall be deemed to be made by him or them under a power conferred by this Act.

(6) This section applies to deeds of appointment or discharge executed on or after the first day of January, eighteen hundred and eighty-two.

NOTE: A person can only be appointed to act as a trustee if they are adult and are of full capacity (having 'legal competency or qualification' (OED), which includes 'mental capacity' (Mental Capacity Act 2005 Sch. 6, s.3(3)—which came into force on 1 October 2007)). A person should not be appointed to act as a trustee if they are unfit (e.g. if they are an undischarged bankrupt).

B: Termination of trusteeship

TRUSTEE ACT 1925

39. Retirement of trustee without a new appointment

(1) Where a trustee is desirous of being discharged from the trust, and after his discharge there will be either a trust corporation or at least two individuals to act as trustees to perform the trust, then, if such trustee as aforesaid by deed declares that he is desirous of being discharged from the trust, and if his co-trustees and such other person, if any, as is empowered to appoint trustees, by deed consent to the discharge of the trustee, and to the vesting in the co-trustees alone of the trust property, the trustee desirous of being discharged shall be deemed to have retired from the trust, and shall, by the deed, be discharged therefrom under this Act, without any new trustee being appointed in his place.

(2) Any assurance or thing requisite for vesting the trust property in the continuing trustees alone shall be executed or done.

NOTE: In cases of hostility between trustees or between trustees and beneficiaries, a trustee can be removed. The leading case, *Letterstedt* v *Broers* (1884) LR 9 App Cas 371, was followed in *The Thomas and Agnes Carvel Foundation* v *Carvel* [2007] EWHC 1314 (Ch) (where 'intense hostility' led to the removal of a personal representative from office) and in *Jones* v *Firkin-Flood* [2008] EWHC 2417 (Ch). The dispute in the latter case arose when a millionaire left the vast majority of his wealth to his youngest son whom he also appointed to act as a trustee. The testator's daughter and eldest son failed in their action to acquire an equal share of the inheritance, but did succeed in having their brother and two other of the four trustees removed. The judge found that they had been guilty of 'total abdication of their duties'. Hostility between siblings seems to be a common cause of such cases (see, by way of further example, *Re E A Scott (1991 Children's Settlement No.1)*; *Scott* v *Scott* [2012] EWHC 2397 (Ch)).

C: The role of beneficiaries

Where a sole beneficiary is absolutely entitled to the entirety of the trust property, or where all the beneficiaries are *sui iuris* and together so entitled, the rule in *Saunders* v *Vautier*, considered in greater detail in Chapter 9, permits the beneficiaries to terminate the trust. They may then, if they so wish, set up a new trust to which they, now as settlors, have the right to appoint the trustees. This course of action, however, will require transfers, which may well give rise to liability for capital transfer or other tax upon the dissolution and fresh settlement. It was in response to this problem that the following statutory provisions were enacted.

TRUSTS OF LAND AND APPOINTMENT OF TRUSTEES ACT 1996

19. **Appointment** and retirement of trustee at instance of beneficiaries

  (1) This section applies in the case of a trust where—

    (a) there is no person nominated for the purpose of appointing new trustees by the instrument, if any, creating the trust, and

    (b) the beneficiaries under the trust are of full age and capacity and (taken together) are absolutely entitled to the property subject to the trust.

  (2) The beneficiaries may give a direction or directions of either or both of the following descriptions—

    (a) a written direction to a trustee or trustees to retire from the trust, and

    (b) a written direction to the trustees or trustee for the time being (or, if there are none, to the personal representative of the last person who was a trustee) to appoint by writing to be a trustee or trustees the person or persons specified in the direction.

  (3) Where—

    (a) a trustee has been given a direction under subsection (2)(a),

    (b) reasonable arrangements have been made for the protection of any rights of his in connection with the trust,

    (c) after he has retired there will be either a trust corporation or at least two persons to act as trustees to perform the trust, and

    (d) either another person is to be appointed to be a new trustee on his retirement (whether in compliance with a direction under subsection (2)(b) or otherwise) or the continuing trustees by deed consent to his retirement,

      he shall make a deed declaring his retirement and shall be deemed to have retired and be discharged from the trust.

  (4) Where a trustee retires under subsection (3) he and the continuing trustees (together with any new trustee) shall (subject to any arrangements for the protection of his rights) do anything necessary to vest the trust property in the continuing trustees (or the continuing and new trustees).

  (5) This section has effect subject to the restrictions imposed by the Trustee Act 1925 on the number of trustees.

20. Appointment of substitute for incapable trustee

[as amended by the Mental Capacity Act 2005, which came into force on 1 October 2007]

 (1) This section applies where—

  (a) a trustee lacks capacity (within the meaning of the Mental Capacity Act 2005) to exercise his functions as trustee,

  (b) there is no person who is both entitled and willing and able to appoint a trustee in place of him under section 36(1) of the Trustee Act 1925, and

  (c) the beneficiaries under the trust are of full age and capacity and (taken together) are absolutely entitled to the property subject to the trust.

 (2) The beneficiaries may give to—

  (a) a deputy appointed for the trustee by the Court of Protection,

  (b) an attorney acting for him under the authority of an enduring power of attorney or lasting power of attorney registered under the Mental Capacity Act 2005, or

  (c) a person authorised for the purpose by the Court of Protection, a written direction to appoint by writing the person or persons specified in the direction to be a trustee or trustees in place of the incapable trustee.

Re May's WT

[1941] 1 Ch 109, Chancery Division

Facts: A testator appointed three trustees in his will. One of the trustees, his widow, happened to have been in Belgium at the date of the German invasion. The other two trustees took out a summons to establish whether they were empowered to appoint a new trustee in her place.

Held: The continuing trustees did not have the power to appoint new trustees, because there was nothing to suggest that the widow was 'incapable of acting' within the meaning of the Trustee Act 1925, s.36(1). The court would appoint a new trustee under s.41(1) of the Act, it being otherwise inexpedient, difficult, or impractical to make an appointment.

CROSSMAN J: I feel that there is some danger in declaring that the plaintiffs, as continuing trustees, have power, pursuant to the Trustee Act 1925, to appoint a new trustee of the will in the place of the widow. Especially do I feel that there is danger in laying down any rule, as a rule may well be susceptible of misuse. I cannot come to any conclusion covering more than this particular case. I can find no evidence that the lady is really 'incapable of acting' within the meaning of s.36, sub-s.1.

 The case seems to be one in which the right course is for the Court to appoint a new trustee. The evidence is enough to justify the Court's doing so under s.41, sub-s.1. Therefore, subject to the production of the proper affidavit of fitness, I will appoint the person whom the summons asks may be appointed to be a trustee in the place of the widow, and will make the necessary vesting orders. I will dispense with service of this application on the widow.

D: Disclaimer of the trust

Re Lord and Fullerton's Contract

[1896] 1 Ch 228, Court of Appeal

Facts: A testator having real and personal property in England and abroad left his residuary estate to trustees upon trust for sale. One of the trustees disclaimed the trusts of the will except as to the property abroad. The remaining trustees sold land of the testator in England.

Held: That the disclaimer had no effect, and that the disclaiming trustee was a necessary party to the conveyance.

LINDLEY LJ:…Treating this, therefore, as a partial disclaimer—as a disclaimer of the offices of trustee and executor so far as the property in this country is concerned—the point is reduced to this: Will that enable the three trustees who are the vendors to make a good title? Now, although the point, so far as I know, is new in species, I think the purchaser is right—that is to say, that according to our law it is not competent for a trustee to execute or to rely on a partial disclaimer of the office either of executor or of trustee, or of the property devised to him. Let us consider what his position is in this case. It is to be observed that he is executor as well as trustee. What would be the position under this document if he remitted personal estate from America to this country? Would not he be responsible for it? Would this disclaimer by him affect him in any way? I should say, obviously not. He would be clearly responsible for the property in respect of his office if he accepts the office at all—in other words, from a purchaser's point of view, if he is not proved not to have accepted he must be deemed to have accepted the office of the trust; and then the ordinary principle applies, that it is not competent for a man to do that partially: he must either do it altogether or not at all…

NOTE: See *Re Lysaght (dec'd)* [1966] 1 Ch 191 (ChD) in Chapter 9.

■ QUESTIONS

1. Is the extent of the duties of fulfilling the office of trustee determined by the need to ensure that the office is filled?

2. The present rule governing the judicial review of trustees' discretions appears to be a rule of economic efficiency—is it appropriate that an efficient rule should be employed when exemplary standards are at stake?

■ SUMMATIVE QUESTION

Trudy has been appointed trustee. The trust deed contains the following clause:

online
resource
centre

> The trustees shall be entitled to all professional charges incurred in the execution of the trust and shall be entitled to delegate all or any of their duties in accordance with the general law.

Trudy has accepted the trust, even though she is a total amateur and rather ignorant of business affairs. She purchases a large quantity of office equipment and stationery to facilitate the smooth running of her tasks but still finds that the job is too complicated. After putting in several months of work in service of the trust, she eventually enlists the assistance of a friend who, having run his own betting office for many years, is more at ease with commercial matters. She transfers the trust fund into the friend's bank account with the instruction that he should invest it wisely for the benefit of the trust. In fact, the friend 'invests' the money on Lucky Laddie, the favourite to win a greyhound race. Lucky Laddie loses the race and the trust fund is lost.

Is Trudy liable for breach of her trust, and why? If she is liable, will she be required to reinstate the full value of the fund, or can she claim remuneration or expenses?

FURTHER READING

Bell, C., 'Some Reflections on Choosing Trustees' (1988) *Trust Law & Practice* 86.

Davies, P. S., 'Correcting mistakes: wither the rule in *Re Hastings-Bass*' (2011) 5 *Conv* 406–421.

Fox, D. M., 'Disclosure of a Settlor's Wish Letter in a Discretionary Trust' (2008) 67(2) *Cambridge Law Journal* 252.

Herbert, M., 'Attacking Trustee Decisions—Grounds for Complaint' (2005) 4 *Private Client Business* 219.

Kirkland, K., 'Recruiting, Selecting and Inducing Charity Trustees' (2002) 4 *Private Client Business* 253.

Lightman, Sir Gavin, 'The Trustees' Duty to Provide Information to Beneficiaries' [2004] *PCB* 23

Matthews, P., 'The Constitution of Disclaimed Trusts Inter Vivos' (1981) 45 *Conv* 141.

Mitchell, C., 'Reining in the Rule in *Re Hastings-Bass*' (2006) 122 *LQR* 35.

Morris, J. and O'Sullivan, C., 'Jasmine Trustees: Tangles in the Trusteeship Chain: Part 1' (2007) 5 *Private Client Business* 347.

Paling, D. R., 'The Trustee's Duty of Skill and Care' (1973) 37 *Conv* 48.

Reed, P., 'The death of the so-called rule in *Hastings-Bass*' (2011) 4 *Private Client Business* 179.

Walker, R., 'The Limits of the Principle in *Re Hastings Bass*' (2002) 4 *Private Client Business* 226.

12

Investment

KEY AIMS

To contrast trustees' very wide power to invest in any type of investment they choose with their duty to choose particular investments prudently. To appreciate that, in accordance with modern portfolio theory and the modern paradigm of prudence, the prudence of trustee investments cannot be assessed by viewing individual investments in isolation but only by assessing the portfolio as a whole. To identify the scope of the trustees' duty to invest the fund so as to achieve fairness between beneficiaries with competing interests in the fund.

SECTION 1: INTRODUCTION

Trustees must invest in a manner that is prudent in the light of current investment practice and fair as between beneficiaries with competing interests in the fund. If they breach their trust in either of these respects, they may be personally liable to compensate for any loss caused. This sounds straightforward enough. The authorities suggest, however, that disappointed beneficiaries find it hard to establish that their trustees have invested improperly, let alone that improper investment has actually caused the trust fund to suffer a quantifiable loss. It is difficult to prove a breach of trust because prudent trustees choose to invest similar funds in widely divergent ways, and because it is reasonable for trustees to have quite different views as to which investments are likely to achieve a fair balance between beneficiaries with competing interests in the fund. Even if it were conceded that trustees had invested imprudently and that the trust fund had suffered a loss, the significant obstacle would remain of proving that the trustees' imprudence had caused the loss. In short, as the law currently stands, there will, in many cases, be no effective remedy for improper trustee investment. Given the vast amount of social wealth that is held in trust this should be a cause for concern, but we will see that the modern trend in trustee investment is towards liberalisation, towards freedom of choice and the free participation of trust funds in investment markets. In such a climate, a weak regulatory scheme will be tolerated, and may even be desired.

In *Nestle* v *National Westminster Bank plc* [1993] 1 WLR 1260, Court of Appeal, Leggatt LJ asserted that 'the importance of preservation of a trust fund will always outweigh success in its advancement', which at first sight suggests a bias in favour of stability and against growth. However, the statement begs at least two further questions. First, is the real value of the fund to be preserved, or merely its nominal value? Secondly, what qualifies as 'success' in the advancement of a trust fund? On the facts of *Nestle*, the nominal value of the fund increased five-fold over a 60-year period, but in the same period, its real value decreased four-fold. Is that success? Leggatt LJ's question is unhelpful because it suggests that the trustees' duty is to achieve particular outcomes. This ought not to be the case, as Hoffmann J stated at first instance in the same case:

> Preservation of real values can be no more than an aspiration which some trustees may have the good fortune to achieve ... a rule that real capital values must be maintained would be unfair to both income beneficiaries and trustees.

The trustees' investment duty is not to achieve a particular outcome, but rather to invest the fund in a particular way, namely prudently and fairly. However, before we consider trustees' duties in detail, we must first examine the scope of their powers.

SECTION 2: THE MEANING OF INVESTMENT

A: The need for direct financial benefits

Investments are acquired for financial return, not for mere use or enjoyment. At one time, investments had to be income-producing, but it now seems that capital return will suffice, subject to the need to 'balance' the interests of life and remainder beneficiaries. Note, also, that the Law Commission for England and Wales has recommended that in the longer term HM Revenue and Customs and HM Treasury should enter into discussions with the trust industry regarding the feasibility of 'total return' investment, i.e. investment which ignores the distinction between income and capital, so far as consistent with current tax policy (Law Com No. 315, *Capital and Income in Trusts: Classification and Apportionment*, 7 May 2009, para. [5.104]). In the case of charities, it is recommended that a statutory provision should be enacted to enable the trustees to free the endowment fund, or a portion of it, from restrictions with respect to expenditure of capital in order that they might operate total return investment in accordance with regulations made by the Charity Commission, without having to seek authorisation under Charities Act 1993, s.26. This reform would avoid the litigation that may arise where it is uncertain whether a special dividend declared on company shares, say, should be treated as income or capital (e.g. see *Trustees of the Bessie Taube Discretionary Settlement Trust* v *HMRC* [2010] UKFTT 473 (First-Tier Tribunal Tax)).

Re Peczenik's ST
[1964] 1 WLR 720, Chancery Division

Facts: The terms of a settlement authorised the trustees to invest the trust funds 'in any shares stocks property or property holding company as the trustees in their discretion shall consider to be in the best interests of [the beneficiary]'. The question arose on the construction of this clause, whether the trustees were permitted to invest as they thought fit.

Held: On the natural construction of the clause, the trustees would be permitted to invest in any 'property' capable of being treated as an investment. They would not, however, be permitted to 'invest' on mere 'personal' security.

BUCKLEY J: I have been referred to the decision of Jenkins J in *In re Harari's Settlement Trusts* [1949] 1 All ER 430, and I recognise that there is a general rule that clauses in trust settlements which enlarge the power of trustees to invest beyond the class of investment which is authorised by the general law ought to be construed strictly. Nevertheless, I have to apply my mind to what is the proper construction to be placed upon the particular settlement before me, and that rule is not one which in any way imposes upon me the duty of putting any unduly restrictive construction upon the language which I have to consider. That was the view which Jenkins J took. He had to consider a settlement in which the trustees were authorised to invest 'in or upon such investments as to them may seem fit'. He came to the conclusion that those words conferred upon the trustees a general wide discretion, and that, on the plain meaning of those words, they could invest in any investments which they honestly thought desirable whether or not authorised by the general law for the investment of trust funds.

I have, therefore, to consider, what is the meaning of the language used in this particular document which is before me. I agree with the suggestion which was made that the term 'property holding company,' which is not any kind of term of art, is one to which, in this context, I really can give no precise meaning, and I think I should ignore the reference to 'property holding company,' for I cannot see how those words, whatever meaning is given to them, could really extend what is already covered by the words 'shares stocks property' in clause (1). Any investment in a company, whether a property holding company or a company of any other kind, must, it seems to me, be either a share, or stock, or some other form of property. I do not take the view, which was also urged before me, that 'property' here should be confined to real property. I see no reason for putting such a confined interpretation upon the words. Taking clause (1) by itself, it appears to me that the clause authorises the trustees to invest in any shares, any stock, or any property. It must, of course, be property of a kind capable of being treated as an investment, not property which is acquired merely for use and enjoyment. But, apart from that, it seems to me that clause (1) places no restriction upon the discretion of the trustees beyond saying that the investments must be investments in stocks or shares or something which can properly be described as property. The clause would not, I think, authorise investments merely upon personal security ... .

NOTE: The last reference to investments on personal security echoes the observation of Lord Russell of Killowen in *Khoo Tek Keon* v *Ch'ng Joo Tuan Neoh* [1934] AC 529 that 'loans on no security beyond the liability of the borrower to repay ... are not investments'. However, there is authority to show that a trustee will be permitted to 'invest' on personal security if the trust expressly and precisely authorises such an investment (in *Re Laing's Settlement* [1899] 1 Ch 593 the instrument authorised investment 'upon such personal credit without security as the trustees ... think fit'). If Lord Russell was correct, investments on personal security are not really investments at all, and they will therefore remain unauthorised despite the general investment power provided by the Trustee Act 2000. However, a better approach under the 2000 Act may be to allow this type of investment, but to presume that such investments will not satisfy the standard investment criterion of 'suitability' unless specifically authorised by the trust instrument.

SECTION 3: EXPRESS AND GENERAL POWERS OF INVESTMENT

The first guide to a trustee's investment powers is the trust instrument governing his particular trust (Trustee Act 2000 (s.6(1)(b))). The terms of the trust instrument in relation to investment powers are always to be given their natural construction (*Re Harari's ST* [1949] 1 All ER 430). Where a pre-Trustee Act 2000 trust authorised trustees to invest without limitation in accordance with the Trustee Investments Act 1961, such trustees will now be authorised to invest without limit in accordance with the Trustee Act 2000 (s.7(6)). However, any limitations set out in trust instruments prior to the 2000 Act will still apply unless made before 3 August 1961 (s.7(5)).

TRUSTEE ACT 2000

7 Existing trusts

(1)   This Part applies in relation to trusts whether created before or after its commencement.

(2)   No provision relating to the powers of a trustee contained in a trust instrument made before 3rd August 1961 is to be treated (for the purposes of section 6(1)(b)) as restricting or excluding the general power of investment.

(3)   A provision contained in a trust instrument made before the commencement of this Part which—

      (a)   has effect under section 3(2) of the Trustee Investments Act 1961 as a power to invest under that Act, or

      (b)   confers power to invest under that Act,

is to be treated as conferring the general power of investment on a trustee.

NOTE: The explanatory note to this provision explains that it 'ensures that an intention of a settlor to provide ample powers of investment is not frustrated by this liberalisation of the general law'.

■ QUESTIONS

1. What if the settlor of a trust executed on 10 April 1997 included the clause 'My trustees' powers of investment are those currently permitted by the general law'? Are the trustees of that trust restricted to the general law as at 10 April 1997, or can they take advantage of the wider investment powers introduced by the 2000 Act?

    Hint: See the Trustee Act 2000, s.7(3)(a).

2. What if the settlor of a trust executed on 10 April 1997 included the clause 'My trustees are permitted to invest in nothing other than government bonds'? Are the trustees of that trust bound by that restriction, or can they take advantage of the wider investment powers introduced by the 2000 Act?

3. What if the settlor of a trust executed on 10 April 1997 included the clause 'My trustees are permitted to invest in shares quoted on the London Stock Exchange, but not in shares of X plc'? Can the trustees take advantage of the general investment power provided by the 2000 Act?

    Hint: See the Trustee Act 2000, s.6(1) (see extract in subsection A. General investment powers.

A: General investment powers

Subject to the particular powers set out in the trust instrument, one would expect a trustee, as legal owner of the trust property, to have the same powers as any other legal owner of property. In fact, it was only with the coming into force of the Trustee Act 2000 (see extract) that the law was reformed to allow trustees to make 'any kind of investment', as if they were 'absolutely entitled to the assets' of the trust. The Trustee Investments Act 1961, which was repealed by the Trustee Act 2000, had restricted trustees to certain types of so-called 'safe' investments, such as gilt-edged securities, bank accounts, and shares in quoted public limited companies with a good track record and a strong financial base. More creative investment had been permitted only if authorised by the trust instrument or by the court. The 'authorised list' approach laid down by the 1961 Act denied conscientious trustees the freedom to invest positively in accordance with the best available techniques (and, in particular, in accordance with modern portfolio theory), it also encouraged the indolent to restrict themselves to investments on the 'authorised list' even when they had express authority to invest beyond it (see the *Nestle* case).

TRUSTEE ACT 2000

PART II INVESTMENT

3. General power of investment

(1)   Subject to the provisions of this Part, a trustee may make any kind of investment that he could make if he were absolutely entitled to the assets of the trust.

(2)   In this Act the power under subsection (1) is called 'the general power of investment'.

(3)   The general power of investment does not permit a trustee to make investments in land other than in loans secured on land (but see also section 8).

(4)   A person invests in a loan secured on land if he has rights under any contract under which—

(a)   one person provides another with credit, and

(b)   the obligation of the borrower to repay is secured on land.

(5)   'Credit' includes any cash loan or other financial accommodation.

(6)   'Cash' includes money in any form.

NOTE: As things turned out, the timing of the Trustee Act 2000 could not have been much worse. It changed the law to allow trustees unrestricted power to invest in stock markets just as stock markets reached historical all-time highs. (By the end of 2010 stock markets had still failed to attain the levels they had achieved at the very end of 1999.)

B: Investment in land

TRUSTEE ACT 2000

PART III ACQUISITION OF LAND

8. Power to acquire freehold and leasehold land

(1)   A trustee may acquire freehold or leasehold land in the United Kingdom—

(a)   as an investment,

(b)   for occupation by a beneficiary, or

(c)   for any other reason.

(2)   'Freehold or leasehold land' means—

(a)   in relation to England and Wales, a legal estate in land,

(b)   in relation to Scotland—

(i)   the estate or interest of the proprietor of the dominium utile or, in the case of land not held on feudal tenure, the estate or interest of the owner, or

(ii)   a tenancy, and

(c)   in relation to Northern Ireland, a legal estate in land, including land held under a fee farm grant.

(3)   For the purpose of exercising his functions as a trustee, a trustee who acquires land under this section has all the powers of an absolute owner in relation to the land.

9. Restriction or exclusion of this Part

The powers conferred by this Part are—

(a)   in addition to powers conferred on trustees otherwise than by this Part, but

(b) subject to any restriction or exclusion imposed by the trust instrument or by any enactment or any provision of subordinate legislation.

10. Existing trusts

(1) This Part does not apply in relation to—

(a) a trust of property which consists of or includes land which (despite section 2 of the Trusts of Land and Appointment of Trustees Act 1996) is settled land, or

(b) a trust to which the Universities and College Estates Act 1925 applies.

(2) Subject to subsection (1), this Part applies in relation to trusts whether created before or after its commencement.

C: Powers of trustees of land

TRUSTS OF LAND AND APPOINTMENT OF TRUSTEES ACT 1996

6. General powers of trustees

(1) For the purpose of exercising their functions as trustees, the trustees of land have in relation to the land subject to the trust all the powers of an absolute owner.

(2) Where in the case of any land subject to a trust of land each of the beneficiaries interested in the land is a person of full age and capacity who is absolutely entitled to the land, the powers conferred on the trustees by subsection (1) include the power to convey the land to the beneficiaries even though they have not required the trustees to do so; and where land is conveyed by virtue of this subsection—

(a) the beneficiaries shall do whatever is necessary to secure that it vests in them, and

(b) if they fail to do so, the court may make an order requiring them to do so.

(3) The trustees of land have power to acquire land under the power conferred by section 8 of the Trustee Act 2000.

[subsection (4) is repealed by Trustee Act 2000]

(5) In exercising the powers conferred by this section trustees shall have regard to the rights of the beneficiaries.

(6) The powers conferred by this section shall not be exercised in contravention of, or of any order made in pursuance of, any other enactment or any rule of law or equity.

(7) The reference in subsection (6) to an order includes an order of any court or of the Charity Commissioners.

(8) Where any enactment other than this section confers on trustees authority to act subject to any restriction, limitation or condition, trustees of land may not exercise the powers conferred by this section to do any act which they are prevented from doing under the other enactment by reason of the restriction, limitation or condition.

(9) The duty of care under section 1 of the Trustee Act 2000 applies to trustees of land when exercising the powers conferred by this section.

SECTION 4: GENERAL INVESTMENT DUTIES

The law recognises trustees to have the same investment powers as absolute owners, but whereas an absolute owner may use his property as he pleases—choosing, if he wishes, to gamble and speculate—trustees' legal powers are constrained by their duty to invest prudently and fairly. Absolute owners invest on their own account; trustees are accountable to beneficiaries. This does not mean that trustees are required to make up from their own funds every loss that befalls the trust fund. They are not insurers of the fund.

Harvard College v *Amory*

26 Mass (9 Pick) 446 (1830)

JUSTICE PUTMAN (at 461): All that can be required of a trustee to invest, is, that he shall conduct himself faithfully and exercise a sound discretion. He is to observe how men of prudence, discretion and intelligence manage their own affairs, not in regard to speculation, but in regard to the permanent disposition of their funds, considering the probable income, as well as the probable safety of the capital to be invested.

NOTE: This passage sets out the essential trustee duties in relation to investment. First, the trustee must be faithful: he must not invest in companies he owns or otherwise place himself in a position of conflict. Secondly, he must exercise a positive discretion: he must make choices in relation to all aspects of investment management, such as when to sell and acquire investments; which investments to sell and acquire; whether or not to delegate investment functions; when to delegate, and to whom. Thirdly, the discretion he exercises must be a sound one. This is judged objectively, the question being whether the trustee exercised his discretion prudently and fairly. Fourthly, speculation is *ipso facto* imprudent and is not permitted. It is sometimes said that one must 'speculate to accumulate' but 'select to protect' is a more appropriate motto for the trustee. Fifthly, the trustee should have regard to both income and capital returns. This latter requirement is especially relevant to traditional trusts where there is a life tenant and remainderman. Generally speaking, the life tenant is interested in income and the remainderman is interested in capital.

TRUSTEE ACT 2000

4. Standard investment criteria

(1)   In exercising any power of investment, whether arising under this Part or otherwise, a trustee must have regard to the standard investment criteria.

(2)   A trustee must from time to time review the investments of the trust and consider whether, having regard to the standard investment criteria, they should be varied.

(3)   The standard investment criteria, in relation to a trust, are—

    (a)   the suitability to the trust of investments of the same kind as any particular investment proposed to be made or retained and of that particular investment as an investment of that kind, and

    (b)   the need for diversification of investments of the trust, in so far as is appropriate to the circumstances of the trust.

■ QUESTIONS

1.   Can it be said that 'investment' under the new 'general investment power' (Trustee Act 2000, s.3) now includes financial outlay which is expected to realise returns in the form of capital growth alone? Does this spell the end of the traditional requirement that an investment must be income-producing?

2.   Like the old Trustee Investments Act 1961, s.6(1)(a), the Trustee Act 2000 provides that trustees should have regard to 'the need for diversification of investments of the trust, in so far as is appropriate to the circumstances of the trust' (s.4(3)(b)). What are the 'circumstances' of the trust?

NOTE: In *Cowan* v *Scargill*, Megarry V-C stated that:

the reference to 'circumstances of the trust' plainly includes matters such as the size of the trust funds: the degree of diversification that is practicable and desirable for a large fund may plainly be impracticable or undesirable (or both) in the case of a small fund.

TRUSTEE ACT 2000

5. Advice

(1)   Before exercising any power of investment, whether arising under this Part or otherwise, a trustee must (unless the exception applies) obtain and consider proper advice about the way in which, having regard to the standard investment criteria, the power should be exercised.

(2)   When reviewing the investments of the trust, a trustee must (unless the exception applies) obtain and consider proper advice about whether, having regard to the standard investment criteria, the investments should be varied.

(3)   The exception is that a trustee need not obtain such advice if he reasonably concludes that in all the circumstances it is unnecessary or inappropriate to do so.

(4)   Proper advice is the advice of a person who is reasonably believed by the trustee to be qualified to give it by his ability in and practical experience of financial and other matters relating to the proposed investment.

NOTE: The explanatory notes accompanying the Act suggest that if the proposed investment is small, the cost of obtaining advice might be disproportionate to the benefit to be gained from doing so; in such a case it would therefore be reasonable not to seek the advice (note 26).

6. Restriction or exclusion of this Part

(1)   The general power of investment is—
   (a) in addition to powers conferred on trustees otherwise than by this Act, but
   (b) subject to any restriction or exclusion imposed by the trust instrument or by any enactment or any provision of subordinate legislation.

(2)   For the purposes or this Act, an enactment or a provision of subordinate legislation is not to be regarded as being, or as being part of, a trust instrument.

(3)   In this Act 'subordinate legislation' has the same meaning as in the Interpretation Act 1978.

7. Existing trusts

(1)   This Part applies in relation to trusts whether created before or after its commencement.

(2)   No provision relating to the powers of a trustee contained in a trust instrument made before 3rd August 1961 is to be treated (for the purposes of section 6(1)(b)) as restricting or excluding the general power of investment.

(3)   A provision contained in a trust instrument made before the commencement of this Part which—
   (a) has effect under section 3(2) of the M1Trustee Investments Act 1961 as a power to invest under that Act, or
   (b) confers power to invest under that Act,
is to be treated as conferring the general power of investment on a trustee

---

Nestle v *National Westminster Bank plc*
(1996) 10(4) *TLI* 11

Facts: A testator died in 1922 leaving a fund worth approximately £54,000 on trust for various descendants. The claimant, the testator's only granddaughter, became solely and absolutely entitled to the fund in 1986, at which time it was valued at approximately £270,000. She claimed that, with proper investment, the present value of the fund should have been more than £1 million.

Held: The bank had misinterpreted the powers of investment granted to it by the terms of the will trust and should have taken legal advice as to them. The bank should also have made regular reviews of the investments under its control. However, the claimant had failed to show that the bank's breaches of duty had resulted in a loss to the fund and on that basis the appeal was dismissed.

HOFFMANN J: …

IV. The Investment Duties of Trustees

1. The Law

There was no dispute over the general principles to be applied. First, there is the prudence principle. The classic statement is that of Lindley LJ:

> The duty of a trustee is not to take such care only as a prudent man would take if he had only himself to consider; the duty rather is to take such care as an ordinary prudent man would take if he were minded to make an investment for the benefit of other people for whom he felt morally bound to provide.

This is an extremely flexible standard capable of adaptation to current economic conditions and contemporary understanding of markets and investments. For example, investments which were imprudent in the days of the gold standard may be sound and sensible in times of high inflation. Modern trustees acting within their investment powers are entitled to be judged by the standards of current portfolio theory, which emphasises the risk level of the entire portfolio rather than the risk attaching to each investment taken in isolation. But in reviewing the conduct of trustees over a period of more than 60 years, one must be careful not to endow the prudent trustee with prophetic vision or expect him to have ignored the received wisdom of his time.

Mr Gerard Wright, who appeared for Miss Nestle, referred me to another passage in *Re Whiteley* (1887) 12 App Cas 727 in which Cotton LJ said:

> Trustees are bound to preserve the money for those entitled to the *corpus* in remainder, and they are bound to invest it in such a way as will produce a reasonable income for those enjoying the income for the present.

In 1886 what Cotton LJ had in mind was the safety of the capital in purely monetary terms. But Mr Wright submitted that in the conditions which prevail a century later, the trustees were under an overriding duty to preserve the *real* value of the capital. In my judgment this cannot be right. The preservation of the monetary value of the capital requires no skill or luck. The trustees can discharge their duties, as they often did until 1961, by investing the whole fund in gilt-edged securities. Preservation of real values can be no more than an aspiration which some trustees may have the good fortune to achieve. Plainly they must have regard to the interests of those entitled in the future to capital and such regard will require them to take into consideration the potential effects of inflation, but a rule that real capital values must be maintained would be unfair to both income beneficiaries and trustees.

This brings me to the second principle on which there was general agreement, namely that the trustee must act fairly in making investment decisions which may have different consequences for different classes of beneficiaries. There are two reasons why I prefer this formulation to the traditional image of holding the scales equally between tenant for life and remainderman. The first is that the image of the scales suggests a weighing of known quantities whereas investment decisions are concerned with predictions of the future. Investments will carry current expectations of their future income yield and capital appreciation and these expectations will be reflected in their current market price, but there is always a greater or lesser risk that the outcome will deviate from those expectations. A judgment on the fairness of the choices made by the trustees must have regard to these imponderables. The second reason is that the image of the scales suggests a more mechanistic process than I believe the law requires. The trustees have in my judgment a wide discretion. They are for example entitled to take into account the income needs of the tenant for life or the fact that the tenant for life was a person known to the settlor and a primary object of the trust whereas the remainderman is a remoter relative or a stranger. Of course these cannot be allowed to become the overriding considerations but the concept of fairness between classes of beneficiaries does not require them to be excluded. It would be an inhuman law which required trustees to adhere to some mechanical rule for preserving the real value of the capital when the tenant for life was the testator's widow who had fallen upon hard times and the remainderman was young and well off.

NOTES
1. In his judgment, Hoffmann J refers to portfolio theory. This is a reference to so-called 'modern portfolio theory'. It is significant that his judgment appeared in 1988 (although not reported in full until 1996) and so came just two years after the deregulation of investment business in the UK (the so-called 'Big Bang' brought about by the Financial Services Act 1986) and the publication in the US in 1986 of Bevis Longstreth's seminal work, *Modern Investment Management and the Prudent Man Rule*, which applied modern portfolio theory to trustees' investment duties to produce a new modern paradigm of prudence. The major insight offered by modern portfolio theory is that risks specific to investment in any particular company may be virtually eliminated by holding a diverse portfolio of shares in other companies. Portfolios containing investments other than shares also benefit from diversification, but the theory is most applicable to shares, and especially shares in public companies. The values of shares in public companies are quoted on the stock exchange so the market in such shares is efficient relative to other markets, in the sense that the quoted value of the shares ought to be an accurate reflection of all published information relating to those shares. The theory, therefore, is that a prudent investor will not avoid risk, since no investment is risk free, but will manage his risk by spreading his investments across the market and thereby matching (so far as possible) the performance of the market as a whole. If the market collapses, his investments will collapse, but in the meantime he is not exposed to the sort of specific risks to which he would have been exposed if he had invested selectively in just a few quoted companies. To counter the risk of market collapse, he should invest in other markets (e.g. property and overseas shares).
2. According to the explanatory notes accompanying the Trustee Act 2000, the Act is intended to facilitate trustee investment in accordance with modern portfolio theory (note 25).

Nestle v National Westminster Bank plc
[1993] 1 WLR 1260, Court of Appeal

For the facts, and the decision at first instance, see above.

DILLON LJ: ... It was the duty of the bank to acquaint itself with the scope of its powers under the will ... . It is inexcusable that the bank took no step at any time to obtain legal advice as to the scope of its power to invest in ordinary shares. Instead the bank administered the trusts, until the enactment of the Trustee Investments Act 1961, on the basis that while it could continue to retain ordinary shares which had been held by the testator at the date of his death, the power it had to invest in further ordinary shares was limited to investment in further ordinary shares in the companies in which it still retained ordinary shares which had been held by the testator at the date of his death, or ordinary shares in 'similar companies' e.g. ordinary shares in a further insurance company at a time when the bank still retained insurance shares which the testator had held at his death.

After the enactment of the Trustee Investments Act 1961, the bank erroneously assumed that its powers of investment were wholly governed by that Act.

On 25 November 1959 an official of the bank told John Nestle, in a spuriously knowledgable way, that this seemed to the bank to be a case where the bank should apply to the court under the Variation of Trusts Act 1958 for a widening of its investment powers. But again nothing was ever done, and no advice as to the scope of the bank's investment powers was ever sought ... The bank should, in my judgment, have appreciated the true scope of its powers of investment and should have reviewed the investments in the annuity fund regularly (if not necessarily strictly annually) with that in mind.

Mr Lyndon-Stanford submits that, if the bank had done that, the equities would have been diversified and the equities in the annuity fund in 1960 would have been substantially higher in value by 1960 than they actually were ...

The difficulty about that approach is however, as Hoffmann J pointed out, that the evidence showed that if the BZW Equity Index was applied over the period from July 1974 to December 1986 to 'growth' unit trusts (as opposed to 'income' unit trusts) it appeared that 12 of the 'growth' trusts had done better than the index, but 21 had done worse. It is impossible to say that those 21 unit trusts must have been managed with a degree of incompetence which, in a trustee like the bank, would have amounted to a breach of trust ... Mr Nugee for the bank rightly stressed the duty of a trustee to act prudently.

... This principle remains applicable however wide, or even unlimited, the scope of the investment clause in a trust instrument may be. Trustees should not be reckless with trust money. But what the prudent man should do at any time depends on the economic and financial conditions of that time—not on what judges of the past, however eminent, have held to be the prudent course in the conditions of 50 or 100 years before. It has seemed to me that Mr Nugee's submissions placed far too much weight on the actual decisions of the courts in the last century, when investment conditions were very different. Indeed Mr Nugee's submissions accorded scant justice to such common sense and initiative as his client the bank actually displayed in the management of the Nestle trust funds.

If what had happened in the present case had been that the bank, through failure to inform itself as to the true scope of its investment powers, had invested the whole of the annuity fund in fixed interest securities, and no part in equities, for the whole period from 1922 to 1960, then, as on the evidence loss would clearly have been proved to have been suffered, the appropriate course would have been to require the bank to make good to the trust fair compensation—and not just the minimum that might have got by without challenge ... .

The case for the plaintiff in the court below seems largely to have been founded on the BZW Equity Index and the opinions of her expert witnesses, as against the opinion of the bank's expert witnesses, on the desirability or prudence of investment in equities at various stages between 1922 and 1986. On that controversy the judge made his findings, and those findings have not really been challenged on this appeal. Mr Lyndon-Stanford has concentrated instead on the practicalities of what the bank was actually doing, or failing to do, with the trust funds, rather than on the expert evidence. Mr Lyndon-Stanford has put his case with very considerable skill, and there is at the end of the day not much for the bank to be proud of in its administration of the Nestle trusts ... But I am unable to see that any breach of trust which has caused loss to the plaintiff has been proved. Accordingly this appeal must, in my judgment, be dismissed.

STAUGHTON LJ: ... the misunderstanding of the investment clause and the failure to conduct periodic reviews do not by themselves, whether separately or together, afford the plaintiff a remedy. They were symptoms of incompetence or idleness—not on the part of National Westminster Bank but of their predecessors; they were not, without more, breaches of trust. The plaintiff must show that, through one or other or both of those causes, the trustees made decisions which they should not have made or failed to make decisions which they should have made. If that were proved, and if at first sight loss resulted, it would be appropriate to order an inquiry as to the loss suffered by the trust fund.

... I would dismiss the appeal. The judge took the view that 'the bank had acted conscientiously, fairly and carefully throughout the administration of [the] trust.' I cannot join in that accolade. But it is not shown that there was loss arising from a breach of trust for which the trustees ought to compensate the trust fund.

LEGGATT LJ: ... A breach of duty will not be actionable, and therefore will be immaterial, if it does not cause loss. In this context I would endorse the concession of Mr Nugee for the bank that 'loss' will be incurred by a trust fund when it makes a gain less than would have been made by a prudent businessman. A claimant will therefore fail who cannot prove a loss in this sense caused by breach of duty. So here in order to make a case for an inquiry, the plaintiff must show that loss was caused by breach of duty on the part of the bank ... . it does not follow from the fact that a wider power of investment was available to the bank than it realised either that it would have been exercised or that, if it had been, the exercise of it would have produced a result more beneficial to the bank than actually was produced. Loss cannot be presumed, if none would necessarily have resulted. Until it was proved that there was a loss, no attempt could be made to assess the amount of it ... .

No testator, in the light of this example, would choose this bank for the effective management of his investment. But the bank's engagement was as a trustee; and as such, it is to be judged not so much by success as by absence of proven default. The importance of preservation of a trust fund will always outweigh success in its advancement. Inevitably, a trustee in the bank's position wears a complacent air, because the virtue of safety will in practice put a premium on inactivity. Until the 1950s active management of the portfolio might have been seen as speculative, and even in these days such dealing would have to be notably successful before the expense would be justified. The very process of attempting to achieve a balance, or (if that be old-fashioned) fairness, as between the interests of life-tenants and those of a remainderman inevitably means that each can complain of being less well served than he or she ought to have been. But by the undemanding standard of prudence the bank is not shown to have committed any breach of trust resulting in loss.

I am therefore constrained to agree that the appeal must be dismissed.

■ QUESTIONS

1. Do you think trustees should be judged according to the prudence of their invest-ment choices or by the success of the investments they choose? (Note *Jeffrey* v *Gretton and Russell* [2011] WTLR 809 (Ch), in which a trustee escaped liability after impru-dently making an investment which by pure chance happened to do well.)

2. Does the *Nestle* case bear out the statement made by Jesse Dukeminier and James E. Krier, in their article 'The Rise of the Perpetual Trust' (2003) 50 *UCLA L Rev* 1303, p. 1335, where they wrote: 'How do you make a small fortune? Give a bank a large one to manage in trust'?

NOTE: Contrast the outcome in *Nestle* with the outcome in the *Re Mulligan (dec'd)* case.

Re Mulligan (dec'd)

[1998] 1 NZLR 481

Facts: The testator had died in 1949 leaving his widow a substantial legacy and a life interest in a farm. The widow was one of the trustees of the estate. The farm was sold in 1965 and the estate invested in fixed-interest securities until the widow died in 1990. The other trustee had, between 1965 and 1990, tried to persuade the widow to invest in shares to counter inflation but she had adamantly refused to do so.

Held: The latter trustee (a trust corporation) was held to be in breach of trust because it had appreciated the corrosive effect of inflation on the estate capital (which was held to be reliable evidence of the standard of prudence in the industry at the time), but had nevertheless deferred to the widow's wishes.

SECTION 5: **SPECIAL INVESTMENT DUTIES**

TRUSTEE ACT 1925

(Note that sections 8 and 9 of the Trustee Act 1925 only affect loans and investments made before the coming into force of the Trustee Act 2000.)

8. Loans and investments by trustees not chargeable as breaches of trust

(1) A trustee lending money on the security of any property on which he can properly lend shall not be chargeable with breach of trust by reason only of the proportion borne by the amount of the loan to the value of the property at the time when the loan was made, if it appears to the court—

(a) that in making the loan the trustee was acting upon a report as to the value of the prop-erty made by a person whom he reasonably believed to be an able practical surveyor or valuer instructed and employed independently of any owner of the property, whether such surveyor or valuer carried on business in the locality where the property is situate or else-where; and

(b) that the amount of the loan does not exceed two third parts of the value of the property as stated in the report; and

(c) that the loan was made under the advice of the surveyor or valuer expressed in the report.

(2) A trustee lending money on the security of any leasehold property shall not be chargeable with breach of trust only upon the ground that in making such loan he dispensed either wholly or partly with the production or investigation of the lessor's title.

(3)   A trustee shall not be chargeable with breach of trust only upon the ground that in effecting the purchase, or in lending money upon the security, of any property he has accepted a shorter title than the title which a purchaser is, in the absence of a special contract, entitled to require, if in the opinion of the court the title accepted be such as a person acting with prudence and caution would have accepted.

(4)   This section applies to transfers of existing securities as well as to new securities and to investments made before as well as after the commencement of this Act.

9. Liability for loss by reason of improper investment

(1)   Where a trustee improperly advances trust money on a mortgage security which would at the time of the investment be a proper investment in all respects for a smaller sum than is actually advanced thereon, the security shall be deemed an authorised investment for the smaller sum, and the trustee shall only be liable to make good the sum advanced in excess thereof with interest.

(2)   This section applies to investments made before as well as after the commencement of this Act.

■ QUESTION

What will be the extent of a trustee's liability for advancing a £200,000 loan on the security of freehold land worth £270,000 without having taken expert advice?

PENSIONS ACT 1995

33. Investment powers duty of care

(1)   Liability for breach of an obligation under any rule of law to take care or exercise skill in the performance of any investment functions, where the function is exercisable—
    (a) by a trustee of a trust scheme, or
    (b) by a person to whom the function has been delegated under section 34,
    cannot be excluded or restricted by any instrument or agreement.

34. Power of investment and delegation

(1)   The trustees of a trust scheme have, subject to any restriction imposed by the scheme, the same power to make an investment of any kind as if they were absolutely entitled to the assets of the scheme.
    ...
[The remainder of section 34 permits pension trustees to delegate their investment powers to some of their number, or to an authorised fund manager, and outlines the circumstances in which they will be liable for the defaults of the delegate.]

35. Investment principles

(1)   The trustees of a trust scheme must secure that there is prepared, maintained and from time to time revised a written statement of the principles governing decisions about investments for the purposes of the scheme.

(2)   The statement must cover, among other things—
    (a) the trustees' policy for securing compliance with sections 36 and 56, and
    (b) their policy about the following matters.

(3)   Those matters are—
    (a) the kinds of investments to be held,
    (b) the balance between different kinds of investments,
    (c) risk,
    (d) the expected return on investments,
    (e) the realisation of investments, and
    (f) such other matters as may be prescribed.

(4)   Neither the trust scheme nor the statement may impose restrictions (however expressed) on any power to make investments by reference to the consent of the employer.

(5) The trustees of a trust scheme must, before a statement under this section is prepared or revised—

  (a) obtain and consider the written advice of a person who is reasonably believed by the trustees to be qualified by his ability in and practical experience of financial matters and to have the appropriate knowledge and experience of the management of the investments of such schemes, and

  (b) consult the employer.

(6) If in the case of any trust scheme—

  (a) a statement under this section has not been prepared or is not being maintained, or

  (b) the trustees have not obtained and considered advice in accordance with subsection (5), section 3 [Prohibition Orders] and 10 [Civil penalties] apply to any trustee who has failed to take all steps as are reasonable to secure compliance.

SECTION 6: INVESTMENT POLICY

Where a trust exists for the purpose of financial provision (as most private trusts do) the trustees are obliged to pursue the beneficiaries' best *financial* interests. At present, the only exceptions to this are where the trust instrument authorises ethical investments, or the beneficiaries are unanimously opposed to particular investments. However, reform may be in the air. The Trustee Act 2000 requires trustees to consider the 'suitability' of investments when exercising their investment powers, and the explanatory notes accompanying the Act confirm that suitability 'will … include any relevant ethical considerations as to the kind of investments which it is appropriate for the trust to make' (note 23).

Cowan v Scargill

[1985] 1 Ch 270, Chancery Division

Facts: One half of the management committee of the National Coal Board's pension fund trusts brought an action against the members of the other half; the former having being appointed by the National Coal Board, the latter by the National Union of Mineworkers (NUM). The committee members appointed by the NUM included Mr Arthur Scargill, president of the union. The committee members were the trustees of pension funds worth approximately £3,000 million, with a responsibility to invest £200 million on an annual basis. Because the planned investment scheme included investments in overseas industries and in oil and gas, the union trustees refused to adopt the scheme. The union trustees justified their actions as being in the beneficiaries' best interests, although they admitted that they had also been motivated by union policy. The National Coal Board trustees brought proceedings to determine whether the refusal of the union trustees had been in breach of trust.

Held: The purpose of the trust was the provision of financial benefits, and it was therefore the duty of the trustees to invest with a view to securing those benefits. The trustees must set their personal views to one side, although they could in rare cases take into account personal views unanimously held by the beneficiaries. In the present case, the union trustees had put their political views before the best financial interests of the beneficiaries. Further, they had been motivated not by the interests of the beneficiaries (retired miners), but by the contributors to the pension funds (working miners). They were, accordingly, in breach of trust for refusing to adopt the proposed investment scheme.

SIR ROBERT MEGARRY V-C: The starting point is the duty of trustees to exercise their powers in the best interests of the present and future beneficiaries of the trust, holding the scales impartially between different classes of beneficiaries. This duty of the trustees towards their beneficiaries is paramount. They must, of course, obey the law; but subject to that, they must put the interests of their beneficiaries first. When the purpose of the trust is to provide financial benefits for the beneficiaries, as is usually the case, the best interests of the beneficiaries are normally their best financial interests. In the case of a power of investment, as in the present case, the power must be exercised so as to yield the best return for the beneficiaries, judged in relation to the risks of the investments in question; and the prospects of the yield of income and capital appreciation both have to be considered in judging the return from the investment.

The legal memorandum that the union obtained from their solicitors is generally in accord with these views. In considering the possibility of investment for 'socially beneficial reasons which may result in lower returns to the fund,' the memorandum states that 'the trustees' only concern is to ensure that the return is the maximum possible consistent with security'; and then refers to the need for diversification. However, it continues by saying:

> Trustees cannot be criticised for failing to make a particular investment for social or political reasons, such as in South African stock for example, but may be held liable for investing in assets which yield a poor return or for disinvesting in stock at inappropriate times for nonfinancial criteria.

This last sentence must be considered in the light of subsequent passages in the memorandum which indicate that the sale of South African securities by trustees might be justified on the ground of doubts about political stability in South Africa and the long-term financial soundness of its economy, whereas trustees could not properly support motions at a company meeting dealing with pay levels in South Africa, work accidents, pollution control, employment conditions for minorities, military contracting and consumer protection. The assertion that trustees could not be criticised for failing to make a particular investment for social or political reasons is one that I would not accept in its full width. If the investment in fact made is equally beneficial to the beneficiaries, then criticism would be difficult to sustain in practice, whatever the position in theory. But if the investment in fact made is less beneficial, then both in theory and in practice the trustees would normally be open to criticism.

This leads me to the second point, which is a corollary of the first. In considering what investments to make trustees must put on one side their own personal views. Trustees may have strongly held social or political views. They may be firmly opposed to any investment in South Africa or other countries, or they may object to any form of investment in companies concerned with alcohol, tobacco, armaments or many other things. In the conduct of their own affairs, of course, they are free to abstain from making any such investments. Yet under a trust, if investments of this type would be more beneficial to the beneficiaries than other investments, the trustees must not refrain from making the investments by reason of the views that they hold.

Trustees may even have to act dishonourably (though not illegally) if the interests of their beneficiaries require it. Thus where trustees for sale had struck a bargain for the sale of trust property but had not bound themselves by a legally enforceable contract, they were held to be under a duty to consider and explore a better offer that they received, and not to carry through the bargain to which they felt in honour bound: *Buttle* v *Saunders* [1950] 2 All ER 193. In other words, the duty of trustees to their beneficiaries may include a duty to 'gazump,' however honourable the trustees. As Wynn-Parry J said at p. 195, trustees 'have an overriding duty to obtain the best price which they can for their beneficiaries.' In applying this to an official receiver in *In re Wyvern Developments Ltd* [1974] 1 WLR 1097, 1106, Templeman J said that he 'must do his best by his creditors and contributories. He is in a fiduciary capacity and cannot make moral gestures, nor can the court authorise him to do so.' In the words of Sir James Wigram V-C in *Balls* v *Strutt* (1841) 1 Hare 146, 149:

> It is a principle in this court, that a trustee shall not be permitted to use the powers which the trust may confer upon him at law, except for the legitimate purposes of his trust; ...

Powers must be exercised fairly and honestly for the purposes for which they are given and not so as to accomplish any ulterior purpose, whether for the benefit of the trustees or otherwise: see *Duke of Portland* v *Topham* (1864) 11 HL Cas. 32, a case on a power of appointment that must apply a fortiori to a power given to trustees as such.

Third, by way of caveat I should say that I am not asserting that the benefit of the beneficiaries which a trustee must make his paramount concern inevitably and solely means their financial benefit, even if the only object of the trust is to provide financial benefits. Thus if the only actual or potential beneficiaries of a trust are all adults with very strict views on moral and social matters, condemning all forms of alcohol, tobacco and popular entertainment, as well as armaments, I can well understand that it might not be for the 'benefit' of such beneficiaries to know that they are obtaining rather larger financial returns under the trust by reason of investments in those activities than they would have received if the trustees had invested the trust funds in other investments. The beneficiaries might well consider that it was far better to receive less than to receive more money from what they consider to be evil and tainted sources. 'Benefit' is a word with a very wide meaning, and there are circumstances in which arrangements which work to the financial disadvantage of a beneficiary may yet be for his benefit: see, for example, *In re T.'s Settlement Trusts* [1964] Ch 158 and *In re C.L.* [1969] 1 Ch 587. But I would emphasise that such cases are likely to be very rare, and in any case I think that under a trust for the provision of financial benefits the burden would rest, and rest heavy, on him who asserts that it is for the benefit of the beneficiaries as a whole to receive less by reason of the exclusion of some of the possibly more profitable forms of investment. Plainly the present case is not one of this rare type of case. Subject to such matters, under a trust for the provision of financial benefits, the paramount duty of the trustees is to provide the greatest financial benefits for the present and future beneficiaries.

Fourth, the standard required of a trustee in exercising his powers of investment is that he must 'take such care as an ordinary prudent man would take if he were minded to make an investment for the benefit of other people for whom he felt morally bound to provide': *per* Lindley LJ in *In re Whiteley* (1886) 33 ChD 347, 355; see also at pp. 350, 358; and see *Learoyd* v *Whiteley* (1887) 12 App Cas 727. That duty includes the duty to seek advice on matters which the trustee does not understand, such as the making of investments, and on receiving that advice to act with the same degree of prudence. This requirement is not discharged merely by showing that the trustee has acted in good faith and with sincerity. Honesty and sincerity are not the same as prudence and reasonableness. Some of the most sincere people are the most unreasonable; and Mr. Scargill told me that he had met quite a few of them. Accordingly, although a trustee who takes advice on investments is not bound to accept and act on that advice, he is not entitled to reject it merely because he sincerely disagrees with it, unless in addition to being sincere he is acting as an ordinary prudent man would act.

Fifth, trustees have a duty to consider the need for diversification of investments. By s.6(1) of the Trustee Investments Act 1961:

> In the exercise of his powers of investment a trustee shall have regard—(a) to the need for diversification of investments of the trust, in so far as is appropriate to the circumstances of the trust; (b) to the suitability to the trust of investments of the description of investment proposed and of the investment proposed as an investment of that description.

The reference to the 'circumstances of the trust' plainly include matters such as the size of the trust funds: the degree of diversification that is practicable and desirable for a large fund may plainly be impracticable or undesirable (or both) in the case of a small fund. In the case before me, it is not in issue that there ought to be diversification of the investments held by the fund. The contention of the defendants, put very shortly, is that there can be a sufficient degree of diversification without any investment overseas or in oil, and that in any case there is no need to increase the level of overseas investments beyond the existing level. Other pension funds got on well enough without overseas investments, it was said, and in particular the NUM's own scheme had, in 1982, produced better results than the scheme here in question. This was not so, said Mr Jenkins, if you compared like with like, and excluded investments in property, which figure substantially in the mineworkers' scheme but not at all in the NUM scheme: and in any case the latter scheme was much smaller, being of the order of £7 million ...

■ **QUESTION**

Which situations did the Vice-Chancellor acknowledge might justify investment with a view to non-financial benefits? Can you think of any others?

A: Ethical considerations

Harries v *The Church Commissioners for England*
[1992] 1 WLR 1241, Chancery Division

Facts: The Right Reverend Richard Harries, Bishop of Oxford, was one of the Church Commissioners. The Commissioners control and invest large sums of money on behalf of the Church of England, such funds being held under charitable trusts. The Bishop of Oxford, together with certain other Church of England clergy, brought proceedings against the other Commissioners, seeking declarations clarifying the Commissioners' obligation to invest in a manner compatible with Christian morality.

Held: The declarations were refused. Charity trustees were required to invest with a view to securing the maximum financial return compatible with ordinary prudence. 'Christian morality' covered a range of divergent views which should not be accommodated if to do so would create significant financial prejudice to the funds. However, if some of those views could be accommodated without financial detriment, such an ethical investment policy would be proper.

SIR DONALD NICHOLLS V-C: The Church Commissioners for England administer vast estates and large funds. At the end of 1990 their holdings of land were valued at about £1.7bn, their mortgages and loans at about £165m, and their stock exchange investments at about £780m. In 1990 these items yielded altogether an investment income of £164m. The Commissioners' income included also some £66m derived principally from parish and diocesan contributions to clergy stipends. So the commissioners' total income last year was £230m ...

... For some time there have been voices in the Church of England expressing disquiet at the investment policy of the commissioners. They do not question either the good faith or the investment expertise of the commissioners. Their concern is not that the commissioners have failed to get the best financial return from their property and investments. Their concern is that, in making investment decisions, the commissioners are guided too rigorously by purely financial considerations, and that the commissioners give insufficient weight to what are now called 'ethical' considerations.

... In most cases the best interests of the charity require that the trustees' choice of investments should be made solely on the basis of well-established criteria, having taken expert advice where appropriate and having due regard to such matters as the need to diversify, the need to balance income against capital growth, and the need to balance risk against return.

In a minority of cases the position will not be so straightforward. There will be some cases, I suspect comparatively rare, when the objects of the charity are such that investments of a particular type would conflict with the aims of the charity. Much-cited examples are those of cancer research companies and tobacco shares, trustees of temperance charities and brewery and distillery shares, and trustees of charities of the Society of Friends and shares in companies engaged in production of armaments. If, as would be likely in those examples, trustees were satisfied that investing in a company engaged in a particular type of business would conflict with the very objects their charity is seeking to achieve, they should not so invest. Carried to its logical conclusion the trustees should take this course even if it would be likely to result in significant financial detriment to the charity. The logical conclusion, whilst sound as a matter of legal analysis, is unlikely to arise in practice. It is not easy to think of an instance where in practice the exclusion for this reason of one or more companies or sectors from the whole range of investments open to trustees would be likely to leave them without an adequately wide range of investments from which to choose a properly diversified portfolio.

There will also be some cases, again I suspect comparatively rare, when trustees' holdings of particular investments might hamper a charity's work either by making potential recipients of aid unwilling to be helped because of the source of the charity's money, or by alienating some of those who support the charity financially. In these cases the trustees will need to balance the difficulties they would encounter, or likely financial loss they would sustain, if they were to hold the investments against the risk of financial detriment if those investments were excluded from their portfolio. The greater the risk of financial detriment, the more certain the trustees should be of countervailing disadvantages to the charity before they incur that risk. Another circumstance where trustees would be entitled, or even required, to take into account non-financial criteria would be where the trust deed so provides.

... The instances I have given are not comprehensive. But I must emphasise that of their very nature, and by definition, investments are held by trustees to aid the work of the charity in a particular way: by generating money. That is the purpose for which they are held. That is their raison d'être. Trustees cannot properly use assets held as an investment for other, viz., non-investment, purposes.

... Those who wish may do so with their own property, but that is not a proper function of trustees with trust assets held as an investment ... .

Trustees may, if they wish, accommodate the views of those who consider that on moral grounds a particular investment would be in conflict with the objects of the charity, so long as the trustees are satisfied that course would not involve a risk of significant financial detriment. But when they are not so satisfied trustees should not make investment decisions on the basis of preferring one view of whether on moral grounds in investment conflicts with the objects of the charity over another. This is so even when one view is more widely supported than the other.

I have sought above to consider charity trustees' duties in relation to investment as a matter of basic principle. I was referred to no authority bearing directly on these matters. My attention was drawn to *Cowan* v *Scargill* [1985] Ch 270, a case concerning a pension fund. I believe the views I have set out accord with those expressed by Sir Robert Megarry V-C in that case, bearing in mind that he was considering trusts for the provision of financial benefits for individuals. In this case I am concerned with trusts of charities, whose purposes are multifarious.

The evidence does show that the commissioners have declined to adopt financially disadvantageous policies advocated by, among others, the Bishop of Oxford. In October 1989 his bishop's council passed a resolution urging his diocesan board of finance to adopt certain specific criteria in relation to South Africa. For example, investments should not be directly or indirectly in groups of companies (other than banks, for the time being) which derived more than £10m in annual profits from South Africa or more than three per cent of their worldwide profits from South African activities. As to that, the commissioners' ethical policy excludes about 13 per cent of listed United Kingdom companies (by value) from consideration. The companies in which the commissioners hold shares that would be excluded under the suggested criteria would comprise a further 24 per cent (by value) of listed United Kingdom companies, making a total exclusion of about 37 per cent. The part of the market excluded by the criteria would include some of the largest United Kingdom companies whose shares make up a very important part of the commissioners' total portfolio. The criteria would exclude two companies which make up 65 per cent of the oil sector, and a further two companies which make up 62 per cent of the chemical sector of the United Kingdom equity market. Not surprisingly, the commissioners' view is that a portfolio thus restricted would be much less balanced and diversified, and they would not regard it as prudent or in the interests of those for whom they provide.

The investment issue raised by this resolution is another example of a moral question to which there can be no certain answer. The commissioners do not invest in a company where more than a small part of its business is in South Africa. The policy advocated by the Bishop of Oxford's council does not seek to exclude every company which has a South African business connection. The councils' policy embodies fixed, and to this extent, artificial limits on the degree of South African involvement which is acceptable. As between these two alternatives, there can be no right or wrong answer. This is a question of degree, and whether Christian ethics require a more restrictive policy than that adopted by the commissioners is a matter on which there can be literally endless argument and debate. The commissioners are therefore right not to prefer one view over the other beyond the point at which they would incur a risk of significant financial detriment.

Another example raised before me concerned land owned by the commissioners in a village where local young people are finding housing impossible to afford. Such land, it was suggested by the plaintiffs, could be made available for low-cost housing at a price below open-market value. Investing instead in a more expensive housing development with a higher rate of return would undermine the credibility of the Christian message by the affront such a policy would cause to the needs and consciences of local people. I do not think this example advances the plaintiffs' case. The commissioners are not a housing charity. There is force in the commissioners' contention that local housing needs are or should be reflected in local planning policies. When planning permission is available for a particular type of development, it is not a proper function for the commissioners to sell their land at an under-value in order to further a social objective on which the local planning authority has taken a different view. This, once more, is an illustration of a circumstance in which different minds within the Church of England, applying the highest moral standards, will reach different conclusions. If the commissioners' land is to be disposed of at an undervalue, they need an express power to do so. Such a disposition cannot properly be made in exercise of their power to make and change investments ...

■ **QUESTION**

The rule is that private trusts must be invested for the beneficiaries' best financial benefits. Do you think different principles should apply to the investment of charitable funds? See, generally, Richard Nobles, 'Charities and Ethical Investment' (1992) 56 *Conv* 115.

Lord Nicholls of Birkenhead, 'Trustees and their Broader Community: Where Duty, Morality and Ethics Converge'

(1995) 9(3) *TLI* 71

Preferring ethical ends to financial gain

Whether an expert or not, the ordinary prudent person is not to be regarded as wholly lacking in moral sensitivity. This person, the creation of equity, is surely as anxious as the next person to do all he can to promote good and to remedy injustices, whatever form they take. But this laudable characteristic is not easily translated into practice in the investment field. In the absence of a generally accepted attitude to the morality of investing in this or that investment, it cannot be right for moral considerations to displace beneficiaries' financial interests. Some people disapprove of investments in the armaments industry, others do not. Many people feel passionately about animal welfare, and the fur trade and the conditions in which some animals are still reared, others less so. Increasing numbers of people are anxious about the environment and wish to support companies with an enlightened attitude on green issues, others' cares lie elsewhere …

A further complication is that, increasingly, businesses are interdependent, so that clear-cut demarcation is often not possible. Instead there are questions of degree when considering investments, for example, in a food supermarket which sells cigarettes, or in a car manufacturer one of whose components is imported from a country with an oppressive regime. In these circumstances equity's creature, the ordinary prudent person looking after another's financial affairs, would surely take the view that it is not for him to foist onto his beneficiaries his own particular views about ethical or green investments. He should not let his views, or the views of some of the fund members, despite being held very deeply, affect his investment policy decisions to the financial detriment of all the fund members. He should exercise a power of investment for the purpose for which it was created.

This is not a pusillanimous abdication of responsibilities in the modern world. Rather, it is a recognition that on moral issues on which there is no consensus, it is no part of the function of a trustee to reject one view and prefer another, whether his own or that of some of the beneficiaries, when to do so would be contrary to the financial interests of the beneficiaries. A pension fund trustee is not the guardian of the moral welfare of the fund members, and modern developments in social conditions do not compel the conclusion that he should assume this role. The fund exists to confer financial benefits on the members. The money in the fund represents part of the overall pay package of the members, in the form of deferred remuneration. It is not for the trustee to decide that, although it might mean a reduction in their income, the members ought to play their part in, say, encouraging investment in emerging markets or discouraging smoking, or that they should do so by the trustee seeking or shunning particular classes of investments. It is not for the trustee to decide that would be for the benefit of the beneficiaries. The trust fund was not set up for the purpose either of promoting or of discouraging these activities. If the trustee were to use his investment powers to one or other of these ends regardless of the financial consequences, he would be departing from the only purpose for which he holds the trust's funds …

This analysis, however, by no means leads to the conclusion that trustees are precluded from having any regard to moral considerations. The range of sound investments available to trustees is so extensive that very frequently there is scope for trustees to give effect to moral considerations, either by positively preferring certain investments or negatively avoiding others, without thereby prejudicing beneficiaries' financial interests. In practice, the inclusion or exclusion of particular investments or types of investment will often be possible without incurring the risk of a lower rate of return or reducing the desirable spread of investments. When this is so, there is no reason in principle why trustees should not have regard to moral and ethical considerations, vague and uncertain though these are. The trustees would not be departing from the purpose of the trust or hindering its fulfilment. The ordinary prudent person would surely feel no inhibitions in this situation, where the beneficiaries are not required to pay a financial price.

Take the simple example of dedicated employees who have worked for years seeking a cure for lung cancer. They would be horrified if their pension fund included shares in tobacco companies. Again, employees of a chain of hotels would be surprised were their pension fund trustee to invest in their keenest competitor. In practice, in these and most other cases where trustees or members of a pension fund have strong views about particular investments on non-financial grounds, it should be possible for trustees to exercise their investment powers in a manner avoiding embarrassment to all concerned without upsetting the balance of the portfolio. In other words, in most cases trustees may adopt an ethical investment policy. This may not always be so rigorous as they or some beneficiaries might wish. However, the very lack of consensus on many of these issues should cause trustees to take care lest they become involved in controversies to which no certain outcome is possible. Here, as always, trustees should make use of two further attributes with which equity's ordinary prudent person is liberally endowed: tact and common sense ...

■ QUESTIONS

1. Certain of the trustees of a charitable trust 'for the promotion of health education and compassion through vegetarianism' wish to invest in a highly profitable British public limited company, one subsidiary business of which is to export live veal calves. Two of the trustees object to such an investment. Advise them.

2. Does the breadth of trustees' investment choices make it difficult to prove a breach of the trustees' investment duties? Can you see how this might provide an opportunity for trustees to escape liability even where they prefer ethical investment to investment for best financial returns?

■ SUMMATIVE QUESTION

**online
resource
centre**

Steve and Jane are trustees of a £300,000 cash fund for the benefit of their sister Joanne for her life remainder to her sons Mark and Peter. Joanne is a widow and her only source of income is the trust.

The trust instrument, dated 1 March 2010, states that the trustees are 'subject to the default powers of investment for the time being permitted by the general law'.

Steve and Jane propose to purchase freehold premises for Joanne to live in. The freehold is valued at £50,000. They also propose to put aside £10,000 for investment in Chelsea porcelain figurines, because Jane collects these, and the remainder is to be put in a bank account.

Advise Steve and Jane as to the validity of the proposed investments.

FURTHER READING

American Law Institute, *Restatement of the Law of Trusts (3rd): The Prudent Investor Rule* (St Paul, MN: American Law Publishers, 1992).

Dale, H. P. and Gwinell, M., 'Time for Change: Charity Investment and Modern Portfolio Theory' (1995) 3(2) *Charity Law and Practice Review* 65.

David, E. M., 'Principal and Income—Obsolete Concepts' (1972) 43 *Penn Bar Association Quarterly* 247.

Docking, P. and Pittaway, I., 'Social Investment by English Pension Funds: Can it Be Done?' (1990) *Trust Law and Practice* 25.

HM Treasury, *Investment Powers of Trustees: A Consultation Document*, May 1996.

Longstreth, B., *Modern Investment Management and the Prudent Man Rule* (New York, Oxford: Oxford University Press, 1986).

Lord Nicholls of Birkenhead, 'Trustees and their Broader Community: Where Duty, Morality and Ethics Converge' (1995) 9(3) *TLI* 71.

McCormack, G., 'Sexy but not Sleazy: Trustee Investments and Ethical Considerations' (1998) 19(2) *Company Law* 39.

McCormack, G., 'OEICS and Trusts: The Changing Face of English Investment Law' (2000) 21(1) *Company Law* 2.

Nobles, R., 'Charities and Ethical Investment' (1992) 56 *Conv* 115.

Richardson, B. J., *Socially Responsible Investment Law: Regulating the Unseen Polluters* (New York, Oxford: Oxford University Press, 2008).

Watt, G. and Stauch, M., 'Is there Liability for Imprudent Trustee Investment?' (1998) 62 *Conv* 352.

13

Breach of Trust: The Personal Liability of Trustees

KEY AIMS

To identify the basic extent of trustees' liability to reinstate the trust fund, compensate losses, and account for unauthorised gains. To identify the range of possible defences to breach of trust. To identify the scope for relief from liability for breach of trust. To appreciate the possibility that there might be a technical or judicious breach of trust without incurring any liability for breach. To distinguish traditional settlement trusts (where the trust fund must be reinstated) from bare trusts in commercial contexts (where the trustee or fiduciary must compensate the beneficiary or principal directly).

SECTION 1: INTRODUCTION

The beneficiary of any trust, even if it is a discretionary trust, has *locus standi* to bring an action against his trustees for breach of trust, and all the trustees are presumed jointly and severally liable for all breaches. Where there is more than one beneficiary interested in the action, the court may, in the interests of efficient justice, make a representation order allowing one or more claimants to represent the interests of the others with whom they have an identity of interest. An order of this type was made to protect the interests of the 800 or so mail-order customers in *Re Kayford Ltd (In liq.)* (see Chapter 3). However, it is not only the beneficiaries who have *locus standi* to bring action against trustees who have breached their trust. Trustees have *locus standi* to bring claims against their co-trustees. Nevertheless, for all this talk of bringing actions for breach of trust, one must not lose sight of the fact that trustees frequently breach their trust without incurring liability (see the *Nestle* case in the Chapter 12 for a stark illustration of this point). In fact, even when a trustee *deliberately* breaches his trust, by making an investment he knows he has no authority to make, he will escape liability unless loss is proved. It has even been suggested, somewhat tongue in cheek, that 'the main duty' of a trustee is to commit 'judicious' breaches of trust (attributed to Selwyn LJ by Sir Nathaniel Lindley MR in *Perrins* v *Bellamy* [1899] 1 Ch 797, 798, CA).

Target Holdings Ltd v *Redferns (a firm)*

[1996] 1 AC 421, House of Lords

(See Section 2: Beneficiaries' remedies, B: Compensation in settlement trusts for the facts and decision in this important case.)

LORD BROWNE-WILKINSON: Say, as often occurs, a trustee commits a judicious breach of trust by investing in an unauthorised investment which proves to be very profitable to the trust. A carping beneficiary could insist that the unauthorised investment be sold and the proceeds invested in authorised investments: but the trustee would be under no liability to pay compensation either to the trust fund or to the beneficiary because the breach has caused no loss to the trust fund (at 433G).

Even where there is no difficulty in establishing that a breach of trust has produced a loss to the trust or an unauthorised gain for the trustee, the trustee might still escape liability if he can successfully raise a defence to the beneficiary's claim. The defendant may plead statutory limitation or 'laches', both of which are concerned to prevent claims being brought too long after the occurrence of the alleged breach. Appropriately worded exculpatory clauses in trust instruments may also be relied upon to defend allegations of breach. Most defences operate merely to excuse a breach of trust but defences which might be said actually to justify the breach include the advance authority of a court and the advance unanimous consent of the beneficiaries. The various defences are considered in Section 3 of this chapter. We will also consider the possibility of a trustee being relieved of some or all of his liability in cases where he does not have a defence as such.

SECTION 2: BENEFICIARIES' REMEDIES

Distinguished counsel in *Bartlett* v *Barclays Bank Trust Co. Ltd (Nos 1 and 2)* [1980] Ch 515 summarised perfectly the precise nature of the trustees' liability to the beneficiaries. It is first and foremost a duty to account (which is a procedure whereby the trustee explains himself to the beneficiaries, and produces proper accounts), secondly, a duty to reconstitute the fund, and thirdly, a duty to compensate:

Equity does not award damages: it requires the trustee to account, and if necessary to reconstitute the trust fund, or if that is not literally possible, to restore to the trust estate the monetary value of what should have been there had there been no breach of trust.

In his judgment in that case (a case involving loss caused by poor investment—see Chapters 11 and 12), Brightman LJ acknowledged that reconstituting the trust fund (so-called 'restitution') 'is in reality compensation for loss suffered'.

■ QUESTION

Suppose a trustee misappropriates assets from the trust to his own use. Applying your common sense, can you see why an award of compensation (for loss suffered by the trust) would be inconsistent with an order requiring the trustee to disgorge (account for) his unauthorised fiduciary gains? The beneficiary must elect between these two mutually inconsistent claims (see A: Election between inconsistent remedies).

A: Election between inconsistent remedies

An election is the choice that any claimant must make when presented with two 'mutually exclusive' courses of action. It is relevant here because English law permits a claimant to bring all his claims at once, even though they may be mutually inconsistent, provided he elects at the moment of judgment between any claims that are mutually inconsistent. This is in order to prevent the claimant being overcompensated (so-called 'double satisfaction') and to prevent a logically inconsistent judgment from appearing on the court record.

Tang Man Sit (dec'd) (Personal Representative) v Capacious Investments Ltd
[1996] 1 All ER 193, Privy Council

Facts: Mr Tang, the owner of land, was party to a joint venture for the building of houses on the land. He agreed to assign some of the houses to the claimant after completion of the building works. No assignment was made. Instead, Mr Tang let out the houses as homes for the elderly without the claimant's knowledge or approval. The claimant's claim was, on the one hand, for damages for loss of use and occupation and diminution of the value of the property due to wrongful use and occupation, and on the other hand for an account of unauthorised profits and for compensation for breach of trust.

Held: The two sides of the claimant's claim were mutually exclusive, and the claimant would have to elect between the two remedies.

LORD NICHOLLS OF BIRKENHEAD: ... The law frequently affords an injured person more than one remedy for the wrong he has suffered. Sometimes the two remedies are alternative and inconsistent. The classic example, indeed, is (1) an account of the profits made by a defendant in breach of his fiduciary obligations and (2) damages for the loss suffered by the plaintiff by reason of the same breach. The former is measured by the wrongdoer's gain, the latter by the injured party's loss ...

Alternative remedies
Faced with alternative and inconsistent remedies a plaintiff must choose, or elect, between them. He cannot have both. The basic principle governing when a plaintiff must make his choice is simple and clear. He is required to choose when, but not before, judgment is given in his favour and the judge is asked to make orders against the defendant. A plaintiff is not required to make his choice when he launches his proceedings. He may claim one remedy initially, and then by amendment of his writ and his pleadings abandon that claim in favour of the other. He may claim both remedies, as alternatives. But he must make up his mind when judgment is being entered against the defendant. Court orders are intended to be obeyed. In the nature of things, therefore, the court should not make orders which would afford a plaintiff both of two alternative remedies. In the ordinary course, by the time the trial is concluded a plaintiff will know which remedy is more advantageous to him. By then, if not before, he will know enough of the facts to assess where his best interests lie. There will be nothing unfair in requiring him to elect at that stage. Occasionally this may not be so. This is more likely to happen when the judgment is a default judgment or a summary judgment than at the conclusion of a trial. A plaintiff may not know how much money the defendant has made from the wrongful use of his property. It may be unreasonable to require the plaintiff to make his choice without further information. To meet this difficulty, the court may make discovery and other orders designed to give the plaintiff the information he needs, and which in fairness he ought to have, before deciding upon his remedy. In the ordinary course the decision made when judgment is entered is made once and for all. That is the normal rule. The order is a final order, and the interests of the parties and the public interest alike dictate that there should be finality. The principle, however, is not rigid and unbending. Like all procedural principles, the established principles regarding election between alternative remedies are not fixed and unyielding rules. These principles are the means to an end, not the end in themselves. They are no more than particular applications of a general and overriding principle governing the conduct of legal proceedings, namely that proceedings should be conducted in a manner which strikes a fair and reasonable balance between the interests of the parties, having proper regard also to the wider public interest in the conduct of court proceedings. Thus in *Johnson v Agnew* [1979] 1 All ER 883 the House of Lords held that when specific performance fails to be realised, an order for specific performance may subsequently be discharged and an inquiry as to damages ordered. Lord Wilberforce observed ([1979] 1 All ER 883 at 894): 'Election, though the subject of much learning and refinement, is in the end a doctrine based on simple considerations of common sense and equity.' ...

B: Compensation in settlement trusts

Where the trust is of the sort to A for life and B in remainder, a fund must be maintained to achieve a fair balance (see Chapter 11) between the interests of A and B (which have traditionally been considered to be in competition with each other—A being assumed to want investments which will produce income, B being presumed to want investment which will maintain capital and produce capital growth). The fact that a fund must be maintained means that the trustee who causes loss by his breach must reinstate (reconstitute) the fund or compensate the fund. He does not compensate individual beneficiaries. So if the trustee's breach reduces the level of trust income and thereby has the incidental effect of reducing the tax burden on individual beneficiaries, the trustee's liability is not reduced to take the beneficiaries' tax savings into account (*Bartlett* v *Barclays Bank Trust Co. Ltd (Nos 1 and 2)* [1980] Ch 515).

C: Equitable compensation in bare trusts

Target Holdings Ltd v *Redferns (a firm)*

[1996] 1 AC 421, House of Lords

Facts: The defendants were a firm of solicitors acting on behalf of a mortgagor (an established client) and a mortgagee on the creation of a mortgage. The defendants held the loan moneys on trust for the mortgagee, but paid them over to the mortgagor before the mortgage had been completed. This was in breach of trust. The mortgagee sued the firm of solicitors. In their defence, the solicitors argued that they had committed only a technical breach of trust and that the claimants had not suffered any loss because the solicitors had acquired the mortgages to which the claimants were entitled.

Held: The Court of Appeal had held that when the 'trustees' (solicitors) had paid away the 'trust' moneys to the stranger (mortgagor) they came under a duty to reinstate the trust fund immediately. An inquiry into whether the breach of trust actually *caused* loss to the trust fund was unnecessary; the causal connection being obvious. The defendants appealed to the House of Lords. The appeal was allowed.

LORD BROWNE-WILKINSON: My Lords, this appeal raises a novel point on the liability of a trustee who commits a breach of trust to compensate beneficiaries for such breach. Is the trustee liable to compensate the beneficiary not only for losses caused by the breach but also for losses which the beneficiary would, in any event, have suffered even if there had been no such breach?

...

... the decision of the Court of Appeal in this case can only be maintained on the basis that, even if there is no causal link between the breach of trust and the actual loss eventually suffered by Target (i.e. the sum advanced less the sum recovered) the trustee in breach is liable to bear (at least in part) the loss suffered by Target.

The transaction in the present case is redolent of fraud and negligence. But, in considering the principles involved, suspicions of such wrongdoing must be put on one side. If the law as stated by the Court of Appeal is correct, it applies to cases where the breach of trust involves no suspicion of fraud or negligence. For example, say an advance is made by a lender to an honest borrower in reliance on an entirely honest and accurate valuation. The sum to be advanced is paid into the client account of the lender's solicitors. Due to an honest and non-negligent error (e.g. an unforeseeable failure in the solicitors' computer) the moneys in client account are transferred by the solicitors to the borrower one day before the mortgage is executed. That is a breach of trust. Then the property market collapses and when the lender realises his security by sale he recovers only half the sum advanced. As I understand the Court of Appeal decision, the solicitors would bear the loss flowing from the collapse in the market value: subject to the court's discretionary power to relieve a trustee from liability under s.61 of the Trustee Act 1925, the solicitors would be bound to repay the total amount wrongly paid out of the client account in breach of trust receiving credit only for the sum received on the sale of the security.

To my mind in the case of an unimpeachable transaction this would be an unjust and surprising conclusion. At common law there are two principles fundamental to the award of damages. First, that the defendant's wrongful act must cause the damage complained of. Second, that the plaintiff is to be put 'in the same position as he would have been in if he had not sustained the wrong for which he is now getting his compensation or reparation' (see *Livingstone* v *Rawyards Coal Co.* (1880) 5 App Cas 25 at 39 *per* Lord Blackburn). Although, as will appear, in many ways equity approaches liability for making good a breach of trust from a different starting point, in my judgment those two principles are applicable as much in equity as at common law. Under both systems liability is fault based: the defendant is only liable for the consequences of the legal wrong he has done to the plaintiff and to make good the damage caused by such wrong. He is not responsible for damage not caused by his wrong or to pay by way of compensation more than the loss suffered from such wrong. The detailed rules of equity as to causation and the quantification of loss differ, at least ostensibly, from those applicable at common law. But the principles underlying both systems are the same. On the assumptions that had to be made in the present case until the factual issues are resolved (i.e. that the transaction would have gone through even if there had been no breach of trust), the result reached by the Court of Appeal does not accord with those principles. Redferns as trustees have been held liable to compensate Target for a loss caused otherwise than by the breach of trust. I approach the consideration of the relevant rules of equity with a strong predisposition against such a conclusion ...

... The basic right of a beneficiary is to have the trust duly administered in accordance with the provisions of the trust instrument, if any, and the general law. Thus, in relation to a traditional trust where the fund is held in trust for a number of beneficiaries having different, usually successive, equitable interests, (e.g. A for life with remainder to B), the right of each beneficiary is to have the whole fund vested in the trustees so as to be available to satisfy his equitable interest when, and if, it falls into possession. Accordingly, in the case of a breach of such a trust involving the wrongful paying away of trust assets, the liability of the trustee is to restore to the trust fund, often called 'the trust estate', what ought to have been there.

The equitable rules of compensation for breach of trust have been largely developed in relation to such traditional trusts, where the only way in which all the beneficiaries' rights can be protected is to restore to the trust fund what ought to be there. In such a case the basic rule is that a trustee in breach of trust must restore or pay to the trust estate either the assets which have been lost to the estate by reason of the breach or compensation for such loss. Courts of Equity did not award damages but, acting in personam, ordered the defaulting trustee to restore the trust estate (see *Nocton* v *Lord Ashburton* [1914] AC 932 at 952, 958, *per* Viscount Haldane LC). If specific restitution of the trust property is not possible, then the liability of the trustee is to pay sufficient compensation to the trust estate to put it back to what it would have been had the breach not been committed (see *Caffrey* v *Darby* (1801) 6 Ves 488 and *Clough* v *Bond* (1838) 3 My & Cr 490). Even if the immediate cause of the loss is the dishonesty or failure of a third party, the trustee is liable to make good that loss to the trust estate if, but for the breach, such loss would not have occurred (see Underhill and Hayton *Law of Trusts and Trustees* (14th edn, 1987) pp. 734–736, *Re Dawson (dec'd), Union Fidelity Trustee Co. Ltd* v *Perpetual Trustee Co. Ltd* [1966] 2 NSWR 211 and *Bartlett* v *Barclays Bank Trust Co. Ltd (No. 2)* [1980] 2 All ER 92). Thus the common law rules of remoteness of damage and causation do not apply. However, there does have to be some causal connection between the breach of trust and the loss to the trust estate for which compensation is recoverable, viz the fact that the loss would not have occurred but for the breach (see also *Re Miller's Deed Trusts* (1978) 75 LS Gaz 454 and *Nestle* v *National Westminster Bank plc* [1994] 1 All ER 118).

Hitherto I have been considering the rights of beneficiaries under traditional trusts where the trusts are still subsisting and therefore the right of each beneficiary, and his only right, is to have the trust fund reconstituted as it should be. But what if at the time of the action claiming compensation for breach of trust those trusts have come to an end? Take as an example again the trust for A for life with remainder to B. During A's lifetime B's only right is to have the trust duly administered and, in the event of a breach, to have the trust fund restored. After A's death, B becomes absolutely entitled. He of course has the right to have the trust assets retained by the trustees until they have fully accounted for them to him. But if the trustees commit a breach of trust, there is no reason for compensating the breach of trust by way of an order for restitution and compensation *to the trust fund* as opposed to the beneficiary himself. The beneficiary's right is no longer simply to have the trust duly administered: he is, in equity, the sole owner of the trust estate. Nor, for the same reason, is restitution to the trust fund necessary to protect other beneficiaries. Therefore, although I do not wholly rule out the possibility that even in those circumstances an order to reconstitute the fund may be appropriate, in the ordinary case where a beneficiary becomes absolutely entitled to the trust fund the court orders, not restitution to the trust estate, but the payment of compensation directly to the beneficiary. The measure of such compensation is the same, i.e. the difference between what the beneficiary has in fact received and the amount he would have received but for the breach of trust ... .

For these reasons I reach the conclusion that, on the facts which must currently be assumed, Target has not demonstrated that it is entitled to any compensation for breach of trust. Assuming that moneys would have been forthcoming from some other source to complete the purchase from Mirage if the moneys had not been wrongly provided by Redferns in breach of trust, Target obtained exactly what it would have obtained had no breach occurred, i.e. a valid security for the sum advanced. Therefore, on the assumption made, Target has suffered no compensatable loss. Redferns are entitled to leave to defend the breach of trust claim ....

■ QUESTION

1. What was the nature of the trust, and of the breach of trust, in *Target*?

2. Would the decision have been different in the case of a more traditional trust, where, for example, trustees are appointed to hold a fund on trust for A for life and B in remainder?

Bristol and West Building Society v *Mothew*

[1998] 1 Ch 1

For the facts and decision, see Chapter 10.

MILLETT LJ: ... Although the remedy which equity makes available for breach of the equitable duty of skill and care is equitable compensation rather than damages, this is merely the product of history and in this context is in my opinion a distinction without a difference. Equitable compensation for breach of the duty of skill and care resembles common law damages in that it is awarded by way of compensation to the plaintiff for his loss. There is no reason in principle why the common law rules of causation, remoteness of damage and measure of damages should not be applied by analogy in such a case. It should not be confused with equitable compensation for breach of fiduciary duty, which may be awarded in lieu of rescission or specific restitution ...

D: Interest on the judgment

Wallersteiner v *Moir (No. 2)*

[1975] QB 373, 397

BUCKLEY LJ: Where a trustee has retained trust money in his own hands, he will be accountable for the profit which he has made or which he is assumed to have made from the use of the money. In *Attorney-General* v *Alford* 4 De GM & G 843, 851 Lord Cranworth LC said: 'What the court ought to do, I think, is to charge him only with the interest which he has received, or which it is justly entitled to say he ought to have received, or which it is so fairly to be presumed that he did receive that he is estopped from saying that he did not receive it.' This is an application of the doctrine that the court will not allow a trustee to make any profit from his trust. The defaulting trustee is normally charged with simple interest only, but if it is established that he has used the money in trade he may be charged compound interest .... The justification for charging compound interest normally lies in the fact that profits earned in trade would be likely to be used as working capital for earning further profits. Precisely similar equitable principles apply to an agent who has retained moneys of his principal in his hands and used them for his own purposes: *Burdick* v *Garrick*.

NOTES

1. The Court does not have jurisdiction to award compound interest against a fiduciary on damages for deceit except where the deceit relates to the use of a fund held by the fiduciary, since the purpose of the award of compound interest is to ensure the defendant does not profit from his breach (*Black* v *Davies* [2004] EWHC 1464 (QB), (Transcript) Queen's Bench Division). Although

Primlake Ltd v *Matthews* [2006] EWHC 1227 (Ch) suggests that compound interest can be awarded if a trustee dishonestly assists in a breach of trust—and in such a case the trustee, by definition (see Chapter 15), never holds trust property for his own benefit.

2. In *Sempra Metals Ltd (formerly Metallgesellschaft Ltd)* v *IRC* [2008] 1 AC 561, it was held by a bare majority of the House of Lords that courts have power to make an award of compound interest in a claim for restitution where such an award is necessary to achieve full justice for the claimant. As a result of a decision of the Court of Justice of the European Communities which had held certain UK tax provisions to be in contravention of Art. 52 (now Art. 43) of the EC Treaty, numerous taxpayers sought restitution of tax paid. It was held that the detriment suffered by a taxpayer by the premature payment of tax was loss of use of the money for the period of prematurity and such loss included interest paid on borrowing substitute money during that period. Alternatively, if the taxpayer's reparation claim was framed in restitution, the Inland Revenue had been unjustly enriched by the tax and by interest earned on it. Accordingly, an award of compound interest 'was necessary to achieve full restitution and, hence, a just result' (at 605).

SECTION 3: DEFENCES

When a trustee is called upon to account for unauthorised gains, it is no defence for him to show that the trust has suffered no loss (see Chapter 10), and when a trustee is called upon to compensate a loss caused to the trust, it is no defence for the trustee to show that he has made no gain. There are, however, a number of defences that trustees may raise to actions for breach of trust.

A: Statutory time-bar

LIMITATION ACT 1980

21. Time limit for actions in respect of trust property

(1) No period of limitation prescribed by this Act shall apply to an action by a beneficiary under a trust, being an action—

    (a) in respect of any fraud or fraudulent breach of trust to which the trustee was a party or privy; or

    (b) to recover from the trustee property or the proceeds of trust property in the possession of the trustee, or previously received by the trustee and converted to his use.

(2) Where a trustee who is also a beneficiary under the trust receives or retains trust property or its proceeds as his share on a distribution of trust property under the trust, his liability in any action brought by virtue of subsection (1)(b) above to recover that property or its proceeds after the expiration of the period of limitation prescribed by this Act for bringing an action to recover trust property shall be limited to the excess over his proper share.

This subsection only applies if the trustee acted honestly and reasonably in making the distribution.

(3) Subject to the preceding provisions of this section, an action by a beneficiary to recover trust property or in respect of any breach of trust, not being an action for which a period of limitation is prescribed by any other provision of this Act, shall not be brought after the expiration of six years from the date on which the right of action accrued.

For the purposes of this subsection, the right of action shall not be treated as having accrued to any beneficiary entitled to a future interest in the trust property until the interest fell into possession.

(4) No beneficiary as against whom there would be a good defence under this Act shall derive any greater or other benefit from a judgment or order obtained by any other beneficiary than he could have obtained if he had brought the action and this Act had been pleaded in defence.

22. Time limit for actions claiming personal estate of a deceased person

Subject to section 21(1) and (2) of this Act—

    (a) no action in respect of any claim to the personal estate of a deceased person or to any share or interest in any such estate (whether under a will or on intestacy) shall be brought after the expiration of twelve years from the date on which the right to receive the share or interest accrued; and

    (b) no action to recover arrears of interest in respect of any legacy, or damages in respect of such arrears, shall be brought after the expiration of six years from the date on which the interest became due.

23. Time limit in respect of actions for an account

An action for an account shall not be brought after the expiration of any time limit under this Act which is applicable to the claim which is the basis of the duty to account.

24. Time limit for actions to enforce judgments

(1)   An action shall not be brought upon any judgment after the expiration of six years from the date on which the judgment became enforceable.

(2)   No arrears of interest in respect of any judgment debt shall be recovered after the expiration of six years from the date on which the interest became due.

    ...

28. Extension of limitation period in case of disability

(1)   Subject to the following provisions of this section, if on the date when any right of action accrued for which a period of limitation is prescribed by this Act, the person to whom it accrued was under a disability, the action may be brought at any time before the expiration of six years from the date on which he ceased to be under a disability or died (whichever first occurred) notwithstanding that the period of limitation has expired.

(2)   This section shall not affect any case where the right of action first accrued to some person (not under a disability) through whom the person under a disability claims.

(3)   When a right of action which has accrued to a person under a disability accrues, on the death of that person while still under a disability, to another person under a disability, no further extension of time shall be allowed by reason of the disability of the second person.

(4)   No action to recover land or money charged on land shall be brought by virtue of this section by any person after the expiration of thirty years from the date on which the right of action accrued to that person or some person through whom he claims.

(4A) If the action is one to which section 4A of this Act applies subsection (1) above shall have effect as if for the words from 'at any time' to '(occurred)' there were substituted the words 'by him at any time before the expiration of three years from the date when he ceased to be under a disability'.

(5)   If the action is one to which section 10 of this Act applies, subsection (1) above shall have effect as if for the words 'six years' there were substituted the words 'two years'.

(6)   If the action is one to which section 11 or 12(2) of this Act applies, subsection (1) above shall have effect as if for the words 'six years' there were substituted the words 'three years' ...

    ...

32. Postponement of limitation period in case of fraud, concealment or mistake

(1)   Subject to subsections (3) and (4A) below, where in the case of any action for which a period of limitation is prescribed by this Act, either—

    (a) the action is based upon the fraud of the defendant; or

    (b) any fact relevant to the plaintiff's right of action has been deliberately concealed from him by the defendant; or

    (c) action is for relief from the consequences of a mistake;

the period of limitation shall not begin to run until the plaintiff has discovered the fraud, concealment or mistake (as the case may be) or could with reasonable diligence have discovered it.

References in this subsection to the defendant include references to the defendant's agent and to any person through whom the defendant claims and his agent.

(2) For the purposes of subsection (1) above, deliberate commission of a breach of duty in circumstances in which it is unlikely to be discovered for some time amounts to deliberate concealment of the facts involved in that breach of duty.

(3) Nothing in this section shall enable any action—

(a) to recover, or recover the value of, any property; or

(b) to enforce any charge against, or set aside any transaction affecting, any property;

to be brought against the purchaser of the property or any person claiming through him in any case where the property has been purchased for valuable consideration by an innocent third party since the fraud or concealment or (as the case may be) the transaction in which the mistake was made took place.

(4) A purchaser is an innocent third party for the purposes of this section—

(a) in the case of fraud or concealment of any fact relevant to the plaintiff's right of action, if he was not a party to the fraud or (as the case may be) to the concealment of that fact and did not at the time of the purchase know or have reason to believe that the fraud or concealment had taken place; and

(b) in the case of mistake, if he did not at the time of the purchase know or have reason to believe that the mistake had been made.

(4A) Subsection (1) above shall not apply in relation to the time limit prescribed by section 11A(3) of this Act or in relation to that time limit as applied by virtue of section 2(1) of this Act.

(5) Sections 14A and 14B of this Act shall not apply to any action to which subsection (1)(b) above applies (and accordingly the period of limitation referred to in that subsection, in any case to which either of those sections would otherwise apply, is the period applicable under section 2 of this Act).

36. Equitable jurisdiction and remedies

(1) The following time limits under this Act, that is to say—

(a) the time limit under section 2 for actions founded on tort;

(aa) the time limit under section 4A for actions for libel or slander;

(b) the time limit under section 5 for actions founded on simple contract;

(c) the time limit under section 7 for actions to enforce awards where the submission is not by an instrument under seal;

(d) the time limit under section 8 for actions on a specialty;

(e) the time limit under section 9 for action to recover a sum recoverable by virtue of any enactment; and

(f) the time limit under section 24 for actions to enforce a judgment;

shall not apply to any claim for specific performance of a contract or for an injunction or for other equitable relief, except in so far as any such time limit may be applied by the court by analogy in like manner as the corresponding time limit under any enactment repealed by the Limitation Act 1939 was applied before 1st July 1940.

(2) Nothing in this Act shall affect any equitable jurisdiction to refuse relief on the ground of acquiescence or otherwise

NOTES

1. In *Gwembe Valley Development Company Ltd* v *Koshy* [2003] EWCA Civ 1478, a trustee dishonestly concealed the fact that he had a personal interest in a transaction carried out on behalf of the trust; this amounted to fraud for the purposes of Limitation Act 1980, s.21(1)(a). In *Halton International Inc* v *Guernroy Ltd* [2006] EWCA Civ 801, Gwembe was said to have been decided not on the ground of simple fraud, but upon fraudulent concealment. (Note that certain other aspects of the decision in *Gwembe* have since been disapproved by the Court of Appeal, in *Green* v *Gaul* [2007] 1 WLR 591.)

2. It is not always straightforward to identify who is, and who is not, a constructive trustee for the purposes of the Limitation Act. See *Martin* v *Myers* [2004] EWHC 1947 (Ch) (below).

3   In *Davies* v *Sharples* [2006] EWHC 362 (Ch), the question arose whether s.22(a) has any application to cases of trusts created by a will once the administration of an estate is complete and the

personal representatives continue in office only as trustees. It was held that s.22 is not intended 'to deal with breaches of trust committed by trustees long after the period of administration has come to an end'. Section 22 does apply to the special personal action established by *Re Diplock's Estate* [1948] Ch 465 (see Chapter 15).

4. In *Attorney-General* v *Cocke* [1988] 1 Ch 414, ChD, the Attorney-General brought an action for an account against the trustees of a charitable trust. The defendant trustees sought to show that the Attorney-General was time-barred from bringing the action. It was held that the Limitation Act 1980, s.21(3) had no application because a charitable trust has no beneficiary capable of bringing an action which could be time-barred.

5. In *P&O Nedlloyd B.V.* v *Arab Metals Co* [2006] EWCA Civ 1717, the Court of Appeal concluded that in claims for specific performance it is never appropriate to apply a limitation period in equity by analogy to the common law, because specific performance has no common law counterpart. Whilst logical, this is hard to reconcile with the wording of s.36(1).

6. *Cattley* v *Pollard* [2006] EWHC 3130 (Ch), [2007] Ch 353 establishes that a person who dishonestly assists in a fraudulent breach of trust (for dishonest assistance, see Chapter 15) is subject to the general six-year limitation period, even though the trustee in such a case would not be subject to a limitation period. (For an argument that the dishonest assistant should not be permitted to take advantage of a limitation period in such a case, see *obiter dicta* in *Statek Corporation* v *Alford* [2008] EWHC 32 (Ch), [2008] BCC 266.)

■ **QUESTIONS**

1. Lindsey, an adult beneficiary, has a life interest under a trust of which Roger is remainderman. Eleven years ago, the trustees of the settlement had placed the trust fund in unauthorised investments. Lindsey died four years ago, having never got around to suing the trustees for their breach. Advise Roger who now wishes to sue.

2. Laura, an adult beneficiary, has a life interest under a trust of which Richard is remainderman. Sixteen years ago, the trustees of the settlement placed the trust fund in unauthorised investments. Laura died nine years ago, never having got around to suing the trustees for their breach. Advise Richard, aged 20, who now wishes to sue.

Williams v *Central Bank of Nigeria*

[2012] EWCA Civ 415; [2012] 3 All ER 579, Court of Appeal (Civil Division)

Facts: The claimant alleged that money held in a solicitor's client account, and therefore held in trust, had been paid into an account of the defendant bank as part of a fraud conducted by the solicitor trustee. The question was whether an action against the bank for dishonest assistance in the fraud could be brought after the end of the general limitation period.

Held: A trust beneficiary is permitted to bring an action (even after the expiration of the usual limitation period for breach of trust) against a person who dishonestly assists in a fraud or fraudulent breach of trust.

SIR ANDREW MORRITT (Chancellor of the High Court): Is it implicit in s.21(1)(a) that the cause of action there described may only be pursued outside the primary limitation period against the trustee (the singular including the plural) who was party or privy to the fraud or fraudulent breach of trust? The only words which could import that requirement is the passage reading 'being an action … in respect of any fraud or fraudulent breach of trust to which the trustee was a party or privy … '. The definite article preceding the word 'trustee' connotes the trustee of the relevant trust, but the phrase of which it forms a part is descriptive of and a limitation on the generality of the phrase 'any fraud or fraudulent breach of trust'. Of itself it cannot in my view justify any implication that 'the action' may only be brought against that trustee.

■ QUESTION

In *Paragon Finance plc* v *D B Thakerar & Co (a firm)* [1999] 1 All ER 400, Court of Appeal, Millett LJ stated, *obiter*, that '[a] claim for an account in equity, absent any trust, has no equitable element; it is based on legal, not equitable rights'. His lordship also stated that a claim against a third party who dishonestly assists in a breach of trust is not, as some have said, a claim under a 'constructive trust' because the defendant never holds property as a trustee, but merely assists in the trustee's breach (see, further, Chapter 15). Does this suggest that *Williams* v *Central Bank of Nigeria* [2012] EWCA Civ 415; [2012] 3 All ER 579 was wrongly decided?

Martin v *Myers*

[2004] EWHC 1947 (Ch), Chancery Division

Facts: A couple had lived as husband and wife for many years without it being certain to anyone outside the relationship that they were married. The man died and the woman remained in the 'matrimonial' home for 24 years. When she died, she left the house to one son by her will. This action was brought by her four daughters, who claimed that their mother had never been married and (which is the point that concerns us) must therefore have held the house on constructive trust for all her 'husband's' children after his death, with the result that she could not have acquired title to the land by 12 years' adverse possession against her children under the Limitation Act 1980.

Held: The couple were not married but the mother never became a constructive trustee for her children because her conscience was never affected by knowledge of any entitlement her children might have in the house.

MR STRAUSS QC: Until the passing of s 19 of the Limitation Act 1939, which is in substantially the same terms as s 21 of the 1980 Act, only an express trustee was prevented, by s 8 of the Trustee Act 1888, from relying upon the provisions of the Limitation Acts. The effect of this is explained in an article by Mr Frank Hinks in 38 The Conveyancer p 176 entitled 'Executors De Son Tort And The Limitation Of Actions'. As he explains, in general neither an executor nor an executor de son tort was an express trustee, and therefore both could establish title to property of a deceased person against those interested in the estate by adverse possession. However, in some circumstances, especially where infants were involved, the executor or the executor de son tort were regarded as express trustees. This was so, for example, where on the death intestate of her husband, the widow remained in possession of the property without obtaining grant of letters of administration; she could not acquire a possessory title to the property as against infant children entitled to an interest in the estate. This was because she was regarded as the equivalent of a guardian to the children, and therefore as an express trustee. This was apparently something which occurred quite often in Ireland. However, the position was different where all the other persons interested in the estate were adults. The widow was then not a trustee, and could establish a possessory title: see *Doyle* v *Foley* [1903] 2 LR. 95. [para. [28]]

... at what point time in time does the constructive trust, if there is one, arise? At least two answers are possible, namely when the occupation starts or at the expiration of the 12-year period. In Mr Hinks's article, he seems to have envisaged that in this kind of case a constructive trust would be likely to arise at the time when title would otherwise be acquired by adverse possession: see the passage referred to earlier in which it is said that 'whenever an executor de son tort claims title by lapse of time against his relatives' the courts ought to consider whether to impose a constructive trust so as to prevent him from relying upon possession. Similarly, in Paragon, Millett LJ stated at 408 that a constructive trust arises [para. [38]]

'... whenever the circumstances are such that it would be unconscionable for the owner of property ... to assert his own beneficial interest in the property and deny the beneficial interests of another.'

This approach has the advantage of enabling the court to take into account all the events which have occurred during the period of occupation, and to consider whether in all the circumstances then obtaining it would be unconscionable for the person who has occupied the property to acquire a possessory title. This seems right as a matter of principle, and it is preferable to the alternative, which may give rise to complications if the circumstances have altered over time, so that it has at some times during a long period of occupation been 'unconscionable' for the occupier to be acquiring a possessory title and at other times not. [para. [39]]

In addition, there is the difficulty that, at the beginning of the period of occupation, the occupier by definition has no title to the property but is simply in possession in circumstances in which, until letters of administration had been taken out, legal title is nowadays vested in the Public Trustee (until 1994 in the probate judge). As was said by Kekewich J in *Re Barney* [1892] 2 Ch 265 at 272–273: [para. [40]]

> '[I]t is essential to the character of the trustee that he should have trust property actually vested in him or so far under his control that he has nothing to do but require that, perhaps by one process, perhaps by another, it should be vested in him.'

Nevertheless, in *James* v *Williams* the Court of Appeal held that the constructive trust commenced at the beginning of the period of occupation, basing its decision principally on the failure by the brother to take out letters of administration, in circumstances in which not to do so while taking the benefit of the property was unconscionable. The fact that the brother, as one of the persons competent to take out letters of administration, was in a position to require that the property be vested in him, was sufficient to make the property trust property and to justify the imposition of a trust. However, it does not follow that the only time when a constructive trust can arise, in any case of this kind, is the time when the period of occupation begins; it is necessary to consider the question as at the end of the period as well. [para. [41]]

In the present case, I do not consider that any constructive trust arose in 1977 on the death of Edward Myers. Amy Myers did nothing other than to remain in the property in circumstances in which title was vested in the probate judge.

As the unmarried partner of Edward Myers, she had no standing to obtain a grant of administration, and was therefore not in a position to have the property vested in her. Even if her conduct had been unconscionable she was not in control of the property. *James* v *Williams* is clearly distinguishable. [para. [42]]

In any event, the basic principle underlying the imposition of a constructive trust is that the owner of the legal interest should not be entitled to hold property, where the circumstances are such as to make it inequitable or unconscionable for him to do so. There must be factors which 'affect his conscience': see per Lord Browne-Wilkinson in Westdeutsche *Landesbank* v *Islington LBC* [1996] AC 669, [1996] 2 All ER 961 at 705, 709. It seems to me quite artificial to suggest that any such factors affected Amy Myers' conscience immediately on Edward Myers's death. She simply remained in her home, as no doubt all her children wished her to do whatever suspicions they might have held as to whether or not there had been a marriage. [para. [43]]

The appropriate question to ask, in my view, is whether a constructive trust arose in April 1989 so as to prevent Amy Myers from acquiring a possessory title. I have not found it easy to answer it, but I have come to the conclusion that it has not been established on the evidence that the circumstances in April 1989 were such as to make it inequitable or unconscionable for Amy Myers to rely on her 12 years' possession of the house. [para. [44]]

NOTE: For the meaning of *'trustee de son tort'*, see Chapter 15.

B: Laches

See *Frawley* v *Neill* [2000] CP Rep 20 (CA), in Chapter 16.

Re Sharpe

[1892] 1 Ch 154, Court of Appeal

Facts: The liquidator of an insolvent company brought an action against one of the former directors of the company, seeking to recover moneys which had been paid (in the form of interest payments) to the shareholders of the company in the years prior to its insolvency.

Held: The directors were to be treated as being in the position of trustees, accordingly the defendant could not raise the Statute of Limitations as a bar to the action. Neither would the action be barred as a 'stale demand'.

LINDLEY LJ: ... That staleness of demand as distinguished from the Statute of Limitations and analogy to it may furnish a defence in Equity to an equitable claim was settled at least as early as *Smith* v *Clay* 3 Bn CC 639n. The principles on which the doctrine is based will be found clearly set forth by the Privy Council in *Lindsay Petroleum Company* v *Hurd* Law Rep 5 PC 221, and in the judgment of Lord Blackburn in *Erlanger* v *New Sombrero Phosphate Company* (1878) 3 App Cas 1218. Whether these principles are applicable to the case of a company seeking relief in respect of a misapplication of its money which neither the directors nor the company could authorise or ratify has not, I believe, been decided, and need not be decided on the present occasion, for the circumstances of this case are insufficient to support a defence founded on the equitable doctrine in question. A defence based on staleness of demand renders it necessary to consider the time which has elapsed and the balance of justice or injustice in affording or refusing relief. I do not disregard, but I do not attach much importance to, the time which elapsed before Captain Bennett's death, nor, for reasons already given, to that which has elapsed between the winding up of the company and the commencement of the action. The remaining time is about two years and a quarter, which I do not consider long ...

NOTES

1. In *Patel* v *Shah* [2005] EWCA Civ 157, CA, a claim to a beneficial interest in certain properties was barred by laches because the defendant had borne all the risk of negative equity during the property recession of the early 1990s and the claimant had waited until the market improved to claim his share. (*Frawley* v *Neill* followed.)
2. Laches applies where the Act expressly disapplies the usual statutory limitation period, as it does, for example, where the trustee is still in possession of trust property (*Green* v *Gaul* [2007] 1 WLR 591, Court of Appeal, dismissing an appeal from the decision of Lawrence Collins J in *Re Loftus (deceased)* [2005] EWHC 406 (Ch), [2007] 1 WLR 591).
3. A very clear example of a defendant who is said to be a constructive trustee, but never holds trust property and never commits a breach of trust, is the person who dishonestly assists in a breach of trust and is held liable to account *as if he were* a constructive trustee (see Chapter 15). He is not in fact a trustee and is not subject to the limitation period for breach of trust. (*Cattley* v *Pollard* [2006] EWHC 3130 (Ch), [2007] 2 All ER 1086.)

C: Beneficiary's instigation of (or consent to) the breach

Re Somerset v *Earl Poulett*

[1894] 1 ChD 231, Court of Appeal

Facts: Trustees of a settlement committed an innocent breach of trust when they invested in an undersecured mortgage. One of the beneficiaries had consented in writing to investing by way of mortgage, the question therefore arose whether the trustees should for that reason be indemnified by the beneficiaries for the consequences of their breach.

Held: If the beneficiary has instigated, requested, or consented to an investment which amounts to a breach of trust, the beneficiary will be liable to indemnify the trustee for any liability arising from that breach. If, however, the beneficiary has instigated, requested, or consented to an investment which is not of itself a breach of trust, the beneficiary will not be liable if the trustee proceeds to make that investment with a lack of ordinary prudence. In the present case, the beneficiary had consented to an investment within the terms of the trust and the trustees would therefore be liable in full. When considering whether a beneficiary had instigated, requested, or consented to a breach of trust it was not necessary to show that the beneficiary knew the investment was, in law, a breach of trust.

LINDLEY LJ: ... If a *cestui que trust* instigates, requests, or consents in writing to an investment not in terms authorised by the power of investment, he clearly falls within the section; and in such a case his ignorance or forgetfulness of the terms of the power would not, I think, protect him—at all events, not unless he could give some good reason why it should, e.g. that it was caused by the trustee. But if all that a *cestui que trust* does is to instigate, request, or consent in writing to an investment which is authorised by the terms of the power, the case is, I think, very different. He has a right to expect that the trustees will act with proper care in making the investment, and if they do not they cannot throw the consequences on him unless they can show that he instigated, requested, or consented in writing to their non-performance of their duty in this respect....

D: Exemption clause

An exemption clause is a clause in a trust instrument that excludes or limits a trustee's liability for breaches of trust. According to *Wight* v *Olswang, The Times*, 18 May 1999, any ambiguity in the wording of such a clause is construed strictly *contra proferentem* (against the one who seeks to benefit from it). There was no ambiguity in the wording of the clause in the leading case *Armitage* v *Nurse*, so the court simply had to determine whether it was proper as a matter of law, principle, and policy that such a wide exculpatory clause should be permitted to operate according to its natural construction.

Armitage v *Nurse*

[1998] Ch 241, Court of Appeal

Facts: By a settlement made on 11 October 1984, the claimant, who was then aged 17, became entitled in remainder to settled agricultural land of which her mother was tenant for life. Her portion was to be held on certain trusts until she reached the age of 40. Clause 15 of the settlement provided that no trustee should be liable for any loss or damage to the claimant's fund or the income thereof at any time or from any case unless it was caused by his own actual fraud. On appeal by the claimant from the judge's decision that the trustees were absolved by clause 15.

Held (dismissing the appeal): Since it was open to contracting parties to exclude liability for ordinary or even gross negligence, such an exclusion was also open to the parties to a settlement; that, by referring to 'actual' fraud, clause 15 of the settlement excluded constructive fraud or equitable fraud and was apt to exclude liability for breach of trust in the absence of a dishonest intention; that, although trustees might deliberately commit a breach of trust by consciously acting beyond their powers, their conduct was not fraudulent if they did so in good faith and in the honest belief that they were acting in the interest of the beneficiaries; that a clause excluding the liability of a trustee for equitable fraud or unconscionable behaviour was not so repugnant to the trust or contrary to public policy as to be liable to be set aside at the suit of a beneficiary; and that, accordingly, since without amendment the pleadings could not support a plea of fraud, clause 15 of the settlement operated to absolve the trustees from liability for the alleged breaches so long as they had not acted dishonestly; but that the claimant would be allowed to examine the trust documents and investigate the trustees' management in order to re-amend her statement of claim.

Per curiam: The view is widely held that trustee exemption clauses have gone too far, and that trustees who charge for their services and who, as professional men, would not dream of excluding liability for ordinary professional negligence should not be able to rely on an exemption clause excluding liability for gross negligence. If such clauses are to be denied effect, however, it should be done by Parliament.

MILLETT LJ: ... In my judgment clause 15 exempts the trustee from liability for loss or damage to the trust property no matter how indolent, imprudent, lacking in diligence, negligent or wilful he may have been, so long as he has not acted dishonestly.

The permitted scope of trustee exemption clauses

It is submitted on behalf of [the claimant] that a trustee exemption clause which purports to exclude all liability except for actual fraud is void, either for repugnancy or as contrary to public policy. There is some academic support for the submission (notably an article by Professor Matthews, 'The Efficacy of Trustee Exemption Clauses in English Law' [1989] Conv. 42 and *Hanbury & Martin's Modern Equity*, 14th edn (1993), pp. 473–474) that liability for gross negligence cannot be excluded, but this is not the view taken in *Underhill and Hayton's Law of Trusts and Trustees*, 15th edn (1995), pp. 560–561 (where it appears to be taken only because the editor confusingly uses the term 'gross negligence' to mean reckless indifference to the interests of the beneficiaries). In its consultation paper Fiduciary Duties and Regulatory Rules, A Summary (1992) (Law Com. No. 124), para. 3.3.41 the Law Commission states:

> Beyond this, trustees and fiduciaries cannot exempt themselves from liability for fraud, bad faith and wilful default. It is not, however, clear whether the prohibition on exclusion of liability for 'fraud' in this context only prohibits the exclusion of common law fraud or extends to the much broader doctrine of equitable fraud. It is also not altogether clear whether the prohibition on the exclusion of liability for 'wilful default' also prohibits exclusion of liability for gross negligence although we incline to the view that it does.

... the expression 'wilful default' is used in the cases in two senses. A trustee is said to be accountable on the footing of wilful default when he is accountable not only for money which he has in fact received but also for money which he could with reasonable diligence have received. It is sufficient that the trustee has been guilty of a want of ordinary prudence: see, e.g. *In re Chapman; Cocks v Chapman* [1896] 2 Ch 763. In the context of a trustee exclusion clause, however, such as s.30 of the Trustee Act 1925, it means a deliberate breach of trust: *In re Vickery: Vickery v Stephens* [1931] 1 Ch 572. The decision has been criticised, but it is in line with earlier authority: see *Lewis v Great Western Railway Co.* (1877) 3 QBD 195; *In re Trusts of Leeds City Brewery Ltd's Debenture Stock Trust Deed, Leeds City Brewery Ltd v Platts (Note)* [1925] Ch 532 and *In re City Equitable Fire Insurance Co. Ltd* [1925] Ch 407. Nothing less than conscious, and wilful misconduct is sufficient. The trustee must be conscious that, in doing the act which is complained of or in omitting to do the act which it said he ought to have done, he is committing a breach of his duty, or is recklessly careless whether it is a breach of his duty or not: see *In re Vickery* [1931] 1 Ch 572, 583, *per* Maugham J.

A trustee who is guilty of such conduct either consciously takes a risk that loss will result, or is recklessly indifferent whether it will or not. If the risk eventuates he is personally liable. But if he consciously takes the risk in good faith and with the best intentions, honestly believing that the risk is one which ought to be taken in the interests of the beneficiaries, there is no reason why he should not be protected by an exemption clause which excludes liability for wilful default ...

There can be no question of the clause being repugnant to the trust. In *Wilkins v Hogg* (1861) 31 LJ Ch 41, 42 Lord Westbury LC challenged counsel to cite a case where an indemnity clause protecting the trustee from his ordinary duty had been held so repugnant as to be rejected. Counsel was unable to do so. No such case has occurred in England or Scotland since.

I accept the submission made on behalf of [the claimant] that there is an irreducible core of obligations owed by the trustees to the beneficiaries and enforceable by them which is fundamental to the concept of a trust. If the beneficiaries have no rights enforceable against the trustees there are no trusts. But I do not accept the further submission that these core obligations include the duties of skill and care, prudence and diligence. The duty of the trustees to perform the trusts honestly and in good faith for the benefit of the beneficiaries is the minimum necessary to give substance to the trusts, but in my opinion it is sufficient. As Mr Hill pertinently pointed out in his able argument, a trustee who relied on the presence of a trustee exemption clause to justify what he proposed to do would thereby lose its protection: he would be acting recklessly in the proper sense of the term ...

The submission that it is contrary to public policy to exclude the liability of a trustee for gross negligence is not supported by any English or Scottish authority ...

At the same time, it must be acknowledged that the view is widely held that these clauses have gone too far, and that trustees who charge for their services and who, as professional men, would not dream of excluding liability for ordinary professional negligence should not be able to rely on a trustee exemption clause excluding liability for gross negligence. Jersey introduced a law in 1989 which denies effect to a trustee exemption clause which purports to absolve a trustee from liability for his own 'fraud, wilful mis conduct or gross negligence.' The subject is presently under consideration in this country by the Trust Law Committee under the chairmanship of Sir John Vinelott. If clauses such as clause 15 of the settlement are to be denied effect, then in my opinion this should be done by Parliament, which will have the advantage of wide consultation with interested bodies and the advice of the Trust Law Committee ...

NOTES

1. Their Lordships declined to strike out the clause as being repugnant to the public interest, on the ground that a clause excluding liability for 'ordinary negligence or want of care' had never been deemed contrary to public policy in the law of contract'. However, if such similar policies apply to trust deeds as apply to contracts, it may be wondered why the Court of Appeal in *Re Duke of Norfolk's Settlement Trusts* [1982] Ch 61 held that the Unfair Contract Terms Act 1977 does not apply to exculpatory clauses in trusts and cautioned against taking the contractual analysis of the deal between settlor and trustee too far.

2. On 19 July 2006, the Law Commission for England and Wales published a Report (No. 301) containing its recommendations for the reform of the law governing trustee exemption clauses. The recommended reform takes the form of a rule to be adopted by regulatory and professional bodies, to the effect that: 'Any paid trustee who causes a settlor to include a clause in a trust instrument which has the effect of excluding or limiting liability for negligence must before the creation of the trust take such steps as are reasonable to ensure that the settlor is aware of the meaning and effect of the clause.' The Law Commission expects that this will ensure that exemption clauses will in future 'represent a proper and fully informed expression of the terms on which settlors are willing to dispose of their property on trust' (para. 1.19).

   The report follows a consultation paper on the same subject (*Trustee Exemption Clauses* (2003) Law Com Consultation Paper No. 171).

3. *Bonham* v *David Fishwick* [2008] EWCA Civ 373, Court of Appeal, suggests that trustees who follow legal advice will be able to rely on a clause exempting them from liability for wilful default.

4. The honesty of a trustee's conduct is judged according to what an objective trustee, looking on, would make of it—it is not judged subjectively according to the trustee's own beliefs (*Barnes* v *Tomlinson* [2006] EWHC 3115 (Ch), [2007] WTLR 377).

5. Trustee exemption clauses are construed fairly without preference for either party (*Bogg* v *Raper*, *The Times*, 22 April 1998, CA), but any ambiguity in the wording of an exemption clause is construed strictly *contra proferentem* (against the one who seeks to benefit from it (*Wight* v *Olswang*, *The Times*, 18 May 1999)).

Spread Trustee Company Ltd v *Hutcheson*

[2011] UKPC 13, Privy Council

LORD KERR: If ... placing of reliance on a responsible person to manage property so as to promote the interests of the beneficiaries of a trust is central to the concept of trusteeship, denying trustees the opportunity to avoid liability for their gross negligence seems to be entirely in keeping with that essential aim. (para [180]).

SECTION 4: RELIEF FROM LIABILITY

If trustees are unable to raise a defence to a breach of trust, or if the defence can only be raised against some of the beneficiaries, trustees may nevertheless be relieved of all or some of their liability.

A: Set-off

The general rule is that if a trustee makes a gain in one breach of trust, he cannot set off that gain against a loss arising out of another breach of trust (*Dimes* v *Scott* (1828)

4 Russ 195), but if transactions are connected as part of a larger transaction, as is the case where individual investments form part of a portfolio of investments, a loss in one transaction may be set off against a gain in another transaction.

■ QUESTION

In *Bartlett* v *Barclays Trust (No. 1)* [1980] 1 All ER 139 (see Chapter 11) a property develop-ment company, which was almost wholly owned by the trust corporation (the bank), made a loss on one speculative property investment and made a gain on another. What was the result of that case? Did the result infringe the general rule against set-off of one breach against another?

B: Contribution

CIVIL LIABILITY (CONTRIBUTION) ACT 1978

1. Entitlement to contribution

(1)   Subject to the following provisions of this section, any person liable in respect of any damage suffered by another person may recover contribution from any other person liable in respect of the same damage (whether jointly with him or otherwise).

(2)   A person shall be entitled to recover contribution by virtue of subsection (1) above notwith-standing that he has ceased to be liable in respect of the damage in question since the time when the damage occurred, provided that he was so liable immediately before he made or was ordered or agreed to make the payment in respect of which the contribution is sought.

(3)   A person shall be liable to make contribution by virtue of subsection (1) above notwith-standing that he has ceased to be liable in respect of the damage in question since the time when the damage occurred, unless he ceased to be liable by virtue of the expiry of a period of limitation or prescription which extinguished the right on which the claim against him in respect of the damage was based ...

2. Assessment of contribution

(1)   Subject to subsection (3) below, in any proceedings for contribution under section 1 above the amount of the contribution recoverable from any person shall be such as may be found by the court to be just and equitable having regard to the extent of that person's responsibility for the damage in question ...

NOTE: Section 6(1) of the Act confirms that a person is liable to contribute under the Act whether his liability is based in 'tort, breach of contract, breach of trust or otherwise'. A person who is liable for knowing receipt of property misapplied in breach of trust (see Chapter 15) is also liable to contribute under the Act (*Charter plc and another* v *City Index Ltd* [2007] 1 WLR 26, Ch D).

C: Indemnity

Re Towndrow

[1911] 1 Ch 662, Chancery Division

Facts: A trustee who was entitled to a specific legacy under the trust of which he was trustee misappropriated part of the residue of the trust fund. The residuary beneficiaries brought an action seeking to make good their loss out of the trustee's legacy, which had been assigned to a third party.

Held: The legacy and residue were held upon entirely separate trusts, therefore the residu-ary beneficiaries could not take advantage of the principle that a trustee who had caused a loss to his trust could not assert his entitlement to a share in the trust fund. The trustee's assignees took the legacy free from any equitable charge or lien in favour of the residuary beneficiaries.

PARKER J: ... I think that the real principle is stated by Stirling J in *Doering* v *Doering* 42 ChD 203 where he says, 'The law has gone to this extent, that though the breach of trust is committed after the assignment, nevertheless, the rule applies, and the assignee or mortgagee is not entitled to any share in the estate until the default is made good. The theory on which that rule is based is that the Court treats the trustee as having received his share by anticipation, and the answer to any claim made by the trustee is this: "You have already received your share; you have it in your own hands."' Therefore you must, I take it, have a defaulting trustee claiming a share in the aggregate amount of a certain fund, and the answer to him is, 'You cannot have it; you have already had it.' But that cannot apply to a case like the present, where the only interest which the trustee has is in another fund in which the *cestuis que trust* whose property has been misappropriated have no interest at all; it cannot apply so as to give them a lien on that other fund. The trustee in this case is not claiming a share in the residue, and, therefore, his default has no effect on the distribution of that residue, and, in my opinion, his assigns under the settlement, there being no default at the date of the assignment, take clear of and are entitled to hold the settled fund free from any equity against them ...

D: Statutory power to relieve trustee from personal liability

---

TRUSTEE ACT 1925

61. Power to relieve trustee from personal liability

If it appears to the court that a trustee, whether appointed by the court or otherwise, is or may be personally liable for any breach of trust, whether the transaction alleged to be a breach of trust occurred before or after the commencement of this Act, but has acted honestly and reasonably, and ought fairly to be excused for the breach of trust and for omitting to obtain the directions of the court in the matter in which he committed such breach, then the court may relieve him either wholly or partly from personal liability for the same.

NOTES

1. The trustees were protected by this section in *Re Wightwick* [1950] 1 Ch 260. They had paid income from dividends to the National Anti-Vivisection Society, believing this to be a valid donation to charity. The House of Lords held the society non-charitable in 1947 (see further Chapter 7). Wynn-Parry J observed:

   > In paying the income, as they have done, to the association and then to the National Anti-Vivisection Society up till now, the plaintiffs have acted throughout *bona fide* and in accordance with the generally held view that the primary gift was a good charitable trust: see *Re Foveaux* [1895] 2 Ch 501. It will, therefore, be proper to declare under the Trustee Act 1925, s.61, that they acted honestly and reasonably and ought fairly to be excused for any breach of trust which they may have committed and for omitting to obtain the directions of the court in the matter, and that they should be wholly relieved from personal liability.

2. In *Bartlett* v *Barclays Bank Trust Co. Ltd (No. 1)* [1980] Ch 515 (see Chapter 12), the bank could not use this section as a defence, since it protects only trustees who had acted honestly and reasonably. The bank had acted honestly, but not reasonably.

3. In *Re Evans* [1999] 2 All ER 777, a trustee was relieved from liability for underinsurance. Discussed in J. Lowry and R. Edmonds, 'Excuses', in P. Birks and A. Pretto (eds), *Breach of Trust* (Oxford: Hart Publishing, 2002), p. 269. In *Re St Andrew's (Cheam) Lawn Tennis Club Trust (sub nom Philippe* v *Cameron)* [2012] EWHC 1040 (Ch); [2012] 3 All ER 746, trustees of land used by a tennis club omitted to charge rent because they (erroneously) believed that the land was held on charitable trusts for the benefit of the club members. The trustees were relieved of liability under s.61.

4. Section 61 offers a possible (although not the only, or best) basis for reducing trustee liability to take account of a beneficiary's contributory fault, but it has been said that Parliament 'could have provided for the conduct of the beneficiary to be taken into account' so as to reduce the defendant's liability for breach of trust under s.61, but '[i]t did not and it is not for the Court to extend the law in a way that was not done by the legislature' (*Lloyds TSB Bank Plc* v *Markandan & Uddin (A Firm)* [2010] EWHC 2840 (Ch)). The prevailing view in English law is that the plea of contributory negligence 'has no application to liability for breach of trust or for breach of fiduciary duty'

(*De Beer* v *Kanaar & Co. (A Firm)* [2002] EWHC 688 (Ch), *per* Patten J at para. [92]). This can be contrasted with the approach taken in New Zealand (*per* Sir Robin Cooke P in *Day* v *Mead* [1987] 2 NZLR 443, New Zealand Court of Appeal, at 451):

> Whether or not there are reported cases in which compensation for breach of a fiduciary obliga-tion has been assessed on the footing that the plaintiff should accept some share of the respon-sibility, there appears to be no solid reason for denying jurisdiction to follow that obviously just course, especially now that law and equity have mingled or are interacting.

See, further, R. Mulheron, 'Contributory Negligence in Equity: Should Fiduciaries Accept all the Blame?' (2003) 19(3) *Professional Negligence* 422. Matthew Conaglen contends that '[i]t would be anathema to the nature and function of fiduciary liability for [contributory fault] pleas to be accepted' to reduce a fiduciary's liability ('Remedial ramifications of conflicts between a fidu-ciary's duties' (2010) 126 *LQR* 72–101). But this is too absolute, and is somewhat at odds with Conaglen's own theory that fiduciary duties are merely protective of non-fiduciary duties (see Chapter 10). If fiduciary duties are utterly free-standing duties established in the public interest to prevent abuse of trust, to reduce a fiduciary's liability on account of the principal's fault ought then to be prohibited or wholly exceptional, but if, as Conaglen argues, the core duties owed by a fiduciary to their principal are non-fiduciary duties, it is then not difficult to imagine cases in which the fiduciary's personal liability ought in fairness to be reduced to take account of the prin-cipal's contribution to their own loss.

G.Watt, 'Contributory Fault and Breach of Trust'
(2005) 5(2) *Oxford University Commonwealth Law Journal* 205–224, p. 224

> [T]here are a number of obstacles of principle in the way of apportionment of liability between trustee and beneficiary on the ground of contributory fault. One significant obstacle is the basic difference between the compensatory aim of tortious liability and the traditional aim of trustee liability to reinstate the trust fund by means of the action for account. Another is the exemplary nature of trustee liability, which favours the enforcement of trust obligations even where this might over compensate individual beneficiaries. Significant though these obstacles are…they can be overcome in the case of a careless breach by the trustee of a bare trust. In such a case there is no significant difference between the conceptual basis for, and remedies for, negligently caused harm in tort actions and actions for breach of trust. The trustee's fault-based liability in such a case should therefore be capable of reduction to take account of the beneficiary's own fault. Furthermore, the current outright refusal to take account of contributory fault represents an allocation to the trustee of all risk of loss even where his conduct was merely one contribu-tory factual cause of the loss. Such an allocation may be appropriate to trustees who breach their fiduciary duty or recklessly run the risk of breach of fiduciary duty, but justice requires that the presumption against apportionment should be rebuttable in the case of a merely careless trustee. Until this is accepted, trustees will continue to pay for the careless conduct of trust beneficiaries.

E: Impounding a beneficiary's share

The court has an inherent power to impound the interest of a beneficiary, thus providing the trustee with an indemnity to the extent that the beneficiary's interest will suffice to replace the loss to the trust.

The power can arise where a beneficiary has merely consented to the breach, but only if some benefit to him can be proved, and then only to the extent of that benefit. If the beneficiary has gone further, and actually requested or instigated a breach, the power can be exercised whether or not he has received a personal benefit from the breach.

Needless to say, the trustee has to show that the beneficiary acted in full knowledge of the facts, but it is not necessary to show that he knew that the acts he was instigating or consenting to amounted to a breach.

There is also a statutory discretion to impound.

TRUSTEE ACT 1925

62. Power to make beneficiary indemnify for breach of trust

(1) Where a trustee commits a breach of trust at the instigation or request or with the consent in writing of a beneficiary, the court may, if it thinks fit [and notwithstanding that the beneficiary may be a married woman restrained from anticipation,] make such order as to the court seems just, for impounding all or any part of the interest of the beneficiary in the trust estate by way of indemnity to the trustee or persons claiming through him.

(2) This section applies to breaches of trust committed as well before as after the commencement of this Act.

NOTE: The words in square brackets were repealed by the Married Women (Restraint upon Anticipation) Act 1949, but are set out here to explain Wilberforce J's view of the purpose of this section, set out in *Re Pauling's ST (No. 2)* [1963] Ch 576.

This section replaced an earlier enactment, and has been treated as a consolidating section.

Re Pauling's ST (No. 2)
[1963] Ch 576, Chancery Division

Facts: In *Re Pauling's ST*, the Court of Appeal largely upheld a decision of Wilberforce J [1962] 1 WLR 86. Pursuant to that decision, the claimants took out a summons for the appointment of new trustees. The defendants resisted the appointment on the grounds that they were entitled to impound the interests of the tenant for life, Mrs Younghusband, both under equitable jurisdiction apart from statute, and under the Trustee Act 1925, s.62, and their removal as trustees would imperil their right to impound Mrs Younghusband's interest.

Note that Mrs Younghusband's interest as life tenant would have been in the form of continuing income (interest on the fund invested), so that it would have been impossible, for example, for the bank simply to have impounded a single capital sum.

Held: The trustees had no right to continue in office merely to impound Mrs Younghusband's interest. In any case, neither the equitable nor the statutory right to impound was limited to the case where the trustee continued in office, so that the appointment of new trustees would not imperil the right. However, in the light of various undertakings entered into by the bank, and the appeal on liability (eventually heard in *Re Pauling's ST*), the new appointments should not be made in the circumstances.

WILBERFORCE J: [Wilberforce J considered the general equitable jurisdiction, and continued:] As regards the statutory right, that depends on the language of s.62 of the Trustee Act 1925, and at first sight it might look as if that right only exists in favour of a person who is actually a trustee. But, on consideration, that seems to me to be a misconstruction of the section. In the first place, the same objection against limiting the right in this way applies to the statutory jurisdiction. It seems to me an absurdity that it is required as a condition of exercising the right to obtain an impounding order, that the trustee who, *ex hypothesi*, is in breach of trust, must remain as trustee in order to acquire a right of indemnity. Further, it seems to me on the authorities, and, indeed, on the very terms of the section, that the section is giving an additional right, among other things, to deal with the case of a married woman beneficiary; that the statutory right is extending the equitable right and not limiting it, and that it is not right to read the section so as to apply only to a person who was formerly a trustee. The section begins with the words: 'Where a trustee commits a breach of trust', thereby indicating that at the time the breach of trust is committed the person in question must be a trustee. Then further down in the section there is a reference to a trustee and that appears to me to be merely a reference back to the same person as the person who committed the breach of trust and not as an indication that the person in question must be a trustee at the date of the order.

NOTES

1. Wilberforce J treats the right under s.62 as extending the equitable jurisdiction. There are probably no circumstances where the equitable jurisdiction is wider than the jurisdiction under the statute.

2. The courts seem to have treated this largely as a consolidating section, rather than extending their powers, except that Wilberforce J in *Re Pauling's ST (No. 2)* [1963] Ch 576 thought that it gave an additional right, among other things, to deal with a married woman beneficiary. This additional right is no longer necessary, because of changes in legislation on family property, and that part of the section was repealed in 1949.

3. The effect of the court making such an order is that the beneficiary is not only debarred from pursuing his own claim against the trustee, but is also liable to replace the losses suffered by the other beneficiaries, to the extent ordered by the court, and perhaps up to the full value of his own interest. To this extent, the trustee is protected at the beneficiary's expense.

4. The discretion is a judicial discretion, and although the section appears to extend the inherent power of the court by giving a discretion to impound a beneficiary's interest regardless of whether he obtained a benefit, it has received a restrictive interpretation. It seems that the court will make an impounding order in any case where it would have done so before the Act; generally speaking, in any case where the beneficiary has actively induced the breach (for which it has never been necessary to show benefit).

5. It must, of course, be shown that the beneficiary was fully aware of what was being done. In *Re Somerset* [1894] 1 Ch 231, a beneficiary had urged the trustees to invest in a mortgage of a particular property, but had left them to decide how much money they were prepared to invest. Lindley MR said (at 265):

   > In order to bring a case within this section the cestui que trust must instigate, or request, or consent in writing to some act or omission which in itself is a breach of trust, and not to some act or omission which only becomes a breach of trust by reason of want of care on the part of the trustees.

   The words 'in writing' have been held to apply only to consent, and not to instigation or request: *Griffith* v *Hughes* [1892] 3 Ch 105. So it is necessary only for a request or instigation to be oral.

6. The power to impound will not be lost upon an assignment of the beneficial interest. Nor is it lost when the court replaces the trustees in consequence of the breach. In *Re Pauling's ST* [1962] 1 WLR 86, the trustees resisted removal because they were claiming an indemnity out of the interests of the parents. Wilberforce J held that they were entitled to such indemnity and that this would be unaffected by their replacement. They were therefore unable to use this as a ground for continuing in office: see *Re Pauling's ST (No. 2)* [1963] Ch 576.

7. Apart from statute, it is the practice, where trustees have under an honest mistake overpaid a beneficiary, for the court to make allowance for the mistake in order to allow the trustee to recoup as far as possible: *Re Musgrave* [1916] 2 Ch 417. An overpaid beneficiary is not compelled to return the excess, but further payment may be withheld until the accounts are adjusted.

   If a payment is made by mistake to someone who is not entitled, the trustee may recover on an action for money had and received if the mistake was one of fact, but not if it was a mistake of law: *Re Diplock* [1947] Ch 716. It is also certain that the error must be corrected where trustee–beneficiaries overpay themselves.

■ QUESTION

To what extent does the trustee's duty to reinstate the trust fund resemble an equitable hybrid of contractual and tortious measures of damages?

■ SUMMATIVE QUESTION

Theresa died in 1993. By her will, she settled a trust of £20,000 cash on trustees for the benefit of her nephew Bill and her niece Barbara, 'in equal shares upon their attaining the age of 21'. At the date of Theresa's death, Bill was 13 and Barbara was 14. Theresa had also made a gift in her will of £10,000 to another nephew, Barry.

The trustees are Tricia, Tracy, and Barry. Tricia is a solicitor.

online
resource
centre

In 1996, Tricia urged Tracy and Barry to join her in investing in a private limited company which, she said, promised to be a very profitable investment. She explained to the trustees that although the investment was 'technically unauthorised' (the trust instrument prohibited investment in private companies) it was very secure. In the event, the trustees went ahead with the investment in the company, having first obtained the consent of Bill and Barbara, who had been told that the investment was a 'secure one'.

Shortly after making the investment, the shares rose in value and yielded large dividends to the trust, but later they fell in value and today they are practically worthless.

It is now April 2003 and Bill and Barbara have issued proceedings against the trustees. Advise the trustees as to the possible extent of their liability to the trust and any defences which might be open to them.

FURTHER READING

Birks, P. and Pretto, A. (eds), *Breach of Trust* (Oxford: Hart Publishing, 2002).

Brunyate, J., *The Limitation of Actions in Equity* (London: Stevens & Sons, 1932).

Capper, D., 'Compensation for Breach of Trusts' (1997) 61 *Conv* 14.

Conaglen, M. D. J., 'Equitable Compensation for Breach of Fiduciary Dealing Rules' (2003) 119 *LQR* 246.

Dal Pont, G., 'Wilful Default Revisited—Liability for a Co-trustee's Defaults' (2001) 65 *Conv* 376.

Elliott, S. and Edelman, J., 'Target Holdings Considered in Australia' (2003) 119 *LQR* 545.

Hayton, D., 'The Irreducable Core Content of Trusteeship', in A. J. Oakley (ed.), *Trends in Contemporary Trust Law* (Oxford: Clarendon Press, 1996), p. 47.

Mather, J., 'Fiduciaries and the law of limitation' [2008] JBL 344.

McCormack, G., 'The Liability of Trustees for Gross Negligence' (1998) 62 *Conv* 100.

Oakley, A. J., 'The Liberalising Nature of Remedies for Breach of Trust', in A. J. Oakley (ed.), *Trends in Contemporary Trusts Law* (Oxford: Clarendon Press, 1996), p. 217.

Paling, D. R., 'The Trustee's Duty of Skill and Care' (1973) 37 *Conv* 48.

PART IV

Trusts and Third Parties

14

Tracing and Recovering Trust Property

KEY AIMS

To distinguish the process of following trust property from the process of tracing the value of trust property. To distinguish the processes of following and tracing from the ultimate remedies employed to recover misapplied trust property. To distinguish remedies at common law, remedies in equity, and restitutionary remedies from each other.

SECTION 1: INTRODUCTION

Tracing is the process of proving that a defendant has received trust property. The rules of tracing raise presumptions for or against a finding that the claimant's property or its substitute (its value represented in a new form) has passed into the defendant's hands. Most of the tracing presumptions are rebuttable by contrary evidence in the form of written accounts, memoranda, and similar documentary statements, but such evidence is, of course, usually absent when trust property is misapplied. At its simplest, tracing involves following a trust asset, such as an antique vase, as it passes from the trustee to 'stranger A' to 'stranger B' to 'stranger C' and so on. In fact, this simple process is usually referred to as 'following' in order to distinguish it from the more sophisticated process of 'tracing' the value of an asset into substitute assets for which the original asset has been exchanged. Of course, the 'simple' process of following becomes impossible when the thing itself is effectively destroyed. Thus in *Borden (UK) Ltd* v *Scottish Timber Products* [1981] Ch 25, the claimant was unable to recover resin which had been used in an irreversible process of manufacturing chipboard (see the details at Section 2: Common law remedies, A: Express retention of legal title to a transferred asset).

It is crucial to be aware that tracing is a process of acquiring evidence to support an ultimate claim against the defendant. Tracing is not the remedy itself. The ultimate remedies are considered next and in the following sections. Having considered remedies at law, we will examine the tracing process at law; having considered remedies in equity we will consider the tracing process in equity. In theory, there should not be separate tracing processes at law and in equity (given that tracing is merely an evidential process), but the different ultimate remedies in law and equity have, for many years, drawn the courts into the trap of distinguishing the common law tracing process from the equitable tracing process, and it is a trap from which extrication does not seem imminent.

A successful proprietary claim in equity requires the claimant to identify his property in the hands of the defendant. It is necessary for the defendant not only to have received but also to retain the claimant's property. So, if the defendant no longer has the property, a proprietary claim will not be available. (The requirement to show that the claimant's property is in the defendant's hands, and that it can be traced from the claimant to the defendant by an unbroken chain of connections, applies just as rigorously in the context of claims against criminal assets 'frozen' under the Proceeds of Crime Act 2002—see *The Serious Fraud Office* v *Lexi Holdings PLC (In Administration)* [2008] EWCA Crim 1443.) A proprietary claim is essential if the defendant is bankrupt, and is also useful if the property has increased in value, since the claimant by identifying the property can benefit from its increase in value. A 'freezing injunction' is a means by which a claimant bringing a proprietary claim can prevent the defendant from disposing of 'target' assets prior to the court hearing. (The 'freezing injunction' was formerly known as the '*Mareva*' injunction: *Mareva Compania Naviera SA* v *International Bulk Carriers SA* [1975] 2 Lloyd's Rep 509, Court of Appeal.) One reason why an injunction is so effective is because breach of its terms is contempt of court (see Chapter 1). Another reason for the effectiveness of the injunction is that it operates *in personam*, which is to say that it binds a defendant to proceedings in a domestic court personally, even if his assets are held in a foreign jurisdiction (see Chapter 1). However, a freezing injunction will only be granted against a foreign-resident defendant if the injunction against the foreign-resident is incidental to and dependent upon a substantive claim against a defendant within the English jurisdiction. In *Cardille* v *LED Builders Pty Ltd* (1999) ALR 294, an injunction was granted on this basis against a husband resident abroad whose wife, the defendant to a substantive claim within the English jurisdiction, held certain assets in the English jurisdiction on trust for her husband.

At common law, there is also the claim for money had and received. This is a personal claim, which requires the claimant to show only (subject to the complete and partial defences described throughout this chapter that the defendant received the claimant's property, and not necessarily that he still retains it. There is even a personal form of equitable claim (see *Re Diplock's Estate* (discussed throughout this chapter)).

It is important to appreciate that in a tracing action, the claimant can trace the money 'not because it is the claimant's, but because it is derived from a fund which is treated as if it were subject to a charge in the claimant's favour' (*London Allied Holdings Ltd* v *Lee* [2007] EWHC 2061 (Ch), *per* Etherton J at para. [257] citing *El Ajou* v *Dollar Land Holdings* [1993] 3 All ER 717, *per* Millett J at 735j–736a).

SECTION 2: COMMON LAW REMEDIES

A: Express retention of legal title to a transferred asset

Borden (UK) Ltd v *Scottish Timber Products Ltd*
[1981] Ch 25, Court of Appeal

Facts: The contract by which the claimants supplied resin to the defendants for use in the manufacture of chipboard stated that property in the resin would only pass when the defendants had paid in full, even though it was implied that the resin could be used before payment. In fact, the manufacturing process was such that the resin could not be removed from the chipboard after use. The defendants became insolvent before payment had been paid. At first instance, the claimants succeeded (on the ground that they still had a property right in the resin) in establishing a charge over the chipboard, and proceeds of sale of any chipboard, containing their resin.

Held: Allowing the appeal, that once used in the manufacture of the chipboard, pursuant to the intention of the parties, the resin as such ceased to exist and with it the claimants' title thereto; that, as the resin had lost its identity in the manufacturing process, the chipboard being a wholly new product, it could not be traced into the chipboard.

BRIDGE LJ: In the instant case, even if I assume that so long as the resin remained resin the beneficial ownership of the resin remained in the plaintiffs, I do not see how the concept of the beneficial ownership remaining in the plaintiffs after use in manufacture can here possibly be reconciled with the liberty which the plaintiffs gave to the defendants to use that resin in the manufacturing process for the defendants' benefit, producing their own chipboard and in the process destroying the very existence of the resin ...

Some extreme examples were canvassed in argument. Suppose cattle cake is sold to a farmer, or fuel to a steel manufacturer, in each case with a reservation of title clause, but on terms which permit the farmer to feed the cattle cake to his herd and the steelmaker to fuel his furnaces, before paying the purchase price. Mr. Mowbray concedes that in these cases the seller cannot trace into the cattle or the steel. He says that the difference is that the goods have been consumed. But once this concession is made, I find it impossible to draw an intelligible line of distinction in principle which would give the plaintiffs a right to trace the resin into the chipboard in the instant case. What has happened in the manufacturing process is much more akin to the process of consumption than to any simple process of admixture of goods. To put the point in another way, if the contribution that the resin has made to the chipboard gives rise to a tracing remedy, I find it difficult to see any good reason why, in the steelmaking example, the essential contribution made by the fuel to the steel manufacturing process should not do likewise.

These are the principal considerations which have led me to the conclusion that the plaintiffs are not entitled to the tracing remedy which they claim. But I am fortified in that conclusion by the further consideration that if the remedy were available in such cases, a most intractable problem could, and in many cases would, arise in quantifying the proportion of the value of the manufactured product which the tracer could claim as properly attributable to his ingredient. In the instant case, a breakdown of the actual costings of chipboard over a period of seven months to July 29, 1977, has been agreed, attributing 17 per cent of the total cost to the cost of resin, subject to a reservation with respect to wastage and over-usage. But one can well see that in many cases where the cost of materials and labour involved in a particular production process were constantly fluctuating, it might be quite impossible to assign a proportion of the total cost properly attributable to one particular ingredient with any certainty at all.

The lesson to be learned from these conclusions is a simple one. If a seller of goods to a manufacturer, who knows that his goods are to be used in the manufacturing process before they are paid for, wishes to reserve to himself an effective security for the payment of the price, he cannot rely on a simple reservation of title clause such as that relied upon by the plaintiffs. If he wishes to acquire rights over the finished product, he can only do so by express contractual stipulation. We have seen an elaborate, and presumably effective, example of such a stipulation in *Aluminium Industrie Vaassen B.V.* v *Romalpa Aluminium Ltd.* [1976] 1 W.L.R. 676. An attempt to acquire rights over the finished product by a stipulation which proved ineffective for want of registration under section 95 of the Companies Act 1948 is to be seen in the decision of Slade J. in *In re Bond Worth Ltd* [1980] Ch. 228 to which in the course of argument we were helpfully referred.

For the reasons that I have attempted to explain, I would allow this appeal and set aside the judge's order ...

B: Proprietary remedies at common law

Legal title is, in principle, enforceable against anybody in the world (see Chapter 1), and it might therefore be thought that if the claimant can establish that the defendant has his property, he should be able to recover it. However, whereas the common law developed an action for the recovery of a specific piece of land, it never extended this 'real' remedy to allow a claimant to recover a specific chattel. Although the common law acknowledged the claimant's ownership of the chattel, his action was a personal action in detinue, the remedy for which was damages. The defendant could therefore choose whether to return the claimant's chattel or pay him its full value as damages.

The Common Law Procedure Act 1854, s.78, gave the court a discretion to order specific delivery of the chattel, and this power is retained by the Torts (Interference with Goods) Act 1977, s.3. But there is no absolute right to the return of the chattel. The importance of the proprietary claim lies rather in the fact that it entitles the claimant to the full value of the chattel, in preference to the claims of the defendant's other creditors.

The common law also concluded that the claimant's right should continue even if the defendant has exchanged the claimant's property for some other property, or sold it and purchased other property with the proceeds. So long as it was possible to 'trace' his original property—that is, to show that what the defendant now holds can be regarded as simply a substitute—his claim is unaffected. In *Re Diplock's Estate* [1948] Ch 465 (see below), Lord Greene MR explained the doctrine in terms of the claimant ratifying the wrongful sale of purchase, to enable the legal owner to claim the substitute.

In *Taylor* v *Plumer* (1815) 3 M & S 562, Sir Thomas Plumer had handed over money to a stockbroker with instructions to purchase exchequer bonds, but the stockbroker instead purchased American investments and bullion, and attempted to abscond with these. He was caught before he could leave England, and the investments and bullion were seized by Plumer. The assignees of the stockbroker then brought an action to recover them from Sir Thomas, but failed. The investments and bullion were held to be Sir Thomas's own property. In effect, Plumer's money was traced into the investments and bullion for, according to Lord Ellenborough at 575, 'the product of or substitute for the original thing still follows the nature of the thing itself, as long as it can be ascertained as such'.

As Millett LJ observed in *The Trustees of the Property of F. C. Jones & Sons* v *Anne Jones* [1996] 3 WLR 703, *Taylor* v *Plumer* was actually decided on equitable principles (see also Lionel Smith [1995] *LMCLQ* 240), but claims to substitute assets were upheld in *Banque Belge* v *Hambrouck* [1921] 1 KB 321 and *Lipkin Gorman* v *Karpnale Ltd* [1991] 2 AC 548 (see C: Money had and received in this section), and indeed in *The Trustees of the Property of F. C. Jones & Sons* v *Anne Jones* itself. So it is clear that a substitution doctrine is recognised by the common law.

Two other points need to be made about the substitution doctrine. First, if it depends on ratification, the claimant is equally entitled not to ratify the transaction and instead to claim the original property. Secondly, where, say, money is paid into a bank account, at any rate where it is unmixed with other money, it is exchanged for a chose in action against the bank. In *Diplock*, Lord Greene MR thought that there was no reason why the common law would not allow the substitution of the money into the chose in action, and vice versa:

> If it is possible to identify a principal's money with an asset purchased exclusively by means of it, we see no reason for drawing a distinction between a chose in action such as banker's debt to his customer and any other asset. If the principal can ratify the acquisition of the one, we see no reason for supposing that he cannot ratify the acquisition of the other.

This passage was approved by Millett J in *Agip (Africa) Ltd* v *Jackson* [1990] 1 Ch 265, but he thought that it was limited to following an asset into a changed form in the same hands, rather than following the same asset from one recipient to another. Millett J did not think that it necessarily followed that the common law allowed free tracing of causes of action from one person to another.

C: Money had and received

A proprietary tracing claim depends upon the claimant being able to trace his actual property, or its product or substitute, into the defendant's hands. In the case of currency, title will pass to the recipient, but the law imposes upon the recipient of, say, money stolen from the claimant an obligation to reimburse the claimant with an equivalent sum. From the House of Lords decision in *Lipkin Gorman* v *Karpnale Ltd* [1991] 2 AC 548, and in particular the speech of Lord Goff, the basis of the action appears to be that the defendant has been unjustly enriched at the expense of the claimant. The claim is established merely by showing that the defendant has received the claimant's property. The defendant's knowledge (or lack of it) is irrelevant. Neither is the action defeated by the recipient later disposing of the money, or mixing it with his own money, since the claim is a personal and not a proprietary claim. It is defeated, however, if the recipient has not been unjustly enriched. Innocently to receive stolen money in return for full consideration is not to be unjustly enriched at all, so that, for example, a shop which has innocently taken stolen money to pay for its goods is not liable to the victim of the theft. Consideration recognised by the common law must be provided, however.

Lipkin Gorman (a firm) v Karpnale Ltd
[1992] 4 All ER 512, House of Lords

Facts: Cass, a partner in the appellant firm of solicitors, by cashing cheques of which he was an authorised signatory, stole a large sum of money from their clients' account. He took the cash to the Playboy Club, which was owned by the respondents, whereupon he gambled it away. The appellants successfully claimed the club's winnings from Cass, although property in the money had undoubtedly passed to the respondents, and they no longer had the money.

Held:
  (a) The club was liable in an action for money had and received. It was unable to claim that it had provided consideration for the money, since contracts by way of gaming and wagering were rendered null and void by the Gaming Act 1845, s.18. Gambling contracts were not therefore contracts for consideration.
  (b) There is a change of position defence to the restitutionary common law claim, which limited the appellants' right to recovery of the winnings taken by the casino, rather than all the money gambled by Cass. Paying out money as winnings constituted a change in position by the club.

LORD TEMPLEMAN: My Lords, Cass was a partner in the appellant firm of solicitors, Lipkin Gorman (the solicitors). Cass withdrew £323,222.14 from the solicitors' bank account. The sum of £100,313.16 was replaced, recovered or accounted for, but the balance of £222,908.98 was money which Cass stole from the solicitors and proved to be irrecoverable from him. Cass staked £561,014.06 at the gaming tables of the Playboy Club, a licensed casino owned and operated by the respondents, Karpnale Ltd (the club). Cass won £378,294.06. After making adjustments for certain cheques, the club agreed that the club won and Cass lost overall, in a matter of months, the sum of £174,745. The parties also agreed that the maximum gross personal resources of Cass amounted to £20,050 and that at least the sum of £154,695 won by the club and lost by Cass was derived from money stolen from the solicitors. The club acted innocently throughout and was not aware that it had received £154,695 derived from the solicitors until the solicitors claimed restitution. Conversion does not lie for money, taken and received as currency: see *Orton* v *Butler* (1822) 5 B & Ald 652, 106 ER 1329 and *Foster* v *Green* (1862) 7 H & N 881, 158 ER 726. But the law imposes an obligation on the recipient of stolen money to pay an equivalent sum to the victim if the recipient has been 'unjustly enriched' at the expense of the true owner. In *Fibrosa Spolka Akcyjna* v *Fairbairn Lawson Combe Barbour Ltd* [1942] 2 All ER 122 at 135, [1943] AC 32 at 61 Lord Wright said:

It is clear that any civilised system of law is bound to provide remedies for cases of what has been called unjust enrichment or unjust benefit, that is, to prevent a man from retaining the money of, or some benefit derived from, another which it is against conscience that he should keep.

The club was enriched as and when Cass staked and lost to the club money stolen from the solicitors amounting in the aggregate to £300,000 or more. But the club paid Cass when he won and in the final reckoning the club only retained £154,695, which was admittedly derived from the solicitors' money. The solicitors can recover the sum of £154,695 which was retained by the club if they show that in the circumstances the club was unjustly enriched at the expense of the solicitors.

In the course of argument there was a good deal of discussion concerning tracing in law and in equity. In my opinion, in a claim for money had and received by a thief, the plaintiff victim must show that money belonging to him was paid by the thief to the defendant and that the defendant was unjustly enriched and remained unjustly enriched. An innocent recipient of stolen money may not be enriched at all; if Cass had paid £20,000 derived from the solicitors to a car dealer for a motor car priced at £20,000, the car dealer would not have been enriched. The car dealer would have received £20,000 for a car worth £20,000. But an innocent recipient of stolen money will be enriched if the recipient has not given full consideration. If Cass had given £20,000 of the solicitors' money to a friend as a gift, the friend would have been enriched and unjustly enriched because a donee of stolen money cannot in good conscience rely on the bounty of the thief to deny restitution to the victim of the theft. Complications arise if the donee innocently expends the stolen money in reliance on the validity of the gift before the donee receives notice of the victim's claim for restitution. Thus, if the donee spent £20,000 in the purchase of a motor car which he would not have purchased but for the gift, it seems to me that the donee has altered his position on the faith of the gift and has only been unjustly enriched to the extent of the secondhand value of the motor car at the date when the victim of the theft seeks restitution. If the donee spends the £20,000 in a trip round the world, which he would not have undertaken without the gift, it seems to me that the donee has altered his position on the faith of the gift and that he is not unjustly enriched when the victim of the theft seeks restitution. In the present case Cass stole and the club received £229,908.48 of the solicitors' money. If the club was in the same position as a donee, the club nevertheless in good faith allowed Cass to gamble with the solicitors' money and paid his winnings from time to time so that, when the solicitors sought restitution, the club only retained £154,695 derived from the solicitors. The question is whether the club which was enriched by £154,695 at the date when the solicitors sought restitution was unjustly enriched.

[Lord Templeman went on to consider whether the club had provided consideration for the money.]

LORD GOFF OF CHIEVELEY (on the change of position defence): I turn then to the last point on which the club relied to defeat the solicitors' claim for the money. This was that the claim advanced by the solicitors was in the form of an action for money had and received, and that such a claim should only succeed where the defendant was unjustly enriched at the expense of the plaintiff. If it would be unjust or unfair to order restitution, the claim should fail. It was for the court to consider the question of injustice or unfairness, on broad grounds. If the court thought that it would be unjust or unfair to hold the club liable to the solicitors, it should deny the solicitors recovery. Mr Lightman QC, for the club, listed a number of reasons why, in his submission, it would be unfair to hold the club liable. These were: (1) the club acted throughout in good faith, ignorant of the fact that the money had been stolen by Cass; (2) although the gaming contracts entered into by the club with Cass were all void, nevertheless the club honoured all those contracts; (3) Cass was allowed to keep his winnings (to the extent that he did not gamble them away); (4) the gaming contracts were merely void not illegal; and (5) the solicitors' claim was no different in principle from a claim to recover against an innocent third party to whom the money was given and who no longer retained it.

I accept that the solicitors' claim in the present case is founded upon the unjust enrichment of the club, and can only succeed if, in accordance with the principles of the law of restitution, the club were indeed unjustly enriched at the expense of the solicitors. The claim for money had and received is not, as I have previously mentioned, founded upon any wrong committed by the club against the solicitors. But it does not, in my opinion, follow that the court has carte blanche to reject the solicitors' claim simply because it thinks it unfair or unjust in the circumstances to grant recovery. The recovery of money in restitution is not, as a general rule, a matter of discretion for the court. A claim to recover money at common law is made as a matter of right; and, even though the underlying principle of recovery is the principle of unjust enrichment, nevertheless, where recovery is denied, it is denied on the basis of legal principle.

It is therefore necessary to consider whether Mr Lightman's submission [for the club] can be upheld on the basis of legal principle. In my opinion it is plain, from the nature of his submission, that he is in fact seeking to invoke a principle of change of position, asserting that recovery should be denied because of the change in position of the club, who acted in good faith throughout.

Whether change of position is, or should be, recognised as a defence to claims in restitution is a subject which has been much debated in the books. It is, however, a matter on which there is a remarkable unanimity of view, the consensus being to the effect that such a defence should be recognised in English law. I myself am under no doubt that this is right.

...

In these circumstances, it is right that we should ask ourselves: why do we feel that it would be unjust to allow restitution in cases such as these? The answer must be that, where an innocent defendant's position is so changed that he will suffer an injustice if called upon to repay or to repay in full, the injustice of requiring him so to repay outweighs the injustice of denying the plaintiff restitution. If the plaintiff pays money to the defendant under a mistake of fact, and the defendant then, acting in good faith, pays the money or part of it to charity, it is unjust to require the defendant to make restitution to the extent that he has so changed his position. Likewise, on facts such as those in the present case, if a thief steals my money and pays it to a third party who gives it away to charity, that third party should have a good defence to an action for money had and received. In other words, bona fide change of position should of itself be a good defence in such cases as these. The principle is widely recognised throughout the common law world ... The time for its recognition in this country is, in my opinion, long overdue.

...

I wish to add two further footnotes. The defence of change of position is akin to the defence of bona fide purchase; but we cannot simply say that bona fide purchase is a species of change of position. This is because change of position will only avail a defendant to the extent that his position has been changed; whereas, where bona fide purchase is invoked, no inquiry is made (in most cases) into the adequacy of the consideration. Even so, the recognition of change of position as a defence should be doubly beneficial. It will enable a more generous approach to be taken to the recognition of the right to restitution, in the knowledge that the defence is, in appropriate cases, available; and, while recognising the different functions of property at law and in equity, there may also in due course develop a more consistent approach to tracing claims, in which common defences are recognised as available to such claims, whether advanced at law or in equity.

[Lord Goff then turned to the application of this principle to the present case.]

■ QUESTIONS

1. Did the claimants have property rights in the money in the client account? If not, what property is being traced? (See note 1 at the end of this list of questions.)

2. Is what is being traced in fact a chose in action against the bank (see Millett LJ (1991) 107 *LQR* 71, but also Margaret Halliwell (1992) 56 *Conv* 124)?

3. When Cass withdrew the money from the solicitors' bank account, whose money was it? Did the money belong to Cass? Did the money belong to the claimants?

4. Are Lord Goff's views on the change of position defence limited to the action for money had and received? If not, to what type of action is change of position a defence?

NOTES

1. Lionel Smith has advanced an analysis of *Lipkin* which, if accepted, would greatly simplify our conceptual understanding of the action for money had and received. Smith notes that, because the action for money had and received is a common law action, courts usually seek to explain it without relying on the (equitable) law of trusts. This, he says, is a 'misunderstanding', for 'all of the cases in which the action for money had and received is deployed in relation to the surviving proceeds of an unauthorised disposition can be understood as allowing a common law claim in respect of a determined sum of money held in trust for the claimant, being the traceable proceeds of an unauthorised disposition of trust property or of the claimant's legal property'. Hence, 'the only kinds of rights held in the proceeds of an unauthorised disposition are equitable rights arising under a trust'. In short, 'the law in these cases follows equity ... by allowing claimants to use common law claims to vindicate equitable interests under a trust' ('Simplifying Claims to Traceable Proceeds' (2009) 125 *LQR* 338, pp. 346–7).

2. The change of position defence was applied by Tuckey J in *Bank Tejarat v Hong Kong and Shanghai Banking Corporation (Ci) Ltd and Hong Kong and Shanghai Bank Trustee (Jersey) Ltd* [1995] 1 Lloyd's Rep 239. Bank Tejarat had been induced, by a fraudulent transaction, to advance money (under a bankers' documentary credit) to the account of the fraudsters (CAK) at Hong Kong and Shanghai Banking Corporation (Ci) Ltd. Hong Kong later paid the money, in pursuance of an apparently legitimate instruction, to one Madame Parvin Farzaneh, a lady in Paris. When the fraud was discovered, Bank Tejarat sued Hong Kong for money had and received. It failed because it was unable to establish that Hong Kong had ever received any of its money (see below), but also because Hong Kong had a change of position defence, having paid the money away, in good faith, before receiving any notice of Tejarat's claim. It is not yet clear whether the change of position defence applies only to money had and received. The essential questions of principle in regard to restitutionary remedies were set out by Lord Hoffmann in *Banque Financiere de la Cite v Parc (Battersea) Ltd* [1999] 1 AC 221, 234: 'first, whether the defendant would be enriched at the plaintiff's expense; secondly, whether such enrichment would be unjust; and thirdly, whether there was nevertheless reasons of policy for denying a remedy'. It is also not clear what happens when money is paid to a second recipient, but Millett argues in (1991) 107 *LQR* 71, p. 79, that since the action is personal and not proprietary, what happens to the money after it has been received by the first recipient is irrelevant, it becomes the property of the first recipient, and any subsequent recipient will be receiving the first recipient's money rather than that of the claimant. It ought also to follow that the first recipient will only be liable to reimburse the value of what was received, and if he makes a favourable investment with it, he should be able to keep the benefit of that. Authority to the contrary can be found in Nourse LJ's judgment in *Trustee of the Property of F. C. Jones and Sons (a firm) v Jones* [1996] 3 WLR 703, [1996] 4 All ER 721, but this looks incorrect in principle, and it is in any case weak authority as Millett and Beldam LJJ reasoned on the basis of a proprietary tracing claim.

SECTION 3: COMMON LAW TRACING

The main constraint on common law tracing is establishing that what the defendant received was in fact the claimant's property. While *Taylor v Plumer* shows that tracing is available where a straightforward exchange of the property has occurred, the position is more complicated where the property or its proceeds have been placed into a bank account, and it is in this area where equitable rules appear to be more generous. The leading authority is *Banque Belge pour L'Etranger v Hambrouck* [1921] 1 KB 321.

Banque Belge pour L'Etranger v *Hambrouck*

[1921] 1 KB 321, Court of Appeal

Facts: Hambrouck, who was a cashier, stole cheques from his employer, altered them so as to make it appear that they were drawn by his employer on the claimant bank to Hambrouck's order, and used them to pay money into a new account (at Farrow's Bank) which he opened specifically for the purpose. Farrow's Bank collected the proceeds from the claimant bank and credited them to Hambrouck's account. Hambrouck then paid various sums from this account to Mlle Spanoghe, with whom he was living, and she paid these sums (and no other sums) into a deposit account of her own at a different bank. Mlle Spanoghe later spent most of the money in this account, but £315 remained.

Held: The Court of Appeal held that the claimant bank was entitled to trace this money.

BANKES LJ: Had the claim been for the recovery of a chattel sold instead of for a sum of money alleged to be given, the appellant's [i.e. Mlle Spanoghe's] counsel do not dispute that, in order to retain the chattel, the appellant must establish that she gave value for it without notice that it had been obtained by the vendor by fraud; but they attempt to distinguish the present case from the case of a chattel by saying: (a) that the appellant, who had no notice of Hambrouck's fraud, obtained a good title to the money, because it was a gift to her from Hambrouck; (b) that the rule applicable to a chattel has no application to currency; (c) that the fact that the appellant had paid the money into her banking account prevented the following of the money by the plaintiff Bank, and that an action for money had and received would therefore not lie.

In my opinion the first contention cannot be supported either upon the facts or in law. The facts show that the payments made by Hambrouck to the appellant were made without valuable consideration, and for an immoral consideration. Even if they could appropriately be described as gifts, a gift without valuable consideration would not give the appellant any title as against the plaintiff Bank.

The second contention also cannot be supported in law. It rests upon a misconception as to the meaning which has been attached to the expression 'currency' in some of the decisions which have been referred to ... Where the word 'currency' is used merely as the equivalent of coin of the realm, then for present purposes the difference between currency and a chattel personal is one of fact and not of law. This was the view of Lord Ellenborough in *Taylor* v *Plumer* ... Dealing with this point in *Sinclair* v *Brougham* [1914] AC 398, 420, Lord Haldane says: 'The common law, which we are now considering, did not take cognisance of such duties. It looked simply to the question whether the property had passed, and if it had not, for instance, where no relationship of debtor and creditor had intervened, the money could be followed, notwithstanding its normal character as currency, provided it could be earmarked or traced into assets acquired with it.' ...

The last contention for the appellant cannot in my opinion be supported ...

The facts in the present case in my opinion remove any difficulty in the way of the plaintiff Bank recovering, without having recourse to the equity rule. The money which the Bank seeks to recover is capable of being traced, as the appellant never paid any money into the Bank except money which was part of the proceeds of Hambrouck's frauds, and the appellant Bank have paid all the money standing to the appellant's credit into Court, where it now is. Even if it had been necessary to apply the rule in *Hallett's Case* [see Section 5: Tracing in equity, C: Mixing by trustee or fiduciary and the rest of this extract] to enable the plaintiff Bank to establish their right to the money they claim, I see no difficulty in applying the rule to the facts as found by the learned judge in the Court below.

ATKIN LJ: ... I notice that in *Sinclair* v *Brougham* [1914] AC 398, 419 Lord Haldane LC in dealing with [*Taylor* v *Plumer*] says: 'Lord Ellenborough laid down, as a limit to this proposition, that if the money had become incapable of being traced, as, for instance, when it had been paid into the broker's general account with his banker, the principal had no remedy excepting to prove as a creditor for money had and received,' and proceeds to say 'you can, even at law, follow, but only so long as the relation of debtor and creditor has not superseded the right *in rem*.' The words above 'as for instance' *et seq.* do not represent and doubtless do not purport to represent Lord Ellenborough's actual words; and I venture to doubt whether the common law ever so restricted the right as to hold that the money became incapable of being traced, merely because paid into the broker's general account with his banker. The question always was, Had the means of ascertainment failed? But if in 1815 the common law halted outside the bankers' door, by 1879 equity had had the courage to lift the latch, walk in and examine the books: *Re Hallett's Estate* (1880) 13 ChD 696. I see no reason why the means of ascertainment so provided should not now be available both for common law and equity proceedings. If, following the principles laid down in *Re Hallett's Estate*, it can be ascertained either that the money in the bank, or the commodity which it has bought, is 'the product of, or substitute for, the original thing,' then it still follows 'the nature of the thing itself.' On these principles it would follow that as the money paid into the bank can be identified as the product of the original money, the plaintiffs have the common law right to claim it, and can sue for money had and received. In the present case less difficulty than usual is experienced in tracing the descent of the money, for substantially no other money has ever been mixed with the proceeds of the fraud ...

NOTES

1. Atkin LJ's views were not shared by the other two judges, and it is difficult precisely to ascertain the *ratio* of *Banque Belge*. Scrutton LJ apparently took the view that the money could not be traced at common law, since it changed its identity when paid into the account at Farrow's Bank, but could be traced in equity (as is undoubtedly the case: see Section 5). Bankes LJ felt that tracing at common law was permissible, but only because the proceeds of Hambrouck's fraud had never been mixed with any other money, either at Farrow's or Mlle Spanoghe's bank. In the passage quoted above, Atkin LJ appeared to take the view that the question of the property's

identification was the same in common law and equity, in which case common law tracing would be possible even into mixed funds (on the same basis as in equitable tracing).

The orthodox view is probably that of Bankes LJ, that if the property has been converted into money, and this money mixed with other funds belonging to the defendant, it is no longer possible at common law to identify the subject matter of the claimant's claim, and he is thereafter limited to his personal remedy in damages. In any case, only Bankes LJ's view is supported by later authorities. Since mixing will often occur in the case where funds are misappropriated, the usefulness of tracing at common law is rather limited in breach of trust situations.

2. It is also necessary to be able to follow the property at every stage from its original form into its current form. Tracing will not be possible if there is a break in the chain at any stage.

3. The claim by the bank was for a declaration that the £315 in Mlle Spanoghe's account was their property, and it is clear from Bankes LJ's judgment, above, that no property ever passed to Mlle Spanoghe. This must therefore be a proprietary tracing claim, not an action for money had and received (since in the latter case, property passes to the recipient).

4. The actual decision in *Sinclair* v *Brougham*, that a fiduciary relationship arose giving rise to a proprietary equitable tracing claim, was overruled in *Westdeutsche Landesbank Girozentrale* v *Islington London Borough Council* [1996] AC 669, but this probably does not affect any views expressed therein on tracing at common law.

Trustee of the Property of F. C. Jones and Sons (a firm) v Jones

[1996] 3 WLR 703, Court of Appeal

Facts: A supplier of F. C. Jones and Sons obtained judgment against the firm. The judgment was not satisfied and a bankruptcy notice was issued. The partners, Messrs F. C. Jones, F. W. J. Jones, and A. C. Jones, failed to comply with the notice and thereby committed an act of bankruptcy. Between the act of bankruptcy and the adjudication, Mrs Anne Jones, the wife of Mr F. W. J. Jones, opened an account with a firm of commodity brokers in order to deal on the London Potato Futures Market, and paid into it three cheques totalling £11,700, drawn on the firm's partners' account.

Mrs Jones's dealings in potato futures proved to be highly profitable. She received two cheques totalling £50,760 from the commodity brokers and paid them into a call deposit account (at Raphaels), in which there was remaining a balance of £49,860. This money was claimed by the trustee in bankruptcy, on the grounds that the legal title was vested in him, and had been since the time of the act of bankruptcy.

Held: The trustee in bankruptcy was entitled to the entirety of the £49,860 remaining in the call deposit account, and hence the profit element. In Millett LJ's view, this was a proprietary claim, none of the money having been mixed with other money, and no property having passed to Mrs Jones. He thought that in contrast, a money had and received action ought, in principle, to be limited to the amount of the money received, but that the trustee had made a proprietary rather than a personal claim. Nourse LJ agreed with Millett LJ, but also (apparently) took the view that the same result could be reached on the basis of a money had and received claim.

It was necessary to trace the money at common law, because Mrs Jones did not receive the money in a fiduciary capacity, and did not become a constructive trustee (see Section 5 Tracing in equity, E: Requirement for fiduciary relationship).

MILLETT LJ: What is the result? If the cheques had passed the legal title to Mrs Jones but not the beneficial ownership, she would have received the money as constructive trustee and be liable to a proprietary restitutionary claim in equity (sometimes though inaccurately described as a tracing claim). Mrs Jones would have been obliged, not merely to account for the £11,700 which she had received, but to hand over the £11,700 *in specie* to the trustee. Her position would have been no different from that of an express trustee who held the money in trust for the trustee; or from that of Mr Reid in *A-G for Hong Kong* v *Reid* [1994] 1 AC 324 [see Chapter 8], whose liability to account for the profits which he made from investing a bribe was based on his obligation to pay it over to his principal as soon as he received it: see p. 331 D–E.

The existence of any such obligation has been disputed by commentators, but no one disputes that, if the obligation exists, it carries with it the duty to pay over or account for any profits made by the use of the money.

But Mrs Jones was not a constructive trustee. She had no legal title to the money. She had no title to it at all. She was merely in possession, that is to say, in a position to deal with it even though it did not belong to her. Counsel for Mrs Jones says that it follows that she cannot be made liable to any kind of proprietary claim. He relies strongly for this purpose on *Ex parte Hooson, ex parte Chapman* (1872) Ch App 231, followed in *Re Bishop, ex parte Claxton* (1891) Morr Bankruptcy Reports 221, which were both cases concerned with fraudulent preference …

But those were cases in which the payment was valid when made and passed a good though defeasible title to the recipient. He obtained legal title to the money and, since he was not a trustee, equitable title as well. He was free to deal with the money on his own account as he pleased. If he made a profit from the use of his own money, he was entitled to keep it. If he became bankrupt, the money would form part of his estate, and the debtor's trustee would have to prove in his bankruptcy for the amount claimed. The present case is entirely different. Mrs Jones had no title at all, at law or in equity. If she became bankrupt, the money would not vest in her trustee. But this would not be because it was trust property. It would be because it was not her property at all. If she made a profit, how could she have any claim to the profit made by the use of someone else's money?

In my judgment she could not. If she were to retain the profit made by the use of the trustee's money, then in the language of the modern law of restitution she would be unjustly enriched at the expense of the trustee. If she were a constructive trustee of the money, a Court of Equity as a court of conscience would say that it was unconscionable for her to lay claim to the profit made by the use of her beneficiary's money. It would, however, be a mistake to suppose that, because the common law courts were not courts of conscience, they disregarded such considerations. Lord Mansfield CJ, who did much to develop the early law of restitution, founded it firmly on the basis of good conscience and unjust enrichment.

It would in my judgment be absurd if a person with no title at all were in a stronger position to resist a proprietary claim by the true owner than one with a bare legal title. In the present case equity has no role to play. The trustee must bring his claim at common law. It follows that, if he has to trace his money, he must rely on the common law tracing rules; and that he has no proprietary remedy. But it does not follow that he has no proprietary claim. His claim is exclusively proprietary. He claims the money because it belongs to him at law, or represents profits made by the use of money which belonged to him at law.

The trustee submits that he has no need to trace, since the facts are clear and undisputed. Mrs Jones did not mix the money with her own. The trustee's money remained identifiable as such throughout. But of course he does have to trace it in order to establish that the money which he claims represents his money. Counsel for Mrs Jones acknowledges that the trustee can successfully trace his money into her account at Raphaels, for his concession in respect of the £11,700 acknowledges this. I do not understand how his concession that the trustee is entitled to £11,700 of the money in Court is reconcilable with his submission that the only cause of action available to the trustee is an action for money he had and received. I say this for two reasons. In the first place, the trustee has never brought such an action, and any such action would now be long out of time. In the second place, in an action for money had and received it would be irrelevant what Mrs Jones had done with the money after she received it. Her liability would be based on her receipt of the money, and she would be personally liable to a money judgment for £11,700. But while the trustee would be entitled to a money judgment for that sum, he would not be entitled to any particular sum of £11,700 *in specie*.

But in my judgment the concession that the trustee can trace the money at common law is rightly made. There are no factual difficulties of the kind which proved fatal to the common law claim in *Agip (Africa) Ltd* v *Jackson* [1991] Ch 547 [see the case study in this subsection]. It is not necessary to trace the passage of the money through the clearing system or the London Potato Futures Market. The money which Mrs Jones paid into her account with the commodity brokers represented the proceeds of cheques which she received from her husband. Those cheques represented money in the bankrupts' joint account at the Midland Bank which belonged to the trustee.

In *Lipkin Gorman (a firm)* v *Karpnale Ltd* [1991] 2 AC 548 at p. 573, Lord Goff held that the plaintiffs could trace or follow their 'property into its product' for this 'involves a decision by the owner of the original property to assert title to the produce in place of his original property'. In that case the original property was the plaintiffs' chose in action, a debt owed by the bank to the plaintiffs. Lord Goff held that the plaintiffs could:

> ... trace their property at common law in that chose in action, or in any part of it, into its product, i.e. cash drawn by Cass from their client account at the bank.

Accordingly, the trustee can follow the money in the joint account at Midland Bank, which had been vested by statute in him, into the proceeds of the three cheques which Mrs Jones received from her husband. The trustee does not need to follow the money from one recipient to another or follow it through the clearing system; he can follow the cheques as they pass from hand to hand. It is sufficient for him to be able to trace the money into the cheques and the cheques into their proceeds.

In *Agip (Africa) Ltd* v *Jackson* [1990] Ch 265 at p. 285, I said that the ability of the common law to trace an asset into a changed form in the same hands was established in *Taylor* v *Plumer* (1815) M & S 562. Lord Ellenborough CJ in that case had said:

> The product of or substitute for the original thing still follows the nature of the thing itself as long as it can be ascertained to be such and the right only ceases when the means of ascertainment fails, which is the case when the subject is turned into money and confined within the general mass of the same description.

In this it appears that I fell into a common error, for it has since been convincingly demonstrated that although *Taylor* v *Plumer* was decided by a common law court, the court was in fact applying the rules of equity: see Lionel Smith: 'Tracing in *Taylor* v *Plumer*: Equity in the King's Bench' [1995] LMCLQ 240.

But this is no reason for concluding that the common law does not recognise claims to substitute assets. Such claims were upheld by this Court in *Banque Belge* v *Hambrouck* [1921] 1 KB 321 [also discussed in this section] and by the House of Lords in *Lipkin Gorman* v *Karpnale Ltd* [1991] 2 AC 548 [see Section 2:Common law remedies, C: Money had and received]. It has been suggested by commentators that these cases are undermined by their misunderstanding of *Taylor* v *Plumer*, but that is not how the English doctrine of *stare decisis* operates. It would be more consistent with that doctrine to say that in recognising claims to substituted assets, equity must be taken to have followed the law, even though the law was not declared until later. Lord Ellenborough CJ gave no indication that, in following assets into their exchange products, equity had adopted a rule which was peculiar to itself or which went further than the common law.

There is no merit in having distinct and differing tracing rules at law and in equity, given that tracing is neither a right nor a remedy but merely the process by which the plaintiff establishes what has happened to his property and makes good his claim that the assets which he claims can properly be regarded as representing his property. The fact that there are different tracing rules at law and in equity is unfortunate though probably inevitable, but unnecessary differences should not be created where they are not required by the differing nature of legal and equitable doctrines and remedies. There is, in my view, even less merit in the present rule which precludes the invocation of the equitable tracing rules to support a common law claim; until that rule is swept away unnecessary obstacles to the development of a rational and coherent law of restitution will remain.

Given that the trustee can trace his money at Midland Bank into the money in Mrs Jones' account with the commodity brokers, can he successfully assert a claim to that part of the money which represents the profit made by the use of his money? I have no doubt that, in the particular circumstances of this case, he can. There is no need to trace through the dealings on the London Potato Futures Market. If Mrs Jones, as the nominal account holder, had any entitlement to demand payment from the brokers, this was because of the terms of the contract which she made with them. Under the terms of that contract it is reasonable to infer that the brokers were authorised to deal in potato futures on her account, to debit her account with losses and to credit it with profits, and to pay her only the balance standing to her account. It is, in my opinion, impossible to separate the chose in action constituted by the deposit of the trustee's money on those terms from the terms upon which it was deposited. The chose in action, which was vested in Mrs Jones' name but which in reality belonged to the trustee, was not a right to payment from the brokers of the original amount deposited but a right to claim the balance, whether greater or less than the amount deposited; and it is to that chose in action that the trustee now lays claim.

Given, then, that the trustee has established his legal claim to the £11,700 and the profits earned by the use of his money, and has located the money, first, in Mrs Jones' account with the commodity brokers and, later, in Mrs Jones' account at Raphaels, I am satisfied that the common law has adequate remedies to enable him to recover his property ...

In my judgment the trustee was entitled at law to the money in the joint account of the bankrupts at Midland Bank, which had vested in him by statute. He was similarly entitled to the balance of the money in Mrs Jones' account with the commodity brokers, and the fact that it included profits made by the use of that money is immaterial. He was similarly entitled to the money in Mrs Jones' account at Raphaels and able to give them a good receipt for the money. Mrs Jones never had any interest, legal or equitable, in any of those moneys. The trustee is plainly entitled to the money in court and the judge was right to order that it be paid out to him.

NOURSE LJ: I also agree that the appeal must be dismissed.

I recognise that our decision goes further than that of the House of Lords in *Lipkin Gorman (a firm)* v *Karpnale Ltd* [1991] 2 AC 548, in that it holds that the action for money had and received entitles the legal owner to trace his property into its product, not only in the sense of property for which it is exchanged, but also in the sense of property representing the original and the profit made by the defendant's use of it.

Millett LJ has explained how that extension is justified on the particular facts of this case. But there is, I think, a broader justification to be found in the seminal judgment of Lord Mansfield in *Clarke* v *Shee and Johnson* (1774) 1 Cowp 197 at p. 199, where he said of the action for money had and received:

> This is a liberal action in the nature of a bill in equity; and if, under the circumstances of the case, it appears that the defendant cannot in conscience retain what is the subject matter of it, the plaintiff may well support this action.

In my view Mrs Jones cannot in conscience retain the profit any more than the original £11,700. She had no title to the original. She could not, by making a profit through the use of money to which she had no title, acquire some better title to the profit.

[Beldam LJ's reasoning was essentially similar to that of Millett LJ.]

NOTE: Millett LJ's reasoning in *F. C. Jones* can apply only where the money is not mixed. If Anne Jones had mixed the money with her own before investing it, legal title would have passed to her, in which case the only action at common law would have been for money had and received (for £11,700). Only if she had the requisite knowledge for a knowing receipt claim (see Chapter 15, Section 3) would the claimants then have been able to claim the profit element, in equity rather than at common law. It might be thought that since Mrs Jones was a volunteer, the claimants would also have been able to trace in equity, whatever the state of her knowledge, on the principles in *Re Diplock's Estate*, but this is not correct because the claimants originally had only legal but not equitable title to the money: no fiduciary relationship could therefore be established.

Agip (Africa) Ltd v *Jackson*
[1991] Ch 547, Court of Appeal

Facts: The case involved the last of a series of frauds, totalling some US$10 million, committed on Agip (Africa), an oil exploration company. In each case, companies were set up as 'cut-offs' to launder the money and hide its destination. In most cases, the ultimate destination was Euro-Arabian Jewellery Ltd and its subsidiary, Kinz (a French jewellery business), and thereafter presumably the fraudsters. For the last of the frauds, of around US$518,000, Euro-Arabian was not used, the money being paid instead through two clients' accounts of Jackson & Co., a firm of accountants.

The claimant company's chief accountant (Mr Zdiri) fraudulently altered payment orders which had been signed by an authorised signatory of the claimant, altering the name of the payee to that of a company (Baker Oil), of which the defendants were directors and shareholders. The forged payment order (for over US$ half a million) was taken to the Banque du Sud in Tunis, which debited the claimant's account and sent telexed instructions to a London bank (Lloyds) to credit the account which Baker Oil had there. The Banque du Sud also instructed its correspondent bank (Citibank) in New York to reimburse Lloyds with an equivalent sum. However, Lloyds credited Baker Oil before themselves being reimbursed by Citibank.

Baker Oil subsequently disposed of the money, but about US$45,000 remained identifiable, and was paid into court. Baker Oil did no trading, and was set up entirely for the purpose of laundering the proceeds of this fraud.

After the money left the Baker Oil account, it was paid into an account of Jackson & Co. in the same bank, thence to another of their accounts (a clients' account) in the Isle of Man, which was newly opened for the purpose, thence to Kinz (a French jewellery business) and elsewhere. From Kinz, it was presumably dissipated to the fraudsters and their associates.

Movement of the money, after receipt by Baker Oil

The Baker Oil money was paid out into an account (which was being used as a clients' account) Jackson & Co. had with the same bank, thence to Jackson & Co.'s clients' account at the Isle of Man Bank Ltd in the Isle of Man, thence to Kinz and others. The money had and received claim was against Jackson & Co.

It is probable that the money was originally moved to another account at the same bank as the Baker Oil account because it would then be difficult to follow without examining the records of Lloyds Bank.

The defendants

Jackson (the first defendant) and Bowers (the second defendant) were partners in Jackson & Co., a firm of accountants practising in the Isle of Man. Griffin (the third defendant) was an employee of the firm.

Bowers did not participate in the furtherance of the fraud at all; although he was a partner in Jackson & Co., he played no part in the movement of the money and gave no instructions about it. (He had, however, acted as liquidator for some of the earlier laundering companies.)

Jackson set up the company structures. None of the companies used to launder the money from any of the frauds had any assets or carried on any business activity. None of them was known to, or had any dealings or contact with, the claimants.

Jackson was a director of Euro-Arabian Jewellery Ltd, whose dollar account at Lloyds Bank had been used in previous frauds against the claimants—not the last one, however (this time they used Jackson & Co.'s account instead). There was no evidence that Euro-Arabian carried on any genuine business activity, or that it was known to or had any dealings or contact with the claimants.

Jackson was a director of Kinz, the ultimate recipient of most of the money and a wholly-owned subsidiary of Euro-Arabian.

Jackson and Griffin were the only directors and shareholders of Baker Oil, and signatories of Baker Oil at Lloyds Bank. Jackson and Griffin were signatories of Jackson & Co.'s account at Lloyds Bank. Jackson and Griffin therefore controlled the movement of the money from the time it reached Baker Oil to the time it was paid out of the account of Jackson & Co. in the Isle of Man Bank.

Liability of the defendants

The money could not be traced at common law into Baker Oil's hands, and hence could not be traced from there into the hands of any of the defendants. Therefore all common law claims, based on money had and received, failed.

The claimants succeeded, however, in an equitable tracing claim, but only in respect of the $45,000 which was still identifiable and which had been paid into court.

On the knowing receipt claim, based on receipt by Jackson & Co., Griffin (the employee) did not receive the money at all, and Jackson and Bowers did not receive or apply it for their own use and benefit. In Millett J's judgment (upheld in the Court of Appeal), none of them could be made liable to account as a constructive trustee on the basis of knowing receipt.

Jackson and Griffin were liable for knowing assistance. Bowers was innocent of the fraud, but was liable for the acts of Jackson, who was his partner, and of Griffin, who was employed by the partnership.

Held: (on the tracing claims): The money could not be traced at common law. The claimants succeeded, however, in an equitable tracing claim, and in a claim for knowing assistance (now referred to as 'dishonest assistance', see Chapter 15, Section 4).

MILLETT J (whose decision was upheld by the Court of Appeal): The common law has always been able to follow a physical asset from one recipient to another. Its ability to follow an asset in the same hands into a changed form was established in *Taylor* v *Plumer*. In following the plaintiff's money into an asset purchased exclusively with it, no distinction is drawn between a chose in action such as the debt of a bank to its customer and any other asset: *Re Diplock's Estate* [1948] 2 All ER 318 at 346, [1948] Ch 465 at 519. But it can only follow a physical asset, such as a cheque or its proceeds, from one person to another. It can follow money but not a chose in action. Money can be followed at common law into and out of a bank account and into the hands of a subsequent transferee, provided that it does not cease to be identifiable by being mixed with other money in the bank account derived from some other source: *Banque Belge pour L'Etranger* v *Hambrouck* [1921] 1 KB 321. Applying these principles, the plaintiffs claim to follow their money through Baker Oil's account, where it was not mixed with any other money, and into Jackson & Co.'s account at Lloyds Bank.

The defendants deny this. They contend that tracing is not possible at common law because the money was mixed, first when it was handled in New York and secondly in Jackson & Co.'s own account at Lloyds Bank.

The latter objection is easily disposed of. The cause of action for money had and received is complete when the plaintiff's money is received by the defendant. It does not depend on the continued retention of the money by the defendant. Save in strictly limited circumstances it is no defence that he has parted with it. A fortiori it can be no defence for him to show that he has so mixed it with his own money that he cannot tell whether he still has it or not. Mixing by the defendant himself must, therefore, be distinguished from mixing by a prior recipient. The former is irrelevant, but the latter will destroy the claim for it will prevent proof that the money received by the defendant was the money paid by the plaintiff.

In my judgment, however, the former objection is insuperable. The money cannot be followed by treating it as the proceeds of a cheque presented by the collecting bank in exchange for payment by the paying bank. The money was transmitted by telegraphic transfer. There was no cheque or any equivalent. The payment order was not a cheque or its equivalent. It remained throughout in the possession of the Banque du Sud. No copy was sent to Lloyds Bank or Baker Oil or presented to the Banque du Sud in exchange for the money. It was normally the plaintiffs' practice to forward a copy of the payment order to the supplier when paying an invoice but this was for information only. It did not authorise or enable the supplier to obtain payment. There is no evidence that this practice was followed in the case of forged payment orders and it is exceedingly unlikely that it was.

Nothing passed between Tunisia and London but a stream of electrons. It is not possible to treat the money received by Lloyds Bank in London or its correspondent bank in New York as representing the proceeds of the payment order or of any other physical asset previously in its hands and delivered by it in exchange for the money. The Banque du Sud merely telexed a request to Lloyds Bank to make a payment to Baker Oil against its own undertaking to reimburse Lloyds Bank in New York. Lloyds Bank complied with the request by paying Baker Oil with its own money. It thereby took a delivery risk. In due course it was no doubt reimbursed, but it is not possible to identify the source of the money with which it was reimbursed without attempting to follow the money through the New York clearing system. Unless Lloyds Bank's correspondent bank in New York was also Citibank, this involves tracing the money through the accounts of Citibank and Lloyds Bank's correspondent bank with the Federal Reserve Bank, where it must have been mixed with other money. The money with which Lloyds Bank was reimbursed cannot therefore, without recourse to equity, be identified as being that of the Banque du Sud. There is no evidence that Lloyds Bank's correspondent bank in New York was Citibank, and accordingly the plaintiffs' attempt to trace the money at common law must fail.

FOX LJ: Now in the present case the course of events was as follows. (1) The original payment order was in December signed by an authorised signatory. (2) The name of the payee was then altered to Baker Oil. (3) The altered order was then taken to BdS [Banque du Sud], who complied with it by debiting the account of Agip with $US 518,822.92 and then instructing Lloyds Bank to pay Baker Oil. BdS also instructed Citibank in New York to debit its account with Citibank and credit Lloyds with the amount of the order. (4) Lloyds credited the money to Baker Oil's account on the morning of 7 January. (5) On 8 January Lloyds in pursuance of instructions from Baker Oil transferred the $US 518,822.92 which was the only sum standing to the credit of Baker Oil's account to an account in the name of Jackson & Co. (6) Immediately before the transfer from Baker Oil, Jackson & Co.'s account was $US 7,911.80 in credit. In consequence of the transfer it became $US 526,734.72 in credit.

The inquiry which has to be made is whether the money paid to Jackson & Co.'s account 'was the product of, or substitute for, the original thing'. In answering that question I do not think that it matters that the order was not a cheque. It was a direction by the account holder to the bank.

When Atkin LJ refers in *Banque Belge Pour l'Etranger* v *Hambrouck* [1921] 1 KB 321 to the 'original money' he is, I assume, referring to the money credited by Banque Belge (the plaintiff) to Hambrouck's account. Money from that account was the only money in Mlle Spanoghe's deposit account. It was not, therefore, difficult to say that the money in issue (i.e. the residue of Mlle Spanoghe's account) could be identified as the product of the original money. There were no complexities of tracing at all. Everything in Mlle Spanoghe's account came from Hambrouck's account and everything in Hambrouck's account came from the credit in respect of the fraudulent cheque.

The position in the present case is much more difficult. BdS can be regarded as having paid with Agip's money but Lloyds (acting as directed by BdS) paid Baker Oil with its own money. It had no other (and accordingly took a delivery risk). It was, in the end, put in funds, but it is difficult to see how the origin of those funds can be identified without tracing the money through the New York clearing system.

The money in the present case did get mixed on two occasions. The first was in the New York clearing system and the second was in Jackson & Co.'s own account. The judge held that the latter was of no consequence. I agree. The common law remedy attached to the recipient and its subsequent transposition does not alter his liability. The problem arises at an earlier stage. What did Jackson & Co. receive which was the product of Agip's asset?

Baker Oil was controlled for present purposes by Jackson & Co. but Baker Oil was paid by Lloyds, which had not been put in funds from New York. It was subsequently recouped. But it is not possible to show the source from which it was recouped without tracing the money through the New York clearing system. The judge said ([1992] 4 All ER 385 at 399, [1990] Ch 265 at 286):

> Unless Lloyds Bank's correspondent bank in New York was also Citibank, this involves tracing the money through the accounts of Citibank and Lloyd's Bank's correspondent bank with the Federal Reserve Bank, where it must have been mixed with other money. The money with which Lloyds Bank was reimbursed cannot therefore, without recourse to equity, be identified as being that of the Banque du Sud.

I respectfully agree with that view. Accordingly, it seems to me that the common law remedy is not available.

I should add this. Atkin LJ's approach in the *Banque Belge* case amounts virtually to saying that there is now no difference between the common law and equitable remedies. Indeed, the common law remedy might be wider because of the absence of any requirement of a fiduciary relationship. There may be a good deal to be said for that view but it goes well beyond any other case and well beyond the views of Bankes and Scrutton LJJ. And in the 70 years since the *Banque Belge* decision it has not been applied. Whether, short of the House of Lords, it is now open to the courts to adopt it I need not consider. I would in any event feel difficulty in doing so in the present case, where, as I indicate later, it seems to me that the established equitable rules provide an adequate remedy.

NOTES

1. Millett J makes clear that the claim for money had and received does not depend on the continued retention of the money by the defendant.
2. Both Millett J and Fox LJ held that the money could not be traced through the New York clearing bank system, since there it clearly became mixed with other money.
3. Since Lloyds must surely have had a contractual claim against the Banque du Sud at the latest when they had received and acted upon the telexed payment order, and Baker Oil a cause of action against Lloyds, the alternative would have been to trace the causes of action from

Agip to Baker Oil, but at first instance, Millett J distinguished between a payment order and a cheque, commenting that the payment order never moved from Tunisia, and that nothing passed between Tunisia and London but a stream of electrons. The common law can only follow a physical asset, such as a cheque.

4. Fox LJ did not adopt Millett J's distinction, relying instead upon the fact that Lloyds had credited the money to Baker Oil before it was reimbursed with the claimants' money. They thereby took a delivery risk, Fox LJ commenting that whereas the Banque du Sud could be regarded as having paid with the claimants' money, Lloyds must be regarded as having paid Baker Oil with its own (Lloyds') money, since at the time of payment it had no other money with which to pay. The money in Baker Oil's account could not therefore be identified as the claimants' money. This, however, would seem to be merely an additional reason why the *money* could not be traced through the New York banks. It does not explain why Agip could not follow the causes of action, and it is necessary to adopt Millett J's distinction to do that.

5. Millett J's reasoning was applied by Tuckey J in *Bank Tejarat* v *Hong Kong and Shanghai Banking Corporation (Ci) Ltd and Hong Kong and Shanghai Bank Trustee (Jersey) Ltd* [1995] 1 Lloyd's Rep 239 (above). As in *Agip (Africa)*, the money was paid by telegraphic transfer, through clearing banks, and for the same reason, a common law tracing claim failed. Bank Tejarat also failed to argue that since (as is common in documentary credit transactions) they had paid against presentation of a draft (i.e. a bill of exchange), that operated similarly to a cheque. The draft was not being used as a cheque would be, as the method of making the payment. Its presentation to the claimant bank was merely the trigger for payment, so the analogy with the cheque failed. Tuckey J observed that:

> The simple answer to this submission is that the drafts were not the means by which Tejarat paid their money to CAK. The payment out of Tejarat's account ... was probably made by telex instructions ... (a stream of electrons). It was certainly not made by the drafts, so there is nothing from which Tejarat can trace.

6. Since the common law does not recognise equitable interests in property, a beneficiary under a trust cannot follow trust property in the hands of a trustee, although he can in equity compel the trustee to trace the property at common law, where it has fallen into the hands of a third party.

SECTION 4: **EQUITABLE PROPRIETARY REMEDIES**

Where a trustee misappropriates trust property and uses it to acquire other property the beneficiary may elect to claim ownership of that portion of the new asset acquired with his trust property or to bring a personal claim against the trustee for breach of trust and to impose an equitable lien or charge on the new assets as a way of securing the personal claim. Both claims (proportionate beneficial share or equitable lien) are proprietary, which means they are unaffected by the trustee's insolvency. The fact that the remedies are proprietary does mean, however, that they will only be effective against a defendant (the trustee or his successor) who still has the target assets in his possession. To prevent disposal of the assets prior to trial the claimant should seek an *ex parte* freezing injunction.

Foskett v *McKeown*

[2001] 1 AC 102, House of Lords

Facts: Following the entry into contracts by a large number of purchasers for the purchase of plots of land on a site to be developed in the Algarve, M held the purchasers' money in respect of the purchase price on trust for them until the land was developed and then transferred. In the event, the land was never developed and M, in breach of trust, used the purchasers' money to pay several annual premiums of £10,220 payable under a life assurance policy. M committed suicide and the sum of £1,000,589.04 was paid to certain of his relatives under the policy. The claimant, one of the prospective purchasers, issued proceedings against the defendants, purporting to sue on his own behalf and on behalf of all the other prospective purchasers, claiming the policy money paid to the defendants, contending that it was the purchasers' money which had kept the policy on foot and that they could trace their money into the proceeds of the policy.

Held: The parties were entitled to the proceeds of the policy in the proportions in which those proceeds represented their respective contributions.

LORD MILLETT: My Lords, this is a textbook example of tracing through mixed substitutions. At the beginning of the story the plaintiffs were beneficially entitled under an express trust to a sum standing in the name of Mr Murphy in a bank account. From there the money moved into and out of various bank accounts where in breach of trust it was inextricably mixed by Mr Murphy with his own money. After each transaction was completed the plaintiffs' money formed an indistinguishable part of the balance standing to Mr Murphy's credit in his bank account. The amount of that balance represented a debt due from the bank to Mr Murphy, that is to say a chose in action. At the penultimate stage the plaintiff's money was represented by an indistinguishable part of a different chose in action, viz the debt prospectively and contingently due from an insurance company to its policyholders, being the trustees of a settlement made by Mr Murphy for the benefit of his children. At the present and final stage it forms an indistinguishable part of the balance standing to the credit of the respondent trustees in their bank account.

Tracing and following

The process of ascertaining what happened to the plaintiff's money involves both tracing and following. These are both exercises in locating assets which are or may be taken to represent an asset belonging to the plaintiffs and to which they assert ownership. The processes of following and tracing are, however, distinct. Following is the process of following the same asset as it moves from hand to hand. Tracing is the process of identifying a new asset as the substitute for the old. Where one asset is exchanged for another, a claimant can elect whether to follow the original asset into the hands of the new owner or to trace its value into the new asset in the hands of the same owner. In practice his choice is often dictated by the circumstances. In the present case the plaintiffs do not seek to follow the money any further once it reached the bank or insurance company, since its identity was lost in the hands of the recipient (which in any case obtained an unassailable title as a bona fide purchaser for value without notice of the plaintiff's beneficial interest). Instead the plaintiffs have chosen at each stage to trace the money into its proceeds, viz the debt presently due from the bank to the account holder or the debt prospectively and contingently due from the insurance company to the policy holders.

Having completed this exercise, the plaintiffs claim a continuing beneficial interest in the insurance money. Since this represents the product of Mr Murphy's own money as well as theirs, which Mr Murphy mingled indistinguishably in a single chose in action, they claim a beneficial interest in a proportionate part of the money only. The transmission of a claimant's property rights from one asset to its traceable proceeds is part of our law of property, not of the law of unjust enrichment. There is no 'unjust factor' to justify restitution (unless 'want of title' be one, which makes the point). The claimant succeeds if at all by virtue of his own title, not to reverse unjust enrichment. Property rights are determined by fixed rules and settled principles. They are not discretionary. They do not depend upon ideas of what is 'fair, just and reasonable'. Such concepts, which in reality mask decisions of legal policy, have no place in the law of property.

A beneficiary of a trust is entitled to a continuing beneficial interest not merely in the trust property but in its traceable proceeds also, and his interest binds every one who takes the property or its traceable proceeds except a bona fide purchaser for value without notice. In the present case the plaintiffs' beneficial interest plainly bound Mr Murphy, a trustee who wrongfully mixed the trust money with his own and whose every dealing with the money (including the payment of the premiums) was in breach of trust. It similarly binds his successors, the trustees of the children's settlement, who claim no beneficial interest of their own, and Mr Murphy's children, who are volunteers. They gave no value for what they received and derive their interest from Mr. Murphy by way of gift.

Tracing

We speak of money at the bank, and of money passing into and out of a bank account. But of course the account holder has no money at the bank. Money paid into a bank account belongs legally and beneficially to the bank and not to the account holder. The bank gives value for it, and it is accordingly not usually possible to make the money itself the subject of an adverse claim. Instead a claimant normally sues the account holder rather than the bank and lays claim to the proceeds of the money in his hands. These consist of the debt or part of the debt due to him from the bank. We speak of tracing money into and out of the account, but there is no money in the account. There is merely a single debt of an amount equal to the final balance standing to the credit of the account holder. No money passes from paying bank to receiving bank or through the clearing system (where the money flows may be in the opposite direction). There is simply a series of debits and credits which are causally and transactionally linked. We also speak of tracing one asset into another, but this too is inaccurate. The original asset still exists in the hands of the new owner, or it may have become untraceable. The claimant claims the new asset because it was acquired in whole or in part with the original asset. What he traces, therefore, is not the physical asset itself but the value inherent in it.

Tracing is thus neither a claim nor a remedy. It is merely the process by which a claimant demonstrates what has happened to his property, identifies its proceeds and the persons who have handled or received them, and justifies his claim that the proceeds can properly be regarded as representing his property. Tracing is also distinct from claiming. It identifies the traceable proceeds of the claimant's property. It enables the claimant to substitute the traceable proceeds for the original asset as the subject matter of his claim. But it does not affect or establish his claim. That will depend on a number of factors including the nature of his interest in the original asset. He will normally be able to maintain the same claim to the substituted asset as he could have maintained to the original asset. If he held only a security interest in the original asset, he cannot claim more than a security interest in its proceeds. But his claim may also be exposed to potential defences as a result of intervening transactions. Even if the plaintiffs could demonstrate what the bank had done with their money, for example, and could thus identify its traceable proceeds in the hands of the bank, any claim by them to assert ownership of those proceeds would be defeated by the bona fide purchaser defence. The successful completion of a tracing exercise may be preliminary to a personal claim (as in *El Ajou* v *Dollar Land Holdings* [1993] 3 All ER 717) or a proprietary one, to the enforcement of a legal right (as in *Trustees of the Property of F.C. Jones & Sons* v *Jones* [1997] Ch. 159) or an equitable one.

Given its nature, there is nothing inherently legal or equitable about the tracing exercise. There is thus no sense in maintaining different rules for tracing at law and in equity. One set of tracing rules is enough. The existence of two has never formed part of the law in the United States: see Scott *The Law of Trusts* 4th ed. (1989), pp. 605–609. There is certainly no logical justification for allowing any distinction between them to produce capricious results in cases of mixed substitutions by insisting on the existence of a fiduciary relationship as a precondition for applying equity's tracing rules. The existence of such a relationship may be relevant to the nature of the claim which the plaintiff can maintain, whether personal or proprietary, but that is a different matter. I agree with the passages which my noble and learned friend Lord Steyn has cited from Professor Birks' essay 'The Necessity of a Unitary Law of Tracing', and with Dr Lionel Smith's exposition in his comprehensive monograph. 'The Law of Tracing' (1997) see particularly, pp. 120–30, 277–79 and 342–47.

This is not, however, the occasion to explore these matters further, for the present is a straightforward case of a trustee who wrongfully misappropriated trust money, mixed it with his own, and used it to pay for an asset for the benefit of his children. Even on the traditional approach, the equitable tracing rules are available to the plaintiffs. There are only two complicating factors. The first is that the wrong-doer used their money to pay premiums on an equity linked policy of life assurance on his own life. The nature of the policy should make no difference in principle, though it may complicate the accounting. The second is that he had previously settled the policy for the benefit of his children. This should also make no difference. The claimant's rights cannot depend on whether the wrongdoer gave the policy to his children during his lifetime or left the proceeds to them by his will; or if during his lifetime whether he did so before or after he had recourse to the claimant's money to pay the premiums. The order of events does not affect the fact that the children are not contributors but volunteers who have received the gift of an asset paid for in part with misappropriated trust moneys.

The cause of action

As I have already pointed out, the plaintiffs seek to vindicate their property rights, not to reverse unjust enrichment. The correct classification of the plaintiffs' cause of action may appear to be academic, but it has important consequences. The two causes of action have different requirements and may attract different defences.

A plaintiff who brings an action in unjust enrichment must show that the defendant has been enriched at the plaintiff's expense, for he cannot have been unjustly enriched if he has not been enriched at all. But the plaintiff is not concerned to show that the defendant is in receipt of property belonging beneficially to the plaintiff or its traceable proceeds. The fact that the beneficial ownership of the property has passed to the defendant provides no defence; indeed, it is usually the very fact which founds the claim. Conversely, a plaintiff who brings an action like the present must show that the defendant is in receipt of property which belongs beneficially to him or its traceable proceeds, but he need not show that the defendant has been enriched by its receipt. He may, for example, have paid full value for the property, but he is still required to disgorge it if he received it with notice of the plaintiff's interest.

Furthermore, a claim in unjust enrichment is subject to a change of position defence, which usually operates by reducing or extinguishing the element of enrichment. An action like the present is subject to the bona fide purchaser for value defence, which operates to clear the defendant's title.

The tracing rules

... The simplest case is where a trustee wrongfully misappropriates trust property and uses it exclusively to acquire other property for his own benefit. In such a case the beneficiary is entitled at his option either to assert his beneficial ownership of the proceeds or to bring a personal claim against the trustee for breach of trust and enforce an equitable lien or charge on the proceeds to secure restoration of the trust fund. He will normally exercise the option in the way most advantageous to himself. If the traceable proceeds have increased in value and are worth more than the original asset, he will assert his beneficial ownership and obtain the profit for himself. There is nothing unfair in this. The trustee cannot be permitted to keep any profit resulting from his misappropriation for himself, and his donees cannot obtain a better title than their donor. If the traceable proceeds are worth less than the original asset, it does not usually matter how the beneficiary exercises his option. He will take the whole of the proceeds on either basis. This is why it is not possible to identify the basis on which the claim succeeded in some of the cases.

Both remedies are proprietary and depend on successfully tracing the trust property into its proceeds. A beneficiary's claim against a trustee for breach of trust is a personal claim. It does not entitle him to priority over the trustee's general creditors unless he can trace the trust property into its product and establish a proprietary interest in the proceeds. If the beneficiary is unable to trace the trust property into its proceeds, he still has a personal claim against the trustee, but his claim will be unsecured. The beneficiary's proprietary claims to the trust property or its traceable proceeds can be maintained against the wrongdoer and anyone who derives title from him except a bona fide purchaser for value without notice of the breach of trust. The same rules apply even where there have been numerous successive transactions, so long as the tracing exercise is successful and no bona fide purchaser for value without notice has intervened.

A more complicated case is where there is a mixed substitution. This occurs where the trust money represents only part of the cost of acquiring the new asset ...

In *In re Hallett's Estate, Knatchbull v Hallett* (1880) 13 ChD 696, 709 Sir George Jessel MR acknowledged that where an asset was acquired exclusively with trust money, the beneficiary could either assert equitable ownership of the asset or enforce a lien or charge over it to recover the trust money. But he appeared to suggest that in the case of a mixed substitution the beneficiary is confined to a lien. Any authority that this *dictum* might otherwise have is weakened by the fact that Jessel MR gave no reason for the existence of any such rule, and none is readily apparent. The *dictum* was plainly *obiter*, for the fund was deficient and the plaintiff was only claiming a lien. It has usually been cited only to be explained away (see for example *In re Tilley's Will Trusts* [1967] Ch 1179, 1186 *per* Ungoed-Thomas J; Burrows *The Law of Restitution* (1993), p. 368). It was rejected by the High Court of Australia in *Scott v Scott* (1963) 109 CLR 649 (see the passage at pp. 661–2 cited by Morritt LJ below at [1998] Ch 265, 300–301). It has not been adopted in the United States: see the American Law Institute, Restatement of the Law, Trusts, 2d (1959) at section 202(h). In *Primeau v Granfield* (1911) 184 F. 480 (SDNY) at p. 184 Learned Hand J expressed himself in forthright terms: 'On principle there can be no excuse for such a rule'.

In my view the time has come to state unequivocally that English law has no such rule. It conflicts with the rule that a trustee must not benefit from his trust. I agree with Burrows that the beneficiary's right to elect to have a proportionate share of a mixed substitution necessarily follows once one accepts, as English law does, (i) that a claimant can trace in equity into a mixed fund and (ii) that he can trace unmixed money into its proceeds and assert ownership of the proceeds.

Accordingly, I would state the basic rule as follows. Where a trustee wrongfully uses trust money to provide part of the cost of acquiring an asset, the beneficiary is entitled at his option either to claim a proportionate share of the asset or to enforce a lien upon it to secure his personal claim against the trustee for the amount of the misapplied money. It does not matter whether the trustee mixed the trust money with his own in a single fund before using it to acquire the asset, or made separate payments (whether simultaneously or sequentially) out of the differently owned funds to acquire a single asset.

Two observations are necessary at this point. First, there is a mixed substitution (with the results already described) whenever the claimant's property has contributed in part only towards the acquisition of the new asset. It is not necessary for the claimant to show in addition that his property has contributed to any increase in the value of the new asset. This is because, as I have already pointed out, this branch of the law is concerned with vindicating rights of property and not with reversing unjust enrichment. Secondly, the beneficiary's right to claim a lien is available only against a wrongdoer and those deriving title under him otherwise than for value. It is not available against competing contributors who are innocent of any wrongdoing. The tracing rules are not the result of any presumption or principle peculiar to equity. They correspond to the common law rules for following into physical mixtures (though the consequences may not be identical). Common to both is the principle that the interests of the wrongdoer who was responsible for the mixing and those who derive title under him otherwise than for value are subordinated to those of innocent contributors. As against the wrongdoer and his successors, the beneficiary is entitled to locate his contribution in any part of the mixture and to subordinate their claims to share in the mixture until his own contribution has been satisfied. This has the effect of giving the beneficiary a lien for his contribution if the mixture is deficient.

Innocent contributors, however, must be treated equally *inter se*. Where the beneficiary's claim is in competition with the claims of other innocent contributors, there is no basis upon which any of the claims can be subordinated to any of the others. Where the fund is deficient, the beneficiary is not entitled to enforce a lien for his contributions; all must share rateably in the fund. The primary rule in regard to a mixed fund, therefore, is that gains and losses are borne by the contributors rateably. The beneficiary's right to elect instead to enforce a lien to obtain repayment is an exception to the primary rule, exercisable where the fund is deficient and the claim is made against the wrongdoer and those claiming through him. It is not necessary to consider whether there are any circumstances in which the beneficiary is confined to a lien in cases where the fund is more than sufficient to repay the contributions of all parties. It is sufficient to say that he is not so confined in a case like the present. It is not enough that those defending the claim are innocent of any wrongdoing if they are not themselves contributors but, like the trustees and Mr Murphy's children in the present case, are volunteers who derive title under the wrongdoer otherwise than for value. On ordinary principles such persons are in no better position than the wrongdoer, and are liable to suffer the same subordination of their interests to those of the claimant as the wrongdoer would have been. They certainly cannot do better than the claimant by confining him to a lien and keeping any profit for themselves ...

Insurance policies

... if a claimant can show that premiums were paid with his money, he can claim a proportionate share of the policy. His interest arises by reason of and immediately upon the payment of the premiums, and the extent of his share is ascertainable at once. He does not have to wait until the policy matures in order to claim his property. His share in the policy and its proceeds may increase or decrease as further premiums are paid; but it is not affected by the realisation of the policy. His share remains the same whether the policy is sold or surrendered or held until maturity; these are merely different methods of realising the policy. They may affect the amount of the proceeds received on realisation but they cannot affect the extent of his share in the proceeds. In principle the plaintiffs are entitled to the insurance money which was paid on Mr Murphy's death in the same shares and proportions as they were entitled in the policy immediately before his death.

... In my opinion there is no reason to differentiate between the first premium or premiums and later premiums. Such a distinction is not based on any principle. Why should the policy belong to the party who paid the first premium, without which there would have been no policy, rather than to the party who paid the last premium, without which it would normally have lapsed? Moreover, any such distinction would lead to the most capricious results. If only four annual premiums are paid, why should it matter whether A paid the first two premiums and B the second two, or B paid the first two and A the second two, or they each paid half of each of the four premiums? Why should the children obtain the whole of the sum assured if Mr Murphy used his own money before he began to use the plaintiffs' money, and only a return of the premiums if Mr Murphy happened to use the plaintiffs' money first? Why should the proceeds of the policy be attributed to the first premium when the policy itself is expressed to be in consideration of all the premiums? There is no analogy with the case where trust money is used to maintain or improve property of a third party. The nearest analogy is with an instalment purchase.

... In the course of argument it was submitted that if the children, who were innocent of any wrong-doing themselves, had been aware that their father was using stolen funds to pay the premiums, they could have insisted that the premiums should not be paid, and in the events which happened would still have received the same death benefit. But the fact is that Mr Murphy concealed his wrongdoing from both parties. The proper response is to treat them both alike, that is to say rateably. It is morally offensive as well as contrary to principle to subordinate the claims of the victims of a fraud to those of the objects of the fraudster's bounty on the ground that he concealed his wrongdoing from both of them.

... The Court of Appeal held that the plaintiffs were entitled by way of subrogation to Mr Murphy's lien to be repaid the premiums. He was, they thought, entitled to the trustee's ordinary lien to indemnify him for expenditure laid out in the preservation of the trust property: see *In re Leslie* (1883) 23 ChD 560. Had Mr Murphy used his own money, they said, it would have been treated as a gift to his children; but the fact that he used stolen funds rebutted any presumption of advancement.

With all due respect, I do not agree that Mr Murphy had any lien to which the plaintiffs can be subrogated. He was one of the trustees of his children's settlement, but he did not pay any of the premiums in that capacity. He settled a life policy on his children but without the funds to enable the trustees to pay the premiums. He obviously intended to add further property to the settlement by paying the premiums. When he paid the premiums with his own money he did so as settlor, not as trustee. He must be taken to have paid the later premiums in the same capacity as he paid the earlier ones. I do not for my own part see how his intention to make further advancements into the settlement can be rebutted by showing that he was not using his own money; as between himself and his children the source of the funds is immaterial. He could not demand repayment from the trustees by saying: 'I used stolen money; now that I have been found out you must pay me back so that I can repay the money'. Moreover, even if the presumption of advancement were rebutted, there would be no resulting trust. Mr Murphy was either (as I would hold) a father using stolen money to make further gifts to his children or a stranger paying a premium on another's policy without request: see *Falcke v Scottish Imperial Insurance Co.* (1886) 34 ChD 234.

But perhaps the strongest ground for rejecting the argument is that it makes the plaintiffs' rights depend on the circumstance that Mr Murphy happened to be one of the trustees of his children's settlement. That is adventitious. If he had not been a trustee then, on the reasoning of the majority of the Court of Appeal, the plaintiffs would have had no proprietary remedy at all, and would be left with a worthless personal claim against Mr Murphy's estate. The plaintiffs' rights cannot turn on such chances as this ...

Conclusion

... the money should be divided between the parties in proportions in which they contributed to the premiums.

SECTION 5: TRACING IN EQUITY

The courts of equity have themselves developed a method of tracing property which acknowledges and protects equitable interests. Equitable tracing also has the advantage that it applies where the defendant has mixed the trust money with his own. There are respects, however, in which tracing in equity is less extensive than at common law. Thus it is a requirement of equitable tracing that the property had at some time been held by a fiduciary, and in accordance with ordinary equitable principles, the right is lost if the property comes into the hands of a bona fide purchaser for value who has no notice of the claimant's right, whereas the common law recognises no such limitation.

Equity acts *in personam* (see Chapter 16). In *El Ajou v Dollar Land Holdings plc* [1993] 3 All ER 717, Millett J, whose decision on this point was upheld by the Court of Appeal ([1994] 2 All ER 685), held that it was possible to trace property through civil jurisdictions, such as Panama, which did not recognise equitable tracing, so long as the defendant was within the jurisdiction. It does not matter where the property actually is, therefore.

A: Identification of property as belonging to the claimant

When tracing in equity, it is easier than at common law to establish that what the defendant has is the claimant's property. Thus, the equitable right is available not only in the common law situations where the claimant can identify his property *in specie*, or point to a fund representing its proceeds, but also where the defendant has created a mixed fund, and possibly even when this fund has itself been converted into other property. The courts are also less concerned in equity to be able to follow the property at every stage.

Agip (Africa) Ltd v *Jackson*

[1991] Ch 547, Court of Appeal

Facts: The facts have already been stated in Section 3: Common law tracing. In addition to their claim at common law (which failed), the claimants also claimed that they were entitled to trace in equity.

Held: The plaintiffs were entitled to claim the money in equity.

MILLETT J (whose decision was upheld by the Court of Appeal): There is no difficulty in tracing the plaintiffs' property in equity, which can follow the money as it passed through the accounts of the correspondent banks in New York or, more realistically, follow the chose in action through its transmutation as a direct result of forged instructions from a debt owed by the Banque du Sud to the plaintiffs in Tunis into a debt owed by Lloyds Bank to Baker Oil in London.

The only restriction on the ability of equity to follow assets is the requirement that there must be some fiduciary relationship which permits the assistance of equity to be invoked. The requirement has been widely condemned and depends on authority rather than principle, but the law was settled by *Re Diplock's Estate* [1948] Ch 465. It may need to be reconsidered but not, I venture to think, at first instance. The requirement is easily circumvented since it is not necessary that there should be an initial fiduciary relationship in order to start the tracing process. It is sufficient that the payment to the defendant itself gives rise to a fiduciary relationship: *Chase Manhattan Bank N.A.* v *Israel-British Bank (London) Ltd* [1981] Ch 105 [see Section 5: Tracing in equity, E: Requirement for fiduciary relationship].

The requirement is also readily satisfied in most cases of commercial fraud, since the embezzlement of a company's funds almost inevitably involves a breach of fiduciary duty on the part of one of the company's employees or agents. That was so in the present case. There was clearly a fiduciary relationship between Mr Zdiri and the plaintiffs. Mr Zdiri [the chief accountant] was not a director or a signatory on the plaintiffs' bank account, but he was a senior and responsible officer. As such he was entrusted with possession of the signed payment orders to have them taken to the bank and implemented. He took advantage of his possession of them to divert the money and cause the separation between its legal ownership which passed to the payees and its beneficial ownership which remained in the plaintiffs. There is clear authority that there is a receipt of trust property when a company's funds are misapplied by a director and, in my judgment, this is equally the case when a company's funds are misapplied by any person whose fiduciary position gave him control of them or enabled him to misapply them.

...

The tracing claim in equity gives rise to a proprietary remedy which depends on the continued existence of the trust property in the hands of the defendant. Unless he is a *bona fide* purchaser for value without notice, he must restore the trust property to its rightful owner if he still has it. But even a volunteer who has received trust property cannot be made subject to a personal liability to account for it as a constructive trustee if he has parted with it without having previously acquired some knowledge of the existence of the trust: *Re Montagu's Settlement Trusts* [1987] Ch 264.

The plaintiffs are entitled to the money in court which rightfully belongs to them. To recover the money which the defendants have paid away the plaintiffs must subject them to a personal liability to account as constructive trustees and prove the requisite degree of knowledge to establish the liability.

FOX LJ: Both common law and equity accepted the right of the true owner to trace his property into the hands of others while it was in an identifiable form. The common law treated property as identified if it had not been mixed with other property. Equity, on the other hand, will follow money into a mixed fund and charge the fund. There is, in the present case, no difficulty about the mechanics of tracing in equity. The money can be traced through the various bank accounts to Baker Oil and onwards. It is, however, a prerequisite to the operation of the remedy in equity that there must be a fiduciary relationship which calls the equitable jurisdiction into being. There is no difficulty about that in the present case since Zdiri must have been in a fiduciary relationship with Agip. He was the chief accountant of Agip and was entrusted with the signed drafts or orders upon Banque du Sud.

NOTES

1. The case clearly suggests that it is easier to establish that the defendant has received the claimant's property in equity than it is at common law.
2. Because (unlike the action for money had and received) tracing in equity is a proprietary claim, it depends on retention of the money by the defendant. Baker Oil had retained only about US$45,000, and only this amount could be traced in equity, but the plaintiffs also succeeded in respect of the amount dissipated by Baker Oil, on the basis of knowing assistance (now referred to as 'dishonest assistance', see Chapter 15, Section 4).

■ QUESTIONS

1. X steals a car from Y and gives it to his friend Z. Who has property in the car?
2. X steals £500 cash from Y and gives it to his friend Z. Who has property in the cash? What, if any, is the nature of Z's liability to Y?
3. X steals £500 cash from Y and gives it to his friend Z. Z spends £300 and has £200 of it left. Y sues Z for money had and received. For how much is Z liable? Would your answer be different if Z had paid any or all of the money into his general bank account? Does it matter whether Z knows of its origin?

   Hint: Consider possible defences.

B: Quantifying shares in mixed funds: *pari passu* and *Clayton's case*

Once it is accepted that equity can trace into mixed funds, it is necessary to consider the basis upon which the fund is apportioned between rival claimants. Usually, the problem is that payments have been made out of the fund, leaving insufficient moneys to satisfy all the claimants. But another possibility is that the payments out have been wisely invested, in which case claimants may prefer to claim a share of the payments out, rather than what remains in the fund.

The leading authority is the Court of Appeal decision in *Re Diplock's Estate* [1948] Ch 465. The testator, Caleb Diplock, gave the residue of his property 'to such charitable institutions or other charitable or benevolent object or objects in England' as his executors should, in their absolute discretion, select. In the belief that this created a valid charitable trust, the executors distributed some £203,000 among 139 different charities. Then the next of kin successfully challenged its validity in *Chichester Diocesan Fund and Board of Finance* v *Simpson* [1944] AC 341. The next of kin, having exhausted their remedy against the executors, successfully recovered money from the various charities. The personal claim is considered at the end of the chapter, but a proprietary claim also succeeded against some of the charities. The advantage of the proprietary claim was that it allowed the next of kin to claim interest.

On the proprietary claim, the Court of Appeal, extending the principles derived from *Re Hallett's Estate* and *Sinclair* v *Brougham*, held that the right to trace into a mixed fund is not limited to cases where the defendant is the person who has mixed the funds. Neither does there need to be a fiduciary relationship as between the parties to the action. The right to trace is available against an innocent volunteer. A volunteer is not a purchaser, and provides no value. Here, the volunteer charities had mixed Diplock money with their own, and hence the question of apportionment arose.

Where a trustee wrongly mixes trust money with his own, the principles in *Hallett's Estate*, below, apply, essentially to the disadvantage of the trustee, but the volunteers in *Diplock* were innocent, and the Court of Appeal did not apply the same harsh principles to them. They were treated just like any other innocent claimant to a share in a mixed fund, and in particular, as being no less deserving than the next of kin. The volunteer's duty of conscience is regarded as akin to that of a person having an equitable interest in a mixed fund towards the other equitable owners, and so, for example, where Diplock money was used to purchase stocks, where the charity already had similar stocks, the charity ranked *pari passu* with the next of kin (i.e. in proportion to the amount each has contributed to the amalgam). This is clearly the fairest method of apportionment in such a case.

For current bank accounts, however, the Court of Appeal in *Diplock* applied the rule developed in *Clayton's case* (1816) 1 Mer 572, which enshrines the principle of 'first in, first out'. The first payment in is appropriated to satisfy the earliest debt. The basis of the rule is said to be the presumed intention of the person operating the account. A preferable solution, in the opinion of the authors of the *Report of the Review Committee on Insolvency Law and Practice* (Cork Report 1982, Cmnd 8558), paras 1076–80, would be to divide the mixed fund rateably (i.e. *in pari passu*). However, in *Barlow Clowes International Ltd* v *Vaughan* [1992] 4 All ER 22, noted (1993) 57 *Conv* 370, the Court of Appeal held that *Clayton's case* normally applied, the court being bound by the *ratio* of *Diplock*. Actually, in *Barlow Clowes* itself, the presumption in *Clayton's case* was rebutted (see the note to this discussion), but it would normally be very difficult to operate *pari passu* distribution with a running bank account, because *pari passu* distribution assumes a starting date for the fund (otherwise how can you determine how much each has contributed to the amalgam).

NOTE: The so-called 'rule' in *Clayton's case* is so often disapplied in the interests of justice that Lindsay J referred to it as the 'exception' in *Clayton's case* (*Russell-Cooke Trust Co* v *Prentis* [2002] All ER (D) 22 (Nov)).

■ **QUESTION**

Suppose Paul pays £10 into a fund, then Michael pays in £10, then £10 is spent, then Karen pays in £10, then a further £10 is spent, leaving £10 in the fund. What is the share of each under:

    (a) *pari passu*; and

    (b) *Clayton's case*?

Would your answer be different if the £10 withdrawals, instead of being dissipated, are used for an investment which increases in value, to £50?

NOTE: Before the final £10 is spent, *pari passu* gives Paul, Michael, and Karen an equal share of the £20 in the fund, or £6.67 each. After the final transaction, each has an equal share in the £10 remaining, or £3.33 each.

If *Clayton's case* applies, the first withdrawal will be attributed to Paul alone, on the 'first in first out' principle, leaving him with no share in the fund. When Karen pays in her £10, Michael and Karen will have a share of £10 each. So at this stage, Paul is doing worse, and Michael and Karen better, than under *pari passu*. The final withdrawal is attributed to Michael, leaving Karen sole owner of the remaining £10. Clearly, then, *Clayton's case* benefits the late investor.

However, the positions are reversed if the £10 withdrawals, instead of being dissipated, are used for an investment which increases in value, to £50. Here *Clayton's case* benefits the early investor into the fund, *pari passu* the later. Before the final withdrawal and purchase, *pari passu* gives Paul, Michael, and Karen equal shares in the first £50 investment, and the £20 remaining in the fund, or a share worth £23.33 each. After the final withdrawal and purchase, they have equal shares in the two £50 investments and the £10 remaining in the fund, each therefore having a share worth £36.67.

Under *Clayton's case*, the entirety of the first investment, worth £50, is owned by Paul, whose total share is therefore £50. Michael and Karen are worse off immediately before the final purchase, each with just a £10 share in the fund. But the second investment will belong to Michael, who therefore ends up, like Paul, with an investment worth £50. Karen's share is the whole of the remaining fund, or £10. So Karen is far worse off under the rule in *Clayton's case* than under *pari passu*.

It is arguable that neither of these positions is fair. In the first case, *pari passu* leads to everyone's share, including Karen's, being reduced by the first withdrawal, but that withdrawal occurred before Karen had invested anything. Surely that is unfair? (Is it always unfair though? Suppose everyone regarded this as a common fund.) Also in the first case, after the first withdrawal but before Karen's investment, Paul's share under *Clayton's case* is zero, whereas Michael has lost none of his investment, yet surely their equities are equal?

Similarly in the second case, *pari passu* gives Karen the benefit of the first investment, in which she was in no meaningful sense involved. Under *Clayton's case*, Paul gets the entire benefit of the first investment, yet surely his equity is the same as Michael's?

For an argument that the North American rolling charge is fairer than either of these distribution methods, and could still have a place in UK law, see Lowrie and Todd [1997] *Denning LJ* 43.

C: Mixing by trustee or fiduciary

The principles discussed at B assume that all claimants are equally innocent, or at any rate are treated as such, but as against a trustee who is in breach of trust, who has mixed trust money with his own, the beneficiary is entitled to a first charge over a mixed fund or property purchased with it. This will generally operate against the interests of the trustee.

Re Hallett's Estate, Knatchbull v *Hallett*
(1880) 13 ChD 696, Court of Appeal

Facts: Hallett, a solicitor, was a trustee of his own marriage settlement. He had paid some of the money from that trust into his own bank account, into which he also paid money which had been entrusted to him for investment by a client. He made various payments in and out of the account, which at his death contained sufficient funds to meet the claims of the trust and his client, but not those of his personal creditors as well.

Held: The Court of Appeal held that both the trust and the client were entitled to a charge in priority to the general creditors, and that the various payments out of the account must be treated as payments of Hallett's own money.

SIR GEORGE JESSEL MR: ... There is no doubt ... that Mr Hallett stood in a fiduciary position towards Mrs Cotterill. Mr Hallett, before his death, ... improperly sold the bonds and put the money to his general account at his bankers. It is not disputed that the money remained at his bankers mixed with his own money at the time of his death; that is, he had not drawn out that money from his bankers. In that position of matters Mrs Cotterill claimed to be entitled to receive the proceeds, or the amount of the proceeds, of the bonds out of the money in the hands of Mr Hallett's bankers at the time of his death, and that claim was allowed by the learned judge of the court below, and I think was properly so allowed ... The modern doctrine of Equity as regards property disposed of by persons in a fiduciary position is a very clear and well-established doctrine. You can, if the sale was rightful, take the proceeds of the sale, if you can identify them. If the sale was wrongful, you can still take the proceeds of the sale, in a sense adopting the sale for the purpose of taking the proceeds, if you can identify them. There is no distinction, therefore, between a rightful and a wrongful disposition of the property, so far as regards the right of the beneficial owner to follow the proceeds. But it very often happens that you cannot identify the proceeds. The proceeds may have been invested together with money belonging to the person in a fiduciary position, in a purchase. He may have bought land with it, for instance, or he may have bought chattels with it. Now, what is the position of the beneficial owner as regards such purchases? I will, first of all, take his position when the purchase is clearly made with what I will call, for shortness, the trust money, although it is not confined, as I will show presently, to express trusts. In that case, according to the now well-established doctrine of Equity, the beneficial owner has a right to elect either to take the property purchased, or to hold it as a security for the amount of the trust money laid out in the purchase; or, as we generally express it, he is entitled at his election either to take the property, or to have a charge on the property for the amount of the trust money. But … where a trustee has mixed the money with his own, there is this distinction, that the *cestui que trust*, or beneficial owner, can no longer elect to take the property, because it is no longer bought with the trust money simply and purely, but with a mixed fund. He is, however, still entitled to a charge on the property purchased, for the amount of the trust money laid out in the purchase; and that charge is quite independent of the fact of the amount laid out by the trustee. The moment you get a substantial portion of it furnished by the trustee, using the word 'trustee' in the sense I have mentioned, as including all persons in a fiduciary relation, the right to the charge follows …

When we come to apply that principle to the case of a trustee who has blended trust moneys with his own, it seems to me perfectly plain that he cannot be heard to say that he took away the trust money when he had a right to take away his own money … What difference does it make if, instead of putting the trust money into a bag, he deposits it with his banker, then pays in other money of his own, and then draws out some money for his own purposes? Could he say that he had actually drawn out anything but his own money? His money was there, and he had a right to draw it out, and why should the natural act of simply drawing out the money be attributed to anything except to his ownership of money which was at his bankers?

NOTE: The principle is that where an act can be done rightly, the trustee is not allowed to say that he did it wrongfully. Hallett was not entitled to use the trust money for his personal benefit, so it was assumed that he had spent his own money, rather than the trust funds. The principle does not restrict the beneficiaries to a claim on money in the bank account, however: they have first claim on any identifiable property that can be traced back to the trust.

Re Oatway

[1903] 2 Ch 356, Chancery Division

Facts: The trustee had withdrawn money from the mixed account and invested it in shares, leaving a balance in the account which at that time was ample to meet the claims of the beneficiaries. Subsequently, however, he exhausted the account, so that it was useless to proceed against the account.

Held: The argument that he must be treated as withdrawing his own money first (so that his shares would be treated as his own property) was rejected. The beneficiaries' claim must be satisfied out of any identifiable part of the fund before the trustee could set up his own claim. They were entitled to the proceeds from the sale of the shares in priority to the general creditors. (The assumption made here is that the trustee was not entitled to draw out for his personal benefit the money used to buy the shares.)

NOTES

1. The cases depend on the trust moneys remaining always identifiable. Once it is clear that all money belonging to the trustee has been withdrawn, so that any further withdrawals must have been from trust money, they cannot claim that any subsequent payments in must be taken as intended to replace the trust money, unless the trustee shows an intention to make such repayment. In such a case, the right to trace will apply up to the lowest balance of the account in the period between the trust fund being paid into the account and the time when the remedy is sought. For example, if the trustee mixes £1,000 of his own money with £3,000 of trust money and later withdraws £2,000, the right to trace will not extend beyond the £2,000 which is thereby left in the account, even if the trustee later pays in further sums of his own. (In such a case, of course, the beneficiaries will have a personal claim against the trustee for any outstanding sum.)

2. The 'lowest intermediate balance' rule suggests that it would be highly unorthodox to allow tracing into an asset which the defendant acquired before the claimant's money had been misappropriated (this is so-called 'backwards tracing'. See *Bishopsgate Investment Management Ltd (in liquidation)* v *Homan* [1995] Ch 211), and yet, where a debt is incurred to acquire an asset (such as a loan to acquire a car), and the debt is incurred with the intention of repaying it with misapplied trust money and the debt is actually repaid in whole or in part with misapplied trust money, it is arguable that the beneficiaries of the trust should be permitted to trace their money into the asset, to the extent that it has been redeemed (from the debt) by their money.

3. In *Re Oatway*, the shares had increased in value, but were still worth less than the trust moneys paid into the account. If they are regarded as trust property, then in principle, the beneficiary ought also to be entitled to any profit made on the sale of the shares, even if they had ended up being worth more than the trust moneys paid into the account. This depends on it being established that trust money was used to purchase the shares. In the *Tilley's WT* case, it could not be established that the trustee had done more than mix trust money with her own, and the beneficiaries were not entitled to any of the profit later made by her on her investments.

■ **QUESTION**

Is there merit in the argument that a trustee who wrongfully mixes his own property with trust property should forfeit the entirety of any increase in value of the mixed fund or asset, in accordance with the rule that a trustee must account for unauthorised gains?

Re Tilley's WT

[1967] Ch 1179, Chancery Division

Facts: A sole trustee who was also the life tenant had mixed a small amount of trust money (£2,237) in her own bank account before embarking on a series of property speculations which were so successful that upon her death her estate was worth £94,000. The beneficiaries entitled in remainder claimed a share of this wealth in the proportion which the trust money in the account bore to the balance of the account at that time.

Held: Ungoed-Thomas J held them entitled only to the return of the trust money with interest.

UNGOED-THOMAS J: For the defendants it has been rightly admitted that, if a trustee wrongly uses trust money to pay the whole of the purchase price in respect of the purchase of an asset, a beneficiary can elect either to treat the purchased asset as trust property or to treat the purchased asset as security for the recouping of the trust money. It was further conceded that this right of election by a beneficiary also applies where the asset is purchased by a trustee in part out of his own money and in part out of the trust moneys, so that he may, if he wishes, require the asset to be treated as trust property with regard to that proportion of it which the trust moneys contributed to its purchase ...

[Ungoed-Thomas J reviewed the facts and continued ...] If, of course, a trustee deliberately uses trust money to contribute with his own money to buy property in his own name, then I would see no difficulty in enabling a beneficiary to adopt the purchase and claim a share of any resulting profits; but the subjective test does not appear to me to be exclusive, or indeed adequate, if it is the only test.

It seems to me that if, having regard to all the circumstances of the case objectively considered, it appears that if the trustee has in fact, whatever his intention, laid out trust moneys in or towards a purchase then the beneficiaries are entitled to the property purchased and any profits which it produces to the extent to which it has been paid for out of the trust moneys. Even by this objective test, it appears to me, however, that the trust moneys were not in this case so laid out. On a proper appraisal of the facts of this particular case, the trustee's breach halted at the mixing of the funds in her bank account. Although properties bought out of those funds would, like the bank account itself, at any rate if the moneys in the bank account were inadequate, be charged with repayment of the trust moneys which then would stand in the same position as the bank account, yet the trust moneys were not invested in properties at all but merely went in reduction of the trustee's overdraft which was in reality the source of the purchase moneys.

NOTES

1. It is clear from the above passage that the decision was based on a finding of fact that Mrs Tilley had not invested the trust money in property but merely used it to reduce her overdraft. If a trustee has in fact laid out trust money towards a purchase, the beneficiaries would then be entitled to the property and any profit to the extent that it had been paid for with trust money.

   The reasoning is that if the trustee draws on a mixed fund to purchase property but leaves enough in the account to cover the trust funds, the rule in *Re Hallett's Estate* requires that the purchase be treated as made entirely with his own money, in which case, should no further dissipations to the mixed fund occur, the property, and any profit, belong to him. But should he then go further and dissipate the remaining balance, the beneficiaries will have a charge on the property (*Re Oatway*), and this may be for the proportionate part of the increased value, and not merely for the original amount of the trust fund. This solution allows the beneficiaries the choice of a charge for an amount of the trust money, which will be to their advantage where the funds are depleted, or a share in the property where its value has risen.

2. None of the above applies where the rival claims to the mixed fund arise between two or more trusts, or between the beneficiaries under a trust and an innocent volunteer, where the rule developed in *Clayton's case* (1816) 1 Mer 572 (see Section B above: Quantifying shares in mixed funds: *pari passu* and *Clayton's case*) is normally applied. However, *Clayton's case* operates on presumed intention, which can therefore be rebutted. Indeed, it was rebutted in *Re Hallett's Estate*, considered in the last section. The courts have been reluctant to apply it outside the realm of current bank accounts. In *Re Hobourn Aero Components Air Raid Distress Fund* [1946] Ch 86, for example, where contributions had been made into, and moneys paid out of, a non-charitable unincorporated association, *Clayton's case* was argued by later contributors (who, as explained, generally benefit from the application of *Clayton's case*), to suggest that all payments out were attributable to the earlier contributions. Cohen J rejected the argument, preferring what was, in effect, a *pari passu* distribution. There was, of course, a definite start date to the fund in *Hobourn Aero* so it was easy to make a *pari passu* calculation.

   Barlow Clowes International Ltd v *Vaughan* [1992] 4 All ER 22, noted (1993) 57 *Conv* 370, concerned the collapse of a deposit-taking company, where money had been invested in portfolios. Because the fund available for distribution was so much smaller than the totality of claims, *Clayton's case* would benefit only a few, late depositors. The Court of Appeal held that *Clayton's case* applied in principle to this type of case, Woolf LJ with some reluctance, and only because he felt constrained by authority. However, Dillon LJ showed less reluctance, at any rate to the adoption of *Clayton's case* as a starting point, observing (at 32 and 33) that:

   > If the application of *Clayton's case* is unfair to early investors *pari passu* distribution among all seems unfair to late investors ...
   >
   > It is indeed correct that the precise situation in the present case did not arise in the reported cases. In *Re Hallett's Estate* there were indeed two separate beneficiaries claiming, but both were paid in full when it was ruled that the account holder must be deemed to have exhausted his own moneys first ...
   >
   > None the less the decisions of this court, in my judgment, establish and recognise a general rule of practice that *Clayton's case* is to be applied when several beneficiaries' moneys have been blended in one bank account and there is a deficiency. It is not, in my judgment, for this court to reject that long-established general practice.

   The rule in *Clayton's case* is only the starting point, however, and applies only where it provides a convenient method of determining competing claims. In the particular case, the presumed intention (from the application of the rule) was rebutted as being impractical and unjust, because a small number of investors would get most of the funds, and the fund was divided in *pari passu*.

D: Assets misapplied by the trustee and recovered by the trustee

It had been thought that a trustee was precluded from recovering assets which he had misapplied in breach of trust, because the trustee would be relying in his cause of action on the very fact of his own breach. However, this notion has been rejected by the Court of Appeal (*Montrose Investment Ltd* v *Orion Nominees Ltd* [2004] EWCA Civ 1032).

E: Requirement for fiduciary relationship

Unlike tracing at common law, tracing in equity requires that at some stage, there must have existed a fiduciary relationship of some sort which was sufficient to give rise to an equitable proprietary right in the claimant. The clearest case is that of the relationship of trustee and beneficiary, so that in breach of trust cases there is no problem. As we saw in Chapter 2, agents and bailees (and others) may also occupy a fiduciary position. See further on this requirement the passages from *Agip (Africa)* v *Jackson*, quoted in this chapter.

The requirement of a fiduciary relationship for tracing in equity is often thought to be not easy to justify in principle, because it means that a mere equitable owner may have a better action than someone who is both legal and equitable owner of property (since there will always be a fiduciary relationship in the former case, with the trustee). Thus a beneficiary can always trace in equity—someone who is both legal and equitable owner (if such a person can exist, see discussion on *Westdeutsche* in this section) can do so only if he can find an additional fiduciary relationship.

The requirement appears to have arisen by historical accident. The original authority for tracing into mixed funds was *Re Hallett's Estate* (1880) 13 ChD 696, above, which involved mixing by a trustee. The principle was extended in *Sinclair* v *Brougham* [1914] AC 398, from which (because the speeches of their Lordships differ substantially) it has always been difficult to extract a clear *ratio*, and indeed the case has recently been overruled in *Westdeutsche Landesbank Girozentrale* v *Islington London Borough Council* [1996] AC 669. However, as the case was interpreted in *Re Diplock's Estate*, the mixing was done by a fiduciary, and the case was interpreted as authority for the requirement of an initial fiduciary relationship. In *Re Diplock's Estate*, the claimants also succeeded on a personal claim, so it might be thought arguable that remarks on the proprietary tracing claim were obiter, except that the proprietary remedy was necessary for the interest claim.

Re Diplock's Estate was accepted by Millett J in *Agip (Africa)* as Court of Appeal authority for the requirement, and it has in any case been reiterated by the Privy Council in *Re Goldcorp Exchange* [1995] 1 AC 74, and most recently by the House of Lords in *Westdeutsche Landesbank Girozentrale* v *Islington London Borough Council* [1996] AC 669 (despite the overruling of *Sinclair* v *Brougham*) and the Court of Appeal in *Trustee of the Property of F. C. Jones and Sons (a firm)* v *Jones* [1996] 3 WLR 703 (see Section 3: Common law tracing), so the requirement appears to be entrenched.

In *Westdeutsche*, Lord Browne-Wilkinson doubted the very concept of someone being both legal and equitable owner, on the ground that the equitable ownership would have no existence in the absence of separation of legal and equitable titles (for example, on the creation of a trust). Since he also appears to take the view that if there is a trust there will inevitably be a fiduciary relationship, this may also justify the *Diplock* conclusion in principle, since it will be difficult to conceive of an equitable title existing in the absence of a fiduciary relationship.

Chase Manhattan Bank v *Israel-British Bank*

[1981] Ch 105, Chancery Division

Facts: The claimant, a bank in New York, was instructed to pay a substantial sum of money to another bank for the account of the defendant. The defendant was not a customer of the claimant bank. By mistake, the money was paid twice. The defendant was later wound up in proceedings in the English High Court. The claimant bank claimed to trace the sum mistakenly paid into the hands of the liquidators (had it merely proved as a general creditor in the winding-up, it could not have hoped to recover the whole of the sum paid).

It was accepted that whereas the legal effects of the mistaken payment were determined in accordance with the law of the State of New York, the procedural rights and remedies were governed by English law.

Held: Under both systems of law, the claimant had the right to trace the sum paid into the hands of the liquidators. It was not fatal that there was no fiduciary relationship between claimant and defendant before the money got into the wrong hands, but was sufficient that a fiduciary relationship came into being as a result of the mistaken payment being made. The existence of a fiduciary relationship at some stage is essential to the right to trace in equity in English law, however, whatever may be the position in the United States.

GOULDING J: The plaintiff's claim, viewed in the first place without reference to any system of positive law, raises problems to which the answers, if not always difficult, are at any rate not obvious. If one party P pays money to another party D by reason of a factual mistake, either common to both parties or made by P alone, few conscientious persons would doubt that D ought to return it. But suppose that D is, or becomes, insolvent before repayment is made, so that P comes into competition with D's general creditors, what then? If the money can still be traced, either in its original form or through successive conversions, and is found among D's remaining assets, ought not P to be able to claim it, or what represents it, as his own? If he ought, and if in a particular case the money has been blended with other assets and is represented by a mixed fund, no longer as valuable as the sum total of its original constituents, what priorities or equalities should govern the distribution of the mixed fund? If the money can no longer be traced, either separate or in mixture, should P have any priority over ordinary creditors of D? In any of these cases, does it make any difference whether the mistake was inevitable, or was caused by P's carelessness, or was contributed to by some fault, short of dishonesty, on the part of D?

At this stage I am asked to take only one step forward, and to answer the initial question of principle, whether the plaintiff is entitled in equity to trace the mistaken payment and to recover what now properly represents the money.

[There being no English authorities, Goulding J cited a number of American cases, and a passage from Professor A. W. Scott's *The Law of Trusts*, 27th edn. (1973), p. 289. He continued:]

Counsel for the defendant says that … there is no equitable right to trace property unless some initial fiduciary relationship exists, the right being founded on the existence of a beneficial owner with an equitable proprietary interest in property in the hands of a trustee or other fiduciary agent. Counsel says further that the essential fiduciary relationship must initially arise from some consensual arrangement.

The facts and decisions in *Sinclair v Brougham* [1914] AC 398, and in *Re Diplock's Estate* [1948] Ch 465 are well known and I shall not take time to recite them. I summarise my view of the *Diplock* judgment as follows. 1. The Court of Appeal's interpretation of *Sinclair v Brougham* was an essential part of their decision and is binding on me. 2. The court thought that the majority of the House of Lords in *Sinclair v Brougham* had not accepted Lord Dunedin's opinion in that case, and themselves rejected it. 3. The court … held that an initial fiduciary relationship is a necessary foundation of the equitable right of tracing. 4. They also held that the relationship between the building society directors and depositors in *Sinclair v Brougham* was a sufficient fiduciary relationship for the purpose. The latter passage reads ([1948] Ch 465 at 540–1):

> … a sufficient fiduciary relationship was found to exist between the depositors and the directors by reason of the fact that the purposes for which the depositors had handed their money to the directors were by law incapable of fulfilment.

It is founded, I think, on the observations of Lord Parker in *Sinclair v Brougham*.

This fourth point shows that the fund to be traced need not (as was the case in *Re Diplock's Estate* itself) have been the subject of fiduciary obligations before it got into the wrong hands. It is enough that, as in *Sinclair v Brougham*, the payment into wrong hands itself gave rise to a fiduciary relationship. The same point also throws considerable doubt on counsel's submission for the defendants that the necessary fiduciary relationship must originate in a consensual transaction. It was not the intention of the depositors or of the directors in *Sinclair v Brougham* to create any relationship at all between the depositors and the directors as principals. Their object, which unfortunately disregarded the statutory limitations of the building society's powers, was to establish contractual relationships between the depositors and the society. In the circumstances, however, the depositors retained an equitable property in the funds they parted with, and fiduciary relationships arose between them and the directors. In the same way, I would suppose, a person who pays money to another under a factual mistake retains an equitable property in it and the conscience of that other is subjected to a fiduciary duty to respect his proprietary right.

I am fortified in my opinion by the speech in *Sinclair* v *Brougham* of Lord Haldane LC, who, unlike Lord Dunedin, was not suspected of heresy in *Re Diplock's Estate*. Lord Haldane LC (who spoke for Lord Atkinson as well as himself) includes money paid under mistake of fact among the cases where money could be followed at common law, and he proceeds to the auxiliary tracing remedy, available (as he said) wherever money was held to belong in equity to the plaintiff, without making any relevant exception ...

Thus, in the belief that the point is not expressly covered by English authority and that *Re Diplock's Estate* does not conclude it by necessary implication, I hold that the equitable remedy of tracing is in principle available, on the ground of continuing proprietary interest, to a party who has paid money under a mistake of fact. On that prime question, I see no relevant difference between the law of England and the law of New York and there is no conflict of laws to be resolved.

NOTES

1. There was no fiduciary relationship initially between claimant and defendant, but Goulding J held it sufficient that a fiduciary relationship arose as a result of the mistaken payment. Nor need the fiduciary relationship exist between the parties to the action, so long as it originally existed. This follows from *Re Diplock's Estate* [1948] Ch 465, where an action was successful against a volunteer.

2. In *Agip (Africa)*, Millett J observed that:

   In [*Chase Manhattan*] however, equity's assistance was not needed in order to trace the plaintiff's money into the hands of the defendant; it was needed in order to ascertain whether it had any of the plaintiff's money left. The case cannot, therefore, be used to circumvent the requirement that there should be an initial fiduciary relationship in order to start the tracing process in equity.

   The general proposition, then, is that it is necessary for the fiduciary relationship to exist before the tracing process starts. In *Agip* itself, therefore, it was necessary to show a fiduciary relationship before the money got into the New York clearing system.

3. Unfortunately, Goulding J's reasoning in *Chase Manhattan* led Tuckey J into error in *Bank Tejarat* v *Hong Kong and Shanghai Banking Corporation (Ci) Ltd and Hong Kong and Shanghai Bank Trustee (Jersey) Ltd* [1995] 1 Lloyd's Rep 239. He observed that Millett J's analysis of *Chase Manhattan* is wrong, since the money became mixed (in another bank account) before it reached the defendant. Tuckey J therefore concluded (wrongly, as we now know) that where a payment is made under a mistake of fact (in *Bank Tejarat* itself, the bank had been deceived into thinking that the shipping documents tendered to it represented goods that had been shipped, whereas in fact they were simply forgeries), a fiduciary relationship arises as soon as the money has been paid out; it is not delayed until it has been actually received by the recipient.

■ QUESTIONS

1. Is the remedy for recovery of misapplied trust property based on the claimant's continuing property right in the misapplied property, or is it designed to reverse the unjust enrichment of the defendant?

2. Is it a valid criticism of the property law analysis of tracing that the claimant's property notionally 'multiplies' during the period when it is unclear which of several potential defendants is in possession of it?

NOTE: R. C. Nolan has argued, on the basis of recent judicial statements (which, being either first-instance, '*obiter*', or made in the Judicial Committee of the Privy Council, are technically unable to change the orthodox law) that there is an error in the orthodox understanding of a beneficiary's proprietary rights under a trust. He argues that they are not to be considered co-extensive with the beneficiary's rights against a properly appointed trustee for him, but that it is 'better to regard the proprietary rights inherent in a beneficiary's interest under a trust as basically negative and exclusionary, yielding a claim to recover misapplied trust assets, or their traceable proceeds, or an interest in such proceeds'. ('Equitable Property' (2006) 122 *LQR* 232.)

■ SUMMATIVE QUESTION

Trevor is a trustee of two trusts, Black's Settlement and White's Settlement, each comprising £50,000 in cash. The trust monies are kept in separate bank accounts. Trevor also has a private bank account in which he holds £100,000. Suppose that the following events take place, in the following order:

- Trevor withdraws all the monies from the Black's Settlement account and places them in his own private account.
- Trevor withdraws all the monies from the White's Settlement account and places them in his own private bank account.
- Trevor withdraws £100,000 from his own account in order to purchase a piece of fine art.
- Trevor withdraws £50,000 from his account and uses the monies to pay off the building society mortgage on his house.
- Trevor withdraws the balance of his private account and spends the monies on a luxury world cruise.
- Trevor finally pays £10,000 into his private account.

Trevor has just been declared bankrupt. His general creditors claim the work of fine art which is now worth £150,000, and the balance of monies in Trevor's private account. Advise the beneficiaries of the two trusts, who wish to recover the value of their misappropriated funds.

FURTHER READING

Bant, E., *The Change of Position Defence* (Oxford: Hart Publishing, 2009).

Birks, P. (ed.), *Laundering and Tracing* (Oxford: Clarendon Press, 1995).

Conaglen, M., 'Difficulties with tracing backwards' (2011) 127 *LQR* 432.

Fox, D., *Property Rights in Money* (Oxford: Oxford University Press, 2008).

Matthews, P., 'The Legal and Moral Limits of Common Law Tracing', in P. Birks (ed.), *Laundering and Tracing* (Oxford: Clarendon Press, 1995), p. 23.

Millett, Sir Peter, 'Tracing the Proceeds of Fraud' (1991) 107 *LQR* 71.

Oakley, A. J., 'The Prerequisites of an Equitable Tracing Claim' (1975) 28 *CLP* 64.

Pawlowski, M., 'Constructive Trusts, Tracing and the Requirement of a Fiduciary Obligation' (2005) 11 *Trusts and Trustees* 10.

Pearce, R. A., 'A Tracing Paper' (1976) 40 *Conv* 277.

Penner, J., 'Value, Property and Unjust Enrichment: Trusts of Traceable Proceeds' in R. Chambers, C. Mitchell and J. Penner (eds), *Philosophical Foundations of Unjust Enrichment* (Oxford: Oxford University Press, 2009).

Smith, L., 'Tracing in *Taylor* v *Plumer*: Equity in the Court of King's Bench' [1995] *LMCLQ* 240.

Smith, L., 'Tracing into the Payment of a Debt' [1995] *CLJ* 290.

Smith, L., *Tracing* (Oxford: Clarendon Press, 1997).

Smith, L., 'Simplifying Claims to Traceable Proceeds' (2009) 125 *LQR* 338.

Stevens, J., 'Vindicating the Proprietary Nature of Tracing' (2001) 65 *Conv* 94.

15

The Equitable Liability of Strangers to the Trust

KEY AIMS

To identify the ingredients of personal liability in equity for receipt of trust property in breach of the terms of the trust. To identify the ingredients of personal liability in equity for assistance in a breach of trust—and in particular, whether the accessory should be liable for knowing assistance or liable only where he was dishonest.

SECTION 1: INTRODUCTION

For an equitable tracing action to operate, the trust property must still be identifiable in some form, albeit that at least in equity it need not be *physically* identifiable, so that if, for example, the trust property has been sold, it may still be possible to trace the *proceeds* of sale. There are also rules in equity for the tracing of trust money which has become mixed with other money (see Chapter 14).

Suppose, however, that the property no longer exists in any identifiable form. Trust money may have been spent, for example, with nothing identifiable to show for it. If the trust property no longer exists, then clearly it is not traceable. Alternatively, it may be that it has been mixed with other funds in such a way as no longer to be traceable on the principles elaborated above. We saw in Chapter 14 that the common law 'money had and received' action depends only on receipt of the money by the defendant and that liability is unaffected by anything that later happens to the property, but that is not the case with tracing in equity. That is not necessarily the end of the matter, however, even in equity, as there is still the possibility that a stranger could be liable as if they were a constructive trustee. Such liability is not trustee liability properly-so-called, for it is merely personal liability against the stranger and gives no direct proprietary right in assets held by the stranger. Such personal actions in equity are very useful to trust beneficiaries, because they are unable to bring personal claims at common law (trustees can bring common law actions on behalf of trust beneficiaries: *Roberts* v *Gill & Co* [2010] UKSC 22; [2010] 2 WLR 1227, Supreme Court; *Colour Quest Ltd* v *Total Downstream UK Plc* [2010] EWCA Civ 180; [2010] 3 All ER 793, Court of Appeal).

Re Montagu's ST

[1987] Ch 264

> SIR ROBERT MEGARRY V-C: The equitable doctrine of tracing and the imposition of a constructive trust by reason of the knowing receipt of trust property are governed by different rules and must be kept distinct. Tracing is primarily a means of determining the rights of property, whereas the imposition of a constructive trust creates personal obligations which go beyond mere property rights.

SECTION 2: TRUSTEE DE SON TORT

Mara v Browne

(1896) 1 Ch 199, Court of Appeal

> SMITH LJ: ... if one, not being a trustee and not having authority from a trustee, takes upon himself to intermeddle with the trust matters or to do acts characteristic of the office of trustee, he may thereby make himself what is called in law a trustee of his own wrong—i.e. a *trustee de son tort*, or, as it is also termed, a constructive trustee.

SECTION 3: KNOWING RECEIPT

A person will be personally liable in equity if he receives property for his own benefit knowing that someone else is entitled to the property under a trust. In *Agip (Africa) Ltd v Jackson*, Millett J stated that a recipient would not be liable as a constructive trustee for knowing receipt until they *know* about the breach of trust. This was confirmed in *Papamichael* v *National Westminster Bank plc* [2003] 1 Lloyd's Rep 341, 375 and *Criterion Properties plc* v *Stratford UK Properties LLC* [2003] 1 WLR 2108, CA.

Bank of Credit and Commerce International (Overseas) Ltd v Akindele

[2001] Ch 437, Court of Appeal

Facts: The liquidators of the bank had sought to recover US$6.79 million from the defendant on the basis of personal liability for assistance in a breach of trust or wrongful receipt of trust property. In 1985, A had advanced US$10 million to a company controlled by the bank under a false loan agreement. In 1988, A received US$16.79 million under the agreement. The claimants argued that A's dishonesty could be inferred from his knowledge of the artificial character of the loan and from his receipt of an unusually high rate of return of 15 per cent compound interest.

Held: At first instance, the court dismissed the claim on the ground that the claimant had failed to prove that the defendant had been dishonest. The Court of Appeal held that it is not necessary to prove that a defendant was dishonest in order to fix him with liability for knowing receipt, but dismissed the appeal on the ground that the state of the defendant's knowledge in 1985 was not such as to make it unconscionable for him to enter into the transaction. Furthermore, it was not unconscionable for him to receive the benefits of the transaction in 1988, notwithstanding the rumours that were then circulating about the integrity of the bank's management. There was nothing to alert the defendant to the fact that his transaction, entered into three years earlier, might be tainted.

NOURSE LJ: This is a claim by liquidators under both the knowing assistance and knowing receipt heads of constructive trust. The argument in this court has been mainly directed to two questions arising in relation to liability under the latter head. What must be the recipient's state of knowledge? Must he be dishonest? ...

Knowing receipt

The essential requirements of knowing receipt were stated by Hoffmann LJ in *El Ajou* v *Dollar Land Holdings plc* [1994] 2 All ER 685, 700:

> For this purpose the plaintiff must show, first, a disposal of his assets in breach of fiduciary duty; secondly, the beneficial receipt by the defendant of assets which are traceable as representing the assets of the plaintiff; and thirdly, knowledge on the part of the defendant that the assets he received are traceable to a breach of fiduciary duty.

In the present case the first two requirements were satisfied in relation to the defendant's receipt of the US$16.679m paid to him pursuant to the divestiture agreement ...

So far as the law is concerned, the comprehensive arguments of Mr Sheldon and Mr Moss have demonstrated that there are two questions which, though closely related, are distinct: first, what, in this context, is meant by knowledge; second, is it necessary for the recipient to act dishonestly? Because the answer to it is the simpler, the convenient course is to deal with the second of those questions first.

Knowing receipt—dishonesty

As appears from the penultimate sentence of his judgment, Carnwath J proceeded on an assumption that dishonesty in one form or another was the essential foundation of the claimants' case, whether in knowing assistance or knowing receipt. That was no doubt caused by the acceptance before him (though not at any higher level) by Mr Sheldon, recorded at p. 677f, that the thrust of the recent authorities at first instance was that the recipient's state of knowledge must fall into one of the first three categories listed by Peter Gibson J in *Baden* v *Société Générale pour Favoriser le Développment du Commerce et de l'Industrie en France SA* (Note) [1993] 1 WLR 509, 575–76, on which basis, said Carnwath J, it was doubtful whether the test differed materially in practice from that for knowing assistance. However, the assumption on which the judge proceeded, derived as I believe from an omission to distinguish between the questions of knowledge and dishonesty, was incorrect in law. While a knowing recipient will often be found to have acted dishonestly, it has never been a prerequisite of the liability that he should.

An authoritiative decision on this question, the complexity of whose subject transactions has sometimes caused it to be overlooked in this particular context, is *Belmont Finance Corpn Ltd* v *Williams Furniture Ltd (No. 2)* [1980] 1 All ER 393, where the plaintiff ('Belmont') was the wholly-owned subsidiary of the second defendant ('City'), which in turn was the wholly-owned subsidiary of the first defendant ('Williams'). The chairman of all three companies and the sole effective force in the management of their affairs was Mr John James.

Reduced to its essentials, what had happened there was that the shareholders of a fourth company ('Maximum') had agreed to sell its shares to Belmont for £500,000 and to buy the share capital of Belmont from City for £489,000, a transaction which, as carried out, constituted a contravention of section 54 of the Companies Act 1948 (prohibition of provision of financial assistance by a company for the purchase of its own shares) and was thus a misapplication of Belmont's funds.

Belmont having subsequently become insolvent, its receiver obtained an independent valuation of the shares in Maximum as at the date of the transaction which suggested that, instead of being worth £500,000, they were only worth some £60,000. The receiver brought an action in Belmont's name principally against Williams, City and the shareholders of Maximum, claiming that they were liable to Belmont, first, for damages for conspiracy and, secondly, as constructive trustees on the grounds of both knowing assistance and knowing receipt. At the trial, Foster J found that Mr James genuinely believed that to buy the capital of Maximum for £500,000 was a good commercial proposition for Belmont. He held that there had been no contravention of section 54 and dismissed the action.

On Belmont's successful appeal to this court Buckley LJ is recorded, at p. 403a–b, as having pointed out that Mr James had genuinely believed that the transaction was a good commercial proposition for Belmont without having any good grounds for that belief. He continued:

> After careful consideration I do not feel that we should be justified in disturbing the judge's finding that Mr James genuinely believed that the agreement was a good commercial proposition for Belmont. It was a belief which, on his view of the commercial aspects of the case, Mr James could have sincerely held.

Having observed, at p. 404e, that Mr James, as a director of both Williams and City, knew perfectly well what the objects of the transaction were, that other officers of City had the same knowledge and that their knowledge must be 'imputed' to the respective companies, and having referred, at p. 405c, to the judgment of Lord Selborne LC in *Barnes v Addy* (1874) LR 9 Ch App 244, 251–52, Buckley LJ dealt with the claim in constructive trust [1980] 1 All ER 393, 405:

> In the present case, the payment of the £500,000 by Belmont to [the shareholders of Maximum], being an unlawful contravention of section 54, was a misapplication of Belmont's money and was in breach of the duties of the directors of Belmont. £489,000 of the £500,000 so misapplied found their way into the hands of City with City's knowledge of the whole circumstances of the transaction. It must follow, in my opinion, that City is accountable to Belmont as a constructive trustee of the £489,000 under the first of Lord Selborne LC's two heads. There remains the question whether City is chargeable as a constructive trustee under Lord Selborne LC's second head on the ground that Belmont's directors were guilty of dishonesty in buying the shares of Maximum and that City with knowledge of the facts assisted them in that dishonest design. As I understand Lord Selborne LC's second head, a stranger to a trust notwithstanding that he may not have received any of the trust fund which has been misapplied will be treated as accountable as a constructive trustee if he has knowingly participated in a dishonest design on the part of the trustees to misapply the fund; he must himself have been in some way a party to the dishonesty of the trustees. It follows from what I have already held that the directors of Belmont were guilty of misfeasance but not that they acted dishonestly.

Goff LJ also held that City was liable in knowing receipt: see pp 410–12. Waller LJ did not add anything of his own on the question of constructive trust. Accordingly, though the claim in knowing assistance failed because the directors of Belmont did not act dishonestly, the claim in knowing receipt succeeded. I will return to that decision when dealing with the question of knowledge.

Belmont Finance Corpn Ltd v Williams Furniture Ltd (No. 2) [1980] 1 All ER 393 is clear authority for the proposition that dishonesty is not a necessary ingredient of liability in knowing receipt. There have been other, more recent, judicial pronouncements to the same effect. Thus in *Polly Peck International plc v Nadir (No. 2)* [1992] 4 All ER 769, 777d Scott LJ said that liability in a knowing receipt case did not require that the misapplication of the trust funds should be fraudulent. While in theory it is possible for a misapplication not to be fraudulent and the recipient to be dishonest, in practice such a combination must be rare. Similarly, in *Agip (Africa) Ltd v Jackson* [1990] Ch 265, 292a Millett J said that in knowing receipt it was immaterial whether the breach of trust was fraudulent or not. The point was made most clearly by Vinelott J in *Eagle Trust plc v SBC Securities Ltd* [1993] 1 WLR 484, 497:

> What the decision in *Belmont (No. 2)* [1980] 1 All ER 393 shows is that in a 'knowing receipt' case it is only necessary to show that the defendant knew that the moneys paid to him were trust moneys and of circumstances which made the payment a misapplication of them. Unlike a 'knowing assistance' case it is not necessary, and never has been necessary, to show that the defendant was in any sense a participator in a fraud.

Knowing receipt—the authorities on knowledge

With the proliferation in the last 20 years or so of cases in which the misapplied assets of companies have come into the hands of third parties, there has been a sustained judicial and extrajudicial debate as to the knowledge on the part of the recipient which is required in order to found liability in knowing receipt. Expressed in its simplest terms, the question is whether the recipient must have actual knowledge (or the equivalent) that the assets received are traceable to a breach of trust or whether constructive knowledge is enough. The instinctive approach of most equity judges, especially in this court, has been to assume that constructive knowledge is enough. But there is now a series of decisions of eminent first instance judges who, after considering the question in greater depth, have come to the contrary conclusion, at all events when commercial transactions are in point. In the Commonwealth, on the other hand, the preponderance of authority has been in favour of the view that constructive knowledge is enough ...

[His Lordship referred to the following English authorities: *Karak Rubber Co. Ltd v Burden (No. 2)* [1972] 1 WLR 602, 632h; *Belmont Finance Corpn Ltd v Williams Furniture Ltd (No. 2)* [1980] 1 All ER 393, 405, CA; *Rolled Steel Products (Holdings) Ltd v British Steel Corporation* [1986] Ch 246, 306–7, CA; In *Agip (Africa) Ltd v Jackson* [1990] Ch 265, 291; In *Houghton v Fayers* [2000] 1 BCLC 511, 516, CA]

Collectively, those observations might be thought to provide strong support for the view that constructive knowledge is enough. But it must at once be said that in each of the three cases in this court (including, despite some apparent uncertainty in the judgment of Goff LJ in *Belmont Finance Corpn Ltd v Williams Furniture Ltd (No. 2)* [1980] 1 All ER 393, 412f) actual knowledge was found and, further, that the decisions in *Karak Rubber Co. Ltd* v *Burden (No. 2)* [1972] 1 WLR 602 and *Agip (Africa) Ltd* v *Jackson* [1990] Ch 265 were based on knowing assistance, not knowing receipt. Thus in none of the five cases was it necessary for the question to be examined in any depth and there appears to be no case in which such an examination has been conducted in this court. The groundwork has been done in other cases at first instance. I will refer to those of them in which the question has been considered in depth.

The seminal judgment, characteristically penetrative in its treatment of authority and, in the best sense, argumentative, is that of Sir Robert Megarry V-C in *In re Montagu's Settlement Trusts* [1987] Ch 264. It was he who first plumbed the distinction between notice and knowledge. It was he who, building on a passage in the judgment of this court in *In re Diplock* [1948] Ch 465, 478–79, first emphasised the fundamental difference between the questions which arise in respect of the doctrine of purchaser without notice on the one hand and the doctrine of constructive trusts on the other. Reading from his earlier judgment in the same case, he said [1987] Ch 264, 278:

> The former is concerned with the question whether a person takes property subject to or free from some equity. The latter is concerned with whether or not a person is to have imposed upon him the personal burdens and obligations of trusteeship. I do not see why one of the touch-stones for determining the burdens on property should be the same as that for deciding whether to impose a personal obligation on a [person]. The cold calculus of constructive and imputed notice does not seem to me to be an appropriate instrument for deciding whether a [person's] conscience is sufficiently affected for it to be right to bind him by the obligations of a constructive trustee.

He added that there is more to being made a trustee than merely taking property subject to an equity.

The practical importance of that distinction had been explained by Sir Robert Megarry V-C in his earlier judgment. The question in that case was whether the widow and executrix of the will of the 10th Duke of Manchester was liable to account to the 11th Duke in respect of certain settled chattels or the proceeds of sale thereof. Having found that the 10th Duke had had no knowledge that the chattels received by him were still subject to any trust and that he believed that they had been lawfully and properly released to him by the trustees, Sir Robert Megarry V-C continued, at p. 272:

> If liability as a constructive trustee depended on his knowledge, then he was not liable as a constructive trustee, and his estate is not liable for any chattels that have been disposed of, as distinct from any traceable proceeds of them. Even if he was not a constructive trustee and was a mere volunteer, his estate is liable to yield up any chattels that remain, or the traceable proceeds of any that have gone … But unless he was a constructive trustee, there appears to be no liability if the chattels have gone and there are no traceable proceeds.

Sir Robert Megarry V-C summarised his conclusions in eight subparagraphs, at p. 285. I read the first three:

(1) The equitable doctrine of tracing and the imposition of a constructive trust by reason of the knowing receipt of trust property are governed by different rules and must be kept distinct. Tracing is primarily a means of determining the rights of property, whereas the imposition of a constructive trust creates personal obligations that go beyond mere property rights.

(2) In considering whether a constructive trust has arisen in a case of the knowing receipt of trust property, the basic question is whether the conscience of the recipient is sufficiently affected to justify the imposition of such a trust.

(3) Whether a constructive trust arises in such a case primarily depends on the knowledge of the recipient, and not on notice to him; and for clarity it is desirable to use the word 'knowledge' and avoid the word 'notice' in such cases.

The effect of Sir Robert Megarry V-C's decision, broadly stated, was that, in order to establish liability in knowing receipt, the recipient must have actual knowledge (or the equivalent) that the assets received are traceable to a breach of trust and that constructive knowledge is not enough.

In *Eagle Trust plc* v *SBC Securities Ltd* [1993] 1 WLR 484, 503e Vinelott J did not think it would be right to found a decision that the statement of claim in that case disclosed no cause of action solely on the authority of *In re Montagu's Settlement Trusts* [1987] Ch 264. However, on the ground that he (unlike Sir Robert Megarry V-C) was dealing with a commercial transaction, he arrived at the same conclusion and held that in such a transaction constructive knowledge is not enough. He cited [1993] 1 WLR 484, 504d, a well known passage in the judgment of Lindley LJ in *Manchester Trust* v *Furness* [1895] 2 QB 539, 545, the latter part of which reads thus:

> In dealing with estates in land title is everything, and it can be leisurely investigated; in commercial transactions possession is everything, and there is no time to investigate title; and if we were to extend the doctrine of constructive notice to commercial transactions we should be doing infinite mischief and paralysing the trade of the country.

The decision of Vinelott J was followed by Knox J in *Cowan de Groot Properties Ltd* v *Eagle Trust plc* [1992] 4 All ER 700 (another case of a commercial transaction) and the decisions of both of them by Arden J at the trial of the action in Eagle Trust case: see *Eagle Trust plc* v *SBC Securities Ltd (No. 2)* [1996] 1 BCLC 121.

We were also referred to three decisions in New Zealand and one in Canada. In each of *Westpac Banking Corpn* v *Savin* [1985] 2 NZLR 41; *Equiticorp Industries Group Ltd* v *Hawkins* [1991] 3 NZLR 700 and *Lankshean* v *ANZ Banking Group (New Zealand) Ltd* [1993] 1 NZLR 481 the preferred view was that constructive knowledge was enough, although in the last-named case the point went by concession. All of them were cases of commercial transactions. In *Westpac Banking Corpn* v *Savin* [1985] 2 NZLR 41, a decision of the Court of Appeal, Richardson J, having expressed a provisional preference for the view that constructive knowledge was enough, said at p. 53:

> Clearly courts would not readily import a duty to inquire in the case of commercial transactions where they must be conscious of the seriously inhibiting effects of a wide application of the doctrine. Nevertheless there must be cases where there is no justification on the known facts for allowing a commercial man who has received funds paid to him in breach of trust to plead the shelter of the exigencies of commercial life.

In *Citadel General Assurance Co* v *Lloyds Bank Canada* (1997) 152 DLR (4th) 411, another case of a commercial transaction, the Supreme Court of Canada held, as a matter of decision, that constructive knowledge was enough.

The *Baden* case

It will have been observed that up to this stage I have made no more than a passing reference to the five-fold categorisation of knowledge accepted by Peter Gibson J in *Baden* v *Société Générale pour Favoriser le Développment du Commerce et de l'Industrie en France SA* (Note) [1993] 1 WLR 509, 575–76:

> (i) actual knowledge; (ii) wilfully shutting one's eyes to the obvious; (iii) wilfully and recklessly failing to make such inquiries as an honest and reasonable man would make; (iv) knowledge of circumstances which would indicate the facts to an honest and reasonable man; (v) knowledge of circumstances which will put an honest and reasonable man on inquiry. Reference to the categorisation has been made in most of the knowing receipt cases to which I have referred from *In re Montagu's Settlement Trusts* [1987] Ch 264 onwards. In many of them it has been influential in the decision. In general, the first three categories have been taken to constitute actual knowledge (or its equivalent) and the last two constructive knowledge.

Two important points must be made about the *Baden* categorisation. First, it appears to have been propounded by counsel for the plaintiffs, accepted by counsel for the defendant and then put to the judge on an agreed basis. Secondly, though both counsel accepted that all five categories of knowledge were relevant and neither sought to submit that there was any distinction for that purpose between knowing receipt and knowing assistance (a view with which the judge expressed his agreement: see [1993] 1 WLR 509, 582e–f), the claim in constructive trust was based squarely on knowing assistance and not on knowing receipt: see p. 572d. In the circumstances, whatever may have been agreed between counsel, it is natural to assume that the categorisation was not formulated with knowing receipt primarily in mind. This, I think, may be confirmed by the references to 'an honest and reasonable man' in categories (iv) and (v). Moreover, in *Agip (Africa) Ltd* v *Jackson* [1990] Ch 265, 293 Millett J warned against over-refinement or a too ready assumption that categories (iv) and (v) are necessarily cases of constructive knowledge only, reservations which were shared by Knox J in *Cowan de Groot Properties Ltd* v *Eagle Trust plc* [1992] 4 All ER 700, 761g.

Knowing receipt—the recipient's state of knowledge

In *Royal Brunei Airlines Sdn Bhd* v *Tan* [1995] 2 AC 378, which is now the leading authority on knowing assistance, Lord Nicholls of Birkenhead, in delivering the judgment of the Privy Council, said, at p. 392g, that 'knowingly was better avoided as a defining ingredient of the liability, and that in that context the

Baden categorisation was best forgotten. Although my own view is that the categorisation is often helpful in identifying different states of knowledge which may or may not result in a finding of dishonesty for the purposes of knowing assistance, I have grave doubts about its utility in cases of knowing receipt. Quite apart from its origins in a context of knowing assistance and the reservations of Knox and Millett JJ, any categorisation is of little value unless the purpose it is to serve is adequately defined, whether it be fivefold, as in the *Baden* case [1993] 1 WLR 509, or twofold, as in the classical division between actual and constructive knowledge, a division which has itself become blurred in recent authorities.

What then, in the context of knowing receipt, is the purpose to be served by a categorisation of knowledge? It can only be to enable the court of determine whether, in the words of Buckley LJ in *Belmont Finance Corpn Ltd v Williams Furniture Ltd (No. 2)* [1980] 1 All ER 393, 405, the recipient can 'conscientiously retain [the] funds against the company' or, in the words of Sir Robert Megarry V-C in *In re Montagu's Settlement Trusts* [1987] Ch 264, 273, '[the recipient's] conscience is sufficiently affected for it to be right to bind him by the obligations of a constructive trustee'. But, if that is the purpose, there is no need for categorisation. All that is necessary is that the recipient's state of knowledge should be such as to make it unconscionable for him to retain the benefit of the receipt.

For these reasons I have come to the view that, just as there is now a single test of dishonesty for knowing assistance, so ought there to be a single test of knowledge for knowing receipt. The recipient's state of knowledge must be such as to make it unconscionable for him to retain the benefit of the receipt. A test in that form, though it cannot, any more than any other, avoid difficulties of application, ought to avoid those of definition and allocation to which the previous categorisations have led. Moreover, it should better enable the courts to give commonsense decisions in the commercial context in which claims in knowing receipt are now frequently made, paying equal regard to the wisdom of Lindley LJ on the one hand and of Richardson J on the other.

Knowing receipt—a footnote

We were referred in argument to 'Knowing Receipt: The Need for a New Landmark', an essay by Lord Nicholls of Birkenhead in *Restitution Past, Present and Future* (1998) p. 231, a work of insight and scholarship taking forward the writings of academic authors, in particular those of Professor Birks, Professor Burrows and Professor Gareth Jones. It is impossible to do justice to such a work within the compass of a judgment such as this. Most pertinent for present purposes is the suggestion made by Lord Nicholls, at p. 238, in reference to the decision of the House of Lords in *Lipkin Gorman v Karpnale Ltd* [1991] 2 AC 548:

> In this respect equity should now follow the law. Restitutionary liability, applicable regardless of fault but subject to a defence of change of position, would be a better-tailored response to the underlying mischief of misapplied property than personal liability which is exclusively fault-based. Personal liability would flow from having received the property of another, from having been unjustly enriched at the expense of another. It would be triggered by the mere fact of receipt, thus recognising the endurance of property rights. But fairness would be ensured by the need to identify a gain, and by making change of position available as a defence in suitable cases when, for instance, the recipient had changed his position in reliance on the receipt.

Lord Nicholls goes on to examine the *In re Diplock* [1948] Ch 465 principle, suggesting, at p. 241, that it could be reshaped by being extended to all trusts but in a form modified to take proper account of the decision in *Lipkin Gorman v Karpnale Ltd* [1991] 2 AC 548.

No argument before us was based on the suggestions made in Lord Nicholls's essay. Indeed, at this level of decision, it would have been a fruitless exercise. We must continue to do our best with the accepted formulation of the liability in knowing receipt, seeking to simplify and improve it where we may. While in general it may be possible to sympathise with a tendency to subsume a further part of our law of restitution under the principles of unjust enrichment, I beg leave to doubt whether strict liability coupled with a change of position defence would be preferable to fault-based liability in many commercial transactions, for example where, as here, the receipt is of a company's funds which have been misapplied by its directors. Without having heard argument it is unwise to be dogmatic, but in such a case it would appear to be commercially unworkable and contrary to the spirit of the rule in *Royal British Bank v Turquand* (1856) 6 E & B 327 that, simply on proof of an internal misapplication of the company's funds, the burden should shift to the recipient to defend the receipt either by a change of position or perhaps in some other way. Moreover, if the circumstances of the receipt are such as to make it unconscionable for the recipient to retain the benefit of it, there is an obvious difficulty in saying that it is equitable for a change of position to afford him a defence.

Knowing receipt—the facts of the present case

... There having been no evidence that the defendant was aware of the internal arrangements within BCCI which led to the payment to him of the US$16.679m pursuant to the divestiture agreement, did the additional knowledge which he acquired between July 1985 and December 1988 make it unconscionable for him to retain the benefit of the receipt? In my judgment it did not. The additional knowledge went to the general reputation of the BCCI group from late 1987 onwards. It was not a sufficient reason for questioning the propriety of a particular transaction entered into more than two years earlier, at a time when no one outside BCCI had reason to doubt the integrity of its management and in a form which the defendant had no reason to question. The judge said that the defendant was entitled to take steps to protect his own interest, and that there was nothing dishonest in his seeking to enforce the 1985 agreement. Nor was there anything unconscionable in his seeking to do so. Equally, had I thought that that was still the appropriate test, I would have held that the defendant did not have actual or constructive knowledge that his receipt of the US$6.79m was traceable to a breach or breaches of fiduciary duty by Mr Naqvi, Mr Hafeez and Mr Kazmi.

■ QUESTIONS

1. Is the equitable jurisdiction to prevent unconscionable reliance on a legal right or power an appropriate basis, as held in *BCCI (Overseas) Ltd* v *Akindele*, for establishing liability for knowing receipt of trust property? Does it erroneously assume that the defendant has some right in or power over the property which is being abused?

2. Should a recipient of trust property in breach of trust be strictly liable to account for it to the trust beneficiary, or should liability be restricted to cases in which the receipt was dishonest, or to situations in which it would be unconscionable not to account?

NOTES

1. After *Akindele*, the test for liability was whether the recipient's state of knowledge of the breach of trust was such as to make it 'unconscionable for him to retain the benefit of the receipt'. (See *Arthur v AG Turks and Caicos Islands* [2012] UKPC 30, Privy Council; *Armstrong DLW GmbH* v *Winnington Networks Ltd* [2012] EWHC 10 (Ch); [2012] 3 WLR 835; *Glen Dimplex Home Appliances Ltd* v *Smith* [2011] EWHC 3392 (Comm)). In the House of Lords in *Criterion Properties Plc v Stratford UK Properties LLC* [2004] 1 WLR 1846, Lord Scott of Foscote acknowledged that the law relating to knowing receipt of assets may be applicable where assets have been transferred by a fully executed contract. Lord Scott of Foscote dismissed the appeal in *Criterion* on the basis that the contract in the case was merely executory (the subject of the contract had not yet been transferred). However, Lord Nicholls (who supports strict liability for receipt of trust property) expressed his opinion that the Court of Appeal in *Akindele* had been wrong to consider the law of knowing receipt in relation to the fully executed contractual transfer of assets in that case.

2. Liability for knowing receipt probably requires more than mere possession of the trust property. In *Agip (Africa) Ltd* v *Jackson* [1990] 1 Ch 265, Millett J said of liability for knowing receipt that 'the recipient must have received the property for his own use and benefit'. It followed that a bank was not liable as a knowing recipient merely because money had been deposited in a customer's account. Professor Birks has argued that a stranger who receives another's wealth, whether in the form of equitable or legal benefits, is unjustly enriched and personally liable to make restitution to the person at whose expense the unjust enrichment was acquired. The liability to make restitution is strict, but subject to the usual restitutionary defences including the recipient's innocent change of position and the claimant's consent (Peter Birks, 'Receipt', in P. Birks and A. Pretto (eds), *Breach of Trust* (Oxford: Hart Publishing, 2002); see also (1989) 105 *LQR* 352 and 528; [1989] *LMCLQ* 296). *Charter plc and another* v *City Index Ltd* [2007] 1 WLR 26, ChD, confirms that the remedy for knowing receipt is compensatory 'notwithstanding that it may also be described as restitutionary'.

3. For the purposes of liability for knowing receipt, the defendant will not be deemed to 'know' facts which he has genuinely forgotten. (*AON Pension Trustees Ltd* v *MCP Pension Trustees Ltd* [2010] EWCA Civ 377; [2011] 3 WLR 455, applying *Re Montagu's Settlement Trusts* [1987] 1 Ch 264, 284.)

4. Despite the *Akindele* approach, which judges the defendant according to the 'unconscionability' of their conduct, some courts still prefer the older formulation which asks whether the

defendant's conscience became 'sufficiently affected for it to be right to bind him by the obligations of a constructive trustee'. (*Relfo Ltd (In Liquidation)* v *Varsani* [2012] EWHC 2168 (Ch), applying *Re Montagu's Settlement Trusts* [1987] Ch 264.)

5. In *Goldspan Ltd* v *Patel* [2012] EWHC 1447 (Ch) a third party recipient was permitted to retain £100,000 received as part of a money laundering transaction because the recipient had been owed £100,000 by the transferor. Suppose that, in another case, a fake 'loan' were fabricated as part of a money laundering scam? Do decisions such as this have the potential to play into the hands of fraudsters?

L. D. Smith, 'Unjust Enrichment, Property and the Structure of Trusts'
(2000) 116 *LQR* 412, pp. 430–1

The argument which suggests that personal claims based on receipt of trust property must line up with the strict liability in Lipkin Gorman seems to ignore a very basic truth: a beneficiary's interest under a trust is not legal ownership. Equitable proprietary rights are not protected in the same way as legal ones. In general, they are protected less well. They are always subject to destruction by bona fide purchase of a legal interest or overreaching, and wrongful interference with them is dependent on fault. Beneficiaries cannot generally sue in conversion when a defendant interferes with the trust property; nor are they owed the duties of care which are owed to the legal owner. The argument for strict liability would make the most sense as part of an agenda which sought the abolition of the trust, and the return to a regime in which only one person can claim to be the owner of a given asset. That would be an odd agenda to pursue, when civilian systems all over the world, aware of the flexibility which the trust device offers, are introducing it in various forms. Certainly as the law is now, the beneficiary's interest under a trust attracts incidents different from legal ownership. It is not clear that it would make sense to abolish some of the characteristics of equitable proprietary rights while leaving others intact. If liability for receiving trust property is strict, why should equitable interests be subject to destruction by the defence of bona fide purchase of a legal interest?

The trustee is (usually) the legal owner. If he makes, for example, a mistaken payment, or is defrauded like the plaintiffs in Lipkin Gorman, he will have at his disposal all of the strict liability claims which protect his legal title and protect him from defective transfers. On the other hand, he might not have a claim; he might have given trust money away in breach of trust. But it does not follow from this that we must give the beneficiaries the same rights that the trustee would have had, had he acted properly. It is in the nature of the trust institution that beneficiaries are vulnerable to breaches of trust, in ways which they would not be if they were the legal owners of the trust property. To complain about this is to complain about the incidents of the institution of the trust.

NOTES

1. Professor Smith accepts that there can be a personal, strict, unjust enrichment claim, not at the moment of receipt, but in the event of the recipient subsequently consuming the trust property or otherwise acting to deprive the beneficiary whilst enriching himself. He argues that this is the rule at common law, too, contrary to the usual assumption that liability at common law is strict at the moment of mere receipt. See L. D. Smith, 'Restitution: The Heart of Corrective Justice' (2001) 79 *Texas L Rev* 2115, pp. 2172–4.

2. There is, it is submitted, one context in which proof of fault should certainly be a prerequisite to liability for receipt of trust property. Namely, where the claimant is claiming under a trust which was a bare trust at the time of misapplication of the trust property. In such a case the claimant, as beneficiary of a bare trust, had the power to bring the trust to an end before the misapplication of the fund. The beneficiary must therefore be taken to have run the risk of misapplication. Having run the risk that third parties might receive misapplied trust property, the onus should be on the claimant to prove that the recipient received with knowledge of the misapplication. See G. Watt, 'Personal Liability for Receipt of Trust Property: Allocating the Risks', in E. Cooke (ed.), *Modern Studies in Property Law—Volume III* (Oxford: Hart Publishing, 2005), pp. 91–110. This concern for the allocation of risk and responsibility explains why in one recent case there was an attempt to shift responsibility to the beneficiaries of a pension trust by arguing that they held their shares as sole beneficiaries under bare sub-trusts (*Dalriada Trustees Ltd* v *Woodward* [2012] EWHC 21626 (Ch)). That argument was rejected in favour of the more orthodox conclusion that beneficiaries hold shares in a single trust fund.

3. In Australia the argument in favour of strict liability based on the reversal of unjust enrichment has been expressly disapproved (*Farah Constructions Pty Ltd* v *Say-Dee Pty Ltd* [2007] HCA 22).

4. In a note on *City Index Ltd* v *Gawler* [2007] EWCA Civ 1382, [2008] Ch 313 CA (Civ Div), Simon Gardner argues that knowing receipt should be seen to be 'simply the usual liability for failure to preserve trust property, applicable to all trustees, given particular application to those who are trustees because they receive illicitly transferred trust property' (2009) 125 *LQR* 20, p. 23. In the event, the case did not proceed to the House of Lords, so an opportunity to clarify the law relating to knowing receipt was lost.

P. D. Finn, 'The Liability of Third Parties for Knowing Receipt or Assistance'

in D. W. N. Waters (ed.), *Equity, Fiduciaries and Trusts* (Ontario: Carswell, 1993), p. 195 and pp. 210–11

I would seriously question ... the ... appropriateness in the present context of insisting today upon property protection with the consequential imposition of a near strict liability upon a third party who, though not guilty of any unconscientious conduct in the receipt or later dealing with the property, has had the misfortune to deal with a disloyal fiduciary. Why that third party and not the fiduciary's beneficiaries should be asked, in effect, to bear the risk of that disloyalty ... is not at all apparent to this writer.

SECTION 4: DISHONEST ASSISTANCE

Royal Brunei Airlines Sdn Bhd v *Philip Tan Kok Ming*

[1995] 2 AC 378, Privy Council

Facts: An insolvent travel agency owed money to the claimant airline. The present action was brought against the principal director and shareholder in the travel agency. The claimants sought to fix the defendant with liability as a constructive trustee on the basis of the defendant's knowing assistance in a dishonest and fraudulent design. The 'design' was the use of the airline's moneys by the travel agency for its own business purposes in breach of the trust under which those moneys were held.

Held: The defendant would be liable on the basis of his 'dishonest assistance in or procurement of the breach of trust'.

LORD NICHOLLS OF BIRKENHEAD: The proper role of equity in commercial transactions is a topical question. Increasingly plaintiffs have recourse to equity for an effective remedy when the person in default, typically a company, is insolvent. Plaintiffs seek to obtain relief from others who were involved in the transactions, such as directors of the company or its bankers or its legal or other advisers. They seek to fasten fiduciary obligations directly onto the company's officers or agents or advisers, or to have them held personally liable for assisting the company in breaches of trust or fiduciary obligations. This is such a case. An insolvent travel agent company owed money to an airline. The airline seeks a remedy against the travel agent's principal director and shareholder. Its claim is based on the much-quoted *dictum* of Lord Selborne LC, sitting in the Court of Appeal in Chancery, in *Barnes* v *Addy* (1874) LR 9 Ch App 244 at 251–52:

That responsibility [of a trustee] may no doubt be extended in equity to others who are not properly trustees, if they are found ... actually participating in any fraudulent conduct of the trustee to the injury of the *cestui que trust*. But ... strangers are not to be made constructive trustees merely because they act as the agents of trustees in transactions within their legal powers, transactions, perhaps of which a Court of Equity may disapprove, unless those agents receive and become chargeable with some part of the trust property, or unless they assist with knowledge in a dishonest and fraudulent design on the part of the trustees.

In the conventional shorthand the first of these two circumstances in which third parties (non-trustees) may become liable to account in equity is 'knowing receipt', as distinct from the second where liability arises from 'knowing receipt', as distinct from the second where liability arises from 'knowing assistance'.

Stated even more shortly, the first limb of Lord Selborne LC's formulation is concerned with the liability of a person as a *recipient* of trust property or its traceable proceeds. The second limb is concerned with what, for want of a better compendious description, can be called the liability of an *accessory* to a trustee's breach of trust. Liability as an accessory is not dependent upon receipt of trust property. It arises even though no trust property has reached the hands of the accessory. It is a form of secondary liability in the sense that it only arises where there has been a breach of trust. In the present case the plaintiff relies on the accessory limb. The particular point in issue arises from the expression 'a dishonest and fraudulent design on the part of the trustees' ...

The honest trustee and the dishonest third party

It must be noted at once that there is a difficulty with the approach adopted on this point in the *Belmont* case. Take the simple example of an honest trustee and a dishonest third party. Take a case where a dishonest solicitor persuades a trustee to apply trust property in a way the trustee honestly believes is permissible but which the solicitor knows full well is a clear breach of trust. The solicitor deliberately conceals this from the trustee. In consequence, the beneficiaries suffer a substantial loss. It cannot be right that in such a case the accessory liability principle would be inapplicable because of the innocence of the trustee. In ordinary parlance, the beneficiaries have been defrauded by the solicitor. If there is to be an accessory liability principle at all, whereby in appropriate circumstances beneficiaries may have direct recourse against a third party, the principle must surely be applicable in such a case, just as much as in a case where both the trustee and the third party have been dishonest. Indeed, if anything, the case for liability of the dishonest third party seems stronger where the trustee is innocent, because in such a case the third party alone was dishonest and that was the case of the subsequent misapplication of the trust property.

The position would be the same if, instead of *procuring* the breach the third party dishonestly *assisted* in the breach ... what matters is the state of mind of the third party sought to be made liable, not the state of mind of the trustee ... there has been a tendency to cite, interpret and apply Lord Selborne LC's formulation as though it were a statute. This has particularly been so with the accessory limb of Lord Selborne's apothegm. This approach has been inimical to analysis of the underlying concept. Working within this constraint, the courts have found themselves wrestling with the interpretation of the individual ingredients, especially 'knowingly' but also 'dishonest and fraudulent design on the part of the trustees', without examining the underlying reason why a third party who has received no trust property is being made liable at all. One notable exception is the judgment of Thomas J in *Powell* v *Thompson* [1991] 1 NZLR 597 at 610–615. On this point he observed (at 613):

> 'Once a breach of trust has been committed, the commission of which has involved a third party, the question which arises is one as between the beneficiary and that third party. If the third party's conduct has been unconscionable, then irrespective of the degree of impropriety in the trustee's conduct, the third party is liable to be held accountable to the beneficiary as if he or she were a trustee.'

To resolve this issue it is necessary to take an overall look at the accessory liability principle. A conclusion cannot be reached on the nature of the breach of trust which may trigger accessory liability without at the same time considering the other ingredients including, in particular, the state of mind of the third party. It is not necessary, however, to look even more widely and consider the essential ingredients of recipient liability. The issue on this appeal concerns only the accessory liability principle. Different considerations apply to the two heads of liability. Recipient liability is restitution-based, accessory liability is not.

No liability

The starting point for any analysis must be to consider the extreme possibility: that a third party who does not receive trust property ought never to be liable directly to the beneficiaries merely because he assisted the trustee to commit a breach of trust or procured him to do so. This possibility can be dismissed summarily. On this the position which the law has long adopted is clear and makes good sense. Stated in the simplest terms, a trust is a relationship which exists when one person holds property on behalf of another. If, for his own purposes, a third party deliberately interferes in that relationship by assisting the trustee in depriving the beneficiary of the property held for him by the trustee, the beneficiary should be able to look for recompense to the third party as well as the trustee. Affording the beneficiary a remedy against the third party serves the dual purpose of making good the beneficiary's loss should the trustee lack financial means and imposing a liability which will discourage others from behaving in a similar fashion ...

Strict liability

The other extreme possibility can also be rejected out of hand. This is the case where a third party deals with a trustee without knowing, or having any reason to suspect, that he is a trustee. Or the case where a third party is aware he is dealing with a trustee but has no reason to know or suspect that their transaction is inconsistent with the terms of the trust. The law has never gone so far as to give a beneficiary a remedy against a non-recipient third party in such circumstances. Within defined limits, proprietary rights, whether legal or equitable, endure against third parties who were unaware of their existence. But accessory liability is concerned with the liability of a person who has not received any property. His liability is not property-based. His only sin is that he interfered with the due performance by the trustee of the fiduciary obligations under-taken by the trustee. These are personal obligations. They are, in this respect, analogous to the personal obligations undertaken by the parties to a contract. But ordinary, everyday business would become impossible if third parties were to be held liable for *unknowingly* interfering in the due performance of such personal obligations. Beneficiaries could not reasonably expect that third parties should deal with trustees at their peril, to the extent that they should become liable to the beneficiaries even when they received no trust property and even when they were unaware and had no reason to suppose that they were dealing with trustees.

Fault-based liability

Given, then, that in some circumstances a third party may be liable direct to a beneficiary, but given also that the liability is not so strict that there would be liability even when the third party was wholly unaware of the existence of the trust, the next step is to seek to identify the touchstone of liability. By common accord dishonesty fulfils this role ...

Dishonesty

Before considering this issue further it will be helpful to define the terms being used by looking more closely at what dishonesty means in this context. Whatever may be the position in some criminal or other contexts (see, for instance, *R v Ghosh* [1982] 2 All ER 689), in the context of the accessory liability principle acting dishonestly, or with a lack of probity, which is synonymous, means simply not acting as an honest person would in the circumstances. This is an objective standard. At first sight this may seem surprising. Honesty has a connotation of subjectivity, as distinct from the objectivity of negligence. Honesty, indeed, does have a strong subjective element in that it is a description of a type of conduct assessed in the light of what a person actually knew at the time, as distinct from what a reasonable person would have known or appreciated. Further, honesty and its counterpart dishonesty are mostly concerned with advertent conduct, not inadvertent conduct. Carelessness is not dishonesty. Thus for the most part dishonesty is to be equated with conscious impropriety ...

In most situations there is little difficulty in identifying how an honest person would behave. Honest people do not intentionally deceive others to their detriment. Honest people do not knowingly take others' property. Unless there is a very good and compelling reason, an honest person does not participate in a transaction if he knows it involves a misapplication of trust assets to the detriment of the beneficiaries. Nor does an honest person in such a case deliberately close his eyes and ears, or deliberately not ask questions, lest he learn something he would rather not know, and then proceed regardless.

Negligence

It is against this background that the question of negligence is to be addressed. This question, it should be remembered, is directed at whether an honest third party who receives no trust property should be liable if he procures or assists in a breach of trust of which he would have become aware had he exercised reasonable diligence. Should he be liable to the beneficiaries for the loss they suffer from the breach of trust? The majority of persons falling into this category will be the hosts of people who act for trustees in various ways: as advisers, consultants, bankers and agents of many kinds. This category also includes officers and employees of companies in respect of the application of company funds. All these people will be accountable to the trustees for their conduct. For the most part they will owe to the trustees a duty to exercise reasonable skill and care. When that is so, the rights flowing from that duty form part of the trust property. As such they can be enforced by the beneficiaries in a suitable case if the trustees are unable or unwilling to do so. That being so, it is difficult to identify a compelling reason why, in addition to the duty of skill and care vis-à-vis the trustees which the third parties have accepted, or which the law has imposed upon them, third parties should also owe a duty of care directly to the beneficiaries. They have undertaken work for the trustees. They must carry out that work properly. If they fail to do so, they will be liable to make good the loss suffered by the trustees in consequence. This will include, where appropriate, the loss suffered by the trustees being exposed to claims for breach of trust.

Outside this category of persons who owe duties of skill and care to the trustees, there are others who will deal with trustees. If they have not accepted, and the law has not imposed upon them, any such duties in favour of the trustees, it is difficult to discern a good reason why they should nevertheless owe such duties to the beneficiaries ...

Unconscionable conduct

Mention, finally, must be made of the suggestion that the test for liability is that of unconscionable conduct. Unconscionable is a word of immediate appeal to an equity lawyer. Equity is rooted historically in the concept of the Lord Chancellor, as the keeper of the royal conscience, concerning himself with conduct which was contrary to good conscience. It must be recognised, however, that unconscionable is not a word in everyday use by non-lawyers. If it is to be used in this context, and if it is to be the touchstone for liability as an accessory, it is essential to be clear on what, *in this context*, unconscionable *means*. If unconscionable means no more than dishonesty, then dishonesty is the preferable label. If unconscionable means something different, it must be said that it is not clear what that something different is. Either way, therefore, the term is better avoided in this context.

The accessory liability principle

Drawing the threads together, their Lordships' overall conclusion is that dishonesty is a necessary ingredient of accessory liability. It is also a sufficient ingredient. A liability in equity to make good resulting loss attaches to a person who dishonestly procures or assists in a breach of trust or fiduciary obligation. It is not necessary that, in addition, the trustee or fiduciary was acting dishonestly, although this will usually be so where the third party who is assisting him is acting dishonestly. 'Knowingly' is better avoided as a defining ingredient of the principle, and in the context of this principle the *Baden* scale of knowledge is best forgotten.

Conclusion

From this statement of the principle it follows that this appeal succeeds. The money paid to BLT on the sale of tickets for Royal Brunei Airlines was held by BLT upon trust for the airline. This trust, on its face, conferred no power on BLT to use the money in the conduct of its business. The trust gave no authority to BLT to relieve its cash flow problems by utilising this rolling 30-day credit afforded by the airline. Thus BLT committed a breach of trust by using the money instead of simply deducting its commission and holding the money intact until it paid the airline, Mr Tan accepted that he knowingly assisted in that breach of trust. In other words, he caused or permitted his company to apply the money in a way he knew was not authorised by the trust of which the company was trustee. Set out in these bald terms, Mr Tan's conduct was dishonest. By the same token, and for good measure, BLT also acted dishonestly. Mr Tan was the company and his state of mind is to be imputed to the company ...

■ QUESTIONS

1. *Tan* has made the stranger's 'dishonesty' and not that of the principal/trustee/fiduciary, the trigger of liability. Can you think of any justification for this change of emphasis?

2. Do you detect any conceptual difficulty in creating liability as a constructive *trustee* for 'dishonest assistance'?

NOTE: If a stranger is fixed with liability as a constructive trustee by reason of their dishonest assistance in a fraudulent design, they are a very 'strange' trustee indeed. As Millett J observed in *Agip (Africa) Ltd* v *Jackson* [1990] Ch 265: 'The basis of the stranger's liability is not receipt of trust property but participation in a fraud.' If the strangers are truly 'trustees', it must be asked: 'What is the trust property to which they hold the legal title?' It may be simple enough, in most cases, to identify the trust property, namely the property held on the original trusts (or the property subject to the original fiduciary obligations), but this still begs the question whether the stranger can ever be said to have held or controlled the legal title to that property to such a degree that it is right to call them trustees of any sort. The fact is that they are not trustees, but that they are subject to liability *as if they were* constructive trustees. Constructive trusteeship of this sort is therefore not trusteeship at all, but merely a 'formula' for granting relief (see the *Paragon* case, in Chapters 8 and 13). It may be that these unresolved conceptual difficulties are no bad thing as equity seeks flexible tools to rationalise the complex transactional environment of the modern commercial world. (See S. Gardner, 'Knowing Assistance and Knowing Receipt: Taking Stock' (1996) 112 *LQR* 56.)

Twinsectra Ltd v *Yardley*
[2002] 2 AC 164, House of Lords

Facts: Mr Yardley borrowed £1m from Twinsectra Limited. Leach, a solicitor, acted for Mr Yardley in connection with the loan, but did not deal directly with Twinsectra. Twinsectra dealt with another firm of solicitors, 'Sims', which represented themselves as acting on behalf of Mr Yardley. Sims paid the money to Leach and he paid it on to Yardley. Sims gave the following undertaking to Twinsectra:

1. The loan monies will be retained by us until such time as they are applied in the acquisition of property on behalf of our client.
2. The loan monies will be utilised solely for the acquisition of property on behalf our client and for no other purposes.
3. We will repay to you the said sum of £1,000,000 together with interest calculated at £657.53 such payment to be made within four calendar months after receipt of the loan monies by us.

Contrary to the terms of the undertaking, Sims did not retain the money until it was applied in the acquisition of property by Yardley. On being given an assurance by Yardley that it would be so applied, they paid it to Leach. He in turn did not take steps to ensure that it was utilised solely for the acquisition of property on behalf of Yardley. He simply paid it out upon Yardley's instructions. The result was that £357,720.11 was used by Yardley for purposes other than the acquisition of property. The loan was not repaid. Twinsectra sued all the parties involved, including Leach. The claim against him was for the £357,720.11 which had not been used to buy property. The basis of the claim was that the payment by Sims to Leach in breach of the undertaking was a breach of trust and that Leach was liable for dishonestly assisting in that breach of trust.

Held: The appeal was allowed (Lord Millett dissenting). The majority of Their Lordships applied the test for dishonest assistance and concluded that Mr Leach had not been dishonest. Lord Millett, rejecting dishonest assistance as a basis of liability, held that Mr Leach was liable for knowing assistance.

LORD HUTTON: ... My Lords, in my opinion, the issue whether the Court of Appeal was right to hold that Mr Leach had acted dishonestly depends on the meaning to be given to that term in the judgment of Lord Nicholls of Birkenhead in *Royal Brunei Airlines Snd Bhd* v *Tan* [1995] 2 AC 378, [1995] 3 All ER 97. In approaching this question it will be helpful to consider the place of dishonesty in the pattern of that judgment. Lord Nicholls considered, at pp. 384 and 385, the position of the honest trustee and the dishonest third party and stated that dishonesty on the part of the third party was a sufficient basis for his liability notwithstanding that the trustee, although mistaken and in breach of trust, was honest. He then turned to consider the basis on which the third party, who does not receive trust property but who assists the trustee to commit a breach, should be held liable. He rejected the possibility that such a third party should never be liable and he also rejected the possibility that the liability of a third party should be strict so that he would be liable even if he did not know or had no reason to suspect that he was dealing with a trustee. Therefore Lord Nicholls concluded that the liability of the accessory must be fault-based and in identifying the touchstone of liability he stated, at p. 387 H: 'By common accord dishonesty fulfils this role'. Then, at pp. 388 and 389, he cited a number of authorities and the views of commentators and observed that the tide of authority in England had flowed strongly in favour of the test of dishonesty and that most, but not all, commentators also preferred that test.

Whilst in discussing the term 'dishonesty' the courts often draw a distinction between subjective dishonesty and objective dishonesty, there are three possible standards which can be applied to determine whether a person has acted dishonestly. There is a purely subjective standard, whereby a person is only regarded as dishonest if he transgresses his own standard of honesty, even if that standard is contrary to that of reasonable and honest people. This has been termed the 'Robin Hood test' and has been rejected by the courts. As Sir Christopher Slade stated in *Walker* v *Stones* [2001] 2 WLR 623, [2000] Lloyds Rep PN 864, p. 877 of the latter report para. 164:

> A person may in some cases act dishonestly, according to the ordinary use of language, even though he genuinely believes that his action is morally justified. The penniless thief, for example, who picks the pocket of the multi-millionaire is dishonest even though he genuinely considers that theft is morally justified as a fair redistribution of wealth and that he is not therefore being dishonest.

Secondly, there is a purely objective standard whereby a person acts dishonestly if his conduct is dishonest by the ordinary standards of reasonable and honest people, even if he does not realise this. Thirdly, there is a standard which combines an objective test and a subjective test, and which requires that before there can be a finding of dishonesty it must be established that the defendant's conduct was dishonest by the ordinary standards of reasonable and honest people and that he himself realised that by those standards his conduct was dishonest. I will term this 'the combined test'.

There is a passage in the earlier part of the judgment in *Royal Brunei* which suggests that Lord Nicholls considered that dishonesty has a subjective element. Thus in discussing the honest trustee and the dishonest third party at [1995] 2 AC 378, 385 A–C he stated:

> These examples suggest that what matters is the state of mind of the third party ... But [the trustee's] state of mind is essentially irrelevant to the question whether the third party should be made liable to the beneficiaries for breach of trust.

However, after stating, at p. 387 H, that the touchstone of liability is dishonesty, Lord Nicholls went on at p. 389 B–C to discuss the meaning of dishonesty:

> Before considering this issue further it will be helpful to define the terms being used by looking more closely at what dishonesty means in this context. Whatever may be the position in some criminal or other contexts (see, for instance, *R* v *Ghosh* [1982] QB 1053), in the context of the accessory liability principle acting dishonestly, or with a lack of probity, which is synonymous, means simply not acting as an honest person would in the circumstances. This is an objective standard.

My noble and learned friend Lord Millett has subjected this passage and subsequent passages in the judgment to detailed analysis and is of the opinion that Lord Nicholls used the term 'dishonesty' in a purely objective sense so that in this area of the law a person can be held to be dishonest even though he does not realise that what he is doing is dishonest by the ordinary standards of honest people. This leads Lord Millett on to the conclusion that in determining the liability of an accessory dishonesty is not necessary and that liability depends on knowledge.

In *R* v *Ghosh* [1982] QB 1053: [1982] 2 All ER 689 Lord Lane CJ held that in the law of theft dishonesty required that the defendant himself must have realised that what he was doing was dishonest by the ordinary standards of reasonable and honest people. The three sentences in Lord Nicholl's judgment, at p. 389 B–C of the former report, which appear to draw a distinction between the position in criminal law and the position in equity, do give support to Lord Millett's view. But considering those sentences in the context of the remainder of the paragraph and taking account of other passages in the judgment, I think that in referring to an objective standard Lord Nicholls was contrasting it with the purely subjective standard whereby a man sets his own standard of honesty and does not regard as dishonest what upright and responsible people would regard as dishonest. Thus after stating that dishonesty is assessed on an objective standard he continued, at p. 389 C of the former report:

> At first sight this may seem surprising. Honesty has a connotation of subjectivity, as distinct from the objectivity of negligence. Honesty, indeed, does have a strong subjective element in that it is a description of a type of conduct assessed in the light of what a person actually knew at the time, as distinct from what a reasonable person would have known or appreciated. Further, honesty and its counterpart dishonesty are mostly concerned with advertent conduct, not inadvertent conduct. Carelessness is not dishonesty. Thus for the most part dishonesty is to be equated with conscious impropriety. However, these subjective characteristics of honesty do not mean that individuals are free to set their own standards of honesty in particular circumstances. The standard of what constitutes honest conduct is not subjective. Honesty is not an optional scale, with higher or lower values according to the moral standards of each individual. If a person knowingly appropriates another's property, he will not escape a finding of dishonesty simply because he sees nothing wrong in such behaviour.

Further, at p. 391 A–C of the former report, Lord Nicholls said:

> Ultimately, in most, cases, an honest person should have little difficulty in knowing whether a proposed transaction, or his participation in it, would offend the normally accepted standards of honest conduct.

Likewise, when called upon to decide whether a person was acting honestly, a court will look at all the circumstances known to the third party at the time. The court will also have regard to personal attributes of the third party, such as his experience and intelligence, and the reason why he acted as he did.

The use of the word 'knowing' in the first sentence would be superfluous if the defendant did not have to be aware that what he was doing would offend the normally accepted standards of honest conduct, and the need to look at the experience and intelligence of the defendant would also appear superfluous if all that was required was a purely objective standard of dishonesty. Therefore I do not think that Lord Nicholls was stating that in this sphere of equity a man can be dishonest even if he does not know that what he is doing would be regarded as dishonest by honest people.

Then, at p. 392 F–G of the former report, Lord Nicholls stated the general principle that dishonesty is a necessary ingredient of accessory liability and that knowledge is not an appropriate test:

The accessory liability principle

Drawing the threads together, their Lordships' overall conclusion is that dishonesty is a necessary ingredient of accessory liability. It is also a sufficient ingredient. A liability in equity to make good resulting loss attaches to a person who dishonestly procures or assists in a breach of trust or fiduciary obligation. It is not necessary that, in addition, the trustee or fiduciary was acting dishonestly, although this will usually be so where the third party who is assisting him is acting dishonestly. 'Knowingly' is better avoided as a defining ingredient of the principle, and in the context of this principle the *Baden* [1993] 1 WLR 509 scale of knowledge is best forgotten.

I consider that this was a statement of general principle and was not confined to the doubtful case when the propriety of the transaction in question was uncertain ...

There is, in my opinion, a further consideration which supports the view that for liability as an accessory to arise the defendant must himself appreciate that what he was doing was dishonest by the standards of honest and reasonable men. A finding by a judge that a defendant has been dishonest is a grave finding, and it is particularly grave against a professional man, such as a solicitor. Notwithstanding that the issue arises in equity law and not in a criminal context, I think that it would be less than just for the law to permit a finding that a defendant had been 'dishonest' in assisting in a breach of trust where he knew of the facts which created the trust and its breach but had not been aware that what he was doing would be regarded by honest men as being dishonest.

It would be open to your Lordships to depart from the principle stated by Lord Nicholls that dishonesty is a necessary ingredient of accessory liability and to hold that knowledge is a sufficient ingredient. But the statement of that principle by Lord Nicholls has been widely regarded as clarifying this area of the law and, as he observed, the tide of authority in England has flowed strongly in favour of the test of dishonesty. Therefore I consider that the courts should continue to apply that test and that your Lordships should state that dishonesty requires knowledge by the defendant that what he was doing would be regarded as dishonest by honest people, although he should not escape a finding of dishonesty because he sets his own standards of honesty and does not regard as dishonest what he knows would offend the normally accepted standards of honest conduct ...

For the reasons which I have given I would allow Mr Leach's appeal and set aside the judgment of the Court of Appeal.

LORD MILLETT (dissenting): In my opinion the Court of Appeal were correct to find that the terms of paras 1 and 2 of the undertaking created a *Quistclose* trust. The money was never at Mr Yardley's free disposal. It was never held to his order by Mr Sims. The money belonged throughout to Twinsectra, subject only to Mr Yardley's right to apply it for the acquisition of property. Twinsectra parted with the money to Mr Sims, relying on him to ensure that the money was properly applied or returned to it. Mr Sims act in paying the money over to Mr Leach was a breach of trust, but it did not in itself render the money incapable of being applied for the stated purpose. Insofar as Mr Leach applied the money in the acquisition of property, the purpose was achieved ...

Knowing (or dishonest) assistance

Before turning to the critical questions concerning the extent of the knowledge required and whether a finding of dishonesty is a necessary condition of liability, I ought to say a word about the distinction between the 'knowing receipt' of trust money and 'knowing (or dishonest) assistance' in a breach of trust; and about the meaning of 'assistance' in this context.

Liability for 'knowing receipt' is receipt-based. It does not depend on fault. The cause of action is restitutionary and is available only where the defendant received or applied the money in breach of trust for his own use and benefit: see *Agip (Africa) Ltd v Jackson* [1990] Ch 265, [1992] 4 All ER 385 at pp. 291–92 of the former report; *Royal Brunei Airlines Sdn Bhd v Tan* [1995] 2 AC 378, [1995] 3 All ER 97 at p. 386 of the former report. There is no basis for requiring actual knowledge of the breach of trust, let alone dishonesty, as a condition of liability. Constructive notice is sufficient, and may not even be necessary. There is powerful academic support for the proposition that the liability of the recipient is the same as in other cases of restitution, that is to say strict but subject to a change of position defence.

Mr Leach received sums totalling £22,000 in payment of his costs for his own use and benefit, and Twinsectra seek their repayment on the ground of knowing receipt. But he did not receive the rest of the money for his own benefit at all. He never regarded himself as beneficially entitled to the money. He held it to Mr Yardley's order and paid it out to Mr Yardley or his companies. Twinsectra cannot and does not base its claim in respect of these moneys in knowing receipt, not for want of knowledge, but for want of the necessary receipt. It sues in respect of knowing (or dishonest) assistance.

The accessory's liability for having assisted in a breach of trust is quite different. It is fault-based, not receipt-based. The defendant is not charged with having received trust moneys for his own benefit, but with having acted as an accessory to a breach of trust. The action is not restitutionary; the claimant seeks compensation for wrongdoing. The cause of action is concerned with attributing liability for mis-directed funds. Liability is not restricted to the person whose breach of trust or fiduciary duty caused their original diversion. His liability is strict. Nor is it limited to those who assist him in the original breach. It extends to everyone who consciously assists in the continuing diversion of the money. Most of the cases have been concerned, not with assisting in the original breach, but in covering it up afterwards by helping to launder the money. Mr Leach's wrongdoing is not confined to the assistance he gave Mr Sims to commit a breach of trust by receiving the money from him knowing that Mr Sims should not have paid it to him (though this is sufficient to render him liable for any resulting loss); it extends to the assistance he gave in the subsequent misdirection of the money by paying it out to Mr Yardley's order without seeing to its proper application.

The meaning of dishonesty in this context …

In my opinion Lord Nicholls was adopting an objective standard of dishonesty by which the defendant is expected to attain the standard which would be observed by an honest person placed in similar circumstances. Account must be taken of subjective considerations such as the defendant's experience and intelligence and his actual state of knowledge at the relevant time. But it is not necessary that he should actually have appreciated that he was acting dishonestly; it is sufficient that he was.

… The question is whether an honest person would appreciate that what he was doing was wrong or improper, not whether the defendant himself actually appreciated this …

Should subjective dishonesty be required?

The question for your Lordships is not whether Lord Nicholls was using the word dishonesty in a subjective or objective sense in *Royal Brunei Airlines Sdn Bhd v Tan* [1995] 2 AC 378. The question is whether a plaintiff should be required to establish that an accessory to a breach of trust had a dishonest state of mind (so that he was subjectively dishonest in the *R v Ghosh* sense); or whether it should be sufficient to establish that he acted with the requisite knowledge (so that his conduct was objectively dishonest). This question is at large for us, and we are free to resolve it either way.

I would resolve it by adopting the objective approach. I would do so because:

(1) consciousness of wrongdoing is an aspect of *mens rea* and an appropriate condition of criminal liability: it is not an appropriate condition of civil liability. This generally results from negligent or intentional conduct. For the purpose of civil liability, it should not be necessary that the defendant realised that his conduct was dishonest; it should be sufficient that it constituted intentional wrongdoing.

(2) The objective test is in accordance with Lord Selborne's statement in *Barnes v Addy* LR 9 Ch App 244 and traditional doctrine. This taught that a person who knowingly participates in the misdirection of money is liable to compensate the injured party. While negligence is not a sufficient condition of liability, intentional wrongdoing is. Such conduct is culpable and falls below the objective standards of honesty adopted by ordinary people.

(3) The claim for 'knowing assistance' is the equitable counterpart of the economic torts. These are intentional torts; negligence is not sufficient and dishonesty is not necessary. Liability depends on knowledge. A requirement of subjective dishonesty introduces an unnecessary and unjustified distinction between the elements of the equitable claim and those of the tort of wrongful interference with the performance of a contract ...

It would be most undesirable if we were to introduce a distinction between the equitable claim and the tort, thereby inducing the claimant to attempt to spell a contractual obligation out of a fiduciary relationship in order to avoid the need to establish that the defendant had a dishonest state of mind. It would, moreover, be strange if equity made liability depend on subjective dishonesty when in a comparable situation the common law did not. This would be a reversal of the general rule that equity demands higher standards of behaviour than the common law.

If we were to reject subjective dishonesty as a requirement of civil liability in this branch of the law, the remaining question is merely a semantic one. Should we return to the traditional description of the claim as 'knowing assistance', reminding ourselves that nothing less than actual knowledge is sufficient; or should we adopt Lord Nicholls' description of the claim as 'dishonest assistance', reminding ourselves that the test is an objective one?

For my own part, I have no difficulty in equating the knowing mishandling of money with dishonest conduct. But the introduction of dishonesty is an unnecessary distraction, and conducive to error. Many judges would be reluctant to brand a professional man as dishonest where he was unaware that honest people would consider his conduct to be so. If the condition of liability is intentional wrongdoing and not conscious dishonesty as understood in the criminal courts, I think that we should return to the traditional description of this head of equitable liability as arising from 'knowing assistance'.

Knowledge

The question here is whether it is sufficient that the accessory should have actual knowledge of the facts which created the trust, or must he also have appreciated that they did so? It is obviously not necessary that he should know the details of the trust or the identity of the beneficiary. It is sufficient that he knows that the money is not at the free disposal of the principal. In some circumstances it may not even be necessary that his knowledge should extend this far. It may be sufficient that he knows that he is assisting in a dishonest scheme.

That is not this case, for in the absence of knowledge that his client is not entitled to receive it there is nothing intrinsically dishonest in a solicitor paying money to him. But I am satisfied that knowledge of the arrangements which constitute the trust is sufficient; it is not necessary that the defendant should appreciate that they do so. Of course, if they do not create a trust, then he will not liable for having assisted in a breach of trust. But he takes the risk that they do.

The gravamen of the charge against the principal is not that he has broken his word, but that having been entrusted with the control of a fund with limited powers of disposal he has betrayed the confidence placed in him by disposing of the money in an unauthorised manner. The gravamen of the charge against the accessory is not that he is handling stolen property, but that he is assisting a person who has been entrusted with the control of a fund to dispose of the fund in an unauthorised manner. He should be liable if he knows of the arrangements by which that person obtained control of the money and that his authority to deal with the money was limited, and participates in a dealing with the money in a manner which he knows is unauthorised. I do not believe that the man in the street would have any doubt that such conduct was culpable ...

Conclusion

I do not think that this was a case of wilful blindness, or that the judge overlooked the possibility of imputed knowledge. There was no need to impute knowledge to Mr Leach, for there was no relevant fact of which he was unaware. He did not shut his eyes to any fact in case he might learn the truth. He knew of the terms of the undertaking, that the money was not to be at Mr Yardley's free disposal. He knew (i) that Mr Sims was not entitled to pay the money over to him (Mr Leach), and was only prepared to do so against confirmation that it was proposed to apply the money for the acquisition of property; and (ii) that it could not be paid to Mr Yardley except for the acquisition of property. There were no enquiries which Mr Leach needed to make to satisfy himself that the money could properly be put at Mr Yardley's free disposal. He knew it could not. The only thing that he did not know was that the terms of the undertaking created a trust, still less a trust in favour of Twinsectra. He believed that Mr Sims' obligations to Twinsectra sounded in contract only. That was not an unreasonable belief; certainly not a dishonest one; though if true it would not have absolved him from liability.

Yet from the very first moment that he received the money he treated it as held to Mr Yardley's order and at Mr Yardley's free disposition. He did not shut his eyes to the facts, but to 'the implications', that is to say the impropriety of putting the money at Mr Yardley's disposal. His explanation was that this was Mr Sims' problem, not his.

Mr Leach knew that Twinsectra had entrusted the money to Mr Sims with only limited authority to dispose of it; that Twinsectra trusted Mr Sims to ensure that the money was not used except for the acquisition of property; that Mr Sims had betrayed the confidence placed in him by paying the money to him (Mr Leach) without seeing to its further application; and that by putting it at Mr Yardley's free disposal he took the risk that the money would be applied for an unauthorised purpose and place Mr Sims in breach of his undertaking. But all that was Mr Sims' responsibility.

In my opinion this is enough to make Mr Leach civilly liable as an accessory (i) for the tort of wrongful interference with the performance of Mr Sims' contractual obligations if this had been pleaded and the undertaking was contractual as well as fiduciary; and (ii) for assisting in a breach of trust. It is unnecessary to consider whether Mr Leach realised that honest people would regard his conduct as dishonest. His knowledge that he was assisting Mr Sims to default in his undertaking to Twinsectra is sufficient …

I would reduce the sum for which judgment was entered by the Court of Appeal by £22,000, and subject thereto dismiss the appeal.

NOTE: An attempt to apply *Twinsectra* against solicitors failed in the case of *Gabriel* v *Little* [2012] EWHC 1193 (Ch) because the documents drawn up by the solicitors to pass funds for a particular purpose were held not to create a *Quistclose* trust.

Barlow Clowes International Ltd (In Liquidation) v Eurotrust International Limited

[2006] 1 All ER 333, Privy Council

Facts: In the mid-1980s, Mr Clowes operated a fraudulent offshore investment scheme through Barlow Clowes International Ltd. He attracted about £140 million, mainly from small UK investors. Most of the money was spent for the personal benefit of Mr Clowes and his associates. Mr Clowes was eventually convicted and sent to prison. Some of the investors' funds were paid away during 1987 through bank accounts maintained by a company called International Trust Corporation (Isle of Man) Ltd ('ITC'). In proceedings in the High Court of the Isle of Man, Barlow Clowes (now in liquidation) claimed that the directors of ITC and, through them, ITC itself, dishonestly assisted Mr Clowes and one of his principal associates, Mr Cramer, to misappropriate the investors' funds.

Held: The defendants were liable. Their claim that that they did not realise they were assisting in a breach of trust was to no avail. It was held (following *Twinsectra Ltd* v *Yardley* [2002] 2 AC 164) that '[s]omeone can know, and can certainly suspect, that he is assisting in a misappropriation of money without knowing that the money is held on trust or what a trust means' and 'it was not necessary to know the "precise involvement" of Mr Cramer in the group's affairs in order to suspect that neither he nor anyone else had the right to use Barlow Clowes money for speculative investments of their own'.

LORD HOFFMANN: Their Lordships accept that there is an element of ambiguity in [Lord Hutton's speech in *Twinsectra*] which may have encouraged a belief, expressed in some academic writing, that *Twinsectra* had departed from the law as previously understood and invited inquiry not merely into the defendant's mental state about the nature of the transaction in which he was participating but also into his views about generally acceptable standards of honesty. But they do not consider that this is what Lord Hutton meant. The reference to 'what he knows would offend normally accepted standards of honest conduct' meant only that his knowledge of the transaction had to be such as to render his participation contrary to normally acceptable standards of honest conduct. It did not require that he should have had reflections about what those normally acceptable standards were.

NOTE: *Barlow Clowes* was followed in *Abou-Rahmah* v *Abacha* [2006] EWCA Civ 1492, [2006] All ER 80, Court of Appeal. In this case, Arden LJ held that *Barlow Clowes* 'shows how the *Royal Brunei* case and the *Twinsectra* case can be read together to form a consistent corpus of law'. Does that appear to be a rather hopeful reading of *Barlow Clowes*? Surely it is the case that *Royal Brunei* advocated a purely objective test of a stranger's liability, albeit an objective test which varies according to the type of defendant (e.g. the conduct of a senior partner in a law firm will be weighed against a heavier standard than that applied to judge the conduct of a trainee solicitor), whereas *Twinsectra* advocates a standard which, because it takes account of the individual defendant's personal opinion as to the honesty of their own behaviour, cannot be said to be wholly objective. In *Starglade Properties Ltd* v *Nash* [2010] EWCA Civ 1314), the Court of Appeal (whilst purporting to follow *Abou-Rahmah* and *Barlow Clowes*) stated that the standard by which 'dishonesty' is tested does not vary just because some people might think that the standard is set too high: 'There is a single standard of honesty objectively determined by the court. That standard is applied to specific conduct of a specific individual possessing the knowledge and qualities he actually enjoyed'.

Republic of Zambia v Meer Care & Desai (a firm)

[2008] EWCA Civ 1007, Court of Appeal

Facts: A solicitor assisted in the disbursement of certain funds which had been stolen from the Republic of Zambia. The question was whether the solicitor had assisted dishonestly. The judge at first instance held that he must have been suspicious about the source of the funds and dishonestly chose not to make appropriate inquiries of his client.

Held: Allowing the appeal. The solicitor was very incompetent but not dishonest. It was stated that no amount of negligence will amount to dishonesty.

LORD JUSTICE LLOYD: ... we would question the comment that the difference between negligence and dishonesty is a question of degree. Either the person in question does know (or clearly suspect) the facts which show that the relevant conduct is dishonest, or he does not. It may not be easy to tell on which side of the line a particular defendant stands as a matter of fact, but the dividing line is clear ... it is one thing to throw caution to the winds; that is likely to lead to negligent conduct. But even to do that to the nth degree does not involve crossing the dividing line and passing over to dishonesty.

In our judgment, the judge's conclusion that Mr Meer was liable on the basis of dishonest assistance and of conspiracy is undermined by several misdirections and errors as regards the evidence, the contentions and in one respect also the law. The misdirection of law is as to the burden of proof in relation to the propriety of disbursements. As we have said at paragraph [147] above, where a defendant's liability depends (as here) on showing that he knew that a disbursement was for an improper purpose, it is not for that party to disprove the impropriety, but for the Claimant to prove both the fact, and also the defendant's knowledge, of the impropriety.

... According to the judge's finding, by 7 December 1995, when he was given the first instruction as to a relevant payment out of his client account, Mr Meer had not merely thrown caution to the wind (paragraph 567) but had come to know, or at least to have a clear suspicion, that the disbursements which Mr Kabwe instructed him to make were improper and showed that Mr Kabwe (together with Mr Chungu) was in the process of stealing money from Zambia. That would involve a dramatic and sudden change of position from honesty to dishonesty, which was unexplained. As the judge accepted, no motive for Mr Meer to act dishonestly was proved, and he had to proceed on the basis that there was no such motive. That being so, a sudden conversion of Mr Meer from his established background of honesty and integrity to a position of unmotivated dishonesty seems to defy probability.

... the judge relied heavily on the test of what an honest solicitor would have done, or, to put the test more accurately (as the judge did at some points), whether an honest solicitor could have done that which Mr Meer did, given the knowledge of the facts that he had. At some points, however, the judge used the benchmark of the honest and competent solicitor ... that hypothetical comparator is not appropriate, because it assumes that Mr Meer was competent. Of course Mr Meer would have wished to be thought competent, but there were many indications to the judge that, in relevant respects, he was not. It seems to us that the judge failed to give adequate consideration to the possibility that Mr Meer was honest but not competent, and was not in truth knowledgeable or experienced in relation to the sort of transaction with which he was faced, and in particular did not really understand what was involved in money-laundering.

The question, was he dishonest or not, is to be answered in favour of honesty unless fraud is proved on the balance of probabilities, bearing in mind the need for cogent evidence for an allegation as serious as fraud. In our judgment, on the material that was before the judge, the more probable explanation for Mr Meer's conduct is that he was honest, albeit foolish, sometimes very foolish, and far from competent in his understanding, as well as in his application and observance, of relevant professional duties, above all the need to comply with the warnings about money-laundering. We agree with the judge that Mr Meer should have acted differently, more cautiously and with a more suspicious mind. We do not agree with him that Mr Meer's failure to do so shows that he knew or suspected what was going on, and chose not to ask questions in order not to be told the truth.

NOTES

1. In *Governor and Company of the Bank of Scotland* v *A Ltd and others* [2001] 1 WLR 751, Lord Woolf CJ observed that it is 'almost inconceivable that a bank which takes the initiative in seeking the court's guidance should subsequently be held to have acted dishonestly so as to incur accessory liability'. See, also, *Tayeb* v *HSBC Bank plc* [2004] EWHC 1529 (Comm).

2. Should liability for dishonest assistance in a breach of trust be reframed as a tort? In support of this view, it has recently been held that 'in a case for accessory liability there is no requirement for there to be trust property' and that '[s]uch a requirement wrongly associates accessory liability with trust concepts' (*JD Wetherspoon Plc* v *Van de Berg & Co Ltd* [2009] EWHC 639 (Ch) (following *Satnam Investments Ltd* v *Dunlop Heywood & Co Ltd* [1999] 3 All ER 652, CA (Civ Div)), per Peter Smith J at para. [518]). Even more clearly, it has been stated that the equitable wrong should only be distinguished from tort for the purposes of domestic law and that 'its proper characterisation for the purposes of private international law is as a tort' (*OJSC Oil Company Yugraneft (in liquidation)* v *Abramovich* [2008] EWHC 2613 (Comm)).

SECTION 5: THE PERSONAL ACTION IN *DIPLOCK*

In *Re Diplock's Estate* [1948] Ch 465, which was affirmed by the House of Lords on this issue in *Ministry of Health* v *Simpson* [1951] AC 251, the next of kin also succeeded in a personal action against charities that had received distributions from the estate to which they were not entitled. Unlike knowing receipt, however, liability was strict. The defendants were innocent volunteers who took in good faith with no notice of the next of kin's title.

In *Diplock*, the executors had made the payments to the charities under a mistake of law. The charities argued unsuccessfully that the personal action was limited to payments made under a mistake of fact (on analogy with the common law money had and received action), and where the administration of the estate had been made by the direction of the court. It is arguable that the action applies only to the administration of estates, but it seems more probable that it applies generally against volunteers. There is a requirement, however, that remedies against the wrongdoers (in this case, the executors) should be exhausted first. It is also possible (but not certain) that the change of position defence in *Lipkin Gorman* v *Karpnale Ltd* [1991] 2 AC 548 (as discussed in *BCCI* v *Akindele* at Section 3) applies to this equitable action also.

SECTION 6: MULTIPLICITY OF CLAIMS

It is important always to keep in mind that in English law even the simplest sets of facts can give rise to a multiplicity of claims. We have seen that claims can be legal or equitable and they can be personal or proprietary. We have also seen that not only the trustee and fiduciary, but third parties also, can be subject to the various claims available to recover misapplied wealth. Crucially, we have seen that claims may be brought even where they are mutually inconsistent, provided the claimant elects between alternate inconsistent claims before judgment is entered in his favour. The following passage, taken from the typical case of a company director who misapplied company wealth to his own benefit, typifies the range of claims to which a defendant might be answerable.

Primlake Limited (In Liquidation) v *Matthews Associates et al.*

No. HC 03 C 04314 (TLC 137/05) [2006] EWHC 1227 (Ch), paras [333]–[335]

MR JUSTICE LAWRENCE COLLINS: On my findings Mr Matthews is liable under several possible heads ... Plainly Mr Matthews is liable, on my findings, as constructive trustee of funds which he procured in breach of his own fiduciary duty, or by virtue of his dishonest assistance and knowing receipt. If, as I have found, Mr Matthews was a de facto director, it follows that he was in breach of duty by enriching himself at its expense in paying large sums to himself to which he was not, and knew he was not, entitled. That gives rise both to a personal remedy and a proprietary remedy: *Clark* v *Cutland* [2004] 1 WLR 783, paras 23 and 26. If my conclusion that Mr Matthews was a de facto director is wrong, he is any event liable as a constructive trustee on the basis of dishonest assistance and knowing receipt: *El Ajou* v *Dollar Land Holdings* [1994] 2 All ER 685, 700; *Brown* v *Bennett* [1999] BCC 525, 530; *BCCI* v *Akindele* [2001] Ch 437, 455.

The prevailing view is that there is no separate cause of action for unjust enrichment as such, and that it is necessary for the case to be brought within one of the recognised restitutionary heads, such as money had and received, constructive trust, and resulting trust. In my judgment the authorities would justify the conclusion that Mr Matthews is liable for money had and received (and also, probably, as a trustee on resulting trust) on the basis of an absence of consideration in the sense of no legal basis for the payments: *Woolwich Equitable Building Society* v *Commissioners of Inland Revenue* [1993] AC 70, 197; *Westdeutsche Landesbank Girozentrale* v *Islington LBC* [1996] AC 669, 683 and 710; *Guinness Mahon & Co Ltd* v *Kensington and Chelsea RLBC* [1999] QB 215; Goff & Jones, Restitution, 6th ed., para 1–055.

online
resource
centre

■ **SUMMATIVE QUESTION**

Mr Sleeson, a solicitor, is a sole practitioner with access to his clients' accounts. He withdraws money from 'the client account' and places it in his own private bank account which he holds with the Nelson Westminster bank. Later, he withdraws monies from his private account and plays it at a casino in the city. He places the winnings and the original withdrawals in his private account at the bank. This happens regularly and the bank manager suspects that something may be amiss, but turns a blind eye to Mr Sleeson's activities. Eventually, Mr Sleeson 'went for the big gamble', lost all his money, and was declared bankrupt. The casino manager had accepted his bets because he 'knew that solicitors made a lot of money'.

Advise Mr Sleeson's clients who now seek to recover their lost funds.

FURTHER READING

Elliott, S. B. and Mitchell, C., 'Remedies for Dishonest Assistance' (2004) 67(1) *MLR* 16.

Gardner, S., 'Knowing Assistance and Knowing Receipt: Taking Stock' (1996) 112 *LQR* 56.

Harpum, C., 'Accessory Liability for Procuring or Assisting a Breach of Trust' (1995) 111 *LQR* 545.

Lord Nicholls of Birkenhead, 'Knowing Receipt: The Need for a New Landmark', in W. R. Cornish et al. (eds), *Restitution: Past, Present and Future: Essays in Honour of Gareth Jones* (Oxford: Hart Publishing, 1998), p. 231.

Loughlan, P., 'Liability for Assistance in a Breach of Fiduciary Duty' (1989) 9 *OJLS* 260.

Mitchell, C., 'Dishonest Assistance, Knowing Receipt, and the Law of Limitation' (2008) 72 *Conv* 226.

Ridge, P., 'Justifying the Remedies for Dishonest Assistance' (2008) 124 *LQR* 445.

Sales, P., 'The Tort of Conspiracy and Civil Secondary Liability' (1990) 49 *CLJ* 491.

Smith, L. D., 'Unjust Enrichment, Property and the Structure of Trusts' (2000) 116 *LQR* 412.

Thomas, S. B., 'Goodbye Knowing Receipt, Hello Unconscientious Receipt' (2001) 21 *OJLS* 239.

Watt, G., 'Personal Liability for Receipt of Trust Property: Allocating the Risks', in E. Cooke (ed.), *Modern Studies in Property Law*, Vol. 3 (Oxford: Hart Publishing, 2005), pp. 91–109.

Woodcock, A., 'Claims for dishonest assistance with breach of trust, and changes made by *Twinsectra v Yardley*' (2006) 57(3) *NILQ* 494.

PART V

Equity

16

Equity: Maxims, Doctrines, and Remedies

KEY AIMS

To examine the utility of equitable maxims, the operation of equitable doctrines, and the award of equitable remedies.

SECTION 1: INTRODUCTION

Equity is a body of law developed originally by the old Court of Chancery in constructive competition with the common law courts, but now applied (since the Judicature Acts 1873–75) by the unified Supreme Court of England and Wales. The abolition of the old Court of Chancery and Courts of Common Law has led to the suggestion that the distinction between law and equity is now obsolete; that the two systems of law have become 'fused'. The better view is that the common law and equity remain distinct but mutually dependent aspects of law. They 'are working in different ways towards the same ends' (as discussed in Chapter 1). The function of the common law is to establish rules to govern the generality of cases, the effect of those rules being to recognise that certain persons will acquire certain legal rights and powers in certain circumstances. Legal rules allow the holders of legal rights and powers to exercise them in the confidence that they are entitled to do so. The function of equity is to restrain or restrict the exercise of legal rights and powers in particular cases, whenever it would be unconscionable for them to be exercised to the full. Here it is necessary to exercise great caution, for 'unconscionable' cannot be defined in the abstract; it can only be understood in connection to the facts of particular cases. The question is always whether it would be unconscionable to exercise this legal right or power in the particular context. It is important to bear in mind the contextual specificity of equitable intervention as we proceed to consider the maxims, doctrine, and remedies through which equitable intervention is given effect.

SECTION 2: THE MAXIMS OF EQUITY

In the exercise of discretion, a principle or maxim is a more flexible and useful tool than a rule. It is true that some maxims, particularly those that relate to title and property, lay down something equivalent to a rule. A common law maxim of this sort is the maxim *nemo dat non quod habet*, which roughly translated provides that no one can transfer title which he does not have. An equitable maxim of this sort is the maxim *qui prior tempore est potior est*, which provides that where equitable claims or interests are equal, priority will go to whichever claim or interest arose first in time. Nevertheless, for the most part, maxims tend to guide the exercise of discretion without stultifying it in the way that rules do. Maxims should, however, be employed with caution. The most useful feature of equitable maxims—that they will sometimes outweigh a rule where there is a conflict between a maxim and a rule—is also their most dangerous feature. Maxims have no objectively assayable weight. They have, as Simon Gardner has observed, 'a peculiarly Delphic quality, wrapped as they are in metaphor, grandly unqualified, and acknowledging no authority but transcendent wisdom' ('Two Maxims of Equity' (1995) 54(1) *Cambridge Law Journal* 60).

Christopher St. German, *Dialogue in English between a Doctor of Divinity and a Student in the Laws of England*
(London: Robert Wyer, c.1530), Chapter 8

The first Ground of the Law of England is the Law of Reason ...
The second Ground of the Law of England is the Law of God ...
The third Ground of the Law of England standeth upon divers general customs of old time used through all the Realm ...
The fourth Ground of the Law of England standeth in divers Principles that be called in the Law Maximes, the which have been always taken for Law in this Realm, so that it is not lawful for any that is learned to deny them: for every one of those maxims is sufficient authority to himself. And which is a Maxime, and which is not, shall always be determined by the Judges, and not by 12 men. And it needeth not to assign any reason why they were first received for maximes, for it sufficeth that they be not against the Law of Reason, nor the Law of God, and that they have always been taken for a Law.

A: Equity will not suffer a wrong without a remedy

Where an activity is one with which the law is concerned, and in relation to which the law provides no sufficient remedy, equity will endeavour to supplement the shortcomings of the common law.

B: Equity follows the law

This maxim applies to equitable remedies (see (i)) and to equitable property rights.

(i) Equitable remedies

Leech v *Schweder*
(1873) 9 LR Ch App 463

SIR G. MELLISH LJ: I always supposed that where a right existed at law and a person only came into equity because the Court of Equity had a more convenient remedy than a court of law ... there equity followed the law, and the person entitled to the right had no greater right in equity than at law (at 475).

(ii) Equitable property rights

All interests which are recognised at common law are also recognised in equity (and as a result of the Law of Property Act 1925, s.1, many estates in land which once existed at law can now exist only in equity). Thus, in the case of land, if a legal estate (a freehold or lease) or interest (e.g. an easement or mortgage) is created without the perfect formality required by the law, there may still be an equitable estate (see the example of the equitable lease in *Walsh* v *Lonsdale* (at C: Equity looks to substance not form). However, in the context of property rights equity came to recognise certain rights not recognised at law. Perhaps the most significant example is the restrictive covenant. A 'covenant' is a promise made in a deed, and the typical restrictive covenant is a promise made in a deed of purchase by the purchaser of a part of the vendor's land whereby the purchaser (covenantor) promises not to build on the land. According to the usual legal rule the contract between the vendor and purchaser is entirely private, so there is nothing to stop the purchaser selling the land at great profit the next day to a stranger who is not bound by the building restriction. It was to prevent the covenantor taking such unconscionable advantage of the legal rule of privity of contract that equity permitted the original vendor (covenantee) to enforce the restrictive covenant against any ultimate purchaser who acquired the burdened land with notice of the covenant (*Tulk* v *Moxhay* (1848) [1843–60] All ER Rep 9, Lord Chancellor's Court).

LAW OF PROPERTY ACT 1925

1. Legal estates and equitable interests

   (1) The only estates in land which are capable of subsisting or of being conveyed or created at law are—

       (a) An estate in fee simple absolute in possession;

       (b) A term of years absolute.

   (2) The only interests or charges in or over land which are capable of subsisting or of being conveyed or created at law are—

       (a) An easement, right, or privilege in or over land for an interest equivalent to an estate in fee simple absolute in possession or a term of years absolute;

       (b) A rentcharge in possession issuing out of or charged on land being either perpetual or for a term of years absolute;

       (c) A charge by way of legal mortgage;

       (d) ... and any other similar charge on land which is not created by an instrument;

       (e) Rights of entry exercisable over or in respect of a legal term of years absolute, or annexed, for any purpose, to a legal rentcharge.

   (3) All other estates, interests, and charges in or over land take effect as equitable interests.

C: Equity looks to substance not form

Walsh v *Lonsdale*

(1882) 21 ChD 9, Court of Appeal

Facts: A landlord and tenant had entered into a contract for a seven-year lease and the tenant had gone into possession, but the parties had forgotten to execute the formal deed needed for a valid legal lease. The rent clause in the contract provided that under the lease the rent should be payable in advance at the beginning of each year (the precise figure would depend upon the number of looms run by the tenant for his business). Despite the absence of a deed granting a legal lease, the landlord demanded the rent in advance in accordance with the contractual term. Indeed, he attempted to recover the rent due by exercising his right of distress. The tenant claimed that as there was no deed and therefore no proper lease, any rent should be payable in arrear. He therefore claimed an injunction against the action for distress.

Held: The landlord could claim rent in advance. The contract had created an equitable lease enforceable between the parties. The terms of this lease would correspond to the terms of the contract.

> JESSEL MR: ... The question is one of some nicety. There is an agreement for a lease under which possession has been given. Now since the *Judicature Act* the possession is held under the agreement. There are not two estates as there were formerly, one estate at common law by reason of the payment of the rent from year to year, and an estate in equity under the agreement. There is only one Court, and the equity rules prevail in it. The tenant holds under an agreement for a lease. He holds, therefore, under the same terms in equity as if a lease had been granted, it being a case in which both parties admit that relief is capable of being given by specific performance. That being so, he cannot complain of the exercise by the landlord of the same rights as the landlord would have had if a lease had been granted. On the other hand, he is protected in the same way as if a lease had been granted; he cannot be turned out by six months' notice as a tenant from year to year. He has a right to say, 'I have a lease in equity, and you can only re-enter if I have committed such a breach of covenant as would if a lease had been granted have entitled you to re-enter according to the terms of a proper proviso for re-entry.' That being so, it appears to me that being a lessee in equity he cannot complain of the exercise of the right of distress merely because the actual parchment has not been signed and sealed.

D: Equity will not permit a statute to be used as an instrument of fraud

This principle was developed by the courts of equity to prevent people from taking unfair advantage of statutory formality provisions, which are, of course, intended to prevent, rather than to encourage, fraud.

Hodgson v *Marks*

[1970] 3 WLR 956, Chancery Division

Facts: The claimant transferred her legal title in certain land to her lodger on the understanding, orally agreed, that the claimant would remain equitable owner of the property. In course of time, the lodger sold the house to the first defendant. The first defendant then raised a mortgage on the security of the house, the mortgagee being the second defendant to this action. The claimant commenced the present proceedings for a declaration that the house should be transferred to her and that the second defendant's mortgage should not be binding on her.

Held: Ungoed-Thomas J held against the claimant. (His decision was reversed on other grounds by the Court of Appeal [1971] 1 Ch 892.)

> UNGOED-THOMAS J: In the leading case *Rochefoucauld* v *Boustead* [1897] 1 Ch 196, the defendant bought property on an express oral trust for the plaintiff, subject to specified advances. The defendant subsequently spent money on developing the property. He also raised money for himself personally by mortgages of the property; and later he or his mortgagees sold the property without the plaintiff's knowledge. Despite the absence of writing required by the Statute of Frauds, the plaintiff successfully contended that the property was bought in trust for her, subject to the specified advances and the defendant's outlays on the property; and for an account on that footing. The purchaser and mortgagees, from whom the defendant raised money, for his personal purposes, were not parties to the proceedings. No order was made with regard to the property itself; and as the property is said to have been sold by the defendant or his mortgagees, presumably those mortgagees were paid off out of the proceeds of sale.
>
>   The evidential character of the writing is emphasised, at p. 206:

But it is not necessary that the trust should have been declared by such a writing in the first instance; it is sufficient if the trust can be proved by some writing signed by the defendant, and the date of the writing is immaterial.

Then the judgment goes on to state the principle on which oral evidence of the trust is admitted.

It is further established by a series of cases, the propriety of which cannot now be questioned, that the Statute of Frauds does not prevent the proof of a fraud; and that it is a fraud on the part of a person to whom land is conveyed as a trustee, and who knows it was so conveyed, to deny the trust and claim the land himself. Consequently, notwithstanding the statute, it is competent for a person claiming land conveyed to another to prove by parol evidence that it was so conveyed upon trust for the claimant, and that the grantee, knowing the facts, is denying the trust and relying upon the form of conveyance and the statute, in order to keep the land himself.

It was submitted for the defendants that the principle was limited to cases in which the person relying on the statute was himself the person who had accepted the conveyance of the land as trustee and who nevertheless claimed the land free from the trust. The quoted statement of the principle is expressed in terms compatible with this submission and so lends colour to it. But such statements have to be considered in the light of their facts. In *Rochefoucauld v Boustead* [1897] 1 Ch 196 the grantee who himself took the land on the oral trust had transferred the land in breach of the trust and in fraud of the plaintiff. So there was no occasion in that case to state the principle, except with reference to such a person. In *In re Duke of Marlborough* [1894] Ch 133 the principle was stated at p. 145 in terms of the same effect as in *Rochefoucauld v Boustead* [1897] 1 Ch 196 but those who unsuccessfully relied on the statute in that case were not the original grantee trustee but his executors. So either the principle applies to them as standing in the original grantee's place or it is to be understood more widely than the defendants submit.

Whoever relies upon the statutory requirement of writing is himself using the statute as an instrument to avoid cognisance being taken of the trust. This might occur in circumstances in which establishment of the trust would establish fraud, for example, where, as here, a transfer on oral trust would be taken free of the trust. No other defence is in the least affected by thus dispensing with the statutory requirement of writing. The oral evidence in our case is directed to establishing the trust, i.e. the true nature of the transfer to Mr Evans, and does not affect such defences as those which have been based upon what subsequently happened and estoppel. The statute is thus only a material defence when there is no other effective defence. So if there is other effective defence, the defendant is not defeated; and if there is none, then if he succeeds by relying on the statute, he succeeds only by excluding the evidence of the trust and thus of the fraud. This is so, whether the defendant be, for example, a volunteer or a purchaser for value without notice. So to the extent to which a person relies on the statutory defence to exclude the establishment of fraud, he uses the statute as an instrument of fraud—to succeed by using the statute to exclude evidence of fraud.

In *Rochefoucauld v Boustead* [1897] 1 Ch 196 such a case as that now before me was treated as falling exclusively within the section corresponding to section 53(1)(b) of the Law of Property Act 1925, and the defendants did not attempt to rely on any of the other provisions of section 53 to escape the operation of the principle.

It was further submitted for the defendants that the inclusion in the transfer by Mrs Hodgson to Mr Evans of its being made in consideration of her love and affection for him excluded any resulting trust. Lord Upjohn's observations in *Vandervell v Inland Revenue Commissioners* [1967] 2 AC 291, 312 were referred to. Those observations were made in reference exclusively to resulting trusts; but, as I have said, Mrs Hodgson expressly disclaimed relying on any resulting trust. It did not appear to me that the defendants relied on this reference to consideration of love and affection to defeat the admission of oral evidence of the trust, although counsel for Mrs Hodgson did seem concerned at one stage to rebut such an argument. It seems to me that such a submission would be contrary to the well-established principle that extrinsic evidence is always admissible of the true nature of any transaction, for example, to establish that conveyances, despite their terms, are according to the true nature of the transaction mortgages. *Lincoln v Wright* (1859) 4 De G & J 16, itself a Statute of Frauds case, was a conveyance in form which it was agreed should operate as a mortgage. In *Haigh v Kaye* (1872) 7 Ch App 469 a conveyance was expressed to be in consideration of a money payment and was of an estate described as absolute. There was in fact no consideration. (The plaintiff thus conveyed the estate, because he had feared an adverse decision in a pending suit, but it was held that that did not affect the position.) It was held that, although the defendant invoked the Statute of Frauds, the plaintiff was entitled to have the estate reconveyed to him.

My conclusion, therefore, is that the defendants are not entitled to exclude parol evidence of the trust.

E: Equity acts *in personam*

One feature of equitable jurisdiction has always been that it is exercised against specific persons—equity acts *in personam*. This is on account of equity's traditional concern to address unconscionability in particular cases. Even under a modern trust, where the beneficiary has a property right in the trust assets (a so-called right in the thing or a right *in rem*) enforceable against the trustee and third party recipients from the trustee, the beneficiary also has the right to bring an action against the trustee personally (a right *in personam*) to ensure that the trust property is properly cared for and the trust properly discharged. There are other contexts in which the personal nature of equitable jurisdiction remains of significance. One is where land is situated abroad.

Richard West and Partners (Inverness) Ltd v *Dick*

[1969] 2 Ch 424, Court of Appeal

Held: The English courts had jurisdiction to grant a decree of specific performance of a contract for the sale of land abroad (in Scotland).

MEGARRY J (whose decision was approved by the Court of Appeal): By the writ in this action, issued on 9 August 1967, the plaintiffs, who are the vendors under a contract for the sale of land, claim specific performance of the contract against the defendant, the purchaser ...

The main point in the case turns on the fact that the land in question is situate in Scotland ...

Mr Godfrey [for the purchaser] ... challenged much of the alleged jurisdiction to decree specific performance of contracts relating to foreign land. Such a jurisdiction, he said, might be appropriate in cases where the land was subject to no civilised jurisdiction, or where it was subject to a jurisdiction similar to or derived from the English jurisdiction. But where, as in Scotland, the land was subject to an entirely different system, this made it inappropriate to grant a remedy which might involve grave difficulties in working out the decree. Scottish land law is probably no less obscure to the English lawyer than English land law is to the Scot.

...

The existence of the jurisdiction to decree specific performance of a contract for the sale of foreign land against a defendant within the jurisdiction has been laid down by high authority for over two centuries. An odd feature, however, is that [counsel for the vendors] has been able to refer me to no reported case in which such a decree has actually been made. The leading authority is, of course, *Penn* v *Lord Baltimore* (1750) 1 Ves Sen 444, where Lord Hardwicke LC decreed specific performance of an English agreement relating to the boundaries between Pennsylvania and Maryland, despite the inability of the court to enforce its decree *in rem*. Lord Hardwicke said at p. 447:

> The conscience of the party was bound by this agreement; and being within the jurisdiction of this court ... , which acts *in personam*, the court may properly decree it as an agreement, if a foundation for it.

Of the many subsequent pronouncements on the subject, I will select two, merely mentioning *Fry on Specific Performance of Contracts*, 6th ed. (1921), pp. 56–59. In *Ewing* v *Orr Ewing* (1883) 9 App Cas 34, 40, the Earl of Selborne LC said:

> The jurisdiction of the English court is established upon elementary principles. The courts of equity in England are, and always have been, courts of conscience, operating *in personam* and not *in rem*; and in the exercise of this personal jurisdiction they have always been accustomed to compel the performance of contracts and trusts as to subjects which were not either locally or *ratione domicilii* within their jurisdiction. They have done so as to land, in Scotland, in Ireland, in the Colonies, in foreign countries.

He then cited *Penn* v *Lord Baltimore* (1750) 1 Ves Sen 444, and the notes to it in 2 LC Eq, 4th ed., pp. 939, 940, 941. In the judgment of Byrne J in *Duder* v *Amsterdamsch Trustees Kantoor* [1902] 2 Ch 132 at 140, 141, there is conveniently set out an extensive quotation from the judgment of Lord Cottenham LC in [*Re Courtney*], *ex parte Pollard* (1840) Mont & Ch 239 at 251. The quotation includes this passage:

> Bills for specific performance of contracts for the sale of lands, or respecting mortgages of estates, in the colonies and elsewhere out of the jurisdiction of this Court, are of familiar occurrence. Why

then, consistently with these principles and these authorities, should the fact, that by the law of Scotland no lien or equitable mortgage was created by the deposit and memorandum in this case, prevent the Courts of this country from giving such effect to the transactions between the parties as it would have given if the land had been in England? If the contract had been to sell the lands a specific performance would have been decreed; and why is all relief to be refused because the contract is to sell, subject to a condition for redemption? The substance of the agreement is to charge the debt upon the estates, and to do and perfect all such acts as may be necessary for the purpose; and if the Court would decree specific performance of this contract, and the completion of the security according to the forms of law in Scotland, it will give effect to this equity by paying out of the proceeds of the estate (which being part of the bankrupt's estate must be sold) what is found to be the amount of the debt so agreed to be charged upon it, which is what the creditor asks.

It is, of course, curious that neither of these cases nor any other case that has been cited to me relates to an actual decree of specific performance of a contract for the sale of foreign land; but when it has been asserted on such high authority that the grant of such decrees is of familiar occurrence and of long standing, and Scotland is in terms mentioned, I do not think it is for me to question the doctrine, even if (as is not the case) I had any inclination to do so. It may be that one reason why there is no report of any such decree is that no such case has been thought reportable. Certainly I do not think that I can treat the absence of such a report as throwing doubt on the principle that equity, acting *in personam*, may decree specific performance against a defendant within the jurisdiction whose conscience is bound by some trust or contract. Any inability of the court to enforce the decree *in rem* is no reason for refusing the plaintiff such rights and means of enforcement as equity can afford him. In the present case, of course, the vendors stand ready and willing to convey the land; and the fact that it is in Scotland provides no reason why the purchaser should not pay the money that he contracted to pay.

...

Mr Godfrey took two other points. [Megarry J went on to discuss peripheral points relating to fire precautions and planning consent.]

HARMAN LJ: ... There remains the point on which Megarry J, learned man that he is, exhibited a very interesting and powerful judgment, whereby he expressed the view that there is no objection to a grant of specific performance of a contract for foreign land by an English court. As far as I am concerned I am content to adopt the elaborate reasoning by which he reached that conclusion. I have always thought, and I still think, that the Court of Chancery, acting as it does *in personam*, is well able to grant specific performance of a contract to buy or sell foreign land, provided the defendant is domiciled within its jurisdiction. I say nothing about a case where the defendant is domiciled outside; but the purchaser here lives at Enfield: the vendors have their registered office in England (if that be relevant; I do not think it is): and I see nothing difficult about a vendors' decree of specific performance in the circumstances. There might be difficulties raised by matters of Scottish title; but here the title was accepted. The decree contains the usual recital that the purchaser has accepted the vendors' title to the property, about which I gather there is no doubt ...

NOTES

1. See also *Ewing* v *Orr-Ewing* (1883) 9 App Cas 34.
2. Reasoning along similar lines was adopted in *Webb* v *Webb* [1991] 1 WLR 1410, [1992] 1 All ER 17, where a father had purchased a property in France in his son's name. The father successfully brought proceedings in England against the son for a declaration that the son held the property as trustee and for an order to execute the documents necessary for vesting the legal title in the father. The resulting trust recognised under English law was enforceable against a defendant who was subject to the jurisdiction of the English courts.
3. The ability of equity to act *in personam* can be useful in any case where the property is situate abroad. The worldwide freezing order (*Mareva* injunction) depends on equity acting *in personam*, as does equity's ability to trace property through civil law jurisdictions (see Chapter 14).
4. For another example of equity enforcing a right in another jurisdiction, see *R. Griggs Group Ltd* v *Evans* [2004] All ER (D) 155 (Chancery Division), where the right was equitable copyright.

5. Despite all the talk of 'conscience' as a basis for equity's *in personam* intervention, it must be borne in mind that courts of law are not concerned with moral conscience in the abstract, but with conduct that is deemed to be unconscionable in the particular context: 'Conscience for the purposes of the law of equity denotes an objective standard of right and wrong, as understood by the reasonable person: If the court were obliged to give effect to any view claimed to be an expression of conscience, it would not be law but anarchy' (*Commissioner of Police of the Metropolis v Times Newspapers Ltd* [2011] EWHC 2705 (QB), para. [103]).

F: Those who come to equity must come with clean hands

This maxim applies in the case of injunctions and on applications for specific performance, because the award of such remedies lies in the discretion of the court. The maxim will not be applied to prevent a claimant from bringing an action under an established equitable right (see *Rowan* v *Dann* (1992) 64 P & CR 202 and *Tinsley* v *Milligan* in Chapter 5).

Lee v Haley

(1869) 5 LR Ch App 155, Court of Appeal in Chancery

Facts: The plaintiffs sought an injunction to protect their trade as coal merchants.

Held: The injunction would be refused because the plaintiffs had unclean hands (not because of the coal, but because they had been dishonestly selling their customers short).

SIR G. M. GIFFARD LJ: ... if the Plaintiffs had been systematically and knowingly carrying on a fraudulent trade, and delivering short weight [of coal], it is beyond all question that this court would not interfere to protect them in carrying on such trade.

Coatsworth v Johnson

[1886–90] All ER Rep 547, Court of Appeal

Facts: Johnson entered into an agreement to lease a farm to Coatsworth for 21 years. The agreement contained a clause to farm 'in good and husband-like manner'. Coatsworth took possession of the farm without a formal deed being executed in his favour. Within a few months of his taking possession, he had allowed the condition of the land to deteriorate very badly. Johnson took the rather drastic step of evicting Coatsworth from the farm. Coatsworth sued for wrongful eviction, contending that the agreement created an equitable lease lasting 21 years.

Held: Coatsworth's failure to take good care of the farm was a substantial breach of the contract which meant that he had 'unclean hands' in the sight of equity. He would therefore be denied the discretionary remedy of specific performance of the contract. He was evicted.

LORD ESHER MR: ... The moment the plaintiff went into equity, and asked for specific performance, and it was proved that he himself was guilty of the breach of contract, which the defendant says he is by not cultivating, the court of equity would refuse to grant specific performance, and would leave the parties to their other rights. Then, if the court of equity would not grant specific performance, we are not to consider specific performance as granted. Then the case is at an end. It is a lease at will ...

G: Those who come to equity must do equity

J. W. Perry (ed.), *Story's Commentaries on Equity Jurisprudence*
12th edn (Boston: Little, Brown & Co, 1877)

[T]he interference of a court of equity is a matter of mere discretion ... And in all cases of this sort ... the court will, in granting relief, impose such terms upon the party as it deems the real justice of the case to require ... The maxim here is emphatically applied—he who seeks equity must do equity.

O'sullivan v *Management Agency and Music Ltd*
[1985] 3 All ER 351, Court of Appeal

Facts: When still an unknown artist, Gilbert O'sullivan, a composer and performer of pop music, signed management agreements with companies controlled by Mr Mills, a music agent. The terms of the agreements were not as favourable to O'sullivan as they would have been had he had independent legal advice. O'sullivan had trusted Mills and had not negotiated the agreements in the usual 'arm's-length' way. Nevertheless, the management and marketing prowess of Mills's companies brought O'sullivan great success and the wealth that accompanies such success. In due course, however, their working relationship deteriorated, and ultimately O'sullivan brought an action against Mills and his companies, seeking to have his management contracts declared void on the basis that they had been obtained by undue influence. The trial judge set the contracts aside and ordered that Mills and his companies should account for profits made on O'sullivan's music, together with compound interest on those profits. The defendants conceded that there had been undue influence on the part of Mills, but appealed against the companies' liability and against the remedies awarded against the companies and against Mills.

Held: The companies were subject to the same liability as Mills as they were under the de facto control of Mills. It had therefore been proper to set aside all the contracts. However, in determining the appropriate remedy for the claimant, it was necessary to make allowance for the work done by the companies on behalf of O'sullivan. This would include allowing the companies to retain a reasonable profit even though they were in a fiduciary position in relation to O'sullivan.

DUNN LJ: ... It is true that in this case moral blame does lie on the defendants, as the judge's findings of fact show. On the other hand it is significant that until O'sullivan met Mills he had achieved no success, and that after he effectively parted company with Mills in 1976 he achieved no success either. During the years that he was working with Mills his success was phenomenal. Although equity looks at the advantage gained by the wrongdoer rather than the loss to the victim, the cases show that in assessing the advantage gained the court will look at the whole situation in the round. And it is relevant that if the approach of counsel for O'sullivan is applied O'sullivan would be much better off than if he had received separate legal advice and signed agreements negotiated at arm's length on reasonable terms current in the trade at the time. This point was made forcibly by counsel for the first five defendants at the conclusion of his address in reply, when he relied on the maxim 'He who seeks equity must do equity' and submitted that equity required that the position of O'sullivan was relevant in considering the appropriate remedy.

In my judgment the judge was right to set the agreements aside and to order an account of the profits and payment of the sums found due on the taking of the account. But in taking the account the defendants are entitled to an allowance as proposed by Fox LJ, whose judgment I have read in draft, for reasonable remuneration, including a profit element, for all work done in promoting and exploiting O'sullivan and his compositions, whether such work was done pursuant to a contractual obligation or gratuitously. What constitutes 'reasonable remuneration' will depend on evidence on the taking of the account, but not the evidence of Mr Levison (an expert witness) who approached the question on a different basis ...

... Looking at the position in equity, that the defendants are bound to account for their actual profits, with the credits to which I have referred, their actual profits do not include tax paid and irrecoverable. In my opinion therefore it is right that, in computing the sums payable to O'sullivan for the years during which tax was actually paid and is not reclaimable, credit should be given to the defendants for all sums paid to any tax authority or which would have been paid but for the utilisation of tax losses or group relief or advanced corporation tax surrendered. Sums payable to O'sullivan in subsequent years should be paid without regard to tax.

NOTE: For further illustrations of the maxim, see *Sledmore* v *Dalby* (1996) 72 P & CR 196, *Cheese* v *Thomas* [1994] 1 WLR 129, 136, and *Vadasz* v *Pioneer Concrete (SA) Pty Ltd* [1995] 69 ALR 678.

H: Equity sees as done that which ought to be done

Although normally applied to private transactions (see *Walsh* v *Lonsdale* (1882) 21 ChD 9, CA, above) this maxim has occasionally been applied to treat a court order to transfer property as taking immediate effect in equity, so as to impose a constructive trust on the person subject to the order (*Mountney* v *Treharne* [2003] Ch 135, CA; *Re Flint (A Bankrupt)* [1993] Ch 319). The maxim was applied in *HR Trustees Ltd* v *Wembley plc (in liquidation)* [2011] EWHC 2974 (Ch) to ratify a transaction that had been author-ised by four trustees, but which should have been ratified by all five of the trustees. The judge agreed, however, that equitable maxims should be 'strictly confined to the areas in which they can be seen to have been previously applied' (*per* Vos J at para [59]).

I: Equity imputes an intention to fulfil an obligation

It is important to recall that equity is not a form of morality. Equity is an aspect of law, so equity only imputes an intention to fulfil a *legal* obligation. See *Re Hallett's Estate* (1880) 13 ChD 696, CA (Chapter 14).

J: Where the equities are equal, the first in time prevails

This maxim is sometimes paraphrased *the first in time is the first in right*. Its use can be illustrated by taking the straightforward case of equitable mortgagees competing against each other for priority. Suppose that A grants an equitable mortgage of property to B and later grants a mortgage of the same property to C. In the usual course of events, B's mortgage will have priority over C's, in accordance with the maxim. In theory, the maxim only applies if the competing equities are equal, but Kay J in *Taylor* v *Russell* [1890] 1 Ch 8, 17 stated that nothing less than 'gross negligence' must be proved by a later equitable mortgagee against a prior mortgagee to give priority to a later one. Earlier authorities which appear to suggest that B might cede priority to C, if C's equity is merely *technically* superior to B's must be doubtful.

K: Where the equities are equal, the law prevails

This maxim, like the previous one, operates more like a rule than a principle and oper-ates in the context of determining priority between competing equitable claims. If we take our previous hypothetical case, where A granted an equitable mortgage to B and then another to C, the present maxim allows C to gain priority over B by the simple expedient of purchasing the legal title from A (see *Bailey* v *Barnes* [1894] 1 Ch 25 and *Taylor* v *Russell* [1893] AC 244).

One exception to this maxim is the rule in *Dearle* v *Hall* (1828) 3 Russ 1. According to this rule, priority between competing assignees of a *debt* is awarded to the first one to give notice to the debtor. It does not matter that one of the competitors has a legal interest and the other merely an equitable one.

L: Where equity and law conflict, equity shall prevail

This maxim, established in *The Earl of Oxford's Case* (1615) 1 Rep Ch 1, is now enshrined in statute:

SENIOR COURTS ACT 1981

Section 49

Every Court exercising jurisdiction in England and Wales in any civil cause or matter shall continue to administer law and equity on the basis that, wherever there is any conflict or variance between the rules of equity and the rules of common law with reference to the same matter, the rules of equity shall prevail.

M: Equality is equity

For illustrations of the application of this maxim, see *IRC* v *Broadway Cottages Trust* [1955] Ch 20, CA (Chapter 3) and *Midland Bank plc* v *Cooke* [1995] 4 All ER 562, CA (Chapter 8).

N: Delay defeats equities

The processes of law are notorious for delay. Shakespeare's *Hamlet* lists 'the law's delay' among the chief woes of life in his famous 'to be, or not to be' soliloquy. More than two centuries later, administrative delay effectively crippled Chancery procedure. This may in part explain the requirement, enshrined in this maxim, that a person seeking an equitable remedy should not be lax in bringing their claim. In practice, however, the maxim is little used and the doctrine of laches (pronounced 'lay-cheese') is the usual means of defeating stale equitable claims. The doctrine is concerned with the private interest of preventing prejudice to the particular defendant and the public interest in bringing civil dispute to an end (see G. Watt, 'Laches, Cause of Action Estoppel and Election in Breach of Trust', in P. Birks and A. Pretto (eds), *Breach of Trust* (Oxford: Hart Publishing, 2002)).

Smith v *Clay*
(1767) 3 BRO CC 639n, House of Lords

LORD CAMDEN: ... A Court of Equity, which is never active in relief against conscience, or public convenience, has always refused its aid to stale demands, where the party has slept upon his right, and acquiesced for a great length of time ... '*Expedit reipublicae ut sit finis litium*,' is a maxim that has prevailed in this court in all times, without the help of an act of parliament.

Frawley v *Neill*

[2000] CP Rep 20, Court of Appeal

Facts: Frawley and Neill purchased a property in their joint names in 1974. F paid two-thirds of the deposit, and N paid the other third. The balance was provided by a mortgage with the Halifax Building Society. When their cohabitation ended in 1975, N agreed (orally) that she would sell her interest to F. The judge found that this agreement had been finalised and that F had paid the defendant the agreed sum. Arrangements to convey the property into F's sole name were made but never completed. In 1986, the building society repossessed and sold the house, paying surplus proceeds of sale into a bank account. F claimed that he was entitled to this entire sum, as he had purchased N's share. Against this, N raised the defence of delay or laches, claiming that F was too late to claim specific performance of the purchase agreement. In spite of this argument, the judge awarded a declaration in favour of F. N appealed.

Held: (Dismissing the appeal): F's agreement with N had been performed and therefore F had no need of specific performance. N was a bare trustee of the legal title until it had been extinguished by the building society's sale. The proceeds of sale belonged beneficially to the claimant after repayment of the mortgage and the mortgagee's expenses. Delay and laches would not, in any event, have prevented an award of specific performance, as F had acted upon the agreement and N had acquiesced in it. There were no circumstances which would bar the enforcement of his equitable right. It was held *per curiam* that the modern approach to the doctrine of laches should not entail slavish adherence to formulae derived from earlier cases. Each case should be decided on its facts applying a broad approach directed to ascertaining whether, in all the circumstances it would be unconscionable for a party to be permitted to exercise his beneficial right.

ALDOUS LJ: In my judgment, there are no circumstances which would act as a bar in this case to the court granting specific performance. To the contrary, it would be inequitable not to do so.

The contract between Mr. Frawley and Miss Lindley had in essence been performed. The money was paid. Mr. Frawley became the sole occupant. What more was needed? Nothing more was needed to perfect Mr. Frawley's beneficial interest but to perfect his legal title he needed Miss Lindley's signature on the conveyance. In my view, that did not require specific performance because she became a bare trustee of her share on behalf of Mr. Frawley. I can see no reason why a lapse of time or, to use the technical word, laches, should enable a bare trustee to avoid signing a conveyance to perfect a legal title. In any case, the Halifax had under the mortgage a right to possession and exercised that right, and upon sale conveyed the legal title to the purchaser. There remained the net proceeds of sale. They belonged beneficially to Mr. Frawley, and there can be no need, as is demonstrated by the order made in this case, for specific performance to be ordered to enable Mr. Frawley's right to them to become clear. Miss Lindley had no interest. Her legal interest in the property had become extinguished on sale, and all that remained was the beneficial interest in the net proceeds. That belonged to Mr. Frawley.

I draw comfort from the written reasons given by Millett LJ when he refused Miss Lindley leave to appeal against the judgment of Chadwick J refusing to strike out this action. He said this:

'Payment. Once the purchaser pays the whole of the purchase price, the vendor becomes a bare trustee of the land for the purchaser. The basis of the purchaser's beneficial interest changes; it is no longer dependent on the availability of a decree of specific performance: see Williams Vendor & Purchaser p. 572–3l, *Re Cumming* (1869) 5 Ch.App. 72 and other cases to like effect; and *Bridget* v *Mills* (1957) Ch. 475, which seems to me to be on all fours with the present. By the time the building society sold, the plaintiff did not need to enforce the agreement, which was fully executed. He was in possession and had paid the full purchase price (on his case); the vendor was his nominee and could not resist a vesting order, without the necessity for a decree of specific performance; and in any case her legal title was probably barred anyway.'

Mr. Taylor also sought to rely by analogy on section 36 of the Limitation Act 1980. I can see no justification for such a submission. Mr. Frawley had had an equitable interest in the house since 1975 and in the proceeds of sale when the house was sold. Why he should be barred from claiming the money by a claim from Miss Lindley, who sold her interest in the house in 1975, I cannot understand.

The principles of law applied in *Mills* v *Haywood* and *Williams* v *Greatrex* are instances of a wider principle applied in the last 20 or so years to the doctrine of laches, estoppel and acquiescence, which were identified by Oliver J in such cases as *Taylor Fashions* v *Liverpool Victoria Trustees Co. Ltd* [1981] 2 WLR and *Habib Bank Ltd* v *Habib Bank A.G.* [1981] 1 WLR 1265. That wider principle was enunciated by Sir Barnes Peacock in *Lindsay Petroleum Company* v *Hurd* 1874 L.R. 5 Privy Council 221 and 229, and cited with approval by Lord Blackburn in *Erlanger* v *New Sombrero Phosphate Co* (1878) 3 App.Cas. 1218, 1279:

> 'The doctrine of laches in courts of equity is not an arbitrary or a technical doctrine. Where it would be practically unjust to give a remedy, either because the party has, by his conduct done that which might fairly be regarded as equivalent to a waiver of it, or where, by his conduct and neglect he has, though perhaps not waiving that remedy, yet put the other party in a situation in which it would not be reasonable to place him if the remedy were afterwards to be asserted, in either of these cases lapse of time and delay are most material. But in every case if any argument against relief, which otherwise would be just, is founded upon mere delay, that delay of course not amounting to a bar by any statute of limitations, the validity of that defence must be tried upon principles substantially equitable. Two circumstances always important in such cases are the length of the delay and the nature of the acts done during the interval, which might affect either party and cause a balance of justice or injustice in taking the one course or the other, so far as relates to the remedy.'

Lord Blackburn in Erlanger quoted that passage from the judgment of Sir Barnes Peacock and continued:

> 'I have looked in vain for any authority which gives a more distinct and definite rule than this; and I think, from the nature of the inquiry, it must always be a question of more or less, depending on the degree of diligence which might reasonably be required, and the degree of change which has occurred, whether the balance of justice or injustice is in favour of granting the remedy or withholding it. The determination of such a question must largely depend on the turn of mind of those who have to decide, and must therefore be subject to uncertainty; but that, I think, is inherent in the nature of the inquiry.'

In my view, the more modern approach should not require an inquiry as to whether the circumstances can be fitted within the confines of a preconceived formula derived from earlier cases. The inquiry should require a broad approach, directed to ascertaining whether it would in all the circumstances be unconscionable for a party to be permitted to assert his beneficial right. No doubt the circumstances which gave rise to a particular result in decided cases are relevant to the question whether or not it would be conscionable or unconscionable for the relief to be asserted, but each case has to be decided on its facts applying the broad approach.

Applying those principles to the present case, there can be no doubt that Mr. Frawley should not be prevented from being paid that to which he is beneficially entitled. He bought out Miss Lindley. He paid the money. He continued to live in the house and, as owner, paid the mortgage instalments. It would not be unconscionable to prevent him obtaining the proceeds of sale. In fact, in my view, it would be unconscionable for Miss Lindley to assert any right to the money. She has accepted payment. She allowed Mr. Frawley to pay the mortgage instalments and should not be entitled to any of the proceeds. The judge came to the right conclusion, and I believe for the right reasons. I would dismiss this appeal.

NOTE: Subsequent cases confirm that delay will not give rise to laches if the delay causes no prejudice to the defendant (e.g. *Brudnell-Bruce* v *Moore* [2012] EWHC 1024 (Ch); [2012] 2 P & CR DG8).

O: Equity will not assist a volunteer

See Chapter 4, where this maxim is considered in detail.

P: There is no equity to perfect an imperfect gift

See Chapter 4, where this maxim is considered in detail.

Q: Equity abhors a vacuum in ownership

See Chapter 5, especially on the topic of 'automatic resulting trusts'.

SECTION 3: EQUITABLE DOCTRINES

The equitable doctrines are rigid traditional precepts by which equitable discretion is guided and restrained. They are ultimately derived from the application of equitable maxims, most of the doctrines owing a good deal to the twin maxims 'equity imputes an intention to fulfil an obligation' and 'equity sees as done that which ought to be done', but over time, they have lost virtually all contact with the forces of principle and pragmatism which first gave rise to the maxims themselves. With the benefit of hindsight, the development of the equitable doctrines can be seen to be a project quite out of character for such a pragmatic branch of law as equity, since equity is not doctrinaire.

A: Conversion

According to this doctrine, equity will in certain circumstances regard personal property as real property and real property as personal. We considered an important instance of this process earlier, when we examined the specific performance of a contract for the sale of land. We saw that, whereas at law the contract entitles the purchaser to a personal monetary remedy, equity will order specific performance of the contract and since specific performance ought to be done in the future, equity will consider it as done now. By this feat of imagination, equity converts the purchaser's right to personal property (monetary damages) into a right in real property (the land).

Fletcher v Ashburner

(1779) 1 Bro CC 497, 499

SIR THOMAS SEWELL MR: 'money directed to be employed in the purchase of land, and land directed to be sold and turned into money, are to be considered as that species of property into which they are directed to be converted ... The owner of the fund, or the contracting parties, may make land money, or money land.'

The doctrine of conversion as it applies to convert land into money is now of reduced relevance since the Trusts and Land and Appointment of Trustees Act 1996 abolished the traditional application of the doctrine to trusts of land where the trustee is under an obligation to sell the land (what was known as a 'trust for sale'), although a trust for sale of land created in a will taking effect before 1 January 1997 will still operate to convert the land into money.

TRUSTS OF LAND AND APPOINTMENT OF TRUSTEES ACT 1996

3. Abolition of doctrine of conversion

(1)   Where land is held by trustees subject to a trust for sale, the land is not to be regarded as personal property; and where personal property is subject to a trust for sale in order that the trustees may acquire land, the personal property is not to be regarded as land.

(2)   Subsection (1) does not apply to a trust created by a will if the testator died before the commencement of this Act.

(3)   Subject to that, subsection (1) applies to a trust whether it is created, or arises, before or after that commencement.

B: Satisfaction

Where A owes a sum of money to B, equity will require A to pay the debt while he is alive. However, if the debt has not been paid by the time of A's death and A's will contains no clause requiring his executors to repay his debts, a legacy (a bequest of a sum of money) left by A to B in his will is presumed to satisfy any outstanding debt for an equal or lesser sum owed by A to B prior to making his will. Equity sees as done that which ought to be done and imputes to A an intention to fulfil his obligation to B, provided the legacy is on terms which are as beneficial to B as repayment of the debt.

C: Performance

If A promises B that he will leave a sum of money to B in his will, but A dies intestate (without making a valid will), any money received by B on A's intestacy will be deemed a performance of A's promise. A leading authority for this is *Blandy* v *Widmore* (1716) 1 P Wms 324, even though the doctrine of performance was in that case mistakenly referred to as the doctrine of satisfaction. The error is understandable. The doctrine of performance is a close relation of the doctrine of satisfaction and both doctrines share a common root in the maxim 'equity imputes an intention to fulfil an obligation'. However, whereas the doctrine of satisfaction presumes an intention to pay based on a completely adequate payment, the doctrine of performance regards a partial payment as evidence of an intention to fulfil a promise to pay the full amount. Thus if A promises to acquire freehold land of a certain value and settle it on trust for the benefit of his wife to be, the purchase of freehold land of a lesser value may be held to be a partial performance of the promise (*Lechmere* v *Lady Lechmere* (1735) Cas t Talb 80).

D: Election

The doctrine of election requires a party to choose between mutually exclusive courses of action. The common law version of the doctrine requires a claimant to choose between mutually inconsistent remedies before judgment is entered in his favour; this is, in part, with a view to achieving justice between the parties, but also with a view to maintaining public confidence in legal proceedings by ensuring that no internally inconsistent judgment becomes a matter of public record (on this form of election, see Chapter 13). In equity, the doctrine is concerned solely with fairness between the parties. It provides, for example, that where a court judgment or a written instrument such as a will (*Codrington* v *Codrington* (1875) LR 7 HL 854) or trust deed confers a benefit on a certain person, that person must choose to take the benefit subject to all the requirements of the judgment or instrument or else to reject the judgment or instrument and lose the benefits conferred by it. Despite its name, the equitable doctrine does not confer a right to choose; rather, it restricts the right to choose in the interest of fairness between the parties by ensuring that no party takes a benefit without taking an associated burden (*Nexus Communications Group Ltd* v *Lambert* [2005] EWHC 345 (Ch)).

First National Bank Plc v *Walker*
[2001] 1 FLR 505

Facts: A wife who was awarded the matrimonial home in divorce proceedings, and in doing so accepted the validity of the mortgage on the home, was not permitted in subsequent repossession proceedings brought by the bank to allege that the mortgage was invalid. She had elected to take the house and could not in conscience take it free of the mortgage.

> LORD JUSTICE RIX: ... she knew all she had to know to put her to her election as to the course down which she wished to proceed. She was facing in two directions. She had obtained relief in the matrimonial proceedings on the basis that the charge was a subsisting charge which bound her as well as her husband. However, in the possession action, she sought to set that charge aside on the basis that it did not bind her but only her husband. As such her stand might be said to be equivocal. In my judgment she could not in good conscience maintain both those positions.

SECTION 4: EQUITABLE REMEDIES

The usual common law remedy for breach of contract or commission of a tort is an award of damages, but where in a particular case, or in a particular type of case, it would be unconscionable for the defendant to restrict the claimant to common law damages, the court may award an equitable remedy against the defendant. For example, an injunction may be awarded to remedy the tort of trespass and the court may decree specific performance of a contract to acquire land, for in both these cases, an award of damages is insufficient to achieve a just outcome. In the former case, because an award of damages will be nominal unless real harm has been caused, and in any event, an award of damages does not prevent future trespass; in the latter case, because even if an award of damages were competent to meet the purchaser's legitimate expectations as to the investment value of the land, no amount of money will assist the purchaser to buy identical substitute land, since all land is unique.

Evans Marshall & Co. Ltd v *Bertola SA*
[1973] 1 WLR 349

> SACHS LJ: The standard question in relation to the grant of an injunction 'Are damages an adequate remedy?' might perhaps, in the light of the authorities of recent years, be rewritten: 'Is it just, in all the circumstances, that a plaintiff should be confined to his remedy in damages?'

A: The discretionary nature of equitable remedies

Whereas common law remedies are available as of right, equitable remedies retain the discretionary nature of the early equitable jurisdiction; although the onset over the last two centuries or so of defined systems of precedent and law reporting have curtailed the early discretion somewhat so that discretion is now exercised in accordance with fairly clear and even rigid principles. We have already noted that the discretionary nature of equitable remedies can lead to the refusal of a remedy where the defendant comes to equity with unclean hands, but entirely innocent claimants may also be denied a remedy where to grant it would put the other party in breach of a contract with a third party (see *Warmington v Miller* [1973] QB 877). Other grounds for refusing the remedy are that severe hardship might be caused to the defendant (reflected in the maxim, *those who come to equity must do equity*), or, as in a contract action, that the contract has been forced upon the defendant through unfair pressure (whether or not actual undue influence or duress were also present).

Warmington v *Miller*

[1973] QB 877, Court of Appeal

Held: The court would not grant specific performance of an oral contract for an under-lease where to do so would result in the landlord of the underlease breaking a term of the head-lease (the head-lease contained a prohibition on assigning, under-letting, or parting with possession of part only of the premises). The claimants were therefore left to their common law remedy of damages.

STAMP LJ: … I turn to consider the alternative submission advanced on behalf of the defendant that the judge ought not to have ordered specific performance. Counsel for the defendant submits that the judge ought not to have ordered specific performance requiring the defendant to do that which he cannot do under the terms of the lease under which he holds the premises and which, if he did, would expose him to proceedings for forfeiture. In my judgment that submission is well founded. I can see nothing in this case to take it outside the practice of the court, in determining whether to exercise its discretionary power to grant the equitable remedy of specific performance, not to do so where the result would necessitate a breach by the defendant of a contract with a third party or would compel the defendant to do that which he is not lawfully competent to do: see *Fry's Specific Performance*, 6th ed. (1921), p. 194 and *Willmott* v *Barber* (1880) 15 ChD 96 per Fry J at p. 107. Here the landlord is under an unqualified covenant in his lease not to underlet or part with possession of part only of the premises demised to him. To order him specifically to perform the contract by granting an underlease and so allowing the plaintiffs to retain possession would be to order him to do something he cannot do or, if he did it, would expose him to a forfeiture. As Lord Redesdale LC remarked in a passage in *Harnett* v *Yielding* (1805) 2 Sch. & Lef 549, 554, quoted in *Fry's Specific Performance*, at p. 194:

> [The plaintiff] must also show that, in seeking the performance, he does not call upon the other party to do an act which he is not lawfully competent to do; for, if he does, a consequence is produced that quite passes by the object of the court in exercising the jurisdiction, which is to do more complete justice.

During the course of the argument I suggested to counsel that the position of the [plaintiffs] might be sufficiently and properly protected by a declaration that [the plaintiffs] were in possession of the workshop under the terms of the agreement of 3 August 1971. That suggestion was supported by [counsel for the plaintiffs] with enthusiasm and I must deal with it. I have, for the following reasons, come to the clear conclusion that the suggestion was misconceived, and I regret having made it.

It is not and never has been the contention of the [plaintiffs] that they are lessees at law under the agreement: and [counsel for the defendant] submitted, as I think correctly, that the *Walsh* v *Lonsdale* situation, where the intended lessee is treated as having the same rights as if a lease had in fact been granted to him, applies only if the lessee is entitled to specific performance: see the judgment of Sir George Jessel MR in *Walsh* v *Lonsdale* (1882) 21 ChD 9, 14. The equitable interests which the intended lessee has under an agreement for a lease do not exist *in vacuo* but arise because the intended lessee has an equitable right to specific performance of the agreement. In such a situation that which is agreed to be and ought to be done is treated as having been done and carrying with it in equity the attendant rights. But the intended lessee's equitable rights do not in general arise when that which is agreed to be done would not be ordered to be done. The suggested declaration would thus not be justified.

There is, I think, another objection to the making of such a declaration as I am discussing—or perhaps it is putting the same point in another way. The equitable right to be in possession under the agreement could be protected only by an injunction, and, if after the making of such a declaration, the [plaintiffs] sought the equitable remedy of an injunction to protect their right to remain in possession it would be an invitation to the court to grant part specific performance of the agreement. Such an injunction, like the order for specific performance itself, would in its effect compel the [defendant] to continue to break the covenant not to part with possession of part only of the premises demised to him and be open to the same objection as an order for specific performance. The suggested declaration would be a misleading nuisance.

For these reasons, the [plaintiffs] ought, in my judgment, to be left with their remedy at law, namely, damages for the repudiation by the [defendant] of his agreement to grant the [plaintiffs] a lease.

B: The equitable remedy of specific performance

The common law gives a contracting party the option of performing his contract or paying damages to compensate for its breach, but where it would be unconscionable to restrict the other party to the common law remedy of damages, a court may order that the contract be performed. The order is described as a 'decree of specific performance'. Because it is an equitable remedy, specific performance will be refused if the claimant has not kept his side of the bargain (in accordance with the maxim that those who come to equity must come with clean hands, see Section 2: The maxims of equity, F: Those who come to equity must come with clean hands). The availability of specific performance also varies according to the subject matter of the contract.

(i) Land

See *Walsh* v *Lonsdale* at A: The discretionary nature of equitable remedies.

(ii) Sale of goods

THE SALE OF GOODS ACT 1979

52 Specific performance

　　(1)　In any action for breach of contract to deliver specific or ascertained goods the court may, if it thinks fit, on the plaintiff's application, by its judgment or decree direct that the contract shall be performed specifically, without giving the defendant the option of retaining the goods on payment of damages.

　　(2)　The plaintiff's application may be made at any time before judgment or decree.

　　(3)　The judgment or decree may be unconditional, or on such terms and conditions as to damages, payment of the price and otherwise as seem just to the court.

　　(4)　...

(iii) Shares

See *Oughtred* v *IRC* and *Neville* v *Wilson* in Chapter 6.

(iv) Contract of employment

TRADE UNION AND LABOUR RELATIONS (CONSOLIDATION) ACT 1992

236 No compulsion to work

No court shall, whether by way of:

　　(a)　an order for specific performance ... of a contract of employment, or

　　(b)　an injunction ... restraining a breach or threatened breach of such a contract,

compel an employee to do any work or attend at any place for the doing of any work.

C. H. Giles & Co. Ltd v *Morris and Others*

[1972] 1 WLR 307, Chancery Division

MEGARRY J: One day, perhaps, the courts will look again at the so-called rule that contracts for personal services or involving the continuous performance of services will not be specifically enforced. Such a rule is plainly not absolute and without exception, nor do I think that it can be based on any narrow consideration such as difficulties of constant superintendence by the court. Mandatory injunctions are by no means unknown, and there is normally no question of the court having to send its officers to supervise the performance of the order of the court. Prohibitory injunctions are common, and again there is no direct supervision by the court. Performance of each type of injunction is normally secured by the realisation of the person enjoined that he is liable to be punished for contempt if evidence of his disobedience to the order is put before the court; and if the injunction is prohibitory, actual committal will usually, so long as it continues, make disobedience impossible. If instead the order is for specific performance of a contract for personal services, a similar machinery of enforcement could be employed, again without there being any question of supervision by any officer of the court. The reasons why the court is reluctant to decree specific performance of a contract for personal services (and I would regard it as a strong reluctance rather than a rule) are, I think, more complex and more firmly bottomed on human nature. If a singer contracts to sing, there could no doubt be proceedings for committal if, ordered to sing, the singer remained obstinately dumb. But if instead the singer sang flat, or sharp, or too fast, or too slowly, or too loudly, or too quietly, or resorted to a dozen of the manifestations of temperament traditionally associated with some singers, the threat of committal would reveal itself as a most unsatisfactory weapon: for who could say whether the imperfections of performance were natural or self-induced? To make an order with such possibilities of evasion would be vain; and so the order will not be made. [Note the maxim 'equity will not act in vain' (e,g. *Redcard Ltd* v *Roger Williams* [2010] EWHC 1078 (Ch)).] However, not all contracts of personal service or for the continuous performance of services are as dependent as this on matters of opinion and judgment, nor do all such contracts involve the same degree of the daily impact of person upon person. In general, no doubt, the inconvenience and mischief of decreeing specific performance of most of such contracts will greatly outweigh the advantages, and specific performance will be refused. But I do not think that it should be assumed that as soon as any element of personal service or continuous services can be discerned in a contract the court will, without more, refuse specific performance. [Compare *Araci* v *Fallon* [2011] EWCA Civ 668, in which champion jockey Kieren Fallon was held to an agreement to ride the claimant's horse in 'The Derby' and to ride no competitor horse.]

(v) Contract to run a business

Co-Operative Insurance Society Ltd v Argyll Stores (Holdings) Ltd
[1998] AC 1, House of Lords

Facts: The claimants were landlords of a shopping centre and the defendant's supermarket was the main tenant. In the defendant's lease, the defendant had covenanted to keep its premises open for retail trade during the usual hours of business in the locality, but when the supermarket became unprofitable, the defendant closed the supermarket having given the claimants only one month's notice to find a new tenant. At first instance, the judge granted an order for damages to be assessed but refused an order for specific performance. The Court of Appeal, by a majority, allowed an appeal by the claimants and ordered specific performance.

Held: The settled judicial practice *not* to grant specific performance of an agreement to carry on a business was affirmed, although it was recognised that the grant or refusal of specific performance remains a matter for the discretion of the judge and the settled practice might be departed from in exceptional circumstances. Appeal allowed.

LORD HOFFMANN: A decree of specific performance is of course a discretionary remedy and the question for your Lordships is whether the Court of Appeal was entitled to set aside the exercise of the judge's discretion. There are well-established principles which govern the exercise of the discretion but these, like all equitable principles, are flexible and adaptable to achieve the ends of equity, which is, as Lord Selborne L.C. once remarked, to 'do more perfect and complete justice' than would be the result of leaving the parties to their remedies at common law: *Wilson* v *Northampton and Banbury Junction Railway Co.* (1874) L.R. 9 Ch.App. 279, 284. Much therefore depends upon the facts of the particular case ...

 Specific performance is traditionally regarded in English law as an exceptional remedy, as opposed to the common law damages to which a successful plaintiff is entitled as of right. There may have been some element of later rationalisation of an untidier history, but by the 19th century it was orthodox doctrine that the power to decree specific performance was part of the discretionary jurisdiction of the Court of Chancery to do justice in cases in which the remedies available at common law were inadequate. This is the basis of the general principle that specific performance will not be ordered when damages are an adequate remedy. By contrast, in countries with legal systems based on civil law, such as France, Germany and Scotland, the plaintiff is prima facie entitled to specific performance. The cases in which he is confined to a claim for damages are regarded as the exceptions. In practice, however, there is less difference between common law and civilian systems than these general statements might lead one to suppose. The principles upon which English judges exercise the discretion to grant specific performance are reasonably well settled and depend upon a number of considerations, mostly of a practical nature, which are of very general application. I have made no investigation of civilian systems, but a priori I would expect that judges take much the same matters into account in deciding whether specific performance would be inappropriate in a particular case.

The practice of not ordering a defendant to carry on a business is not entirely dependent upon damages being an adequate remedy. In *Dowty Boulton Paul Ltd v Wolverhampton Corporation* [1971] 1 WLR 204, Sir John Pennycuick V-C. refused to order the corporation to maintain an airfield as a going concern because: 'It is very well established that the court will not order specific performance of an obligation to carry on a business': see p. 211. He added: 'It is unnecessary in the circumstances to discuss whether damages would be an adequate remedy to the company': see p. 212. Thus the reasons which underlie the established practice may justify a refusal of specific performance even when damages are not an adequate remedy.

The most frequent reason given in the cases for declining to order someone to carry on a business is that it would require constant supervision by the court. In *J. C. Williamson Ltd v Lukey and Mulholland* (1931) 45 C.L.R. 282, 297–298, Dixon J. said flatly: 'Specific performance is inapplicable when the continued supervision of the court is necessary in order to ensure the fulfilment of the contract.'

There has, I think, been some misunderstanding about what is meant by continued superintendence. It may at first sight suggest that the judge (or some other officer of the court) would literally have to supervise the execution of the order. In *C. H. Giles Co. Ltd v Morris* [1972] 1 WLR 307, 318 Megarry J. said that 'difficulties of constant superintendence' were a 'narrow consideration' because:

> 'there is normally no question of the court having to send its officers to supervise the performance of the order ... Performance ... is normally secured by the realisation of the person enjoined that he is liable to be punished for contempt if evidence of his disobedience to the order is put before the court; ... '

This is, of course, true but does not really meet the point. The judges who have said that the need for constant supervision was an objection to such orders were no doubt well aware that supervision would in practice take the form of rulings by the court, on applications made by the parties, as to whether there had been a breach of the order. It is the possibility of the court having to give an indefinite series of such rulings in order to ensure the execution of the order which has been regarded as undesirable.

Why should this be so? A principal reason is that, as Megarry J. pointed out in the passage to which I have referred, the only means available to the court to enforce its order is the quasi-criminal procedure of punishment for contempt. This is a powerful weapon; so powerful, in fact, as often to be unsuitable as an instrument for adjudicating upon the disputes which may arise over whether a business is being run in accordance with the terms of the court's order. The heavy-handed nature of the enforcement mechanism is a consideration which may go to the exercise of the court's discretion in other cases as well, but its use to compel the running of a business is perhaps the paradigm case of its disadvantages and it is in this context that I shall discuss them.

... the seriousness of a finding of contempt for the defendant means that any application to enforce the order is likely to be a heavy and expensive piece of litigation. The possibility of repeated applications over a period of time means that, in comparison with a once-and-for-all inquiry as to damages, the enforcement of the remedy is likely to be expensive in terms of cost to the parties and the resources of the judicial system.

This is a convenient point at which to distinguish between orders which require a defendant to carry on an activity, such as running a business over a more or less extended period of time, and orders which require him to achieve a result. The possibility of repeated applications for rulings on compliance with the order which arises in the former case does not exist to anything like the same extent in the latter. Even if the achievement of the result is a complicated matter which will take some time, the court, if called upon to rule, only has to examine the finished work and say whether it complies with the order. This point was made in the context of relief against forfeiture in *Shiloh Spinners Ltd* v *Harding* [1973] AC 691. If it is a condition of relief that the tenant should have complied with a repairing covenant, difficulty of supervision need not be an objection. As Lord Wilberforce said, at p. 724:

> 'what the court has to do is to satisfy itself, ex post facto, that the covenanted work has been done, and it has ample machinery, through certificates, or by inquiry, to do precisely this.'

This distinction between orders to carry on activities and orders to achieve results explains why the courts have in appropriate circumstances ordered specific performance of building contracts and repairing covenants: see *Wolverhampton Corporation* v *Emmons* [1901] 1 KB 515 (building contract) and *Jeune* v *Queens Cross Properties Ltd* [1974] Ch. 97 (repairing covenant). It by no means follows, however, that even obligations to achieve a result will always be enforced by specific performance ...

There is a further objection to an order requiring the defendant to carry on a business, which was emphasised by Millett L.J. in the Court of Appeal. This is that it may cause injustice by allowing the plaintiff to enrich himself at the defendant's expense. The loss which the defendant may suffer through having to comply with the order (for example, by running a business at a loss for an indefinite period) may be far greater than the plaintiff would suffer from the contract being broken. As Professor R. J. Sharpe explains in 'Specific Relief for Contract Breach,' ch. 5 of *Studies in Contract Law* (1980), edited by Reiter and Swan, p. 129:

> In such circumstances, a specific decree in favour of the plaintiff will put him in a bargaining position vis-à-vis the defendant whereby the measure of what he will receive will be the value to the defendant of being released from performance. If the plaintiff bargains effectively, the amount he will set will exceed the value to him of performance and will approach the cost to the defendant to complete.'

This was the reason given by Lord Westbury L. C. in *Isenberg* v *East India House Estate Co. Ltd* (1863) 3 De G.J. S. 263, 273 for refusing a mandatory injunction to compel the defendant to pull down part of a new building which interfered with the plaintiff's light and exercising instead the Court of Chancery's recently-acquired jurisdiction under Lord Cairns's Act 1858 (21 22 Vict. c. 27) to order payment of damages:

> ... I hold it ... to be the duty of the court in such a case as the present not, by granting a mandatory injunction, to deliver over the defendants to the plaintiff bound hand and foot, in order to be made subject to any extortionate demand that he may by possibility make, but to substitute for such mandatory injunction an inquiry before itself, in order to ascertain the measure of damage that has been actually sustained.'

It is true that the defendant has, by his own breach of contract, put himself in such an unfortunate position. But the purpose of the law of contract is not to punish wrongdoing but to satisfy the expectations of the party entitled to performance. A remedy which enables him to secure, in money terms, more than the performance due to him is unjust. From a wider perspective, it cannot be in the public interest for the courts to require someone to carry on business at a loss if there is any plausible alternative by which the other party can be given compensation. It is not only a waste of resources but yokes the parties together in a continuing hostile relationship. The order for specific performance prolongs the battle. If the defendant is ordered to run a business, its conduct becomes the subject of a flow of complaints, solicitors' letters and affidavits. This is wasteful for both parties and the legal system.

An award of damages, on the other hand, brings the litigation to an end. The defendant pays damages, the forensic link between them is severed, they go their separate ways and the wounds of conflict can heal.

The cumulative effect of these various reasons, none of which would necessarily be sufficient on its own, seems to me to show that the settled practice is based upon sound sense. Of course the grant or refusal of specific performance remains a matter for the judge's discretion. There are no binding rules, but this does not mean that there cannot be settled principles, founded upon practical considerations of the kind which I have discussed, which do not have to be re-examined in every case, but which the courts will apply in all but exceptional circumstances ....

NOTE: Equity will decree specific performance in the place of ('in lieu of') a common law remedy of damages to achieve more perfect justice, but where a decree of specific performance is just but impracticable, equity has been permitted since Lord Cairns' Chancery Amendment Act of 1858 to award common law-type damages in lieu of specific performance (see now Senior Courts Act 1981, s.50, and *Jaggard* v *Sawyer* [1995] 1 WLR 269, CA). The same is true of the award of an injunction (see C: Injunctions), so, for example, if an injunction to restrain building work is awarded too late to stop it the court may award damages in lieu of an injunction.

C: Injunctions

Injunctions are an equitable order of the court directed at an individual defendant, with the result that to breach an injunction is not to break a legal rule but, rather, to act in contempt of court—an offence that is punishable by fine or even imprisonment. In *Shalson* v *Russo* [2003] EWHC 1637 (Ch), a fraudster was imprisoned for two years for breaching an equitable injunction that had frozen his assets.

Injunctions may be made at the final hearing of a matter, in which case they will often be made on detailed terms designed to ensure that the parties do not have to resort to litigation in the future, or an 'interlocutory' ('between hearings') injunction may be made in a preliminary hearing before the merits of the case on both sides. Interlocutory injunctions are frequently made to deal with some emergency and for this reason some may be sought by an 'application without notice' to the other party (previously called an *ex parte* application). This is especially true of injunctions to freeze a defendant's assets (for consideration of 'freezing injunctions'—formerly known as *Mareva* injunctions—see Chapter 14, and below) and so-called 'search orders' (formerly known as *Anton Piller* orders) which permit inspection and seizure of evidence which is at risk of being destroyed, concealed, or removed, and which is needed to prove the applicants claim.

The effect of an injunction will be to stop the defendant from doing something (a 'prohibitory' injunction) or to require the defendant to do something (a 'mandatory' injunction) or, exceptionally, to prevent the defendant from committing a tort which has not yet been committed, but is threatened. The latter is the so-called *'quia timet'* (tr. 'because he fears') injunction. An example of a prohibitory injunction is one which prevents a trespasser from entering onto the claimant's land. An example of mandatory injunction is one which requires a person to pull down a wall that was built on another person's land (or, as in the case of *City of London Corp* v *Samede* [2012] EWHC 34 (QB), an order to remove tents erected outside St Paul's Cathedral by protesters).

■ QUESTION

Can you see the close similarity between a decree of specific performance and a mandatory injunction? What, if any, is the difference between them?

SENIOR COURTS ACT 1981

37. **Powers of High Court with respect to injunctions and receivers**

(1)   The High Court may by order (whether interlocutory or final) grant an injunction or appoint a receiver in all cases in which it appears to the court to be just and convenient to do so.

(2)   Any such order may be made either unconditionally or on such terms and conditions as the court thinks just.

(3)   The power of the High Court under subsection (1) to grant an interlocutory injunction restraining a party to any proceedings from removing from the jurisdiction of the High Court, or otherwise dealing with, assets located within that jurisdiction shall be exercisable in cases where that party is, as well as in cases where he is not, domiciled resident or present within that jurisdiction ...

(i) Interim (formerly 'interlocutory') injunction

American Cyanamid Co. v *Ethicon Ltd*

[1975] 2 WLR 316, House of Lords

Facts: The plaintiffs, an American company, owned a patent covering certain medical products. The defendants, also an American company, were about to launch on the British market a product which the plaintiffs claimed infringed their patent. The plaintiffs applied for an interlocutory injunction which was granted by the judge at first instance with the usual undertaking in damages by the plaintiffs. The Court of Appeal reversed his decision on the ground that no prima facie case of infringement had been made out.

Held: Appeal allowed.

LORD DIPLOCK: MY Lords, when an application for an interlocutory injunction to restrain a defendant from doing acts alleged to be in violation of the plaintiff's legal right is made upon contested facts, the decision whether or not to grant an interlocutory injunction has to be taken at a time when *ex hypothesi* the existence of the right or the violation of it, or both, is uncertain and will remain uncertain until final judgment is given in the action. It was to mitigate the risk of injustice to the plaintiff during the period before that uncertainty could be resolved that the practice arose of granting him relief by way of interlocutory injunction; but since the middle of the 19th century this has been made subject to his undertaking to pay damages to the defendant for any loss sustained by reason of the injunction if it should be held at the trial that the plaintiff had not been entitled to restrain the defendant from doing what he was threatening to do. The object of the interlocutory injunction is to protect the plaintiff against injury by violation of his right for which he could not be adequately compensated in damages recoverable in the action if the uncertainty were resolved in his favour at the trial; but the plaintiff's need for such protection must be weighed against the corresponding need of the defendant to be protected against injury resulting from his having been prevented from exercising his own legal rights for which he could not be adequately compensated under the plaintiff's undertaking in damages if the uncertainty were resolved in the defendant's favour at the trial. The court must weigh one need against another and determine where 'the balance of convenience' lies …

The use of such expressions as 'a probability,' 'a prima facie case,' or 'a strong prima facie case' in the context of the exercise of a discretionary power to grant an interlocutory injunction leads to confusion as to the object sought to be achieved by this form of temporary relief. The court no doubt must be satisfied that the claim is not frivolous or vexatious, in other words, that there is a serious question to be tried. It is no part of the court's function at this stage of the litigation to try to resolve conflicts of evidence on affidavit as to facts on which the claims of either party may ultimately depend nor to decide difficult questions of law which call for detailed argument and mature considerations. These are matters to be dealt with at the trial … So unless the material available to the court at the hearing of the application for an interlocutory injunction fails to disclose that the plaintiff has any real prospect of succeeding in his claim for a permanent injunction at the trial, the court should go on to consider whether the balance of convenience lies in favour of granting or refusing the interlocutory relief that is sought … As to that, the governing principle is that the court should first consider whether, if the plaintiff were to succeed at the trial in establishing his right to a permanent injunction, he would be adequately compensated by an award of damages for the loss he would have sustained as a result of the defendant's continuing to do what was sought to be enjoined between the time of the application and the time of the trial. If damages in the measure recoverable at common law would be adequate remedy and the defendant would be in a financial position to pay them, no interlocutory injunction should normally be granted, however strong the plaintiff's claim appeared to be at that stage. If, on the other hand, damages would not provide an adequate remedy for the plaintiff in the event of his succeeding at the trial, the court should then consider whether, on the contrary hypothesis that the defendant were to succeed at the trial in establishing his right to do that which was sought to be enjoined, he would be adequately compensated under the plaintiff's undertaking as to damages for the loss he would have sustained by being prevented from doing so between the time of the application and the time of the trial. If damages in the measure recoverable under such an undertaking would be an adequate remedy and the plaintiff would be in a financial position to pay them, there would be no reason upon this ground to refuse an interlocutory injunction.

It is where there is doubt as to the adequacy of the respective remedies in damages available to either party or to both, that the question of balance of convenience arises. It would be unwise to attempt even to list all the various matters which may need to be taken into consideration in deciding where the balance lies, let alone to suggest the relative weight to be attached to them. These will vary from case to case. Where other factors appear to be evenly balanced it is a counsel of prudence to take such measures as are calculated to preserve the status quo. If the defendant is enjoined temporarily from doing something that he has not done before, the only effect of the interlocutory injunction in the event of his succeeding at the trial is to postpone the date at which he is able to embark upon a course of action which he has not previously found it necessary to undertake; whereas to interrupt him in the conduct of an established enterprise would cause much greater inconvenience to him since he would have to start again to establish it in the event of his succeeding at the trial. Save in the simplest cases, the decision to grant or to refuse an interlocutory injunction will cause to whichever party is unsuccessful on the application some disadvantages which his ultimate success at the trial may show he ought to have been spared and the disadvantages may be such that the recovery of damages to which he would then be entitled either in the action or under the plaintiff's undertaking would not be sufficient to compensate him fully for all of them. The extent to which the disadvantages to each party would be incapable of being compensated in damages in the event of his succeeding at the trial is always a significant factor in assessing where the balance of convenience lies, and if the extent of the uncompensatable disadvantage to each party would not differ widely, it may not be improper to take into account in tipping the balance the relative strength of each party's case as revealed by the affidavit evidence adduced on the hearing of the application. This, however, should be done only where it is apparent upon the facts disclosed by evidence as to which there is no credible dispute that the strength of one party's case is disproportionate to that of the other party. The court is not justified in embarking upon anything resembling a trial of the action upon conflicting affidavits in order to evaluate the strength of either party's case.

Page One Records Ltd v *Britton and others (Trading As 'The Troggs')*

[1968] 1 WLR 157, Chancery Division

Facts: The manager of sixties pop-group 'The Troggs' asked the court to award him an interim injunction to restrain the group from engaging any other manager.

Held: Application refused. The court will not grant an interim mandatory injunction if it would have an effect equivalent to specific performance, unless specific performance would itself be an appropriate order. The applicant's request for an injunction to prevent the employment of another manager was interpreted as being in effect, a mandatory injunction compelling the group to continue to employ the applicant, which would in turn be tantamount to ordering the applicant to specifically perform his contract for personal services. The applicant was therefore refused his injunction ... for his own protection!

NOTES

1. It is permitted to seek an interim injunction even when the defendant's name is unknown, provided the defendant can be adequately described. See, for example, *Hampshire Waste Services Ltd v Intending Trespassers upon Chineham Incinerator Site* [2003] EWHC 1738 (Ch), [2004] Env LR 9, Ch D.

2. Lord Diplock states that the claimant must demonstrate a 'real prospect of succeeding in his claim for a permanent injunction'. Something more than this is usually required where the injunction will restrict freedom of expression, although exceptions may be admitted (see *Cream Holdings Ltd* v *Banerjee* [2004] UKHL 44, [2005] 1 AC 253, House of Lords and *Douglas* v *Hello! Ltd (No. 3)* [2005] EWCA Civ 595, [2006] QB 125, Court of Appeal). In *BBC* v *Harpercollins Publishers Limited, Ben Collins, Collins Autosport Limited* [2010] EWHC 2424 (Ch), the BBC sought an interlocutory injunction on the grounds of breach of 'equitable duty of confidence', to prevent publication of a book in which the racing driver Ben Collins reveals that he had been 'The Stig' (a mysterious driver always concealed beneath a racing suit and helmet) on the hit TV programme *Top Gear*. The BBC failed. As the judge said: 'the identity of Mr Collins as The Stig is [already] in the public domain. If that has caused and/or will cause harm to the BBC, I do not see how any further harm will be caused to the BBC if Mr Collins is allowed to publish his autobiography in time for the 2010 Christmas market'.

3. According to Megarry J in *Shepherd Homes Ltd* v *Sandham* [1971] Ch 340, Chancery Division (approved in *Locabail International Finance Ltd* v *Agroexport 'The Sea Hawk'* [1986] 1 WLR 657, the Court of Appeal):

   'the court is far more reluctant to grant a mandatory injunction than it would be to grant a comparable prohibitory injunction. In a normal case the court must, inter alia, feel a high degree of assurance that at the trial it will appear that the injunction was rightly granted and this is a higher standard than is required for a prohibitory injunction.'

4. The standard form of court order for an interim injunction contains the following fearsome warning to the defendant:

Practice Direction on Interim Injunctions 25PD.10

'(1) This Order [prohibits you from doing] [obliges you to do] the acts set out in this Order. [You should read it all carefully. You are advised to consult a Solicitor as soon as possible.] You have a right to ask the Court to vary or discharge this Order.

(2) If you disobey this Order you may be found guilty of Contempt of Court and [any of your directors] may be sent to prison or fined [and you may be fined] or your assets may be seized.'

(ii) Final injunction

Redland Bricks Ltd v *Morris*

[1970] AC 652, House of Lords

Facts: A judge awarded a mandatory injunction requiring the defendant clay-digging company to fill in a pit so as to restore support to the claimant's neighbouring land. The defendant appealed.

Held: Allowing the appeal, that albeit there was a strong probability of grave damage to the claimant's land in the future and damages were not a sufficient remedy, the appellants had not behaved unreasonably, and since the mandatory injunction imposed upon them an unqualified obligation to restore support without any indication of what work was to be done, the injunction would be discharged.

LORD UPJOHN: My Lords, *quia timet* actions are broadly applicable to two types of cases. First, where the defendant has as yet done no hurt to the plantiff but is threatening and intending (so the plaintiff alleges) to do works which will render irreparable harm to him or his property if carried to completion. Your Lordships are not concerned with that and those cases are normally, though not exclusively, concerned with negative injunctions. Secondly, the type of case where the plaintiff has been fully recompensed both at law and in equity for the damage he has suffered but where he alleges that the earlier actions of the defendant may lead to future cases of action. It is in this field that undoubted jurisdiction of equity to grant a mandatory injunction, that is an injunction ordering the defendant to carry out positive works, finds its main expression, though of course it is equally applicable to many other cases. Thus, to take the simplest example, if the defendant, the owner of land, including a metalled road over which the plaintiff has a right of way, ploughs up that land so that it is no longer usable, no doubt a mandatory injunction will go to restore it; damages are not a sufficient remedy, for the plaintiff has no right to go on the defend-ant's land to remake his right of way.

... The grant of a mandatory injunction is, of course, entirely discretionary and unlike a negative injunction can never be 'as of course'. Every case must depend essentially on its own particular circumstances. Any general principles for its application can only be laid down in the most general terms:

1. A mandatory injunction can only be granted where the plaintiff shows a very strong probability on the facts that grave damages will accrue to him in the future. As Lord Dunedin said [*A-G for the Dominion of Canada* v *Ritchie Contracting and Supply Co. Ltd* [1919] AC 999, 1005] it is not sufficient to say 'timeo'. It is a jurisdiction to be exercised sparingly and with caution but, in the proper case, unhesitatingly.

2. Damages will not be a sufficient or adequate remedy if such damage does happen. This is only the application of a general principle of equity; it has nothing to do with Lord Cairns' Act (the Chancery Amendment Act 1858) or Meux's case.

3. Unlike the case where a negative injunction is granted to prevent the continuance or recurrence of a wrongful act the question of the cost to the defendant to do works to prevent or lessen the likelihood of a future apprehended wrong must be an element to be taken into account: (a) where the defendant has acted without regard to his neighbour's rights, or has tried to steal a march on him or has tried to evade the jurisdiction of the court or, to sum it up, has acted wantonly and quite unreasonably in relation to his neighbour he may be ordered to repair his wanton and unreasonable acts by doing positive work to restore the status quo even if the expense to him is out of all proportion to the advantage thereby accruing to the plaintiff ... ; (b) but where the defendant has acted reasonably, although in the event wrongly,

the cost of remedying by positive action his earlier activities is most important for two reasons. First, because no legal wrong has yet occurred (for which he has not been recompensed at law and in equity) and, in spite of gloomy expert opinion, may never occur or possibly only on a much smaller scale than anticipated. Secondly, because if ultimately heavy damage does occur the plaintiff is in no way prejudiced for he has his action at law and all his consequential remedies in equity.

So the amount to be expended under a mandatory order by the defendant must be balanced with these considerations in mind against the anticipated possible damages to the plaintiff and if, on such balance, it seems unreasonable to inflict such expenditure on one who for this purpose is no more than a potential wrongdoer then the court must exercise its jurisdiction accordingly. Of course, the court does not have to order such works as on the evidence before it will remedy the wrong but may think it proper to impose on the defendant the obligation of doing certain works may on expert opinion merely lessen the likelihood of any further injury to the plaintiff's land ...

4. If in the exercise of its discretion the court decides that it is a proper case to grant a mandatory injunction, then the court must be careful to see that the defendant knows exactly in fact what he has to do and this means not as a matter of law but as a matter of fact, so that in carrying out an order he can give his contractors the proper instructions ...

Shelfer v *City of London Electric Lighting*

[1895] 1 Ch 287, Court of Appeal

Facts: An electric lighting company erected powerful engines and other works on land near to a house which was subject to a lease. Owing to excavations for the foundations of the engines, and to vibration and noise from the working of them, structural injury was caused to the house, and annoyance and discomfort to the lessee. The lessee and the reversioners brought separate actions against the company for an injunction and damages in respect of the nuisance and injury thus occasioned.

Held: There is nothing in the Electric Lighting Act 1882, to relieve undertakers thereunder from liability to an action at common law for nuisance to their neighbours caused by their works.

LINDLEY LJ: ... It is very true that Lord Cairns' Act (21 & 22 Vict c 27), s 2, conferred upon the Court of Chancery jurisdiction which it had not before to award damages in lieu of an injunction. That section enacts that 'in all cases in which the Court of Chancery has jurisdiction to entertain an application for an injunction ... against the commission or continuance of any wrongful act ... it shall be lawful for the same Court, if it shall think fit, to award damages to the party injured, either in addition to or in substitution for such injunction ... '

The jurisdiction to give damages instead of an injunction is in words given in all cases; but the use of the word 'damages' has led to a doubt whether the Act applies to cases where no injury at all has yet been inflicted, but where injury is threatened only. Subject, however, to this doubt, there appears to be no limit to the jurisdiction. But in exercising the jurisdiction thus given attention ought to be paid to well settled principles; and ever since Lord Cairns' Act was passed the Court of Chancery has repudiated the notion that the Legislature intended to turn that Court into a tribunal for legalising wrongful acts; or in other words, the Court has always protested against the notion that it ought to allow a wrong to continue simply because the wrongdoer is able and willing to pay for the injury he may inflict. Neither has the circumstance that the wrongdoer is in some sense a public benefactor (eg, a gas or water company or a sewer authority) ever been considered a sufficient reason for refusing to protect by injunction an individual whose rights are being persistently infringed. Expropriation, even for a money consideration, is only justifiable when Parliament has sanctioned it. Courts of Justice are not like Parliament, which considers whether proposed works will be so beneficial to the public as to justify exceptional legislation, and the deprivation of people of their rights with or without compensation. Lord Cairns' Act was not passed in order to supersede legislation for public purposes, but to enable the Court of Chancery to administer justice between litigants more effectually than it could before the Act ...

Without denying the jurisdiction to award damages instead of an injunction, even in cases of continuing actionable nuisances, such jurisdiction ought not to be exercised in such cases except under very exceptional circumstances. I will not attempt to specify them, or to lay down rules for the exercise of judicial discretion. It is sufficient to refer, by way of example, to trivial and occasional nuisances: cases in which a plaintiff has shown that he only wants money; vexatious and oppressive cases; and cases where the plaintiff has so conducted himself as to render it unjust to give him more than pecuniary relief. In all such cases as these, and in all others where an action for damages is really an adequate remedy—as where the acts complained of are already finished—an injunction can be properly refused. There are no circumstances here which, according to recognised principles, justify the refusal of an injunction; and in my opinion, therefore, an injunction ought to have been granted in the action brought by the tenant.

Wrotham Park Estate Company v *Parkside Homes Ltd*

[1974] 2 All ER 321, Chancery Division

Facts: In 1935, the Wrotham Park Estate, then owed by the Earl of Strafford, extended to about 4,000 acres. In that year, the Earl sold 47 acres out of the estate. This land was subject to a restrictive covenant 'not to develop the ... land for building purposes except in strict accordance with plans [approved by the owners of Wrotham Park Estate]'. The covenant was expressed to be for the benefit of 'Wrotham Park Estate'. The claimant company later acquired Wrotham Park Estate. The defendant, Parkside Homes Ltd, acquired a small part of the servient land. The defendant obtained planning permission from the local authority to build 13 'middle class' houses on the land. It did not, however, submit its plans to the claimant for approval. It believed that the claimant was not entitled to enforce the covenant. In January 1972, the defendant started to lay the foundations. On 14 February, the claimant issued a writ claiming an injunction to restrain building. The claimant failed, however, to seek an 'interlocutory' (temporary) injunction to restrain development pending the full trial of the dispute. Parkside, accordingly, completed the building operations and the first residents moved into their new homes.

Held: The judge refused to order that the houses should be demolished. Instead, he awarded the claimant damages equivalent to the 'price' it could reasonably have asked for releasing the covenant.

BRIGHTMAN J: ...I must now consider the relief to which the plaintiffs are entitled, that is to say a mandatory injunction or damages (both are not sought): if damages, whether substantial or nominal; or a declaration of the plaintiffs' rights as the sole relief. The plaintiffs made it abundantly clear at the outset of the case that the relief they primarily sought was a mandatory injunction. This did not spring from outraged feelings or from indifference to the welfare of those who have made the offending houses their homes. It sprang from the belief, sincerely held, that there was no other effective way of preserving the integrity of the planning restrictions imposed by the terms of the Blake conveyance. Quite apart from the benefit to the Wrotham Park estate, the plaintiffs, as I have already said, take the view that they have a moral obligation towards the residents of the building estates to enforce the restrictive covenants so far as they are lawfully entitled to do so. I agree. The plaintiffs do not seek to bulldoze the occupiers out of their homes but are content that they shall have a period of two years in which to acquire other homes with the help of the £20,000 or so that will come to each of them under the indemnity assurance that has been arranged ...

Counsel for the plaintiffs submitted, and I accept, that it is no answer to a claim for a mandatory injunction that the plaintiffs, having issued proceedings, deliberately held their hand and did not seek the assistance of the court for the purpose of preserving the status quo. On the other hand, it is, in my view, equally true that a plaintiff is not entitled 'as of course' to have everything pulled down that was built after the issue of the writ. The erection of the houses, whether one likes it or not, is a fait accompli and the houses are now the homes of people. I accept that this particular fait accompli is reversible and could be undone. But I cannot close my eyes to the fact that the houses now exist. It would, in my opinion, be an unpardonable waste of much needed houses to direct that they now be pulled down and I have never had a moment's doubt during the hearing of this case that such an order ought to be refused. No damage of a financial nature has been done to the plaintiffs by the breach of the layout stipulation. The plaintiffs' use of the Wrotham Park estate has not been and will not be impeded. It is totally unnecessary to demolish the houses in order to preserve the integrity of the restrictive covenants imposed on the rest of area 14. Without hesitation I decline to grant a mandatory injunction. But the fact that these houses will remain does not spell out a charter entitling others to despoil adjacent areas of land in breach of valid restrictions imposed by the conveyances. A developer who tries that course may be in for a rude awakening.

... In my judgment a just substitute for a mandatory injunction would be such a sum of money as might reasonably have been demanded by the plaintiffs from Parkside as a quid pro quo for relaxing the covenant. The plaintiffs submitted that that sum should be a substantial proportion of the development value of the land. This is currently put at no less than £10,000 per plot, i.e. £140,000 on the assumption that the plots are undeveloped. Mr Parker gave evidence that a half or a third of the development value was commonly demanded by a landowner whose property stood in the way of a development. I do not agree with that approach to damages in this type of case. I bear in mind the following factors: (1) The layout covenant is not an asset which the estate owner ever contemplated he would have either the opportunity or the desire to turn to account. It has no commercial or even nuisance value. For it cannot be turned to account except to the detriment of the existing residents who are people the estate owner professes to protect. (2) The breach of covenant which has actually taken place is over a very small area and the impact of this particular breach on the Wrotham Park estate is insignificant. The validity of the covenant over the rest of area 14 is unaffected.

... I think that damages must be assessed in such a case on a basis which is fair and, in all the circumstances, in my judgment a sum equal to 5 per cent of Parkside's anticipated profit is the most that is fair. I accordingly award the sum of £2,500 in substitution for mandatory injunctions ...

NOTE: The Court of Appeal in *Mortimer v Bailey* [2004] EWCA Civ 1514 (noted Watt (2005) 69 *Conv* 14) confirmed that developers build at their own risk and should not assume that damages will be awarded in lieu of a mandatory injunction to remove a completed building. The claimant's failure to apply for an interim injunction does not prevent a final injunction. In *Regan v Paul Properties DPF No 1 Ltd* [2006] EWHC 2052 (Ch), the fact that the defendant continued development in the face of the applicant's strong protests was given as a reason for refusing to enforce the applicant's undertaking to pay the defendant's damages. Usually, though, the court will enforce an undertaking to pay damages if at the final hearing it appears that the injunction should not have been awarded in the first place (*SmithKline Beecham plc v Apotex Europe Ltd* [2006] EWCA Civ 658).

(iii) *Quia timet* injunction

Angela Drury v *The Secretary of State for the Environment, Food and Rural Affairs*
[2004] EWCA Civ 200, Court of Appeal

WILSON J: If a claimant entitled to an order for possession of a certain area of land contends that its occupants are likely to decamp to a separate area of land owned by him, the separate area should in my view be included in the order for possession if, but only if, he would have been entitled to an injunction *quia timet* against the occupants in relation to the separate area .... in [*Ministry of Agriculture, Fisheries & Food v Hayman* (1990) 59 P. & C. R. 48, 50] Saville J. [held] the threshold requirement [to be] convincing evidence of real danger of actual violation. I consider, if I may say so with respect, that Saville J's test represents a fair summary of what nowadays would be required for the grant of an injunction *quia timet*, such being conveniently summarised in Snell's Equity, 30th ed., 45–13 as follows:—

'Although the claimant must establish his right, he may be entitled to an injunction even though an infringement has not taken place but is merely feared or threatened; for "preventing justice excelleth punishing justice". This class of action, known as *quia timet*, has long been established, but the claimant must establish a strong case; "no one can obtain a *quia timet* order by merely saying 'Timeo'". He must prove that there is an imminent danger of very substantial damage ... '

(iv) Freezing order (formerly *'Mareva* injunction')

This is a prohibitory interim injunction by which the defendant is prevented from dealing with his assets in any way which might defeat the claimant's prospects of enforcing a legal judgment against the defendant. Originally developed in judicial decisions, including the decision of the Court of Appeal in *Mareva Compania Naviera SA* v *International Bulkcarriers SA* [1975] 2 Lloyd's Rep 509, the order now has statutory force. The Civil Procedure Rules 1999 describe it as an order 'restraining a party from removing from the jurisdiction assets located there' or 'restraining a party from dealing with any assets whether located within the jurisdiction or not' (r.25.1(f)). It is not the purpose of the order to give a claimant security for his claim or to give him any proprietary interest in the 'frozen' assets (*Fourie* v *Le Roux* [2007] UKHL 1, House of Lords). As Lord Bingham of Cornhill put it recently: 'The ownership of the assets does not change. All that changes is the right to deal with them' (*Customs and Excise Commissioners* v *Barclays Bank plc* (see discussion in this subsection). A freezing order will not be awarded on an interim basis unless the claimant issues, or undertakes to issue, definable substantive proceedings (*Fourie* v *Le Roux*). In *Fourie*, it was held that the applicant should have failed at first instance because when he applied for the injunction he had not even 'worked out what proceedings he was going to bring to which the freezing order would be relevant'.

Customs and Excise Commissioners v Barclays Bank plc

[2006] UKHL 28, [2006] 1 CLC 1096, House of Lords

Facts: The House of Lords was called upon to determine whether a bank, notified by a third party of a freezing order granted to the third party against one of the bank's customers, affecting an account held by the customer with the bank, owes a duty to the third party to take reasonable care to comply with the terms of the injunction.

LORD BINGHAM OF CORNHILL: It would be 'unjust and unreasonable that the Bank should, on being notified of an order which it had no opportunity to resist, become exposed to a liability which was in this case for a few million pounds only, but might in another case be for very much more' [para. [23]].

NOTES
1. In *Independent Trustee Services Ltd* v *GP Noble Trustees Ltd* [2009] EWHC 161 (Ch), the applicant company applied to vary a freezing order made on a without notice application by the respondent company. The applicant wanted to release funds to help it to defend an action brought by the respondent company. It was held that a balance had to be found between permitting the applicant to spend funds which might belong to the respondent and refusing to allow the applicant to spend the funds. On the evidence, the respondent had an arguable proprietary claim to the monies and it was arguable that F was a vehicle for fraud. The variation was refused.
2. A freezing order may be made against assets in a foreign jurisdiction, when it is known as a 'Worldwide Freezing Order' (WFO) (see *Derby & Co. Ltd* v *Weldon (Nos 3 & 4)*).

Derby & Co. Ltd v Weldon (Nos 3 & 4)

[1990] Ch 65, Court of Appeal

Facts: the claimant sought a *Mareva* injunction against a number of defendants, including a Panamanian company and a Luxembourg company, neither of which appeared to have any assets within the UK.

Held: the purpose of the Mareva injunction was to prevent frustration of a court order and, although normally confined to assets within the jurisdiction, it could be used in relation to foreign assets, subject to the ordinary principles of international law. Because the injunction operated *in personam* it did not offend against the principle that courts should not make orders to take effect in foreign jurisdictions. Their Lordships did suggest, however, that the existence of sufficient assets within the jurisdiction would be an excellent reason for refusing a worldwide injunction.

Lord Chief Justice's Practice Direction on Mareva Injunctions and Anton Piller Orders

[1994] 1 WLR 1233, High Court (Lord Taylor of Gosforth CJ, Sir Stephen Brown P, and Sir Donald Nicholls V-C)

' … The Terms of this order do not affect or concern anyone outside the jurisdiction of this court until it is declared enforceable or is enforced by a court in the relevant country and then they are to effect him only to the extent that they have been declared enforceable or have been enforced UNLESS such person is: (a) a person to whom this order is addressed or an officer or an agent appointed by power of attorney of such a person; or (b) a person who is subject to the jurisdiction of this Court and (i) has been given written notice of this order at his residence or place of business within the jurisdiction of this Court and (ii) is able to prevent acts or omissions outside the jurisdiction of this Court which constitute or assist in a breach of the terms of this order.'

NOTE: When a WFO is made, the claimant is usually required to give an undertaking to seek the permission of the English court before actually enforcing it in a foreign jurisdiction. Detailed guidelines governing the grant of that permission were set down in *Dadourian Group International Inc* v *Simms*.

Dadourian Group International Inc. v Simms

[2006] 1 WLR 2499, Court of Appeal

Held: It was held that when the judge at first instance had given permission to enforce a WFO in Switzerland, he had failed to take adequate account of the law governing proceedings underway in Switzerland and of the possible oppression of a third party whom the claimant proposed to join to those proceedings. Nevertheless, the WFO was allowed to stand because of the real prospect that the defendant had assets in Switzerland and that it was reasonable and proportionate for it to seek to enforce the WFO there.

The 'Dadourian Guidelines'

1) the grant of permission should be 'just and convenient' and 'not oppressive to the parties to the English proceedings or to third parties who may be joined to the foreign proceedings';
2) consideration should be given to 'granting relief on terms' (for example, extending to third parties the requirement of giving an undertaking for costs) and to 'the proportionality of the steps proposed to be taken abroad' and to 'the form of any order';
3) 'The interests of the applicant should be balanced against the interests of the other parties … and any new party likely to be joined to the foreign proceedings';
4) 'Permission should not normally be given in terms that would enable the applicant to obtain relief in the foreign proceedings which is superior to the relief given by the WFO';
5) the decision, whether or not to grant permission, should be based on all the relevant information reasonably obtainable in the available time such as the judge would require to reach an informed decision (including evidence as to the applicable law and practice in the foreign court, the nature of the proposed proceedings to be commenced, the assets believed to be located in the jurisdiction of the foreign court and the names of the parties by whom such assets are held).
6) The standard of proof requires proof of a 'real prospect' that such assets are located within the jurisdiction of the foreign court in question;
7) the risk of dissipation of the assets;
8) 'Normally the application should be made on notice to the respondent, but in cases of urgency, where it is just to do so, the permission may be given without notice to the party against whom relief will be sought in the foreign proceedings but that party should have the earliest practicable opportunity of having the matter reconsidered by the court at a hearing of which he is given notice'.

NOTES

1. Interim freezing injunctions (domestic and worldwide) may be made in the UK to support foreign courts, provided that the foreign state is a Regulation State within the meaning of the Civil Jurisdiction and Judgments Act 1982, s.25(1), or is a signatory to the Brussels Convention or the Lugano Convention.

2. In *Fourie* v *Le Roux* [2007] UKHL 1, House of Lords, it was held that an interim injunction may be made in support of foreign litigation only if the injunction is genuinely acting as relief relevant to the final remedy sought. There must also be a genuine nexus between UK territory and the interim relief sought.

   Compare *Banco Nacional de Comercio Exterior SNC* v *Empresa de Telecomunicationes de Cuba SA* [2007] EWCA Civ 723, Court of Appeal, in which two orders were made at first instance: one to freeze the defendant's assets in England and another (a WFO) to freeze assets elsewhere. The orders were made to support a judgment made by a court in Turin. The Court of Appeal set aside the WFO on the basis that there was no connection between the UK-based assets and assets which might be covered by the WFO.

3. A freezing order will frequently permit the party subject to the order to continue to deal with or dispose of any of its assets in the ordinary and proper course of business (*Mobile Telesystems Finance SA* v *Nomihold Securities Inc* [2011] EWCA Civ 1040; [2012] Lloyd's Rep 6).

(v) Search order (formerly *'Anton Piller* order')

This order allows a claimant to search the defendant's premises and seize things, especially documents, which the claimant will need to prove a legal claim against the defendant. In theory the search is not forcible, but the defendant is ordered to give his permission to be searched and is provided with the incentive of prison for contempt of court if he refuses. The Civil Procedure Rules 1999 summarise it as being an 'order requiring a party to admit another party to premises for the purpose of preserving evidence etc.' (r.25.1).

Anton Piller KG v *Manufacturing Processes Ltd*

[1976] Ch 55, Court of Appeal

Facts: AP Ltd, a German Company, claimed that MP Ltd, its English agent, had been passing on confidential information to certain of AP's rival German companies. AP Ltd applied for an interim injunction to permit, *inter alia*, entry of MP's premises to inspect documentation and to remove documentation to the custody of AP's solicitors. AP undertook to issue a writ forthwith to support the action for breach of confidence and AP was granted its injunction. MP appealed.

Held: Appeal allowed. Lord Denning MR held that in very exceptional circumstances, where the plaintiff has a very strong prima facie case to show that the defendant has caused or will cause very serious damage to the plaintiff, and where there is clear evidence that the defendant possesses vital evidence which might be disposed of so as to defeat justice, the court could by order permit the plaintiff's representatives to enter the defendant's premises to inspect and remove such material. The order could in such very exceptional circumstances be made without notice to the other party (at that time called an '*ex parte*' application). It was stated that where such an injunction is granted the plaintiff must act carefully and with full respect for the defendant's rights. One aspect of this is that the applicant's solicitors should photocopy confiscated documentation and return the originals to their owner.

NOTE: From this and subsequent cases, it is possible to identify the following factors as general prerequisites to an order: an extremely strong prima facie claim against the defendant; a real risk of serious damage to the defendant if the search order is refused; clear evidence that the defendant has the target assets in his possession; clear risk that the defendant will destroy, conceal or dispose of the target assets.

THE CIVIL PROCEDURE ACT 1997

Section 7 of this statute provides that in the case of any existing or proposed proceedings the court may make an order for the purpose of securing (a) the preservation of evidence which is or may be relevant, or (b) the preservation of property which is or may be the subject-matter of the proceedings or as to which any question arises or may arise in the proceedings. Such an order may direct any person to permit any person described in the order to enter premises in England and Wales, and while on the premises, to take any of the following steps, so far as the terms of the order allow: to carry out a search for or inspection of anything described in the order; and to make or obtain a copy, photograph, sample or other record of anything so described; and to retain for safe keeping anything described in the order.

NOTES

1. The beneficiary of a search order is not allowed to use force (even when seeking to recover pirated *Star Wars* films, see *Rank Film Distributors Ltd* v *Video Information Centre* [1982] AC 380). Where a search order has been executed in an excessive and oppressive manner the court may order aggravated damages against the applicants and possibly, since solicitors executing such orders do so as officers of the court, exemplary damages.
2. As a result of the Human Rights Act 1998, we can add to the applicant's worries the risk that a disproportionate search may be a potential breach of Article 8 of the European Convention on Human Rights; *Chappell* v *United Kingdom* 10461/83 [1989] ECHR 4 (30 March 1989).

D: Rescission

Rescission is an equitable remedy by which a specific contract or other transaction can be set aside, and the parties restored to their original positions. It is, in a sense, a decree of specific non-performance. It directly and comprehensively prevents unconscionable assertion of legal rights and has therefore been described as 'one of the most common and natural occasions for the exercise of equitable jurisdiction' (R. Wooddeson, *A Systematical View of the Laws of England* (Dublin, 1794)). Rescission may be ordered on a number of grounds, including mistake and undue influence.

The circumstances in which a transaction may be rescinded for mistake depend upon whether the transaction is contractual or non-contractual. In the case of a contract, a fundamental mistake as to the facts or their legal consequences may be a ground for rescission (*Bell* v *Lever Bros Ltd* [1932] AC 161, HL). In the case of a non-contractual transaction, a mistake as to the 'effect' of the transaction may be a ground for rescission, but a mistake as to the 'consequences or the advantages to be gained by entering into it' will not be (*Gibbon* v *Mitchell* [1990] 1 WLR 1304). This rather difficult distinction between 'effect' and 'consequence' has been criticised (see J. Hilliard, '*Gibbon* v *Mitchell* Reconsidered: Mistakes as to Effects and Mistakes as to Consequences', Parts 1 and 2 (2004) 6 *PCB* 357; (2005) 1 *PCB* 31. *Gibbon* v *Mitchell* continues to be followed nevertheless—see, for example, *Smithson* v *Hamilton* [2007] EWHC 2900 (Ch)).

Undue influence is a ground for rescinding many types of transaction including contracts, mortgages and even, as in a recent case, the resignation of a trustee *Daniel* v *Drew* [2005] EWCA Civ 507, CA (Civ Div). There are two broad forms of unacceptable conduct amounting to undue influence. The first comprises overt acts of improper pressure and coercion, the second is a relationship in which one party has taken unfair advantage of a position of strength (*Royal Bank of Scotland Plc* v *Etridge (No. 2)* [2002] 2 AC 773). In certain types of relationship, such as those in which it is 'the duty of one party to advise the other or to manage his property for him', undue influence is presumed, provided the complainant can prove as a matter of fact that the trust-like relationship existed and that the transaction was exceptional and therefore calls for an explanation. Benefits conferred by the vulnerable party will not be examined if they are unexceptional, otherwise no parent could confidently accept so much as a birthday present from their child (*Royal Bank of Scotland* v *Etridge* [2002] 2 AC 773, *per* Lord Nicholls of Birkenhead at 798, approving *Allcard* v *Skinner* (1887) 36 Ch D 145).

A typical situation might be where Mr and Mrs X are beneficial joint tenants (or tenants in common) of the matrimonial home. Mr X wishes to raise money from a bank for a business venture, on the security of the matrimonial home, and induces his wife to allow her share, as well as his, to be subject to the charge. The business fails and the bank brings possession or other proceedings. Mr X has used undue influence to obtain his wife's consent; and no doubt as against him, Mrs X could unravel the transaction. The problem is that she needs to unravel the transaction as against the bank.

In early cases, such as *Kingsnorth Trust Ltd* v *Bell* [1986] 1 All ER 423, the bank asked the husband to obtain the wife's signature on its behalf, and the Court of Appeal held that the husband was then acting as the bank's agent; if he had obtained the signature through undue influence, as was indeed the case, his acts would also bind the bank. The problem with the agency view was that it hardly ever worked (see, e.g. *National Westminster Bank plc* v *Morgan* [1985] AC 686; *Coldunell Ltd* v *Gallon* [1986] 1 All ER 429), and the agency was also generally regarded as artificial.

Barclays Bank plc v O'Brien

[1994] 1 AC 180, House of Lords

Held: The facts were essentially as described at the start of this section. The bank was bound as being fixed with constructive notice of Mrs O'Brien's surety's right to set aside the transaction.

LORD BROWNE-WILKINSON (on the position of the bank as third party): ... Up to this point I have been considering the right of a claimant wife to set aside a transaction as against the wrongdoing husband when the transaction has been procured by his undue influence. But in surety cases the decisive question is whether the claimant wife can set aside the transaction, not against the wrongdoing husband, but against the creditor bank. Of course, if the wrongdoing husband is acting as agent for the creditor bank in obtaining the surety from the wife, the creditor will be fixed with the wrongdoing of its own agent and the surety contract can be set aside as against the creditor. Apart from this, if the creditor bank has notice, actual or constructive, of the undue influence exercised by the husband (and consequentially of the wife's equity to set aside the transaction) the creditor will take subject to that equity and the wife can set aside the transaction against the creditor (albeit a purchaser for value) as well as against the husband: see *Bainbrigge* v *Browne* (1881) 18 ChD 188 and *BCCI* v *Aboody* [1990] 1 QB 923 at 973. Similarly, in cases such as the present where the wife has been induced to enter into the transaction by the husband's misrepresentation, her equity to set aside the transaction will be enforceable against the creditor if either the husband was acting as the creditor's agent or the creditor had actual or constructive notice.

NOTE: The problem is in assessing the nature of the wife's equity to set aside the transaction. The above analysis appears to be in terms of a third-party bank with notice being bound by a wife's equity against her husband (to set aside a transaction which she had been induced to enter by his undue influence). This analysis suggests that the wife has an equity as against her husband, which binds the bank as successor in title to the husband: the bank would take free, as a bona fide purchaser for value, only in the absence of notice.

If this is the correct analysis, there is a problem with the nature of the wife's interest. It could not have been a mere equity, like the interest in *Ainsworth*, since a third party was bound; but almost certainly, the wife did not obtain a full equitable interest in the land, since otherwise, had the land been registered, the bank would have been bound regardless of notice under Land Registration Act 1925, s.70(1)(g) (reformed by the Land Registration Act 2002) (see Dixon and Harpum (1994) 58 *Conv* 421, p. 423, in reply to Professor Thompson (1994) 58 *Conv* 140).

However, *Barclays Bank* v *O'Brien* was reanalysed by Millett LJ in *Royal Bank of Scotland* v *Etridge (No. 2)* [1998] 2 FLR 843, in terms which suggest that the bank is not really a third party at all.

Royal Bank of Scotland v *Etridge (No. 2)*

[1998] 2 FLR 843, Court of Appeal

(reversed in part on other grounds—[2001] 3 WLR 1021, House of Lords)

MILLETT LJ: A transaction may be set aside for misrepresentation or undue influence whether it was procured by the misrepresentation or undue influence of the party seeking to uphold the transaction or that of a third party: ... Until *O'Brien* the basis upon which a transaction could be set aside as against a third party who was not himself guilty of any impropriety was obscure. Two principal theories competed for supremacy. One was based on agency, the other on notice. If the husband could be treated as acting as agent for the bank when procuring his wife to become surety for the debt then the bank could not be in any better position than its agent the husband. But the theory is now almost totally discredited. As Lord Browne-Wilkinson pointed out ([1994] AC 180, 193–4) the supposed agency is highly artificial. In most cases the reality of the relationship is that the creditor stipulates for security, and in order to raise the necessary finance the principal debtor seeks to procure the support of the surety. In doing so he is acting on his own account and not as agent for the creditor.

Since *O'Brien* the doctrine of notice has gained the upper hand. Although there may be cases where, without artificiality, the husband can properly be treated as acting as the agent of the bank in procuring the wife to give security, such cases will be very rare. We doubt that it will ever be possible to treat him as the creditor's agent where he or his company is the principal debtor. But a person who has been induced to enter into a transaction by undue influence, misrepresentation or some other vitiating factor has an equity to have the transaction set aside, and the equity is enforceable against third parties, including third parties who have given value, with notice, actual constructive or imputed, of the equity: see *Bainbrigge* v *Browne* (1881) 18 ChD 188. That was a straightforward application of the ordinary priority rules, for the third party was a successor in title of the wrongdoer. But a similar rule applies whenever a party to a transaction has notice that the consent of the other party has been procured by the impropriety of a third party. There is no voidable transaction between husband and wife which is prior in time to the security which is impugned. The contract of guarantee or collateral charge is entered into by the wife directly with the bank; it is not entered into with the husband and later given by him to the bank. Normally ... there is only one transaction, not two in competition with one another; and there is no question of clearing the title, which is the function performed by the *bona fide* purchaser defence. But the transaction is liable to be set aside as against the bank if the bank had notice, actual constructive or imputed, that it was procured by improper means. This is not, we think, a true application of the *bona fide* purchaser defence, but the effect appears to be much the same ...

It seems, therefore, that the wife has an equity directly against the bank, as the other party to the transaction, and that no intermediate category is created by the undue influence cases.

As a precondition to rescission it must be possible to effect *restitutio in integrum* (which means to put the parties back into the position they were in prior to entering the rescinded agreement), but rescission will be ordered where the court can 'do what is practically just, though it cannot restore the parties precisely to the state they were in before the contract', as appears from the following extract.

O'sullivan v *Management Agency and Music Ltd*

[1985] 3 All ER 351, Court of Appeal

For the facts and the decision see Section 2: The maxims of equity, G: Those who come to equity must do equity, above.

DUNN LJ... In *Erlanger* v *New Sombrero Phosphate Co* (1878) 3 App Cas 1218, a contract for the purchase of an island containing valuable mines by the company from a syndicate was set aside on the ground that the members of the syndicate were in a confidential relationship with the company, notwithstanding that since the contract had been made the mines had been extensively worked so that they were much less valuable. Although Lord Blackburn's speech was expressed to be limited to the question of laches, which was the principal issue in the House of Lords, he said, at p. 1278:

> 'It is, I think, clear on principles of general justice, that as a condition to a rescission there must be a restitutio in integrum. The parties must be put in statu quo. See per Lord Cranworth in *Western Bank of Scotland* v *Addie* (1867) LR 1 Sc. & Div 145, 165. It is a doctrine which has often been acted upon both at law and in equity. But there is a considerable difference in the mode in which it is applied in courts of law and equity, owing, as I think, to the difference of the machinery which the courts have at command. I speak of these courts as they were at the time this suit commenced, without inquiring whether the Judicature Acts make any, or if any, what difference. It would be obviously unjust that a person who has been in possession of property under the contract which he seeks to repudiate should be allowed to throw that back on the other party's hands without accounting for any benefit he may have derived from the use of the property, or if the property, though not destroyed, has been in the interval deteriorated, without making compensation for that deterioration. But as a court of law has no machinery at its command for taking an account of such matters, the defrauded party, if he sought his remedy at law, must in such cases keep the property and sue in an action for deceit, in which the jury, if properly directed, can do complete justice by giving as damages a full indemnity for all that the party has lost: see *Clarke* v *Dickson* (1858) EB. & E 148, and the cases there cited. But a court of equity could not give damages, and, unless it can rescind the contract, can give no relief. And, on the other hand, it can take account of profits, and make allowance for deterioration. And I think the practice has always been for a court of equity to give this relief whenever, by the exercise of its powers, it can do what is practically just, though it cannot restore the parties precisely to the state they were in before the contract.'

This statement, although obiter, has been approved by the House of Lords in subsequent cases and must be regarded as of high authority. The order in that case (sub nom. *New Sombrero Phosphate Co* v *Erlanger* (1877) 5 ChD 73, per Sir George Jessel MR, at p. 125) was that the contract should be set aside; that the purchase price should be repaid with interest at four per cent.; that those shares forming part of the sale consideration which had not been parted with should be returned to the defendants; and that the company should account for any profit derived from the mines …

[Nevertheless] analysis of the cases shows that the principles of restitutio in integrum is not applied with its full rigour in equity in relation to transactions entered into by persons in breach of a fiduciary relationship, and that such transactions may be set aside even though it is impossible to place the parties precisely in the position in which they were before, provided that the court can achieve practical justice between the parties by obliging the wrongdoer to give up his profits and advantages, while at the same time compensating him for any work that he has actually performed pursuant to the transaction …

In my judgment the judge was right to set the agreements aside and to order an account of the profits and payment of the sums found due on the taking of the account. But in taking the account the defendants are entitled to an allowance as proposed by Fox LJ, whose judgment I have read in draft, for reasonable remuneration including a profit element for all work done in promoting and exploiting O'Sullivan and his compositions, whether such work was done pursuant to a contractual obligation or gratuitously. What constitutes 'reasonable remuneration' will depend on evidence on the taking of the account …

Re Edwards (deceased)

[2007] EWHC 1119 (Ch), Chancery Division

Facts: A mother and her three sons lived in the Rhondda Valley, Wales. One son was married and lived nearby. The other sons lived with their mother until one of them died. The mother went to live with her married son and daughter-in-law, apparently because of the bad behaviour of the unmarried son. Her daughter-in-law drafted a letter for her by which she sought to evict the unmarried son from her home. The mother had a fall and admitted herself to a nursing home, but the unmarried son discharged her and took her back to her home against medical advice and there, in apparent revenge against the married couple who had sought his eviction, he unduly influenced his mother to write them out of her will.

Held: The will was set aside. His Lordship observed that there is, in contrast with lifetime dispositions, no presumption of undue influence. It is determined as a matter of fact in the particular case whether or not the will was made under undue influence and the burden of proving undue influence lies on the person who asserts it. Proof requires a high civil standard burden of proof, which means proof of facts which cannot be explained except by positing undue influence. Undue influence might take the form of coercion which overbears the will of the testator.

> LEWISON J: 'Pressure which causes a testator to succumb for the sake of a quiet life, if carried to an extent that overbears the testator's free judgment, discretion or wishes, is enough to amount to coercion in this sense ... The question, in the end, is whether in making his dispositions, the testator has acted as a free agent'.

NOTES

1. William Swadling has argued that it is an 'error ... to assume that where the contract is avoided, the instrument which transferred title is avoided too'. If there was no mistake as to the subject matter of the transfer or as to the identity of the transferee 'a defrauded vendor should be allowed to rescind his contract of sale' but 'it should not carry with it any revesting of title' ('Rescission, Property, and the Common Law' (2005) 121 LQR 123–53).

2. A will may be set aside, without proof of undue influence, if the court is satisfied that the testator/testatrix did not understand and approve the contents of the will. This occured in recent cases of people with severe anxiety disorder (*Gill v RSPCA* [2010] EWCA Civ 1430) and poor grasp of the English language (*Bhatt v Bhatt* [2009] EWHC 734 (Ch)).

E: Rectification

The equitable remedy of rectification is one aspect of the general equitable jurisdiction to relieve from the consequences of mistake (*Gibbon v Mitchell* [1990] 1 WLR 1304, *per* Millett J at 1307; *Gallaher Limited v Gallaher Pensions Limited* [2005] EWHC 42 (Ch)) or fraud (*Collins v Elstone* [1893] P 1). The remedy continues to be useful, especially in the case of mistakes in contracts and wills, but it must be specifically pleaded and proved (*Chartbrook Ltd v Persimmon Homes Ltd* [2009] UKHL 38, [2009] 1 AC 1101, House of Lords; *Cherry Tree Investments Ltd v Landmain Ltd* [2012] EWCA Civ 736, [2012] 2 P & CR 10, Court of Appeal). Sometimes quite extraordinary mistakes are corrected, as in *Lawie v Lawie* [2012] EWHC 2940 (Ch), where a discretionary trust established for the benefit of the settlors' grandchildren accidentally omitted to include the settlors' children with the class of potential beneficiaries. Rectification was ordered in part because the trust, as initially created, gave the trustees no practical choice of potential beneficiaires.

(i) Contracts

Contracts may be rectified in favour of one party, where 'it is inequitable that [the other party] should be allowed to object to the rectification', as might occur if the former party entered the contract under a unilateral mistake of which the latter party was aware (*Thomas Bates & Son Ltd v Windham's (Lingerie) Ltd* [1981] 1 WLR 505, *per* Buckley LJ at 515–16). For rectification to be ordered in such a case, the defendant's conduct in suppressing his knowledge of the mistake must be 'such as to affect the conscience' (*George Wimpey UK Ltd v V I Construction Ltd* [2005] EWCA Civ 77, CA (Civ Div)). The defendant's conscience is unlikely to be affected unless the mistake was one which was to his benefit.

(ii) Wills

ADMINISTRATION OF JUSTICE ACT 1982

20 Rectification

(1) If a court is satisfied that a will is so expressed that it fails to carry out the testator's intentions, in consequence—

(a) of a clerical error; or

(b) of a failure to understand his instructions,

it may order that the will shall be rectified so as to carry out his intentions.

Re Segelman (dec'd)

[1996] 2 WLR 173

Facts: A solicitor who drafted a will failed to remove a drafting inconsistency between the will and a schedule to it.

Held: The test to be applied is whether or not the solicitor had applied his mind to the significance and effect of the words used. Chadwick J held that the solicitor in the instant case had not, so he had committed an error through mere inadvertence with the result that the will should be rectified.

CHADWICK J: Substantially the same principles apply to inter vivos trusts as apply to will trusts, with one obvious and important distinction, namely that the settlor can give evidence of his true intentions in setting up the trust.

F: Account

Account is a process by which the court assesses the sum due from one person to another; it also describes the remedy of payment that is ordered at the end of the assessment process. An action for an account was at one time available at common law, but Chancery procedure for taking accounts, was 'so superior that by the 18th century the common law action for an account had come to be superseded by equitable proceedings for an account' (*Tito* v *Waddell (No. 2)* [1977] Ch 106). Account is most significant for present purposes as a remedy that may be ordered in favour of a beneficiary against a defaulting trustee. The fiduciary duty to account for unauthorised profits is particularly important and is considered in depth in Chapter 10.

NOTE: As a result of Lord Woolf's radical review and reform of civil procedure in England and Wales carried out at the very end of the twentieth century, the remedy of account is now listed as one of the 'interim' (formerly 'interlocutory') remedies that a court may order to facilitate the expeditious resolution of litigation. Read CPR r.25.1 (set out in this subsection) and see if you can identify in the list of 'interim remedies' some of the other equitable remedies we considered earlier.

CIVIL PROCEDURE RULES 1999

Rule 25.1

(1) The court may grant the following interim remedies—

(a) an interim injunction;

(b) an interim declaration;

(c) an order—

(i) for the detention, custody or preservation of relevant property;

(ii) for the inspection of relevant property;

   (iii) for the taking of a sample of relevant property;

   (iv) for the carrying out of an experiment on or with relevant property;

   (v) for the sale of relevant property which is of a perishable nature or which for any other good reason it is desirable to sell quickly; and

   (vi) for the payment of income from relevant property until a claim is decided;

(d) an order authorising a person to enter any land or building in the possession of a party to the proceedings for the purposes of carrying out an order under sub-paragraph (c);

(e) an order under section 4 of the Torts (Interference with Goods) Act 1977 to deliver up goods;

(f) an order (referred to as a 'freezing injunction') —

   (i) restraining a party from removing from the jurisdiction assets located there; or

   (ii) restraining a party from dealing with any assets whether located within the jurisdiction or not;

(g) an order directing a party to provide information about the location of relevant property or assets or to provide information about relevant property or assets which are or may be the subject of an application for a freezing injunction;

(h) an order (referred to as a 'search order') under section 7 of the Civil Procedure Act 1997 (order requiring a party to admit another party to premises for the purpose of preserving evidence etc.);

(i) an order under section 33 of the Supreme Court Act 1981 or section 52 of the County Courts Act 1984 (order for disclosure of documents or inspection of property before a claim has been made);

(j) an order under section 34 of the Supreme Court Act 1981 or section 53 of the County Courts Act 1984 (order in certain proceedings for disclosure of documents or inspection of property against a non-party);

(k) an order (referred to as an order for interim payment) under rule 25.6 for payment by a defendant on account of any damages, debt or other sum (except costs) which the court may hold the defendant liable to pay;

(l) an order for a specified fund to be paid into court or otherwise secured, where there is a dispute over a party's right to the fund;

(m) an order permitting a party seeking to recover personal property to pay money into court pending the outcome of the proceedings and directing that, if he does so, the property shall be given up to him;

(n) an order directing a party to prepare and file accounts relating to the dispute;

(o) an order directing any account to be taken or inquiry to be made by the court; and

(p) an order under Article 9 of Council Directive (EC) 2004/48 on the enforcement of intellectual property.

(2) In paragraph (1)(c) and (g), 'relevant property' means property (including land) which is the subject of a claim or as to which any question may arise on a claim.

(3) The fact that a particular kind of interim remedy is not listed in paragraph (1) does not affect any power that the court may have to grant that remedy.

(4) The court may grant an interim remedy whether or not there has been a claim for a final remedy of that kind.

G: Subrogation

Burston Finance Ltd v *Speirway Ltd*

[1974] 1 WLR 1648

WALTON J (at 1652B–C):... where A's money is used to pay off the claim of B, who is a secured creditor, A is entitled to be regarded in equity as having had an assignment to him of B's rights as a secured creditor ... [subrogation] finds one of its chief uses in the situation where one person advances money on the understanding that he is to have a certain security for the money he has advanced, and, for one reason or another, he does not receive the promised security. In such a case he is nevertheless to be subrogated to the rights of any other person who at the relevant time had any security over the same property and whose debts have been discharged, in whole or in part, by the money so provided by him, but of course only to the extent to which his money has, in fact, discharged their claim.

Boscawen v *Bajwa*

[1996] 1 WLR 328, Court of Appeal

Facts: A building society made an advance for the purchase of a property to be secured by a first legal charge. The purchase fell through after the vendor's solicitors, to whom the purchasers' solicitors had transferred the money, had used it to discharge a mortgage on the property. The claimants, the vendor's judgment creditors, having obtained a charging order against the property, claimed against the vendor and the building society an order for possession and sale of the property. The building society counter-claimed that it was entitled, by way of subrogation, to the rights of the mortgagee and, therefore, to a charge on the proceeds of sale of the property in priority to the claimants. The deputy judge made the order sought.

Held: (Dismissing the appeal): The money used by the vendor's solicitors to discharge the mortgage had been held by the purchasers' solicitors as trust money for the building society and by the vendor's solicitors to the purchasers' solicitors' order pending completion of the purchase; that, therefore, the money could be traced into the payment and the vendor's solicitors in making it had to be taken to have intended to keep the mortgage alive for the benefit of the building society; and that, accordingly, the building society was entitled, by way of subrogation, to a charge on the proceeds of sale of the property in priority to the claimants.

MILLETT LJ:

Tracing and subrogation

[For tracing, see Chapter 14]
Subrogation ... is a remedy, not a cause of action: see Goff & Jones, *Law of Restitution*, 4th ed (1993), pp 589 et seq; *Orakpo* v *Manson Investments Ltd* [1978] AC 95, 104, per Lord Diplock and *In re T H Knitwear (Wholesale) Ltd* [1988] Ch 275, 284. It is available in a wide variety of different factual situations in which it is required in order to reverse the defendant's unjust enrichment. Equity lawyers speak of a right of subrogation, or of an equity of subrogation, but this merely reflects the fact that it is not a remedy which the court has a general discretion to impose whenever it thinks it just to do so. The equity arises from the conduct of the parties on well settled principles and in defined circumstances which make it unconscionable for the defendant to deny the proprietary interest claimed by the plaintiff. A constructive trust arises in the same way. Once the equity is established the court satisfies it by declaring that the property in question is subject to a charge by way of subrogation in the one case or a constructive trust in the other.

Accordingly, there was nothing illegitimate in the deputy judge's invocation of the two doctrines of tracing and subrogation in the same case. They arose at different stages of the proceedings. Tracing was the process by which the Abbey National sought to establish that its money was applied in the discharge of the Halifax's charge; subrogation was the remedy which it sought in order to deprive Mr Bajwa (through whom the appellants claim) of the unjust enrichment which he would thereby otherwise obtain at the Abbey National's expense.

...

Subrogation

The appellants submit that the mere fact that the claimant's money is used to discharge someone else's debt does not entitle him to be subrogated to the creditor whose debt is paid. There must be 'something more:' *Paul* v *Speirway Ltd* [1976] Ch 220, 230, per Oliver J; and see *Orakpo* v *Manson Investments Ltd* [1978] AC 95, 105, where Lord Diplock said:

'The mere fact that money lent has been expended upon discharging a secured liability of the borrower does not give rise to any implication of subrogation unless the contract under which the money was borrowed provides that the money is to be applied for this purpose: *Wylie* v *Carlyon* [1922] 1 Ch 51.'

From this the appellants derive the proposition that in order to be subrogated to the creditor's security the claimant must prove (i) that the claimant intended that his money should be used to discharge the security in question (that being the 'something more' required by Oliver J.) and (ii) that he intended to obtain the benefit of the security by subrogation.

 ... It is perilous to extrapolate from one set of circumstances where the court has required a particular precondition to be satisfied before the remedy of subrogation can be granted a general rule which makes that requirement a precondition which must be satisfied in other and different circumstances. In the present case there was no relevant transaction between Abbey National ('the payer of the money') and Mr Bajwa ('the person at whose instigation it was paid'). This does not mean that the test laid down by Oliver J in *Paul* v *Speirway Ltd* has not been satisfied; it means that the test is not applicable. In *Butler* v *Rice* [1910] 2 Ch 277 the fact that the debtor had not requested the claimant to make the payment and did not know of the transaction was held to be immaterial. This is not to say that intention is necessarily irrelevant in a case of the present kind; it is to say only that where the payment was made by a third party and the claimant had no intention to make any payment to or for the benefit of the recipient the relevant intention must be that of the third party.

Banque Financière de la Cité v Parc (Battersea) Ltd

[1999] 1 AC 221, 234, para. [84]

In this case, Lord Hoffmann categorised the equitable remedy of subrogation as a restitutionary remedy for the reversal of unjust enrichment.

LORD HOFFMANN: I think it should be recognised that one is here concerned with a restitutionary remedy and that the appropriate questions are therefore, first, whether the defendant would be enriched at the plaintiff's expense; secondly, whether such enrichment would be unjust; and thirdly, whether there are nevertheless reasons of policy for denying a remedy.

Filby v Mortgage Express (No. 2) Ltd

[2004] EWCA Civ 759, Court of Appeal

Facts: The appellant, Mrs Filby, had divorced from her husband. When they were married, he had forged her name on a mortgage deed and the mortgage moneys were used, in part, to pay off an earlier mortgage. Mrs Filby claimed that she was not bound by the terms of the later mortgage (the one she had not signed), but the later mortgagee, having redeemed the earlier mortgage, claimed to be subrogated to the earlier mortgagee's unsecured personal rights against Mrs Filby.

 Held: Mrs Filby's appeal was dismissed and the later mortgagee was awarded subrogation to the earlier mortgagee's claim plus 13 years of unpaid interest on the claim.

MAY LJ: The remedy of equitable subrogation is a restitutionary remedy available to reverse what would otherwise be unjust enrichment of a defendant at the expense of the claimant. The defendant is enriched if his financial position is materially improved, usually as here where the defendant is relieved of a financial burden—see Peter Birks, *An Introduction to The Law of Restitution* page 93. The enrichment will be at the expense of the claimant if in reality it was the claimant's money which effected the improvement. Subject to special defences, questions of policy or exceptional circumstances affecting the balance of justice, the enrichment will be unjust if the claimant did not get the security he bargained for when he advanced the money which in reality effected the improvement, and if the defendant's financial improvement is properly seen as a windfall. The remedy does not extend to giving the claimant more than he bargained for. The remedy is not limited to cases where either or both the claimant and defendant intended that the money advanced should be used to effect the improvement. It is sufficient that it was in fact in reality so used. The remedy is flexible and adaptable to produce a just result.

■ QUESTION

In the extract from *Boscawen* v *Bajwa* set out in this subsection, Millett LJ described subrogation as an equitable remedy that 'arises from the conduct of the parties on well settled principles and in defined circumstances which make it unconscionable for the defendant to deny the proprietary interest claimed by the plaintiff'. Is it necessary or desirable to re-frame established equitable doctrine of this sort in terms of a top-down taxonomical scheme that would define the remedy in terms of the reversal of unjust enrichment subject to possible defences (notably 'change of position')? Lord Hoffmann seems to think so, but the High Court of Australia disagrees.

Bofinger v *Kingsway Group Limited*

[2009] HCA 44 (13 October 2009), High Court of Australia

GUMMOW, HAYNE, HEYDON, KIEFEL AND BELL JJ:

90. Subrogation, like other equitable doctrines, is applicable to a variety of circumstances...But that is not to say that subrogation is...in need of the imposition of the 'top-down' reasoning which is a characteristic of some all-embracing theories of unjust enrichment.

91. Such all-embracing theories may conflict in a fundamental way with well-settled equitable doctrines and remedies....

92. Equity has been said to lack the necessary 'exacting taxonomic mentality' when providing an appropriate remedy for unconscientious activity. [Birks, 'Equity in the Modern Law: An Exercise in Taxonomy', (1996) 26 *University of Western Australia Law Review* 1, pp 16–17.] The better view is said to be that liability in 'unjust enrichment' is strict, subject to particular defences [Birks (ibid.), pp 67–8] while '[t]he unreliability of conscience' offends the precept that like cases must be decided alike and not by 'a private and intuitive evaluation' [Birks (ibid.), p. 17].

93. But the experience of the law does not suggest debilitation by absence of a sufficiently rigid taxonomy in the application of equitable doctrines and remedies...

94.... the relevant principles of equity do not operate at large and in an idiosyncratic fashion.

The judgment of the High Court of Australia reminds us that true science is not the servant of theory, but the product of the experiment of experience. It reminds us, also, of the on-going rich variety and vitality of English conceptions of equity and trusts in jurisdictions far from their native shore.

H: Equitable set-off

It seems appropriate to conclude this book with the example of an equitable remedy which can work on a 'self-help' basis without judicial intervention.

Gary Fearns (trading as 'Autopaint International') v *Anglo-Dutch Paint & Chemical Company Limited (and others)*

[2010] EWHC 2366 (Ch), Chancery Division

MR G. LEGGATT QC (Sitting as a Deputy Judge of the Chancery Division):

[17]....[The] limitation of legal set-off to circumstances where both claims are for ascertained or readily ascertainable amounts severely diminishes its utility. Historically, two doctrines were developed by the courts which mitigated this position.

[18] One was the doctrine of abatement which was developed by the courts of common law...

[19] The second doctrine was that of equitable set-off. The definitive account of the evolution of this doctrine is contained in the judgment of Morris LJ in *Hanak* v *Green* [1958] 2 QB 9, described as 'masterly' by Lord Diplock in *Gilbert-Ash (Northern) Ltd* v *Modern Engineering (Bristol) Ltd* [1974] AC 689 at 717. As explained in that judgment, before the passing of the Judicature Acts there were circumstances

in which a court of equity would restrain someone who had brought an action at law from proceeding with the trial of the action or from levying execution of a judgment obtained in the action until further order. Such circumstances included the existence of a cross-claim which the court regarded as entitling the defendant to be protected against the plaintiff's claim, even though no legal set-off was available. After the Judicature Acts were passed, it was no longer necessary (or permissible) to obtain an injunction to restrain a pending action but in those circumstances in which a court of equity would formerly have granted such an injunction a defence to the claim was available. The basis for such a defence of set-off is thus that 'a court of equity would say that neither of these claims ought to be insisted upon without taking the other into account' (per Morris LJ at 26).

[20] The correct test for equitable set-off has been further considered in later cases, most recently by the Court of Appeal in *Geldof Metallconstructie NV v Simon Carves Ltd* [2010] EWCA Civ 667. In *Geldof*, at para 43(vi), the Court of Appeal has endorsed as the best statement of the test, and the one most frequently referred to and applied, that formulated by Lord Denning in *Federal Commerce & Navigation Co Ltd v Molena Alpha Inc (The 'Nanfri')* [1978] 2 QB 927 at 975, namely that equitable set-off is available where a cross-claim is 'so closely connected with [the claim] that it would be manifestly unjust to allow [the claimant] to enforce payment without taking into account the cross-claim'.

Is Equitable Set-off Procedural or Substantive?

[21] As the doctrine of equitable set-off has developed, it has ceased to be regarded simply as a procedural defence, in the way that legal set-off undoubtedly is, and has come be seen as affecting substantive rights. In particular, it is now generally accepted that an equitable set-off can be relied on outside the context of legal proceedings and that, where such a set-off is properly asserted, it can prevent a person from exercising contractual or other legal rights which that person would otherwise have.

[22] The case which most clearly establishes this point is *The Nanfri*, supra, which concerned a dispute about the payment of hire under three time charters. The terms of the charters required hire to be paid twice monthly in advance; in default of payment the owners had the right to withdraw the vessel. The charterers made various deductions from hire, some of which were disputed by the owners. One of the questions on which the court was asked to rule (on a special case stated by arbitrators) was whether the charterers were entitled to deduct from hire without the consent of the owners valid claims which constituted an equitable set-off. A majority of the Court of Appeal (Lord Denning MR and Goff LJ, Cumming-Bruce LJ dissenting on this point) held that they were.

[23] The importance of this decision is that it establishes that an equitable set-off can be relied on outside the context of proceedings as an immediate answer to a liability to pay money otherwise due and to the exercise of rights, such as a right to terminate a contract, which are contingent on such non-payment.

■ **SUMMATIVE QUESTION**

Barry Garlowe is the lead artist in the pop group 'Give This'. Two years ago, the band members entered into a contract with Moni Cowbell, a famous music manager in which they granted her the exclusive right to produce and promote their work for five years and promised to work for no other manager during that time. The contract also provided that Barry would retain copyright to his compositions. Barry has now fallen out with the rest of the band and has told Moni that he wishes to engage Louise Welsh to launch him as a solo artist. He has also told Moni that his first solo release will be a song, 'Love for Now', in which Moni has already invested some effort. Moni therefore takes preliminary steps to appoint William Robbs to be the new face of Give This and it becomes common knowledge in the industry that, if Barry leaves, Moni intends to produce 'Love for Now' with William on guitar. Barry has written to William to warn him that he will be in breach of Barry's copyright if he performs 'Love for Now', but William says that he has seen a signed document transferring Barry's rights to Moni. Barry never signed any such document and is convinced that Moni must have forged his signature. Barry tries to contact Moni, but without success.

online resource centre

Eventually, Barry decides to pay a visit to Moni's mansion house. On arrival, Barry finds a removals firm packing Moni's belongings into a huge van. The driver informs Barry that Moni is moving back to her native Switzerland.

Advise Barry.

FURTHER READING

Bant, E., 'Reconsidering the Role of Election in Rescission' (2012) 32 (3) *OJLS* 467.

Biscoe, P., *Mareva and Anton Piller Orders: Freezing and Search Orders* (Australia: Butterworth's, 2005).

Davies, P.S., 'Rectifying the course of rectification' (2012) 75(3) *MLR* 387.

Devenney J. and Chandler A., 'Unconscionability and the Taxonomy of Undue Influence' (2007) *Journal of Business Law* 541.

Gardner, S. 'Two Maxims of Equity' (1995) 54(1) *CLJ* 60.

Gee, S., *Commercial Injunctions*, 6th revd edn (London: Sweet & Maxwell, 2013).

Goldrein, I., *Privacy Injunctions and the Media* (Oxford: Hart, 2012)

Harris, D. R., 'Specific Performance—A Regular Remedy for Consumers' (2003) 119 *LQR* 541.

Kerridge, R., 'Undue influence and testamentary dispositions: a response' (2012) 2 *Conv* 129–144.
    [A response to the 2011 article by Lee Mason, also included in this list]

Kodilinye, G., 'A Fresh Approach to the *ex turpi causa* and "Clean Hands" Maxims' (1992) *Denning LJ* 93.

Mason, L., 'Undue Influence and Testamentary Dispositions: An Equitable Jurisdiction in Probate Law?' (2011) 75(2) *Conv* 115.

Master of the Rolls, *Report of the Committee on Super-Injunctions: Super-Injunctions, Anonymised Injunctions and Open Justice*, 20 May 2011.

Mitchell, C. and Watterson, S., 'Subrogation: Law and Practice' (Oxford: Oxford University Press, 2007).

Ridge, P., 'Equitable Undue Influence and Wills' (2004) 120 *LQR* 617.

Swadling, W., 'Rescission, Property, and the Common Law' (2005) 121 *LQR* 123–53.

INDEX